Notable Black American Women

Book II

To black American women who paved the way
and to those black women who are searching for a way.

Notable Black American Women

Book II

Jessie Carney Smith
Editor

Gale Research

An ITP Information/Reference Group Company

I(T)P
Changing the Way the World Learns

NEW YORK • LONDON • BONN • BOSTON • DETROIT
MADRID • MELBOURNE • MEXICO CITY • PARIS
SINGAPORE • TOKYO • TORONTO • WASHINGTON
ALBANY NY • BELMONT CA • CINCINNATI OH

Notable Black American Women, Book II

Jessie Carney Smith, *Editor*

Gale Research Inc. Staff:

Marie Ellavich, *Developmental Editor;* Lawrence W. Baker, *Managing Editor;* Jolen Gedridge, Camille Killens, *Associate Editors;* Andrea Kovacs, Jessica Proctor, *Assistant Editors*

Mary Beth Trimper, *Production Director;* Evi Seoud, *Assistant Production Manager;* Shanna Heilveil, *Production Assistant*

Cynthia Baldwin, *Product Design Manager;* Pamela A. E. Galbreath, *Art Director;* Steffan Duerr, Brushstrokes Studio, *Cover Design;* Barbara J. Yarrow, *Graphic Services Supervisor;* Pamela Hayes, *Photography Coordinator;* Willie Mathis, *Camera Operator*

Benita L. Spight, *Manager, Data Entry Services;* Gwendolyn S. Tucker, *Data Entry Coordinator;* LySandra Davis, *Data Entry Associate*

The Library of Congress has cataloged volume 1 as follows:

Notable Black American Women / edited by Jessie Carney Smith
p. cm.
Includes bibliographical references and index.
ISBN 0-8103-4749-0
1. Afro-American women—Biography. I. Smith, Jessie Carney.
E185.96.N68 1991
920.72'08996073—dc20
      [B] 91-35074
      CIP

I(T)P™ Gale Research Inc., an International Thomson Publishing Company.
ITP logo is a trademark under license.

10 9 8 7 6 5 4 3 2 1

Contents

Introduction

"We have many estimable women of our variety, but not any famous ones," the abolitionist and orator Frederick Douglass wrote more than one hundred years ago. He was answering a request from Monroe Majors, who was gathering information for his pioneering book *Notable Negro Women,* published in 1893. Majors had asked Douglass, the most famous black man of his era, to suggest additions to the list of women to be included in the book. In his reply, Douglass defined a famous person as one who was "celebrated in fame or public" and "much talked of." He cautioned: "It is not well to claim too much for ourselves before the public." Douglass continued in his letter, now in the possession of Majors's great-granddaughter, Eleanor Boswell-Raine of El Sobrante, California, that he had seen "no book of importance written by a Negro woman" and that he knew "of no one among us who can appreciably be called famous." Obviously he dismissed Phillis Wheatley, who in 1773 published *Poems on Various Subjects, Religious and Moral* and was the first black woman and the second woman in America to publish a book of poems. It is inconceivable that Douglass considered unimportant the works of Frances E. W. Harper, writer and fellow activist, whose books included *Poems on Miscellaneous Subjects* (1854) and *Iola Leroy; or Shadows Uplifted* (1892); the writing of Frances Anne Rollin Whipper, who in 1868 published *Life and Public Service of Martin R. Delany;* and the well-known Anna Julia Cooper, who wrote *A Voice from the South* (1890).

That Douglass could not recognize the fame of Sojourner Truth and Harriet Tubman, who doubtlessly were "much talked of" during his lifetime, causes further concern. Both Douglass and Truth were abolitionists and proponents of women's rights and had even appeared at the same gatherings on occasion. In her work as underground railroad conductor, Harriet Tubman led over two hundred of Douglass's black brothers and sisters from bondage to freedom. Refusing to acknowledge that the lack of recognition for women reflected a prevailing male chauvinism, Douglass excused himself from expanding Majors's list and said that, while many of the women listed were admirable, "it does not follow that they are famous." Thus one of the nation's most renowned black leaders, Frederick Douglass, demonstrated a limited view of the importance of black women and passed up an opportunity to contribute to an important area of research—black American women's biography.

Thirty-three years later, in 1926, Hallie Quinn Brown published her seminal work, *Homespun Heroines and Other Women of Distinction.* The biographical sketches written by various women for the book presented information on other notable black American women, some of whom may not have been widely known at the time. In one of these sketches, a biography of Elizabeth N. Smith, contributor Maritcha Lyons questioned Frederick Douglass's advice "not to claim too much for ourselves before the public." In fact, Lyons pointed out that "we know so little about ourselves" that we have neglected our history and failed to preserve facts and incidents especially of those who "lived lives of strenuous endurance." Prominent in this category have been black women. Since their stories remained untold, many black American women, enslaved and free, died "unhonored and unsung." In the pre-Civil War era, black women founded schools and trained other young women and men who would, in turn, train others and become educators of renown. We also find among black women of that era concert musicians, linguists, and elocutionists. These women began a tradition of strenuous effort which continues to the present day.

For example, Elizabeth Smith, a nineteenth-century educator, is an unsung exceptional woman. Lyons said that conversation with Smith was "supreme" and continued: "She lived when conversation was an art." Smith read widely, was graceful and charming, and adapted herself to different situations. "She had the faculty of drawing out the best in each"; she was a good listener as well as an engaging conversationalist. Her major claim to fame is heading the best school open to blacks in her hometown of Providence, Rhode Island, yet her reputation extended beyond that place. As a young girl Lyons had met Smith, but, even as she attempted to document the educator's life, information about Smith was disappearing. The result was an unfortunate lack of specific dates in the *Homespun Heroines* sketch on Smith.

Lyons praised the work of black women throughout the country. She recognized African American women of the South who "fought the stars in their course, to step out of the darkness of bondage into the light of personal liberty." She said those of the North and other sections of the country "lived clouded lives, made dim by the tales of the indescribable sufferings endured by their sisters by blood and lineage. Their tears have flowed in sympathy and their characters have been molded by large sacrifices cheerfully made upon demand to alleviate distress which at best could only be surmised."

The history of black women in America is the history of such strife and success. Lyons's conclusion in *Homespun Heroines* is a fitting tribute to the black women profiled in this book and other accomplished women not presented here. As she said, "they all have done their duty, much better than they knew. They have left a broad foundation upon which their successors are obligated to raise an enduring superstructure of character, one that will exhibit the progress of the much maligned 'black woman of America,' and so conserve the toils, vigils and prayers of the many whose lives have been lived in shade, who only in lives of others saw 'the shine of distant suns.'"

A century after Majors's pioneering biographical work and nearly seventy years after Brown continued the search, the history of pre-twentieth-century black American women remains incomplete. In some cases it is still surprisingly difficult to find information about important contemporary and near-contemporary women. This second volume of *Notable Black American Women* represents more than twenty-five years of research and extends the work on women—on the abolitionists, educators, doctors, journalists, writers, and women of many other professions—begun in the first volume. Some of those included here were identified earlier and excluded from the first volume only because of space limitation or because of the editor's aim to present women with a wide range of experiences. Following the focus of the first volume, this work defines the lives of women from colonial times to the present. Of the three-hundred women included, over one-third are historical. The earliest known birthdate in this volume is about 1686, when Alice of Dunk's Ferry was born, while the latest is 1970, when Queen Latifah was born. The aim was to balance the length of the essays with a rough estimate of importance. In a few instances the essays are much briefer than desired, as, for example, in the entries for Alice of Dunk's Ferry and Aurelia Brazeal (1943-) due to the difficulty in locating biographical information. Other entries became longer than planned as research turned up new or neglected sources.

Focus on Diversity Continues

Women in the first volume are not ranked in importance over those in the second. Nor do the entries in either volume—altogether eight hundred—represent a selection of all the most important and the most famous African American women. Rather, the aim of the editor, the advisory board, and the scholars throughout the country who were consulted was to give the reader an important assemblage of biographies of women who are diverse by geography, history, and profession. The editors and the advisors screened a list of approximately eight hundred women for this volume. The final selection produced a list that fits the primary aim for diversity. The initial list was compiled both from works with a local focus, such as W. D. Johnson's *Biographical Sketches of Prominent Negro Men and Women in Kentucky* and the Georgia edition of Arthur Bunyan Caldwell's *History of the American Negro in His Institutions,* as well as from sources more widely known. Again the researchers relied heavily on such works as Monroe Majors's *Noted Negro Women;* Hallie Quinn Brown's *Homespun Heroines and Other Women of Distinction;* and Lawson A. Scruggs's *Women of Distinction.* General biographical directories used included *Who's Who in Colored America, Black Biographies,* and *Who's Who in Black America.* For women known for their work in specific subject areas the researchers consulted works such as Edward Mapp's *Directory of Blacks in the Performing Arts* and I. Garland Penn's *The Afro-American Press and Its Editors.* Additional names were suggested as research in individual biography proceeded. Women were selected when they met one or more of the following criteria:

> a pioneer in a particular area, such as first black woman elected to public office in a state or first black woman editor of a newspaper, or

> an important entrepreneur, such as a manufacturer of cosmetics for black women or developer of hair care products, or

> a leading businesswoman, such as president of an advertising firm, or vice-president of a major bank, or

> a literary or creative figure of stature, such as an outstanding poet, well-known writer, author of works on a unique theme, important artist, outstanding sculptor, or

> a leader of social or human justice, such as abolitionist, freedom fighter, suffragist, outstanding participant in the civil rights movement, or

> a major governmental or organizational official, such as the director of the Women's Bureau, president of the National Medical Association, president of the National Education Association, first black president of the American Library Association, or

> a creative figure in the performing arts, such as the first black to perform at the Metropolitan Opera, outstanding popular singer or performer, prima ballerina, actress, or composer, or

> a noted orator, elocutionist, or public speaker (particularly for nineteenth- and early twentieth-century women), or

> a distinguished educator, such as first woman principal of an early high school, president of a college, founder of a college, first black woman to receive a doctoral degree, or

> a noted scholar, such as a scientist, mathematician, historian, or sociologist, or

> a leader, pioneer, or contributor in other fields or areas who meets the basic criteria suggested above for selection as an outstanding black American woman.

The authors of the entries were asked to be as inclusive as possible in recording references to women of earlier periods to help capture for future scholarship the scarce or scattered biographical reference sources, especially since local resources may be obscure and not readily available to researchers. The intention was to make the entries as accurate as possible, but frequently the researchers and authors were hampered by inaccurate, incomplete, or conflicting information. When possible, the authors interviewed the subjects, their descendants, or those who had an affiliation with the women. Many of the essays contain quotations from works written by the biographees, from works written about them, and/or from interviews with them, their relatives, or others who knew them. The editor's special concern in choosing quotations was for the subject's views on women and issues they faced. Primary materials, such as diaries, letters, and census reports, were sought out and used when found.

Other features of the work include wherever possible the description of primary sources in archival repositories, libraries, and in private hands at the conclusion of many of the entries as a guide for future researchers. Although photographs were unavailable for some of the subjects, every effort was made to publish a photograph of each woman. For convenience, the subject index identifies the women whose lives were chronicled in the first volume. Two new features in this volume are the publication of addresses for the living biographees and a geographical index that includes both the birthplace and places of residence. The subject index will guide the reader to important people, places, and events referenced in the entries. For the benefit of future scholarship, readers are invited to provide leads to additional primary or secondary sources, as well as information to correct, clarify, or expand that presented in the entries.

Arrangement of Entries

The entries in this volume are arranged alphabetically by surname or, when appropriate, by a single name (for example, Belinda). Preference is given to the name by which the woman was generally known (for example, Sarah Willie Layten is listed under S. Willie Layten). Women with compound surnames are arranged under the first of these names whether or not the names are hyphenated. For example, Ida Gray Nelson Rollins is treated as Nelson Rollins.

Contributions to *Notable Black American Women* Acknowledged

Notable Black American Women, Book II, is the work of one hundred writers who conducted research and wrote painstakingly so that the lives of the women chronicled here could be available to advance scholarship in this subject area. In many instances the writers pieced together fragments of information, wrote a history that seemed to be lost, and produced a portrait that both enlightens and informs. The editor recognizes that this volume would not have been possible without their important contributions.

As well, this work is the product of countless researchers in libraries and repositories throughout the country. The many who worked with the writers are unrecognized individually in this book, and they remain silent contributors to black women's scholarship. While those libraries and repositories that provided generous support to the project and to the individual writer are too numerous to mention, three of the leading supporters, however, deserve special recognition: Moorland-Spingarn Research Center, Howard University, Washington, D.C.; Schomburg Center for Research in Black Culture, New York Public Library; and Special Collections Department, Fisk University, Nashville, Tennessee. James Huffman at Schomburg, Donna Wells at Moorland-Spingarn, Prince Rivers, Elaine Williams, and Elisha Miller at Clark-Atlanta University, Beth Howse at Fisk University, and Charles Blockson at Temple University aided in the search for photographs. As well, Marcia Lein of Associated Press/Wide World Photos and Jocelyn Clapp of the Bettman Archives eased the editor's search for illustrations.

The Advisory Committee for the project deserves praise for guiding the project in its early stages and for lending support as the work progressed.

Researchers and assistants who worked directly with the editor were Betty Gubert, New York City; Helena Carney Lambeth, Washington, D.C.; Duane P. Lambeth, Detroit, Michigan; Karen Carney Filmore, Oakland, California; Sharon Hull, Fletcher Moon, and Murle Kennerson of Tennessee State University; and John Henderson, Dorothy Lake, and Frederick Smith Jr. of Fisk University. I am grateful to each of them for their diligent support and attention to project requirements.

I place in a separate category three people who continue to support, encourage, and facilitate this series of works on African American women. Vallie Pursley, Tennessee State University, provided research and computer assistance and handled other special project activities. Robert L. Johns, my Fisk colleague, created useful computer files, edited each of the three hundred essays, wrote many himself, conducted bibliographical and biographical research, and offered a sympathetic ear and comforting words as I faced the usual obstacles encountered in such a research project. President Henry Ponder of Fisk University made possible the completion of the project while I was involved in administrative duties. To these three supporters I am especially grateful.

The staff at Gale Research provided advisory, editorial, and technical expertise. They are all to be recognized for their efforts, particularly Christine Nasso, Leah Knight, and, for working diligently to pull it all together, editors Lawrence Baker and Marie Ellavich.

Finally, I acknowledge the gifts of patience, encouragement, and understanding from my family and friends, who share my enthusiasm for scholarship about African American women and who allowed me time from activities we usually share so that I might complete this work.

Jessie Carney Smith

Entrants

Occupation Index

Individuals Profiled in
Notable Black American Women

These profiles appear in the first *Notable Black American Women,*
edited by Jessie Carney Smith and published by Gale Research Inc. in 1992.

Clara Leach Adams-Ender
Cecelia Adkins
Octavia Albert
Sadie Alexander
Elreta Alexander Ralston
Debbie Allen
Caroline Still Anderson
Marian Anderson
Regina M. Anderson
Maya Angelou
Lillian Hardin Armstrong
Gertrude Elise Ayer
Pearl Bailey
Augusta Baker
Ella Baker
Josephine Baker
Maria Louise Baldwin
Carnella Barnes
Etta Moten Barnett
Marguerite Ross Barnett
Janie Porter Barrett
Willie B. Barrow
Charlotta Spears Bass
Daisy Bates
Flora Batson
Bessye Bearden
Delilah Leontium Beasley
Phoebe Beasley
Louise Beavers
Gwendolyn Bennett
Mary Francis Berry
Mary McLeod Bethune
Camille Billops
Jane M. Bolin
Margaret Bonds
Matilda Booker
Eva del Vakia Bowles
Mary Elizabeth Bowser

Mary E. Branch
Carol Brice
Gwendolyn Brooks
Charlotte Hawkins Brown
Dorothy Brown
Hallie Brown
Letitia Brown
Josephine Beall Bruce
Grace Ann Bumbry
Selma Hortense Burke
Yvonne Braithwaite Burke
Margaret Taylor Burroughs
Nannie Helen Burroughs
Vinie Burrows
Anita Bush
Octavia E. Butler
Selena Sloan Butler
Shirley Caesar
Blanche Calloway
Lucie Campbell Williams
Alexa Canady
Mary Elizabeth Carnegie
Diahann Carroll
Betty Carter
Eunice Hunton Carter
Elizabeth Carter Brooks
Alice Dugged Cary
Melnea Cass
Elizabeth Catlett
Barbara Chase-Riboud
Alice Childress
May Edward Chinn
Shirley Chisholm
Septima Clark
Alice Coachman
Jewell Plummer Cobb
Johnnetta Betsch Cole
Rebecca J. Cole

Bessie Coleman
Cardiss Collins
Janet Collins
Marva Collins
Coralie Cook
Anna J. Cooper
Fanny Jackson Coppin
Camille Cosby
Julia Ringwood Coston
Elizabeth "Libba" Cotten
Marie Bernard Couvent
Ida Cox
Ellen Craft
Otelia Cromwell
Maud Cuney Hare
Marion Vera Cuthbert
Dorothy Dandridge
Margaret Danner
Angela Davis
Elizabeth Lindsay Davis
Henrietta Vinton Davis
Hilda Davis
Jennie Dean
Ruby Dee
Lucy A. Delaney
Sara "Sadie" P. Delaney
Clarissa Scott Delany
Wilhelmina R. Delco
Henriette Delille and the Sisters of the Holy Family
Bernadine Newsom Denning
Juliette Derricotte
Irene Diggs
Sharon Pratt Dixon
Mattiwilda Dobbs
Dorothy Donegan
Anna Murray Douglass
Sarah Mapps Douglass
Rita Dove
Shirley Graham Du Bois
Alice Dunbar-Nelson
Katherine Dunham
Alice Dunnigan
Alfreda M. Duster
Eva B. Dykes
Ramona Hoage Edelin
Marian Wright Edelman

Helen G. Edmonds
Ophelia Settle Egypt
Zilpha Elaw
Elleanor Eldridge
Daisy Elliott
Effie O'Neal Ellis
Evelyn Ellis
Mari Evans
Matilda Arabella Evans
Lillian Evanti
Sarah Webster Fabio
Crystal Dreda Bird Fauset
Jessie Redmon Fauset
Dorothy Boulding Ferebee
Catherine Ferguson
Mary Fields
Ada L. Fisher
Ella Fitzgerald
Lethia C. Fleming
Kay Stewart Flippin
Ida Forsyne
Margaretta Forten
Charlotte L. Forten Grimké
Aretha Franklin
Charlotte White Franklin
J. E. Franklin
Martha Minerva Franklin
Elizabeth Freeman
Meta Warrick Fuller
Mary Hatwood Futrell
Marie D. Gadsden
Irene McCoy Gaines
Phillis "Phyl" T. Garland
Sarah Garnet
Frances Joseph Gaudet
Zelma Watson George
Althea Gibson
Paula Giddings
Nikki Giovanni
Eliza Gleason
Whoopi Goldberg
Nora Antonia Gordon
Elizabeth T. Greenfield
Angelina Weld Grimké
Verta Mae Grosvenor
Lucille C. Gunning

Marjorie McKenzie Lawson
Jarena Lee
Edmonia Lewis
Elma Lewis
Ida Elizabeth Lewis
Samella Sanders Lewis
Abbey Lincoln
Inabel Burns Lindsay
Adella Hunt Logan
Audre Lorde
Josephine Harreld Love
Ruth B. Love
Jackie "Moms" Mabley
Jane Ellen McAllister
Gertrude P. McBrown
Jewell Jackson McCabe
Rosalie "Rose" McClendon
Mary Eleanora McCoy
Viola McCoy
M. A. McCurdy
Hattie McDaniel
Alice Woodby McKane
Nina Mae McKinney
Enolia Pettigen McMillan
Thelma "Butterfly" McQueen
Carmen McRae
Naomi Long Madgett
Mary Mahoney
Gerri Major
Arenia C. Mallory
Annie Turnbo Malone
Vivian Malone
Paule Burke Marshall
Sara Martin
Biddy Mason
Lena Doolin Mason
Victoria Earle Matthews
Dorothy Maynor
Adah Isaacs Menken
Louise Meriwether
Lydia Moore Merrick
Emma F. G. Merritt
May Miller
Florence Mills
Abbie Mitchell
Juanita Mitchell

Mollie Moon
Melba Moore
Queen Mother Audley Moore
Undine Smith Moore
Rose Morgan
Toni Morrison
Gertrude Bustill Mossell
Lucy Ellen Moten
Constance Baker Motley
Joan Murray
Pauli Murray
Ethel Ray Nance
Nettie Langston Napier
Diane Nash
Annie Greene Nelson
Effie Lee Newsome
Camille Nickerson
Jessye Norman
Eleanor Holmes Norton
Oblate Sisters of Providence
Odetta
Nell Irvin Painter
Rosa Parks
Mary Parrish (G. Ermine)
Mary Jane Patterson
Georgia E. L. Patton
Ethel Payne
Carolyn Robertson Payton
Mary S. Peake
Anna Belle Rhodes Penn
Carrie Saxon Perry
Julia Perry
Dorothy Peterson
Ann Petry
L. Eudora Pettigrew
Vel R. Phillips
Annette L. Phinazee
Ann Plato
Willa B. Player
Mary Ellen Pleasant
Dorothy Porter
Ersa Hines Poston
Renee Francine Poussaint
Georgia M. Powers
Evelyn Preer
Frances E. L. Preston

Florence Price
Leontyne Price
Amelia Perry Pride
Pearl Primus
Lucy Terry Prince
Nancy Gardner Prince
Ernesta G. Procope
Barbara Gardner Proctor
Elizabeth Prophet
Mary Ann Prout
Harriet Forten Purvis
Sarah Forten Purvis
Norma Quarles
Muriel Rahn
Ma Rainey (G. Pridgett)
Amanda Randolph
Virginia Randolph
Charlotte E. Ray
H. Cordelia Ray
Bernice J. Reagon
Sarah P. Remond
Beah Richards
Fannie M. Richards
Gloria Richardson
Florida Ruffin Ridley
Eslanda Goode Robeson
Rubye Doris Robinson
Charlemae Hill Rollins
Diana Ross
Wilma Rudolph
Josephine St. Pierre Ruffin
Betye Saar
Edith S. Sampson
Deborah Sampson (Shurtleff)
Sonia Sanchez
Doris Saunders
Augusta Savage
Philippa Schuyler
Esther Mae Scott
Gloria Scott
Hazel Scott
Mary Ann Shadd
Ntosake Shange
Ella Sheppard Moore
Olivia Shipp (O. Porter)
Modjeska Simkins

Althea T. L. Simmons
Judy Simmons
Hilda Simms
Nina Simone
Carole Simpson
Naomi Sims
Barbara Sizemore
Norma Merrick Sklarek
Edith Barksdale Sloan
Lucy Diggs Slowe
Ada Smith
Amanda Berry Smith
Bessie Smith
Clara Smith
Lucie Wilmot Smith
Mamie Smith
Willie Mae Ford Smith
Mabel Murphy Smythe-Haithe
Valaida Snow
Eileen Southern
Eulalie Spence
Anne Spencer
Isabele Taliaferro Spiller
Hortense Spillers
Victoria Spivey
Jeanne Spurlock
Mabel Keaton Staupers
Susan McKinney Steward
Ella P. Stewart
Maria W. Stewart
Juanita Kidd Stout
Niara Sudarkasa
Madame Sul-Te-Wan
Mary Morris Talbert
Ann Tanneyhill
Ellen Tarry
Anna Diggs Taylor
Eva Taylor
Susan King Taylor
Susan L. Taylor
Mary Church Terrell
Sister Rosetta Tharpe
Alma Thomas
Edna Thomas
Lillian May Thomas
Eloise Bibb Thompson

Era Bell Thompson
Louise Thompson
Adah Thoms
Lucinda Thurman
Sue Thurman
Jackie Torrence
Geraldine Pindell Trotter
Sojourner Truth
Harriet Tubman
C. DeLores Tucker
Tina Turner
Cicely Tyson
Susan Paul Vashon
Sarah Vaughan
Mother Charleszetta Waddles
A(i)da Overton Walker
A'Lelia Walker
Alice Walker
Lelia Walker
Madame C. J. Walker
Maggie L. Walker
Margaret Walker
Joan Scott Wallace
Phyllis Ann Wallace
Sippie Wallace
Clara Mae Ward
Laura Wheeler Waring
Dionne Warwick
Dinah Washington

Fredi Washington
Josephine Washington
Margaret M. Washington
Olivia D. Washington
Sarah Spencer Washington
Ethel Waters
Faye Wattleton
Ida B. Wells Barnett
Dorothy West
Doris L. Wethers
Laura Frances Wheatley
Phillis Wheatley
Ionia Rollin Whipper
Eartha White
Fannie B. Williams
Lorraine A. Williams
Maria Selika Williams
Mamie Williams
Mary Lou Williams
Edith Wilson
Harriet E. A. Wilson
Margaret Bush Wilson
Nancy Wilson
Oprah Winfrey
Deborah C. P. Wolfe
Geraldine Pittman Woods
Elizabeth Wright
Jane C. Wright
Josephine Silone Yates

Advisory Board

Arlene Clift-Pellow
Director, Humanities Division, North Carolina Central University

Johnnetta B. Cole (Robinson)
President, Spelman College

Bettye Collier-Thomas
Director, Center for Black Culture and History, Temple University

Nikki Giovanni
Writer; professor of English, Virginia Polytechnic Institute and State University

Beverly Guy-Sheftall
Director, Women's Research & Resource Center, Spelman College

Jean Blackwell Hutson
Retired director, Schomburg Center for Research in Black Culture

Karen Jefferson
Program officer, National Endowment for the Humanities

Julianne Malveaux
Talk show host, WPFM, Washington, D.C.

Genna Rae McNeil
Professor of history, University of North Carolina, Chapel Hill

Dorothy Porter (Wesley)
Director emerita, Moorland-Spingarn Research Center

Gloria Randall Scott
President, Bennett College

Susan L. Taylor
Editor-in-chief, *Essence* magazine

Contributors

Yvette Marie Alex-Assensoh, *Indiana University*
A. B. Assensoh, *Southern University, Baton Rouge, Louisiana*
Tandy Avant, *Louisiana State University*
Kathleen E. Bethel, *Northwestern University*
Charles L. Blockson, *Temple University*
Lisa Boyd, *University of Georgia*
Jacqueline Brice-Finch, *James Madison University*
Walton L. Brown, *Central Connecticut State University*
Phiefer L. Browne, *Fisk University*
T. J. Bryant, *Coppin State College*
Lauretta Flynn Byars, *University of Kentucky*
Linda M. Carter, *Morgan State University*
Arlene Clift-Pellow, *North Carolina Central University*
Bettye Collier-Thomas, *Temple University*
Grace E. Collins, *Howard Community College*
Beverly A. Cook, *Chicago Public Library*
Dawn Cooper-Barnes, *Howard Community College*
Sarah A. Crest, *Towson State University*
Sandra D. Davis, *Detroit Free Press*
Margaret Duckworth, *Virginia Union University*
De Witt S. Dykes, Jr., *Oakland University*
Derek Elliott, *Tennessee State University*
Joan Curl Elliott, *Tennessee State University*
Nicole D. Elliott, *Longwood College*
Sharynn Owens Etheridge, *University of Tennessee*
Kathleen Flanagan, *Longwood College*
Michael Flug, *Carter G. Woodson Library, Chicago*
Vonita W. Foster, *Virginia Union University*
V. P. Franklin, *Drexel University*
Eiling Freeman, *Oberlin College*
Elizabeth Hadley Freydberg, *Northeastern University*
Phyl Garland, *Columbia University*
Marie Garrett, *University of Tennessee*
Martia Graham Goodson, *Baruch College*
Sandra Y. Govan, *University of North Carolina, Charlotte*
Barbara L. J. Griffin, *Howard University*
Erica L. Griffin, *University of Tennessee*
D. Antoinette Handy, *Jackson, Mississippi*

Janie Greenwood Harris, *St. Louis, Missouri*
Ruth Edmonds Hill, *Radcliffe College*
Ruth A. Hodges, *Howard University*
Felicia Harris Felder Hoehne, *University of Tennessee*
Helen R. Houston, *Tennessee State University*
Juanita Howard, *Baruch College*
Dona L. Irvin, *Oakland, California*
Lucilla Hiomara Iturralde, *Oberlin College*
Jacquelyn L. Jackson, *Middle Tennessee State University*
Joyce Marie Jackson, *Louisiana State University*
Laura C. Jarmon, *Middle Tennessee State University*
Barbara Williams Jenkins, *South Carolina State University*
Robert L. Johns, *Fisk University*
Adrienne Lash Jones, *Oberlin College*
Carolyn Jones, *Louisiana State University*
Casper LeRoy Jordan, *Atlanta, Georgia*
Juanita Karpf, *University of Georgia*
Ellen Kirschman, *Oakland, California*
Jo Ann Lahmon, *University of Tennessee*
Helena Carney Lambeth, *Washington, D.C.*
Candis La Prade, *Longwood College*
Nadya J. Lawson, *University at Albany, State University of New York*
Margaret C. Lee, *Spelman College*
Theresa Leininger-Miller, *University of Cincinnati*
Thura Mack, *University of Tennessee*
Umaimah Mahmud, *Oberlin College*
John McClendon, III, *University of Missouri*
Phyllis McClure, *NAACP Legal Defense Fund*
Karen Cotton McDaniel, *Kentucky State University*
Edward B. McDonald, *Xavier University, New Orleans*
Genna Rae McNeil, *University of North Carolina, Chapel Hill*
Denis Mercer, *Rowan College*
Alyson Myers, *Baruch College*
Jessica A. Nelson, *Oberlin College*
Dolores Nicholson, *Head Middle School, Nashville, Tennessee*
Kathy A. Perkins, *University of Illinois*
Margaret Perry, *Thompsonville, Michigan*
Patsy B. Perry, *North Carolina Central University*
Bobbie Pollard, *Baruch College*
Janet Prescod, *University of Tennessee*
Marlo Price, *Oberlin College*
Margaret A. Reid, *Morgan State University*
Marva Rudolph, *University of Tennessee*
Vivian O. Sammons, *Adelphi, Maryland*
Brenda R. Shaw, *North Carolina Central University*
Susan J. Sierra, *Oberlin College*

Simona Simmons-Hodo, *University of Maryland, Baltimore County*
Janet Sims-Wood, *Howard University*
Jessie Carney Smith, *Fisk University*
Benjamin F. Speller, Jr., *North Carolina Central University*
Robert Stephens, *Montclair State University*
Claire Taft, *Texas A & M University, Kingsville*
Darius L. Thieme, *Fisk University*
Mia Nwaka Thompson, *Oberlin College*
John Mark Tucker, *Purdue University*
Laura D. Turner, *Xavier University, New Orleans*
Nagueyalti Warren, *Emory University*
Judith Weisenfeld, *Barnard College*
Audrey Williams, *Baruch College*
Phyllis Wood, *Garner, North Carolina*
Linda Wynn, *Tennessee Historical Society*
Dhyana Ziegler, *University of Tennessee*

Photo Credits

Photographs appearing in *Notable Black American Women, Book II,* were received from the following sources:

Cover photos (clockwise from top right): **Robert W. Woodruff Library; Meharry Medical College Archives; Reuters/ Bettmann; Leslie E. Spatt, Dance Theatre of Harlem.**

Charles L. Blockson Afro-American Collection, Temple University: 1; City of Philadelphia, Department of Records, City Archives: 2; Del Marie Anderson: 6; Schomburg Center for Research in Black Culture: 8; Fisk University Library: 11; Fisk University Library: 13; Fisk University Library: 15; Fisk University Library: 17; AP/Wide World Photos: 19; Gwendolyn Calvert Baker: 21; Fisk University Library: 24; AP/Wide World Photos: 26; Cirrincione Lee Entertainment, Inc.: 31; South Carolina State University: 33; Juliann Stephanie Bluitt: 34; Thelma Boozer Baxter: 39; Fisk University Library: 42; Fisk University Library: 44; Fisk University Library: 46; Bowen Agency Ltd.: 49; Fisk University Library: 52; U.S. Department of State, Bureau of African Affairs: 53; Fisk University Library: 56; Fisk University Library: 57; Colorado Historical Society: 61; AP/Wide World Photos: 63; UPI/Bettmann: 65; Fisk University Library: 67; Schomburg Center for Research in Black Culture: 69; AP/Wide World Photos: 74; Fisk University Library: 76; Fisk University Library: 78; UPI/Bettmann: 81; Mae Bertha Carter: 83; *The London Guardian:* **85; Reuters/Bettmann: 88; Fisk University Library: 90; AP/Wide World Photos: 92; Turner Broadcasting System Management: 97; Barry Forbus: 99; Corky Gallo, Emory University: 101; Ruth C. Bond: 103; Fisk University Library: 105; Michael S. Glaser: 108; New York Public Library for the Performing Arts: 112; UPI/Bettmann: 116; AP/Wide World Photos: 119; Tougaloo College: 123; Fisk University Library: 124; Fisk University Library: 125; Johnnie Colemon: 129; Fisk University Library: 131; Barbara-Rose Collins: 134; Fisk University Library: 137; Fisk University Library: 141; Robert W. Woodruff Library, Atlanta University Center: 144; Ellen Banner: 149; Patricia Cowings: 151; North Carolina Department of Cultural Resources, Historic Sites Section, Charlotte Hawkins Brown Collection: 153; Fisk University Library: 156; Geechee Girls Productions: 159; Hatch-Billops Collection: 162; Fisk University Library: 165; Lois Marie DeBerry: 167; Suzanne De Chillo, New York Times Pictures: 171; Fisk University Library: 174; Rachel McCallister & Associates: 177; Helen Octavia Dickens: 179; Fisk University Library: 183; Abbeville Press: 186; Hazel Nell Dukes: 190; Digging It Up: 196; Fisk University Library: 198; Office of the Surgeon General: 200; Mercedes Ellington: 203; Jack Dermid, courtesy of Jo Kallenborn: 205; AP/Wide World Photos: 207; Tennessee State University: 211; Southern Education Foundation, courtesy of Judy Ondrey: 213; Wide World Photos: 215; Fisk University Library: 218; Archival and Museum Collection, Hampton University: 221; AP/Wide World Photos: 223; Trevor Leighton/ Magic Lady: 225; Robert W. Woodruff Library, Atlanta University Center: 228; Black American West Museum: 229; Burton Historical Collection, Detroit Public Library: 235; Frankie Muse Freeman: 237; Percy A. Garland, courtesy of Phyllis Garland: 241; International Public Relations and Marketing for Athletes: 244; Schomburg Center for Research in Black Culture: 246; Robert W. Woodruff Library, Atlanta University Center: 250; Darryl Gorham: 251; Detroit Public Library: 254; Micki Grant: 256; AP/Wide World Photos: 259; AP/Wide World Photos: 262; Bonnie Guiton: 264; Fisk University Library: 266; Mabel Dole Haden: 268; Robert W. Woodruff Library: 270; Scurlock Studios, from the collections of the Moorland-Springarn Research Center, Howard University: 272; D. Antoinette Handy: 277; John W. Moseley, courtesy of Charles L. Blockson Afro-American Collection, Temple University: 280; Jessie Mae Hemphill: 283; Fisk University Library: 285; The White House: 287; AP/Wide World Photos: 289; Susan Wilson: 292; Fisk University Library: 295; Pinderhughes: 297; Schomburg Center for Research in Black Culture: 302; AP/Wide World Photos: 305; Fisk University Library: 307; AP/Wide World Photos: 309; Oberlin College Archives: 312; John I. Lattany, Sr.: 314; Kentucky State University: 317; Northern California Center for Afro-American History and Life: 320; AP/Wide World Photos: 323; Fisk University Library: 327; Louise E. Jefferson: 329; Fisk University Library: 331; Sebetha Lee Jenkins: 333; Patricia Prattis Jennings: 335; Fisk University Library: 338; Eddie Bernice Johnson: 340; Leslie E. Spatt, Dance Theatre of Harlem: 341; AP/Wide World Photos: 343; Edith Irby Jones: 347; AP/Wide World Photos: 349; Elayne Kaufman Jones: 350; AP/ Wide World Photos: 353; Fisk University Library: 355; Fisk University Library: 360; UPI/Bettmann: 363; Vivian Harsh Collection, Carter G. Woodson Library: 366; Reuters/Bettmann: 371; AP/Wide World Photos: 374; Yvonne Kennedy: 379; AP/Wide World Photos: 382; Higher Ground Productions: 384; AP/Wide World Photos: 387; AP/Wide World Photos: 390; AP/Wide World Photos: 393; © Chad Lawson: 395; James J. Lawson, courtesy of Anacostia Museum: 398; Fisk University Library: 401; Fisk University Library: 403; North Carolina Central University: 406; Shirley A. R. Lewis: 409; Eleanor**

Young Love: 416; **Fisk University Library:** 417; **Meharry Medical College Archives:** 421; **Julianne Malveaux:** 425; **Northern California Center for Afro-American History and Life:** 429; **Scurlock Studios, from the collections of Moorland-Springarn Research Center, Howard University:** 432; **Bennett College:** 433; **Dementia-Foster Studio:** 437; **New York Public Library for the Performing Arts:** 440; **Dana Smith:** 442; **Viola McFerren:** 445; **Doris Evans McGinty:** 449; **Leatrice B. McKissack:** 451; **All-Writing Services:** 455; **Marion Ettlinger:** 458; **AP/Wide World Photos:** 463; **New York Public Library for the Performing Arts:** 465; **Carrie Meek:** 468; **Fisk University Library:** 470; **AP/Wide World Photos:** 473; **AP/Wide World Photos:** 477; **Fisk University Library:** 479; **Florida Agricultural and Mechanical University:** 480; **Carol E. Moseley-Braun:** 482; **Fisk University Library:** 485; **Robert W. Woodruff Library, Atlanta University Center:** 486; **Reuters/Bettmann:** 490; **Fisk University Library:** 492; **AP/Wide World Photos:** 494; **Fisk University Library:** 497; **Smithsonian Institution:** 498; **Robert W. Woodruff Library, Atlanta University Center:** 500; **Office of the Secretary of Energy:** 507; **Lillian Adams Parks:** 510; **Lillian Rogers Parks:** 512; **Labadie Collection, University of Michigan:** 515; **Jennie R. Patrick:** 517; **Dorothy Smith Patterson:** 519; **Fisk University Library:** 522; **Louisiana State Museum:** 523; **Ponchitta Pierce:** 526; **Lou Jones:** 530; **Fisk University Library:** 535; **Fisk University Library:** 537; **Robert W. Woodruff Library, Atlanta University Library:** 541; **AP/Wide World Photos:** 543; **AP/Wide World Photos:** 546; **Fisk University Library:** 548; **Ken Barbos:** 550; **AP/Wide World Photos:** 553; **Johnson Publishing Company:** 554; **Helen Caldwell Day Riley:** 556; **Wilhelmina Jackson Rolark:** 568; **AP/Wide World Photos:** 571; **AP/Wide World Photos:** 573; **J. Clay Smith:** 575; **Russell-McCloud & Associates:** 578; **Northern California Center for Afro-American History and Life:** 580; **Xavier University Archives and Special Collections:** 582; **Oberlin College Archives:** 589; **AP/Wide World Photos:** 591; **Alumni Office, Fisk University:** 593; **Fisk University Library:** 596; **Jean C. Sinkford:** 598; **Library of Congress:** 601; **Edwin and Camie Smith:** 603; **Kentucky State University:** 605; **Mary Perry Smith:** 607; **Fisk University Library:** 609; **Fisk University Library:** 613; **Fisk University Library:** 615; **Thura Mack:** 616; **AP/Wide World Photos:** 620; **Scurlock Studios, from the collections of the Moorland-Sprigarn Research Center, Howard University:** 624; **Fisk University Library:** 626; **Scurlock Studios, from the collections of the Moorland-Springarn Research Center, Howard University:** 628; **University Publications of America:** 631; **AP/Wide World Photos:** 635; **Ellen F. Kirschman:** 638; **AP/Wide World Photos:** 641; **Fisk University Library:** 644; **Vivian Harsh Collection, Carter G. Woodson Library:** 647; **Fisk University Library:** 650; **Melba Tolliver:** 652; **UPI/Bettmann:** 654; **Schomburg Center for Research in Black Culture:** 656; **Smithsonian Institution:** 659; **Tennessee State University:** 661; **AP/Wide World Photos:** 664; **AP/Wide World Photos:** 667; **Yvonne Walker-Taylor:** 670; **Northern California Center for Afro-American History and Life:** 673; **Lincoln Center, Billy Rose Theatre Collection:** 675; **Juanita Karpf:** 677; **Fisk University Library:** 680; **Tuskegee University:** 684; **Schomburg Center for Research in Black Culture:** 686; **Maxine Waters:** 688; **Schomburg Center for Research in Black Culture:** 691; **Joann Watson:** 694; **Joseph Solomon, Carl Van Vechten Estate:** 696; **Mary Welcome:** 699; **AP/Wide World Photos:** 701; **Linda Wynn:** 702; **Schomburg Center for Research in Black Culture:** 705; **New York Public Library for the Performing Arts:** 708; **South Carolina State University:** 711; **UPI/Bettmann:** 713; **AP/Wide World Photos:** 717; **California State University, Northridge:** 720; **Schomburg Center for Research in Black Culture:** 722; **United Food and Commercial Workers International Union:** 724; *Atlanta Constitution:* 728.

Notable
Black
American
Women

Book II

Alice of Dunk's Ferry
(c. 1686-1802)
Oral historian, slave, toll collector

Although little is known about this curious figure, Alice of Dunk's Ferry was one of black America's early oral historians—a memory source for those whose lives overlapped with hers. A centenarian, she told firsthand accounts of people and places in early Philadelphia and nearby areas. This amazing woman, who is said to have lived to the age of 116, lit the pipe of William Penn, the "proprietor" of Pennsylvania.

Alice was born around 1686 in Philadelphia, Pennsylvania, to slave parents who had been brought from Barbados; she lived in Philadelphia until the age of ten. Her master then moved her to Dunk's Ferry, seventeen miles up the Delaware River in Bucks County. She lived as a slave in the Dunk's Ferry vicinity until the end of her life, collecting tolls at a bridge for some forty years.

Alice of Dunk's Ferry, as she became known, was a lively woman who enjoyed sharing her many vivid memories of the early days of the colony. She was respected by her contemporaries as an oral historian and they liked to hear her graphic recollections of people, places, and events. She herself was remembered as galloping on horseback to Christ Church in Philadelphia at the age of ninety-five. When she returned to Philadelphia for visits, Alice frequently described to those who would listen the original wooden structure of her beloved Christ Church. She said she could touch the ceiling with her hands. The bell to call the people was hung in the crotch of a tree close by. Alice loved to hear the Bible read and had a great regard for the truth. She remembered the ground on which Philadelphia stands when it was a wilderness, when native Americans hunted wild game in the woods while panthers, wolves, and other beasts of the forest prowled about the wigwams and cabins in which they lived.

Alice gradually lost her sight between the ages of ninety-six and one hundred. Miraculously, it returned. While blind, Alice was still skillful at catching fish and would row herself out into the stream to do so. She seldom returned without a

Alice of Dunk's Ferry

handsome supply of fish for her master's table. Her hair was perfectly white before she died, and the last of her teeth fell out when she was one hundred and sixteen years old, her supposed age when she died a few miles from Philadelphia at Bristol in Buck's County, Pennsylvania in 1802.

REFERENCES:

Blockson, Charles L. *Pennsylvania's Black History.* Philadelphia: Portfolio Associates, 1975.

Kaplan, Sidney. *The Black Presence in the Era of the American Revolution, 1770-1800.* Washington, D.C.: Smithsonian Institution, 1975.

Thomas, Isaiah. *Eccentric Biography; or Memoirs of Remarkable Female Characters, Ancient and Modern.* Worcester, Mass.: Isaiah Thomas, 1803.

Watson, John. *Annals of Philadelphia and Pennsylvania in the Olden Times.* Philadelphia: Edwin S. Stuart, 1900.

Charles L. Blockson

Ethel D. Allen
(1929-1981)
Physician, politician, women's rights advocate

From early on, Ethel D. Allen courted two loves—politics and medicine. As Philadelphia's first black woman Republican councilmember and later Pennsylvania's secretary of the commonwealth, she reigned as a clever, street-smart representative for her political constituents. As an osteopath, she was gentle and caring, especially when it came to Philadelphia's indigent community. Dubbed by others as "Doc" and self-proclaimed a "ghetto practitioner," Allen combined both of her interests to become a champion of women's and minority rights and health care for the poor. From that base, Allen evolved to become Pennsylvania's highest-ranking black female politician.

Allen once dreamed of becoming mayor of Philadelphia, but put the thought aside after she was appointed to the Pennsylvania cabinet post. By then, she thought that maybe one day she would find herself a Republican candidate for vice-president of the United States. That, she figured, would give her a natural progression to becoming president of the United States. Fate did not deem it so. Following complications from diabetes and heart surgery, Ethel Allen died December 16, 1981, at the age of fifty-two.

Allen was born in Philadelphia on May 8, 1929, one of three children in her family. She would live in Philadelphia for most of her life. Her father, Sidney S. Allen, Sr., born in Georgia, went as far as the seventh grade in school. He left the South and headed north at about age seventeen or eighteen. Sidney Allen grew up wanting to become a physician, but with rampant racism and the lack of educational opportunities for a black man, he became a self-employed tailor. His dream would later be realized by his daughter. Allen described her mother in the *Philadelphia Inquirer* as the proverbial housewife, a woman who took care of home and husband and was proud of being identified as Mrs. Sidney S. Allen, Sr.

Allen said in "A Minority of One," published in the *Philadelphia Inquirer,* that she had a sheltered childhood. "I had been exposed only to my relatives and white schoolmates. I spent all my spare time—virtually every day—at the Free Library. . . . There weren't that many children in my neighborhood and I very seldom ventured off our block." Allen helped her father by delivering clothes for him. Even though her parents were Baptists, Allen attended Catholic schools and throughout her life remained a Roman Catholic.

As a youngster, Allen found herself intrigued with and inspired by science and politics. She is quoted in "A Minority of One" as saying that she remembered wanting to be a physician from the time she was three and liking politics since age six. The article also states: "As a child, Ethel wanted to understand how things work—to make sense out of a universe that could hardly make sense to a sensitive black child in

Ethel D. Allen

North Philadelphia going to a white [Catholic] school. She had to understand why. How."

In the September 7, 1973, *Philadelphia Inquirer,* Allen said that during her childhood she "was always interested in science from age five up. I had an uncle who was a dentist. He motivated me tremendously toward the scientific field. He used to take me to his office, and even though I was never keen on pulling teeth, I was interested in his patient's reactions and fascinated by the camaraderie between him and his patients."

Still, it was politics that Allen seemed drawn to more and more. Her parents, who logged years of service as Democratic committee members in the twenty-ninth ward, got her a job as a page at the national conventions held in Philadelphia in the late 1940s. Elected officials and various political aspirants became her heroes. "Like most people thought about movie stars, I thought about politicians," Allen said in an interview with the *Philadelphia Inquirer*'s *Today* magazine. "Franklin Roosevelt was the man, and to see him first-hand, close-up, was just. . . . Well, he was my Number One man. And Mrs. Roosevelt was my Number Two gal." Mary McLeod Bethune, an advisor to President Roosevelt, was Allen's number one gal. During a time when few black women were recognized for their achievements, Bethune was Allen's role model.

While attending John W. Haliahan Girls Catholic High School, Allen managed the student council president campaign of another student. Always exploring new avenues, Allen also learned to play the trumpet and the piano. During her senior year at West Virginia State College, then an all-black school, she ran for council president and lost by two votes, one being her own. In the meantime, with a major in chemistry and biology and a minor in mathematics, Allen concentrated on schoolwork.

College was an exciting time for Allen, and West Virginia State College offered her an opportunity to see life from a different perspective. Up to that point, Allen's education had been in a predominantly white environment. "And although the discipline of Catholic schools does not permit open manifestations of racism, there were times when it was made very clear you were not expected to have intellectual achievement because black people were supposed to have smaller brains and all of that," Allen explained in "A Minority of One." Allen squeezed as much into her college years as she could, which included being a Latin scholar and a drama student. Following graduation, she worked as a chemist on an Atomic Energy Commission project.

Combines Medical Career with Politics

As a young woman, Allen continued attending Democratic and Republican national conventions and eventually became what was almost unheard of in those days—a black woman Republican. Eventually, Allen would introduce herself as a "BFR—a black female Republican, an entity as rare as a black elephant and just as smart." According to the *Philadelphia Inquirer's Today* magazine, the young politician stuffed envelopes and addressed flyers for local and national campaigns. In 1952, during the Dwight Eisenhower presidential campaign, "I got promoted from the mail department to scheduling and appointments for the Philadelphia area," Allen explained in *Today*.

Allen became a diligent worker, but always in the background. She had no aspirations for office at the time; politics was purely an avocation. Allen felt the need to pursue her lifelong ambition to become a physician, though in those times racism made it very hard for blacks to break into the medical field—twice as hard for a black man, even harder for a black woman. For seven years after graduation, Allen tried to get into medical school. Instead of opening, doors seemed to snap shut. She said of that experience in the *Philadelphia Inquirer:* "I was turned down many times with the usual response that they had 'no facilities for women physicians.'"

When she was finally accepted at the Philadelphia College of Osteopathic Medicine, Allen juggled her studies with fighting racism and sexism. She received her degree in osteopathic medicine in 1963, served an internship in Grand Rapids, Michigan, and then in 1964 returned to Philadelphia and began work in community medicine. Although she had an office, Allen saw many of her patients in the streets—literally—at Fifteenth Street and Columbia Avenue.

Allen was an aggressive and assertive advocate for the poor and disadvantaged. She referred to herself as a "ghetto practitioner." She faced incredibly difficult situations while trying to serve Philadelphia's poorest patients. For instance, her private practice was located in a neighborhood that was so rough that once drug addicts came into her office waiting room and asked her patients to stand up so they could cart off all her furniture.

Later, as medical director at the Spring Garden Community Center for the federally-funded Model Cities program, a job that paid $32,000 a year, Allen carried a gun on house calls. According to "A Minority of One," "One time when she answered a house call to examine a woman, she found herself in a trap. Four men came into the room to rob her because they assumed she would have drugs in her little black medicine satchel. Instead of getting drugs, all four found themselves looking into the barrel of Dr. Allen's conveniently-placed gun. She made them all undress and ordered them out into the street naked before making her getaway."

After that, Allen refused to answer house calls without a police escort. Eventually, Allen decided that she would try to help Philadelphia by fighting street crime from a council seat. In November of 1971 she ran for office against three-term city councilman Thomas McIntosh, a Democrat. During the campaign, she and McIntosh had one debate. According to the *Today* article, she stood and spoke first: "In the interest of brevity," she told the audience, "let me just say that I am a candidate. Whatever my opponent hasn't done, I will do. Whatever he has done, I will do better." Allen sat down.

McIntosh rose. He sputtered, then sat down. Allen beat him by some four thousand votes. The post paid $24,000 a year less that what she had been making, but Allen didn't seem to mind the cut in salary. The woman who stood just a whisper shy of five feet represented the city's fifth council district. The district's population was 60 percent black and included sections of Center City, Kensington, and North Philadelphia, which contained young middle-income and wealthy whites, Puerto Ricans, Slavs, Poles, and Lithuanians.

Allen, a stout woman with short hair, a booming voice, and an attention-grabbing manner, was a Republican in a chamber controlled by Democrats. She was a passionate advocate of women's rights and a champion of her black constituents. She was a liberal Republican who supported legal abortions. Her primary concerns also included the environment, housing, gang warfare, and drug problems. As a council member, she was studious yet sometimes theatrical, and still other times, she was somber and serious. She felt that one of her strong points was her scientific approach to her council work. "I do take a relatively scientific approach to politics," she said in "A Minority of One." "It's my research background coming out. I always do research. People don't always tell you the whole story, so you have to research." Away from city hall, she filled in for vacationing doctor friends, taught community medicine at Hahnemann Medical College, and acted as an advisor to black medical students.

As a councilmember Allen did not mince words or sugarcoat her feelings. According to the same article, when Philadelphia city council president George X. Schwartz was "expounding his gut feelings" on a proposed tunnel, Allen shot back: "As a physician, Mr. President, I'd say your gut was anesthetized." Another time, when a male councilman beat Allen and another female council member to introducing a sex discrimination bill, Allen called it "legislative plagiarism'' and told *Today* magazine: "We're going to make him an honorary member of women's liberation, and that's 'honorary' spelled O-R-N-E-R-Y.''

A Woman of Boundless Energy

In 1973 Allen was still single and lived at home with her parents in the house that she grew up in near Twenty-third Street and Ridge Avenue. Known as a woman of boundless energy, she remained unmarried and never had any children, though she acted as the legal guardian for a child named Kathy Ann, whose parents died shortly after her birth. She spent a lot of time making speeches, talking to church groups and students, and attending community and civic association meetings. She continued to devote three nights a week to her medical practice. A variety of interests filled her free time.

Allen loved political novels, once saying that she read "everything I can get my hands on about Richard Nixon, before and after Watergate,'' and was a fan of mysteries and good detective stories. According to the *Today* article, her other hobbies included photography ("I'm good at animals''), cooking ("I once beat a gourmet chef in a popover-baking contest''), art, music (both listening to and playing the piano, organ, and trumpet), clothes ("I have a real fetish for shoes''), and soap operas ("I'm an addict'').

After serving her first city council term, in 1975 Allen ran for council again, but this time for an at-large seat. She triumphed as the first black councilwoman elected to an at-large seat on the Philadelphia City Council. Allen became the GOP's top vote-getter in Philadelphia. *Esquire* magazine listed her as one of the nation's twelve outstanding women politicians. She remained a politician who did not bite her tongue. At a city council meeting she once spoke out against Mayor Frank L. Rizzo's position on a Puerto Rican housing project, warning him, "Una scupa nuova scazzivane,'' which in Italian means "a new broom sweeps clean.'' She further challenged him by stating, "If you push me, I may have to run against you, Mr. Mayor. And when I run, I win.''

In late 1975, upon self-examination, Allen found a lump in her left breast. A few days later she underwent a radical mastectomy. Always fun-loving, Allen tossed a champagne party in her hospital room. When her friends arrived, the chubby politician was sitting on Santa's lap and answering questions from reporters. Two days later, she appeared at a city council meeting in a wheelchair to cast the only opposing vote against a street vendors bill.

In 1976 the nation focused on Allen as the black female Republican who delivered a seconding speech for President Gerald Ford at the GOP national convention. Two years later, she was mentioned as a possible candidate and a two-to-one favorite for the Second Congressional District seat, but she decided against running.

Appointed Secretary of the Commonwealth

In January 1979, Allen told the press that Pennsylvania's newly elected governor, Richard Thornburgh, had first dis-

cussed the job of secretary of the commonwealth with her a few weeks earlier at the Pennsylvania Society dinner in New York City, where Allen was sounding out fellow Republicans and large political contributors to see if she would have enough political and financial support to run for mayor of Philadelphia. She had asked a Republican city leader for his assurance that she would be the sole GOP mayoral candidate in a closed primary in May. Allen said that without that pledge, she would not run for mayor. GOP officials did not give her the nod, so nothing was standing in the way of Allen making a change in political direction when Thornburgh officially offered her the job of secretary of the commonwealth. Allen accepted the $38,500-a-year appointment. The next day, while sitting in her office at Philadelphia City Hall, Allen celebrated in her down-to-earth fashion: she ordered out for a hamburger.

As secretary of the commonwealth, Allen was in charge of the state's election machinery, supervised the regulation of charities, and registered lobbyists and corporations. It was also her responsibility to license twenty-two professions and occupations. Though largely a ceremonial post, the job also required Allen to attend functions in the governor's stead.

Always popular in Pennsylvania, Allen began receiving widespread national media attention. All around the country, she became a role model for black youngsters. She was considered one of the nation's most influential and powerful black politicians.

Shortly following the appointment, a close friend of Allen artistically recreated the first moon landing with Allen's smiling face on a figure wearing a space suit and holding an American flag. It was published in the *Ebony* magazine article "Two States Choose Black Women as Secretaries.'' The caption to the picture originally read: "One giant leap for mankind.'' But the artist drew an "X'' across the word man and changed the caption to read: "One giant leap for WOM-ANkind.'' Allen hung the work on a wall in her office.

But the high tide Allen was riding as secretary of the commonwealth ebbed quickly. Governor Richard Thornburgh, who had eagerly embraced her, told Allen that she had violated procedures and must resign immediately. When Allen refused, the governor fired her, saying that Allen had accepted honorariums for speeches that had been prepared by state employees, and he linked that with a charge of absenteeism. Reportedly she had been absent twenty-one days during a forty-day stretch. Allen admitted that she had used a state worker to help write two speeches for which she earned one thousand dollars. She said that during her term, from February to October, she had delivered one hundred eighteen speeches and had received two thousand dollars for twelve of the appearances.

Community leaders said the governor's actions were "sexist'' and "racist.'' Black leaders said the firing reflected a double standard since the governor's office had admitted that three other cabinet members also had a large number of absences because they traveled extensively to perform daily administrative duties. In contrast, Allen told the press that she was not bitter about the incident. According to the *Philadelphia Daily News* for November 1, 1979, she called the situation "a most unusual affair that could have been handled differently," and she said that she remained "unbossed and unbowed."

Ironically, the reasons Thornburgh offered for Allen's dismissal matched those offered in 1977 by then governor Milton Shapp, who dismissed another black woman secretary of the commonwealth, C. Delores Tucker, who was accused of using state staff to help prepare speeches for which she was paid. At that time, C. Delores Tucker had been the highest ranking black woman in government in the United States.

After leaving the job, Allen worked for the Philadelphia School District as a school clinician. Her tenure there ended abruptly in October 1981 when she underwent open heart surgery at Hahnemann Hospital, where she had previously been a member of the staff. On December 3, she was transferred to the intensive care unit at Albert Einstein Medical Center, Northern Division. She remained in intensive care until December 16, when she died at the age of fifty-two. An editorial published in the *Philadelphia Inquirer* on December 19, 1981, summed up Allen's life by stating, "When Dr. Ethel D. Allen tackled a problem, which was often, she did so with enthusiasm and vigor that inspired others to join in the endeavor. When she sought to remedy an injustice, which was frequently, she held unwaveringly to the view that this world can be made a better place if people work hard enough and resolve firmly to make it so."

REFERENCES:

"Allen Not Bitter." *Philadelphia Daily News,* November 1, 1979.

"Council Pays Tribute to Dr. Ethel Allen." *Philadelphia Daily News,* December 18, 1981.

"Doc's Party Favorite." *Philadelphia Daily News,* January 3, 1979.

"Dr. Allen Tapped for Top D.A. Post." *Philadelphia Daily News,* January 2, 1979.

"Dr. Allen's Newest Patient: The City of Philadelphia." *Ebony* 28 (May 1973): 124-26, 128, 130-31.

"Dr. Ethel Allen Dies; Held Pennsylvania Job." *New York Times,* December 18, 1981.

"Dr. Ethel Allen Named to Pennsylvania Cabinet Post." *Jet* 55 (January 25, 1979): 7.

"Ethel Allen's Example: A Life Devoted to Service." *Philadelphia Inquirer,* December 19, 1981.

"I've Learned to Survive. . . ." *Philadelphia Inquirer, Today* section, January 1976.

"A Minority of One." *Philadelphia Inquirer,* September 7, 1973.

"Two States Choose Black Women as Secretaries." *Ebony* 34 (October 1979): 74-76.

Sandra D. Davis

Del Marie Neely Anderson
(1937-)
College president, educator, model

In July 1991, Del Marie Neely Anderson was appointed president of San Jose City College in San Jose, California. She became one of the small group of black women college presidents who call themselves "sister presidents" along with Johnetta Cole of Atlanta's Spelman College and Niara Sudarkasa of Lincoln University in Pennsylvania. She joined the ranks of new black college presidents heading predominantly nonblack institutions of higher education: John Slaughter (Occidental), Vera Farris (Stockton State), David Carter (Eastern Connecticut State), Adam Herbert (University of North Florida), and Josephine Davis (York College of the City University of New York). For sixteen years prior to her appointment as president, Anderson was a college professor and administrator at various schools in California. To finance her own education, Anderson worked a variety of jobs. Her decision to pursue a career in academia may seem somewhat unusual because she was once a highly successful *Ebony* Fashion Fair Model who graced the cover of the December 7, 1961, issue of *Jet* magazine.

Anderson was born on November 6, 1937, in the Deep South. The Vicksburg, Mississippi, native grew up in urban and rural southern environments. Her parents, Frank and Emma Williams, worked as laborers, and her great-grandmother lived on a farm where the young girl spent her summers. Reminiscing about her childhood, Anderson said in *Ebony* that she "did everything from cutting down trees to slaughtering animals and curing meats and canning foods."

Anderson graduated from the Cherry Street Elementary School and Bowman High School, both in Vicksburg, and was an honor student. Anderson attended Alcorn Agricultural and Mechanical College for two years, and she supported herself by working as a secretary there, all the while continuing to be an honor student. Realizing that remaining in Mississippi would not prepare her for the future she envisioned, Anderson went to California to further her education. She attended school on a part-time basis, again financing her studies by working. She obtained secretarial positions and was also employed at the San Diego Navy Electronic Laboratory and at the Veterans Administration Hospital Nursing Department and Speech and Hearing Clinic in San Francisco.

Anderson once considered a nursing career but decided that it would be too taxing physically and emotionally. Although it took her ten years, she completed her undergraduate degree in 1965 and then earned a master's degree in social work in 1967, both at San Diego State University. In a recent interview, Anderson humorously related that she still does her own personal correspondence and can still type faster than the average secretary.

Anderson's most interesting and unique job experience was as an *Ebony* Fashion Fair model. She had previously

Del Marie Neely Anderson

attended modeling school in San Francisco as a self-improvement project. When the Fashion Fair came to that city, she applied for a modeling job and, after an initial interview, was immediately hired. In an April 1992 *Ebony* article, Anderson discussed how excited she was to meet President John F. Kennedy at a White House luncheon and to learn that he knew about the organization because of his wife's involvement with the Fashion Fair in Boston. Although Anderson gave up her modeling career to complete her college degree, she still values the experience: "It has helped me a lot subsequently to be at ease in public situations, to feel comfortable with my body and in presenting myself."

Anderson loves being the "Boss" because it enables her to create opportunities to help people grow personally and professionally. She is proud of being a mentor and a frequently tough supervisor who has "carried a lot of people with her." This is most assuredly a carryover from her recollections of the many people who helped her when she was struggling to support herself and reach her educational goals. Anderson has no specific role models but has always admired certain strengths and qualities of successful people, especially the schoolteachers who reached out to her when she was a young girl, recognizing that she had the drive and potential to get ahead in life. She is quick to credit significant people who opened doors that furthered her career ambitions.

Anderson's Academic Career Begins

Anderson began her academic career in 1969 as assistant professor of social work at her alma mater, San Diego State

University, and then in 1972 moved to Grossmont College in El Cajon, California, as dean of counseling services, where she also worked with nursing students. Her next career move was to Los Angeles Harbor College in 1981 as dean of student services and later dean of students. While at Grossmont, she had served as mentor to a younger female colleague, Linda G. Salter, who later became president of Skyline College in San Bruno, California. The two had promised that the first one to "make it" would reach back and help the other, and that promise was kept. Salter was instrumental in Anderson's hiring in 1986 at Skyline as vice-president for instruction, a position enabling her to gain valuable management and administrative skills that enhanced her growing reputation and contributed to her being selected for the presidency at San Jose City College.

Anderson Becomes College President

Anderson survived a nationwide search for a president of San Jose City College and emerged as the top candidate from a field of 167 applicants. San Jose City College, a two-year public community college that was founded in 1921, has nearly 13,000 students and 390 faculty members. Unlike many other community colleges with a 100 percent commuter student population, San Jose City College provides student life activities and athletics, in addition to a full array of student services. Anderson has the same top priority as most other community college presidents, that of lowering dropout rates. She is also committed to upgrading physical facilities on the old campus and attracting young teachers to replace older faculty members nearing retirement. Her sixteen-year tenure as a community college administrator, extensive networking background, and continuous development of innovative educational programs will stand her in good stead as Anderson moves toward her goals.

Anderson's reputation was largely based on the highly innovative Model Matriculation Program she designed and implemented at Los Angeles Harbor College. She had long been disturbed over the negative results of the open-door policy of California community colleges. Since eight of every ten black California students are enrolled in community colleges, she was especially concerned about the negative effects on black students, many of whom were not receiving the education they needed to compete in the job market. "I turned the corner philosophically to end the 'revolving door syndrome,'" said Anderson. She created a new system designed to enable students to succeed academically and to be qualified to transfer to four-year colleges or to obtain worthwhile jobs. Strict requirements were expected of all prospective students at Harbor College, including orientation and placement testing. Anderson was severely criticized for raising academic standards and making mandatory the new procedures, especially by some blacks, who accused her of discriminating against black students. Because of the visible success of Anderson's model program, the California legislature took notice and appointed a blue ribbon commission to study it. The outcome was the passage of a state law mandating that all California community colleges implement the Model Matriculation Program.

Anderson is also proud of the strides made by California women in higher education: 33 percent of community college presidents are women; the same percentage holds for women at the dean's level, on boards of trustees, and in management positions. This record surpasses comparative figures for other higher education institutions and the corporate world, where women in California hold one of every eight top level positions.

Anderson is also involved in a unique civic endeavor that further illustrates the power of women. As her first major political initiative, the female mayor of San Jose, Susan Hammer, asked Anderson to chair Project Diversity, a policy-making body designed to promote equity among people of different race, gender, age, and physicality in city government. The group was commissioned to recruit applicants, review applications for city government commissions, and make recommendations for an approved list required by law to be used within a year. Anderson allowed no publicity about Project Diversity until the success of the plan was evident, then, the mayor could take full credit for the achievement. To date, San Jose is the only city to entrust such a project to a policy-making body, as opposed to an advisory body with no power for implementation.

Anderson is now embarking on a career as a writer. She has just completed a chapter on ''Non-Traditional Paths to Advancement'' for the book *Cracking the Wall: Women in Higher Education,* edited by Patricia Turner Mitchell, a professor at the University of San Francisco. Anderson is currently preparing to edit a book about the changing face of community colleges for Jossey-Bass Publishers.

Seemingly tireless and possessed of an enormous amount of energy, Anderson has even more professional and personal goals. She plans to continue writing and to learn more about corporate fund raising. Buying a piano and taking piano lessons are more immediate personal goals. Anderson is not a ''social joiner'' because her job entails chairing and attending meetings on a regular basis. Although she has no children from a previous sixteen-year marriage, she has always taken an interest in her nieces and nephews, participating in such activities as Little League and chaperoning duties. When her sister's husband was in the military, Anderson lived with her and helped raise her two children. She is happy that both of her parents are still living, her father in Oakland, California, and her mother in Vicksburg, Mississippi. Although she has no hobbies, Anderson is a big fan of jazz music, an avowed chocoholic, and a lover of haute couture clothes. Before career demands became so time consuming, she made most of her clothes, and she is known by her friends as the best bargain shopper around. Reading is also a favorite pastime.

Del Marie Anderson is unique as a person and as an educator. Once a high-fashion model, she is now a role model for thirteen thousand San Jose City College students and a mentor to those she believes have the drive and potential to achieve their goals. As Anderson pursued her own dreams, many people assisted her because they viewed her as having that same kind of initiative and capability. Now she is returning the favor by helping others.

REFERENCES:

Anderson, Del Marie. Telephone interview with Dolores Nicholson. July 22, 1992.

The College Handbook, 1993. 30th ed. New York: College Entrance Examination Board, 1993.

''From Fashion Fair Model to Role Model.'' *Ebony* 47 (April 1992): 112-17.

Peterson's Guide to Two-Year Colleges, 1993. 23rd edition. Princeton: Peterson's Guides, 1992.

''San Jose City College Gets First Woman Prexy, Educator Del Anderson.'' *Jet* 81 (October 21, 1991): 21.

Williams, Jeannette. Telephone interview with Dolores Nicholson. January 30, 1995.

Dolores Nicholson

Ivie Anderson
(1905-1949)
Singer

I vie Anderson, according to most critics, was the best and most important vocalist Duke Ellington ever had, musically on a par with the legendary top soloists of her era. She was already an established singer when she joined Ellington's band in February 1931, and she spent the most active part of the remainder of her career with him. Because Anderson suffered from severe asthma attacks, she eventually had to leave the Ellington band in 1942 on her doctor's advice that she refrain from keeping a rigorous touring schedule. During the few years left in her short life, she sang occasionally on the West Coast but concentrated her efforts first on her Los Angeles restaurant and then on real estate.

Ivie Marie Anderson was born in Gilroy, California, on July 10, 1905. (One dissenting source says she was born in Oklahoma, and one other gives 1904 for her birth date.) Little is known of her family, but it has been stated that her parents were named Smith. She was educated at a local convent, St. Mary's, until she was thirteen years old. Then she seems to have spent two years in Washington, D.C., where she studied voice with Sara Ritt. She returned to the West Coast and there began her professional career, possibly in 1921, as most sources have it; in a July 15, 1942, interview for *Down Beat* magazine, she herself said she began singing professionally in 1923, but she may have preferred to gloss over the fact that she was only fifteen or just over sixteen when she began to sing professionally in clubs.

Anderson Sings in Ellington Band

Anderson's first professional engagement was at Tait's Club in Los Angeles, and another early venue was Mike Lyman's Tent Cafe. She was then discovered by the produc-

Ivie Anderson

ing team of Fanchon and Marco and hired as a dancer in a show featuring Mamie Smith that they were sending out on a white vaudeville circuit. The soubrette in the revue fell ill, and Anderson gained a vocal spot. In 1925 she worked at the Cotton Club in New York and then toured with a *Shuffle Along* company. Upon her return to the West Coast, she worked with the bands of such musicians as Curtis Mosby, Paul Howard, and Sonny Clay. Anderson was probably the first black to sing backed by a white band—that of Anson Weeks—when she had a brief engagement with them at the Mark Hopkins Hotel in San Francisco in 1928. She sang at the West Coast Cotton Club in Culver City and, beginning in January 1928, went on a five-month tour with Sonny Clay in Australia. After this foreign tour, Anderson had a twenty-week tour of the West Coast as the star of her own revue. In 1930 she had a twenty-week engagement at the Grand Terrace in Chicago, where Earl Hines led the orchestra. Just after she finished the engagement, she was asked to join Duke Ellington's orchestra for a fourteen-week tour. She had a sensational opening with the band at the Oriental Theater in Chicago on Friday, February 13, 1931—they performed live between showings of a movie—and she remained with the Ellington organization until August 1942.

There is disagreement about how closely Ellington was involved in Anderson's hiring. Some sources imply that he actively pursued her, but in his memoir *Music Is My Mistress* he says that there was considerable discussion of the choice between May Alix and Ivie Anderson. May Alix was better known because she had had several quite successful records, but the producer chose Anderson. Ellington later found out

that the deciding factor was skin color. The producer felt that May Alix looked too white and that this could cause trouble on the road if someone decided she really was white. Ellington said in tribute to Ivie Anderson,

> I soon found that she was really an extraordinary artist and an extraordinary person as well. She had great dignity, and she was greatly admired by everybody everywhere we went, at home and abroad. She became one of our mainstays and highlights, and she gave some unforgettable performances. . . . They still talk about Ivie, and every girl singer we've had since has had to try to prevail over the Ivie Anderson image.

Anderson was the first African American singer to join a black band on a permanent basis. Black bands had regularly backed singers, as Ellington had done at the Cotton Club, but the singers were not part of the organization. Up to this time the singing in the Ellington band was done by drummer Sonny Greer or, reluctantly, by trumpeter Cootie Williams. Anderson, who quickly accepted Ellington's suggestion that she dress in white, fit in well with the organization. She and Sonny Greer developed a crowd-pleasing routine of verbal and musical interplay. In public she always behaved with propriety. Offstage with the band, however, it appears that her behavior was not always so angelic. In *Beyond Category*, John Hasse quotes onetime band member Rex Stuart, who describes her as "bossing the poker game, cussing out Ellington, playing practical jokes or giving some girl advice about love and life." It is also reported that Anderson was a consistent winner at poker.

The routine of dances and stage shows in the United States was broken by a fifty-five day tour of Great Britain, Holland, and France in 1933. Ivie Anderson's performance of "Stormy Weather" was a sensation, as was the entire show. With the Ellington orchestra, Anderson was a definite hit. While one British critic was vehement in his denunciation of Anderson—a jazz buff, he wanted to hear only the orchestra—Ellington was shrewd enough to realize that she was a drawing card with the public, both abroad and in the States, as well as a singer uniquely suited to his music.

Of course it was as a musician that she made her mark. Among her performances on important records are "It Don't Mean a Thing (If It Ain't Got That Swing)" (1932); "Raising the Rent" and "Stormy Weather" (both 1933); "Solitude" and "Mood Indigo" (both 1941); and "I Got It Bad (and That Ain't Good)" (1941). But, as Will Friedwald notes in *Jazz Singing,* "we remember her mainly for dozens of unimportant and wonderfully insignificant little songs that seemed to exist only for Anderson to sing: since many were in fact written by Ellington, this could well have been the case." Friedwald's favorites are "Love Is Like a Cigarette," "When My Sugar Walks down the Street," "Oh, Babe, Maybe Someday," and "The Chocolate Shake." To summarize Anderson's achievement, Donald Bogle, in *Brown Sugar*, quotes music critic Ralph Gleason, who was writing of Ellington's band in the 1960s.

In only one respect has this band lost with the years: There never was, nor will there ever be again, a vocalist of the caliber of Ivie Anderson. She was unique and irreplaceable. There have been other good singers with the band, but only Ivie sounded as if she was born to sing this music.

Ivie Anderson can be seen in two films. In the ten-minute short *A Bundle of Blues* (1933), which features Duke Ellington's orchestra, she sings "Stormy Weather." In the Marx Brothers' movie *A Day at the Races* (1937), she performs "All God's Chillun Got Rhythm."

Anderson's last important appearance on stage was in Ellington's *Jump for Joy* (1941), a musical show he produced in Los Angeles. In that year she opened a restaurant, Ivie's Chicken Shack, in Los Angeles, with the help of her first husband, Marques Neal. The following year ill health led her to leave Ellington's orchestra. Her restaurant was a success. In 1944, in a long list of his favorite eating places across the country, Ellington said, "Then there's Ivy Anderson's chicken shack in Los Angeles, where they have hot biscuits with honey and very fine chicken-liver omelets." Anderson also continued to do some singing locally and had a final recording session in 1946, when she was accompanied by musicians of the caliber of Charles Mingus, Willie Smith, and Lucky Thompson. At the time of her death, on December 28, 1949, she was married to Walter Collins and involved in real estate ventures. She had no will, so Collins and her former husband went to court to settle her estate.

Ivie Anderson never became a big recording star on her own, but she achieved success as a singer with the Duke Ellington orchestra. Both her work with the band and her 1946 recording session have been reissued. These performances stand as monuments to her musical talent.

REFERENCES:

Bogle, Donald. *Brown Sugar.* New York: Harmony Books, 1980.

Boyer, Richard O. "The Hot Bach." *New Yorker* (June 24, July 1, and July 8, 1944). Reprinted in *The Duke Ellington Reader,* edited by Mark Tucker. New York: Oxford University Press, 1993.

Chilton, John. *Who's Who of Jazz.* Philadelphia: Chilton, 1972.

Collier, James Lincoln. *Duke Ellington.* New York: Oxford University Press, 1987.

Dahl, Linda. *Stormy Weather.* New York: Pantheon, 1984.

Ellington, Edward Kennedy. *Music Is My Mistress.* Garden City, N.Y.: Doubleday, 1973.

Friedwald, Will. *Jazz Singing.* New York: Charles Scribner's Sons, 1990.

Gammond, Peter. *The Oxford Companion to Popular Music.* New York: Oxford University Press, 1991.

Hasse, John Edward. *Beyond Category.* New York: Simon and Schuster, 1993.

Kernfeld, Barry, ed. *The New Grove Dictionary of Jazz.* New York: Macmillan, 1988.

Larkin, Colin, ed. *The Guinness Encyclopedia of Popular Music.* Chester, Conn.: New England Press Associates, 1992.

Miller, Paul Edward. "Ivie Joined the Duke for Four Weeks, Stays with Band for Twelve Years." *Down Beat* (July 15, 1942). Reprinted in *The Duke Ellington Reader,* edited by Mark Tucker. New York: Oxford University Press, 1993.

Robert L. Johns

Leafy Anderson
(c. 1887-1927)
Religious leader

Leafy Anderson, also known to her religious followers as Mother Leafy Anderson, is celebrated as the originator of the numerous Spiritual churches in New Orleans. Current Spiritualism is a syncretistic religious movement that often incorporates a large amount of Voodoo; some leaders of present-day churches trace their origins to Marie Laveau, the nineteenth-century Voodoo leader. More leaders trace their founding to Leafy Anderson, and some of these are very emphatic in repudiating any connection with Voodoo, just as Anderson herself did. It is certain that Anderson was very influential in developing the movement and in training its leaders. Part of the attraction of Spiritualism was its provision of large opportunities for women to assume prominent roles. During the first fifteen years of the religion's existence in New Orleans, its leadership was almost exclusively made up of women. Little of Anderson's life and activities can now be traced, but enough information exists to confirm her significance.

Black and white Spiritual churches in the United States ultimately trace their modern ancestry to American Spiritualism, which arose from the spirit rappings that Kate Fox claimed she began to understand on March 31, 1848. Spirit rappings are sounds supposed to have been made by ghosts. The Fox sisters said that the rappings came from their spirit contact, Mr. Splitfoot (Charles B. Roena, who had been murdered in their house earlier). In reality, the Fox sisters were cracking the joints in their big toes. Experimentation with and belief in spiritualism became widespread, and in the late nineteenth century, believers began to organize churches with services much like those of Protestant churches, except for the differences resulting from such practices as receiving spirit greetings and messages during the service. Other important activities were the holding of seances and the organization of development classes to further psychic ability.

Black Spiritual churches began to be organized in the first two decades of the twentieth century. One of the earliest known advertisements for a Spiritual church in a black newspaper appeared in the *Chicago Defender* on August 28,

1915. Although little is known of the early life and background of Anderson, she appears to have been born around 1887 in Wisconsin; she was of black and Native American ancestry. Some of her followers say that she claimed to be half Mohawk. She established the Eternal Life Christian Spiritualist Church in Chicago in 1913, when she would have been about twenty-six years old.

In 1920 Anderson moved to New Orleans to establish a new church. This seems to be the most accurate date, although Zora Neale Hurston said the church was founded in 1918 and Robert Tallant, in *Voodoo in New Orleans,* cited 1921. Either before or after coming to New Orleans, Anderson also worked in Little Rock, Memphis, Pensacola, Biloxi, and Houston, as well as in smaller towns. At her death she was head of an association of churches based in these places. When she arrived in New Orleans, she was accompanied by her spirit contact, an Indian named Black Hawk. There is a historic Black Hawk, a leader of the Sauk and Fox who was particularly prominent in an 1832 uprising. The authenticity of his 1882 autobiography is disputed, but Anderson was quite probably familiar with it. According to Anderson, Black Hawk was the saint for the South and White Hawk was the saint for the North. Black Hawk made his way into successor Spiritual and Voodoo churches, where his image may occupy a place alongside Jesus, the saints, angels, and Moses. He is also celebrated in rituals and ceremonies. Another popular spirit guide associated with Anderson is Father John (also known as Father Jones—it is not always easy to distinguish the pronunciation of the two in New Orleans). Father John could derive from a famous mid-nineteenth-century practitioner of Voodoo or from a patent medicine called Father John's Medicine. Claude Jacobs and Andrew Kaslow, in their *The Spiritual Churches of New Orleans,* quote the Tallant archive for an explanation given by two followers:

> Leafy Anderson said Father John was a great doctor and a great minister. Call him and pay him and see if you won't get over it. Just like they say "Heal me. I'm going to St. Jude to be healed." Tell Father John to heal me. . . . [Father John] was a spirit, somebody that she knew in spirit that came to her, like Black Hawk did, like a guide.

Queen Esther, another important guide also introduced by Anderson, has a strong appeal to current churches, whose leadership is still two-thirds women.

Church Flourishes in New Orleans

On October 25, 1920, Anderson was able to get a Louisiana state charter for her organization, which eventually occupied Eternal Life Christian Spiritualist Church Number 12 on Amelia Street. She is said to have experienced considerable difficulty obtaining official recognition; at one point she was under police surveillance and even jailed. It is claimed that she overcame her difficulties by giving a reading to the judge and telling him things about himself that were not widely known. Her church developed a large congregation, and both blacks and whites visited her for readings. (Spiritual churches in New Orleans in the 1920s and 1930s often had

interracial congregations that drew large numbers of Italian Americans.) Not only were Anderson's readings popular, her training classes also enrolled some eighty aspiring leaders. Her first year of classes seems to have earned her fifteen hundred dollars. Jacobs and Kaslow list Mothers L. Crosier, Lena Scovotto, Alice Mancuso, Dora Tyson, and Bessie S. Johnson, and Father Lloyde Thomas as being noted followers of Anderson. Mother Catherine Seals also trained with Anderson. Tallant quotes a Mother Doris (Dora Tyson?), who was then head of her own church and also in Anderson's first class, as saying,

> There was eighty-five to one hundred of us in her first class and she charged a dollar a lesson. She taught healin' and prophesyin' and callin' up spirits. Of course most of 'em didn't ever finish 'cause everybody ain't got the *power,* but most of the Mothers in New Orleans now learned what they know from Mother Anderson.

There are few contemporary printed sources about Anderson and the movement, but the 1926 Eternal Life Spiritual Church Association convention did receive press coverage in the *Louisiana Weekly,* December 4, 1926, as reported by Jacobs and Kaslow. Two special events highlighted the conference. Since the convention took place near Thanksgiving, there was a skit about the Mayflower complete with spirit messages from the ship. Later, during the final session, there was a special Black Hawk service, during which Anderson presented four spirits, Father Jones, White Hawk, the Virgin Mary, and finally Black Hawk. The only other contemporary source for church activities found by Jacobs and Kaslow tells of a lecture given by white Spiritual leader Dr. F. Robertson of Lily Dale, New York, in early 1927. On this occasion there was also another dramatic presentation, *A White Man's Sin and a Squaw's Revenge.* Anderson played the woman, who was taken possession of by a powerful spirit.

Anderson's activities were lucrative from the beginning of her work in New Orleans, and according to Jacobs and Kaslow, she "dressed lavishly, favoring lace, sequins, expensive shoes, and lots of jewelry." On her dress for church services, Tallant cites Mother Doris, who said,

> "Sometimes she wore all white wit' a purple veil, but other times she wore a gold gown wit' a Black Hawk mantle over her shoulders; it had a picture of Black Hawk sewed on it. Once in a while she wore a man's full dress suit, but that was only for special occasions." Church services, classes, and readings were not Anderson's only source of income. Additional fund-raisers included parties on the roof of the building, featuring dancing to jazz bands. Dances included the shimmy and the jitterbug.

Mother Leafy Anderson's death was announced on the front page of the *Louisiana Weekly* of December 17, 1927. She had been sick for only a few days and died of complications from a cold. Her followers believe that she still appears to them to express her wishes. Anderson, like most Spiritual leaders, owned the church property, which passed on to her niece, A. Price Bennett, who became the new pastor. The inventory of her estate lists few assets: $36 in two banks, two pianos valued at $75, and six lots valued at $8,800. Bennett ran into financial difficulties by 1930, lost a building through foreclosure, and was accused by church members of mismanagement of church funds. Despite the failure of Mother Leafy Anderson to leave a strong institution behind, the religious impulses she both responded to and originated are still influential. She is also an exemplar of the response of some black women to traditional male domination of visible leadership roles in church organizations.

REFERENCES:

Baer, Hans A. *The Black Spiritual Movement: A Religious Response to Racism.* Knoxville: University of Tennessee Press, 1984.

Jacobs, Claude F., and Andrew J. Kaslow. *The Spiritual Churches of New Orleans.* Knoxville: University of Tennessee Press, 1991.

Melton, J. Gordon. *The Encyclopedia of American Religions.* 3 vols. Reprint. Tarrytown, N.Y.: Triumph Books, 1991.

Tallant, Robert. *Voodoo in New Orleans.* 1946. Reprint. New York: Collier Books, 1962.

COLLECTIONS:

Materials on Leafy Anderson are also found in the Robert Tallant Collection, Federal Writers Project, in the New Orleans Public Library.

Robert L. Johns

Naomi Bowman Talbert Anderson

Naomi Bowman Talbert Anderson

(1843-?)

Temperance leader, suffragist, civil rights activist, writer

Naomi Bowman Talbert Anderson is an example of a black American woman whose insight and selflessness benefitted her family, gender, and race. She wrote on temperance and women's rights, lectured and campaigned on behalf of women's suffrage, and was a staunch advocate of human rights.

Anderson was born on March 1, 1843, in Michigan City, Indiana, one of three children born to Elijah and Guilly Ann Bowman, who were natives of Ohio. They were a family of moderate means, but, more importantly, the Bowmans were free blacks.

Naomi Anderson was effectively barred from the segregated Indiana public schools. Since there were only two black families, including the Bowmans, in Michigan City, there was no school for black children. As a result, Anderson's mother hired a private teacher. This reaction to discrimination served as an early lesson to young Naomi that determined individuals can overcome barriers. Ironically, the white community noticed Anderson's poetic talent and unlocked the door to a public education by admitting the twelve-year-old to a previously all-white school. Her mother's dream was that both of her daughters would graduate from Oberlin College (the first college in the United States to admit students regardless of race or gender); however, her father did not share that dream. When his wife died during Naomi's seventeenth year, he dismissed additional education for Naomi as unnecessary.

Her mother's death and the lack of opportunity to attend college were only two of the misfortunes Anderson experienced within a relatively brief period of time. Before her twenty-first birthday, she also mourned the deaths of her brother and sister. Prior to her sister's death, Anderson married William Talbert, a barber from Valparaiso, Indiana. Several months later, she returned to Michigan City to care for her dying sister. The Talberts remained in Michigan City for five years, and during that time they buried their first-born, a son. In 1868, along with their second son and Elijah Bowman, they moved to Chicago.

Begins Temperance Work and Public Opposition to Discrimination

Anderson became a public figure while in Chicago. She was involved with the temperance work of the International

Organization of Grand Templars, and in 1869 Anderson spoke in favor of suffrage at the first Woman's Rights Convention. In 1869 and throughout the 1870s she wrote articles for newspapers, including the *Chicago Tribune* and the *Dayton Journal,* and lectured in Illinois, Indiana, and Ohio advancing the causes of women, Christianity, and temperance. Terborg-Penn wrote in *Black Women in America* that Anderson "was part of a growing number of African American women who felt the sting of both racism and sexism and decided to speak against them."

In 1869 the family moved to Dayton, Ohio. Over the years, the Talberts had two more children before William became ill. After he got sick, Anderson moved with her family to Portsmouth, Ohio, and supported her dependents by working first as a hairdresser, then as an organizer and manager of an orphanage for blacks, and finally as a teacher. William Talbert died in December 1877.

In 1879 Anderson moved with her children and father to Columbus, Ohio, where she continued to work as a hairdresser in addition to writing articles in favor of temperance and women's rights. In May 1881 she married Lewis Anderson; they lived on a farm near Columbus for the next three years. In 1884 they moved to Wichita, Kansas, where Lewis Anderson became a bank employee.

In Wichita, Anderson continued to write poetry, lecture, support temperance, and advocate women's rights. As a member of the Women's Christian Temperance Union, she campaigned along with her white peers for the state woman suffrage referendum. In addition, Anderson continued to criticize what she considered the misguided notions of blacks who wanted equality along with separatism and whites who viewed blacks as foreigners. As noted by Monroe Majors in *Noted Negro Women,* she wrote:

> Our leaders are wrong in fighting and clamoring for "social equality" and at the same time holding themselves aloof and claiming to be a separate people. . . . We are one and the same people, made so by the strongest ties of nature, bone and flesh of every nationality of white men in this country. . . . We are not Negroes, but Americans, because we were born here in America. Negroes are foreigners, we are not foreigners, hence not Negroes, but Americans, and not until we walk side by side with the white people claiming no nationality save that of American citizens and knowing no people but God's people, will we ever get our rights.

During the late 1880s, a children's home was established in Wichita. When Anderson discovered that black children were excluded, she convinced other black women to help her establish a home for black children. Their efforts were successful: by 1890 their home was operational and received monthly city and county stipends.

Subsequent events of Anderson's life included a move to California by 1895, where she continued to promote the suffrage movement. Her sisters in suffrage, including Susan B. Anthony, praised her work in San Francisco. However,

according to *Black Women in America,* Anderson's name did not appear in the National American Woman Suffrage Association proceedings after 1895.

Anderson had expressed an interest in writing her autobiography; whether she even began this effort apparently is yet to be determined. The details of her life from the 1890s on have received little documentation, and the exact year of her death is not known. Nevertheless, Anderson's contributions to nineteenth-century America are significant. She was a pioneer in the areas of temperance, women's rights, and civil rights, daring to voice her discontent about the mistreatment of individuals because of their race, gender, or age. She was eloquent and steadfast in her written and spoken opposition. Anderson was also a literary pioneer; her newspaper articles are a rare, early example of published protest by a black woman. Her verses also represent unusual published examples of a nineteenth-century black woman's poetic voice.

Several lines from Anderson's "Centennial Poem," published initially in 1876 and again in Majors's *Noted Negro Women,* aptly describe her philosophy. "We're free to do, as all are free . . . And we will serve both Nation and State / As justice doth command." Anderson wanted individuals to take advantage of their freedom, seek their rights, and improve their communities and the nation. Whether lecturing, writing articles, creating poetry, or directly helping others, Naomi Bowman Anderson's objective was empowerment.

REFERENCES:

Hine, Darlene Clark, ed. *Black Women in America.* Brooklyn: Carlson Publishing, 1993.

Majors, Monroe A. *Noted Negro Women.* Chicago: Donohue & Henneberry, 1893.

Linda M. Carter

Violette Neatley Anderson
(1882-1937)
Lawyer, reformer, clubwoman

Violette N. Anderson's legal career was punctuated by a whole series of "firsts" for which she is best known. The entire fabric of her life, however, was innovative. As a businesswoman, lawyer, and clubwoman, she expanded the traditional roles of women.

Violette N. Anderson was born in London, England, on July 16, 1882. Her mother, Marie Jordi Neatley, was German, while her father, Richard Neatley, was of West Indian descent. Not much is known about her parents except that they

Violette Neatley Anderson

arrived in the United States while Violette was still a young child. The family settled in Chicago. Violette Neatley was educated in the Chicago public schools, graduating from the North Division High School in 1899. She also attended Chicago Antheneum from 1902 to 1903 and the Chicago Seminar of Sciences from 1912 to 1915.

Neatley was a member of Saint Thomas Episcopal Church, which was founded in 1879. The first predominantly black Episcopal church in Illinois, it numbered among its congregants some of the most prominent black citizens of Chicago, including a number of those who later formed the Old Settlers Club, an influential organization composed of Chicago's earliest black settlers and their descendants. The Old Settlers Club, formed around 1900, was known both for its exclusivity and for its social and political weight. By 1916, it was located on South Indiana Avenue and boasted an enrollment of over six hundred members. Political activism also characterized Saint Thomas's history; several Illinois supporters of the Niagara Movement, the organization founded by W. E. B. Du Bois as a more radical alternative to Booker T. Washington's cautious positions on civil rights, were among the members. In 1909 the movement merged with the NAACP.

Neatley married Amos Preston Blackwell on June 21, 1899. That marriage lasted a stormy seven years. Violette Blackwell put a notice in the *Broad Ax,* September 15, 1906, signifying her intentions of dissolving her marriage. She cited her husband's cruelty as the main reason for its failure. In December of 1906 she remarried, this time to a Dr. D. H. Anderson.

The year before Anderson's first marriage dissolved, she began her career in the legal field as a court reporter. She worked as a court reporter from 1905 to 1920, operating a successful stenography, shorthand, and court reporting business in the downtown district. According to *Crisis* magazine, "all the colored lawyers and many noted white lawyers" were among her patrons. At a time when the only professions open to black women were as nurses, musicians, and teachers, Anderson stood out. As late as 1910, the United States census showed 65 percent of black women working as domestic servants. Anderson was evidently not satisfied with successfully running a business; she wanted more. She decided to become a lawyer.

Anderson Becomes a First for Illinois

Anderson was part of a rising group of young black women who dared to make the jump from being court reporters, stenographers, and wives of lawyers to being lawyers themselves. She began studies at Chicago Law School in 1917 and graduated in 1920, having passed the Illinois state bar examination in the spring of that year. At the graduation exercises of the Chicago Law School on June 20, 1920, Anderson received two honorary citations—one for scholarship and one for her thesis on marriage and divorce. She was the only woman member of the class of 1920 and the first black woman to graduate from any law school in the state of Illinois. She was also one of the class officers for that year. The *Broad Ax* praised her as the "colored woman disciple of the great Blackstone in the Sucker State."

In the summer of 1920 Anderson married again, this time to Albert E. Johnson, a pharmacist. While the fate of her second husband is not documented, she continued to carry his name throughout her professional career after her remarriage. Anderson's third marriage was widely reported as a major social event. According to the *Broad Ax,* Anderson and Johnson had the distinction of being the "first couple to be married at Idlewild." Idlewild, Michigan, was America's first and most famous summer resort for blacks north of the Ohio River. Located in northern Michigan on some thirty-five hundred acres of woodland, Idlewild became a "Black Eden" or haven for the black elite, who were prohibited from vacationing with their white brethren. It was founded by four white middle-aged men who used advertisements and articles in black newspapers to lure blacks into buying the lots. Idlewild numbered among its owners Daniel Hale Williams, Edward H. Wright, Louis B. Anderson, and many others who had purchased the land for development. Violette N. Anderson served as secretary of the Idlewild Lot Owners Association. Later, such dignitaries as Madame C. J. Walker, Charles Chestnut, and social reformer Irene McCoy Gaines purchased their own lots and built summer cottages there. Anderson and Johnson fit easily into the social circle at Idlewild.

Anderson and Johnson's marriage was a gala occasion. The service was read by H. Franklin Bray, a minister. The couple's cottage, Miramar, had been decorated for their honeymoon. The bride was attended by the elite of the social matrons of Chicago. Evelyn Casey later described the bride in the *Broad Ax* as "dressed in a simple lingerie frock of white and yellow with a garden hat covered with goldenrod and carried a wonderful bouquet of the same flowers." At the midnight hour the guests formed a party with fife and drums, bells and whistles, and "rent the night air around Miramar" with revelry.

Fame in the Legal Profession Mounts

Violette N. Anderson began her extensive and successful career as an attorney in that same year. Thus began a series of "firsts" for which Anderson is best known. She served as the first legal adviser for the Northern District of Federated Women's Clubs. She was the first black woman to be admitted to practice in the United States District Court, Eastern Division. In 1922 she was appointed as the first black woman assistant city prosecutor in Chicago. She made history in January 1926 when she became the first black woman admitted to practice before the Supreme Court of the United States, after proving that she had practiced for more than five years before the highest court of Illinois. Judge James A. Cobb of Washington, D.C., approved her application.

One has only to read through the papers of the day to see that Anderson's law practice kept her busy. Her practice ran the gamut from criminal to contractual law. She had an office in the downtown lawyer's district for several years before moving her practice to her Southside home on Fifty-third at Michigan Avenue. The newspapers of the day also described her as a very civic-oriented clubwoman.

The objections of Chicago's white lawyers to black membership in the Chicago Bar Association resulted in black lawyers, under the leadership of men like Edward H. Wright, forming an association of their own in 1915. It was called the Cook County Bar Association. Its membership ranged from 50 to 150, and it took an active part in judicial elections. Anderson was elected as its first vice-president.

She was also active as a member of the Friendly Big Sisters League of Chicago. The Friendly Big Sisters League was organized in 1913 with ten members. Social reform and charity work were but two of its objectives. In 1918 the club began buying a seven-room house to be used as a home for dependent black women and children. It was simply called the "Home." Anderson was president of the organization during the year of 1926. According to the papers of Irene McCoy Gaines, Anderson listed in her annual report some of her goals and accomplishments: "It has been my aim during the past year to bring to the notice of the public The Friendly Big Sisters League and its work; we have made a $1500 payment on our mortgage; we have sheltered 32 girls." She concluded her report by reminding the club members not to stop working. She urged them to keep on striving and working together and to try to establish a permanent office in Springfield to lobby for reform.

Anderson's other activities included serving as chairwoman of the legal status bureau of the League of Women Voters; holding the position of secretary of the Pan-Hellenic Conference; and acting as a member of the executive board of the Chicago Council of Social Agencies. She devoted the most time, however, to her work as an active member of Zeta Zeta Chapter, Zeta Phi Beta Sorority.

Addresses Plight of Tenant Farmers

Anderson was the national president of the sorority from 1933 until her death in 1937. She used her formidable legal experience and her organizational skills developed in club work to lobby the congressmen of Illinois to urge passage of the controversial Bankhead-Jones Bill in 1936. She also urged the heads of the other forty-two chapters of Zeta Phi Beta Sorority to do the same with their congressmen. The Bankhead-Jones Bill was designed to help black tenant farmers and sharecroppers who lived in abject poverty in a system that kept them virtual slaves due to the expenses they were required to pay to the owners of the land they worked. The bill proposed lending them money to buy small farms of their own with repayment set on a long-term scale with low interest rates. Due in large part to the efforts of individuals like Anderson, who lobbied tirelessly on behalf of the tenant farmers, President Roosevelt appointed a special task force to investigate the problem of farm tenancy and to recommend a program to help landless farmers. In February 1937, the President's Committee on Tenancy issued their report and suggestions. Their suggestions read suspiciously like the Bankhead-Jones Bill introduced the year before. In July 1937, Congress passed the Bankhead-Jones Act.

Anderson lived long enough to see her efforts on behalf of the tenant farmers result in the passage of the Bankhead-Jones Act. She died of colon cancer on December 21, 1937, in Provident Hospital. She was to have presided at the boule of the Zeta Phi Beta Sorority that was being held in Houston, Texas, December 27-30, 1937. As she lay on her sick bed, she continued working right up to the end. Her last words to Claude Barnett were:

> Tell the girls to keep on going ahead. Put over the boule with a bang. Don't let my passing throw the slightest shadow of gloom. The organization has a grand mission before it.

Violette N. Anderson was buried in Lincoln Cemetery on December 24, 1937. She left only one surviving family member, her widower, Albert E. Johnson. In January 1938 the Zetas held a memorial for Anderson in Houston, Texas. They donated to the Chicago Public Library a portrait of her that now hangs in the Vivian G. Harsh Research Collection at Carter G. Woodson Regional Library.

REFERENCES:

"Attorney Violette N. Anderson. 1st Colored Woman Graduate from Any Law School." *Broad Ax,* June 26, 1920.

Brawley, Benjamin. *Negro Builders and Heroes.* Chapel Hill: University of North Carolina Press, 1937.

Buckler, Helen. *Doctor Dan.* Boston: Little, Brown, 1954.

Davis, Elizabeth. *The Story of the Illinois Federation of Colored Women's Club.* Chicago: n.p., 1922.

DeZutter, Hank. "Black Eden." *Reader* (June 4, 1993): 12-18.

Drake, St. Clair. *Churches and Voluntary Associations in the Chicago Negro Community.* Chicago: Illinois Writers Project, 1940.

"Famous Woman Attorney Dies." *Amsterdam News* (New York), January 1, 1938.

Gosnell, Harold. *Negro Politicians.* Chicago: University of Chicago Press, 1967.

"Miss Violette N. Anderson Will Soon Become a Full Fledged Lawyer." *Broad Ax,* March 13, 1920.

Negro in Chicago, 1779-1927. Chicago: Washington Intercollegiate Club of Chicago, 1927.

"Rites Friday for Atty. V. M. Anderson." *Chicago Defender,* December 25, 1937.

"Some Chicagoans of Note." *Crisis* 20 (August 1920): 237-42.

Spear, Allan F. *Black Chicago: The Making of a Negro Ghetto, 1890-1920.* Chicago: University of Chicago Press, 1967.

Turner, Geneva. "Zeta Phi Beta Sorority, Inc." *Negro History Bulletin* 15 (May 1952): 156-59.

"Violette N. Anderson: 1st Colored Woman to Pass the Bar Examination." *Broad Ax,* August 21, 1920.

Who's Who in Colored America, 1928. Yonkers on the Hudson, N.Y.: Christine E. Burckel, 1927.

Who's Who in Colored America. 5th ed. Brooklyn: Thomas Yenser, 1940.

"Zetas Hold Memorial for Miss Anderson." *Norfolk Journal and Guide,* January 8, 1938.

COLLECTIONS:

Documents relating to the life and work of Violette Neatley Anderson are located in the Claude A. Barnett Papers and the Irene McCoy Gaines Papers at the Chicago Historical Society; and in the Illinois Writers Project/"Negro in Illinois" Papers, Vivian G. Harsh Research Collection of Afro-American History and Literature, Box 43, Chicago Public Library.

Beverly A. Cook

Lucie Bragg Anthony
(1870-1932)
Physician, educator, temperance leader, musician, writer

Trained as a physician, Lucie Bragg Anthony made her contribution to society in education. She left an immeasurable mark in Sumter County, South Carolina, where she was known as Dr. Bragg. The first supervisor of Sumter County Colored Schools, she recognized the many needs of

Lucie Bragg Anthony

students, teachers and the community. Establishing schools as well as improving teaching, teacher salaries, and health conditions became her primary focus. For sixteen years, from 1915 to 1931, Bragg worked tirelessly and relentlessly in Sumter County. Rather than practice medicine, she spent her life in the field of education and incorporated her medical training in teaching adults and youth good health practices. The motivation that fueled her life's work is expressed in her book, *Little Clusters:*

> In the vineyard of our Father
> Daily work we find to do.
> Scattered gleanings we may gather
> Tho we are but young and few,
> Little Clusters, Little Clusters
> Help to fill the garners, too.

Lucie Bragg Anthony was born in Warrenton, North Carolina, on December 4, 1870. Her parents, George Freeman and Mary Bragg, later moved to Petersburg, Virginia, where they were active in the Episcopal Church and where Lucie's father served as junior warden. The Braggs also had a son, George Freeman Jr.

Anthony enrolled at Oberlin College and Conservatory in 1889 and graduated in 1893. Still looking for a way to serve humanity, she entered Meharry Medical College in 1902 and graduated in 1907. She married Francis W. Anthony, an African Methodist Episcopal Zion minister, on September 4, 1908. He died February 20, 1928, in Sumter, South Carolina. They had no children. Francis Anthony's church assignments may account for their moves to Kentucky, where Lucie

Anthony was principal of the Saint Clemens School in Henderson, and to Texas, where she was principal of a church school in San Antonio. She was also a kindergarten teacher at the John Hopkins Home for Colored Children in Charlotte, North Carolina. Later she established the industrial department at Clinton College, Rock Hill, South Carolina. There is no evidence that she ever practiced medicine.

In the early 1910s, Francis and Lucie Anthony moved to Sumter, South Carolina, where he was minister of the Clinton Chapel AME Zion Church. Their home was located at the corner of Oakland and Purdy Streets.

Vision Becomes Reality

Still imbued with the zeal of serving others, in 1915 Lucie Anthony became the first county supervisor for black rural schools in Sumter County. Her goals for the schools were published in her book, *A Concise History of Sumter County Colored Schools 1915-1931*. She said:

> We had in the beginning four things in our vision
> for the work. The first, to extend the terms, second
> to increase the salary; third to get better school
> buildings, fourth to help make better teachers.

Anthony's tasks as county supervisor were not deterred when school superintendent J. H. Haynesworth stated, "he had very little, if anything" to assist her. She raised funds at events such as field days. Anthony identified home conditions and social issues of the county and sought improvements. Between 1918 and 1920, she formed demonstration clubs to improve the family health through better diets. Not only were food preservation projects initiated, but in 1920 and 1921, milk was provided to families. The Milk Campaign resulted in the state matching a dollar for every dollar raised. The campaign improved the number of milk-producing cows owned by families and raised the milk consumption level for adults and undernourished children. Still concentrating on the home, Anthony oversaw the construction by and for students of nine hundred garments for everyday use. Useful items of wood such as chairs and stools were made for home.

Anthony knew that in order to have good schools, teachers had to be trained and rewarded for their work. She began a summer school program where teachers could be trained and skills upgraded. She also sought salary increases for them. Prizes and awards were offered as incentives for the teachers to accomplish the various programs that were part of Anthony's initiative.

In 1930 and 1931, temperance work became a part of her mission in the county, and she organized thirty-one temperance clubs and received hundreds of signed pledges from those who would abstain from drinking alcohol. She gave a prize for the essay "Why I Should Not Drink Alcohol."

The talented, petite, and light-brown-complexioned Anthony wrote *Little Clusters* for use in instruction. It was termed "a mixed method for beginners" by the author. The text demonstrated lessons with stories and also gave health notes and information on child study, psychology, and child astrology, which described personality traits of children born in each month of the year. There were spelling lessons and instruction in numbers, language and geography. Included for character building were the Ten Commandments and the Lord's Prayer. Anthony also included motion songs with words and music which she had written, such as "Paper Cutting, Weaving Songs" and "Busy Little Fingers."

Little Clusters was endorsed for public use by outstanding members of the community and state in 1925, although it had already been used in the Sumter County Schools for ten years. Letters of endorsement published in the book were from a college president, school principal, vice president of Palmetto State Teachers Association of South Carolina, ministers, and teachers of Sumter County.

Anthony's accomplishments from 1915 to 1931 as county supervisor were recorded in her reports which noted that her goals had been met. The school term was extended, teachers' salaries were increased, schools supported by the Julius Rosenwald Fund were erected, and the summer school term continued.

Church work was a part of Lucie Anthony's life. Her love of inspiring youth led to a long friendship when she noticed a young girl, Lillie B. Moore, singing in the choir of Clinton AME Zion Church in Sumter. Anthony gave music lessons to Moore and later sent her to Barber Scotia College to earn a teacher's certificate. Anthony was a great role model for Moore. In an interview, Lillie Moore Nelson confirmed that "Anthony was firm, dedicated and liked to inspire." Anthony advised her to "be a good Christian woman."

Educated as a musician and physician, Anthony used many of those skills to make outstanding contributions to the black community through the school and church. Her lifetime devotion to racial uplift wherever she lived and worked left an indelible mark on the generations that followed. Anthony died in 1932 in Baltimore, Maryland.

REFERENCES:

Anthony, Lucie Bragg. *A Concise History of Sumter County Colored Schools, 1915-1931*. Sumter, S.C.: Knight Brothers Printers, n.d.

———. *Little Clusters*. Baltimore: James A. Murray Press, 1925.

Logan, Rayford, and Michael R. Winston, eds. *Dictionary of American Negro Biography*. New York: Norton, 1982.

Nelson, Lillie B. Moore. Interview with Barbara Williams Jenkins. May 21, 1993.

COLLECTIONS:

Personal books, publications, and photographs of Lucie Bragg Anthony are in the possession of Lillie B. Moore Nelson, Sumter, South Carolina, and the Sumter Historical Society.

Barbara Williams Jenkins

Hannah Diggs Atkins

(1923-)

Librarian, educator, state legislator

As a politician in Oklahoma, Hannah Diggs Atkins worked to reform legislation for human rights, mental health, employment, housing, education, women's rights, and child care. When she took on the role of Secretary of State in 1987, she became the highest ranking woman in Oklahoma state government. Jewel Prestage in Darlene Clark Hine's *Black Women in America* called her "a gadfly poised to prick the moral conscience of law makers." She had seen first-hand the injustices surrounding American politics and the insanity of unjust laws. As a child in North Carolina she had watched her father come home bloody and beaten for merely attempting to exercise his right to vote. She would not rest until her presence helped produce a change in American politics.

Atkins was born November 1, 1923, in Winston-Salem, North Carolina, to Mabel Kennedy Diggs and James Thackery Diggs. She grew up during the Great Depression and consequently developed a strong work ethic. She also learned to appreciate the value of family and the creative ways in which women were able to get things done. She observed the way her mother managed the family on an inadequate budget, supervised children, cooked, cleaned, and worked outside the home, if necessary.

A member of the Episcopal Church, Atkins chose to attend Saint Augustine College, an Episcopal college in Raleigh, North Carolina, where she became a member of the Alpha Kappa Alpha Sorority and graduated in 1943, having earned a bachelor of science degree. In the year following her graduation Atkins worked as a cub reporter for the *Winston-Salem Journal and Sentinel*. In 1944 and 1945 she taught French at Atkins High School in Winston-Salem. In 1943 she had married Charles N. Atkins, a physician, and in 1948, they moved to Nashville, Tennessee, where he was employed at Meharry Medical College and she worked as a research assistant in biochemistry.

Hannah Atkins received a bachelor of library science degree from the University of Chicago in 1949 and was inducted into Phi Beta Kappa. In the fall of 1949, she became a reference librarian at Fisk University in Nashville. In 1950, the couple moved back to Winston-Salem, where Hannah Atkins became the librarian at Kimberly Park Elementary School.

In 1953, the Atkins family, which now consisted of three children—Edmund Earl, Charles N., and Valerie Ann—moved west to Oklahoma. Atkins became a branch librarian for the Oklahoma City Public Library. She retained this position until 1956. It was in Oklahoma City that Atkins became most productive. In 1962, she became a reference librarian for the Oklahoma State Library and by 1963, she had worked her way up to chief of general reference and acting law librarian. She became an instructor of library science, as

Hannah Diggs Atkins

well as an instructor of law, at Oklahoma City University. She studied at Oklahoma City University Law School (1963-64) and later at the University of Oklahoma, receiving a master of public administration degree in 1989, when she was sixty-six years old.

Although she had often worked behind the scenes in politics, working voter registration drives and aiding others in their campaigns, Atkins, at the age of forty-six, decided to throw her own hat into the political ring. In 1969, she campaigned for a position as Oklahoma state representative and won, thus becoming the first African American woman to sit in the state's legislature. Not only did she join the ranks of Oklahoma's lawmakers, she became the first African American woman in the history of the Oklahoma legislature to chair a committee. Atkins chaired both the Mental Health and Retardation Committee and the Oklahoma County House Delegation.

Political Work Makes a Difference

Dissatisfied with the laws affecting human rights, mental health, employment, housing, education, women's rights, and child care, Hannah Diggs Atkins worked for legislative reform in these areas. She brought a vision and experience that had been missing in the State House, that of an African American, a woman, a wife, a mother, and a professional wage earner.

As chair of the Mental Health and Retardation Committee, Atkins handled legislation concerning drug and alcohol abuse, which were serious concerns in her Oklahoma City district. She was appointed to the Governor's Advisory Committee on Health Sciences and the Governor's Commission on the Status of Women, served as delegate to the National Conference of State Legislatures, and was a member of the powerful Appropriations and Budget Committee and the Committee on Public Health.

Atkins convened the Oklahoma Women's Political Caucus and was instrumental in the passage of a bill that forbids sex discrimination in the hiring practices of state agencies. She also was largely responsible for changing the House rules that prohibited women from serving as pages. Constantly fighting any injustice, Atkins demanded the removal of sex designation from state protective labor laws and worked unceasingly for the ratification of the Equal Rights Amendment. Clearly understanding the problems of both racism and sexism, Atkins said in *Ms.* magazine, "Although being black is my first priority, I realized a long time ago that you can't separate being black and being a woman. Feminism means both to me. What it finally boils down to is liberating people."

Atkins served in the Oklahoma state legislature from 1969 to 1983. During her tenure she had many firsts: she was the first black woman to serve in the Oklahoma state legislature and the first chairperson of Oklahoma's Advisory Committee of the U.S. Commission on Civil Rights. After leaving the legislature, she became the director of human resources for the state of Oklahoma in 1983. In 1987, she became the Secretary of Human Resources, then Secretary of State, a position that made her the highest ranking woman in Oklahoma state government.

President Jimmy Carter, aware of Hannah Diggs Atkins's contributions not just to the state of Oklahoma, but to the cause of justice for all people, in 1980 appointed her delegate to the United Nations Thirty-fifth Assembly. In 1991, Atkins retired at the age of sixty-eight.

During her career, Atkins served as a member of the National Board of the American Civil Liberties Union, president of the Special Libraries Association, executive board member of Sunbeam Home and Family Services, member of the NAACP, president of the Visiting Nurses Association, member of the National Black Child Development Institute, founder and president emeritus of NTU Art Gallery in Oklahoma City, vice-president of the Oklahoma City chapter of People to People, secretary of Oklahoma Sister Cities, and member of the executive committee of the Oklahoma Chapter of UN/USA.

Her awards date back to 1964, when Atkins was named reference librarian by Library USA at the New York World's Fair. Atkins has received a number of other awards, including: Rutgers University Eagleton Institute of Politics Award, 1972; National Public Citizen, 1975; National Association of Social Workers Award, 1975; Oklahoma Woman's Hall of Fame, 1982; Afro-American Hall of Fame of Oklahoma, 1983; Phi Beta Kappan of the Year, University of Oklahoma Chapter of Phi Beta Kappa, 1983; and the Humanitarian Award, Oklahoma Chapter, National Conference of Christians and Jews, 1990. Benedict College awarded Atkins the doctor of humane letters in 1983. In 1990, Oklahoma State University established an endowed chair in her honor, the Hannah Atkins Endowed Chair in Public Service.

Hannah Diggs Atkins is known both as a librarian and as a politician. Perhaps her greatest achievements have been in her successful work for legislative reform in Oklahoma, which affected housing, women, children, human rights, and education. Although retired, Atkins now is a volunteer at the NTU Art Gallery in Oklahoma City.

Current Address: Oklahoma City.

REFERENCES:

Hine, Darlene Clark, ed. *Black Women in America.* Brooklyn: Carlson Publishing, 1993.

Phelps, Shirelle, ed. *Who's Who among Black Americans, 1994-95.* 8th ed. Detroit: Gale Research, 1994.

Who's Who in American Politics, 1991-92, Vol. 2. 13th ed. New York: Bowker, 1992.

Nagueyalti Warren

Anita Baker

(1958-)

Singer

Since the appearance of her album *Rapture* in 1986, Anita Baker has been recognized as a major recording star. The album won two Grammys, as did its successor, *Giving You the Best That I Got,* which came out in 1988. In the early 1990s, Baker slowed down her recording and touring schedule and gave birth to two children. In 1994 she released a new album, *Rhythm of Love.*

Anita Baker was born on December 20, 1958, in Toledo, Ohio. She grew up as the youngest in a family of four girls. She did not learn that she had been abandoned by her biological mother at the age of two until her foster parents died when Baker was twelve. Then an older foster sister, who took over responsibility for her, began telling Baker about her biological family. Shortly thereafter, Baker met her mother, who had been sixteen when Baker was born. Contact between the two has continued over the years, although the relationship is still not entirely relaxed.

Anita Baker grew up in Detroit, where her foster mother ran a beauty shop and managed to instill the work ethic in her daughters by requiring them to work in the shop to earn money for their clothes and makeup. In addition, she saw to it that her daughters attended a church that emphasized spontaneity and the workings of the spirit. It was the music of the church that made Baker wish to become a singer when she was twelve. Her voice was already deep, and her idol was Mahalia Jackson, since Jackson was the only singer Baker knew about whose vocal timbre resembled hers. Until she was about sixteen, Baker's singing followed a familiar pattern: for church, gospel; with her friends, rhythm-and-blues and soul. Then she became aware of jazz and acquired a new favorite, Sarah Vaughan, whom Baker still idolizes.

Anita Baker began to sing in Detroit clubs when she was sixteen. Thinking that Baker was using poor judgement, her family prayed for her. In 1978 Baker became lead singer for a hard-core funk band, Chapter Eight. The popularity of the band in Detroit led to concert tours and to a contract with the now defunct Ariola Records in Los Angeles. They recorded an album in 1980, and the single "I Just Want to Be Your Girl" was a regional hit, but the band's sound did not match the styles popular at the moment. Executives at Ariola apparently decided that Baker did not have the potential to be a star.

Discouraged, Anita Baker returned to Detroit and stopped singing. At first she waited on tables in a club, and then her

Anita Baker

speaking voice won her a job as a receptionist at a law firm. In 1982 she heard from Otis Smith, formerly with Ariola, who had established the Beverly Glen independent label. Since she had a secure job, her own apartment, and a mother happy to see her out of clubs, it took considerable persuasion to convince Baker to return to Los Angeles and resume a recording career. But she finally acquiesced, recording the 1983 album *The Songstress,* for Beverly Glen. The ballads Baker sang on the album filled an empty niche in the market. It was on the rhythm-and-blues charts for over a year, and a single, "Angel," made the top ten. Baker, however, was having difficulties with the label; she was receiving no royalties and her next album was delayed.

Baker began to look for a new company, but Otis Smith threatened to sue. After spending a considerable amount of time in court due to an action brought by Smith, Baker was free to sign with a new company. She chose Elektra, which allowed her the unusual privilege for a beginner of being the executive producer of her first album for them. After much haggling with the recording company, Baker chose Michael J. Powell, former guitarist with Chapter Eight, as her producer. She then had difficulty coming up with material and eventually wrote three of her own songs to add to the five songs by other people she had chosen. A perfectionist, she also went $100,000 over budget, an expense she was glad to pay.

Baker Scores Major Recording Hit

The album *Rapture* appeared on the Elektra label in late summer 1986. It was well received by critics and had two hit singles, ''Sweet Love'' and ''You Bring Me Joy.'' In that year Baker won an NAACP Image Award, and in 1987 she received two Grammys for the album. Sales of *Rapture* had not been impressive initially, but by the end of 1988 the album had sold five million copies.

Although she was recording primarily love songs, Baker was also keeping in touch with other types of music. She sang gospel at Trinity Baptist Church from time to time, and in the summer of 1988, she opened for Al Jarreau at Switzerland's Montreux Jazz Festival, singing jazz. Baker's jazz singing brought to the fore comparisons of her voice to that of Sarah Vaughan. Baker now rejects any comparison with Vaughan or with another favorite singer, Nancy Wilson, saying it will be years before she has trained her voice to the point where the comparison could have any real basis. *Current Biography* cites a *New York Times* interview in 1988 in which Baker expressed her feelings about her musicianship in connection with her upcoming album: ''It wouldn't have been good business for me to rush off and make a jazz album. But I know I've got to expand. My musicianship is limited, and the first thing on my list of things to do is to take some theory classes and learn more harmonies on the piano.''

Baker's next album, *Giving You the Best That I Got* of 1988, showed more jazz influence than her previous recordings. It was very popular and sold two million copies in the first month. Her performance on the album earned her Grammys for best female singer and best record. Critics had mixed feelings, however, generally praising Baker's voice and delivery but questioning her choice of material. Baker's 1990 album, *Compositions,* was basically recorded live in the studio with some overdubs. This album inspired Phyl Garland to write in *Stereo Review,* December 1990: ''She embraces you with her voice, a lustrously textured contralto that she uses like an instrument, carefully shaping the contours of each note to produce a sculptured sound. She then bends these melodic fragments into fresh forms with absolute control and amazing fluidity. And she devotes just as much thought to a song's lyrics, investing them with a mesmerizing intensity.''

Baker's *Rhythm of Love* appeared in September 1994, with a single, ''Body and Soul,'' released in mid-August. The bulk of the album was recorded at a studio at her old home near Detroit, with Baker as executive producer. Although Baker was executive producer on her earlier albums for Elektra, *Rhythm of Love* was the first on which she did not work with producer Michael Powell.

In concert and in videos, the barely five-foot Baker wears designer gowns and light makeup in a simple setting. This image contrasts sharply with that of her contemporaries Janet Jackson, Madonna, and Whitney Houston. She also contrasts sharply in the amount of publicity she generates; she keeps a very low profile for a major recording star.

Since the summer of 1987 Baker has been living in a home on Lake St. Clair in Michigan. In 1989 she married Walter Bridgforth, who once worked for IBM in the area of marketing but is now a real estate developer. Her first child, Walter Baker Bridgforth, was born in January 1993; a second, Edward Carlton Bridgforth, was born in May 1994.

Despite the four years between her latest albums, Baker retains her popularity. In an article in the *Tennessean Showcase* of August 7, 1994, David Bither of Elektra says of the sampler of her three previous albums issued in mid-July, 1994: ''We want to remind people of her stature and influential role in music. She introduced a specific kind of vocal style which other performers have picked up and found success with. Yet she has such a distinctive sound that there is no way she can be confused with anyone else.''

Current Address: c/o Sherwin Bass, 804 North Crescent Blvd., Beverly Hills, CA 90210.

REFERENCES:

Current Biography. New York: H. W. Wilson, 1989.

Garland, Phyl. ''Anita Baker's Love Songs.'' *Stereo Review* 55 (December 1990): 118.

Larkin, Colin, ed. *The Guiness Encyclopedia of Popular Music.* Chester, Conn.: New England Publishing Associates, 1992.

Leavy, Walter. ''Who's the Greatest.'' *Ebony* 42 (October 1987): 140-46.

Mapp, Edward. *Directory of Blacks in the Performing Arts.* 2d ed. Metuchen, N.J.: Scarecrow Press, 1990.

Norment, Lynn. ''Anita Baker Returns with a Bang.'' *Ebony* 49 (September 1994): 44-50.

Waldron, Clarence. ''Anita Baker Makes Comeback with World Tour, Hit Album.'' *Jet* 87 (March 13, 1995): 60-63.

Who's Who among Black Americans, 1994-95. 8th ed. Detroit: Gale Research, 1994.

Robert L. Johns

Gwendolyn Calvert Baker
(1931-)
Administrator, educator, activist

Gwendolyn Baker is highly regarded for her leadership in academics, government, and the nonprofit and private arenas, as well as for championing women, children, and minorities. She has been a teacher in elementary classrooms

Gwendolyn Calvert Baker

and a professor and administrator at the university level, chief executive of the National Institute of Education and of the national YWCA, and president of the New York City Board of Education. She is now president of the United States Committee for the United Nations Children's Fund (UNICEF).

Baker was born in Ann Arbor, Michigan, on December 31, 1931, and attended public schools there. Baker's father, Burges Edward Calvert, who was born in Windsor, Canada, worked for Ford Motor Company in Ann Arbor, Michigan, for many years before leaving to fulfill his dream of entrepreneurship. He bought a pickup truck and established a rubbish collection business that eventually netted nearly a quarter of a million dollars a year. When he retired he sold the business to his youngest son, Russell, who has developed it into a million-dollar recycling enterprise. Viola Lee Calvert, Baker's mother, was born in Ypsilanti, Michigan. Although she spent her married years primarily as a homemaker and mother, she worked for a while in a printing shop and enjoyed using her cosmetology skills in her home for her daughters and friends.

Growing up in a Strong Community

When she was young, Baker was closer to her mother than to her father. Her mother's travels around the world as a Jehovah's Witness gave Baker an awareness of activities beyond her home sphere and kindled her interest in persons of various cultural and economic backgrounds. This proved a key to her later career success. After her father's death, Baker recalled his particular contributions to her development, espe-

cially how he encouraged her to complete her education; she recognizes that without academic preparation, her career would have taken a much different course.

Baker remembers her paternal grandmother, Olive Levi, as a close, understanding friend during her formative years. Until her death in 1955, Baker spent many hours at her house, across the street from the Calvert home. Grandmother Levi was a gracious lady from whom Baker learned about the niceties of keeping a home. In her house there were no paper napkins. She used linen napkins and tablecloths, with sterling silver napkin rings, and a silver crumb scraper for the table. Baker's grandmother taught her to wear white gloves to church and gave her a polish and finish she found useful when she entered the professional world.

There were three boys and two girls in the Calvert family, with Gwendolyn being the oldest. The Calvert home was a warm, loving, comfortable place, where the family sat at a round oak table to eat dinner at six o'clock every evening and talked about the events of the day. Theirs was a middle class, Christian family. The Calverts owned their home and had nice cars; the children had hot cereal for breakfast and would come home at noon to enjoy their mother's homemade soups. On Thanksgiving and Christmas the house was filled with relatives and friends to celebrate in the traditional way.

Until her parents joined the Jehovah's Witnesses, the Calverts attended Second Baptist Church as a family. Baker was baptized there when she was nine, sang in the choir, taught Sunday school, and was church bookkeeper. She is grateful to the minister, Charles Carpenter, and his wife, Linnia, for their part in setting the tone of her present lifestyle. They were well-educated people whose attitudes, actions, and encouragement made a lasting impression on her. In the environment of Second Baptist she discovered a belief in God and developed a conviction that her life had divine guidance that would insure success in all of her undertakings. Now she is a member of Riverside Church in New York City.

In 1950, when she was eighteen and in her first year at the University of Michigan, Gwendolyn Calvert married James Baker, her childhood sweetheart. James is the son of Charlie Baker, co-owner of an iron foundry in Ann Arbor. Gwendolyn worked at the foundry as a bookkeeper for one summer when she was an undergraduate, and her husband was employed there for several years before he started teaching in a state school for boys. Gwendolyn and James Baker were divorced in 1978.

Finishing her first academic degree was not easy for Baker, who had withdrawn from college after she was married in her freshman year. The original intention had been for the bride and groom to continue study without interruption. However, with the arrival of their first child, they decided that Gwendolyn should remain at home to care for the infant, and she did not reenter the university until their family of three children was complete.

More than ten years after her original matriculation, when she was about twenty-eight, Baker undertook the simultaneous challenges of being a wife, mother, student, and worker outside the home. Her daily schedule began with taking the children to school and driving to the university to attend two morning classes. Then she picked up the children to take them home for lunch. After they ate, she took them back to school and returned to the university for her two afternoon classes. Somewhere in the day she found time to work as a part-time bookkeeper. With assistance from her husband with the household duties and the support of some women classmates around her own age with similar family responsibilities, she received her first degree, a bachelor's in elementary education, from the University of Michigan in 1964.

Educator Has Multicultural Interests

Baker chose teaching as a vocation because she wanted to motivate students in the manner she had been inspired, and because she wanted to help fill the void of African American representation in the public schools of Ann Arbor. She took all the courses required for teacher certification, ensuring that she would not be disappointed to learn she was not qualified to teach. She accepted an elementary teaching position in Ann Arbor and taught there from 1964 to 1969.

After four years of teaching, Baker received the University of Michigan's Ann Arbor Teacher of the Year award in recognition of her efficiency in supervising student teachers in her classroom. The award included assignment to the university's faculty for the next year, teaching a methods course and supervising student teachers in the Ann Arbor area. In 1968 Baker completed a master's in elementary administration.

That initial university experience sparked her interest in teacher education in relation to racial issues and in the subject of multicultural education in general. She thought that a multicultural approach to teaching, with an awareness of racial issues and differences, would be a way to help improve the lives and behavior of young children. At the end of the year she joined the faculty on a full-time basis as a lecturer. Eventually she became an associate professor in the School of Education. In the interim she conducted research in multiethnic education for a dissertation and was awarded a Ph.D. in education in 1972. She taught at the University of Michigan from 1970 to 1976.

After receiving tenure as associate professor, Baker became the university's director of affirmative action programs, making her the only woman and only the second black person to sit on the president's executive cabinet. In this very sensitive position, from 1976 to 1978, she helped to reduce racism and sexism on campus by bringing about changes in the university's policies and curriculum, and by helping the university become more aware of the needs of all of its students. In 1978, during the Carter administration, Baker went to Washington, D.C., to become chief of Minorities and Women's Programs for the National Institute of Education. She remained in this position until 1981. This project, which provided funds to help minorities and women finish educational research and complete doctoral programs, allowed her

to continue to concentrate on her interest in multicultural education.

In the early years of her career, Baker's goal was to be an elementary school principal, but when that opportunity came, her sights had shifted to a college presidency, so she opted to remain at the university. However, when she was a finalist in one competition to become head of a college, she was refused an interview because the selection committee thought her experience, which was limited to the interests of women and minorities, was too specialized.

The perfect chance to broaden her involvement came with an offer from Bank Street College of Education in New York City. She served as vice-president and dean of Graduate and Children's Programs at this highly rated teacher training institution from 1981 to 1984. Not only did this position afford more extensive exposure, it let her put to use the theories that she had outlined in her book *Planning and Organizing for Multicultural Instruction* and begin the revisions for its second edition.

Administrator Committed to Women, Children, and Minorities

In the 1940s Baker had been denied summer employment at the Ann Arbor YWCA because of race, but was later employed as a receptionist on a trial basis. No one knew then that impending changes in the social climate of the country would be reflected in the philosophy and operation of the organization—or that Gwendolyn Calvert Baker would later become national executive director of the YWCA of the United States of America in 1984. At the YWCA she used her training as an educator and her experience as an administrator to better the status of girls and women through the elimination of racism and sexism.

Project Redesign was one of Baker's greatest successes with the YWCA. During the 1992-93 year she initiated this reorganization, which resulted in a balanced budget with reduced staff, while providing better services to the four hundred local associations. After a survey of the associations, Baker developed new strategies to offer the quality of support that the local boards wanted from the national office. The work of field specialists is now done through state and regional councils; there is a computer network for electronic communication with each association; the New York office is no longer involved in local programs; a private firm has been hired to manage the huge annual convention; and consultants write proposals, leaving the executive director free to cope with the tasks requiring more professional experience, primarily those relating to helping women and minorities. Her work with the YWCA continued until 1993, when she accepted a position with UNICEF.

Baker welcomed her 1986 appointment to the New York City Board of Education when she was still at the YWCA because she could then address issues not restricted to the concerns of women. She used her expertise to secure adequate funding for all children in the multicultural district of a million students, 80 percent African American, Latino, and Asian. She had been appointed to the board in 1986 by David Dinkins, then Manhattan Borough president, and in 1990 was sworn in as president of the board by Mayor Dinkins.

After five years on the board of education, Baker resigned to lessen the long hours of board-related duties and devote full time to the increasing demands of the YWCA. She had contributed to the administration of the schools and through board membership had made helpful contacts for the YWCA that would have otherwise been unattainable.

On September 13, 1993, Baker became president of the United States Committee for UNICEF, an ideal placement to bring together aspects of her personal and professional philosophy about children, women, and people of differing ethnic and cultural groups. She broke the forty-seven-year history of UNICEF's white male leadership and assumed a role that enabled her to consider the needs of people globally. She is now responsible for a staff of 120 and for a fifty million dollar budget, which she hopes to double in five years.

One of Baker's ambitions at UNICEF is to help children throughout the world understand the cultures of their counterparts in other lands. Thinking of the value of person-to-person interaction, Baker stated in the *Ann Arbor News,* ''Wouldn't it be wonderful to be able to send two elementary school children, two junior high and two high school children to Cambodia or Mozambique? What they bring back could promote better understanding, help reduce hate and bigotry by showing the linkage and connection between people of all countries.''

Baker has received repeated recognition for her administrative ability. Aside from the earned Ph.D. from the University of Michigan, she holds honorary doctorates from Medgar Evers College of the City University of New York; King's College, Pennsylvania; and Southeastern Massachusetts University. Baker has served on many boards, councils, and commissions, has extensive affiliation with professional organizations, and has participated in many civic activities. She was selected in 1992 to be on the board of the Greater New York Saving Bank, the first woman and the first African American ever chosen. This honor came not only because of her effective administrative ability, but also because of her familiarity with the politics and the needs of the city. She is on the Board of Trustees of the Fashion Institute of Technology, a State University of New York college for design and business professions. The New York Alliance of Black School Educators created a five-thousand-dollar scholarship in her name.

Other honors and awards accorded Baker include the Athena Award of the University of Michigan, the Women's Forum, Strength of the City Award, and a place on *Working Women's Magazine*'s 1993 list of the ten best managers in the United States. Organizations often select Baker as an honored guest and speaker and she has appeared in national television presentations.

Besides more than a dozen articles for professional publications, she has written two books. *Planning and Organ-*

izing for Multicultural Instruction advocates and presents a multicultural curriculum that addresses sexism as well as racism. Baker wants school personnel to give serious attention to political and social changes, not only in the former Soviet Union, South Africa, Central America, China, and the Middle East, but in our country as well. Her book is a useful text and reference book for classroom teachers and undergraduate and graduate students in education. Baker wrote her other book, *How Vision, Leadership and Planning Helped One Nonprofit Redesign Itself,* at the request of the National Center for Nonprofit Boards, to be used as a guide for other nonprofits that have similar problems.

Despite her demanding schedule Baker manages to indulge in her hobbies of reading, traveling, and tennis. Whenever she is free on a weekend in New York or during her frequent travels, she plays tennis for the sheer enjoyment of the game and for its physical fitness value. Her best opportunity for tennis comes when she goes to Ixtapan De La Sal, a small town in the mountains near Mexico City. Here she has the luxury to relax with a favorite book, enjoy the hot mineral baths, massages, and facials, and spend hours on the tennis courts. After a week in Ixtapan De La Sal, she can return to her office with renewed vigor.

Baker has two daughters: JoAnn Elizabeth Baker Gomez, a teacher of reading and social studies in a junior high school, and Claudia Jayne Baker, a chef. Her son, James Grady Baker, Jr., is a technical engineer at a diesel repair shop. The only grandchild, Marshall Baker, aged ten, lives with his mother, Claudia. Baker is proud of, and very close to, her children and grandson. They visit as often as their schedules permit and communicate regularly by mail or phone.

Gwendolyn Calvert Baker is an attractive, poised woman who has taken to heart the teachings and examples of her family, friends, and colleagues. She still maintains the enthusiasm and stamina that made it possible for her to conquer the simultaneous challenges of being a wife, mother, student, and part-time bookkeeper when she returned to the University of Michigan to complete her first academic degree. This determination, as well as her dedication to improving people's lives, has led her to the internationally influential leadership position she holds today.

REFERENCES:

''At UNICEF, Black President Stresses Global Responsibility.'' *Bay State Banner,* August 5, 1993.

Baker, Gwendolyn C. Taped interview with Dona L. Irwin, September 8, 1993.

———. *Planning and Organizing for Multicultural Instruction.* 2nd ed. Menlo Park, Calif.: Addison-Wesley Publishing Co., 1994.

''Bank Appoints Dr. Baker as Board Member.'' *New York Amsterdam News,* December 26, 1992.

''Ex-teacher U.S. Leader for UNICEF.'' *Ann Arbor News,* July 21, 1993.

''Job Strategies.'' *Glamour* 91 (April 1993): 117.

"Wiping the Slate Clean: How the YWCA of the USA Redefined Itself." *Board Member* 2, no. 3 (1993): 4.

Dona L. Irvin

Harriet Ann Baker
(c. 1829-?)
Evangelist

Harriet Ann Baker

During the latter part of the nineteenth century, Harriet A. Baker became a highly persuasive preacher in great demand by both white and black congregations, overcoming the discouragement of her family, friends, and church from entering evangelist work on the grounds that God did not intend women to preach. Since childhood, she had known that her mission was to preach the Gospel and she held on to this vision. Through her preaching, she won the admiration and respect of ministers and congregations in a number of states in the eastern part of the country.

Harriet Ann Cole Baker was born about 1829, in Havre de Grace, Harford County, Maryland, then a town of about 2,500 residents situated on the Susquehanna River at the entrance to Chesapeake Bay. The year of her death is not known. Baker was one of seven children born to William and Harriet Cole. Her maternal great-grandmother was an Indian woman who married an Englishman. Their daughter married a man named Lego, a native of Guinea, and gave birth to a daughter, Harriet Baker's mother. Baker's paternal grandmother, whose name was Bradford, was a slave and a cook for her master's family. Although she married a man named Cole, she was best known by the name Bradford. A high-spirited, gentle, reliable, and industrious woman, she would not consent to whippings. Bradford was sold to another slaveholder whose mistress had her whipped for some trivial cause. Bradford's rebellious spirit was aroused, and she struck her mistress with the cowhide which had been used for beating slaves. Angered, the master directed the overseer to tie her to a post. The master then beat her with such dreadful power that parts of her skin and flesh were torn from her body. At the end, her insides were left protruding.

As she suffered, a passerby heard Bradford's cries and cut her down. With superhuman energy, she sprang to her feet, seized a nearby axe, and split the master's skull, killing him instantly. Then she struck the overseer who witnessed the beating, and he died two days later. Bradford was jailed in Baltimore, and five weeks later gave birth to a son, William. Citizens who heard about her experiences came to her support. At trial time, she was carried into court on a couch, acquitted, released from jail and freed from slavery.

Life was difficult for Bradford and her son, but as the child became old enough, she felt obliged to indenture him and bound him to a slave owner where he was to stay until he was twenty-five years old. He grew over six feet tall and was proportionately stout and strong. William Cole, known as Bill Bradford, became a noted prize fighter. When Bradford was nineteen years old and had won a considerable amount of money from his fights, the owner set him free. He lived with his mother in Baltimore until he met and married Harriet Lego.

Harriet Baker never attended school. At that time there were no public black schools and teaching a black to read was a legal offense. Harriet Baker told her biographer, John H. Acornley,

> No mortal man or woman on earth has taught me a letter, I grew up without it. After I married, I studied to learn the letters. I cannot forget how, at one time, when I was living at a rich gentleman's house, and I was obliged to clean out his office. I saw a letter on his table, and wanted to write very much, I took up the pen, and copied from his letter, and put the duplicate in my pocket, but I could not read it, so I carried it around in my pocket until it was work out. I did not know A from B, but I could copy all I saw, and I was very quick to learn.

Although born free, Baker met many hardships in her early life. When she was eleven years old, her father, who had been an indentured servant, died. By custom, when a man serving an indenture died the owner would come to the house immediately to claim children who were old enough and bind them out. By law, however, if the home contained generous food and clothing, the owners could not take the children.

Some of William (Bradford) Cole's former employers and friends were slaveowners and knew the law, but had compassion for the family and supplied five bushels of corn, three bushels of wheat, and some meat every winter. After the house was searched on about a dozen separate occasions and found well-stocked with barrels of meals, flour, potatoes, meat, and fish, all seven of the children were saved. The larger children were hired out in service, but none were enslaved.

Agents of slaveholders watched free blacks constantly, and given the opportunity, they would kidnap a young person and quickly sell him or her into slavery. If challenged, the agents would accuse the black of being a thief or having escaped slavery. To secure Baker from kidnappers or of being wrongly accused, Baker's mother hired her out for one dollar per month, and when she changed workplaces the mother would strip the child in the presence of the employer to assure him or her that nothing had been stolen or hidden in the clothes. At one time, Baker's mother hired her out to a Mrs. Bailey, who paid one dollar and twenty-five cents per month. She remained there for some time. She found the work pleasant and the woman and her children warm and accepting. Bailey would take her silk dresses and tuck them up for young Baker, which made the girl feel good about herself. White women visitors wondered why Bailey "made such a fuss over a little colored girl."

On October 25, 1845, when she was sixteen or seventeen years old, Harriet married William Baker, a slave. Since Harriet Baker was ambitious, an excellent worker, and in great demand, her employer arranged for a notice of the marriage to appear in the local paper. Baker told John Acornley that she rejoiced to see her name in the paper, "especially as two of the first families in the town were to be married, and the notice of their marriage would appear at the same time."

The next year William Baker's owner decided to sell him to a Georgia trader. He was scheduled to depart on a Monday morning, but at midnight Saturday the couple and their seven-week-old baby escaped across the Maryland border into Pennsylvania. They settled in Columbia, Lancaster County, where William Baker found new employment. Since work in the lumber region was plentiful and the workers were paid well, they were able to save enough to build a house in the spring of 1848. In three years they had paid off all their debts, except a small amount on the land.

The fugitive slave bill of 1850 gave slave holders the right to pursue their slaves who had escaped into free states. The Bakers left Pennsylvania and lived in New York for a time, then returned to Columbia on the assurance from friends that they would protect William Baker from slave catchers. William Baker was caught, however, then tried, condemned as a fugitive, and returned to his master. Several hundred friends raised enough money to buy his freedom.

The Bakers met other difficulties. In 1872, two of their daughters died within two weeks of each other: Hannah Rebecca, fifteen, on March 20, 1872, and Rulletta, thirteen, on April 9. The Bakers had three other children who in 1872 were aged four, six, and eight.

Baker Becomes an Evangelist

In 1842, when Baker was about twelve or thirteen years old, she accompanied her mother to a band-meeting (a prayer meeting for women and their children) and experienced a religious conversion. From then on she was persuaded she should enter some distinctive religious work. When Baker expressed an interest in the ministry, members of her church in Columbia, her minister, her friends, and her husband, opposed her on the basis that God never intended women to preach the gospel. Baker yielded to their persuasion for a while. Then, while attending her church one day, Baker had a vision that convinced her to embark on her religious mission. About the time of the deaths of her two daughters, in the winter of 1872, she set out to become an evangelist and appears to have preached her first sermon in Brownstown, Pennsylvania, a German settlement, where she was warmly received. After three weeks in the area, she and a Reverend Brown of the white Evangelical church had converted seventy-two people and added them to church membership. White churches received her warmly, but some time was to pass before her own church and black people accepted a woman evangelist.

A black camp meeting held in the vicinity of Cressona, Schuylkill County, Pennsylvania, in the summer of 1874 attracted large crowds. At the meeting Baker was invited to work in the St. Clain, Pottsville, and Mahanoy City Primitive Methodist churches, where she remained for two months. Following that, she preached in Pennsylvania, Ohio, Virginia, Maryland, Delaware, New Jersey, New York, and Connecticut in connection with a number of denominations—Methodist Episcopal, Primitive Methodist, Baptist, African Methodist Episcopal, and others. She also preached in a number of white churches.

By that time, her work had been endorsed by several AME bishops, including the renowned Henry McNeal Turner, all of whom had given her authority to preach the Gospel. In 1889 the AME Conference of Philadelphia appointed Baker to St. Paul's Church on Tenth Street in Lebanon, Pennsylvania. After eighteen years of labor she had converted about five thousand people to the church. Still, larger and richer congregations sought her services.

Baker's life was not free from trials. She had faced serious illnesses when she contracted a fever that had raged through Pennsylvania, and she once accidentally took a dose of poison. Her husband suffered from a prolonged illness and became blind and almost a helpless cripple. By then, one of her children had enlisted in the United States Army, another had married and left home, and the remaining daughter was at home attending school and ministering to the ailing father. Baker continued to support her family financially, and as her limited time permitted, and emotionally, by making visits home. No information is available on the date or circumstances of Baker's death.

Several of Baker's sermons are printed in John Acornley's biographical work on Baker, *The Colored Lady Evangelist; Being the Life, Labors, and Experiences, of Mrs. Harriet A.*

Baker, published in 1892, which is the single known source of information on her life.

The life of Harriet Ann Baker reflects the struggles of nineteenth-century black women who would not be bound by slavery or gender. Baker, a highly spiritual woman, shared her preaching with people regardless of race and religious denomination and quenched the spiritual thirst of thousands who heard her message.

REFERENCES:

Acornley, John H. *The Colored Lady Evangelist; Being the Life, Labors and Experiences, of Mrs. Harriet A. Baker.* Brooklyn: 1892. Reprinted. New York: Garland, 1897.

Jessie Carney Smith

Kathleen Battle

Kathleen Battle

(1948-)

Opera singer

From her debut in 1972 at the *Spoleto Festival of Two Worlds* in Italy, Kathleen Battle has emerged as an internationally renowned operatic singer possessing a light lyric coloratura voice ideal for roles of ingenues and soubrettes. Battle respects the limitations of her voice, which lacks the steel quality in its middle range to portray the traditional grand opera heroines. According to Bernard Holland of the *New York Times Magazine,* Battle's voice "actually challenges the definition of 'small'. . . . There is a shimmer, a gleam, above all, a heart, which together convey the elusive 'ping'—that purity of intonation and sheer musical caring." In addition to her performances in German and Italian, Battle frequently includes spirituals in her recitals. She and Jessye Norman, another African American, have been hailed as two of the nation's finest contemporary sopranos. According to Thomas H. Stahel, writing for *America,* Battle and Norman in March 1990, during a recorded concert at Carnegie Hall, "gave a performance of their people's spirituals that will live in the nation's memory, and on its videotapes, as a new standard of American excellence."

Kathleen Deanne Battle was born on August 13, 1948, in Portsmouth, a small industrial city in the southern part of Ohio. In *Current Biography Yearbook, 1984,* Battle describes her family as "wonderfully close" and the source of her strength. The youngest of seven children of a steel worker from Alabama, Grady Battle, and Ollie Lane Battle, Kathleen Battle has three brothers and three sisters, including a teacher,

an accountant, a welder, a secretary, a carpenter, and a personnel supervisor.

Kathleen Battle learned to sing listening to her father, a gospel singer in a quartet. A sister taught her how to read music, and on her own she began to experiment on the piano while looking over the shoulders of others. She has always enjoyed performing. At the African Methodist Episcopal Church that her family attended, Battle would often be placed on a table when she was quite young to sing at civic functions, banquets, and church activities. As she grew older, she began playing the organ and piano at summer services.

At the public schools of her hometown, Battle excelled in all subject areas. Thus, her special musical talent was not immediately recognized when she began formal piano lessons at age thirteen. In high school, Battle continued to study piano and began voice lessons. A person with a practical approach to life, she also enrolled in secretarial courses and studied typing and shorthand. Charles Varney, Battle's music teacher at Portsmouth High School, encouraged her to go to Cincinnati to study music and gave her first classical music scores, "Bist du bei mir" and two familiar Ave Marias. Upon her graduation from Portsmouth High School in 1966, Battle received a Ford Foundation National Achievement Scholarship.

Battle's intention after high school was to attend college and major in mathematics. However, persuaded by Varney, she decided to major in music instead. In her characteristically practical manner, when Battle entered the University of Cincinnati College Conservatory of Music at the University of Cincinnati, she elected to specialize in music education rather than performance. Having little prior knowledge of the classical vocal repertory and not fully understanding her own capabilities, Battle immersed herself in a program of music studies, art, dance, and languages. By 1971 Battle had earned both her bachelor's and master's degrees in music education from the University of Cincinnati.

Upon completing her formal education, Battle began teaching music to fourth-, fifth-, and sixth-graders at the Garfield School in inner-city Cincinnati. She spent her evenings studying second-year German at night school and taking private voice lessons, emphasizing the oratorio literature, with Franklin Bens.

Opera Singer's Career Launched

After a year of private lessons, Battle auditioned for Thomas Schippers, a cofounder with Gian-Carlo Menotti of the *Spoleto Festival of Two Worlds* held annually in Italy. Schippers, who was also director of the Cincinnati Symphony Orchestra at that time, hired Battle to sing the soprano part in Brahms's *Ein Deutsches Requiem,* as well as several Handel arias, at the 1972 Spoleto Festival. Since she had previously sung only in local church choirs, this festival effectively launched Battle's professional career.

Although she returned to the elementary school classroom in the fall of 1972, Battle was certain after her experience in Spoleto that she wanted to be a professional singer. She spent much of her leisure time studying opera interpretation, song literature, and acting.

In 1973, through her association with Schippers and the Cincinnati Symphony Orchestra, Battle was introduced to pianist/conductor James Levine, who was then director of the Cincinnati May Festival. She told *Current Biography Yearbook* that Levine would become "the cornerstone of my career—my mentor, coach, adviser and friend."

Not only did Levine hire Battle to appear with him at the Cincinnati and Ravinia (Illinois) festivals, he supervised her training and developed her repertory to include Mozart's *Mass in C Minor,* Haydn's *The Creation,* and Bach's *Cantata No. 202/Weichet nur* (Wedding Cantata).

In March 1974, Battle won first place in the WGN-Illinois Opera Guild Auditions of the Air. As first place winner, she received three thousand dollars and an appearance as featured soloist in the annual Chicago Grant Park Summer Concert Series.

In April 1975, Battle's talent was further recognized when she received the top prize in the Young Artists Awards, a national competition at the Kennedy Center for the Performing Arts in Washington, D.C. Also in 1975 she won the Martha Baird Rockefeller Fund for Music Award.

Battle spent part of the summer of 1975 at the Ravinia Festival and was considering spending the next several months auditioning in Europe. Offered the opportunity to understudy

and eventually succeed Carmen Balthrop in the title role of *Treemonisha,* the Scott Joplin folk opera on Broadway, Battle altered her plans to audition in Europe in favor of the Broadway role. When Battle eventually took over the role of Treemonisha, her performance was described as one of rare quality.

Singing with increasing confidence, Battle appeared in operas and recitals across the United States. She made her New York City Opera debut as Susanna in Mozart's *Le Nozze di Figaro,* conducted by David Effron, in September of 1976. She made her first appearance at the Metropolitan Opera as the Shepherd in a production of Wagner's *Tannhäuser.* During the following opera season, Battle performed the roles of Sophie in Jules Massenet's *Werther,* at the Metropolitan Opera; Nanetta in Verdi's *Falstaff,* for the Houston Grand Opera; and the page, Oscar, in Verdi's *Un Ballo in maschera,* for the San Francisco Opera. During the 1981-82 Metropolitan Opera season, she performed the parts of Bionde in Mozart's *Die Entführung aus dem Serail* and Pamina in Mozart's *Die Zauberflöte.* In addition to singing in various operas, in January 1982 Battle performed a recital of Brahms, Schumann, and Schubert staged by James Levine at New York City's Alice Tully Hall.

Since then Battle has earned an international reputation. She made her Washington, D.C., recital debut in November 1982, singing songs by Purcell, Schubert, Mozart, and Fauré. During that same month she sang the roles of Solomon's Queen and Queen of Sheba in Handel's *Solomon,* presented by the Toronto Mendelssohn Choir. In September of 1983, Battle performed the difficult role of Zerbinetta in Richard Strauss's *Ariadne auf Naxos* with the San Francisco Opera. For the Metropolitan Opera 1983-84 season, she sang the roles of Zdenka in Strauss's *Arabella;* Sophie, in his *Der Rosenkavalier;* and Zerlina in Mozart's *Don Giovanni.*

Perhaps more challenging, during the same season, was her three-concert recital series at Alice Tully Hall entitled "Kathleen Battle and Friends." Assisted by her manager, Samuel Niefeld, Battle selected music by Bach, George Gershwin, and Duke Ellington and invited pianist James Levine, trumpeter Wynton Marsalis, and flutist Hubert Laws to accompany her.

The Friends recital notwithstanding, Battle's greatest acclaim, for the 1983-84 season, was for her performance of the familiar roles of Solomon's Queen and Queen of Sheba in Handel's *Solomon* with the Musica Sacra Chorus and Orchestra at Avery Fischer Hall in New York City. Of this performance *New Yorker* music critic Andrew Porter wrote: "Miss Battle's singing of the two queens was so exquisitely beautiful and distinguished that one wanted to hear as much of her as possible. . . . I thought her account of the Queen of Sheba's 'Will the sun forget to streak Eastern skies with amber ray' the most ravishing performance of a Handel air I have ever heard."

Battle has won recognition abroad. During the summer of 1984, she went to Paris to sing the role of Susanna in *Le*

Nozze di Figaro and to Salzburg to perform Despina in *Così fan tutte.* A live recording grew out of her 1988 Tokyo performance.

A disciplined performer, Battle is said to exude professionalism. Bernard Holland of the *New York Times* observed that in contrast to many singers, including some celebrities, who use rehearsals to learn what they will perform, Battle arrives at her first rehearsal "scrupulously prepared." Asked by *Esquire* magazine, "Whom are you trying to please?" Battle replied: "Sometimes you try to put all thoughts out of your head and try to become closer to the music. At those moments . . . you soar with the music. Then, of course, you would be singing to the deities."

Battle expresses her thoughts readily where expectations are unclear. She told Bernard Holland: "I've earned my right to ask questions. I'm interested in what others have to give me, but if someone asks me to do something that has none of my strong points, I'm not going to die trying to make it work."

Battle's career continues to be closely followed by members of the music world. A high point in her career has been the videotaped performance entitled *Kathleen Battle and Jessye Norman Sing Spirituals,* aired on PBS in December 1990 as a part of the Great Performances series.

During the 1992-93 season, Battle joined Kurt Masur, music director, and the New York Philharmonic Orchestra in a benefit performance at Avery Fischer Hall celebrating the Philharmonic's 150th season. Later in the season, she appeared with Frederica von Stade and the Boston Symphony Orchestra at Carnegie Hall performing Mendelssohn's *Incidental Music* for *A Midsummer Night's Dream.* In November 1992, Battle appeared at Alice Tully Hall singing music from Mozart, Schumann, Strauss, Bizet, and Victor Herbert.

Battle's career with the Metropolitan Opera ended on Monday, February 7, 1994, when the opera cancelled all of its contracts with what the *Washington Post* labeled a "tempestuous mega-soprano." She has been compared with other difficult artists in "the world's major leagues of vocal drama," and was characterized as one who cancels performances and storms out of rehearsals. Battle's management company said in a public statement that she had not been told about unprofessional actions. Already a diva and overbooked for performances, her career is not expected to suffer and might benefit from the notoriety.

A widely recorded soprano, Battle is featured on *Ariadne auf Naxos,* directed by James Levine; *Cosi fan tutte,* directed by Raccardo Muti; *Un Ballo in maschera,* directed by Georg Solti; *Don Giovanni,* directed by Herbert von Karajan; *Pleasures of Their Company* with guitarist Christopher Parkening; *Salzburg Recital* with James Levine; and other recordings.

In 1992, Battle was among the recipients of Candace awards given by the National Coalition of 100 Black Women. The award, which is named for the ancient Ethiopian title for empress or queen, is given in recognition of black women who embody the coalition's goal of empowering black women through programs focused upon volunteering, building leadership, role modeling, and mentoring.

Battle, an attractive woman both on and off stage, maintains a striking, model-like figure and dresses in designer clothes. She is said to possess sensuality and sophistication uncommon among soubrettes. In general, Battle may be described as somewhat reserved with strangers yet very confident about herself and her objectives. She told Bernard Holland, "I've accepted my reality. . . . I was meant to sound the way I do."

Current Address: c/o Epstein Division, Columbia Artists, 165 West 57th Street, New York, NY 10019.

REFERENCES:

"The Age of the Black Diva." *Ebony* 46 (August 1991): 74-76.

"Camille Cosby, Kathleen Battle Win Candace Awards." *Jet* 82 (July 20, 1992): 16-17.

Current Biography Yearbook, 1984. New York: H. W. Wilson Company, 1985.

Davis, Peter G. "The Ascent of Mann." *New York* 27 (February 21, 1994): 57-58.

Hine, Darlene Clark, ed. *Black Women in America.* New York: Carlson Publishing, 1993.

Holland, Bernard. "Classical Music in Review." *New York Times,* November 10, 1992.

———. "Kathleen Battle Pulls out of *Rosenkavalier* at Met." *New York Times,* January 30, 1993.

———. "A Very Special Soprano." *New York Times Magazine,* November 17, 1985.

Jellinek, George. "Kathleen Battle: At Carnegie Hall." *Stereo Review* 67 (December 1992): 123.

Keller, James M. "Kathleen Battle and Jessye Norman: Spirituals." *Musical America* 110 (July 1990): 62-63.

Marsh, Carole S. *The Color Purple and All That Jazz! Black Music, Poetry, Writing and Art.* Bath, N.C.: Gallopade Publishing Group, 1989.

"The Met's Battle Royal." *Washington Post,* February 9, 1994.

Musical America, International Directory of the Performing Arts. New York: Musical America Publishing, 1992.

Oestreich, James R. "Classical Music in Review." *New York Times,* October 17, 1992.

Porter, Andrew. "Musical Events." *New Yorker* 60 (April 9, 1984): 114-16.

Rothstein, Edward. "With Emphasis on the Upbeat, the Philharmonic Turns 150." *New York Times,* September 17, 1992.

Stahel, Thomas H. "Lessons in Song and Slaughter." *America* 164 (January 12, 1991): 17.

"Whom Are You Trying to Please?" *Esquire* 106 (December 1986): 208.

Dawn Cooper Barnes

Belinda

(c. 1713-?)

Slave

The sparse biographical information available on Belinda appears in a petition to the General Court of Massachusetts dated February 14, 1783. Written in the third person and signed with an X as her mark beside the name Belinda, the document appears to have been dictated. It states that the petitioner was born "on the banks of the Rio De Volta" and that she was kidnapped before she had "twelve years enjoyed the fragrance of the native groves." Her abductors are identified as "an armed band of white men." There is no indication of her African name, and it may be that Belinda is not the name by which she was known as a slave. The reference to the Volta River suggests that she was taken from the area known broadly during the slave trade era as the Gold Coast (now Ghana).

The petition states that after surviving the horrors of the middle passage, Belinda was enslaved to the Isaac Royall family for fifty years. Approximately eight more years passed before the petition was filed; during that time the Royall property was administered by the state of Massachusetts. This information suggests that she was abducted in the 1720s. The dating is plausible in light of the history of the Isaac Royall family and in the wider outline of the history of the slave trade. Although little is known about Belinda, much is known about the Royalls. An examination of the Royall family is helpful in providing a framework for understanding the atmosphere in which Belinda most likely lived.

One of the owners cited on the petition, Isaac Royall, Sr., was born around 1672 in Maine. He lived in Massachusetts for most of his life before he went to Antigua (around 1700), one of the Leeward Islands. Even before he moved to the Caribbean, Royall often visited Antigua and other West Indian islands, according to James H. Stark in his *The Loyalists of Massachusetts and the Other Side of the American Revolution.* This type of travel suggests his involvement in the interconnected slave, sugar, and rum economy. In any case, the move to Antigua assured Isaac Royall, Sr.'s fortune, which grew substantially between 1704 and 1710. According to Gladys Hoover in her *The Elegant Royalls of Colonial New England,* Royall owned a sugar plantation, ran a distillery, and engaged in some slave trading.

The general history of the Caribbean reflects the significance of the slave economy. In *The Atlantic Slave Trade: A Census,* Philip Curtin notes that the slave population of the Leeward Islands increased steadily between 1672 and 1707 and that the number continued to rise, although more slowly, between 1707 and 1733, the period of Belinda's likely arrival. Curtin has also established that about 38 percent of the Africans transported to the Americas in 1724 were taken from the Gold Coast. If the petition is accurate, then Belinda very likely belonged initially to Isaac Royall, Sr. Royall's first wife had

died before he relocated to Antigua. His second wife was Elizabeth Browne, a widow, whom he married in Antigua in 1707. They were the parents of two children who survived to adulthood, Isaac, Jr., born in 1719, and Penelope, born in 1724. In 1737 Isaac Royall, Sr. returned with his family to New England, settling in Charlestown (now Medford), Massachusetts. In December of that year, he petitioned the General Court that he not be taxed on the twenty-seven slaves he brought with him from Antigua.

Isaac Royall, Sr. died in 1739. In that year, Isaac Royall, Jr. made an inventory of his father's property for the probate court. Nine slave men and four slave women are included in the inventory, but none of the women is named Belinda, according to the information supplied by Hoover.

Isaac Royall, Jr. had been married about a year when his father died. A portrait of the Isaac Royall, Jr. family was painted by Robert Feke in 1741. Along with Royall himself, the painting includes his wife, Elizabeth; their daughter, also named Elizabeth; Isaac's sister, Penelope; and his sister-in-law, Mary (McIntosh) Palmer.

For more than twenty years, Isaac Royall, Jr. was a representative of the Massachusetts General Court (the same court that received Belinda's petition) and a member of its council. He was appointed a brigadier general in 1761. According to a source quoted in Lorenzo Sabine's *Biographical Sketches of Loyalists of the American Revolution,* Isaac Royall, Jr. was "kind to his slaves, charitable to the poor, and friendly to everybody." Unfortunately, the very detailed journal Royall kept has been lost.

Maintaining allegiance to Great Britain during the Revolutionary War, Royall fled Massachusetts in 1775, and he subsequently sailed to England from Nova Scotia. His property in Massachusetts was taken over by the state. He died in England in 1781. His will established the first law professorship at Harvard, which has continued to the present.

The petition made on Belinda's behalf requests financial assistance based on her long service to the Royall family. The document also asks for monetary aid for her "more infirm daughter." This detail is helpful, for it suggests that Isaac Royall, Sr.'s March 12, 1776, letter to a family friend, cited in Hoover's study of the Royalls, may be referring to Belinda in its close:

> As to Betsey, and her daughter Nancy, the former may tarry, or take her freedom, as she may choose; and Nancy you may put out to some good family by the year.

The General Court granted Belinda a yearly annual pension of close to fifteen pounds from Royall's estate, but she received nothing after the first year. She made another request in 1787. The original appeal was printed in Mathew Carey's Philadelphia-based journal, the *American Museum.* (The date of the original petition is given erroneously there as 1782.) The court awarded her another year's pension in November 1787. There is no additional record found to date that gives any information about her life after this time.

At the time of the original petition, Belinda's age is given as approximately seventy. She is described as "marked with the furrows of time, and her frame feebly bending under the oppression of years . . . [unable to enjoy] one morsel of that immense wealth of part whereof hath been accumulated by her own industry, and the whole augmented by her servitude." There is no portrait of the petitioner, but the Royalls' colonial mansion, shown in Stark's work, and the 1741 portrait of the Isaac Royall, Jr. family, reproduced in E. Alfred Jones's *The Loyalists of Massachusetts,* serve to capture visually the prosperity to which Belinda and her fellow slaves contributed significantly.

REFERENCES:

Braxton, Joanne M. *Black Women Writing Autobiography.* Philadelphia: Temple University Press, 1989.

Curtin, Philip D. *The Atlantic Slave Trade: A Census.* Madison: University of Wisconsin Press, 1969.

Dunn, Richard S. *Sugar and Slaves: The Rise of the Planter Class in the English West Indies, 1624-1713.* Chapel Hill: University of North Carolina Press, 1972.

Hoover, Gladys N. *The Elegant Royalls of Colonial New England.* New York: Vantage Press, 1974.

Jones, E. Alfred. *The Loyalists of Massachusetts: Their Memorials, Petitions, and Claims.* 1930. Reprint. Baltimore: Genealogical Publishing Co., 1969.

Kaplan, Sydney, and Emma Nogrady Kaplan. *The Black Presence in the Era of the American Revolution.* Rev. ed. Amherst: University of Massachusetts Press, 1989.

Loggins, Vernon. *The Negro Author.* 1931. Reprint. Port Washington, N.Y.: Kennikat Press, 1959.

Mott, Abigail Field. *Biographical Sketches and Interesting Anecdotes of Persons of Color.* New York: Mahlon Day, 1839.

"Petition of an African Slave, to the Legislature of Massachusetts." *American Museum or Repository of Ancient and Modern Fugitive Pieces &C. Prose and Poetical* 1 (June 1787): 463-65. Printed by Mathew Carey, 1788.

"Royall, Isaac." *Appleton's Cylopedia of American Biography.* Edited by James Grant Wilson and John Fisk. 1888. Reprint. Detroit: Gale Research, 1968.

"Royall, Isaac." *Dictionary of American Biography.* Edited by Francis S. Drake. Boston: James R. Osgood and Co., 1872.

Sabine, Lorenzo. *Biographical Sketches of Loyalists of the American Revolution with an Historical Essay.* Vol. 2. 1864. Reprint. Port Washington, N.Y.: Kennikat Press, 1966.

Stark, James H. *The Loyalists of Massachusetts and the Other Side of the American Revolution.* 1910. Reprint. Clifton, N.J.: Augustus M. Kelley, 1972.

Arlene Clift-Pellow

Halle Berry
(c. 1967-)
Actress, model, activist

Halle Berry, considered one of Hollywood's hottest black actresses and one of the fifty most beautiful women in the world, gained fame first as a beauty queen, then for her roles in film and on television. Since her film debut in 1991, she has had a high-profile rise to success. While she may be best known for her lead role as Alex Haley's grandmother in the television miniseries *Queen,* Berry calls herself an activist for the integration of the film industry.

Berry was born around 1967 in Cleveland to a white mother and a black father. Her father, who was an alcoholic and abusive to his wife, left the family when Berry was four years old. Berry and her sister, Heidi, were raised by their mother, Judith (Judy) Berry, a registered nurse. Life in a racist society was not easy for the young, biracial child. At first Judy Berry and her daughters lived in Cleveland's inner-city neighborhood where race was not an issue. But when they moved to the racially mixed suburban neighborhood of Bedford, race became an issue. Such taunts as "half-breed," "mulatto," and "Oreo cookie" were often hurled at Berry, who was totally unaware of their meaning.

Berry attended the predominantly white Bedford High School, where she was constantly confronted with racial discrimination. Her schoolmates rejected her, often engaging her in fights. She told Laura Randolph for the April 1993 *Ebony,*

> The Black kids assumed I thought I was better than they were, and the White kids didn't like me because I was Black. And I didn't know who I felt comfortable with, Black people or White people.

She added that her mother had cleared up any uncertainty about whether she was white or black when Berry was very young. Berry paraphrased her mother's remark for Randolph: "When you look in the mirror you're going to see a Black woman. You're going to be discriminated against as a Black woman so ultimately, in this society, that's who you will be." Berry continued:

> And that's made my life very easy. . . . I think if you're an interracial child and you're strong enough to live "I'm neither Black nor White but in the middle," then more power. But I *needed* to make a choice and feel part of this culture. I feel a lot of pride in being a Black woman.

Judith Berry's warnings were in fact accurate predictions of the future and helped to shape Halle Berry's thought on matters of race. After she was elected prom queen in her senior year in high school, she was accused of stealing the crown. "They weren't about to have a Black prom queen, so they accused me of stuffing the ballot box," she related to

Halle Berry

Berry Makes Mark as Actress

Since making her first film, Spike Lee's *Jungle Fever,* in 1991, Berry's rise as an actress has seemed effortless. Berry starred as Vivien, a crazed crack addict, in Lee's movie, which helped her win fans on the big screen. To prepare for the role, she trained to become an emotional and physical wreck, interviewing more than eighty recovering cocaine addicts. She deliberately delayed taking a bath for ten days to "get into character." She felt that the role enabled her viewers to see her as more than a beauty queen or a pretty face. Berry's performance established her as a talented character actress.

Also in 1991, she appeared as a sexy, aloof entertainer in the movie *Strictly Business,* and with Damon Wayans and Bruce Willis in *The Last Boy Scout.* In 1992 she appeared as Eddie Murphy's friend and lover in the film *Boomerang.* She had a recurring role in the popular nighttime soap opera, *Knots Landing,* but left the show to work on Murphy's movie. She told Trudy Moore for *Jet* magazine that the script for *Knots Landing* had been written "to allow her character, Debbie, to return at any time"; she had taken the part for financial reasons.

Berry gained popular attention again in 1993 with the television miniseries *Queen,* in which she played Alex Haley's grandmother. Until the series was filmed, she had spent little time in the South. The character that she played enabled her to get in touch with her feelings about the internal turmoil she had known early in life because of the confusion over her racial identity. "I saw a lot of the young me in *Queen,*" she told Laura Randolph. "The confusion, the uncertainty, not really knowing if you should be Black or White." The film also led to emotional difficulties afterward, as Berry examined the continued oppression of blacks and other racist practices. She told Lisa Jones for *Essence,* "Racism can give you the blues."

Berry has since appeared in other movies. In *Honor among Thieves* she played opposite Patrick Swayze as a journalist, and she played a college student in *The Program,* with James Caan. She won praise for her work in *Halle-lujha.* She appeared as a seductive Stone Age secretary in *The Flintstones* (1994), having studied old tapes of Mae West to prepare for the role. After completing shooting on *Losing Isaiah,* filmed in Chicago, she was off to Morocco to play Queen of Sheba in the film *Solomon and Sheba.* Beyond this, Berry has been working quietly studying the life of educator and activist Angela Davis, gearing up to convince the studios that Davis's work affected all Americans regardless of race. In addition, Suzanne de Passe of de Passe Entertainment approached Berry about a film on the life of Elaine Brown, who headed the Black Panther Party. Considering both possibilities, Berry told Trudy Moore for *Jet,* "I'd just like to have good work that I can be proud of and hope that I've crossed the color line and opened doors for others who come behind me."

While Berry has worked with black film directors and independents, since 1993 she has focused on projects "to open doors to the mainstream," as she told Lisa Jones for *Jet.*

Randolph in 1993. The racist students could accept the fact that she was an A student, "but when it came to being the queen, that was something different," she said. Backed by the administration, the students forced her to share the crown. According to Berry, the co-queens were "me and this White, blond, blue-eyed, all-American girl." Devastated by the decision to have two queens, Berry said, "It made me feel like I wasn't beautiful; that they don't see *us* as beautiful."

Challenges were a part of Berry's life. When she was seventeen years old, a high school boyfriend entered her name in the Miss Teen Ohio Pageant. She won that title in 1985 as well as the Miss Ohio Pageant. The state title qualified her for competition in the 1985 Miss USA contest, in which she was named first runner-up. In 1986 she was winner of the dress competition in the Miss World Pageant.

In 1986 Berry entered Cuyahoga Community College in Cleveland, where she studied broadcast journalism. However, she soon turned her attention to modeling and left college that year, moving to Chicago to pursue modeling and to study acting. Berry auditioned for a role in Aaron Spelling's television pilot *Charlie's Angels '88,* a show that never aired. Impressed with her Los Angeles screen test, Spelling encouraged her to continue to pursue acting. Berry's career began to take off. She did a three-week USO tour with Bob Hope and also signed with a manager, Vincent Cirrincione. She moved to New York City and landed a role as a brainy model in ABC's situation comedy *Living Dolls,* which premiered on September 26, 1989. When the show was canceled (it was last telecast on December 30, 1989), Berry worried that people weren't taking her seriously as an actress.

She further stated that she would like to see blacks in the industry depart from stereotypical roles: "I'd like to see us change the picture of ourselves that we're presenting to the public. It's something that *we* have to do because the studios won't."

A compassionate woman, in 1993 Berry shared an apartment with Paul Kirkpatrick, a gay white male who was dying of AIDS. She called him "the best friend I have," and their relationship gave her a new perspective on life and a new understanding of AIDS. She told Laura Randolph in 1993 that, through Kirkpatrick, she learned "the real meaning of love and friendship" and about "the value of life. . . . I've learned how short and precious life is."

Berry already knew pain, suffering, and disease. The pain and suffering had come through abusive relationships with males. First she observed her father's abusive behavior in the home, then she entered more than one romantic relationship of her own in which her partners became abusive or destructive. Admitting that she always wanted an honest, romantic relationship, she told Laura Randolph in 1993 that she allowed herself "to get in some strange relationships because I was searching for that." She had turned to men who needed to be "rescued" but in time they left her "holding all their baggage." One highly abusive relationship left her permanently damaged. "One guy hit me in the eardrum and I lost 80 percent of my hearing in my left ear," she told Randolph. She remembered her mother's teaching: "If a man hits you, you get out as fast as you can. You leave smoke." And she did. Although she should wear a hearing aid, often she is too self-conscious to do so.

While filming *Living Dolls,* Berry collapsed, having entered a diabetic coma. Her doctors noted that stress probably caused the disease to manifest itself early in her life rather than in her later years. Although doctors told her that she would be insulin-dependent the rest of her life, she has improved her health through diet, exercise, meditation, and low-stress activities. Exercise is a "vital part of feeling good and staying healthy," she told *Ebony* in July 1993. At that time she had a state-of-the-art gym at home that she used to work out four times a week for sixty to ninety minutes; she also had a personal trainer to work with her when she was filming away from home.

Berry sees as one of the most personally rewarding events in her life her marriage to Atlanta Braves outfielder David Justice, a native of Cincinnati. After a courtship of ten months, Justice accepted Berry's marriage proposal. When asked how she "got the nerve" to propose, Berry told Lisa Jones, "I felt good about it. It was part of my taking control of my love life and relationships." It freed her from the unfortunate interpersonal relationships she had known earlier. Berry and Justice married in the early hours on New Year's Day 1993, in their Atlanta home. Judith Berry was the maid of honor, and Nettie Justice, David's mother, was his "best woman." Both mothers shared common experiences: they were single parents of high-profile offspring whose fathers left home when their children were four years old. Although

Berry and Justice have busy careers and they must deal with being apart, they respect each other's work. The marriage has resulted in greater calm and internal peace for Berry.

Halle Berry is constantly in the news because of her talent, her film work, and her beauty. In 1993 *People* magazine named her one of their "50 Most Beautiful People in the World." *Ebony*'s Annual Readers Poll, published in the September 1993 issue, called Berry and Denzel Washington the "hottest stars in Black America." Readers called the two "the most attractive Black female and male" as well as the ones they would "like most to spend an evening with." Berry is committed to addressing the problems that destroy black communities—guns and drugs. Her mission is also to protest the work of a color-biased film industry, to force the industry to stop portraying black women as nannies, prostitutes, and crackheads. She continues to support new roles for the black woman in films. She told Lisa Jones, "I feel that this is *our* time to break new ground, to make statements."

Berry's professional life continues on the upswing. She has formed her own production company. She has also signed on to star in a Disney-funded movie, *Eden Close.* Halle Berry and her husband David Justice now live in the Hollywood Hills section of Los Angeles.

Current Address: c/o Cirrincione Lee Entertainment, Inc., 300 West 55th St., New York, NY 10019, and 8721 Sunset Blvd., P-8, Los Angeles, CA 90069.

REFERENCES:

"Annual Readers Poll." *Ebony* 50 (September 1993): 92-94, 96.

Collier, Aldore D. "Halle Berry Plays Seductive, Stone Age Secretary in Movie *The Flintstones.*" *Jet* 86 (June 6, 1994): 36-38, 40.

Contemporary Black Biography. Vol. 4. Detroit: Gale Research, 1993.

"Halle Berry and David Justice Purchase New Home in Los Angeles." *Jet* 87 (November 28, 1994): 15.

"Halle Berry: Strictly Business about Show Business." *Ebony* 47 (February 1992): 36, 38, 40-41.

Jones, Lisa. "The Blacker the Berry: Not Just Another High-Toned Ingenue, Halle Berry Is an Activist Actress Who Speaks Her Mind." *Essence* 25 (June 1994): 60-62, 114-16.

Moore, Trudy S. "Halle Berry: Actress Tells Why She Sticks by Male Friend with Aids." *Jet* 81 (June 20, 1992): 34-37.

Randolph, Laura B. "Halle Berry: Hollywood's Hottest Black Actress Has a New Husband, a New Home and a New Attitude." *Ebony* 48 (April 1993): 118-20, 122.

———. "Halle Berry: On Her Roles, Her Regrets and Her Real-Life Nightmare." *Ebony* 50 (December 1994): 114-15, 118-22.

"Running in the Fast Lane." *Ebony* 48 (July 1993): 68, 70, 74.

"Summer Movies Doing Bang-Up Business." *USA Today,* July 10, 1992.

Jessie Carney Smith

Ruth Gardena Birnie

Ruth Gardena Birnie
(1884-1956)
Pharmacist, clubwoman

Ruth Gardena Birnie was one of the earliest African American pharmacists in South Carolina, male or female. In the early to mid-1900s, health care among blacks in Sumter and the surrounding rural areas was improved as the result of Birnie's work as a pharmacist. She also helped enhance the social life of local blacks by making her drugstore available as a gathering place for those whose social outlets were restricted.

On August 15, 1884, Ruth Gardena Birnie was born to Moses and Louise Harrison in Sumter, South Carolina. The Harrisons had six other children—Louise, Katie, Melinda, Rosa, Page, and William. Since her parents died while she was very young, Birnie was reared by Martha A. Savage, a teacher.

Birnie graduated from Lincoln School, an early African American school in Sumter. Later she taught there for a short period of time. As was customary for women during the early twentieth century, she learned to sew, and she used her talents as a seamstress while teaching school.

In 1902, when she was eighteen years old, she married Charles Wainwright Birnie, who came to Sumter as its first African American physician. Charles W. Birnie, a native of Charleston, South Carolina, was educated at Avery Institute, Wilbraham Academy, Oberlin College, and the University of Pennsylvania School of Medicine. Sixteen years after their marriage, the Birnies gave birth to a daughter, Anna.

As Charles W. Birnie's practice grew, he and Martha Savage, Ruth Birnie's foster mother, encouraged Ruth to pursue pharmacy as a profession. She entered Benedict College, then went on to Temple University and received her degree in pharmacy.

Upon her return to South Carolina, Birnie became one of the earliest female African American pharmacists in the state. About 1912, she opened her drugstore, People's Pharmacy, on West Liberty Street. Ruth Birnie worked in close proximity to her husband. Charles Birnie's office was located upstairs and the People's Pharmacy was located downstairs in the same building on West Liberty Street.

Ruth Birnie's drugstore was open for service Monday through Friday from 8:00 A.M. to 9:00 P.M. and Saturday from 8:00 A.M. to 11:00 P.M. In addition to medicine, the store sold ice cream, sodas, and sundries and was a social gathering place for African Americans, most especially for those from the rural areas on weekends—hence, the late hours on Saturday night. One can imagine conversations on farming, church, social activities, and family well-being and the exchange of recipes and child rearing techniques as people sat around the store's marble tables.

Ruth Birnie often accompanied her husband to rural areas when he was summoned to deliver children or to treat illnesses. Their working relationship appears to have been strong, and both were committed to medicine and had respect for professional responsibility.

Ruth and Charles Birnie also had a strong commitment to the community. According to Anna Birnie McDonald, their daughter, "They were very interested in young people getting an education." The Birnies entertained the graduates of Lincoln High School in their home annually for many years and gave scholarships to students. The couple loved people and arranged parties to celebrate various occasions.

After Charles W. Birnie died in 1938, Ruth Birnie closed People's Pharmacy. She was active in the Good Shepherd Episcopal Church, the Federated Club, "One More Effort" (a club participating in the South Carolina Federation of Colored Women), and the Palmetto Medical, Dental and Pharmaceutical Association. Birnie became an avid reader of the classics. After an extended illness, she died on June 10, 1956.

REFERENCES:

"Black Women Pharmacist Served Others." *The Sumter Item,* March 9, 1983.

McDonald, Anna Birnie. Interview with Barbara Williams Jenkins. Sumter, South Carolina, May 22, 1993.

———. "Recollections of Dr. C. W. Birnie," unpublished paper, 1979. Sumter Historical Society, Sumter, South Carolina.

Barbara Williams Jenkins

Juliann S. Bluitt

(1938-)

Dentist, college administrator, educator, writer, lecturer

Juliann S. Bluitt

Juliann S. Bluitt is a doctor of dental surgery, a dental school administrator, an advocate of organized dentistry, a teacher, and an author. For over thirty years Bluitt has strived to advance the philosophy of comprehensive dentistry and total patient care for all citizens, particularly children, through dental education. The first woman president of the Chicago Dental Society and Northwestern University Dental School's first full-time African American teacher, Bluitt is an inspiration to aspiring dentists because of her community involvement and high standards. Bluitt has opened doors not only for women and minorities to become dentists but also for advocates of the profession and patients. She told the *Chicago Sun-Times,* February 15, 1991, "I may never pass this way again. Whatever good that I do, let me do it now."

Juliann Stephanie Bluitt was born on June 14, 1938, in Washington, D.C., the daughter of Stephen Bernard Bluitt, a hospital payroll clerk, and Marion Eugene Hughes, an elementary school teacher. Bluitt married orthodontist Roscoe C. Foster, a former Chicago Dental Society director, on January 27, 1973. Their nuptials were described in great detail in the *Chicago Defender,* February 17, 1973. They have two children, Barbara and David.

Growing up, Bluitt had wanted to be a veterinarian. The recipient of the Louis Ball Scholarship from 1955 to 1959, Bluitt graduated with a bachelor of science degree from Howard University in Washington, D.C., in 1958. In 1955, she received the Daughters of the American Revolution Citizenship Award. Bluitt had applied and been accepted to schools of veterinary medicine, but in the spring before she was to enter graduate school, she decided that she did not want to leave home. As there were no veterinary schools in Washington, D.C., she attended Howard University Dental School.

Bluitt told the *Chicago Tribune,* June 26, 1988, that when she enrolled in the dental school of Howard University in 1958, she wanted "to do something I could believe in, to be independent, to have a challenge and do something that was different for a woman. I liked science and working with my hands." She was also driven by her desire to bring dentistry to people who didn't have it, especially children. While the science of dentistry was her motivation, Bluitt's childhood orthodontist was her greatest professional role model. He improved her appearance greatly with the braces he put on her teeth when she was a teenager. Bluitt said in *Ebony,* March 1973, "I was highly impressed by the orthodontic care I received as a child. There was a wide opening between my front teeth—wide enough to fit in another tooth. And I was a finger sucker for a long time. So when I saw what my parents sacrificed for me to have this work done and the end results, I was amazed."

Bluitt had the benefit of studying bridge and crown work under Jeanne Sinkford, whose appointment at Howard University in 1968 made her the first woman associate dean of any dental school in the United States. Bluitt received her doctor of dental surgery degree from Howard University's College of Dentistry in 1962. She was a LaVerne Noyes Foundation Fellow and a member of the Omicron Kappa Upsilon Honorary Dental Fraternity. Bluitt remained at Howard University for a few years to teach in the department of oral diagnosis.

The lack of access to medical services persists as a national concern, but the lack of access to dental care has proven to be even more acute. What is most alarming about the lack of access to dental services is that teeth problems are progressive in nature: for example, problems overlooked among children tend to worsen as they grow older. In an attempt to reach this underserved populace, Bluitt practiced with the Chicago Board of Health as a dentist in the public schools and in forty free clinics in Chicago's Englewood community from 1964 to 1967. She also contributed her services to "Project Headstart," a community program that took dentistry to Chicago neighborhoods during the summers from 1964 to 1966.

Bluitt Joins Northwestern University Dental School

Bluitt was one of only a handful of African American female dental professionals who lived or practiced in Chicago in the 1960s. When the dean of the Northwestern University Dental School decided to upgrade the dental hygiene program to departmental status within the institution, Bluitt was chosen to direct the program. She joined the faculty in 1967 as director of dental hygiene and became the first full-time African American teacher at the Northwestern University Dental School (NUDS).

The transition from practicing dentistry on young children to educating older students to become dental professionals was very satisfying. In her new position, Bluitt was able to help train students to provide dental care for hundreds of people. Continuing her focus on improving the dental health of children, Bluitt guided the dental school in a comprehensive, community-oriented program of dental care. She sponsored several projects, getting the students to participate in dental health education programs involving children from orphanages, Upward Bound programs, churches, and the Jane Addams Center of Chicago's Hull House Association. The dental school's community program was also extended with a mobile van dental clinic facility.

In 1970, Bluitt was appointed assistant dean for auxiliary and community programs and patient relations at Norwestern University Dental School. The 1970s witnessed a change in many dental school curriculums, with added emphasis on the dentist's responsibility to provide quality health care to the indigent community. Implementing one of the suggestions of the dental students at Northwestern, Bluitt instituted a free dental clinic on Saturday mornings as part of the dental school's program to serve the community. Students and faculty volunteered their time and services at the clinic, which accommodated an average of twenty patients each week. Bluitt arranged for guest lecturers to discuss community dental care. Under Bluitt's leadership, the People's Clinic provided young patients with oral health rehabilitation and maintenance at very low cost. She designed and wrote the *Hector and Timmy Coloring Book* to motivate children and give them a sense of participation in the dental care process. These services were accomplished in conjunction with Bluitt's responsibilities for the NUDS dental hygiene program and her other assignments as an assistant professor in the medical school's Department of Community Medicine. From 1972 to 1978, Bluitt served as associate dean of auxiliary and community programs for the dental school.

Dentist Committed to Service

A strong advocate for the health of the nation's young people, Bluitt exhorted her colleagues to work for a national dental health program that would give priority to youth. The *Ladies Home Journal,* September 1972, quotes her on this issue: "At least for children [dental health] is a human right." Her efforts in this regard did not go unnoticed. In April 1973, associate dean Bluitt was named Dentist of the Year by the Illinois chapter of the American Society of Dentistry for Children. The Chicago Area Council of Boy Scouts of America awarded her its Good Scout Award in 1973. In 1974, Bluitt received a fellowship from the American College of Dentists.

Approximately eleven hundred women in the United States were engaged in the private practice of dentistry in 1976, comprising 1.2 percent of the total profession. However, less than one percent of these women were African American. Bluitt is tireless in her efforts to recruit women and minority students for dental professions. From 1979 to 1989, she served as head of the combined Office of Student Affairs and Dental Admissions at Northwestern's dental school. "In 1970, only 2 percent of first year dental students were women," said Bluitt in the May 13, 1993, issue of the *Chicago Tribune.* "By 1990 the figure was 38 percent, and by 2000 it's expected to be at least 40 percent." Bluitt has always believed that dentistry is ideal for women. She told the *Chicago Tribune,* April 1, 1973, "Women have definite assets for this job. They have a sensitivity for people, manual dexterity, and an ability to work in a limited space."

Bluitt addressed her own continuing education needs by acquiring a certificate in personnel administration from Northwestern University's University College in 1984. As part of a university review in 1988, the NUDS dean gave Bluitt the task of developing a recruitment program and admission policies that would attract highly qualified students. In her new capacity as associate dean for student affairs, Bluitt supervises all aspects of the nonacademic life of students, including student government, counseling, housing, parking, health issues, and protection of student rights. In addition, she monitors the Faculty and Clinical Adviser programs, another important responsibility in assisting a diverse student body.

Bluitt's list of awards and honors is impressive. They include the Alumni Award for Distinguished Postgraduate Achievement, Howard University, 1974; Outstanding Service Award, American Dental Association and Colgate-Palmolive Company, 1983; and Outstanding Service to the Community and to the Profession of Dentistry Award, Howard University, 1988. In August of 1975, Bluitt received the Citation Award from Phi Delta Kappa. The national sorority cited her "for distinguished achievement in Dental Education and Human Welfare through preventive dental hygiene and recruitment of women and minorities for dental professions."

Devotion to Organizations

Committee appointments and consultant work require that Bluitt devote a great deal of her time and energy to a variety of institutions and organizations. At each stage of her professional development, Bluitt has published numerous articles in scholarly journals and given speeches and presentations at a wide array of medical, educational, and community forums on many aspects of dental health, dental education, and the dental profession. She was a contributing author to *The Profile of the Negro in American Dentistry,* edited by Foster Kidd (1979). She cochaired the dental education plenary session for the national workshop/conference on ''Black Dentistry in the Twenty-first Century,'' June 23-27, 1991, in Ann Arbor, Michigan. In 1991, she completed a four-year term as regent for the American College of Dentists.

In recognition of her involvement in dental care and dental education in the city, Bluitt was inducted into the Chicago Women's Hall of Fame in December 1991. She was recognized for her work with children as a past member of the Chicago Board of Health and for her promotion of the Donna Olsen People's Clinic at NUDS. Bluitt has made numerous appearances on television and radio shows presenting information about proper dental care for young people, preventive dental concepts, innovations in dentistry, and careers in dentistry.

Bluitt became the first woman to head the Chicago Dental Society (CDS) in the group's 128-year history, becoming president-elect in May 1991. Her term of office lasted until 1993. As CDS president, Bluitt led the management team responsible for formulating policies and conducting business for the forty-five-hundred-member organization. The CDS's mid-winter meeting draws tens of thousands of dental professionals from around the world and is the largest gathering of its kind. During her presidency, Bluitt gave visibility to the overlooked problems affecting the general health and well-being of women.

For over twenty years, Bluitt has served as a member of a variety of boards of directors, including the editorial boards of the *Journal of Dental Education* and the *Journal of the American Dental Hygienists' Association;* the board of the Health Care Service Corporation (Blue Cross/Blue Shield of Illinois); the board of the Johnson Rehabilitation Nursing Home; and the board of Urban Gateways, the Center for Arts in Education. She has also served as a trustee of the American Fund for Dental Health and as a governor of the Odontographic Society. She is active in the Alpha Gamma Pi philanthropic sorority. Bluitt is a member of the American College of Dentists, American Association of Dental Schools, National Dental Association, Federation Dentaire Internationale, American Society of Dentistry for Children, American Association of Women Dentists, Pierre Fauchard Academy, the Odontographic Society of Chicago, International College of Dentists, and the American Society of Association Executives.

In a statement on file at Fisk University, Bluitt summarized a career that is still evolving:

> What I have done, directly or indirectly, in fostering the delivery of dental health care for people, especially children, and impressing upon adults and children the importance of dental home care, has given me the greatest professional satisfaction. I have been involved in programs for adults and children, using various methods of communication to demonstrate and inform. Another area of major interest in which I have actively engaged is in the recruitment of minorities and women into the health professions. I have spoken at career days in schools, and to organizations stressing the advantages of a career in the dental health professions.

Bluitt no longer has a private practice but she continues in her position as associate dean for student affairs at NUDS and serves as a professor in the Department of Dental Hygiene and Community Dentistry at NUDS. She is a lecturer in the departments of Community Health and Preventive Medicine at Northwestern University's medical school and teaches courses from introductory dentistry to dental ethics. Bluitt's interests include travel, theater, the outdoors, golf, knitting, collecting crystal and porcelain, and domestic animals. She enjoys playing the organ and the piano. A woman with a warm wit, she fails to allow her hectic schedule to shatter her poise or ruin her enjoyment of life. One of her favorite anecdotes, published in the April 12, 1973, issue of the *Chicago Tribune,* is about a woman who worried more about how her teeth looked than how they felt: ''She asked me just to clean the front ones because the back ones don't show.''

Current Address: Associate Dean for Student Affairs, Northwestern University Dental School, 311 East Chicago Avenue, Chicago, IL 60611.

REFERENCES:

Bluitt, Juliann S. *Curriculum Vitae.* 1988.
———. ''Female Dental Students.'' *Journal of the American College of Dentists* 58 (Fall 1991): 24-26.
———. *Hector and Timmy Coloring Book.* Chicago: American Association of Dentistry for Children, 1970.
———.''Hull House and Northwestern Join Forces.'' *Journal of the American Dental Hygienists Association* 43 (Fourth Quarter 1969): 205-6.
———. ''Women Power in Dentistry.'' *Dental Assistant* 43 (September 1974): 10-12.
''Bluitt Makes Dental History.'' *Chicago Defender,* July 13, 1992.
''Chicago Profile: Juliann S. Bluitt.'' *Chicago Sun-Times,* February 15, 1991.
''Dental Dean.'' *Ebony* 28 (March 1973): 84-92.
Dummett, Clifton O., and Lois Doyle Dummett. *Culture and Education in Dentistry at Northwestern University (1891-1993).* Chicago: Northwestern University Dental School, 1993.
''For Dentistry, It's the Brushoff—At Least for Now.'' *Chicago Tribune,* June 26, 1988.
''Juliann S. Bluitt, CDS President 1992-93.'' *CDS Review* 85 (June 1992): 14-20.
Kidd, Foster, ed. *The Profile of the Negro in American Dentistry.* Washington, D.C.: Howard University Press, 1979.
''Putting Children First.'' *Ladies Home Journal* 89 (September 1972): 78.

"She's Fighting the Battle for Better Teeth for Everyone."
Chicago Tribune, April 1, 1973.

"Simplicity Keys Wedding of Drs. Bluitt, Foster." *Chicago Defender,* February 17, 1973.

"Women Sinking Teeth in Dentistry." *Chicago Tribune,* May 13, 1993.

COLLECTIONS:

Biographical information on Juliann S. Bluitt, including a questionnaire, is located in the Fisk University Library, Nashville, Tennessee.

Kathleen E. Bethel

Dorothy Lee Bolden
(1923-)
Labor organizer

After becoming familiar with the plight of domestic workers, Dorothy Lee Bolden founded the National Domestic Workers Union to improve work conditions and the wage system for its members. Training programs for maids, counseling, and job placement were among its primary activities. Bolden's work touched the lives of domestic workers on a national scale and changed the direction that their lives took. She received national recognition for her work as a community leader of consequence.

Born on October 13, 1923, in Atlanta, Georgia, Dorothy Lee Bolden was the daughter of Raymond Bolden and Georgia Mae Patterson Bolden. While her father worked as a chauffeur, her mother migrated to Atlanta from Madison, Georgia, to work as a domestic cook.

For various reasons, formal education did not come to the young Bolden easily. Her initial handicap stemmed from the fact that, at the age of three years, Bolden was blinded when her optical nerve was damaged in a fall. It was between the ages of seven and nine that she regained her sight. Bolden then attended E. P. Johnson Elementary School and David T. Howard High School in Atlanta, Georgia, but her formal education terminated at the ninth grade as she needed a job to support herself.

In 1930, barely seven years old, Bolden took her first job, cleaning baby diapers after school for one dollar and twenty-five cents per week. At the age of twelve, she began to clean house for a Jewish family for a weekly wage of one dollar and fifty cents.

Bolden's first marriage took place in 1941. She married a man named Frank Smith; the relationship did not produce any children and ended in divorce within a short time. Bolden said little about Smith, although her friends and relatives could discern a lot from her description of her ex-husband as "just a good looking man coming." Her second marriage, to Abram Thompson, produced six children. To earn enough money to support her family, Bolden took various jobs, including employment with the Greyhound bus station, Linen Supply Company, Sears Roebuck, and Railroad Express.

In order to have ample time to be with her six children and husband, Bolden had the habit of leaving her salaried jobs after working for a brief period. However, compelled by the necessity of having an income to contribute to the family's budget, Bolden would invariably take domestic jobs in the interim. For her future retirement and social security needs, she made sure that she had regular company jobs that contributed adequately to her Social Security. According to Darlene Clark Hine, Bolden once stated, "I would quit when I got ready and take a domestic because of the excitement of going."

It could be true that Bolden found excitement in her domestic jobs because she worked as a maid from 1930 until 1968. Also, she had her share of problems with some of her employers. For example, it is on record that she was jailed for five days for allegedly talking back to one of her employers. As she was to explain in later life, Bolden was considered mentally ill for talking back to the employer, but her own explanation for her conduct was, according to Hine, that "no one had ever talked as nasty to me as she did."

Bolden took pride in the fact that the late civil rights leader Martin Luther King, Jr. was her neighbor in Atlanta. Consequently, she became a faithful follower of King's teachings and, in the 1960s, was actively involved in civil rights and labor issues. For example, when the Atlanta School Board decided to move the eighth grade class out of her community to a dilapidated school building in downtown Atlanta, Bolden led the organized protest to stop the move and to demand quality as well as equal education. Bolden's tough civil rights stance prompted the school board to construct an ultra-modern school building in her area of the city.

By 1964, Bolden's civil rights involvement led her to become painfully aware of the poor service conditions endured by domestic workers. Therefore, she decided to come to grips with the need for an avenue through which her hardworking colleagues could enjoy improved conditions. What prompted her immediate reaction was the fact that, during that period, the official hourly minimum wage was supposed to be one dollar and twenty-five cents. Yet, according to the *Atlanta Constitution* and Bolden's records at Georgia State University, African Americans who served as domestic hands were paid a flat rate of between three dollars and five dollars a day, working no less than twelve to thirteen hours daily.

Joins Ranks in Organized Labor

In 1968, Bolden took the plunge into the ranks of organized labor. She decided to utilize her organizing and leadership capabilities as well as rely on her close association with Martin Luther King's Atlanta-based civil rights movement. Consequently, Bolden approached organized labor officials for guidance in her efforts to organize her fellow domestic workers, and her efforts culminated in the creation of the National Domestic Workers Union (NDWU). NDWU's immediate goal was to help its Atlanta-based members to achieve better conditions, including increased wages. Other goals of the union included the development of training programs for maids and the creation of a nonprofit employee service to offer job placement as well as counseling for its active members. The efforts of the Atlanta organization offered the yardstick by which domestic workers outside of Atlanta measured their own predicament and service conditions. Although Bolden's new union, of which she became the president in September 1968, was not affiliated with the AFL-CIO, the NDWU worked very closely with organized labor leaders.

The NDWU succeeded in recruiting almost all area-based domestic workers into its membership under the able leadership of Bolden. Some of the union's achievements included the fact that it received its union charter, wages for its members increased, and their general working conditions quickly improved. In fact, toward the end of the 1960s, NDWU had succeeded in getting between thirteen dollars and fifty cents and fifteen dollars per day and busfare or carfare for the maids. Also, members of the union were taught methods of bargaining and working out differences amicably with their employers. In the end, the union became a force to reckon with and Bolden received national recognition as a community leader. She became so powerful that in the 1970s, Bolden was consulted on matters dealing with workers by presidents Richard Nixon and Gerald Ford and her fellow Georgian, President Jimmy Carter. Her numerous national honors included membership on the advisory committee to Department of Health, Education and Welfare Secretary Elliot L. Richardson. Back in Georgia, in 1975 Bolden was appointed by Governor George Busbee to the Georgia Commission on the Status of Women.

By the early 1980s, the local and national standing of NDWU was to be undermined by the detailed investigation of the National Domestic Workers Emergency Assistance Fund by a federal grand jury. That investigation followed a negative audit report, whose findings included the allegation that much more money had been spent than its funding grants allowed. The only vindication for Bolden was that she had, in fact, utilized personal funds to supplement limited federal funds in the day-to-day operations of the organization for which she had so much love. Although in partial retirement, Bolden continues to work with the National Domestic Workers Union.

Current Address: 52 Fairlee Street, N.W., Atlanta, Georgia 30303.

REFERENCES:

"Bolden: The Fighter." *The Atlanta Constitution,* January 6, 1983.
Hine, Darlene Clark, ed. *Black Women in America.* Brooklyn: Carlson Publishing, 1993.
King, Coretta Scott. *My Life with Martin Luther King, Jr.* New York: Holt, Rinehart and Winston, 1969.

COLLECTIONS:

Records of Dorothy Lee Bolden are located at Georgia State University Library, Atlanta.

A. B. Assensoh

Bonner, Marita
    See Occomy, Marita Bonner

Thelma Berlack Boozer
(1906-)
Journalist, public relations official, government official

Thelma Berlack Boozer, a nationally known public relations official and government administrator in New York City, was also a leading black journalist and feminist writer. After a long and very successful association with the *New York Amsterdam Star News,* where she eventually became assistant managing editor, she moved on to set up the school of Journalism at Lincoln University in Jefferson City, Missouri. Returning to New York, she made her feminist views known in articles in such magazines as the *New York Age.* She then made a career change, deciding to pursue public and community relations work. Praised for her work as Community Relations Director of Manhattan, she was asked to join the New York City Office of Civil Defense. She served them for twelve years in a variety of public relations positions. She later took on the difficult job of director of public relations for Harlem Hospital Center in Manhattan, which was in a crisis situation with mounting costs and little community support.

Boozer was born in Ocala, Florida, on September 26, 1906, to Leonard Berlack, a chief of clerks for the Seaboard Railroad, and Sallie Smith Berlack, a dietitian. Although she was the child of a broken home, Thelma Boozer loved and respected her father. "My parents were divorced shortly before I turned 5 years old," she recalled in a column in the *New York Age* on June 18, 1949, "but I knew for a long time the love and devotion of both my parents." They remained in Ocala and young Thelma lived with her mother, grandmother, and great-grandmother. "But my father visited me there whenever he pleased," she said. Boozer visited her father's new family "and was friendly with my stepmother." Boozer

Thelma Berlack Boozer

was quite proud of her father's accomplishments. "My dad was a plugger. Perhaps that trait alone was responsible for the job he held—an exceptional one for a Negro in the deep South. At his death on January 16, 1931, he was clerk-in-charge, U.S. Railway Mail Service, on a run between Jacksonville and Tampa." The salary for this position was quite high, so much so that in 1949 Boozer was able to say, "I am told it is too much now for a Negro!"

Boozer came to New York City with her mother and grandmother, Josephine Smith, in the summer of 1920, as part of the great migration of southern blacks to northern cities during and after World War I. They lived in Manhattan, but Boozer enrolled in Theodore Roosevelt High School in the Bronx and graduated in June 1924 with the highest scholastic average for any student in the school's history. During her senior year in high school, Boozer won the *New York World's* contest for high school students in the New York area for "The Best News Item of the Week." Selected from over eighteen hundred entries, Boozer's article examined "The Proposed Child Labor Amendment" then under consideration in the U.S. Congress.

Upon graduation from high school, Boozer enrolled in New York University, majoring in journalism. She received her bachelor's degree in commercial science with honors in June 1928. While working for several newspapers in the city, she attended New York University for her master's degree in journalism, which she received in February 1931. Her master's thesis examined "The Evolution of Negro Journalism in the United States."

As an undergraduate, Boozer joined Alpha Kappa Alpha Sorority and was editor of its official publication, *Ivy Leaf,* in 1928 and 1929. She became the first director of the North Atlantic Region for Alpha Kappa Alpha, serving from 1930 to 1935. On June 28, 1930, she married James C. Boozer, who worked for the U.S. Postal Service. The couple had two children, Barbara, born in 1937, and Thelma, born in 1946.

Journalism Career Begins

Boozer began her professional career in journalism while she was still an undergraduate student at New York University. She worked as a reporter and columnist for the New York City edition of the *Pittsburgh Courier* between 1924 and 1926. Then she moved to the *New York Amsterdam Star News,* working as reporter, columnist, women's page and feature editor, and finally assistant managing editor. She remained there over fifteen years. In the late 1930s and early 1940s she wrote the society column "Chatter and Chimes," in which she reported the latest goings-on among the Sugar Hill set and other socially connected black New Yorkers. But "TEB," as she was known, was also the author of the "Woman of the Week" column, which highlighted the accomplishments of African American professional women, primarily in the New York area. Nurses, social workers, businesswomen, educators, government employees, and other outstanding black women professionals were profiled, and the elements important for their professional success were examined and disseminated throughout the black community.

In September 1941, due partly to her experiences as a journalist and managing editor, the administrators at Lincoln University asked Boozer to come to Jefferson City, Missouri, to set up its School of Journalism. At the time she was one of a handful of college-trained newspaper journalists who also had years of extensive experience in the field. In her farewell column in the *New York Amsterdam Star News,* December 20, 1941, she admitted, "If I remain in New York, I would continue a life of service. In Missouri, I shall attempt to be of service." At a luncheon held in her honor that served as both celebration and send-off to her new position, over 350 people were in attendance. They heard letters of congratulations and appreciation from Eleanor Roosevelt, Mary McLeod Bethune, and Sherman D. Skruggs, president of Lincoln University. Between January 1942 and March 1944, Boozer served as Lincoln University's first acting director and assistant professor of journalism. During that time she established the program of study, organized the department, hired additional faculty, and placed the fledgling institution well on the road to accreditation. After two years, Boozer was offered the directorship of the school on a permanent basis, but she decided to return to New York City, primarily because she wished to be close to her family and friends. She was a New Yorker at heart.

Upon her return she became a writer for the New York edition of the *Pittsburgh Courier* and a columnist for the *Labor Vanguard,* a monthly magazine published for local trade unionists. Between August 1948 and August 1949, Boozer was an editor and columnist for the *New York Age*. For the two newspapers she wrote for the society page, but in the magazine she wrote stories about the conditions and circumstances for professional and working women. Boozer was committed to reporting the life and times of African American working men and women and she made this clear in the column "The Feminist Viewpoint," published in the *New York Age* between January and August 1949.

Boozer always considered herself a feminist, and in her newspaper columns she often emphasized the accomplishments of African American women in the black community. In her column in the *New York Age* on April 9, 1949, for example, she applauded the social service work of Alberta T. Kline, who had worked for twenty-five years at the New York Mission Society, located on Convent Avenue in Harlem. "The pattern fashioning the lives of more than 15,000 children in religion, education, and recreation has stemmed from Mrs. Kline, who for 22 years was the worker in charge of the girls' program and who for the past 3 years has been executive in charge."

Boozer's feminism also meant "defending the name" and reputation of African American women. At the annual meeting of the Child Study Association of America, held in New York City in March 1949, in a session on "Sex Education—A Critical Evaluation," Bernard Wortis, professor of psychiatry and neurology at New York University's School of Medicine, opened the discussion with "an off-color joke about a 'Negress.'" While admitting that Wortis was a well-respected psychiatrist, in her *New York Age* column on April 2, 1949, Boozer stated, "He is not too learned nor too successful to be told in no uncertain terms that his joke might have gone over better if he had not identified it specifically with a race." Boozer went on to say, "It is a pity that he does not know that the time has long passed since women of the Negro race were referred to as 'Negress' and 'Negresses.'" But more importantly, "Dr. Wortis and everybody else ought to know and admit that loose morals have never been nor never will be restricted to any particular race or creed. Only colossally ignorant persons think, believe, accept, and say offending things about one race to the exclusion of other races, especially in interracial situations."

Boozer's "feminist viewpoint" encompassed the belief that African American men and women who want to maintain a strong marriage or relationship must envelope it in "a cycle of tenderness." "If you expect and accept tenderness," she wrote in her column in the *New York Age* on March 9, 1949, "in turn you should give tenderness, in bountiful doses. In fact, it is possible and advisable to 'jump the gun' and give tenderness without a definite hope of having it meted out to you. Before you know it, however, a cycle of tenderness will be heaped upon you—and all because you set the sparks yourself." Because her parents were divorced when she was quite young, Boozer understood that "divorce, like marriage, may be a mistake," and she advised couples having troubles "to find the courage to stay married." In the current debate

over the black feminist theories, the inclusion of the perspectives of black female journalists such as Thelma Boozer would very likely expand our understanding of the parameters and issues addressed by African American women who considered themselves "feminists" during the early decades of the twentieth century.

Serves Community in New Roles

While serving as a journalist for the *Pittsburgh Courier* and *New York Age,* Boozer began public relations work for the New York office of the National Foundation for Infantile Paralysis and also became head of fund-raising in New York City for the United Negro College Fund. These experiences were very helpful when she assumed the position of director of community relations in the Office of the Borough President of Manhattan, Robert F. Wagner. In this position, which she began in January 1950, Boozer worked to establish and then directed the twelve "Borough of Manhattan Community Planning Boards." These community boards were created to obtain local input in the development of government programs and agencies in the various neighborhoods in Manhattan. When Wagner became mayor of New York City in 1953, this innovative program for community development was expanded throughout New York City's five boroughs.

Partly as a result of the outstanding work Boozer had done as community relations director in Manhattan, in January 1954 newly elected Mayor Wagner decided to appoint Boozer to the New York City Office of Civil Defense. Initially appointed as chief of publications and reports, over the next twelve years she would work in a number of specific areas within the Civil Defense Department. Boozer headed numerous civil defense educational projects and public relations programs. She also served as the director of recruiting information and assisted in hiring staff for the Civil Defense Program. Most important, as chief of publications, Boozer was responsible for disseminating to all residents of New York City information necessary in case of armed attack or other civil defense emergencies.

When Mayor John Lindsay decided to reorganize New York City's Civil Defense Program in July 1966, Boozer left the department for an equally challenging and responsible position. She was appointed by the New York City Health and Hospital Corporation to serve as the director of public relations for the Harlem Hospital Center in Manhattan. The most important medical facility in the largest urban black community in the United States, Harlem Hospital had fallen onto hard times. While the demand for health services increased exponentially, there was no corresponding increase in financial support coming from the city or state governments, and the result was a deterioration in patient services. Moreover, those who were most likely to come to Harlem Hospital for medical services were the poor and lower working class, who not only had nowhere else to turn but also were unable to pay for medical services they received.

As director of public relations at Harlem Hospital beginning in July 1966, Boozer's job was to develop educational programs and materials that fostered a more positive attitude in the community about the hospital. Her office was responsible for issuing press releases and public statements about hospital activities, and it served as a liaison with local newspapers, radio, and television. For seven years, until her retirement in March 1973, Boozer worked with health administrators, city officials, the media, and the public in improving the relations between Harlem Hospital and the residents of New York City.

Over her long and distinguished career, Boozer received numerous awards and certificates of recognition. Named as one of the Ten Leading Newsmen in the nation by *Color Magazine* in 1946, she received awards for journalism from the Brooklyn Service Women's Organization in 1935 and Omega Psi Phi Fraternity in 1938. In May 1954 Boozer received the Sojourner Truth Award from the New York chapter of the National Association of Negro Business and Professional Women's Clubs, and she was honored by the National Association of Colored Women in July 1962 for distinguished achievement. The United Negro College Fund's Greater New York Alumni Division honored Boozer in October 1966 for her "dedicated, unselfish, and effective service to the Fund" for over two decades and for "her leadership in New York Alumni activities." And in April 1981 at the Fiftieth Anniversary Conference of the North Atlantic Region of Alpha Kappa Alpha Sorority, Boozer received an award for her distinguished service and leadership. The professional experiences of Thelma Berlack Boozer represent the heights achieved by African American women who understood that black feminism meant the dedication of one's life to valuable and committed service to their community and the entire nation.

Current Address: 479 West 152nd Street, Number 7N, New York, NY 10031.

REFERENCES:

Boozer, Thelma Berlack. "Evolution of Negro Journalism in the United States." Master's thesis, New York University, 1931.

Boozer, Thelma Berlack, Thelma Boozer Baxter, and Barbara Boozer. Interview with V. P. Franklin, September 26, 1993.

New York Age, March 8, 1924; April 19, 1924; May 10, 1924; July 5, 1924; June 28, 1930; August 6, 1932; January 15, 1949; August 20, 1949; January 23, 1954; April 10, 1954; September 10, 1955.

New York Amsterdam Star News, December 13, 1941; December 17, 1941; December 20, 1941; May 26, 1956; November 12, 1966.

Pittsburgh Courier, June 28, 1930.

United Negro College Fund, Testimonial Dinner in Honor of Thelma Berlack Boozer (pamphlet), October 30, 1966.

Who's Who in Colored America, 1950. 7th ed. Yonkers, N.Y.: C. E. Burckel Publishers, 1950.

                                            V. P. Franklin

Maudelle Brown Bousfield
(1885-1971)
Educator, reformer, club leader

A soft-spoken woman with an unassuming manner, an indomitable will to succeed, and an unquenchable thirst for knowledge, Maudelle Brown Bousfield was a child of the post-Reconstruction era. She carved out a career for herself in education, paved the way for other black women in that field, and offered her expertise in civic and charitable endeavors.

Maudelle Brown was born to Charles Hugh and Arrena Isabella Tanner Brown on June 1, 1885, in Saint Louis, Missouri. The family was part of the rising middle class: Charles Brown himself was a teacher in the Saint Louis public schools for over fifty-two years. He spent the latter part of those years as the principal of L'Ouverture School. Bousfield's mother, Arrena Isabella Tanner, was the niece of Benjamin Tanner, a bishop in the African Methodist Episcopal church. She was also first cousin to Henry O. Tanner, an outstanding painter. Bousfield and her siblings were educated in the public schools of Saint Louis. She graduated from Summer High School and the Charles Kunkel Conservatory of Music in 1903. She holds the distinction of being the first black woman admitted to the conservatory.

Bousfield entered the University of Illinois in 1903 and majored in mathematics and astronomy. She subsidized her education by tutoring other students in mathematics for fifteen cents an hour. In 1906, she became the first black woman to graduate from the University of Illinois. So outstanding was her college record and her subsequent career that she was asked to return to her alma mater in 1965 to be inducted into Phi Beta Kappa. She graduated from Chicago's Mendelssohn Conservatory of Music in 1920.

Begins Professional Career

Bousfield professional career began in East Saint Louis, Illinois, in 1906. She taught mathematics there for a year before moving on to the Colored High School in Baltimore, Maryland. She taught there seven years, 1907-14. She then moved back to Saint Louis and briefly taught mathematics at her old high school, Summer.

She married Midian O. Bousfield, a physician from Kansas, on September 9, 1914. Before marrying Maudelle, Midian Bousfield had graduated from the University of Kansas in 1907 and received his medical degree from Northwestern University in 1909. He practiced medicine in Kansas City, Missouri, and was one of the first black men to be appointed to the staff of the Old General Hospital in that city. After their marriage, the couple moved to Chicago in 1914, and Midian Bousfield continued to practice there until World War II. In 1939 he became the first black member of the Chicago Board of Education. During World War II, Midian Bousfield, along with thirty-five other black officers, organized a large, well-

Maudelle Brown Bousfield

equipped hospital in the Arizona desert for the all-black Ninety-third Division located at Fort Huachuca. Midian Bousfield, who was born in 1885, died of a heart attack on February 16, 1948.

Maudelle Bousfield gave birth to a daughter, to whom she gave her own name, on October 22, 1915. She put her career on hold for seven years to raise her. Her daughter later became a teacher and married W. Leonard Evans, a Chicago publisher and businessman. Maudelle B. Bousfield returned to the classroom in 1922 to teach mathematics at Chicago's Wendell Phillips Senior High School.

The early schools in Chicago were racially mixed. The city was willing to lure black teachers from other northern schools to Chicago, but this all changed during the early years of the twentieth century. Rising racial tension and prejudice culminated in a violent race riot in the summer of 1919. By this time the black population was scattered throughout enclaves on the south and west sides of the city. Even neighborhood schools that were predominantly black were filled with overwhelming numbers of white teachers and administrators. It was in this tense racial atmosphere that Bousfield returned to her first career.

At Wendell Phillips High School, Bousfield's teaching style won her wide support from students and faculty members alike. According to Benjamin Brawley in *Negro Builders and Heroes,* "the enthusiasm she created for a subject [mathematics] often avoided by young people directed attention to the personal element in her teaching and her ability to enlist the cooperation of students for their own discipline." In

March of 1926, she became the first black dean of girls at Phillips Senior High School, holding that position until 1928.

Bousfield, like many of her colleagues, was lighter in complexion than most of her students. While Bousfield's career ambitions were certainly not impeded either by her light complexion or by her husband's prominence, the extent to which these characteristics helped her advance is in question. Surely, much of her breakthrough career in the Chicago public schools was of her own making.

Bousfield Becomes Chicago's First Black Public School Principal

Bousfield became the first black principal in the Chicago public schools when she was assigned to Keith School in January 1928. Later she was assigned as principal to Stephen A. Douglas from 1931 to 1939 and still later to Wendell Phillips High School from 1939 until her retirement. She thus became both Chicago's first black elementary school principal and first black high school principal. Bousfield had passed a difficult written examination and was given a succession of oral examinations and visits by committees of principals and assistant superintendents before her assignment to Keith School. Regarding her first appointment as principal, she told Harold Gosnell in *Negro Politicians:*

> During my last two years of teaching at Phillips I was a dean. At that time the dean was selected by the principal, or rather the candidates for the positions were selected, for we all had to take an examination, the only one in fact that has been given for this position. I was assigned principal at the Keith school in 1928 and at the Douglas school in 1931. Most persons think that the Douglas assignment was a move up but it really wasn't for there was no increase in salary at all, only more work.
>
> If there has been any politics in the school system, I haven't come into contact with it. I know in my own case there hasn't been any. There was only one time when I was determined to bring very definite political influence to bear and that was when my turn for assignment as principal came. I was determined that if they skipped me I would make trouble. They didn't skip me so I didn't have to do anything.

This may not be completely accurate. A number of organizations and individuals wrote letters on Bousfield's behalf. According to the Irene McCoy Gaines Papers, the black women's clubs of Chicago were solidly behind her appointment.

By the 1930s, elements in the black community expressed concern with the growing trend of placing black teachers and assistant principals in predominantly black schools, creating a segregated school system. Bousfield did not share this view. She argued that the school board had properly placed black teachers. Later she said that she had no trouble securing cooperation between black and white teachers in the schools under her command.

While teaching at Phillips Senior High School, Bousfield decided to return to school to enhance her education and career. She did graduate work at the University of Chicago in 1923-24 and in 1925-26. She took three courses in administration there during the summer of 1930 and received her M.A. in 1931.

The theme of her master's thesis was the measurement of the mental ability and achievement of black children in school. She performed this study while she was at Keith School. She tested 252 students between the fifth and eighth grades. The students were given questionnaires to fill out detailing information about their personal lives and home situations. She concluded that even though the black children tested below normal in reading and arithmetic, further studies with more refined techniques needed to be developed.

She published her findings in the *Journal of Negro Education* in 1932. There she wrote: "until machinery is set up which will yield objective results determining the question as to whether the Negro faces distinct and peculiar social problems which demand special educational objectives and procedures" no accurate judgment can be reached.

She pursued this issue throughout the 1930s, finally concluding: "My own personal opinion is . . . that the Negro's distinct social problems are not being served either in kind or degree by the type of education he is receiving at any level in his training." The education of Negro children, she argued, calls for a curriculum embodying training in "practical activities."

Community Activities Keep Bousfield Busy

Bousfield was a member of Alpha Kappa Alpha Sorority; serving as the organization's national president from 1929 to 1931. At the sorority's California Boule in 1932, Bousfield was the speaker at the public meeting. Her subject, health, was the forerunner of the Health Program established a few years later for which she served on the Advisory Committee for the project. Marjorie Parker characterized her sojourn as one of "morality, scholarship, dependability and service." Her activities in later years were severely curtailed by her failing eyesight. She also held membership in the Central Association of Science and Mathematics Teachers, the National Education Association, and the National Association of Dean of Women.

Bousfield retired from Wendell Phillips in 1950. She remained an active chairwoman of the board of Saint Edmund's Episcopal parochial school that she organized in 1947. She was a member of Mayor Richard Daley's Commission on Juvenile Delinquency and vice-president of the Board of Trustees of Provident Hospital.

After retiring, she gave more time and attention to her organizations, hobbies, and two grandchildren. She was an avid collector of early American glass and a gardening enthusiast at her West Chester home. Bousfield maintained her lifelong interest in music. She was a charter member of the National Association of Negro Musicians that was formed in Chicago after World War I.

She never forgot the children of Chicago and fought tirelessly on their behalf, first in the Chicago public schools and then later as an examiner on the Chicago Board of Education. She never ceased her cry that education should begin in the home and the school's job should be simply to enhance that knowledge and experience.

Maudelle B. Bousfield was truly a role model for teachers and reformers of the twentieth century. She believed that it is never enough to say that one's work is complete, because the job is never finished as long as there are children out there to be educated. Bousfield died on October 14, 1971. A portrait of her hangs in the social room of Wendell Phillips High School and in the board room of the Chicago chapter of Alpha Kappa Alpha.

REFERENCES:

Bousfield, Maudelle B. "A Study of the Intelligence and School Achievement of Negro Children." Master's thesis, University of Chicago, 1931.
———. "The Intelligence and School Achievement of Negro Children." *Journal of Negro Education* 1 (October 1932): 388-95.
———. "Redirection of the Education of Negroes in Terms of Social Needs." *Journal of Negro Education* 5 (July 1936): 412-19.
———. "In High School." *Ebony* 6 (December 1950): 24-32.
Brawley, Benjamin. *Negro Builders and Heroes.* Chapel Hill: University of North Carolina Press, 1937.
Chicago Negro Almanac and Reference Book. Chicago: Chicago Negro Almanac Publishing Company, 1972.
Gosnell, Harold. *Negro Politicians.* Chicago: University of Chicago Press, 1937.
Herrick, Mary. "Negro Employees of the Chicago Board of Education." Master's thesis, University of Chicago, 1931.
Homel, Michael. *Down from Equality: Black Chicagoans and the Public Schools, 1920-1940.* Chicago: University of Illinois Press, 1984.
"Maudelle B. Bousfield Dies." *Jet* 41 (November 4, 1971): 48.
Ottley, Roi. "Woman Leads Way for Negro in Education." *Chicago Tribune,* October 29, 1955.
Parker, Marjorie. *Alpha Kappa Alpha Sorority, 1908-1958.* Washington, D.C.: Alpha Kappa Alpha Sorority, 1958.
"Set Rites for Pioneer Principal." *Chicago Tribune,* October 17, 1971.
Spear, Allan H. *Black Chicago: The Making of a Negro Ghetto.* Chicago: University of Chicago Press, 1967.
Who's Who in Colored America. 6th ed. Brooklyn: Thomas Yenser, 1942.
Who's Who in Colored America. 7th ed. New York: Christine E. Burckel and Associates, 1950.

Ariel Serena Hedges Bowen

Ariel Serena Hedges Bowen
(c. 1862-1904)
Educator, temperance leader, writer, lecturer

A multi-talented woman, Ariel Serena Hedges Bowen began her professional life as an educator and soon became an organizer of black women's organizations in the church and community. Her competencies as vocalist, pianist, organist, writer, and public speaker caused her to become known as one of the most cultured black women of her time. She had a short but rich life of service to her community.

Ariel Serena Hedges Bowen was born about 1862 in Newark, New Jersey, the oldest of three children born to Charles E. Hedges and his wife, whose name is not known. Charles Hedges was a graduate of Lincoln University in Pennsylvania and organized churches in New York before becoming a Presbyterian minister in Newark. Apparently when he was in New York Bowen met his future wife, who was a member of one of the oldest Presbyterian families there. Ariel Bowen's grandfather was a bugler in the Mexican War and a Guard of Honor during Lafayette's visit to the United States.

Bowen's parents moved to Pittsburgh, Pennsylvania. She completed the academic course at Avery Institute, Allegheny City, Pennsylvania. The family then moved to Baltimore, Maryland, where Charles Hedges was pastor of the Madison Avenue Presbyterian Church from 1873 to 1880. In 1880 Hedges became pastor of the Grace Presbyterian Church, which was founded by former members of the Madison Avenue Presbyterian Church. Bowen studied in the parochial school of Madison Avenue Presbyterian Church and Massachusetts's Springfield High School, where in 1883 she graduated with honors in a large class. Although the dates of her continued studies are unknown, the musical education that she began in Pittsburgh was completed at the New York Conservatory of Music. According to Daniel Culp in *Twentieth Century Negro Literature,* after completing the Teacher's Course and Examination, Bowen accepted a teaching position in Springfield. She later moved to Alabama and taught history, elocution, and music at Tuskegee Normal and Industrial Institute. For two years she was professor of music at Clark University in Atlanta.

On September 14, 1886, Bowen married John Wesley E. Bowen, Sr. (1855-1933). Two years later J. W. E. Bowen, as he was known, became the first black American to receive a doctorate in religion from Boston University and the second black to earn a Ph.D. degree. Ariel Hedges Bowen shared in his pastoral duties at St. John's Methodist Episcopal Church in Newark, New Jersey, and Centennial Methodist Episcopal Church in Washington, D.C. She organized the Woman's Home Missionary Society in the Washington Methodist Episcopal Conference and was its first president. While in Washington she also was one of the organizers of the Woman's League. The Bowens moved to Atlanta in 1893, when J. W. E. became the first black to hold a regular professorship (and later was the first black president) at Gammon Theological Seminary. He became coeditor of *Voice of the Negro* and *The Negro.* In Atlanta, Ariel Bowen organized a society similar to the one in Washington in the local Methodist Episcopal Conference. She was also active in temperance work and was president of the Women's Christian Temperance Union (WCTU) No. 2 of Georgia and of the Woman's Club of Atlanta. Bowen remained true to her upbringing as the daughter of a minister and was active in many phases of church work, including missionary work. She was a life member of the Woman's Home Missionary Society.

Bowen organized and advanced many mother's clubs and young women's societies. In 1895, at the second national conference of black women, known as the Atlanta Congress of Colored Women, she was a member of the Committee on Courtesies, along with Nettie Langston Napier, Frances E. Preston, Fannie Barrier Williams, Frances E. W. Harper, and others. She was a member of the Georgia Federation of Colored Women's Clubs, organized in 1902, and was associate editor of the *Women's Advocate*—the official organ of the state federation.

An enlightening and convincing platform speaker, Bowen was called on frequently to address large assemblies on such topics as moral and social reform. She reached a wide audience through the publication of her numerous articles in various black journals. Among her published works, which were primarily related to music and ethics, were "Music in the Home," "The Convict Lease System," "The Ethics of Reform," "Home Literary Table," "The Influence of Daughters," "Mother's Meetings," and "Is the Young Negro an Improvement, Morally, on His Father?" In the latter article, published in Culp's *Twentieth Century Negro Literature,* Bowen expressed her views on women as educators, homemakers, and reformers:

> The noble army of teachers, most of whom are women, are not to be overlooked or underestimated. Next to the faithful mother, these noble women have lived and worked for the race. They have proved themselves ever against untoward conditions. Their work and worth should not be reflected against because of the few whose lives are not up to the standards of true womanhood. It is undeniably true that the virtues of Solomon's virtuous women may be duplicated in multitudes of our women teachers.

Her views on the black woman were also published in Sylvia Dannett's *Profiles of Negro Womanhood:*

> The Negro woman is asserting herself also and is building for herself a character that rests upon a foundation of personal purity. This she is doing not only for herself, but for others. The building up of pure homes is her chief concern and in them she reigns with womanly queenliness.

> Social reform receives her attention, and in these walks she may be found teaching the young the single standard of purity for both sexes. Her way is the roughest, her path most closely beset with snares, but her works show for themselves.

Bowen emphasized the black woman's role in improving the black individual, whether female or male, as she recognized the black youth who possessed physical strength, intelligence, and morality as the hope for the race's future.

Bowen's classrooms, home, community, and church benefitted from her many talents. In addition to "living and working for the race" by educating and training college students, according to Culp, Bowen trained and fitted her family for life. Culp called her a superb housekeeper and "one of the foremost and best cultured women of her race." She was well-educated, competent in history, English, music, and perhaps ethics, as demonstrated by her college teaching career, and read Greek, Latin, and German. She was an accomplished vocalist, pianist, and organist.

At the time of her death, Ariel Bowen was in St. Louis to attend the World's Fair, after having traveled with her husband to the West Coast, where they attended the General Conference of the Methodist Episcopal Church. Her mother and children had joined her to wait for J. W. E. Bowen's return from the General Conference. She died on July 7, 1904, at 3:00 A.M., at the age of forty-two. In addition to her husband and mother, her survivors included three children: Irene, Juanita, and John Wesley Edward, Jr., also a minister. A third daughter, Portia Edmonia, died in early childhood. In his tribute to Bowen, William H. Weaver wrote in *Voice of the Negro* that she was a woman "buoyant in spirit, full of sunshine and cheerfulness and most pleasing in manners. There was a look of love in her eye, there was a generality in her converse, there was a cordiality in the grasp of her hand, there was an urbanity in her whole demeanor that told you of the warmth of her heart." Bowen was a woman of resolute firmness who would not compromise principle for worldly expedience. Called a noble woman, Ariel Hedges Bowen demonstrated a commitment to service throughout her short life in the variety of ways in which she worked.

REFERENCES:

Britt, William H., comp. "History of Madison Avenue Presbyterian Church" (church pamphlet). N.d.

Culp, Daniel W., ed. *Twentieth Century Negro Literature.* Atlanta: J. L. Nichols and Co., 1902.

Dannett, Sylvia G. *Profiles of Negro Womanhood.* Vol. 1. Philadelphia: M. W. Lads, 1964.

"John Wesley Edward Bowen." *Journal of Negro History* 19 (April 1934): 214-21.

Logan, Rayford W., and Michael R. Winston, eds. *Dictionary of American Negro Biography.* New York: Norton, 1982.

Rywell, Martin, ed. *Afro-American Encyclopedia.* Vol. 2. North Miami: Educational Book Publisher, 1974.

Salem, Dorothy. *To Better Our World: Black Women in Organized Reform, 1890-1920.* Brooklyn: Carlson Publishing, 1993.

Weaver, William H. "A Tribute to Mrs. J. W. E. Bowen." *Voice of the Negro* (August 1904): 335-38.

Wesley, Charles Harris. *History of the National Association of Colored Women's Clubs.* Washington, D.C.: NACW, 1984.

Linda M. Carter

Cornelia Bowen
(1858-1934)
School founder, educator, clubwoman, writer

Cornelia Bowen, also known as Nellie Bowen, was a tireless educator, clubwoman, and writer whose work in the late 1800s and early 1900s uplifted the lives of countless African Americans in rural Alabama. She founded Mt. Meigs

Cornelia Bowen

Institute, a smaller version of Tuskegee Institute, and used the school to teach the self-help concept that she had learned at Tuskegee by offering agricultural and industrial training to rural blacks. She supported family values and community renewal, and she persuaded the Alabama courts to improve conditions for black juveniles who were institutionalized for delinquency. She promoted her views on the education of blacks by traveling extensively and lecturing throughout the United States and Europe.

Bowen's mother was born a slave in Baltimore, Maryland, but spent the greater part of her life on Colonel William Bowen's plantation in Macon County, Alabama. In Baltimore, the master's daughter taught Bowen's mother to read and, despite laws to prohibit it, the Bowens allowed her to continue to read. While a slave on the Bowen plantation, Bowen's mother was a servant in her mistress's home and, as was custom, was prohibited from mingling with the plantation slaves. Nothing is known of Bowen's father. Cornelia Bowen's birthplace was on the Bowen plantation in a house that later became the industrial building for girls at Tuskegee Institute. This building and two smaller ones on the Bowen plantation became the school's founding site. On Sundays Bowen and her several sisters gathered about her mother's knees to listen to the church hymns she read to them. The frightful stories of slavery were never told. Why her mother could read so well but was unable to write was a mystery to Bowen. She remembered these as days of freedom and knew nothing of those of slavery.

Bowen's first teacher was a white woman who lived in Tuskegee and knew her mother well. She recognized the

child's talent and wanted her to read properly; therefore, she devoted herself to teaching her from *McGuffey's First Reader* when Bowen was very young. Later Bowen and her sisters began formal education in Tuskegee's public schools. She developed a competitive spirit early on and resented classmates who appeared to be ahead of her in class.

Having been brought up in the Methodist Sunday school, Bowen later joined the Methodist Church, where Lewis Adams, a former slave, a trustee of Tuskegee Institute, and an influential leader among the town's black residents, was superintendent of the Sunday school. He encouraged the class members to take an active part in the work. Although the older girls expected they would teach the younger ones, Bowen was assigned as teacher because she was an excellent reader. While the other girls in the class, including one of her sisters, resented her and rebelled, Bowen was never discouraged by their conduct.

The public school for blacks on Zion Hill, where Bowen began her education, closed when Booker T. Washington established Tuskegee Normal School. She was one of the first students examined for entrance—by a test that Washington gave in arithmetic, grammar, and history—and received junior standing. With Washington as her teacher, she soon learned that she had never heard of a sentence or its subject or verb and that she barely understood the meaning and use of the grammar that she did know. Washington was precise in spelling and in the use of verbs.

The industrial departments that developed at Tuskegee later on were less elaborate during Bowen's four years there. Her training came largely from the classroom. She and her classmates graduated in 1885, in the first class, and she won one of the Peabody medals for excellence in scholarship. After graduation she became principal of the campus training school, later known as Children's House. She resigned the position after several terms, to pursue what she called "a broader field of usefulness."

Mt. Meigs Institute for Rural Blacks Founded

When E. N. Pierce of Plainfield, Connecticut, resolved to provide better school facilities for blacks living on a large plantation that came into his possession, he asked Booker T. Washington in 1888 to find him a teacher to work in the vicinity of Mt. Meigs, Alabama, geographically close to Tuskegee, to carry on a smaller version of the work of Tuskegee. Washington telegraphed Bowen from Boston, where he was visiting, and stated that she was the proper person to meet the challenge and carry on the work that Pierce and his friends envisioned.

With Pierce's financial backing, Bowen went to Mt. Meigs to examine conditions. She found no evidence of hope for local support, for the residents were poor and burdened with heavily mortgaged crops as well. Considering the fact that no one in the community owned their land, they were probably sharecroppers. Homes were neglected and family values were lacking. An air of gloom pervaded the town. Older people gathered for worship in a badly deteriorated

Baptist church. Bowen first established a connection with the townspeople through the Sunday school, where she taught each week. She also organized a class of older residents and encouraged them to attend the Sunday sessions with their children.

Since none of the parents were literate, Bowen taught them the Scriptures by repeating verse after verse until they memorized them. Through the class she taught many people to read and they studied topics other than the Scriptures that were applicable to daily life. Bowen was ombudsman for disputes and difficulties in family relationships and served as church leader in the minister's absence.

Bowen's main concern paralleled that of the parent institution, Tuskegee: to teach people self-help. She began to plan for the erection of a main school building for the Mt. Meigs Colored Institution that was also to serve as a community center. Although crops were bad and conditions in general were poor, the residents paid the two thousand dollars required to build the two-story structure. Agriculture was introduced into the curriculum immediately, and later, when a large trades building was erected, Tuskegee teachers assisted the school by teaching trades such as blacksmithing, wheelwrighting, carpentry, and painting to the men, and cooking, laundering, housekeeping, and sewing to the young women. Still later, other buildings were added—a girls' dormitory, a blacksmithing shop, and a teachers' home.

Bowen kept abreast of developments in the black communities of Alabama, particularly through attending the annual Negro conferences held at Tuskegee. The conferences, which attracted the interest of black leaders throughout the country, including Victoria E. Mathews of New York City, H. H. Proctor of Atlanta, and Benjamin T. Tanner of Philadelphia, demonstrated firsthand what the people themselves were doing, what was being done to assist them, and how they were improving the educational, moral, and religious fabric of their lives. A portion of the 1896 meeting was devoted to a woman's conference. In a report about Mt. Meigs that year, Bowen indicated that blacks, whether just a man and wife or a family with children, were no longer content to live in the one-room cabins where many were forced to stay. She also noted that the cabins were quickly disappearing.

By 1906 Bowen had been in charge of the school for most of the previous seventeen years. Her absences occurred while she studied at Teachers College, Columbia University and, through the generosity of a friend, at Queen Margaret's College, Glasgow, Scotland, where she spent a year. At some point in her career she had obtained a B.A. from Straight University (now Dillard University) in New Orleans, and an M.A. from Battle Creek College in Michigan, where she wrote a thesis on "Juvenile Crime among Negroes in Alabama." Biographical information in *History of the Alabama State Teachers Association* notes that she was still the school's president between 1927 and 1929, during which time she had become the first woman president of the association. Mt. Meigs changed names several times during its history to become the Montgomery County Training School and then George Washington High School.

Bowen was pleased with the progress blacks had made in the Mt. Meigs community. This trend was to continue. Some of the residents had become home owners and others had moved out of their one-room cabins. She had held regular mothers' meetings, like those that Margaret Murray Washington held so successfully at Tuskegee, which resulted in a higher quality of home life for the people. The women had been taught how to rear children and were persuaded to discontinue habits such as dipping snuff and smoking and chewing tobacco. The men were better farmers, cleaner in their habits, and more ambitious in their ideals. The sanctity of the family came to be recognized as the men and women defined their roles and expectations of each other and as they formed cleaner ideals about home and family. Church life became less emotional and the minister preached only forty minutes rather than two hours as had been the practice. Many of the farmers were debt free.

The United States Bureau of Education's study *Negro Education,* published in 1916, noted that the teaching force and physical plant of the Mt. Meigs Colored Institution, valued at twenty thousand dollars, were inadequate, but that the school had "exerted considerable influence on the neighborhood." At that time, most of its board members lived in the North. There were 206 students in the school; the academic curriculum included grammar, algebra, writing, reading, and other subjects; and limited time was allotted to the trades. School support came from general donations, tuition and fees, and boarding of students. The first school of its kind in Alabama, Mt. Meigs Colored Institution demonstrated clearly that a school established among blacks in the rural South could indeed enhance the quality of life for the people in the community. Similar schools had been started elsewhere in Alabama and in other parts of the South, including Voorhees College in Denmark, South Carolina, founded by Elizabeth "Lizzie" Wright, another Tuskegee graduate. Former students and graduates of Mt. Meigs had made great progress. The graduates had continued their studies at Tuskegee or other schools, and those who could not afford further education used the trades they had learned to help improve not only their own lives but the lives of others as well.

Bowen Takes Active Role in Women's Organizations

Bowen took an early interest in the women's club movement. She was an active member of the National Association of Colored Women (NACW). Before the association held its fourth biennial meeting at Saint Louis, Missouri, the national president, Josephine Silone Yates, organized the association into departments, and Bowen became head of the social science division. By the time of the meeting in Detroit in 1904, she had been elected delegate from Alabama and, along with Mary Church Terrell, Josephine Beall Bruce, Margaret Murray Washington, and Nannie Helen Burroughs, was one of the presenters at the session, where the women discussed the convict-lease system, lynching, education, home life, and other topics. When officers were elected for the 1906-08 term, she became corresponding secretary. The association authorized Bowen to greet the Nurses Training Association during their August 1908 session in New York City, at which time the NACW would also be meeting there. Bowen, Fannie Barrier Williams, Emma Ransom, and Verina Morton Jones were among the women who were presenters at the session.

Black women in Alabama had been involved in organized club work since 1899. Bowen was elected president of the Alabama State Federation of Colored Women's Clubs, the state affiliate of NACW, and served in that capacity from 1905 to 1918—longer than any other president. The Alabama women supported the founding and development of the Mt. Meigs Industrial School for Boys, named in some sources as the Alabama Reform School for Juvenile Negro Lawbreakers, which later became the Alabama Industrial School for Negro Children. In 1907 the association purchased twenty acres of land at Mt. Meigs to house delinquent black boys. Bowen and Margaret Murray Washington spoke during the mass meetings held to raise funds for the reformatory. As a result of successful lobbying, the state assumed control of the reform school in 1911, and Bowen served on the board of trustees for fourteen years. A similar home for girls, the Girls Rescue Home, was erected under the administration of Margaret Murray Washington between 1919 and 1921, when it was dedicated and its named changed to Girls' Home.

Bowen was a multifaceted woman who gave selflessly to the cause of improving the quality of life for black people. Throughout her career she petitioned the courts in Alabama to improve conditions for juveniles. She campaigned for self-help among blacks, a concept that Booker T. Washington and Margaret Murray Washington taught her at Tuskegee and that she practiced at her Mt. Meigs school. She fought to instill moral values in young people and pushed for family solidarity. She lectured widely and traveled throughout the United States and Europe to study educational programs, particularly those for maladjusted youth. An entrepreneur, Bowen sold or donated to the state much of the land for the Alabama Industrial School. For five years she also taught at Alabama State Teachers College. She wrote extensively, including some works of poetry. She died in 1934.

REFERENCES:

Bowen, Cornelia. "A Woman's Work." In *Tuskegee and Its People.* Edited by Booker T. Washington. New York: D. Appleton and Co., 1906.

Gray, Jerome A., Joe L. Reed, and Norman W. Walton. *History of the Alabama State Teachers Association.* Washington, D.C.: National Education Association, 1987.

Harlan, Louis R., ed. *The Booker T. Washington Papers.* Vol. 2, 1860-89; Vol. 3, 1889-95. Urbana: University of Illinois Press, 1972.

Hartshorn, W. N., ed. *An Era of Progress and Promise, 1863-1910.* Boston: Princilla Publishing Co., 1910.

Johnson, John Quincy. *Report of the Fifth Tuskegee Negro Conference, 1896.* Trustees of the John F. Slater Fund,

Occasional Papers, no. 8. Baltimore: Trustees of the John F. Slater Fund, 1896.

Richardson, Clement. *The National Cyclopedia of the Colored Race.* Montgomery, Ala.: National Publishing Co., 1919.

Thrasher, Max Bennett. *Tuskegee: Its Story and Its Work.* Boston: Small, Maynard, and Co., 1900.

U.S. Department of Interior, Bureau of Education. *Negro Education: A Study of the Private and Higher Schools for Colored People in the United States.* Bulletin 1916, nos. 38, 39. 1916. Reprint. New York: Negro Universities Press, 1969.

Wesley, Charles Harris. *The History of the National Association of Colored Women's Clubs.* Washington, D.C.: NACW, 1984.

Jessie Carney Smith

Ruth Jean Bowen
(1924-)
Entertainment booking agent, business executive

R uth Bowen has guided the careers of some of the most well-known and successful entertainers in the world. Interested in making success possible for black performers, Bowen founded Queen Booking Corporation, once the largest black-owned talent agency in the world. In working with such artists as Aretha Franklin, Sammy Davis, Jr., Ray Charles, and others, she has changed the face of the entertainment industry, a field she entered nearly fifty years ago, when she first became Dinah Washington's publicist.

Ruth Jean Baskerville Bowen was born in Danville, Virginia, on September 13, 1924, to Marion Baskerville and Claude Carlton. She attended Westmoreland Elementary School and Langston High School in Danville; later, when her family moved to New York, she graduated from Girls High School in Brooklyn. She studied at New York University for two years before marrying Wallace "Billy" Bowen, one of the original Ink Spots, in 1944. The singing group is renowned as one of the first black acts to break the racial barrier of the 1950s by performing for white audiences across the United States. The Bowens remained married until his death in 1982.

Ruth Bowen initially gained hands-on experience in the entertainment industry by handling her husband's business affairs. This provided her with much of the background and practical know-how that led to her long and successful career in the entertainment industry. She spent a great deal of time traveling around the country with the Ink Spots in the 1940s and 1950s, during which time she also learned firsthand about

Ruth Jean Bowen

racism and the treatment of African Americans as second-class citizens.

After World War II, segregation continued to dominate the lives of African Americans. In most cities, hotels denied rooms to black people, including the Ink Spots and their party. Black performers were expected to stay in guest houses or in black-owned private homes where rooms could be rented overnight. On one occasion the Bowens and the Ink Spots were scheduled to stay in a guest house in Salt Lake City. Bowen refused the accommodations and demanded that her husband take her to the best hotel in the city instead. He complied, and although scared to death herself, Ruth Bowen marched into the hotel and asked for two rooms. The party was offered two rooms without difficulty.

Bowen Manages Dinah Washington

While traveling through Pittsburgh on a tour of the country with her husband and the Ink Spots, Bowen spotted a painted sign on a tour bus that said, "Dinah Washington—Queen of the Blues." When they caught up with the bus, Billy Bowen introduced his wife to Dinah Washington. The two women conversed and vowed to keep in touch. Shortly thereafter, Washington offered Bowen a job as her personal publicist, which Bowen accepted. The two women became friends and Washington encouraged Bowen to pursue publicity work. Before long, Bowen was doing both publicity and management for Dinah Washington. But she was not booking Washington for engagements.

Bowen wanted and needed to learn the nuts and bolts of how the entertainment industry worked. She found out all she could from an established booking agent, Joe Glaser, who handled Dinah Washington's bookings. When he worked in his office on weekends, Bowen took the opportunity to observe him—his meticulous attention to details, how he carefully read letters before signing them, the way he handled his acts. In addition, she witnessed firsthand how the entertainment industry routinely limited the earning potential of black performers by restricting the places where they could appear.

When Glaser failed to book Dinah Washington for European engagements, Bowen used her own contacts to arrange for Washington to go to Europe to perform. That, according to Bowen, suggested to Dinah Washington that she had no more use for Glaser's services. With the success of Bowen's initial effort at entertainment booking, Washington and Bowen decided to start their own booking agency. Ruth would do the legwork—she borrowed five hundred dollars to rent office space—and Dinah would provide some contacts and the name: Queen Artists. They would find acts themselves and book them. It was 1959.

Washington had insisted that Bowen get a booking license from the State of New York; when Bowen applied, she had as her references the impressive names of Joe Glaser and Jules Podell, of the Copacabana, and she had retained David Dinkins, later to become mayor of New York, as her attorney. She got the license and has been booking ever since.

As Dinah Washington's career grew, she requested that Bowen give up other clients and become her personal manager. Bowen, however, hired some help for the business so she could spend more time with Dinah.

Once she had established herself as a booking agent, Bowen never looked back. She had walked into a world dominated by men, but her money had been invested and she would remain. The business had begun with a staff of four. The Queen Artists office was so tiny that, according to Bowen, you had to back in and out. To help the business, Washington referred to Bowen acts that she had come across while on the road. Those early referrals included the Dells and Lola Falana.

Before the establishment of Queen Booking, Bowen had never had any serious intentions of entering business in a big way, but the booking work took on a life of its own. The staff at Queen had to be trained to become good agents. As salespeople, their products were the artists themselves. At the beginning, Queen Artists was booking acts at the Howard in Washington, D.C., the Apollo in Harlem, and the Regal in Chicago. In addition, bookings for jazz clubs across the country were arranged by Queens Artists for their organ trios. By listening to and learning from Bowen herself, the Queen agents—black and white—grew to understand the business of entertainment booking. Combining what she calls "street intelligence" and traditional experience, the business expanded. Before long, Queen Artists began handling the press and bookings for Earl Bostic, Johnny Lyttle, Kenny Burrell, and the Basin Street East Nightclub.

Bowen Founds Booking Agency

When Dinah Washington died, Queen Artists was only a few years old. By 1964, Queen Artists had become Queen Booking Corporation (QBC), with Ruth Bowen as founder and president. The number of clients grew and the staff increased to thirty. By 1969, Queen Booking had become the largest black-owned entertainment agency in the world. The more than one hundred acts handled by Queen Booking ran the gamut from individual singers to soul-rock groups to gospel choirs to comedians. In the presence of competitors like the William Morris Agency and Creative Management Associates, QBC thrived. Through Bowen's work with Dinah Washington, she had become wise to entertainment industry tactics. She learned how to hold her own against those nightclubs that were known to discriminate against blacks and how to demand and receive top dollar and top billing for her clients.

Bowen had dispelled the initial doubts of those performers who wondered if a woman could transact their business; some performers she talked to showed their confidence in her ability by switching to QBC when their contracts expired with their agents.

Helping the artists to succeed required that Bowen get close to her acts. She thought of them as family and worked hard to nurture them. Young artists were sometimes no more than eighteen years old. They were new to the entertainment business and wanted her guidance. Bowen accompanied them to engagements, where she studied them and the audiences' reactions. Her acts played in the clubs, auditoriums, theaters, and armories where black performers appeared at that time. In some instances Bowen arranged for promoters to meet an act when it arrived in town and to chauffeur the artists around. She also managed costuming, travel arrangements, publicity, and finances. For her work with her staff, whom Bowen trained to treat all clients with respect, and for her own care in developing the artists, she earned the nickname "Mother Goose."

Finding work for the many artists she had signed proved a challenge to Bowen. The entertainment world was still male-dominated and some men were unwilling to give Bowen the opportunity to book her artists. Sometimes club owners would only let her try one time to book performers; others were more generous. QBC felt pressure from a competing major talent agency, which was then in control of most major nightclubs and many international television shows. This company would blacklist QBC acts in the hopes of forcing the talent to desert Bowen and join their agency. They wanted her to fail and tried to ensure that she did. Her work kept her so busy and her traveling was so frequent that Bowen often kept two suitcases packed at home: one for warm weather and one for cold.

As an agent, Bowen had a reputation for being very serious about her clients' demands. She said in the June 1974 issue of *Ebony,* "When a QBC act is bought, the purchaser pays the same money and provides the respectful comforts he would give a white one. No one bargains with my black acts' price. Take it or leave it."

As rock and roll and rhythm and blues grew in popularity, Queen was representing most of the Motown acts, from the Supremes to Stevie Wonder. But, as reported by Bowen in the *Ebony* article, one by one, as soon as the Motown acts got big, they were yanked from QBC and "placed with a white agency."

Despite the discrimination she faced, Bowen was able to build her vision into a three-million-dollar business. Her stature was recognized when Wednesday, March 14, 1973, was declared "Ruth Bowen Day" in New York City by Manhattan Borough president Percy Sutton in a special proclamation. A star-studded tribute was held to honor Bowen for her work as president of QBC.

Popular Acts Represented

The roster of soul singers and musicians handled by Queen Booking is enormously impressive. The company represented Aretha Franklin, The Drifters, Harold Melvin and the Bluenotes, Patti LaBelle and the Bluebells, Curtis Mayfield and the Impressions, Gladys Knight and the Pips, the Isley Brothers, Kool & the Gang, the Dells, the Chi-Lites, the Sweet Inspirations, the O'Jays, the Intruders, Gene Chandler, Teddy Pendergrass, Smokey Robinson, Bobby Womack, Marvin Gaye, Millie Jackson, Ike and Tina Turner, the Four Tops, the Marvelettes, Dee Dee Warwick, Dee Dee Sharpe, the Delfonics, the Manhattans, the Ohio Players, Jerry Butler, Tyrone Davis, the Staples Singers, the Stylistics, Barbara Mason, Ben E. King, Al Green, Tavares, Gwen McRae, Stanley Turrentine, Bobbi Humphrey, and others.

Bowen has displayed a special talent for boosting the careers of artists who had previously been told that their audience appeal had disappeared. For example, Ray Charles's former agent insisted that Charles's career had played itself out. Bowen rejected that notion. Within a year, she had tripled Charles's earnings by increasing his exposure to include talk shows, widening his appeal by introducing him to segments of the population that had never before heard of him, and increasing his possibilities for first-rate playdates.

Likewise, Gladys Knight and the Pips had been told that, despite their number-one hit, "I Heard It through the Grapevine," there was no demand for their kind of act. The group watched with amazement as Bowen, in the two weeks she asked for to prove the agency's worth, arranged six months of work for the group.

The list of gospel singers Bowen has handled is also impressive. It includes the Reverend James Cleveland, Inez Andrews, Shirley Caesar, Clara Ward and the Famous Ward Singers, the Mighty Clouds of Joy, the Barrett Sisters, Sara Jordan Powell, the Soul Stirrers, the Gospelaires, the Reverend Isaac Douglas, and the Stars of Faith. Comedians associated with QBC have included Richard Pryor, Slappy White, Willie Tyler and Lester, Hi Fi White, Gilliam, and Redd Foxx.

In addition to her work in the entertainment business, Bowen has served as president of the Rinky Dinks, a social and civic club of the 1950s and 1960s made up primarily of the wives of New York musicians. The names Bowen, Basie, Hawkins, Jacquet, Bostic, and Hinton were among those found on the Rinky Dinks' roster. The club conducted service projects that benefited the African American community. Their fund-raisers allowed the club to donate to such charitable organizations as day-care centers for black children. For a time, Harlem's Savoy Ballroom was the site of the Rinky Dinks' fund-raisers. Later, with Bowen's influence, the Hotel Americana and the Waldorf-Astoria opened their doors for the Rinky Dinks' formal dances.

Bowen retired once, when her health seemed to be declining. However, her artists kept after her to continue booking for them. So before long, she came out of retirement, founded the Bowen Agency, and resumed work. As CEO of Bowen Agency, Ltd., she admits to thriving on challenge and the wheeling and dealing of the business. Ruth Bowen has earned a place among the power brokers in the multi-billion-dollar entertainment field. She is now active with Aretha Franklin, the Isley Brothers, Smokey Robinson, Illinois Jacquet Orchestra, Bobby Womack, and Ray Charles.

Current Address: Bowen Agency Ltd., 504 West 168th St., New York, NY 10032.

REFERENCES:

Bowen, Ruth. Interview with Martia Graham Goodson, November 1993.
"First Lady of Talent Booking." *Ebony* 29 (June 1974): 73-80.
George, Nelson. *The Death of Rhythm and Blues.* New York: Pantheon Books, 1988.
Hine, Darlene Clark, ed. *Black Women in America: An Historical Encyclopedia.* Brooklyn: Carlson Publishing, 1993.
Mapp, Edward. *Directory of Blacks in the Performing Arts.* 2d ed. Metuchen, N.J.: Scarecrow Press, 1990.
Maultsby, Portia. "Africanisms in African-American Music." In *Africanisms in American Culture.* Edited by Joseph H. Holloway, Bloomington: University of Indiana Press, 1990.
Ploski, Harry A., and James Williams, comps. and eds. *The Negro Almanac.* Detroit: Gale Research, 1989.
"Ruth Bowen Shows a Woman Can Do It." *New York Amsterdam News,* June 26, 1965.
"A Toast to Entertainment Impresario Ruth Bowen." *New York Amsterdam News,* March 24, 1973.
Who's Who among Black Americans, 1992-93. 7th ed. Detroit: Gale Research, 1993.

Martia Graham Goodson

Rosa Dixon Bowser
(1885-1931)
Educator, clubwoman

Rosa Bowser had a long and successful career as a teacher in the public schools of Richmond, Virginia. In Monroe A. Majors's *Noted Negro Women,* she is described by Joseph E. Jones as

> a born teacher. She has in herself the element of a true teacher. That element is sympathy, a sympathy ... which flows from a community of life. This shows itself that she endeavors to help her pupils to become something in the world. This very effort upon her part has done much to enshrine her name in the hearts of hundreds of pupils whom she has taught.

Bowser was also involved in a number of educational associations, as well as other organizations that worked to improve social, spiritual, and educational conditions for blacks, most notably the National Association of Colored Women.

Rosa Dixon Bowser was born at Clay Hill Plantation in Amelia County, Virginia, in 1885. Her parents were Augusta and Henry Dixon. Her father, also born in Amelia County, was a cabinetmaker by trade. He apparently had some education and was able to read. The Dixons moved to Richmond, Virginia, when Rosa was quite small. There, she entered the free primary school and went through all grades of the public school system. According to L. A. Scruggs in *Women of Distinction,* when she was still young "her teachers were convinced that she would be no mean leader of her people." Bowser then attended the Richmond Normal and High School, which was headed by Ralsa Morse Manly of Vermont. Daniel Wallace Culp, who included an essay by Bowser in his collection of writings by black authors, said that Manly was recognized for his work as an educator in the North as well as for being a "pioneer educator in Virginia among the Negro race." Bowser graduated with distinction and then spent an additional year with Manly studying Latin and higher mathematics.

Soon after completing her studies, Bowser was appointed by the Richmond School Board to teach in the Navy Hill group of schools—until 1883 the only schools in Richmond that had black teachers. She taught school for seven years and then married James H. Bowser, a former schoolmate. Scruggs describes James Bowser as "scholarly, refined, and worthy," and Majors portrays him as "a scholarly gentleman, and a man of most upright Christian character." Early in her life Rosa Bowser became a Christian and thereafter a Sunday school teacher, sometimes acting as a representative for her school at state conventions. As was the custom of the day, married women could not teach, so it was necessary for Bowser to resign from her position.

Rosa Dixon Bowser

As noted by Scruggs, at this time Ralsa Manly wrote Bowser a letter of reference for future use should she decide to reenter the teaching profession.

Mrs. Rosa Bowser graduated with honor from the Normal School while it was under my charge, and then, with others, was a member of an "ex-senior" class, and pursued more advanced studies for one year under my own instruction. She was always a studious, faithful and intelligent scholar, her character always above criticism, and her deportment marked by a dignity, sobriety and respectfulness not common with girls of her age. She had a very successful experience as teacher in the service of the city, and should she wish to teach again I recommend her to you with entire confidence that she would do her work not only faithfully, but wisely, and with the approval of herself and School Board.

Very respectfully, R. M. Manly

Bowser had been married for only two years when her husband died. Shortly afterwards, the Richmond School Board invited her to teach again. In 1887 and for several summers after she taught at the Peabody Normal Institute in Lynchburg, Virginia, where she devoted most of her time to instructing the honors class. After 1887, Bowser taught in the Richmond Public School System for more than twenty-five years.

Community Activities Advance the Race

Bowser had many interests outside her teaching activities and was blessed with creative abilities. She made wax flowers, fine laces, and did other needlework; she enjoyed drawing, painting, and music, and taught music to young students; and she read much and had an excellent library in her home.

Bowser supported numerous projects for the betterment of her race, and her organizational affiliations were many. She was a member of the Negro Educational Society of Virginia, and served as president of the Woman's Educational Convention of Richmond for a time. For at least two years, she was president of the Richmond Normal School Alumni and of the Virginia Teachers' Association. She was also active in the Ladies' Auxiliary of the YMCA. From 1891 to 1893 she managed the Woman's Department of the Colored Fairs in Virginia and West Virginia. She founded the Woman's League of Richmond and was president of the Richmond Mothers' Club. Bowser was active in the Southern Federation of Colored Women and at one time was a member of the executive board. She also chaired the executive board of the Women's Educational and Missionary Association of Virginia, and for several years she chaired the standing Committee of Domestic Economy for the Hampton Negro Conference. Finally, she was president of the Woman's Department of the Negro Reformatory Association of Virginia.

In 1896 Bowser was a member of a committee of seven representing the Federation of Afro-American Women when it met with seven women from the Colored Women's League to consider how the two organizations might work together. The groups decided to organize as one and became the National Association of Colored Women (NACW). When it came time to elect a president for the organization, the name of every committee member, including Bowser's, was brought up until finally Mary Church Terrell received a majority vote. Bowser was one of the members of the NACW who edited the information on the group that appeared in *Woman's Era,* and she reported on NACW activities in Virginia for the publication.

Bowser wrote a paper that was published in Daniel Culp's *Twentieth Century Negro Literature.* She and three other women, including Mary Church Terrell, had been asked to write on the subject "What Role Is the Educated Negro Woman to Play in the Uplifting of Her Race?" In her essay, Bowser strongly expressed her ideas on the important role of women in society.

The character of the homes of the land, the moral and immoral bearing of every settlement, town, and city, in a large measure depend upon the class of women. . . . That society is ruled by women cannot be questioned. The age of complete dependence of women upon the stronger sex, has so far passed to be foreign to the minds of the present generation. . . . [I]t is of such common occurrence that women are thrown upon their own resources in the maintenance of the home, that they of necessity rather than from choice assume a degree of independence in various avenues of life. . . . She stands beside her brother as a partner, sharing equally with him in the world's work for humanity.

Rosa Dixon Bowser lived in Richmond until her death in 1931. She is remembered as an outstanding teacher and as a supporter of community causes who enhanced the lives of blacks.

REFERENCES:

Bowser, Rosa D. "Report of the Committee on Domestic Economy." *Hampton Negro Conference,* no. IV, July 1900.

————. "Report of the Committee on Domestic Science." *Hampton Negro Conference,* no. VI, July 1902.

————. "What Role Is the Educated Negro Woman to Play in the Uplifting of Her Race?" In *Twentieth Century Negro Literature,* edited by Daniel Wallace Culp. Naperville, Ill.: J. L. Nichols, 1902.

Dannett, Sylvia G. L. *Profiles of Negro Womanhood.* 2 vols. Yonkers, N.Y.: Educational Heritage, 1964-66.

Giddings, Paula. *When and Where I Enter.* New York: Morrow, 1984.

Hine, Darlene Clark, ed. *Black Women in America.* Brooklyn: Carlson Publishing, 1993.

————. *Black Women in United States History.* Vols. 13-14. Brooklyn: Carlson Publishing, 1990.

Majors, Monroe A. *Noted Negro Women, Their Triumphs and Activities.* Chicago: Donohue and Henneberry, 1893.

Rywell, Martin, ed. *Afro-American Encyclopedia.* Vol. 2. North Miami, Fla.: Educational Book Publishers, 1974.

Salem, Dorothy. *To Better Our World: Black Women in Organized Reform, 1890-1920.* Brooklyn: Carlson Publishing, 1990.

Scruggs, L. A. *Women of Distinction.* Raleigh, N.C.: L. A. Scruggs, 1893.

Wesley, Charles Harris. *The History of the National Association of Colored Women's Clubs.* Washington, D.C.: National Association of Colored Women's Clubs, 1984.

Ruth Edmonds Hill

Aurelia E. Brazeal

(1943-)

Ambassador, government official

A career foreign service officer since 1968, Aurelia E. Brazeal is known for the numerous diplomatic positions she has held. She was named ambassador to the Federated States of Micronesia in 1990, and then in 1993 she was appointed ambassador to Kenya. During her career, Brazeal has also worked in Argentina, Uruguay, Paraguay, and Japan,

Aurelia E. Brazeal

with the added distinction of being the first black ever to serve as an economic counselor in Japan.

Born in Chicago on November 24, 1943, Aurelia Erskine Brazeal is one of two daughters of Brallsford Reese Brazeal and Ernestine Vivian Erskine Brazeal. Her father was an outstanding educator who held various positions at Morehouse College in Atlanta, Georgia, and who was especially known for his expertise as an economist. Aurelia Brazeal grew up in Atlanta. She graduated from Northfield School for Girls in East Northfield, Massachusetts. She earned a B.A. degree from Spelman College in Atlanta in 1965 and an M.I.A. degree from Columbia University in 1967. She later did independent study at the John F. Kennedy School at Harvard University during the 1972-73 academic year.

Brazeal applied to join the Foreign Service, a program the U.S. State Department describes as "a career professional corps of men and women who were selected and prepared to carry out the foreign service policy of the United States." She took the Service's highly competitive written and oral examinations, which she passed successfully. A July 1968 news release from the U.S. State Department, quoted in the Spelman *Messenger,* announced Brazeal's official entrance into the Foreign Service. She was sworn in at a ceremony held in Washington, D. C.

Fluent in Spanish and Japanese, Brazeal has served in a number of countries since 1968. Brazeal was a consular and economic officer in Buenos Aires, Argentina, from 1969 to 1971. The next year she was assigned as economic reports officer in the Economic Bureau. She took leave from Foreign

Service when she studied at Harvard from 1972 to 1973, then returned as a watch officer in the Operations Center. She was line officer in the Office of the Secretariat from 1973 to 1974, after which she attended the Foreign Service Institute's six-month economic course. Upon completion of the course, Brazeal became desk officer for Uruguay and Paraguay serving for three years, 1974 to 1977. In 1977 she was chosen as review officer in the newly created Treasury Department Secretariat, where she remained until 1979. She then was assigned as economic officer in Tokyo, Japan, from 1979 to 1982.

Brazeal returned to Washington, D.C., after the Tokyo assignment, and from 1982 to 1984 was in the Economic Bureau's Office of Development and Finance. Then she served in the newly created position on the Japan Desk, deputy director for economics, from 1984 to 1986. She attended the senior seminar from 1986 to 1987 and became minister counselor for economic affairs in Tokyo from 1987 to 1990.

Civil Servant Becomes Ambassador

Her rich, invaluable, and successful experience in Foreign Service earned Brazeal the position of ambassador to the Federated States of Micronesia, where she served from September 7, 1990, to the summer of 1993. In 1993 Brazeal received a new assignment as ambassador to Kenya, where she currently serves.

Her current and previous affiliations include the Foreign Service Association, League of Women Voters, National Association of University Women, the American Civil Liberties Union, the Urban League, the NAACP, and the YWCA.

As a career foreign servant, Aurelia Brazeal has served her country well and has carried the image of strong, black women leaders with her wherever she has gone.

Current Address: Bureau of East African Affairs, U.S. Department of State, Washington, D.C. 20502.

REFERENCES:

"Aurelia Erskine Brazeal." Spelman *Messenger* 84 (August 1968): 41.

Jet 84 (May 17, 1993): 12.

Who's Who among Black Americans, 1975-76. 1st ed. Northbrook, Ill. *Who's Who among Black Americans,* 1976.

Who's Who in America. 48th ed. New Providence, N.J.: Marquis Who's Who, 1993.

Who's Who of American Women. 18th ed. New Providence, N.J.: Marquis Who's Who, 1993.

COLLECTIONS:

Biographical information on Aurelia Brazeal may be found at the Bureau of African Affairs, U.S. Department of State, Washington, D.C.

Jessie Carney Smith

Martha Bailey Briggs
(1838-1889)
Educator, school administrator

Martha Bailey Briggs's life was a true testimony to the kind of dedicated leadership that was provided by African American women in the field of education during the nineteenth century. Besides overcoming obstacles to her own education, she helped prepare other teachers who would in turn give students with limited opportunities the greatest gift of all, the development of their minds.

Martha Bailey Briggs was born on March 31, 1838, in New Bedford, Massachusetts, to John Briggs of Tiverton, Rhode Island, and Fanny Bassett Briggs of Vineyard Haven, Martha's Vineyard, Massachusetts. Her mother died early in Briggs's life, and she was left to be raised by her father and an aunt. She died at the age of fifty on March 28, 1889, in Washington, D.C.

Because his own education was limited, John Briggs encouraged his only child to take advantage of the few opportunities available in New Bedford to obtain an education. After receiving private tutoring, Martha entered New Bedford High School in 1850, at the age of twelve, and finished the course with honors, the first African American girl to graduate from the school. Shortly afterward, she began conducting day classes for young pupils at her father's home and evening classes for adult former slaves and fugitive slaves. Subsequently she taught at a private school in Christiantown, Martha's Vineyard, Massachusetts, as an employee of George T. Downing, who donated a house and paid tuition for his own children to avoid subjecting them to the city's segregated public schools. Later, she taught in the public schools in Newport, Rhode Island.

While she was teaching in Newport, Briggs was recruited in 1859 by Myrtilla Miner to come to Washington, D.C., to join the faculty of her own Miner Normal School. However, because of her father's reluctance for her to travel south, she declined the invitation. Ten years later, after briefly pursuing nurse's training at Boston Medical College and teaching for two years (1866-69) in Easton, Maryland, she finally applied and was appointed to teach in the public schools in Washington, D.C. There, her leadership skills were quickly recognized, and she became principal of the Anthony Bowen School from 1869 until 1873.

Briggs became well known as an experienced instructor and leader in the Washington, D.C., area. She was offered a teaching position in the Normal and Preparatory Department of Howard University in 1873, where she remained for six years. During that time she was identified in the school's catalog at different times as instructor in mathematics and instructor in the Normal Department. In 1879, when the board of trustees took over authority for the Miner Normal School—some twenty years after Briggs was first invited to teach there—she was chosen as its third principal. The school, then also referred to as Washington Normal No. 2, was later known as Miner Teachers' College. Her work was praised by the board of trustees after her first year, and they rewarded her with a handsome annual salary of $1,350. During her four years as principal (1879-83), she graduated as many as eighty teachers to help fill the critical demands for African American teachers in the district as well as in other southern locations.

In September 1883 Briggs returned to Howard University. Her extensive experience as a teacher and administrator served her well as she performed her duties as principal of Howard's Normal Department until 1889. She had voluntarily relinquished her post at Miner because of health problems, choosing instead the less demanding role at the university.

Martha Bailey Briggs's death on March 28, 1889, was a tragic loss to the black community. Not only was the loss felt keenly by the educational community, but she had also extended her sphere of influence to include several organizations. She was active in the Monday Night Literary Club and, just prior to her death, had been elected president of the Industrial Institute Association of Washington, D.C., an education organization.

At a memorial service held in Washington on May 14, 1889, by the Bethel Historical and Literary Society, Briggs was eulogized as one of the most outstanding educators of her time. As a tribute to her work, the District of Columbia Board of Education named a new school building on 27th Street the Martha B. Briggs Building. The school's first principal was one of her normal graduates, Miss M. E. Gibbs. An additional memorial service at Howard University ended with a marble tablet being inserted into the wall of the university's Andrew Rankin Chapel. The tablet is inscribed, "Her works do follow her." Briggs was returned to her birthplace, New Bedford, for burial.

REFERENCES:

Hine, Darlene Clark, ed. *Black Women in America.* New York: Carlson Publishing, 1993.

O'Connor, Ellen M. *Myrtilla Miner: A Memoir.* Cambridge, Mass.: Houghton Mifflin, 1885.

Scruggs, Lawson A. *Women of Distinction.* Raleigh, N.C.: L. A. Scruggs, 1893.

Turner, Geneva C. "For Whom Is Your School Named?" *Negro History Bulletin* 22 (April 1959): 165.

Lucilla Hiomara Iturralde and Adrienne Lash Jones

Mary Elizabeth Britton
(1858-1925)
Physician, educator, journalist, social activist, church worker

Mary Britton distinguished herself as the first African American woman licensed to practice medicine in Lexington, Kentucky. As an educator and reformer, she touched the lives of many young people. Button was also a journalist, and her writings provide insight into the social, cultural, educational, and religious activities of African Americans, particularly in Lexington, around the turn of the century.

Mary Elizabeth Britton was born free in Lexington, Kentucky, in 1858. Perhaps much of Britton's success can be attributed to the motivation she received from her parents, Laura and Henry Britton. Henry H. Britton was a free man, born in Kentucky around 1824. Laura Marshall Britton, born a slave, was fathered by her master, Thomas F. Marshall, a member of one of the state's most distinguished families; his slave mistress was Laura Britton's mother. Henry and Laura Britton were highly respected in the Lexington community where Mary Britton was born. The Brittons encouraged each of their seven children—Julia, Susan J., Hattie, Mary, Josiah, Robert, and William—to acquire an education. Mary and her siblings were educated in Lexington's private schools for African Americans, mostly those operated by the American Missionary Association (AMA). The family later moved to Berea, Kentucky, where the children attended Berea College. Mary studied there from 1871 to 1874. Laura Britton was employed as a matron at Berea College while Henry Britton worked as a barber. Following their deaths, which occurred within a few months of each other in 1874, the children went on to pursue their different goals. Mary's sister, Julia, inherited her mother's musical talent. She became the first African American teacher at Berea College and later was known as the Angel of Beale Street in Memphis, Tennessee. She married Charles Hooks, and they became the grandparents of Benjamin Hooks, who served for many years as the executive director of the NAACP.

Mary Britton never married or had children. She spent her life in service to others and accomplished much before her death in 1925. After leaving Berea, she held teaching positions in several schools in central Kentucky, going to Lexington to teach in 1876. An article that appeared in the *Louisville Defender* on February 17, 1983, spoke of her scholarly nature, public speaking ability, and interest in the education of youth. The article also stated that in 1894 she presented a paper entitled "History and Science of Teaching" before the American Association of Educators of Colored Youth in Baltimore, Maryland, and that it met "with great approval."

Britton received part of her medical training at the Battle Creek Sanitarium in Michigan. She later attended the American Missionary Medical College of Chicago, from which she graduated in 1903. According to Doris Y. Wilkinson in the

Mary Elizabeth Britton

October 1988 *Think Newsletter,* in 1904 Britton became the first African American woman licensed to practice medicine in Lexington. Her specialties were hydrotherapy, electrotherapy, and massage.

Britton the Social Reformer

Britton promoted her ideas on important social issues in such local newspapers as the *Lexington American Citizen* and the *Lexington Daily Transcript.* In the *Lexington Herald,* she wrote a regular women's column calling for social reform that focused on abstinence from alcohol and tobacco. Her writings also appeared in newspapers across the country, including the *Cleveland Gazette,* the *Indianapolis World,* the *Ivy* in Baltimore, and the *American Catholic Tribune* in Cincinnati.

In W. D. Johnson's collection of biographies of prominent African Americans from Kentucky, Britton discusses the importance of the written word as a legacy and the progress being made by African Americans:

> Races, as well as individuals, are estimated according to their achievements in religion, literature and the arts. Without a record of their progress along these lines the world would be ignorant of those characters, both male and female, who have made history. We are told that this glorious continent was named to honor Amerigo Vespucci because he printed an account of his voyages, and that Columbus lost the honor because little was known of him until after the continent was named. . . .

> The present as compared to the past shows an intelligent and material advance [for the African American race]. Their dwellings, schools, churches and public institutions testify to their progress. Negro children are being educated and trained by men and women of their own race in letters, in mechanics, and in the arts. It is not necessary to enumerate the opportunities which they create or improve; it is enough to say there is no standing still for them, no falling behind, their daily watchword being progression.

Johnson provides an assessment of Britton's public activities and her character:

> As a thinker and writer, Miss Britton is deep and logical, impressive and instructive; as a speaker, fluent and forcible. She is strictly a temperate woman, and of strong, conscientious convictions, with marked individuality and a firm will, yet kind and tender hearted. She is industrious, frugal, honest, faithful and charitable. She is unostentatious, and is often seen and heard of, giving alms and doing good deeds for and among the poor and needy.

Britton served as a charter member of the Ladies Orphans Society, which founded the Colored Orphan Industrial Home in Lexington in 1892 to provide food, shelter, education, and training to destitute orphans and elderly homeless women. Britton was an original member of the Kentucky Negro Education Association, which formed in 1877 to improve "the condition of colored people through legislative action." At its second meeting in Louisville in 1879, she presented a paper entitled "Literary Culture of the Teacher." Britton served as president of the Lexington Woman's Improvement Club, whose goal, according to W. D. Johnson, was the "elevation of woman, the enriching and betterment of home, and the incitement of proper pride and interest in the race."

Britton became well known in the community for her religious work. For many years she was an Episcopalian, but in 1893, she joined the Seventh Day Adventist Church, where she remained a faithful worker until her death. An avid reader, Britton accumulated on extensive library that she bequeathed to her church. Despite her significant accomplishments and dedication to social reform, she has remained virtually absent from historical texts. She is, as Wilkinson described her, a "forgotten pioneer," and her life and achievements need further exploration.

REFERENCES:

Burnside, Jacqueline Grisby. "Black Symbols: Extraordinary Achievements by Ordinary Women." *Appalachian Heritage* 15 (Summer 1987): 11-16.

Dunnigan, Alice Allison. *The Fascinating Story of Black Kentuckians: Their Heritage and Traditions.* Washington, D.C.: Associated Publishers, 1982.

Harris, Lawrence. *The Negro Population of Lexington in the Professions, Business, Education and Religion.* Lexington: Lawrence Harris, 1907.

Johnson, W. D. *Biographical Sketches of Prominent Negro Men and Women in Kentucky.* Lexington: Standard Printing, 1897.

Louisville Defender, February 17, 1983.

Sears, Richard. "Early Berea History." *The Pinnacle,* February 20, 1988.

State of Kentucky. Fayette County Clerk. Will Book, 13, Type W, p. 581.

Wilkinson, Doris Y. "Forgotten Pioneers." *Think Newsletter* (Kentucky Humanities Council), October 1988.

Wilson, A. S. *Proceedings of the Kentucky Negro Education Association, 1877-1913,* Vol. 1. N.p., n.d.

Lauretta Flynn Byars

Virginia E. Walker Broughton

Virginia E. Walker Broughton
(c. 1856-1934)
Feminist, missionary, educator, lecturer, writer

Virginia Walker Broughton was an important figure in the religious life of blacks in Tennessee. A missionary who placed her divine calling before all else, she traveled throughout the state, encouraging black Baptist women to form Bible bands to study and interpret the Scriptures. She organized the Tennessee Women's Convention, a statewide association for black Baptist women and a part of the national convention of black Baptist women, which was in turn a part of the male-dominated National Baptist Convention, U.S.A. A highly effective speaker, Broughton was influential in raising funds for the black Baptist women's convention movement and was a successful crusader for the uplift of the black family. She advocated the high visibility of women in the Baptist conventions and argued that they should belong to state and national executive boards. She knew the Scriptures well and was a Bible teacher of marked ability—one of the best in the Baptist church. She was called on to represent her church denomination at various church and religious conferences.

Born in Tennessee in about 1856 to Nelson and Eliza Smart Walker, Virginia E. Walker Broughton was named for her father's home state. Nelson Walker had been a slave; his master allowed him to work elsewhere and he earned enough money to purchase his freedom and also that of his wife. Broughton spent her early years in Nashville, where she entered a private school taught by Daniel Watkins. When Fisk University opened in 1866, young Virginia was one of its first pupils and one of the most advanced. She studied at Fisk for ten years and received her B.A. in May 1875, as one of four members of the first graduating class. She is said to have been the first black woman in the South to graduate from college.

She also received an honorary M.A. from Fisk in 1878. Immediately after her graduation, she went to Memphis and passed an examination for a teaching position in the public schools. She taught in Memphis for twelve years, received various promotions, and became principal of the North Memphis School. Sometime during this period she married John Broughton, a Republican lawyer who served in the County Register's office in Memphis and later in the state legislature. The marriage produced at least five children, four of whom were alive when she died in 1934.

As a teacher Broughton experienced gender bias when a less experienced black male teacher was promoted over her; in 1885, with her husband's support, she entered a successful complaint and became head teacher (assistant principal) of the Kortrecht Grammar School. Kortrecht was the city's most advanced public school for blacks—the only one to offer one year of high school instruction.

Broughton Becomes a Missionary

As a teacher Broughton was fulfilling the expectations of the founders of schools of higher education for blacks in the South; she was enlightening and uplifting students from the perspective of a committed Christian. But in about 1882 she became more active in Christian work. The initial stimulus for this involvement came from her contact with Joanna Moore, the white missionary who was popular and influential among blacks because of her strong commitment to egalitarian views. Under her influence, Broughton became a member of a Bible band, a woman's group formed for daily Bible study. The groups were very popular, and in 1887, Midwestern Auxiliary of the American Baptist Home Mission Society sponsored a permanent missionary station in Memphis and soon engaged Broughton as a missionary. At first she had no interest in becoming a missionary. She enjoyed a comfortable salary as a teacher and was content with her home and school duties. But the death of her mother was an intensely traumatic experience. Broughton, then in poor health, felt that she would soon die. In 1887 she was seriously ill again. She prepared for death as she felt God's call to work. Once her health was restored, she became a full-time missionary and was sent on her first missionary journey to areas beyond Memphis—up the Mississippi River, to points in Tennessee, Arkansas, and Missouri. In 1892 she was appointed a missionary by the Women's Baptist Home Mission Society, and by 1894 she could report that Bible bands existed in fifty-seven places in Tennessee and ran twenty industrial schools. In 1895 she attended the mission society's meeting in Saratoga, New York, and spoke very successfully in the North from Massachusetts to Illinois.

Broughton's work did not go unopposed by the men she came in contact with, many of whom did not take kindly to literate women using the Bible to refute the pretensions of males, especially illiterate preachers. The first male Broughton had to confront may have been her own husband. By her choosing, Broughton's work was fully consuming and continued to separate her from her family. She placed God and missionary work above all else. As Broughton wrote in her autobiography, *Twenty Years' Experience of a Missionary* (1907), initially John Broughton was opposed to his wife's frequent absences from home and protested, "When is this business going to stop?" She replied, "I don't know; but I belong to God first, and you next; so you two must settle it." Her family was definitely of secondary consideration. In fact, after canceling a missionary event to return home to nurse a dying daughter, she vowed to never again allow family concerns to cause her to cancel a meeting—God would dispose of her family as He saw fit in spite of all her actions. In time, John Broughton became interested in the work of the church and supported his wife's missionary activities. A strong woman who believed in her divine calling, Broughton was difficult to stop since she viewed opposition to her mission as the work of the devil: "While men opposed and Satan strove our progress to retard, God was with us and was only permitting those trials our dross to consume and our gold to refine," she wrote in her autobiography.

Black women throughout the state went to the meetings to hear the new doctrines. According to Broughton, they wanted to hear what the women were teaching and what the men were discussing and opposing. Some men, including ministers, deeply resented the women missionaries and were jealous of their successful work. Black men in Tennessee were disturbed at the women's progress and feared that since so many of them had Bibles and were becoming so adept at interpreting the Scriptures they would demand to become preachers. To them a woman's place was not at the pulpit.

Evelyn Higginbotham, in her *Righteous Discontent: The Women's Movement in the Black Baptist Church, 1880-1920,* states that the greatest opposition to organized womanhood was among the rural, uneducated ministry and that churches in urban areas were fertile ground for the growth of the black women's convention movement. So confident was Broughton in her speeches and her work that her male adversaries labeled her a "mannish woman." Some of the bands actually dissolved because of the men's attitudes, yet Broughton and other women like her persevered. To get the word to the people, Broughton at different times promoted *The Women's Messenger* and *The Missionary Helper,* both of which aided in the development of the women's work. Gender agitation in Tennessee's black Baptist church had begun.

Involvement in Schools

In 1888 the State Baptist Convention of Tennessee, with the financial support of white missionaries, founded the Bible and Normal Institute (later the Howe Bible and Normal Institute, named so for a benefactor) in a black church in Memphis to accommodate the dense black population in and around the city in Tennessee and neighboring Arkansas and Mississippi. Broughton took a keen interest in the Howe school and became a field-worker to stimulate interest among the church women in the school and to raise funds to help support the school's dormitory and buy kitchen supplies. That year the board sent Broughton and another black women, E. B. King, throughout the state to organize Bible bands and to elicit support for the school.

One of the Howe school's most interesting features was a Bible training class for women, which by 1908 reached a membership of 216 students, representing thirty churches and several religious denominations. That September black women throughout the state met at the Mt. Zion Baptist Church in Stanton, Tennessee, and organized a separate association to address women's rights, Bible study, and other issues. Broughton taught a women's missionary training course at Howe in 1890 and taught Bible studies there throughout the 1890s. She also supervised the Christian Home and Training School for Women, which served women who came from the rural areas.

The Broughton family moved to Nashville in December 1899, and Virginia Broughton became a secretary in Joanna P. Moore's Fireside School program. Fireside schools were not formal institutions; rather, they were study groups about the fireside in the home and placed under the care of the church. The goal of the schools was to improve home life and encourage daily prayer and home Bible study. They taught parents and children how to live daily and to help neighbors. They promoted temperance and industry, the provision of good books to homes to stimulate reading, religious and secular education, and support of the church. Moore, a white missionary, developed the program to forestall white opposition to organized schools for blacks, which had resulted in a week of violence in November 1890 and had forced her to close her Baton Rouge training school. Given the purpose of Moore's Fireside schools, Broughton could fill her own mission of service through this outlet. Broughton also became assistant editor of *Hope,* the official organ of the Fireside

School program, a monthly magazine founded by Joanna Moore that published Sunday school lessons, guides for Bible bands, discussions of various issues, and letters from ministers and black women. Some of Broughton's writings were published in the magazine. For six months when Moore was ill Broughton acted as supervisor of the Fireside School program. While in the position she visited local churches of all denominations and attended minister's conferences at the state and national levels. After the temporary appointment ended, Broughton was called to state mission work. She traveled throughout Tennessee, teaching the biblical view of women's work, organizing missionary societies, and encouraging women to join the spiritual effort to evangelize the world.

Black Baptist Women United

Broughton worked with other women who were vocal in defense of women's rights to organize separate state conventions for black Baptist women. These women promoted middle-class values among the masses, garnered financial support for the churches, and spearheaded numerous social service programs. Their gender agitation developed about the same time that women across the nation were uniting in women's clubs and promoting the uplift of black people through their work.

Broughton attended the National Baptist Convention held in Louisville in 1890 and spoke on the subject of "The Ideal Woman." She called for a separate and distinct organization for women. The movement was sidetracked, however, by the drive to create the National Baptist Convention, U.S.A., which came about in 1895. A Woman's Auxiliary was unofficially formed the same year with Broughton as recording secretary, but it was disbanded the next year at the St. Louis meeting and women were placed on various boards of the National Baptist Convention. The women continued to work on behalf of their own interests, and at the Richmond, Virginia, meeting in 1900, the national Women's Convention became a recognized body of the National Baptist Convention. From then on the two groups usually held their annual conferences simultaneously; however, their sessions were held in separate buildings. While the male-dominated convention spoke for the denomination, the women's organization formed a valuable forum for women to discuss their own concerns. Significantly, the Women's Convention did not split when the National Baptist Convention divided into two major factions in 1915.

Among the original officers of the Women's Convention were Mrs. S. W. (Sarah Willie) Layton of Philadelphia, president; the very young Nannie Helen

Burroughs, of Louisville, corresponding secretary; and Broughton, recording secretary. In late 1902 and much of 1903, Broughton and Burroughs competed for editorship of the "Woman's Column" published in the *National Baptist Union.* By August 1903, however, the women and the convention put the controversy behind them and Broughton edited the column.

Journals of the annual sessions of the Women's Convention published between 1900 and 1915 indicate that the Women's Auxiliary was involved in numerous activities, including temperance, work with children, the promotion of reading black literature in the home, Bible study, and foreign and domestic missions. Broughton expressed her views, and doubtless those of the Women's Convention, when, in 1902, she called for blacks to publish "distinctive literature" that would instill pride in the race. She and the women also harshly criticized women's fashions. Broughton found "gaudy colors and conspicuous trimmings" distasteful, and, by 1913, the Woman's Convention attacked the décolleté dress and slit skirt, advising mothers that their daughter's dresses should be made wide enough to make a slit unnecessary. Both the Women's Convention and the National Baptist Convention raised money to support the development of the National Training School for Women and Girls located in Washington, D.C. Nannie Helen Burroughs (1879-1961), corresponding secretary of the Woman's Convention for nearly fifty years, mobilized the convention to underwrite the school, and when it opened on October 19, 1909, she was its president.

For one year, beginning in September 1906, Broughton was Bible teacher at Alabama Agricultural and Mechanical College in Normal. She became superintendent of the Sunday school and supervised the YWCA. The school's president, William H. Councill, and students contributed money for her to travel to the World's International Sunday School Congress held in Rome, Italy, which she attended as a delegate of the Women's Convention. The National Baptist Publishing Board underwrote a large portion of the expenses. Further recognition of her stature as a leader came when she was the first black person appointed by the Associated Charities of Memphis to assist in flood relief. Her position was enhanced by her continuing role in the Women's Convention at the state and national levels.

Richard Henry Boyd (1843-1922), cofounder of the National Baptist Publishing Board and an influential black religious and business leader, became unofficial advisor to the Women's Convention. He was particularly close to Broughton, who was an editor for the board's *Missionary Herald* and contributed much toward its success. To help the women in their initial efforts, Boyd and the publishing board gave them literature and offered printing services without charge. Broughton was highly regarded in the council of the auxiliary and was still recording secretary at the time of her death—she held the position for thirty-three years.

During Broughton's lifetime, the black male Baptists of Tennessee and the South eventually encouraged the work of women, finding it valuable to the uplift of black people, and they supported women's organizations, particularly the auxiliary to the National Baptist Convention. Black male Baptists accepted Broughton because she found outlets beyond the pulpit for her religious teachings. As other black women leaders of that time had done, for example, Margaret Murray Washington and Cornelia Bowen in Alabama, Broughton advocated programs of uplift for mothers to help them improve themselves and family life as well. Baptist women worked with mothers, visited the sick, consoled the bereaved, and were largely responsible for the church's missionary work.

Lectures and Publications

Virginia Broughton was a religious feminist and one of several black Baptist women of the 1880s, 1890s, and early 1900s who developed her own views on women's rights in the church and society. These women used the Bible to defend women's rights in and beyond the church, taking positions that challenged traditional male religious chauvinism. Broughton's views on women and the Bible were published in 1904 in her book, *Women's Work, as Gleaned from the Women of the Bible.* She expounds on her missionary activities in her book, *Twenty Years' Experience of a Missionary.* Her public lectures given throughout the state of Tennessee, her missionary work, and her correspondence gave her other forums for expressing her feminist views.

An excellent writer, she also published, through the National Baptist Publishing Board in Nashville, a number of tracts and pamphlets that she distributed to supplement her lectures. Her writings were valuable contributions to Baptist denominational literature. As early as the 1890s she was editor of *Women's Messenger.* Her interests also included social and civic work. When Tennessee prepared to celebrate its centennial for a six-month period in 1897 and plans were made for a Negro Building at the exposition, Broughton became chair of the Negro Department's Educational Committee.

In Memphis, Broughton divided her church connection between First Baptist Church on Saint Paul Avenue and Tabernacle Baptist Church, where writer Sutton E. Griggs was minister. When she returned to Nashville, Broughton worshipped as a member of the black First Baptist Church, which had arisen from the white First Baptist Church.

Broughton died a widow in Memphis on September 21, 1934, when she was about seventy-eight years old. The cause of death was diabetes mellitus, complicated by old age. She was survived by her children, Emma O. Broughton, Elizabeth Branson, and Julius A. Broughton, all of Memphis, and Virginia Cameron of Los Angeles; and her brothers Robert and Rufus Walker, of Nashville. Another daughter, Selena, had died as a young child. At the time of her death she lived at 392 South Lauderdale. She was buried in Zion Cemetery on September 24.

REFERENCES:

Alumni Directory of Fisk University. Nashville: Office of Alumni Affairs, 1971.

Broughton, Virginia. *Twenty Years' Experience of a Missionary.* Chicago: Pony Press, 1907. Reprinted in *Spiritual Narratives.* New York: Oxford University Press, 1988.

Certificate of Death. Tennessee State Library and Archives, Nashville.

Death Notice. Files of the Memphis County Public Library and Information Center, Memphis, Tennessee.

Fuller, Thomas Oscar. *History of Negro Baptists in Tennessee.* Memphis: Haskins Print, Roger Williams University, 1936.

Haley, James T. *Sparkling Gems of Race Knowledge Worth Reading.* Nashville: J. T. Haley and Co., 1897.

Hartshorn, W. N., ed. *An Era of Progress and Promise, 1863-1910.* Boston: Priscilla Publishing Co., 1910.

Higginbotham, Evelyn Brooks. *Righteous Discontent: The Women's Movement in the Black Baptist Church, 1880-1920.* Cambridge: Harvard University Press, 1993.

Journal of the Eighth Annual Session of the Assembly of the Woman's Convention, Washington, D.C., September 19-23, 1907. In *Journal of the National Baptist Convention, 27th Annual Session, Washington, D.C., September 11-16, 1907.*

Journal of the Second Annual Session of the Women's Convention, Auxiliary to the National Baptist Convention, Held in the Mound Street Baptist Church, Cincinnati, Ohio, September 11-16, 1901. In *Journal of the Annual Session of the National Baptist Convention, Cincinnati, Ohio, September 11-16, 1901.*

Lovett, Bobby L. *A Black Man's Dream. The First 100 Years: Richard Henry Boyd and the National Baptist Publishing Board.* Nashville: Mega Corporation, 1993.

U.S. Department of the Interior. Bureau of Education. *Negro Education: A Study of the Private and Higher Schools for Colored People in the United States.* Vol. 2. Bulletin 1916, no. 39. Washington, D.C.: Government Printing Office, 1916.

Jessie Carney Smith

Clara Brown
(1800-1885)
Philanthropist, pioneer

Clara Brown, known by her friends as "Aunt," was eulogized by the Society of Colorado Pioneers, according to Kathleen Bruyn's account of her life, *'Aunt' Clara Brown: Story of a Black Pioneer,* as "the kind old friend whose heart always responded to the cry of distress, and who, rising from the humble position of slave to the angelic type of a noble woman, won our sympathy and commanded our respect." Assuming nobility of heart as a more powerful determinant for quality of life than status of birth, one is compelled to remember Brown as worthy of great respect. She was devoted to Christian ideals and expressed them by sharing the good things of life with others. She displayed a great commitment to family and sought constantly, with every resource at her disposal, to reestablish her family ties, which were brutally severed by slavery. Freed from slavery in 1857, Brown traveled west, eventually settling in the boomtown of

Clara Brown

Central City, Colorado, where she operated a laundry and wisely invested in property. In Central City, she engaged in a number of philanthropic activities, including contributing money to churches, converting her home into a makeshift hospital, and providing travelers with food and shelter. Brown overcame the limitations imposed by illiteracy and human bondage to emerge as a successful businesswoman and to take her rightful place among those public-spirited citizens who provide courage and hope to others.

Clara Brown was born a slave in 1800. Her immediate family unit was shattered when various members were sold to different slaveholders. Customarily, children aged ten and under were allowed to remain with their mothers. Such was young Clara's case when, at age three, she and her mother were acquired by Ambrose Smith, a tobacco farmer living in Spotsylvania County, Virginia, near Fredericksburg. In 1809 they moved with the Smith family to Logan County, Kentucky, where her mother assisted Myra Smith with domestic chores while Clara, even at an early age, joined two other slaves and the two Smith sons in clearing fields and planting crops. In 1810, when the Smith family attended a Methodist revival, young Clara traveled along with them and pledged her life to Jesus.

As Brown grew to maturity, her life was marked for a time by harmony and tranquility. Ambrose Smith acquired a slave named Richard, an accomplished carpenter, to whom Brown was married in 1818. The couple had four children: Richard; Margaret; and twin girls, Paulina Ann and Eliza Jane. Circumstances dealt the family a severe blow when Paulina Ann died in a swimming accident. This was a harbin-

ger of the cruel events of 1835. In that year the economic structure that had brought Clara and Richard together collapsed. Ambrose Smith died abruptly of pneumonia, and his widow settled his estate in order to move nearer to her family. One of the Smith boys had become a doctor and the other had become an attorney, so neither one was interested in maintaining their father's farm or in keeping slaves.

Brown's family was dissolved on the auction block in Russellville, Kentucky. She was sold to George Brown, a Russellville hatter and lodge brother of Ambrose Smith. She likely fared much better than did other members of her family. Her husband was sold, probably to a trader, and was never heard from again. Brown always believed that Richard's destination was one of the large plantations in the deep South where living conditions were inhumane and where economic interests permeated every aspect of slave existence. Her son, Richard, was sold and resold numerous times and, over the years, George Brown gradually lost track of his whereabouts. Margaret was sold to Bednigo Shelton of Morgantown, Kentucky, and died at a young age of a respiratory disease. According to Kathleen Bruyn, Eliza Jane was sold to James Covington in Logan County, which was "too far distant from Russellville to permit communication. She then left, but why or for where, George Brown could not learn." Many of the decisions that Clara Brown would make throughout the remainder of her life were guided by her attempts to find her family, to rebuild that which economic policy and race hatred had destroyed.

Brown Finds the Way West

Brown's dreams of a better life began to be realized in 1857. Following the death of her owner, George Brown, she was given her freedom by his daughters, Mary Prue, Lucinda, and Evaline. Brown wanted to stay in Kentucky, where she had spent her entire adult life. Kentucky state law, however, required that manumitted slaves leave the state within one year following receipt of their freedom or become slaves once again. Clara had served the Browns faithfully for twenty-two years and had earned their trust and appreciation. They, in turn, sought to secure for her a suitable working and living arrangement. They transported her to a St. Louis merchant who had agreed to hire her as a domestic servant. Within two years she had moved with her new family to Leavenworth, Kansas. With help from her employer, she purchased irons, tubs, and a boiler and opened her own laundry. Yet, Brown did not remain in Leavenworth. Upon hearing that other blacks had migrated further west, she was stirred by the promise of economic opportunity and by the dim but undying hope that she might somehow find Eliza Jane.

Brown hired on as a cook for a wagon train of gold prospectors headed for the Pike's Peak region of Colorado. Since the wagons were needed for provisions and supplies, Brown and the other travelers walked the full distance of more than six hundred miles, a journey lasting approximately eight weeks. In the summer of 1859 she arrived in Auraria in the Cherry Creek region near Denver and, for a small sum, was able to occupy one of the rough-hewn cabins that had been vacated by dispirited prospectors. She worked in a local bakery and, once again, took in laundry.

At Auraria, Brown's commitment to community interests became apparent to her neighbors. Her industrious nature soon earned her the respect and appreciation of her laundry customers and patrons at the bakery. She also demonstrated a gift for hospitality by making a home for the local Methodist church, which met in her cabin during 1859 and 1860. Brown's Christian faith was all-encompassing, and she showed no concern for sectarian issues. At various times in her life she attended services of the Baptist, Disciples of Christ, Episcopal, Methodist, and Presbyterian denominations.

The promise of a still better economic situation and the undiminished desire to reunite with Eliza Jane drew Brown higher into the Rocky Mountains to Mountain City, later to be known as Central City, Colorado. She had established herself in one of the territory's most volatile regions. John Gregory struck gold in May 1860 and, within another month, ten thousand people were camped within an eight-mile radius. Brown was part of this movement, which overwhelmed the mining camps in Central City, Black Hawk, Nevadaville, and Russell Gulch. Yet her goal was not wealth, simply economic security and opportunities for service.

Brown made friends easily, becoming a central figure in the boomtown's philanthropic endeavors. Just as she had at Auraria, she made her home available for church services, she frequently took in weary and misplaced travelers, and she converted her cabin into a hospital to nurse injured miners and to serve as a midwife. Having once again opened a small laundry service, she worked hard, used her income frugally, and, throughout the 1860s, invested in rental property and shared mining claims at Central City, Idaho Springs, Boulder, Denver, and Clear Creek County. With these assets she contributed funds toward the construction of a building for the St. James Methodist Church on Eureka Street as well as for buildings for the local Roman Catholic and Congregational churches. Yet she was not content merely to contribute her own money. She also collected money for St. James Methodist, where she attended services for many years and whose building was dedicated in 1872.

Brown Goes Home Again

After the Civil War, travel became easier for African Americans. With some wealth at her disposal, Brown returned to Kentucky to renew her search for Eliza Jane. George Brown's oldest daughter, Mary Prue, and her husband, Richard Higgins, gave her a place to stay and solicited the aid of a number of former slaves, church members, ministers, and others who conceivably could help. But memories were dim and some courthouse records had been destroyed in the war. Brown journeyed to Gallatin, Tennessee, the birthplace of her parents, but could find no clues that would lead her to Eliza Jane. Not wanting to return to Colorado alone, she decided to offer passage to anyone who might be interested in economic opportunity further west. Sixteen blacks, most of them former slaves, followed her back to Colorado from Gallatin and Russellville. She would provide them food, shelter, employ-

ment, and the supportive community she had come to enjoy in Central City.

One of the worst facts of life for American slaves was the absence of educational opportunity. Rare was the owner who, whether from economic or philanthropic motives, taught slaves to read or write. Brown was born and reared in this adverse environment. Though a shrewd businesswoman, she was constantly forced to rely on friends, neighbors, business partners, or fellow church members to prepare correspondence or to calculate debits and credits. She was particularly vulnerable to unscrupulous activity when away from home. On the trip east to Kentucky, probably while encamped in Leavenworth, Brown and her companions were swindled of approximately four thousand dollars. This amount represented much of what she had accumulated through the years, and its loss, when coupled with her obligations to settle and reestablish those who had migrated to Colorado, proved a financial blow from which she would never fully recover.

Brown battled the adverse circumstances common to many pioneer villages. In 1864, floodwaters destroyed the houses she owned in Denver, sweeping away with them the deeds that proved her ownership. In 1873, fire destroyed three of her Central City properties and, the next year, her cabin on Lawrence Street. Thereafter, her economic security declined.

Brown's generosity, her desire to nurture, and her impulse to serve drew her inexorably to the aid of others. Symbolic of her humanitarian instincts was her offer at age seventy-nine to aid the "exodusters," migrants who had been attracted from numerous locations in the South to the Wyandotte region of Kansas in a movement that offered them a sense of community and the hope of inexpensive land.

Movement organizers solicited funds from around the nation. When Frederick W. Pitkin, governor of Colorado, took an interest in the plight of the exodusters and considered committing funds for that purpose, he dispatched Brown to investigate. According to Robert Athearn's *In Search of Canaan*, Pitkin's letter of introduction to migration organizers noted that Brown had "accumulated quite a large fortune, but has spent most of it for the relief of her own race. She is one of the best old souls that ever lived and is respected by all who know her. She goes to Kansas to see the destitute freedmen and to report here upon their condition."

Reunion Comes At Last

By 1880, with both her fortune and her health in serious decline, Brown moved to Denver to occupy a small cabin on Arapahoe Street. Yet some of her most amazing moments lay ahead. At age eighty-one she was honored by induction into the society of Colorado Pioneers in recognition of her authenticity as a "fifty-niner," the society having earlier lifted its ban against blacks and women. Word came in 1882 that Eliza Jane was living in Council Bluffs, Iowa, although contemporary reports conflict wildly as to how Brown learned this vital information. Friends collected money to provide for Brown's day-and-a-half journey. Following an emotional reunion and the completely unexpected realization of a lifelong dream,

Brown returned to Denver accompanied by a granddaughter, who took care of her until she died. Her remains were interred in Riverside Cemetery in Denver. Remarkably, her body was exhumed eleven years later and reburied in the lot of Harriet Mason (wife of prominent miner Andrew Mason), according to the stipulations of Mrs. Mason's will. Why the reburial held such importance for Harriet Mason remains unclear. Perhaps she was the beneficiary of one or more of the thousands of kindnesses bestowed by Clara Brown as she lived out her eighty-five years.

REFERENCES:

Armitage, Sue, Theresa Banfield, and Sarah Jacobus. "Black Women and Their Communities in Colorado." *Frontiers* 2 (1977): 45-51.

Athearn, Robert G. *In Search of Canaan: Black Migration to Kansas, 1879-80.* Lawrence: Regents Press of Kansas, 1978.

Bancroft, Caroline. *Historic Central City: Its Complete Story as Guide and Souvenir.* 9th ed. Boulder, Colo.: Johnson Publishing Co., 1974.

Bruyn, Kathleen. *'Aunt' Clara Brown: Story of a Black Pioneer.* Boulder, Colo.: Pruett Publishing Co., 1970.

Jackson, George F. *Black Women, Makers of History: A Portrait.* Oakland, Calif.: GRT Book Print, 1975.

Katz, William Loren. *The Black West.* Garden City, N.Y.: Doubleday, 1971.

Metcalf, Kenneth E. "The Beginnings of Methodism in Colorado." Ph.D. diss., Iliff School of Theology, 1948.

Riley, Glenda. "American Daughters: Black Women in the West." *Montana: The Magazine of Western History* 38 (Spring 1988): 14-27.

Savage, W. Sherman. *Blacks in the West.* Westport, Conn.: Greenwood Press, 1976.

John Mark Tucker

Cora M. Brown

Cora M. Brown
(1914-1972)
Social worker, police officer, lawyer, politician

In 1952, thirty-two years after American women won the right to vote and thirteen years before the Voting Rights Act of 1965 provided the legal means to enforce and protect each American citizen's voting rights, Cora M. Brown was elected to the Michigan State Senate. She was the first female to be elected rather than appointed to fulfill an unexpired term and the first black woman to be elected to a state senate. Thus Cora Brown was a political pioneer.

Brown was born on April 16, 1914, in Bessemer, Alabama; she was Richard and Alice Brown's only child. When

Brown was seven years old, her family moved to Detroit, where her father established a tailor's shop. In 1931 Brown graduated from Detroit's Cass Technical High School and enrolled in Fisk University in Nashville.

In an effort to help pay college expenses, she worked at a Detroit Urban League summer camp for underprivileged children, and her mother accepted a job as a cook for a family. In spite of these efforts to generate additional income, sometimes Brown had to wear the same dress to classes each day and the same evening gown to all the dances. However, in *The Negro Politician,* Edward T. Clayton characterized Brown's years at Fisk by her ability to remain "diligent in her pursuit of an education" as well as by her willingness to battle injustice. Brown left Fisk in 1935 with a degree in sociology, yet she could not leave behind the memory of the 1933 lynching in Columbia, Tennessee, of a young African American who was accused of an attempted rape although the evidence was inconclusive. Brown participated in a campus demonstration that members of the community and Fisk faculty unsuccessfully tried to discourage. The *Detroit Free Press* of February 25, 1956, noted that Brown's involvement in the demonstration marked the debut of her lifelong campaign against "injustice and inhumanity."

After graduating from Fisk, Brown returned to Detroit and became a social worker for the Old Age Assistance Bureau, the Children's Aid Society, and the Works Progress Administration (WPA). From 1941 to 1946 Brown worked as a policewoman in the Women's Division; her assignments involving the preparation of legal cases motivated her to study law. Brown enrolled in Wayne State University in 1946, received a law degree in 1948, and passed the bar examination within two weeks after graduation. She entered the firm of Morris and Brown where she practiced general law and maintained an interest in criminal law. Brown's friend Geraldine Bledsoe summarized her nonpolitical years in the *Michigan Chronicle,* December 30, 1972:

> As a social worker . . . giving help to the needy and disparaged in those dark depression years; as a policewoman, dealing understandingly with those in conflict with the law and society, and as a counselor at law . . . she gave wise counsel, guidance and defense to those continuing to be caught in the confusing maze of the system.

Brown's political career began with her involvement in district activities. Then in 1950 she ran for the state senate in Detroit's Second District and lost the election by six hundred votes. When A. J. Wilkowski was denied his state senate seat in 1951, a special election was called, and Brown campaigned again. She was defeated by a disc jockey. Brown, still possessing the determination she displayed during her undergraduate years at Fisk, ran for the same office in 1952.

Elected Michigan's First Woman Senator

Brown, after winning the Democratic nomination from a field of eight opponents in the primary, told the *Detroit News* on August 10, 1952, "It wasn't too hard to sell the women on voting for me. I found there is a little loyalty in our sex. The men were a little more stand-offish." Her opponent in the general election was a black man, an assistant city corporation counsel. They campaigned for the senate seat in Detroit's Second District, where a significant number of blacks lived. Brown won the general election in November, and after analyzing the election results, she commented in the November 6, 1952, issue of the *Detroit News:*

> These women voters have awakened and they expect their views to be properly represented. Women have always been able to bring sound and humane reasoning into everyday life. I believe they are the hope of the country.

Before assuming office, Brown stated, as reported by Clayton in *The Negro Politician:*

> I don't expect much opposition because I am a woman. I haven't found that too difficult a 'handicap' to overcome. I was surprised and pleased that after I was elected a number of senators wrote me letters saying they were happy that I was going to work with them.

However, after her first term, during which the *Detroit News* of December 6, 1952, found her "seated in lonely feminine determination" among thirty-two senators, Brown voiced a different opinion in the *Michigan Chronicle,* December 11, 1958: "I have found sex a greater handicap than ever."

Ebony magazine regarded Brown as "energetic and able" during her two terms in the Michigan Senate from 1953

to 1957. Another article in *Ebony* called her a "rather aggressive legislator" with a keen sense of public relations who did not fear controversy. Brown would openly disagree with other blacks when she deemed it necessary. Whether representing minority populations in the Second or Third districts (the district change resulted from a boundary readjustment), the *Detroit Free Press* of February 25, 1956, said that Brown was known as a "champion of the underprivileged," and a December 19, 1972, issue of the newspaper called her the "perennial thorn in the conscience" of Michigan's Democratic party because of Brown's focus on such issues as civil rights, community, education, health, and labor.

Civil rights was the stimulus for many of Brown's actions, especially in 1956. She co-introduced a bill with a Republican senator that called for revoking or suspending all state and local licenses held by businesses that discriminated on the basis of race; this bill was passed in February 1956. During that same month, Brown, who was selected as the Outstanding Woman Legislator of 1956, announced her candidacy for the Democratic nomination for Congress in the First District after accusing the incumbent of favoring his Polish constituents at the expense of his black constituents. In her effort to become the United States' first black congresswoman, Brown lacked support from the Democratic organization and lost the August election by 6,491 votes. In October, she shocked her Democratic colleagues when she endorsed President Eisenhower's bid for reelection. At a news conference held after her White House meeting with Eisenhower, Brown asserted that her decision was based on civil rights; she opposed Adlai Stevenson, the Democratic candidate, because of his support from pro-segregationists. As a result, Brown, along with black New York congressman Adam Clayton Powell, urged blacks to vote for Democratic local and state candidates and for the Republican president.

Eisenhower was reelected, and, according to Clayton in *The Negro Politician,* Brown was ignored by the Michigan Democratic Party:

> Having relinquished her senatorial post to make a bid for Congress, then defying party leadership to support Eisenhower, she now found herself without political office or favor. Even when she topped a civil service list of eligibles for appointment as a referee in the Court of Probate Judge Nathan J. Kaufman . . . she saw herself bypassed for the job. . . . It remained for the Republicans to reward her politically for her efforts in Eisenhower's behalf.

In August 1957, Brown was appointed as the special associate general counsel of the United States Post Office. She was the first black woman to serve on the post office's legal staff. Brown held the position until 1960, when John F. Kennedy's election to the presidency returned the Democrats to power.

Brown moved to Los Angeles, opened an office, and practiced law for nearly ten years before returning to Detroit in 1970. She was appointed to the Michigan Employment Security Commission, becoming the first black woman referee in thirty-five years. When Brown was appointed, she told the *Detroit Free Press,* December 19, 1972, ''My hobby used to be politics. . . . But those days are over.''

In addition to her career activities, Brown was a member of the Detroit chapter of the National Council of Negro Women, NAACP, YWCA, Alpha Kappa Alpha Sorority, Order of the Eastern Star, Improved Benevolent Order of Elks of the World, and New Calvary Baptist Church.

Brown died on December 17, 1972, at Detroit's Grace Central Hospital and was buried in Elmwood Cemetery four days later. The *Michigan Chronicle* of December 30, 1972, eulogized her as ''a servant of the people.''

REFERENCES:

Brown, Nadine. ''Eulogize Cora Brown as 'Servant of the People.'''
Michigan Chronicle, December 30, 1972.
Clayton, Edward T. *The Negro Politician, His Success and Failure.* Chicago: Johnson Publishing Co., 1964.
Cousins, Fred W. ''Women Take 2 State Seats.'' *Detroit News,* November 6, 1952.
George, Hub M. ''Friends to Honor Senator Cora Brown.'' *Detroit Free Press,* February 25, 1956.
Hushen, Wallace. ''Portia to Wear Senate Toga.'' *Detroit News,* August 10, 1952.
Michigan Chronicle, December 11, 1958.
''Pioneering Legislator Is Dead.'' *Detroit Free Press,* December 19, 1972.
''Women in Politics.'' *Ebony* 11 (August 1956): 81-84.
''Women Who Make State Laws.'' *Ebony* 22 (September 1967): 27-34.

COLLECTIONS:

The main branch of the Detroit Public Library has a clipping file on Brown in its History and Travel Department.

Linda M. Carter

Elaine Brown
(1943-)
Political activist, civic activist, musician

A member of the Black Panther party, Elaine Brown moved up the ranks to the helm as chairperson in 1974—the highest-ranking woman in the party and second in command only to the party's founder, Huey P. Newton. Her rise from obscurity in Philadelphia's ghetto to notoriety as a political activist is a story of a black woman's struggle for change.

Elaine Brown

An only child, Elaine Brown was born on March 3, 1943, in Philadelphia, Pennsylvania. Her unwed mother, Dorothy Clark, raised her young daughter with the assistance of her sister and mother. Despite Clark's limited income and resources as a manual laborer, she had high aspirations for her daughter and provided Elaine with very rich educational opportunities. Brown's early years as a child were spent in the ghetto environment of North Philadelphia.

Brown says in her autobiography that she is the daughter of Horace Scott, a claim her mother could not prove in court. She received very meager support from Scott, even though he was a neurosurgeon and a member of a very prominent black family. He was the son of Emmett Scott, Sr., who had been the secretary of the black educator and political leader Booker T. Washington and held several distinguished positions, including secretary of the National Negro Business League and special assistant to the Secretary of War during World War I. Horace Scott and the Scott family were embarrassed by the presence of an out-of-wedlock child. Furthermore, Horace Scott's elitism and snobbishness could not allow him to marry a woman of Dorothy Clark's class. Clark constantly sought to gain child support but the social connections of the Scott family influenced the courts to rule against her.

The financial constraints did not stop Clark from providing a good education for her daughter. Brown attended a special experimental school, Thaddeus Stevens School of Practice, and began private piano lessons at age six. She also had ballet lessons and was exposed to other cultural activities such as plays and musicals. She was a student at the Philadelphia High School for Girls from 1957 to 1961, where she graduated with a B-plus average. After high school, Brown attended Temple University as a prelaw student and pursued her musical interest at the Philadelphia Conservatory of Music. Through her teen years, she sang in the Jones Tabernacle AME Church choir and wrote a number of musical selections.

Brown Embraces Leftist Ideas

Brown dropped out of Temple University and moved to California in 1965. In search of a new life and the possibility of becoming a professional songwriter, she settled in Los Angeles. She worked as a waitress at Hollywood's Pink Pussycat, where she met Jay Kennedy, the former manager of singer Harry Belafonte and a noted writer. He introduced Brown to various political and social philosophies. During her romantic relationship with Kennedy, Brown began to discuss Communism, Socialism, Marxism, Leninism, and other leftist ideas. She also began to think about the emerging black power movement.

It was, however, an African American woman, Beverlee Bruce, who introduced Brown to the actual black power movement and the ideas of Malcolm X, Langston Hughes, Ralph Ellison, and Richard Wright. Bruce facilitated Brown's personal engagement in the black community as a piano teacher to young African American women in the Watts section of Los Angeles.

Brown became an active member of the Los Angeles Black Congress, a united front organization of various black groups. She worked as a staff member of the Black Congress newspaper, *Harambee,* in 1967 and was involved in various other activities in California, including working with Angela Davis, who would herself later join the Communist party.

In April 1968 Brown joined the Black Panther party (BPP) and by 1969 served as the Los Angeles chapter's minister of information. In November 1969 she and Ericka Huggins went to Bridgeport, Connecticut, where they started a new chapter of the BPP. About thirty people attended the organizational meeting. Two sisters, Peggy and Frances Carter of Bridgeport, were meticulously dressed for the meeting and wore big natural hairstyles, fur jackets—everything carefully matched. On the contrary, the Panthers, who were dressed in fatigues, looked like urban guerrillas. Frances Carter told Hilliard and Cole,

> That led to an immediate class distinction between us and them because Elaine Brown made reference to these ''little china dolls, little kewpie dolls.'' We . . . told her not to put any distinction between herself and us, that we were black women, not kewpie dolls, and that we would not be categorized as china dolls, and assured her that if we wanted to come next time in a Oscar de la Renta we would come through that door and be totally accepted. . . . She seemed really genuine, spaced out, but genuine.

During Brown's BPP days she worked in the Panther's breakfast program, led voter registration drives, ran for city

council of Oakland, and was a delegate to the Democratic National Convention in 1976.

In 1974 Brown became chairperson of the BPP and second in command only to its founder, Huey P. Newton, which made her the highest ranking black woman in the party. David Hilliard and Lewis Cole wrote in *This Side of Glory* that Newton ''had provided himself with an incredible array of talent'' that included Brown and leaders from the Boston chapter and the Chicago branch. The bright, quick witted, highly articulate Brown caused friction between Newton and other members. Further,

> She used her fast tongue against other Party members; many gave her a wide berth because she was so quick to detect slights against Huey and then use the supposedly offending comment to score a point against the comrade who made it. . . . Her loyalty was very valuable to Huey. Her weakness was her strength: she had no place to go, could organize no independent base. Huey would chuckle that she might be a son of a bitch, but she was his son of a bitch.

Brown's tenure as BPP chairperson from 1974 to 1977 signaled a shift in the direction of BPP's initiatives. The early image of the party was marred by paramilitarism and constant shootouts with police. This image greatly reduced the effectiveness of the BPP's functioning as an organization that served the interests of the African American masses. When Brown gained the helm of the party, which was during Huey Newton's exile in Cuba, she expanded the scope of the party's programs to include electoral politics, education of black youth, civic issues, and the internal elevation of the role of women in the BPP.

In the realm of electoral politics, Brown engineered voter registration efforts in Oakland, which led to the election of Lionel Wilson, a black Superior Court Judge, to the office of mayor in 1977. Earlier she had assisted John George to the position of Alameda County supervisor in November 1976. Brown, along with fellow Panther member Phyllis Jackson, served on George's committee, while Panther member Joan Kelly was a member of the Alameda County Juvenile Delinquency Prevention Committee.

The Panthers' efforts to promote education of black youth through its school, the Oakland Community Learning Center, were enriched during Brown's leadership and in 1977 it gained a commendation for its work from the California State Assembly. The school was principally run by women in the BPP; Ericka Huggins was director and Regina Davis was responsible for daily operations. Brown even taught a class consisting of many who had been labeled by the public school system as special education students.

Departure from the Black Panther Party

The increased role of women in the BPP caused concern among a number of men in the party. Many of the men complained about the power delegated to women, including Brown's chairing the BPP. According to Brown, when Newton returned to the United States from Cuba in July 1977, he yielded to the men's complaints. When Regina Davis was beaten by men in the party, Brown remarked, ''The beating of Regina would be taken as a clear signal that the words 'Panther' and 'comrade' had taken a gender on gender connotation, denoting an inferiority in the female half of us.'' Brown's departure from the BPP came in the wake of both the attack on black women in the party and its general decline into gang activity.

Brown departed from the Black Panthers in 1977 and returned to her musical career. She previously had two albums, *Seize the Time* in 1969 and *Until We're Free* on the Motown label in 1973.

Elaine Brown has one daughter, Ericka, named after Black Panther Ericka Huggins. In 1992, she wrote her autobiography, *A Taste of Power*—a candid and self-revealing account of her rise from North Philadelphia's black ghetto to fame and power as the highest ranking woman in the Black Panther party.

REFERENCES:

Brown, Elaine. ''Tough Love.'' *Essence* 19 (December 1988): 69-71, 117-18, 121.
———. *A Taste of Power: A Black Woman's Story.* New York: Pantheon Books, 1992.
Churchill, Ward, and Jim Vander Wall. *Agents of Repression: The FBI Secret War against the Black Panther Party and the American Indian Movement.* Boston: South End Press, 1990.
Hampton, Henry, and Steve Fayer. *Voices of Freedom: An Oral History of the Civil Rights Movement from the 1950's through the 1980's.* New York: Bantam Books, 1990.
Hilliard, David, and Lewis Cole. *This Side of Glory.* Boston: Little, Brown and Co., 1993.
Hine, Darlene Clark. *Black Women in America.* Brooklyn: Carlson Publishing, 1993.
Pearson, Hugh. *The Shadow of the Panther.* New York: Addison-Wesley Publishing Co., 1994.

John H. McClendon III

Sue M. Wilson Brown
(1877-1941)
Clubwoman, writer, editor, political activist, suffragist, church worker

S ue M. Wilson Brown was known throughout the state of Iowa as an important clubwoman. She also actively campaigned for civil rights, was a leader of the women's suffrage movement, and played a prominent role in Republi-

Sue M. Wilson Brown

can politics. Her husband, a respected lawyer, took up many of the same causes. Together they devoted their lives to the uplift of the people of Iowa and worked tirelessly to foster positive race relations.

Sue M. Wilson Brown was born in Staunton, Virginia, on September 8, 1877, to Jacob and Maria Harris Wilson. She attended public schools in Iowa, completing her high school education in Oskaloosa. On December 31, 1902, she married Samuel Joe Brown, a native of Iowa who had just opened a law practice. He was well-known as the first black male graduate of Ottumwa High School and, a Phi Beta Kappan, the first black liberal arts graduate of the State University of Iowa (1898). After serving as a school principal in Muchakinock, Iowa, and professor of Greek at Bishop College in Marshall, Texas, Samuel Joe Brown returned to the State University of Iowa and earned bachelor of laws and master of arts degrees. The newlyweds were well matched in their desire to join civic, political, and religious organizations dedicated to improving the quality of life for blacks in Iowa.

A Prominent Clubwoman

By 1914, Brown had founded the Intellectual Improvement and Mary V. Talbert clubs for women and begun to edit *Iowa Colored Women,* the official publication of the Iowa Federation of Colored Women. Her husband shared her interest in promoting culture. He founded the Des Moines Negro Lyceum Association and presided over the Inter-State Literary Association of Kansas and the West, for which Brown served as historian.

Brown made her most notable contribution as a civic leader when, as president of the Iowa Federation of Colored Women (1915-17), she spearheaded efforts to secure a dormitory for black women students at the State University of Iowa. When Brown's husband was a student there, only two black men and no black women were enrolled. By 1917, seven black women students were enrolled, and the number increased to twenty-five some twelve years later. Within two years of appointing an investigative committee, Brown's efforts came to fruition with the purchase of a twelve-room, two-story residence. By 1929 it was clear that the purchase of the home by the women of the Iowa federation was a good idea, based on university enrollment and housing data. Of a total enrollment of nine thousand, four thousand students were women, with access to only two campus dormitories that could house around four hundred women. It was clear that black women students would require much assistance in securing safe and comfortable housing near the university. The federation made improvements on their investment by remodeling and beautifying the home, selecting a matron to oversee living arrangements, hiring a house secretary in addition to a staff of workers and a winter custodian, equipping the facility with the basic amenities of home, and securing the approval of the university dean of women to operate under the same rules as regular university dormitories. Brown also served as chairperson of the Trustee Board of the Iowa Federation Home.

As a devoted and productive member of the turn-of-the-century federated clubs for black women, Brown and her activities exemplified the first objective of the National Federation of Afro-American Women, as stated in the minutes of the federation's 1896 convention:

> [To consolidate] the dormant energies of the women of the Afro-American race into one broad band of sisterhood . . . [for] the practical encouragement of all efforts being put forth by various agencies, religious, educational, ethical, and otherwise, for the upbuilding, ennobling, and advancement of the race.

Although the federated clubs placed a heavy emphasis on homemaking, motherhood, industrial and reform school training, and temperance issues, Brown had enough foresight to see that young black women would need their support in gaining access to higher education. She recognized that they would be the future leaders of the federated clubs in America and abroad. In recognition of her club activities, she was elected Life Trustee of the National Association of Colored Women in 1921.

Sue and Joe Brown were affiliated with fraternal organizations that afforded them opportunities to exercise their writing talents. In addition to editing *Iowa Colored Women*, Brown wrote for *American Social Science* and the *Social Science Bulletin*. She served a four-year term as international matron of the Order of the Eastern Star and also wrote the *History of the Order of the Eastern Star Among Colored People*, published in 1925. Her husband was simultaneously serving in high-ranking positions in the Eastern Star (grand patron), Knights Templar (grand commander and International Conference treasurer), and Masons (grand master and various International Conference positions). Joe Brown's writings focused on civil rights for black Americans; he also wrote and published ritual manuals for the Knights Templars.

Brown Works for Women's Suffrage and Civil Rights

Sue Brown was a tireless worker for women's suffrage and civil rights at both local and state levels. She founded the Des Moines League of Colored Women Voters and chaired the Precinct Board of Registration. A leading Republican, she was a member of the Polk County Central Commission, a delegate to the Republican county and state conventions, and first vice-president of the National League of Republican Colored Women. Her husband was a Republican committeeman for Polk County (1918-24) who had served an earlier political apprenticeship as candidate for district court judge (1906) and councilman (1910). In 1928, Attorney Brown was nominated for the position of municipal court judge. The Browns were early supporters of interracial efforts to improve race relations in Des Moines and in the church. Brown was a member of the executive committee of the Des Moines Interracial Commission. A member of the African Methodist Episcopal (AME) Church, she was also on the Interracial Commission of Federated Council Churches and president of the Des Moines branch of the Church Women's Interracial Commission. Brown founded the Richard Allen Aid Society of the AME Church and served as superintendent of AME Sunday Schools of Iowa. Joe Brown served as vice-chairman of the local interracial commission and as a delegate to the First National Inter-Racial Commission. Brown also directed her attention toward young people, organizing the Mothers' Congress of Des Moines, the High School Girls' Club, and the Boys Social Center. In recognition of her contributions to her race, Brown was elected a trustee of the Monrovia College and Industrial School in Monrovia, Liberia.

In Sylvia G. L. Dannett's *Profiles of Negro Womanhood*, a line drawing of Brown depicts a serene, well-groomed woman of culture wearing a double strand of pearls. What the illustration does not reveal is Brown's energy, which she channelled into a variety of worthy causes. In tandem with her husband, she succeeded in uplifting the black race, improving the lot of women and young people, strengthening the AME Church, and promoting racial harmony.

REFERENCES:

Dannett, Sylvia G. L. *Profiles of Negro Womanhood.* Vol. 1. Yonkers, N.Y.: Educational Heritage, 1964.

Davis, Elizabeth Lindsay. *Lifting as They Climb.* Washington, D.C.: National Association of Colored Women, 1933.

A History of the Club Movement among the Colored Women of the United States of America as Contained in the Minutes of the Conventions, Held in Boston, July 19, 20, 21, 1895 and of the National Federation of Afro-American Women, Held in Washington, D.C., July 20, 21, 22,

1896. Washington, D.C.: National Association of Colored Women's Clubs, 1902.

Mather, Frank Lincoln, ed. *Who's Who of the Colored Race.* Vol. 1. Chicago: n.p., 1915.

Who's Who in Colored America. 2d ed. New York: Who's Who in Colored America Corporation, 1929.

Who's Who in Colored America. 5th ed. New York: Thomas Yenser, 1940.

Dolores Nicholson

Willa Brown

Willa Brown
(1906-1992)
Aviator, activist, educator

A pioneering aviator, Willa Brown was the first African American officer in the Civil Air Patrol (CAP). In 1943, she was the only woman in the United States who simultaneously possessed a mechanic's license and a commercial license in aviation. She was employed as president of the National Airmen's Association, the Pioneer Branch, located in Chicago. A tireless advocate of aviation, Brown was instrumental in integrating the aviation industry; she is also remembered for training some of the most celebrated African American pilots of World War II.

Willa Beatrice Brown was born on January 22, 1906, in Glasgow, Kentucky, to Eric B. Brown, a minister, and Hallie Mae Carpenter Brown. Her parents moved the family to Indianapolis, Indiana, when Brown was about six years old. They later moved to Terre Haute, Indiana, where Brown received most of her education, graduating from Sarah Scott Junior High School in 1920, and from Wiley High School in 1923. After high school she attended Indiana State Teachers College, where she received a bachelor of science degree in business in 1927. Brown began to teach in Gary, Indiana, immediately after graduating from college. Five years later, she moved to Chicago and began teaching in the city's public schools. In 1934, Brown began postgraduate studies at Northwestern University. Three years later she obtained a master's degree in business administration. Brown was married three times, first to Wilbur Hardaway, an alderman in Gary, Indiana; then to Cornelius R. Coffey, a certified flight instructor and an expert aviation and engine mechanic; and finally to the Reverend J. H. Chappell. After marrying Chappell in 1955, she became very active in the West Side Community Church in Chicago. Brown had no children. She retired as a public school teacher in 1971.

In addition to her various teaching positions, Brown secured numerous other jobs in Indiana and Chicago after receiving her college degree. She served as head of the commercial department for Roosevelt High School in Gary, Indiana, (1927-32); secretary to Calar Paul Page, director of the Chicago Relief Administration (1932-33); social service worker, Cook County Bureau of Public Welfare (1933); and cashier for Walgreen Drug Company (1933-35). Brown held two federal civil service positions—clerk-stenographer for the U.S. Department of Immigration and Naturalization (1936-37), and clerk-typist for the U.S. Post Office Department (1936-37). She was also secretary and laboratory assistant to Julian H. Lewis, the first African American to serve on the faculty of the University of Chicago's medical school, in the Department of Pathology at the University of Chicago (1937-38); secretary and receptionist to Theodore K. Lawless, a dermatologist (1938-39); and secretary to Horace R. Cayton, director of the Works Project Administration (WPA) Sociological Study of the Negro in Chicago (1939).

Brown had begun to pursue her interest in aviation while attending Northwestern University in the mid-1930s. She signed up for flight lessons with a man named Fred Schumacher, who gave lessons at the Harlem Airport in Oak Lawn, a Chicago suburb. She exercised her business acumen there by managing Brown's Lunch Room, a small sandwich shop. She undertook additional training from Dorothy Darby and Colonel John C. Robinson and received a master mechanic's certificate in 1935 from the Aeronautical University, located in the Chicago Loop.

Subsequently, she studied aviation with Lieutenant Cornelius R. Coffey (who was to become her second husband), earning her private pilot's license, which permitted her to carry passengers, on June 22, 1938. She passed her examination with a grade of 96 percent. Brown became affiliated with a flight service located at Harlem Airport, for which she provided ten-minute entertainment jaunts for curious adventurers who paid a dollar to go up in an airplane. Her involvement with aviation soon expanded into administration and activism. Brown became a member of the Challenger Air Pilots Association, one of the first African American pilot organizations, founded in 1931 by Colonel John C. Robinson. The pilots owned their own hangar, located at the Harlem Airport. Brown served as chairperson of the education committee of the group, which included, among others, some of Robinson's students who graduated from Curtiss Wright Aeronautical University in Chicago. Robinson, one of the first African American graduates of Curtiss Wright Aeronautical University, had earlier succeeded in convincing the school to train African American pilots. The school, recognizing his outstanding record, also agreed to let him teach, with the stipulation that he only have African American students.

School of Aeronautics Founded

Brown along with her husband Cornelius R. Coffey and journalist Enoc P. Waters, Jr. founded the National Airmen's Association of America in 1939. The same year the association elected her as its national secretary, and she also began to teach aviation subjects for the Works Progress Administration (WPA) Adult Education Program (1939-40). She received her Civil Aeronautics Authority (CAA, now FAA) ground school instructor's rating in 1940. Also in 1940, Brown and Coffey established the Coffey School of Aeronautics. Brown was director of the school during its first two years of existence. Brown's education in business administration served her well because, in addition to teaching at the school, she handled administrative and promotional responsibilities. The Coffey School of Aeronautics became defunct in 1945 after World War II.

During this same period, Brown taught aviation mechanics for the Chicago Board of Education and was elected president of the Chicago branch of the National Airmen's Association of America and vice-president of the Aeronautical Association of Negro Schools. Brown, an activist for racial equality, used her administrative positions to successfully petition a reluctant U.S. government to integrate African Americans into the U.S. Army Air Corps. She was also an advocate for the inclusion of African Americans in the Civilian Pilot Training Program (CPTP), a government-funded aviation training program initiated in 1939 and designed to prepare a reserve supply of civilian pilots who could be called upon in the event of a national emergency.

Brown was widely respected in the white male-dominated field of aviation. This is attested to by the fact that in 1940 she was chosen by the U.S. Army Air Corps and the Civil Aeronautics Administration to participate in an experimental program for the admission of African Americans to the U.S. Army Air Corps. Admiration for her abilities was demonstrated again when the U.S. government appointed her federal coordinator for two Chicago units of the CPTP. Brown achieved the rank of lieutenant in Squadron 613-6 of Illinois in 1942, making her the first African American officer in the Civil Air Patrol. In her capacity as lieutenant in this squadron,

as noted by Jesse J. Johnson in *Black Women in the Armed Forces*, "she organized more than 1,000 young people who also marched in military and civilian parades. Brown was adjutant of this squadron; Captain Coffey was commander."

The majority of the CPTP government contracts that went to blacks were awarded to black colleges between 1939 and 1945, among them West Virginia State College, Delaware State College, Hampton Institute, Howard University, North Carolina Agricultural and Technical State College, Lincoln University (Missouri), Lincoln University (Pennsylvania), and Tuskegee Institute, the only school to train African American officers. Brown, however, was awarded contracts to train African American pilots at the Coffey School of Aeronautics and Wendell Phillips High School, two non-college units. As director of the Coffey School of Aeronautics, she administered federal contracts valuing sixty thousand to one hundred thousand dollars annually.

Advocacy Career in Aviation Launched

Inspired by the life of her late predecessor, aviator Bessie Coleman (1896-1929), Brown enlisted the assistance of *Chicago Defender* editor Robert Abbott when she embarked upon her career as an aviation advocate. During the early 1930s Abbott was financially sponsoring tours of African American aviators to African American colleges and universities, where they encouraged students to get involved in aviation. He was also lobbying Congress to include African Americans in federally sponsored aviation programs. The U.S. military forces were segregated; African Americans were denied enlistment in the Air Corps, and there was no indication that the government would award contracts for the training of African American pilots. Brown also promoted the efforts of Chauncey Spencer (son of Anne Spencer, poet and Virginia's literary salon queen of the Harlem Renaissance), and Dale White, two licensed pilots and members of the National Airmen's Association (a black organization) who flew from Chicago to Washington in an outmoded airplane and lobbied for the inclusion of African Americans in the CPTP. Brown traveled throughout the country encouraging young African Americans to take up aviation, and she also went to Washington, D.C., to persuade the federal government to award CPTP contracts for the training of African American pilots. *Chicago Defender* city editor Enoc P. Waters, Jr. covered the majority of her recruitment activities and the air shows she performed to stimulate the interest of prospective aviators.

Brown trained some of the most distinguished African American pilots of World War II; several of the men she trained in aviation mechanics went on to become members of the now legendary Tuskegee Airmen of the Ninety-ninth Pursuit Squadron, the military's first African American pilots.

From 1935 when Willa Beatrice Brown joined other supporters in organizing a memorial flight to Bessie Coleman to pay homage to the first internationally licensed American pilot until her death, she was an advocate for aviation. After the closing of the Coffey School in 1945, she established children's flight clubs to stimulate interest in careers in aviation. For many years she remained active in the National Airmen's Association, the Civil Air Patrol (Illinois wing), Women Flyers of America, the National Aviation Training Association, the International Women's Air and Space Museum, the OX-5 Pioneer Aviation Club, and the Tuskegee Airman's Association. In addition to her other efforts, Brown was the first African American woman to run for a U.S. congressional seat, making an unsuccessful bid as a Republican in 1946 and then again in 1948 and 1950. In 1947, Brown campaigned for the position of Chicago alderman, also unsuccessfully. Remarkably, she continued to teach in the Chicago Public School System until 1971. In 1972, she was appointed to the Federal Aviation Administration's Women's Advisory Board in recognition of her contributions to aviation in the United States. Brown was proud of her accomplishments, and she clearly had a very positive effect on African Americans in the field through her achievements as aviator, aviation instructor, and aviation activist.

Brown died of a stroke at the University of Chicago's Bernard Mitchell Hospital on July 18, 1992. She was eighty-six years old. She is survived by three brothers, one of whom remained by her side until her death.

REFERENCES:

"The Afro-American Airman in World War II." *Aviation Education,* April 1971.

Dixon, Walter T., Jr. *The Negro in Aviation.* Baltimore: Clarke Press, 1950.

Downs, Karl E. "Willa B. Brown: Vivacious Aviatrix." In *Meet the Negro.* Pasadena, Calif.: Login Press, 1943.

Hunt, Rufus A. *The Coffey Intersection.* Chicago: J.R. D.B. Enterprises, 1982.

Johnson, Jesse J., ed. *Black Women in the Armed Forces, 1942-74.* Hampton, Va.: Johnson Publishing, 1974.

Locke, Theresa A. "Willa Brown-Chappell, Mother of Black Aviation." *Negro History Bulletin* 50 (January-June 1987): 5-6.

Naulty, Bernard C., and Morris J. MacGregor, eds. *Blacks in the Military: Essential Documents.* Wilmington, Del.: Scholarly Resources, 1981.

Rose, Robert A. *Lonely Eagles: The Story of America's Black Air Force in World War II.* Los Angeles: Tuskegee Airmen, 1976.

"School for Willa." *Time* (September 25, 1939): 16.

Travis, Dempsey J. *An Autobiography of Black Chicago.* Chicago: Urban Research Institute, 1981.

Waters, Enoc P. "Little Air Show becomes a National Crusade." In *American Diary: A Personal History of the Black Press.* Chicago: Path Press, 1987.

Who's Who in Aviation, 1942-43. Chicago: Ziff-Davis Publishing, 1942.

"Young Aviatrix To Teach Air-Minded Billikens the Principles of Aviation." *Chicago Defender,* May 16, 1936.

"Young Woman Flyer Gets Pilot's License: Willa Brown, Chicago Aviatrix, Can Carry Passengers, Give Instruc-

tions or Make Cross-Country Flights." *Pittsburgh Courier,* July 2, 1938.

Elizabeth Hadley Freydberg

Marie Bryant
(1919-1978)
Dancer, singer, choreographer, dance instructor

Mississippi-born Marie Bryant was one of the most vivacious black dancers in the United States. Her career soared just before and during the early years of World War II, a period in entertainment characterized by exciting bands playing in big cities like Los Angeles and New York. Bryant did not become a superstar, but not for lack of talent, drive, or ambition. She and Lena Horne are examples of Cotton Club performers of the 1940s whose screen careers were limited by Hollywood. At that time, the film industry was afraid to use black actors in large parts for fear of displeasing white audiences, particularly in the South. Blacks were given parts as domestics, slapstick comedians, or solo performers whose spots could easily be eliminated in areas where their presence might offend. Along with her work as a Cotton Club performer, Bryant had a very successful career as a singer and dancer in such musical shows as *Jump for Joy* and *Beggar's Holiday.* Other aspects of Bryant's talent are preserved in the many film performances of stars whom she worked with as teacher, coach, and choreographer.

Marie Bryant was born in 1919, in Meridian, Mississippi, where she spent the first six years of her childhood. Her father, John R. Bryant, was a railroad chef. The Bryant family left Meridian for New Orleans, where Bryant grew up surrounded by the sights and sounds of jazz. It is no wonder that she learned to sing and dance at a very early age. Singing in church and at socials gave Bryant the practice and exposure she needed to excel. At age ten, she made her debut at a church social doing an impersonation of her idol, Josephine Baker. Baker later became Bryant's good friend, confidante, and mentor. Mary Bruce was her dancing teacher, and as a child she danced in Bruce's annual Regal Theater show in Chicago.

Cotton Club Performances Begin

In 1934, at age fifteen, Bryant made her professional debut with Louis Armstrong at Chicago's Grand Terrace Cafe. The Grand Terrace was to Chicago what the Cotton Club was to New York, and she became a featured performer in the spectacular floor shows that were the club's major attractions. In 1935, singer-dancer Bryant was apprearing regularly in a Los Angeles club, making seventeen dollars a week. She was working with the then-unknown Lionel Hampton. Her dancing, singing, and acting made her one of the most versatile performers in show business. Bryant was a resident performer at the Cotton Club in New York when Duke Ellington, whose band was working there, offered her a three-year contract. She remained at the Cotton Club until Duke Ellington left in 1938. While at the Cotton Club she met another attractive performer trying to make it big in show business—Lena Horne. They became friends and remained so over the years.

By 1939, Bryant was a star attraction at Harlem's famous Apollo Theater on 125th Street. Then Duke Ellington offered her another opportunity to work with him, this time in Los Angeles. En route to Los Angeles the band played two-, three-, and four-week engagements in major hotels, ballrooms, and theaters. The band had lengthy stays at Casa Manana, which was originally Frank Sebastian's Cotton Club, and later at the Meadowbrook.

Once in Los Angeles, Duke Ellington and a group of Hollywood notables created the musical revue *Jump for Joy*. The show featured Ivie Anderson introducing "I Got It Bad and That Ain't Good" and Bryant exuberantly belting out songs and dancing up a storm in the show-stopping "Bli-Blip" number. According to the *Los Angeles Times Calendar* in 1978, "Marie projected a kind of savage, wanton innocence in her performances. Her style was considered 'hip.'" According to *Ebony*, April 1950, Duke Ellington called her "one of the world's greatest dancers." *Jump for Joy* ran for three months before World War II came along to claim most of the young men in the cast, forcing the show to fold.

Makes Screen Appearances

In 1944 Bryant headed a black dance troupe in the movie *Carolina Blues*. In 1945 she appeared in the sensational one-reel Warner Brothers movie short *Jammin' the Blues*. This ten-minute movie employed the genius of crack photographer Gjon Mili and the wisdom of musical adviser Norman Granz to catch the intimacy, informality, and improvisations of a genuine jam session. The cast consisted of black musicians and one white guitarist who was photographed so that his complexion could not be determined. Bryant was a big hit with her gut-voiced, blues-style vocals on songs like "On the Sunny Side of the Street."

In December 1946 Bryant starred as the Cocao Girl in the musical show *Beggar's Holiday*, which was based on the English classic *The Beggar's Opera*. Produced by her friend Dale Wasserman, the book and lyrics were written by John LaTouche and the music was by Duke Ellington. Bryant's rendition of "The Wrong Side of the Railroad Tracks" brought wild cheers from the crowd. Like *Jump For Joy*, *Beggar's Holiday* was far ahead of its time. It provided a good illustration of black-white collaboration in the theater. Bryant also appeared in shows such as *The Twisted Road* and *They Live by Night* (1948); *Wabash Avenue* (1950); *Return of Gilbert and Sullivan* (1952); and *Cross-Up* (1955).

Becomes Dance Instructor and Choreographer

During the run of the play *Beggar's Holiday*, Bryant taught tap and jazz dancing at Katherine Dunham's Dance School. Among her pupils were Marlon Brando and Peter Gennaro. After the show closed Bryant intermittently assisted choreographers Hermes Pan and Jack Cole and taught at Eugene Loring's American School of Dance, where her pupils included Debbie Reynolds, Vera-Ellen, Cyd Charisse, Ava Gardner, and Mitzi Gaynor.

In 1948, Bryant was living in Los Angeles with her mother and her daughter, Julia Nance, when several Hollywood show producers reopened the formerly bankrupt landmark Florentine Gardens as a new Cotton Club. Bryant was a headliner there, but the club folded again within two months. Out of work, she was contacted by a local burlesque house in Los Angeles, the Belasco. She took a job there teaching new routines to the chorus lines each week. Soon she had another class going in which she taught Afro-Cuban, blues, and striptease work to some of the girls working at the Cotton Club. According to *Ebony* in April 1950, her theory was "to make the strip more of a dance and less of a come-on, to give the stripper more art and more dignity."

Bryant became a popular recording star during the 1940s. She made two recordings for Keynote. She sang the title song for RKO's *Your Red Wagon,* a story about juveniles who get pushed around. In 1950 she had a dancing and singing role in RKO's *They Live by Night*. Happiest in front of the footlights, Bryant toured the United States in *The Big Show of 1951*. This revue starred Ethel Waters, Sarah Vaughan, Nat King Cole and the Nat King Cole Trio, and Marie Bryant and the Marie Bryant Dancers.

Bryant became the first black to crack the technical side of Hollywood when she began another aspect of her career as movie dance director, teaching dancing routines to Hollywood stars. It all began when movie star Gene Kelly asked her to come to Metro and help his dancing partner, Vera-Ellen, work on a number. According to *Ebony* in April 1950, Kelly called Bryant "one of the finest dancers I've ever seen in my life." Bryant could dance everything from boogie to ballet. She became a frequent employee of the three major motion-picture studios—Paramount, MGM, and Twentieth Century Fox—coaching their stars and choreographing dance routines. She worked for Columbia and RKO as well, and others requested her services as a dance instructor. She instructed Paulette Goddard on shimmy dancing in *Anna Lucasta* and staged the dances for Betty Grable in the film *On Wabash Avenue*. Her other students included Lucille Ball, Ava Gardner, Cyd Charisse, and Bob Hope.

Bryant developed her own teaching style and method called "controlled release," which her eager pupils found to be so body-freeing they wanted to work with her to limber up before facing the day's grueling camera work. Bryant told *Ebony*, April 1950, of her technique:

> My style is based on the work of the well-known Negro teachers Mary Bruce and Katherine Dunham. Miss Bruce taught me when I was six years old and gave me a basic education in dance. Later I studied the Dunham method and then worked on my own in clubs and shows all over the country. From all this, I've built a dancing style of my own that can best be

described as "controlled release." This consists in finding the natural line in each body and the favorite ways it likes to move about—then controlling these movements.

Bryant objected to her dancing being characterized as the kind of dancing only blacks can do. To Bryant, it was the pure, undiluted music, controlled and artfully routined. Billy Daniels, a top Hollywood dance director who hired Bryant as part of his team to teach movie stars dance routines for pictures, told *Ebony* in April 1950, "I have never had to sell Marie to anyone. Stars usually ask for her." Nick Castle, a famed dancer, included Bryant on his list of ten best dancers.

Bryant Makes International Performances

In 1953 Bryant starred with Cyril Ritchard and Diana Churchill in the English revue *High Spirits,* which opened in London's Hippodrome Theater to standing-room audiences. With the success of *High Spirits,* offers poured in for Bryant, who was booked for theater appearances in Paris, Glasgow, Brussels, and Hamburg. In another revue, *Harlem Blackbirds,* Bryant toured India and Ceylon. It was during this time that she fell in love with the manager of the show, East Indian John A. Rajakumar. They were married on the boat to Bombay. After a honeymoon that took them across the Indian subcontinent, they were off on a successful tour of Australia and New Zealand. The tour had to be cut short when Rajakumar fell ill, and the couple returned to the United States. He died in 1965.

During the 1970s Bryant operated her own dance studio, the Marie Bryant Dance Studios. In addition, she was an understudy to Pearl Bailey in the stage show *Hello, Dolly!* She choreographed acts for the Bing Crosby and Perry Como Christmas specials. Alternating between Hollywood and Las Vegas, she worked with Gower and Marge Champion and helped choreograph Las Vegas acts for Wayne Newton and Leslie Uggams.

Marie Bryant died of cancer in Los Angeles, California, on May 23, 1978, at the age of fifty-nine. She is survived by her daughter and three grandchildren. Her talent and success opened many doors for African Americans in the entertainment industry and her performances touched the lives of people across the globe.

REFERENCES:

"An Homage to Marie Bryant." *Los Angeles Times Calendar,* October 22, 1978.

"Jam Session in Movieland: Jamming Jumps the Color Line." *Ebony* 1 (November 1945): 6-9.

Marston, Alan. "Marie Bryant—She Always Jumped for Joy." *Los Angeles Times Calendar,* October 8, 1978.

"Movie Dance Director." *Ebony* 5 (April 1950): 22-26.

"Movie Maids." *Ebony* 3 (August 1948): 58.

Obituary. *Variety* (June 7, 1978): 91.

"Rajkumari Marie Bryant." *Our World* (June 1953): 28.

Truitt, Evelyn Mack. *Who Was Who on Screen.* 3d ed. New York: Bowker, 1983.

Janette Prescod

Bessie Allison Buchanan
(1902-1980)
State politician, singer, dancer

Bessie Allison Buchanan was the first African American woman to serve in the New York state legislature. After several years as a dancer and singer on the Broadway stage, she became active in social and civic activities and was chosen by Democratic leaders in New York City to run for a state assembly seat representing the people of Harlem. As a legislator, Buchanan championed social welfare and civil rights issues, and in the 1960s she served on the New York State Human Rights Commission, where she worked for the improvement of social conditions for citizens throughout the Empire State.

Buchanan was born in New York City on March 7, 1902. Her parents, Charles and Evelyn Allison, came to the north at the turn of the century from Petersburg, Virginia. Her mother was a schoolteacher and her father eventually became the first black "Redcap" porter in Grand Central Station. She had five sisters and one brother, Charles Allison, Jr., who became the first black parole officer in New York City. From a very young age Buchanan was interested in a career on the stage and studied dance and voice. In an interview in the *New York Post* in March 1960, she recalled that having grown up in New York City's theatrical district, "ever since I was a little child my aspirations had been to some day go in the theatrical field. I started out as a singer. My first show was called 'Shuffle Along,' then I went into a number of Dillingham shows and to the dramatic theater, where I was with Alan Dinehart in 'Creole.' I was in a musical called 'Deep Water,' and I was in the original version of 'Showboat.'" In the 1920s Bessie Allison became one of the dancers in the chorus line at the Cotton Club in Harlem. During this time she met Charles Buchanan, who was then the director of the newly built Savoy Ballroom. They were married in 1929, and at that time she retired from the stage and became a fixture in Harlem's most elite social circle, but she also worked as a volunteer in numerous social and civic organizations. Her husband also became the president and chairman of the board of directors for United Mutual Life Insurance Company, New York state's only black-owned and operated life insurance company.

Political Career Begins in Harlem

Buchanan traced her interest in politics to black educator Mary McLeod Bethune, who in 1949 asked her to work in the campaign offices of New York governor Herbert Lehman,

Bessie Allison Buchanan

who was then seeking the nomination for United States senator on the Democratic ticket. Lehman was elected. Buchanan was delighted by the opportunity to become more involved in Democratic party politics and continued working within the organization in its Harlem districts. In 1954 Carmine DeSapio, the leader of the New York Democratic County Committee ("Tammany Hall"), asked her to run for the New York state assembly from Harlem's Twelfth District. The current Twelfth District assemblyman, Leslie Turner, had been supported by Tammany Hall when it was headed by Edward Flynn, and Turner had received his nomination under the old rules: that is, he was chosen by the local Democratic district leaders. When Carmine DeSapio took over as leader of the Democratic County Committee following the death of Flynn in 1953, he reformed the nomination process and allowed the direct election of the party's candidates to the Congress and the state legislature in citywide primaries. Assemblyman Turner was too closely allied with Flynn and the "old regime," so DeSapio decided to ask Buchanan to be the candidate of the regular Democratic party in the primary election. Leslie Turner lost to Buchanan because he lacked the support of the Democratic machine. According to published reports, Buchanan received 3,832 votes to Turner's 2,586 in that primary.

Buchanan began campaigning in the middle of September 1954, pledging to work "to secure a greater participation of Negro women in government." But her Republican opponent in the November election was also a black woman, Lucille Pickett, who made the same pledge. According to a campaign report in the November 6, 1954, issue of the *New York Amsterdam News,* Buchanan declared that she was "for increased workmen's compensation and unemployment benefits, curbs on juvenile delinquency, and for greater care for foster children." But the reporter also noted that Buchanan's election "was almost assured last September after she won the primary race in the strongly Democratic district; and in the closing weeks state Democratic leaders used Mrs. Buchanan in radio, television and street corner speeches for the state ticket." In addition, Buchanan was endorsed as the candidate for the Liberal party. In the November 1954 election Lucille Pickett received 6,177 votes to Buchanan's 22,401 on the Democratic ticket plus 2,201 from the Liberal party.

"I hadn't thought in terms of elective office," assemblywoman Buchanan recalled in the March 23, 1960, *New York Post,* "but I was thrilled to run and won overwhelmingly. I ran ahead of the ticket. It was both amazing and gratifying." As the first black woman elected to the New York state legislature, Buchanan received national attention. She appeared on the cover of *Ebony* magazine in April 1956 and was featured in the article on "Women in Politics." In that article she recalled that at first her husband opposed the idea of a career in politics, and even stopped speaking to her. At the press conference announcing her candidacy, however, Charles Buchanan appeared, a show of support that affected Buchanan greatly. "I broke down and cried," she told the *Post.*

Legislative and Human Rights Activities

Bessie A. Buchanan began serving in the New York State Assembly in January 1955 and was reelected to three more terms, serving for eight years. Considered by many "the first lady of Harlem," it has been estimated that she introduced over 150 bills aimed at the improvement of the community services available to her Harlem constituents and those in need throughout the state. She introduced legislation to bar discrimination in private housing and to end the practice of requiring the indication of one's race on applications for marriage licenses. She called for the elimination of certain residency requirements for receiving New York State welfare benefits and other social services, and, following several fascist attacks upon Jews and other minority groups in the state, introduced a bill to make the desecration and defacement of cemeteries and religious institutions subject to federal as well as state prosecution. In the 1959-60 legislative session she submitted a bill authorizing the state commissioner of education to investigate any educational institution that received private endowments to support the teaching of white supremacist beliefs. Buchanan also served on the Joint Legislative Committee on the Problems of the Aged and attended White House conferences on the aged during the presidency of John F. Kennedy in the early 1960s.

When questioned about her legislative record by a reporter from the *New York Age* in January 1960, Buchanan responded, "I have always tried to introduce the kind of bills which would most vitally help the people in my district and correct the abuses of regulations which work against a people who are doing an effective job in their work.'' When asked about how she voted on the numerous pieces of legislation that came before each assemblyperson, Buchanan replied, ''I vote according to my conscience and in the very best interests of the people whom I represent.''

Buchanan wrote an official song for the state of New York and tried to get it adopted by the state legislature. Although the measure passed the state assembly by a vote of 147-0, the Democratic leadership in the state senate made little effort to counter Republican attempts to allow the measure to die in committee. Buchanan decided not to run for reelection in November 1962, perhaps because of difficulties she experienced trying to get the Democratic leadership in the state senate to support various pieces of legislation. Assemblywoman Buchanan also decided not to endorse Robert Morganthau, Jr., the Democratic gubernatorial candidate, and threw her support behind the incumbent Republican governor, Nelson A. Rockefeller. Buchanan believed that Governor Rockefeller had demonstrated ''a deep concern for the problems of minorities.'' In November 1962 Rockefeller was reelected in a landslide, and in April 1963, Buchanan was rewarded for her support with an appointment by Governor Rockefeller to the New York State Human Rights Commission. She was the first black woman on the seven-member commission and her term lasted until July 1967.

Before, during, and after her years as state legislator and state commissioner for human rights, Buchanan belonged to and was honored by a wide range of social, political, and cultural institutions. She was a life member of the Negro Actors Equity and Screen Writers Guild. She served on the board of directors of the Wiltwick School, which worked with fatherless delinquent boys in Harlem and Brooklyn. She was involved with the Harlem Serviceman's Center during and after the Second World War. Buchanan received certificates of award for outstanding achievement from the American Cancer Society, National Council of Negro Women, National Foundation for Infantile Paralysis, and the New York Mission Society. She chaired local committees for the National Urban League, American Red Cross, the Young Men's Christian Association, and, in 1953, Mayor Robert Wagner's Uptown Women's Committee.

Shortly after being appointed to the New York State Human Rights Commission in April 1963, Buchanan declared in an interview in the *New York Amsterdam News,* ''I am honored to be the first Negro Woman Commissioner and I am determined to do a conscientious job in this most vitally important work in the field of human rights, human dignity . . . and the problems of minorities.'' This same commitment to the struggle for civil and human rights had taken Bessie Buchanan to the New York state legislature earlier in her political career.

Buchanan retired from public office following her years of service on the state human rights commission but remained active in numerous social and civil organizations. She died at home on September 7, 1980, after a brief illness. She is remembered for her rich career in the political, civic, and social life of Harlem and New York State.

REFERENCES:

Hamilton, Charles. *Adam Clayton Powell, Jr.: The Political Biography of an American Dilemma.* New York: Atheneum, 1991.

Haney, Lynn. *Naked at the Feast.* New York: Dodd, Mead and Co., 1981.

Haygood, Wil. *The King of the Cats: The Life and Times of Adam Clayton Powell, Jr.* New York: Houghton-Mifflin, 1993.

McNickle, Chris. *To Be Mayor of New York: Ethnic Politics in the City.* New York: Columbia University Press, 1993.

New York Age, January 2, 1960; January 30, 1960.

New York Amsterdam News, September 11, 1954; September 18, 1954; November 6, 1954; February 11, 1962; May 5, 1962; May 12, 1962; December 24, 1962; May 4, 1963.

New York Post, March 23, 1960.

New York State Red Book. Albany: State of New York, 1955-62.

New York Times, September 11, 1980.

New York World Telegram, February 1, 1961.

                                                    V. P. Franklin

Olivia Ward Bush-Banks
(1869-1944)
Writer, educator

Olivia Ward Bush-Banks was a poet, a teacher of dramatic interpretation, and a patron of the arts. Although her last published poetry dates from 1916 and for the most part does not escape the limits imposed by the conventions of her times, she was a member of the generation that laid a foundation for the New Negro movement. She was not wealthy, but she supported the movement to the limits of her meager funds. In addition, she is noteworthy for her attempts to uphold her two major ethnic identities, African American and Native American.

Olivia Ward Bush-Banks was born on February 27, 1869, in Sag Harbor, New York, a village on Long Island. Both parents, Abraham and Elizabeth Ward, were of mixed African American and Montauk Indian descent. She was the youngest of three children. In November of 1869, Elizabeth Ward died, and Abraham Ward moved to Providence, Rhode Island, with his children. He remarried in 1871, and in the subsequent alteration of family arrangements, Bush-Banks was placed under the guardianship of Maria Draper, her mother's sister.

Bush-Banks credits Draper with giving her a sense of her Native American heritage. Throughout her life Bush-Banks attended meetings of Native American groups and powwows. Her involvement was probably all the more spirit-

Olivia Ward Bush-Banks

ed due to a government legal assault on the Montauks: a 1910 New York State court decision declared the tribe legally extinct. Until 1916, when she moved to Chicago, she was Montauk tribal historian. Several poems and the fragments of a play *Indian Trails; or, Trail of the Montauk* also testify to her interest. When she was on a literary tour of the South sometime between 1919 and 1929, this play was performed at Booker T. Washington High School in Norfolk, Virginia.

Draper was herself uneducated, but she saw that Bush-Banks attended Providence schools through high school. In 1889 or early 1890, when she was twenty, Bush-Banks married Frank Bush and later had two children, Rosa Olivia (Rosamund) and Marie. In an autobiographical statement first published by Bernice F. Guillaume, Bush-Banks writes "domestic misfortune followed" the marriage and refers to "that portion of my life which proved most extremely unfortunate." She became her two children's sole support. Bush-Banks's family responsibilities apparently increased even more when Maria Draper became dependent upon her niece in 1890. The couple divorced sometime between 1895 and 1910.

To support her family Bush-Banks took whatever work was available, moving between Providence and Boston as necessary until 1916. Traces of her activities in Boston remain. In 1914 she was assistant drama director for the Robert Gould Shaw Community House, a Boston settlement. Between 1900 and 1904 she contributed to the *Colored American* magazine, and she was later literary editor of Boston's *Citizen* magazine. She was also active in the Northeastern Federation of Women's Clubs.

In 1916 Bush-Banks moved to Chicago, where she lived until 1928. Sometime during this period she married Anthony Banks, a Pullman car porter. Little is known of this marriage although at the very least the two remained in contact; Banks sent her money at Christmas 1942. Bush-Banks and her daughter Rosa Olivia (Rosamund) Bush Lockhart became estranged, apparently because of personality clashes and differences over Rosa's choice of husband. Rosa Lockhart died in 1929 before any reconciliation.

Between 1928 and the early 1940s, Bush-Banks lived in both Chicago and New York, although the exact dates of the moves between the cities are not known. In New York she lived with her daughter Marie Bush Horton and her granddaughter Helen. The influence of these two women determined her final religious affiliation. Her father may have been a Mormon; it is alleged that he was a polygamist who had two wives between 1865 and 1869. Whatever religious upbringing she received as a child does not seem to have satisfied her when she became an adult. From Bush-Banks's writings she appears early on to have been in sympathy with the Debbsian socialism popular among the pre-World War I avant-garde and also to have been attracted by the Baha'i faith. Still she seems to have maintained contact with liberal Christian churches. She left a number of unpublished Sunday school plays, and, for seven years in the late 1920s and early 1930s, she was a member of white minister John Haynes Holmes's Community Church in New York City. Her daughter and granddaughter became Seventh Day Adventists, and she converted to this faith shortly before her death in 1944.

Bush-Banks's artistic interest was awakened in her second-year high school literature course by a teacher named Miss Dodge, who also ran the Dodge School of Dramatics. Dodge taught something called Behavior Drama. This is not clearly defined in Bush-Banks's notations, but it involved emotional behavior in interpretation of texts. Hearing Bush-Banks recite Coleridge's *Rime of the Ancient Mariner,* Dodge knew she had found a prize student, and she gave Bush-Banks private lessons during that year. Bush-Banks later taught Behavior Drama in studios in Chicago and New York. Her work with children led to a job in the Chicago public schools' enrichment courses. In January 1936 she earned a certificate of completion from an adult teacher education program in New York, and from 1936 to 1939 she worked under the auspices of the WPA Community Drama Unit to demonstrate Behavior Drama at Adam Powell's Abyssinia Community Center. She also taught extension courses elsewhere in New York City.

Works of Poetry Published

Bush-Banks published her first booklet of poems, *Original Poems,* in Providence, Rhode Island, in 1899. This first effort reveals little that goes beyond the literary conventions of her time. Her second volume, *Driftwood,* of 1914, is a longer and more successful collection. It includes twenty-five poems and two prose pieces. The remainder of the work published during her lifetime is slight: another poem, a dramatic Easter sketch, and three short essays. There is also a substantial amount of unpublished work now available in Bernice F. Guillaume's edition of the works. (Literary scholar Guillaume is Bush-Bank's great-granddaughter.) One work, *Aunt Viney's Sketches* (c.1920-32), presents a black woman from the folk tradition commenting on the contemporary scene. Guillaume points out that "in contrast to nearly all other black dialect characters Aunt Viney is an assertive, positive figure," and that she "precedes the appearance of Langston Hughes's 'Jesse B. Simple' character by at least six years."

The effects of Bush-Bank's life go beyond her teaching and her writing. As a member of the avant-garde in both Chicago and New York, she helped create an artistic milieu and through her activities, limited as they were by paucity of her financial resources, she was a patron of the New Negro movement. In Chicago she became closely involved with the artists of Chicago's Lincoln Center. In both Chicago and New York, her studios served as places for dramatic renditions by herself and others, musical recitals, and intellectual evenings. In the early 1930s, she was "Cultural Art" columnist for the *New Rochelle Westchester Record-Courier.* Black artist Richmond Barthé knew her well, and Elizabeth Bowser, granddaughter of *New York Age* editor T. Thomas Fortune, remembered her as well-known in Harlem.

Olivia Ward Bush-Banks is in many ways a representative African American author of her generation. She also has the distinction of being cognizant of the Native American element of her ethnic heritage. During her life, she was associated with an avant-garde which formed a milieu supportive of authors and artists, some of whom have greater contemporary fame than she does. Still, to overlook her completely would impoverish our understanding of her era.

REFERENCES:

Guillaume, Bernice F. *The Collected Works of Olivia Ward Bush-Banks.* New York: Oxford University Press, 1991.
Shockley, Ann Allen. *Afro-American Women Writers 1746-1933.* Boston: G. K. Hall and Co., 1988.

COLLECTIONS:

The principal location of Olivia Ward Bank's personal papers is the Amistad Research Center, Tulane University, New Orleans, Louisiana.

Robert L. Johns

DeVerne Lee Calloway
(1916-1993)

State representative, educator, civil rights activist, editor

DeVerne Lee Calloway became involved with the civil rights movement and was totally committed to making life better for the poor and minorities. She first made her stand against racism by organizing a chapter of Congress on Racial Equality (CORE) in St. Louis, Missouri. She continued her fight against the inequities in the system by participating in the political process as a legislator in the Missouri House of Representatives for ten consecutive terms.

DeVerne Lee Calloway, the oldest of four children, was born on June 17, 1916, to Charles Howard and Sadie Mae White Lee in Memphis, Tennessee. Growing up during the era of segregation, she experienced the indignities and humiliations of discrimination then common in the South. She sat on the back of the street car, bus, or train. When she went downtown in Memphis, she drank from ''colored'' water fountains, used ''colored'' rest rooms, sat in ''colored'' waiting rooms in the bus or train stations, and attended segregated movie houses.

From the beginning of her education in Memphis, she was an excellent student. She attended the Seventh Day Adventist Grammar School, Booker T. Washington High School, and LeMoyne-Owen College in Memphis. She received an A.B. degree from LeMoyne in 1938 with a double major in sociology and English. While in college, she was a volunteer worker with a settlement house in Memphis and with the Southern Tenant Farmers Union, where she helped organize sharecroppers. This work stirred her interest in social problems. She later did graduate work at Atlanta University and at Northwestern University in Evanston, Illinois.

After completing her undergraduate studies, Calloway taught school in Vicksburg, Mississippi, and at the Hasley Institute in Cordele, Georgia. Following these positions, she moved to Pennsylvania and worked as a secretary. She studied at the Pioneer Business Institute and at a Quaker school, Pendle Hill, both in Philadelphia. While working as secretary for a Republican judge, she developed an interest in politics. Calloway worked on the judge's reelection campaign in the role typical for women at the time: stuffing envelopes, answering the telephone, and arranging precinct meetings. Eventually, this experience proved valuable for her own campaigns.

During World War II, Calloway served her country by working for the United Service Organization (USO) in Phila-

DeVerne Lee Calloway

delphia and at Fort Huachuca, Arizona. She joined the American Red Cross in 1942 and worked in Calcutta, India, the headquarters of the China-Burma-India theater during the war. Sensitive to the discriminatory practices against black soldiers by the Red Cross, she expressed her outrage by leading a protest against segregation in the Red Cross Clubs.

At the end of the war, Calloway migrated to Chicago and worked as a writer. As a contributor to *Our World,* she provided stories to the New York headquarters until the magazine folded. Remaining in Chicago, she found employment as a secretary and bookkeeper for the Fair Employment Practices Council, the Jewish Welfare Fund, and the Department of Health.

Political and Civil Rights Activities Begin

In Chicago she met Ernest Calloway, a union organizer, whom she married in 1948. They moved to St. Louis, Missouri, in 1950 when Ernest Calloway became director of research for Teamsters Local 699; he eventually became a professor of urban studies at St. Louis University. After moving to St. Louis, DeVerne Calloway became more actively involved in Democratic party politics, the NAACP, and civil rights activities. In 1952, she became a volunteer for the presidential campaign of Adlai Stevenson. Ernest Calloway was also active in civic activities. He was elected president of the NAACP in St. Louis in 1955. From 1961 to 1962, the Calloways published the *New Citizen,* a newspaper which focused on political and civic activities in the black community. By that time the civil rights movement of the late fifties and early sixties was in full gear, and the couple participated in the movement's leadership. "My husband and I both saw that it was not enough to be in a protest or demonstration," she told the *St. Louis Dispatch.* "To be effective, it was necessary to get into greater participation."

Through the urging of her husband, Calloway decided to run for the Missouri House of Representatives. She said in the *Dispatch,* "If I had been left to my own devices, I'd probably have gone into interior decorating." DeVerne Calloway took up the political challenge and ran for state representative from the Thirteenth district (later the Seventieth and Eighty-first districts) in November 1962. She won the election and remained in the Missouri House until 1982. An eloquent speaker, she focused on legislation that dealt with education, civil rights, social welfare, and women's issues. Once she said in the *Dispatch,* "I consider myself a militant. And I'll not hesitate to vocalize a position." She fought for passage of bills that she thought were best for the people. She did not just go along to get along. In the *Dispatch,* Melba Sweets, Calloway's longtime friend and former co-owner of the *St. Louis American* newspaper, said, "She was way above the politicians. She was a stateswoman. She wasn't the kind who went into it for money or political influence."

Sensitive to the plight of blacks, Calloway became an organizer of Congress on Racial Equality (CORE), a leading civil rights activist group. CORE was one of the first civil rights groups to sponsor freedom rides in the late 1930s and early 1940s to protest the segregated policies of the bus and train companies. Moreover, she was always in the forefront in the fight to desegregate public accommodations as well as the school system in St. Louis.

Because her interests were rooted in social issues, Calloway twice sponsored fair housing bills in the Missouri House of Representatives. Aware that limiting blacks to certain areas of the city denied them equal rights under the law, she worked on behalf of black citizens to remove barriers in housing. In the 1960s, most banks redlined areas in which they would not approve loans for improvement or erection of houses or businesses. Black neighborhoods frequently fell within these areas. Without capital, the black neighborhoods deteriorated and declined in value. For Calloway, open housing was the only solution to the inequities experienced by blacks.

Calloway was equally active in the battle to win fair employment for black citizens. Victimized by discrimination in employment, blacks experienced more than their share of poverty. Calloway constantly prodded the Missouri legislature to enact laws which would give black citizens equal access to employment. She insisted the state offer a variety of opportunities to ethnic minorities who sought jobs above the

most menial positions. She was aware of the lack of minority representation in the Missouri House of Representatives. While serving on the Education Committee in the state house, she actively pressed for the needs of higher education and the public school system. In Calloway's view, the state legislature's role was to exercise its full power to provide opportunities for all citizens. Calloway was persistent in improving the lot of black children in schools in the ghetto. She encouraged community participation in the operation of the St. Louis school board. Sensitive to black children's needs, she recognized the urgency of this task and supported education for minorities.

In 1967 she led a successful fight to create a Congressional district from which Missouri might elect a black Congressperson. Two years later she fought for the establishment of a state commission on the status of women. She stated in the *St. Louis Dispatch:* "Basic rights of women have long been ignored or inadequately addressed. You can defend women's rights if you know where you are and how much ground you must cover." Calloway felt that the victories of women candidates represented meaningful changes for all women of this country. She was interested in the passage of basic laws to protect the rights of all women. An advocate of reproductive rights for women, she cosponsored a bill to reform Missouri's abortion law in 1970. She indicated that women have demonstrated their power both to put legislators in office and to eliminate them from office, and that women as voters have the leverage needed to secure their rights from future backlash.

The Calloways were commended by the St. Louis community for guiding, assisting, and facilitating the education of citizens in the political process. On these issues, DeVerne Calloway said in the *St. Louis Dispatch,* "Black people cannot meet their goals until they participate effectively politically on the local, state and federal levels."

Calloway was active as a member of many city and state committees. She was a life member of the NAACP, a member of the National Council of Negro Women, the Congress on Racial Equality, the Greater St. Louis Community Council, United Church Women, and the Missouri Association for Social Welfare.

Calloway won her tenth consecutive term to the Missouri house in November 1980. After twenty years of public service, she retired. She always demonstrated her sensitivity toward the victimization of the poor, the elderly, blacks, and women. Concerned about the inferior status of these groups, she constantly worked against negative practices embedded in the laws of the legislature. For her civic work, she received over fifty awards and an honorary Doctor of Laws degree from the University of Missouri, St. Louis.

In 1990, Calloway's sister, Evelyn Lee Iles of Memphis, moved Calloway to Memphis after she suffered a stroke. She remained bedridden for three years until her death. DeVerne Lee Calloway, the first black woman to serve in the Missouri Legislature, died January 23, 1993, at the age of seventy-six.

REFERENCES:

Dains, Mary K., ed. *Show Me Missouri Women: Selected Biographies.* Kirksville, Mo.: Thomas Jefferson University Press, 1989.

"DeVerne Lee Calloway." *AKA Heritage Series II.* Chicago: Alpha Kappa Alpha Sorority, 1976.

"DeVerne Calloway Dead at 76." *St. Louis Post Dispatch,* January 25, 1993.

Ebony Success Library. Vol. 1. Nashville: Southwestern Publishing, 1973.

Smith, JoAnn A. "DeVerne Calloway." *Neighbors and Neighborhoods of North St. Louis.* St. Louis: Friends of Vaughn Cultural Center, 1988.

Who's Who among Black Americans, 1980-81. Lake Forest, Ill.: Who's Who among Black Americans, 1980.

COLLECTIONS:

The DeVerne Calloway papers as well as oral history interviews are in the Western Historical Manuscript Collection, University of Missouri, St. Louis.

Joan C. Elliott

Mary Ann Campbell

(c. 1817-1910)

Philanthropist, community and church worker

Mary Ann Campbell was an early African American philanthropist who furthered the development of the black race through her support of various institutions and charities, including two schools, a health care facility, a home for the aged and infirm, and a women's religious organization. She and her husband, Jabez P. Campbell, a bishop in the African Methodist Episcopal (AME) church, were widely known for their charities and highly respected for their work.

Mary Ann Akins Shire Campbell was born in Philadelphia on January 10, 1817 or 1818, and died there in January 1910. She grew up in a Christian home and lived for many years on Philadelphia's South Side. She married Joseph Shire when she was quite young and gave birth to four children, but she was later widowed. In 1855 she married again, this time to Jabez Pitt Campbell, a bishop in the AME church.

Jabez Campbell was born in Slaughter Neck, Delaware, on February 5, 1815. His early years were quite eventful. His father was a preacher in the Methodist Episcopal church and later in the AME church. Jabez Campbell ran away from home at a young age and went to Philadelphia, where his mother lived, to escape being taken for a mortgage his father had incurred using his son as collateral. He was captured and sold in Philadelphia for a term of years. He served over four and a half years, then bought two of the years from his master. At the age of eighteen he was free.

Jabez Campbell was licensed to preach in the AME church on September 10, 1839. He became an ordained elder in 1843, filled stations in Albany and New York City, and preached and taught school in New York and Philadelphia from 1847 to 1854. Like Mary Ann Campbell, he had a previous marriage. From 1855 to 1860 he was general book steward and editor of the *Christian Recorder.* He pastored churches in Philadelphia and Baltimore before being elected eighth bishop in the AME church in May 1864. The Baltimore Conference granted him a doctor of divinity degree. The first AME bishop to visit California, he organized the California Conference. During the 1880s, at a campsite outside of Ocean Grove, New Jersey, he founded the Ocean Grove Conference, known also as an Annual Missionary Jubilee—a type of religious holiday. Bishops from New York and Philadelphia met with local authorities and the Pennsylvania Railroad to coordinate special excursion trains for celebrants, singers, and bands who came together for several days of evangelism. As his wife, Mary Ann Shire Campbell most likely attended the celebrations.

Mary A. Campbell was a devoted Christian woman who worked diligently on behalf of the community and her church. On August 11, 1874 she co-founded the Woman's Parent Mite Missionary Society. Among the other founders were Mrs. C. M. Burley and Harriette A. Wayman. In the years 1824 to 1827, Richard Allen, bishop in the AME church, organized the first missionary society for the women, known as the Dorcas Society, and later his wife, Sarah Allen, organized the Daughters of Conference, the women's second missionary group. She was president of the society from 1874 to 1878, and then treasurer for a decade.

Campbell Supports Charities

The Campbells were widely known for their works of charity. They were life members of the Board of Managers of the Home for Aged and Infirm Colored Persons in west Philadelphia. Mary Campbell was one of the founders of the Frederick Douglass Hospital, also in Philadelphia. One source, *The Centennial Retrospective History of the African Methodist Episcopal Church,* reports that she was active in home and foreign missions. While she made financial contributions to a number of charities, the recipients of her largest gifts were the home for the aged in Philadelphia, the Woman's Parent Mite Missionary Society, and two AME schools—Wilberforce University, in Wilberforce, Ohio, and Jabez Pitt Campbell College in Jackson, Mississippi.

When Gertrude Mossell interviewed Mary Campbell to get information for a biographical essay to be published in Monroe A. Majors's *Noted Negro Women,* Campbell asked: "What have I done, my child, that I should appear among the distinguished women of the race?" Mossell, with whom Campbell had a friendship of more than a quarter of a century, described Mary Campbell as of average height with soft brown skin. She wore her hair bound with a black velvet band and her smile was a "benediction." Her home was neat, beautifully furnished, and comfortable. She was intelligent and educated, and perhaps had financial and philanthropic aspirations that exceeded most of those of her day. Well-loved by her peers, she was almost idolized by the young and the less well-to-do.

Mary Ann Shire Campbell lived and worked at a time when blacks were struggling for economic independence and for ways to improve the quality of life for themselves and the race. Campbell made a difference in the lives of those she touched by her spirituality and her generosity.

REFERENCES:

Handy, James A. *Scraps of African Methodist Episcopal History.* Philadelphia: AME Book Concern, n.d.

Jenifer, John Thomas. *The Centennial Retrospective History of the African Methodist Episcopal Church.* Nashville: Sunday School Union, 1916.

Lane, Roger. *William Dorsey's Philadelphia and Ours.* New York: Oxford University Press, 1991.

Majors, Monroe A. *Noted Negro Women.* Chicago: Donohue and Henneberry, 1893.

Murphy, Larry G., J. Gordon Melton, and Gary L. Ward. *Encyclopedia of African American Religions.* New York: Garland Publishing, 1993.

Wright, R. R., comp. *The Encyclopaedia of the African Methodist Episcopal Church.* 2d ed. Philadelphia: Book Concern of the AME Church, 1947.

Jessie Carney Smith

Vinnette Justine Carroll

Vinnette Justine Carroll
(1922-)
Actress, stage director, playwright, educator

Vinnette Justine Carroll is best known for her significant contributions to black theater and her support of young minority artists. She has been the artistic director of the Urban Arts Corps in New York City since 1967 and also maintains her own production company in Fort Lauderdale, Florida, where she also makes her home. In 1976 Carroll made theater history when she became the first black woman to direct a Broadway musical.

Carroll was born on March 11, 1922, in New York City, the younger of two daughters of Florence Morris Carroll and Edgar Carroll, a dentist. When Vinnette was three, the family moved to Jamaica, West Indies, where she spent most of her childhood years.

After graduating from high school, Carroll earned a B.A. in 1944 from Long Island University and an M.A. in 1946 from New York University, followed by doctoral work in psychology at Columbia University. Carroll's father encouraged his daughters to become physicians and, as she recalled in an interview with Loften Mitchell, "To satisfy my father, [I] did all the work for my Ph.D. in psychology. You see, I compromised. I knew I'd never be a physician, the profession he wished for me, because the sight of blood bothered me, so I chose clinical psychology." While employed as a psychologist with the Bureau of Child Guidance of the New York City Board of Education, Carroll began studying acting. In 1948 she accepted a two-year scholarship as a post-graduate night student in Erwin Piscator's Dramatic Workshop at the New School for Social Research. While a participant in the workshop, Carroll studied acting with Margaret Barker, Lee Strasberg, and Stella Adler, and voice with Susan Steele.

Carroll made her professional acting debut in 1948 at the Falmouth (Massachusetts) Playhouse in George Bernard Shaw's *Androcles and the Lion.* After completing her post-graduate studies in theater, she was cast as Ftatateeta in Shaw's *Caesar and Cleopatra,* becoming the first black woman to play the role. When additional roles became scarce, Carroll developed a one-woman show and successfully toured throughout the United States and the West Indies. In 1955 she accepted a position on the faculty of the High School of Performing Arts in New York City, where she taught theater arts and directed productions for eleven years. She made her Broadway acting debut in 1956 in a revival of *A Streetcar Named Desire,* and her directing debut in 1958 when she staged *Dark of the Moon* with an all-black cast. She also directed Langston Hughes's *Black Nativity* in New York City and London, England.

Carroll entered the world of television and film in 1962 with the CBS production of *Black Nativity.* Subsequent television appearances included her Emmy Award-winning *Beyond the Blues* in 1964, and in 1974, she played the part of Sojourner Truth in the CBS presentation of *We the Women.* Carroll made her film debut in 1960 in *A Morning for Jimmy,* with additional credits in *One Potato, Two Potato* (1964); *Up the Down Staircase* (1967); and *Alice's Restaurant* (1969).

Establishes Urban Arts Corps

For six months in 1967, Carroll was associate director of the Inner City Repertory Company in Los Angeles. Returning to New York City that same year, she founded and became artistic director of the Urban Arts Corps, a pilot project of the Ghetto Arts Program and the New York Council on the Arts. Designed to assist minority performers in all theatrical disciplines, the Corps was "enriched by drawing on the resources of the entire artistic community—relentless in its pursuit of excellence, and in its pursuit of values that will sustain the artist," Carroll commented in *Theatre Profiles.* "The Urban Arts Corps is multi-racial," she told Loften Mitchell for his book *Voices of the Black Theatre,* "because we feel the need for input from other peoples and from other groups. . . . If we can all get to be a part of a more universal experience, we will get to see our similarities more than we see our differences." As artistic director, Carroll selected and directed all productions, specializing in works by black playwrights and composers. When it became difficult to find material by minority writers suitable for her cast, Carroll created her own.

In 1972, Carroll began a successful collaboration with songwriter Micki Grant with the quasi-religious *Don't Bother Me, I Can't Cope,* which Carroll directed and coauthored. Another of their well-known musicals, *Your Arms Too Short to Box with God,* was commissioned for the Spoleto (Italy) Festival during the summer of 1975. The show opened to rave reviews in New York City in 1976, and Carroll became the first black woman to direct a Broadway musical.

Forms Own Repertory Company

Widening her audience still farther, Carroll established her own production company in southern Florida in 1985, the Vinnette Carroll Repertory Company. The company moved into its permanent home in 1988 in a renovated church in Fort Lauderdale. "This is just what I was looking for," Carroll told Carolyn Jack in an interview. "The idea that it was a church we were going to convert to a theatre was like a sign to me, because I do so much religious drama."

Carroll's fifty-year career has served as a guiding light for the growth of black theater in the United States. As a theater innovator, Carroll sees her work as an important chapter in the history of black artistic growth and accomplishment. Speaking to Loften Mitchell, she commented,

> The whole thing of black people liking themselves . . . undoubtedly helped because it made one feel that it was possible to happen, that it was important that we say things in our way and that rhythm and

sounds and ways of working are valid and important. If I had to discuss major changes in the black theatre during my time, I would have to point out the sense of self, that black people feel that what they have to say creatively is important. Black artists don't have to use white criteria for judging their work.

Carroll holds memberships in the Actors' Equity Association, the Screen Actors Guild, and the American Federation of Television and Radio Artists. She has received some of the most prestigious awards and honors in theater and film. Among these are an Obie Award for *Moon on a Rainbow Shawl* in 1961 and an Emmy Award in 1964 for *Beyond the Blues.* She has received three Tony nominations, including one for *Don't Bother Me, I Can't Cope* in 1975. In 1979 Carroll was inducted into the Black Film Makers Hall of Fame, and that same year she was given the Black Achievement Award by *Ebony* magazine. Her other awards are numerous and include the Los Angeles Drama Critics Award in 1967, the New York Outer Critics Circle Award in 1972, the Harold Jackman Memorial Award in 1973, and the Audelso Achievement Award in 1975.

Through her theatrical company, Carroll continues to promote the work of black playwrights and to provide opportunities for aspiring black actors and directors. During her long career Carroll has sought state repertoire that brings the black experience to theater. Her success at reaching a wide audience on stage, in films, and on television has enabled her to support the careers of gifted writers, actors, and directors who might otherwise remain unknown. The many awards and honors bestowed upon Carroll stand as testimony to the undeniable significance and role of the black voice in the history of twentieth-century American theater.

Current Address: Vinnette Carroll Repertory Theater, P.O. Box 030473, Fort Lauderdale, FL 33303.

REFERENCES:

"Actress Vinnette Carroll to Star in London." *Jet* 14 (August 1958): 60.

Amsterdam (New York) News, September 30, 1978.

Anderson, Addell Austin, ed. *The Black Theatre Directory.* 2d ed. Detroit: Black Theatre Network, 1990.

"At 10, Urban Arts Corps Keeps Pace." *New York Times,* June 24, 1979.

"Black Repertory Troup Is 'Coping' with Success." *New York Times,* March 23, 1975.

Black Stars. (December 1972): 66; (May 1973): 66-73.

Bordman, Gerald, ed. *The Oxford Companion to American Theatre.* 2d ed. New York: Oxford University Press, 1992.

Calta, Louis. "Vinnette Carroll Gets a State Post." *New York Times,* March 23, 1968.

Charles, Jill, ed. *Regional Theatre Directory.* Dorset, Vt.: American Theatre Works, 1991.

Cumming, Marsue, ed. *Theatre Profiles.* Vol. 3. New York: Theatre Communications, 1977.

Harris, Jessica. "Broadway's New Breed." *Essence* 8 (December 1977): 72.

Hine, Darlene Clark, ed. *Black Women in America.* Brooklyn: Carlson, 1993.

Hubbard, Monica O'Donnell, and Owen O'Donnell, eds. *Contemporary Theatre, Film, and Television.* Vol. 5. Detroit: Gale Research, 1988.

Jack, Carolyn. "Carroll Has a Mission, a New Home." *American Theatre* 5 (November 1988): 42-43.

King, Woodie, Jr. *Black Theatre, Present Condition.* New York: National Black Theatre Touring Circuit, 1981.

Mitchell, Loften. *Voices of the Black Theatre.* Clifton, N.J.: James T. White, 1975.

New York Times, December 10, 1976; November 17, 1979.

Peterson, Maurice. "Spotlight on Vinnette Carroll." *Essence* 7 (March 1977): 8.

Ploski, Harry, ed. *The Negro Almanac.* 5th ed. Detroit: Gale Research, 1989.

Ragan, David, ed. *Who's Who in Hollywood.* New York: Facts on File, 1992.

Robinson, Alice M., Vera Mowry Roberts, and Milly S. Barranger, eds. *Notable Women in American Theatre.* Westport, Conn.: Greenwood Press, 1989.

Spradling, Mary Mace, ed. *In Black and White.* 3d ed. Detroit: Gale Research, 1980.

Who's Who among Black Americans, 1994-1995. 8th ed. Detroit: Gale Research, 1992.

Williams, Mance. *Theatre in the 1960s and 1970s.* Westport, Conn.: Greenwood Press, 1985.

Woll, Allen L., ed. *Dictionary of Black Theatre: Broadway, Off-Broadway, and Selected Harlem Theatre.* Westport, Conn.: Greenwood Press, 1983.

COLLECTIONS:

The Billy Rose Theatre Collection at the New York Public Library, Performing Arts Research Center at Lincoln Center, maintains a clipping file on Vinnette Carroll.

Juanita Karpf

Mae Bertha Carter

(1923-)

Civil rights activist, educator, sharecropper

Denied the right to a quality education and exposed to the cruelties of white mob violence in rural Mississippi, where she grew up, Mae Bertha Carter developed the courage and commitment to improve the lives of blacks in her home state. Her work in voter registration drives greatly

Mae Bertha Carter

enhanced the voting power of blacks in Mississippi, and through her work as a teacher with the Head Start program, she battled the injustices black students suffered during desegregation.

The second of LouVenia and Isaiah Slaughter's nine children, Mae Bertha Carter was born on January 13, 1923, on a plantation in Sunflower County, Mississippi. She started picking cotton at the early age of six, but she was unable to use the customary sack, worn over one shoulder and holding one hundred pounds of cotton, because she was so small. Instead, she was given a sixteen-pound lard can to empty into her mother's sack.

The school year for black children in Mississippi began in November when cotton picking was over and ended as soon as the cotton was ready to be chopped, usually the end of March or the beginning of April. The little education Carter received was provided by the church she attended, where one teacher taught all grades for the short school year. Carter has always regretted that circumstances did not allow her to receive more formal schooling; she said in an October 1, 1993, interview with Vonita White Foster, "I always wanted an education, but it passed me by." When Carter was quite young, she vowed to herself that when and if she had children of her own, she would devote herself to creating a life for them that would offer better educational opportunities than she had been afforded.

During her life, Carter has witnessed white mobs carry out many acts of racial injustice against blacks. The Spring 1992 issue of *Southern Changes,* for which Connie Curry interviewed Carter, reports several such events that still remain indelibly impressed on Carter's mind. Carter recalled:

> Right over there . . . is where they shot down my uncle. Right in that field. A mob crew shot him down like a rabbit. I was 'bout seven years old but my momma says that when they shot him, it blew that hat right off his head. No one would even go pick up poor old son Ham's hat. The people were too afraid. That hat it just blew and blew across the fields.

Connie Curry cites another conversation she had with Carter during a car ride, near a place called Hitchin' Hill on the outskirts of the town of Drew, Mississippi. Carter pointed to a collapsing barn and said:

> "You know that's where they actually murdered that Emmett Till boy. It belonged to a cousin of one of those white people who killed him." [Emmett Till was a fourteen-year-old black boy from Chicago who was brutally murdered in 1955 for allegedly whistling at a white woman. The all-white, all-male jury took one hour and seven minutes to acquit the two white men accused of the crime.] "They put him in a truck," Mae Bertha said, "and they put him in the Tallahatchie River. Some black peoples near Hitchin' Hill heard him holler, but they all left a long time ago."

Such memories inspired Carter to endure—and fight—the racial prejudice she encountered daily. Through it all she persevered, maintaining her courage and commitment to her race. She always fought valiantly for what she believed was right.

In 1943 Mae Bertha married Matthew Carter, with whom she had thirteen children. Matthew was a farmer and the family sharecropped on different plantations in Mississippi. Mae Bertha Carter credits a woman named Hattie Leggett with being the person who most influenced her life. She writes, "Mrs. Leggett was my neighbor on the farm, who had 14 children. She worked very hard in order to send all of her children to school. Seeing her do what she did motivated me. I realized that with hard work and persistence, I, too, could educate my children—all 13 of them." All of Carter's children graduated from high school. Seven graduated from the University of Mississippi. Three of her sons enlisted in the United States Air Force and one made a career in the military.

Challenges Racism and Racial Terror

In 1955, shortly after the U.S. Supreme Court's 1954 *Brown v. Board of Education* ruling, which outlawed segregation in public schools, Carter decided to join the NAACP. This was a risky choice in many areas of the South, where antisegregation protests and violence against blacks were common.

Indeed, most of her life Carter demonstrated that she was a risk taker. In the 1960s, the Carter family was confronted with an enormous decision. Many southern school districts implemented Freedom of Choice plans to comply with federal regulations to desegregate public schools under Title VI of the Civil Rights Act of 1964. Freedom of Choice plans provided that all parents could send their children to any school they desired. On August 11, 1965, the Carters officially decided to send their seven school-age children to the local white schools. Three of the children would be attending elementary school and four would be attending high school. This decision exposed the family to immediate physical danger and resulted in economic hardship and social ostracism. The Carter home was riddled with gunfire and one shot entered the room where Ruth, one of the children, was sleeping. White backlash spread rapidly. Credit from the plantation store was refused to the Carters. Mae Bertha Carter wrote: "The man at the store said, 'You withdraw your children out of the school, then you can have credit.'" People in the community were afraid to help. Eventually the Carters were evicted from the plantation where they were living. The family was without shelter or food until they received assistance from the American Friends Service.

Carter only wanted for her children something that had been denied her and her eight siblings—a quality education. She believed that, by attending white schools, her children would be exposed to the kind of education and opportunities that would ensure them good jobs and happy, productive lives.

Head Start Teacher Becomes Activist

In 1966, when no one else would offer her a job, a courageous black man hired Carter as a teacher for Head Start, a national program sponsored by the federal government which was designed to provide the underprivileged children of poor families with a better start in school and in life. While working for Head Start, Carter became even more committed to civil rights and expanded her activist activities. She focused on the many problems black students faced during desegregation, such as higher rates of suspension for black male students than white male students, different conduct rules for black students, and the disproportionate number of blacks assigned to special education programs in comparison with whites.

Carter was equally concerned about limited voter registration programs for blacks. Her activities in this area greatly enhanced the voting power of black people in Drew, Mississippi. Later she formed the Drew Improvement Association, became its president, and was very active in voter registration. The primary focus of the association was to coordinate and provide transportation, enabling many people to get to the polls to vote. Her tireless efforts were rewarded when Willie Simmons was elected the first black state senator from Sunflower County in 1992.

In addition to educating her thirteen children, Carter found time to earn her General Education Diploma (GED). Today she says there is civil rights work still to be done, and she wants to devote more time to registering eighteen- and nineteen-year-old blacks to vote. When asked during the October 1, 1993, interview what advice she would give today's African American youth, Carter said,

I would tell today's African American youth to stay in school and stay off drugs. Above everything, get a good education because education is the key to success. Sure there are prejudice and racism in this country, but do not let prejudice and racism stop you from accomplishing your goals.... Try to always be the best you can be, and never stop until the job is done. Be persistent in your goals and put your whole self in whatever you plan to do and do it well.

Carter believes that racism still plagues blacks. "I see it every day and everywhere. You don't have to look for racism. It stares black folk in the face all the time." She deplores black-on-black crime and believes that it has a negative effect not just on blacks but on the country as a whole. "I feel that if we can stop the crime, and start focusing on education, then opportunities will be there for African Americans. The challenge is to convince African Americans to believe strongly in education."

For her willingness to continually confront danger and hostility over the years Carter received an award in the category "Women Taking Risks" from the Wonder Women Foundation in 1982. She also received an award of distinction from the University of Mississippi on February 11, 1993.

Mae Bertha Carter is a courageous black woman of the South whose commitment to human rights and education is so strong that she has risked her life and the safety of her family to affect change. Her efforts in Mississippi were successful.

Current Address: 116 Broadway, Drew, MS 38737.

REFERENCES:

Carter, Mae Bertha. Interview with Vonita White Foster. October 1, 1993.
———. Letters to Vonita W. Foster, October 12, 1993; October 26, 1993.
Curry, Connie. "Son Ham's Hat." *Southern Changes* 14 (Spring 1992): 16.

Vonita White Foster

Sara Lou Harris Carter
(1926-)
Educator, entertainer, model, humanitarian

Sara Lou Harris Carter turned her early desire "to make something" of herself into a career as a well-known fashion model, entertainer, educator, and humanitarian. She broke the color barrier several times. She was the first African American model in the New York buyers fashion show and

Sara Lou Harris Carter

the first national poster model for Lucky Strike cigarettes. Her second husband, a barrister from Guyana named John Carter, was knighted by Queen Elizabeth II in 1966, and she became known as Lady Sara Lou. When John Carter became ambassador to the United States, Canada, and the United Nations, Lady Sara Lou filled in for him in his absence. She became famous for her charm and elegance and was recognized as the first African American to serve as chatelaine of the embassy. Throughout her life, Carter has organized fund-raisers for charities. Her continuous desire to help her own people has been realized time and time again, most recently when she became a teacher for inner-city children in a drug-plagued area of the District of Columbia.

The daughter of a house painter and a cotton mill worker, Sara Lou Harris Carter was born in Wilkesboro, North Carolina, in 1926. Her parents, James W. and Esther Park Harris, had two other daughters, Rhina (a Cafe Zanzibar "Zanzibeaut" and now deceased) and Esther (a teacher), and a son, James W. Harris, Jr. (a retired fireman). Carter graduated with a B.A. from Bennett College in Greensboro, North Carolina, in 1943. According to Dyl Bishop in a 1974 article in *Ebony,* her classmates said, "We prophesy that you, Sara Lou Harris, will become a successful high fashion model and the best hat mannequin in the industry." Although James and Esther Harris gave their daughter the name Sarah at birth, Esther Harris began omitting the "h" at the end of Sarah in letters to her daughter while she was studying at Bennett, saying that she was saving the "h" for Harris. Carter preferred the spelling without the final "h" and continued her mother's practice. After teaching third grade for a year in her hometown of Wilkesboro, Carter went to Columbia University in New York to study for a master's degree. Her eventual multifaceted career grew out of the modeling, dancing, acting, and radio and television work she did to help support her studies.

Breaks Race Barriers in Modeling

In a *New York Times* interview in 1966, Carter recalled, "I always wanted to make something of myself—to help my own people." Carter broke the color barrier and also changed the image of the black woman model from servant to glamour girl in high fashion modeling when she became the first black model in the New York buyers fashion show. She was one of the original twelve Branford Lovelies of the Branford Modeling Agency, the first licensed African American modeling agency in the United States. In the late 1940s and early 1950s she also broke the stereotype of African American women when she was featured as a glamour girl on Lucky Strike (American Tobacco Company) cigarette posters. She noted in the *New York Times* interview that "those posters appeared only in Negro neighborhoods. . . . There is still so much room for improvement. It's so gratifying to see people of color given dignified jobs." According to Darlene Clark Hine in *Black Women in America,* Carter appeared on the cover of national black publications, including *Jet, Ebony, Tan,* and *Hue,* at least thirty times over the course of her modeling career. In the November 1949 *Ebony* article "The Most Beautiful Negro Women in America," John Powers, former owner of one of the largest and most well-known modeling agencies in the world, included Carter among the women he discussed. He called her "The best example of the 'You' look, which is highly individual and distinct from the New Look. She is altogether warm, attractive and intelligent." Six years later, the National Association of Fashion and Accessory Designers published in the May issue of *Ebony* magazine its "Ten Best Dressed Women" and included her "among 1955's crop of best dressed Negro women." The women represented "the quintessence of good clothes sense." The caption under the accompanying photograph notes that "Sara Lou Harris, New York . . . of new Branford Models, illustrates 'built-up look' with pink satin, hand-beaded sheath gown, featuring high-necked Chinese influence, nylon pouffed fishtail. Popular model likes pastels, says they 'make me feel alive.'"

The famous model also excelled in singing, dancing, and acting. The Sy Oliver Orchestra featured Carter as vocalist. Touring Europe in 1946 with the Noble Sissle United Service Organizations troupe, Carter was part of a girls' quartet and had a solo part in *Shuffle Along.* She also played the love interest in the Astor movie *Rhythm in a Riff* starring singer Billy Eckstine and featuring music by Dizzie Gillespie. She began a career in radio, hosting a daily "Mr. and Mrs." radio interview show with comedian Buddy Bowser, her first husband. Her sister Rhina appeared in a Louis Jordan picture, *Reet, Petite, and Gone,* to have been released in spring 1947 by Astor Pictures. Looking back in 1966, one of Carter's favorite memories was appearing with Juanita Hall (Bloody Mary of *South Pacific*) in the radio soap opera *The Story of Ruby Valentine,* in which she played the part of a young girl who comes up from the South and makes good—a story not far from her own experience.

Sara Lou Becomes a "Lady"

In 1958 Carter traveled to British Guiana as part of a fashion show. Her official escort, barrister John Carter, who was educated at the University of London, became her second husband a year later. In 1963 John Carter received the special honor of being made queen's counsel. In June 1966, less than a month after his country became independent and changed its name to Guyana, Queen Elizabeth II knighted him, so Sara Lou, as his wife, received the title "Lady." In Guyana, Lady Sara Lou, as she was known from then on, continued in radio with an interview program, "Sara's Salon," which featured famous people like Miriam Makeba, a South African singer. Carter also put on fashion shows and in the process learned the Guyanese were current in their styles. In the *New York Times* interview, Carter noted, "I thought I was introducing new fashions. I remember the sack was in, and there they were, out-sacking me all over the place. I really had to keep on my toes. Almost everyone sews and they are wonderful designers. They do beautiful bead work." She took several beaded cocktail dresses with her when she moved back to the United States. Carter also established a charm school for young girls in Guyana, teaching the manners, etiquette, and poise for which she had long been recognized. She also planned and directed various entertainment fund-raisers for charity, helping to raise money for a leprosarium and a hospital laboratory.

Many new directions for Carter's talents opened up in 1966, when Guyana made Sir John Carter its first ambassador to the United States, Canada, and the United Nations. Washington recognized Lady Sara Lou Carter as the first African American woman to serve as chatelaine of an embassy, and she filled in for her husband in his absence. Her charming personality and elegance served her well as she performed his ambassadorial duties: she has been credited with shaking more hands in one day than Robert Kennedy during the height of his New York campaign, which, according to *Ebony,* July 1967, led one veteran State Department diplomat to exclaim, "She does more with a smile to win friends than many embassies with huge sums to entertain." Another person said of her conquest: "She's to the diplomatic set what Jackie Robinson was to baseball."

In Washington, D.C., New York, London, and all the other cities in which the Carters appeared, they were always seen in the most fashionable and elegant circles—with various members of the State Department in social gatherings in D.C., with Sammy Davis, Jr. at Washington's famous Shoreland Hotel, with permanent representatives to the United Nations at the United Nations Ball in the Grand Ballroom of New York's Waldorf-Astoria, in Westminster Abbey at the wedding of Her Royal Highness Princess Anne and Lieutenant Mark Phillips, at a lively celebration with steel-band calypso music in London's luxurious Commonwealth Institute honoring Guyana's independence (which the Carters hosted), and as guests of Frederick Bennett, M.P., at a riverboat party marking the opening of parliament in London.

In June 1968 Carter was appointed liaison to the Diplomatic Corps for Shady Grove Music Fair and assigned to coordinate the weekly Ambassador Theatre Parties celebrating opening night. She and Sir John also appeared on the Merv Griffin television show demonstrating the preparation of what the *Evening Star,* March 17, 1968, called their famous 'Ambassador's Punch.'

As noted in the *Washington Post,* February 19, 1967, Carter often talked in Washington, D.C., public schools to groups of teenagers, "giving them advice on charm, beauty, and manners. . . . Her beauty advice to young girls is, 'Go for the natural look.'" Her "Leadership Improvement Course" gave advice "on what to wear on your first dinner date, how to stand when talking to 'important grown-ups,' and other self-improvement and etiquette questions." She has taught self-improvement courses in Guyana, Harlem, the District of Columbia, and Alexandria, Virginia. She did the fashion show commentary for the Co-Ette Club, an organization of high school girls involved in civic, cultural, educational, and charitable work, when they modeled for the Negro College Fund benefit on March 29, 1968, in Trinity Episcopal Church and, according to the *Evening Star,* March 17, 1968, gave reasons for involving herself: "Being a woman of color, I particularly love working with young people and showing them ways that they can be proud of their appearance." Carter also did the commentary for the Junior Village fashion show with young children modeling Easter outfits; the Co-Ettes helped by buying the clothes for the youngsters.

Gives Advice to the Young

The title of a June 1947 *Our World* article, "Cover Girl Sara Lou Harris Reads the Bible—Dances, Sings Too," describes the expected combination of traits people found in her—a "simple, beautiful girl who neither drinks nor smokes." A February 1953 article in *Color* quotes her advice to those who wished to follow a career in the limelight as she did:

A pretty girl has the same chance to develop her character as an ordinary girl. Being a pretty girl gives one no excuse for being an immoral or careless girl. It is no more difficult for a pretty girl to be nice than it is for an ordinary one. Unfortunately a pretty girl too many times falls easy prey to the abnormal social pressures. It is probably because she is sought after a little more than her ordinary sister.

Most of the time temptations cause a pretty girl to lose her perspective in normal living. A life of glamour looks more inviting, mainly because it is easy for her to have. When material things come too easily, they are oftimes appreciated less. Now this does not apply to all pretty girls because there are some girls that are just normal human beings and have no desire at all for special attention.

Her mother had advised her to finish her education before going on to a glamorous career, and, as noted in *Ebony,* May 1955, Carter always passed that advice on to young women: "First, I tell them to get an education. . . . So many of them want to go straight into the field of fashion. I tell them to prepare to support themselves and to model as a sideline. And I tell them not to feel that they have to be one of the crowd, to stick by their guns, set their own standards and stick by them."

The Carters moved to London when Sir John was appointed there as Guyana's High Commissioner in Britain and ambassador-delegate to France, then Europe—Germany, the Netherlands, Yugoslavia, and Russia. (He was later sent to several other countries, eighteen in all, including India, China, and finally Jamaica.) While in London, Lady Sara Lou Carter was very active in assisting its young West Indian community, particularly those in The Moonshot Club. Also in London, she produced fund-raising shows at the Commonwealth Institute to buy a "Sunshine Coach" for the mentally challenged children in Guyana, a cancer detection unit for the public hospital there, and many other useful items. She organized and participated in an international cultural show involving over fifty embassies in Peking as a fund-raiser for charities. In Jamaica, she organized and presented "Stars Over Kingston" for a home for the physically challenged; the show featured Carter in a duet. The Doll League in New York, which she helped establish, grew from giving dolls to children in hospitals at Christmas to establishing a center for unwed Hispanic and African American mothers.

The Carters now make their home in Chevy Chase, Maryland, near her married daughter, Robin Bowser Marston, and their sons, John, a paralegal clerk, and Brian, a lawyer. Carter is very active in the Chevy Chase United Methodist Church and many other groups, including the YMCA International Committee of the Board of Directors, United Nation's Association for Coordinating Fund-raiser Dinners, the Bethesda Academy of Performing Arts, the Women's Committee for the Performing Arts, the "Hillbillies" Inc. (a group of friends who give money to organizations), and Delta Sigma Theta Sorority. She continues to assist The Doll League in its expansion outside of New York. In a letter to Claire Taft in 1993, Carter wrote about experiences outside of her family life:

Nothing has given me more pleasure than working in a small group tutoring or one-to-one teaching reading skills to those children at Cleveland Elementary School, a school right smack in the middle of a drug area of [the District of Columbia]. I found those children working hard under sad conditions at home, yet they were bright and eager to learn. That was my most rewarding experience.

In "making something" of herself, Lady Sara Lou Carter has changed the image of the African American woman. "Helping her people," as she challenged herself early in life, she has broadened the career options of women to include not only education, the arena in which she began, but also high fashion modeling and other glamorous careers as well as charitable work, making herself a role model to women of different cultural and ethnic backgrounds throughout the world.

REFERENCES:

"Best Dressed Ambassadress." *Sepia* 16 (July 1967): 24-29.

Bishop, Dyl. "Lady Sara of Guyana; Former Fashion Model Is the Busy Wife of South American Envoy." *Ebony* 92 (March 1974): 128-30, 132, 134, 136.

Carter, Sara Lou Harris. Interviews with Claire Taft. June 1993 through January 1995.

———. Letter to Claire Taft. July 6, 1993.

"Cover Girl Sara Lou Harris Reads the Bible—Dances, Sings Too." *Our World* 2 (June 1947): 31-32.

"Fashion Notebook: Lady Carter Helping with College Benefit." *Evening Star,* March 17, 1968.

"The Fruitful Life of Lady Carter." *Ebony* 22 (July 1967): 40-48.

Hine, Darlene Clark, ed. *Black Women in America.* 2 vols. Brooklyn: Carlson, 1993.

"Lady Carter Gets Theater Post." *Evening Star,* June 26, 1968.

MacPherson, Myra. "Envoy's Wife from Wilkesboro, N.C." *New York Times,* October 30, 1966.

McLendon, Winzola. "New Embassy Has No Need for New Broom—Lady Carter Still Gives Advice on Charm." *Washington Post,* February 19, 1967.

Powers, John. "The Most Beautiful Negro Women in America." *Ebony* 5 (November 1949): 42-44.

Reid, James M. "Is Beauty a Curse?" *Color* (February 1953): 24-29.

"Ten Best Dressed Women." *Ebony* 10 (May 1955): 94-96.

Claire Taft

Carwell, L'Ann
    See McKissack, Patricia C.

Tracy Chapman
(1964-)
Folksinger, songwriter

Heralded as "the new artist of the year" in *Rolling Stone* magazine, September 22, 1988, Tracy Chapman had become one of the most exciting and fastest rising talents in pop mainstream. In the October 5, 1989, issue of *Rolling Stone,* Fred Goodman noted that Chapman's rise to superstar prominence on the music scene was breathtaking in its speed. Just three months after releasing her first album, Chapman performed at the Nelson Mandela Freedomfest for a world-

Tracy Chapman

wide television audience of millions. In September 1988 she headlined Amnesty International's Global Human Rights Now! tour with Bruce Springsteen, Peter Gabriel, and Sting. "That Chapman could move such a broad audience on the strength of one album is testimony to the power of her vision and clarity of style," Goodman concluded in *Rolling Stone.* Though her songs are linked to the folk rock of the late 1960s and early 1970s by their strong vocal sound, compelling lyrics, and often biting social messages, Chapman is difficult to categorize. John Milward, a critic for *Mademoiselle* magazine, September 1988, credited Chapman, along with other new female songwriters, such as Toni Childs, Natalie Merchant, and Suzanne Vega, with beginning

> [a] mini-revolution among female singer-songwriters: Chapman has firmly switched their traditional plaint to a very 80s demand, and is as likely to apply it to a lover as to a social issue. But it's not a 60s rehash. Chapman's music is very personal, very emotional even when it quietly rages over poverty.

Chapman has alternately been labeled a protest singer, a classic folk singer, and an urban folk singer, but her repertoire is much broader, ranging from rhythm and blues, rock, reggae, and pop to blues and folk. "Her sound is not wholly new," reported Steve Pond in *Rolling Stone* on June 2, 1988, "but at its best it feels that way because modern pop—as opposed to folk, a genre far too restricted for Chapman—rarely accommodates women who sing with this much open political anger." Chapman is said to be partly responsible for the revival of protest music. When she emerged in the spring of 1988, recalled Stephen Holden, writing for *Rolling Stone,*

May 14, 1992, "the music world held its breath. Was it possible that a singer-songwriter with the vision and moral authority of the young Bob Dylan had finally arrived to rekindle folk rock's flame?" By the summer of 1988, Chapman was "one of the most highly touted debut artists in America."

Chapman quickly became a cultural icon. She wore her hair in short spiky dreadlocks, quite different from the styles traditionally used in pop glitter. Since her emergence on the music scene, she has continued to capture an international audience with her hauntingly rich contralto and flawless performances. Richard Stengel in *Time,* March 12, 1990, said:

> Her music pared down, almost willfully naive, was an antidote to the synthesized sound of the 1980s. In an age when pop singers seemed more like musical M.B.A.'s than recording artists, she seemed genuine. . . . She was an urban folksinger without the fragility of the genre.

Tracy Chapman was born on March 30, 1964, in Cleveland, Ohio. She was four years old when her parents, George and Hazel Winters Chapman, divorced. From early childhood, she and her sister were exposed to their mother's extensive record collection, and young Tracy started playing the ukelele in grade school and later the organ and clarinet. She also acquired a guitar and started writing songs at the age of eight. Chapman penned her first socially conscious song, "Cleveland 78," when she was fourteen. She said in *Rolling Stone,* September 22, 1988,

> As a child, I always had a sense of social conditions and political situations. I think it had to do with the fact that my mother was always discussing things with my sister and me—also because I read a lot.

Attending high school at the Wooster School in Danbury, Connecticut, to which she had won a scholarship, Chapman wrote and performed her own songs at school functions and at the school's coffeehouse. During her sophomore year, Robert Tate, the chaplain, took up a collection among students and faculty to buy Chapman a new Fender guitar in recognition of her talent; he received a thank-you credit in her debut album. Although music was her first love in school, Chapman distinguished herself in extracurricular activities as star of the basketball team and captain of the varsity soccer team. Following her graduation from Wooster in 1982, she enrolled at Tufts University in Medford, Massachusetts. Though she originally intended to become a veterinarian, Chapman changed her major to cultural anthropology with a concentration in West African cultures and ethnomusicology. Performing on the folk circuit in Boston coffeehouses and at local clubs and colleges, as well as on the streets in Harvard Square, she soon "became a force on the folk scene around Boston and Cambridge" and developed an ardent following, according to Richard Stengel in *Time.* Fellow student Brian Koppelman introduced her to his father, Charles Koppelman, president of the JBK publishing house, who signed her to JBK after she graduated in 1986 and helped her get a record contract with Elektra records later that year. Chapman acquired a manager, Elliot Roberts, who also managed Joni

Mitchell, and a producer, David Kershenbaum, who fell in love with her voice. Kershenbaum said in the March 12, 1990, issue of *Time,*

> The timbre of it is rare to find. It instantly disarms you. She's able to sit there and produce an almost flawless performance. Normally today's producers take tracks and build them and then put in the voice. We wrapped the tracks around the voice.

First Album Brings Success

Several months before the scheduled release of her first album, Elektra Records kicked off a promotional tour to launch it and to introduce Chapman to the media and to an international audience. In March 1987 she made her debut at the Donmar Warehouse in London, performing with labelmates Natalie Merchant and the 10,000 Maniacs; she later played at the Bitter End Club in New York. Attracting widespread critical acclaim, her first album, *Tracy Chapman,* climbed to number one on Billboard's pop album chart, and her breakthrough "Fast Car" single from the album made top ten on the charts. Chapman produced what Steve Pond called in *Rolling Stone,* September 22, 1988, "a stunning debut, a collection of songs that sketch the lives of the disenfranchised with vivid clarity and bluntly insist that a change had come." By the end of the year, the album had sold ten million copies.

The instant success of this album, observed Pond in *Rolling Stone,* June 2, 1988, was due to "a mixture of defiantly optimistic, big-scale political statements, as in 'Talkin' bout a Revolution,' and 'Why?' and grim, knowing urban stories, 'Fast Car' and 'Behind the Wall.'" "At the heart of the blunt realism," he continued, "is a deliberate naive realism." Armand White, quoted in the July 1988 *Essence,* states that the album explores love, racism, and sexism, "delivering poetic images of pain and passion in a potent, husky voice." Garr Gillion, in *She's a Rebel: The History of Women in Rock and Roll,* contends that the success of the album was due in part to Chapman's willingness to address issues that the U.S. government dismissed during the 1980s: "the growing ranks of the homeless, the ever-rising crime rate, and a failing education system." Explaining that she never believed any record company would be interested in songs about revolution because they are about life, Chapman asserted in *Life,* August 1988,

> Things are not as they should be. Too many people are homeless, don't have jobs, don't have food. I think that right now, with everything from large-scale wars to the smaller wars people have in their homes, it's become more convenient to kill people than to sit down and talk to them.

Chapman has received numerous awards and honors. In 1988 she won a Grammy for Best New Artist. That same year, she was also the recipient of awards for Best New Artist, Best Contemporary Folk Recording, and Best Female Pop Vocalist; she also received the National Award of Recording Arts and Sciences. Chapman won in the Pop, New Artist category at the 1989 American Music Awards. In the same year, she was named Best International Artist, Female, and Best International Newcomer at the eighth annual BRIT Awards in London.

Less successful than her debut album, Chapman's *Crossroads* (1989) and *Matters of the Heart* (1990) received mixed reviews. Stephen Holden wrote in *Rolling Stone,* May 14, 1992, that the second and third albums are not bad records, but "in light of 'Fast Car' and a couple of other vignettes on her first album, they are terribly mundane. *Matters of the Heart* is somewhat weaker than *Crossroads,* with most of its ten songs mimicking the simplistic vocabulary of generic sixties folk-pop anthems." Chapman's second album has, however, been praised as displaying the same brilliance as her debut work, with equally "compelling songs of social commentary" but with less anger. Her tone is softer, and she even includes love songs. Like *Crossroads, Matters of the Heart* speaks simple truths about complex feelings. Chapman changed musical directions in *Matters of the Heart,* taking an introspective turn. Chapman remains insistent about issues of love and corruption.

Since 1990, Tracy Chapman has lived in San Francisco. A very private person, she said in *Emerge,* August 1992, that what is most important to her is that the world "return to decent values and look beyond this generation by respecting the earth."

Current Address: c/o Elektra Entertainment, Warner Communications, 345 North Maple, Beverly Hills, CA 90210.

REFERENCES:

Ash, Jennifer, and Mary Frakes. "Good 'n' Gritty." *Life* (August 1988): 60-61.

DeLurhs, Anthony. "Tracy Chapman's Black and White World." *Rolling Stone* (June 30, 1988): 46.

Gaar, Gillian G. *She's a Rebel: The History of Women in Rock and Roll.* Seattle: Seal Press Feminist, 1992.

George, Nelson. "Tracy Chapman." *Essence* 19 (July 1988): 27.

Goodman, Fred. "Tracy Chapman at the Crossroads." *Rolling Stone* (October 5, 1989): 135.

Holden, Stephen. Review of *Matters of the Heart. Rolling Stone* (May 14, 1992): 103.

Light, Alan. "Singing from the Heart." *Rolling Stone* (April 16, 1992): 26.

Milward, John. "The New Singer-Songwriter: These Big Girls Don't Cry." *Mademoiselle* 94 (September 1988): 108-12.

Moss, Knolly. "Tracy: Matters of the Heart and Universe." *Emerge* (August 1992): 48.

Pond, Steve. "Singer-Songwriter Is Not a Dirty Word." *Rolling Stone* (June 2, 1988): 70.

———. "On Her Own Terms." *Rolling Stone* (September 22, 1988): 54-56.

Stengel, Richard. "Singing for Herself." *Time* 135 (March 12, 1990): 70-72.

Jacquelyn L. Jackson

Emma Carolyn Chappell
(1941-)
Banking executive

Emma Chappell set high goals early in her life. Beginning her career in banking when she was a teenager, she set her sights on a top executive position in the field. She has devoted her entire career to the banking industry, concentrating her efforts on minority economic development. She took a step closer to her goal when she became the first woman vice-president of Continental Bank of Philadelphia. She then fulfilled her career plans when she became chair and chief executive officer of the black-controlled United Bank of Philadelphia.

Emma Carolyn Bayton Chappell was born February 18, 1941, in Philadelphia, Pennsylvania, the daughter of George Bayton Sr. and Emma Lewis Bayton. She married Verdayne Chappell and had two daughters, Tracey and Verdaynea. Emma Chappell was educated at Berean Business Institute, Temple University, the American Institute of Banking, and Stonier Graduate School of Banking at Rutgers University.

The field of banking became a part of Chappell's life after she graduated from West Philadelphia High School. Leon H. Sullivan, noted civil rights leader and the pastor of her church, Zion Hill Baptist Church, was impressed with her ability and in 1959 helped her obtain a position as clerk-photographer at Continental Bank in Philadelphia. Before she could move to a higher position in the bank, Chappell knew that she should get a college degree. From 1962 to 1967 she attended night school at Temple University and continued to work in various positions at the bank. She set her goals on a top management position. "At that time all a woman could be was a secretary," she told *Essence* magazine. Equipped with ambition, determination, and skill, in 1971 she became one of the first two women to complete an executive banking program. This qualified her to work in every department in the bank.

In 1974 she was granted a leave of absence from Continental Bank to develop and implement the Model Cities Business and Commercial Project, now renamed the Philadelphia Commercial Development Project. Through this project, the bank assisted minority entrepreneurs in establishing businesses in Philadelphia's inner city. The work of these new business leaders impressed Chappell: "I'm amazed at the stamina of Black entrepreneurs who in the last six years have implemented their ideas into potential million dollar businesses," she told *Essence.* She was also one of the founders of the Delaware Valley Mortgage Plan that enabled residents with low and moderate incomes to buy homes with small down payments and interest rates that were below the current market. Chappell was promoted to vice-president of Continental Bank in 1977, becoming the first woman to hold this position. In this role, she was in charge of the urban develop-

Emma Carolyn Chappell

ment services department. In addition she managed a sizeable portfolio of business loans and became a lobbyist as well.

She found marriage and banking a good mix. "My husband gave me the extra push I needed to hang in there and stick to my goal of reaching the top in banking," she told *Essence*. She had the support of her daughters as well. "I see many young girls who have already given up, and I'd like to prove to them that job opportunities can happen for women if we prepare ourselves."

Banker Reaches the Top

In 1990 Chappell became chair and chief executive officer of the United Bank of Philadelphia, which opened in 1991. She heads a staff of thirty and watches over the management, organization, and leadership of the bank. In 1993, the bank's assets exceeded twelve million dollars. When United Bank of Philadelphia was chartered, Chappell saw it as a milestone for the African American community of Philadelphia.

She described to Franklin Smith in *American Banker* the strength of the new bank's management team: "The president and I have 50 years of experience in lending and making commercial loans to minorities and small businesses." It was a bank whose time had come: "United Bank is long overdue, and our primary mission is to serve the community. . . . We plan to branch out into the community where the major banks have closed." The bank was aggressive in its capital development plan and had the support of business and financial leaders in the community. The African American community

was anxious to have its own bank and they were ready to support it. Organizers had raised over half of the five million dollars targeted for the initial capital. Chappell told Franklin Smith: "United Bank will be a neighborhood bank. It's time for the community to be in charge of its economic destiny . . . I understand the needs of the community through my involvement serving a number of boards and civic organizations." For its pioneering efforts in neighborhood expansion, *Black Enterprise* named United Bank of Philadelphia its 1994 Financial Company of the Year.

Chappell has been active in a number of organizations. Her current and previous affiliations include the American Bankers Association, National Bankers Association, Robert Morris Association, National Business League, National Association of Bank Women, and the Philadelphia Urban League. A founding president of the National Rainbow Coalition, in 1984 she took a leave of absence from the Continental Bank to become national treasurer for Jesse Jackson's presidential campaign. She has served as a board member of PUSH (People United to Save Humanity), Girl Scouts of Greater Philadelphia, Philadelphia Industrial Development Corporation, United Way of Southern Pennsylvania, and the March of Dimes, Delaware Valley Chapter. She has co-chaired Philadelphia's advisory committee on economic development.

In 1988 Robert P. Casey, governor of Pennsylvania, recognized Chappell's commitment and service to minority economic development. He named Chappell to the state's Economic Development Partnership board and three of its panels: the International Development Advisory Committee, the Committee on Housing, and the Statewide Advisory Committee on Minority Economic Development. Chappell has been vice-president for administration and treasurer of the National Rainbow Coalition and vice-chairperson of the African Development Foundation. She founded and served as chair of the Women's Network for Good Government. In the area of higher education, she has been a board member of Temple University's College of Arts and Sciences, Chestnut Hill College President's Council, Cheyney State University Foundation, and the United Negro College Fund.

In recognition of her contributions, Chappell has received a number of honors, including an achievement award from the Philadelphia Police Department; a certificate of appreciation from the Society for Advancement of Management; an achievement award from the North Philadelphia Action Branch of the NAACP; and the President's Award from the National Association of Colored Women's Clubs. In 1986 *Dollars and Sense Magazine* placed her on its list of America's Top 100 Black Business and Professional Women. The next year *Blackbook Magazine* honored her with its Business and Professional Award, and that same year she received the Bishop R. R. Wright Humanitarian Award from Ward AME Church. In 1988 Chappell received the Achievement Award from the West Philadelphia Economic Development Corporation.

Emma Chappell has greatly contributed to the economic development of the black community in Philadelphia. Her keen insight into local development and a lifetime of experience in the banking industry have contributed to her success. Her rise to the top came from her ambition, determination, and vision, all of which enabled her to fulfill a lifelong dream. In the process, her work in minority economic development enabled others to help fulfill their dreams.

Current Address: United Bank of Philadelphia, 714 Market Street, Philadelphia, PA 19106.

REFERENCES:

"Bank Founder and CEO." *Ebony* 48 (March 1993): 7.
Black Business Digest (January 1972): 46.
Black Enterprise (May 1978): 53.
Brown, Carolyn M. "A Bank Grows in Philly." *Black Enterprise* 25 (June 1995): 166-74.
Davis, James R., Jr. "Emma Chappell." *Essence* 6 (May 1976): 11.
Davis, Marianna W., ed. *Contributions of Black Women to America.* Vol. 1. Columbia, S.C.: Kenday Press, 1982.
Who's Who among Black Americans, 1994-95. 8th ed. Detroit: Gale Research, 1994.
Smith, Franklin. "Dream Is Becoming Reality for Philadelphia's Chappell." *American Banker* 155 (October 16, 1990): 2.

Helena Carney Lambeth

Michele Clark

Michele Clark
(1941-1972)
Television correspondent

A talented and ambitious black woman, Michele Clark quickly established herself as one of the best and brightest reporters on CBS television in the early 1970s. Within two years of completing her journalism training, she had become a reporter for the Democratic and Republican conventions, and then rose to a position as a national reporter on the network. She was the first black woman network news correspondent on CBS. Working at a time when television networks were trying to bring minorities and women into visible positions, Clark's rise was swift, her career brief, and her life "a promise unfilled."

Michele Clark was born December 8, 1941, in Gary, Indiana, to Harvey E. Clark and his wife. Clark and her younger brother, Harvey, grew up in Chicago. The Clark family had a harrowing racial experience when Michele was only ten years old. In 1951, the family was driven from their home in the previously all-white Chicago suburb of Cicero by an angry white mob. The mob destroyed their furniture and other property in the twenty-family building where they had rented an apartment. The Chicago Branch of the NAACP came to the family's aid, and NAACP executive secretary Walter White made an investigation of the riot.

Clark graduated from Roosevelt University in Chicago. After graduation, she worked in a variety of jobs: she was a model, telephone company employee, narrator of commercials, and a reservations clerk for United Airlines. In 1969, she was named "Performance Theme Queen" at a Los Angeles auto show. Little else is known of Clark's personal life. She considered becoming a lawyer, but decided to enter the field of journalism. In May 1970, she joined CBS at its Chicago affiliate, WBBM-TV, as a newswriter. That summer, she completed a program at Columbia University called Broadcast and Print Journalism for Minorities, and she returned to the WBBM station as a general assignment reporter. She was the only woman reporter at the station, a position she held for about one year. In 1971, *Ebony* magazine took a look at television's African American "news girls," including Norma Quarles, Melba Tolliver, Carol Simpson, and Michele Clark, publishing brief interviews with each of them. At that time, these women covered stories related to blacks, but none was totally restricted to black news developments. Clark told *Ebony* she objected to the tendency of men at the television stations to "put women in assignments that are less 'hard' than ones given men." She was clear about her position in media and her commitment to her race:

> My preference is to be judged simply as a good reporter, without the "black" attached. Still, though, I want to cover some black stories because I have a lot that most whites lack. My roots are in the black community.

Richard Salant of CBS recalled a visit she made to a school and her response to a question about her entry into broadcast journalism. She stated she had gone to an interview and at the end the news director offered her the job, saying "she had come to the right place at the right time." Clark added that she was "the right sex and the right color" as well.

Journalist Becomes Television Correspondent

The CBS news staff was immediately impressed with Clark's performance and considered her a good reporter. She received the kind of difficult and prestigious assignments that were usually restricted to men. Still based in Chicago, she was assigned to cover the 1972 presidential primaries in New Hampshire, Wisconsin, and California. While on the campaign trail she covered political events for the Walter Cronkite evening news and other broadcasts. In summer 1972, she was assigned to cover the Democratic and Republication Conventions. At the Democratic Convention in Miami Beach, she was promoted to correspondent. Clearly, CBS had big plans for Clark.

In 1972, Clark was reassigned to Washington, D.C., where she was CBS News Washington correspondent and had a quasi-anchor slot for that summer and fall. When Washington correspondent Nelson Benton was away, she took over the "Morning News" and was well on her way to the top echelon of network correspondents. She often commuted to Chicago where her family still lived. When she headed home for Christmas in 1972 to spend a month's vacation with her family, she was one of forty-four people killed when a United Air Lines plane crashed on December 8 near Chicago's Midway Airport. She was only thirty-one years old. According to *Jet* magazine the flight that December was to have been her last commute, for she was returning to work permanently at the CBS bureau in Chicago.

Tributes from Her Peers

Clark's death was widely felt. Her death brought tributes from CBS, as well as from her vast television audiences. Richard Salant's tribute to Clark, published in *Ms.* magazine, reflected the widespread consensus of what she meant to her family, friends, colleagues, and the public:

> Like Ed Murrow, who without early training in the craft was suddenly plunged into journalism from other pursuits and was a towering figure from the start, so, too, Michele Clark confirmed that the best of journalists are born and not made, and that they await only self-discovery and an opportunity from others. . . . She knew what and who she was. She was all of one piece. . . . She had put it all together. . . . She was to us what she was to herself— honest, lovely, gracious, candid, tough, and tender. She was not all things to all people. She was the same to all.

An editorial in *Crisis* magazine put into focus the meaning of Clark's life. The editorial called her "exceptionally articulate, brilliant, poised, and [a] gracious lady of the

television screen." *Encore* noted that "she mastered the tools of her trade—the special grammar of electronic journalism." Though her life was brief, it was eventful and influential. She was an inspiration to many young black people throughout the country. Although Clark and her family had experienced the racism of a white mob, according to the *Crisis* editorial, she remained "a person singularly free of racist poison." Her racial pride was not equated with racism. The editorial continued,

> She believed in America and had faith in her country's potential for achieving equality of opportunity and color-blind justice. For Michele Clark these were notable attributes, for she, far more than most of her generation of Negro Americans, had sound cause to hate her fellow white citizens and to question the validity of the American promise of equal opportunity for all.

Those who knew Clark well or worked with her knew her personal and professional qualities. "That she succeeded so magnificently," said *Crisis,* "is a tribute to her own inner resources as well as to the dedication, commitment and understanding of her courageous parents who dared face the mob."

Although a tragic accident ended a seemingly unlimited career, Clark was not to be forgotten. The journalism program she had completed at Columbia University, funded by CBS, NBC, and the Ford Foundation, was renamed the Michele Clark Fellowship Program for Minority Journalists in her honor. From its inception to 1974, when the program closed, 227 minority women and men were trained for employment in print and electronic media. The program produced nearly twenty percent of the nation's minority journalists employed in 1974. The next year, with a grant from the Gannett Foundation and guided by noted black journalist Earl Caldwell, the program was reinstated and relocated at the University of California at Berkeley and renamed the Institute for Journalism Education.

When Clark completed her application in 1970 for the Columbia journalism program, she was not to know that her statement would become a credo for journalists of the future. According to *Encore,* she wrote:

> My vanity requires public recognition; my confidence requires a mode of expression; my intelligence and training require an intellectual challenge; my fear of boredom requires that routine be avoided; my ego requires that I contribute something and become involved, and my great mistrust and dislike for do-gooders requires that I be paid well for my services. . . .

Clark chose journalism over law because she felt the newsroom provided a better chance for her to effect change. She said further in her application:

> Truth and accuracy of reporting and writing, courage to expose unpleasant realities where necessary, good judgment to determine where to draw the line and to separate the thought-provoking from the

merely dramatic and sensational, are all more effective ways of stimulating change and are the ways I have chosen.

Michele Clark, an able journalist, had a brief, though enriching and impressive career, which doubtless helped to pave the way for minority television journalists who followed. As Richard Salant of CBS said in *Ms.* magazine, "we do have a right to weep for what she might have been. But also we can smile and remember what she already had become."

REFERENCES:

"Columbia University Minority Journalism Program Closes." *Jet* 46 (September 24, 1974): 14.

Dates, Jannette L., and William Barlow, eds. *Split Image.* Washington, D.C.: Howard University Press, 1990.

The Ebony Handbook. Chicago: Johnson Publishing Company, 1974.

Friendly, Fred W. "Lady Encore." *Encore* 2 (March 1973): 36-37.

"Her Death Is a Loss to Us All." *Jet* 43 (December 28, 1972): 22.

"In Memoriam." *Crisis* 80 (February 1973): 70.

"In Memoriam." *Ms.* 7 (April 1973): 117.

"Michele Clark." *Crisis* 80 (February 1973): 41.

"Michele Clark." *Jet* 46 (September 5, 1974): 14.

"Upsurge in TV News Girls." *Ebony* 26 (June 1971): 168-70.

COLLECTIONS:

A clippings file in Special Collections, Fisk University Library, contains information on Michele Clark.

Jessie Carney Smith

Constance E. Clayton

(1937-)

Educator, school superintendent, reformer

Constance E. Clayton faced the challenge of heading the sixth-largest school system in the nation for a decade. At a time when urban school heads ran into great difficulties marked by frequent changes in leadership, she has been conspicuously successful. Even her critics, who charge her with being autocratic and abrasive, concede that her vision of what is possible in the Philadelphia school system has improved public support for the schools. Beginning as an elementary school teacher in the city in which she spent all but one year of her entire career, she brought an insider's knowledge of the system and a broad vision to her task. The president of the Philadelphia Board of Education, Rotan E. Lee, paid this tribute to her in the *P R Newswire* in response to the notice of her retirement in 1993:

> You have become—few would argue—the nation's most prominent superintendent of an urban school district. In 1982, your administration began, albeit saddled by a legacy of debt; labor unrest; disconnected curricula; poor self-image . . . a decade later, the school district's infrastructure is well-grounded and is readied to meet the challenges of educational reformation and postured to prepare a generation of children for the twenty-first century.

Constance Elaine Clayton was born in Philadelphia in 1937, the only child of Levi Clayton, a plumber, and Willabell Harris Clayton, a social worker. When Clayton was two her parents divorced and she was subsequently raised by her mother and her grandmother. She attended Paul Lawrence Dunbar Elementary School and the Philadelphia High School for Girls. Clayton earned B.S. and M.Ed. degrees from Temple University. Initially she intended to be a physician, but decided that since she loved children so much she would become a teacher. In addition, the amount of discrimination that she would have had to endure as a woman and as a person of color in medicine, a vocation then more commmon for males, made a teaching career more appealing. She received her Ed.D. in Educational Leadership from the University of Pennsylvania, where she was a Rockefeller Scholar. She has also received honorary doctorates from seventeen colleges and universities.

Clayton Becomes School Superintendent

Clayton joined the Philadelphia school system in 1955 as a teacher at Harrison Elementary School, a predominantly black school in northeast Philadelphia. In 1964, she became a collaborating teacher in the Social Studies Department of the Curriculum and Instruction Division. In 1969, she worked as a project director of the Staff Development Program in African and Afro-American Studies. In 1971, she tried something new and served as regional director of the Women's Bureau, United States Department of Labor. Her job was to deal with women's issues in the region consisting of Pennsylvania, Delaware, Virginia, West Virginia, and Maryland. As director she had to coordinate seminars about women's work-related issues. By the end of one year she returned to her first love, the Philadelphia school system. Clayton served successfully as director and executive director of Early Childhood Education Programs and associate superintendent of Early Childhood Education, School District of Philadelphia. Then she was chosen to be superintendent of Philadelphia's school system in 1982. Clayton was faced with a multitude of problems. For example, as a superintendent of urban schools, she has been plagued with financial problems. In 1982 when Constance Clayton became superintendent of the Philadelphia Public

Schools, she started with a deficit of twenty-five million dollars. In a cost-cutting measure that netted a savings of three million dollars, Clayton ordered the temperature in all schools be turned down from seventy-six degrees to sixty-eight degrees. In addition, she faced the problems of meeting the needs of a changing school population as the middle class fled urban schools. She fostered programs to meet the new challenge.

The programs developed during Clayton's tenure reflect her creativity and awareness of social conditions that plague many of the children in the Philadelphia schools. She said in the *Boston Globe,* "The mission of education is to educate all kids and not just the middle class and the mainstream. . . . We must educate the kids born into poverty and despair. We must value all kids and not just a select few." She has been particularly successful in getting large businesses to invest in the children of Philadelphia—and in the future—with such programs as the Homeless Student Initiative and the Take Stock in Education program. The Homeless Student Initiative is an example of a program that meets the students on their own ground. It is an effort to provide educational continuity to an estimated fifteen hundred to two thousand homeless children and to minimize the impersonal aspects of daily shelter life. A large company has donated encyclopedias, educational games, VCR's, and tokens for transportation for students to use all year. Funds are provided for the children to visit museums and other cultural institutions that require an entry fee. Two shelters have been "adopted" (by another large company). Part of the company's responsibility is to create a quiet homework center for the children.

Another program that Clayton has woven into the Philadelphia school system is America 2000, which is a plan for urban school districts in the United States to implement radical changes in school systems by the year 2000. The goals are to raise the level of encouragement for urban students so that they can excel and feel motivated to compete with other students, raise school spirit in students to make them happy to go to school, raise graduation rates to those of nonurban schools, enable students to graduate with honors and skills so that they can successfully join the job market, hire teachers who care about students and who are willing to teach them properly, and improve the health of students by getting rid of drugs and alcohol. Members of the Council of Great City Schools (CGCS), of which Clayton was president in 1992, must work hard to make these changes. She refers to the meeting of the council as a summit in the *P R Newswire* for January 4, 1991: "This summit will result in the development of consensus recommendations for specific actions by which to confront the challenges facing urban education in our country."

Television has brought the failures and some successes of urban education to the attention of the public. In a special program entitled "America's Schools: Pass or Fail?" schools that were succeeding despite the social and economic problems were cited. Simon Gatz High School in Philadelphia was spotlighted because it uses a team teaching approach that seems to be working. The team approach gives the teachers

more control and reduces the bureaucracy. Clayton joined a group of panelists at the end of the program to discuss America 2000 and school choice plans. In her comments, cited in *Daily Report Card* for August 31, 1992, she said: "[America 2000] is not going to solve the problems in Philadelphia unless we can have the kind of support from our federal government and state government and city government in terms of understanding and realizing how important it is to make a concrete investment in education."

Clayton Promotes Sex Education

One of the turbulent issues in education of the last decade has been the issue of sex education in the public schools. Clayton, who was initially criticized by the AIDS activist group ACT-UP, was able to broaden the Philadelphia sex education program. After pressure from ACT-UP, she established a condom distribution program. She and the school board then agreed to change the curriculum from teaching only abstinence to teaching the dangers of AIDS and the risks of getting pregnant. Although this is seen as an improvement by Clayton's critics, they still are dissatisfied with the Philadelphia schools for not teaching how to use the condoms and have safe sex.

Prior to Clayton's administration young women who became pregnant while they were still high school students were not allowed to participate in graduation. Clayton, in stressing the need for youth to have an education to be able to take care of their families and themselves, adamantly encouraged four young women who were pregnant to complete their studies and participate in graduation.

Clayton's dedication to education is never-ending. Though she retired from her position as superintendent of schools, she plans to remain active in "the continuing quest to provide for all the children the education and the future to which they are entitled." She is active in community affairs and serves on a number of boards, including PNC Corporation, Connecticut Mutual Life Insurance Company, Public Broadcasting Service, Private Industry Council, Research for Better Schools, Area Council for Economic Education, and the National Board of Medical Examiners. She is also a board member of the Philadelphia Museum of Art, Widener University, Drexel University, and Bryn Mawr College, as well as a member of the American Association of School Administrators and the Committee to Support Philadelphia's Public Schools. She served from September 1988 until September 1989 on the Secretary of Labor's Commission on Workforce Quality and Labor Market Efficiency. She was the guest lecturer for the 1986 Hanify-Howland Memorial Lecture at the College of Holy Cross. In March 1989, Clayton was guest lecturer for the Horace Mann Lecture Series at the University of Pennsylvania.

Clayton has received many awards for her work. The Constance E. Clayton Chair on Urban Education at the Graduate School of Education, University of Pennsylvania, was named in her honor. This is the first endowed professorship in the United States that was named for a black woman. She has also received the Gimbel Award, the Police Athletic

League Award, the Humanitarian Service Award presented by the Philadelphia Commission on Human Relations, the Distinguished Daughters of Pennsylvania Award, and the United States Air Force Recruiting Service American Spirit Award.

Clayton resides in Mount Airy, Pennsylvania, with her mother. She consented to be interim superintendent of the Philadelphia schools while the Board of Education conducts a search for her replacement.

Current Address: Philadelphia Board Office of the Superintendent, Parkway at Twenty-first Street, Philadelphia, PA, 19103.

REFERENCES:

"America's Schools: Will Our System Pass or Fail?" *Daily Report Card,* August 31, 1992.

Clayton, Constance. "We Can Educate All Our Children." *Nation* 249 (July 24-31, 1989): 132-34.

"Clayton: Four Pregnant Students of the Philadelphia High School for Girls to Graduate, Despite Reports." *P R Newswire,* June 10, 1991.

Contemporary Black Biography. Vol. 1. Detroit: Gale Research, 1992.

"Educators Set Rescue Plan for Urban Schools." *Boston Globe,* January 15, 1991.

"Lynn Yeakel to Present MCP/Gimbel Philadelphia Award to Sister Mary Scullion, Advocate for the Homeless." *P R Newswire,* December 1, 1992.

"New York's Schools: Profiles of Chancellor Finalists." *New York Times,* December 28, 1987.

"Pennsylvania: Acting Up on Condom Distribution." *Abortion Report,* March 26, 1992.

"Philadelphia School Officials to Have Key Roles in Urban Education Summit." *P R Newswire,* January 4, 1991.

"Philadelphia School Superintendent Receives Maalox Moment Award; Surprise Party Held to Honor a Decade of Service." *P R Newswire,* October 7, 1992.

"Philadelphia Superintendent of Schools Dr. Constance E. Clayton Announces Retirement." *P R Newswire,* July 16, 1993.

"Recession Forces Sharp School Cuts." *New York Times,* January 16, 1991.

"School Beat: Philly Police Lend Top Officials to Schools." *P R Newswire,* February 24, 1993.

"Shelter Adoptions Bring New Hope to Homeless Students." *P R Newswire,* June 10, 1993.

Stout, Kate. "Shaking Up the System (Constance Clayton, Philadelphia School Superintendent)." *Working Woman* 9 (April 1984): 114-18.

"Student Stockholders Gain More than Dividends from New Educational Program." *P R Newswire,* March 1, 1993.

"Three Recommended for Schools Chancellor." *New York Times,* December 22, 1987.

Audrey Williams and Alyson Myers

Xernona Clayton

(1930-)

Television executive, television producer, television host, educator, civil rights activist, civic leader

Xernona Clayton demonstrates the vision, strength, wisdom, and determination of the black woman in U.S. history. She exposed job discrimination in Chicago for the Urban League, fought the school dropout problem in Los Angeles public schools, joined Martin Luther King's civil rights crusade through her work with the Southern Christian Leadership Conference (SCLC), spoke out against racial inequality in local activities in Atlanta, and worked to enlighten and uplift black people through civic activism. The first black woman in the South to host a regular prime time television talk show, Xernona Clayton continues to influence black community development through her executive position with Turner Broadcasting System (TBS).

Xernona Brewster Clayton was born August 30, 1930, in Muskogee, Oklahoma, to James M. Brewster, a Baptist minister, and Lillie Elliott Brewster. She and her identical twin sister Xenobia, were the youngest of four children—they had a sister, Vera, who was the oldest child in the family, and a brother, James, who was born four years after Vera. Reverend Brewster was well known and widely respected in both the white and black communities. Community members often sought his counsel and backing, and it was common practice for those seeking political office to visit the Brewster home to ask for his endorsement. According to Xernona Clayton's autobiography, *I've Been Marching All the Time,* her father was the strongest influence in her early life and the source of the family's stability. Lillie Brewster contrasted greatly with the gregarious Reverend Brewster. Xernona Clayton recognized her mother's contemplative nature, which reflected her Cherokee Indian heritage. She was a homebody who thought long and hard before she befriended others and was slow both with her words and warmth. She rejected the traditional role of the minister's wife and rarely attended church services.

The Brewsters aimed to develop wholesome values in their children. Xernona grew up at a time when many blacks considered a light complexion a sign of beauty and judged how "good" someone's hair was on the basis of its length, equating long hair with quality. Reverend Brewster taught the youngsters to disregard such frivolous things over which they had no control and always to treat others well. He also taught the family to share. Xernona Clayton recalls that he encouraged her to have a sense of responsibility. He instilled in her the importance of reliability, a trait that is now one of her characteristics.

After graduating from high school in Muskogee, Xernona and Xenobia attended Tennessee State University in Nashville and graduated in June 1952. Reverend Brewster's dream that he live long enough to see the only two of his children to pursue college educations receive their degrees was barely

Xernona Clayton

realized, for he died six months after they graduated. Since she had received a scholarship to attend graduate school at the University of Chicago, Xernona moved to Chicago immediately after completing her college work; her twin sister moved to Chicago as well. Since school would not start until fall, Xernona needed a summer job. The Chicago Urban League, whose mission, in part, is the search for employment for black people, hired Xernona and her sister as undercover agents to assist the Urban League in breaking down racial barriers in employment, especially in major companies.

Xernona entered the University of Chicago in the fall of 1952 but discontinued her studies to teach music education full-time in the Chicago public school system. Although by this time the U.S. Supreme Court had declared public school segregation unconstitutional, she found the system practiced the "separate but equal" doctrine. The white and black schools reflected the ethnic makeup of the neighborhoods. For a while she studied at Ru-Jac School of Modeling in Chicago and did some modeling locally. During this period Xernona met Edward T. Clayton, executive editor of *Jet* magazine, whom she would later marry. Her spiritual upbringing and its strong influence upon her were apparent in her decision to become the organist and choir director for of one of the largest Baptist churches in Chicago, South Shore Baptist Church. By this time Xernona had become very popular in the city and had met a number of well-known people. Wherever she went, she invited her new friends and acquaintances to her church. Sugar Ray Robinson, the boxer, was among those who accepted her offer, and he brought with him Jersey Joe Walcott, another professional fighter.

Racial Barrier Broken Down in Louisville

Edward and Xernona Clayton soon married. Both were very active in Chicago's social and civic activities and were vital members of the religious community. Ed Clayton's father, Eugene Clayton, the first black alderman and one of the first black elected officials in the South, still lived in Louisville, Ed Clayton's hometown. Eugene Clayton was a respected civic leader. When he died, Xernona went shopping in Louisville for a black hat to wear to the funeral. When Xernona was denied the privilege of trying on a hat in the millinery department of a store because of her race, it was the first time she had faced blatant racial discrimination. She noted in her autobiography that she was aware of racial discrimination as a child in Oklahoma and had witnessed it while working for the Chicago Urban League, but added, "I was a twenty-nine-year-old married woman when I first faced racial discrimination in a way that seemed personally hurtful. It was in Louisville, Kentucky." When the clerk refused to give Xernona Clayton the help she needed, she reported the matter to the executive offices. Clayton told the one of the store's officers that her father-in-law had shopped at the store often and sent her gifts from the store, so the officer asked who he was. Once the officer learned that Eugene Clayton was her father-in-law, the matter was resolved quickly and Clayton was escorted to the millinery department where the better hats were displayed. Rather than responding to the racial affront with rage, Clayton had responded with dignity. She learned later that her action broke down the racial barrier in the Louisville store and that black women from that time on were able to try on hats, shoes, and dresses when they shopped there.

Increased Social Activism

Ed and Xernona Clayton moved to Los Angeles in 1960, where Ed was assigned to *Jet* magazine's West Coast office. Because of the magazine's national reputation, they were accepted immediately into the Los Angeles community and aspiring politicians sought their support. One of these was future mayor Tom Bradley, who was then on the city council. The Claytons were politically active—Ed as a dyed-in-the-wool Democrat and Xernona as an elected member of the state Republican Committee.

Concerned over the high dropout rate in the Los Angeles schools, Xernona Clayton became interested in the school dropout program. Following President John F. Kennedy's call for volunteers to work with dropouts, she offered her services and helped guide the Los Angeles program to national attention. During this period, she also became a member of the Los Angeles Urban League's board.

Early in 1963 the Claytons moved to Atlanta, where they worked with the Southern Christian Leadership Conference. Ed Clayton worked to improve the SCLC's public relations system and wrote speeches and compiled materials for Martin Luther King, Jr. He died three years later. Xernona Clayton worked as Coretta Scott King's traveling companion and the organizer for her singing engagements. Though Xernona Clayton was closely allied with Martin Luther King and his civil rights activities, King needled her about the fact that she never participated in a civil rights march. As she drove him to the Atlanta airport for his final trip to Memphis, she responded to his teasing with, "I've been marching all the time," a sentiment which summed up her activism. All along she fought racism in her own way. Clayton was a leading facilitator of activities associated with King's family at the time of his death in April 1968.

Her social activism continued. Xernona Clayton became director of the Model Cities program, which led her to housing projects, direct work with the poor, and continued work with school dropouts. The position created some curious contacts for Clayton, including meetings with the Grand Dragon of the Ku Klux Klan. They developed a dialogue and her persuasive conversations with the Grand Dragon led him to resign from the Klan.

Xernona Clayton's social activism was also demonstrated through her work with the NAACP. She had been with the committee in the mid-1960s when they formed the Southwest Atlantans for Progress (SWAP) and became community relations director for the American Friends Service Committee. Through these activities she established a close professional relationship with Ralph McGill, then editor of the *Atlanta Constitution*.

Early in 1966, Clayton became involved in the desegregation of Atlanta's hospitals, working with a group of local black physicians on the Doctor's Committee on Implementation. The U.S. Department of Health, Education, and Welfare had set a deadline for eighteen area hospitals to desegregate, and if they did not comply, they would lose federal funding. When the deadline was extended, the committee went to Washington to protest. The hospitals finally complied, and black patients and physicians then had free and equal access to most of the hospitals in Atlanta—and in the South, since the project had become the inspiration for a national movement to desegregate hospitals across the nation.

Career in Television Develops

Xernona Clayton's friendship with Ralph McGill led her to break another racial barrier: in 1968 she became the first black woman in the South to host a regular television program. McGill liked her confrontational style and the manner in which she pricked the white conscience, and he had recommended her to participate in programs and panels. He also recommended her to host a talk show for WAGA-TV filmed at a local hotel, which had a wide, receptive audience that would enable her to break the color barrier in Atlanta television programming. The first show aired on Sunday evening, July 21, 1968. Initially called *Theme and Variations,* the name changed later to *The Xernona Clayton Show*. In late 1969 the program expanded to an hour and was syndicated. It aired until 1975. Clayton also originated "Moments in History," the popular one-minute daily broadcasts aired during Black History Month.

In 1974 Clayton married Paul L. Brady, a local judge whose great-uncle, Bass Reeves, became a federal deputy marshal in Fort Smith, Arkansas, in 1875 and served for thirty-two years. For twenty-one of those years he served Judge Isaac C. Parker, popularly known as the "Hanging Judge." Reeves, who drove outlaws and desperadoes from the old Indian Territory in Oklahoma, was an important figure in Oklahoma history. Clayton read and advised Paul Brady on the manuscript for his autobiographical work in which Reeves is featured.

For a while Xernona Clayton wrote a regular column for the *Atlanta Voice*. She returned to television in 1979, assuming a part-time position in programming and producing documentaries for Ted Turner's superstation, WTBS. Beginning in the early 1980s she hosted weekly public affairs shows, then became coordinator of minority affairs, director of public affairs, and vice-president for public affairs, all for WTBS. When Turner and Turner Broadcasting planned the Goodwill Games, which were held in Moscow in 1986, Clayton became a member of the Turner delegation. In 1988 Clayton became the assistant corporate vice-president for urban affairs for the Turner Broadcasting System.

Despite her successes, overt racial prejudice in the South was far from dead. Clayton was invited to speak before the Business and Professional Women's Club in Rome, Georgia, in 1987, but the group of white women rescinded the invitation when they learned that she was black. Some of the women denied that the change was due to race, but the local press published the real story. She was invited to speak before the national group at its meeting in Hawaii in mid-July.

Clayton's civic and professional activities include memberships in the Atlanta Chamber of Commerce, the National Association of Market Developers, the Arts Alliance Guild, America in Women in Radio and Television, the National Association of Media Women, the National Association of Press Women, the National Academy of Television Arts and Sciences, the Atlanta Broadcast Executive Club, the Atlanta chapter of Sigma Delta Chi, and Alpha Kappa Alpha Sorority. She is the founder of the Atlanta chapter of Media Women, a member of the State and Manpower Advisory Committee for the Georgia Department of Labor, and a member of the board of directors of the Greater Atlanta Multiple Sclerosis Society. Clayton has been recognized for her outstanding work on a number of occasions. She received the National Association of Market Developers' Leadership Award of 1968 and in 1969 was named Phi Delta Kappa's Bronze Woman of the Year in Human Relations. She received the Georgia Associated Press Award for Superior Television Programming, 1969-71, and the American Spirit Award, 1987. In 1991 *Ebony* magazine included her in their "Top 100 Most Promising Black Women in Corporate America."

Religion has remained central to Xernona Clayton's life, and she is an active member of Ebenezer Baptist Church. Protest, too, has remained an integral part of her life. Clayton is still affected by the pain of racism when she faces it or sees others face it. She said in her autobiography that the time will come when people realize that "there is no victory in separation—no victory in racial or sexual discrimination," and people will rid themselves of ''certain blindness'' and enjoy a free and just society.

Xernona Clayton has worked through television, the press, civic activities, and civil rights programs to promote cultural uplift and the rights of black people. Her final statement in her autobiography, a message to Martin Luther King, Jr., sums up her view of herself as a civil rights activist: ''I am still marching. I will keep marching until we achieve justice and equality for all people.''

Current Address: c/o Turner Broadcasting System, One CNN Center, Atlanta, Georgia 30303.

REFERENCES:

Clayton, Xernona, with Hal Gulliver. *I've Been Marching All the Time.* Atlanta: Longstreet Press, 1991.

Contemporary Black Biography. Vol. 3. Detroit: Gale Research, 1993.

Ebony Success Library. Vol. 1. Nashville: Southwestern Co., 1973.

Estell, Kenneth, ed. *The African-American Almanac.* 6th ed. Detroit: Gale Research, 1994.

Smart, Monica. ''Southern Exposure.'' *Essence* 17 (March 1987): 97-98, 122.

Who's Who among Black Americans, 1993-94. 8th ed. Detroit: Gale Research, 1993.

Wortham, Jacob. ''In with the Big Boys.'' *Black Enterprise* 5 (September 1974): 22-25.

Jessie Carney Smith

Pearl Cleage
(1948-)
Playwright, poet

Pearl Cleage is a multifaceted writer of essays, short stories, and poems, as well as a performance artist and the author of award-winning plays. In her collection of essays *Deals with the Devil: And Other Reasons to Riot* (1993), she describes herself as a ''womanist'' and a ''third generation black nationalist.'' The purpose of her writing, she says, is often ''to expose the point where racism and sexism meet.''

Pearl Michelle Cleage was born December 7, 1948, in Springfield, Massachusetts, the younger of two daughters of Albert Buford Cleage, a charismatic minister, and Doris Graham Cleage, an elementary school teacher. Her older sister is Kristin Cleage Williams. In *Deals with the Devil,* she describes her family as ''politically radical and highly opinionated.'' Her parents instilled in her the idea that because she

Pearl Cleage

came from a relatively privileged background, on becoming an adult, she had the responsibility to engage in racial uplift.

Cleage grew up on the west side of Detroit, where by the age of eight or nine, she was aware of how racism impacted the lives of African Americans. In elementary school, she refused to say the Pledge of Allegiance because it contained the line ''with liberty and justice for all.'' She also refused to stand for the singing of the national anthem, since civil rights demonstrations made her highly conscious of the injustices borne by African Americans.

Cleage's race consciousness was undoubtedly heightened by her politically active, black nationalist father, the Reverend Albert Cleage, who later renamed himself Abebe Agyeman. In 1962, he ran for governor of Michigan on the Freedom Now ticket, and in 1966, his Central Congregational Church formed the Inner Organizing Committee. Also in 1966, Albert Cleage preached a sermon that made him, according to *Black Firsts,* ''the first proponent of Black Theology to attract national attention.'' His church, decorated with a fifteen-foot painting of the Black Madonna and Child, became known as the ''Shrine of the Black Madonna.''

Despite her racial awareness, her light complexion and blue eyes confused some of her classmates. In *Deals with the Devil,* she describes herself as belonging to a ''racial subgroup that is both punished and rewarded for the genes it shares with its former masters.''

At age thirteen, she experienced such an intense emotional response to the inaugural activities of President John F. Kennedy, whose idealism impressed her, that she wanted to join the Peace Corps upon graduating from high school. As stated in *Deals with the Devil,* her mother's response to this idealism was, "We're Negroes.... We don't have to go anywhere to find somebody who needs help. All we have to do is walk out the door." Subsequently, the political upheaval of the 1960s changed everything. She saw that her mother's comment made sense in the light of ghetto supermarkets in Detroit selling tainted meat, automobile plants permanently laying off workers, and policemen shooting civilians in the back.

After graduating from high school, Cleage studied play writing at Howard University from 1966 to 1969. In 1969, at the age of twenty, after a brief courtship, she married Michael Lucius Lomax, an elected official of Fulton County, Georgia. Cleage then studied drama and play writing at Spelman College in Atlanta, obtaining a B.A. degree in 1971. After five years of marriage, she had a daughter, Deignan Njeri.

In 1971, a collection of Cleage's poems, *We Don't Need No Music,* was published by Broadside Press. In this volume she states:

> I believe that a Black Poet has a responsibility to contribute his [or her] art toward the strengthening and unifying of the Black Nation.... One way is to explore the relationships of brothers and sisters inside the nation in hopes of reflecting positive values and exposing negative ones. This is what I hope to do with my poems. I hope that the reflection of positive Black images will help us to see ourselves and eliminate the psychological sickness that we have been infected with after so many years of slavery and oppression. I would hope to write healing poems that show Black people their beauty as a group and help to move us from a collection of individuals to a cohesive force dedicated to the liberation struggle.

The period from 1974 to 1976 was busy and stressful for Cleage. During this period she served as director of communications for Atlanta, becoming the press secretary for Maynard Jackson, the city's first African American mayor. In an *Essence* article, "Is Your Life Making You Sick?" she admits, "This was not just a job, but a cause, a mission." She further stated,

> I was convinced [at twenty-five] that I could, and should, perform well at an incredibly demanding job, satisfy my boss's perfectionism, love my husband, entertain and be entertained regularly, nurture and enjoy my three-month-old daughter and write a little poetry on the side.

The grind of this lifestyle caused her to start taking "preventive" painkillers and to develop a nervous tic. The admission that her life was out of control was the prelude to the acknowledgement that she had to quit her job. After she did so, she took a part-time position allowing her to spend more time with her daughter and to develop her writing. Soon she was earning enough money from freelance writing to set up a home office.

Cleage's mother died of cancer, her death so traumatic an event that Cleage forgot its exact date. She describes the months immediately preceding her mother's death as the worst period of her life, because in addition to her mother's dying, her marriage of ten years was also falling apart. After her divorce, she entered into a period of heightened sexual activity and overdrinking. Her daughter, sympathetic friends, and writing, however, pulled her out of this temporary slump.

Creativity Widely Demonstrated

After this brief setback, Cleage has enjoyed a long period of abundant creativity and has found a variety of outlets for her artistic abilities. In addition to her freelance writing, she has engaged in television work. In the 1970s, she was an associate producer for WQXI-TV, Channel 11, in Atlanta, and staff writer and interviewer for *Ebony Beat Journal,* for WQXI. In 1983, she produced a privately printed collection of short fiction, *One for the Brothers.*

Presently Cleage is playwright-in-residence at Spelman College, editor of *Catalyst* magazine, a columnist for the *Atlanta Tribune,* and the artistic director of Just Us Theater Company. She has written a number of plays first produced by Just Us Theater, and has been the author-performer of several performance pieces. She has coauthored several works with her "life's companion," Zaron (Zeke) W. Burnett, Jr. Her play *Hospice* won five Audelco awards in 1983 for Outstanding Off-Broadway Achievement. *Puppetplay,* premiering at the Just Us Theater in 1981, opened the seventh season of the Negro Ensemble Company. In 1991, *The Brass Bed and Other Stories,* a collection of autobiographical sketches interspersed with poems, was published by Third World Press. Cleage has also regularly contributed to *Essence* and many other periodicals.

In 1993, she published a collection of essays, *Deals with the Devil: And Other Reasons to Riot.* These essays are on a wide range of topics such as Arsenio Hall, Malcolm X, Clarence Thomas, and the movies *Driving Miss Daisy* and *Daughters of the Dust.* Several of the essays are specifically addressed to women and issues of particular concern to them. Cleage says, "I wanted to see if I could talk about things black women writers address in our novels in a form that was more direct and invited political analysis and discussion rather than literary criticism." Especially concerned about the violence perpetrated against women, she admonishes them, "All men are capable of abusing women, no matter what they tell you or what they call it, so don't kid yourself about this or that one being different." One essay offers women ten warning signs of potential male violent behavior along with concrete suggestions for protecting themselves against rape by either strangers or acquaintances.

In *Deals with the Devil,* Cleage describes herself as an African American Urban Nationalist Feminist Warrior. Indeed, she sees most African Americans as belonging to one or two ideological camps. They are either African American Urban Integrationists, "who believe in both the desirability *and the possibility* of racial integration," or African American

Urban Nationalists, who believe they "must reclaim and revitalize . . . African American communities."

Cleage sees no conflict between being a black feminist and a black nationalist. She explains:

> In fact, I don't think you can be a true Black Nationalist, dedicated to the freedom of Black people, *without* being a feminist, black *people* being made up of both men and *women,* after all, and feminist being nothing more or less than a belief in the political, social, and legal equality of women.

Pearl Cleage is a prolific writer in various genres who believes the African American writer must be a warrior in the collective struggle for African American equality. Her heroes are the African American women who have been in the forefront of that struggle, such as Ida B. Wells, antilynching activist; Ruby Doris Robinson, civil rights activist and driving force of the Student Nonviolent Coordinating Committee; and Fannie Lou Hamer, founder of the Mississippi Freedom Democratic Party. In *Deals with the Devil,* Cleage credits such sister writers as Alice Walker, Maya Angelou, Sonia Sanchez, Toni Morrison, and Ntozake Shange as standing "beside [her] shoulder offering advice for correct living." She joins their ranks as a proponent of freedom and equality.

Current Address: 1665 Havilon Drive, S.W., Atlanta, Georgia 30311.

REFERENCES:

Black Writers. 2nd ed. Detroit: Gale Research, 1994.
Cleage, Pearl. *Deals with the Devil: And Other Reasons to Riot.* New York: Ballantine Books, 1993.
———. "Is Your Life Making You Sick?" *Essence* 21 (June 1990): 55-58, 105-7.
———. *We Don't Need No Music.* Detroit: Broadside Press, 1972.
Smith, Jessie Carney, ed. *Black Firsts.* Detroit: Gale Research, 1994.

Phiefer L. Browne

Kathleen Neal Cleaver

(1945-)

Educator, writer, lawyer, activist

Although Kathleen Neal Cleaver first came to the attention of the public because of her relationship with Eldridge Cleaver and the Black Panther Party, she has many accomplishments outside of her relationship with Cleaver for which she is well known. She is widely viewed as a gifted lawyer and educator who speaks out ardently against racism.

Kathleen Neal Cleaver

She is greatly in demand as a lecturer and has published numerous articles in newspapers and magazines.

Born on May 13, 1945, in Dallas, Texas, Cleaver was the first child of Ernest Neal and Juette Johnson Neal. Her father was at that time a sociology professor at Wiley College in Marshall, Texas. Her mother held a master's degree in mathematics. Shortly after Cleaver's birth, Ernest Neal accepted a position as director of the Rural Life Council of Tuskegee Institute in Alabama. After six years teaching sociology and designing community development projects, Ernest Neal joined the Foreign Service and moved the family abroad. The Neals would spend the next years in such locations as India, Liberia, Sierra Leone, and the Philippines.

While her parents remained in West Africa, Cleaver returned to the United States and enrolled in the George School, a Quaker boarding school near Philadelphia, Pennsylvania. There she completed high school in 1963, graduating with honors. Cleaver began her college education at Oberlin College in Ohio and later transferred to prestigious Barnard College in New York. In 1966, she left college to work in the New York office of the Student Nonviolent Coordinating Committee (SNCC).

Cleaver's January 1967 arrival at SNCC's Atlanta, Georgia, headquarters set off a series of life-altering events. As secretary of SNCC's campus program, she assisted in organizing a black student conference at Fisk University in Nashville, Tennessee. One of the attendees at the March conference was the minister of information for the Black Panther Party (the Party), Eldridge Cleaver. Eldridge Cleaver's intense oratory about black nationalism and revolution captivated Kathleen Neal Cleaver. Attracted by the Party's more radical approach to social change, she left SNCC and joined the Black Panther Party and Eldridge Cleaver in San Francisco in November 1967. The couple was married on December 27, 1967.

Speaks for Black Panther Party

Kathleen Neal Cleaver's impact on the Party was immediate. As the national communications secretary she became the first female member of the Party's decision-making body, the Central Committee. In that role, she served as the Party's spokesperson and press secretary, delivering speeches across the country. In 1968, she organized the national campaign to free the Party's jailed minister of defense, Huey Newton. In that same year she ran unsuccessfully for the California state assembly on the ticket of the Peace and Freedom party.

The Black Panther Party also impacted Kathleen Neal Cleaver's private life. On January 16, 1968, the eve of a scheduled Panther rally, the Cleavers' apartment was raided by the San Francisco Tactical Squad, who claimed to have been informed about a cache of guns and ammunition. On April 6 of that year, Eldridge Cleaver was wounded in a "shoot-out" between several Panthers and the San Francisco police; only one of the Panthers was armed. As a result of the confrontation, Eldridge Cleaver was charged with parole violations—he had been on parole since November 1966 for a 1958 conviction for assault with intent to kill—and scheduled to report to the parole board to be returned to prison on November 27, 1968. Unwilling to face another term of incarceration, Cleaver left the country on November 26, leaving his wife behind, and arrived by a rather circuitous route in Cuba on Christmas day, 1968.

Eldridge Cleaver lived under guard in Havana, Cuba, for seven months waiting for Cuban authorities to fulfill promises to bring over his wife and other members of the Party. By summer 1969, a mutual distrust had developed between the Cubans and Cleaver. Additionally, the press had discovered his whereabouts and sought interviews. The combined situations served as a catalyst for the Cubans to request that Kathleen and Eldridge Cleaver meet elsewhere.

The Cleavers were reunited in Algiers, Algeria, in July 1969. Their son, Maceo, named for the black Cuban general Antonio Maceo, was born on July 29. One year later, Kathleen gave birth to their second child, Jojuyounghi (Korean for young heroine), while the couple and other members of the Party were in North Korea.

After a disagreement between Huey Newton and Eldridge Cleaver during a live talk show on February 26, 1971 (Cleaver spoke long distance from Algiers), the International Branch of the Black Panther Party was expelled from the Party. The Cleavers and the former international members formed the Revolutionary People's Communication Network (the Network). Kathleen Neal Cleaver was again called on to use her public relations talents to promote the organization.

In the fall of 1971, Kathleen Neal Cleaver and the children returned to the United States to set up a headquarters for the new organization in New York. With the children in the care of her mother, she traveled the country explaining the position of the Network. She returned to Algiers in the spring of 1972.

The government of Algeria was becoming increasingly unhappy with Eldridge Cleaver and the Party remnant. Eldridge Cleaver had become disillusioned with the government's decision to give back money obtained by hijackers and with the move to align more closely with the United States. As relations cooled and financial support from the Algerian government, other countries, and individuals ceased, the group sought another location. Without a valid passport, Eldridge Cleaver had to leave Algiers secretly. His rendezvous with his wife took place in Paris, France, in January 1973.

While living underground in Paris, Eldridge Cleaver made several unsuccessful appeals for asylum. In the fall of 1973, Kathleen Neal Cleaver returned to the United States to try to arrange her husband's return as a parolee on bail and to raise a defense fund to cover legal fees. By 1974, the French government, under the direct influence of French President Valery Giscard d'Estaing, granted legal residency to the Cleavers and the family was reunited in Paris.

During the year in Paris, Eldridge Cleaver became increasingly unhappy with his life as an expatriate and finally decided to return to the United States. On November 15, 1975, the Cleaver children were sent to Pasadena, California, to stay with their paternal grandmother. Eldridge Cleaver arrived in New York on November 18 and was immediately jailed.

Having stayed on in Paris to conclude matters, Kathleen Neal Cleaver returned to the United States in late 1975 and began to work full time on the Eldridge Cleaver Defense Fund. Eldridge was finally freed on bail on August 13, 1976. The family was reunited in Los Angeles on August 16.

Eldridge Cleaver's legal situation was finally settled in 1980 when he agreed to plead guilty to three counts of assault in return for having the charge of attempted murder dropped. Once her husband's legal problems were resolved, Kathleen Neal Cleaver returned to college. In August 1981, having received a full scholarship to Yale University, she moved the children to New Haven, Connecticut, leaving Eldridge in California. She graduated in 1983, *summa cum laude* and Phi Beta Kappa, with a bachelor of arts degree in history.

Becomes Lawyer and Educator

In 1987, Kathleen Neal Cleaver divorced Eldridge Cleaver. After receiving her law degree in June 1988 from Yale Law School, she joined the New York City law firm of Cravath, Swaine and Moore. In 1991, she accepted a position as a law clerk in the United States Court of Appeals for the Third Circuit in Philadelphia, Pennsylvania. In 1992, Cleaver joined the faculty of Emory University in Atlanta, Georgia, where she teaches law.

Of her experiences with the Black Panther Party, Cleaver told the *New York Times Magazine,* "It was thrilling to be able to challenge the circumstances in which blacks were confined; to mobilize and raise consciousness, to change the way people saw themselves, blacks could express themselves."

Cleaver continues to have a very active life. As an advocate for the elimination of racism from our culture, she has published articles in magazines and newspapers since 1968 and is much in demand on the lecture circuit. She has also been featured in a number of film documentaries.

Current Address: School of Law, Emory University, Gamball Hall, Atlanta, GA 30322-2770.

REFERENCES:

Bray, Rosemary L. "A Black Panther's Long Journey." *New York Times Magazine,* January 31, 1993.

Cleaver, Kathleen Neal. Interview with Sarah Elizabeth Crest. April 23, 1993.

————. Letter to Sarah Elizabeth Crest, July 26, 1993.

Heath, G. Louis, ed. *Black Panther Leaders Speak.* Metuchen, N.J.: Scarecrow Press, 1976.

Hilliard, David, and Lewis Cole. *This Side of Glory: The Autobiography of David Hilliard and the Story of the Black Panther Party.* Boston: Little, Brown, 1993.

Hine, Darlene Clark, ed. *Black Women in America: An Historical Encyclopedia.* Brooklyn: Carlson Publishing, 1993.

Sarah Elizabeth Crest

Emma C. Clement
(1874-1952)
Church leader, clubwoman, social and civil rights activist

In 1946, Emma Clarissa Clement became the first African American woman to be selected American Mother of the Year by the American Mothers Committee of the Golden Rule Foundation in New York. The granddaughter of a slave, she was seventy-one years old at the time of this honor. Clement was not only the first African American to win this award, she was also the first African American nominated. A minister's wife and the mother of seven successful children, all of whom were devoted to serving their communities and the country at large, Clement gained national prominence through her church work and served as the national president of the Women's Society of the African Methodist Episcopal (AME) Zion

Emma C. Clement

Church. In Kentucky, she was parliamentarian of the Kentucky Federation of Women's Clubs and secretary of the Kentucky (Negro) Division of the American Field Army Cancer Society. She was also a charter member of the Southern Commission on Interracial Cooperation.

Although she considered herself a Kentuckian, Emma Clarissa Clement was born in Providence, Rhode Island, on December 6, 1874, to John and Abby Early Williams. She had a younger brother, Frederick, and a younger sister, Mayme. Their father was the supervisor of the loading crew for a piano company.

Clement grew up and was educated in Providence. She graduated from high school in 1894. At the urging of the president of Livingston College in Salisbury, North Carolina, she enrolled at the school, an institution sponsored by the AME Zion Church. There she met George Clinton Clement, whom she married on her college commencement day in 1898. Her husband had been ordained a minister in the AME Zion Church in 1893 and together they shared a lifelong commitment to serving the needs of others through church work.

From 1894 to 1900 George Clement pastored churches in five different communities in North Carolina. He was then transferred to Kentucky for a four-year period. In 1904 he became editor of the AME Zion's *Star of Zion* and in 1914 the manager of their publication house in his native state of North Carolina. In 1916, when he was elected bishop of the AME Zion Church's third district, the family moved again, this time to Louisville. He died in 1934.

Seven Outstanding Children

The couple had seven children—four boys and three girls—all of whom graduated from Livingston College. With the exception of the time she spent as an assistant teacher at Livingston College in 1899, Clement's entire life was devoted to her husband's ministry, raising her family, and her involvement in numerous civic, women's, and religious clubs.

Clement taught her seven children to work and play together harmoniously. Her daughter Abbie Clement Jackson said in the May 2, 1946, *Louisville Times,*

> The Clement family has always stuck together. . . .
> One Clement's problem is the whole family's problem and one's good fortune is shared with the rest.
> We have always worked and played in the closest relationship.

Clement's other daughters, Ruth and Emma, revealed in interviews on October 29, 1994, that she prided herself on her appearance and was always stylishly attired. The first thing each morning, she appeared to her family fully dressed and in high heels, never in house shoes and housecoat. She made some of the clothing worn by her daughters. An accomplished pianist and vocalist, Clement taught music lessons in the community, sang in and directed church choirs, and served as the church organist. All of her daughters were required to take music lessons. She viewed herself as an old-fashioned mother: she was very strict, yet affectionate, supportive, and kind. Because she always wanted to know where her children were, she never allowed them to have house keys until they had grown up and left home. She insisted that they share with each other and with friends and that they respect the rights and property of everyone. The Clements always had a family prayer service in the morning and a family conference each evening at dinner.

Clement was a pious, energetic, and gentle woman who never spoke ill of anyone. According to the *Louisville Courier Journal* of May 2, 1946, she was known among her friends as the "most church-going, charitable woman ever." It was not uncommon for her to attend as many as four church services plus Sunday school on any given Sunday.

First Black Mother of the Year Named

In 1946, while attending a district conference of the AME Zion Church in Springfield, Kentucky, news came that Clement had been selected as the 1946 American Mother of the Year. Because there was only one phone in Springfield's black community at that time, Clement had to go to the telephone company's office to receive the notification call from her daughter, who was at her home in Louisville.

In a bold move for the times, the *Louisville Courier Journal* of May 2, 1946, ran a front-page article titled "Louisville Negro Is Chosen American Mother of 1946," including a photograph, announcing Clement's selection for the award. Nominated by the executive secretary of the United Council of Churchwomen, Clement was recognized by the American Mothers Committee of the Golden Rule Foundation for her "great personal qualities as a mother of children who are devotedly serving their country and their people, as a partner in her husband's ministry in his life time, as a social and community worker in her own right." They also acknowledged that she embodied "the great spirit of America."

When Clement received this honor, her seven children were engaged as follows: Abbie Clement Jackson was serving as executive secretary of the Woman's Home and Foreign Mission Society of the AME Zion Church; Rufus Early Clement was president of Atlanta University; Frederick A. Clement was professor of physics at West Virginia State College; Ruth Clement Bond was the wife of the director of the Inter-American Education Foundation in Haiti; George W. Clement was a Red Cross recreation director in Italy; James A. Clement was a chaplain in the army; and Emma Clement Walker was an English professor at Tuskegee Institute.

On May 12, 1946, in New York City's Central Park, Clement gave her acceptance speech, which was broadcast nationwide. She accepted the award in the name of the millions of African Americans in the United States and in the name of all mothers. She further stated,

> In other years Mother's Day has been largely a day of sentiment, eulogizing mothers, giving them gifts and flowers. This year, and in years to follow, let us make it also a day of sharing—sharing with those of other countries. The best investment in world peace at this juncture is sacrificial gifts from America to other lands of food, clothing, medicines, and life's necessities.

After receiving the award, much of Clement's time was spent on speaking tours from New York to California. She gained the reverence and admiration of all who met her. Clement also received other honors and awards. She was named to the 1946 Honor Roll of Race Relations and received the keys to the cities of Philadelphia, Atlantic City, and Louisville. Her speaking engagements gave her numerous opportunities to address the topic of racial equality and issues relating to equitable funding for black education and health-care facilities. In 1947 her alma mater, Livingston College, presented her with an honorary doctorate of philosophy in humanitarianism.

In 1951, having been ill as a result of diabetes, Clement underwent two operations, one of which resulted in the amputation of her right leg. This, however, did not prevent her from regularly attending church. In fact, when she died on December 26, 1952, she had most recently attended church services on Christmas Eve. Her burial place is Louisville Cemetery, Louisville, Kentucky.

In 1971 the Kentucky Commission on Human Rights honored Clement in their poster series of Kentucky's outstanding African Americans. The selection of the high-spirited, determined, and well-respected Clement as Mother of the Year for 1946 not only honored the race but was another inroad in opening up opportunities for all African Americans.

REFERENCES:

"American Mother." *Time* 47 (May 13, 1946): 25.

Bond, Ruth Clement. Telephone interview with Karen Cotton McDaniel, October 29, 1994.

Dunnigan, Alice A. *The Fascinating Story of Black Kentuckians: Their Heritage and Tradition.* Washington, D.C.: Associated Publishers, 1982.

Kentucky Commission on Human Rights. *A Gallery of Great Black Kentuckians.* Frankfort: Kentucky Commission on Human Rights, 1971.

————. *Kentucky's Black Heritage.* Frankfort: Kentucky Commission on Human Rights, 1971.

"Louisville Negro Is Chosen American Mother of 1946." *Louisville Courier Journal,* May 2, 1946.

"Louisville's Mother of the Year Named on 1946 Race Relations Honor Roll." *Louisville Courier Journal,* February 10, 1947.

"Mother." *Newsweek* 27 (May 13, 1946): 28.

"Mothers Extolled in Day of Tributes." *New York Times,* May 13, 1946.

"Proud Welcome Given 1946 American Mother." *Louisville Times,* May 2, 1946.

Walker, Emma Clement. Telephone interview with Karen Cotton McDaniel, October 29, 1994.

Who's Who in Colored America. Brooklyn, N.Y.: Thomas Yenser, 1933.

Who's Who in Colored America. Yonkers, N.Y.: Christian E. Burckel, 1950.

COLLECTIONS:

Emma Clarissa Clement's personal papers and photographs are in the possession of her daughter, Ruth Clement Bond, Washington, D.C.

Karen Cotton McDaniel

Carrie Williams Clifford

and civil rights activist produced substantial benefits for her people regardless of their gender or age.

Details about Clifford's personal life are scarce. She was born in Chillicothe, Ohio, in 1862. She grew up in Ohio, and, during her high school years in Columbus, she was recognized as a brilliant student. It is apparent that her family and educational background more than adequately prepared her for the years ahead. Before leaving Columbus, she married William H. Clifford, a lawyer and influential Republican member of the Ohio State Legislature. The Cliffords lived in Cleveland, and the couple had two sons.

Women's Club Activities Begin

In addition to caring for her family, Clifford consistently demonstrated her community concern. She founded the Minerva Reading Club. According to Dorothy Salem in *To Better Our World: Black Women in Organized Reform, 1890-1920,* a typical literary club during the late nineteenth century was more than an opportunity for poetry readings and musical performances; it functioned as a social improvement association that developed black women's leadership skills "and increased educational awareness of racial issues." Clifford's Minerva Club activities led to her involvement with the National Association of Colored Women (NACW). Her diligent work and considerable abilities benefited the Cleveland organization, and when the need for a state organization was realized, Clifford was the major force responsible for the founding in 1901 of the Ohio Federation of Colored Women's

Carrie Williams Clifford

(1862-1934)

Clubwoman, writer, editor, women's and civil rights activist

The mythic King Midas had the ability to turn everything he touched to gold. Yet Midas was limited; his transformations did not improve his subjects' lives. Carrie Clifford's golden touch in organizing and inspiring others aided her nation and the communities she lived in. Her significant endeavors as a clubwoman, writer, women's rights activist,

Clubs (OFCWC); it was the first of at least sixteen such organizations in the United States.

The organization's motto was "Deeds, Not Words." Excerpts from "Marching to Conquest," one of the OFCWC's songs written by Clifford and published in *Alexander's Magazine,* vol. 2, announced the ladies' mission:

> We are battling for the right with
> purpose strong and true,
> Tis a mighty struggle, but we've
> pledged to dare and do;
> Pledged to conquer evil, and we'll see
> the conflict thro',
> Marching and marching to conquest.
> All the noble things of life we'll teach
> our girls and boys,
> Warn them of its pitfalls, and reveal
> its purest joys;
> Counsel, guide and keep them from
> the evil that destroys. . . ,
> Ignorance and vice and hate at our
> approach shall flee,
> As we go marching to conquest.

Indeed the members of the OFCWC were determined to make a better world for their children as well as battle the racism that black men, women, and children encountered.

As president of the OFCWC, Clifford was an exceptional executive who focused the organization's efforts on family, community, women's rights, and racial issues. Whether delivering a dramatic reading, lecturing, or writing, she sought society's improvement; for example, her "Love's Way (A Christmas Story)" advocated temperance.

Clifford was editor-in-chief of the women's edition of the *Cleveland Journal* and a contributor to publications, including *Alexander's Magazine.* She also created several publications that highlighted the thoughts and activities of other black women. In addition to establishing vehicles for black, feminine voices, Clifford ensured that national black voices were heard in her city by arranging the Cleveland appearances of such luminaries as W. E. B. Du Bois and Booker T. Washington. Clifford was instrumental in the OFCWC's promotion of suffrage. The National American Woman Suffrage Association (NAWSA) gained the support of Clifford and other organizers of black women's clubs. Clifford was among the black and white women who participated in suffrage demonstrations.

Under Clifford's competent leadership, the OFCWC blossomed; there were more than one hundred delegates to the fifth annual convention. Clifford's efforts on behalf of the OFCWC were appreciated by the organization's members to the extent that when she attempted to decline reelection, the women would not allow her to relinquish the presidency. Her accomplishments were also recognized by Charles Alexander in *Alexander's Magazine,* vol. 2, in "Editorial: Mrs. Carrie W. Clifford:"

There are very few women in this country who are accomplishing larger purposes for the uplift of mankind, or who are expending more mental and moral energy in unselfish endeavors, or who have achieved greater distinction on account of a liberal show of exceptional elocutionary talent and rare literary gifts or greater forcefulness of personality as an organizer and leader of her sex than Mrs. Carrie W. Clifford of Cleveland, Ohio.

Washington D.C. and the NAACP

When the Cliffords left Cleveland, Carrie Clifford's literary and humanitarian activities did not decrease. The family moved to Washington, D.C., where the Cliffords associated with other members of the black intelligentsia, including W. E. B. Du Bois, Charles W. Chesnutt, Georgia Douglas Johnson, Alain Locke, and Mary Church Terrell. Rosemary Clifford Wilson, in her introduction to Clifford's *The Widening Light,* noted that on Sunday evenings "the most vital black figures of the day . . . [who] were creating the cultural and political heritage for black Americans which preceded and gave impetus to the so-called 'Harlem Renaissance' of the 1930's" would gather at the Clifford home.

Clifford remained active in charitable and social reform work and became a member of the Niagara Movement. The first meeting of this civil rights organization, spearheaded by W. E. B. Du Bois, was held in Ontario, Canada, in 1905. In his biography of Du Bois, David Levering Lewis cited the "irony . . . that the first collective attempt by African Americans to demand full citizenship rights in the twentieth century (without even indirect support of influential whites) had been forced to spring to life on Canadian soil."

Dynamic black women such as Clifford, who sought to participate in collaborative civil rights efforts with their black male peers, had to wait for acceptance. In 1906, Du Bois asked several women to head a national committee for a female auxiliary of the Niagara Movement. Clifford assumed responsibility for encouraging women to join. Later that year, members of the auxiliary were present at the Niagarites' second meeting, held in Harper's Ferry, West Virginia. Although denied admission to the sessions until the third meeting held in Boston the following year, they met among themselves. At the Niagara Night program, William Monroe Trotter and Max Barber spoke prior to Clifford's recital of Du Bois's "Credo." In 1907 at the Boston meeting, half of the eight hundred delegates were women. Thus, it is obvious that the campaign led by Clifford to persuade more women to join the Niagara Movement was most successful.

The Niagara Movement was a victim of internal problems and the strenuous opposition of Booker T. Washington and his supporters; when Du Bois encouraged the Niagarites to join the NAACP, founded in 1910, most of them did so. As a result, the Niagara Movement became defunct. The Niagarites, including Clifford, were among the NAACP's earliest and most faithful members. In her essay, "National Association for the Advancement of Colored People," published in 1993 in *Black Women in America,* Darlene Clark Hine wrote: "Until recently, few scholars have focused on the importance of women's roles in the association. Usually historical accounts of the NAACP focused on the male membership—most noticeably on the prominent scholar W. E. B. Du Bois. However there is a growing body of work documenting the crucial early contributions of women to this organization.'' Hine identified Nannie Helen Burroughs, Mary McLeod Bethune, Mary Church Terrell, and Ida B. Wells-Barnett as the NAACP's ''more well-known Black women activists.'' Although Clifford's name is not well-known today, her efforts on behalf of the NAACP and blacks in general appear equally impressive as those of her famous male and female contemporaries.

Clifford's contributions to the NAACP were diverse. She was a member of the NAACP's National Committee of One Hundred, later known as the General Committee; membership on this committee reinforced her leadership position in the organization. In 1911 Clifford, along with Mary Church Terrell, represented the NAACP when presenting antilynching resolutions to the President of the United States, William Howard Taft. Salem commented that it was appropriate for Clifford and Terrell to undertake this responsibility since they ''were married to political appointees in Washington, they were able to use their connections to promote the NAACP resolutions reflecting principles of justice.'' In 1912 Clifford, aided by Addie D. Waites Hunton, created a women's fund-raising and speakers' committee for the NAACP.

Clifford, in addition to assuming national responsibilities for the NAACP, exercised great influence in the activities of the Washington branch. Children were of special interest to Clifford, who headed the NAACP's Juvenile Department. While providing Washington's children with numerous cultural and educational opportunities to increase awareness of their heritage, she created a card game that contained information about influential blacks in various fields that was sold in the *Crisis,* a publication of the NAACP. In 1912 Addie Hunton and Clifford collaborated again to form a second committee that produced the branch's women leaders. In 1913 the male president of the Washington chapter unsuccessfully attempted to exploit his position in order to gain a political appointment; as a result, Clifford and other women were elected to administrative positions. During the next two years, membership increased from four hundred to fifteen hundred, making it the largest chapter.

Clifford's Writing Talent Surfaces

Clifford worked for the NAACP in still another capacity; she contributed articles to the *Crisis* that focused on various types of discrimination. ''Votes for Children,'' for example, is an eloquent expression of her discontent that women were not allowed to vote:

[T]he wonder grows that her voice is not first heard in planning for the ideal State in which her child, as future citizen, is to play his part. . . . Yes, it is the great mother-heart reaching out to save her children from war, famine, and pestilence; from death, degradation and destruction, that induces her to

demand ''Votes for Women,'' knowing well that fundamentally it is really a campaign for ''Votes for Children.''

In addition to writing a number of articles for the *Crisis,* Clifford published two volumes of poetry: *Race Rhymes* (1911) and *The Widening Light* (1922). Topics of her poetry included Africa; slavery; discrimination; injustice; protest; democracy; religion; famous black individuals such as William Stanley Braithwaite, Paul Laurence Dunbar, Frederick Douglass, and Phyllis Wheatley; black institutions such as Howard University; and black Broadway actors. In the ''Preface'' to *The Widening Light,* Clifford announced her purpose in writing poetry:

The author makes no claim to unusual poetic excellence or literary brilliance. She is seeking to call attention to a condition which she, at least, considers serious. Knowing that this may often be done more impressively through rhyme than in an elegant prose dissertation, she has taken this method to accomplish this end. Each poem has been called forth by some significant event or condition in the history of the Negro in America. The theme of the group here presented—the uplift of humanity—is the loftiest that can animate the heart and pen of man; the treatment, she trusts, is not wholly unworthy . . . she sends these lines forth with the prayer that they may change some heart, or right some wrong.

Clifford's writing, whether prose or poetry, received little critical attention during her lifetime. One exception was Robert T. Kerlin, who included Clifford's ''An Easter Message,'' from *The Widening Light,* in his *Negro Poets and Their Poems* (1923). He commented that Clifford's sonnet contained ''discord . . . of the kind that stabs you.'' In the poem's octave, Clifford crafted majestic images of spring and renewal while in the sestet, she painted a picture of black despair. The poem is reminiscent of the contrast and despair found in Frederick Douglass's famous Fourth of July speech delivered in Rochester, New York, in 1852.

Carrie Clifford is one of the lesser known writers of the Harlem Renaissance. Just as historical researchers are beginning to investigate the contributions of Clifford and other women to the NAACP during its earliest years, literary scholars are beginning to investigate the contributions of Clifford and other women to the Harlem Renaissance. For example, Lorraine Roses, writing in *Black Women in America,* acknowledged the significance of Clifford's work when she described her as ''a poet activist whose commentaries on the injustices and sufferings specific to women of color (such as sexual harassment and abuse), foreshadow late-twentieth-century protests.''

Additional details of Clifford's remarkable life are scarce. She died in 1934. As a clubwoman, writer, women's rights activist, and civil rights activist, Carrie Clifford may be best remembered by Rosemary Clifford Wilson's vision of her: ''She was a black woman who lived and spoke and wrote and worked ceaselessly for the rights of all black people.''

REFERENCES:

Alexander, Charles. "Editorial: Mrs. Carrie W. Clifford." *Alexander's Magazine* 1 (1905-06): 39.

——. "The Ohio Federation at Dayton." *Alexander's Magazine* 1 (1905-06): 7.

Clifford, Carrie W. "Lines to Garrison." *Alexander's Magazine* 1 (1905-06): 8-9.

——. "Love's Way (A Christmas Story)." *Alexander's Magazine* 1 (1906-07): 55-58.

——. "Marching to Conquest." *Alexander's Magazine* 2 and 3 (1906-1907): 60.

——. "Votes for Children." *Crisis* 10 (August 1915): 8.

——. *The Widening Light.* Introduction by Rosemary Clifford Wilson. Boston: Walter Reid Co., 1922.

Hine, Darlene Clark, ed. *Black Women in America.* Brooklyn: Carlson Publishing, 1993.

Kerlin, Robert. *Negro Poets and Their Poems.* Washington, D.C.: Associate Publishers, 1923.

Lewis, David Levering. *W. E. B. Du Bois: Biography of a Race 1868-1919.* New York: Henry Holt and Co., 1993.

Salem, Dorothy. *To Better Our World: Black Women in Organized Reform, 1890-1920.* Brooklyn: Carlson Publishing, 1990.

Stetson, Erlene, ed. *Black Sister: Poetry by Black Women, 1746-1980.* Bloomington: Indiana University Press, 1981.

                                                    Linda M. Carter

Lucille Clifton

Lucille Clifton

(1936-)

Poet, children's author, educator

An author of poetry and prose works for adults and children, Lucille Clifton has been published extensively since 1966. Her canon includes nineteen children's books, nine volumes of poetry written for adults, and a memoir. Over the years, Clifton's poetry and prose have appeared in more than one hundred anthologies, magazines, and journals. Characterized by a feminine sensibility rooted in the history of African American women, Clifton's works treat children, family, domesticity, and the concerns of ordinary women. Her characters and speakers dwell mainly in urban settings—usually inner-city African American neighborhoods and occasionally multicultural American neighborhoods. Affirmative, her works have a political agenda. They exude black racial pride and celebrate black womanhood.

The vision that pervades Clifton's works is summarized in her memoir *Generations* (1976). Implicitly countering the cataclysmic vision of Chinua Achebe's *Things Fall Apart* (1959), Clifton proclaims in *Generations,* "Things don't fall apart. Things hold. Lines connect in thin ways that last and

last and lives become generations made out of pictures and words just kept." The recurring theme in her works is that hope exists alongside despair and that personal or racial suffering does not necessarily translate into individual or collective defeat. Consistently hopeful, her works posit that humans determine their own fates and can conquer evil if they are strong and if they have the support of their families. As her frequent recourse to biblical allusions implies, Clifton's hopefulness is rooted in Christian optimism.

Born to Samuel Louis Sayles, Sr. (1902-1969) and his second wife, Thelma Moore Sayles (1914-1959), on June 27, 1936, in Depew, New York—a small, primarily Polish town twelve miles from Buffalo, New York—Clifton was named Thelma Lucille Sayles by her father. She is a descendent of Caroline Donald Sale, a Dahomey woman who was "born free in Africa" in 1822 and who "died free in America" in 1910, and of Sam Louis Sale, who was born a slave in America in 1777 and who died a slave in America around 1860. Clifton appears to have been guided through much of her life by the mantra of her foremother Caroline, who, Clifton says in *Generations,* urged her family, "Get what you want, you from Dahomey women." Owned by the Sale family of Bedford, Virginia, Clifton's ancestors changed their name to Sayle after the Civil War so that they could be distinguished from the white Sale family. After the war, her grandfather Gene Sayle was born to Harvey Nichols, a white man from Connecticut, and Clifton's namesake, Lucille Sayle, whose distinct place in family history was won when as punishment for killing Nichols, she allegedly became the first black woman hanged legally in the state of Virginia. Clifton says in *Generations* that her father Samuel changed his surname from Sayle to Sayles "after finding a part of a textbook in which the plural was explained. There will be more than one of me, my father thought, and he added the *s* to his name." Lucille Clifton's father had three children in addition to Lucille: Josephine, an older daughter who was born to his first wife, Edna Bell Sayles; Elaine, a daughter born to a neighbor woman six months after Clifton's birth; and Samuel, Jr., a son born to his second wife, Thelma Moore Sayles, two years after Clifton's birth.

Neither of Clifton's parents completed elementary school. A coal miner and a laborer in the South, her father worked in a steel mill after he migrated to the North. Her mother worked in a laundry. The family was poor; however, because their love sustained them, they were not worn down by penury. She attributes her interest in writing and reading to her parents, both of whom were voracious readers. Her mother, who wrote verse during her spare moments, was her only role model as a poet other than the white male poets whose works were traditionally taught then in schools. Her mother's poetry was good enough to warrant acceptance by a publisher, but the family disapproved. In response, her mother burned her poems and ceased writing.

When Clifton was a small child, her family moved to Purdy Street in Buffalo. As her poetry and prose reflect, her childhood years there were happy—so happy that they are the foundation of her first book of poems, *Good Times* (1969). Academically talented, Clifton left Buffalo when she was sixteen years old to attend Howard University in Washington, D.C. Supported by a full scholarship provided by her church, she attended Howard from 1953 to 1955, a period during which Leroi Jones (Amiri Baraka), A. B. Spellman, Owen Dodson, and Sterling Brown were there. Pursuing a major in drama at Howard, Clifton appeared in the first performance of James Baldwin's *The Amen Corner*. In *Generations*, Clifton explains that when she went to college she was frightened. She had never been away from home before; she had little knowledge of what to expect, for neither of her parents and no one in her church had attended college. Seeing herself as a special person and believing that she did not have to study, she did not—a decision that in time cost her the scholarship that made her university education possible.

After returning to Buffalo, Clifton entered Fredonia State Teachers College (now the State University of New York at Fredonia) in 1955, where she joined a group of African American students who met to read and perform plays. During this period, she was coming into her own as a writer, but publication was not uppermost in her mind. Ishmael Reed, a member of the group, showed some of her poems to Langston Hughes, who included a few in his anthology *Poetry of the Negro, 1746-1970* (1970).

In 1958, Clifton wed Fred James Clifton (1935-1984), a philosophy teacher at the University of Buffalo who was also a member of the Fredonia State group of black intellectuals. In seven years, they had six children—four daughters (Sidney, Fredrica, Gillian, and Alexia) and two sons (Channing and Graham). A busy wife and mother during these years, Clifton

was also writing. Additionally, she was employed from 1958 to 1960 as a claims clerk in the New York State Division of Employment in Buffalo.

Writer's Works in Print

During the late 1960s, Clifton's works began to appear in print. In 1966, she saw a prose dialogue, "It's All in the Game," published in *Negro Digest*. In 1969, her short story "The Magic Mama," parts of which appeared later in *Generations,* was published in *Redbook;* the focus of the story is Clifton's mother's epileptic seizures and their effect on the family. Later that year, a poem, "In the Inner City," appeared in the *Massachusetts Review*. Also in 1969, Clifton sent some of her poems to poet Robert Hayden, who showed them to poet Carolyn Kizer, who sent them, in turn, to the YW-YMHA Poetry Center in New York City. That year Clifton won the center's Discovery Award, presented annually to a promising but undiscovered poet, and Random House published *Good Times,* her first book of poems, which was subsequently cited by *The New York Times* as one of the ten best books of the year. She also received a National Endowment for the Arts grant. While winning accolades for her accomplishments as a published writer, Clifton began employment as a literature assistant at the United States Office of Education in Washington, D.C., where she remained until 1971.

In 1974, she became poet-in-residence at Baltimore's Coppin State College; she held this position until 1979. During her first year at Coppin, Clifton was selected as Maryland's poet laureate, a governor-appointed position that paid an annual stipend of one thousand dollars and that had as its only official duty the creation of new poems for specific state occasions. Widowed in 1984, Clifton assumed the position of professor of literature and creative writing in 1985 at the University of California at Santa Cruz, where she remained on the faculty until 1989. That year she returned to Maryland, where she assumed the position of visiting distinguished professor of literature at St. Mary's College of Maryland; she held the position for two years. Since 1991, she has held the rank of distinguished professor of humanities at St. Mary's College of Maryland. Since fall 1994, Clifton has taught at St. Mary's College one semester during the academic year and at Columbia University in New York City one semester.

Over the years, Clifton has written for two audiences—children and adults. According to critic Audrey McCluskey, in *Black Women Writers, 1950-1980,* Clifton's children's books are "her most prolific literary product, and no analysis of her work could ignore their overall importance." Her universe is one in which self-love and self-acceptance reign and self-abnegation is subordinated. It is a world in which children experience joy and pain and in which they learn to accept both emotions; it is a literary world that children visit and leave reassured. Characterized by Christian values, racial pride, and an affirmative perception of "uncelebrated man and woman,'' according to McCluskey, Clifton's vision in her works for children as well as in those for adults is akin to that of African American writer Gwendolyn Brooks, whose canon is grounded in a similar ''racial and spiritual legacy.'' Also, states McCluskey, Clifton's Christian optimism resembles that of early twentieth-century African American women writers Effie Lee Newsome, primarily a children's writer, and Anne Spencer, a writer for adults.

Works for Children Published

Among Clifton's best-known children's books are those that focus on Everett Anderson, a young African American boy. The first book in this series, *Some of the Days of Everett Anderson,* published in 1970, was selected for the American Institute of Graphic Arts's Children's Book Show and was chosen as one of the *School Library Journal*'s Best Books of 1970. The following year, the second Everett Anderson book, *Everett Anderson's Christmas Coming,* appeared. Additional books on Everett Anderson and other children followed in subsequent years. Having had six children of her own, who attracted other children, Clifton has indicated that she saw so many children that she got ideas from observing them and was thus inspired to write about them.

Her Everett Anderson books present stages in the title character's changing life. Rudine Sims in *Language Arts,* February 1982, quotes Clifton as saying the works in this series are not poetry in the purest sense but are instead ''very good verse'' that may serve as useful and valuable means of introducing poetry to children. Among the series' assets are the free-flowing rhythm of the lines and the succinct presentation of themes. A faithful adherence to African American vernacular, a straightforward manner, and an understanding and accurate depiction of children's psychology lend authenticity and immediacy to the works.

Clifton's other books for children include *The Black BC's* (1970), which teaches the ABC's from an Afro-centric perspective. In the tradition of Langston Hughes's *A Pictorial History of the Negro in America* (1956), *The Black BC's* refigures American history by invoking black contributors such as cowboys, inventors, and musicians. Fostering black pride, Clifton's work clearly has a political agenda. Similar to *The Black BC's* are Clifton's children's books such as *Don't You Remember?* (1973); *All Us Come Cross the Water* (1973); *The Times They Used to Be* (1974); *Good, Says Jerome* (1974); and *Amifika* (1978). These books also celebrate the African American experience, proclaim the beauty of blackness, and insist that poverty need not mean a lack of love, warmth, or dignity.

In some of Clifton's children's books, including *The Boy Who Didn't Believe in Spring, My Friend Jacob,* and *Sonora Beautiful,* white children are the protagonists. However, most of her major characters are African Americans and have names children can associate with. According to Sims, the abundance of black protagonists in Clifton's works is consistent with her unequivocal proclamation that her ''whole *thing* is geared to black children.''

Works for Adults Published

During the years when her children's books were being published steadily, Clifton was also writing for adults. *Good Times,* her first collection of poems for adults, was published in 1969. Described by Haki Madhubuti in *Black Women Writers, 1950-1980* as ''unusually compacted and memory-evoking,'' the poems in this collection treat black lives that are rescued from desperation by love. Three years later, in 1972, her second volume of poetry for adults, *Good News about the Earth,* appeared. *Good News* is a group of brief, powerful, and simply expressed poems that place biblical stories in black and contemporary contexts.

A prolific writer, Clifton has published seven additional books of poetry for adults and one prose work for adults since *Good News about the Earth* appeared in 1972. The poems in *An Ordinary Woman,* published in 1974, celebrate everyday things—marriage, motherhood, sisterhood, continuity, and blackness. According to Madhubuti, it is in this work that Clifton achieves her promise as a writer. The major images in the poems are bones, which represent strength and connection among generations, and light, which represents knowledge, existence, and life.

Generations, Clifton's only prose work for adults, was published in 1976. An ode to the survival of the African American family that is indebted to Walt Whitman's *Song of Myself* for its inscriptions and its structure, *Generations* chronicles and celebrates Clifton's family history through five generations while also recording her own journey of self-discovery.

Four years later, in 1980, *Two-Headed Woman* appeared. It was the winner that year of the Juniper Prize, an annual poetry award given by the University of Massachusetts Press. Characterized by dramatic tautness, simple language, and original groupings of words, the poems are tributes to blackness, celebrations of women in general and black women in particular, and testimonies to familial love.

Both *Good Woman* and *Next* were published in 1987. *Good Woman* contains 177 poems and a fifty-three page memoir in which the writer ''celebrates the beauty and strength of a creation that endures,'' according to the February 5, 1988, *Christian Science Monitor,* and ''challenges her readers . . . to do more than grieve over life's inconsistencies.'' Among the major themes in *Next,* a collection of sixty-five poems, are women's strength and sisterhood, war's cruelties, the horrors of the African American experience, the deleterious effects of racism on African Americans' self-esteem, and death and dying. According to the *Christian Science Monitor,* the poems collectively denounce finality, denounce endings.

Ten Oxherding Pictures (1988) and *Quilting* (1991) were followed in 1993 by *The Book of Light* (1993), in which light signifies creativity, spirituality, and love. As in her earlier writings, the work celebrates African American womanhood, here in poems such as ''daughters'' and ''won't you celebrate with me.'' Also, in *The Book of Light,* the speaker pays tribute to dearly departed family members in poems such as "thel," in which the speaker describes her mother as a "sweet attic of a woman," and "sam," in which the speaker laments her father's being denied an opportunity to go to school, where "he would have learned to write / his story and not live it." Additionally, *The Book of Light* has a social agenda; "move" and "samson predicts from gaza the philadelphia fire" protest the 1985 bombing in Philadelphia of a house occupied by dreadlocked members of an Afro-centric back-to-nature group, while "seeker of visions" resurrects the destruction of Native Americans by white men, "the pale ghosts" of the Indian speaker's "future." As "brothers" indicates, Christianity is another major theme in *The Book of Light;* in this eight-part poem, an aged Lucifer explains God's silence in the face of change on Earth.

Throughout her career as a writer, Clifton has won laurels. As recently as 1992, she received the Shelley Memorial Prize from the Poetry Society of America. In 1991 she won the Charity Randall Citation from the International Poetry Forum. In 1988 she received the Shestack Poetry Prize from the *American Poetry Review.* That same year she received the Woman of Words Award from the Women's Foundation. In 1987 she was one of three finalists for the Pulitzer Prize for Poetry. Additionally, over the years, she has received honorary doctorate degrees from three Maryland institutions—the University of Maryland at Baltimore County, Towson State University, and Washington College—and from Albright College in Pennsylvania.

These honors and awards have been acknowledgments of a vision and a style that have made Clifton's works both meritorious and accessible. Regardless of their genres, her works have been characterized by a deceptively simple language, by frequent reliance on African American dialect, by understatement and subtlety, by concreteness, by wittiness, by economy, and by musicality. In the main, Clifton's major thesis has consistently been that African Americans have triumphed because of inner strength that has its genesis in familial love and self-love. Her works have consistently proclaimed that African Americans, even the most "ordinary," possess the stuff of greatness, for without this capacity they would not have triumphed—by surviving—in the Western world.

Current Address: St. Mary's College of Maryland, St. Mary's City, MD 20686.

REFERENCES:

Amini, Johari [Jewel C. Latimore]. "Books Noted." *Black World* 19 (July 1970): 51-52.

Beckles, Frances N. "Thelma Lucille Sayles Clifton." In *20 Black Women: A Profile of Contemporary Black Maryland Women.* Baltimore: Gateway Press, 1978.

"Books for Young People." *Journal of Reading* 20 (February 1977): 432-35.

"Classroom Choices for 1978: Books Chosen by Children." *The Reading Teacher* 32 (October 1978): 28-46.

Clifton, Lucille. *Generations.* New York: Random House, 1976.

———. "A Simple Language." In *Black Women Writers, 1950-1980: A Critical Evaluation.* Edited by Mari Evans. Garden City, N.Y.: Anchor-Doubleday, 1984.

———. *The Book of Light.* Port Townsend, Wash.: Copper Canyon Press, 1993.

Cripps, Edward J. "Home Scene." *America* 134 (May 1, 1976): 393.

"Critically Speaking." *The Reading Teacher* 34 (March 1981): 732-47.

Fuller, Hoyt W. "For Young Readers." *New York Times Book Review,* September 6, 1970.

"Girlchild in the Promised Land." *Washington Post Book World,* November 10, 1974.

Heins, Ethel L., et al. "Fall Booklist." *Horn Book Magazine* 53 (October 1977): 522-54.

Hull, Gloria T. "Black Women Poets from Wheatley to Walker." In *Sturdy Black Bridges: Visions of Black Women in Literature.* Edited by Roseann P. Bell, Bettye J. Parker, and Beverly Guy-Sheftall. Garden City, N.Y.: Anchor-Doubleday, 1979.

Jackson, Angela. Review of *Good News about the Earth. Black World* 22 (February 1973): 77-78.

Jordan, June. "The Boy Who Didn't Believe in Spring. . . ." *New York Times Book Review,* November 4, 1973.

Kazemek, Frances E., and Pat Rigg. "Four Poets: Modern Poetry in the Adult Literacy Classroom." *Journal of Reading* 30 (December 1986): 218-25.

Kirkpatrick, D. L., ed. *Twentieth-Century Children's Writers.* New York: St. Martin's Press, 1983.

Lazer, Hank. "Blackness Blessed: The Writings of Lucille Clifton." *Southern Review* 25 (July 1989): 760-70.

Lehmann-Haupt, Christopher. "Books of the Times." *New York Times,* December 20, 1976.

Madhubuti, Haki. "Lucille Clifton: Warm Water, Greased Legs, and Dangerous Poetry." In *Black Women Writers, 1950-1980: A Critical Evaluation.* Edited by Mari Evans. Garden City, N.Y.: Anchor-Doubleday, 1984.

McCluskey, Audrey T. "Tell the Good News: A View of the Works of Lucille Clifton." In *Black Women Writers, 1950-1980: A Critical Evaluation.* Edited by Mari Evans. Garden City, N.Y.: Anchor-Doubleday, 1984.

McHargue, Georgess. "Children's Books." *New York Times Book Review,* May 15, 1977.

"A New Kind of Laureate: No Greeting Cards for This Maryland Poet." *Washington Post,* August 9, 1979.

O'Reilly, Jane. "For Young Readers: 'Tis the Season." *New York Times Book Review,* December 5, 1971.

Price, Reynolds. Review of *Generations. New York Times Book Review,* March 14, 1976.

Redmond, Eugene. *Drumvoices: The Mission of Afro-American Poetry.* Garden City, N.Y.: Anchor-Doubleday, 1976.

Review of *Generations.* "Books." *New Yorker* 52 (April 5, 1976): 138-39.

Richardson, Judy. "Black Children's Books: An Overview." *Journal of Negro Education* 43 (Summer 1974): 380-400.

Rush, Theressa Gunnels, Carol Fairbanks Myers, and Esther
Spring Arata. *Black American Writers Past and Present:
A Biographical and Bibliographical Dictionary.* Metuchen,
N.J.: Scarecrow Press, 1975.

Scarupa, Harriet Jackson. "Lucille Clifton: Making the World
'Poem Up.'" *Ms.* 5 (October 1976): 118, 120, 123.

Sims, Rudine. "Profile: Lucille Clifton." *Language Arts* 59
(February 1982): 160-67.

Slung, Michele. "Young Bookshelf." *Washington Post Book
World,* February 10, 1980.

Vendler, Helen. "A Quarter of Poetry." *New York Times
Book Review,* April 6, 1975.

"The Voice of a Visionary, Not a Victim." *Christian Science
Monitor,* February 5, 1988.

T. J. Bryan

Inez Clough

Inez Clough
(c. 1870-1933)
Singer, dancer, actress

I nez Clough was one of a number of black actresses whose
career was launched around the beginning of the twentieth
century. Clough, like the other actresses, began on the musical
stage because that was the only form of theater open to
African Americans. Nonetheless, she was a participant in a
landmark event. On April 5, 1917, Clough was one of the
actresses featured in white author Frederick Ridgely Torrence's
Three Plays for a Negro Theatre, the first sympathetic plays
about blacks with black casts to be produced in a Broadway
theater. Her talent was such that she was named one of that
year's ten best actresses by famed theater critic George Jean
Nathan for her role as Procula in "Simon the Cyrenian."
Although this is her most celebrated achievement, Clough had
a long theatrical career during which she helped to make room
for blacks on the legitimate stage.

Clough was born in Worcester, Massachusetts, sometime around 1870. One of the most recent sources of information on Clough states that she was educated in Worcester and
Boston, becoming a trained concert singer and pianist. She is
further said to have begun singing concerts in Worcester in the
1880s. Little is known at present of her family and education,
and her birth date is a learned guess based on the year she
began her professional career. There is also the possibility that
the reason so little information about her early years can be
stated with certainty is that her life is often confused with that
of a near contemporary, concert singer and pianist Estella
Pickney Clough, also of Worcester, who gave concerts in
New England and sang in Drury Opera Company productions
in New York during the early 1900s.

Artist Joins the Professional Stage

The path of Clough's career can be traced with certainty
after she began to appear on the professional stage. Clough's
first professional appearance was in a production of *Oriental
America,* in which she sang in the section entitled "Forty
Minutes of Grand and Comic Opera." *Oriental America* was
the first black show to appear in a legitimate rather than a
burlesque theater. Besides marking the debut of Clough, this
show also marked the initial performance of Ada (Aida)
Overton. The show opened in New York in 1896 and went to
London in 1897. Clough remained in Europe until 1906. She
sang in the chorus of the London run of *In Dahomey* in 1903,
but during most of her time abroad she sang alone in music
halls. She also found employment in the pantomimes presented in English theaters during the holiday season, twice appearing as a fairy queen and three times as principal boy—in
Robinson Crusoe, Red Riding Hood, and *Dick Whittington.*
(The leading male pantomime role is traditionally played by a
woman.)

Upon returning to the United States in 1906, Clough
found work in *Shoo-Fly Regiment* (1906, Bob Cole and J.
Rosamond Johnson), *Abyssinia* (1907, Bert Williams and
George Walker), *Bandana Land* (1908, Williams and Walker), and *Mr. Lode of Koal* (1909, the last all-black show of
Bert Williams). As productions of black musicals declined
after 1909, Clough sang concerts in major eastern cities and
worked in vaudeville.

In 1916 Clough joined the Lafayette Players, founded by
Anita Bush in that year. This was the first black stock

company with a repertory of straight dramas. Because of the lack of black dramatists, the company presented successful plays by white authors. Clough played in such dramas as Clyde Fitch's *The City, Sherlock Holmes in Sign of the Four,* and *The Lure,* a play about white slavery; in farces like *Charlie's Aunt;* and in operettas like *The Chocolate Soldier.* Her activity with the Lafayette Players continued through the rest of the decade. It was interrupted by her appearance in *Three Plays for a Negro Theatre* in 1917.

Movies and Radio Appearances

In 1921 Clough appeared in two movies for the Reol Company, *The Simp* and *Ties of Blood.* In the early 1920s opportunities were once more available in black musicals. Unfortunately, one of her first shows during the decade, *Dumb Luck,* closed after several performances on the road in 1922, stranding the company, which included Alberta Hunter as a featured artist. She had much better luck playing the role of Mrs. Hez Brown in *Chocolate Dandies* (1924), a show created by Eubie Blake and Noble Sissle and featuring a talented cast, including Josephine Baker, Valaida Snow, and Elizabeth Welch.

In 1927 Clough had the chance to play the lead in a serious drama, *Earth,* by Em Jo Basshe. The play centers on the conflict between Voodoo and Christianity among rural blacks in the 1880s. In the role of Deborah, Clough prays to God for the return of one of her six dead children and then turns to Voodoo. Finally she is struck dead after killing the Voodoo priest. Among the reviews cited in Jo A. Tanner's book *Dusky Maidens* are those of the *New York Graphic* and the *Amsterdam News.* The *Graphic* said, "Inez Clough, the grief-stricken and blasphemous Deborah, gave an uncommonly fine performance." The *Amsterdam News* reported that, "The chief feature of the evening was the stirring acting of Inez Clough as Deborah. She revealed herself to be an emotional actress of splendid ability." The show was produced by The New Playwrights Theatre on February 9, 1927, and it ran for twenty-six performances before being transferred to another theater.

Clough did not always escape the inevitable role for black women performers in legitimate drama at this time. She played a maid in the comedy *Wanted,* which ran for sixteen performances in July 1928. In February 1929 Clough played the mother in *Harlem, an Episode of Life in New York's Black Belt,* by Jourdon Rapp and Wallace Thurman. The play ran for ninety-four performances at New York's Apollo Theater. That same year she appeared in a presentation of the New Negro Art Theatre, *Wade in the Water,* a play by Jeroline Hemsely set on a Georgia plantation in 1885. Clough and Hemsely Winfield were the only professionals in a cast of amateurs. In May 1930 she appeared in a two-act pageant with dialogue by Jeroline Hemsely and music by Russell Wooding. *De Promis' Land,* which was presented by the National Negro Pageant Association of Chicago, had one performance at Carnegie Hall before a small audience.

In late 1930 Clough put her speaking voice, which by all accounts was magnificent, to use as a cast member in a weekly radio program on the NBC network. This depiction of "life among colored folk" was written by F. Carlton Moss, also one of the featured actors. The show's time slot was 2:15 P.M. on Sundays, and it ran for more than a year. The last play in which Clough appeared was *Savage Rhythm* by Harry Hamilton and Norman Foster, which opened on December 31, 1931, and ran for twelve performances. The play was a depiction of "primitive" life among rural blacks—Clough's character found it was her religious duty to stab her wayward, adulterous husband, Sweetback, who had earlier murdered a granddaughter of the Conjur-Woman during a party. There was a third and final movie appearance for Clough in Paragon Pictures' 1932 feature *The Crimson Fog.*

Inez Clough died of peritonitis on November 24, 1933, in the Cook County Hospital in Chicago after a long illness. Her career is a demonstration of talent and perseverance in the face of the great obstacles that were placed in the way of black actors and actresses. She was instrumental in establishing acting in the legitimate theater as a possible option for African Americans.

REFERENCES:

Johnson, James Weldon. *Black Manhattan.* 1940. Reprint. New York: Arno Press and the *New York Times,* 1968.

Kellner, Bruce, ed. *The Harlem Renaissance.* New York: Methuen, 1984.

Klotman, Phyllis Rauch. *Frame by Frame.* Bloomington, Ind.: Indiana University Press, 1979.

Patterson, Lindsay, ed. *Anthology of the American Negro in the Theatre.* New York: Publishers Co., 1970.

Tanner, Jo A. *Dusky Maidens.* Westport, Conn.: Greenwood, 1992.

Robert L. Johns

Helena Brown Cobb
(1870-c. 1918)
Educator, missionary, editor, writer, feminist

During her time, Helena Brown Cobb was the most widely known and most influential woman in the Colored Methodist Episcopal (CME) Church, now known as the Christian Methodist Episcopal Church. She served her race as a teacher, school principal, editor, and missionary. Cobb agitated for the formation of a missionary department for women in the CME Church; although it was not established during her lifetime, she was an inspiration to her successors, who continued her crusade. By 1918, the Women's Conventional Missionary Society had been founded.

The only daughter of Jonah and Louvonia Brown, Helena Maud Brown Cobb was born January 24, 1870, in the southwestern part of Monroe County, Georgia. Since the Browns were a very religious couple, from the start they gave their daughter a Christian upbringing. Cobb attended elementary school in Monroe and Pike counties, and in the fall of 1883 she enrolled in Stoors School, located in Atlanta. She entered Atlanta University in 1885 and graduated with high honors on May 28, 1891.

Cobb entered the field of education and for nearly a quarter of a century was among the foremost black educators in Georgia. She loved the classroom and believed that training young people was her calling. She was principal of Milner public schools for six years, and then for one year held the position of assistant principal of the public school in Columbus, Georgia. Her next move was to Haines Normal and Industrial School in Augusta, a private school for black children founded by Laney in 1883 and chartered by the state of Georgia in 1886. Cobb served Haines first as a teacher for seven years, then as principal for three years. From there she became mathematics teacher at Lampson Normal School in Marshallville and headed that school for three years. She resigned in May 1903. On December 19, 1899, while still teaching at Haines, she married Andrew J. Cobb, a minister; he died on September 7, 1915.

Helena Brown Cobb became an active and influential member of the Colored Methodist Episcopal Church, as it was known then, and began a career in missionary work. She became known as one of the most active missionary workers in the church as well as one of the first women to promote the development of a missionary department exclusively for women within the CME Church. When the General Conference convened in Nashville, Tennessee, in 1902, a group of women including Sarah J. McAfee, Mrs. M. J. Dinkins, and Cobb fought for the churchwomen's right to their own department. While the Missionary Council rejected the petition, Cobb had agitated enough to persuade the women who succeeded her to continue the fight, and a Missionary Council for women was established at the Chicago Conference in 1918. The group was at first known as the Woman's Connectional Missionary Council. Mattie E. Coleman of Tennessee—a physician, religious feminist, and apparently an advocate of woman's suffrage—was its first president. While *The Encyclopedia of African American Religions* reports that Cobb died on September 15, 1915, before she could see the results of her labor, she is listed as a vice-president of the council when the first roll call was taken in 1918.

Cobb was also known for her missionary work at the local level in Georgia. When the Georgia Conference met at Milledgeville, Georgia, on November 29, 1902, in her absence, she was unanimously elected president of the Woman's Home Missionary Society, as it was known then. At once she set in motion plans to stimulate men and women of the church to become involved in missionary activities. By planning and working, the whole church became involved in educational and missionary work.

Bishop Lucius H. Holsey suggested in 1904 that the church publish a magazine to be known as the *Woman's Missionary Age*. When the General Conference met in Memphis, Tennessee, in May 1906, members responded by unanimously electing Cobb editor-in-chief and naming the journal the official organ of the Woman's Missionary Society. As result of her management and writings, the *Age* soon enjoyed nationwide circulation. Cobb used her writing skills to produce another publication, a pamphlet called *Our Women—A Sketch of Their Work*. After she became editor, Cobb was often called on to write articles for leading black publications. In addition to her editorial work and publications, Cobb, though not known as a great orator, gave many public lectures.

Founds School for Girls

In 1908 the CME Church opened the Helena B. Cobb Industrial Institute for Girls in Barnesville, Georgia. She was the school's first principal. Later the school was renamed the Helena B. Cobb Home and School. The school's mission was to provide religious, moral, intellectual, domestic, and social training for black girls. The enrollment each year reached almost two hundred. According to Sara J. McAfee's *History of the Woman's Missionary Society,* published in *The Revised Edition of the Woman's Missionary Society,* "the school was unique in that it was the only school of its kind owned and operated purely by Colored people in the South." In December 1913 the U.S. government visited the school as a part of its survey of black education and reported in 1917 that the Helena B. Cobb Home and School was a small home for girls that was engaged in effective work. Although it was still nominally controlled by the CME Church, the management was vested in the principal. There were five teachers, all of whom were black, and 183 students. Cobb's attendance in the 1917 report was 150 day pupils and 33 boarders. While the day school students worked with children through the town of Barnesville, the boarding students were assigned such daily chores as cleaning, bed making, cooking, and sewing.

The school's plant value was estimated at four thousand dollars, and the plant consisted of about three acres of land, a two-story frame school building, two small cottages, and limited equipment for classes and dormitories. The school became a vital part of Cobb's life and was as important in the CME Church as Nannie Burroughs's National Training School for Women and Girls, founded in 1909 in Washington, D.C., was to the Baptist Church. Cobb Institute had opened a year earlier. Perhaps because of its location and the smaller size of the CME Church, Cobb Institute never enjoyed the popularity of the Burroughs school. Yet the love between Cobb and her students was mutual; the students affectionately called her "Mother Cobb." Her love for young people was demonstrated again as she took into her home several underprivileged girls and provided for their education.

In 1914 Cobb was elected conference lecturer for her church and was also in charge of the Georgia and Florida conferences. Though she did not live very long, Helena Brown Cobb was a role model for black women who worked with her and for those who carried on her fight for women's rights in the CME Church. She was also a dedicated teacher who made a great contribution to the education of young people of her race in rural Georgia.

REFERENCES:

Caldwell, Arthur Bunyan. *History of the American Negro and His Institutions.* Georgia Edition. Vol. 1. Atlanta: A. B. Caldwell Publishing Co., 1917.

Duncan, Sarah J. *Progressive Missions in the South and Addresses; with Illustrations and Sketches of Missionary Workers and Ministers and Bishops' Wives.* Atlanta: Franklin Printing and Publishing Co., 1906.

Harris, Eula Wallace, and Naomi Ruth Patterson. *Christian Methodist Episcopal Church Through the Years.* Jackson, Tenn.: Publishing House C.M.E. Church, 1949.

McAfee, Sara J. *The Revised Edition of the Woman's Missionary Society, Colored Methodist Episcopal Church.* Phenix City, Ala.: Phenix City Herald, 1945.

Murphy, Larry G., J. Gordon Melton, and Gary L. Ward, eds. *Encyclopedia of African American Religions.* New York: Garland Publishing, 1993.

Pegues, Ann. "A Brief History of the Woman's Missionary Council." *Missionary Messenger* 48 (October 1994): 7-8.

U.S. Bureau of Education. *Negro Education: A Study of Private and Higher Schools for Colored People in the United States.* Bulletin 1916, Vol. 2, no. 39. Washington, D.C.: U.S. Government Printing Office, 1917.

Jessie Carney Smith

Maria Cole

(1922-)

Singer, business manager, charity worker, producer, writer

Maria Cole, once a singer with Duke Ellington's band, is best known as the elegant wife of legendary entertainer Nat "King" Cole. Growing up in a privileged African American family from Massachusetts and attending a finishing school in North Carolina, Cole, from an early age, dreamed of being wealthy, well known, and married to a famous man. She was also willing to risk the security of the genteel lifestyle her family wanted for her in favor of pursuing her dream of becoming a jazz singer. Cole achieved some recognition in her personal career; however, more significantly, she is credited with being a major influence on the career of Nat King Cole, who died of lung cancer in 1965. Cole has kept her husband's legacy alive, while contributing to such causes as the American Cancer Society. Cole is the mother of five children, including popular vocalist Natalie Cole.

The second of three girls in her family, Cole was born Marie Hawkins in the Roxbury section of Boston, Massachusetts, on August 1, 1922. Her father, Mingo Hawkins, was a letter carrier for the post office at a time when civil service positions were among the most prestigious for African Americans. When Cole was two years old, her mother died while giving birth to Carol, her youngest sister. At age seven or eight, Cole and her elder sister, Charlotte, were sent to live with their father's sister, Charlotte Hawkins Brown, at the Palmer Memorial Institute in Sedalia, North Carolina, which was founded and directed by Brown. Cole grew up at the institute, a finishing school for African Americans, and recalls such visitors as Eleanor Roosevelt, W. E. B. Du Bois, Langston Hughes, and Mary McLeod Bethune. Despite the segregation that Cole and her sister Charlotte were subjected to in public places such as the Carolina Theater in nearby Greensboro, where they had to sit in the balcony, the Hawkins girls led a sheltered life. Their aunt's two-story house had a large living room, four upstairs bedrooms, and the luxuries of two baths and a telephone.

Cole's youth consisted primarily of studying, attending Episcopalian church services, and Wednesday night prayers. She listened to the radio, particularly enjoying Friday nights and a program that featured singer Frances Langford. There were occasional dances at the institute that were strictly supervised. Most memorable for Cole was Christmas, a very special time for the Hawkins girls and their aunt. When she returned to Boston during the summer months of her youth, Cole remembers avidly reading movie magazines and attending movies, which cost eight cents. Describing her childhood in a biography of Nat Cole that she coauthored with Louie Robinson, Cole stated: "Christmas and travel were the rare fun times, however, when we were in my aunt's charge. She ruled supreme over our lives, demanding discipline, rigorous school work, love of God and attention to our manners."

Singing Career Begins

Cole has always been intrigued by the world of entertainment. Although she received formal vocal and piano lessons as a child, they were not the kind of music that the young girl had in mind. After high school, her aunt Charlotte, who did not approve of the entertainment business, offered to send Cole to the college of her choice as long as she did not stay in Boston with her father. However, Cole, who wanted to become a jazz singer, chose to stay in Boston, attending Boston Clerical College in the mornings and working with a local orchestra led by Sabby Lewis at night. Later, when band

Duke Ellington and Maria Cole rehearse for a 1966 musical reunion.

leader Blanche Calloway needed a replacement singer for four weeks during the summer, Cole got the job.

During her third year at Boston Clerical, band leader Phil Edmond offered Cole a job singing for two weeks in New York. Her father agreed only because it was for a short time. Once the two weeks were over, Cole again pleaded with her father to remain in New York where she would live with an aunt and uncle while pursuing a career in show business.

Cole's aunt, Charlotte Hawkins Brown, had other plans for her. Brown arranged a job for her niece with the help of Mordecai Johnson, a friend and the president of Howard University in Washington, D.C. Cole went to work as secretary to the purchasing agent at Howard University.

Continuing her pursuit of a singing career, she returned to New York with Benny Carter's band using the name Marie Winter, presumably because of her family's disapproval. In 1943, she married Spurgeon Neal Ellington, a lieutenant in the army air corps. A member of the famous African American 332d Fighter Group during World War II, Ellington earned the Distinguished Flying Cross and returned to the United States in 1945. Cole was living in New York, and Lieutenant

Ellington had just returned from visiting her when he was killed during a routine training flight in Tuskegee on December 10, 1945.

Cole performed briefly with Count Basie and Fletcher Henderson. However, her major break came when she was offered a job with Duke Ellington's orchestra. Calling herself Maria Ellington (her married name), she came to Duke Ellington's attention when her sister Charlotte gave some tapes of Cole's voice to Freddie Guy, who was a guitar player in Duke Ellington's orchestra. Cole was working as a secretary at the Harlem YMCA when arranger Billy Strayhorn was sent by Duke Ellington to offer her a job as a singer in the orchestra. She accepted and became part of a trio including Joya Sherrill and Kay Davis, a trained lyric soprano with a master's degree from Northwestern University. Cole, whom critics found attractive and sophisticated, frequently had to clarify that she and Duke Ellington were not related. In 1946, Duke Ellington fired Cole after he learned that she was planning to leave the orchestra to become a solo performer.

Cole was doing her first solo performance singing two songs per show at Club Zanzibar before the Mills Brothers' show when she first encountered her future husband. Nat King

Cole, replacing the Mills Brothers with his trio, was reputedly enamored the first time he saw Cole singing at the microphone during a rehearsal at Club Zanzibar.

Maria and Nat Cole first became friends when he was able to get her tickets to see the Joe Louis-Billy Conn fight on June 19, 1946, in Yankee Stadium. Nat Cole was still married to his first wife, Nadine, at the time; however, he and Maria became engaged and began spending considerable time together.

His divorce from Nadine settled, Nat Cole and Maria were married on Easter Sunday 1948 in a widely publicized ceremony officiated by prominent politician and minister Adam Clayton Powell, Jr. at the Abyssian Baptist Church in Harlem. Wedding guests included pianist Hazel Scott, Powell's wife, actor Canada Lee, dancer Bill "Bojangles" Robinson, band leader Andy Kirk, and singers Nellie Lutcher and Sarah Vaughan. Bridesmaids were Duke Ellington's daughter-in-law, Mrs. Mercer Ellington, Mrs. Bill Robinson, and Maria's younger sister, Carol Lane. Her matron of honor was her elder sister, Charlotte Charity, and her young niece, Carol—later adopted by the Coles—was the flower girl. Cole's father gave her away and her aunt, Charlotte Hawkins Brown, was present despite her disapproval. The wedding reception, which was arranged by Marvin Cane, a song plugger for Shapiro Berstein, a music publishing company, took place at the Moderne Room of the Belmont Plaza Hotel. This event was controversial because, at that time, many of the hotels in mid-town New York City still discriminated against African Americans. The couple honeymooned in Acapulco, Mexico, and were such a media attraction that they were accompanied on their honeymoon by *Ebony* photographer Griffith Davis.

In 1948 Nat King Cole became one of the first African American stars on radio. His soaring career as a ballad singer and particularly the success of "Nature Boy," his hit song released on the Capitol Record label in 1948, afforded the Coles the opportunity to purchase a twenty-room Tudor mansion in Los Angeles' Hancock Park area. The couple came under attack because the neighborhood was exclusively white, Christian, and comprised of families with money and influence acquired over generations. The Coles withstood the controversy by using police protection during the closing on their home.

Not long after her marriage to Nat Cole, Maria Cole learned of the death of her younger sister, Carol. Carol's husband died a few months later, leaving a young daughter, also named Carol, born on October 17, 1944. The Coles decided to adopt Carol (called Cookie) even though this involved a court battle with Maria's aunt, Charlotte Brown, who also wanted the child.

Life with Nat King Cole

During the 1950s the Coles became increasingly affluent and socially prominent largely because of Nat King Cole's hit

songs "Nature Boy," "Mona Lisa," "Too Young," "The Christmas Song," "Answer Me, My Love," and "Unforgettable." As Nat Cole's wealth and reputation grew, so did attention to Maria Cole's sophisticated style and her forceful and sometimes criticized influence over her husband.

Cole concerned herself with the details of Nat King Cole from his skin care to his business arrangements. She designed a flashier, more distinctive wardrobe for him, including a lace tuxedo shirt, a mohair tuxedo, and file-top shoes. Some observers felt that Maria Cole also influenced the salaries earned by Nat Cole's sidemen.

Cole gave birth to their first child on February 6, 1950, a baby girl named Natalie Maria. From a very young age, Natalie demonstrated musical ability, mimicking her father's songs. Cole did not encourage this interest at first, preferring to protect her children from the stresses of the entertainment business.

In March 1951, the Internal Revenue Service ordered the $85,000 home of the Coles in Hancock Park seized and sold for nonpayment of income taxes. Nat Cole reportedly owed the government $146,000 for income taxes in 1947, 1948, and 1949. The Coles were able to save their home by borrowing the necessary funds from Maria's aunt Charlotte Hawkins Brown and through arrangements with Capitol Records to pay the IRS against future earnings on Cole's records. Their affairs were managed by the firm of Braunstein, Plant, and Chernin throughout the tax crisis, and Harold Plant, of the same firm, continued to counsel Maria Cole into the 1990s even after his retirement.

In 1950 Maria and Nat Cole took their first trip to England. That same year, Maria recorded several songs with Nat on the Capitol Records label. Pete Rugulo led the orchestra and arranged several songs for Nat and Maria Cole, most notably "Get Out, Get Under the Moon." Their tax problems and restricted budget may have curtailed this joint venture.

During the 1950s Maria Cole took up performing for a very short time, perhaps to alleviate financial problems. She performed at Ciro's in Los Angeles, the Fairmount Hotel in San Francisco, and at several East Coast locations.

On April 5, 1953, Nat Cole became seriously ill during a performance at Carnegie Hall. He was admitted to New York Hospital-Cornell Medical Center, where he underwent surgery to repair stomach ulcers. By 1954, he had fully recovered and Maria went with him on a tour of France, England, Ireland, Scotland, Holland, Denmark, Sweden, and Norway, where Nat King Cole was extremely well received.

During the next decade, Nat King Cole became involved with diverse entertainment ventures, including seven motion pictures and guest appearances on several television programs. In October 1956, he became the first African American to host a program on a national television network (National Broadcasting Company). The program lasted only one season because of southern white viewers' opposition to African American performers in Nat Cole's position. Early in

1959 Nat Cole took Maria and daughters Carol and Natalie with him on a tour of Latin America after the release of his popular album featuring songs in Spanish and Portuguese, *Señor Cole Espanol.* In July of the same year, the Coles adopted a son and named him Nat Kelly Cole. On September 26, 1961, Cole gave birth to identical twin girls, Timolin and Casey.

At the height of his career, Nat King Cole earned over two million dollars in royalties on the sale of recordings made for Capitol Records and an additional million for songs published by a firm created by Cole, Kell-Cole Productions. He also created a widely acclaimed musical revue, *Sights and Sounds,* which toured nightclubs and theaters in one hundred cities.

Nat King Cole was criticized by some African American political activists during the early 1960s for failing to use his status to assist in the struggle for civil rights. In an interview in the *Washington Post* in August 1963, Cole stated that he would not participate in the March on Washington because of an engagement in Pittsburgh, but that he thought it was a worthwhile activity. Maria agreed, stating that the march was a good thing as long as it was done ''in a dignified manner.''

In December 1964, doctors at Saint John's Hospital in Santa Monica, California, announced a diagnosis of an advanced stage of cancer, which began as a tumor in Nat Cole's lungs and spread to his liver. Cole died on February 25, 1965. Episcopalian funeral rites were held at St. James's Church in Los Angeles and he was buried in Forest Lawn Memorial Park in Glendale, California.

Maria Cole Becomes Producer, Keeps Nat Cole's Legacy Alive

Since Nat King Cole's death, Maria Cole has come to public attention on several occasions. She produced James Baldwin's play *Amen Corner* on Broadway in 1965, a project that her husband had encouraged before his death. In January 1966, in an article in *Ebony* magazine entitled ''Why I Am Returning to Show Business,'' Maria Cole explained her desire for self-fulfillment and to support the Cole Cancer Foundation. In 1971 Maria Cole published a book about her husband, *Nat King Cole: An Intimate Biography,* written with Louie Robinson.

Cole married television producer Gary Devore in 1969 and moved with her younger children to her native Massachusetts. She purchased an estate in the village of Tyringham in the Berkshires of western Massachusetts and a condominium in Boston's Back Bay area. Her marriage to Devore later ended; however, Cole continued to live in Massachusetts and serve on various boards and as director of the Massachusetts division of the American Cancer Society. Of her life up to that point, Cole told Charles L. Sanders in an article for *Ebony* in 1981, ''Not everyone may want my particular style of life, but if they do, I want them to know that it's something you have to work very hard to get and manage very wisely to keep.''

Maria Cole and her daughter Natalie Cole have remained dedicated to preserving the legacy of Nat King Cole. In 1987, Natalie Cole and Johnny Mathis starred in a PBS tribute to Nat King Cole. Maria Cole was interviewed and discussed her life with Nat Cole during a PBS special, ''The Unforgettable Nat King Cole,'' which premiered in March 1990. When Nat Cole was selected posthumously to receive the Lifetime Achievement Award during the thirty-second Grammy Awards ceremony in 1990, Maria and Natalie Cole were pleased to accept the award. Maria Cole reminisced about the good and bad times of her husband's life when Capitol Records named the month of February 1990 Nat King Cole Month. While his music attracted people of all racial backgrounds, Maria Cole remembered that African American performers of her husband's generation had a difficult time because of racial bigotry. She credited Nat King Cole and others with easing the way for African American artists who have followed and stated that although she was not the sort of person to live in the past or spend much time listening to her late husband's music, her favorite song by Nat King Cole was ''Our Love Is Here to Stay.''

While some entertainers and their families have failed to manage their fame and fortunes effectively, Maria Cole has prospered. When he was alive, Maria Cole steered Nat King Cole's career in positive directions. Since his death, she has kept his music vibrant while maintaining, for herself, an influential position in American society. She travels, spending time with her children and participating in various civic activities.

Current Address: c/o William Morrow and Company, 105 Madison Avenue, New York, NY 10016.

REFERENCES:

Cole, Maria (as Mrs. Nat King Cole). ''Why I Am Returning to Show Business.'' *Ebony* 21 (January 1966): 45-52.

Cole, Maria, with Louie Robinson. *Nat King Cole: An Intimate Biography.* New York: William Morrow and Co., 1971.

Colier, Aldore. ''Maria and Natalie Cole Keep Alive the Legacy of Nat King Cole.'' *Jet* 77 (February 22, 1990): 16-18.

Gourse, Leslie. *Unforgettable: The Life and Mystique of Nat King Cole.* New York: St. Martin's Press, 1991.

''Great Catches for the Over-40 Crowd.'' *Ebony* 45 (September 1990): 68-74.

Haskins, James, with Kathleen Benson. *Nat King Cole: A Personal and Professional Biography of a Man as Unforgettable as His Music.* New York: Stein and Day, 1984.

Logan, Rayford W., and Michael R. Winston, eds. *Dictionary of American Negro Biography.* New York: Norton, 1982.

Sanders, Charles L. ''The Elegant and Busy World of Maria Cole.'' *Ebony* 36 (October 1981): 58-64.

''She Likes to Travel Along Rather Than Sing Along.'' *Washington Post,* August 22, 1963.

"Two Decades of the Duke." *Ebony* 2 (January 1946): 11-19.

Dawn Cooper Barnes

Natalie Maria Cole

(1950-)
Singer

Natalie Maria Cole

Singer Natalie Cole, the daughter of Nat "King" Cole, rocketed to stardom of her own with her 1975 album, *Inseparable,* which won two Grammy awards. Cole's success continued throughout the 1970s, with another Grammy award-winning album, *Natalie,* gold and platinum records, and several hit singles. However, in the early 1980s, problems with her personal and professional relationships, combined with the pressure of constantly being compared to her famous father, resulted in Cole's addiction to drugs and alcohol. She eventually sought treatment and, once rehabilitated, she changed record companies and staged a successful comeback. When her 1991 album *Unforgettable—With Love* reaped seven Grammy awards, she proved to herself and to her critics that she had met and conquered the ghost of Nat King Cole, a spectre that had haunted her since his 1965 death. On this album, Natalie and her father sing twenty-two of his songs together by means of recording industry technology. The album incorporates Nat King Cole's incomparable musical gifts with Natalie's own inimitable vocal style. In a January 13, 1992, *Jet* interview, Cole characterized the *Unforgettable* album as one "that has allowed [me] to make my peace with his memory. . . . These songs are a gift from my father. The best gift. In a way, I'm finally free." Further vindication came from a music reviewer in the June 20, 1993, *New York Times* who said: "As a singer, she has accomplished exactly the kind of fusion her father might have achieved had he been a little younger and lived a little longer."

Cole is the daughter and first-born child of Maria (Marie) Hawkins Ellington Cole and the late Nathaniel Adams Cole, best known as Nat King Cole. She was born on February 6, 1950, at Cedars of Lebanon Hospital in Los Angeles, California. Her sister, Cookie, is really her cousin who was adopted by the Coles in 1949 after her mother's youngest sister died. Cole's brother, Kelly, was adopted in 1959 after her mother miscarried and believed she could not conceive another child. The next year, Maria and Nat Cole were quite surprised to learn of her pregnancy, which resulted in the birth of twin girls, Casey and Timolin, on January 26, 1961.

The Cole's marriage was performed by the Reverend Adam Clayton Powell, Jr. at Abyssinian Baptist Church, a Harlem landmark, despite Maria's being a staunch Episcopalian. In a November 22, 1993, *Jet* interview, Cole said that Maria's family considered Nat King Cole "too black for them." Charlotte Hawkins Brown, Maria's aunt, did not approve of the marriage because Nat Cole was a divorced musician. Many friends, onlookers, and relatives felt that the two were from completely different worlds.

Nat King Cole was born in Montgomery, Alabama, on March 17, 1919, and reared in Chicago, Illinois. His father, Edward James Coles, Sr., was a pastor of his own storefront church on Chicago's South Side. His mother, Perlina Adams Coles, was the daughter of a Baptist minister. Nat Cole later dropped the "s" from the family name. The Coles family was close-knit and highly religious; they were viewed as unpretentious, plain-spoken, "down-home" folk who lived simply and within their means. Edward Coles abhorred the influence of popular music on his children, especially the boys. But his wife Perlina Coles, his long-time organist, was Nat Cole's first piano teacher and ally; she persuaded her husband to let the teenager play jazz as long as he played for his father's Sunday services. When Nat Cole first met Maria Ellington at the Club Zanzibar, a popular Broadway nightspot, his trio was established as a first-class and highly successful musical ensemble. He had come through the lean years and hard times of a novice musician. Their romance rapidly intensified and once his divorce was granted, they were free to marry and begin a life together that was largely fast paced and exciting because of his fame and status as a premier song stylist and Maria Cole's desire for a lifestyle that her aunt's influence and tutelage had prepared her to assume.

Natalie Cole and her siblings grew up in an atmosphere of privilege and luxurious comfort. The Cole home was in the exclusive Hancock Park neighborhood of Los Angeles, a formerly whites-only enclave. When Natalie was just five weeks old, Maria Cole hired a nurse to care for her and Cookie and resumed traveling with her husband, a pattern that would continue throughout most of their marriage. When the children were older, they joined their parents on the road when their schooling would permit it. Since their education did come first, their aunt Charlotte, Maria's older sister, became their main caretaker, as well as Nat's personal secretary. The Cole children attended private schools or the "best" public schools: Cookie integrated the Thirty-second Street Elementary School; Kelly attended the University of California, Los Angeles, Experimental University Elementary School and Buckley private school; Natalie attended a preparatory school in Massachusetts.

Makes First Public Appearance

Natalie Cole's first public appearance was on *Kids Say the Darndest Things,* the popular Art Linkletter show of the 1950s. Her first professional appearance was in 1960 in a musical partially underwritten by and starring her father. Cole sang "It's a Bore" in the revised version of the original *I'm With You,* a black version of *Gigi;* the "new" version was entitled *Sights and Sounds: The Merry World of Nat King Cole.* By this time, Cole and her sister realized that their carefully planned and rehearsed home performances could get their parents' attention when they returned home after Nat's extended road engagements. Cole began to practice singing with a tape recorder her father had given her and finally felt she was good enough for him to hear her sing. After an a capella rendition of an Ella Fitzgerald song, he was stunned and said: "By gosh! You've got it!" When she was twelve years old, Cole formed the Malibu Music Men, a jazz trio, with two peers. One was Daryl Dragon, later the "Captain" of the Captain and Tenille, and the other was Skip Riddle, whose father was Nelson Riddle, the noted conductor and composer. Even Dragon was the offspring of a famous musician; his father was Carmen Dragon, also a conductor.

When her father died of lung cancer in 1965, Cole was in that awkward post-adolescent period when most teenagers feel gawky and insecure. His death caused her to feel cheated and angry because their times together had been too few; Cole has spoken of not crying about her father until years after his death. Still, his delight in her growing singing talent certainly prodded her in the direction of a singing career. Physically and talent-wise, she was the Cole child who most resembled Nat King Cole. But there would be no immediate professional career because her mother insisted that she, like all her siblings, attend college.

At the University of Massachusetts at Amherst, Cole decided on a career that did not involve performing. Her plans were to complete her degree in psychology with a German minor, get a medical degree and a post-baccalaureate degree at the University of Heidelberg (Germany), and open a children's clinic that would have a music therapy component.

But the music would not let go. Cole came under the spell of the noted black folksinger Taj Mahal because of his musical philosophies and synthesis of musical influences and styles. Soon, she was singing with a bar band, Black Magic, of which she was the only black member. Although she was never a "wild-eyed" radical during her college years, Cole did sport the required "big Afro" hairdo and participated in some black-oriented student programs. She worked with a local Black Panther food program for underprivileged children and demonstrated to urge the creation of a black studies program. During her junior year, Cole transferred to the University of Southern California in Los Angeles but was dissatisfied with the low level of political activism and the sparsity of black students who were not "star" athletes. She returned to Amherst and graduated in 1972 with a bachelor of arts degree in child psychology. Cole remained in Amherst and worked as a waitress and local singer until she began to be noticed by industry people of influence.

Singing Career Launched

Cole's career began to slowly take off as she appeared in higher calibre clubs. Her New York debut was in 1973, and her big break came in 1974 when she met Marvin Yancey and Chuck Jackson, two black producer-songwriters who heard her at Mr. Kelley's, a noted Chicago nightspot. Although they were more interested in Aretha Franklin singing their songs, they settled on Cole when their original efforts were thwarted. Cole's manager negotiated a contract with the Capitol record company, with whom her father had worked, and Cole's first album, *Inseparable* (1975), went to the top of the charts. From that point on, the Cole-Yancey-Jackson alliance was pure gold and the beginning of Grammy history.

A constantly recurring problem for Cole was simply being the daughter of Nat King Cole and being expected to sing the songs he had made classics. During this time, her efforts were geared toward finding her own style in her own way, not as her father's female clone. Not surprisingly, she remained professionally insecure and constantly wondered if she was really good enough to have earned so much so soon. Cole and Yancey also had a personal relationship that resulted in their marriage in 1976. Their son, Robert Adam (Robbie), was born in 1978, and they continued their working relationship, which was still successful. However, the marriage began to deteriorate because, as Cole said in *Essence* magazine, "Marvin wasn't ready to be domesticated. His roots were still in Chicago. I wasn't ready to move to Chicago. My roots were here in California."

Yancey was not only a producer/songwriter, but also a minister at the Fountain of Life Baptist Church in Chicago. During her courtship with Yancey, Cole had become acquainted with her father's side of the family, who were still in Chicago. As they became closer, her perspective on her religious life changed, and she left the Episcopal Church to undergo baptism at the Third Baptist Church in Chicago. She would need her reborn faith to sustain her as the decade of the 1980s approached.

Drug Crisis Affects Personal Life and Career

Although Cole was still successful in her career, her personal life was becoming a shambles and this, in turn, began to affect her professional relationships. While she loved her husband, the marriage had really never been on solid ground and she and Yancey separated in 1979 and later divorced. Cole's dealings with her manager and record company were becoming less productive and, for her, nerve-racking. Then, her drug use developed into drug abuse. Like many college students of the 1970s, she had experimented with hallucinogenic drugs, and as her career escalated, so did the amount and kinds of drugs she used. She became addicted to alcohol, prescription drugs, and cocaine. Cole said in *Rolling Stone* of her dilemma, "Once I started using drugs, I just didn't stop. My first marriage was ruined by that. I almost lost my son for being a negligent mother. My mother and I weren't speaking."

She was involved in a few car accidents but was never seriously injured and was placed on two years probation and fined for driving under the influence. In a serious attempt to overcome her problem, Cole entered a drug rehabilitation program but it was unsuccessful. When she was released, she resumed her drug use and kept on until even she could see that she was totally out of control. Other events were also taking their toll on her mental and physical health. In 1981 she and her entourage were trapped in the Las Vegas Hilton Hotel during a fire that claimed eight lives. Although she was not physically injured, she was hospitalized for shock. Later, her constant hoarseness was diagnosed as being the result of throat polyps, an all-too familiar ailment of singers who overextend their throats and vocal cords. When Cole voluntarily entered the Hazelden Hospital in Minnesota for drug and alcohol rehabilitation, her mother petitioned the Los Angeles Superior Court for conservatorship of her daughter's financial estate and it was granted. From late 1983 until May 16, 1984, Cole underwent a successful six-month treatment program. After her release, she had surgery to remove the polyps and that, too, was successful. According to Leslie Gourse in her autobiography of Nat King Cole, she said of her mother's support: "My mother was really my first support system, but I didn't know it. My mother has been in my corner forever."

Cole still celebrates the date of the last day she used drugs and relies on her mother and son and her faith in God to sustain her. She has said that when she was at her lowest, it was her son who was the first family member to forgive her. It would take all of these resources to keep her from resorting to drugs again. In 1985, Marvin Yancey died from a heart attack and Cole had to mend fences and prove herself trustworthy to record companies before she could resume her recording career.

Back on the Right Track

Cole changed record companies and recorded a successful comeback album on the EMI Manhattan label that had three hit singles. Romance again came into her life by way of a longtime acquaintance. Cole and Andre Fischer had met in 1976 at the Tokyo Music Festival. He was then founder and drummer for Rufus, a popular band fronted by Chaka Khan. Although Fischer had married three times since then, he admitted that he had loved Cole since that first meeting. After an intense courtship, they married on September 17, 1989, in Los Angeles, at Bethany Baptist Church. Before their marriage, Cole told *Ebony* magazine of him: "I'd never had a best friend in a man I was in a relationship with and I never knew that was possible."

The Cole-Fischer union, like the Cole-Yancey alliance, hit pay dirt in record time. Within two years, Fischer produced the Elektra album *Unforgettable—With Love,* which earned seven Grammies. It is ironic that Maria Cole was the one person to have reservations about the album described as "a gift from my father" by Cole. According to the January 13, 1992, issue of *Jet,* her mother stated: "On one hand, I'm very happy about what it's done for her career and for my husband's . . . a whole new generation is going to hear him now, and I love that. But still, I don't like to listen to (Natalie's version). I just feel that everything belonged to him."

Maria Cole also admitted to having been overcome while listening to her daughter record her track over her husband's tape in the recording studio. Cole, however, in *Jet,* expressed her thoughts about the album this way: "I feel like I'm sharing this one with my dad, definitely. I think he would have been tickled that not only did I go on to sing, but that I recorded not one, but twenty-something songs 30 years later."

In the same *Jet* article, Cole spoke of her father's spiritual presence as having been a major factor in helping her regain her career momentum during her struggles against drug abuse. Cole had high hopes for her second marriage since Fischer was successful in his own right as a professional musician and respected producer. It was very important to her that she had kicked the drug habit on her own and that her husband had nothing to do with it; therefore, they had started their married life with a clean slate. But they separated in 1992 on a temporary basis. Fischer is one of the producers of Cole's 1993 album, *Take a Look,* an eighteen-song offering of both well-known and somewhat obscure standards. In an interview with the *Los Angeles Times* Cole discussed the option she exercised in selecting the songs: "I had an option to do 'Unforgettable Vol. II,' I had an option to go back to R&B and pop, or I had the option of segueing into something similar to 'Unforgettable' but taking it maybe a couple of levels further. And I chose the last one."

In 1994 Natalie Cole released a new Christmas album, *Holly and Ivy,* produced by long-time collaborator Andre Fisher, her husband, and Tomy LiPuma. The album includes some of the traditional holiday tunes her father recorded on his classic album *The Christmas Song.* According to Clarence Waldron in the December 19, 1994, issue of *Jet,* sometime in 1995 Cole plans to release another album, this time to include "soulful tunes."

In referring to 1993 as the tenth anniversary of her efforts to conquer her drug problems, Cole discussed her plans to celebrate by thanking God for now being able to make the choice to stay sober. She mentioned that she and singer Bonnie Raitt, another survivor of the war on drugs, equate themselves to cats with nine lives and believe that their successful recoveries mean that evidently God has some "grand plan" for them. One reviewer of the 1993 album wrote in the *New York Times* on June 20, 1993: "'Take a Look' is ultimately a showcase for Ms. Cole's musical identity, as distinct from that of her father. If their stylistic kinship is as pronounced as before, this time Ms. Cole sounds emotionally liberated from the constricting role of worshipful daughter."

Cole was the featured guest on the July 21, 1993, *Arsenio Hall Show* where she was allotted a record number of performances that introduced her new album to the viewing public. She praised her husband and son Robbie, now fifteen years old and a professional drummer who played on the album. In December 1994 she starred in a Christmas special on PBS-TV's "Great Performances" and also made her movie debut when she was on the USA Cable Network film *Lily in Winter*.

An outstanding and courageous young woman, Cole has been honored by the NAACP with Image Awards in 1976, 1977, and 1992 and with the American Musical Award in 1978 and 1992. Cole is a member of such music industry associations as AFTRA and NARAS and of the Delta Sigma Theta Sorority. During the Thirty-fourth Annual Grammy Week events in 1991, Cole presented a Grammy Week benefit concert at the historic Apollo Theatre. The performance netted $100,000 to help keep the cultural landmark open. She later sang at a benefit for the NARAS MusiCares program that honored Bonnie Raitt for her efforts in promoting the careers of veteran artists, particularly that of the brilliant singer-pianist Charles Brown. This benefit raised $300,000 for the NARAS Foundation, which promotes the health and welfare of the music community. In 1994, a Natalie Cole Scholarship Award was established by the entertainment industry's Permanent Charities Committee. It will be administered by the Shelter Partnership of Los Angeles as a means of training and educating teachers of homeless children.

Cole is a successful song stylist and artist. She is on good terms with her relatives and she and her mother have a relationship built on mutual trust, respect, and love. Best of all, as noted in the *New York Times,* she has "stepped out of her father's shadow" into her own spotlight where she shines as "a mature performer who blends pop, jazz and soul with an ease and fluency that ... seem practically effortless." Her words in the *Los Angeles Times* speak about her new life:

> Even when you end up in the process of recovery, it's not a given that you're gonna be happy. And I'm happy, and that's a blessing, too. There are all kinds of ways of getting back, but the best way to come back is 100%.

REFERENCES:

Cole, Natalie. Television Interview, *The Arsenio Hall Show.* Fox Broadcasting Network. July 21, 1993.
Current Biography Yearbook, 1991. New York: H. W. Wilson Co., 1992.

Futrell, Jon. *The Illustrated Encyclopedia of Black Music.* New York: Harmony Books, 1982.
Gourse, Leslie. *Unforgettable—The Life and Mystique of Nat King Cole.* New York: St. Martin's Press, 1991.
The Grammy Winners Book. Burbank: National Academy of Recording Arts and Sciences, 1993.
Gregory, Hugh. *Soul Music A-Z.* London: Blandford, 1991.
Haskins, James, with Kathleen Benson. *Nat King Cole: A Personal and Professional Biography.* Chelsea: Scarborough House, Publishers, 1990.
"Music." *Jet* 81 (February 24, 1991): 34-38.
"Nat Cole's Widow Voices Objections with Their Daughter's 'Unforgettable.'" *Jet* 81 (January 13, 1992): 52.
"Natalie Cole and Andre Fischer: Singer Talks about Her Marriage, Son and Career." *Jet* 77 (October 16, 1989): 54-57.
"Natalie Cole and Husband Separate after Two Years." *Jet* 82 (May 4,1991): 34.
"Natalie Cole Says 'Take a Look' Album Celebrates Songs by Famous Black Singers." *Jet* 84 (July 5, 1993): 56-57, 60.
"Natalie Cole Steps out of Her Father's Shadow." *New York Times,* June 20, 1993.
"Natalie Cole To Appear at Caesar's Palace July 9-11." *Los Angeles Times,* June 13, 1993.
"Natalie Cole's Unforgettable Journey." *GRAMMY Magazine* 10 (May 1992): 12-17, 24-25.
"Natalie Says Mother Kept Her from Other Blacks." *Jet* 85 (November 22, 1993): 60.
Randolph, Laura B. "The Untold Story of Natalie Cole's Comeback Tribute to Her Father, Nat King Cole." *Ebony* 46 (October 1991): 112, 114, 116, 118.
Slater, Jack. "Natalie Cole." *Essence* 14 (October 1983): 86, 148, 150.
"So What's Next, Natalie?" *Los Angeles Times,* June 13, 1993.
Waldron, Clarence. "Natalie Cole." *Jet* 87 (December 19, 1994): 36-40.
Who's Who in Entertainment. 2d ed. Wilmette, Ill.: Marquis Who's Who, 1992.
Wild, David. "Natalie Cole's Unlikely Smash." *Rolling Stone* 13 (September 19, 1991): 19, 21.

Dolores Nicholson

L. Zenobia Coleman
(1901-)
Librarian

L. Zenobia Coleman became one of the most notable and widely recognized librarians in the state of Mississippi. Many librarians and educators were motivated and counseled by her because of her awareness of the essentials of

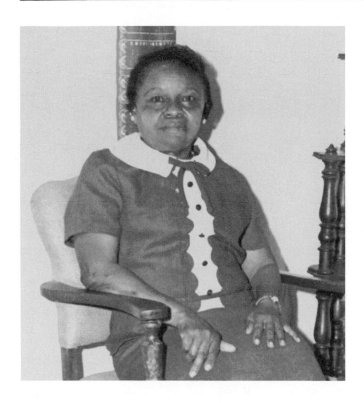

L. Zenobia Coleman

librarianship. Librarians and schools both in and out of the state of Mississippi valued her counsel and wisdom.

Coleman fought in the mid-1930s for a chance to become a part of the Mississippi Library Association. Though blacks were greatly discriminated against, Coleman nonetheless tried to make her voice heard by attending association meetings. In this way, she paved the way for future generations of black librarians. The drive of this uncommon woman to refute the view that blacks were inferior and non-achievers transformed not only her life but the lives of many others. For thirty-six years, from 1933 to 1969, Coleman served as librarian at Tougaloo College. After her retirement she helped plan the new library building.

The daughter of Joseph and Alice Hunter Coleman, Louie Zenobia Coleman was born in Childerburg, Alabama, on January 21, 1901. In 1921 Coleman received her bachelor of arts degree from Talladega College in Alabama. Talladega was one of the prestigious colleges founded by the American Missionary Association (AMA) at the end of the Civil War. Coleman did further study in education at the University of Chicago in 1925, 1926, and 1929. Columbia University and the University of Illinois library schools had become the principal producers of black librarians, graduating over fifty before 1937. Coleman received a bachelor of science in library service degree from Columbia University in 1936. In 1943 she received a master's degree in library science from Columbia University—a special feat for a black woman in this period. The subject of her master's thesis was "Changes Needed in the Library of the Small Liberal Arts College to Meet the Needs of the New Curriculum."

Coleman's first professional appointment came in 1924, a position as teacher-librarian at Brick Junior College, Brick, North Carolina. She held this position until 1932. Coleman's distinguished career as a librarian in Mississippi began at Tougaloo College in 1933, where she stayed until her retirement in 1969.

Participation by blacks in the programs of local and national library associations was limited during this era. Thus, Coleman was refused acceptance to become a part of the mainstream of library activities in Mississippi. Like a good soldier though, Coleman kept fighting. Under the most dehumanizing conditions, a few blacks made it a habit to attend library association meetings as regularly as possible. Utilizing freight elevators and service entrances to gain access to convention activities and "missing" luncheons and banquets did not shake Coleman's determination to continue to battle for the right to be heard. Black librarians today are beneficiaries of Coleman's courageous and selfless efforts.

Coleman's other career experiences included being assistant in cataloging at Alabama State College, Montgomery, Alabama, summer 1954; instructor in library science at Southern University, Baton Rouge, Louisiana, summer 1943; and visiting librarian at North Carolina College for Negroes (as it was known then), Durham, North Carolina, summer 1942. She published articles for library and education journals, including "Book Week as Motivation for a College Reading Program," *Wilson Library Bulletin,* 1945, and "Needed Program of Library Development," *Mississippi Educational Journal for Teachers in Colored Schools,* 1949.

Coleman was a member of the American Library Association; the American Association of University Professors; the Mississippi Association of Teachers in Colored Schools; the advisory board of the Carver Branch Library, Jackson Public Library; the National Education Association; and the Mississippi Library Association. She was also a member of the Women's Fellowship Club. In 1934 she founded the local chapter of Alpha Kappa Alpha—a national sorority for black women. She was a member of the Congregational Church. The American Library Association in July 1973 informed Coleman that "in recognition of your long and unbroken period of membership in the American Library Association you have been made a Continuing Member for life."

The L. Zenobia Coleman Library Named

The new library at Tougaloo College was named in honor of Coleman in 1974. She started the L. Zenobia Coleman Library Endowment Fund when she learned that the new library was being named in her honor. Clara Bedenfield, a protegeé of Coleman's, along with Jeanetta Roach, Tougaloo's library director, formed an endowment committee to further her efforts. Consisting of fifteen members, the committee, along with Coleman, raised $5,283 by June 15, 1974.

Believing in her own proficiency and proud of her legacy, during her career Coleman was willing to combat racial prejudice in the education and library professions and to bring books and readers together in rural Mississippi—often for the first time. Though her cry was often singular, in time librarians and educators in Mississippi and elsewhere were able to break down racial barriers and work toward common goals. Coleman helped to make possible the progress of generations of librarians. Zenobia Coleman is retired and is living in Tougaloo, Mississippi.

REFERENCES:

Coleman, Louie Zenobia. "Book Week as Motivation for a College Reading Program." *Wilson Library Bulletin* 20 (October 1945): 144-45.

A Directory of Negro Graduates of Accredited Library Schools, 1900-1936. Washington, D.C.: Columbia Civic Library Association, 1937.

Dunlap, Mollie E., and Anna O'H. Williamson, eds. "Institutions of Higher Learning among Negroes in the United States: A Compendium." *Negro College Quarterly* 5 (June 1947).

Rhodes, Lelia G. "'See How They Ran': Black Librarians in Mississippi." In *The Black Librarian in the Southeast: Reminiscences, Activities, Challenges.* Edited by Annette L. Phinazee. Durham, N.C.: North Carolina Central University School of Library Science, 1980.

Tougaloo News, June 1975.

Who's Who in Colored America. 7th ed. Yonkers-on-Hudson, N.Y.: Christian E. Burckel, 1950.

Casper L. Jordan

Lucretia Newman Coleman

Lucretia Newman Coleman
(18??-?)
Writer, educator, secretary, bookkeeper

Lucretia Newman Coleman contributed to the history of black journals in this country through her articles and essays on scientific topics. She also produced a biography and a popular poem. In addition, Coleman taught school. In 1893, Monroe Majors wrote in *Noted Negro Women* that Coleman had added to black journals of the time with her "usual fascination for saying things in her own way."

The details of Lucretia Newman Coleman's life and career are not well documented. The fourth child of William and Nancy Newman, Coleman was born in Canada in Dresden, Ontario, sometime during the mid-nineteenth century. Her exact birth and death dates are unknown. She accompanied her father to the West Indies, where he worked for a number of years as a missionary. When they returned to the United States, he became a pastor at a church in Cincinnati, Ohio. Early in her life, Lucretia Coleman was faced with the deaths of both her parents. Her father died in Cincinnati, and she and her mother moved to Appleton, Wisconsin. Shortly after-

wards, her mother became an invalid. Coleman spent thirteen months caring for her mother before her death; the young girl became head of the household and took charge of her siblings.

After completing her early education, Coleman went on to finish a scientific course of study at Lawrence University in Appleton. Her first job after graduation was as a high school music teacher. Her other occupations included clerking in dry goods stores.

Literary Works Published

In 1883, Coleman became the assistant secretary and bookkeeper for the African Methodist Episcopal (AME) Church. This was also the year that she published her first literary piece, a poem entitled "Lucille of Montana," which ran in several issues of the journal *Our Women and Children.* In *The Black Press, 1827-1890,* Martin Dann writes that the poem was praised by one contemporary as being "full of ardor, eloquence, and noble thought." According to Irvine Penn in *The Afro-American Press and Its Editors,* by 1884, Coleman's work was already being recognized by journals such as *The American Baptist,* which commented, "As a writer, her fame is spreading, not only in one or two states, but throughout the United States." Alice Dunnigan notes in the summer 1965 issue of the *Negro History Bulletin* that Coleman aimed her journalistic work "more at scholars than the people."

Coleman also published a biographical work sometime around 1890 through the AME Sunday School Union. *Poor Ben: A Story of Real Life* traced the life of Benjamin William

Arnett (1838-1906), the seventeenth bishop of the AME Church. Coleman dedicated the work to the "colored young men and women of America," whom she hoped would benefit from Arnett's knowledge of Christianity, which she called "the very breath of true nobility." Coleman also produced several articles for the *A.M.E. Review.* Thus, Coleman's association with the church was beneficial for two reasons: she was able to gain employment as well as recognition as a writer through the religious institution.

Lucretia Newman Coleman remains an obscure figure, and scholars of black history have written relatively little about her life. However, she should be remembered for her contributions to early black journals. Irvine Penn asserts in *The Afro-American Press and Its Editors* that her writings were "rich in minute comparisons, philosophic terms, and scientific principles." He writes further that she was a "painstaking" writer who wrote for scholars, and that she helped to raise the standards for the black press.

REFERENCES:

Coleman, Lucretia Newman. *Poor Ben: A Story of Real Life.* Nashville: A.M.E. Sunday School Union, [1890].

Dann, Martin E. *The Black Press, 1827-1890.* New York: G.P. Putnam's Sons, 1977.

Dunnigan, Alice E. "Early History of Negro Journalism." *Negro History Bulletin* 28 (Summer 1965): 178.

Majors, Monroe A. *Noted Negro Women.* Chicago: Donohue and Henneberry, 1893.

Mossell, Mrs. N. F. *The Work of the Afro-American Woman.* Philadelphia: G. S. Ferguson Co., 1894.

Penn, Irvine Garland. *The Afro-American Press and Its Editors.* Springfield, Mass.: Wiley, 1891.

Scruggs, Lawson A. *Women of Distinction.* Raleigh, N.C.: L. A. Scruggs, 1893.

Jessica A. Nelson

Mattie E. Coleman

(1870-1942)

Physician, missionary, school administrator, activist, lecturer, feminist, suffragist

Mattie E. Coleman was one of Tennessee's first black women doctors and one of a group of religious feminists who early in the history of the Colored Methodist Episcopal (CME) Church, now the Christian Methodist Episcopal Church, agitated for women's rights within the organization. A highly visible and influential woman in the CME Church, she was the founding president of its Woman's Missionary Council, an organization which has been known

Mattie E. Coleman

under a variety of names, including the Woman's Connectional Missionary Society. Coleman became known as well for her work on behalf of women's suffrage, and she played a large part in getting over two thousand black women to vote in the 1919 municipal elections in Nashville.

Born in Sumner County near Gallatin, Tennessee, a town that neighbors Nashville, on July 3, 1870, Mattie Elizabeth Howard Coleman was the oldest of four children. Ironically, it was also in 1870 that the CME Church was organized. The identity of Coleman's mother has not yet been uncovered; however, it is known that her father, referred to in published sources simply as Reverend Howard, was a minister in the African Methodist Episcopal (AME) Church. Mattie Coleman was born and reared in an AME Church parsonage; after experiencing a religious conversion, she joined the church when she was twelve years old.

Coleman graduated from high school at age fifteen, then studied at Central Tennessee College in Nashville. It is said that she had a beautiful voice, and she sang in the College's Walden Chorale Society as well as in the women's quartet. In 1900 Central Tennessee College was renamed Walden University in honor of John M. Walden, a bishop in the Methodist Church, a founder of the Freedmen's Aid Society, and the new school's first president. Meharry Medical College grew out of Walden in 1876.

In 1902 Mattie E. Howard married P. J. Coleman. A minister in the CME Church, P. J. Coleman no doubt influenced her decision to join his denomination. Mattie Coleman studied medicine at Meharry Medical College, graduating in

1906. She received a second degree from Meharry in 1932, becoming the first graduate of its dental hygiene program.

Around 1906, Coleman's husband was appointed pastor of Wesley Chapel CME Church in Clarksville, Tennessee, about forty-five miles northwest of Nashville. Coleman established a medical practice in Clarksville and operated what was in effect a mission for the needy. She was a woman with great concern for the poor and donated her time and knowledge to providing health care to those who could not afford it. From her own funds she also provided food, clothing, and shelter.

Coleman had a zeal for missionary work. The humanitarian nature of her medical practice in Clarksville, combined with her devotion to many aspects of church work and intense desire to help those in need, led to her election as president of the Clarksville District Missionary Society. From her Clarksville experiences on, Coleman's missionary vision was clear. The March 1, 1994, *Christian Index* quotes Coleman on the subject of missionary work. She is reported to have said in 1909:

> We can lend a helping hand to a fallen brother or sister. We can help the helpless. There are many bright boys and girls in humble homes that need a kind home and need to be brought to Christ. There are many homes that are dark and polluted, that may be light and pure by letting the sunshine of God's life in by a loving word and kind deed. Does that commission . . . appeal to us which says, "Go into the hedges and highways and compel them to come?" The gospel must be preached everywhere, and we must not only send the light we must carry it.

Coleman Joins Religious Feminists

Coleman became active in the struggle among women in the CME Church to change official rules that excluded women from helping to formulate the church's national program. At this time, in fact, women were barred from participating as members of conference delegations and were only allowed visitors' status at conference meetings. The problem of women's rights in the church extended beyond the absence of a Connectional Woman's Missionary Society, as the organization came to be known, and into the matter of women in the pulpit. In 1894 the bishops recommended that women be licensed to preach and carry on evangelistic work, but apparently it was not until the 1918 General Conference that the church leaders actually licensed women as local preachers, after which time several women made significant contributions to the church as preachers and evangelists.

Along with several other religious feminists in the CME Church, including Helena Brown Cobb and Sara J. McAfee, Coleman agitated for the establishment of a national women's missionary society. They made unsuccessful appeals to the General Conference at its meeting held in Memphis on May 2, 1906, and again at its 1910 session. In the October 1994 *Missionary Messenger,* P. Ann Pegues wrote that the women said, "We'll take low, saw wood, and plan another healthy battle." The women requested another hearing at the 1916 meeting and asked Helena B. Cobb to serve as spokesperson. When Cobb became ill, Coleman became the leader of the women's committee for the petition.

The women continued their fight. They attended a late night session of the Bishops' Conference held in 1918 and gave their presentation. According to Pegues, at the opening session in Chicago on May 2, 1918, C. H. Phillips, one of the bishops, presented the Episcopal Address, in which he recognized the women's plight:

> Our women furnished an example of consecration, zeal and efficiency without parallel in any period of the Church. Their Missionary efforts have been realized and localized for enterprises in charges, districts, and Annual Conference. But in a Connections sense, their value has been negligible. . . . It is fair to say that the fault is not with them. They have never been organized by the church of initiative. . . . An open door and opportunities most vast would challenge their best endeavors, really give them a larger vision of their worth in the Church, and an enlarged view of their relation to all its multiple interests and people conception of their own latent possibilities.

CME Bishops Approve Organization

The bishops as a group supported this view and believed that a general women's society would give the women a greater opportunity to exercise their gifts and talents. The women would raise money and use it for what they called connectional work, thus helping to move the church forward. The women and the bishops finally convinced the membership to approve the women's request. Yet the conference still had among its participants male skeptics who believed that the move was inconsistent with the church's program.

While the women now had their own organization, the Woman's Connectional Missionary Society, they functioned under a patron bishop whose charge was to help coordinate affairs. The new group of forty-one women held its first meeting in Nashville, Tennessee, and elected Coleman president and Helena B. Cobb first vice-president. Other officers included a second vice-president, secretary, treasurer, community director, chairman of literature, chairman of the art department, editor, and chaplain.

Coleman called the group to action on September 3, 1918, at 4:30 P.M. at Capers Chapel CME Church. She gave a glowing tribute to the women, setting forth the various ways in which they helped advance the women's movement within the church. The constitution and by-laws for governing the council were drawn. In her first address to the Woman's Connectional Missionary Society, published in McAfee's *Revised Edition of the Woman's Missionary Society,* Coleman quoted a loud cry that she had heard at the organizational meeting a year before: "Surely this is the age of women."

"And a most remarkable age it is," she added. Still speaking on women's progress, she said,

> In the records of woman's progress within the last few years there have been some notable events, which tend to show that her sphere is widening. Her ability to do things is being admitted; her loyalty and fitness unquestioned. . . . A number of states have passed laws providing pensions for mothers, some have passed new labor laws for women and children, limiting their hours for work. Other states have passed a law forbidding discrimination in salaries between male and female public school teachers.

Women's Suffrage Addressed

While accounts of Coleman's work concentrate on her church activities, she was also concerned about women's suffrage. In her research on the roles of gender, race, and class in the 1919 municipal elections in Nashville, historian Anita Goodstein of the University of the South in Sewanee discusses Coleman and Frankie R. Pierce as organizers of black women voters. They joined forces with the white women suffragists of the period and helped to change the course of history. Speaking about Coleman and Pierce's efforts to encourage black women to vote, Goodstein said in a November 7, 1994, interview that the two of them "got the women out in a notable way." Through their efforts, twenty-five hundred black women voted for the first time in the 1919 municipal elections in Nashville.

In her speeches before the women of the CME Church Coleman addressed the issue of suffrage and the need for increased opportunities for women in the church. In her first speech before the Women of the CME Church in Nashville on September 3, 1918, according to Sara J. McAffee's history of the missionary society, Coleman said: "The right of suffrage has been given her and lately rights in the great Methodist Episcopal, North and South, and the A. M. E. Zion, the Baptist and Episcopal, thus it is seen that woman's opportunities are growing larger and larger."

Coleman saw a need for the church to address other critical issues of the time, including social service and temperance. After identifying the critical need for social service workers throughout the world, she suggested that the church should serve as a center for social activities. Not only should the church "work to denominational needs and among those having monetary, education and other outstanding prominences," but it should serve the whole of society. She believed that the church should lead young people to engage in social service work. She asked the women in session at the second Woman's Connectional Missionary Society meeting to unite across religious denominational lines and join their sisters in the Methodist Episcopal Church in building more Bethlehem Centers to serve the social needs of young people.

Coleman's speech went on to discuss the issue of temperance, which had been a focus of missionary societies.

Coleman said that as temperance agents women had worked to bring about nationwide prohibition. Women were successful civic workers who helped to enforce the laws of the nation's great cities with untold results, Coleman continued. She noted the long-standing and close relationship between the sisters of the Methodist Episcopal and the CME Church in the South and acknowledged their interdependency. She urged women and men to serve as volunteers and "fill places in the Church and community" made vacant by World War I.

Coleman wrote to the women members of the church prior to the 1922 General Conference, where the Woman's Connectional Missionary Society would hold its first quadrennial session. She commented on a letter she had received from the Bishops' Council that endorsed their work and expressed an interest in their meeting. According to Othal Hawthorne Lakey's *History of the CME Church,* she stated that, in order to keep the council's support, she would need delegates who would be their "best and most interested women" and who would come to the conference "with a mind filled with plans and a heart filled with love" for their work. Although their organization was still subservient to the bishops, according to Lakey the bishops "were by no means negative or antagonistic" toward the women. Their attitude, however, was paternalistic and condescending. Lakey quotes the Episcopal Address for 1922, which reflects the bishops' patronizing attitude:

> It will be well for this General Conference to assist them (the women) in perfecting their connectional organization so that it will function harmoniously in our local and general work. We recommend that you rearrange your constitution so that there will be no conflict with any of our laws and customs.

Many years would pass before the women gained full recognition as a connectional organization and were no longer subservient to other departments of the church. As Lakey points out, however, in time the Woman's Connectional Missionary Society "evolved into the strongest and most viable organization of the CME Church." Coleman was one of the women whose exceptional leadership and commitment made this possible.

Madame President

Coleman's work as president is documented in reports of the women's meetings. She headed the council from 1918 to 1939, when she was succeeded by Rossie Thompson Hollis, whom she had inspired. Hollis and Coleman began their connectional work together during the 1920 meeting in Dallas. At the Connectional meeting in Louisville in 1930, the name of the organization was changed from Connectional Missionary Society to Connectional Council. Women of the CME Church established summer schools for the members; they also established a "literature headquarters" located at Paine College, Augusta, Georgia.

Around 1909, Coleman became the first dean of women and medical advisor at Lane College, Jackson, Tennessee. She also served as lecturer at the school. She was highly admired for her work at the college by other administrators, faculty, and students, and by the community residents as well. She was appointed medical examiner of the Court of Calanthe in Tennessee, a position she held for twenty years. Coleman was also the first black woman physician to serve as a state tuberculosis advisor and counselor. From 1939 until her death in July 1942, she headed the State Vocational School for Girls in Nashville, which had been founded by Frankie Pierce, organizer of the City Federation of Colored Women's Clubs, the foundation that supported the school. While superintendent, Coleman promoted the school's choir, which performed on campus and held concerts in the area. During her administration the girls attended Haynes School, where one became valedictorian and another salutatorian.

Although she was highly active in the church, Coleman was diligent in her medical practice and very involved in civic and social work as well. She gave medical attention to children and indigents. She provided food, clothing, and shelter for the homeless. She aided Mother Sallie Sawyer and Estelle Haskins in establishing the Nashville Bethlehem Center in 1894, and she was highly in demand as a speaker—at churches, at conferences to aid children, and before organizations such as the Red Cross and the NAACP. The work of Mattie E. Coleman is important to the history of women in medicine, the history of black women in the church, and the history of women's rights.

REFERENCES:

Cooke, Anna L. *Lane College: Its Heritage and Outreach, 1882-1982.* Jackson, Tenn.: Lane College, 1987.

Craig, Mazie Harris, and Eula Wallace Harris. *Colored Methodist Episcopal Church through the Years.* Jackson, Tenn.: Publishing House C.M.E. Church, 1949.

"Dr. Mattie E. Coleman." *Christian Index* 127 (March 1, 1994): 6.

Edmondson, Virginia. "Frankie J. Pierce and the Tennessee Vocational School for Colored Girls." In *Leaders of Afro-American History,* Nashville: Conference on Afro-American Culture and History, 1985.

Goodstein, Anita. Telephone interview with Jessie Carney Smith, November 7, 1994.

Harmon, Nolan, ed. *The Encyclopedia of World Methodism.* Nashville: United Methodist Publishing House, 1974.

Harris, Eula Wallace, and Naomi Ruth Patterson. *Christian Methodist Episcopal Church through the Years.* Rev. ed. Jackson, Tenn.: Christian Methodist Episcopal Church Publishing House, 1965.

Hartshorn, W. N. *An Era of Progress and Promise, 1863-1910.* Boston: Priscilla Publishing Co., 1910.

Lakey, Othal Hawthorne. *The History of the CME Church.* Memphis, Tenn.: CME Publishing House, 1985.

McAfee, Sara J. *The Revised Edition of the Woman's Missionary Society, Colored Methodist Episcopal Church.* Phenix City, Ala.: Phenix City Herald, 1945.

Murphy, Larry G., J. Gordon Melton, and Gary L. Ward, eds. *Encyclopedia of African American Religions.* New York: Garland Publishing, 1993.

Pegues, P. Ann. "A Brief History of the Women's Missionary Council." *Missionary Messenger* 48 (October 1994): 7-8.

Jessie Carney Smith

Johnnie Colemon

Minister, evangelist, church founder, educator

Johnnie Colemon is an ordained Unity minister who founded and heads one of the largest churches in Chicago, the nondenominational Christ Universal Temple, where she espouses the New Thought philosophy of a here-and-now religion rather than one that makes its followers wait for rewards until they get to heaven. Her disciples are taught how to improve the quality of life, to believe in the power of positive thinking, and to find Christ within themselves. Her philosophy is practiced by twenty-two study groups and churches nationally and internationally. Colemon rides a crest of success and has been recognized widely for her work.

Born in Centerville, Alabama, Johnnie Colemon is the daughter of John Haley and Lula Haley (Parker). Her father had wanted a son when she was born, but had a daughter instead, and named her Johnnie, after himself. During her childhood Colemon was troubled with an inferiority complex that stemmed from her appearance as well as from her struggle to win her father's approval. She told Shawn D. Lewis for *Ebony,*

> I spent my entire childhood trying to excel in everything, hoping to win his appreciation and affection. And on top of that, I was a very skinny child, very homely and jet black. I used to ask God why he had sent me here looking like this.

Colemon spent her college years at Wiley College in Marshall, Texas, where her feelings of inferiority intensified as she felt the pain of discrimination by her own black sisters. The leading sorority at the historically black college denied her admission because, in her view, she was the wrong shade of black. She graduated from Wiley in 1943 with a B.A. degree. Later, in 1977, she received her Doctor of Divinity degree from Wiley.

The educator taught school in Canton, Mississippi, and later in Chicago's public schools. Then a serious illness that doctors had diagnosed as incurable led her to the ministry. Although she grew up Methodist, she turned to the Unity church and sought a spiritual healing. Having read Unity's positive-thought literature and been influenced by it, she

Johnnie Colemon

enrolled in Unity School, located in Unity Village's headquarters in Lee's Summit, Missouri.

Colemon soon felt the sting of discrimination again, this time during her training for the ministry at Unity Village. Both inside and outside the church she had been called arrogant; in reality, her arrogance was a camouflage for the persistent pain rejection and discrimination caused her. Although blacks had trained at Unity Village before, they were forbidden to live there or to eat in the village restaurant; they sat in a roped-off balcony in the Kansas City church that they attended. Colemon became the first black to live at the village, although her cottage was set apart from those of the white residents.

In 1956 Colemon became an ordained minister in the Unity School of Christianity and opened her first church, known as Christ Unity Center, in a YWCA building in Chicago. Twelve years later, Colemon became the first black president of the Association of Unity Churches. Anxious to leave an indelible mark on the association, Colemon took advantage of the fact that fifty-two years had passed since the association had held a formal convention. In 1970, after some member churches withdrew their support, Colemon led a successful convention in Kansas City.

When Unity's bylaws were changed in 1974, Colemon's church withdrew from the association. She renamed her congregation Christ Universal Temple, and she founded and became president of the Universal Foundation for Better Living (UFBL). This service organization includes twenty-two study groups and churches in the United States, South America, Canada, and the West Indies, as well as the Johnnie

Colemon Institute in Chicago, where Bible classes, training programs, and classes for teachers and ministers are held. The institute teaches ministers to run a church like a business, with a worldly side as well as a spiritual one. In 1978 the first ministers graduated and were ordained. The UFBL also operates a bookstore housed in Christ Universal Temple and publishes an inspirational booklet each month called *Daily Inspiration for Better Living.* Colemon began a television ministry in 1981 known as *Better Living with Johnnie Colemon,* which for several years was broadcast on thirteen stations in the United States.

Christ Universal Temple, the church in Chicago that Colemon serves as minister, promotes a ministry of "teaching rather than preaching." According to Lewis, New Thought philosophy or Truth philosophy, as it is sometimes called, is not actually new; the philosophy was expressed by such believers as Buddha in the sixth century B.C., Ralph Waldo Emerson, Norman Vincent Peale, and others who embraced "positive thought." Hans Baer and Merrill Singer, in their *African-American Religion in the Twentieth Century,* note that Colemon is not as well known as the black minister Reverend Ike (Frederick J. Eikerenkoetter II), yet both preach "the gospel of material prosperity." Describing Colemon's teachings in greater detail, Baer and Merrill state that she preaches "Holy Materialism, positive thinking, and Practical Christianity." A number of other black churches had also begun to follow this trend. New Thought believers such as Colemon affirm the "right here, right now" philosophy as opposed to waiting for rewards in heaven. "You make your own heaven or hell on earth. There is no other heaven or hell," Colemon and her followers believe. In addition, Colemon uses no water to baptize her followers, believing that "water is only a symbol." She told Lewis that in her church "we call forth the Christ that is within each person, which is the *real* spiritual baptism." Her baptism is taken from the Bible, Mark 1:7, 8 and John 20: 19-22.

Colemon's church was first a study group that met in a YWCA building, but in 1963 the congregation moved to the relatively affluent Chatham section of South Side Chicago. In 1973 Colemon's church expanded to a two-building complex with closed-circuit television to provide multiple services. In 1985 Colemon and her growing number of parishioners moved into a new, four-thousand-seat facility on Chicago's far South Side, the largest New Thought Unity church in the world. The facility, located on thirty-two acres of land, also houses the UFBL bookstore and a Prayer Ministry, which offers a twenty-four-hour call-in service. The building was expanded in 1994 to accommodate the four thousand people who attend, and plans are underway to build a prayer tower, dormitory, the Johnnie Colemon Elementary School, a performing arts center, and a fitness center.

Colemon's experiences extend beyond the church. She has been a guest lecturer at a number of conferences, including the Festival of Mind and Body in London, England, the 1986 Boule of the Alpha Kappa Alpha Sorority, and the Prayer Breakfast held in Atlanta, Georgia. She has also been a guest speaker and consultant on radio and television shows. She is a member of the International New Thought Alliance (INTA) and was district president and chair of the board of directors for the sixtieth annual INTA Congress. Among the numerous honors and awards Colemon has received are the Tremendous "Ten Years" of the Unity Chicagoland Association; Deep Appreciation of Unity, Association of Unity Churches; Golden Anniversary Award, Alpha Kappa Alpha Sorority; Recognition Award for Service to Humanity, First CP Church; Service to Youth Award, YMCA; and Outstanding Achievement in Gospel Ministry, Youth for Christ. Colemon also received the Women's Day Annual Black Excel Operation PUSH (People United to Serve Humanity) Award, as well as the Year of the Woman Award, and the Excellence in Religion Award, both from the PUSH Foundation. She was named one of 100 Outstanding Black Women in Dallas in 1985. Keys to the cities of Brooklyn, Atlanta, Detroit, and Chicago have been awarded to Colemon.

Colemon was first married to Richard Colemon, who managed a delicatessen in Chicago. After he died she married Don Nedd, who was a minister at the Brooklyn Truth Center for Better Living, a New York branch of her church. He died in December of 1985. They had no children. Colemon overcame her inferiority complex and survived an "incurable disease" to become a highly effective and successful spiritual leader of New Thought philosophy. She summarized her thoughts in a statement she made in a September 1, 1994, interview:

> What my mind can conceive, I can achieve. In other words, if my mind conceives lack and limited thoughts, poverty, inflation, I will achieve just that. If my mind conceives this statement: "You can have anything you want, if you desire it badly enough." I can be anything I desire to be. You can accomplish anything you set out to accomplish if you hold to that desire with singleness of purpose. Health, Joy, Love and Prosperity will be yours. God is waiting for you to recognize and accept what you desire. Remember, it works if you work it.

Current Address: Christ Universal Temple for Better Living, 11901 South Ashland Avenue, Chicago, IL 60643.

REFERENCES:

Baer, Hans A., and Merrill Singer. *African-American Religion in the Twentieth Century*. Knoxville: University of Tennessee Press, 1992.

Colemon, Johnnie. Questionnaire. Fisk University, Nashville, Tennessee.

———. Telephone interview with Jessie Carney Smith, September 1, 1994.

Lewis, Shawn D. "Dawning of a New Day." *Ebony* 33 (July 1978): 84-86, 88, 90, 92.

Melton, J. Gordon, ed. *The Encyclopedia of American Religions*. Vol. 2. New York: Triumph Books, 1991.

Murphy, Larry G., J. Gordon Melton, and Gary L. Ward, eds. *Encyclopedia of African American Religions*. New York: Garland Publishing, 1993.

Poinsette, Alex. "Rev. Johnnie Colemon's Dream Church." *Ebony* 40 (December 1985): 74-80.

Who's Who among Black Americans, 1994-95. 8th ed. Detroit: Gale Research, 1994.

Jessie Carney Smith

Florence O. Cole-Talbert
(1890-1961)
Opera singer, educator

Florence O. Cole-Talbert has been hailed as the first African American woman to play the demanding title role in Verdi's *Aida*. Called the Leontyne Price of her day, she is a legendary figure in the annals of African American music history. The *Chicago Defender* for January 1916 described Cole-Talbert as "an artist who sings with volume, sweetness and clearness." Not only did she contribute to the African American community through performance, she was also a teacher and active member of several cultural and music organizations, including the National Association of Negro Musicians (NANM). She prepared herself for success through years of severe and unremitting study that allowed her to dominate the opera scene as a black woman. She was one of a few black vocalists performing operatic roles abroad and her singing earned her great acclaim during her career.

Cole-Talbert was born to Thomas A. and Sadie Chandler Cole on June 17, 1890. At an early age, she began her studies in piano and dramatic reading. She came from a musically talented family. Her father was an excellent basso and a fine dramatic reader. Her mother was a talented mezzo-soprano, and by the time of Florence Cole-Talbert's birth, she had traveled extensively with the Fisk Jubilee Singers and had become quite well-known.

Cole-Talbert's maternal grandmother, Mrs. Hatfield-Chandler, a patron of music with a high soprano voice, was the organizer of and a singer in the first "colored" Baptist Choir in Cincinnati, Ohio. Her maternal grandfather Hatfield was an active member of the Underground Railroad. At age six, Cole-Talbert began to study piano performance, which became her initial career ambition. Even after her family's move to California when she was eight years old, she continued to learn the piano at a rapid rate. As a teenager, she taught instrumental music to help pay for her vocal lessons with her first teacher, Gloria Mayne Windsor, and accompanied her mother in public concerts.

Florence O. Cole-Talbert

Ambition Becomes Singing

As a student at Los Angeles High School, Cole-Talbert studied ancient and modern languages as well as music theory. She participated in music programs and was the first black soloist for the Glee Club. She won most of her praise through her piano performances. At age fifteen, after viewing a performance of *Aida,* she changed her career ambitions to singing. In an interview with Ruby Goodwin, as quoted by Patricia Turner's "In Retrospect: Florence Cole-Talbert," Cole-Talbert recalled:

> I was impressed by the opera as nothing had ever moved me before. I sat breathlessly watching the artists, and as the opera progressed, a desire (an impossible desire, so it seemed at the time) took possession of me. I wanted to sing the title role in *Aida.* I could see myself thrilling large audiences as I myself was thrilled.

At the age sixteen, Cole-Talbert was chosen to accompany the famous Madam E. Azalia Hackley, a black classical soprano, at a recital in Los Angeles. Hackley and Cole-Talbert's high school teachers recognized her exceptional talent and encouraged her to concentrate on developing her voice. With this encouragement, Cole-Talbert studied voice with John B. Miller, Herman Devries, and Oscar Saenger in Los Angeles. Maud Cuney-Hare quotes Sanger in *Negro Musicians and Their Music* as saying, "her voice [was] a beautiful soprano, which she [used] with consummate skill."

Eusebio Concialdi, an Italian baritone, urged Cole-Talbert to study Italian operatic roles and sang duets with her at

several concerts. In the 1910s she was the only black in her high school graduating class of over two hundred. She was also selected soloist for the commencement exercises. Cole-Talbert was the first black woman to take part in a high school commencement program in Los Angeles.

After high school graduation, Cole-Talbert went to the University of Southern California (USC) College of Music, where she specialized in the study of oratorio under Mrs. Rockhold-Robbins. After graduation from USC, she joined Hahn's Jubilee Singers, a group promoted by the Midland Lyceum Bureau, with whom she spent about a year. The singers toured extensively in the middle and western parts of the United States and Canada. Through this experience, Cole-Talbert had the chance to work with musicians who would become famous in their own right, such as organist Walter Gossette and lyricist, bandleader, and singer Noble Sissle. During her stint with Hahn's Jubilee Singers, she met and married musician Wendall P. Talbert. He was a graduate of Wilberforce College, who also studied at the Oberlin College Conservatory of Music. He studied piano and composition and subsequently became known as a jazz band leader and pianist. The couple performed together until the end of 1915.

When Wendall Talbert switched to jazz, their careers took different routes. By 1916 the Talberts had separated, and Cole-Talbert left Hahn's Jubilee Singers. She settled in Chicago, Illinois, where she became a vocal student at the Chicago Musical College. Her talents were recognized early in her attendance there, and she was encouraged to sing in student programs.

Talbert was the first black person to appear on a student program at Chicago's Musical College. As a first year student, she proved her training and technique to be far superior to that of any of the other students. In her first performance, she rendered the difficult "Indian Bell Song" from *Lakmé* by Delibes, which was met with roaring applause. According to the article "Praises Mme. Talbert" published in the *Chicago Defender,* for the most difficult selection of coloratura style, "her voice was clear and [had the] flexibility necessary for the song and her expression and understanding of the text gave the audience a splendid interpretation." The audience could not deny Cole-Talbert's exceptional gift of song, as noted by J. B. Miller, who said in the same article that "color has no bar to an artist and . . . when they have the ability to sing as Madame Talbert they should always be encouraged." Cole-Talbert's talent and perseverance provided her with the determination to complete her musical studies in a year instead of the average four.

At her graduation in 1916, she was awarded Musical College's coveted Diamond Medal for outstanding achievement in vocal studies and for having the highest average in her class. As the graduation soloist (she was the first black to receive this honor), she performed "Caro Nome" from Verdi's *Rigoletto* in Italian, accompanied by the Chicago Symphony Orchestra. Her achievements earned her a cover story in the first issue of *Half Century Magazine,* which began publication in August 1916, in Chicago.

Extensive Concert Tours Begin

After graduation, Cole-Talbert went on to do an extensive series of concerts between 1916 and the early 1920s. She traveled throughout the United States and became a great favorite in all parts of the country. Reviews of her concerts and reports on her activities appeared regularly in contemporary publications such as the *Chicago Defender* and the *Competitor*. Turner noted in "In Retrospect" that the latter publication hailed Cole-Talbert as "An Idol of the Concert Stage." Her base cities were Chicago, Detroit, and Los Angeles, where she participated in various community activities. In Chicago, Cole-Talbert was a charter member of the National Association of Negro Musicians, and in Detroit she was president of the Detroit Etude Society.

Throughout her concert years, Cole-Talbert studied under Oscar Saenger and other great voice teachers and shared many recital programs with the contralto Daisy Tapley. In 1918, Cole-Talbert was a soloist with the Chicago Symphony Orchestra, and on April 16, 1918, she made her New York recital debut at Aeolian Hall. During this period, Cole-Talbert also performed at various colleges. On January 22, 1919, at the First Congregational Church, she, along with the Howard University Choral Society, rendered Handel's *Messiah* under the direction of Lulu Vere Childers. Along with a solo in Handels' *Messiah,* she was also the soloist in "Hiawatha" and "Laughing Water-Minnehaha." The *Competitor,* June 1920, quotes a critic from the *Washington Times,* who wrote that Cole-Talbert's "voice was pure and high and held appealing expression that was exquisite at times, then full of the sunlight of spring, or again told this gripping tale with pathos and sympathy."

Like many other American artists of her time, Cole-Talbert decided to go to Europe for further study. Before leaving, she was given a farewell reception by the Cosmopolitan Arts Society of Los Angeles on June 22, 1925. On July 18, 1925, she left for Europe on a two year tour for additional vocal studies under Delia Valeri and Vito Carnevale in Italy at the Summer School for Americans at the Villa d'Este. Continuing with her studies, she spent a year in Rome studying with Julian Quexada, a Chilean, who coached her in voice and dramatic interpretation. Furthering her training, Cole-Talbert went to Milan and was coached by Sylvo Puccetti and Mario Bellini. In Paris, she received further operatic coaching from M. Marcel Picheran of the Opéra Comique, placing special emphasis on Verdi's *Aida* and Meyerbeer's *L'Africaine.*

Makes Debut in Italy

Cole-Talbert's true breakthrough came in March 1927 when she debuted—to critical acclaim—in the title role of Verdi's *Aida* at the Communale Theater in Cozenza, Italy. According to Raoul Dodd in *Blacks in Classical Music,* it is believed that she was the first black woman to perform the role with considerable success with a professional company. The role of *Aida* is a difficult one to perform successfully, especially in front of a critical audience. And the audience in Cozenza, Italy, was known for its strong reactions—either angry hisses or fervid acclamation. She won the audiences' approval, however, and was hailed by Italy's newspapers as a premier opera singer with a bright future. Calabria's newspaper, *Fascista,* was quoted in the *Competitor* for June 1920 as reporting: "The title role was taken by Signorina Florence Talbert in a praiseworthy manner. Her beautiful voice and expressive acting won her hearty applause from the large audience." Through that performance, she was invited to become the first black American to become a member of the Facista Group of Lyric Artists. After three performances of *Aida,* Cole-Talbert continued to share her vocal talent with various concert appearances in Rome and Paris. During a concert before the Sicilian Society, she sang "some Indian and Negro melodies which were greatly appreciated" by her admiring audience, according to the October 29, 1927, *New York Age. Blacks in Classical Music* quotes the *Il Messagero* in Rome, which reported on another occasion: "All of the artists did well, but the greater success was won by Florence Talbert in the arias from *Aida* and *L'Africaine.* Her voice of velvety quality was such as to overwhelm the audience."

In the fall of 1927, Cole-Talbert returned to the United States. She continued performing in concerts, becoming one of the more popular concert singers in the African American community. One critic quoted in Turner's "In Retrospect" noted that although "her singing won her much praise in Europe, she never was able to break into organized opera in the United States of America." She was honored in July 1953 by the National Negro Opera Guild with a Certificate of Merit as "The First Lady in Grand Opera."

As she toured the United States, she began to accept voice students and eventually moved from the role of performer to that of teacher. In 1930, she began teaching at Bishop College in Marshall, Texas, where she became the first black director of music.

On one of her tours through the South, Cole-Talbert met Benjamin F. McCleave, a physician and dentist from Memphis, Tennessee. After a long courtship with the widower, she married him on August 27, 1930. At that time, she reduced her touring activities, opened her own studio, and continued teaching at various Southern colleges. With no children of her own, she helped to rear her husband's four children. At Fisk University, she was the head of the voice department, and in later years she was a member of the music faculty and head of the voice department at Tuskegee Institute when William L. Dawson expanded the school's music program.

Educator and Mentor

Cole-Talbert's greatest joy came from teaching voice to young people in her Memphis studio. One of her esteemed students was the opera singer Vera Little, a mezzo soprano who made her debut as Carmen at the State Opera House in Berlin in 1957. Not only did she serve as a teacher, but Cole-Talbert also served as a mentor to young musicians. She was one of the first to encourage Marian Anderson, who later became a world-famous opera singer, to study voice. In an *Atlanta Daily World* article published at her death, it was said that Cole-Talbert heard Anderson sing once and told her, "Child, child, you must be a singer." Through a benefit concert given by Cole-Talbert, money was raised for a scholarship to train Anderson's voice.

Although she cut back on concert touring, Cole-Talbert remained musically and culturally active in other ways. She became an active charter member (1919) of the National Association of Negro Musicians, often serving as chairperson of the Conference of Artists and the Voice Conference. She, along with Mrs. T. H. Watkins, organized the Memphis Music Association. At a historic convention in 1924, Cole-Talbert and her sorority sister Alice Dunbar-Nelson presented the national hymn for Delta Sigma Theta Sorority that they had written together. Besides composing her sorority's national hymn, Cole-Talbert's musical arrangements of spirituals were often used in her recitals. In Memphis, Cole-Talbert was an active member and one of the founders of the Christian Science Society Church, as well as a member of the Elite Club and the Women's Medical Auxiliary.

In spite of rigid racial barriers, Cole-Talbert found a high place in the music and entertainment fields. Many warned her that her race was a serious handicap to her survival in the operatic world, but she did not waiver from her dreams. Instead, she continuously reminded herself of her favorite motto, which was: "Aim at the stars if you just hit the chimney tops." In an interview, she once told Ruby Berkley Goodwin:

> I have found this [psychology] an invaluable help to me in my art. The understanding of its basic laws and adherence to the same has enabled me to rise above every unpleasant situation which has confronted me. I know beyond a shadow of a doubt that no one can hurt me but myself. I alone am responsible for my success or failure.

Cole-Talbert died on April 3, 1961, in Memphis, Tennessee, at age 70. She was survived by her husband and her stepchildren, Gladys V. Johnson, Compton, California; Benjamin F. McCleave Jr., Detroit; and Richard McCleave, Los Angeles. Services were held at the Chapel of the Palms on April 10, 1961, in Los Angeles, where she was admired and known as "Our Divine Florence."

Her repertoire, which was large and varied, included operatic arias from French, Italian and English composers; songs from contemporary composers like Charles Wakefield Cadman, Thurlow Lieurance, and William Grant Still; and spirituals arranged by Harry T. Burleigh, Hall Johnson and J. Rosamond Johnson. Possessed with a strong, compelling drive to succeed, despite hardships, trials, tribulations and disappointments, Cole-Talbert persevered through it all. In the interview with Goodwin, she stated that "Art is not racial. Art is universal. And to be an artist one must aim not only to rank with those of a certain group but to rank with all of those who have ever accomplished anything worth while in that line

of endeavor." Her story is inspirational and shows how one black woman broke through barriers with the strength of her talent and achieved success.

REFERENCES:

Beasley, Delilah. *The Negro Trailblazers of California.* Los Angeles: Privately printed, 1919.

Cuney-Hare, Maud. *Negro Musicians and Their Music.* New York: DeCapo Press, 1974.

Dodd, Raoul Abdul. *Blacks in Classical Music.* New York: Dodd, Mead and Company, 1977.

"Florence Cole-Talbert Back from Europe." *New York Age,* October 29, 1927.

"Florence Cole-Talbert on KECA Broadcast." *Sentinel,* January 28, 1954.

Giddings, Paula. *In Search of Sisterhood: Delta Sigma Theta and the Challenge of the Black Sorority Movement.* New York: Morrow, 1988.

Goodwin, Rudy Berkely. "She Aimed at the Stars and Hit Her Mark: An Inspirational Gem Concerning the Rise and Fame of One of America's First Colored Artists." *The Bronzeman* (c. 1930). Reprinted in *Black Perspective in Music* 12 (Spring 1984): 72-75.

Half Century Magazine, August 16, 1916. Reprinted in *Black Perspective in Music* 12 (Spring 1984): 63-65.

Logan, Rayford W. *Howard University: The First Hundred Years (1867-1967).* New York: New York University Press, 1969.

"Madame Florence Cole-Talbert McCleave: Grand Opera's First Negro Soprano Dies at Age 70." *Atlanta Daily World,* April 16, 1961.

"Madame Florence Cole Talbert Met Challenge and Became Opera Star." *Chicago Defender,* August 1, 1953.

"Madame Florence Cole Talbert Returns After Three Years in Europe." *Amsterdam News,* October 26, 1927.

"Madame Florence Cole-Talbert to be Heard in Sunday Afternoon Recital." *Amsterdam News,* November 2, 1927.

"Mme. Florence Cole Talbert, Famed Soprano, Dies in Tennessee." *Los Angeles Sentinel,* April 17, 1961.

"Mme. McCleave's Great Voice is Silent Forever." *Kansas City Call,* April 14, 1961.

"Mrs. Florence Talbert, Pioneer Opera Singer is Buried In L.A." *Baltimore Afro-American,* April 22, 1961.

"Praises Madame Talbert." *Chicago Defender,* January 1916.

Turner, Patricia. *Dictionary of Afro-American Performers.* New York: Garland Publishing, 1990.

———. "In Retrospect: Florence Cole Talbert." *Black Perspective in Music* 12 (Spring 1984): 57-79.

COLLECTIONS:

Cole-Talbert's scrapbook and other materials are held by her stepdaughter, Gladys McCleave Johnson. Her niece, Florence Cole Berg, has photographs and clippings.

Marlo Price

Barbara-Rose Collins

(1939-)

Community activist, state representative, U.S. representative

Motivated to help improve her neighborhood and the public school system, Barbara-Rose Collins became a community activist and a regional Detroit school board member. To accomplish more on a larger scale, she moved to the state legislature and was successful in advancing women's issues, passing consumer-oriented legislation, and promoting the interests of the economically and socially disadvantaged. Eight years of service on the Detroit City Council prepared her for her 1990 election to the U.S. Congress.

Barbara-Rose Richardson Collins was born on April 13, 1939, in Detroit, Michigan, the oldest of four children (she has two sisters and one brother) born to Lamar Nathaniel Richardson Sr. and Lou Versa Jones Richardson. Lamar Richardson Sr. was a longtime Ford Motor Co. employee who by the mid-1970s worked as a contractor specializing in home improvement. Lou Versa Richardson was a full-time homemaker. Barbara-Rose grew up in a neighborhood where other family members also lived, including grandparents, aunts, and uncles. After graduating from Cass Technical High School in Detroit in 1957, she attended Wayne State University, studying political science and anthropology. She completed approximately two years of academic credit. At the age of eighteen, she married Virgil Gary Collins, a chemistry student who later worked as a pharmaceutical salesman. After a few years, the marriage broke up and Barbara-Rose Collins obtained a divorce in the 1960s. Virgil Collins died in 1971. Barbara-Rose Collins is the mother of three children, one of whom died at the age of two months. The others are Cynthia Lynn and Christopher Lauren.

To support her family, Collins worked at a variety of jobs but still needed to receive public aid—food stamps and medical benefits for seven months—to meet her family's needs. She achieved job stability in the 1960s and 1970s when she worked at Wayne State University, serving for nine years as business manager of the physics department and for approximately a year and a half as an assistant in the office of Equal Opportunity and Neighborhood Relations.

About 1966 or 1967, Collins heard a speech by Stokeley Carmichael that greatly influenced the future direction of her life. Carmichael mentioned that large numbers of whites were leaving the cities for the suburbs and that if educated, middle-class blacks also moved away from the poorer areas of the cities, low-income blacks would not have the inspiration or the resources to improve their lives. Carmichael stressed the need for blacks to upgrade their own neighborhoods and to use society's resources to better themselves. Shortly after hearing this speech at the Shrine of the Black Madonna in Detroit, Collins joined the Shrine Church, and she later moved back to the neighborhood of her youth, purchasing a home

Barbara-Rose Collins

near the one in which she was born. She became committed to community development and race advancement.

The Shrine of the Black Madonna, while affiliated with the United Church of Christ, also developed its own Pan African Orthodox Christian theology (also called Black Christian Nationalist theology) and stressed a church mission to use social and political means to elevate the living standards of blacks. Collins's involvement with the Shrine of the Black Madonna led her to investigate community issues from the point of view of low-income blacks and motivated her to enter politics to help increase and allocate the resources available for community advancement. The Shrine's pastor, Jaramogi Abebe Agyeman (the Reverend Albert Cleage, Jr.), played a key role as a mentor and advisor over the years.

Collins became chair of a church group that investigated and discussed school decentralization and other community issues and sought solutions to the city's problems. Improving the quality of public schools was a major concern, and school decentralization would allow citizens more opportunity to influence the quality of education in their local schools. At a 1969 rally to petition the state legislature to increase state funding for Detroit schools, Collins met the influential state senator Coleman A. Young, who in 1974 became the first black mayor of Detroit. In later years Collins would take Young's advice to heart and support most of his political positions. Collins's work with the church study group so impressed Agyeman that he suggested that she run for election to a position on the newly created Region One School Board. Elected in 1970, she served from 1971 to 1973. For each of the forty-two schools in Region One, she was credited with helping to form community councils that worked to reduce vandalism and promoted policies that increased student academic achievement. She found the amount of time spent attending supplementary meetings in the community and talking to concerned parents too demanding, so she decided not to seek reelection.

Elected Michigan State Representative

Encouraged by Agyeman, Collins decided to seek higher office, setting her sights on election to either the Detroit City Council or the state legislature. To get the attention of a large number of voters, she began to use her middle name "Rose" as a symbol to distinguish her from other candidates. She carried a rose to all campaign appearances, hyphenated her name as Barbara-Rose, and, as a member of the Michigan state legislature, named her constituent's newsletter *The Rose Illustrated.*

In 1973 and 1974 Collins was defeated in three elections before winning a primary election for state representative in August 1974. In 1973 she was a candidate for the Detroit City Council; in a citywide vote with 114 candidates, she qualified in the primary as one of eighteen finalists for the nine positions on the city council. Lack of money to advertise was a factor in her losing the general election in November 1973. In 1974 Collins entered two special elections to fill vacancies in the state legislature. In February 1974, in a primary election for the Michigan state senate, Collins was the second largest vote-getter, losing to David S. Holmes, Jr., a fifteen-year veteran state representative. Collins then sought election to the state house of representatives seat vacated by Holmes's election to the state senate. Though Collins was endorsed by the *Detroit Free Press* in the primary election in May 1974, she lost in a low turnout election by sixty-three votes to a political newcomer, Clifford D. Gary.

Somewhat discouraged but undaunted, Collins decided to try again. Gary's victory allowed him to occupy the seat until the end of the year. In the August primary election for the full term starting in 1975, Collins beat Gary by sixty-eight votes, becoming the Democratic party nominee for the Michigan House of Representatives. Winning the general election in November, Collins was subsequently reelected three times, serving through 1981.

In the state legislature, Collins developed a reputation as a coalition builder and sponsor of significant consumer and civil rights legislation. In her first term, she was appointed chair of the Constitutional Revision and Women's Rights Committee, a position she held for six years. That committee not only issued the first analytical report on the history and current status of women in the Michigan state legislature, entitled *Women in the Legislative Process* (1977), but also was instrumental in the passage of laws on sex education and sexual harassment. Collins also served as chair of both the Subcommittee on Spouse Abuse, which investigated the problem of domestic violence, and the Committee on Urban Affairs. She was chosen chair of the Black Caucus and vice-chair of the Democratic Caucus in the Michigan legislature.

Collins was the principal sponsor of several significant laws adopted by the state legislature. The Food Dating Bill required grocery stores to label products with a recommended last day of sale, the Pituitary Gland Retrieval Bill facilitated donations of organs for medical research, the Sex Education Bill allowed teaching about birth control and family planning in public schools, the Sexual Harassment Bill prohibited sexual harassment and discrimination based on gender, and the Pension Bill required employers to give equal insurance and sick leave benefits for pregnancy and childbirth conditions. Collins became well-known as a strong and effective advocate for civil rights and consumer issues as well as for the city of Detroit. She frequently reminded the legislature that she represented more poor black constituents than anyone else in the House.

Election to City Council

By the end of the 1970s, Collins believed that her time on the school board and in the state legislature had provided her with both the experience and the knowledge to be an effective member of the U.S. Congress. She considered running against Charles Diggs, Jr., the longtime black representative from Detroit, but after consulting with both Diggs and Detroit mayor Coleman A. Young, Collins instead decided to seek election to the Detroit City Council in 1981. She was elected, resigned from the state legislature, and assumed her city council office in January 1982. She was reelected two times and served until her resignation in January 1991.

Collins approached her city council position as if it were the state legislature, working hard to serve constituents' needs and pass city ordinances. She sponsored and secured passage of ordinances on South African divestiture, toxic waste cleanup, and single-room occupancy housing for the homeless. She also supported black business development through the awarding of city contracts and college scholarships for Detroit high school seniors. Collins also served as chair of the Task Force on Teenage Violence and Juvenile Crime, chair of the Task Force on Homelessness, and vice-chair of the Task Force on Litter and Clean-Up Detroit.

During her years on the city council, Collins's interest in election to Congress continued. In the 1980s she became known citywide for her community activities and work on the council, building name recognition and voter support. When Diggs resigned from Congress in 1980, a highly respected former judge and ally of Coleman A. Young, George W. Crockett, Jr., had been elected to the seat. Many assumed that because of his age Crockett would serve only a short time. But when Crockett announced his candidacy for a fifth consecutive term, Collins decided to wait no longer for a vacancy. In 1988 Collins challenged Crockett in the Democratic primary. Collins realized that it would be difficult to defeat an incumbent who had earned considerable respect and admiration in a predominantly black congressional district. Her campaign was a strategic move with minimum risk. If she made a strong showing, her success might be a preview of future challenges; if she lost, she would still have a year to go in her Detroit City Council position. Both Crockett and Collins ran strong campaigns, with Collins coming in a near second and holding Crockett to less than 49 percent of the vote. Though he was reelected in 1988, Crockett reportedly did not like the close vote in the primary and chose to retire rather than seek reelection in 1990.

Collins Elected to Congress

Collins's campaign for the open seat in 1990 had the personal endorsement and the organizational support of Detroit's major, Coleman A. Young. In an eight-candidate field in the Democratic primary, Collins attracted 34 percent of the vote, receiving over five thousand more votes than her closest competitor. She won the general election with 80 percent of the vote. Resigning her city council position, Collins was sworn in as a member of Congress in January 1991.

Collins declared that her goals and concerns in Congress would be to bring more federal dollars to Detroit, to help shape a federal urban policy of long term assistance to cities, to "save the black male," and to strengthen black families. Collins credits the strength and closeness of her extended family for her own success but also notes that in many families with no strong black male role model, young black males tend to go astray. Her teenage son, Christopher, went to prison in 1989 for armed robbery, leading Collins to conclude in the *Detroit Free Press* on October 8, 1993, "I could teach a girl how to be a woman, but I could not teach a boy how to be a man." Though help to cities can be legislated, Collins believes that aid to families must include not only financial support to social work agencies and programs, but also better jobs as well as moral leadership and the involvement of churches and social groups.

Reflecting on her experience in the Michigan legislature, Collins drew up a strategy for achieving her goals in the U.S. Congress. First, she asked Representative John Dingell, D-Michigan, a veteran of thirty-six years in Congress, to be her mentor. He agreed. Next, with his influence, she was able to win a seat on the House Public Works and Transportation Committee, where she could champion her aid-to-cities plans. Other committee service included membership on the Select Committee on Children, Youth, and Families, the Government Operations Committee, and the Post Office and Civil Service Committee; she also chaired the Subcommittee on Postal Operations and Services. Her voting record in 1991-92 was decidedly liberal, receiving positive ratings of 90 to 100 percent by the AFL-CIO labor union and the Americans for Democratic Action and negative ratings of 0 percent by the American Conservative Union and 20 percent by the national Chamber of Commerce. Collins was reelected in 1992 with 80 percent of the vote.

Over the years, Collins has received her share of criticism. While a member of the Detroit City Council, it was said that she was not as effective in getting legislation passed as she had been in the state legislature and that she was frequently absent from council meetings. She was also accused of being overly dependent upon Mayor Coleman Young, automatically supporting his recommendations because he had aided her election to the city council. Finally, some charged that Collins did not have the "smarts" or intelligence to be a good member of Congress. In reply, Collins has pointed out that she authored fewer laws on the city council because the council has less power and is more dependent upon the mayor's cooperation than the state legislature is upon the governor's cooperation. Collins claimed to have often disagreed with Mayor Young in private but said she did not need to make those disagreements public since she is against "Mayor-bashing." Also, in her 1988 challenge to George Crockett, she opposed the Coleman Young political organization that backed Crockett. Several believe that Collins will show greater independence in Congress and that her intellectual ability, experience, and personal drive will make her a success there. John Dingell told the *Detroit News* for May 12, 1991, "Barbara-Rose is going to be a good congresswoman because she wants to be good. She works hard, she is smart . . . and she is learning her lessons early."

Collins was appointed majority whip-at-large for the 1993-94 Congress and is a member of the Congressional Black Caucus and the Congressional Caucus for Women's Issues. A board member of the Detroit Symphony Orchestra, she is also active in the National Political Congress of Black Women and a member of Gamma Phi Delta Sorority and the American Business Women's Association. In 1974-75 she served on the Detroit Human Rights Commission and in 1985 she was regional coordinator for the National Black Caucus of Local Elected Officials.

Collins is a full-figured woman of average height with an attractive face. Photographs reveal her as stylishly dressed in suits with a smiling, cheerful countenance and a changing hair style: an Afro in the 1970s, braids in the 1980s, and shoulder length straight hair in the 1990s. Her hobbies include playing classical music on the piano and harp, listening to opera and symphony music, reading novels and science fiction, and portrait painting.

Barbara-Rose Collins is a seasoned politician whose dissatisfaction with the public education system in Detroit catapulted her into a career in politics as city councilwoman, state legislator, and U.S. congresswoman. As a goal-oriented politician, she has positioned herself to become as effective in Congress as she has been in Michigan.

Current Address: 317 Cannon House Office Building, Washington, DC 20515.

REFERENCES:

"Barbara-Rose Collins, U.S. Representative." *Detroit Free Press,* March 31, 1991.

"Barbara-Rose Collins Wins in Motown." *Ebony* 46 (January 1991): 104, 106.

"Candidate with Old Fashioned Views." *Detroit Free Press,* October 23, 1973.

"Cause Is Close to Home." *Detroit Free Press,* October 8, 1993.

"Climbing the Hill." *Detroit News,* May 12, 1991.

"Collins' Career Rose under Young's Star." *Detroit Free Press,* August 9, 1990.

"Collins Wants a 'Rose' in Washington." *Michigan Chronicle,* June 25, 1988.

"Collins: You Don't Know Me." *Michigan Chronicle,* June 6-12, 1990.

"Congressional Candidates Both Think Big." *Detroit Free Press,* September 18, 1990.

Congressional Directory, 102 Congress, 1991-1992. Washington, D.C.: Government Printing Office, 1991.

"Detroit's Rep. Collins Likes Exciting Roles, Believes in Mayor Young." *Lansing State Journal,* April 16, 1975.

"Four Women Make Council Ballot." *Detroit Free Press,* September 13, 1973.

"Fragrance and Fire: Barbara-Rose Collins." *City* (Detroit) 2 (April 1988): 33-36, 38.

"From Cass to the Capital." *Detroit Free Press,* November 13, 1977.

"Making It Happen in Michigan." *Redbook* 150 (April 1978): 49, 51.

Michigan Manual, 1975-1976. Lansing: Michigan Department of Management and Budget, 1975.

Michigan Manual, 1991-1992. Lansing: Michigan Legislative Service Bureau, 1991.

Michigan Manual, 1993-1994. Lansing: Michigan Legislative Service Bureau, 1993.

"Rep. Collins Talks of Fight for Powerless." *Detroit News,* March 10, 1980.

"Scenes of Struggle and Success." *Detroit Free Press,* March 31, 1991.

"Welcome to Washington: A Bumpy Ride for Rep. Collins." *Detroit News,* September 15, 1991.

Who's Who among Black Americans, 1992-93. 7th ed. Detroit: Gale Research, 1993.

Who's Who in Congress, 1993. Washington, D.C.: Congressional Quarterly, 1993.

Women in the Legislative Process. Lansing: Legislative Service Bureau, State Legislature, October 1977.

Women in the Legislative Process. Lansing: Legislative Service Bureau, State Legislature, 1985.

Young, Coleman A., and Lonnie Wheeler. *Hard Stuff: The Autobiography of Coleman Young.* New York: Viking, 1994.

　　　　　　　　　　　　　　　　　De Witt S. Dykes, Jr.

Helen Appo Cook

Helen Appo Cook

(1837-1913)

Club leader, civic worker

" "Mrs. Cook was not only the president of the League, but was the mother of organizations among colored women in the country." These were the words used in the *Washington Colored American* by Anna Evans Murray, a clubwoman, to describe Helen Appo Cook, president of the Colored Women's League of Washington, D.C. (CWL). Cook was also a woman of considerable wealth; there were many high achievers in her family and in her husband's as well. A caption under her picture in the February 25, 1899, *Washington Colored American* reads, "President Women's League and mother of the Organization movement among Afro-American women of the country." The Colored Women's League was the older of two organizations, the CWL and the National Federation of Afro-American Women, which merged to found the National Association of Colored Women (NACW). Cook was head of the CWL at the time of the merger. During her tenure, the league provided day nurseries, kindergartens, and night schools for the care and development of women and children. Cook worked with a number of other distinguished women, including Charlotte Forten Grimké, Anna J. Cooper, Lucy E. Moten, Mary Church Terrell, and Josephine B. Bruce.

Helen Elizabeth Appo Cook was born in 1837 in New York to William Appo and Elizabeth Brady Appo. Her certificate of death showed that she died of pneumonia and heart failure in the District of Columbia on November 20, 1913, at the age of seventy-six; she was buried at Harmony Cemetery in Washington, D.C., on November 24, 1913. Her name is given as Ellen in the United States Census of 1850 in Philadelphia and in the 1880 census of the District of Columbia. However, this may possibly be attributed to spelling errors by the census takers, which were not uncommon at the time. Also listed in the 1850 United States Census were the Appos' other children: Catherine, the oldest, born about 1833;

William, born about 1842 and, according to the Cook Family Papers, killed during the Civil War; and John (St. John), born about 1848 and described in the Cook Family Papers as assimilating into the white race. Garnet, the youngest son of William and Elizabeth Appo, was born about 1855 and died at age eighteen. He was living with his sister Helen and her husband, John Francis Cook, Jr., in the District of Columbia at the age of fifteen.

Two Prominent Families

Although official records show that Helen Appo Cook was born in New York, other sources list Philadelphia as her birthplace. This is understandable, considering her musician father William Appo's frequent travel between several cities during the 1820s and 1840s. Eileen Southern's *Music of Black Americans* indicates that in the 1840s William Appo combined performing with teaching music in both Philadelphia and Baltimore and later in New York, where he settled permanently. According to Martin R. Delany in *Condition, Elevation, Emigration, and Destiny of the Colored People of the United States,* teaching French was among Appo's other occupations. Daniel Payne referred to William Appo as "the most learned musician of the race." William and his brother Joseph Appo played with the Walnut Street Orchestra and the once-famous Frank Johnson Band of Philadelphia. Among his many accomplishments, William Appo was one of the earliest performers of instrumental music in an African Methodist Episcopal (AME) church: in Baltimore in 1848 Appo directed a seven-piece string ensemble at Bethel Church. Around that time black congregations were introducing choirs and instrumental music into their churches over the strenuous objections of some of their members.

During the period 1837 to 1840 in New York, William and Elizabeth Appo actively sought customers—he for his music and she for her millinery businesses—by advertising in the *New York Colored American.* Cook's family included other entrepreneurs: her paternal grandfather, St. John Appo, who was born in 1779 or 1789 in Pondicherry, India, was a confectioner at Sixth and Spruce Street in Philadelphia, where his French wife's original recipe for ice cream was the *specialité de la maison.*

Helen Appo married John Francis Cook, Jr., educator and District of Columbia tax collector, about 1863. They had five children: Elizabeth Appo, John Francis III, George Frederick, Charles Chaveau, and Ralph Victor. Paul Sluby's *Appo, Fisher, Hawkins* genealogy indicates that Elizabeth Appo Cook was born in 1864 and died in 1953; she served as professor of romance languages at Howard University. The 1880 United States Census showed that John Francis III was born about 1868 in the district. He accepted a federal appointment as postmaster of Bonner's Ferry, and he was married to Elizabeth Rebecca Abele; however, he went to Oregon or Washington state where he became mayor of a city. Charles Chaveau Cook was born in 1871 or 1872 in the district and died in 1910 or 1911 in a swimming accident at Sea Isle City, New Jersey, at age thirty-eight. George Frederick was born about 1874 and died in 1927. Ralph Victor Cook, the youngest

son, was born in 1875 in the district and died in 1949; he was a mechanical engineer and teacher.

John Francis Cook, Jr., the husband of Helen Appo Cook, was born in the District of Columbia in September 1833. He belonged to one of the district's most prominent and wealthy families. His family members were known throughout the nineteenth century for their work in education, religion, politics, and community service. Among them were John F. Cook, Sr. and John F. Cook, Jr.'s brother, George F. T. Cook. The father was a successful educator, clergyman, and community leader before the Civil War. George, a member of the District of Columbia Board of Trade, was the first superintendent of Washington's colored public schools.

In addition to serving as the district's tax collector, John F. Cook, Jr. was a member of the Board of Aldermen, a trustee of the colored public schools, a trustee of Howard University, and a member of the university's executive committee.

The Cook family was prominent in Washington's black society. According to *A Study of Historic Sites in the District of Columbia,*

> They were among the few Blacks listed in Washington's *Elite List* for 1888; they were considered as some of the city's wealthiest Blacks. In 1884 John F. Cook, Jr. was cited in the *Age* as a member of the Black "four hundred", Blacks reportedly worth $70,000.

Also, an undated newspaper from the Cook Family Papers identified Mrs. John F. Cook, Jr. as the wife of the wealthy owner of the Langham Hotel building.

Helps Found the Colored Women's League

Although little is known about Cook's education before she moved to the District of Columbia and began work in the Colored Women's League, several early sources state that she was a well-educated woman possessing linguistic abilities, and probably speaking French. An undated newspaper in the Cook Family Papers reported, "Her complexion was that of a Spaniard and she was a Miss Appo of Philadelphia, a woman of fine education and remarkable acquirements as a linguist." The November 26, 1946, *Washington Pittsburgh Courier* stated, "She learned to speak French almost as soon as she could talk, having a mother who was of French and Spanish origin"; and Martin R. Delany wrote, "[William Appo's] young daughter, Helen, a miss of fourteen years of age, inherits the musical talents of her father and is now organist in the Central Presbyterian Church."

Cook's work in the Colored Women's League of Washington, D.C., began with its inception in June 1892 and its incorporation on January 11, 1894. It was considered the first organization of black women established for the definite purpose of becoming national, according to Mary Church Terrell in *Aframerican Woman's Journal.* Terrell wrote that incorporators of the CWL were herself, Helen Appo Cook, Charlotte Forten Grimké, Josephine B. Bruce, Anna J. Cooper, Mary J. Patterson, Evelyn Shaw, and Ida D. Bailey. The mission of the organization was to collect facts concerning the moral, intellectual, and social development of blacks; to foster unity among them; to encourage progress; and to determine methods of promoting the best interests of black people in directions that would be suggested by the members of the organization. Cook was elected first president of the league and probably held the position until the early 1900s. Her presidency is documented in the *National Notes of the NACW* and the *Washington Colored American* for the years 1892, 1894-96, 1899-1900, and 1903.

In 1895 the CWL became one of first groups to respond to the appeal of Josephine St. Pierce Ruffin, president of the Woman's Era Club, to form a national organization. Reacting to an assault on the character of black women by the president of the Missouri Press Association, Ruffin called a meeting in Boston for the purpose of establishing a national organization among black women. The first national conference assembled by black women was held in Boston, July 29-31, 1895. Approximately one hundred delegates attended, representing twenty clubs from sixteen states and the District of Columbia. Elected officers of the convention were Josephine St. Pierce Ruffin, president; Helen Appo Cook, vice-president; Margaret Murray Washington, vice-president; and Eliza Carter, secretary.

Cook addressed the conference on July 29, 1895, defining the goals and purpose of a national league and calling for unity among women. In 1896 the two national women's groups, the CWL and the National Federation of Afro-American Women, held their conventions in Washington, D.C. (As noted, the CWL was the first women's club organized with the intention of becoming a national group.) The CWL's convention was held at the Fifteenth Street Presbyterian Church in the district on July 14-16, 1896, with Cook as presiding officer. The next week the federation held its convention at the Nineteenth Street Baptist Church with Margaret Murray Washington the presiding officer. Joint committees were appointed and a program of unity for the two associations was envisioned. Mary Church Terrell was elected chair of the joint committee, and the committee stipulated that they would consolidate under the name National Association of Colored Women.

Referring to the effectiveness of Cook's leadership abilities, a caption in the May 27, 1899, *Washington Colored American* read, "Under her intelligent, tactful and energetic leadership a magnificent organization has been perfected, and many reforms helpful to our women, have been instituted." Perhaps this explains why women like Charlotte Grimké and Lucy E. Moten were still serving under Cook in the early 1900s. The CWL appeared to be at the forefront among NACW clubs in providing kindergartens and day nurseries. The club held night education classes, sewing classes, and mother's meetings, which dealt with the everyday problems of motherhood and homemaking. It worked to improve conditions for the city's alley dwellers and sponsored garden parties and receptions to raise funds for its day nurseries. The league was recognized as a champion of every cause of special interest to black women and children in the district. Membership in the league consisted primarily of teachers and other cultured and influential black women. Willard Gatewood

cites a clubwoman who explained the membership composition of the club in this way:

> As a woman of culture, refinement and financial independence, Mrs. John F. Cook has been, and is a noted example and inspiration to women of her own social standing in the serious work of social reform. Helen Cook and other female aristocrats of color avail themselves of the opportunities offered by the club movement to make use of their superior training in behalf of the race; they served to combat the notion that "colored women of education and refinement" had no sympathetic interest in their own race.

Cook spoke at the Congress of Mothers Conference in 1898 along with W. E. B. Du Bois. She defended the character of blacks, arguing that whites too had their share of problems and that the "race traits and tendencies" of blacks were not the cause of their plight. Her speech was entitled "We Have Been Hindered: How Can We Be Help?" The June 4, 1898, *Washington Colored American* summarized her speech:

> The efforts of so-called scientists to fix upon colored people, under the guise of "race traits and tendencies," the responsibility, as the result of their vices, for the excessive mortality among the Negroes in large cities.... [T]hese "race traits and tendencies" are due, in part, to their poverty-stricken and unhealthy surroundings, and, in part, by the reflex influence by the American people toward them.

> "Imitation" ... is the goal toward which destiny drives us; imitation, whether willing or unconscious.... [T]he same generation that produced a Webster, a Calhoun, a Sumner, and a Wendell Phillips produced also our great orator, Frederick Douglass.

> It is inevitable that the Negroes should copy the bad as well as the good, and that a few should follow the example set by duelling, ku klux klans [sic] and lynchings. When a learned Judge ... declared hanging too good for a hardened Negro murderer, did he forget that the same year had produced a Luetgert, a Holmes and a Martin Thorn?

Although Cook is not discussed in historical literature as much as her contemporaries Charlotte Grimké, Lucy Moten, Anna Cooper, and Mary Terrell, obviously she played a major role in the progress of nineteenth-century women. Her contributions are documented in history as a long-term president of the Colored Women's League, an organizer in the establishment of the NACW, and a community worker for the welfare of women and children.

REFERENCES:

Advertisement by William Appo. *New York Colored American,* September 2, 1837.

Afro-American Bicentennial Corporation. "Cook Family, 16th and K Street, N.W." In *A Study of Historic Sites in the District of Columbia of Special Significance to Afro-Americans*. Pt. II. Washington, D.C.: Afro-American Bicentennial Corporation, 1974.

"Brilliant Garden Party. Favored by the Elements; the Woman's League Give Joy to the Elite and Net a Handsome Sum for Day Nursery—Devotees to Pleasure al Fresco." *Washington Colored American*, September 30, 1899.

"Congress of Mothers . . . Mrs. Helen A. Cook's Eloquent Defense of Negro Character—the Spirit of Imitation and Environment Responsible for Alleged Race Traits and Tendencies." *Washington Colored American*, June 4, 1898.

"Congress of Mothers. Praiseworthy Interest Shown by the Women of the Negro Race—Warmly Welcomed." *Washington Colored American*, February 25, 1899.

Cuney-Hare, Maud. *Negro Musicians and Their Music*. New York: Da Capo Press, 1974.

Delany, Martin R. *Condition, Elevation, Emigration, and Destiny of the Colored People of the United States*. Philadelphia: Martin R. Delany, 1852.

Family History and Pedigree Charts. Cook Family Papers.

"For Charity's Sake. Benevolent Women of the Nation's Capital Work for Sweet Charity's Sake—The Election of Officers." *Washington Colored American*, January 31, 1903.

"Francis Johnson (1792-1844)." *Black Perspectives in Music* 4 (1976): 209-12.

Gatewood, Willard B. *Aristocrats of Color: The Black Elite, 1880-1920*. Bloomington: Indiana University Press, 1990.

Hutchinson, Louise Daniel. *Anna J. Cooper*. Washington, D.C.: Smithsonian Institution Press, 1981.

Logan, Rayford W., and Michael R. Winston, eds. *Dictionary of American Negro Biography*. New York: Norton, 1982.

Majors, Gerri. *Black Society*. Chicago: Johnson Publishing Co., 1976.

"Mrs. E. A. Appo. Plain and Fashionable Milliner and Dress Maker." *New York Colored American*, July 11, 1840.

National Notes (NACW), 3 (November 1899); 4 (January 1900). Mary Church Terrell Papers.

"Negroes of High Rank . . . Mrs. Langston and Mrs. Shad—Other Ladies of Talent and Prominence Who Are Factors in Society." Unnamed newspaper about 1890. Cook Family Papers.

"Remarks at Dinner Given by the NACW," October 17, 1949. Mary Church Terrell Papers.

"Retired D.C. Teacher Casts Ballot Here." *Pittsburgh Courier*, November 26, 1946.

Sluby, Paul E., Jr., and Stanton L. Wormley, eds. *Appo, Fisher, Hawkins*. Genealogy of Dr. Annette Hawkins Eaton and Dr. Walter Lincoln Hawkins. Washington, D.C.: Columbian Harmony Society, 1983.

Southern, Eileen. *Biographical Dictionary of Afro-American and African Musicians*. Westport, Conn.: Greenwood Press, 1982.

———. *The Music of Black Americans: A History*. New York: Norton, 1971.

———, ed. *Readings in Black American Music*. New York: Norton, 1971.

Terrell, Mary Church. "History of the Club Women's Movement." *Aframerican Woman's Journal* 1 (Summer & Fall 1940): 34-38.

"Town Topic." *Washington Colored American*, October 27, 1900.

Trotter, James M. *Music and Some Highly Musical People*. Boston: Lee and Shepard, 1881.

U.S. Census 1850. William Appo. Philadelphia, Pa.

U.S. Census 1870; U.S. Census 1880. John F. Cook. Washington, D.C.

Washington, Booker T. "Club Movement among Colored Women of America." In *A New Negro for a New Century*. Chicago: American Publishing House, 1900.

Wesley, Charles Harris. *History of the National Association of Colored Women's Clubs*. Washington, D.C.: NACW, 1984.

"Women of the Hour (Mrs. Helen A. Cook)." *Colored American* (Washington), May 27, 1899.

COLLECTIONS:

The Cook Family Papers and the Mary Church Terrell Papers are located at the Noorland-Spingarn Research Center, Howard University, Washington, D.C.

Ruth A. Hodges

Myrtle Foster Cook
(1870-1951)
Editor, clubwoman, educator, civic worker, political worker

As a member of an affluent immigrant Canadian family, Myrtle Foster Cook was privileged with many educational, religious, social, and cultural advantages. Her early experiences resulted in her lifelong devotion to civic and women's club work at both the local and national level. She also held leadership positions with the Republican party. Cook served for many years as the national program chair of the National Association for Colored Women (NACW), the premier women's organization of her time, and in 1922 she became the second editor of the association's newsletter, eventually transforming the one-page leaflet *National Notes* into a magazine. During her years as a leader in the NACW she worked with such notable women as Mary McLeod Bethune, Hallie Quinn Brown, and Mary Church Terrell, with whom she frequently corresponded.

Myrtle Foster Cook was born in Canada on April 17, 1870, to James William and Elizabeth Butler Foster. She died of bronchopneumonia on August 31, 1951, in Los Angeles,

Myrtle Foster Cook

California, at the age of eighty-one. Funeral services were held at Peoples Funeral Home in Los Angeles. Cook's family immigrated to the United States in 1877 or 1879 from Amherstburg, Canada, and settled in Monroe, Michigan. She became a citizen of the United States as a child, when her parents became naturalized residents of Monroe. James E. Devries, in *Race and Kinship in a Midwestern Town: The Black Experience in Monroe, Michigan, 1900-1915,* discusses the ambiguity in classifying the racial status of the Foster family. He indicates that several Monroe County records classified them as mulattos; the U.S. census lists the Fosters as black in 1880, white in 1900, and mulatto in 1910; and Grace Foster Schmitt died "white" in 1954 according to Devries, who also indicates that the Fosters denied their African heritage and lived as if they were members of the white majority.

The fathers of James and Elizabeth Foster were both slaves who escaped to Canada, presumably on the Underground Railroad during the abolitionist years. Elizabeth's father, William H. Butler, was a native of South Carolina and her mother, Ann Calvert, was English and white. James Foster's father, Levi, a leading black figure in Amherstburg, was originally from Ohio or Virginia, and James's mother was Elizabeth Waring, a native of Virginia. It appears that Levi Foster was not pleased with life in Canada between 1866 and 1873. He petitioned several times to end the separate school department for "coloreds" in his community, but each time the trustees turned down his request. Daniel G. Hill, in *The Freedom Seekers: Blacks in Early Canada,* states that Mrs. Levi Foster also appealed to the district school board to allow her to send her children to the common school but was refused. According to the board, the separate school "was sufficient for the wants of the colored people."

Hill also writes that Levi Foster was a tavern owner in Amherstburg when he attended a public debate at the Sons of Temperance Hall, where it was resolved, "The slave holder is better than a tavern keeper." The day after the debate Levi Foster hung a notice on his closed tavern stating that, since he was a former slave himself, he could not let it be said that he was worse than a slave holder. Levi Foster was affluent in Amherstburg, operating, in addition to a livery business, a successful stage line and hotel from 1848 to 1873. After closing the tavern, he continued his livery business and built up large holdings of valuable real estate, eventually owning several houses and farms in Amherstburg. In 1861 his property included livestock valued at one thousand dollars, seven carriages worth seven thousand dollars, and forty-four acres of land. When James and Elizabeth Foster arrived in Monroe, they had the cash and the know-how to thrive in their new surroundings.

The Foster family pedigree chart in Devries's *Race and Kinship in a Midwestern Town* shows that Myrtle Foster Cook had six siblings. Ella was born May 16, 1873, and was married to Marion Arthur. In October 1899 the Foster family backed Ella in a candy store enterprise in Monroe, says Devries in "Home Grown: The Black Experience in the City of Monroe, Michigan, 1900-1915." Another sister, Mae, later joined Ella in the candy store business; she was born on December 29, 1876, and was married to John Fields. Grace was born on April 30, 1879, and remained in Monroe with her aging mother; in 1921, after her mother's death, she married Carl Schmitt, the family's German hired hand. Grace died in May 1954. Jay was born in 1883 and was murdered in Toledo, Ohio, on January 13, 1911. The Foster's two other children, William and an unnamed daughter on the pedigree chart, apparently died at young ages.

Shortly after James and Elizabeth Foster arrived in Monroe, they purchased a home and a livery stable business, which was operated at a profit until 1893 when James Foster retired and sold the concern; the family then bought a homestead of twenty-three acres on the outskirts of the city and ran a successful fruit and dairy farm for several years. As an affluent family in Monroe, they resided in two of the community's better homes. At the time of his death in 1900, according to Devries in "Home Grown," James Foster's estate was valued at over $10,000, which included real estate assessed at $5,500 and bank savings and credit totaling $4,530.02. Because of the Fosters' standing in the community, they participated fully in Monroe's economic, political, school, and church activities.

While James Foster never ran for political office, he was a dependable and committed Republican. Both Myrtle and Ella Foster were elected as speakers for their high school graduation exercises in 1889 and 1893, respectively. In his Baptist church James Foster was elected several times to positions of deacon, treasurer, and trustee; he also chaired annual meetings when the church was without an ordained leader. All of the Foster children were baptized in the Baptist church, and the daughters took leading roles in the Baptist Young People's Union. Meetings of this group and the Ladies' Aid Society were held at the Fosters' home. On more than one occasion conflicts arose in the congregation involving the Fosters and a white person, and each time the Fosters prevailed. For example, in 1890 the pastor accused Myrtle Foster Cook of writing an anonymous and defamatory letter to him. On May 1, 1890, the pastor, his witness, and Cook were summoned to a classroom in the church to give testimony. After discussions it was concluded that nothing could be proven and the matter should be dropped. However, bitter feelings lingered, resulting in the congregation's dismissal of the pastor. Another incident in which the Foster family triumphed occurred when Jay Foster killed a white male trying to burglarize the Fosters' home on June 22, 1901. According to Devries, the Monroe press reported that citizens supported the Fosters and referred to them as among the city's most highly respected people. The incident concluded with Jay Foster being completely exonerated on all charges by the public and the jury. Throughout the entire affair there was no race baiting or cry for lynching.

Combines Teaching Career with Club Work

Myrtle Foster Cook attended the University of Michigan. She served as a part-time teacher in Monroe for a few years before a desire to do missionary work led her to Kentucky, where she served as principal of a small normal school supported by the Baptist district association. She then accepted a position offering professional advancement at a high school in Frankfort. It was in Frankfort that she met and married Dr. Louis G. Todd, a descendant of a prominent Kentucky family. The Todds settled in Muskogee, Oklahoma, around the early 1900s. Cook was immediately asked to teach in the government high school for black children of American Indians. Responding to the generally poor health of blacks in the community, she organized the Dorcas Club in order to establish a hospital, which was completed by others who continued her work after she left Oklahoma. In Oklahoma Cook also organized a series of lectures and recitals, arranging statewide tours with the assistance of the State Teachers' Association. Coming to Oklahoma were individuals such as Richard B. Harrison, who played the "De Lawd" in *Green Pastures* and Dr. Kelly Miller, educator, lecturer, and scientist.

Cook was a charter member in the writing of the constitution of the Oklahoma State Federation. Louis Todd died on December 23, 1911. In 1916 Cook moved to Kansas City, Missouri, to head the English department of Lincoln High School. There she joined the Book Lover's Club, the City Federation, and the Woman's League. After four years of teaching, Cook married Hugh Oliver Cook, head of the mathematics department and later principal of Lincoln High. Myrtle Cook laughingly told the NACW that she had married a family, for Hugh Cook had two young sons, Hugh Oliver and Hartwell Cook, and a foster daughter, Chloe, in college. The Cooks supported and aided dozens of other children; some were adopted, reared as their own children and sent to college, and others were given financial aid to help them

finish high school or college. Through the Woman's League of Kansas City, Cook initiated a movement to found a home for "colored" boys. She was the organizer and secretary of the Colored Children's Association, working nine years to secure the erection, equipment, and staffing of the Jackson County Home for Negro Boys in Jackson County, Missouri. After Hugh Cook retired from the school system in January 1944, he and Myrtle Cook moved to Los Angeles, where Hugh Cook died in 1949.

Named Editor-Manager of *National Notes*

Myrtle Foster Cook's numerous social and charitable activities began in Monroe, Michigan, and continued in Kentucky, Oklahoma, and Missouri. Cook held a number of positions within the NACW, including teller, national program chairperson, editor-manager of the *National Notes,* and chairperson of the Publicity Committee. From 1918 to 1928, while serving as national program chairperson and as editor-manager of the *National Notes,* Cook frequently corresponded with Mary Church Terrell, the first president of NACW, soliciting articles and pictures for the *Notes* and outlining special programs. Cook succeeded Margaret Murray Washington in 1922 as editor-manager of the *National Notes.* Conceived by Washington, *Notes* was adopted as the official organ of the association in 1897 and was circulated at a subscription price of twenty-five cents a year. It was originally a small sheet of facts published by Washington at her own expense at Tuskegee Institute and distributed at the national conventions. Cook expanded the newsletter into a sixteen-page magazine full of a variety of reports, articles, and personal comments, along with illustrations of clubwomen, convention groups, and projects.

With the expansion of national projects—the restoration of the Frederick Douglass Home in the District of Columbia, the scholarship loan fund, plans for a national headquarters—*Notes* functioned effectively in disseminating information, inspiring enthusiasm, unifying sentiments, and coordinating state and national support. In addition, *Notes* prospered financially under the management of Cook, who was able to return $619.28 of the association's subsidy as projected in her Second Biennial Report of the NACW for 1924-26, the NACW's fifteenth biennial session. In 1926 Myrtle Foster Cook resigned as editor of *Notes.* Mary McLeod Bethune, the NACW president at the time, stated in the "Special Notice" section of the *National Notes,* "We hope that our splendid organ will go forward in the future with the same interest and efficiency as it has in the past. The standard has been set very high and we hope the succeeding editor will keep it so." Cook's expression of appreciation to the organization also appeared in the same issue of the *Notes.*

Cook was nationally known for her work with the Republican party. She served as chairperson of the Women's Division in Jackson county during the 1920 presidential campaign, and in 1924 she was designated national chairperson of the Black Division and a member of the National Speakers' Bureau. During the 1924 campaign she assisted

Hallie Quinn Brown, who was director of Colored Republican Women in the Republican National Committee. In the early 1920s Cook was appointed by the governor as a committee member of the Missouri Negro Educational and Industrial Commission and served for six years. Cook, along with her husband, was involved in other activities as well. Myrtle Foster Cook helped organize the NAACP branch in Kansas City and served as its secretary and treasurer for many years; she also organized the Paseo branch of the YWCA, serving as a member of its first Committee of Management and chair of the Public Affairs Committee. Both of the Cooks were pioneer workers in the Peoples Finance Corporation, of which Myrtle Cook was the major stockholder. The couple also helped organize the Home Seekers Savings and Loan Company in 1926.

Myrtle Cook spent a lifetime in the service of organizations that sought to improve the conditions of blacks. She was a clubwoman, educator, businesswoman, and civic and political worker. Her keen intellect enabled her to contribute much to the development of *National Notes* and to the realization of the NACW's goals of self-improvement, woman's suffrage, and the uplift of the black community. More research is needed to further examine her role in organizations such as the Home Seekers' Savings and Loan Company, the Peoples Finance Corporation, the Republican National party, the NAACP, and the YWCA.

REFERENCES:

Buckley, John M. *History of Monroe County, Michigan.* Chicago: Lewis, 1913.

Davis, Elizabeth L. *Lifting as They Climb.* Washington, D.C.: National Association of Colored Women, 1933.

Devries, James E. "Home Grown: The Black Experience in the City of Monroe, Michigan, 1900-1915." Ph.D. diss., Ball State University, 1978.

———. *Race and Kinship in a Midwestern Town: The Black Experience in Monroe, Michigan, 1900-1915.* Chicago: University of Illinois Press, 1984.

Hill, Daniel G. *The Freedom Seekers: Blacks in Early Canada.* Agincourt, Can.: Book Society of Canada, 1981.

"Hold Funeral Rites for Mrs. H. O. Cook." *Kansas City Call,* September 7, 1951.

"Jay W. Foster Murdered Friday the 13th." *Monroe Record-Commercial,* January 19, 1911.

"Mrs. Karl Schmidt." Obituary. *Monroe Evening News,* May 31, 1954.

"Myrtle Foster Cook." Certificate of Death. Los Angeles, California, August 31, 1951.

National Association of Colored Women. *Minutes of the Tenth Biennial Convention.* Baltimore, Maryland, August 7-10, 1916. *Minutes of the Thirteenth Biennial Convention.* Richmond, Virginia, August 6-12, 1922. *Minutes of the Fifteenth Biennial Convention.* Oakland, California, August 1-5, 1926.

National Association of Colored Women, Inc., 1896-1952. Washington, D.C.: NACW, 1952.

Second Report of the Missouri Negro Educational and Industrial Commission. Jefferson City: Missouri Negro Educational and Industrial Commission, 1920.

Semi-Annual Report of the Missouri Negro Industrial Commission. Jefferson City: Missouri Negro Industrial Commission, 1921.

"Special Notice." *National Notes* 28 (September-October 1926): 3.

COLLECTIONS:

Correspondence of Myrtle Foster Cook, 1918, 1922, 1924-28, Reels 4-6, can be found in the Mary Church Terrell Papers, Manuscript Division of the Library of Congress, Washington, D.C., and in the Mary Church Terrell Papers. Box 102-13, Moorland-Spingarn Research Center, Howard University, Washington, D.C. See also "Myrtle Foster Cook," Works Projects Administration, Historical Records Survey, Folder 18844, Western Historical Manuscript Collection, a joint collection of the University of Missouri and the State Historical Society of Missouri in Columbia.

Ruth A. Hodges

Anne Margaret Cooke
(1907-)
Theater educator, director

For nearly four decades, Anne Margaret Cooke has been a pioneering director, teacher, and administrator in theater education. In 1934, Cooke founded the first black summer theater in America, and in 1949 she brought international acclaim to the Howard Players of Howard University when they became the first undergraduate group in America to be invited to perform abroad with State Department sponsorship. Cooke brought a professional quality to theater programs on predominantly black campuses. She achieved distinction for her excellence wherever she worked, and many of the students and individuals she mentored, including Amiri Baraka, Earl Hyman, Roxie Roker, Shauneille Perry, Zaida Coles, Richard Wesley, Ted Shine, and Joseph Walker, became prominent figures in the theater.

Anna Margaret Cook (she later changed her name to Anne) was born on October 6, 1907, in Washington, D.C., but spent her early years in over a dozen cities before settling in Gary, Indiana, for high school. She is the daughter of Mr. and Mrs. William W. Cooke. Her father was an architect who taught at Wilberforce University in Ohio. Cooke's grandfather, Thomas E. Miller, was a United States congressman from South Carolina and later the first president of South Carolina State College.

Anne Margaret Cooke

Cooke graduated from Emerson High School in Gary, Indiana, in 1924, and that same year, at age sixteen, she entered Oberlin College, where she earned her A.B. in English and art history in 1928. Cooke received her Ph.D. in theater from Yale University in 1944, making her the second known black to receive a Ph.D. in theater in America. (Thomas Poag, later of Tennessee State University, was the first in 1943 with a degree from Cornell.)

Known for her perfect diction, the five-foot-ten-inch, slim, light-complexioned Cooke landed her first job as a teacher of speech and English at Spelman College in Atlanta at the young age of twenty in 1928. In a 1988 interview Cooke spoke about how sophisticated her Spelman students were about life. Cooke felt that she knew very little compared to these women, even though she had traveled a great deal and had read extensively. Many of her students were as old and often older than she was. Cooke also spoke about Atlanta being her first real experience in the South among such large numbers of blacks, having been exposed to primarily integrated situations in the Midwest. In the same interview Cooke stated: "It was my first experience with what today we call blacks, and I was overwhelmed by the blackness and being black." In an April 25, 1993, interview with Shauneille Perry, conducted in New York City at the Hatch-Billops Collection, Cooke indicated that it was during her years at Oberlin that she actually became conscious of race and color:

> I became conscious of race, not from anything the college did, but the handful of black students who were at Oberlin then clustered together and that sort of surprised me. I saw this little huddle, hither and

yon, all pigmented. The Asians didn't all get together. I became very conscious of the behavior of my colleagues and classmates.

Introduces Theater to Black Community

During her first few months at Spelman, Cooke realized that there was virtually no legitimate theater in the city. She viewed this as a gold mine and seized the rare opportunity to organize a small group on the campus. Since there were no existing community theater groups, she had no competition.

Up until this point in her career, Cooke had had very little experience in live theater, particularly as a director. She had, however, seen numerous productions as a young woman because her father, William Cooke, enjoyed the theater. Since they lived near Chicago, the Cookes attended shows regularly. For Cooke, going to the theater was just another part of life. She had desired to major in theater as an undergraduate, but her father persuaded her to pursue English and study theater later, should she consider graduate studies. Before arriving in Spelman, Cooke had taken an eight-week acting course taught by Ivan Lazareff at the Chicago Art Theatre. In addition, during the summer of 1927, she had studied speech for six weeks at the University of Iowa, where she was exposed to theater. Even with her limited work in the theater, Cooke was convinced she knew more about the business than the people in Atlanta.

Equipped with strong organizational skills and a vision, Cooke made theater an integral part of the Atlanta black college community. She started the drama program at Spelman and became its first director. A little theater was created on the campus when Howe Memorial Hall was remodeled in the summer of 1929. One of the first plays Cooke directed was *The Passing of the Third Floor Back*.

For the academic year 1930-31, Cooke took a leave of absence. She studied at the American Academy of Dramatic Arts in New York City and also took courses at Columbia University. The summer prior to enrolling at the academy, she traveled to Europe to observe theater in various countries.

Returning to Spelman in 1931 after a year of intensive theater training, Cooke organized the University Players, composed of students from Spelman, Morehouse, and Atlanta University. The players produced excellent productions, which were attended by blacks and whites. Plays chosen represented modern and classical dramatic works by Sophocles, George Bernard Shaw, Anton Checkov, and Leo Tolstoy. In addition to the productions, Cooke added formal courses, such as theater history, stage lighting, scene design, and writing.

With the strong support of Spelman's president, Florence M. Read, Cooke launched the Atlanta University Summer Theatre in 1934, making it the first black summer theater in the country. In her 1938 fellowship application to the Julius Rosenwald Foundation, Cooke stated the three-fold purpose of the summer theater:

> 1) to provide regular dramatic entertainment to Summer School students and the general public in a community where there are no opportunities for

attending the legitimate theater; 2) to offer a selected group of students and faculty the benefits derived from working a repertory company; 3) to establish a community theater consciousness and to build a permanent, dynamic audience.

The theater ran for six weeks and mounted four full-length productions. These productions, often elaborately executed, included such modern and classical dramas as *Antigone, Medea, Le bourgeois gentilhomme, The Cherry Orchard,* and works by William Shakespeare, Victor Hugo, George Bernard Shaw, and Leo Tolstoy. Referring to the schedule in a 1984 interview, Cooke stated:

Four productions! And they played five nights a week. We'd come at 10:00 in the morning to rehearse next week's show and stop at 3:00 and then have line rehearsal for a show that's going to go on at 8:00 o'clock. And we all got about an hour and a half break.

During the early years Cooke directed as well as designed many of the productions, but as time progressed she brought in such outstanding blacks as director Owen Dodson and designer and technical director John Ross, both Yale graduates; Ella Haith Weaver, director of the Basement Players in Washington, D.C.; Thomas Pawley, professor of speech and theater at Lincoln University in Missouri; James Butcher from Howard University; and Baldwin W. Burroughs, director of dramatics at Houston-Tillotson College in Texas, who later succeeded Cooke as head of Spelman's drama department.

Aside from producing classics, original scripts by students and faculty were added to the season, such as Thomas Pawley's *Smokey,* produced in 1939, which explored the topic of lynching in the South. To encourage more writings by blacks, the University Players sponsored a contest for original scripts based on "Negro life."

The Atlanta Summer Theatre gained a reputation for excellence in dramatics. For many years, the summer theater was the only place where black students were afforded an opportunity to have a concentrated semiprofessional theater experience. Students and teachers from across the country converged on Atlanta to work under Cooke and her outstanding staff. High school teachers came to the theater, and though most of them had no prior theater experience, they were required to produce and direct two or three one-act plays. As the needs of the students and teachers increased, other programs were introduced to the summer theater. In 1937, the theater's summer school was added. Designed for teachers, the program enabled its participants to attend classes in the morning and work on productions during the evening. These teachers would leave Atlanta and be better prepared to raise the quality of performances in institutions located throughout the country.

Cooke's outstanding talents came to the attention of the General Board of Education of the Rockefeller Foundation. With a fellowship from the organization, Cooke entered Yale Drama School in 1936 to pursue an M.F.A. in directing. She attended Yale from 1936 to 1937, and from 1938 to 1940 with assistance from the Rosenwald Foundation. During her years at Yale, she continued as director of the Atlanta Summer Theatre. With strong urging by one of her professors at Yale, Cooke switched from the M.F.A. program in the drama school to the graduate school in 1942 to pursue her Ph.D. in theater. Because of her years of teaching, combined with her course work from the American Academy of Dramatic Arts and Columbia, Cooke needed barely two years of class work toward the Ph.D.

During her period at Yale, Cooke met three other black students pursuing graduate degrees in theater—Fannin Belcher, who wrote the landmark dissertation "The Place of the Negro in the Evolution of the American Theatre, 1767-1940" (1945); Owen Dodson, who would later work with Cooke at Atlanta Summer School and Howard University as well as succeed her as chair of Howard's Department of Drama; and Shirley Graham, who staged the first professional opera composed by a black in America (1932) and was the second wife of W. E. B. Du Bois.

While at Yale, Cooke directed a one-act production entitled *Hospital Scene* in 1940 under the supervision of famed film director Otto Preminger. Through her association with Preminger, Cooke was able to do some directing during the early years of television on NBC. She and Preminger directed *Hospital Scene* for prime time NBC.

In 1942, Cooke left Spelman to become director of the Communications Center at Hampton Institute, a historically black college located in Hampton, Virginia. The center was new and Cooke was brought in to structure the program. Working mainly in an administrative position, Cooke succeeded in launching a new era for Hampton—the beginning of television. She continued to return to Atlanta, however, to direct the summer theater for several years after her departure. When she was not engaged in her administrative and teaching duties at Hampton, Cooke was busy completing her dissertation. Her topic was "The Acting Styles of Garrick, Siddons and Edmund Kean in Relationship to English Taste." During a 1984 interview, Cooke spoke about the difficulty she had writing the dissertation, because at the time, she had a block for academic writing. Much later, a friend finally convinced her to first use a tape recorder to discuss the works and then write the paper, which she found tremendously helpful. Cooke also indicated that she was writing on a subject that was unrelated to what she wanted to do, which was direct, but the dissertation taught her a great deal in terms of eighteenth-century acting and how it also related to furniture and clothing. In 1944 Cooke earned her Ph.D. in theater history. That same year, the president of Howard University invited Cooke to Howard to create a Department of Drama.

The Howard University Years Bring Wide Acclaim

From 1944 to 1958, Cooke organized and chaired Howard University's first drama department, making it the premiere black institution for drama. Before resigning in 1958, Cooke was instrumental in the construction of a new fine arts center on the campus, housing the famed Ira Aldridge Theatre.

The new Department of Drama consisted of Cooke, whose strengths were in administration, history, and the classics; Cooke's Yale classmate, Owen Dodson, who taught directing and playwriting; and James "Beanie" Butcher, a graduate of the University of Iowa, who taught acting and design. Cooke's goal was to create a professional program patterned primarily after the one at Yale. Cooke also believed that students should experience total theater, which meant being exposed to all areas of theater—acting, directing, design, technical matters, and administration. Cooke continued to promote classical drama, including at least one Shakespeare play each season. She also included new works by black writers such as Owen Dodson's *Bayou Legend* (1948) and the premiere of James Baldwin's *The Amen Corner* (1955).

Often referred to as "Queen Anne," Cooke was highly regarded by her students. Many described Cooke's appearance as smooth, with chiseled features and snow white hair, although she appeared very young. She was always immaculately dressed, appearing quite regal. She often seemed much taller than five feet ten inches and always held her head very high. Cooke was perceived as an excellent role model in terms of her intelligence and teaching ability. A firm teacher and somewhat blunt in manner, Cooke administered praise only when she felt it was well deserved. Some students felt that getting praise from Cooke was like hearing from God. Maintaining a professional posture at all times, Cooke rarely socialized with students.

Howard Players Perform Abroad

One of Cooke's monumental accomplishments during her decades in education occurred at Howard during the late 1940s. In the summer of 1948, Washington, D.C.'s only major professional theater, the National Theatre, was closed due to a strike by the Actors Equity Union, which was protesting the National Theatre's refusal to eliminate the color bar and admit black audiences. White theater goers in substantial numbers sought out alternative dramatic entertainment at college productions at such institutions as Howard and Catholic universities. At this time, the Norwegian delegate to the United States, Fredrik Haslund, was in town and was looking for a live performance to attend. That particular week, the Howard Players were performing a production of *The Wild Duck* by Norwegian playwright Henrik Ibsen. The idea of a black cast performing Ibsen intrigued Haslund. He attended, and after the show, he approached Cooke and invited her to come to Norway. With the backing of the Norwegian Parliament and the United States State Department, the Howard Players became the first undergraduates to be invited by the State Department and a foreign government to perform abroad.

The Howard Players were requested to perform in the Scandinavian country for ten weeks. The State Department also requested that the players perform for troops stationed in Berlin, Munich, Mannheim, Kitzigen, and Frankfurt. In addition to the Ibsen play, the players also took a second production abroad—*Mamba's Daughters* by white playwrights Dorothy and Du Bois Heyward, the authors of *Porgy and*

Bess. Many black critics expressed disappointment about the choice of the play, arguing that the players should have chosen a play by one of their own people.

Despite criticism by several blacks, the Howard Players set sail on August 31, 1949, from New York harbor aboard the SS *Stavangerfjord* with twenty of their students and their three faculty members. At the dock to see them off was Eleanor Roosevelt. The trip was a success and a crowning glory for Cooke and the Howard Players. For almost ninety days the players performed in over a dozen cities and four countries and gave close to sixty performances. Members of the troupe included Graham Brown, Roxie Roker, Zaida Coles, William Brown, Marilyn Berry, and Shauneille Perry, who would all become prominent in theater and television. With international recognition to add to her list of achievements, Cooke and the Howard Players continued to make a name for themselves.

In 1958, Cooke married noted Atlanta University sociologist and author Ira De A. Reid. That same year Cooke resigned from Howard to relocate with her husband, who joined the faculty of Haverford College in Pennsylvania. At Haverford, Cooke became active in campus and community drama. The couple spent a year in Nigeria and Japan, teaching and working. After the death of her husband in 1968, Cooke served as senior preceptor for student affairs at the University of California, Santa Cruz, and after leaving that position she began another career at the University of Maryland, teaching for eight years before she retired. During her career Cooke worked as a consultant to numerous organizations, developed modern drama techniques, and served as judge for new plays.

Cooke has been heralded as a dynamic inspiration, particularly for the black women who studied under her and came in contact with her. She achieved what very few black women could even imagine during this period. Not seeing herself as a feminist, Cooke elaborated in the 1993 interview: "I never fought the battle as a female. Women do have to get together to fight, but evaluating a problem or a situation in terms of sex is not my first item." The phenomenal success of the Atlanta University Summer Theatre and that of the Howard University Drama Department must be attributed to the brilliance of Cooke. Cooke resides in White Plains, New York.

REFERENCES:

Cooke, Anne. Interviews with Kathy A. Perkins. Washington, D.C., July 23, 1984 and June 17, 1988.
———. Interview with Shauneille Perry. New York City, Hatch-Billops Collection, April 25, 1993.
Hatch, James V. *Sorrow Is the Only Faithful One: The Life of Owen Dodson*. Urbana: University of Illinois Press, 1993.
Long, Richard. "Theater at Atlanta University." *Atlanta University Bulletin* (September 1974): 18-24.
Read, Florence Matilda. *The Story of Spelman College*. Princeton: Princeton University Press, 1961.

COLLECTIONS:

Information on Anne Cook may be found in Howard University's Channing Pollock Archives, Theater Collection, Washington, D.C.; Moorland-Spingarn Research Center, Manuscript Division, Howard University; Atlanta University Archives, Manuscript Division, Atlanta, Georgia; Spelman College Archives, the Women's Research and Resource Center (including files of the *Messenger*), and the Theater Collection, Spelman College, Atlanta, Georgia; and Rockefeller General Education Board Archives, Manuscript and Recipients, File Divisions, North Tarrytown, New York.

Kathy A. Perkins

Ada A. Cooper

(1861-?)

Lecturer, educator, poet, writer, journalist, missionary

The work of Ada A. Cooper has been told largely through her autobiographical essay published in Monroe A. Majors's *Noted Negro Women*. She spent most of her life teaching, lecturing, and writing in the South. Lawson Scruggs in *Women of Distinction* called her "a brilliant scholar, a pleasant lecturer, a fine writer and an earnest, energetic Christian woman." She is an example of a courageous and determined black woman who emerged from a troubled home life, overcame illnesses, and became a creative and productive member of the community.

Born on February 6, 1861, in Brooklyn, New York, Ada A. Newton Cooper was the daughter of Alexander H. Newton and Olivia Hamilton Newton. Her father was a minister in the New Jersey Conference of the African Methodist Episcopal (AME) Church. Her mother was the daughter of Robert Hamilton, a singer in New York. Ada Cooper had learned to read prior to entering school at age five. She said in her autobiographical essay, "It seems to me that I have always known." In fact, Cooper had been called exceedingly bright early on. After her mother died when Cooper was seven years old, she was placed in her grandmother's care.

The family exposed Cooper to books, perhaps from the home library, and to music, thus helping her to develop her literary and musical talents. In her autobiography she speaks of having read *Pilgrim's Progress, Swiss Family Robinson,* and *Robinson Crusoe* by the time she was ten, and *David Copperfield* by age fourteen. At fourteen she could also recite the works of various poets. Extensive reading continued, and by eighteen she had read *Paradise Lost* and Pope's *Essay on Man.* Cooper labeled herself a "peculiar child" who had no interest in children's games or in playing with dolls. Although she was unable to identify her specific interest, she knew that she preferred activities that would benefit the world.

An accident at age eleven left Cooper with a disease in her hip joint and unable to walk or attend school for nearly two years. At age thirteen she returned to school and wrote a story that impressed her teacher, who said that if she persevered, in time she might be a good writer. From then on Cooper was determined to become a writer.

By the time she was fifteen, her father had transferred to Little Rock, Arkansas, where he pastored an AME church. Cooper moved to Little Rock and lived with her father. His marriage to a young lady near Cooper's age shortly after her arrival apparently left her void of companionship from either her father or her stepmother. Left alone much of the time, Cooper turned her hand to writing again, this time with a story called "Bride of Death."

She remained in Arkansas one and a half years, spent one year in New Orleans, then with her father and stepmother moved to Raleigh, North Carolina, in about 1878. Then about seventeen years old, she enrolled in Shaw University. Cooper was without equal in elocution and composition. She was assigned to teach all of the reading classes in return for free tuition and fees. Apparently the family was very poor, since Cooper says that she had only three dresses during her nearly three years at Shaw. Her schoolmates often ridiculed her shabby dress and plain clothing, yet her spirit remained undaunted.

Writing and Poetry

Soon after her arrival in Raleigh, Cooper met W. R. Harris, a teacher in the local schools. Their mutual attraction led to a secret courtship for over a year, but when her father learned about the relationship he sent Cooper to New Bern, some forty miles away. He believed she could "not love and study too," she said in her autobiography. Perhaps lonely again, Cooper returned to writing. When she was eighteen, her story "Bride of Death," which she had written three years earlier, was published in the *North Carolina Republican,* a newspaper edited by William V. Turner. She published other stories as well, becoming known statewide. Still in New Bern, she was asked to read the emancipation poem on the Emancipation Day celebration. Without a dress to wear, she borrowed one from a friend and read the poem she had written. Here again her work was well received and was discussed widely for some time.

After a time she returned to school and was reunited with her lover, then a professor at St. Augustine's Institute in Raleigh studying to become an Episcopal minister. Although the couple agreed to wait until he had completed his studies before they were married, Cooper's father was still bitterly opposed to the relationship, this time because of Harris's religious affiliation.

Cooper left school at age twenty and returned to Brooklyn with her father. Life became burdensome: home life was unpleasant, and she felt unwanted there; her health was poor; and her lover seemed to have deserted her. She considered ending her life but when a bottle of prescription medicine fell from her hand and shattered, she suddenly felt a desire to live and to accomplish something in life.

In time, Cooper returned to North Carolina to teach in Haywood, Chatham County, where she was reunited with her lover. Describing herself as a pretty, rosy, brown girl with black eyes and straight black hair, she had already recieved numerous marriage proposals, but was still in love with her friend Harris.

Cooper had an unforgettable experience in Haywood that demonstrated her own militancy and racial and gender pride. As she sought medical attention from a Dr. Budd, a white doctor who treated black patients in his home office, she rang the front bell rather than use a black entrance. "I do not go in back yards to see doctors," she told a woman whom she encountered at the residence. She also heard the wife call to her servant, "Tell the doctor there is a nigger woman out here who desires to see him," and listened as the servant told the doctor, "There is a lady out front who desires to see you." A verbal and nearly physical confrontation followed, which led to her being ordered from the yard. As the news reached the Haywood area, most blacks thought she had committed an unpardonable sin. Simon Green Atkins, the prominent educator and later founder of Winston-Salem State Teachers College, and others asked Budd to keep the matter silent and called Cooper "one of the townspeople trying to put on airs."

Cooper moved to Raleigh shortly afterward and in May 1885 married her lover, W. R. Harris, who had completed his studies and was then an Episcopal minister. After his death, the following January, Cooper taught one year at St. Augustine Normal School in Raleigh and then taught three years in graded schools in Raleigh and in Washington, North Carolina. She also edited the "Woman's Column" in *The Outlook*. She continued to write for local papers, became interested in numerous charitable undertakings, and kept on teaching Sunday school, which she had done since she was fifteen years old.

In 1890 Cooper was seriously ill with "congestion of the brain." She sought treatment at Philadelphia's Woman's Hospital, where she underwent surgery. Prayerful during the ordeal, she vowed to devote her life to God if He would spare her life. When she recovered she moved to Maryland, where she taught for three months, giving herself untiringly to the people among whom she lived and worked, perhaps to meet her vow made during her hospital stay. She left Maryland to become a traveling agent with a western publishing company, traveling from Trenton, New Jersey, to Easton, Pennsylvania, where she became ill again and was unable to work.

Reward through Lecturing

With the encouragement of a Methodist minister, Cooper lectured in his church, then sang and recited. Successful in her presentation, she embarked on a new career as a lecturer, perhaps also singing and giving recitations. The press gave her favorable reviews as did such notable religious leaders as bishops Henry McNeal Turner and Levi Jenkins Coppin.

Cooper continued to travel, lecture, and visit the sick until she reached Winchester, Virginia, where she worked for five months as a missionary in Free Will Baptist Church. It was the experience in Winchester that encouraged her to become a missionary or evangelist in the AME Church.

As a missionary, Cooper felt a need to visit prisons and places of ill repute. She lectured until she reached Raleigh again in 1891, in time to attend the Southern Exposition. On November 5, 1891, she lectured before the North Carolina Industrial Fair on the exposition grounds and was said to have made a presentation far superior to that of Louisiana's black governor Pinckney Benton Stewart Pinchback, who was among the speakers.

She met A. N. Cooper, also a minister in the AME Church, on November 18, 1891. They were married on January 13, 1892. She lived in Washington, North Carolina, and continued her writings, concentrating on a book of poems that she proposed to complete in 1893. Additional research is needed to identify Cooper's works and examine them as early examples of writings by black women. She may be best known for her writings and her missionary work.

REFERENCES:

Majors, Monroe A. *Noted Negro Women.* Chicago: Donohue and Henneberry, 1893.

Scruggs, Lawson. *Women of Distinction.* Raleigh, N.C.: L. A. Scruggs, 1893.

Jessie Carney Smith

J. California Cooper
Short story writer, novelist, playwright

J. California Cooper is one of the most prominent black American fiction writers today. In an interview on August 18, 1994, she said, "I don't really think of myself as being a writer; I just tell stories. . . . I don't know really know how to write; I just do it." Critics and the public have tended to disagree, however. In 1989, her second collection of short stories, *Homemade Love,* won an American Book Award. In 1991, *Family,* her first novel, was bought by the Literary Guild, which gave her much greater visibility and a wider audience.

Cooper was born in Berkeley, California, to Joseph C. and Maxine Rosemary Lincoln Cooper, and she has spent most of her life in the San Francisco Bay area—Oakland and Berkeley. Because she liked the first name that her mother gave her and found it very personal and private, she decided to keep it silent; thus, she uses only the initial of her given name. She adopted the name "California." She refuses to reveal the year she was born because she believes that age is unimportant.

J. California Cooper

From 1987 to 1994, Cooper led a very quiet and almost reclusive life in the small city of Marshall, Texas. She said of herself in the *Dallas Morning News,* "Nobody really knows me, and I'll tell you why. Because I am really extra private for some reason I don't know. My daughter [Paris Williams] knows me more than anybody." Marshall was her father's hometown and Cooper spent a year there with her aunt when she was twelve. She returned to Marshall over the years, so she never forgot the hard work of country life and the bleak realities of jobs such as picking cotton for a penny a pound. The little city of Marshall, where tall, ancient trees formed a canopy over Cooper's bright green house, gave her the peace and tranquility she both desired and needed to write her books. In November 1994, however, Cooper moved back to Oakland, for two reasons: to be close to her daughter, who is working on her master's degree in anthropology and archaeology at Antioch College in San Francisco, and to gain more ready access to larger libraries, which house the research materials she now finds she needs.

The serenity Cooper found in Marshall was indeed a source of creative inspiration. Her second novel, *In Search of Satisfaction,* was published in October 1994, and her fifth collection of short stories, *Some Love, Some Pain, Sometime,* will be published in the fall of 1995. Her earlier short story collections, *A Piece of Mine, Some Soul to Keep, Homemade Love,* and *The Matter Is Life,* brought her recognition and fame as a gifted storyteller. Cooper explained one of the reasons she wrote *Family* in the May 1991 issue of *Essence:* "I wanted to tell people that if you're white, the person you may hate could be your relative, so you should love." As she put it in the *Dallas Morning News,* July 24, 1994, "The family is the nucleus—the center—of life. If you think about it, what else is there in the world?"

Alice Walker Encourages Writer

Cooper credits Alice Walker, the best-selling author of the novel *The Color Purple,* with launching her career as a short story writer. In an August 18, 1994, interview, Cooper stated that, had it not been for Walker, her stories "could still be sitting in the drawer." Before Cooper ever published any of her fiction, she had written seventeen plays. In 1978, she was named San Francisco's Black Playwright of the Year for *Strangers,* and in 1988 she received the James Baldwin Award and the American Library Association's Literary Lion Award. Alice Walker read Cooper's collection of plays and encouraged her to write stories. The result was *A Piece of Mine,* which Walker published through Wild Trees Press, her own company. According to the *Dallas Morning News,* Walker wrote: "In its strong folk flavor, Cooper's work reminds us of Langston Hughes and Zora Neale Hurston. Like theirs, her style is deceptively simple and direct. . . . It is a delight to read her stories."

Of her characters and her own life, Cooper said in an interview:

> I try always to be honest. If one of my characters is acting foolish, well, I write it, [but] I don't like a fool! All of my life I've prayed "Don't let me be a fool." I write about fools and people who have integrity, and God permeates the whole thing, my life and my work. Good always triumphs over evil.

Cooper writes in bed, in longhand, during the early morning hours. She stated in an August 18, 1994, interview that her stories and characters come to her "all at one time, and I just have to get down all the conversations and words they're saying." She writes this way—in longhand—because "this is the only way I can get those voices to come," she continued. She later completes the work on a computer.

In 1987 Cooper made her escape to Marshall, Texas. Away from the noise of the city, she created her own private, eclectic domicile. She kept a pair of goldfinches, two cats, and some chickens, all of which were given special names. She surrounds herself with her books, her music, her plants, and her pets. She said in an August 31, 1994, interview, "Everywhere I look in my house, I can see something that I love—my birds, my cats, my books. My heart is filled with love and I enjoy having something that I love all around me." While Cooper rarely entertains guests, she does occasional public readings and lecture tours to promote her work.

In a September 2, 1994, interview, Cooper said that her mother, Maxine Rosemary Lincoln Cooper, was "a great thinker and a great reader. She was a woman who loved wisdom and wanted her children to use their brains and opportunities to make successful lives for themselves." According to Cooper, her mother was also a woman who wanted to be either "a gun moll or a pioneer." Her zest for life encouraged Cooper's lively imagination. For Cooper, writing dramas was a natural extension of her habit of playing with paper dolls, which she did until she was seventeen. Cooper said in the *Dallas Morning News,* "My mother took them away, but the next year I was married and was getting ready to have a baby. She should have left me alone with those paper dolls! But she took them away—and so I began to write stuff out."

While her youthful imaginary stories always had beautiful endings, Cooper's life has had its ups and downs. Two unsuccessful marriages, the death of her only brother, who was an award-winning artist, in January 1993, and the loss of her mother several years ago have caused her great heartache. For Cooper, the best part of her life now is her daughter, Paris Williams, who is her pride and joy.

During Cooper's very full life, she has reared a child, traveled the world, taken extension courses at San Francisco State College and the University of California at Berkeley, and worked as a secretary, waitress, manicurist, loan officer, and—when she lived with her mother in Alaska—bus and truck driver as a member of the Teamsters Union. She said in the *Dallas Morning News:* "I don't believe people hate to grow old so much as you hate to grow past your opportunities. The way life looks to me is, you can do different chapters." While writing is now her immediate occupation, Cooper would like other possible chapters to be such experiences as taking flying lessons, training as an LPN, and taking art classes and learning to paint.

The idea of time is a recurrent theme in Cooper's works. Her own life embodies her conception of time as she expressed in *Family:* "History, Lived, Not Written, is such a thing not to understand always, but to marvel over. Time is so forever that life has many instances when you can say 'Once upon a time' thousands of times in one life." When asked about her characters in connection with the idea of time, Cooper said in an August 18, 1994, interview: "They are all fictional, and I have no favorites. I just love to come back to these people that I know and love so well, because I've been through all of their pain and their struggles. They are truly old friends." For most readers these characters also become old friends, ones they want to visit again.

Current Address: Arabella Meyer, Doubleday and Company, 1540 Broadway, New York, NY 10036-4094.

REFERENCES:

Cooper, J. California. *Family.* New York: Doubleday, 1991.
———. Telephone interview with Phyllis Wood, August 18 and 31, 1994; September 3, 1994.
"J. California Cooper." *Dallas Morning News,* July 24, 1994.
Oliver, Stephanie Stokes. "J. California Cooper: From Paper Dolls to Paperbacks." *Essence* 21 (May 1991): 52.

Phyllis Wood

Patricia S. Cowings
(1948-)
Psychologist, flight scientist

Solving the condition of motion sickness, the number-one problem that astronauts face as they venture into space, has been the main concern of Patricia Cowings from her earliest days as a scientist. The results of recent space missions in which Cowings's procedures were applied suggest that motion sickness and space motion sickness can be significantly relieved through the use of a technique called Autogenic Feedback Training (AFT). AFT may be an effective alternative to antimotion sickness medication and produces no harmful or uncomfortable side-effects. Research on AFT has been the focus of Cowings's career at the National Aeronautics and Space Administration (NASA) Ames Research Center. This work is crucial to space exploration because a permanent human presence in space requires a thorough understanding of the physiological and behavior indicators of human adaptation to the microgravity environment. AFT is used to facilitate this adaptation process.

Patricia Cowings was born in New York City on December 15, 1948, the only girl among the four children of Sadie B. Cowings and Albert S. Cowings. Albert Cowings owned and operated a neighborhood grocery store in the Bronx for thirty years. Later he worked as a guard at the Metropolitan Museum of Art until his retirement. Sadie B. Cowings obtained an associate degree in psychology at the age of fifty-five and became an assistant teacher for preschoolers for the New York City Board of Education. While Patricia Cowings has become internationally known in the fields of psychology and psychophysiology, her oldest brother, a two-star general, is the Commanding General of Army Aviation and Troops. Another brother is a professional jazz vocalist, and the other one is a professional disc-jockey and a freelance writer.

Patricia S. Cowings grew up in the Bronx, New York, and attended Music and Art High School. Upon graduation, she elected to attend State University of New York at Stony Brook because of the outstanding reputation of its psychology department. In college Cowings majored in psychology, serving as a research assistant for four years, and graduated with honors in psychology in 1970. She enrolled in the doctoral program in psychology at the University of California at Davis and received both her master's and doctorate in psychology in 1973.

Work with NASA

A graduate school summer program first brought Cowings to work at NASA as a research psychologist, beginning a long-term relationship between Cowings and the space agency. While in graduate school, Cowings was a teaching assistant. As guest investigator at Rockefeller University where she studied, she worked with Neal E. Miller, who created the field of visceral learning, now called biofeedback.

Patricia S. Cowings

He was the first person to say this was possible. Cowings received recognition for her distinguished scholarship in graduate school and a National Research Council postdoctoral associateship at the completion of her doctoral work.

Cowings works in collaboration with international space agencies, engineers, astronauts, and other scientists. She particularly enjoys her work with astronauts. Since the beginning of her career, Cowings has published her research findings, often with her co-investigator of twenty-two years, her husband William B. Toscano.

The title of one of Cowings's early projects, for which she was principal investigator, suggests her interest in the problem to which she has devoted most of her time, "A Preventive Method for Zero Gravity Sickness Syndrome" (1976). One of the first publications she coauthored is entitled "Visceral Responses to Opposite Types of Autogenic Training Imagery." In 1976, at their annual scientific meeting, the Space Medicine branch of the Aerospace Medical Association recognized Cowings for her "Learned Control of Multiple Autonomic Responses to Compensate for the Debilitating Effects of Motion Sickness." The association gave her an award for producing the Best Aerospace Medicine Research Paper by a Young Investigator.

In the zero gravity environment in which astronauts work, motion sickness is a frequent problem and it can seriously reduce the crew's efficiency. In order to combat motion sickness, astronauts first learn to recognize its signs. Using the Autogenic Feedback System 2 (AFS-2) developed by Cowings and her associates, astronauts are trained to detect the symptoms and learn what to do to stop them. This training helps to improve the level of performance of cockpit crews on NASA missions and allows the astronauts to stay in space longer.

Among Cowings's recent publications on the topic of motion sickness are "Autogenic Feedback Training as a Countermeasure for Orthostatic Intolerance"; "The Stability of Individual Patterns of Autonomic Responses to Motion Sickness Stimulation"; "Autogenic-Feedback Training: A Preventive Method for Motion and Space Sickness"; "The Effects of Autogenic Feedback Training on Emergency Flight Performance"; and "Autogenic Feedback Training Improves Pilot Performance during Emergency Flying Conditions."

The titles of some of Cowings's other publications reflect additional subjects that have attracted her interest. These include "Observed Differences in Learning Ability of Heart Rate Self-regulation as a Function of Hypnotic Susceptibility" (1977); "Combined Use of Autogenic Therapy and Biofeedback in Training Effective Control of Heart Rate by Humans" (1977); "A Theory on the Evolutionary Significance of Psychosomatic Disease" (1977); and "Psychosomatic Health: Simultaneous Control of Multiple Autonomic Responses by Humans—A Training Method" (1977).

Since her college days, Patricia Cowings has continuously garnered recognition for her work. She has won both individual and group achievement awards from NASA several times for her work on flight experiments on Spacelab missions. In 1985 she was the recipient of the Ames Honors Award for Excellence in the Category of Scientist. She was recognized by the Mid-Peninsula YWCA as Outstanding Black Woman of 1988. The following year she received the Candace Award for Science and Technology from the National Coalition of 100 Black Women. In 1990 Cowings was the recipient of the Innovative Research Award by the Biofeedback Society of California and an award for "Achieving against the Odds" from the Black United Fund of Texas. In 1993 she was appointed professor of psychiatry at the Neuropsychiatric Institute of the University of California, Los Angeles, medical school. Cowings explained that although she was trained in psychology, a field which focuses on the study of behavior, she works as a professor of psychiatry so she can pass along methods she has developed for healing behavior, which falls under the work of psychiatrists.

Recognized for Scientific Achievements

Cowings's work has been the subject of television coverage. Her work on space motion sickness has been featured on the PBS *Discover* series and on *Nova,* as well as on *Walter Cronkite's Universe.* Her work received attention in the NASA film *Space for Women* and the in PBS program *Black Stars in Orbit,* which featured many African American contributors to aerospace. Cowings has also received media coverage in both Australia and Japan.

Additional recognition of Cowings's work has come in the form of memberships in professional societies and in invitations to present papers at national and international gatherings. Cowings has been a member of the Aerospace Medical Association since 1973 and was elected an associate fellow in 1986. She is also a fellow in the American Autogenic Society. She holds memberships in the Society for Psychophysiological Research, American Association for the Advancement of Science, Association for Applied Psychophysiology and Biofeedback of California, and New York Academy of Science. Cowings is a charter member of the Aerospace Human Factors Association and was elected a fellow in 1993. In addition, she holds memberships in the Human Factors and Ergonomics Society and the American Autonomic Society.

Cowings has participated in numerous technical committees and panels both in the United States and internationally, including the U.S./Russia Symposia on the Biomedical Problems of Crewed Spaceflight in Moscow; the ninth annual Symposium on the Role of Psychology in the Department of Defense; the fifteenth annual meeting of the Biofeedback Society of America; and the first Joint NASA Cardiopulmonary Work Shop. More than once she has been part of an Investigators Working Group for Payload Development for Department of Defense Space Shuttle Missions.

At present, Cowings holds the title of research psychologist and director of the Psychophysiological Research Laboratory at NASA's Ames Research Center at Moffett Field, California. She serves as a collaborator on a NASA/U.S. Coast Guard/U.S. Army study of autogenic feedback training to improve the coordination of cockpit crews in high-performance aircraft flight. The success of Autogenic Feedback Training in space flight has suggested new possibilities for its use with airplane pilots and those who navigate on water. Cowings is working in collaboration with the Japanese space agency NASDA on a project to monitor human health in space (Spacelab J) and has provided Japanese astronauts with Autogenic Feedback Training. She is the principal investigator for a Spacelab J experiment entitled Autogenic Feedback Training as a Preventive Method for Space Motion Sickness. She received the Eleventh Annual Lectureship for the Society of Nuclear Medicine in 1994. In that year she also gave four lectures at Mayo Clinic in Rochester, Minnesota.

Cowings has been married for sixteen years to her co-investigator, William B. Toscano. They have a son, Christopher Michael Cowings Toscano.

As a psychologist and space scientist Cowings has made important contributions to the nation's space program. Her work has led to the relief of motion sickness and greater understanding of human adaptation to the microgravity environment.

Current Address: Life Science Division, NASA Ames Research Center, Mail stop 239A-2, Moffett Field, CA 94035.

REFERENCES:

Cowings, Patricia S. Interview with Martia Graham Goodson, July 1993.

————. Telephone interview with Jessie Carney Smith, February 27, 1995.

Graves, Curtis, and Ivan Van Sertima. "Space Science: The African-American Contribution." In *Blacks in Science: Ancient and Modern.* Edited by Ivan Van Sertima. New Brunswick, N.J.: Transaction Books, 1983.

Martia Graham Goodson

Wilhelmina Marguerita Crosson
(1900-1991)
Educator, school administrator, community worker

Known for her pioneering teaching methods, Wilhelmina Marguerita Crosson was one of the first American educators to view reading not as an isolated subject but as a learning skill to be used in all areas of study. She began the first remedial reading program in Boston in 1935, and in 1952 she became the second president of the Alice Freeman Palmer Memorial Institute in Sedalia, North Carolina, one of the country's leading preparatory schools for blacks.

Expressing her views on the teacher's proper role, Crosson told Marie Hart in a February 28, 1981, interview that "all children need a good foundation and each child should be studied individually and then grouped according to their needs." Crosson wanted to share the joy of learning with others in hopes of preparing them for a better life; she felt that children should have a future goal that they needed to work toward, and she sought to develop the self-esteem of her students, believing that pride in oneself is the basis for self-fulfillment and achievement.

Wilhelmina Marguerita Crosson was born on April 26, 1900, in Rutherford, New Jersey. She was the fourth of nine children born to Charles Tasker Crosson, Sr., and Sallie Alice Davis Crosson. Her parents, who were born in Warrenton, North Carolina, in 1872, moved the family to New Jersey around 1900 and to the Cambridge area of Boston in 1906. Charles Crosson, Sr. was a minister, painter, paper hanger, and realtor. They moved to Boston so that he could find better employment and his children could have a better education.

Crosson had three brothers and five sisters (Viola, Susie, Primrose, Nanny, George, Tasker, Archie, and Lorraine). The children were all named for celebrities. Wilhelmina was named for Queen Wilhelmina of the Netherlands. Each child was expected to excel, inspired by his or her famous namesake. All of the children finished high school and some attended college. The family joined the Ebenezer Baptist Church in Boston. Wilhelmina Crosson was baptized at age

Wilhelmina Marguerita Crosson

thirteen, and at age fifteen she joined the Twelfth Baptist Church.

Crosson attended the Boston public schools; her early education took place at Hyde School, and she graduated from Girls' High School in the Roxbury section of Boston. Blacks were just beginning to attend Girls' High but Crosson excelled in her studies and was a star player on the girls' basketball team.

Crosson always wanted to teach and felt it was her God-given talent. As a child she would arrange her dolls and give them lessons. Since she wanted to be an elementary school teacher, Crosson decided to attend Salem Normal School (later Salem Teachers College) because of its elementary school department. Crosson commuted the sixteen miles from Boston to Salem each day, since the school did not have dormitories. She sometimes worked a part-time job in Boston before heading to school. Crosson was the only black student in Salem's elementary section, but two blacks were enrolled in the junior high section.

Black graduates had difficulty getting the necessary experience to qualify for a teaching job in Boston. The distinguished black educator Charlotte Hawkins Brown, a graduate of Salem and the founder of the Palmer Memorial Institute in Sedalia, North Carolina, often offered promising teachers the opportunity to work at the school. Crosson hoped that she would be one of the lucky ones chosen by Brown.

Crosson had always admired Brown. As a child, she remembered hearing Brown speak each April at Ebenezer Baptist Church. Crosson's Sunday school teacher, May E.

Luck, took her to the lectures. The Crosson family had put aside "a penny a meal to help Palmer," and each April Wilhelmina turned over the box of pennies to Brown. Charlotte Hawkins Brown sometimes went to the Salem Normal School to speak with the students, and on occasion she took Crosson to dinner. It was during this period that Crosson hoped Brown would ask her to come to teach at Palmer. When she was not selected, Crosson started her teaching career in Boston.

Crosson received a bachelor's degree from Boston Teachers' College in 1934. She had been working for some ten years before she received her B.S. in education, but felt that it was necessary to get a degree. In 1954 Crosson earned a master's degree from Boston University in educational administration. She took additional education courses at Harvard University, Goddard College, Columbia University, Emerson College of Oratory, and Purdue University. She would often return to Goddard, an experimental college in Plainfield, Vermont, to take courses that would keep her in touch with the latest advances in the field of education. She also took courses at the University of Mexico.

Success as a Reading Specialist

Crosson began her teaching career in the 1920s at the oldest girls' school in Boston, the Hancock School, located on the North End. She was one of the first black women to teach in the Boston public schools. It was at Hancock, in 1935, that she started the first remedial reading program in Boston. One of the first four teachers chosen to teach remedial reading, her first assignment was to teach the children of Italian immigrants. She instilled in her students a desire to learn by appealing to their imaginations. Old teaching methods and equipment were replaced by materials dictated by new concepts. Her program was extremely successful.

Crosson was among the first teachers to see the need for remedial reading courses. Such courses reflected a new pedagogy that viewed reading as an essential learning tool and not just an isolated subject to be taught to students. Crosson's approach was so successful that she was invited to speak on the subject, and teachers, administrators, and students were sent to observe her teaching methods. Children even asked to be sent to Crosson because the learning skills she taught not only helped them with their reading but also their other subjects. Crosson opened the first of four Remedial Centers in Boston at the Paul Revere School, located in the all-white Hancock district. This center served all six schools in the district.

Crosson was known for her ability to work with many ethnic and religious groups. Not only did she teach Italian children, but she worked with Catholic, Baptist, and Methodist groups as well. One of the highlights of her early career came when she was selected as one of the forty-eight best teachers in the Boston school system. School superintendent Jeremiah E. Burke called the honored teachers the "cream of the crop of Boston" and told them how much they were appreciated for their work.

In 1945 Crosson took a sabbatical from the Boston public schools to study the intercultural approach to teaching in the Mexican public schools. She studied at the University of Mexico and worked under the auspices of the Association for the Study of Negro Life and History (now Association for the Study of Afro American Life and History). She also wanted to investigate the persons with African ancestry living in the country. She found this part of her trip a difficult task as blacks, Jews, Japanese, Chinese, Indians, and Spaniards all intermarried, losing many of their own racial characteristics, and they had assimilated into the Mexican culture.

Crosson observed little racial hatred in the country. She found a number of black Cubans and also blacks from the West Indies, most of whom came to Mexico to supply the demand for labor. It was while she was in Mexico that she received a letter asking her to return to teach at the all-black Hyde School and continue her work in remedial education. At first she did not want to leave her school on Boston's North End because she had been there for twenty-five years, but she was encouraged by her family to take the position to help black children.

At the Hyde School in Roxbury, Crosson worked with children in grades one to three. The first grade class had had some twenty substitute teachers before she arrived. After making many changes she was able to get the children to develop a love for reading. She encouraged the parents to purchase books to help the children build their libraries. Crosson did pioneering work on the "Cleveland Plan," which was another method of remedial reading that graded students according to book levels instead of class levels.

Crosson loved her students but also had a concern for the community as a whole. When she learned that some black children were dropping out of school, she took measures to help the students realize the importance of education. She also helped them learn about their heritage and gave them the encouragement and will to stay in school. To this end, she founded and organized the Aristo Club. This group of black professional women met to study black history and to give scholarships to worthy black children. To raise scholarship monies, Aristo members would often write and produce pageants depicting events and personalities in black history.

Crosson was an associate editor of the *Boston Teachers News Letter* and was a member of the League of Women for Community Service, the Boston League of Women Voters, the Alpha Kappa Alpha Sorority, and the Charles Cox Fund Committee, which gave thirty-two thousand dollars yearly to needy students and families. She taught Sunday school at Twelfth Baptist Church and also taught black history to adults and children on Saturdays.

New Era Begins at Palmer Memorial Institute

In 1949 Charlotte Hawkins Brown invited Crosson to teach remedial reading at the Alice Freeman Palmer Memorial Institute in Sedalia, North Carolina—the school that Brown had founded in 1902. Crosson took a leave of absence from the Hyde School and arrived on the Palmer campus in August.

Palmer Memorial Institute, once a finishing school, had become a college preparatory school. Crosson lived with Brown in the house Brown had built on campus, known as Canary Cottage. Most of the students came from prosperous families, many were city children, and some came from foreign countries. The students were exposed to art, literature, and music. Brown would not let segregated facilities stop her students from enjoying recreational and cultural events. She would often rent an entire theater or buy an entire section of a hall or theater so her students could attend performances.

Following the same educational philosophy as Brown, Crosson set up the Learning Aid Center for the full development of honor students at Palmer. In the view of both women, students are educated through all their activities—including those taking place in the classroom, the dining room, and the dormitory—as well as through their cultural, spiritual, financial, and physical lives. This was the basic "Seven Program" that was designed to make the student academically and culturally secure.

After a fire on the campus on October 8, 1950, Brown's health began to fail and she became more dependent on Crosson, who had by then become the administrative assistant to the president. Brown had been grooming Crosson to become the president of Palmer and in 1952 Brown asked her if she could take over the position. The board of trustees also asked her to take on the presidency.

October 5, 1952, marked a turning point at Palmer Memorial Institute. Brown relinquished her responsibilities as president and passed on the torch to her chosen successor, Wilhelmina Marguerita Crosson. Thus Brown ended fifty years of service to the institution she founded, although she stayed on at Palmer as vice-chairperson of the board of trustees and director of finances. She continued to share Canary Cottage with Crosson and was a source of inspiration and counsel for several years.

Mordecai Johnson, president of Howard University, delivered Crosson's inaugural address. He honored Brown and her work at the school that his son had attended. Brown's charge to Crosson upon her inauguration is quoted in Constance Hill Marteena's biography of Brown:

> I want . . . [Palmer] to continue to be a standard school, where good breeding and good English will play a major part. I want the pupils to be courteous; I want them to be good students so that they can become an integral part of this great century; and "Mena" if you preserve these values, that's all I can expect. If you are going to do a good job, you will be dedicated.

With Brown on the campus, along with other dedicated teachers and staff, Crosson was able to ease into her responsibilities. It was during this time that Crosson completed her master's degree at Boston University. As president, Crosson instituted many new programs and received government funding to help with the school. Some of the programs included upgrading the program for high school students with academic problems. This program was funded by the Ford

Foundation. She also initiated the Upward Bound program to help needy high school seniors attend college. She had a training program for students from African countries, and Palmer students also had an opportunity to study in England, Spain, and France for eight weeks during the summer.

As time passed, Crosson had difficulty obtaining more funds for the school, although she did secure $530,000 from the Babcock-Reynolds Foundation for the building program. She retired in 1966 and returned to Boston in 1970 to undertake such volunteer work as tutoring children in reading and helping in homeless shelters.

In 1968 Rose Butler Brown of North Carolina College (now Carolina Central University) asked Crosson to come to the college for four months to help build a curriculum for Peace Corps volunteers. When questioned in an interview with Constance H. Marteena if this request infringed on her retirement, Crosson stated, "I am still concerned with doing all that I can to further Black Awareness. I have given much thought to spending my time in the most advantageous way toward this goal."

Palmer Memorial Institute closed in 1971. On February 14 of that year the Alice Freeman Palmer Building was destroyed by fire. In November Bennett College assumed the debts and took over the site. In the 1981 interview with Marie Hart, Crosson discussed how Palmer had changed over the years. The most dramatic changes were in the student body. She stated that the students attending Palmer after the 1960s did not believe in the old philosophy that she tried to carry on from the Brown administration, needed more freedom, and were not as interested in their cultural development. When asked if there was a place for schools like Palmer in the 1980s and how integration would have affected Palmer, Crosson said that "the school must have good teachers who have a love for their job and children and also believe that children should have freedom to develop. Integration would not have affected the students much since all races were always on campus. There were some white faculty and most of the Board of Trustees was white. There would have been no problems with integration."

In 1983 the Charlotte Hawkins Brown Historical Foundation was incorporated to help establish North Carolina's first historic site to honor a black and a woman. In 1987 the former campus of the Palmer Memorial Institute was designated a historic site. Many of the materials of the school are now housed at the North Carolina State Archives in the Department of Cultural Resources, Historic Sites Section.

Crosson was a quiet woman who took no credit for her many accomplishments. In 1960 Crosson was honored by the Florida Association of Colored Women, and on October 26, 1969, the Boston and Vicinity Negro Business and Professional Women's Clubs honored her at their sixth annual awards luncheon by presenting her with the Sojourner Truth Plaque. In 1971 she was presented with the Dolly Madison Award from the Greensboro, North Carolina, Chamber of Commerce.

Crosson died on Tuesday, May 28, 1991, at her home on West Springfield Street in Boston's South End. Funeral services were held on Saturday, June 1, 1991, at the Twelfth Baptist Church with Michael E. Haynes, pastor of the church, officiating. During the service, many tributes were paid to Crosson. The burial site for Crosson is the Mount Hope Cemetery in Mattapan, Massachusetts. She was survived by her sister Viola. The Wilhelmina M. Crosson Scholarship Fund was established in her honor at the Twelfth Baptist Church.

REFERENCES:

"Annual Meeting at Coliseum Tuesday." *Greensboro Record,* January 6, 1971.

"A Bit of New England in North Carolina." *The Brown American* 1 (Summer 1958): 20-35.

Crosson, Wilhelmina. "Women for Democracy: Harriet G. Hosmer." *Boston Teachers News Letter* (March 1934): 64.

————. *Personally Conducted: A Series of Articles Relating to Historical Spots of Interest in and around Boston.* Reprinted articles from the January-June 1939 issues of *Boston Teachers News Letter.* Boston: Wilhelmina M. Crosson, n.d.

————. Interview with Marie Hart. Boston, Mass., February 28, 1981.

Dannett, Sylvia G., ed. *Profiles of Negro Womanhood.* Vol. II. New York: Educational Heritage, 1966.

Funeral Program. Wilhelmina M. Crosson. Twelfth Baptist Church, Boston, Mass., June 1, 1991.

Marteena, Constance Hill. *The Lengthening Shadow of a Woman: A Biography of Charlotte Hawkins Brown.* Hicksville, N.Y.: Exposition Press, 1977.

"A New Guide." *The Brown American* 1 (Summer 1958): 36-38.

Smith, Jessie Carney, ed. *Notable Black American Women.* Detroit: Gale Research, 1992.

"Wilhelmina M. Crosson, at 91; A Pioneer in Remedial Reading." *Boston Globe,* May 31, 1991.

"Wilhelmina M. Crosson in Mexico." *Negro History Bulletin* 9 (June 1946): 206, 213.

"Wilhelmina M. Crosson Reports on Intercultural Education in Mexico." *Negro History Bulletin* 10 (December 1946): 55-60, 68-71.

COLLECTIONS:

Bennett College Archives, Bennett College, Greensboro, N.C., has articles on Crosson and a copy of her interview with Constance H. Marteena. The North Carolina State Archives, Department of Cultural Resources, Historical Site Section, Raleigh, N.C., has articles, the Marie Hart interview, and the materials on Charlotte Hawkins Brown from the Schlesinger Library, Radcliffe College. Materials on Charlotte Hawkins Brown and the Palmer Memorial Institute can also be found in the following collections: Schlesinger Library, Radcliffe College, Cambridge, Mass.; Bethune Museum and Archives,

Washington, D.C.; Schomburg Center for Research in Black Culture, New York Public Library; North Carolina Historical Room, Greensboro Public Library; W. C. Jackson Library, University of North Carolina, Greensboro; Carol Brice Papers, Amistad Research Center, Tulane University, New Orleans, La.; and the Moorland-Spingarn Research Center, Howard University, Washington, D.C.

Janet Sims-Wood

Minnie Lou Crosthwaite

Minnie Lou Crosthwaite
(1860-1937)
Educator, college registrar, clubwoman

Minnie Lou Crosthwaite became the first black teacher in the segregated public school system of Nashville, Tennessee, in 1879. Finding the standard practice of hiring only white teachers in the "colored" schools of Nashville unacceptable, Crosthwaite decided to try to upset the system and succeeded. As a child, Crosthwaite had witnessed a celebration marking the founding of Fisk University, where for years to come education would be provided for thousands of students regardless of gender or ethnic origin. Highly honored in Nashville and the surrounding vicinity, she was perhaps best known for her work at Fisk University as registrar and in the community as a clubwoman and promoter of human relations.

Born in Nashville, Tennessee, on August 20, 1860, Minnie Lou Scott Crosthwaite was the daughter of Frances McAlister Scott. Her father's name is not known. She began her early education at Fisk when the school offered elementary and high school training, studying there from 1865 to 1867. She then entered the public schools, where she remained until 1874. According to Mary E. Spence in *Fisk News,* May 1922, she had known the Fisk campus from her early childhood. When Crosthwaite gave a tribute to Ruthanna Jackson Cravath at her death in 1922, she recalled watching with her grandmother the celebration held for Erastus Milo Cravath and his wife, Ruthanna Cravath, when they arrived as president and first lady at the opening of the Fisk School, as it was called, in 1865. Along with the carriage that bore the Cravaths and the governor of Tennessee, who represented the founding association, the American Missionary Association, she saw

> a procession of many colored people in all manner of costumes, men, old and young, some in rags, some in cast-off soldiers' uniforms, women in homespun dresses, the older ones with bandanna handkerchiefs tied around their foreheads, all marching up Cedar street, led by a band, everyone very happy over this new opportunity to obtain an education.

Crosthwaite enrolled in the Higher Normal or Teacher Training Department at Fisk in 1874, completing the course in 1877 when she was seventeen years old. On June 12, 1884, Minnie Lou Scott married Scott Washington Crosthwaite. They had four children: Holcome Sinclair, George Scott, Scott Washington, Jr., and Lenida Thomas.

Scott Washington Crosthwaite, Sr. was a physician, clergyman, and educator. Born near Murfreesboro, Rutherford County, Tennessee, on April or May 8, 1856, he was the son of Scott Taylor Crosthwaite and Joyce Elizabeth Keeble Crosthwaite. He worked as a shoe shine boy, barber, bellboy, and waiter to earn enough money for his education. He attended Nashville's public schools and in 1889 graduated from Meharry Medical College in Nashville. Scott Crosthwaite graduated from Chicago Homeopathic Medical College in 1891 and received a Bachelor of Divinity degree from Fisk University in 1909.

Up to 1879 the "colored" schools of Nashville employed only white teachers. In summer 1874 Scott Crosthwaite began to teach in the county schools, continuing to do so a part of each year until 1879. Dissatisfied with the discriminatory practice of hiring only white teachers in the public schools, he and Minnie Crosthwaite sought to determine whether or not black teachers could be appointed to the Nashville public schools. To qualify, applicants were required to pass a teachers' examination. The first black to pass the examination and qualify, Minnie Crosthwaite became the first black teacher in Nashville's schools. She had been reluctant to interrupt her studies—she was now in her junior year in her attempt to get her bachelor's degree—but saw a great opportunity to address the "crisis in the education of colored children." The first four black teachers in Nashville's public schools were, in addition to Minnie Crosthwaite, Scott Crosthwaite, who became the first black principal, Robert White, and another young woman who thus far remains unidentified.

Scott Crosthwaite, who became a prominent citizen, practiced medicine in Nashville and Knoxville from 1891 to 1896. In addition to chairing the Committee of Religious Education for the Middle Tennessee Colored Teachers' Association, he was a member of the Carnegie Library Committee and the Nashville Negro Board of Trade and held other positions devoted to community interests. Minnie Crosthwaite taught fourteen years in the Nashville schools and a few years at Slater Training School in Knoxville when the family relocated there. When the Crosthwaites returned to Nashville, Minnie Crosthwaite resumed her training at Fisk and received a bachelor of arts degree in June 1903. The family lived near the Fisk campus, first at 1815 Morena Street and later at 1025 Eighteenth Avenue, North.

Crosthwaite joined the Fisk faculty in 1905 as instructor in mathematics; she was also in charge of developmental or drill courses in the subject. From 1906 to 1910 she was principal of the Normal Department, then became registrar in 1910. She continued to teach in the Normal Department on a part-time basis until 1916, when she devoted her full attention to the registrar's position. She retired in the 1925-26 academic year. Crosthwaite was responsible for the detailed record-keeping practices for alumni. She recorded alumni news such as births, marriages, deaths, changes in positions and locations, and other information of vital importance to alumnae and the institution. She was named registrar emeritus in the 1927-28 school year. According to Mary D. Shane, who wrote a tribute to Crosthwaite at her death, published in *Fisk News,* January-February 1937, Crosthwaite was best known on the whole as registrar and for her keen interest in students. "She was friend, adviser, counselor and mother. She had time for the little problems to grown-ups, but all important to the student who needed to be guided very carefully during the tempestuous adolescent stage." She was insightful, tactful, courageous, patient, and empathetic, according to Shane. She had a remarkable memory and never forgot past and present events or any student who ever attended Fisk during her tenure. Shane continued in her tribute to Crosthwaite: "Whenever Fiskites get together, both old and new, one figure remains outstanding as a memory of their school days, that of Minnie Lou Crosthwaite." Minerva Hawkins, who was a Fisk student during Crosthwaite's tenure and became her close friend, remembered her in a September 13, 1994, interview as a tall, hefty, proud, and majestic woman who never bowed her head but always held it upright. "I remember watching her during chapel service. Instead of bowing during prayer, she held head back and closed her eyes."

Crosthwaite Works as Humanitarian

Minnie Lou Crosthwaite's commitment to human relations extended beyond the Fisk campus and the classroom. During World War I she headed a movement that raised money for needy soldiers in middle Tennessee. She pioneered the establishment of the YWCA and headed the organization on the Fisk campus. She was also one of the initial workers for the local branch of the YWCA in Nashville. Her interest in race relations was demonstrated by her membership in the Southern Interracial League.

Her community activities brought Crosthwaite into the company of such outstanding local black women professionals and leaders as Nettie Napier, Frankie J. Pierce, and physician Josie Wells. Crosthwaite wrote a moving tribute to Napier, "The Model Woman: A Toast," given during James Carroll Napier's eighty-seventh birthday celebration held in Nashville on June 9, 1932. The women were active in Nashville's black women's organizations, including the City Federation of Colored Women's Clubs. In 1907, Napier founded the Day Home Club in a house located at 618 Fourth Avenue South, later known as Porter homestead. Club president Napier called a meeting on January 14, 1907, for women who were interested in supporting programs for the poor and needy black women and children in Nashville. Josie Wells was appointed physician-in-charge. Crosthwaite reported on the educational activities of blacks in Nashville.

Following a trend established in the federated black women's clubs throughout the country, Crosthwaite worked with several public-spirited black women, including Frankie Pierce, to found the Tennessee Vocational School for Colored Girls which opened on October 9, 1923, with Pierce as superintendent. The aim was to provide wholesome surroundings for the young women and to help them build a new life based on their own "morals and courage."

In 1927 Crosthwaite became the first woman alumni trustee for Fisk University, remaining on the board for eight years. She was elected with two male graduates, Henry Hugh Proctor and F. A. Stewart. The Crosthwaites left Nashville in 1927 and moved to St. Paul, Minnesota, where they lived at 447 Carroll Street. By fall 1928 she had moved to Detroit, Michigan, where she lived with her younger son, whose address at first was 7143 Sarena Street, then 521 Hague Avenue. By the time of Crosthwaite's death she had given thirty years of service to Fisk University. Her continued interest in Fisk was expressed clearly in her letters to Fisk president Thomas Elsa Jones, and he kept her informed about Fisk matters.

Crosthwaite's life was touched by a distasteful aspect of U.S. history. She was deeply concerned about racial problems in Nashville in the mid-1930s and their potential impact on Fisk University. She wrote to Jones on January 22, 1934, to express her concern for the safety of the institution and its students. Forty years earlier she had passed through a crowd on Church Street in downtown Nashville marching into town to lynch Ephraim Grizzard, a black man from nearby Gallatin, Tennessee.

> They went thru Nashville without question at 2 P.M. in the day, marched to the jail, battered down the door, took the prisoner to the bridge leading from Cedar St, and lynched him. My husband stood in the rear of the O'Bryan Bros. Store on the square, and

saw it. Two of my white neighbors, both young ladies, came home, told me about it, and exhibited a bit of his clothing as a treasured souvenir. And, if the people who do those things want to come on the campus of Fisk and do the same thing, they will.

Crosthwaite died at her home in Detroit, Michigan, on January 13, 1937. The university recognized her on October 6, 1963, when it dedicated a new, modern, air-conditioned women's dormitory, Crosthwaite Hall, in her honor. Minnie Lou Crosthwaite, a Congregationalist, was an important educator, college registrar, and community worker whose work has been hidden from view, but who made important contributions to black and women's history.

REFERENCES:

Collins, L. M. *One Hundred Years of Fisk University Presidents: 1875-1975.* Nashville: Hemphill Creative Printing, 1989.

Crosthwaite, Mrs. S. W. [Minnie Lou]. "The Model Woman: A Toast." Paper delivered at the Ira Bryant sponsored celebration of J. C. Napier's Eighty-Seventh Birthday, Nashville, Tennessee, June 9, 1932.

Dedication of Crosthwaite Hall, Fisk University. Program. Ninety-second Jubilee Day. Sunday, October 6, 1963.

Hawkins, Minerva H. Interview with Jessie Carney Smith, September 13, 1994.

Mather, Frank Lincoln. *Who's Who of the Colored Race.* Vol. 1. Chicago: n.p., 1915.

"Meeting of Day Home Club." *Nashville Globe,* October 30, 1908.

Shane, Mary D. "Mrs. Minnie Lou Crosthwaite as a Woman." *Fisk News* 10 (January-February 1937): 3-4.

Spence, Mary E. "Ruthanna Jackson Cravath Called Home." *Fisk News* 12 (May 1922): 1-18.

"Women's Meeting Held in the Interest of 'Day Home' Project." *Nashville Globe,* February 22, 1907.

COLLECTIONS:

Correspondence of Thomas Elsa Jones and Minnie Lou Crosthwaite during her tenure on the board of trustees are in the Thomas Elsa Jones Collection, Special Collections, Fisk University Library.

Jessie Carney Smith

D

Julie Dash
(1952-)
Filmmaker

Julie Dash claims that she never intended to become a filmmaker; indeed, it was serendipity that led her to discover the joys and possibilities inherent in cinematography. Today, she has become an independent filmmaker acclaimed for her fine screen representations of African American women. With the general release of *Daughters of the Dust* in 1992, Julie Dash became the first African American woman to have a full-length general theatrical release.

Born in New York City in 1952, Julie Dash spent her early years in the Queensbridge Housing Projects in Long Island City. She said in her *"Daughters of the Dust": The Making of an African American Women's Film* that her path to filmmaking occurred quite by accident when she was seventeen:

> I was just tagging along with a friend who had heard about a cinematography workshop (at the Studio Museum in Harlem) and thought she could learn to take still photos. We joined the workshop and became members of a group of young African Americans discovering the power of making and redefining our images on the screen.

The challenge of the workshop captured her interest; when she was nineteen years old, she made her first film: *The Legend of Carl Lee DuVall.* Using pictures from *Jet* magazine attached to pipe cleaners and shooting with a super 8 camera, she later said in her book about the making of *Daughters of the Dust* that she created this "animated film about a pimp who goes to an African village and is beaten and dragged out of the village by the people there." She did not know that her career had begun.

Although she loved the creative potential and the sheer fun of cinematography, she did not think of it in terms of her lifetime pursuit. She intended to become a physical education teacher when she entered college; then, as an undergraduate at the City College of New York, she majored in psychology. While still a student, she discovered a special film studies program at the Leonard Davis Center for the Performing Arts. It was her successful interview at this David Picker Film Institute that permitted her to graduate from City College of New York with a degree in film production. Even before graduation, however, she was being productive: in 1974, she wrote and produced *Working Models of Success,* a promotional documentary for the New York Urban Coalition.

Julie Dash

Armed with a bachelor of arts in film production, she immediately set off for the West Coast. Los Angeles was home to many black documentary filmmakers; the promise of camaraderie, mentorship, and support was appealing. She began her career by joining the crew of Larry Clark's film *Passing Through* (1973) as a sound assistant. It was there, in the California desert, that she met Cora Lee Day, who was later to portray Nana Peazant in *Daughters of the Dust.* Julie Dash then received a fellowship to the Center for Advanced Film Studies at the American Film Institute. One of the youngest fellows to attend, she studied under William Friedkin, Jan Kadar, Slavko Vorkapich, and other distinguished filmmakers.

Films Earn Recognition and Awards

During her two-year fellowship, Dash worked diligently and her efforts foreshadowed the quality of her later films. She completed a feature-length screenplay, *Enemy of the Sun.* She also received two auspicious awards. In 1977, she received a Director's Guild Award for a student film that was shown at the Los Angeles film exposition. This adaptation of an Alice Walker short story was titled *Diary of an African Nun* (1977). One year later, she received a Gold Medal for Women in Film at the 1978 Miami International Film Festival for *Four Women*. This award-winning work was an experimental dance film that she conceived and directed.

Dash next worked for the Motion Picture Association of America (MPAA) in Los Angeles. As a member of the Classifications and Rating Administration, she was one of six voting board members who made daily decisions that affected the fortunes of more than 350 movies made each of the years she worked there. As part of her affiliation with the MPAA, she traveled to Europe and attended the Cannes International Film Festival in France. In 1980 she cosponsored a session at the festival; this presentation was comprised of several short films by black Americans.

Dash's fascination with depicting diverse and positive images of black women in film led to a 1981 Guggenheim grant to create a series of films about black women. That grant sparked the films that would bring her wide acclaim.

According to S. V. Hartman and Farah Griffin in the summer 1991 issue of *Black American Literature Forum, Illusions* (1983), a thirty-four minute film set in Hollywood, "raised the difficult question 'How can blackness be truly represented, if at all?'" N. H. Goodall, writing in *Black Women in America* says the film explores issues of race and gender by focusing upon two African American characters:

> Two black women occupy differing spaces in wartime (1942) Hollywood: one has become a studio executive while passing for white; the other is a behind-the-scenes singer, dubbing the voices of the white starlets on the screen. Both illustrate how the film industry specifically and society in general conspire to keep Black women both voiceless and invisible.

This drama was highly acclaimed. It was awarded the 1989 Jury Prize for Best Film of the Decade by the Black Filmmakers Foundation, was nominated for a 1988 Cable Ace Award in Art Direction, was the season opener of the Learning Channel's series on fictional works by independent filmmakers, and won for its creator the 1985 Black Cinema Society Award. Prints of *Four Women* and *Illusions* can be found in the archives of Indiana University and Clark Atlanta University.

During the decade of the 1980s, Dash was extremely busy. She was granted an Individual Artist Grant from the National Endowment for the Humanities in 1981, 1983, and 1985. In 1982, she joined a group of other black American independent filmmakers at a film festival in England; "this festival occasioned the historical meeting of Black American independent filmmakers with their British counterparts," she said in *"Daughters of the Dust": The Making of an African American Women's Film*. Later that year, she was invited to attend the Festival against Racism in Amiens, France. A year later, two of her films were selected as part of the Black Filmmakers Foundation exhibit to introduce African audiences in forty countries to the works of black Americans. In 1986, she moved to Atlanta to work on several projects: she was directing apprentice for *The Leader of the Band* and

became involved in the National Black Women's Health Project, helping to create information videotapes. In 1987, she was involved with two works for the women's health project, *Breaking the Silence: On Reproductive Rights* (director), and *Preventing Cancer* (producer, director, editor).

Daughters of the Dust Takes Form

Dash's *Daughters of the Dust* had begun quite modestly in 1975, but during the 1980s, the filmmaker continued to work on this project that kept growing in scope. Originally, Julie Dash said in her book about the film, she had conceived a different film: ". . . a short silent film about the migration of an African American family from the Sea Islands off of the South Carolina mainland to the mainland and then the North. I envisioned it as a kind of 'Last Supper' before migration and the separation of the family." The birth of hew own daughter, N'zinga, in 1984, was further impetus for the *Daughters of the Dust* project. As a mother, Julie Dash now clearly and personally saw unity of the past, present, and future. N'zinga became the prototype for the unborn spirit child who moves so freely among the film's characters. The film was also, in a sense, a gift to N'zinga, since it is grounded in Julie Dash's own family history.

In 1988, Dash founded Geechee Girls Productions, Inc. This is her own company and is based in Atlanta. She has said that the company "brings to bear the power and the voice of the African American female's spirit into the area of media production." *Daughters of the Dust* is a Geechee Girls production.

Daughters catapulted Julie Dash to national attention. The film enjoyed wide release and critical acclaim. It won first prize in cinematography for dramatic film at the 1991 Sundance Film Festival in Utah where it premiered; it also was nominated for Outstanding Motion Picture of 1992 by the Beverly Hills chapter of the NAACP for the twenty-fifth annual Image Awards. Reviewers found *Daughters* to be truly affecting. Gregory Tate stated in Dash's book that "the film works on . . . emotions in ways that have less to do with what happens in the plot than with the ways the characters personalize the broader traumas, triumphs, tragedies, and anxieties peculiar to the African American experience." The film is a powerful and beautiful statement of the strength of tradition as a sustaining force in the face of disenfranchisement and assimilation. Critics noted that the work is poetic in its voice, stunning in its photography, creative in its structure, and eloquent in its vision. Centering upon a turn-of-the-century African American community belonging to the South Carolina coast culture known as Gullah or Geechee, the film captures the tenacious, independent spirit of these people whose unique society developed in self-imposed, carefully guarded isolation. The sense of cultural unity that transcends time and place is vividly depicted through a complex interaction of character, structure, and symbol.

Despite the film's critical success, however, Dash had difficulty finding a distributor, in part because film executives were concerned that the film's attempts to recreate the Gullah dialect would be incomprehensible to moviegoers. Eventually, in July 1992, *Daughters* was nationally televised as part of the PBS American Playhouse series. Since then, appreciation among scholars has been growing. Toni Cade Bambara said in the preface to Dash's 1992 book about the film that "currently *Daughters* is enjoying cult status. It is not unreasonable to predict that it will shortly achieve the status it deserves—classic.''

Dash has been the recipient of several awards: the American Film Institute selected her to receive the 1993 Maya Deren Award, given annually to independent film and video artists; the National Conference of Black Mayors honored her in 1993 for Literary Excellence at the nineteenth annual President's Luncheon; the Greater New York chapter of the Links presented her with the 1993 "Sojourner Truth Award" in the Visual Arts/Cinema category; and the National Coalition of 100 Black Women presented her in 1992 with a Candace Award, a tribute to achievement among African American women. Most recently, Dash received a Fulbright fellowship for work in London with Maureen Blackwood on a screenplay about the black British film collective Sankofa.

Making twentieth-century American films that speak to the black experience is a task Julie Dash well understands. She has acknowledged this challenge in *"Daughters of the Dust": The Making of an African American Women's Film:*

> One of the ongoing struggles of African American filmmakers is the fight against being pushed, through financial and social pressure, into telling only one kind of story. African Americans have stories as varied as any other people in American society. As varied as any other people in the world. Our lives, our history, our present reality is no more limited to "ghetto" stories, than Italian Americans are to the Mafia, or Jewish Americans to the Holocaust. We have so many stories to tell. It will greatly enrich American filmmaking and American culture if we tell them.

Julie Dash's contributions lie in her achievement as an African American woman filmmaker, in the superior quality of her work as cinematographer, and in the message she offers. Her creation of strong, positive female images, her fusion of reality and spirituality, and her holistic view of African American identity all combine to truly enrich American filmmaking.

Current Address: Geechee Girls Film/Video Productions, 137 North Larchmont Blvd., Suite 244, Los Angeles, CA 90004.

REFERENCES:

Boyd, Valerie. *"Daughters of the Dust." American Visions* 6 (February 1991): 46-48.
Chambers, Veronica. "Finally, a Black Woman behind the Camera." *Glamour* 90 (March 1992): 111.
Dash, Julie. *"Daughters of the Dust": The Making of an African American Women's Film.* Preface by Toni Cade Bambara. New York City: New Press, 1992.
———. Bio. sheet. Geechee Girls Productions.
Flanagan, Sylvia. *"Daughters of the Dust." Jet* 81 (March 23, 1992): 62.
Hartman, S. V., and Farah Jasmine Griffin. "Are You as Colored as That Negro?: The Politics of Being Seen in Julie Dash's *Illusions." Black American Literature Forum* 25 (Summer 1991): 361-73.
Hine, Darlene Clark, ed. *Black Women in America.* Brooklyn: Carlson Publishing, 1993.
"Julie Dash: Geechee Girl." Promotional material. Atlanta: Moorc, Littlc, Inc.
Kauffman, Stanley. Review of *Daughters of the Dust. New Republic* 206 (February 10, 1992): 26-29.
Tate, Gregory. "A Word." In *"Daughters of the Dust": The Making of an African American Women's Film,* by Julie Dash. New York: New Press, 1992.
Thomas, Deborah. "Julie Dash." *Essence* 22 (February 1992): 38.

Margaret Duckworth

Dora Dean
(c. 1872-1949)
Dancer, entertainer

Dora Dean was half of the team of Johnson and Dean, which was one of the most popular vaudeville acts of the pre-World War I era. When the act split up in 1914, both Dean and Charles E. Johnson, her husband, carried on independently with lesser success. They reunited twenty years later to try a comeback just as vaudeville was finally dying out for good. Radio audiences in New York were reminded of her name in 1946 when John Reed King asked his studio audience at WCCO every Saturday morning for weeks, "Who is Dora Dean?" and offered large prizes for a correct answer.

Dora Dean's beauty was legendary. Her looks were such that in the late 1890s Bert Williams wrote a song about her after he saw her perform an acrobatic soft shoe dance while wearing an elegant evening gown. Her partner and husband, Johnson, wore top hat, tails, and kid gloves. The team of Williams and Walker used the song in the New York performances that made them national stars.

> Oh, have you ever seen Miss Dora Dean,
> She is the sweetest gal you ever seen.
> Someday I'm going to make this Gal my Queen.
> On next Sunday morning, I'm going to marry
> Miss Dora Dean.

Little is known of Dean's background. A February 1953 *Ebony* article says that she was born Dora Babbige and was the sister of Clarence Babbige, the first black judge in Kentucky. Covington, Kentucky, is her birthplace according to one source, and another says Owensboro, Kentucky, adding

Dora Dean

that her mother was a former slave. Other efforts to trace the family heritage have not been able to verify this information. She herself referred to working as a nursemaid in Cincinnati, Ohio, before she changed her name and went on the stage. In 1889 she was in the chorus of Sam T. Jack's *Creole Show;* she was living in Indiana when she was hired by Jack as a "statue" girl because of her good figure. Through her involvement in *Creole Show* she met Charles E. Johnson of Minnesota, who had also joined the company, his first experience in traveling on his own and his first experience in a traveling company.

Johnson was the son of Eliza Diggs Johnson, a former slave in Missouri, who told him about cakewalks on the plantation, and her husband, a free black. Born in St. Charles, Missouri, on July 27, 1871, Johnson moved to Minneapolis after his father's death. There he became locally famous as a dancer while he worked as a shoe shine boy at the Nicollet Hotel barber shop for three dollars a week and tips. He then joined the *Creole Show,* where he earned seven dollars a week and room and board. Becoming celebrated as an eccentric dancer, Johnson was soon the star of the show, for which he worked several years.

White entrepreneur Sam T. Jack's *Creole Show* was a minstrel show with a difference: it was a large-scale show that, instead of the traditional row of male performers, featured in the first part beautiful and well-dressed women, who stood in a semicircle with a woman interlocutor. Just two men appeared in the semicircle: they stood on the end telling the jokes and playing the bones and tambourines. Before this show, men had also traditionally played all women's roles,

including those of dancers. In addition to the beautiful women, the *Creole Show* had a supporting cast of singers, dancers, and comedians of both sexes. Not only did the show highlight black women performers for the first time, it also broke with the traditional minstrel show's stereotypical depiction of plantation life in favor of a combination of burlesque and vaudeville. Jack ran the business side and left to veteran black performer Sam Lucas the artistic direction of the company. Lucas gave black writers and composers like Bob Cole the chance to hone their skills by writing songs and skits. The show was a great success and important in opening up new avenues for black entertainers. It was an excellent training ground for Johnson and Dean.

Cakewalk Revived

Johnson said that he fell in love with Dora Dean at first sight, but it would be some time before they actually married. According to Tom Fletcher (1873-1954), a black performer and chronicler of blacks in show business, Johnson used his memories of what his mother told him about the cakewalk to revive the dance for the *Creole Show*. He added fancy steps, and the show launched the tremendous vogue for the dance at the turn of the century. The cakewalk remained a popular feature of later Johnson and Dean acts.

Johnson and Dean were married in Chicago in 1893. Johnson, along with Dean presumably, was still with the *Creole Show* at the end of 1893 when he introduced a new sketch worked up by Bob Cole. There is a reference in one source to Johnson and Dean completing a successful engagement in Minneapolis in July 1894, but Dean was reported to be very ill. This was perhaps a summer tryout for their act, since the two finally left Sam Jack's *Creole* company on May 20, 1895. By 1897 they were reaching the top ranks in vaudeville. From the beginning, their act was innovative. Dean introduced the practice of wearing costly gowns, and Johnson claimed to be the first person of any race to wear evening dress in a theatrical act. Their success was resoundingly affirmed on August 30, 1897, when they were the first black act to receive top billing at Tony Pastor's Theater in New York.

On the technical side, in 1897 Johnson became the first to introduce steel plates, or taps, for dancing shoes. In 1901 the team introduced the flicker spotlight, which they called a kinetoscope; as the team danced against a black background the intermittent light picked out the white accents on their costumes. In addition, Dean pioneered in the use of tights to discretely display her charms. In a foreign tour of 1913 the team took what may have been the first jazz band to reach Europe; it included drummer Peggie Holland and pianist Kid Coles. This tour also provides direct evidence of the influence of Johnson and Dean on subsequent "class" acts. Rufus Greenlee and Teddy Drayton accompanied the team and, inspired by their example of elegance, decided they would both dress up, thereby breaking the tradition that a black male vaudeville team consisted of a rustic blackface comedian and a dandified straight man, as exemplified by Bert Williams and George Walker. By the 1920s the team of Greenlee and

Drayton was fabulously successful in vaudeville and an inspiration for other black performers.

By today's standards, Dean was no sylph, and she picked up more weight during the European tours. A caption from a *Vanity Fair* photo of December 11, 1908, reads: "Dora Dean, of the comedy team of Johnson and Dean, it can plainly be seen is not very lean, and as they have been living on the fat of the land while they were making a big hit abroad it would be a big surprise to the patrons of the Wm. Morris Inc., vaudeville houses if she was lean."

Still, Dean was beautiful, but her charms were not only physical. In their *Jazz Dance* Marshall and Jean Stearns quote from an interview with Rufus Greenlee, who said "Miss Dean had a fabulous personality. Whenever she encouraged us, it made us feel two feet taller."

Vaudeville Team Becomes Internationally Famous

Dean's charms were also displayed on cigarette cards when she became the Sweet Caporal Girl. A vertical file on Johnson and Dean at the Schumburg Library in New York contains a piece of publicity for the 1936 revival of their act in which they list their vaudeville records from 1897 to 1914 in telegraphic style:

> One hundred and fifty consecutive nights at Koster and Bials, New York. Three months every summer for three years at Hammerstein's Roof Garden, New York. Two months every year for five years at Wintergarten, Berlin, Germany. Three months every summer for three years at Os-Budavara, Budapest, Hungary. Six months over Richards Circuit, Australia. Two months every year for three years at Palace Theatre, London, England. [The engagement at Tony Pastor's.] Fifteen years as a feature act over Keith-Proctor and Orpheum Circuits.

By the end of 1901 Johnson and Dean were appearing in Germany. Sometime before August 1902 Dean posed for a full-length portrait by the German painter Ernest Hellman, who paid the team's salary for two weeks so Dean would be free to pose. She is depicted in a cakewalking attitude, and the picture was exhibited at the Paris Exposition of that year. A copy of the portrait was one of Charles E. Johnson's prize possessions in his old age, and as he talked of the possibility of a comeback after her death, he always envisioned having it on stage as he danced.

Johnson and Dean were back performing at Keith's Union Square Theatre in New York City by the middle of November 1902, but their European tour had been such a success that they returned there in the summer of 1903 for a protracted stay. On January 15, 1904, they had a huge success as they topped the bill at the Palace Theatre in London. From the summer of 1904 to the summer of 1905 they played in Germany, France, Austria, and Hungary. They then returned to England to tour. In December 1905 they were in Budapest again. In May 1907 they opened in St. Petersburg, Russia. There may have been a brief return to the United States in

1908 before they returned to the U.S. for a longer period in August 1909.

A rather cool review in the October 2, 1909, *Variety,* reprinted in Henry Sampson's *The Ghost Walks,* gives the most extensive overview of the act to that date. Dean sang a Hungarian song wearing tights that were flesh colored on the right leg between the knee and hip. The song was not much liked, and it was dropped, according to the reviewer, because of the limitations of Dean's voice, which rendered her unable to handle a showy song. The critic felt that Johnson and Dean were getting above themselves because of their European experiences, and he stated that the team should concentrate on "singing Coon songs and dancing." He was also shocked by the simulated display of flesh. He added:

> Besides her splendid figure Miss Dean is showing a handsome lot of jewels. A couple of diamond earrings weigh a ton or so on looks, and a blazing diamond pin lies upon her neck. Her dressing is just a trifle extravagant, especially at first, when a cloak gives a look of overdressing. Just what will be left for Miss Dean to do if the tights are chopped is a query, but they risk considerable by the display. . . . If Johnson and Dean will get down to business, show all the good dressing they want to, be "swell" in every way as becomes colored people on stage, forgetting all about Continental Europe adulation, they will become once again the leaders among the colored mixed acts in vaudeville.

The *Indianapolis Freeman* was more appreciative of the 1909 Johnson and Dean act and went into greater detail when the paper reviewed the act in New York a few days after *Variety,* in a piece also reprinted by Sampson. The reviewer wrote:

> The act ran as follows: First part. Johnson and Dean enter with a pretty little song, "I Wouldn't Leave My Little Wooded Hut for You." Mr. Johnson wore a black full dress suit of the latest pattern, while Miss Dean wore a pretty evening coat of costly appearance, with a beautiful pair of diamond earrings in her ears, and presented a fine appearance. They finished the first part of their present offering with soft-shoe dancing a la Charles Johnson to fine applause. Second part. Mr. Johnson enters in a suit of an English soldier. . . . Miss Dean enters in white tights, and they sing and dance, the song being "I'm an English Coon." Mr. Johnson did some clever and original dancing at the finish of his act that won the team a great many encores.

Neither Dean nor Johnson was a talented singer—they talked their way through songs and put themselves over with personality and elegance. Johnson was not primarily a tap dancer. According to the Stearnses, "He was a strutter in the cakewalk tradition and an eccentric dancer who employed legomania, a rhythmic twisting and turning of the legs." Dean seems to have been famous more for her poses than for her dancing. It was the slowdown of show business with the immanent outbreak of World War I, not any decline in popularity, that led to the breakup of the act in 1914. Rufus Greenlee, on tour with them in Europe that last year, testified that they did not get along very well.

Dean Heads "Pick Act"

On June 26, 1914, *Variety* reviewed the act of Dora Dean and Company. This was a "pick act," which consisted of a woman and black children—pickaninnies. The quality of pick acts depended upon the dancing and singing abilities of the children, and they were usually headed by white women. Dean was the first black woman to lead one. *Variety* predicted, "The act should go very well on the big small time." On July 23, 1914, the *Minneapolis Journal* reported on the appearance of Dora Dean and Her Fancy Phantoms—now with only two girls—and stated that the act had been booked for thirty-five weeks on the Loew's circuit. If Dean was no longer at the very top of vaudeville, she was able to keep performing at a lesser level of success. She continued to dress well. A *Variety* article of February 5, 1915, stated that she opened the act wearing "a pink satin dress with a crystalled tunic of old blue." There was a large black hat with aigrettes. She then changed to a harem costume with pale blue bloomers and purple chiffon dress. Her final outfit was a salmon pink satin dress covered with white net and edged in white fox. This display of expensive dress was a constant in Dean's career. Although Dean has been remembered as having an array of thousand-dollar dresses, there is only one mentioned in sources published during Dean's career. Still the three to five hundred dollar dresses mentioned in one account brought her outlay for one act to over one thousand dollars. This was a very substantial amount of money by the standards of the time, even for a team that probably earned five hundred dollars a week or more—a common rate for a top act.

While there is no doubt about Dean's success as head of the pick act, details of her career become scantier after 1914. In addition to her own act, she is credited with training other pick acts for the European circuit. At some point she left show business for a while and went into business with fellow veteran performer Mattie Wilkes. They set up a lingerie and hat shop in New York City. In 1926 Dean worked as maid to Queen Marie of Romania during the queen's visit to the United States. Dean received a ruby and diamond studded brooch in appreciation of her work. Contemporary interest in the queen was high enough for Dean to have a business card printed up mentioning the connection and to include the event in subsequent publicity, along with an illustration of the brooch.

The February 1953 *Ebony* article says that when Dean went to Los Angeles to work in the black movie *Georgia Rose,* starring Clarence Brooks and Evelyn Preer, she met up with Charles Johnson again and they reconciled. Since Phyllis Klotman in *Frame by Frame: A Black Flimography* dates the movie to 1930 rather than 1934, this would not seem to be the immediate cause of their comeback reunion because Johnson says they got together after a twenty-year separation, that is,

in 1934. The reconciliation inspired thoughts of a comeback despite the pair's age and the rapid decline of the popularity of vaudeville. In March 1936 Johnson and Dean enjoyed short-lived success at Connie's Inn in New York, and they continued to make appearances for a few years. Johnson was dancing as late as 1942, when he injured his leg badly in a Minneapolis nightclub. By then Dean was no longer performing. At the time of her death on December 13, 1949, in Minneapolis, she had been ill for many years and had retired some ten years before.

In any case, Dean and Johnson, who died in 1953, had enough money to live comfortably in their Minneapolis home. At one time they owned all the houses on one side of a block. All but two had to be sold because of the expenses connected with Dean's illness, but those two provided sufficient income to support Johnson after her death.

The presence of black acts on the vaudeville stage has almost been effaced from memory, but Dean and her partner were major stars on the white circuits. They helped increase the range of opportunities in show business for blacks and especially for black women. While Dora Dean and Charles E. Johnson won fame as a team, Dean must be recognized for her special contributions to the success of the partnership.

REFERENCES:

"'Cake Walk' Strutters." *St. Paul (Minnesota) Press,* September 4, 1937.

"Cakewalk King." *Ebony* 8 (February 1953): 99-106.

"Dora Dean and Company." *Variety,* June 26, 1914.

"Dora Dean, of Dance Team Johnson and Dean Is Dead." *New York Amsterdam News,* December 17, 1949.

"Dora Dean's Colored Act." *Minneapolis Journal,* July 23, 1914.

Emery, Lynne Fauley. *Black Dance from 1619 to Today.* Princeton, N.J.: Princeton Book Publishers, 1988.

Fletcher, Tom. *100 Years of the Negro in Show Business.* New York: Da Capo Press, 1984.

Haskins, James. *Black Dance in America.* New York: Harper Trophy, 1992.

Klotman, Phyllis Rauch. *Frame by Frame: A Black Filmography.* Bloomington: Indiana University Press, 1979.

"Miss Dean and Her Fantoms." *Variety,* February 5, 1915.

"Originators of Cake Walk Strutting Their Stuff Again." *St. Paul (Minnesota) News,* September 6, 1937.

Sampson, Henry T. *The Ghost Walks: A Chronological History of Blacks in Show Business.* Metuchen, N.J.: Scarecrow Press, 1988.

Stearns, Marshall, and Jean Stearns. *Jazz Dance.* New York: Macmillan, 1968.

Tanner, Jo A. *Dusky Maidens.* Westport, Conn.: Greenwood Press, 1992.

"Two Dancers Die at Ripe Age." *Dance News,* January, 1950.

"Who's Dora Dean? City Holds Answer to Quiz Program." *Minneapolis Morning Tribune,* October 22, 1946.

COLLECTIONS:

Three repositories in New York have clippings and other materials on Dora Dean. These are the Dance Collection at Lincoln Center, the Billy Rose Theatre Collection at Lincoln Center, and a vertical file at the Schomburg Library. For photos of Dora Dean with captions, see *Vanity Fair,* December 4 and 11, 1908, located in the Robinson Locke Collection of Dramatic Scrapbooks, Billy Rose Theatre Collection. For publicity sheets of Johnson and Dean, c. 1934, see the Schomburg Library vertical file.

Robert L. Johns

Georgia Mabel De Baptiste
(1867-19??)

Social worker, religious worker, educator, journalist

Georgia Mabel De Baptiste

Georgia Mabel De Baptiste (the name also appears as DeBaptiste and DeBaptist) began her career as a teacher and writer for Baptist publications, went to Liberia as a missionary, headed the Women's Auxiliary of the National Baptist Convention of America, and finally became a social worker in Chicago. Her life and work is representative of the experience of many nineteenth-century black women who, through their church and club activities, were inspired to pursue their interests in social work. These trailblazing women are becoming objects of contemporary interest and study, but, unfortunately, knowledge of the life of De Baptiste—and the lives of others like her—remains incomplete.

Georgia Mabel De Baptiste was born on November 24, 1867, in Chicago, Illinois. She was the daughter of Richard H. De Baptiste (1831-?) and Georgiana Bush De Baptiste (?-1872) and apparently one of three children. Georgiana Bush was originally from Cincinnati, and she was married to De Baptiste in 1855. Like his wife, Richard H. De Baptiste was a member of a prominent family, and he became a leading Baptist minister. He was born in Fredericksburg, Virginia, on November 11, 1831. His father and uncle, William and Edward, were bricklayers and plasterers by trade and the largest contractors and builders in the city and its county. Richard De Baptiste followed this trade until his conversion led him to the Baptist ministry. His parents maintained a private school in their home for the education of their children and those of their relatives.

Richard De Baptiste moved to Detroit and later worked as a teacher in Ohio for several years before he was ordained in Mount Pleasant, Ohio, in the late 1850s. From 1863 to 1882 he headed Olivet Baptist Church in Chicago, and under his supervision it underwent spectacular growth: the second church building he erected cost $18,000 and seated 1,200.

During this time he was elected to many offices in Baptist associations, including the presidency of the American Baptist Association—the first black national Baptist association—a position he held for ten years, from the organization's creation in Nashville in 1867 until 1877, except for one year. In 1870 he was elected president of the white Baptist Free Mission Society. In addition to his numerous contributions to religious and secular newspapers, he was co-editor of the *Chicago Conservator* for a year, and editor of the *Western Herald* for over a year. He was corresponding editor of the short-lived *Saint Louis Monitor* and of the *Brooklyn National Monitor* for several years.

Early Life and Experiences

Georgia De Baptiste's mother died when Georgia was six. At the age of twelve, she underwent conversion and was baptized by her father, becoming a member of the Olivet Baptist Church. De Baptiste went to public school in Chicago and began high school at South Division High School but finished at Evanston Township High School, where she completed a course in modern languages. In addition, she also studied music and became a proficient performer. After high school, she was educated at Knox College in Galesburg, Illinois, and also did work at the Chicago Musical College.

Her early work experiences include a period as secretary to William J. Simmons, the president of State University, Louisville, Kentucky; a year-long stint as a teacher of English and music at Selma University in Selma, Alabama; two years spent as a teacher of languages at Lincoln University, Jefferson City, Missouri; and an appointment as a teacher of languages and music at Western College, Kansas City, Missouri. She was unable to accept an appointment for a second year at Selma University because Alabama's warm climate caused her health to fail. Her work won enthusiastic recommendations from her employers. As quoted by L. A. Scruggs in *Women of Distinction,* William J. Simmons wrote,

> With her strict application to duty, her untiring perseverance, and her sweet, lady-like demeanor, she cannot do otherwise than win the hearts of those with whom she comes in contact. Her determination to overcome difficulties and her ambition to accomplish great good attract all whom she meets.

For a five-year period De Baptiste worked as clerk in the Chicago Post Office. Sometime before May 1904 De Baptiste married a Dr. C. H. Faulkner. The couple lived in Liberia. Her husband was a city physician in Monrovia, the capital of Libera, and was trying to establish a hospital for the poor. She had been appointed first assistant principal of the female department of Liberia College. This information comes from a letter De Baptiste wrote, which was printed in the Woman's Convention minutes of 1904, denying the report of her death that had been printed in the Baptist press. Little more is known about this marriage to C. H. Faulkner, nor is it sure that it resulted in her one child, a son named Frederick, who seems to have been alive at least into the 1940s.

Publishes in Religious Journals

By the time De Baptiste published the 1904 letter denying reports of her death, her name would have been familiar to readers of Baptist publications because she had been publishing articles since the time she was in high school. For two years, she was a regular correspondent to the *Baptist Herald.* She wrote for the *Baptist Headlight* and the *African Mission Herald* and was also a regular contributor to *Our Women and Children,* a magazine published in Louisville, Kentucky.

Sometime before 1915 Georgia De Baptiste married a Baptist minister named W. R. Ashburn, pastor of Mount Zion Baptist Church in Evanston, Illinois. The Ashburns supported Richard Henry Boyd, head of the National Baptist Publishing Board in Nashville, Tennessee, during the turmoil that split the National Baptist Convention of America away from the National Baptist Convention, USA, Inc., in 1915. Georgia De Baptiste was the first president of the Women's Auxiliary to the NBCA and was reelected to the position in 1917.

It is not known when and how this marriage ended, but W. R. Ashburn's pastorate at Mount Zion ended in 1918, and by the early 1930s Georgia De Baptiste was using her first husband's name. There appears to have been a third marriage sometime before 1943, when a *Chicago Herald American* article of February 7, 1943, gives her name as Georgia De Baptiste Carr.

Before 1918 De Baptiste appears to have spent time as a social worker in New York City and also apparently held two more teaching assignments: one in the normal department of Clifton Forge Normal and Industrial Institute, Clifton, Virgin-

ia, and another at Virginia Theological Seminary and College in Lynchburg, Virginia. From about 1918 on, she worked as a social worker, a war camp worker, and a community worker, all in Chicago, where she settled for the rest of her life.

De Baptiste received additional schooling at the University of Chicago, and she worked increasingly as a professional community worker. Among the positions she held in the 1920s were social worker and organizer in the Butler Community and superintendent of the Home for Business and Working Young Women, sponsored by the Rock River Conference of the Methodist Episcopal Church. In the 1930s she was supervisor of the educational department of the Youth's Conservation Council and School.

De Baptiste was much involved in organizations and clubs. She served as president of the District Teachers Association of Chicago. She was organizer and president of the Mothers Union, which was connected with the Missionary Society of her church. The formation of the West Side Royal Circle of Friends of the World came about through her efforts. Her other affiliations include St. Lukes, the Jean Baptiste Desaible [sic] Club, the Giles Charity Club, the NAACP, the Urban League, the YWCA, and the World's Fellowship of Faiths. In 1943 she was president of the prestigious and exclusive Old Settlers' Club, which sponsored in that year an exhibit on 111 years of significant black presence in Chicago.

Georgia De Baptiste is remembered for her social work and her activities and writings for religious groups. Her career is typical of that of many black women of her generation who transformed an involvement in church work into a concern for social work and uplift. Along with many of her contemporaries, she has been partially forgotten. It is encouraging that modern researchers are now beginning to pay serious attention to these remarkable women.

REFERENCES:

"Achievements of Negro Race in Chicago Told." *Chicago Herald American,* February 7, 1943.

Journal of the Fifth Annual Assembly of the Woman's Convention, Auxiliary to the National Baptist Convention. Held in the Second Baptist Church, Austin, Texas, September 14-19, 1904.

Journal of the Sixteenth Annual Session of the Woman's Convention, Auxiliary to the National Baptist Convention. Held in the Highland Avenue Baptist Church, Kansas City, Kansas, September 6-12, 1916.

Lovett, Bobby L. *A Black Man's Dream. The First 100 Years: Richard Henry Boyd and the National Baptist Publishing Board.* Nashville: Mega Corporation, 1993.

"Noted Women Return from Southland." *Chicago Defender,* July 13, 1918.

Penn, I. Garland. *The Afro-American Press and Its Editors.* Springfield, Mass.: Willey and Company, 1891.

Proceedings of the Thirty-Seventh Annual Convention of the Women's Auxiliary to the National Baptist Convention (Unincorporated). Held in Atlanta, Georgia, September 5-11, 1917.

Scruggs, L. A. *Women of Distinction.* Raleigh, N.C.: L. A. Scruggs, 1893.

Simmons, William J. *Men of Mark.* Cleveland, Ohio: George M. Rewell and Company, 1887.

Who's Who in Colored America. Brooklyn: Thomas Yenser, 1930-32.

Who's Who in Colored America. 5th ed. Brooklyn: Thomas Yenser, 1940.

Williams, Fred Hart. "Richard De Baptiste." *Negro History Bulletin* 22 (May 1959): 178.

Robert L. Johns

Lois M. DeBerry

Lois M. DeBerry
(1945-)
State representative, political activist

In 1972, when Lois M. DeBerry was elected by the voters of Tennessee's Ninety-first House District, she became the first African American woman elected to the Tennessee General Assembly from the city of Memphis and only the second African American woman to serve in the state's legislative body. Two years later, she became the first woman to chair the Shelby County Democratic Caucus. When the membership of the Tennessee House of Representatives elected DeBerry Speaker Pro Tempore in 1986 during the organizational session of the Tennessee General Assembly, she became the first woman in the state's history to hold this position. All during her twenty-year tenure in Tennessee's lower house, Speaker DeBerry has been known for her unselfish devotion to the residents of her district, her untiring work on various legislative committees, and, most of all, her advocacy for senior citizens, children and youth, the impoverished, minorities, and women.

Lois Marie DeBerry was one of two girls—her sister's name was Edwinna—and three boys—Jasper, Michael, and Ira—born to Samuel DeBerry and Mary Page DeBerry. The second of the five children, DeBerry was born in Memphis, Tennessee, on May 5, 1945. Her father, a self-employed trucker, was born in Senatobia, Mississippi, on February 14, 1917, and her mother, who worked at various jobs, was born on October 15, 1917, in Forest, Mississippi. DeBerry's father, sister, and a brother all died within a seventeen-month period—Jasper, April 1969; Samuel DeBerry, May 1969; and Edwinna, September 1970. On April 1, 1981, DeBerry married Charles Traughber, a member of the Tennessee Board of Paroles. She has one son, Michael Boyer, from a previous marriage. Also considered a member of the family is Mykea Rainey, a child Charles Traughber and Lois DeBerry have cared for since she was two weeks old.

As the DeBerry children grew up in Memphis, their parents imbued in them the principles of hard work and self-respect and the spirit of competition. While teaching them to be competitive, the DeBerrys also taught their children to accept winning with humility and defeat with grace. DeBerry feels that her childhood environs in Memphis epitomized the African proverb that proclaims, "It takes a community to raise a child." She recalled in an interview, "The community was the family—the extended family." DeBerry attended Memphis public schools, and in 1962 she graduated from Hamilton High School. Later, she entered LeMoyne-Owen College in Memphis.

Although her parents objected, DeBerry became an active participant in the civil rights movement of the 1960s, taking part in various student sit-ins and picket lines. On August 28, 1963, she was among those who participated in the March on Washington. Two years later, in 1965, she defied her parents and ran away to Selma, Alabama, to take part in the fifty-mile Selma to Montgomery March, an event planned to dramatize the denial of voting rights to African Americans. She later explained her strong feelings about the movement: "Every time I would read the paper, I would get so mad about what was going on. . . . I felt that I had to be there to make my contribution. . . . they needed me to make the numbers. I knew numbers made the difference. If only I could get to Selma, maybe that would help." Her parents were relieved when DeBerry returned home unharmed, and although she was punished, they understood her strong commitment to the movement. "They sensed my potential to become a leader," she said.

Soon after graduating with a baccalaureate degree in elementary education from LeMoyne-Owen College in 1971,

DeBerry began work as a counselor with a federally funded program. She worked in the housing projects, serving as a liaison between students, parents, and the schools. During her tenure as the only African American counselor in a program primarily administered by whites, with a ninety percent African American service area, DeBerry came to the realization that "it was just a program on paper." She strongly felt the program was failing to meet its mission of intervening in the lives of black children and motivating them to stay in school and receive a good education. After calling on several male politicians and receiving no response to her concerns, DeBerry felt disheartened.

One day when DeBerry went to pick up her car from a repair shop, an elderly woman noticed her distress and said, "Young lady, you look troubled." DeBerry replied, "I am troubled." During the ensuing conversation, the sagacious woman told her, "Baby, the only way you can change the system is to get in the system." This comment inspired DeBerry to enter the political arena.

Campaigns for State Representative

At the age of twenty-seven, DeBerry entered the race for state representative from Memphis's newly created Ninety-first House District. The political hopeful found it difficult to raise campaign funds. She said in a 1993 interview, "I can't tell you how many men told me that politics is not a field for women. A woman's place is at home, in the kitchen, raising babies, and being a wife." There were, however, people like Memphis's Fifth District representative, Harold Ford (Tennessee's first African American elected to serve in the United States Congress), who "with some reluctance" supported the aspiring candidate. Ford's backing, said DeBerry, "allowed other men to feel comfortable voting for me."

DeBerry ran against four men for the Ninety-first House District seat. Her political platform addressed social issues and concerns that were most pertinent to senior citizens, children, and youth. She promised the voters that she would return to the community as frequently as possible and would always be there to listen to their problems. DeBerry won her bid to represent the district's people on Capitol Hill in Nashville, Tennessee.

In January 1973, when DeBerry took the oath of office as state representative and joined the 121 males in the Eighty-eighth General Assembly, she held the distinction of being one of five women in the assembly, the first African-American woman from the city of Memphis, and only the second woman of African descent to serve in the state's legislative body. DeBerry was preceded by Dorothy L. Brown, who represented Nashville's Fifth District from 1967 to 1969. Although Brown's tenure in the state legislature was a short one, "she left her own mark in the House," said DeBerry in the interview. "Brown's legacy to me, as a freshman legislator, was to not be afraid to speak out, to stand on my principles and to stand up for what I believe in."

When Lois DeBerry became a member of the House, she was one of nine African Americans serving in the Tennessee General Assembly. Her African American male colleagues were protective and respectful. It was not long before she acquired the sobriquet "Lady D." The conservative Bible-belt white members of the General Assembly, however, were hardly prepared for the assertive, candid, and Afro-coiffured representative who resembled Angela Davis, the militant civil and social revolutionary of the 1960s.

Soon after beginning as a state representative, DeBerry was submerged in a sea of sexism and racism. Said DeBerry, "I came in at an unusual time—I came in the year after they had passed the Equal Rights Amendment and they rescinded it the year I got there." She was told during her first term, "Politics ain't for women." And when she arose on the floor of the House to join the exchange on including the history of blacks in Tennessee history books, she was told, "Blacks don't have a history." The first statement made her angry and the second statement brought her to tears and a swift departure from the House chamber. "I did just what they expected me to do—I cried and was ushered out," said DeBerry in the interview. "That is when I found out what politics was all about." The last episode was the turning point in her legislative career.

One of the first bills sponsored by Representative DeBerry was a law allowing senior citizens the opportunity to attend any state college or university free of charge; the bill passed. Sensitive to the sacrifices senior citizens made to rear their families and contribute to society, the representative said in the interview, "I just felt we owed them something. That's why I opened the door to give them an opportunity to experience some of the things they had given to us. All that I am today, I owe to [senior citizens]."

Legislative Success

The freshman Memphis Democrat benefitted from her experiences during her first session as a state legislator. When the second session began, "Lady D" possessed a stronger resolve and sponsored a bill to include the heritage of blacks in Tennessee history books. In spite of having to learn the legislative rules and procedures on her own, the lawmaker's first legislative term was a productive one, with three of the four bills she introduced being passed, including the bill to include the heritage of African Americans in Tennessee history books. According to the February 10, 1981, *Nashville Banner,* at the end of the legislative term DeBerry reacted to the way freshman legislators were treated by standing on the House floor and telling her colleagues she "enjoyed serving and if she was reelected she hoped no one would ever have to go through what she went through as a freshman." She feels that, because of her commentary on the floor of the House, today new members of the General Assembly receive an extensive orientation.

The following year DeBerry's constituents sent her back to the state legislature. Her experience working with troubled youth from families at the lower end of the socioeconomic scale stimulated her interest in corrections. In 1976 she became chairperson of the House Special Committee on Corrections. Initially interested in adult corrections, she soon realized that in order to reduce the rate of recidivism, it was necessary to address the problems of young offenders. In 1978, After DeBerry's hard-fought struggle for a facility offering treatment to youthful transgressors with special problems, the DeBerry Institute, a correctional facility in Nashville, was named in her honor.

Five years in the Tennessee General Assembly transformed DeBerry into a savvy student of the political process. "Lady D" became an efficacious team player and a tough one, if the situation demanded. She exhibited an effective combination of wit, integrity, certitude, and charm. DeBerry marched forward with self-assurance and found herself well-suited for the mantle of office.

During the gubernatorial campaign in 1978, while traveling with the House Democratic Caucus through small rural Tennessee towns with few African American residents, DeBerry used mirthful witticism to relax the tension. "To keep everybody from feeling uncomfortable when they introduced me, I whispered in Speaker [now governor of Tennessee] McWherter's ear, 'Tell them I'm here to add a little beauty and color,'" said the tall, thin, attractive, and well-groomed Memphis representative in the February 1981 *Nashville Banner*. "That remark usually drew a laugh from the audiences and the other legislators were put at ease."

While DeBerry made the legislative leadership cognizant of the race issue, she was also in the forefront of sensitizing them to gender equity and special legislative committee appointments. She said in the same *Nashville Banner* article that she penned a brief note to the Speaker in which she stated, "I hope the day will come when you will recognize that there are . . . women in this house and that all committees need a little beauty and color."

Becomes Speaker Pro Tempore of the House of Representatives

Thirteen years after coming to Capitol Hill, DeBerry "felt compelled" to run for the General Assembly's office of House Speaker Pro Tempore. The Speaker Pro Tempore presides over the House of Representatives in the absence of the Speaker and is a voting member of all House committees. Because the number of African American legislators had increased, DeBerry said in the interview that she "could not take an all-white, all-male leadership team. I felt I had to challenge the system for the sake of women and for the sake of children. Even if I lost, I felt I had to run." In January 1986, during the organizational session of the General Assembly, DeBerry was elected by her colleagues to a two-year term as Speaker Pro Tempore of the General Assembly's House of Representatives. With that election, she became the first woman and the first African American in the state's history to hold that position. Two years later, DeBerry demonstrated her political prowess when a white male conservative Republican sought to unseat her as House Speaker Pro Tempore. Refusing

to let race and gender become overt issues, DeBerry aligned her coalition of supporters and retained her position. With the opening of the ninety-eighth legislative session in 1993, DeBerry began serving her fourth consecutive term as Speaker Pro Tempore.

Engaged in legislative concerns during the week, DeBerry reserves Sundays for spiritual renewal. An active communicant of Greater Abyssinia Baptist Church, she is director of the Children's Hour, a member of the women's choir, and a former trustee. DeBerry said in the interview, "I owe my victory in the legislature to the churches in my district. I made a vow that if I got elected, I would never leave the church." Drawing from her reservoir of spirituality, DeBerry admitted: "I would not have been able to deal with all the things I have had to deal with as a woman without my religion."

During her tenure in the House, DeBerry was the first woman to chair the Shelby County Democratic Caucus. She has served as secretary of the General Welfare Committee and as a member of the Education Committee, Calendar Committee, Special Joint Committee on Primary Health Care Services, Special House Committee on Criminal Justice, Select Committee on Juvenile Corrections, Criminal Justice System Committee, Committee on Day Care, Task Force on Teen Problems, and Task Force on Mental Health. Prior to becoming Speaker Pro Tempore, DeBerry served as majority whip in the Ninety-second and Ninety-third General Assemblies. She is the founder of the Tennessee Legislative Retreat and vice-chair of the Tennessee Black Caucus. In addition to her state legislative service, she is a member of the executive committee of the National Conference of State Legislators. A former president of the National Caucus of Black Women and vice-president for the National Black Caucus of State Legislators, on March 25, 1995, DeBerry was elected president of the National Caucus of State Legislators, making her the first woman to serve in that position.

DeBerry has been honored with numerous awards, including Outstanding Woman of the Year by radio station KWAM, the National Organization of Links Service Award, the Outstanding Woman in Community Service Award of the Epsilon Epsilon chapter of Alpha Kappa Alpha Sorority, the Bird Dog Award from Common Cause of Tennessee, the Extra Mile Award of the Tennessee Office of Minority Business Enterprise, the Glorification of the Image of Black Womanhood Award, Tri-State Woman of the Year, and the Outstanding Woman in Politics Award. She is a member of the Memphis chapter of Delta Sigma Theta Sorority, the Memphis chapter of Links, the Rosewood Civic Club, the NAACP, People United to Save Humanity (PUSH), the Shelby County Democratic Club, the Democratic Voters' Council, and the Integrity Voters Registration Committee. She is a former member of the Education Board of the National Baptist Convention U.S.A.

For twelve years DeBerry was the only African American woman in the Tennessee General Assembly. In 1985 she was joined by Nashville's state representative Mary Pruitt. In 1991 the ranks of African American women serving in the Tennessee General Assembly increased by one, with the election of Nashville's state senator Thelma Harper. Harper was the first African American woman elected to the state's upper chamber. In January 1993, these women were joined by newly elected state representatives Tommi F. Brown of Chattanooga and Henri Brooks of Memphis. All of these women replaced men. Three succeeded African American men who retired from legislative service, and one defeated an African American male incumbent who had been in office for more than twenty years. Today, these five African American women comprise one-third of the total number of women serving in the Tennessee General Assembly.

DeBerry has ascended the ranks of a white male-dominated political institution. She is a woman of strong convictions and principles, one who is not afraid to speak out and stand by her beliefs. Sensitive and attentive to the needs of her constituents and colleagues, DeBerry remarked in the interview, "I'm not afraid to speak out, and I'm going to stand on my principles, even if I have to stand by myself." DeBerry is serving her eleventh term as a state representative and her fifth term as Speaker Pro Tempore of the Tennessee House of Representatives. Because she presides in the absence of the Speaker of the House and has a vote on every committee, she is one of the most influential legislators on Capitol Hill in Nashville.

Current Address: Speaker Pro Tempore, 15 Legislative Plaza, Nashville, TN 37243-0191.

REFERENCES:

Cornwell, Ilene J. *Biographical Directory of the Tennessee General Assembly, 1951-1971.* Vol. 5. Nashville: Tennessee Historical Commission, 1990.

———. *Biographical Directory of the Tennessee General Assembly, 1971-1991.* Vol. 6. Nashville: Tennessee Historical Commission, 1991.

"DeBerry Changes Face of Lawmaking." *Tennessean,* February 25, 1991.

DeBerry, Lois M. Interview with Linda T. Wynn. August 27, 1993.

"DeBerry Seems Hooked on Politics: Humor, Persistence, Religion Her Keys to Success." *Nashville Banner,* February 10, 1981.

Tennessee Blue Book. Nashville: Office of the Secretary of State, 1973-74; 1975-76; 1977-78; 1979-80; 1981-82; 1983-84; 1985-86; 1987-88; 1989-90.

Tennessee House of Representatives. House Joint Resolution No. 383. February 26, 1976.

"Urban Minorities May Attend Science Program." *Tennessean,* April 7, 1993.

"Women in Legislature Pushing for Top Posts." *Nashville Banner,* November 23, 1990.

Wynn, Linda T. "List of Tennessee African-American State Legislators: 1873-Present." N.p., January 1993.

Linda T. Wynn

The Delany Sisters

Sadie Delany
(1889-)
Educator, humanitarian

Bessie Delany
(1891-)
Dentist, civil rights activist

Sadie Delany was the first African American domestic science teacher at the high school level in the New York City public schools. Bessie Delany was the second African American woman licensed to practice dentistry in New York City. Both now over one hundred years old, they are the oldest surviving members of one of America's most prominent black families. Born during the post-Reconstruction period, they witnessed many epochs in modern American history. They recently became celebrities through the publication of their autobiography, *Having Our Say* (1993), which chronicles the first one hundred years of their lives.

Sadie (Sarah Louise) Delany, born September 19, 1889, and Bessie (Annie Elizabeth) Delany, born September 3, 1891, were the second and third of the ten children born to Henry Beard Delany and Nanny Logan Delany. Henry Beard Delany had been born into a family of relatively privileged, literate house slaves on a plantation in St. Marys, Georgia, and was just seven years old at the end of the Civil War. Although trained as a mason, he went to St. Augustine's College in Raleigh, North Carolina, to study for the ministry. There he met and married Nanny James Logan, the daughter of James Miliam, a white man, and Martha Logan, a free issue black.

Henry and Nanny Delany stayed on at St. Augustine's, where Henry had become vice principal, and raised their ten children there. The Delany children lived a sheltered but happy life on the campus of St. Augustine's. According to Bessie in the Delany sisters' autobiography, *Having Our Say,* "It was religious faith that formed the backbone of the Delany family." The sisters witnessed their parents putting into practice the family motto: "Your job is to help somebody." The Delanys, for instance, yearly distributed Thanksgiving baskets to the down-on-their-luck former slaves who lived in the neighborhood of St. Augustine's.

Being the second and third oldest of ten children, Sadie and Bessie took on roles of responsibility in the family. As a "mama's child," Sadie became her mother's assistant in her homemaking chores, while Bessie supervised the seven younger children in the family. Although the children had few material possessions, they did have musical instruments and playing music together was a favorite family pastime.

At five and seven years of age Bessie and Sadie were introduced to Jim Crow when they were forced to sit at the

Sadie and Bessie Delany

back of a segregated trolley car. Although their parents tried to shelter them from the brutalities of the southern racial caste system, the girls heard about lynchings from the whisperings of the teachers at school.

Delany Sisters Become Educators

Upon graduating from St. Augustine's, Sadie took a job as supervisor of the domestic science curriculum in the black schools in Wake County, North Carolina, but ended up assuming the duties of the county school superintendent at no extra pay. She proudly recalls driving Booker T. Washington around to show him her schools. She inspired many people she visited to get an education, and many of them ended up at St. Augustine's. Bessie, who also graduated from St. Augustine's, spent a lonely two years as a young, single teacher in Boardman, North Carolina, a mill town. She next got a teaching job in Brunswick, Georgia. She came close to being lynched when she rebuffed a drunken white man on a train while on her way to assume her teaching position in Brunswick. She admits in *Having Our Say,* "I am lucky to be alive. But I would rather die than back down."

The Delany sisters moved to Harlem when they were in their mid-twenties to further their educations. Sadie enrolled in the domestic science program at Pratt Institute in New York, then a two-year college. After graduating from Pratt, she enrolled in Columbia University's Teachers College. In 1920 she graduated from Columbia with a bachelor of science degree. Her first teaching job in New York was at a mostly black elementary school. Continuing her studies, she obtained her master's degree in education from Columbia in 1925. During the depression she landed a job at an all-white high school by being appointed to the position, skipping the required face-to-face interview (which would reveal her race), and then showing up on the first day of class. Thus she became the first black high school domestic science teacher in New York. Sadie taught in various New York high schools from 1930 to 1960, when she retired.

Bessie, who had taken some science courses at Shaw University in Raleigh, enrolled in Columbia University's dental school in 1919. She was awarded her doctor of dental surgery degree in 1923. In *Having Our Say* she recalls,

> The class selected me as the marshall, and I thought it was an honor. And then I found out—I heard

them talking—it was because no one wanted to march beside me in front of their parents. It was a way to get rid of me. The class marshall carried the flag and marched out in front, alone.

Bessie became the second black woman licensed to practice dentistry in New York. (The first was Gertrude Elizabeth Curtis (McPherson), who began practice in 1909.) In her practice, located in the heart of Harlem, Bessie experienced not only discrimination from whites, who wouldn't patronize a black dentist, but also from some blacks, who wouldn't patronize a woman dentist. But she soon earned the reputation of taking any patient, no matter how sick, and she never turned away anyone who didn't have money. When she retired in 1950, her rates were the same as when she started up her practice in 1923. She says in *Having Our Say*, "I never raised my rates because I was getting by OK. I was always proud of my work, and that was enough for me."

By the mid-1920s Bessie's dental office had become a meeting place for black activists such as the sociologist E. Franklin Frazier. At her instigation Frazier, Walter White, the future executive director of the NAACP, and noted educator and writer W. E. B. Du Bois demonstrated, and were arrested, at the 1925 rerelease of the movie *The Birth of a Nation*, which featured black villains, Ku Klux Klan heroes, and whites in blackface. Also in this year Bessie experienced a harrowing encounter with the Ku Klux Klan. She and a boyfriend were on an outing on Long Island when they ran into twenty white-robed clansmen stopping and searching the cars of blacks. Bessie credits the powerful engine of her companion's Cadillac for zooming them right around the clansmen. In *Having Our Say* Bessie says,

> should have seen the look on Mama's face when I told her that night what had happe[n]ed. Here, all those years in the South and they had managed to keep us Delany children out of the hands of the KKK and they'd almost got their hands [on] me—on Long Island.

After this encounter with the Klan, Bessie became a staunch activist for the rights of blacks.

Continuing Familial Closeness

The Delany siblings all moved to Harlem, and by 1926 they all lived together in the same apartment building. Bessie and Sadie proudly maintained in Harlem the wholesome, family-oriented lifestyle that they had in Raleigh. Their favorite pastime was having friends over for dinner, and every Sunday found them at Saint Mark's Episcopal Church. In *Having Our Say* Bessie says, "We were proud of the Delany name, and because of our self-discipline it came to mean in Harlem what it had meant in North Carolina—that is, it stood for integrity." Through the years they met through their brother Hubert, an assistant U.S attorney for the Southern District of New York, such entertainers as Ethel Waters, Duke Ellington, and Lena Horne, but their circle of closest friends consisted mainly of professionals.

Bessie and Sadie's father, who in 1918 had become the first elected black Episcopal bishop, passed away in 1928 after a brief illness. The sisters then persuaded their mother to move to New York. Sadie, who in *Having Our Say* stated that she was "still something of a Mama's child" during this period, when she was at least forty years old, traveled extensively with her mother both in the United States and abroad. The most memorable moment of a European tour was seeing Paul Robeson in a London production of *Othello*. Bessie's dental practice seldom allowed her time off to travel with her sister and mother.

At the end of World War II the sisters and their mother moved from Harlem to a cottage in the Bronx, where they could continue to cultivate the victory garden they had started during the war. At the age of fifty-nine Bessie retired from her dental practice to take care of their mother, who was then over ninety years old. As a special surprise for their mother, their brother Hubert arranged for her to meet Eleanor Roosevelt. In *Having Our Say* Bessie recalls, "It was pretty wonderful to see the former first lady of the United States jump up, so respectful like, to greet Mama, an old colored lady."

After the death of two of the Delany brothers in quick succession, Mama Delany herself died at the age of ninety-five. Then in 1957 the sisters moved to Mount Vernon, New York, joining an exodus of middle-class blacks from New York City to the suburbs. Sadie says in *Having Our Say*, "[Bessie] didn't think I would ever get over Mama's death, and that maybe by moving away and starting over, it would help. I think she was right."

One of Bessie and Sadie's biggest regrets was not going on the March on Washington in 1963 and hearing Martin Luther King's "I Have a Dream" speech. In *Having Our Say* Bessie recalls,

> The civil rights movement was a time when we thought: Maybe now it will finally happen. Maybe now our country will finally grow up, come to terms with this race mess. But it seemed like the momentum was lost when the Vietnam War happened. It was like all the energy of the young people, and the focus of the country, got shifted away from civil rights.

She believes a greater factor in the loss of momentum in the civil rights movement was the leadership void caused by King's assassination.

Bessie says women's rights have always been important to her as well as the rights of blacks. In *Having Our Say* she notes, "But it seems to me no matter how much I had to put up with as a woman, the bigger problem was being colored. People looked at me and the first thing they saw was *Negro*, not *woman*. So racial equality, as a cause, won my heart." One of the happiest days of her life occurred back in 1920 when women finally won the right to vote. She and Sadie immediately registered and haven't missed a chance to vote since.

Although the sisters are registered as Independents, they usually vote Democratic. They hold such Democratic leaders as Presidents Truman, Johnson, Carter, and Clinton in high regard. In an article in the *Washington Post,* November 25, 1993, Bessie was quoted as expressing a desire to meet Hillary Rodham Clinton. She believes that there will be a white woman as president before a black. Describing herself in *Having Our Say* as a "little psychic," she predicts, "And if a Negro is elected president? That person will be a Negro *woman.*"

Sisters Become Authors of Best-Selling Autobiography

In 1993 the Delany sisters became celebrities with the publication of their best-selling autobiography, *Having Our Say: The Delany Sisters' First 100 Years.* The book resulted from eighteen months of interviews with Amy Hill Hearth, a free-lance writer who collaborated with them on the project. Hearth wove thousands of anecdotes into a lively seven-part largely chronological narrative. She also provided before each part a brief overview that placed the narrative in the context of black history. Because of the popularity of the autobiography, the sisters have been featured on a number of television shows, where they have graciously shared their secrets to a long and productive life. They do yoga exercises five days a week, for example, and eat up to seven vegetables a day. Every day they take vitamin supplements, a clove of garlic, and a teaspoon of cod liver oil. Still of keen mind, they regularly read the newspaper and watch *The MacNeil/Lehrer News Hour.* Prayers twice a day are also part of their routine. Sadie says in *Having Our Say,* "We pray for each family member living and dead."

The sisters are still fiercely independent. In an interview on the ABC program *Good Morning America* Bessie said, "We don't owe anybody—if we want anything and haven't got the money, we don't go to the bank—we wait until we can get it." In *Having Our Say* she admits, "If you asked me the secret to longevity I would tell you that you have to work at taking care of your health. But a lot of it's attitude. I'm alive out of sheer determination, honey!" Bessie also attributes their longevity to having never married. In *Having Our Say* she says,

> When people ask me how we lived past one hundred, I say, "Honey, we never had husbands to worry us to death!"... And why would I want to give up my freedom and independence to take care of some man? In those days, a man expected you to be in charge of a perfect household, to look after his every need. Honey, I wasn't interested! I wasn't going to be bossed around by some man!

Camille Cosby has acquired the film, stage, and television rights to the sisters' autobiography. Along with her coproducer, Judith Rutherford James, she plans to bring their story to the stage or motion picture screen. In *Jet* magazine, January 17, 1994, Cosby says, "I consider the Delany sisters' ages to be significant, considering the omnipresent youth [oriented] messages that are communicated from the media. Because of their commendable lives, hopefully, people will value the dynamism, intelligence and knowledge of mature men and women."

The Delany sisters followed their success with *Having Our Say* with the publication of a second book, 1994's *The Delany Sisters' Book of Everybody Wisdom.* The American public continues to be enthralled by the spirit and the stories of the Delanys. Amy Hill Hearth said of the Delany Sisters in a *Good Morning America* interview, "They have to offer us a slice of American history which is pretty much missing from most of our basic textbooks."

Current Address: c/o Kodansha America, Inc., 114 Fifth Avenue, New York, NY 10011.

REFERENCES:

"Camille Cosby Acquires the Film, Stage and Television Rights to Delany Sisters' Life Story." *Jet* 85 (January 17, 1994): 26.
"A Century of Being Sisters." *Washington Post,* November 25, 1993.
Delany, Sarah, and Elizabeth Delany, in collaboration with Amy Hill Hearth. *Having Our Say: The Delany Sisters' First 100 Years.* New York: Kodansha, 1993.
Good Morning America. Interview with Delany Sisters by Terry Row. November 23, 1993.

Phiefer L. Browne

Louise De Mortie
(1833-1867)
Lecturer, missionary, fund-raiser

Louise De Mortie, who lived during the Civil War era of United States history, was well known as a lecturer, reader, and persuasive public speaker who first made her mark in the exclusive social circles of Boston, Massachusetts. At the height of her fame in Boston, however, she left for New Orleans, Louisiana. While she continued to pursue her entertainment career in New Orleans, she moved there with the express purpose of devoting her considerable talents to helping black children who had been left orphaned by the war. Though she appears to have been excluded from recent accounts of the Civil War and from the pages of African American history, she was considered one of the most important black Americans of her time.

De Mortie was born in Norfolk, Virginia, in 1833, and died October 10, 1867, in New Orleans, Louisiana. She was born into a high-achieving family of free people of color. The black struggle for freedom and dignity in the nineteenth century was a prominent aspect of De Mortie's life. De Mortie moved to Boston in 1853, as did her future husband, John Oliver (1821-1899), a free black carpenter and an abolitionist

Louise De Mortie

from Petersburg, Virginia. Oliver, having heard William Roscoe Davis, a former slave and agent of the American Missionary Association (AMA), speak in Boston in 1862, joined the AMA in that year. He became a teacher and relief worker, laboring mainly in Norfolk, Virginia, and the surrounding area. Whether he met De Mortie while working in Norfolk or later in Boston is not known. In 1862, John Oliver moved to California, following the gold rush, and he and De Mortie divorced at that time. Oliver returned to Virginia permanently in 1865, where he achieved prominence as the first black notary public in the state, as a city councilman in Richmond, and as a deputy U.S. marshal. Sources do not indicate that De Mortie ever remarried, and there is no mention of surviving children.

William Wells Brown in *The Rising Son* described De Mortie as

> somewhat taller than the middle height, with a Grecian cast of countenance, eyes dark and sparkling, lips swelling, forehead high, refined manners, and possessing energy which always brings success. In fact, it may be truthfully said, that Louise De Mortie was one of the most beautiful of her sex.

Monroe A. Majors in *Noted Negro Women* said that De Mortie was "an angelic soul" who "portrayed a marvelously kind and genial spirit, which endeared and held all friends." According to Majors, as she grew up in Norfolk, her opportunity for education was limited because of "race restrictions" but, in Boston, she enjoyed the freedom to improve herself

and studied "the higher sciences." George W. Williams in *History of the Negro Race in America from 1619 to 1880* said that she was successful at her education, possessing a "remarkable memory . . . and [taking] high standing as a pupil."

Success as Public Reader and Speaker

Her beautiful face, her remarkable memory, and her "voluminous voice, and elocutionary powers wonderful and puzzling to describe," as Majors characterizes them, were the source of De Mortie's success in Boston. There, beginning in 1862, she made her living as a public speaker and reader. As Brown wrote, "her rare ability, eloquent rendering of the poets, pleasing manner, and good sense, gained for her a host of admiring friends, among whom were some of the leading men and women of the country." De Mortie seemed to be destined for a wonderful public career as a lecturer and reader.

At the height of her fame in Boston, De Mortie learned of the destitute condition of the colored orphans in New Orleans. She may have received this information through any one of several possible sources: her former husband and the AMA, the philanthropic societies of Boston, or the founder of the Colored Orphans Home in New Orleans, General Nathaniel P. Banks, himself a Bostonian. Touched by the plight of the children, she went to that city in 1863 to see what she could do to help them.

Orphan Home for Black Children Founded

George Williams says that in New Orleans De Mortie "labored with an intelligence and zeal which made her a heroine among her people." New Orleans was home to a black population made up of both free—and often wealthy—people, usually Creoles, and of recently freed slaves, usually sick and homeless, who were fleeing the plantations in search of shelter, food, and a new life. De Mortie lived in a city with persons like P. B. S. Pinchback, a wealthy black citizen who later became the only black governor of Louisiana; Victor Eugene Macarthy, a black college professor, public school principal, and musician; and Camille Thierry, an important black poet. The black community of New Orleans was socially and politically active. It had its own bands, including a small symphony orchestra; formed its own social societies and clubs that provided both entertainment and social standing for their members; and established its own newspapers and churches.

De Mortie entered the active black social and political life of this unique American city. She continued to make the kind of public appearances for which she had gained attention in the North. She was a noted and popular singer, performing in concert the popular European and American songs of the day. She also continued her public readings and lectured in the city. John W. Blassingame said in *Black New Orleans: 1860-1880:*

> The most impressive Negro women who delivered lectures in New Orleans were Louise De Mortie and Frances E. W. Harper. Both women had received rave notices for their readings in other cities. *The*

Liberator declared that in her appearances in Boston Miss De Mortie "in reading 'Leap from the Long Bridge,' exhibited [sic], in some of its passages, traits that called to mind the finest display of Fanny Kemble, Miss Glinn, or Mrs. Barrow." When she gave a "Patriotic and Sentimental Reading" in New Orleans in March 1865, Miss De Mortie received "immense applause."

De Mortie entered the city's political life at the request of General Nathaniel Prentice Banks, a Bostonian who had relieved Major General Benjamin F. Butler at the Gulf Department headquarters in New Orleans on December 17, 1862. According to William David Godman, whose history of the Gilbert Academy and Agricultural College traces the development of the Colored Orphans Home in New Orleans, Banks required the commissioner of the Freedman's Bureau in New Orleans to gather the neglected and sick orphans of black Union soldiers and provide them shelter. In a letter of June 25, 1879, which Godman published, Banks said that he established the Colored Orphans Home in 1863 and that it was maintained for three years in prosperous condition. He adds that "Madame de Mortier, a colored lady of high culture and character, well known to philanthropic ladies of Boston, and liberally aided by them in her labors in Louisiana, had charge of the home and managed its affairs with great success." Godman goes on to affirm that De Mortie, "an intelligent colored lady, who came to New Orleans to do something for the orphans, was placed in charge of the children. By her influence considerable sums were collected for the work."

John Blassingame in *Black New Orleans* places the orphanage much more under the control of the black community. And Jacquelyn Slaughter Haywood, in a dissertation on the AMA's activity in Louisiana during Reconstruction, says that the black community had asked Banks to make an appropriation for black orphans, and he did so, budgeting about three thousand dollars for the care of 250 indigent children. When the war ended, army funds most likely ran out. De Mortie may have been involved from 1863 on and then have led efforts to establish the orphanage permanently. In any case, Blassingame says that the orphanage was established by De Mortie herself in March 1865 under the patronage of well-to-do French-speaking blacks, members of a society called the Louisiana Association for the Benefit of Colored Orphans. This group included prominent members of the black New Orleans community like Charles Roundanez, one of five black physicians in the city, whose wife served on the orphanage's committee with De Mortie.

Lavish Fair Marks Orphanage's Opening

The most exciting event surrounding the establishment of the orphanage was a fair held from May 26 to June 6, 1865, to raise funds for the institution. The announcement for the fair, signed by De Mortie and two other members of the orphanage's board, was printed daily by the *New Orleans Tribune* beginning May 25 and stopping with the close of the fair. Held at the Soule Mansion, the fair's events included concerts and an auction, as well as tours of the mansion. The

events were described in detail in the *Tribune,* to whose reporters De Mortie, in a skillful public relations move, sent complimentary tickets. The mansion, equipped for the care of the orphans, contained, among other luxuries, a restaurant, post office, and gardens.

The fair was attended by all strata of the New Orleans community, both aristocratic and common, black and white. General Banks and his wife visited the fair two times. The *Tribune,* on June 8, 1865, dedicated an entire column, "The Closing Scenes of the Fair," to the final night of the event, stressing how crowded the mansion was, particularly with dignitaries—including Banks and the chief justice of the state supreme court. The paper reported that "It was late in the evening when the [great] assemblage dispersed—each visitor carrying home with him the most pleasant recollections, and regretting that the good time was over. . . . we are creditably informed that the Fair was a success." It was. Ultimately, the association raised $2,002 for the orphans, spending $918, clearing, as the *Tribune* reported, $1,083.75.

From 1865 until her death in 1867, De Mortie continued her work as a fund-raiser for the orphanage, traveling in Boston, Philadelphia, and other northern cities in which she was well known, to bring in funds for the institution. This was necessitated by the difficulties the orphanage experienced at the end of the Civil War and after the assassination of Lincoln. Government protection was withdrawn from the orphanage at the Pierre Soule mansion, and, as General Banks, as quoted in David Godman's *Gilbert Academy and Agricultural College,* indicated "the orphans narrowly escaped being apprenticed by the government to their former owners." The orphans were moved to Marine Hospital, still under the protection of the Freedman's Bureau, while funds were raised.

At this point, Godman's book reports, "a division took place in the society. Some of the members wishing to have the children trained up strictly as Roman Catholics, separated and organized a society of their own." Two orphanages seem to have emerged from the split and to have been developed with the funds De Mortie helped raise at the Soule mansion. The first, the Providence Asylum, was established in New Orleans. In 1866, Thomy Lafon gave the Louisiana Association for the Benefit of Colored Orphans two lots for a building, and black workers donated their labor to erect the structure.

A second orphanage, Gilbert Academy and Agricultural College, was established on Bayou Teche in Franklin, Louisiana. According to William David Godwin, a Madame de Bossier of Marseilles, France, offered $10,000 to the orphanage, asking that the "friends of the orphans" raise an additional $20,000 to buy a farm and move the orphans to the country. De Mortie's travels, as Willima Wells Brown indicates, were to help raise these additional funds. Ultimately, a Dr. Newman (no first name given) secured the $20,000 and in 1867, the orphans were moved to Bayou Teche in St. Mary's Parish, Louisiana. Since De Mortie died in October 1867 and the orphans were moved in February 1867, she lived to see the orphanage established at Bayou Teche. What her work with the orphanage might have become, however, we will never know, for she died soon after Gilbert Academy was founded.

New Orleans in 1867 was plagued by an outbreak of yellow fever that, along with other deadly diseases, was ravaging the population. De Mortie's friends in the North urged her to leave New Orleans until the plague had come to an end. De Mortie refused. In 1867, after a fund raising tour in the North, she was struck with yellow fever. She died in New Orleans on October 10, 1867. In her last moments she is supposed to have said, with a childlike simplicity, ''I belong to God, our Father.'' After De Mortie's death and a period of regrouping, the orphanage that she had worked so diligently to found became a school, which boasts of its graduates to this day.

The details of the fascinating life of Louise De Mortie are largely unrecorded. Though her brief biography appears along with those of other prominent black Americans in African American histories written from about 1870 to 1890, she virtually disappears in later works. Compounding the problem of tracing her life is the fact that historical records from this period are incomplete at best. De Mortie's life stands as one of the foundations on which the advancement of African Americans was built. Giving up her prosperous and happy life in Boston, she undertook the selfless and difficult task of caring for homeless and indigent children in a southern city that was foreign to her. As George Williams said of De Mortie, ''Although cut off in the morning of her useful life she is of blessed memory among those for whose improvement and elevation she gave the strength of a brilliant mind and the warmth of a genuine Christian heart.''

REFERENCES:

Blassingame, John W. *Black New Orleans: 1860-1880.* Chicago: University of Chicago Press, 1973.

Brown, William Wells. *The Rising Son; or, The Antecedents and Advancement of the Colored Race.* Boston: A. G. Brown and Co., 1874.

Colored American Magazine 5, 1902. New York: Negro Universities Press, 1969.

Godman, William David. *Gilbert Academy and Agricultural College: Sketches and Incidents.* New York: Hunt and Eaton, 1893.

Harrington, Fred Harvey. *Fighting Politician: Major General N. P. Banks.* London: Oxford University Press, 1948.

Haywood, Jacquelyn Slaughter. *The American Missionary Association in Louisiana during Reconstruction.* Unpublished Ph.D. dissertation, University of California-Los Angeles, 1974.

Majors, Monroe A. *Noted Negro Women.* Chicago: Donohue and Henneberry, 1893.

New Orleans Daily Picayune, October 12, 1867.

New Orleans Tribune, May 25, 1865; May 27, 1865; June 8, 1865.

Porter, Betty. ''The History of Negro Education in Louisiana.'' *Louisiana Historical Quarterly* 25 (July 1942): 728-821.

Ripley, C. Peter, ed. *The Black Abolitionist Papers.* Vol. 5, *The United States, 1859-1865.* Chapel Hill: University of North Carolina Press, 1985.

Williams, George W. *History of the Negro Race in America from 1619 to 1880.* New York: G. P. Putnam's Sons, 1883.

Carolyn M. Jones

Suzanne de Passe

(1948-)

Producer, record and film company executive

Suzanne de Passe has become a powerful executive and one of the dynamic forces in the entertainment industry, first in her work with the Motown Music empire then with her own company, de Passe Entertainment. Using her creative talent and business acumen, she organized Berry Gordy's record and film industry into one of America's most well-known and effective black businesses. Through her company she has produced some of television's outstanding miniseries.

Of West Indian heritage, Suzanne Celeste de Passe was born in 1948 in the Harlem section of New York City, where she grew up and received her early education. Although her parents divorced when she was three years old, her father remarried when she was nine, and he and his second wife provided a strong support network for her. As a child, de Passe modeled designs created by DeVera Edwards for prominent Harlem families. From early on, she pictured herself leading a glamorous life. According to *Great Women in the Struggle,* she stated, ''I actually pictured myself climbing in and out of limousines.'' She attended New York City's New Lincoln School, a private integrated institution. Aspiring to be a writer, she attended Syracuse University and later transferred to Manhattan Community College, where she majored in English. In 1978 she married Paul Le Mat, an actor who played the role of Melvin in the 1980 movie *Melvin and Howard.*

Suzanne de Passe's business career reveals a pattern of steady progress. She worked briefly at several jobs, including, according to Bonnie Allen in *Essence,* ''three days as a Bloomingdale's sales clerk, one month in New York's garment district, part-time horse riding instructor, and talent coordinator of a night club.'' It was the informal work as talent coordinator that presaged de Passe's outstanding career as a business executive in the entertainment industry.

While attending college, de Passe began to observe and critique the performers appearing locally. In 1967 at the Cheetah Disco, a popular Manhattan discotheque, her observations led to her position as talent coordinator. She decided the worth of auditioning performers and learned basic business skills for scheduling performers and negotiating contracts. Following her work for the Cheetah Disco, de Passe was employed as a talent consultant for the Howard Stein

Suzanne de Passe

firm. De Passe's work at Howard Stein led to her position with Berry Gordy and Motown.

Named Motown Executive

Before she was offered a position with Motown, de Passe was introduced to Gordy by Cindy Birdsong, who later performed as one of the Supremes. De Passe describes this occasion in Robert DeLeon's article in *Jet:*

> While I was with Cindy at some affair one night, she introduced me to Berry Gordy. His limousine didn't show up to take him from there for some reason, so I offered him a ride in mine.... A friendship blossomed then, and every time he or some other Motown people would come to town, I'd take them around.

De Passe's position with Motown resulted from her efforts to recruit Motown performers for Howard Stein. She was unable to schedule such performers, and on the occasion of her next meeting with Gordy, in Miami, Florida, she expressed her concern to him. Subsequent to this second meeting, in 1968, Gordy offered de Passe a position as his creative assistant. From that point forward, de Passe became a dynamic part of the evolution of the Motown industry, which was at the time based in Gordy's home in Detroit, Michigan.

Upon joining Motown, de Passe helped to organize and promote the business. Following her first assignment, critiquing a Smokey Robinson performance, de Passe participated in most phases of the company's business. Later in 1968 she moved with Motown to its new home in Los Angeles, California. There, as the business grew, so did de Passe's responsibilities; she advanced in the company from the position of director of Motown's West Coast operation's creative division to the division's vice-president, and she then went on to the vice-presidency of Motown Industries. In 1981 de Passe became president of Motown Productions, Motown's motion picture and film division, which had a ten million dollar budget.

Her principal activities at Motown were varied. In 1970, de Passe became involved in talent acquisition for Motown, and from then on was instrumental in signing and developing some of America's star African American musical talent, including Michael Jackson/the Jackson Five, the Commodores/ Lionel Richie, Stephanie Mills, the Temptations, Smokey Robinson, Stevie Wonder, Rick James, and most of the other performers featured as Motown artists. In her first three years with Motown, not only did she travel extensively with artists such as the Jackson Five, but she also had a substantial hand in the production of the company's television specials. Her writing skills were put to the test first for "Diana," Diana Ross's solo television special in 1970, and soon afterward she served as head writer for "Goin' Back to Indiana," an ABC special featuring the Jackson Five.

In 1972, de Passe and coauthor Chris Clark wrote the screenplay for Motown's first movie, the hugely successful and critically acclaimed *Lady Sings the Blues,* starring Diana Ross and Billie Dee Williams. De Passe had a major role in the writing and production of numerous other Motown productions, including *Mahogany* and *The Wiz,* both of which were somewhat less successful than *Lady* due to problems with directing and distribution, despite being well received by black audiences nationwide.

As president of Motown Productions, de Passe's focus shifted from a concern for the broader interests in both record and film production to a concentration on the film industry, which gave her total control over and full responsibility for the division's status in theater, television, and movie production. Under de Passe's leadership, Motown Productions developed productions in all three genres. These included the successful feature "Berry Gordy's the Last Dragon" and the renowned NBC special "Motown 25: Yesterday, Today, Forever." She presented two television movies of the week on CBS, "Callie and Son," which starred Lindsay Wagner, and "Happy Endings," starring John Schneider, and an ABC Afterschool Special, "Out of Step." She developed two theater works, *Satchmo,* a biography of Louis Armstrong, and *Daddy Goodness,* a musical proposed for the Broadway stage.

De Passe's attitude toward her profession is marked by levelheadedness and a realistic perspective. As noted in *Black Enterprise* in 1974—when she was twenty-six and held the position of vice-president of Motown's creative division—she held a down-to-business view of the company's focus on producing high-quality singles and albums:

> It's a real fight to get to the top ... but the biggest gift of all is staying there. Our artists have enjoyed tremendous staying power. I think we are the only

company in the business that can brag of eight, ten or twelve artists who have been hot for ten years or better. I think that shows the degree of concentration that is exerted on, first of all, picking the right people, those people with enough potential to have that kind of staying power, and then staying with them even through the rough spots, because it's virtually impossible to stay on fire all the time.

Eight years later, as president of Motown Productions, although her focus had shifted away from the record industry, according to an interview with Bonnie Allen, she retained her no-nonsense approach toward successful business practices:

> We understand the creative process at Motown. . . . Everything here is homegrown. When you have the kind of success with creating your own work that we have, it would be silly to throw it away. . . . We're a full-scale entertainment company and we can handle anything.

De Passe Founds Entertainment Company

De Passe left Motown in 1988 and again gained national exposure through her own company, de Passe Entertainment, which she established in January 1992. She was executive producer of *Lonesome Dove,* the critically-acclaimed, landmark eight-hour CBS miniseries, winner of Peabody, Golden Glove, and Emmy awards. The Television Critics Association declared *Lonesome Dove* Program of the Year. She was executive producer again for the celebrated "Motown on Showtime" series featuring "Michael Jackson: The Legend Continues," now a best-selling home video; "Small Sacrifices," the critically-acclaimed Peabody Award-winning four-hour miniseries on ABC, and "Motown 30: What's Going On!," a two-hour CBS special. De Passe's most recent work as producer includes the four-hour ABC miniseries "The Jacksons: An American Dream," "Return to Lonesome Dove," the sequel to "Lonesome Dove," and the ABC series "Sister, Sister."

Her talent and success in the entertainment industry have earned de Passe a number of awards. In 1972, she received an Academy Award nomination for "Lady Sings the Blues," and later she received an Emmy Award and the NAACP Image Award as cowriter and executive producer of "Motown 25." The show itself won the Directors Guild of America and the George Foster Peabody awards. De Passe won a second Emmy and a second Image Award for the highly celebrated NBC three-hour special "Motown Returns to the Apollo."

De Passe has received numerous other recognitions, including the Brotherhood Crusade Black Pioneer Award, 1982; National Coalition of 100 Black Women's Candace Award for Business, 1983, and their Trailblazer Award, 1989; YWCA Silver Achievement Award, 1983; National Urban League Achievement Award, 1983; the Los Angeles Sentinel Woman of the Year Award, 1983; and the Equitable Black Achievement Recognition Award, 1986. Also in 1986, de Passe was named one of twelve Women of the Year by *Ms.* magazine for her "leadership in combining art, business and

history to give us unprecedented television specials on black music as part of our national heritage and joy." In 1988, she received the Women in Film Crystal Award. She was inducted into the Black Filmmakers Hall of Fame in 1990. Other honors have been bestowed on her by *Essence Magazine,* the Kwanza Foundation, and The Trusteeship. She was inducted into the Legacy of Women in Film and Television in 1992, and in 1993 she accepted the Turner Broadcasting Trumpet Award and the Achievement Award from the Executive Leadership Council.

Active in civic and cultural affairs, de Passe is a board member of the New York City Ballet and the Academy of Television Arts and Sciences and its foundation. In Los Angeles, where she lives, she is a board member of the Los Angeles Opera and a member of the Hollywood Radio and Television Society. She holds membership in the Academy of Television Arts and Sciences, Academy of Motion Picture Arts and Sciences, Writers Guild, Women in Film, Women's Trusteeship, and the American Society of Composers, Authors, and Publishers.

Given de Passe's obvious success as a high-profile executive, it is clear she is one of the United States' outstanding black professionals. She has overcome the racism and sexism dominant in both the record industry and Hollywood, arenas that Suzanne de Passe conquered with energy, determination, and hard-won expertise.

Current Address: de Passe Entertainment, 5750 Wiltshire Boulevard, Suite 610, Los Angeles, CA 90036.

REFERENCES:

Allen, Bonnie. "Suzanne De Passe: Motown's $10-Million Boss Lady." *Essence* 12 (September 1981): 89-92; 141-44.

Black Enterprise 5 (June 1974): 77-80.

Burger, Michael. "Women in Business." *Ebony* 32 (August 1977): 122-23.

"Clothes for the Young Miss." *Ebony* 5 (September 1950): 51.

DeLeon, Robert A. "Suzanne de Passe: Woman behind Motown Stars." *Jet* 48 (June 12, 1975): 24-31.

Igus, Toyomi, ed. *Great Women in the Struggle.* New York: Just Us Books, 1991.

Ingham, John N., and Lynne B. Feldman. *African-American Business Leaders: A Biographical Dictionary.* Westport, Conn.: Greenwood Press, 1994.

Rothman, Jill. Fax to Jessie Carney Smith. June 21, 1994.

———. Telephone conversation with Jessie Carney Smith. June 23, 1994.

"Suzanne de Passe. Biography." Los Angeles: Rachel McCallister and Associates, 1994.

Who's Who among Black Americans, 1994-95. 8th ed. Detroit: Gale Research, 1994.

Who's Who of American Women. 18th ed. New Providence, N.J.: Marquis Who's Who, 1993.

Laura C. Jarmon

Helen Octavia Dickens

(1909-)

Physician, surgeon, researcher, educator, health administrator, counselor, lecturer

Helen Octavia Dickens has devoted more than sixty years to addressing issues of health care through her medical practice, hospital administration positions, teaching assignments, advocacy of women's health needs, and counseling of medical students. A specialist in obstetrics and gynecology, Dickens was the first African American woman admitted as a fellow of the American College of Surgeons. In addition, she has long been recognized in the medical profession and education community for her research on the effects of intensive medical, psychological, educational, and social services intervention on pregnant, socially deprived teenagers, their families, and the fathers of the unborn children. Her concern has been with using these services to reduce the rate of teen pregnancies.

Helen Octavia Dickens was born in Dayton, Ohio, on February 21, 1909. The oldest of Charles and Daisy Jane Green Dickens's three children, she is their only surviving offspring. Dickens is the widow of Purvis Sinclair Henderson, who was a pediatric neurosurgeon, and the mother of Helen Jayne Henderson Brown and Norman Sinclair Henderson. Dickens's father, who had been a slave in Tennessee, was about nine years old when the Civil War ended. Given the discouraging and seemingly hopeless conditions of the time, he accepted the offer of a white family to relocate with them to Ohio. Dickens said in an interview on August 2, 1993, "My father thought they were going to educate him. They had no idea of educating him. He, nevertheless, learned to read and write by asking people on the street what words meant. When he was twenty he decided it was time to move on."

For a time, Charles Dickens, who sought to improve himself academically and economically, attended Wilberforce University and Oberlin College. Subsequently, he moved to Dayton, where he met Helen Dickens's mother, Daisy Jane Green. Her family, originally from Canada, had migrated to Paulding, Ohio, then to Dayton. Daisy Jane Dickens was a homemaker at the insistence of her husband, who did not want her to work. Ironically, it was Charles Dickens who encouraged his daughter to pursue medicine—a career that, were she to marry, would necessarily keep her out of the home. Unfortunately, when Dickens was eight years old, her father died from an infection he developed after a dental extraction.

Dickens received her elementary and high school educations in Dayton, remaining faithful to her father's insistence that she attend integrated schools. Charles Dickens understood that a segregated education would put Dickens and her siblings at a disadvantage and would not prepare them for the challenges they would meet in the world at large. This was but a part of his larger philosophy of encouraging his children to keep their goals in mind at all times and to keep working to

Helen Octavia Dickens

achieve them. This advice no doubt contributed to Dickens's determined spirit. For example, when she entered high school she realized that she would be eighteen years old when she graduated. She stated in the August 2, 1993, interview:

> I didn't want to graduate at eighteen, I wanted to do so at seventeen which was the average high school age to graduate. I had to figure out how to graduate at seventeen. By going to night school and summer school I did in fact graduate in three years and at the age of seventeen.

Dickens had decided to pursue a medical career when she was approximately twelve years old. Her family was very supportive of her decision, and she was also encouraged in that direction by her family dentist and by Blanche Arnold, a secretary at the local YWCA. She continued in the interview:

> Blanche had been to Africa and had thought of becoming a missionary. She saw that the missionaries sponsored by the YWCA who were physicians were the most helpful. I had no particular interest in being a missionary. But Blanche talked about physicians and I came to realize that was my interest, and that prospect my inspiration.

Educational Pursuits

After high school Dickens was accepted at Crane Junior College in Chicago, where she enrolled in premedical courses. She explained in the interview, "Crane was a city college and thankfully I didn't have to pay tuition. At the time, people didn't make much money. My mother made only twenty-four dollars a week.'' Academic admission standards at Crane were very competitive but fortunately Dickens's grades qualified her. Crane also required that students be Chicago residents. She managed to meet that requirement by living with her maternal aunt, Pearl Williams. Though her financial burden was eased because she didn't have to pay tuition, Dickens worked occasionally at the local A & P grocery. While at Crane, Dickens kept diligently focused on her studies and pointedly ignored the racism of the student body and faculty. She continued in the interview:

> I sat in the front seat. If other students wanted a good seat they had to sit beside me. If they didn't, it was not my concern because I could clearly see the professor and the blackboard as I was right up there. This way I didn't have to look at them or the gestures made that were directed against me or toward me.

Dickens went on to receive her bachelor of science degree in 1932 from the University of Illinois. In that year she entered the University of Illinois College of Medicine, where she was one of five women in a class of 137 medical students. In 1934 Dickens received her medical degree and was one of two women to graduate in her class.

Dickens did her internship and a residency in obstetrics at Provident Hospital in Chicago from 1933 to 1935. She recalled that women interns or residents could not live in the medical quarters but had to share the nurses' quarters. Dickens gave a brief description of these years in the interview:

> There were no demonstrations. If you wanted the job, you just took it as is. This was true for black women and white women. Provident was a black hospital located on the South side of Chicago. There was tremendous poverty and tuberculosis. The medical residents did not go out into the community much. We actually did more community medicine while in medical school. Even then the faculty went with you as a part of the training. We were very anxious to go into the community.

First Medical Practice

Shortly before completing her residency, Dickens saw a notice about a position in Philadelphia with Virginia Alexander, a Quaker who was practicing medicine alone. Dickens was impressed with Alexander's home practice because it provided an alternative to the usual home or hospital obstetrics care. It was there, on Jefferson Street, in a three-story row house called the Asparanto Health Home, that Dickens began her practice. She said in the interview:

> When I started to practice I delivered babies at home. Sometimes there were difficulties delivering babies in the patients' homes. To assist with these problems, Dr. Alexander provided four beds at Asparanto. It was arranged similar to a hospital with a small room the size of a bathroom which was used

as the delivery room. On a night when we went to deliver a woman at home, we found that there was no electricity. We pushed the bed to the window and used the street light.

After about a year, Dickens was left to carry on the practice alone since Alexander had decided to go to Howard University Medical College for a year. In addition to taking over the medical practice, Dickens assumed the care of Alexander's aged father. Fortunately, they both lived at the Asparanto home and he could care for himself with the help of a housekeeper and a nurse provided by Alexander.

For approximately six years, Dickens was a general practitioner and provided obstetrical care with the support of only one nurse. She was persuaded that she particularly needed to know more about the obstetrical care that she was giving. She learned that the University of Pennsylvania graduate school of medicine offered a master's degree in medical science, and she thought this degree would help her secure a residency in obstetrics and gynecology. In 1941 Dickens enrolled at the University of Pennsylvania School of Medicine to study for a master's in medical science with a specialization in obstetrics and gynecology. ''I went there for the year and did get a residency,'' she said in the interview. ''Well, I didn't get the one I wanted at first. I went back to Provident, in Chicago, for a year.''

Medicine, Marriage, and Motherhood

In 1942, when Dickens returned to Provident Hospital, she met Purvis Sinclair Henderson, a resident in general surgery whose father had practiced medicine in Boston. In 1943, while both were still residents, they married. That same year, Dickens was accepted for a residency in obstetrics and gynecology at Harlem Hospital in New York City. This was a residency that she avidly sought after hearing Peter Marshall Murray, a noted internist and surgeon, give a presentation at Provident Hospital. At the same time, Henderson had to consider returning to his practice in Savannah, Georgia. They agreed to support each other's careers and visit between Georgia and New York until their responsibilities were completed.

Dickens finished her residency at Harlem Hospital in 1946 and in that same year was certified by the American Board of Obstetrics and Gynecology. In 1948 Dickens was appointed director of the Department of Obstetrics and Gynecology at Mercy Douglass Hospital in Philadelphia. It was one of the few hospitals in Philadelphia having both a racially integrated staff and patient population. Sexism was a persistent problem for women physicians at Mercy Douglass. Shortly after her appointment, Henderson joined her in Pennsylvania. He took a residency in neurology at the University of Pittsburgh and subsequently was a resident in neurosurgery at the University of Pennsylvania Medical College.

Dickens and her husband raised two children. Their daughter, Helen Jayne Brown, is an internist who practices in

Philadelphia. Norman Sinclair Henderson works in the field of communications in the Washington, D.C., area. Purvis Henderson died in 1961 before he was able to witness his children's accomplishments.

In 1950, two years after her appointment to Mercy Douglass, Dickens became the first African American woman to be admitted as a fellow of the American College of Surgeons. For this singular achievement, she was honored by the governor as a Distinguished Daughter of Pennsylvania. In 1953 she became a fellow of the American College of Obstetrics and Gynecology, and was later admitted as a fellow of the International College of Surgeons. Dickens served as director of obstetrics and gynecology at Mercy Douglass until 1967. She was also a member of the courtesy staff of the Women's Hospital in Philadelphia from 1951 to 1952 and an associate in that hospital's Department of Obstetrics and Gynecology until 1956. That year, she became chief of the department, serving until 1964 when the University of Pennsylvania School of Medicine acquired the Women's Hospital.

In 1965, Dickens began a long-standing relationship with the University of Pennsylvania School of Medicine and was appointed as an instructor in the Department of Obstetrics and Gynecology. In 1966 she became an associate in the department. During the next ten years she was appointed assistant professor and then associate professor. Dickens was named professor of obstetrics and gynecology in 1976 and professor emeritus in 1985. Dickens was appointed associate dean of the University of Pennsylvania School of Medicine in 1969, a position she presently holds. From 1969 to 1985 she was director of the School of Medicine's Teen Clinic in the Department of Obstetrics and Gynecology.

Dickens has also held faculty appointments at the Medical College of Pennsylvania. Between 1954 and 1957 she held the positions of clinical associate and assistant clinical professor in the Department of Obstetrics at the Medical College of Pennsylvania. In 1958 she was appointed associate clinical professor in the college's Department of Obstetrics and Gynecology and served in that position until 1965.

Women's Illnesses and Teen Pregnancy Studied

Dickens's specialization led her to pursue research in the area of women's illnesses. In particular, her studies have been concerned with the prevention of vaginal cancer. Dickens has also been seriously concerned about the treatment of pregnant teenagers in obstetrics and gynecology clinics. In 1970, while director of the Teen Clinic, Dickens initiated a comparative study of pregnant teenagers' prenatal and postnatal behaviors in the prenatal clinic and teenage obstetrical clinic at the University of Pennsylvania. She sought to determine whether more intensive therapeutic intervention would improve these behaviors.

The study strongly suggested the importance of educational intervention with nonpregnant teens, most especially by their families, the schools, and the community at large. In 1972, as a result of the study, funds from a private foundation were used to support a follow-up program in the Department of Obstetrics and Gynecology at the University of Pennsylvania.

Dickens continues to examine the phenomenon of teen pregnancy and has published extensively on the subject. Her focus has been on prevention. This is of particular concern in light of the possible relationship between cancer, sexually transmitted diseases, and AIDS in women. "I don't know if they are as aware of that relationship as they should be. I guess that will come along with more education and more time," Dickens said in the 1993 interview.

Dickens's articles on teen pregnancy and issues related to obstetrics, gynecology, and public health have appeared in *Pan American Medical Women's Journal, American Practice and Diagnosis of Treatment, American Journal of OB/GYN, American Journal of Public Health, Journal of Marriage and Family Counseling, American Journal of Orthopsychiatry,* and *Women's Wellness.* She has also contributed chapters to several books concerning adolescent health problems, particularly as they relate to teenage pregnancy and prevention. Dickens has lectured extensively in her areas of expertise. She was a consultant for the video documentary "Loving Parents," produced in 1978 by Herman J. Engle for Texture Films, Inc., and a member of the Senior Science Advisory Group of the Health Information Network for their publication "The Facts about AIDS—A Special Guide for NEA Members."

Dickens has received numerous awards for her studies of uterine cancer, teaching and academic counseling, advocacy of women's health needs, and committee service. She has been presented with awards by the American Medical Women's Association, the Board of Auxiliaries of Mercy Douglass Hospital, the American Cancer Society, the University of Illinois Alumni Association, the National Association of Medical Minority Educators, the National Coalition of 100 Black Women, the National Council of Negro Women, the Girl Scouts of Greater Philadelphia, and the Frederick Douglass Society. In 1990, on their Founder's Day, Dickens was inducted into the Women Pioneers Hall of Fame by the Southwest Belmont Branch YWCA of Philadelphia. In 1992 she was warmly honored by the University of Pennsylvania Minority Alumni, Faculty, Housestaff, and Students.

Among her many awards from the medical profession are an honorary doctor of medical science degree, which she received from the Medical College of Pennsylvania in 1979, and an honorary doctor of science degree, which the University of Pennsylvania awarded her in 1982.

Dickens holds membership in numerous national societies, among them the American College of Surgeons, the American College of Obstetrics and Gynecology, the American Medical Association, the Association of American Medical Colleges, and the American Cancer Society. Dickens is also a member of local societies, including the Philadelphia County Medical Society, the Obstetrical Society of Philadelphia, the Children's Aid Society, and the American Foundation for Negro Affairs.

In 1968 Dickens developed the Office of Minority Affairs at the University of Pennsylvania School of Medicine to provide academic counseling to minority students. In 1984, Karen Hamilton, the assistant dean of student affairs and the current director of minority affairs, began a particularly productive collaboration with Dickens. Their efforts have resulted in a 98.5 percent minority student retention rate.

Now in her sixtieth year of medical practice, including almost thirty years with the University of Pennsylvania School of Medicine, Dickens focuses her energies on her office practice and on admissions counseling of minority applicants. Today, as in her youth, Dickens is focused on her goals. She works a full day, five days a week. Retirement is not in her immediate plans.

Dickens has been an inspiration and a positive role model for over sixty years. Today she continues to inspire young women, particularly those who have set their sights on medicine as a profession.

REFERENCES:

Dickens, Helen O. "New Hope for Women in the Fight against Cancer." *New Lady* (June 4, 1971): 29, 33-34.
———. "Teen-Age Pregnancy and Abortion." In *Marital and Sexual Counseling in Medical Practice.* Edited by D. W. Abse, E. M. Nash, and L. M. R. Lauden. Haggerstown, Md.: Harper Row, 1974.
———. Telephone interviews with Juanita R. Howard, August 2, 1993, and March 10, 1994.
Dickens, Helen O., Emily Hartshorne, and others. "One Hundred Pregnant Adolescents: Treatment Approaches in a University Hospital." *American Journal of Public Health* 63 (September 1973): 9.
Dickens, Helen O., Emily Hartshorne Mudd, and George R. Huggins. "Teenagers, Contraception, and Pregnancy." *Journal of Marriage and Family Counseling* 1 (April 1975): 175-81.
Dickens, Helen O., and Dale M. Allison. "Teenage Pregnancy." In *Adolescent Gynecology.* Edited by Alfred M. Bongiovanni. New York: Plenum Publishing Corporation, 1983.
Dinan, Dennis A. "Just Do It. Helen Dickens Speaks Her Mind." *Penn Medicine* 4 (Fall 1990): 9-15.
"Dr. Dickens Says 'No' to Retirement." *Center for the Study of Aging Newsletter* 9 (Fall 1987): 1, 4, 6, 10.
"Drs. Helen Dickens, Margaret Mead Are Recipients of Gimbel Awards." *Philadelphia Evening News Bulletin,* January 14, 1971.
Hamilton, Karen. Telephone interview with Juanita R. Howard, March 10, 1994.
"1962 Medical Women of the Year." *Journal of the American Medical Women's Association* 18 (January 1963): 81-88.
"School Contraceptive Programs Should Include Counseling Often." *OB/GYN News* (July 1, 1974).

Juanita R. Howard

Addie Whiteman Dickerson
(1878-?)
Real estate broker, reformer, clubwoman, civic and political activist

Addie Dickerson achieved prominence as a real estate broker and reformer. She was especially active as a leader in women's organizations. Her social work emphasized international issues—especially world peace—and the improvement of conditions for African Americans.

Addie Whiteman Dickerson was born in Wilmington, North Carolina, in 1878. She was the sixth child and third daughter of John H. and Hester (sometimes spelled as Ester) Leonard Whiteman. Her father's occupation is listed in the 1880 North Carolina census as drayman. The Whitemans are described in Elizabeth Davis's *Lifting as They Climb,* a history of the National Association of Colored Women's Clubs, as "one of the section's best known families." Addie Dickerson was educated at Gregory Institute and at Scotia Seminary (subsequently Scotia Women's College). She spent most of her adult life in Philadelphia, and she pursued additional study in the College of Collateral Teachers at the University of Pennsylvania.

Her husband, G. Edward Dickerson, was a prominent Philadelphia attorney. In *The Negro College Graduate,* Charles S. Johnson includes him among the leading African American lawyers of the early twentieth century. A native of Virginia, G. Edward Dickerson received a law degree from Temple University in 1902. According to Roger Lane in *William Dorsey's Philadelphia and Ours,* Dickerson, John C. Asbury, William Fuller, and Henry W. Bass comprised the second wave of black lawyers who arrived in Philadelphia in the early 1900s. The Dickersons had a son, Edmund Whiteman, who died in 1914.

Addie Dickerson worked as a real estate broker and, relatedly, a notary public. A publicity flyer from the late 1920s, cited in *Lifting as They Climb,* identifies her as "Philadelphia's oldest Negro woman Real Estate Broker," with a specialty in mortgages, and "Philadelphia's first Negro woman Notary Public." John A. Saunders, in his *History of the Philadelphia Negro, 1787-1963,* indicates that at the time of G. Edward Dickerson's death in 1940, the family's assets were estimated to be about $100,000.

Represents Community Interests at the White House

Dickerson was very involved in civic, political, and religious organizations. She was a co-organizer of the Philadelphia YWCA and a member of the Philadelphia Chamber of Commerce. Active in Republican party work, she was a delegate to President Herbert Hoover's conferences with black leaders at the White House in 1931. A Presbyterian, she served as chairperson of the National Council of Church Women.

Addie Whiteman Dickerson

Dickerson's work for international causes is also significant. She represented the Women's International League of Peace and Freedom at its council meeting held in Prague, Czechoslovakia, in 1924. She also represented American women at the fourth Pan-African Conference in New York in 1927.

Her work with the International Council of Women of the Darker Races allowed her to pursue many of her interests through a single organization. The council, founded by Margaret Murray Washington in August 1920, was only active for a decade. Nonetheless, as Herbert Aptheker has noted in his *Documentary History of the Negro People in the United States, 1910-1932,* the organization articulated and pursued a comprehensive program that emphasized world peace and educational, social, and economic reform. The organization set out early to study the history and present conditions of women of darker races worldwide. An article on the council, published in the *Southern Workman* for January 1923, notes that important committees were established soon after the organization was founded and that Dickerson was chairperson of the Committee on Foreign Relations. Dickerson became president of the organization in 1929, after having served as vice-president. Dickerson also served on the council's Committee on Education, which was charged with developing a curriculum and textbooks that would be reviewed by school boards throughout the country; other members of this committee were Nannie Burroughs and Mary Church Terrell.

Dickerson's interest in education is also indicated by her service on many school boards and advisory councils to schools, including Charlotte Hawkins Brown's Palmer Me-

morial Institute in Sedalia, North Carolina, and Mary McLeod Bethune's Bethune-Cookman College in Daytona Beach, Florida. Dickerson also served as a trustee of the Frederick Douglass Memorial Association and as the statistician of the Federation of Colored Women.

Dickerson's involvement in business and civic activities shows her dedication to her community. Many of her service-based activities reflect her special interest in the development of young people and her recognition that women needed to make a concerted effort to address their concerns not only at the local level, but at national and international levels as well.

REFERENCES:

Aptheker, Herbert, ed. *A Documentary History of the Negro People in the United States, 1910-1932.* Secacus, N.J.: Citadel Press, 1973.

Ayers, James Curtiss. Letter to Arlene Clift-Pellow, February 25, 1994.

Barnett, Evelyn Brooks. "Nannie Burroughs and the Education of Black Women." In *The Afro-American Woman: Struggles and Images.* Edited by Sharon Harley and Rosalyn Terborg-Penn. Port Washington, N.Y.: Kennikat Press, 1978.

"Colored Women's International Council." *Southern Workman* 52 (January 1923): 7-10.

Davis, Elizabeth Lindsay. *Lifting as They Climb.* Washington, D.C.: National Association of Colored Women, 1933.

Dunbar-Nelson, Alice. *Give Us Each Day: The Diary of Alice Dunbar-Nelson.* Edited by Gloria T. Hull. New York: W. W. Norton, 1984.

Hoytt, Eleanor Hinton. "International Council of Women of the Darker Races: Historical Notes from Margaret Murray Washington." *Sage* 3 (Fall 1986): 54-55.

Johnson, Charles S. *The Negro College Graduate.* 1938. Reprint. New York: Negro Universities Press, 1969.

Lane, Roger. *William Dorsey's Philadelphia and Ours.* New York: Oxford University Press, 1991.

Saunders, John A. *History of the Philadelphia Negro, 1787-1963.* N.p., 1969.

Tucci, Thomas D. Letters to Arlene Clift-Pellow, April 7, 1994, and June 22, 1994.

U.S. Bureau of the Census. Population Schedules. Vol. 16, 1880, North Carolina, and Vol. 256, 1920, Pennsylvania.

Who's Who in Colored America. 5th ed. Brooklyn: Who's Who in Colored America, 1940.

COLLECTIONS:

Correspondence between Addie Whiteman Dickerson and G. Edward Dickerson and Charles S. Johnson is located in the Charles S. Johnson Collection, Fisk University Library, Nashville, Tennessee.

Arlene Clift-Pellow

Beulah Mae Donald
(1920-1988)
Civil rights activist

Heralded as the woman who beat the Klan, Beulah Mae Donald won a seven-million-dollar judgment against the Ku Klux Klan for the murder of her nineteen-year-old son, Michael Donald. The case attracted widespread notice in civil rights, legal, and law enforcement circles. Beulah Mae Donald, a poor chambermaid with very little formal education, seemed an unlikely combatant for the KKK. However, she was a brave and courageous mother who sought justice. Although her sole intent was to clear her son's name and find out who committed such a horrible crime, a federal jury in Mobile, Alabama, decided that the United Klans of America must pay seven million dollars to her for the brutal beating and strangling of her son, who was left hanging in a tree in 1981. Beulah Mae Donald's victory resulted in an historic settlement in which the Klan headquarters near Tuscaloosa, Alabama, was signed over to her and sold for an undisclosed amount. The property has been appraised at one hundred fifty to two hundred thousand dollars.

Donald was born in De Lisle, Mississippi, in 1920. She was the youngest of eight children. Her father, Marion Gregory, was a saw mill worker and her mother, Mary, took in washing and ironing. Donald and her siblings helped their mother to manage at a time when two dollars was a large sum of money. She was raised in the strict tradition of the Southern Baptist Church; as a result, Donald had very strong religious beliefs. The family moved to Mobile when Donald was a child. Pregnant in the tenth grade, she married, dropped out of school, and went to work cleaning hotels.

Divorced with two children, Mary and Betty Jean, living alone, trying to make ends meet, Beulah Mae met and married David Donald in the early 1960s. Together they had five more children, Leo, Stanley, Cecilia, Cynthia, and Michael. A quiet woman whose life was bounded by work, church, and children, Donald was an excellent mother who used love and religion to teach her children values. On Sunday, she would take her family to church in the morning and remain there all day. She was a strong believer who said, "I don't know about man, but I know what God can do." The couple divorced when David Donald moved to New York City to work. She came north to live with him for a couple of years but became homesick, and went back south to work and to take care of her parents. Donald was fond of children and after raising her seven and constantly taking care of grandchildren, she participated in a foster grandparents plan sponsored by the Mobile Community Action Program and she took the toughest, hardest to handle children.

Klan Suspected of Violent Act

Donald's son, Michael, was nineteen when he was kidnapped from a Mobile street in March 1981 and taken to a rural area where he was beaten and choked. His throat was cut and his body was left hanging from a tree in Mobile. A Klan leader is reported as saying that the sight of the black teenager's hanged body was a "pretty sight."

Michael was the youngest of Donald's seven children and still living at home at the time of his murder. He loved basketball and music and was studying brick masonry at Carver Technical College. He worked part time in the mail room of the local newspaper. Considering the kind of boy he was, Donald knew that Michael had done nothing to provoke his murder. She and other local black leaders suspected that the Klan was involved even though local authorities speculated that Michael Donald might have been having an affair with a white co-worker at the *Mobile Press Register,* or that he might have been involved in a drug deal that went sour.

Donald was determined to clear her son's name and to find out what had really happened to him. Local authorities announced that the killing did not appear to have been racially motivated. They ignored the fact that on the night of the murder, Klansmen had burned a cross on the Mobile County Courthouse lawn. Some local white politicians even saw fit to denounce Donald's attorney, state senator Michael Figures, and the head of the Mobile NAACP, Robert Guilliard, for "fanning the flames of racism" by suggesting that white extremists had probably been involved. The same local authorities later had to admit that Michael Donald had been randomly abducted and killed in response to a mistrial in the case of a black man accused of killing a white policeman.

Donald was a strong woman who endured a tremendous burden. She was determined that her child, so brutally slain, would not become just another black man gone and forgotten. The criminal investigation stalled for two years before the case was finally broken. In December 1983, Henry Francis Hays was sentenced to die in Alabama's electric chair for Michael Donald's murder and James (Tiger) Knowles, who pleaded guilty to violating Michael Donald's civil rights, was sentenced to serve life in a federal prison. Both were members of the Ku Klux Klan. When a judge decided that Hays should be electrocuted for such a heinous crime, Donald, who did not believe in capital punishment, disagreed. She said in *Ms.* magazine, "We cannot make life, so we have no right to take it away."

Mother Sues the Klan

Morris Dees, an attorney with the Southern Poverty Law Center, approached Donald and Michael Figures about the possibility of bringing a civil case against the Klan. "Ms. Donald didn't have to go along with the lawsuit," said Dees in *Ms.* magazine. "I will never know how painful it was for her, but I do know her persistence was critical to the case. At the end of the first day of trial, the Klan lawyer came to me and offered to settle out of court for $100,000. I took that offer to Ms. Donald and she turned it down. She wanted to see it through. This is a woman who lived in a public housing project, below the poverty level, a hardworking woman who has been extremely poor all her life. She was doing this for Michael.''

A private person, Donald did not attend the 1983 murder trial. She pushed herself to attend the civil trial even though it was difficult. She was unable to look at Tiger Knowles, the first witness, as he gave the jurors an unemotional account of the events leading up to the murder. It is reported that she cried silently when Knowles stepped off the witness stand to demonstrate how he helped kill her son. She never testified, but rocked back and forth when the testimony brought too much pain. Knowles admitted that he was acting as a Klansman and in court turned to Donald and begged her forgiveness. According to *Ms.* magazine, Donald replied: ''Son, I forgave you a long time ago. From the day I found out who y'all was, I asked God to take care of y'all, and He has. I turned it over to the Lord.'' The jury and the judge wept. Four hours later, the jury announced its seven-million-dollar judgment. Donald never sought revenge. She told the *New York Times,* ''I wanted to know who all really killed my child. I wasn't even thinking about the money. If I hadn't gotten a cent, it wouldn't have mattered. I wanted to know how and why they did it.''

Donald was considered the rock on which the case was ultimately built. It had consumed the last six years of her life. She never backed away and was not worried about possible vengeance by the Klan. According to *People Weekly,* from the beginning she had faith that ''the truth will come out.'' Donald moved out of a Mobile housing project into a comfortable home just before she died. She died in September of 1988 of natural causes at a hospital in Mobile. She was sixty-seven years old. In 1987, she was named one of *Ms.* magazine's ''Women of the Year'' for her courage and fortitude. In 1988, she received one of the annual *Essence* magazine awards for her ''Courageous Spirit.'' .

REFERENCES:

''Beulah M. Donald, 67, Klan Foe.'' *New York Times,* September 20, 1988.

''Beulah Mae Donald; Sued Klan, Won.'' *Los Angeles Times,* September 20, 1988.

''Black Is Handed Deed to Offices of Klan Group.'' *New York Times,* May 20, 1987.

''Courageous Mother Whose Son Was Lynched by KKK Named 'Woman of the Year'.'' *Jet* 73 (January 11, 1988): 12.

''Damages for a Lynching.'' *New York Times,* February 21, 1988.

Ivins, Molly. ''Beulah Mae Donald. (*Ms.* Magazine Woman of the Year).'' *Ms.* 16 (January 1988): 52-56, 88.

Kunen, James S. ''Seeking Justice for Her Lynched Son, an Alabama Mother Ruins the Klan That Killed Him.'' *People Weekly* (June 8, 1987): 55-57.

Marshall, Marilyn. ''Beulah Mae Donald: The Black Woman Who Beat the Ku Klux Klan.'' *Ebony* 43 (March 1988): 148-49, 152-53.

''A Mother's Struggle with the Klan.'' *New York Times,* March 8, 1987.

''1988 Essence Award Winners.'' *Essence* 19 (October 1988): 72.

''Trial Ends in Alabama Suit against the Klan.'' *New York Times,* February 12, 1987.

''The Woman Who Beat the Klan.'' *New York Times Magazine,* November 1, 1987: 26-34.

''Woman Who Beat KKK Beulah Donald, 67, Dies.'' *Jet* 75 (October 10, 1988): 10.

''Woman Who 'Beat KKK' Dies in Alabama.'' *USA Today,* September 19, 1988.

Bobbie Pollard

Lizzie Douglas
(189?-1973)
Singer, guitarist, songwriter

She could sing, play guitar, and write music as well as any man—and better than most. She could smoke cigarettes, drink whiskey, and belt out tunes all night long—just as the bluesmen bragged about doing. In the rough and coarse world of blues musicianship, Lizzie, or ''Kid,'' Douglas ''leveled the playing field.'' She more than succeeded in what had traditionally been a man's world: she prevailed and predominated. In a 1933 contest with Big Bill Broonzy, considered by some to be the greatest living blues player, she was judged the better of the two musicians by three men known as blues legends. She opened the rhythm and blues and blues worlds to ''down-home'' women artists when before there had only been ''classic'' blues female singers. And none of it was as easy as ''Memphis Minnie,'' as Lizzie Douglas became known, made it look.

Lizzie Douglas was born in Algiers, Louisiana, the last of thirteen children born to Abe Douglas and Gertrude Wells Douglas. Scholars differ as to the exact date and year of Lizzie Douglas's birth. While it is generally agreed that she was born sometime in June, alternate sources have listed 1894, 1896, 1897, 1900, and 1902 as the year of her birth. Like the other children, Lizzie Douglas was expected to help on the family farm. Douglas had three husbands, all musicians: ''Casey'' Bill Weldon, ''Kansas'' Joe McCoy, and Ernest (''Little Son Joe'') Lawlar. She had no children. She died in Memphis on August 6, 1973, and was buried in the New Hope Cemetery in Walls, Mississippi.

''In My Girlish Days''

In those approximately seventy years, Memphis Minnie packed a lot of living. When Lizzie Douglas was seven, the

Lizzie Douglas

family relocated to Walls, Mississippi, fourteen miles from Memphis, to continue farming. From her earliest days, she showed no interest in farm work. What she was interested in was music, and she was determined to learn to play it. All she wanted was a guitar. So emphatic was she that her struggling father bought her one when she was eleven. This was the major incident in her early life, and the defining one. In a few years she was playing with incredible skill. When she was thirteen—old enough to help out on the family farm—she followed the bright lights to the big city of Memphis, where she hung out around Beale Street ("the street that never sleeps") with the hustlers and street musicians. It was quite a change from the relative placidity of farm and family, but "Kid" Douglas seemed to thrive on it.

Untutored and unschooled, she somehow managed to eke out a living from her music. When Beale Street got too crowded, she took her "show" to Church's Park (now W. C. Handy Park) to work that crowd in relative peace. But occasionally she needed a respite from this uncertain and stressful life, so she would return home to Walls, where her family would allow her to rest. They encouraged her in her musical pursuits, and their pride in her accomplishments and unconditional love sustained Douglas through the tough times.

Things improved somewhat when in 1916 Douglas joined the Ringling Brothers Circus at Clarksdale and toured with the company for about seven years. Being able to keep regular hours and the assurance of regular meals enabled her to focus on learning from her fellow troupers how to entertain people. Her powerful voice and good looks added to her remarkable

guitar playing. But eventually she returned to Memphis and became the common-law wife of Casey Bill—short for "K. C." (Kansas City) Bill Weldon. A member of the Memphis Jug Band and a man billed as the "Hawaiian Guitar Wizard," Casey Bill was nine years her junior. Though Weldon is credited with greatly helping Douglas with her music, their relationship did not last long. She soon became involved with Joe McCoy and married him in 1929.

Career Takes Off with "Bumble Bee"

With all this talent, Douglas was yet to be recorded. She had met Joe McCoy when they played in Jed Davenport's Beale Street Jug Band in the streets and parks of Memphis, but the two were literally playing for dimes in Memphis barbershops when a Columbia Record talent scout finally discovered them. And that made all the difference in the world. He listened to their repertoire, changed their names to Memphis Minnie and Kansas Joe, and arranged to record them. After several solid sellers, "Bumble Bee," a double-entendre blues song, proved to be their "breakout" vehicle. Memphis Minnie played lead guitar, Joe taking rhythm. As the record-buying public outside of music-saturated Memphis heard the song, the careers of Memphis Minnie and Kansas Joe took off. Soon Vocalion, a subsidiary of Columbia, was advertising her as their greatest star and selling her records—with such titles as "I'm Gonna Bake My Biscuits," "I'm Talkin' about You," "Can I Do It for You?," and "What Fault You Find of Me?"—by mail with coupons in each of them redeemable for a portable phonograph.

For the next six years Memphis Minnie and Kansas Joe recorded extensively on both mainstream and so-called dime store labels. Memphis Minnie assumed her rightful position among outstanding blues musicians. No longer did she have to hustle on the streets; now she and Joe were sought after to do club gigs—and Chicago, with its recently arrived and growing black population, beckoned. Such was their success and reputation that they moved to Chicago to form their own blues group and to work various South Side clubs, among which was Ruby Lee Gatewood's Tavern (known as "The Gate"), where Memphis Minnie frequently held her famous "Blue Monday" parties designed to showcase new talent.

But all this was still the "blues life," and anything but genteel. Even though Memphis Minnie's Blue Monday parties had put The Gate on the map, Ruby Gatewood was hard to work for. Artists found it difficult if not impossible to get paid for their work. (Some, like Memphis Slim, had to resort to going to the cash register and just taking the money.) Brother John Sellers, in Paul Oliver's *Conversations with the Blues*, gives some insight into the lifestyle and personality of Minnie:

> Memphis Minnie—really those Blue Monday parties in those days were too much! She was a very funny woman and she always wore those great big ear-rings . . . and she was a very fine guitarist. But she was so stern sometimes and Memphis Minnie would always say 'I drink anywhere I please!'

Cause Minnie was used to a rough life. She had a rough life and she lived rough.... With all her greatness and her songs and her Blue Monday parties that she gave she was still a singer to be remembered....

[S]he was big in her heart even though she could be rough.... [T]o be the lone woman in the place you had to be rough and tough in a place and act as they did even if you weren't as tough as they were.

Of course it helps to be talented, too. Perhaps the most celebrated event in Minnie's life occurred on June 26, 1933. Even though Minnie was Vocalion's headliner, many in the business thought Big Bill Broonzy was the finest blues player alive. And so the first contest ever held between two blues players, Minnie and Big Bill, was staged in a Chicago hall that was crowded with every musician who could get in to the place. Minnie and Big Bill were each to play two songs, and though they had brought their own alcohol, the prize was a bottle of whiskey and a bottle of gin. Three giants of blues music were to be the judges. All the other musicians played until it was time for the contest, which didn't start until 1:30 A.M. According to Broonzy, "By that time me and Minnie was really loaded."

Everyone in attendance felt that Broonzy was the better player, and that it might not be fair for a man to square off against a woman—and told him so. And after all, three men were going to judge, all popular and accomplished musicians: Sleepy John Estes, Tampa Red, and Richard Jones. Minnie and her music had been heard in the area, but her husband whisked her in and out of the gigs and took her straight back to Memphis.

White and black folks alike "went wild for ten minutes" as Bill ascended the stage, then waited for relative silence to perform two of his best: "Just a Dream" and "Make My Getaway." When Minnie came to the stand the crowd got quiet. She first sang "Me and My Chauffer," and, according to Yannick Bruynoghe in *Big Bill Blues,* "the house rocked for twenty minutes." After she finished her second song, "Looking the World Over," there was no doubt who had won. Two of the judges picked her up and carried her around until her husband told them, "Put her down; she can walk." Broonzy noted her husband's attitude, then waited until the bottles were presented to Minnie. He grabbed the whiskey, ran off, and drank it. Minnie called him "dirty names."

This scene is revealing for several reasons, not the least of which is Joe McCoy's jealousy and insecurity. After the contest, there was no doubt that Minnie's career had eclipsed his, and around 1935 they split up. The breakup with Joe McCoy did not affect Minnie's popularity and demand as a recording artist. She was so well regarded that she was often asked to record behind weaker guitarists as well as make records of her own.

"Good Girl Blues"

Though she still played rough and ready music with bawdy, hokum lyrics in rough and ready venues, Minnie

Douglas was also playing better clubs and working with established performers such as pianist Black Bob and "Fiddlin'" John Carson. By now Chicago was her town, though she went home to her family in Walls whenever her schedule permitted. Never at a loss for material with which to make new songs, she even named one song after the mule that pulled her father's plow back home, "Frankie Jean." But now when she returned to her family home, she drew crowds of area folks who wanted to hear her sing and play in person. Memphis Minnie always obliged, according to her sister Daisy Johnson.

It was on one of those visits home that she met Ernest Lawlar, known professionally as "Little Son Joe." He was a reasonably prominent musician in his own right, but his association with Memphis Minnie benefited him immensely. His personal relationship with Memphis Minnie was even more important: Memphis Minnie felt at last that she had found a soul mate. They married and were partners in music and in life, doing countless joint and separate gigs in the Chicago area and in Indiana, where they played so they could make more money. It was nice not to have a man who inspired "aggravatin' papa" or "dirty mistreater" blues lyrics as a husband.

When second husband Joe McCoy died in 1949 (some sources record the year of death as 1951), it was the stereotypical "penniless performer" funeral. The occasion was fraught with tragic irony. His all-time best song, "Why Don't You Do Right—Like Some Other Men Do?" was playing big at the Chicago Theatre, still, according to Memphis Slim, quoted in Arnold Shaw's *Honkers and Shouters,* "We had to beg money from all of the musicians ... and he was the writer of this song." There were only twenty people in the funeral parlor, mostly relatives of McCoy's new wife and their two children. Big Bill Broonzy lists a number of prominent blues musicians and record executives who should have been at the funeral, but weren't. Among these was Memphis Minnie. And it was generally thought that Memphis Minnie's best music was made with Joe. It is not known whether she was one of the musicians who chipped in to pay for the funeral. It was no secret then that the musicians who recorded big hits, or even modest ones, were denied royalties, being paid flat rates for recording sessions—usually $50 to $199—and that white performers even then were making covers of black tunes that became very popular. Few actually covered Memphis Minnie's work during her lifetime, but the legendary Muddy Waters (McKinley Morganfield) did rework "Bumble Bee" into his own classic, "Honey Bee." But as rough and tough as Memphis Minnie was—at least on the outside—she had been victimized by the unscrupulous record industry, dishonest club owners, and her own naivete.

And so Minnie, like so many of her peers, had to keep working. She partnered with "Saint Louis Jimmy" in a blues club in Indianapolis, hoping to see show business from the other side. She lived and worked in Detroit for a few years in the hope that things would be better there. All this talent and she was still "paying dues," even though she had already paid in full. While she enjoyed recording and performing during the 1940s, she resented having to do so much of it. It seemed to her that she was still hustling, but on a somewhat higher level than the streets, at least. She even formed her own vaudeville troupe that toured the South in a bus that would drop by Walls when it was in the area, usually on its way to the Palace on Beale Street in Memphis. According to her sister Daisy, she still drew huge audiences, who threw money on the stage. Memphis Minnie would have two or three people picking it up.

Meningitis Blues

Record sales for Minnie and most of her contemporaries declined as rhythm and blues took off on the pop charts. Blues was hopelessly old-fashioned according to the increasingly younger record buyer, and so Minnie was back in Chicago playing club dates in the early 1950s and feeling every bit of her age. The blues life, with its drinking and late hours, caught up with her with a vengeance in the late 1950s. She had been singing about her mysterious physical ailments, which she called "Memphis Minnie-itis" but referred to as "meningitis" in one of her songs. In 1957, her husband, Son Joe, became ill, and she had her first heart attack. They couldn't take care of one another and moved in with Minnie's sister Daisy in Memphis. Memphis Minnie's health improved to the point that she was able to make a couple of records in 1959, but they were never pressed. Son Joe got worse and died in 1962 at the age of sixty-two. After his burial in Walls, Memphis Minnie got worse herself, having a series of heart attacks, strokes, and several other medical complications that kept her paralyzed in a wheelchair. She was in and out of various local nursing homes and had to sell everything, even her precious guitar, to pay for her care.

Memphis Minnie's last days were anything but glamorous. She was not without visitors, mostly white blues aficionados and old cohorts, but their visits only seemed to agitate her because her strokes had rendered her speech nearly unintelligible. She seemed to feel just well enough to be frustrated by each visit. Welfare and the local church paid her nursing home bills, but there was not enough to afford her a few comforts. In Bruce E. Cook's *Listen to the Blues,* bluesman Booker T. Washington ("Bukka") White gives a poignant account of her final days:

> And I see Memphis Minnie sometimes, too. She's in a nursing home now, and I went with a white boy from Washington to see her not long ago. You know, she got as fat as a butterball, that woman did, and all she do is sit in her wheelchair and cry and cry. But in her time she was really something. She was the best thing goin' in the woman line.

After a decade of suffering, Minnie had a fatal stroke at her sister Daisy's home in Memphis.

The memory of Memphis Minnie lives on in the reissued records of Chris Strachwitz of Arhoolie Records, who was quoted as saying, "In my opinion, Memphis Minnie was without doubt the greatest of all female blues singers ever to record." In 1973 Steve LaVere in *Living Blues* magazine noted that she was "the most popular female country blues singer of all time." In 1974 the readers of the United Kingdom's *Blues Unlimited* magazine voted her best female blues singer. And her influence is evident in the performances of John Lee Granderson, Jo-Ann Kelly, Mance Lipscomb, Willie Mae "Big Mama" Thornton, Mama Yancey, and numerous others. But it was one of her contemporaries, fellow performer and longtime friend Big Bill Broonzy who paid her the highest compliment: "Memphis Minnie can pick a guitar and sing as good as any man I've ever heard. [S]he can make a guitar speak words, she can make a guitar cry, moan, talk and whistle the blues. And I know that because I played with her all around."

Memphis Minnie was a powerful and prolific singer who recorded over one hundred songs that defined her as one of the best in the business. Some of her most notable recordings are the various versions of "Bumble Bee," "I Want to Do Something for You," "Meningitis Blues," "Nothing in Rambling," "Queen Bee," "In My Girlish Days," and "Me and My Chauffer."

REFERENCES:

Bruynoghe, Yannick. *Big Bill Blues: William Broonzy's Story.* New York: Oak Publications, 1964.

Cook, Bruce E. *Listen to the Blues.* New York: Charles Scribner's Sons, 1973.

Docks, L. R. *American Premium Record Guide.* 3d ed. Florence, Ala.: Books Americana, 1986.

Handy, D. Antoinette. *Black Women in American Bands and Orchestras.* Metuchen, N.J.: Scarecrow Press, 1981.

Harris, Sheldon. *Blues Who's Who: A Biographical Dictionary of Blues Singers.* New Rochelle, N.Y.: Arlington House, 1979.

LaVere, Steve. "Memphis Minnie." *Living Blues* 14 (Autumn 1973): 5.

Leadbitter, Michael. "My Girlish Days." *Blues Unlimited* 79 (December 1970): 8/9.

Oliver, Paul. *Conversations with the Blues.* New York: Horizon Press, 1965.

———. *The Story of the Blues.* Philadelphia: Chilton Book Co., 1969.

———. *Blues Fell This Morning: Meaning in the Blues.* 2nd ed. Cambridge, England: Cambridge University Press, 1990.

Palmer, Robert. *Deep Blues.* New York: Viking Press, 1981.

Russell, Tony. *Blacks, Whites and Blues.* New York: Stein and Day, 1970.

Shaw, Arnold. *Honkers and Shouters: The Golden Years of Rhythm and Blues.* New York: Collier Books, 1978.

Titon, Jeff Todd. *Early Downhome Blues: A Musical and Cultural Analysis.* Urbana: University of Illinois Press, 1977.

Denis Mercier

Grace Bustill Douglass

(1782-1842)

Abolitionist, milliner

Grace Bustill Douglass was one of the early free black women who combined work with abolitionist societies with community service. In 1833, she was one of a racially mixed group that formed the Philadelphia Female Anti-Slavery Society, and she knew well the work of another group of women who formed the Boston Female Anti-Slavery Society. Not only did the Philadelphia Anti-Slavery Society help bring about the abolition of slavery, but the group supported woman's suffrage, and its work led to improvements in education for black youth in Philadelphia. Douglass's activist activities extended to other organizations, such as the Anti-Slavery Convention of American Women, where she held a leadership position.

Douglass was born in Burlington, New Jersey, into a free interracial family in 1782. Her father, Cyrus Bustill, was born in Burlington, New Jersey, on February 2, 1732, and died in 1806. Her mother, Elizabeth Morey, was a Delaware Indian. Grace was one of eight children: she had four sisters and three brothers. The Bustill family was one of the most prominent free black families of its time. Cyrus Bustill, a Quaker, learned how to make bread and subsequently established a baking business, which became very profitable for his family. The family moved to Philadelphia, where Cyrus continued his baking business at 56 Arch Street. He joined several benevolent societies in Philadelphia, most notably the Free Africa Society, and was a diligent fighter for the cause to end slavery.

Grace Bustill married Robert Douglass of Philadelphia. Grace ran a profitable millinery store next door to her father's baking business. Grace was a Quaker, while her husband was one of the founding members of the First African Presbyterian Church of Philadelphia. She and her husband had two children, Sarah Mapps Douglass (1806-1882) and Robert Douglass, Jr. (1809-1887). Douglass and her husband believed firmly in the value of religion and education. Consequently, they hired private tutors for their children. Douglass, too, had been educated at home. As a result of their excellent home training and education, Sarah and her brother, Robert, became prominent Philadelphia citizens.

Douglass's son, Robert, was a portrait painter who received an education at the Academy of Fine Arts, the National Gallery of Fine Arts, and the British Museum. Having the opportunity to make portraits of many illustrious individuals, Robert had a distinguished career and some of his works are extant. Sarah Mapps Douglass followed in her mother's footsteps and became a Quaker. She was also a member of the Philadelphia Female Anti-Slavery Society, which her mother helped to establish. Sarah Mapps Douglass was an ardent educator for over sixty years and was considered an expert on physiology and hygiene. In the 1830s she opened a school for black children, and she joined the staff of

the Institute for Colored Youth in 1853. Retiring from the institute in 1873, she had spent her lifetime training at least two generations of black women and men in Philadelphia.

Grace Douglass was also a trailblazer for African American women during her time. In 1838 she and her daughter were the only two blacks to attend the wedding of white abolitionist Angelina Grimké and Theodore Weld. The presence of the two black women was cited as an "intolerable incident of abolitionist amalgamation," according to Anna Bustill Smith in a *Journal of Negro History* article. Two days later, rioters burned down the newly built headquarters of the state antislavery society and attempted to torch the Shelter for Colored Orphans.

Although Douglass was a Quaker, she was refused regular membership in the Society of Friends. Reportedly, when she attended the funeral services of a Quaker minister, she had to walk with the family's black servants at the rear of the funeral procession.

Although records are scarce, it appears that as early as the 1790s black women had organized societies for mutual relief. In fact, according to Dorothy Sterling, the earliest women's benevolent society predates the earliest men's benevolent society by two years (1793 vs. 1795). Members' dues were used to pay health benefits and to aid widows and fatherless children. By 1821, Douglass was active in one of these societies and, according to Dorothy Sterling's book, *We Are Your Sisters,* one of Douglass's handwritten notes confirms that "the Committee gave [Mrs. Jones] 50 cts worth of groceries" after she had been "confined for 10 days."

Antislavery Activities

Douglass was a founding member of the racially integrated Philadelphia Female Anti-Slavery Society. Eighteen women signed the organization's constitution in December 1833, and Douglass was one of at least seven free black women to become a charter member of the group. Among the other blacks were Charlotte, Margaretta, and Sarah Louisa Forten, and Sarah McCrummell, wife of the prosperous barber and dentist James McCrummell. From 1833 until it ceased operation in 1870, the society waged a battle against slavery and racial and gender discrimination. The society was active in various ways. It raised money to build an antislavery hall, distributed antislavery literature, and instigated petition campaigns against slavery in Washington, D.C. The women supported the then radical ideas of granting women the right to vote, to become leaders in the American Anti-Slavery Society, and to speak in public. Another priority of the society was the improvement of education, perhaps due in large part to Sarah Mapps Douglass's efforts before and after she joined the education committee. Sarah Mapps Douglass had founded a school in 1836, and two years later the society supported it financially. By 1840 the society monitored educational facilities for black children throughout the Philadelphia area. After the ratification of the Thirteenth Amendment to the U.S. Constitution, in 1865, which abolished slavery, and the Fifteenth Amendment in 1870, which gave all black male U.S. citizens the right to vote, the members dissolved the organization, believing that their goal of ending slavery had been attained.

Grace Douglass's abolitionist activities extended into other organizational memberships. She was a member of the Anti-Slavery Convention of American Women, whose members represented antislavery societies in the free states. The convention met annually from 1837 to 1839, and Douglass was elected a vice president of the conventions held in New York in 1837 and 1839. Perhaps one out of each ten members was black. When the Second African Presbyterian Church held its third annual meeting in Philadelphia in August 1839, Grace Douglass was a delegate, along with her husband, Robert, and sister Mary Bustill. Church members saw moral equality between the sexes and welcomed women into the organization. The women delegates included those who were active in the community and in antislavery societies as well. Grace Bustill Douglass's place in African American history rests firmly on her work as an abolitionist and with abolitionist organizations.

REFERENCES:

Hine, Darlene Clark, ed. *Black Women in America.* Brooklyn: Carlson Publishing, 1993.

James, Edward T. ed. *Notable American Women, 1607-1950.* Vol. 1. Cambridge: Belknap Press, 1971.

Philadelphia Female Anti-Slavery Society. *Thirty-sixth and Final Report.* Philadelphia: Merrihew and Son, Printers, 1870.

Smith, Anna Bustill. "The Bustill Family." *The Journal of Negro History* 10 (October 1925): 638-44.

Sterling, Dorothy, ed. *We Are Your Sisters.* New York: Norton, 1984.

Yee, Shirley J. *Black Women Abolitionists: A Study in Activism, 1828-1860.* Knoxville: University of Tennessee Press, 1992.

Yvette Alex-Assensoh

Hazel Nell Dukes

(1932-)

Civil rights activist

A relentless advocate for the civil and human rights of African Americans, indeed all Americans, Hazel Nell Dukes has been on the front lines of many battles for more than thirty years of her life. Her career as a political and social activist has been one steeped in controversy and marred by recrimination, as well as one that is replete with unheralded victories. Her life has been guided by the motto: "If I can help

Hazel Nell Dukes

somebody as I pass along, then my living will not be in vain." Often described as a modern-day Sojourner Truth, she has already earned her place in history.

Hazel Nell Dukes was born on March 17, 1932, in Montgomery, Alabama, the birthplace of the civil rights movement of the 1960s. She was the only child of Edward and Alice Dukes. Edward Dukes was a porter on the Southwind Railroad. He was a member of A. Philip Randolph's Brotherhood of Sleeping Car Porters' Union. Her paternal grandfather was a Baptist minister. Dukes had an extremely close relationship with her parents. The death of her mother in April 1990 was a heart wrenching experience. She said in an interview that watching her mother battle myeloma cancer—a devastating illness—was one of the most difficult experiences of her life. "All of my life, my mother was an energetic person . . . [and it] was devastating for me. I had not seen my mother, ever in my life, [not] up in the morning time cleaning." The experience was one that increased her concern for the plight of individuals who take care of their aging parents. She often helps people undergoing similar experiences find adequate health care and health-care facilities for their aging parents.

Although an only child, Dukes developed sibling-like relationships with an aunt, uncle, and first cousin who were close to her age. She still maintains very close family ties. While pursuing a career and taking a lead in civil rights activities, Dukes raised a son, Ronald, with the support of her extended family. Her sense of family and compassion for children has led her to become the surrogate mother for the sons of a close friend who passed away. The boys, Andrew and David, are both enrolled in private schools. Dukes takes great pride in her "surrogate sons."

Dukes was profoundly affected by her childhood experiences in Montgomery, and her understanding of the impact of racism upon the condition of African Americans needs little explanation. Her unrelenting fight against racial injustice can be traced to her own familiarity with the American system of apartheid, and the people who nurtured and guided her as a child and youth. In Montgomery, her family lived across the street from Rosa Parks—the "mother" of the modern civil rights movement. Dukes fondly remembered Parks in a *New York Newsday* article: "She would take me to Sunday school and tell me to be polite and courteous, to study hard so I would be somebody one day. She was a great inspiration to me. . . . In my wildest dreams I never had thought that she would be the person to spark such a movement."

Dukes attributes her tenacious spirit to her father, whom she says was a "fighter." Her family gave her the motivation to pursue her goals. She credits many of her teachers for their belief in her potential. One teacher, Ms. Dacus, encouraged her to enter an oratory competition sponsored by the Elks in Montgomery. She won first place. Dukes appreciates another teacher, Ms. Fitts, who inspired her to achieve in the sciences and told her that if she could do well in her science class, she would be able to do most anything.

Dukes migrated to the New York City area in 1955 with her parents. Before permanently relocating, she and her parents had often visited relatives in New York City and the New England area. Following a family tradition, Dukes decided to become a teacher, and she began her college education in 1949 at Alabama State Teachers College (now known as Alabama State University). However, she was not really interested in entering the teaching profession. After moving to the New York City area, she began taking business administration courses at Nassau Community College and working at Macy's Department Store on Thirty-fourth Street in Manhattan. Later she transferred to the store on Long Island. In 1978 Dukes finally completed her education at Adelphi University, Garden City, New York, from which she received a bachelor of arts degree. She was awarded an honorary doctorate from the City University of New York Law School at Queens College in 1990.

In 1966 Dukes became the first African American to work in the Nassau County Attorney's Office. She worked as an administrative assistant for the office's sixty attorneys. She moved on to the Nassau County Economic Opportunity Commission (EOC), an agency that was created by the Great Society Program of the 1960s. Her position there was community organizer. She worked with four communities in Nassau County and was responsible for starting day-care centers, working with parents, children, and school districts, and mediating housing problems. She also worked in the Office of Manpower Development.

In another capacity at the EOC, as transportation supervisor, Dukes encouraged women in the community to go back to school through programs made possible by state grants. She also developed programs that addressed the employment problems of people on public assistance created by inadequate and inaccessible transportation.

Dukes and the people of Roslyn, New York, started a program called the College Fellowship for Disadvantaged Adults, which offered the people in Roslyn opportunities to upgrade their employment skills. Fifty-five students went through the program. Thirteen of the participants went on to achieve bachelor's degrees, and four acquired their master's degrees.

She was also appointed by the Nassau County Attorney's Office to the Nassau County Consumer Commission. In that capacity she worked to help low-income people exercise wiser consumer behavior. Her activities brought her into the media spotlight. The press developed an interest in her for her outspoken articulation of community needs. During Nelson Rockefeller's administration as governor, Dukes was appointed to the Governor's Health Advisory Council for the State of New York. Later, she was appointed to the Board of the State of New York Mortgage Agency by Governor Mario Cuomo. As a member of that board, Dukes has taken on a great responsibility to ensure that minorities participate in every aspect of the real estate industry in New York.

In June of 1990, Dukes was appointed president of the New York City Off Track Betting Corporation (NYCOTB) by then mayor of New York, David Dinkins. She knows the business well. Before the appointment, she had worked at the NYCOTB for twenty-five years. In the mid-1970s she filed a discrimination suit against the corporation on the grounds of pay inequity. She won the case and later organized a NYCOTB employees branch of the NAACP. Her position at the NYCOTB is a notable achievement, because she is an African American woman who is the chief executive officer of a multi-billion dollar gaming corporation, an area traditionally dominated and controlled by white males.

Expands Role as Activist

While pursuing her career in the various social service agencies, Dukes devoted much of her time and energies to the fulfillment of her primary social commitment—the advancement of civil rights. Membership in the NAACP has been a tradition in her family; Dukes, for her part, has remained committed to this organization and its work. She has protested in over one hundred marches and been arrested six times for protesting. For Dukes, the NAACP and its programs are effective vehicles that have inspired people to move forward to become all that they can be.

She became the president of the Great Neck, Manhasset, Port Washington, Roslyn chapter of the NAACP. She went on to become the regional president and president of the New York state conference. From 1989 to 1992 she served as the national president of the organization.

Throughout the years, Dukes has been stalwart in her commitment to the organization. During the roughest of times, when critics accused the organization of being stagnant and ineffective, Dukes responded in *New York Newsday*:

We don't call press conferences after every accomplishment or fruitful meeting, and we don't mail out press releases like some of our state legislators. That is not our job.... We are here, we are visible and we have clout.... No other black organization in the country has a Washington lobbying group that compiles every piece of legislation that affects black folks for all our branches and whoever else wants in.

Along with her social and civil rights activism, Dukes became politically active in the Democratic party. She started her involvement in the party as a Nassau County committeewoman. She became the first African American vice-chair of the Nassau County Democratic Committee. She served as a delegate to the Democratic National Convention in 1972, 1976, and 1992. She served on the Democratic National Committee from 1976 to 1982. She worked with Lyndon Johnson's administration to promote such programs as Head Start. She considers Head Start to be one of the most successful programs that she and the NAACP supported because it opened up opportunities for low-income children and parents. She has been a tireless advocate for education. She believes education gives people the personal skills to deal with problems creatively.

Dukes was an ardent supporter of the Jimmy Carter administration and was very active in his 1980 presidential campaign. Carter's loss was personally devastating for Dukes. She said in an interview, "Jimmy Carter was a good president. He was sensitive.... He had changed the face of government." President Carter appointed her to the National Economic Opportunity Council during his term in office. She dealt with the agony of the defeat of the Democratic party in the presidential elections of 1984 and 1988. As a loyal Democrat, Dukes backed Walter Mondale, whom she regards as a "good friend," in his 1984 bid for the presidency and served as a Clinton delegate in 1992.

Dukes's service to her community, state, and the nation have not gone unappreciated. She has received numerous honors and awards for her efforts and contributions. She received the Social Action Award from Delta Sigma Theta Sorority; the Sojourner Truth Award from the National Association of Negro Business and Professional Women's Clubs; the New York City OIC Community Service Award; and she received recognition at the Salute to African American Women sponsored by *Dollar and Sense* magazine. Dukes was awarded the Outstanding Contribution to Social Justice from the New York Human Rights Commission; the B'nai B'rith Award for Promoting Justice and Interracial Harmony; the Candace Award for community service from the National Coalition of 100 Black Women; and the Guy R. Brewer Humanitarian Award from the New York State Black and Puerto Rican Legislative Caucus. She is a member of the Metro-LINKS and the National Council of Negro Women. She is also a prolific speaker and lecturer.

She sits on the boards of a number of organizations, including the National Coalition of 100 Black Women, the State of New York Martin Luther King, Jr. Commission, and the Board of Trustees of the State University of New York and Stillman College.

Dukes Called Controversial

Dukes's outspoken nature, directness, and steadfast commitment to her beliefs have on many occasions left her vulnerable to attacks from the media and critics. Dukes has displayed true character and courage. Because of her unselfish and devoted commitment to principles of justice, fairness, and equality, she has been willing to express her opinions and take positions on issues that many would deem unpopular or inexpedient.

Dukes led the New York State Conference of the NAACP through some of the most difficult times during the Reagan presidency. She often challenged the Reagan White House's lack of regard for the plight of the poor in American society. She said in *New York Newsday,* "Racism is at its height since Ronald Reagan, a second-class actor, took office." She faults the Reagan-Bush years for the loss of civil rights gains won over the decades. According to *New York Newsday,* during those years she observed: "People now have carte blanche to speak out against blacks, affirmative action and everything we've worked so hard to obtain through the years."

As NAACP spokesperson and Democratic National Committeewoman, she led a major assault on Reagan's nomination of Robert Bork to the Supreme Court. She effectively used her political savvy to challenge the nomination by placing pressure on Senator Patrick Moynihan to vote against Bork or face defeat in his bid for reelection. She was quoted in the *Wall Street Journal* as stating, "I have the votes in New York to defeat him. When I get together with his staff in New York, I'll get what I want. It's strictly politics."

The Howard Beach incident also placed her in opposition to many in the black community who advocated the boycott of jobs, schools, and white-owned businesses in the Howard Beach district of New York City. She virtually stood alone as she denounced the idea. She, however, continued to express her support of New York Police Commissioner Benjamin Ward during the crisis, when other black leaders mounted pressures for him to resign.

Dukes's tenure as the national president of the NAACP was also steeped in controversy. Shortly after her election to office in 1990, Dukes made several statements about the impact of immigrants on the employment prospects of African Americans. According to the *New York Times,* she said: "Why let foreigners, newcomers, have these jobs while blacks, who have been here for hundreds of years, can't support themselves or their families?" The remarks were reported to have stimulated outrage from the Hispanic community in New York, and she was accused of increasing tensions between the black and Hispanic community leaders in New York.

When asked about the statements in the interview, Dukes responded that her statements were taken out of context. She said that her comments were directed towards the African

American community. From her perspective, the loss of jobs by African Americans to newer immigrants is much the fault of African Americans because of the unwillingness of many in the community to take the type of jobs that newcomers have been willing to take. Therefore, problems of unemployment and unproductivity in the African American community continue to worsen. Thus her views reflect the value that she places on the traditional "work ethic." She strongly believes that individuals should, regardless of the type of work, strive to live a productive life—which in turn "will make you feel like a human being."

Dukes's tenure as national president of the NAACP lasted until 1992. The change in leadership at the national level was portrayed in the media as one of the worst cases of institutional infighting that the organization had undergone within recent history. During the process, Dukes vigorously opposed the proposed change in the rule of tenure for board chairpersons. The organizational infighting led to her defeat and loss of the position of national president.

Despite the loss, Dukes's indomitable spirit prevailed. She said in the *New York Amsterdam News,* "I did not come out a loser because I am still president of the New York State Conference of the NAACP." She also did not lose because, although no longer the national president, she maintained her board membership, and most importantly, the support of her constituents in New York never wavered. Her constituency viewed her loss of the national presidency as an attempt to appease the conservative critics of the organization by removing the leading "progressives" from its leadership.

A Guiding Force

Dukes has the heart and soul of a true leader. She has been willing to take risks, and her positions on issues have always been based upon careful assessment of the facts and sound reasoning. To her supporters she is a maverick and a champion fighting for justice. To her critics she is abrasive and arrogant. She views the many controversies associated with her civil rights activities as part of the territory of leadership—"leaders are always attacked."

Dukes is a woman of great confidence; her sense of direction is guided by a core of values that she has been able to preserve amidst all of the controversies that she has encountered. Dukes finds her peace and contacts her spirituality through the daily reading of the Bible. When she needs to, she says she will close her office door and read the Scriptures. She is actively involved in her church, the Assembly of Prayer Baptist Church in Roslyn. She is a political power broker who has used her power responsibly—to help others in need. She has established a national network of friends and associates in the political area and successfully earned a place among the leaders of New York City's blacks and those of the nation, yet she has not lost her ability to relate to the average man and woman on the street. In New York City she is often recognized in public by city residents and looked to as a source of hope. According to *New York Newsday,* one young man reportedly said to her in Times Square, "Yo, Mrs. Dukes,

keep on fighting for our rights. It's tough out here. We need you."

Dukes is greatly concerned about the future of African American children and youth. She believes that if children behave poorly it is a reflection of adults. She knows from her own background that children need adults who are loving and caring, whether they are a part of the extended family or not. One of the concerns that she spoke about in her interview was the fact that in urban areas the notion of the extended family is nearly nonexistent. She contends that there is no concept of community in urban areas like New York. "What you really have are big tall buildings with people strewn all over the place, like warehouses." Housing projects, she maintains, are bound to fail because they produce an inhumane environment.

Reflecting upon the disappointments of the civil rights movement, she bemoans the loss of two generations of African American children to drugs and AIDS. To her the loss of every African American child threatens the future. This failure, she believes, is the responsibility of all adults and leaders in the community. In her interview, she wondered, "Have we turned our backs on our children? Have we forsaken them? Have we spent too much time away from them?" Recognizing the impact of these plagues on the community, she spends much of her time with younger children in the schools and with numerous youth programs sponsored by many organizations.

Unlike many leaders, Dukes is acutely aware of the importance of passing on her knowledge, experience, and information to the next generation. She often wonders who will take her place. "I'm not going to live forever and I wonder where will the next Hazel Dukes really come from." Remembering the many role models in her family and among her teachers, Dukes has actively sought to give something back to young people by serving as mentor and role model. Several of her protégés have gone on to pursue medical and legal careers, and one has begun a tenure of service in the NAACP.

Dukes's love for people and her humanitarian nature have been a source of inspiration to others. Always looking forward, in 1992 Dukes wrote an article entitled, "Crises and Opportunities for the Unfinished Civil Rights Agenda," published in the June 18, 1992, *New York Amsterdam News,* in which she lucidly outlined her vision of the work that the civil rights community must continue to undertake.

We must:

1. Develop and instill in our young people a sense of self-worth and a commitment to self-reliance. We cannot expect help from the outside.

2. The three primary institutions in society—the home, the school, and the church must organize our young people and others to confront the problems in society and develop programs and activities to aid our community. We must recapture the spirit of excellence and achievement.

3. We must return education to center focus. Nothing provides as sure a road out of poverty and

ignorance as good as education. Education prepares young people for the opportunities we are working to create.

4. We must develop linkages between our organizations and our schools and churches so that we can accomplish our objectives.

5. Finally, we must keep hope alive. As Dr. Benjamin Mays has said and as many of us know, "Life's great tragedy is not in failing to meet all of our goals and objectives. Life's failure is in having no goals and objectives to achieve."

REFERENCES:

"At the Helm in Stormy Times." *New York Newsday,* January 29, 1987.

Biographical Statement of Hazel Nell Dukes. Executive offices, New York City Off-Track Betting Corporation, New York.

"Criticisms Aimed at Statements on Immigrants." *New York Times,* October 5, 1990.

Dukes, Hazel. "Crises and Opportunities for the Unfinished Civil Rights Agenda." *New York Amsterdam News,* June 18, 1992.

————. Interview with Walton L. Brown. May 26, 1993.

"Editorial." *Wall Street Journal,* July 14, 1987.

"Internal Dispute Will Not Hamper NAACP Agenda." *Washington Post,* February 20, 1992.

"NAACP Hails Yonkers Accord." *New York Amsterdam News,* September 17, 1988.

"New York State NAACP President Dukes Supports New York City Police Commissioner Ward, but Not Boycott of White Businesses." *New York Amsterdam News,* January 17, 1987.

"Turmoil in the NAACP." *New York Amsterdam News,* March 28, 1992.

"Will Democrats Self-Destruct on Bork?" *Washington Post,* July 11, 1987.

"Women Salute Hazel Dukes as Role Model." *New York Amsterdam News,* March 28, 1992.

Walton L. Brown

Mollie Ernestine Dunlap

(1898-1977)

Librarian, bibliographer, editor

Mollie Ernestine Dunlap spent most of her career as a librarian at Wilberforce University and Central State College, which coexist on the same campus in Wilberforce, Ohio. There she built up the archives and black collection of the present Hallie Q. Brown Memorial Library. She was also assistant editor of the *Negro College Quarterly* and a contributing editor to the *Journal of Human Relations.* She published in 1935 a pioneering study of collections of African American materials and coedited a 1947 compendium of black institutions of higher learning. Beginning in 1950, she and her staff also launched a useful reference tool when they undertook to publish indexes of black publications.

Mollie Ernestine Dunlap was born in Paducah, Kentucky, September 2, 1898. She was the daughter of Robert H. Dunlap and Emma M. Donavan Dunlap. Young Mollie obtained her elementary and secondary education in Paducah, Kentucky, and did her post-secondary education at Wilberforce University and Ohio State University, from which she received an A.B. degree in 1928. She received an A.B. in library science in 1931 and an M.A. in library science in 1932, both from the University of Michigan.

Dunlap was an instructor at Wilberforce University from 1918 until 1923. She then was librarian at Winston-Salem Teachers College in North Carolina from 1925 to 1934. During her stint in North Carolina she received her two degrees in library service. While a student in the Michigan program she held a fellowship from the Rosenwald Foundation. Dunlap returned to Wilberforce University in 1934 as librarian. Her article "Special Collections of Negro Literature in the United States," published in the *Journal of Negro Education* in 1935, was indicative of her involvement in research on the subject early in her career.

Dunlap Becomes Editor

Dunlap was a member of the founding editorial staff of the *Negro College Quarterly,* serving as assistant editor from 1944 to 1947. The *Negro College Quarterly* was published at Wilberforce University beginning in 1944. Vishnu V. Oak, professor of economics and sociology at Wilberforce, was the founding editor. Through the journal the university aimed to contribute to educational development at the black college and to provide contributors an avenue of expression for their views in that field. The *Quarterly* offered such features as articles on education, special bibliographies, annotated lists of books by and about blacks, and book reviews, and it also listed important curricular changes and significant educational events. The editors brought to the public scholarly material on the higher education of African Americans by established authorities as well as by promising but yet unknown writers. The editorial and advisory board included such luminaries as Gilbert Haven Jones, Ambrose Caliver, Walter R. Chivers, Edward A. Jones, Virginia Lacy Jones, Lorenzo Greene, Joseph H. Reason, and Mabel M. Smythe.

In 1946, Dunlap and Anne O'H. Williamson, professor of education at Wilberforce, undertook a notable study of institutions of higher learning for African Americans in the United States. The study was an endeavor to compile pivotal information about existing colleges for blacks as of 1946—such a survey had not been attempted since the 1920s. The data was obtained through a questionnaire sent to all predominantly black colleges and universities listed in the *Educational Directory, 1945-46,* which was issued by the United States

Office of Education. Historical vignettes and notable relationships of the school to the college community were taken from catalogs, bulletins, or other material furnished by the institutions. The appendix to the compendium carried tables that could serve as a basis for comparative studies of the institutions. This study, "Institutions of Higher Learning among Negroes in the United States of America: A Compendium," was published in a special issue of the *Negro College Quarterly* in June 1947.

Dunlap was a professionally committed librarian who held memberships in various organizations. She became a member of the American Library Association in 1931, the Ohio Library Association in 1935, the Ohio Association for Adult Education, and the American Teachers Association in 1946. She was a founding member of the Wilberforce branch of the American Association of University Women.

Black Index Launched at Central State University

In 1947, the state of Ohio attempted to seize control of the Board of Trustees of Wilberforce University. The effort failed, a schism was created, and with the creation of Central State College (now University), two colleges existed on the campus. Dunlap was torn between her loyalty as an alumna of Wilberforce and her loyalty to the newly created state-supported division, which subsidized the Carnegie Library where she had worked as a librarian since her return to the campus.

Dunlap elected to throw her lot in with the state and became director of the library to be built later and named in honor of Hallie Q. Brown. However, she remained on affable terms with those who remained with the AME Church-supported university—she was eminently fair in partitioning the library holdings to insure that all resources belonging to Wilberforce remained there.

Dunlap continued with her writing and produced for the Wilberforce branch of the American Association of University Women *Despite Discrimination: Some Aspects of Negro Life in the United States* in 1949.

In 1950 Dunlap and her staff inaugurated an *Index to Selected Negro Publications Received in the Hallie Q. Brown Library.* This was a precedent-breaking undertaking. It was a pioneering attempt to provide a bibliographical tool to periodical resources featuring matter by and about African Americans. Some earlier attempts had been made to collect this data, notably the indexes of A. P. Marshall in North Carolina. Dunlap relied on the professional skills of her library staff as they joined in the effort to systematically index the vast amount of materials. Later, the staff of the New York Public Library's Schomburg Collection joined in the effort. Today this index is an indispensable reference tool in the area of black studies.

The *Negro College Quarterly* did not survive the split between Wilberforce University and Central State College. However, Dunlap's interest in a scholarly journal persisted, and she was one of the founding members of *Journal of Human Relations,* published by Central State. She was re-

sponsible for "Selected Readings" in the journal beginning in 1952.

Black Archives and Collection Organized

Dunlap remained at Central State until her retirement in 1966. She created and organized the archives and black collection in the Hallie Q. Brown Memorial Library at Central State University after her retirement, working with archival and other special material on blacks that she had collected and organized on a part-time basis over the years. Dunlap devoted two years, from 1966 until 1968, to chairing the Department of Library Education at Central State, then assumed the position of university archivist in 1968.

In 1976 she was the recipient of the Distinguished Alumnus Award of the University of Michigan. On April 2, Russell E. Bidlack, then dean of the School of Library Science, read the citation on the occasion of her recognition, which included the following:

> Mollie Dunlap worked with talent in the place that came to her. Sought by others, she resolved to stay, creating, enlarging, teaching hosts of students of the treasures of her world. She would fit equally the tribute made by one Librarian of Congress for another long ago, for she Toiled long, well, and with small Means effecting Much.

Mollie Dunlap retired to the Lutheran Retirement Center in Ann Arbor, Michigan, where she died July 7, 1977. She was cremated and her remains were returned to Wilberforce for burial at nearby Massie's Creek Cemetery.

REFERENCES:

American Association of University Women. Wilberforce (Ohio) Branch. *Despite Discrimination: Some Aspects of Negro Life in the United States.* Yellow Springs, Ohio: Antioch Press, 1949.

A Directory of Negro Graduates of Accredited Library Schools, 1900-1936. Columbia Civic Library Association. Washington, D.C., 1937.

Dunlap, Mollie E. "Special Collections of Negro Literature in the United States." *Journal of Negro Education* 4 (October 1935): 482-89.

Dunlap, Mollie E. and Anna O'H. Williamson, eds. "Institutions of Higher Learning among Negroes in the United States: A Compendium." *Negro College Quarterly* 2 (June 1947).

Index to Selected Negro Publications Received in the Hallie Q. Brown Library. Ann Arbor, Mich.: Edwards Brothers, 1950.

News Release. University of Michigan School of Library Science, March 11, 1976. Ann Arbor, Michigan.

Phinazee, Annette L., ed. *The Black Librarian in the Southeast: Reminiscences, Activities, Challenges.* Durham, N.C.: North Carolina Central University School of Library Service, 1980.

Who's Who in Colored America. 7th ed. Yonkers-on-the-Hudson, N.Y.: Christian Burckel, 1950.

Who's Who in Library Service. Brooklyn: H. W. Wilson, 1955.

Wilson Library Bulletin 51 (June 1976): 778.

Casper L. Jordan

Georgia R. Dwelle

Georgia R. Dwelle
(c. 1884-1977)
Physician, temperance worker, writer

A pioneer in the area of black women's health, Georgia R. Dwelle became possibly the first black woman physician to practice in Atlanta. She founded the first successful private hospital for blacks in Atlanta and the first obstetrics hospital for black women in the city. She became active in community organizations and had a special interest in temperance work. To share her medical wisdom with others, she wrote occasionally for the local press.

Georgia R. Dwelle was born in Albany, Georgia, on February 27, 1883 or 1884, and died in Augusta, Georgia, on July 28, 1977. The only daughter of George Henry Dwelle, a minister, and Eliza Dickerson Dwelle, she had four brothers—George B., John, Thomas, and Edwin L. George H. Dwelle was born a slave on January 26, 1833, in Columbia County, Georgia. He was the son of C. J. Cook, a white man, and Mary Thomas, who was black. George Dwelle was sold twice, first in Columbus when he was a small boy and later in Alabama. He was relocated to Augusta, Georgia, and later bought his freedom as well as that of his mother.

George Dwelle joined Springfield Baptist Church in Augusta on November 5, 1855, and remained active in the Baptist Church throughout life. He married Emily J. Johnson on February 28, 1855, and after her death he married Eliza Dickerson on September 1, 1870. He was well-known in southwestern Georgia for his interest in uplifting the black race and his work as a great church builder and a Sunday school teacher. In 1869 he moved to Americus, Georgia, and worked there and in adjacent county towns. Throughout his lifetime he served various churches in Georgia, including several churches in Sumter County and in Albany. A founder of the Missionary Baptist Convention of Georgia, he served the convention as corresponding secretary and a member of the executive board. As well, he was a member of the American Baptist National Convention.

After studying at Walker Baptist Institute, Dwelle entered Spelman Seminary in Atlanta where she graduated with an A.B. degree. She pursued a medical degree at Meharry Medical College, Nashville, Tennessee. To compensate for her inadequate premedical preparation, she enrolled in extra courses at Walden University and received special tutoring after school hours. Dwelle overcame her deficiencies and graduated with honors in 1904 with an M.D. Thus far, her study at Meharry cannot be substantiated; however, Spelman recognizes her as its first graduate to attend medical school. Dwelle had been cited for her "unusual ability and thoroughness" which she demonstrated when she took her examination for the Georgia state medical board. She scored one hundred on nine of the ten subjects and well above ninety in the tenth subject. In the *History of the American Negro and His Institutions,* Arthur B. Caldwell quotes the *Woman's Journal* of Boston which noted her high scores and her success "as an indication of what it is possible for a woman to do."

After completing her examinations, Dwelle entered medical practice in Augusta, Georgia, becoming one of three black women physicians in Georgia at that time. When Dwelle began her career, over ninety other black women had earned medical degrees. Of this number, approximately sixty-five were still living and fifty were practicing in twenty different cities in fourteen states. Meharry Medical College in Nashville and Howard University Medical School in Washington, D.C., were the leading producers of black physicians.

First Black Woman Physician in Atlanta

In 1906 Dwelle moved to Atlanta and continued her practice in obstetrics and pediatrics and in time became a successful practitioner. In his brief mention of Georgia Dwelle published in *Going against the Wind,* Herman "Skip" Mason said that she may have been the first African American woman physician in Atlanta. On arrival in Atlanta, Dwelle toured the slums of the black neighborhoods to gain firsthand knowledge of the health conditions of the residents. Appalled by the squalor in which blacks lived, she was determined to set up a practice in obstetrics and pediatrics where conditions would be sanitary. She rented a room, cleaned it well, and added a few beds. This was the beginning of the Dwelle Infirmary, officially established in 1920 as an obstetrical hospital, which became the first successful private hospital for blacks in Atlanta. It was also the first lying-in hospital for the city's black women.

By the late 1920s Dwelle's address was 94 North Boulevard, which was also the address of her infirmary. She operated the hospital successfully for twenty-seven years without a death. Arthur Caldwell's *History of the American Negro and His Institutions* notes her interest in establishing a drug store. Whether or not the drug store became a part of the infirmary is unclear. The infirmary closed on April 30, 1949, and in 1951 it reopened as Beaumont School of Practical Nursing, offering practical nurse training to blacks with a degree in six months.

Dwelle advocated cooperation and exchange of information and advice between people in different geographical locations on matters of common interest and welfare. Thus, she was active in the local and state medical societies open to blacks at that time. Dwelle was also a member of the National Medical Association and served as vice president in 1923. Later she served the association as secretary of the pediatrics section. She also read widely in professional literature and in newspapers and other journals. To share her wisdom with the public, Dwelle wrote occasionally for the *Taborian Banner* and other local papers.

Though fully active in her profession, Dwelle found time to serve community organizations. She was especially concerned with temperance, becoming an active member of the Women's Christian Temperance Union. She was chairperson of the health committee of the Atlanta branch of the YWCA. Her interests also extended to fraternal organizations and led her to become affiliated with the women's sections of the Masons, Odd Fellows, Knights, and Sir Knights. She was also a member of the National Association of Colored Women. For many years she was state medical examiner for the Sir Knights. As well, she was interested in religious work and was an active member of the Baptist Church.

Dwelle made a return visit to Spelman in 1974 when she was about eighty-nine years old. Quoted by Beverly Guy-Sheftall and Patricia Bell-Scott in *SAGE* magazine, she said "The Negro health problem is the greatest we have; therefore, we need to concentrate on it." Dwelle was honored in an exhibit on black women in health professions when Spelman sponsored the First National Conference on Black Women's Health issues on June 24-26, 1983. Conference proceedings were published in *SAGE* 2 (Fall 1985) and the issue editorial by Beverly Guy-Shefall and Patricia Bell-Scott published Dwelle's photograph as well as a biographical note.

At some point in her life Dwelle married, becoming first Rooks then Johnson. No information on either husband is available thus far. Records of her work continue to list her under her maiden name.

Georgia Dwelle is generally omitted from biographical sources and is perhaps unknown beyond her home state. Her concern was for the health of black women as well as for the dissemination of information on health issues. She deserves fuller recognition and wider study for her pioneer work as a health care practitioner.

REFERENCES:

Brown, Sara W. "Colored Women Physicians." *Southern Workman* 52 (December 1923): 580-93.

Caldwell, Arthur Bunyan. *History of the American Negro and His Institutions.* Georgia Edition. Vols. 1-2. Atlanta: A. B. Caldwell Publishing Co., 1917, 1920.

Carter, Edward Randolph. *Biographical Sketches of Our Pulpit.* N.p., 1888.

Guy-Sheftall, Beverly and Patricia Bell-Scott. "I'm Sick and Tired of Being Sick and Tired." *SAGE* 2 (Fall 1985): 2, 7.

Mason, Herman "Skip," Jr. *Going against the Wind: A Pictorial History of African-Americans in Atlanta.* Atlanta: Longstreet Press, 1992.

Who's Who in Colored America. Vol. 1. New York: Who's Who in Colored America Corporation, 1927.

COLLECTIONS:

The archives of Spelman College, Atlanta, Georgia, contain brief biographical information and records on Georgia Dwelle.

Jessie Carney Smith

Sarah Jane Woodson Early
(1825-1907)
Educator, temperance leader, activist, writer, lecturer

A dedicated teacher who believed in the principle of self-help, Sarah Jane Early touched the lives of over six thousand children in the classroom. She had an equal commitment to Christian values and became an activist in the Women's Christian Temperance Union (WCTU) and participated in the temperance activities of the African Methodist Episcopal (AME) Church. She was also the wife of an AME Church minister, a writer of books, pamphlets, inspirational articles, and speeches, and an activist for racial equality and women's rights.

The fifth daughter and eleventh and last child of Thomas and Jemima Riddle Woodson, Sarah Jane Woodson Early was born on November 15, 1825, near Chillicothe, Ohio. Family historians contend that Thomas Woodson, born a slave in 1790, was the child of the controversial relationship between Sally Hemmings and Thomas Jefferson. He was sent to live with the Woodson family as a child. When Thomas Woodson was a young man, he purchased his own and his family's freedom for nine hundred dollars. In 1820, shortly after obtaining free status, the family moved by wagon train from Greenbriar County, Virginia, to Ohio with another free family, the Leaches. After settling in Chillicothe, the two families joined the Methodist church there but quickly found that they were only welcome if they would conform to the local custom of separate seating for blacks. This arrangement was unacceptable to many blacks; according to the *Woodson Source Book,* quoted in Ellen Lawson and Marlene Merrill's *The Three Sarahs,* they felt that "they contributed their share in supporting the ministers and defraying the contingent expenses of the church" and deserved equal rights. Thus, the Woodsons, along with several other black families, soon formed their own church. This church became important in the foundation and growth of the AME denomination in the Midwest.

In 1829 the Woodsons moved to Jackson County, Ohio, where they formed an all-black farming community with some other families. The Woodsons and their neighbors prospered, and within ten years, Thomas owned four hundred acres, worth several thousand dollars. This environment—blacks raising and harvesting their own food, living in homes that they themselves built, practicing religion in their own church, and supporting each other so that the whole communi-

Sarah Jane Woodson Early

ty thrived—created the belief among its dwellers that separatism and self-help were the road to equality for black people.

For the members of the Jackson County community, religion and church life were essential elements of existence. Sarah's father and two of the male children in the family, Lewis and John P., became licensed ministers in the AME Church during her childhood. The church was a place of worship as well as the center of social life, and the community placed a heavy emphasis on values such as temperance and education. This atmosphere made a deep impression on Early. Her mother, who was a pioneer for black women within the AME Church, was also a great influence. Jemima Woodson and other women demonstrated to Early that women's involvement was essential to the existence and growth of the church and the black community.

Early was educated in schools in the Jackson County community until she was fifteen. In 1850, she left home to attend Albany Manual Labor Academy in Athens, Ohio, which, because it was integrated, the AME Church endorsed as one of the schools blacks should attend. During vacations, she taught in schools in Circleville and Portsmouth, Ohio, to help with college expenses. Early then entered Oberlin College, and her sister Hannah enrolled in the school's preparatory program. At that time Oberlin was well known for its focus on reform through evangelism. Although only 2 to 4 percent of the student body was black, Sarah and Hannah were able to identify with the school's Christian orientation. Hannah left after only two years, but Sarah remained, graduating in 1856. Thus, she was well prepared for her teaching career, which lasted for almost four decades.

Joins Wilberforce Faculty

By 1859, Early had taught in various schools endorsed by the AME Church. That year she was asked to teach at Wilberforce University in Ohio, where her brother was a member of the board of trustees. Though she was not officially given the title of professor, she did teach courses in literature at the school. Black women college faculty members were rare in the mid-nineteenth century. Moreover, when the school reopened under the auspices of the AME denomination after the Civil War, Early was appointed "preceptress" of English and Latin and served as lady principal and matron as well. The woman she replaced was a white Oberlin graduate who had a nervous breakdown when someone who objected to the education of African Americans set fire to some of the school's buildings.

In 1868 Early left Wilberforce to teach in an all-black girls school funded by the Freedman's Bureau in Hillsboro, North Carolina. In September of the same year, she married Jordan Winston Early, a widowed AME minister who had several children. At the time, she was forty-three years old. Their marriage lasted until Jordan Early's death in 1903.

For the first nineteen years of the marriage, Early taught wherever her husband's preaching took them. From 1869 until 1888, when she and her husband retired to Nashville, she taught in various cities and towns all over Tennessee. She was a dedicated teacher whose belief in the principle of self-help was best expressed through her efforts to educate the children of her race. Although she married too late to have her own children, by the time she retired, Early had taught over six thousand children and had been principal of several large black schools in four cities.

Early was very dedicated to her position in life as a preacher's wife. Having grown up around ministers and preachers and their wives, she had many role models. She says of herself in her biography of her husband, *The Life and Labors of Reverend Early,* which was published in 1894, that she immersed herself "fully into the work of the Gospel with him, assisting in all of his most arduous duties, and sharing most cheerfully with him all of his hardships, deprivations, and toils."

Early Begins Temperance Activities

As an extension of her religious commitment, Early became an activist in the Women's Christian Temperance Union (WCTU) in 1884, when she succeeded Frances Ellen Watkins Harper as superintendent of the colored division of the organization. When the prohibition movement began in Tennessee, she served the State Prohibition party as a spokeswoman and canvasser, going from door to door to warn people of the evils of liquor and tobacco. She also became a leader in AME temperance efforts, delivering a number of lectures in churches, colleges, and prisons; she also spoke to at least two national church conventions.

Through her work with the WCTU, Early encouraged black women to work for the benefit of their communities. Temperance was only one part of the religiously inspired holistic movement for moral reform. In 1893, Early gained national acclaim when she was named "Representative Woman of the World" at the Chicago World's Fair and was included by Lawson Scruggs in his celebratory work *Women of Distinction.*

Like many of her contemporaries, according to Ellen Lawson, Early was less concerned "with political rights than with elevating the Black woman to the status of 'lady.'" With the growing stereotype of black women as immoral, black women leaders were increasingly convinced that if the race was ever to gain equality, they must exhibit exemplary demeanor, moral standards, and domestic capabilities. However, consistent with her upbringing, Early believed that the entire race had to concentrate on developing self-reliance and high moral principles. These were the common themes in her speeches and writings throughout her life.

Although Early has been overlooked by most historians of African American contributions to society, her work and ideas were very influential during her time. She attended integrated schools when others were available yet still believed in separatism and self-help as the route to racial equality for blacks. She was convinced that women were essential to achieving racial equality and a strong black community. Sarah Jane Woodson Early died at the age of eighty-two in Nashville, Tennessee, on August 15, 1907, of heart disease. She was buried in Nashville's Greenwood Cemetary.

REFERENCES:

Berry, Lewellyn L. *A Century of Missions of the African Methodist Episcopal Church, 1840-1940.* New York: Gutenberg Print Co., 1942.

Boulware, Marcus H. "The Black Women Agent-Lecturer in the American Temperance Crusade, 1848-1920." Manuscript, Oberlin College Archives, n.d.

Early, Sarah Woodson. *The Life and Labors of Reverend Early.* 1894. Reprint. New York: Books for Libraries Press, 1971.

Lawson, Ellen NicKenzie. "Sarah Woodson Early: 19th Century Black Nationalist 'Sister.'" *UMOJA* 2 (Summer 1981): 15-26.

Lawson, Ellen NicKenzie, and Marlene Merrill. *The Three Sarahs: Documents of Antebellum Black College Women.* Lewiston, N.Y.: Edwin Mellen Press, 1984.

Majors, Monroe A. *Noted Negro Women.* Chicago: Donohue and Henneberry, 1893.

Miller, Floyd J. "Father of Black Nationalism: Another Contender." *Civil War History* 17 (December 1971): 310-19.

Payne, Daniel Alexander. *History of the African Methodist Episcopal Church.* Edited by Charles Spencer Smith. Nashville: Publishing House of the AME Sunday School Union, 1891.

Scruggs, Lawson. *Women of Distinction.* Raleigh, N.C.: L. A. Scruggs, 1893.

"The Woodson Family Tree." Oberlin College Archives, Oberlin, Ohio.

Mia Nwaka Thompson and Adrienne Lash Jones

Joycelyn Elders

Joycelyn Elders
(1933-)
Physician, researcher, educator, state health official, U.S. Surgeon General

J oycelyn Elders was named the first woman and first black director of the Department of Health in Arkansas in 1987, and in 1993 she became the first black and the first woman U.S. Surgeon General. The honor came under President Bill Clinton's administration. Elders is a crusader for health reform and advocates health care for all citizens. Her progressive stand on sex education in schools ultimately led to her being dismissed from the federal position late in 1994.

Joycelyn Jones Elders, the oldest of eight children, was born on August 13, 1933, in Schaal, Arkansas, to indigent sharecroppers Curtis and Haller Jones. During her childhood, Elders worked with her parents and sisters and brothers as field hands in this small farming community, a town so small it did not appear on a map. She toiled in the fields and experienced poverty and deprivation; her family had to live in inadequate housing with no plumbing. In rural Arkansas, she suffered the hostilities, humiliations, and indignities of Southern segregation. She walked miles to school, where the children studied in old, dilapidated school buildings with outdated textbooks discarded by white schools. Blacks were restricted to their own restrooms and drinking fountains. While growing up, she never saw a doctor, nor did she seriously think about becoming one.

Her family was astonished when she decided to go to college. Although she had no role models or encouragement from her family, she nevertheless set out to accomplish her goal. Some who knew her, however, were not surprised by her decision to pursue a college degree. She had a way of influencing people, making them feel that their lives could improve. She encouraged her brothers to attend college and to pursue their career goals. One of her brothers is now a preacher, another a veterinarian, and her sister is a linguist.

They have noted the zealousness to encourage progress and change that Elders possesses.

Upon receiving a scholarship at the age of fifteen, Elders entered Philander Smith College in Little Rock, Arkansas. Her sisters and brothers had to pick extra cotton to raise her bus fare to Little Rock. While there, she became attracted to biology and chemistry and decided to become a laboratory technician. After hearing Edith Irby Jones, the first black to study at the University of Arkansas and the first black woman president of the National Medical Association, speak to a college sorority, Elders became more ambitious. After receiving her B.S. in 1952, she joined the army and became a physical therapist. After serving from 1953 to 1956, she was admitted to the University of Arkansas School of Medicine; she was the only black woman and one of only three students of color in her class.

When Elders returned home for a visit from medical school in 1957, she shocked her family and friends by protesting against the segregated practices of a local drive-in theater. Refusing to park her car in the back row of the theater as was then customary for blacks in the area, she drove to the middle of the lot and remained there. At the time, this action was considered radical behavior. This action was the beginning of her social and professional attacks on the discriminatory traditions and customs prevalent in the South.

After graduating from medical school in 1960, Elders worked as a pediatric intern at the University of Minnesota Hospital from 1960 to 1961, and was a resident in pediatrics at the University of Arkansas Medical Center from 1961 to

1964. Because she had a strong interest in research, she began studies for a master's degree in biochemistry at the University of Arkansas Medical Center in 1967, receiving that degree in 1971. From 1971 to 1972, she held an associate professorship at the University of Arkansas Medical College and in 1976 she became a professor in the department of pediatrics. In 1977, Elders was named national advisor to the U.S. Food and Drug Administration as well as to the National Pituitary Agency. By this time, she had done extensive research in metabolism, growth hormones, and somatomedia in acute leukemia. Her research made her an expert in the treatment of juvenile patients with insulin-dependent diabetes. The state's medical community noticed her pioneering work and juveniles with insulin-dependent diabetes were then routinely referred to her.

Volatile Health Care Issues Addressed in Arkansas

Her 1987 appointment to head the Department of Health in Arkansas by then-governor Bill Clinton marked the first time a woman or an African American had held that post. One of her main goals in this position was to lower the rate of teenage births in Arkansas, which was second highest in the nation. She was also concerned about the high abortion rate, the non-marital birthrate, and the pregnancy rate. She advocated wide-ranging sex education, a position that created a great deal of controversy. She outraged many conservatives when she encouraged the distribution of condoms in schools. Elders feels that health services have not responded adequately to the problems of adolescents, which include venereal disease and unwanted pregnancies. She addressed the Arkansas legislature and the public concerning the need for school-based health clinics, where young people may obtain birth control information and the contraceptives needed to avoid unwanted pregnancies. She also supported easy access to abortion for those who make that choice, yet her major goal is that this option not be necessary.

Her forthrightness in defense of her position and her choice of words often roused fierce opposition. Although pro-choice, she discouraged abortion and was in favor of preventing unwanted pregnancies. She condemned right-to-life proponents for having undue concerns about the fetus and blamed male domination in various areas for the prevailing attitudes toward abortion. In the June 3, 1993, issue of *USA Today* she said: "Abortion foes are part of a celibate, male-dominated church, a male-dominated legislature and a male-dominated medical profession."

Elders' opponents blast her school-based clinics as little more than how-to sex clinics that lead to promiscuity and the breakdown of the family. She sees her stand as limiting children having children, while promoting a brand of public health that protects children and society. Liberals applaud her support of a woman's right to an abortion, while some conservatives feel her views threaten the moral fiber of the country.

Opponents also look upon her as a radical doctor because she advocates the use of marijuana for medicinal purposes. Elders stated in the December 20, 1992, *Nashville Tennessean:*

"If physicians feel marijuana would be beneficial for use by patients . . . it should be available. . . . Marijuana could be useful in treating glaucoma, relieving nausea and improving appetite in patients with cancer or AIDS."

In addition to her other professional concerns Elders also supports health care reform, but believes that health insurance is not the only problem. Elders said in her speech before the Group Health Association of America in March 1993 that geography and transportation are also forces to contend with in solving health problems:

> Equally significant and maybe more harassing are barriers due to geography, the lack of availability of professionals and in case of rural America, the constant threat of closure of hospitals and clinics. Lack of providers is a significant problem. If every graduate from medical school were to go into primary care for the next 100 years, we still would not have enough primary physicians.

Elders recommends addressing the shortage of doctors by training of a mix of health care providers for underserved areas and utilizing certified nurse midwives, nurse practitioners, and physician assistants.

Elders Confirmed Surgeon General

President Bill Clinton nominated Elders for the position of U.S. Surgeon General on July 1, 1993. Her nomination was confirmed by the Senate on September 7, 1993, and she was sworn in September 8, 1993. Elders planned to continue as director of the Arkansas Department of Health and also work as a federal consultant at her new job. This was perfectly legal since presidential nominees may work in an intermittent consultant capacity at the federal agency to which they are assigned for up to 130 days without resigning their jobs. However, opponents of her nomination attacked her for her plan, which would have resulted in her receiving double paychecks, and she resigned from the state agency on July 18, 1993.

Facing hearings in the U.S. Senate for nomination as U.S. Surgeon General, Elders said in the July 28, 1993, issue of *USA Today:*

> The government in the 1990s must be prepared to grapple with some very tough challenges as we focus on health care for all the people—not just the rich and privileged. Our work is not socially valuable and satisfactory until the needs of all the poor and indigent are met. We cannot be content with devising a narrowly satisfactory patch-work solution for this dilemma. We must work for a society in which people of all classes find satisfactory health care delivery a priority.

During her confirmation hearings, flare-ups continued over her advocacy of condom distribution in schools. Elders was accused of a cover-up in Arkansas. Tests on four lots of the condoms purchased by the Arkansas Department of Health found a defective rate more than twelve times higher than the limit set by the Food and Drug Administration. State officials in Arkansas decided to withhold the information about possible defects rather than stress the fact that condoms were unreliable. Elders concurred with her staff's decision, and her political opponents used this incident to try to prevent her confirmation.

Elders's confirmation hearings before the Senate were delayed until September 1993 as her nomination came under fire. Senate opponents raised questions about Elders's finances, and anti-abortion groups attacked her outspoken views on abortion and sex education. Her role on the board of an Arkansas bank, which was accused of mismanagement, was examined. In addition, her husband was accused of not paying social security taxes for a nurse who was employed to attend to his mother, a victim of Alzheimer's disease. Elders, however, was backed by the American Medical Association and C. Everett Koop, the conservative former Surgeon General.

As Surgeon General, Elders spoke just as pointedly as she had before on health care issues, sometimes igniting political controversy. She came under fire in December of 1993 for her comments on drug legalization. In what she later called "personal observations" based on experiences of other countries, she stated she believed the United States should undergo a study to legalize drug use, as legalized drugs might reduce crime. The White House press announced that President Clinton did not share her views and distanced itself from her remarks. Elders also called cigarettes addictive, but rather than ban them, she supported the Food and Drug Administration's efforts toward regulating them as delivery systems for nicotine. According to the *Nashville Tennessean* on March 28, 1994, she stated: "Nicotine is essential, it has a taste . . . that's what smokers are looking for." She continued her strong support of sex education in schools and abortion rights, while privately admitting she opposes abortion.

Elders still aroused controversy with conservatives. For example, she stated in *USA Weekend* that the Boy Scouts should admit homosexuals and the Girl Scouts should admit lesbians. She commented on drugs and guns: "With the money we're spending and so many young people involved with drugs in prison—yet the killing and robbing go on—we cannot afford not to study the issue." She continued, "When we say 'legalize,' I'm really talking about gun control." As U.S. Surgeon General, she has made an assault on guns and believes that violence is a public health issue. The June 19, 1994, issue of *USA Today* reported that a drumbeat of criticism against Elders was mounting. Elders reminded the public that President Clinton never asks her to soften her rhetoric. The article quoted a White House communications director who said that "people understood there would be days when she would make the news."

Fired By President Clinton

After a speech delivered during on World AIDS Day at the United Nations, Elders responded to a psychologist who asked if she would urge masturbation as a means of discouraging school children from trying other forms of sexual activity. According to the *U.S. News & World Report* for December 19, 1994, Elders said: "With regard to masturbation, I think that

is something that is part of human sexuality and a part of something that perhaps should be taught." The next day President Clinton demanded and received Elders's resignation, saying in the December 10, 1994, *Washington Post* that her "public statements reflecting differences with administration policy and my own convictions have made it necessary for her to tender her resignation." Although her position demanded a leader who was outspoken, her blunt talks and controversial stands had gone too far. She stated in the *Washington Post,* "I don't regret what I said."

In addition to her work in state and national health care administration, Elders has been active in a number of professional associations. Her memberships include the Academy of Pediatrics, the American Association for the Advancement of Science, the Arkansas Academy of Pediatrics, the American Diabetes Association, the Lawson Wilkins Endocrine Society, the American Federation of Clinical Research, the Endocrine Society, the American Physical Society, and the Society for Pediatric Research. An author of one hundred and forty-seven papers and monographs, Elders served as president of the Southern Society for Pediatric Research, and as president of Sigma Xi, a scientific society.

Until Elders moved to Washington, D.C., she lived in Little Rock, Arkansas, with her husband Oliver, a coach at a local high school. She was seen frequently at the basketball games. Oliver Elders is now a special assistant to the intergovernmental affairs director of the U.S. Education Department. The Elders have two adult sons, Eric and Kevin. In Washington, Elders was also named adjunct professor of pediatrics at George Washington University Medical Center.

Throughout her tenure as Surgeon General, Elders brought a serious commitment to the health care issues of the day. Her convictions are deep and durable. She is a voice of concern for liberals and an outspoken foil to conservatives of the country. Her radical stance reflects her dedication to a new approach to health issues. The principle upon which her medical philosophy is based—the dignity of the individual—carried her to the top health position in the federal government. Now that she has returned to her teaching position at the University of Arkansas Medical Center, she aims to continue her outspoken stance on health care issues.

Current Address: University of Arkansas Medical Center, Little Rock, AR.

REFERENCES:

"Arkansas Gave Out Defective Condoms." *Nashville Tennessean,* July 22, 1993.

"Battle Lines Form for Surgeon General Hearings." *USA Today,* July 7, 1993.

"Battle Looms Over Choice for Health Post." *Nashville Tennessean,* July 14, 1993.

Black, Edwin. "Elders' View on Health Care." *Podiatry Today,* April 1993.

"Clinton Picks Arkansas Official to Be New U.S. Surgeon General." *New York Times,* December 15, 1992.

"Colleges as Health Care Models." *USA Today,* June 3, 1993.

Contemporary Black Biography. Vol. 6. Detroit: Gale Research, 1994.

Current Biography 44 (March 1994): 5.

"Doctor Elders: We Need Her." *Nashville Tennessean,* July 16, 1993.

"Dr. Elders's Prescription for Battle." *Washington Post,* February 16, 1993.

"Drumbeat Growing Against Elders." *USA Today,* June 29, 1994.

"Elders Is Ideal Choice for Surgeon General." *USA Today,* July 28, 1993.

Elders, Joycelyn. Interview in *To the Contrary.* Public Broadcasting System, n.d.

————. Speech at Group Health Association of America. Washington, D.C., March 1993.

Elders, Joycelyn, and Jennifer Hui. "Making a Difference in Adolescent Health." *Journal of American Medical Association* 269 (March 12, 1993): 1425.

"Joycelyn Elders Joins GW Medical Faculty." *Jet* 85 (April 4, 1994): 6.

"Listening to Elders." *USA Weekend,* June 3-5, 1994.

"Meeting Health Issues Head-on." *USA Today,* July 30, 1993.

Miller, Mark. "A Uncompromising Woman." *Harper's Bazaar* (July 1993): 111.

"Pick for Surgeon General Says She'll Support Medicinal Use of Marijuana." *Nashville Tennessean,* December 20, 1992.

Pone, Tom. "U.S. System More Sick Care than Health Care." *Oncology Times,* May 1993.

Popkin, James. "A Case of too Much Candor." *U.S. News & World Report* 117 (December 19, 1994): 31.

"President Clinton Fires Elders." *Washington Post,* December 10, 1994.

"Regulate, Not Ban, Smokes Elders Says." *Nashville Tennessean,* March 28, 1994.

"A Unique Individual." *Nashville Tennessean,* July 20, 1993.

"Will Clinton Fall Down on Job of Protecting Elders." *USA Today,* July 9, 1993.

Joan C. Elliott

Mercedes Ellington

Mercedes Ellington

(1939-)

Dancer, choreographer, art director, educator

Mercedes Ellington, modern-day dance pioneer, gained international attention in 1963 as the first black member of the June Taylor Dancers, a trend-setting accomplishment in the entertainment industry. She has been a dancer and choreographer in Broadway productions and was featured dancer and choreographer of the hit show *Sophisticated Ladies.* As dancer, choreographer, and teacher, she has contributed significantly to artistry in the entertainment world.

The United States has had few notable three-generation families in the performing arts. The Ellington family is one of them. Mercedes Ellington is the daughter of Mercer Ellington, well-known musician, arranger, and band leader. Mercer Ellington's father was the peerless orchestra leader, pianist, and composer Edward Kennedy Ellington, best known as "Duke" Ellington.

Mercedes Ellington was born in 1939 to Ruth V. Silas Ellington and Mercer Ellington, who were divorced within a year of her birth. Ellington inherited her artistic talents from both sides of her family. She has told how her mother, as a teenager, organized a club of her peers devoted to exhibition ballroom dancing for local social events. After her divorce, Ruth Silas married James A. Batts, a prominent Philadelphia obstetrician and gynecologist; Ruth Batts still resides in Philadelphia. Ellington, the only child of her parents' marriage, has several half-brothers and sisters from their subsequent remarriages.

Ellington was reared by her maternal grandparents, Louise and Alfred Silas, in Harlem on Convent Avenue. Ellington entered nursery school when she was eighteen months old and began dance lessons shortly thereafter to correct a circulatory problem. In no time, she was performing in dancing and singing recitals. Raised as a Catholic, Ellington attended Our Lady of Lourdes grammar school in the Convent

Avenue area. Her grandmother enrolled her in the school's Tuesday ballet class taught by a Polish teacher who also had a Saturday class. Despite Louise Silas's efforts to enroll her granddaughter in that class also, the young girl could not enter due to a supposed long waiting list. Ellington later found out that her grandmother battled the Catholic school authorities because the real reason was racial prejudice. To appease her grandmother, Ellington was given a featured role in the school's Saint Patrick's Day program. Ellington always respected and admired her grandmother for her efforts to shield her from prejudicial mistreatment so that she would never feel inferior due to her race. Ellington was also a ballet student of black twin sisters Marian and Marjorie Facey, who were ballerinas trained by a partner of Pavlova. They operated their own school at Carnegie Hall in a rented studio. Ellington continued dance studies at Saint Walburga's Academy and won a prestigious scholarship to the Metropolitan Opera School of Ballet, now defunct. After graduating, she enrolled at Juilliard and graduated in 1960 with a degree in classical and modern dance.

Ellington Makes Television History

In 1963, the *Jackie Gleason Show* was one of the most watched shows on televison, drawing millions of viewers during it Saturday night broadcast. Although Gleason was the star of the show, a major highlight was the June Taylor Dancers, a precision dance troupe as familiar to Americans as the Radio City Music Hall Rockettes. That year, television history was made when Mercedes Ellington appeared as the first black dancer in the June Taylor Dancers. The NAACP and the Urban League had long waged a campaign to force the entertainment industry to hire qualified blacks. A major strategy employed by these organizations was to send carefully screened entertainers to audition for posted openings. Ellington was sent to Radio City Music Hall to audition for the ballet corps before the Gleason show audition. After her successful audition, she rushed to call her mother with the good news, but Ruth Batts, in Philadelphia, had already been contacted by reporters. The event was even covered by the European and Japanese press. Ironically, the CBS network was the last to know that it had made television history. Ellington was a June Taylor dancer for seven years, a position that was not only a professional boon but a financial one as well, due to long-term residual payments.

The Ellington Dynasty—*Sophisticated Ladies*

With all of her education and training, Ellington has gained a sterling reputation in the field of modern dance as a dancer, choreographer, and teacher. As a dancer and assistant choreographer, she appeared in such Broadway productions as *No, No Nanette; Hellzapoppin'; Oh, Kay; Happy New Year; The Grand Tour;* and *The Night That Made America Famous.* In 1981, Ellington made dance history again as a featured dancer and assistant choreographer in the Broadway hit *Sophisticated Ladies.* Not only was this production based on the music of Duke Ellington, but the musical director was

Mercer Ellington. When the show opened in Washington, D.C., the reviews were unfavorable and critics predicted that it would never reach Broadway.

Ellington fought to get a featured role in the Broadway show, which was the original idea of Manny Fox. When asked for suggestions for a Broadway director, Fox recommended the show's original director, who brought in his own assistant choreographer and asked Ellington to become dance captain, a position Ellington did not at all desire. This job entailed conducting rehearsals for understudies, hiring new dancers, demonstrating dance routines, and memorizing the entire show book. As a production/staff person, the dance captain does not dance. Hired originally as an ensemble dancer, Ellington became Judith Jamison's understudy and when Jamison, as the featured star, exercised her right not to do less preferred dances, Ellington stepped in and performed them. She was also an asset when much-needed revisions were made that resulted in deleting the libretto, the weakest part, and emphasizing the strong points, namely, the music and dances. Many of Ellington's suggestions were implemented, including the precision-kick line ups featured in two numbers, "Caravan" and the first act finale, "Rockin' in Rhythm." These were later videotaped to specify her unique contributions to the show. *Sophisticated Ladies,* predicted to be a flop, was a Broadway hit for nearly two years with a 767-performance run; afterwards, it became a pay-television production.

In the decade since *Sophisticated Ladies,* Ellington has used her array of professional skills to further and broaden her career. From 1983 to 1985, she and Maurice Hines were artistic codirectors of Balletap USA. When Hines left, she changed it to DancEllington, a tap dance company. Because grants needed to support such enterprises are difficult to secure, the company is now being dissolved. These two companies provided a transition for Ellington from performing to working as a choreographer, director, and teacher. Ellington has spent the years from 1990 to 1993 working exclusively as a choreographer, most recently in Birmingham, Alabama, with *Tuxedo Junction;* she also went to Saint Louis in July 1993 to do *Peter Pan.* In addition, she has used her talents and skills in *Blues in the Night* (1984, 1985) and *Juba* (1985, 1986) and was jazz tap teacher at the Alvin Ailey American Dance Center. Ellington's professional affiliations include Actor's Equity Council of the Actors' Equity Association, Capezio Dance Awards, American Guild of Musical Artists, Screen Actors' Guild, and Society of Stage Directors and Choreographers; she has served on local and national boards of the American Federation of Television and Radio Artists.

Ellington is a modern-day dance pioneer who earned every position on her own merits. In reminiscing about her grandfather, the "Duke," she told *People* magazine: "In show business, you find a lot of family members who are financially dependent on someone like him, but I wasn't. So he found it comfortable talking to me; he knew I wasn't thinking what can he do for me or what can I get from him." In another indication of her struggles to be taken seriously on her own merits, she told *Ebony* magazine: "Being related to a famous person has definitely been a hindrance in my case . . .

people take it for granted that you had an easy life and often lean over backwards to make things more difficult for you."

Always the consummate professional, Mercedes Ellington has shown the world that she is an accomplished performer and artist in her own right who, while appreciating her family and her musical heritage, has been able to rely on her own skills, talents, and gifts. Once described as a "lithe, hollow-cheeked sophisticated lady with a pro form," Ellington is also a gracious, warm, and well-spoken person. As further expression of her athletic and artistic nature, she enjoys photography, ice skating, knitting, and sewing. She also likes model trains, working crossword puzzles, and playing chess.

Current Address: 3900 Ford Road, Philadelphia, PA 19131.

REFERENCES:

Corry, John. "How a Washington Flop Became a Broadway Hit." *New York Times,* March 3, 1981.
Ellington, Duke. *Music Is My Mistress.* Garden City, N.Y.: Doubleday and Co., 1973.
Ellington, Mercedes. Interviews with Dolores Nicholson. June 27, 1993, October 25, 1993.
Frankl, Ron. *Duke Ellington.* New York: Chelsea House Publishers, 1988.
Jewell, Derek. *Duke: A Portrait of Duke Ellington.* New York: Norton, 1977.
"Show Business' Newest Ellington." *Ebony* 19 (December 1963): 67-73.
Wansley, Joyce. "That Sophisticated Lady in the Chorus Line is Duke Ellington's Granddaughter, Mercedes." *People* 16 (December 14, 1981): 147-48.
Who's Who among Black Americans, 1992-1993. 8th ed. Detroit: Gale Research Inc., 1992.
Who's Who in Entertainment. 2nd ed. Wilmette, Ill.: Marquis Who's Who, 1992.
Woll, Allen. *Black Musical Theater—From Coontown to Dreamgirls.* Baton Rouge: Louisiana State University Press, 1989.

Dolores Nicholson

Minnie Evans
(1892-1987)
Visionary artist

Commanded by a heavenly voice to "Draw or die!," Minnie Evans began drawing at the age of forty-three to relieve the stress that exhausting nightmares and day visions had caused her since she was a child. On Good Friday, 1935, she labored feverishly for hours with pen and ink on paper to produce cryptic signs and symbols. Those first

Minnie Evans

drawings heralded the career of one of the most prolific visionary artists of the twentieth century, who, according to art historian Mitchell D. Kahan, declared, "My whole life has been dreams."

The descendant of a slave brought to Charleston, South Carolina, from Trinidad, Minnie Evans was born to Ella Jones on December 12, 1892, in a log cabin in Long Creek, Pender County, North Carolina. Within several months, her mother took Evans to Wilmington, North Carolina, to live with her grandmother, a seamstress, and her great grandmother. Evans's formal education ended when she left school after getting promoted to the sixth grade. She then worked as a "sounder," selling oysters and clams door to door, until she and her family moved to Wrightsville Beach, North Carolina, in 1908. That year she married Julius Caesar Evans, whom she described as the "body servant" of one Pembroke Jones (no relation to Minnie Evans). Together, they raised three sons named after millionaires who visited her husband's employers, Mr. and Mrs. Jones, at their homes in Pembroke Park and Airlie Gardens. Evans also worked for the Joneses as a domestic servant beginning in 1918.

After her first, brief artistic burst in 1935, Evans apparently did not resume drawing until 1940. Working in graphite, she produced abstract, vertically arranged compositions in a dot and line technique, then began to use crayons to create mysterious creatures. In one early work, *Portrait with Earrings* (c.1943-47), electric lines dance maniacally around a human head. The work evokes the pressure Evans experienced from the invasion of her consciousness by incomprehensible images. Evans's husband was concerned about her visions and drawings until their pastor explained that they were part of God's plan.

Spiritual Visions Inspire Artist

Evans is best known for her mixed media (crayon, graphite, ink, and/or oil on paper or board) drawings, such as *Airlie Garden* (1968), of symmetrical, abstract, floral motifs and hieratic, frontal figures of royal or divine personages. In her mysterious, orderly world, balanced forms of flowers, birds, cornucopias, angels, and floating pairs of eyes reign. She drew angels, prophets, and royalty amid lush green foliage, wild animals, and celestial bodies. These images derive from Evans's spiritual vision and fanciful visions of the exotic. Together, the subjects form a "harmonious beatific vision" and celebrate "her understanding of the miracle of existence," notes Mitchell D. Kahan in *Heavenly Visions*. Mandala-like with their scalloped foliage borders, Evans's drawings evoke the rhythmic elements of certain Tibetan, Mayan, Haitian, and Indian mystical images, the delightful dreamscapes of Marc Chagall's paintings, and the revelatory world of William Blake's drawings and engravings.

A devout Christian, Evans was occasionally invited to speak to her congregation at the Saint Matthew AME Church in Wrightsville Beach and at the Pilgrim's Rest Baptist Church, which she also attended. Evans learned the Bible "by heart" and developed a personal cosmography with biblical imagery from the books of Ezekiel, Samuel, and Revelation. While she insisted, according to art critic Pamela Wye in *Arts Magazine*, that she did not plan her own compositions—"I am without a teacher, a worldly teacher . . . [but] God has sent me teachers, the angel that stands by me and directs me what to do"—she was particularly moved by Ezekiel's vision of the Chariot of God; circular designs abound in her work.

Many characteristics of Evans's art (for example, its symmetry, flatness, skewed perspective, and visionary images) and life (her devoted faith, brief formal education, low income, advanced age, and isolation from an art community) parallel those of other self-taught, African American artists, such as Sister Gertrude Morgan, Elijah Pierce, William Edmonson, Clementine Hunter, and Mary A. Bell. Like Evans, these artists gleaned their imagery from the Bible, books, magazines, movies, their environment, and their own imagination. But what was the source of Evans's first two drawings of indecipherable cryptic signs? According to Kahan, she claimed that the designs "just came to me" and that "my art is as strange to me as it is to others." Art historian Robert Farris Thompson suggests in *Black Art, Ancestral Legacy* that certain African American artists, like Evans, James Hampton, J. B. Murray, and Z. B. Armstrong, carry on a tradition of God-directed literacy or "spirit writing" evident among the Yoruba people in West Africa.

First Exhibition

In 1962 Evans met Nina Howell Starr, a New York photographer and art critic, at Airlie Gardens, where Evans had sold her works to visitors since 1948. Over the years, Starr taped numerous interviews with Evans and communicated with her by mail. She became Evans's representative and arranged for her first exhibition at a church in New York in 1966. In 1969 Evans was the subject of several articles in periodicals, and she was honored by the Wilmington chapter of Links at a testimonial luncheon. Evans was both inspired and wearied by her successful reception in the art world and the subsequent demand for interviews; she told a *Newsweek* writer,

> I love people, to a certain extent, but sometimes I want to get off in the garden to talk with God. I have the blooms, and when the blooms are gone, I love to watch the green. God dressed the world in green.

Impressed by the large size of the paintings at the Metropolitan Museum of Art, Evans returned home and enlarged early pieces by grouping them into collages and adding border elements in brilliant hues. By the 1970s, however, Evans's colors had grown dramatically more subdued and her images had become stiffer, perhaps because of her increasing age and diminishing health.

In 1975, when Evans was eighty-three years old, she had a solo show at the Whitney Museum of American Art. In the late 1970s she moved with her mother to Wilmington to live with her son and his wife. After her mother's death in 1981, Evans moved into a nursing home. Just months before her death there in 1987, she had a solo show at the North Carolina Museum of Art. Since then, her work has been exhibited frequently in galleries and museums throughout the United States. While pleased with the fame that her works received because they gave glory to God's power, according to Wye, Evans always maintained that she was an agent of God rather than an artist: "I didn't paint them at all. They made me."

REFERENCES:

"Beautiful Dreamer." *Newsweek* 74 (August 4, 1969): 85-86.

Kahan, Mitchell D. *Heavenly Visions: The Art of Minnie Evans*. Raleigh, N.C.: North Carolina Museum of Art, 1986.

Light, Allie, and Irving Saraf. *The Angel That Stands By Me: Minnie Evans' Art*. San Francisco: Light-Saraf Films, 1983. Film.

MacAdam, Barbara A. "God's Green." *Art News* 89 (March 1990): 34.

Meyer, Jon. "Minnie Evans." *Art News* 85 (April 1986): 144.

"Minnie Evans, 95, Folk Painter Noted for Visionary Work." *New York Times*, December 19, 1987.

Starr, Nina Howell. "The Lost World of Minnie Evans." *The Bennington Review* 3 (Summer 1969): 40-58.

———. "Minnie Evans: Something Had My Hand." *Ms.* 2 (May 1974): 71-73.

Thompson, Robert Farris. *Black Art, Ancestral Legacy: The African Impulse in African-American Art*. New York: Harry N. Abrams, 1989.

———. *Flash of the Spirit: African and Afro-American Art and Philosophy*. New York: Vintage House, 1984.

Wilson, Emily Herring. "Green Animals around the Moon: Minnie Jones Evans." In *Hope and Dignity: Older Black Women of the South.* Philadelphia: Temple University Press, 1983.

Wye, Pamela. "Minnie Evans." *Arts Magazine* 65 (March 1991): 74.

COLLECTIONS:

Paintings and drawings by Minnie Evans are in the National Museum of American Art (Smithsonian Institution), the Whitney Museum of American Art, the Ackland Art Museum (University of North Carolina at Chapel Hill), the collection of Nina Howell Starr, the North Carolina Museum of History, and the Weatherspoon Art Gallery (University of North Carolina, Greensboro).

Theresa Leininger-Miller

Myrlie B. Evers-Williams

Myrlie B. Evers-Williams

(1933-)

Organization executive, civil rights activist, writer, civic worker

A tireless civil rights activist for over thirty years, Myrlie Evers-Williams is the second woman chairperson of the NAACP's National Board of Directors. Her strength, courage, and dedication to human rights and equality have been exemplified in her work in advertising, corporate philanthropy, and municipal government and in linking business, government, and social causes. Although she first became widely known as the widow of civil rights worker and NAACP official Medgar Evers, who was murdered in 1963, her work as an activist has now catapulted Evers-Williams into the international limelight.

Myrlie Louise Beasley Evers-Williams was born in her maternal grandmother's house on Magnolia Street in Vicksburg, Mississippi, on March 17, 1933, to James Van Dyke Beasley, a delivery man, and Mildred Washington Beasley, who was then sixteen years old. The couple separated before their daughter's first birthday, and Mildred Beasley decided to leave Vicksburg. She felt that her daughter was too young to travel with her, and Mildred Beasley's mother worked all day in service and had no time to raise the young child. So young Myrlie was left with her paternal grandmother, Annie McCain Beasley, and an aunt, Myrlie Beasley Polk, both teachers, and therefore highly respected in the black community.

Evers-Williams began school at age five in the pre-primer grade at Magnolia High School. She also studied piano once a week with her aunt, Myrlie Polk. As she grew up, the talented Evers-Williams appeared on numerous programs at school, in church, or at a local club where she sang, recited poetry, or played the piano. Evers-Williams graduated from Magnolia High School in May 1950. Unable to attend the local colleges due to segregation, in 1950 she enrolled in historically black Alcorn Agricultural and Mechanical College in Lorman, Mississippi, where she was an honor student intent on majoring in education and minoring in music. She and Medgar Evers met on her first day of school, and they married the next year on Christmas Eve. Although Evers-Williams left school before graduating, Medgar Evers, also an honor student, remained and completed his degree in 1952.

The Everses moved to the historic, all-black town of Mound Bayou, Mississippi, where Medgar became an agent with Magnolia Mutual Life Insurance Company and Myrlie became a typist. Medgar's work required extensive travel in the Delta area, where he witnessed the squalor of the life of poor black sharecroppers and the ills of poverty and social and racial injustice. Late in the summer of 1952 Myrlie Evers-Williams had a miscarriage and the medical expense that resulted drained the couple's meager budget. Her second pregnancy was successful: the Everses' son Darsell Kenyatta was born in January 1953. In early 1954 Medgar Evers became the first black to apply to the University of Mississippi's School of Law. Then pregnant with her second child, Myrlie Evers-Williams did not want her husband to apply for fear of violence toward him and their family. His application was rejected. Their daughter, Reena Denise, was born that year, in September 1954. Another son, James Van Dyke, followed in 1960.

In December 1954 Medgar Evers was accepted for training to become a field secretary of the NAACP. On January 23, 1955, the NAACP's Mississippi State Office was formally opened with Medgar Evers as head and Myrlie Evers-Williams as his secretary. NAACP officials Ruby Hurley and Gloster Current attended the ceremony. Soon the Everses were fully engaged in seeking voting rights, economic stability, fair housing, equal education, and equal justice and dignity. However, their work drew the scorn of segregationists, who saw that the Everses lived under constant death threats.

Medgar Evers Murdered

During the remainder of the 1950s and into the 1960s the civil rights movement in Mississippi and elsewhere in the South was in full swing. The Everses understood that the death threats they received because of their civil rights work were very serious, so much so that the family was forced to take extreme precautions. Medgar and Myrlie had discussed moving the family to a safer place, perhaps finding sanctuary in California, but they remained in Jackson, where in 1957 they bought a house. Their children were taught to fall to the floor if they heard unusual noises outside, and the entire family steered clear of windows in their home at night. Nonetheless, their home was firebombed in the spring of 1963. Using a garden hose, Myrlie Evers-Williams was able to contain the fire.

On June 12, 1963, at 12:30 A.M., Evers-Williams and her children listened to the familiar sound of Medgar Evers's car pulling into the driveway and then they heard the car door close. When a shot rang out, the children followed their teaching and sprawled on the floor. A second shot fired from a closer range came as Evers-Williams opened the door to find Medgar Evers lying face down on the porch and drenched in blood. He died less than an hour later at the University of Mississippi Hospital. The next night Evers-Williams attended a mass meeting at Pearl Street Baptist Church. According to her book, *For Us, the Living,* she stood before the hushed crowd and television cameras and said:

> I am left without my husband and my children without a father, but I am left with the strong determination to try to take up where he left off. And I come to make a plea that all of you here and those who are not here will, by his death, be able to draw some of his strength, some of his courage, and some of his determination to finish this fight.

Two days later Byron de la Beckwith, a white salesman from Greenwood, Mississippi, who was a known white supremacist and a member of the White Citizen's Councils, was arrested under suspicion of murdering Medgar Evers. He was later indicted, transferred to a mental hospital, declared competent to stand trial, tried by an all-white jury, and set free. A second trial was held a short time later, but again, Beckwith was not convicted. The persistent Myrlie Evers-Williams urged a new trial for Beckwith after allegations of jury tampering during his second trial. It was not until the end of a third trial on February 5, 1994, that a racially-mixed jury found seventy-three-year-old Beckwith guilty of murder. He was given a sentence of life in prison.

Continues Education and Career in California

Familiar with the record of blacks in Mississippi being killed, beaten, lynched, and raped, Evers-Williams knew hatred well and its effect on people. In *I Dream a World* by Brian Lanker she states: "The first year after Medgar's death, my fuel for survival was hatred. . . . Every time I walked out the door, I saw his blood—the place where he had been shot down. I had to move from Mississippi so that my children and I could start anew." In July 1964 Evers-Williams and her children moved to Claremont, California, where she entered her children in school and enrolled herself in Pomona College.

In July of 1963, Evers-Williams had given the acceptance speech for the Springarn Medal that was awarded posthumously to Medgar Evers by the NAACP. Afterwards, she received numerous requests for speaking engagements, mostly for branches of the NAACP around the country who wanted to hear about the life and work of Medgar Evers. The NAACP supported her as she attended college by continuing her husband's salary of $6100 annually in return for the public speeches that she gave. She graduated from Pomona—one of the six Claremont colleges—with a B.A. degree in sociology in 1968. Some time later she obtained a certificate from the Simmons College School of Management in Boston. From 1968 to 1970 Evers-Williams was director of planning at the Center for Educational Opportunity at Claremont College. She worked with underprivileged high-school dropouts who wanted to receive their diplomas and enter college.

Then Evers-Williams set her sights on corporate America. From 1973 to 1975 Evers-Williams was vice-president for advertising and publicity at the New York-based advertising firm of Seligman and Lapz. She traveled throughout the United States and established a social responsibility policy for the firm. Her career also took her to one of the top fifteen companies of the Fortune 500, the Atlantic Richfield Company (ARCO). She moved to Los Angeles in 1975 to become national director for community affairs for ARCO, with responsibility for developing and managing all the corporate programs. She oversaw funding for community projects and approved millions of dollars for outreach programs developed in the community, public and private partnership programs, and staff development. She secured money for such organizations as the National Women's Education Fund and worked with a group that provided meals to the poor and homeless in the Watts section of Los Angeles. She developed the concept for the first corporate booklet on women in nontraditional jobs, *Women at ARCO.* Women employees at ARCO served as role models for the various occupations covered. In great demand, the booklet was revised and reprinted numerous times; it is now used in schools throughout the nation. It also stimulated other corporations to publish their versions of ARCO's examples of women in nontraditional jobs. Later Evers-Williams was promoted to director of consumer affairs at ARCO, with responsibility for defining and evaluating the corporate role in program implementation, evaluating consumer impact on company-wide activities, and presenting policy considerations to management.

By 1970 Evers-Williams had developed an interest in politics. When U.S. Congressman Glenerd P. Lipscomb died in February 1970, Evers-Williams ran for his seat in California's Twenty-Fourth Congressional District. Her battle was difficult in the heavily Republican district, where she was the only Democrat among nine candidates. In *For Us, the Living,* Evers-Williams had commented on racism and hypocrisy outside the South when she stated "I wonder sometimes at the people who deplore racism in Mississippi and call it by some other name in Illinois." These issues became relevant again as she encountered racial prejudice in her campaign, receiving hate mail that reminded her of the threats she had known in Mississippi. Despite these difficulties, however, she carried thirty-eight percent of the vote—the most respectable showing for a Democrat in the local race in some time.

Continuing to explore her interest in politics, Evers-Williams entered a twelve-way race for a Los Angeles City Council seat in 1987 and finished third. Soon after the three-month campaign ended, Mayor Tom Bradley appointed her to the Los Angeles Board of Public Works. When confirmed by the Los Angeles City Council on June 12, 1987, she became the first black woman to serve as a commissioner on the board. She held the full-time position until 1995. As commissioner, Evers-Williams managed 6,000 employees, including staff of the Bureau of Sanitation, engineers, and accountants, and handled an operating budget of approximately $400 million. She also oversaw construction contracts let by the city. Evers-Williams and her department successfully struggled with problems that many major and smaller cities face: waste water, recycling, solid waste, landfills, air quality, water quality, and improving the quality of life for all residents.

Heads NAACP National Board

Evers-Williams had been affiliated with the NAACP since she was eighteen years old, first as a member and later as a staff member at the Mississippi State Office. She had long been a member of the National Board of Directors and had also served as a vice-chair. By 1994, her fellow members knew that the time had come for her to seek the chairmanship of the board. The organization had its first woman chair from 1974 to 1984, when Margaret Bush Wilson held the powerful post. Evers-Williams found the task appealing but was concerned that the post would take her away from family responsibilities.

By this time as well, the NAACP was in a state of turmoil. Executive Director Benjamin F. Chavis, already in disfavor with conservative members for embracing the controversial Muslim leader Louis Farrakhan, was dismissed from office on August 20, 1994, on charges of financial mismanagement and sexual harassment. Board chairman William F. Gibson was also charged with misuse of $1.4 million.

As supporters withheld funds in light of these charges, debts were unpaid and staff members were furloughed. The board chairmanship might have seemed unattractive to all but the dedicated, determined risk-taker Evers-Williams.

On February 7, 1995, Evers-Williams became a candidate for the board chairmanship because she felt the organization needed a fresh start. After a short-lived campaign, she won a one-vote victory over the incumbent chairman Gibson at the directors' meeting in New York City. After her victory she refused a telephone call from President Bill Clinton and asked him to talk to the entire board by speakerphone. Her immediate plans were to find a new executive director, eliminate the organization's debt of an estimated $3 million, and restore confidence in the organization.

Four days after her election, Evers-Williams became a widow again, this time at the death of civil rights worker, union activist, and former longshoreman Walter Edward Williams, whom she had married in 1976. Though dying of cancer during Evers-Williams's consideration of the NAACP post, he had called her a freedom fighter and encouraged her to seek the chairmanship. According the article "Tempering Troubled Waters" in the *New York Times,* February 20, 1995, Williams told his wife, "Stop procrastinating and do what you must do."

Dorothy Height, president of the National Council of Negro Women, said of Evers-Williams's election in *Crisis* magazine, "It's a great day for the NAACP and especially a great day for women. I know that she brings to it a real dedication and commitment and leadership ability." In the same article, others found the new national chair "well placed to wear that mantle" and her reputation in civil rights "inspiring and appropriate for modern-day struggles."

Evers-Williams has been active in other arenas beyond politics, corporate America, and civil rights. In 1967 she wrote *For Us, the Living,* which recounts the Everses' experiences in Mississippi's civil rights struggle and honors the work of Medgar Evers. PBS's *American Playhouse* presented a ninety-minute treatment of the book on television in March of 1983. From the 1970s until 1984 Evers-Williams was a contributing editor for *Ladies' Home Journal,* for which, along with other editors of the magazine, she covered the Vietnam Peace Talks in Paris. Her articles were widely recognized.

Still sought out as a public speaker, Evers-Williams lectures widely and appears on many radio and television programs. She is active in numerous organizations and remains involved in grassroots work. She lives in Bend, Oregon, where she and her second husband moved in 1989. She is especially fond of the family's dog Sugar, a black labrador retriever.

Quoted in the *Jet* issue for March 6, 1995, Evers-Williams noted, "I have said that Medgar died for the NAACP. I will live for the NAACP." The direction that she has set for the civil rights organization may well mean that the NAACP will also experience a renewed sense of life and purpose.

Current Address: NAACP, 4805 Mt. Hope Drive, Baltimore, MD 21215.

REFERENCES:

"Biography: Myrlie B. Evers-Williams." Baltimore: NAACP, n.d.

Current Biography 56 (August 1995): 19-22.

Evers, Mrs. Medgar. *For Us, the Living.* Garden City, N.Y.: Doubleday, 1967.

"Evers-Williams Promises Return to NAACP's Roots." *Nashville Tennessean,* February 20, 1995.

Lanker, Brian. *I Dream a World.* New York: Stewart, Tabori and Chang, 1989.

"Leadership Struggle Over; N.A.A.C.P. Looks for Unity." *New York Times,* February 20, 1995.

"Myrlie Evers-Williams Elected the New Chair of National NAACP." *Jet* 87 (March 6, 1995): 4-7.

"Tempering Troubled Waters." *New York Times,* February 20, 1995.

Wakhist, Tsi Tsi. "Taking the Helm of the NAACP: The Ever-Ready Evers-Williams." *Crisis* 102 (May/June 1995): 14-19.

Who's Who of American Women. 19th ed. New Providence, N.J.: Marquis Who's Who, 1995.

Jessie Carney Smith

F

Mae Faggs
(1932-)
Track athlete, educator, administrator

Mae Faggs was the first American woman to participate in three Olympic Games. In spite of her small size—five-feet tall and 118 pounds—she became a legendary sprinter and was the first of many award-winning Tennessee State Tigerbelle track athletes. It was not until a runner of Faggs's skill and competitive drive joined the Tennessee State track team that the university began to seriously support the development of track as a viable sport. Track coach Ed Temple, who called her the "mother of the team," credits her with getting the Tigerbelles started and initiating the development of the track program. She was highly regarded by other athletes for her team spirit and her willingness to help others. Track star and Olympic gold medalist Wilma Rudolph, who also attended Tennessee State, credited Faggs with giving her invaluable assistance during her career.

Aeriwentha Mae Faggs was born on April 10, 1932, in Mays Landing, New Jersey. She was the only girl and the second of five children (two now deceased) born to Hepsi Faggs, a domestic worker and a needle maker in a musical instrument plant, and to William Faggs, a factory worker. Mae Faggs is a graduate of Bayside High School in Bayside, Long Island, and of Tennessee State University. In 1958, she married Eddie Starr, who is an associate superintendent of a school district in Ohio. They have two children: a daughter, Evelyn, and a son, Eddie Starr II (known as Starr).

Faggs began running track when she was in elementary school, and in high school she became a member of the Police Athletic League (PAL). Faggs ran for the PAL from 1947 to 1952. In 1947, Sergeant John Brennan decided to form an Amateur Athletic Union (AAU) team using runners from all over the city, including those from Bayside, Long Island, where Faggs was running. He became her coach, her mentor, and her trusted friend. She was the pride of the PAL, Brennan's "ace in the hole" on any relay team in any track meet. He patiently watched her grow in strength and speed. Finally he told her that he felt she was ready to enter the trials for the 1948 U.S. Olympic team that were to take place in Providence, Rhode Island. Thus began her monumental track career, one in which she competed against such talented runners as Patricia Monsanto, Margaret Davis, Barbara Jones, and Isabel Daniels.

Mae Faggs

Enters First Olympics

Mae Faggs qualified for the 1948 U.S. Olympic team. Although she was the youngest member of the squad, she did not feel threatened by the other athletes at the games, who seemed more experienced, or by the huge number of people in London's Wembley Stadium. She competed in the 200-meter dash and the 400-meter relay, but did not take home a medal. Her failure to win at this first Olympic challenge did not daunt her spirits. She vowed she would return and be successful. In 1949 at the AAU national indoor meet she won the 220-yard dash, setting an American record of 25.8 seconds. From 1949 to 1952, according to Michael Davis in his *Black American Women in Olympic Track and Field,* "she ran anchor on the PAL's winning 440-yard relay team at AAU indoor nationals; she kept her 220-yard title."

In 1952, Faggs set an American indoor record in the 100-yard dash at Buffalo, New York, and was a member of the winning 880-yard relay U.S. National Team at the British Empire Games in London, England. As she had predicted, she returned to the Olympic Games a second time and was a member of the winning 400-meter relay team in the Olympic Games at Helsinki, Finland.

Thus, Faggs entered Tennessee State University in 1952 having participated in two Olympics. She attended Tennessee State University because there she could complete an undergraduate degree in four years and she had a four-year athletic scholarship. She entered college not only with a great deal of experience as a track athlete, but also with confidence and a real competitive spirit. Coach Temple points out that although she may have been the smallest competitor wherever they went, she was one of the most courageous. She would survey the opposing team and inquire who intended to run second and who intended to run third, for she intended to win first place. At the time she entered the university, the track program was in its embryonic stages. However, through her efforts on behalf of the program, the selection of Ed Temple as coach, and an intensive development plan, the world-class Tigerbelle track team was born.

In 1953, Mae Faggs won the 100-yard dash in the National AAU Women's Championships setting an AAU championship record. Not content with this, she also ran the 200-meter dash at the same competition and set a new American record. By 1954, the track program at Tennessee State was growing and Faggs was still winning. In this year, she was a member of the winning 800-meter relay team in the National AAU Women's Championships at Harrisburg, where she also took first place in the 220-yard run.

Faggs's achievements were even greater in 1955 than in previous years. She won the 100-meter dash in the Evening Star Games at Washington, D.C. At the AAU outdoor nationals in Ponca City, Oklahoma, she set records in the 100-meter and 220-yard races and ran on Tennessee State's winning relay team, which set a new U.S. record for the 440-meter relay with their time of 49.1 seconds. Fagg's performance at the Alabama State Relays in Montgomery, Alabama, was phenomenal: she won the 100-yard dash, was a member of the winning 440-yard relay and 660-yard relay teams, and was winner of the 220-yard dash.

Successful Track Career Celebrated

In 1956, Faggs and an all-Tennessee State University team won the 440-yard relay at the National AAU Women's Championships at Philadelphia, Pennsylvania, with Faggs also taking gold medals in the 100-yard dash and the 220-yard dash. She was named AAU All-American for the third year in a row. In the Olympic Games in Melbourne, Australia, in 1956, Faggs and an all-Tennessee State team won the bronze in the 400-meter relay. By the end of her track career at Tennessee State University, she had won twenty-six trophies, three plaques, and one hundred medals. In recognition of her achievements she was inducted into the Helms Hall of Fame and the National Track and Field Hall of Fame at Charleston, West Virginia.

Throughout Faggs's years in track, she demonstrated leadership skills and an ability to encourage and inspire. These talents coupled with her desire to increase the opportunities available to young people, led her to embark on a teaching career that lasted thirty-two years. She retired in 1989. However, she remains active in community affairs and

has also assumed a part-time job at Xavier University in Cincinnati, Ohio, where she works in a program that aids freshman athletes. Additionally, she operates Xavier's College Opportunity Program for high school students. Students in this program receive academic aid and have their progress monitored; those who graduate from high school with a 2.4 grade point average or above and at least eight hundred on the SAT are awarded scholarships to Xavier. Thus, even in her life outside track, Faggs has assumed the nurturing role that her coach, Ed Temple, attributed to her early in her career.

Current Address: 10152 Shady Lane, Cincinnati, OH 45215.

REFERENCES:

Ashe, Arthur R., Jr. *A Hard Road to Glory: A History of the African-American Athlete since 1946.* New York: Warner Books, 1988.

Davis, Marianna W., ed. *Contributions of Black Women to America.* Vol. 1. Columbia, S.C.: Kenday Press, 1982.

Davis, Michael D. *Black American Women in Olympic Track and Field.* Jefferson, N.C.: McFarland, 1992.

Page, James A. *Black Olympian Medalists.* Englewood, Colo.: Libraries Unlimited, 1991.

Starr, Mae Faggs. Interview with Helen R. Houston, June 16, 1993.

Temple, Ed. *Only the Pure in Heart Survive.* Nashville, Tenn.: Broadman Press, 1980.

"Temple's First Star Lauds New Facility." *Nashville Tennessean,* April 8, 1978.

"This Man on the Right Track." *Tennessean Magazine,* May 1979.

COLLECTIONS:

Information on Mae Faggs may be found in the Ed Temple Papers, Brown-Daniel Library, Tennessee State University, Nashville, Tennessee.

Helen R. Houston

Jean Fairfax
(1920-)
Civil rights activist, philanthropist

Jean E. Fairfax has had a long and distinguished career in public service as a civil rights worker, an advocate for the rights and welfare of children and the elderly, and a trustee of a wide range of philanthropic and educational institutions. As director of the Division of Legal Information and Community Service of the NAACP Legal Defense and Education Fund for

Jean Fairfax

twenty years, she worked with citizens and the government to see that the Civil Rights Act of 1964 was implemented as fully and fairly as possible. Her work helped promote school lunches for the poor and desegregated systems of higher learning.

Fairfax was born in Cleveland, Ohio, in 1920, to Dan Robert Fairfax and Inez Wood Fairfax. Her father had graduated from Western Reserve University in 1902 and was an administrator for the Cleveland water department. After graduating from the University of Kansas in 1903, her mother became a teacher and then a social worker for the Juvenile Court of Cayahoga County. Daughter Jean attended the Cleveland public schools.

Jean Fairfax's higher education spanned five decades. She obtained her bachelor's degree with honors from the University of Michigan in 1941 and her master's degree from Union Theological Seminary and Columbia University in 1944. Between 1984 and 1986 she completed additional postgraduate studies at Harvard University, where she was a Radcliffe visiting scholar.

Her career began as dean of women at two institutions: Kentucky State College from 1942 to 1944, and Tuskegee Institute from 1944 to 1946. While at Kentucky State she worked to integrate the YWCA and coordinated interracial services as well. She then worked for nineteen years for the American Friends Service Committee (AFSC) as director of various programs abroad and at home. After World War II, Fairfax directed Quaker relief for war refugees in Austria. In 1949, she returned to the United States, where she directed

college programs for the American Friends Service Committee in New England for six years.

Fairfax moved south in 1957 and worked for eight years as director of the Southern Civil Rights Program for the AFSC during the height of the black struggle for equal rights. She assisted black families who were victims of the white supremacists' drive to maintain the racial status quo. When all public schools in Prince Edward County, Virginia, were closed by state order because county officials refused to comply with court orders to integrate, Fairfax found temporary homes in northern states for black children so they could continue their educations.

Joins in Fight for Civil Rights

In 1965, Fairfax began working for the NAACP Legal Defense and Educational Fund (LDF). There she established and for twenty years directed the Division of Legal Information and Community Service. Congress had just enacted the Civil Rights Act of 1964, establishing new legal rights for blacks in the areas of education, employment, and public accommodations and creating government agencies to enforce school desegregation and equal employment opportunity. Fairfax's division at the NAACP was born of the need to inform black Americans of their newly won rights and to monitor federal agencies in the implementation of their responsibilities to enforce the new law. She and her staff worked with black communities across the South in documenting racial discrimination practiced by companies and school systems, laying the foundation for hundreds of lawsuits filed by LDF lawyers. According to the Southern Education Foundation, "Her work to document states' failure to abide by laws for school lunch programs resulted in a substantial increase in the number of poor children who received free lunch and reduced-price lunches." Fairfax was a key strategist in *Adams v. Richardson*—a landmark case that resulted in mandates to dismantle dual systems of public higher education.

Fairfax left the LDF in 1985 to devote more time to philanthropic endeavors. She had already been active as a philanthropist: in 1967 she was a founding member of the Black Women's Community Development Foundation (BWCDF). The fund had been established shortly after Daniel Patrick Moynihan, then assistant secretary of labor and on leave from Harvard University's Kennedy School of Government, wrote a report entitled "The Negro Family: The Case for National Action," in which he said that blacks were at the bottom of the country's socioeconomic ladder. He stated that black males were forced to leave their families, that families disintegrated under the guidance of women, and that children of matriarchal families would remain welfare-dependent and beset by low aspirations. Fairfax told Joyce White, who wrote about BWCDF in the February 1976 issue of *Essence*, "It was foolish to consider the Black family pathological in light of the fact that it has survived until this day. . . . We decided to build affirmatively on the strength of Black women by helping them to make their untapped resources more available to the entire community."

Creates Fund to Honor Parents

In 1987, Fairfax and her sister Betty pledged $125,000 to the Southern Education Foundation to establish the Dan and Inez Wood Fairfax Memorial Fund. Created in honor of their parents, the fund was set up to broaden educational opportunities for minority students. As soon as the fund was in place, the Fairfax sisters adopted the 1987 eighth-grade class of Mary McLeod Bethune School in Phoenix, Arizona, and assured the students scholarships of $1,000 a year to those who completed high school and enrolled in four-year degree-granting colleges. The net income from the fund after 1995 is to be used to recruit African American students into institutions of higher education and to ensure that they do not drop out of school. The Fairfax sisters will serve as advisors to the project.

Fairfax's special interest is in documenting and expanding the involvement of African Americans in private philanthropic institutions as trustees, program officers, and contributors. In 1991, she became the director of Black Presence in Organized Philanthropy, a research project sponsored by the Association of Black Foundation Executives. Fairfax has served on a wide variety of committees and commissions, including the United States National Commission for UNESCO; the Central Committee and Programme to Combat Racism of the World Council of Churches; the Planning Committee of the White House Conference on Food, Nutrition, and Health; the Committee on School Lunch Participation; the Committee on Health Care for the Disadvantaged of the American Hospital Development Foundation; the National Commission on Secondary Schooling for Hispanics; the Task Force on Chicana Rights of the Mexican American Legal Defense and Educational Funds; and the Commonwealth Fund's Commission on Elderly People Living Alone. She has also served as a board member for organizations such as the Urban Institute, National Public Radio, and Union Theological Seminary.

Fairfax has served as a trustee for the Arizona Community Foundation, the Mott Fund, the Hazen Foundation, the Muskiwinni Foundation, the Children's Foundation, Women and Foundations Corporate Philanthropy, the Public Education Fund, the Fund for Theological Education, and the Southern Education Foundation (SEF). Her commitment to education in the South is keenly felt through her work with SEF, where she played a key role in establishing the foundation's higher education program in 1974 to address critical issues affecting blacks in the South as dual systems of public higher education were dismantled.

Career Achievement Honored

Throughout her career, Fairfax has received awards and honors recognizing her academic and professional accomplishments. As a University of Michigan undergraduate, she was Phi Beta Kappa and Phi Kappa Alpha. In 1983, she was awarded the Life Time Achievement Award by Radcliffe College. In 1984, the Fund for Theological Education, under a grant from the Muskiwinni Foundation, honored her for her lifelong advocacy of human rights and educational opportunities by establishing a scholarship in her name—the Jean

Fairfax-Muskiwinni Fellowship for Black Women in Religion. She received the 1989 Distinguished Grantmaker Award for career achievement in philanthropy from the Council on Foundations. She stimulated the council's Pluralism in Philanthropy project, which was begun in 1989 "to encourage minorities to participate in the establishment of organized philanthropy." In 1991, Tougaloo College awarded her an honorary doctorate of laws, and SEF chose her to be the recipient of the John A. Griffin Award for Advancing Equity in Education. In her acceptance speech for the Griffin Award, Fairfax focused her remarks on diversity and said that educational equity is more than a black and white issue. According to the *SEF News,* she said that America will be a nation of minorities by the twenty-first century, and the new agenda for educational equity must address the old issue of "justice for all" in the context of diversity.

Articulate, precise, and fully dedicated to obtaining equal educational opportunities and civil justice for African Americans, Jean Fairfax, though highly recognized in many circles, deserves wider acclaim for her fifty years of outstanding leadership. Her lifelong support of quality education and civil rights for blacks, and the philanthropic activities she has participated in to effect those reforms, attest to her unswerving commitment to her race. Fairfax now lives in Phoenix, Arizona.

REFERENCES:

"Addressing Diversity is Key in New Equity Agenda." *SEF News* 6 (February 1992): 1, 4-5.

"Jean Fairfax." Biographical statement, Southern Education Foundation, Atlanta, Georgia, 1992.

"Scholarship Created for Women in Religion." *Jet* 66 (August 20, 1984): 29.

Southern Education Foundation. *Annual Report for Fiscal Year April 1, 1991-March 31, 1992.* Atlanta: SEF, 1992.

White, Joyce. "Black Women's Community Development Foundation." *Essence* 6 (February 1976): 44-45.

Phyllis McClure

Lola Falana

(1942-)

Entertainer, singer, dancer, actress

Often referred to as the "Sex Queen" of television, "the only black sex goddess in American history," and "the First Lady of Las Vegas entertainment," Lola Falana said in a March 1978 article she wrote with Jason Winters that she refuses to take the label "sexy" seriously, claiming that as

Lola Falana

soon as it's taken seriously, it becomes "tasteless." Sexy but always discreet, Lola Falana dazzled the world with her many talents as an entertainer and, at the summit of her career, earned in excess of two million dollars for a five-month performance in Las Vegas. In the course of her life, however, she discovered that neither money nor talent could heal emotional wounds or physical ailments—a realization that led her from stardom back to her spiritual roots.

Falana was born Loletha Elaine Falana on September 11, 1942, in Camden, New Jersey. She dreamed of becoming a famous dancer from the time she was three years old. In *Jet,* March 19, 1990, she recalled, "When I was growing up, I wanted to be like everything I saw in the movies, on television and in videos—hot, sassy, sexy." With parents of African Indian and Cuban descent, Falana, who adopted her first name from the popular song "Whatever Lola Wants, Lola Gets," considers herself a mongrel. Her parents—father, Bennett, a Cuban-born ex-marine and shipyard welder with an Italian name, and mother, Cleo, a seamstress—wanted desperately to help their daughter fulfill her dream and so they enrolled her in classes to study the piano and violin and added jazz, Afro-Cuban, modern, and tap to her dance training. Lola was, however, the third of her parents' six children; Bennett and Cleo Falana had another daughter and four sons to support. When Lola was nine, the family move from Camden, New Jersey, to Philadelphia forced her to relinquish her extensive musical training, but she continued her dance lessons. To earn money Falana taught local Philadelphia youth at the Germantown dance studio of her teacher, Mrs. Sidney King. At twelve she instructed neighborhood children in jazz, tap, and ballet. By

the age of fourteen she worked in the summers as a hairdresser in Atlantic City. In junior high school Falana choreographed and produced several school plays.

Major Break Seen in Entertainment World

In 1958, blues singer Dinah Washington appeared in Philadelphia and needed a dancer. Falana, sixteen and still in high school, rushed to see Washington and asked her for the job. Washington permitted her to report for the show that very night, telling her, according to *Ebony,* October 1979, "If you're going to make a fool of yourself, do it in front of everybody." Attired in a homemade costume, a swimsuit with sequins and ruffles, Falana appeared on stage with the bravado of an over-eager teenager. In the middle of her dance routine, her swimsuit strap broke. She might have lost her composure had she not heard Washington's laughter. To Falana the laughter sounded like a dismissal, go-home-to-your-mama laugh. Angered, she put the broken strap in her mouth and danced, executing sixteen jetés and sending the audience into wild applause. Falana got the job.

By the time she was seventeen, Falana, with her mother or dance instructor along as chaperon, was dancing in cabarets for ten dollars a show. Performing as an opening act in Atlantic City, New Jersey, Falana attracted the attention of Sammy Davis, Jr. Recognizing talent when he saw it, Davis invited Falana to come to New York and audition for *Golden Boy.* However, her parents would not permit her to drop out of high school to pursue her career; her father already had second thoughts about her entering the world of entertainment.

To please her parents, Falana graduated from Germantown High School in June 1961. At eighteen she left home in search of her own life, happy to be away from the dictates of her parents. She arrived in New York intent on becoming a star. When she appeared for the audition of *Golden Boy,* two hundred other lovely dancing women competed against her. Sammy Davis, Jr. missed the audition but Falana's dancing landed her the job.

Davis became Falana's mentor, helping her develop as a multitalented entertainer. Rumors surfaced in the media and in entertainment circles that theirs was more than a professional relationship. Years later—in 1976—Falana admitted to *Sepia* reporter Doris Black that she had loved and wanted to marry Sammy Davis, Jr. during this time, but he was then married to Mai Britt. Some people blamed Falana for the breakup of Davis's marriage in 1968, but what Falana knew and the public did not was that Davis wanted a woman to be a wife, not both wife and entertainer.

Unwilling to sacrifice her career for any man or marriage, Falana left the United States for Europe in 1965. She settled in Italy, where she performed her way to stardom. She sang and danced "Having a Heat Wave" and was an instant success. Within a short time Falana was starring in television commercials and was featured on the cover of such Italian magazines as *Black Venus.* She learned to speak and read

Italian; however, despite her linguistic achievement, filmmakers saw fit to dub her voice in her two Italian films, *Pop Goes the Weasel* and *Lola Colt.* She was twice voted Number One Performer of the Year by the Italian public.

Homecoming Brings Challenge

European fame came too easily for Falana. After five years in Europe and a few singing engagements in South America, Falana returned to the United States and to the challenge of making a name for herself at home. In 1966 she appeared in the movie *A Man Called Adam* starring Sammy Davis, Jr. By 1969 she was a guest on the *Merv Griffin Show* and was also acting guest roles in the television series *The F.B.I., The Mod Squad,* and *Streets of San Francisco.* Although Falana eagerly accepted a starring role in the 1970 film *The Liberation of L. B. Jones,* the movie did not produce the desired results for her career. *Variety* wrote that *The Liberation of L. B. Jones* was "not much more than an interracial sex exploitation film." Donald Bogle, a leading authority on African Americans in popular culture, agreed, calling the movie a "trashy melodrama" full of "adultery, rape, murder, and castration."

The social and political struggles of African Americans during the 1950s and 1960s produced an audience of black people who expected and demanded from their entertainers more social consciousness, political awareness, and sensitivity to stereotypes than perhaps had any other audience. Falana seems to have misread the script when she accepted the role of Emma Jones in *The Liberation of L. B. Jones.* After the film drew sharp criticism for its portrayal of the whorish wife, as well as other black stereotypes, Falana received eleven film offers. Wiser and more politically conscious, Falana declined, stating, according to Doris Black in *Sepia,* April 1976, that these film offers requested her to depict "promiscuous women who slept with white men." "The sisters have had it with that," she concluded. The film's failure prompted Falana to leave the country again, this time to perform with Bob Hope on the U.S.O. South East Asia Tour in 1972. But by 1974, Falana accepted a role in another movie that proved disastrous to her career. *The Klansman* received a scathing review from noted film critic Judith Crist, who is quoted in Bogle as saying, "There's not a shred of quality, dignity, relevance or impact in this yahoo-oriented bunk."

Falana evaluated her career in light of the film disasters and concluded that she must be seen as more than Sammy Davis, Jr.'s protégée. Urged by her manager, Norman Brokaw of the William Morris Agency, to accept a role in the Broadway show *Dr. Jazz,* Falana decided to take the risk. The show lasted only four nights but, as Brokaw had promised, the role helped make her a star. Praised by the critics for her performance, Falana received a 1975 Tony nomination for best actress. Finally in the right place at the most opportune time, Falana's sensuality, charm, talent, and beauty began to benefit her. A representative from Fabergé asked Falana to become its Tigress spokesperson. ABC Television approached her with an offer to do her own television special and offers

came in for nightclub engagements in Las Vegas and around the world.

In 1970 Falana married popular singer Feliciano (Butch) Tavares. Both were eager to pursue their careers and had little time to nurture their relationship. As a result, they divorced in 1975. Of her marriage Falana stated in *Jet,* September 25, 1975:

> Marriage is not fabulous for all people, and I can only speak for Lola Falana. Marriage is not fabulous in this profession. My husband is fabulous, but because of his profession, he travels up to 10 months of the year. I travel extensively also, so the most we see of each other is two or three days here and there. I'm too young and too healthy to sit sound and say "it was nice seeing my husband 10 months ago."

Marriage, to Falana, was a sacred commitment but not one in which the wife was dominated by her husband. According to Doris Black in *Sepia,* Falana commented, "I told [Tavares] I'd be his wife. I never agreed to be a housewife. I don't like being in a servant role."

For all the good spirits she exhibited during her friendly divorce—she talked of a divorce party and insisted that career and freedom were more important than marriage—Falana lamented in *Jet,* September 20, 1979, "I want to be a well-rounded woman. I think I can do my job like you do your job. . . . Everybody does his job and he still has time for the home, or the man or the woman or the children." She resents the fact that women far more often than men are successful at the price of being alone.

The drive to become Lola Falana, superstar, prevented Falana from being lonely, although alone. The lucrative Fabergé perfume commercial earned the entertainer over one million dollars and the Clio Advertising Award in 1976. Between December 1976 and March 1977, the four one-hour Lola Falana television specials won wide acclaim.

Becomes First Lady of Las Vegas

Neither television nor the movies were to make Lola Falana a superstar. Instead she found her true niche in classy nightclub performances. When her television specials failed to result in a regular series, Falana, who changed managers often, hired Mark Moreno to handle her career and look for other avenues of success. Moreno booked her into Las Vegas as co-star with Wayne Newton, who worked Vegas more than any other entertainer, performing thirty weeks a year and splitting his time between three hotels. From co-starring with Newton, Falana went on to headline her own show at the Aladdin Hotel and Casino. She worked twenty weeks a year, more than any other entertainer except Newton. By 1979, Falana was a superstar earning three million dollars a year.

On top of the world, Falana learned to relax and enjoy stardom. In a December 1978 article written for *Black Stars* magazine entitled "Each Separate Moment Is Important," Falana said she was at perfect peace with herself: "I have no long range plans in my career. I've set no goals that I have to reach do or die. There's no desperation in me. I am going to be ruled by Lola, the Performer.''

Having achieved her dream of stardom, Falana took stock of her personal life. In March 1978 Falana told Jason Winters of *Black Stars* magazine, ''If I thought my career would interfere with my life with a man now, I would put the man first.'' Being ''sexy'' and single posed problems for Falana, who considered herself spiritual and in search of a serious relationship.

''A man is at his best when he is in a psychological state of erection.'' ''Screw sex.'' ''Sex is easy to take. Love is hard to give.'' Such were the statements of Falana, thoughts she had recorded in her diary since she was a young girl of ten, reported *Jet*, April 26, 1982. In 1982 Falana produced her reflections in the form of a typed manuscript to submit for publication. To date, *Thoughts* has not been published. Nonetheless, Falana's ruminations led to introspection and further development of her spirituality, for she stated in the same *Jet* article, ''I came to be made aware of God because I realized I needed something stronger than myself.''

In December 1987, following the taping of a Motown Christmas special, Falana faced her most difficult challenge. She described to Robert Johnson for *Ebony,* May 1988, the details of her harrowing experience:

> I got out of bed and fell down. Then I got up and I went again and I fell, and I continued to fall. I fell five times between my bed and getting to the bathroom, and that is when I said something is wrong with me.

With a crooked face, twisted mouth, and limbs that refused to cooperate, Falana suddenly faced the possibility of being without those gifts on which she had always counted. The person she contacted first was her manager, Joe Schenk, who urged her to call the doctor.

Falana was diagnosed with multiple sclerosis. Chronic and degenerative, multiple sclerosis is a crippling and incurable disease that often results in partial or complete paralysis. Falana knew the disease was capable of ending her career. Rather than entering a hospital, however, Falana called on friends instead of nurses, God in place of doctors. Her secretary, Carol Webster, and other friends and neighbors rallied to meet her needs. Dick Gregory devised a special diet to sustain her energy level, and Brenda and Lionel Richie arranged for her to recuperate at their home in Los Angeles. Abandoned by all her gifts but one, Falana realized that the one remaining was the brightest jewel of all—the gift of faith. Recalling the trauma of first learning of her illness, she said in the May 1988 issue of *Ebony:* ''I lifted that jewel as high as I could, to the glory of God and I said it is whole, it is pure, it is real. I offer this in exchange for Thy grace that the promise of Jesus Christ will come true through me and make me well.''

Less than a month after being totally dependent on others, unable to control even her speech, Falana embarked upon the challenging task of recovery. Her diet consisted of fresh fruits, vegetables, and water. Her exercise regime included lifting weights three times a week and riding a stationary bike, as well as using a trampoline. Falana's recovery was nothing less than remarkable. But coming back to the Las Vegas strip also proved a struggle. Hotels were reluctant to book her because of the uncertainty of the disease. Once in remission, multiple sclerosis can return without warning.

Characteristic of her vibrant and assertive style, Falana refused to give up. By 1989 she was booked at the Sands where she announced to her audience, ''I'm back!'' When asked if she thought she was cured, Falana replied, according to the March 20, 1989, issue of *Jet,* ''I'm not cured, but I am healed. Cure is what medicine does. Heal is what God does.''

Falana saw her illness not only as a test of her faith but as a blessing enabling her to move beyond sex symbol to spiritual sign. Hardly surprising, then, was Falana's 1990 announcement from the pulpit of Chicago's Christ Universal Temple of her celibacy and preparation to become a nun. Giving up her career, following a successful return to the Las Vegas nightclubs, was her way of saying good-bye to the world of entertainment. Her departure from the bright lights recalls the words sung by her late friend and sponsor Sammy Davis, Jr.: she did it her way. Falana said in *Black Stars,* ''When the world gets lost in evil and violence, I will just eliminate my presence from it.'' She has practiced her own philosophy, then, by entering a Catholic convent.

Falana's gift of song and dance and her energy as an entertainer ensure her place among the stars of this century, but her undying faith and spirituality will seal forever her place in the hearts of her fellow Americans.

REFERENCES:

Armstrong, Lois. ''Whatever Lola Falana Wants, Lola's Getting: She's Tigress of Her Own Spots and Specials.'' *People Weekly* 48 (March 29, 1976): 62-63.

Black, Doris. ''Lola: Rising TV Star Rides Her Flops to Stardom to Make Lola Falana a Top Name in Show World.'' *Sepia* 25 (April 1976): 48-57.

Bogle, Donald. *Blacks in American Films and Television.* New York: Simon and Schuster, 1988.

———. ''Celebs Pay Tribute to Lola Falana at Recent Filmmakers Hall Gala.'' *Jet* 24 (March 20, 1989): 24, 28.

———. *Toms, Coons, Mulattoes, Mammies, and Bucks.* New York: Continuum, 1990.

''Dancers Go Dramatic.'' *Ebony* 24 (September 1969): 38-40.

Falana, Lola. ''Each Separate Moment Is Important.'' *Black Stars* 7 (December 1978): 54-56.

Johnson, Robert E. ''Lola Falana's Problems of Being Sexy and Single.'' *Jet* 62 (April 26, 1982): 58-60, 62.

———. ''Lola Falana: On Tour with Sexy Show and Witty Thought.'' *Jet* 64 (July 18, 1983): 58-61.

———. ''Lola Falana's Valiant Fight against Multiple Sclerosis.'' *Ebony* 43 (May 1988): 170-76.

———. ''Lola Falana: Sexy Star Tells Why She Is Giving Up Show Biz to Become a Nun.'' *Jet* 77 (March 19, 1990): 56-58.

Lucas, Bob. "Lola Falana: What Lola Wants Lola Gets." *Black Stars* 2 (December 1972): 60-65.

———. "Lola Falana Talks about Life without a Man." *Jet* 57 (September 20, 1979): 22-25.

Robinson, Louie. "Lola Falana: Shapely Singer and Dancer Is One of the Highest Paid Stars on Famed Las Vegas Strip." *Ebony* 34 (October 1979): 49-54.

Thompson, M. Cordell. "Lola and Butch Want Divorce to Save Their Love." *Jet* 49 (September 25, 1975): 28-29.

———. "Lola Falana: Whatever She Wants She Gets and Deserves." *Black Stars* 5 (July 1976): 40-44.

Turner, Renee D. "Lola's Back!" *Ebony* 45 (January 1990): 82-86.

Winters, Jason, and Lola Falana. "I Want to Be the Best I Can Be." *Black Stars* 7 (March 1978): 32-37.

Nagueyalti Warren

Sarah Harris Fayerweather

Sarah Harris Fayerweather

(1812-1878)

School integrationist

In the course of history, acts by significant individuals are sometimes overshadowed by the magnitude of the events in which they took part. This is true of Sarah Harris Fayerweather. Fayerweather sought to do something that in and of itself was unremarkable: she wanted to go to school so that she could become a teacher for black children. However, the school she desired to attend was an all-white female boarding school. Her admittance to the school caused an uproar not only in the Canterbury, Connecticut, community where the school was located, but throughout the country. The school's teacher, Prudence Crandall, who was responsible for admitting Fayerweather, was arrested. Three trials ensued, with the final result that Crandall's arrest was ruled unlawful on the basis of a technicality. Four years later, the so-called Black Law that had been used to arrest Crandall was declared unconstitutional, clearing the way for the opening of schools for blacks in Connecticut.

Sarah Ann Major Harris Fayerweather was born in Norwich, Connecticut, on April 16, 1812. She was the daughter of William Monteflora Harris and Sally Prentice Harris. Sarah was the second eldest of twelve children, including brothers Charles, William Monteflora, Oliver, John, and William Lloyd Garrison and sisters Celinda, Mary, Olive, Jane, Abby, and Maria.

Fayerweather's family was of African and Indian ancestry. They were industrious, honest people who were willing to work. It was only natural that Sarah and her eleven sisters and brothers received encouragement from their mother and father to advance themselves in any way possible. One of the sources quoted in Carl R. Woodward's "A Profile in Dedica-

tion: Sarah Harris and the Fayerweather Family," published in *New England Galaxy,* Summer 1973, describes her father as "a fine-featured man possessed of a remarkably intelligent face." He came to the United States from the French West Indies to obtain a good education but never realized his goal. Thus, he was determined that his children would be educated.

United States census reports list the family as free persons of color engaging in farming as the source of their livelihood. Records are unclear about when the Harris family moved from Norwich to Canterbury, Connecticut. William Harris's name appears on census lists for Norwich from 1810 to 1830 and also on tax lists in Canterbury as early as 1821. It is also known that in January 1832 William Harris purchased a farm about a mile west of the village of Canterbury. The family was identified with the Congregational church at Westminster, three miles west of Canterbury, where their racial background seemed to offer no barrier to their attendance at services with the predominantly white congregation.

A Simple Decision Makes History

Woodward describes Sarah Harris Fayerweather as an attractive, ambitious girl. She worked for a time as a servant in the house of Jedediah Shepherd. She lived at home with her parents and led a simple, uncomplicated life. According to Hallie Q. Brown in *Homespun Heroines,* the events in Fayerweather's life were the consequences of her racial background:

All the circumstances of heredity and environment, save only one, combined to make Sarah's life honorable, responsible, care-free and independent. She enjoyed all the advantages of the freedom and steadiness of an existence in a rural community. She had come from stock possessing elements of character essential to progress and contentment. . . . Had she been an American by birth and descent . . . her story would have been too commonplace to merit record or comment. But she was in part of African extraction.

In 1832 Fayerweather was twenty years old. She wanted to attend Canterbury Female Boarding School, an all-white selective school for young ladies that had opened in the town the previous year. Prudence Crandall, a Quaker originally from Hopkinton, Rhode Island, had been recruited to become the teacher of the newly established school. She had previously had a brief career as a teacher in Plainfield, Connecticut. The Canterbury Female Boarding School opened in November 1831 and it quickly gained an excellent reputation. Soon young white ladies from distant towns applied to the school and were admitted as boarders.

Canterbury, a small village in Windham County, Connecticut, was relatively prosperous, with many small factories and stores. The town manufactured such items as woolen and cotton goods, hats, axes, and carriages, and it was able to support a social library (a free community library, similar to modern free public libraries) at the then enormous sum of eight hundred dollars. The Canterbury Female Boarding School was another step forward for the townspeople.

School Integration Causes Stir

After hearing about the Canterbury Female Boarding School, Fayerweather began to dream of attending. She saw it as an opportunity to continue her education and to later teach the children of her race. According to the May 25, 1833, issue of *The Liberator,* she visited Prudence Crandall in September 1832 and stated,

> I want to get a little more learning, enough if possible to teach colored children, and if you will admit me to your school, I shall forever be under the greatest obligation to you. If you think it will be the means of injuring you, I will not insist on the favor.

After some deliberation, Prudence Crandall permitted Fayerweather to begin attending the boarding school in January 1833.

Fayerweather's acceptance at the Canterbury Female Boarding School divided the citizens of Connecticut and caused heated debates across the United States. The word spread quickly throughout Canterbury that a black girl was attending school with their white daughters. According to Truman Nelson in *Documents of Upheaval,* citizens of the town protested strongly and demanded that Crandall remove Fayerweather from the school. The townspeople feared that if blacks were allowed to attend school with whites, they would eventually demand equality in other areas as well.

The white parents withdrew their daughters, hoping to change Crandall's mind about keeping Sarah in the school.

However, this only strengthened Crandall's resolve to keep the school afloat and to fight racial prejudice against blacks. In a letter to William Lloyd Garrison's newspaper, *The Liberator,* dated May 25, 1833, Crandall wrote:

> I said in mine heart here are my convictions. What shall I do? Shall I be inactive and permit prejudice, the mother of abominations to remain undisturbed? Or shall I venture to enlist into the rank of those who with the Sword of Truth dare hold combat with prevailing iniquity. I contemplated for a while, the manner in which I might best serve the people of color. As wealth was not mine, I saw no other means of benefitting them, than by imparting to those of my own sex that were anxious to learn, all the instructions I might be able to give, however small the amount.

Prudence Crandall formulated the idea of having a school exclusively for "young ladies and little misses of color." She enlisted the help of Garrison, a famous abolitionist, who agreed to advertise the school in *The Liberator.* Others leaders such as Samuel Joseph May and George E. Benson of Connecticut supported the plan.

The advertisement went out as planned in the April 13, 1833, edition of *The Liberator.* It read:

> Prudence Crandall,
> Principal of the Canterbury, (Conn.) Female Boarding School
>
> Returns her most sincere thanks to those who have patronized her School, and would give information that on the first Monday of April next, her school will be opened for the reception of young ladies and little misses of color. The branches taught are as follows: Reading, Writing, Arithmetic, English Grammar, Geography, History, Natural and Moral Philosophy, Chemistry, Astronomy, Drawing and Painting, Music on the Piano, together with the French language.
>
> The terms include board, washing, and tuition, are $25 per quarter, one half paid in advance.

Crandall Ostracized by Community

After this, Prudence Crandall felt the community's wrath. Local merchants refused to sell goods to her, causing her to travel great distances for various supplies, food, and other essentials. According to Edmund Fuller in *Prudence Crandall,* "even the milk-peddler refused her," and her milk and some other essentials "had to be brought from a distance by her father or some of her tiny band of friends." Local physicians joined the protest and declined to provide services. According to Fuller, the discrimination spread:

> All the pupils, like their teacher, were pious Christians, but the church doors were closed to them in Canterbury, though before the crisis the town's few Negroes had worshipped there regularly. . . . every venture out of doors for the school was a form of

skirmish. . . . when pupils and teachers went for exercise walks, stones, sticks, rotten eggs, pellets of manure, dead cats, chicken heads and other repulsive missiles were flung at them, chiefly by boys with the complaisant tolerance of their parents.

Prudence Crandall and her growing number of students prevailed. She now had students from several surrounding New England cities, including Boston, Philadelphia, Providence, and New York. Some of the young ladies who braved the threats and intimidation alongside Fayerweather were Eliza Glasko, Ann Eliza Hammond, Theodosia Degrass, Ann Elizabeth Wilder, and Catherine Ann Weldon.

On May 24, 1833, opponents secured the passage of an act in the Connecticut state legislature making it illegal for anyone to establish a school for "colored" people who were not inhabitants of the state without the consent of the town in which that school was to be located. Under this law, Prudence Crandall was arrested in July 1833, and imprisoned. She was, however, released due to a legal technicality.

Courts Debate Whether Free Blacks Are Citizens

Abolitionist Arthur Tappan provided the money to hire the ablest lawyer available to defend Crandall in the case, which opened in the Windham County Court on August 23, 1833. The case centered on the constitutionality of the new Connecticut law concerning the education of blacks. The defense argued that Fayerweather and others like her were freed persons and, therefore, citizens and could not be deprived of their rights under the U.S. Constitution. The prosecution denied that free blacks were citizens.

The county court jury failed to reach a decision, but in October 1833, a superior court judge ruled that the "Black Law" was constitutional. Yet the case did not end there. In July 1834, a third trial began, in which Crandall's arrest was ruled unlawful on the technical basis that the school had begun operating prior to the passage of the notorious Black Law. The decision, however, did not determine the law to be unconstitutional.

Fayerweather, along with her other classmates, continued to attend what had been the first black female academy in New England. The students withstood an arson attack in January 1834. On September 9, 1834, at midnight, the school was attacked by a mob. Fearing for the students' safety, Prudence Crandall closed the school the next day. Four years later, in August 1838, the infamous Black Law was repealed by the Connecticut General Assembly.

Sarah Harris married George Fayerweather, Jr. on November 28, 1833. She was twenty-one years old and he was thirty-one. George Fayerweather, Jr., like Sarah, was of mixed ancestry. He was one of eight children born to George Fayerweather, Sr. and Nancy Rodman Fayerweather, the daughter of an Indian sachem. Like his father and grandfather, Fayerweather was a blacksmith. In 1841, following the death of his father, Fayerweather moved his growing family to New London, Connecticut, where he purchased a blacksmith shop.

While living there, he was very active in suffrage for blacks and was a member of the Colored Men's Convention.

George and Sarah Fayerweather had eight children: Prudence, their first born, followed by Sarah, Mary, Isabelle, George, Charles, and Oliver. One of their children, whose name is unknown, died before the age of three. The family moved to Kingston, Rhode Island, in 1855.

Although Fayerweather was the catalyst for the events that made the brief history of the Canterbury Female Boarding School famous, little is known about her reactions to these events. Neither the newspaper articles written at the time nor court documents make mention of her ever having been asked about her interpretation of her rights. There is so far no evidence that Fayerweather finished school or continued to teach as she had done earlier. She was devoutly religious and was a member of the Sunday School class in Kingston's Congregational church. While the details of her life at this time are sketchy, it is known that she was an energetic crusader for the civil rights of black people and her home became a center of antislavery activity. For at least twenty-five years she was an avid reader of William Lloyd Garrison's antislavery newspaper, *The Liberator*. She attended antislavery rallies and meetings of the Anti-Slavery Society in New York, Boston, and other major centers and had a close relationship with leading abolitionists, such as the William Lloyd Garrisons and Frederick Douglass. She was held in high esteem by the Kingston community.

In correspondence between Fayerweather and Prudence Crandall Philleo, found years later at the Philleo home, no mention is made of the struggle that these two women went through in 1833. Their letters reflect two friends inquiring about each other's health and families. Their continued correspondence after so many years, however, suggests a close relationship that had been built upon mutual respect and admiration.

George and Sarah Fayerweather were proud of the educations their children received, particularly considering Sarah's unfortunate, but ultimately worthwhile, confrontation with segregation and racism in Canterbury. Their daughter Sarah is said to have been a teacher in Wilmington, Delaware, and their son George an educator in New Orleans.

According to Carl Woodward's "A Profile in Dedication," Fayerweather survived her husband by nine years and died on November 16, 1878, from a "swelling of the neck." Some people speculated that the goiter trouble she had had earlier reoccurred. The local newspaper's long obituary referred to her "long and trying sickness" and stated that she was unable to speak. Before she died she wrote, "I put my trust in God."

Fayerweather was buried in the Old Fernwood Cemetery, Kingston, Rhode Island. The inscription on her headstone is lasting testimony to her estimable qualities: "Her's was a living example of obedience to faith, devotion to her children and a loving, tender interest in all."

In 1902, a widowed granddaughter, Mabel Mitchell Lewis, brought her two young sons, George and Ralph, to

Kingston, Rhode Island, to occupy the Fayerweather homestead. Mabel Lewis married Arthur Perry while there and they lived in the Fayerweather homestead until their deaths.

The house stood vacant until it was restored by the Kingston Improvement Association to serve as a village craft center. In Kingston today, the name of Sarah Harris Fayerweather is memorialized by two buildings—Fayerweather Hall at Brown University and the Fayerweather Craft Guild. Perhaps these sites will remind those who know the significance of her name that Sarah Fayerweather had a part in making it possible for black youths to realize their right to an education during the nineteenth century.

REFERENCES:

Brown, Barbara W. *Black Roots in Southeastern Connecticut, 1650-1900.* Detroit: Gale Research, 1980.

Brown, Hallie Q., ed. *Homespun Heroines and Other Women of Distinction.* Xenia, Ohio: Aldine Publishing Co., 1926.

Connecticut. General Assembly. Public Statute Laws of the State of Connecticut. Chapter IX, Title 53, Inhabitants. Hartford, Conn.: John B. Eldredge, 1835.

Dannett, Sylvia G. L. *Profiles of Negro Womanhood.* Vol. 1. Yonkers, N.Y.: Educational Heritage, 1964.

Fayerweather House in Kingston, Rhode Island (pamphlet). Kingston, R.I.: n.d.

Foner, Philip S., and Josephine F. Pacheco. *Three Who Dared: Prudence Crandall, Margaret Douglass, & Myrtylla Miner-Champions of Antebellum Black Education.* Westport, Conn.: Greenwood Press, 1984.

Fuller, Edmund. *Prudence Crandall: An Incident of Racism in Nineteenth-Century Connecticut.* Middletown, Conn.: Wesleyan University Press, 1971.

"Letter from Miss Prudence Crandall." *The Liberator,* May 25, 1833.

Nelson, Truman, ed. *Documents of Upheaval: Selections from William Lloyd Garrison's "The Liberator," 1831-1865.* New York: Hill and Wang, 1966.

Woodward, Carl R. "A Profile in Dedication: Sarah Harris and the Fayerweather Family." *New England Galaxy* 15 (Summer 1973): 3-14.

Laura D. Turner

Sarah Collins Fernandis
(1863-1951)
Social activist, educator, poet, civic leader

A tireless crusader for social change, Sarah Fernandis was also a teacher, poet, and civic leader. For over forty years, she worked to improve black communities in Baltimore, Washington, D.C., and other cities on the East

Sarah Collins Fernandis

Coast. She lectured and wrote articles about the plight of black workers, especially females.

Sarah Collins Fernandis was born in Port De Posit, Maryland, on March 8, 1863, the daughter of Caleb Alexander Collins and Mary Jane Driver Collins. Rosa Hunter Moore's biographical essay on Fernandis, "A Pioneer Settlement Worker," published in the July 1923 *Southern Workman,* includes the following statement of the goal Fernandis set for herself as a young woman:

> My aim in life is to do well whatever I find to do; to grow broader and deeper in intellect through reading and study; to keep my heart in sympathy with my fellow-creatures and alive to its duties to them; and to make my life a contradiction to the idea that a Negro is low and groveling in sentiment and purpose. I mean to look up and lift up.

She graduated from Hampton Normal and Agricultural Institute in 1882 and attended the New York School of Philanthropy in 1906. On June 30, 1902, Sarah Collins married John A. Fernandis. During a teaching career that spanned nineteen years, Fernandis taught in public schools in Virginia, Tennessee, and Georgia; in Florida she taught under the auspices of the Woman's Home Missionary Society of Boston. After working in Florida, she taught in Baltimore.

Career in Social Work Launched

In 1902 Fernandis accepted the position of resident in the Colored Social Settlement of Washington, D.C., and, with her husband, moved to 118 M Street, S.W. This five-room building, located near the open sewer of the James Creek Canal, became an oasis for the blacks living in the area infamously known as Bloodfield. With the acquisition of a second house in 1903, Fernandis was instrumental in establishing a public library branch on the M Street premises. By 1904, Fernandis had established a day-care center for infants; a kindergarten; an afternoon class in domestic training, such as sewing, for young girls; and a thrift fund for young boys. In 1905, she inaugurated "Baby Day," an excursion down the Potomac River to Somerset Beach for thirteen hundred children and their mothers.

At the time of Fernandis's departure, the settlement had a fund of one thousand dollars to erect a new building. Her tireless efforts to improve the open spaces of the neighborhood resulted in playground facilities for the children and the elimination of blind alleys. She also succeeded in securing housing with modern fixtures and reasonable rents in the neighborhood.

In 1908 Fernandis was asked to establish another settlement house in East Greenwich, Rhode Island. Again the location of the facility was unsavory: an area called Scalloptown, filled with dump piles and squatters. On December 24, 1909, a house bequeathed by a local resident became a lodging for working women. While in East Greenwich, Fernandis wrote an article, "The Negro and Industrialism," in which she called for more employment opportunities for blacks. She also lectured at the School for Social Work operated by Simmons College and Harvard University.

Fernandis was very involved in civic activities throughout her life. In 1913 the Women's Civic League of Baltimore, a white organization, asked Fernandis to found a corresponding group of black women, the Co-operative Civic League. Fernandis organized the first branch of thirty-five members in fall 1913 and became the president of the organization, which eventually grew to include branches located throughout Baltimore. The Women's Civic League and the Co-operative Civic League were instrumental in improving neighborhoods; they ran street cleaning campaigns and helped meet the nutritional needs of children by providing milk for the young.

After World War I, Fernandis conducted a study in Chester, Pennsylvania, on the sharp increase in black residents. She lectured in the northeast from Pennsylvania to Vermont about the plight of the black female worker. By 1922 she was the executive director of the Baltimore Organized Cooperative Civic League and the social investigator for Provident Hospital in Baltimore. In her 1924 article "A More Excellent Way," she reported on an innovative plan to renovate housing available to blacks and to provide reasonable rents. She also denounced the recent attacks on black homeowners in the city.

Fernandis's Poetry Contributions Span Forty-six Years

In addition to essays about social issues, Fernandis wrote poetry. She published two volumes of poetry in 1925, *Poems* and *Vision*. Many of her occasional poems can be found in the

Southern Workman, to which she contributed from 1891 to 1937. The January 1916 issue eulogizing Booker T. Washington includes the poem "The Torch Bearer" by Fernandis. "The Troops at Carrizal" is her tribute to the black soldiers who fought in Mexico. During World War I, she wrote about the courage of black soldiers in "Our Colored Soldiery," and "Our Allegiance" extols black American citizens for being patriotic in spite of the discrimination they faced.

Other poems deal with Fernandis's commitment to social change. In "Denial," published in the *Southern Workman* in 1927, she reflects on her social work:

> Yet ofttimes as I make the daily round
> Of crowded city by-ways, I have found
> Shining up from the mark and slum of things
> Something so beautiful my spirit sings.

She also discusses the plight of the poor, which can be improved by public facilities, in the poem "The Children's Open Door." Her poem "The Cry Supreme" is dedicated to the Red Cross work of the black women of Baltimore who volunteered during the war.

Fernandis received national recognition for her long career of public service. The surgeon general of the United States in March 1922 invited Fernandis, as one of fifteen women, to form a Women's Advisory Council to the United States Public Health Service in Washington.

Sarah Collins Fernandis died on July 11, 1951, at age eighty-eight. She enjoyed a long, fruitful life as a public servant and writer. Her direct contributions to several black communities in the area of social welfare, as well as her advisory role at the state and national levels, make her a role model in contemporary society.

REFERENCES:

Fernandis, Sara Collins. "A Colored Social Settlement." *Southern Workman* 33 (June 1904): 346-50.
———. "Neighborhood Interpretations of the Social Settlement." *Southern Workman* 35 (January 1906): 46-49.
———. "The Negro and Industrialism." Southern Workman 38 (February 1909): 126.
———. "The Children's Open Door." *Southern Workman* 38 (May 1909): 272.
———. "Hampton's Relation to the Constructive Needs of the Negro." *Southern Workman* 39 (April 1910): 202-5.
———. "The Torch Bearer." *Southern Workman* 45 (January 1916): 49.
———. "The Troops at Carrizal." *Southern Workman* 45 (August 1916): 485.
———. "Our Allegiance." *Southern Workman* 46 (June 1917): 348.
———. "The Cry Supreme." *Southern Workman* 47 (September 1918): 426.
———. "Our Colored Soldiery." *Southern Workman* 47 (October 1918): 501.
———. "A More Excellent Way." *Southern Workman* 53 (November 1924): 526-28.

———. *Poems.* Boston: Badger, 1925.

———. *Vision.* Boston: Gorham, 1925.

———. "Denial." *Southern Workman* 57 (March 1927): 106.

Mather, Frank Lincoln. *Who's Who of the Colored Race.* Vol. 1. Chicago: n.p., 1915.

Moore, Rosa Hunter. "A Pioneer Settlement Worker." *Southern Workman* 52 (July 1923): 320-24.

"Personal Notes." *Southern Workman* 30 (September 1901); 35 (November 1905); 39 (February 1910); 41 (January 1912); 43 (September 1914); 45 (April 1916).

Roses, Lorraine Elena. *The Harlem Renaissance and Beyond.* Boston: G.K. Hall, 1990.

Rush, Theressa Gunnels, Carol Fairbanks Myers, and Esther Spring Arata. *Black American Writers Past and Present.* Vol. 1. Metuchen, N.Y.: Scarecrow Press, 1925.

White, Newman Ivey, and Walter Clinton Jackson. *An Anthology of Verse by American Negroes.* Durham, N.C.: Moore, 1924.

Yenser, Thomas, ed. *Who's Who in Colored America.* Brooklyn: Yenser, 1932.

Jacqueline Brice-Finch

Gail Fisher

Gail Fisher

(1935-)

Actress, model

During the late 1960s and early 1970s, Gail Fisher was one of America's most recognized television personalities. At the time, she was one of a handful of African Americans who appeared as a co-star in a popular weekly television series. Fisher played the role of Peggy Fair beginning in the second season of the long-running CBS show *Mannix,* which starred Mike Connors. The show aired from 1967 to 1975. Fisher's path toward such success was paved with high achievements as a model and theater actress.

Gail Fisher was born on August 15, 1935, in Orange, New Jersey, which was then a poor rural area in the vicinity of Potter's Crossing. Her father, a carpenter, died when she was two years old. Fisher's mother, Ona Fisher, was left virtually penniless to raise five children, of whom Gail was the youngest. Gail Fisher graduated from Metuchen High School in Metuchen, New Jersey. She later studied at the American Academy of Dramatic Arts, Lincoln Arts Center, and the Actors Studio. Fisher married John Levy, a talent manager for whom she was at one time employed as a secretary. She has two daughters, Samara and Jole.

Fisher's acting career developed from a variety of early experiences. One was her leading role in her high school's

senior play when she was seventeen years old. Fisher's success in beauty and acting contests as a young woman also directed her toward an acting career. She was the first African American semifinalist in the New Jersey State Fair beauty contest, and later she won the crown at the fair as Miss Essex County. Fisher attributed her success in such contests to Connie Morris Woodruff, a member of the staff of the *New Jersey News Herald* who gave her encouragement and support. According to *Sepia* magazine, October 1964, another source of encouragement was Moss Kendrix, an African American press agent for Coca Cola. Kendrix's support resulted in Fisher taking first prize in a Coca Cola contest that awarded the winner two years' study at the American Academy of Dramatic Arts. Fisher's involvement in these contests gave her the type of exposure that she needed to enter the entertainment world.

Acting Career Takes Off

During the mid- to late 1950s, Fisher continued her quest for an acting career. She became a successful model with the Grace Del Marco organization, getting both high pay and high visibility. She became well known in African American newspapers and magazines nationwide, modeling in advertisements promoting cosmetics and hair care products for African Americans, as well as such goods as cigarettes and beverages. At the same time, she steadily auditioned for roles in off-Broadway and Broadway productions. She was the first African American to receive the Culpepper Fund Scholarship and the first African American to win a Meyner Award. And in 1960 she became the first African American model to speak in a national television commercial (she appeared as a dental patient whose dentist was white). By 1962 Fisher had become the first African American accepted to New York's Lincoln Arts Center repertory theater, where, according to *Sepia,* October 1964, she was ignored rather than trained.

In 1960 Fisher acted for three months in *The Rocks Cried Out,* the first Ford Grant production by the San Francisco Actors' Workshop. She received high praise for her performance. She was also understudy to Ruby Dee in *Purlie Victorious* and appeared on the road in *Raisin in the Sun.* On television, her signature role as Peggy Fair in *Mannix* was accompanied by roles in *Simply Heavenly,* a television play of the week, *The Defenders, The Nurses,* and the NBC soap opera *The Doctors,* in which she played the role of a hospital patient. Her role in *Simply Heavenly* resulted from having earlier trained with Josh Shelley, the production's director, who knew her work well.

Fisher Becomes "Peggy Fair"

In 1967, Fisher took on the dramatic role for which she is best known, the part of Peggy Fair in *Mannix.* By her own account in the *Negro Almanac,* she "read for the part five times and got it. . . . 'Peggy' replaced a bank of computers and a man to make room for me in the show." As Peggy Fair, Fisher was warmly accepted by television audiences. Her role in the series appealed to viewers: she was always there to extricate leading man Mike Connors, appearing as Joe Mannix, private investigator, from threatening circumstances, either by helping him to untangle illogical evidence or by appearing on the scene to help him physically escape danger. One of Fisher's contemporaries, commenting on Fisher's part in the series in the October 1969 issue of *Ebony,* referred to it as "a role which she has elevated from a near-'bit' to the status of co-star in little more than a single season." For her performance in this series Fisher won an Emmy Award in 1970 for outstanding performance by an actress in a supporting role in drama from the Academy of Television Arts and Sciences; she went on to garner four additional Emmy nominations for her continuing co-starring role as Peggy Fair. Fisher's role on *Mannix* ended in 1975, when the show was canceled.

In the October 1969 issue of *Ebony,* Fisher offered her views on acting and the African American presence on television. Referring to television acting as "a difficult medium," she stated:

> You must establish a character and remain within the framework of that character for weeks, months, even years sometimes. This is hard when you must work before the cameras, perhaps only uttering a phrase or two during a whole morning. Most people don't realize what gruelling, hard work acting is. They only see the glamour in it.

Commenting on the gradually increasing visibility of African Americans in respectable roles on television, she further stated,

> What is happening now in TV . . . should have happened ten years ago. . . . People in small towns in the Midwest and elsewhere who have TV sets are just getting to know we're human beings. They no longer fear Negroes. I'm happy for the success of Diahann Carroll in *Julia.* We need a lot of black heroes and heroines.

Fisher's acting career went into decline following her role in *Mannix.* Even at the height of her career, she led a structured and well-rounded life, enjoying everything from dancing, pool, swimming, biking, and cooking, to Yoga, collecting black art, and painting. She retained her sense of what is important in life, and took time to be with her two daughters and cultivate an appreciation of the self. The impact of Gail Fisher's pioneering work in increasing the presence of blacks on television will be felt for a long time to come.

REFERENCES:

"Gail Fisher's Bid for Stardom." *Sepia* 13 (October 1964): 48-51.

"Gail Fisher: The Girl from *Mannix.*" *Ebony* 24 (October 1969): 140-44.

"Hints on Keeping Slim from Famous Personalities." *Ebony* 30 (November 1974): 76-79.

"How to Survive in Hollywood between Gigs." *Ebony* 33 (October 1978): 33-38, 40.

Ploski, Harry A., and Warren Marr II, eds. *The Negro Almanac: A Reference Work on the Afro American.* New York: Bellwether Co., 1976.

"Private Eye's Girl Friday Is Taking Her Success in Stride." *Ebony* 24 (October 1969): 146-47.

"The Way We Were." *Ebony* 31 (November 1975): 155-58.

Laura C. Jarmon

Roberta Flack

(1940-)

Singer

Roberta Flack is a singer and song stylist who exploded into public awareness as a major star in the early 1970s. Several years of preparation laid the basis for her success, beginning with the study of voice at Howard University. After abandoning classical music and teaching in the field of pop, she spent several years polishing her skills and building a local reputation in Washington, D.C., before her national and international career took off. She fused elements of soul, blues, jazz, and mainstream pop into an appealing personal style that led to her enduring success as a musician.

Roberta Flack was born on February 10, 1940, in Black Mountain, North Carolina, a small mountain town near Ashe-

Roberta Flack

ville. Her parents were Laron and Irene Flack, and she was one of four children—three girls and one boy. Her paternal grandfather was a white German immigrant. In a January 1971 *Sepia* article, Flack said her father "was funny looking. He had coarse red hair, freckles and a terrible identity problem. He couldn't stand to talk about his father, couldn't identify, and it killed him." Both parents played the piano. Her father was self-taught, and her mother had a few lessons. Irene Flack played for a Methodist church while they lived in North Carolina. Her daughter remembers sitting on her lap in the church and picking out tunes.

When Roberta Flack was about five, the family moved first to Richmond and then to Arlington, Virginia, a suburb of Washington, D.C. Her father found work as a draftsman for the Veterans Administration, and her mother worked as a cleaning woman and cook at a high school. Her father discovered an old upright piano, so dilapidated that it had been abandoned, and brought it home. It was on this instrument that Flack learned to play by ear before she began taking piano lessons at the age of nine. Her teacher was Alma Blackmon, a member of their church and an excellent musician. When she was thirteen Flack won second prize among black piano students in the state of Virginia in a contest of renditions of James Bland's "Carry Me Back to Old Virginny," which was the state song. As she entered her teens, Flack was a shy and overweight adolescent, weighing over two hundred pounds. Her interests were restricted to church, school, music, and food.

Flack graduated from high school at fifteen and entered Howard University on a scholarship. She began as a piano

major but switched to music education, which meant she had to study voice. Embarrassment at a picture of herself playing the baritone horn in the band—her puffed up cheeks emphasizing her weight—led her to switch her primary emphasis to vocal music. With her practice teaching, she became the first black other than cooks and janitors to work at Alice Deal Junior High School, where apples were thrown at her the first time she came to teach. She graduated from Howard with a B.A. in music education in 1958.

Laron Flack died in 1959 as his daughter was pursuing a master's degree at Howard. To help the family finances, Flack left school and took a job teaching English at a black school in Farmville, North Carolina. The year was hectic. Not only did she teach English, she taught music, directed the school choir, oversaw the cheerleaders, and taught classes for the mentally retarded and the handicapped. One positive effect of the twelve-hour day was that she lost forty pounds. The following year Flack was able to secure a position in the school system in Washington, D.C. Over the next seven years she taught at three different junior high schools.

Decides to Pursue Popular Music

Around 1960 her voice teacher, Frederick "Wilkie" Wilkerson, suggested that she consider changing from the operatic to the popular field. This advice upset her, and it was a while before she pursued the suggestion. As part of this change of direction, she became increasingly involved in the local popular music scene as time went on. One of her first jobs was as a substitute accompanist doing operatic arias at the Tivoli Opera Restaurant in Georgetown, where Alma Blackmon, her first piano teacher, worked. There she sometimes was persuaded to play jazz for the waiters while she was waiting and practicing in the back room. By the spring of 1967 she was singing five nights a week at a club on K Street. In May of that year she auditioned for Henry Yaffe, who gave her a job singing at Sunday brunches at one of his clubs. Flack gave up teaching at the end of that school year, and in August she was singing at Yaffe's newly opened Mr. Henry's in Georgetown. Her popularity was so great that a new room at Yaffe's Capitol Hill club, Mr. Henry's Upstairs, became a showcase for her talent, and she gained an enthusiastic following among show business people who heard her. Among them was jazz pianist Les McCann, who made a demonstration tape of her singing and took it to Atlantic Records, which signed her.

Career Takes Off

Flack's first album, *First Take,* issued late in 1969, sold between 100,000 and 150,000 copies. Her career took off in spectacular fashion with her second album, *Chapter Two,* issued in late 1970. This album sold over a million copies rather quickly. This success was accompanied by appearances on television and in the top nightclubs and at festivals from the Montreux Pop Festival in Switzerland to Newport Jazz Festival. She quickly appeared on the *Today Show,* the *Merv*

Griffin Show, the *David Frost Show,* the *Tonight Show,* and the *Mike Douglas Show.* One show in particular confirmed her star status. This was the *Third Bill Cosby Special* in March 1970, on which she sang two songs as the only guest artist. The year of 1970 ended with a triumphant concert at Philharmonic Hall in December, and *Downbeat* magazine named her Female Vocalist of the Year. Her predecessor, Ella Fitzgerald, had won the title for the previous eighteen years in a row.

Flack's third album, *Quiet Fire* (1971), was also a hit. Her biggest success that year, however, was the single "The First Time Ever I Saw Your Face," which reached number one on the charts. This song had been used on the soundtrack of Clint Eastwood's film *Play Misty for Me,* and its popularity also took her first album, on which it had first been issued, to the top of the charts. A fourth album, *Roberta Flack and Donny Hathaway* (1972), continued her string of successes. The single "Killing Me Softly with His Song" was another major hit the next year; it was number one in February 1973 and held that position for a total of five weeks. This record also demonstrated Flack's move to a more middle-of-the-road pop style.

These recording triumphs were followed by professional recognition. In March 1973 Flack won two Grammy awards, Record of the Year for "The First Time Ever I Saw Your Face" and, with Donny Hathaway, Best Vocal Performance by a Duet, Group, or Chorus for "Where Is the Love?" She was not in attendance to receive the awards since the National Academy of Recording Arts and Sciences had completely overlooked her the previous year even though "You've Got a Friend," a duet featuring Flack and Hathaway, had sold over a million copies. Further recognition came in November 1974 when Flack received an honorary doctorate from Rust College in Holly Springs, Mississippi, at the same time as Marian Anderson.

In the midst of this escalating success, Flack divorced her husband, Stephen Novosel, a white jazz bass player she had married in 1966. Novosel's family and Flack's brother were strongly opposed to this interracial marriage, which ended in 1972. She left the marriage with a fixed determination to avoid trying to have both a career and a marriage—a vow that she has faithfully maintained.

In 1970 Flack moved into a house in Hollins Hill, Virginia, a Washington suburb, where she kept three pianos and numerous cats and dogs. In 1975 Flack moved into the Dakota, a famous apartment building in New York City, much favored by musicians including the opera singer Teresa Stratas. (The building is old and its solid construction reduces sound transmission markedly.) She was the first black in this cooperative. By this time she had begun developing her interest in the supernatural. She told an interviewer for *Jet,* November 29, 1979, "I do not believe in ghosts, but I do believe in extraterrestrial spirits. I feel that it is possible to create a strong amount of spiritual energy so that you could just about see anything." Among those she "saw" are her father and his father, whom she had never met.

In her interview she also discussed the problems of blacks and especially those of black women musicians:

I feel that as black people only a few of us are allowed to make it. And those of us who do make it have had to struggle so hard to do it, we sometimes get very desperate about holding onto this thing.

You don't see many women producers do you? I produced my album but how many are there? We are not encouraged to move beyond that sexy image of being a woman who has these kind of proportions and stands there and sings her heart out. We are not allowed to be thinkers and move beyond that.

Flack herself became a record producer after a falling out with her longtime producer, Joel Darn. She took charge at a late stage in the production of the album, *Feel Like Makin' Love,* which appeared in 1975. Her next album, *Blue Lights in the Basement,* did not appear until 1977. The delay was connected with her decision to be her own producer and also to explore other avenues in her life. For example, she pursued doctoral studies at the University of Massachusetts—Amherst and opened a business. *Blue Lights in the Basement* did well, placing among the top ten selling albums of the year. "The Closer I Get to You" from the album was a number two single. Her career as a singer, however, seemed less assured to some critics who claimed to discern that she was floundering and unsure of her direction.

Duets Renew Success

Two more duets with Donny Hathaway found her again at the top of her form. These were "The Closer I Get to You" (1978) and "You Are My Heaven" (1980). Hathaway, however, was in considerable mental distress at this point in his life and leaped from the fifteenth floor of a New York hotel on January 13, 1979. Flack had been concerned by her inability to reach him and help him through his problems, and his death was a great blow to her. She assigned her royalties from "The Closer I Get to You" to Hathaway's widow and two children.

In the early 1980s Flack enjoyed another fruitful collaboration in duets with Peabo Bryson. They did a number of albums together. Their duet "Tonight I Celebrate My Love" was a top twenty single in 1983. Her activities in this decade also included title tracks for the films *If Ever I See You Again* and *Making Love.* Her later albums, some with Peabo Bryson, include *Love and More* (1980), *Bustin' Loose* (1981), *I'm the One* (1982), *Born to Love* (1983), *Oasis* (1988), and *Set the Night to Music* (1991). The title song of the last album made the top ten.

Roberta Flack also did work in film and television, but most of her appearances in these mediums were as a singer. She performed in *Soul to Soul,* filmed for the fourteenth anniversary of the independence of Ghana in 1971. In 1973 she appeared in *Brothers and Sisters in Concert* (also known as *Save the Children*), a documentary on the 1972 People United to Save Humanity (PUSH) Expo theme. In that year she also sang for and narrated the short animated film *The Legend of John Henry.* She appeared in *Bustin' Loose* in 1981 and sang the title song as well. In the early seventies she was chosen to play Bessie Smith in a film that was never made, and in June 1973 she had a half-hour special, "The First Time Ever," on ABC.

Roberta Flack has had great success as a singer for more than a quarter of a century. Her strengths are amply documented in numerous albums and singles. Her unique style is her greatest asset and also her greatest weakness for some. She does not quite meet the separate demands of the audiences for soul, blues, or jazz. Her appeal lies in the broad range of pop. Still, in the world of popular music, with its everchanging fashions, she maintains a large following because of her generous musical gifts and artistry.

Current Address: Magic Lady Inc., One West 72nd Street, New York, NY 10023.

REFERENCES:

Adderton, Donald. "The Two Sides of Roberta Flack." *Jet* 57 (November 29, 1979): 44-47.

Current Biography. New York: H. W. Wilson, 1973.

De Ramus, Betty. "The Enduring Spirit of Roberta Flack." *Essence* 13 (December 1982): 58-60, 122-24.

"Dynamic Duos." *Ebony* 37 (January 1982): 64-68.

Gammond, Peter. *The Oxford Companion to Popular Music.* New York: Oxford University Press, 1991.

Garland, Phyl. "Roberta Flack: New Musical Messenger." *Ebony* 26 (January 1971): 54-62.

———. "Soul to Soul." *Ebony* 26 (June 1971): 79-89.

Haynes, Howard. "Roberta Flack: Her Secret Ingredient Is Humanity." *Sepia* 23 (July 1974): 73-77.

Higgin, Chester. "Roberta Flack: Exploding New Show Biz Star." *Jet* 39 (December 17, 1970): 58-60.

Hitchcock, H. Wiley, and Stanley Sadie. *The New Grove Dictionary of American Music.* New York: Macmillan, 1986.

Klotman, Phyllis Rauch. *Frame by Frame—A Black Filmography.* Bloomington, Ind.: Indiana University Press, 1979.

Larkin, Colin, ed. *The Guinness Encyclopedia of Popular Music.* Chester, Conn.: New England Press Associates, 1992.

Mapp, Edward. *Directory of Blacks in the Performing Arts.* 2d ed. Metuchen, N.J.: Scarecrow Press, 1990.

Nite, Norm N., with Ralph M. Newman. *Rock On: The Illustrated Encyclopedia of Rock N' Roll.* Vol. 2. New York: Thomas Y. Crowell, 1978.

"Roberta Flack: Her Own Drumbeat." *Sepia* 20 (January 1971): 52-55.

Southern, Eileen. *Biographical Dictionary of Afro-American and African Musicians.* Westport, Conn.: Greenwood Press, 1982.

Stambler, Irwin. *Encyclopedia of Pop, Rock & Soul.* Rev. ed. New York: St. Martin's Press, 1989.

"What Ever Happened to Rubina Flake?" *Time* 105 (May 12, 1975): 62-63.

Who's Who among Black Americans, 1994-95. 8th ed. Detroit: Gale Research, 1994.

Robert L. Johns

Julia A. J. Foote
(1823-1901)
Evangelist, preacher

"She was a great preacher, an uncompromising advocate of holiness . . . who practiced the gospel she preached." These are the words used by AME Zion Bishop Alexander Walters to describe Julia A. J. Foote, a renowned evangelist. Ignoring the gender conventions of her day, she served for over fifty years as an itinerant evangelist and a pioneering black Methodist holiness preacher, traveling and lecturing widely at camp meetings, revivals, and churches in California, Ohio, Indiana, Pennsylvania, New York, Michigan, New England, and Canada. In the introduction to Julia Foote's autobiography, *A Brand Plucked from the Fire,* Thomas K. Doty, the editor of the *Christian Harvester,* stated that she was guilty of "three great crimes—color, womanhood, and Holiness." Doty made reference to the fact that to be an African American and a woman and to advocate the doctrine of holiness meant that one would be subject to triple discrimination in America. In 1894 Foote became the first woman to be ordained a deacon in the AME Zion Church, and in 1900 was the second woman to be ordained an elder. Until her death in 1901 she forcefully advocated participatory equality and ordination of women in the church. Following her ordination as a deacon, Foote said, "We may be debarred entrance to many pulpits (as some of us now are) and stand at the door or on the street corner in order to preach to men and women. No difference when or where, we must preach a whole gospel."

Julia Foote was born in 1823 in Schnectady, New York, the fourth child of former slaves. Their names are unknown. In 1833 she went to live with a prominent white family who enrolled her in an integrated country school, where she received a rudimentary education. In 1836 she moved with the family to Albany, New York. There she experienced conversion at the age of fifteen in 1838, the year before her marriage. Married at age sixteen to George Foote, Julia moved to Boston, where she joined the AME Zion Church pastored by the Reverend Jehiel C. Beman, a leading antislavery orator and president of the Massachusetts Temperance Society of Colored People. The members of this church, like Foote, were former members of the Methodist Episcopal Church, who, seeking greater religious freedom, withdrew and affiliated with a black denomination.

Julia A. J. Foote

Foote Preaches the Gospel

Although Foote had experienced conversion several years earlier, it was in Boston that she was moved to exhort and pray in public and that she became committed to preaching the gospel. Prior to her conversion, Foote was opposed to women preaching and had spoken against it. She did not relish facing the difficulties that she knew existed for women preachers. But, as Foote later recalled, she was obligated to respond to the call that had come in God's name.

Foote clearly understood the meaning of race and gender in white America and the import of gender in the black community. Her decision to preach placed her in conflict with her family, friends, and black ministers, who challenged the right of women to preach. Choosing to pursue a ministerial career meant that Foote would be in contention for most of her life. However, she possessed great faith in herself and an unyielding determination to speak the truth. Her faith, determination, and eloquence as an evangelist were attested to by legions of whites and blacks who turned out to hear her preach wherever she spoke.

Many previous publications have concluded their discussion of Foote's life with the appearance of her autobiography 1879. Although little is known of Foote's activities during the later years of her life, it is know that from 1884 to 1901 she resided with Bishop Alexander Walters and his family and assisted him in his pastorate. According to Lincoln and Mamiya in *The Black Church in the African American Experience,* Bishop Alexander Walters had ordained two black women in the AME Zion church: Mary J. Small in 1898

and Foote in 1900. They then became "the first women to achieve the rights of full ordination to the ministry by any Methodist denomination, black or white," and preceded by half a century similar action by other black Methodist denominations and the United Methodist Church. In his autobiography Walters states that Foote assisted him during his ministry of the Stockton Street AME Zion Church in San Francisco from 1883 to 1886. Walters later pastored churches in Chattanooga and Knoxville, Tennessee, and New York, New York. This is not to suggest that Foote gave up her own ministry, for she did not. She continued to travel and preach and until her death was listed as a evangelist with the New York Conference. Though Walters pastored Mother Zion Church in New York starting in 1887, he lived in Jersey City, New Jersey. Foote seemingly knew and mentored the Reverend Florence Spearing Randolph, a young woman living in Jersey City who entered the ministry during the late 1890s. Randolph, in her unpublished and incomplete autobiography, written out some time during the 1940s, alludes to visiting holiness missions in Jersey City with Foote. Randolph's feminist views, advocacy of the holiness doctrine, and forcefulness as a minister were undoubtedly influenced by Foote. In addition, Randolph, in her autobiography, used a format similar to that used by Foote in her autobiography.

Speaking of the Reverend Julia A. J. Foote following her death, Bishop Clinton said, "She was a preacher indeed. She knew her Bible and studied human nature, and was therefore, a very intelligent and instructive female preacher and a successful evangelist."

REFERENCES:

Andrews, William L., ed. *Sisters of the Spirit: Three Black Women's Autobiographies of the Nineteenth Century.* Bloomington: Indiana University Press, 1986.

Foote, Julia A. J. *A Brand Plucked from the Fire: An Autobiographical Sketch.* 1879. Reprint. Cleveland: Julia A. J. Foote, 1886.

Gates, Henry Louis, ed. *Spiritual Narratives.* New York: Oxford University Press, 1988.

Hine, Darlene Clark, ed. *Black Women in America.* Brooklyn: Carlson Publishing, 1993.

Lincoln, C. Eric, and Lawrence H. Mamiya. *The Black Church in the African American Experience.* Durham: Duke University Press, 1990.

Walters, Alexander. *My Life and Work.* New York: Fleming H. Revell Company, 1917.

COLLECTIONS:

The Reverend Florence Spearing Randolph's papers, sermons, and memorabilia, in the possession of Bettye Collier-Thomas, contain information on Julia Foote.

Bettye Collier-Thomas

Justina L. Ford
(1871-1952)
Physician, humanitarian

Equipped with courage, determination, and a medical degree, Justina Ford became the first black woman physician licensed to practice medicine in Colorado. She was also the first black woman physician in the entire Rocky Mountain West. A pioneer, she overcame discrimination based on her race and gender and defied those who attempted to prevent her from practicing medicine, beginning with the licensing examiner in Colorado and continuing with administrators of local hospitals who denied her hospital privileges. Ford is important not only for breaking down barriers for blacks and women in the medical field but also for her humanitarianism: she selflessly cared for people of all races as well as indigents, many of whom were denied treatment by other doctors.

The seventh child in her family, Justina Laurena Carter Ford was born January 22, 1871, in Knoxville, Illinois, and grew up in Galesburg, Illinois. Little is known about her family background. However, sources confirm that her mother was a nurse. She refused to play with her brothers and sisters unless the game was hospital, with Ford assuming the role of doctor. "I didn't know the names of any medicines," she told Mark Harris for the *Negro Digest,* March 1950, "so I had one standard prescription: tobacco pills." Admitting that she also did not know the names of diseases, she invented names for the illnesses she diagnosed. Ford's love for medicine was unfaltering. "I remember I used to like to dress chickens for dinner so I could get in there and see what the insides were like," she continued, adding that she would examine the heart, lung, and eyes. She also conducted her exploratory research on frogs. In addition, she tended to the needs of her ill neighbors. "I hope I didn't do them any harm," she confided.

Moves Practice to Colorado

Ford graduated from Hering Medical College in Chicago in 1899, then for two years directed a hospital and was a physician at a state school in Normal, Alabama, probably the forerunner of Alabama Agricultural and Mechanical State University. Some sources erroneously identify Ford as the first black woman physician in Alabama. In reality, a black woman named Halle Tanner Dillon Johnson, who passed the medical boards in Alabama in September or October 1891, was the first woman of any race licensed to practice medicine in the state. From 1891 to 1894 Johnson was resident physician at Tuskegee Institute and also had a private practice. Since the Alabama community rejected Ford as a doctor on the grounds of race and gender, she decided to relocate to an area where blacks might be a more integral part of the community. Although she considered Denver still a pioneer town, she chose the city for her work. "I tell folks I came to

Justina L. Ford

Denver in time to help them build Pike's Peak, and it's almost the truth," she told Mark Harris. Some sources say that she was licensed in Colorado on October 7, 1898, but it is more likely that she moved to Denver in 1902 to begin practice. As a black and a woman, Ford faced great odds and was shielded from acts of discrimination only by her determination and courage. "I fought like a tiger against those things," she stated in the *Negro Digest* article.

During the course of her practice Ford also met obstacles many physicians encounter frequently: irregular hours and pay and periods without sleep. It was not uncommon for her low-income patients to pay her in goods rather than cash—groceries, poultry, and other items, including an Oriental cloth and a hand-woven Mexican blanket. One client paid Ford for delivering her daughter thirteen years after the birth. Ford's specialties, gynecology, obstetrics, and pediatrics, were unusual then for blacks and women. According to her brief biographical statement from the Black American West Museum, when she applied for a medical license in Colorado the medical examiner told her, "I feel dishonest taking a fee from you. First of all you're a lady and second, you're colored." Ford responded that she had thought it through before leaving Alabama and that Denver was where she wanted to establish her practice. Successful in the licensing examination, Ford would now have to face the next obstacle: building a practice in a medical community hostile to black professionals.

Since neither Ford nor black patients had access to Denver General Hospital, Ford's practice began with health care delivery to homes, which she initially reached by horse and buggy and then later by bicycle. In time, she purchased a car and hired a relative to drive her to see her patients. Since few families had cars in those days, whenever her "big limo" pulled into a neighborhood everyone knew that someone was having a baby. Still later, Ford, who never obtained a driver's license, relied on taxicabs for transportation. "I just pick up the phone and say my name and the cab rushes right out," she told Mark Harris. "All the drivers know me." The *Denver Weekly News,* February 9, 1984, quoted Ford's friend and driver Charles E. Jackson, who said: "I was Dr. Ford's personal friend, I came to Denver in 1932 and she called on me through the years to drive her to see patients. . . . I used to drive her around in my 1929 Ford when gas was a mere 13 cents a gallon."

Since Denver and the surrounding counties were mountainous, access to many of her patients was limited to rugged mountain roads. Responding to those who criticized her for delivering babies at her patients' homes, she is reported to have said, according to *Colorado Medicine,* February 1989, that the babies "were probably conceived at home, and have nowhere else to be born but at home." Upon reaching the home, Ford removed her dress and delivered the baby in her slip to protect the infant and mother from germs on her outer clothing.

"The Lady Doctor" Earns Acceptance

Ford had a distinguished practice for fifty years and became known as "The Lady Doctor," a title given her out of respect and affection. She delivered over seven thousand babies to parents who lived around the perimeter of an area called Five Points. Many of her patients preferred to have a woman present while they were giving birth. Her patients came from all classes and races, and Ford is especially known for treating those ignored by the conventional health-care systems of the day—Mexicans, Spaniards, Greeks, Koreans, Hindus, Japanese, Bohemians, and people she called "plain white" and "plain colored." As quoted in an article in the *Denver Post* entitled "Learning about Dr. Justina Ford," she said, "Folks make an appointment and whatever color they turn up, that's the color I take them." Only 15 percent of her deliveries were black. She took a particular interest in poor people, many of whom she cared for without charge. To communicate with her patients, she became fluent in somewhere between eight and eleven languages and dialects.

As racial barriers slowly eroded, Ford was admitted to practice at Denver General Hospital. She also received full membership in the Denver Medical Society, the Colorado Medical Society, and the American Medical Society, which early on had denied her membership. As recently as 1950, Colorado had only seven black doctors, with Ford still the only black woman in the group. Although Denver had a population of half a million by then, she was one of only five black physicians there.

In the interview with Mark Harris, Ford remembered funny incidents, such as when a little boy who came with his mother on a medical visit stood looking around searchingly. When Ford asked what he wanted, the child replied: "Where

do you keep those babies?" She had some difficulty convincing him that she "brought babies [and] . . . wasn't allowed to keep them." She also remembered a patient who had changed doctors because her previous doctor was "getting much too old." Ford chuckled that she was twenty years older than he.

Writing for the *Urban Spectrum,* September 1988, Magdalena Gallegos printed a statement Ford made four months before her death in which she commented on her religious beliefs, which guided her work. Pointing to a baby she had just delivered, she said:

> This one will be of a generation that will really see opportunity. I won't see the day, you very well may, and this one certainly will. Hard feelings between the races, my people will come up from the south, your people will see that come to pass. When all the fears, hate, and even some death is over, we will really be brothers as God intended us to be in this land. This I believe. For this I have worked all my life.

As late as 1950, when Ford was nearly eighty years old, she still liked excitement. "Let me tell you about my hobby," she told Mark Harris for *Negro Digest.* "I like to ride ninety miles an hour in an ambulance. That to me is good fun."

Home and Office Becomes Museum

Ford received a number of awards. In 1951 the Cosmopolitan Club gave her the Human Relations Award. Denver residents now recognize Ford as a pioneering medical doctor and humanitarian. Her home and office, once called a beacon of light during her unselfish years of practice and located at 2335 Arapahoe Street, was relocated on February 6, 1984, to 3091 California Street in Denver, just twenty-four hours before it was scheduled to be demolished but not before the wrecking ball had knocked a hole in the brick house. When Ford died, her husband, Alfred Allen, sold the house, which had been built in the late 1880s of Italiante architecture. It was later resold, then scheduled for demolition. The house serves as a memorial to her work and to other pioneer minority and women physicians in Colorado. In 1984 it was also placed on the National Register of Historic Places. On September 24, 1988, a grand opening and dedication ceremony were held to recognize the home. Now established as the Black America West Museum and Heritage Center, the house contains documentation of the area's history. The office and waiting room that Ford used remain on the first floor as a permanent exhibit. Many of Ford's patients and those she delivered as babies continue to live in the area. The museum attempts to locate people who were delivered by Ford, or their relatives, in an effort to obtain an accurate record of the babies she delivered in Denver and other areas of Colorado. Ford's legacy is witnessed not only through the historic site, but also through the Dr. Justina Ford Medical Society, which was organized in 1987 as a support system for black physicians in training in Denver.

Also in recognition of Ford, the Warren Library in East Denver was renamed the Ford-Warren Library in 1975. The

Colorado Medical Society, which until January 12, 1950, denied her membership, passed a resolution at an interim meeting of the House of Delegates in 1989 honoring Ford posthumously "as an outstanding figure in the development and furtherance of health care in Colorado." The citation further identified Ford as a "Colorado Medical Pioneer."

Sometime early in her career she married a man named Ford, a minister in the Zion Baptist Church. After his death she married Alfred Allen but retained the name by which she had become known professionally, Ford. Mark Harris described Justina Ford as a "tiny, round, gray-haired woman." Gallegos in the *Urban Spectrum* said she was "a stern-visaged woman whose unmistakable authority was sharply defined." She was also remembered as active and brisk-mannered and at the same time good-hearted, one who, according to Charles E. Jackson, quoted in the *Denver Weekly News,* February 9, 1984, "was nice and did things without expecting something in return." Gallegos quoted one of Ford's former patients, Agneda Lopez-Stoner, who said of the doctor, "She had a spiritual quality about her and it showed through her eyes." In her later years Ford began to lose her sight. She died at her home on October 14, 1952, at the age of eighty-one, having treated patients just two weeks before her death. She was survived by her husband, three nephews, one niece, two grandnephews, and nine great-grandnephews. She was a member of Zion Baptist Church.

Steadfast in her determination to be a physician, "The Lady Doctor," Justina L. Ford, refused to allow her race and gender to stand in her way and defied the odds in becoming a pioneer in the medical field in Denver. Her contributions are memorable to blacks and women as well as to disadvantaged and underprivileged people of all races.

REFERENCES:

"AIA Awards Fentress for Ford House." *Historic Denver News,* December 1991/January 1992.

Black American West Museum and Heritage Center, Denver, Colorado. Flier. N.d.

Burton, Frances. "A Legacy Continued: Ford Shaped Hopes and Destiny of the Black Community." *Port Charlotte Florida Sun,* February 1989.

"Colorado Medical Pioneer." Resolution. Interim Meeting of the Colorado Medical Society House of Delegates, March 11, 1989.

Denver Post, October 14, 1952.

Denver Weekly News, October 15, 1952.

"Dr. Justina Ford Honored as First Black Female Physician in Colorado." *Colorado Medicine* 15 (February 1989): 60.

"Dr. Justina Ford-Allen; Colorado's First Doctor of Color Passes after 50 Years of Service." Unidentified newspaper clipping in the files of Jessie Carney Smith.

"Ford House Finds Home." *Denver Weekly News,* February 9, 1984.

"Ford House to be Restored as Black American West Museum." Unidentified newspaper clipping. Black American West Museum.

Gallegos, Magdalena. "Doctor Justina Ford, a Medical Legacy Continues." *Urban Spectrum* 2 (September 1988): 4-5.

Harris, Mark. "The Forty Years of Justina Ford." *Negro Digest* 8 (March 1950): 43-45.

Harris, Ottaw. Letter to Jessie Carney Smith, May 5, 1994.

Hibbard, Bill. "How Blacks Helped Win the West." *Michigan Living.* Undated article.

Johnson, Connie. "Dr. Justina Ford: Preserving the Legacy." *Odyssey West* (March 1988): 4-5.

"Justina L. Ford, M.D. One of Colorado's Medical Pioneers." Biographical sheet. Denver: Black American West Museum, n.d.

"Learning about Dr. Justina Ford." *Denver Post.* Undated article in the files of Jessie Carney Smith.

"She Was Truly 'An Angel of Mercy.'" Guest editorial. *La Voz,* July 27, 1983.

COLLECTIONS:

Biographical information on Justina Ford and a photograph of her home are located in the Denver West Museum and Heritage Center, the Western History Collection of the Denver Public Library, and the Colorado Historical Society.

Jessie Carney Smith

Mary Weston Fordham
(c. 1845-1905)
Educator, school founder, poet

Although she composed verse as early as the 1860s, and later published a volume of poetry, *Magnolia Leaves,* in 1897, it was as a teacher that Mary Weston Fordham made her most substantial contribution to the black community and to African American history and culture. A free person of color, Fordham ran her own school during the Civil War years, despite the fact that, by South Carolina law, she risked imprisonment and physical punishment for doing so. Starting in 1865, Fordham provided her services as a teacher to the American Missionary Association (AMA), which operated many schools in the South.

The basic facts about Fordham's life and career are difficult to obtain, and any biographical sketch must be reconstructed from a very few brief references in printed sources and spare notations in letters and archival documents. Compounding the problem is the fact that some early sources reported incorrect information, which later writers who did only cursory research relied upon. Such critical details as the year of her birth, for example, are not known for certain. Several sources repeat an erroneous report that Fordham was born in 1862. Yet a review of census data, combined with the facts that Fordham was employed by the AMA in 1865 and had taught for several years prior to and during the Civil War, makes the 1862 date of birth impossible.

According to the death records kept by the city of Charleston, South Carolina, and the parish registry of St. Marks Episcopal Church, Mary Weston Fordham died in Charleston on July 4, 1905. Interred in Brotherly Cemetery, one of the city's several long-established African American cemeteries, her precise burial site is unknown because several headstones have been broken and the inscriptions on others have been obscured by time. A funeral notice in the *Charleston News and Courier* indicates that she was survived by her children and a sister, Jennie B. Weston. Fordham was probably born somewhere between 1839 and 1845. The uncertainty exists for several reasons. Death records for the city of Charleston show Fordham was sixty when she died; this would establish her birth year as 1845. However, the Population Schedule for the 1860 federal census reports Fordham as seventeen years of age and living at home with her sister, Jeanette, and her parents, John Furman Weston and Louisa Potter Bonneau Weston. Assuming the census data is accurate, this would mean Fordham was born in 1843. Some sources have incorrectly stated that Fordham was the daughter of Jacob Weston, a prosperous and socially prominent businessman in Charleston. This same census shows that Jacob Weston, whose wife was Sarah Ann Bonneau Weston, had a daughter named Mary living at home with him, but this Mary Weston was only eight in 1860.

It is probable that Jacob Weston was either Mary Weston Fordham's uncle or her cousin. The prosperous and prominent Weston clan of Charleston evidently originated with Toney, later called Anthony, Weston. According to Michael Johnson and James Roark in *Black Masters: A Free Family of Color in the Old South,* Anthony Weston had achieved the singular position of being allowed to function as a free person of color although he was still technically a slave. In 1833 a white plantation owner named Plowden Weston had "freed" Anthony, who subsequently used his training as a millwright and machinist to purchase and marry his wife, Maria, and to buy two additional Weston slaves, Samuel and Jacob, "apparently his brothers." Anthony Weston's financial holdings, including real estate appraised at forty thousand dollars and fourteen slaves, were listed under his wife's name. John Furman Weston, Fordham's father, also a machinist and millwright, may have been the son of Anthony or perhaps a cousin. While the record establishing the exact kinship to Anthony is not clear, the record does show that John Furman Weston and Jacob Weston both married daughters of Thomas Bonneau, thus linking them to most of South Carolina's elite mulatto families, including the Ellisons, the Holloways, and the Dereefs.

Hired to Teach for the American Missionary Association

A June 16, 1865, letter to Reverend M. E. Strieby, corresponding secretary of the AMA, from Thomas W. Cardozo, who hired Fordham to teach under the auspices of the AMA, provides some biographical information about the black or "native" Charleston teachers he had employed. William Weston and Francis Rollin were hired by Cardozo in May 1865. In June he added Fordham, Amelia Shrewbury, Margaret Sasportas, and a Mr. S. Spencer to his staff. But by October 1865, Spencer had been replaced by Virginia Hammond. Cardozo stipulated that he knew each of his colored teachers personally and noted they had all been "schoolmates" of his in Charleston and that Fordham and Rollin were from "two of the best families." Fordham, he asserted, was twenty-six. This assessment would place Fordham's birth year as 1839. While Cardozo would seem to be the most creditable source, he could have been mistaken, for his letter also reports that Fordham's cousin, William O. Weston, "[was] about thirty." However, a June 24, 1865, letter from William Weston to the AMA categorically states that he was thirty-one at the time he was first employed by Cardozo.

Irrespective of her exact age, Fordham worked during the Reconstruction period first for Thomas Cardozo and then for his brother Francis Cardozo at a black AMA school in Charleston which evolved to become the Saxon School in 1865; around 1867, it became the Avery Normal Institute. Additional biographical data can be deduced from Fordham's *Magnolia Leaves*. A somewhat restrained memorial poem suggests that a "Mr. Edward Fordham," who died in 1886, was probably Fordham's husband. The poem's third stanza states: "Now thou'ar safely anchored / In the port above, / Gladly do we offer thee / Symbols of our love." A poem memorializing one of Fordham's children, Alphonse Campbell Fordham, who died at the age of six, is considerably more passionate and more clearly shows a family connection:

Yes, my darling, when life's shadows
Over me do darkly fall,
Meet me surely at the river
As I haste to obey the call.

. . . .

In that land no pain or anguish
Ever can my child enfold
Then my darling meet thy mother
Surely at the "Gates of Gold."

Yet Fordham's verse should be read in the context of other data in order to avoid making inaccurate conclusions. While Fordham dedicated several poems to various family members, including her mother, "Mrs. Louise B. Weston," her paternal grandmother, "Mrs. Mary Furman Weston Byrd," and her maternal grandmother, "Mrs. Jeanette Bonneau," a reading of the lines, "Then Pastor and Leader, fond Parent, adieu, / Till the last, grand trump shall sound," from the poem "Rev. Samuel Weston," could lead readers to infer incorrectly that Samuel Weston was Fordham's father. In fact, he was her uncle and the father of her cousin, William, who was also employed by the Cardozos.

Early Teaching Career

In 1865, when Thomas Cardozo initially hired Fordham to work for the AMA in Charleston, he gained the services of an experienced teacher and a very courageous and capable young woman. Connected to the affluent and influential Westons (her uncles, Jacob and Samuel, had established a very successful Charleston tailoring business), Fordham was one of a select group of pioneering African American women educators. Intelligent, talented, and dedicated, Fordham was considered highly accomplished and quite able, as a native southerner, to hold her own when measured against the northern white teachers who were seemingly preferred by the AMA. Privately tutored, Fordham had anticipated the emphasis upon education as a tool to uplift the race. Consequently, in the early 1860s, she organized her own school and became a teacher despite the danger involved: an 1835 South Carolina law expressly prohibited teaching slaves or free persons of color to read or write. "If any person shall hereafter teach any slave to read or write. . . . And if any free person of color shall keep a school or other place of instruction for teaching any slave or free person of color to read or write, such free person of color shall be liable to [a] fine, imprisonment, and corporeal punishment." Yet as Thomas Cardozo reported in a letter of June 16, 1865, Fordham had, in defiance of this law, "kept [a] school for free colored children for the past six or seven years." Jennie Armstrong, a white colleague of Fordham's, indicated in a letter published on January 15, 1866, that Fordham had been arrested or "taken to the guard house for teaching a little school." Commenting upon the black teachers she encountered, Armstrong found them to be the "aristocracy of the colored community," "well bred," "intelligent," and surprisingly well-educated because "in spite of all, schools were kept, in a very secret way to be sure." The products of these clandestine schools were "advanced enough to pursue intelligently all the common branches of English education." Armstrong maintained that she "never heard better readers anywhere."

Along with Francis Rollin, Fordham was consistently described by Thomas Cardozo and Francis Cardozo, who replaced his brother as head of the school, as one of the "two best native teachers" in Charleston. Fordham impressed everyone with her ability in the classroom as well as with her determination to be self-sufficient and her spirited battle for equal rights. By November 1865, she was part of a staff of eighteen teachers, six of whom were black, training eight hundred students. Fordham and Armstrong taught a first-year class of eighty girls the basic subjects of arithmetic, science, grammar, English, and writing. For her work, Fordham was paid a salary of twenty-five dollars; Armstrong received twice that amount. Pleading for equity, Francis Cardozo protested in a December 2, 1865, letter to the AMA:

> This Young lady is a most excellent and experienced teacher. . . . Miss Weston maintains her equality with Miss Armstrong (both are virtually interchangeable as teachers). Miss Armstrong asks her Association at least $50 a month; Miss Weston gets only $25 for doing the same work, and she has very justly refused to continue, especially when I informed her at first that her salary would not be less than $35, as in one of your earlier letters you said that those who did work equal to Northern teachers would be paid at the same rate. I wish you would give Miss Weston $35 a month. She has informed me that she will leave unless she receives the sum and I know either of the other two societies would very willingly give her that sum.

Apparently the AMA did not agree to the request, but Cardozo added five dollars from his own pocket to Fordham's pay because he considered her a "much above the average" teacher and felt she deserved it. (He also thought that William Weston, "being a male," should receive at least sixty dollars.)

Fordham Shows Writing Talent

During this same period Fordham had also shown signs of development as a poet. At Thomas Cardozo's request, she promised to contribute a poem or two to the missionary journal or newsletter; copies of her verse were requested by others for publication in the North as well. But, perhaps in the 1860s, Fordham understood that she needed more time to develop her poetic talent.

Fordham's only published volume of poetry, *Magnolia Leaves,* appeared in 1897 with an introduction by Booker T. Washington, which suggested that the true value of her volume rested in its service to the race because it demonstrated black talent. She commented in lyric verse upon a diverse array of topics, including shipwrecks; displaced Cherokee Indians driven from the South; exiled wanderers from Italy, Ireland, and Scotland; Christian belief and traditions; patriotism; domestic situations; and nature and the changing of the seasons. She also wrote elegies and memorials for departed friends and relatives; composed occasional poems to celebrate civic, racial, or national successes, as in the "Chicago Exposition Ode" and the "Atlanta Exposition Ode"; and meditated on women's lot in life though both reflective and whimsical pieces. "The Coming Woman" anticipates the restructuring or reversal of domestic arrangements by describing a woman dashing off to work, scolding and giving instructions to a house husband. The second stanza states:

> Now hurry and wake up the children;
> And dress them as fast as you can;
> "Poor dearies" I know they'll be tardy,
> Dear me, "what a slow, poky man!"

Although there is very little hint of a racial consciousness in *Magnolia Leaves,* such feeling does surface when Fordham turns to commemorate a significant historic event, like Booker T. Washington's 1895 Atlanta Exposition speech, or an important African American leader, such as Bishop Daniel A. Payne. The first stanza of her "Atlanta Exposition Ode" takes its initial line from Washington's famous metaphor "Cast down your buckets where you are" and closes with that line. The second stanza is more interesting because it both explicitly and implicitly acknowledges a racial sensibility while advocating forgiveness and optimism; its poetic diction, while conventional, seems more natural.

> What doth it matter if thy years
> Have slowly dragged 'mid sighs and tears?
> What doth it matter, since thy day
> Is brightened now by hope's bright ray.

The morning star will surely rise,
And Ethiop's sons with longing eyes
And outstretched hands, will bless the day,
When old things shall have passed away.

Despite the success of Paul Laurence Dunbar in this same period, Fordham employs neither a dialect voice nor one of strident racial protest. Her poetry primarily relies for its effect upon the conventions of nineteenth-century genteel verse; thus, her poetic diction, tone, imagery, and meter are largely uninspired. In the style of Phillis Wheatley's work, Fordham's poems contain "benighted souls" who go to heaven to take "exalted seats" or sing "seraphic song" in a "celestial home." While Newman Ivy White found her work "rather commonplace," a review in *Colored American Magazine* noted her work showed a "tenderness" of feeling and an "appreciative insight" into nature. What emotional force exists in her lyrics is undercut by sentimentality and a derivative mode. However, Fordham's poetry occasionally rises above these limitations, offering a more authentic poetic voice.

In the preface to *Magnolia Leaves* Fordham noted her goals for the volume. She hoped African American young people, "our youth," would be inspired "to higher and greater efforts"; she wanted her volume to serve as a "harbinger" of the far better work she expected from future generations. Modest, refined, respectful, and respectable, Mary Weston Fordham contributed but a single volume of poetry to the canon of African American letters; she died long before the celebrated Harlem Renaissance but the award-winning African American poets produced in successive years proved her sense of a brighter future for blacks in the arts to be true.

REFERENCES:

Armstrong, Jennie. Letter to the *National Freedman* 2 (January 15, 1866): 7-9.

Braithwaite, William Stanley. Review of *Magnolia Leaves*. *The Colored American Magazine* 3 (November 1901): 73, 74.

City of Charleston. Death Records.

Drago, Edmund L. *Initiative, Paternalism, and Race Relations: Charleston's Avery Normal Institute*. Athens: University of Georgia Press, 1990.

Fordham, Mary Weston. *Magnolia Leaves*. Charleston, S.C.: Walker, Evans and Cogswell Co., 1897.

Johnson, Michael P., and James L. Roark, eds. *Black Masters: A Free Family of Color in the Old South*. New York: Norton, 1984.

———. *No Chariot Let Me Down: Charleston's Free People of Color on the Eve of the Civil War*. Chapel Hill: University of North Carolina Press, 1984.

Loggins, Vernon. *The Negro Author*. New York: Columbia University Press, 1931.

Mary Weston Fordham. Obituary. *Charleston News and Courier*, July 6, 1905.

Morris, Robert C. *Reading, 'Riting, and Reconstruction: The Education of Freedmen in the South, 1861-1870*. Chicago: University of Chicago Press, 1981.

Richardson, Joe M. *Christian Reconstruction: The American Missionary Association and Southern Blacks, 1861-1890*. Athens: University of Georgia Press, 1986.

St. Marks Episcopal Church, Charleston, S.C. Parish Register.

U.S. Bureau of the Census. 1860 United States Census, Population Schedule for Charleston, South Carolina.

White, Newman Ivy. "Racial Feeling in Negro Poetry." *South Atlantic Quarterly* 21 (January 1922): 14-29.

COLLECTIONS:

Letters of Thomas W. Cardozo, Francis L. Cardozo, and William O. Weston to M. E. Strieby and E. Whiting are housed in the American Missionary Archives, Amistad Research Center, Tulane University, New Orleans.

Sandra Y. Govan

Elizabeth Denison Forth
(c. 1793-1866)
Maid, landowner, investor, philanthropist

Elizabeth Denison Forth, a former slave who never learned to read or write, pursued freedom at an early age and became one of the nineteenth century's most remarkable and unlikely philanthropists. Friendly and compassionate, Forth worked as a domestic for prominent Michigan families. She amassed her wealth mostly through investments in stocks and real estate, though she also invested in a bank and a steamboat. When she died, the bulk of her estate went toward a chapel for the Saint James Church in Grosse Ile, an exclusively white Michigan island community. Though the contribution today would be no more than what some professionals earn in a week's pay, Forth's legacy paved the way for whites and blacks to come together in a house of worship.

Information about Elizabeth Denison Forth's life is sketchy, and some confusion is due to the fact that Forth was generally known by her maiden name and in some accounts written after her death she is referred to as Elizabeth Forth Denison. However, it is commonly agreed that most people who knew her referred to her affectionately as Lisette.

According to Isabella E. Swan in *Lisette*, Forth was born sometime before 1793 to slaves Peter and Hannah Denison. During the late 1700s, as native Americans and European settlers fought for territorial rights, young Elizabeth grew up on a farm on the Huron River in Saint Clair, Michigan. Peter Denison worked the farm and helped transport produce along the Detroit River. Hannah Denison worked as a household servant. One of six children, Elizabeth was the second oldest Denison child. Growing up, she played with the white child-

Elizabeth Denison Forth

ren of the house and the native American children who frequented the farm. She seems to have been a friendly and gregarious child who learned to speak the Indian languages and is said to have acted as interpreter occasionally. Around the house, she worked alongside her mother, polishing silver, helping in the kitchen, and gathering herbs and vegetables from the garden.

The Denisons' quest for freedom began on March 7, 1805, when slave owner William Tucker died. In his will, Tucker stipulated that Peter and Hannah would become free upon his wife's death, but he bequeathed the Denison children to his brother. Although Congress had passed the Northwest Ordinance of 1787, which prohibited slavery in the territory that would eventually become the states of Michigan, Ohio, Illinois, Indiana, and Wisconsin, the ordinance did not grant freedom to the Denison children, because it referred to new slaves, not existing slaves.

Children Appeal to Legal System for Freedom

Freed in 1806, Peter and Hannah went to work for Detroit lawyer Elijah Brush. Brush, who one year earlier had been admitted to practice law in the Territorial Supreme Court in the newly designated Michigan Territory, encouraged the couple's children to sue for their freedom. The Michigan Territorial Supreme Court heard the case in September 1807. The court ruled that all but one of the Denison children would be slaves for life. The youngest, Peter Denison, Jr., born shortly before the ordinance took effect, would become free at age twenty-five.

The ruling left Elizabeth and her siblings devastated, but they were encouraged by developments in another court case the next month. In that case, a slave owner sought to have his fugitive slaves, who had established their freedom in Canada, restored into slavery in the states. Judge Augustus B. Woodward ruled that the territory had no obligation to return the fugitives to slavery, and that as long as they remained in the states, their freedom would be protected. The Denison children decided to establish freedom elsewhere so they could return to the territory as free citizens. Shortly after the court's ruling, the Denison children crossed the Detroit River into neighboring Canada. The exact date and circumstances of their return to the Michigan Territory are sketchy, but by the early 1820s, Forth was working as a domestic in the Solomon Sibley household in Detroit.

At some point in her adult life, Forth posed for a daguerreotype. According to biographer Swan, the portrait captures Forth's inner beauty as well as her striking outer features:

> The portrait reflects Lisette's temperament. The deep dark eyes search questioningly, she would not easily be deceived; determination is carved in the firmly held lips; sensitivity to sorrow vies with a lurking smile, sympathy or humor ready to emerge as occasion dictates. Taste in attire and erect posture betoken a modest pride.

Forth worked hard, while enjoying close relationships with her employers. Perhaps it was upon the advice of her employers that she invested in land and property. Perhaps it was at their advice too that Forth made sure her financial transactions were properly documented.

On April 21, 1825, she bought four lots, totaling 48.5 acres, in Pontiac, Michigan. On September 25, 1827, she married Scipio Forth, according to the records of Saint Paul's Protestant Episcopal Church in Detroit. Though the exact date is unknown, it is believed that Scipio Forth died sometime before 1830. His death probably motivated Forth to provide for the disposal of her property upon her own death.

Widowed and childless, Forth began working for the John Biddle family in early 1831. She would remain with them for some thirty years.

Investments Yield Dividends

Continuing to invest her earnings, Forth acquired stock in the steamboat *Michigan* and twenty shares of Farmers and Mechanics' Bank stock. According to Swan, "Due to heavy passenger traffic during the surge in westward migration, the *Michigan* earned enormous profits—as high as 80 per cent in one year. The bank also prospered. Its stock soared to great heights in 1836 when a 30 per cent dividend was paid."

On May 25, 1837, Forth bought a lot in Detroit, paying the mortgage off in installments. Later, it appears that she sold the property in Pontiac and invested those proceeds in stocks. Forth's whereabouts between 1849 and 1854 are uncertain. It is possible that she moved to Philadelphia with the Biddle family.

About 1854, Forth was living in her own home at 14 Macomb Street, on the edge of the business section in old Detroit, when the Biddles sent for her to join them in Paris to attend to the ailing Mrs. Biddle. Forth arrived in Paris in late fall. While there, she learned to speak some French, and her buckwheat cakes made her quite a sensation. Though she was on a once-in-a-lifetime trip, an aging Forth became anxious to return to the United States. She came back to Detroit in late 1856 and remained there until August 7, 1866, when she died alone in a house she had bought with some of the assets she acquired over the years. She was buried in Strangers Ground, in Detroit's Elmwood Cemetery.

Will Provides Gift from the Heart

Forth updated her will several times over the years as her financial picture changed. And though she enjoyed entertaining friends and provided nice things for them, she seems to have become somewhat of a miser late in her life, worrying that there was not enough to live on.

For those who believed her to have very little, her final bequest must have been quite surprising. And even those who knew of her investments must have been highly moved by the generosity and spirit of her wishes for the Protestant Episcopal Church.

In part, her will states:

Having long felt the inadequacy of the provisions made for the poor in our houses of worship, and knowing from sad experience that many devout believers, and humble followers of the lowly Jesus, are excluded from those courts, where the rich and the poor should meet together, shut out from those holy services by the mammon of unrighteousness, from that very church which declares the widow's mite to be more acceptable in the sight of the Lord than the careless offerings of those who give of their "abundance" and wishing to do all in my power as far as God has given me the means to offer to the poor man and the stranger "wine and milk without price and without cost."

Although Forth did not name Saint James Church as the specific beneficiary of her estate, it is clear that she wanted the money to be used to erect a chapel for the Protestant Episcopal Church. The particulars she left to be decided by her long-time employer, William S. Biddle. Ultimately it was his decision that the money, about fifteen hundred dollars, would go to St. James Church in Grosse Ile. The chapel, for which Forth's bequest was the initial fund, was completed in the spring of 1868. A new building was erected in 1958 with a corridor leading to the old chapel, where the doors are dedicated to the memory and benevolence of Elizabeth Denison Forth.

REFERENCES:

Hine, Darlene Clark, ed. *Black Women in America.* Brooklyn: Carlson Publishing, 1993.

Swan, Isabella E. *Lisette.* Grosse Ile, Mich.: Isabella E. Swan, 1965.

Sandra D. Davis

Frankie Muse Freeman
(1916-)
Civil rights activist, community activist, lawyer

Frankie Muse Freeman dedicated her life to breaking down the legal barriers of segregation. In 1954, she was one of the lawyers who won a case challenging segregation in the public housing of Saint Louis. For the next fourteen years she helped implement the decision, first as associate general counsel and then as general counsel for the Saint Louis Housing Authority. In 1964, she began a sixteen-year tenure on the United States Commission on Civil Rights. To her concerns for civil and women's rights she has now added that for the rights of the elderly. Throughout her life she has been continuously involved in a wide range of civic activities.

Frankie Muse Freeman was born on November 24, 1916, in Danville, Virginia. She was one of eight children born to Maude and William B. Muse. Her parents emphasized to Freeman and her siblings that they could reach any goal through education and a willingness to work hard.

Growing up in Danville where all public facilities were segregated, Freeman gained a social consciousness about the evils of segregation at an early age. She recalled that as a child she and other family members walked where they needed to go rather than be forced to sit in the back of the bus. Freeman was never able to accept the institution of segregation and early on made the decision to become a lawyer so that she could effect change. In reflecting on those early years, Freeman said in the *St. Louis American '92 Salute to Excellence:* "I decided when I was young and I used to see how we were treated. . .that I would be a lawyer and do my part to change things."

Freeman Becomes a Lawyer

After graduating from Hampton University in 1937 with a bachelor of arts degree, Freeman moved to New York and applied to law school at St. John's University. But to her disappointment, St. John's refused to accept her credits from Hampton. While she was never told so, Freeman has always felt that her credits were denied because Hampton was a black school and the courses were considered inferior. Ironically, it was the practice of segregation that brought her and Shelby Freeman, Jr., together. He was from Saint Louis and had graduated from Lincoln University, the only Missouri university for blacks. The graduate courses he wanted to take were not offered at Lincoln and he was denied access to them at the

Frankie Muse Freeman

all-white University of Missouri. Instead, as was the common practice, the state of Missouri paid his tuition to attend the graduate school at Columbia Teachers College in New York City, where he met Frankie Muse. They were married in 1938. They remained in New York for three years until early 1941 when they moved to Washington, D.C., to accept jobs with the federal government.

Although her desire to become a lawyer had been put on hold, Frankie Muse Freeman always knew that she would go to law school and realize her goal of becoming a civil rights lawyer. In 1944, she quit her government job and enrolled at Howard University's school of law. She earned a bachelor of laws degree, and later the juris doctor degree, graduating second in her class. During her senior year, with a five-year old daughter, she gave birth to a son. With two small children, she had mixed law school and motherhood well.

In 1947, Freeman passed the District of Columbia bar. She and her husband moved to Saint Louis in 1948. She passed the Missouri bar that same year. She immediately became involved with the NAACP and handled a variety of *pro bono* civil rights cases. Freeman opened her law office in 1949 and she engaged in the general practice of law.

One of the highlights of her career occurred in 1954 when she argued and won the case of *Davis v. Saint Louis Housing Authority* in the United States District Court for the Eastern District of Missouri. The case challenged racial segregation in public housing in the city of Saint Louis. Constance Baker Motley and Robert L. Witherspoon served as her co-counsels, along with Thurgood Marshall, who was

general counsel for the NAACP. The next year Freeman was asked to join the legal staff of the Saint Louis Land Clearance and Housing Authorities to assist in implementing the federal court's order prohibiting public housing segregation. She served fourteen years, first as associate general counsel for both authorities and later as general counsel for the Housing Authority. In 1970, she left the Housing Authority to return to private practice.

Named to Civil Rights Commission

In 1964, President Lyndon B. Johnson nominated Freeman to serve on the United States Commission on Civil Rights. She was the first woman to serve on the commission. Freeman was reappointed by presidents Nixon, Ford, and Carter, serving an unprecedented sixteen years until July 1980. During her tenure, Freeman earned a reputation as a determined fact finder who insisted upon a firsthand assessment of the situations the commission was called upon to investigate. Many of the recommendations that emerged from the hearings conducted during her first years on the commission were later incorporated into the Voting Rights Act of 1965. Freeman traveled to rural Canton, Mississippi, to investigate the bombings of four black churches not long after several civil rights workers had been murdered for attempting to register blacks to vote. President Carter wrote to Freeman and thanked her for her service on the Civil Rights Commission: "You have insisted that the nation must follow policies that reflect our unequivocal commitment to the good of equal opportunity for all in all walks of life. . . . You are one of our nation's truly great leaders in the field of civil rights.'

Norman Seay, a civil rights activist and an administrator with the University of Missouri at Saint Louis, said of Freeman in the *Saint Louis Post Dispatch Magazine:* "She's an effective historical leader who has not only contributed to the nation but St. Louisans well. Of course, there may never be another person like her on the Civil Rights Commission."

In October 1979, Freeman was confirmed by the United States Senate as Inspector General of the Community Services Administration, having been nominated by President Jimmy Carter. That appointment lasted until January 26, 1981, when President Ronald Reagan fired all fifteen of the inspector generals appointed by President Carter.

In an interview for the *Saint Louis Post-Dispatch* in 1988, Freeman said: "I have always said that I have two handicaps being black and a woman. I have scar tissue from both. Now I have a third, age. But I've said I would never let that stop me."

Champions Rights for the Elderly

And it has not. From 1991 to 1993, she served as chairperson of the National Council on the Aging, a powerful organization that fights to protect the rights and opportunities of older men and women and their families. When she was elected to the chair, the president of the council characterized Freeman as "an ardent advocate, an activist for many good causes, and an astute analyst of social progress in our nation."

She continues to work with the council as a member of the board. Freeman served as a member of the American Bar Association's Commission on Legal Problems of the Elderly. She helped establish a National Center on Aging Issues at Howard University because of the need "to have a national policy with respect to all of the basic needs of people. . .young and old, and in-between."

Freeman's involvement in community and civic affairs as a volunteer has become legendary. She has served on the Board of Trustees of Howard University for sixteen years. She is now a Trustee Emeritus. Freeman became the fourteenth national president of Delta Sigma Theta Sorority in 1967 and served until 1971. She is a director of the Urban League of Metropolitan Saint Louis and was its first female board chairman. She also serves on the boards of the United Way of Greater Saint Louis and the Greater Saint Louis Chapter of the United Nations Association. Freeman is a life member of the NAACP.

Freeman is determined that all African Americans, particularly young people, understand the place of the civil rights movement in United States history. To that end, she has established a Civil Rights Library at the Harris-Stowe State College in Saint Louis. The library is comprised of civil rights documents and presidential papers collected from four administrations over nearly two decades. When the library was opened to the public in 1983, Freeman said in the *St. Louis American:* "I wanted these books to be where they would be used. Young people don't know what people endured to have the right to vote."

Civil Rights Activist Earns Awards

Although Freeman no longer practices civil rights law, she continues in her role as an activist as a member of the bipartisan Citizens Commission on Civil Rights, a group of fifteen former federal officials that monitors federal enforcement of antidiscrimination laws.

Freeman's unwavering commitment to civil rights and social justice has earned her many honors and awards during her career including honors from the Links, Common Cause, United Nations Association, and the National Council of Negro Women. She holds honorary degrees from Hampton University, Washington University, University of Missouri-Saint Louis, and Harris-Stowe State College.

Freeman's stance on civil rights and her continuous dedication to the struggle for equality was summarized by a statement she made in the *Saint Louis Post-Dispatch Magazine* in 1988:

> My commitment was to work for elimination of discrimination. I could not accept the segregation that existed while I was growing up, even though I had to at least comply with it. But I never emotionally acquiesced to it. I really do believe in the Declaration of Independence. I really believe that all men, all women are created equally. . . . The total commitment to civil rights—we have never had it. The struggle continues. As long as I'm breathing, I'll be a part of it.

Freeman was married for fifty-two years to Shelby T. Freeman, Jr., who died in July 1991. She is the mother of one daughter, Shelbe Patricia Bullock. A son, Shelby, died as a youth. Freeman still practices law in Saint Louis, limiting her practice primarily to probate matters. Freeman is associated with the Saint Louis law firm of Whitfield, Montgomery and Staples, P.C.

Current Address: Attorney at Law, 3900 Lindell Boulevard, St. Louis, MO 63112.

REFERENCES:

Carter, Jimmy. Letter to Frankie Muse Freeman, February 20, 1980.

Freeman, Frankie Muse. Interview with Jane Greenwood Harris. May 20, 1993.

"Perspective on Aging." *The National Council on The Aging* 20 (July-October 1992): 6.

Saint Louis American, December 15, 1983.

Saint Louis American '92 Salute to Excellence, 1992.

Saint Louis Post-Dispatch Magazine, March 27, 1988.

Janie Greenwood Harris

Eliza Ann Gardner
(1831-1922)
Abolitionist, clubwoman, dressmaker, reformer, religious leader

Eliza Ann Gardner's long life spanned nine turbulent decades, during which she was involved in many of the most pressing causes of her time. She was born in New York City thirty years before the start of the Civil War and became active in the abolition movement in Boston when she was quite young; the Gardner family home, in fact, was a station on the Underground Railroad. Throughout most of her life she was a member of the African Methodist Episcopal (AME) Zion Church in Boston. As a religious leader, she was influential locally, nationally, and internationally. She was known in the denomination as the "Mother" of the AME Zion Missionary Society, which raised money for the first church missionaries to visit Africa, and she also served as vice-president of the society's New England Conference.

Known as the "Julia Ward Howe" of her race, Gardner, like many of her female contemporaries, was a strong advocate of temperance. She was also an active clubwoman. Although her name and achievements have been largely forgotten over time, and information about her life is scarce, her antislavery efforts, advocacy of women's rights within the church, and early activism in women's organizations place her among the most important race leaders of the nineteenth century.

Eliza Ann Gardner (also variously spelled Eliza Anne, Gardener, or Gardiner) was born in New York City on May 28, 1831. Her parents were James and Eliza Gardner of New York City. The family moved to Boston during her youth, where her father became a successful contractor for sailing vessels. According to author Sarah L. Fleming in *Homespun Heroines,* her family was always comfortably situated. Gardner never married, and she had no children.

The Gardner family's involvement in the AME Zion Church most likely began during the time of their residency in New York. As early as 1843, Eliza Ann's father was a member of the board of trustees of the Boston church, serving as second treasurer. At that time, and for most of the remainder of her life, Gardner lived in the predominately black West End section of the city. In Boston, Gardner attended the only public school for black children in the city. Her teachers were antislavery leaders. She was an extremely good student, with a keen mind and an excellent memory. Because of her scholastic achievements, she won several scholarships during her student years.

Abolitionist and Church Activities

After leaving school Gardner became active in church and abolitionist circles. She supported herself by dressmaking, and she also turned her sewing skills to the cause of racial uplift when she helped to produce the first banner for the Plymouth Rock Lodge of Odd Fellows. Gardner attributed her independent spirit to having been raised in a home that served as a station on the Underground Railroad, where she became personally acquainted with such outstanding antislavery leaders as William Lloyd Garrison, John Brown, Wendell Phillips, Charles Sumner, Lewis Hayden, Frederick Douglass, Harriet Tubman, and Sojourner Truth. According to some reports, Gardner once shared a speaking platform with Douglass, Garrison, and Sumner at an abolitionist meeting. She also had a "hobby," according to Fleming, of finding work in white homes and businesses for black girls with whom she was acquainted.

In 1865, when the Boston AME Zion Church congregation began a drive to purchase a larger facility, Gardner and her mother became founding contributors. At about this time she also launched a lifetime career of teaching Sunday school. In 1883 she became the Sunday school superintendent for Boston, the first female to hold this position in the city and the only one to do so until 1918. At her church, Gardner organized the first Zion Missionary Society in New England, known as the Mother Conference of Missions. Through this society, which later became known nationally as the Ladies' Home and Foreign Missionary Society, funds were raised to send missionary Andrew Cartwright and his wife to Liberia in 1876.

In 1884, during the seventeenth Quadrennial Conference of the AME Zion Church, fund-raising activities of the Ladies' Home and Foreign Missionary Society, and the prominent role of women in missionary fund-raising in general, came under attack: the church's ministers did not support women trying to raise these funds. According to William J. Walls in *The African Methodist Episcopal Zion Church,* Gardner, then vice-president of the New England Conference of the Ladies' Home and Foreign Missionary Society, spoke in defense of women in the church:

> I do not think I felt quite so Christian-like as my dear sisters. I come from Old Massachusetts, where we have declared that all, not only men, but women, too, are created free and equal. . . .

> If I would go back to Boston and tell the people that some of the members of this conference were

against the women, it might have a tendency to prejudice our interests in that city. . . .

If you commence to talk about the superiority of men, if you persist in telling us that after the fall of man we were put under your feet and that we are intended to be subject to your will, we cannot help you in New England one bit.

Her address and the "stirring appeals" of the other women who spoke were successful in turning around the course of fund-raising. Inspired by Gardner's eloquent address, the members of the Ladies' Home and Foreign Missionary Society reorganized their efforts, making fund-raising more successful.

Involvement in the Club Movement Begins

In 1893 Gardner's social activism and reform work took a new turn with the founding of the Woman's Era Club of Boston. Gardner was one of the 113 founding members of this organization, the first black women's club in Boston. She served as chaplain and as a member of the organizing committee at the founding convention of the National Federation of Afro-American Women in 1895. In 1896, she was registered as president of the E. M. Thomas Lodge at the Washington convention of the National Federation of Afro-American Women, which voted to merge with the National League of Colored Women, forming the National Association of Colored Women. At the 1908 biennial convention of the organization in Brooklyn, the seventy-seven-year-old Gardner was featured as an "honored guest."

In 1903, the Boston AME Zion Church decided to move once again, from the old North Russell Street building to a new site, and five years later Gardner also moved. She left her childhood home for a house at 42 Irving Street, where she took in lodgers. The house was on the fringes of her old neighborhood. By this time, the West End, which had been an African American neighborhood for all of Gardner's life, was changing. More and more immigrants were moving in, and the black residents were relocating to other sections of the city.

In 1909, Gardner founded the Butler Club of the Boston AME Zion Church, named for Joseph Butler, one of the founding members of the Boston church. She remained president of this organization until her death. She continued to be influential in the church in other ways as well, principally as a fund-raiser for the missionary society. In 1916, when she was eighty-five years old, one of the featured exhibits at the twenty-fifth General Conference of the AME Zion Church was a handsome quilt of one hundred squares that she sent. The quilt netted ten dollars for missionary work, and she requested that the quilt itself be presented to the first newborn baby at the mission. At that time she was the oldest living member of the Boston AME Zion Church.

In his book on the Boston AME Zion Church, published in 1918, the Reverend Jacob Powell described Eliza Ann Gardner as the "only living link binding the Zion of the present with the Zion of the remote past." She died in Boston on January 4, 1922.

REFERENCES:

Boston City Directory, 1862, 1870, 1879, 1897, 1908.
Brown, Hallie Quinn, ed. *Homespun Heroines and Other Women of Distinction*. Xenia, Ohio: Aldine Publishing Co., 1926.
Davis, Elizabeth Lindsay. *Lifting as They Climb*. Washington, D.C.: National Association of Colored Women, 1933.
Giddings, Paula. *When and Where I Enter*. New York: Morrow, 1984.
National Association of Colored Women's Clubs. *A History of the Club Movement among the Colored Women of the United States of America, as Contained in the Minutes of the Conventions, Held in Boston, July 29, 30, 31, 1895, and the National Federation of Afro-American Women, Held in Washington, D.C., July 20, 21, 22, 1896*. National Association of Colored Women's Clubs, 1902. Reprint. Washington, D.C.: National Association of Colored Women's Clubs, 1978.
Powell, Jacob W. *Bird's Eye View of the General Conference of the African Methodist Episcopal Zion Church, with Observations on the Progress of the Colored People of Louisville, Kentucky and a History of the Movement Looking toward the Elevation of Rev. Benjamin W. Swain, D.D. to the Bishopric in 1920*. Boston: Lavalle Press, 1918.
United States Census Records for Boston, 1860, 1870, 1910.
Walls, William J. *The African Methodist Episcopal Zion Church: Reality of the Black Church*. Charlotte, N.C.: AME Zion Publishing House, 1974.

Susan J. Sierra and Adrienne Lash Jones

Hazel B. Garland
(1913-1988)
Journalist, editor

A pioneering journalist who championed the cause of the black press, Hazel B. Garland was the first African American woman to serve as editor-in-chief of a nationally circulated newspaper chain. Her popular columns appeared in various editions of the *Pittsburgh Courier* for more than forty years, from 1943 to 1988. She launched her career in the golden age of the black press, which began during World War I and ended in the early 1960s, when mainstream media began covering the Civil Rights Movement. During that period, black newspapers had been crusading organs extolling racial justice and providing, with few exceptions, the only outlet for black journalistic talent. Due to the length of Garland's career and the fact that she achieved her greatest prominence in later life, she was a vital link between that golden age and the latter twentieth century, when most of those going into journalism used the black press primarily as a stepping stone to the

Hazel B. Garland

mainstream. As an editor during the 1960s and 1970s, Garland made some of her most significant contributions behind the scenes, where she determined newspaper policy, shaped staff assignments to reflect social needs, and trained those who would carry on her torch.

Hazel Barbara Maxine Hill Garland was born on January 28, 1913, on a farm outside Terre Haute, Indiana. She died on April 5, 1988, in McKeesport, Pennsylvania, where she had lived for fifty-three years with her husband. She was the oldest of sixteen children born to George and Hazel Hill. After the family moved to Pennsylvania in the early 1920s, her father supported his growing brood by working as a coal miner. Garland assisted her mother in caring for her younger siblings, often amusing them by telling stories.

Although Garland was a bright student who loved reading and yearned for more education, she had to drop out of high school, at her father's urging, so that a younger brother might continue. While she worked as a maid, her father obtained a senatorial scholarship for her brother who did not accept it and did not go to college due to his transient love for a girl whom he never married. Recalling this incident in 1980, Garland told Jean E. Collins in an interview for the book *She Was There: Stories of Pioneering Women Journalists:*

> My father was a dear soul. I loved him dearly. But his idea was, "Why waste your money on sending a girl to college? She's going to get married. Save your money for the boys." I used to go to the library where I would read and read. They didn't have student loans for young people as they do today. I

lived in libraries. I read everything. That's why I say there's no excuse for a person today not to take advantage of all the opportunities that are available. There's no excuse for ignorance.

Career in Journalism Begins

During those years, Garland also considered becoming an entertainer. She found relief from her maid's job after hours by dancing, singing, and playing the drums with local bands, but on January 26, 1935, she married Percy A. Garland, a photographer and businessman and settled down to a life as a homemaker in McKeesport, a suburb of Pittsburgh. In October of that year, she gave birth to her only child, a daughter named Phyllis. Meanwhile, she came under the influence of her mother-in-law, Janey Garland, who encouraged her to become active in local organizations. Since Garland liked to write, she usually was asked to serve as the club reporter. She was on the publicity committee of the local YWCA in 1943 when a reporter for the *Pittsburgh Courier* was supposed to cover a tea honoring the Y's first black staff worker. The reporter got lost and was so late in arriving that the affair was over. Since Garland had written down all the details, it was suggested that she submit the materials herself. The *Courier* editors were impressed by her eye for details and asked her to cover events in nearby communities, working as a stringer, meaning she would be paid two dollars for each news item the paper used. She produced so much material that the editors suggested that she combine them into a column called "Tri-City News," which began appearing that year. Community columns were a common feature of black newspapers in those days. Mainstream publications included little news about African Americans and most of what they did carry was negative.

When *Courier* editors offered to train stringers who came into the office on Saturday mornings, Garland took advantage of the opportunity. Eventually she was asked to substitute when staff reporters went on vacation. One editor, who resented seeing a woman do what he considered a man's job, sent her to cover a murder in a brothel. Somewhat alarmed, since she had never been in such a place, Garland paid a male reporter a dollar to enter the building with her, then proceeded to get the necessary information for her story.

Garland joined the full-time staff of the *Pittsburgh Courier* in 1946. At that time, the name of her column was changed to "Things to Talk About." In it she covered events that highlighted the lives of her readers: marriages, births, new jobs, parties, honors, visits from friends, even tragedy when it struck. She also wrote about her own family and shared her reflections on current events or social trends. Starting out as assistant women's editor, she built her following on her close association with community people. In an interview, Frank E. Bolden, who was city editor and one of her colleagues on the *Courier,* analyzed the philosophy that underscored Garland's work throughout her career:

> She would give a wedding in the housing projects the same attention she would give a wedding that occurred in the upper echelon of what was then

called Negro society. When I asked her about it, she'd say, ''They're all human, and as long as I'm doing this, that's the way it's going to be.'' The clubs relied heavily on Hazel to write about them, and the religious people, too. Family allegiance also was a hallmark of her work. She had come from a small town where life centered on the family. I think she wrote with such compassion because she had such strong feeling for her own family.

Garland had joined the staff at a time when the *Courier* was the most widely read black newspaper in the country, with thirteen editions, including local and national editions. The paper maintained branch offices in major cities with correspondents throughout the nation and abroad. The *Courier*'s popularity stemmed from its emphasis on stories that combined social protest with human interest, along with extensive coverage of black social life, religion, sports, and entertainment.

New Dimensions Explored

One of the high points of Garland's career came in 1952 when she was sent to a rural South Carolina community to do a story on a nurse-midwife named Maude Cullum, who often worked without pay and had delivered most of the babies, black and white, in her community. Bolden recalled the circumstances that led to that assignment:

The press promoted male writers, but nobody paid much attention to what women were saying in the nation back then. In journalism, the women had to just make do with the social tidbits. But when this story came up, the *Courier* didn't have anyone else to send. What did the men know about midwifery? So they sent Hazel.

She was appalled by the poverty and lack of social conditioning she witnessed in Cullum's community and wrote a series of articles based on what she called ''The Three I's: Ignorance, Illiteracy and Illegitimacy.'' *Courier* editors submitted the series in a regional journalism competition judged by the writers from the nation's leading daily newspapers. The *Courier* was the only black newspaper entering the competition. Garland later recalled for Jean Collins in *She Was There: Stories of Pioneering Women Journalists:*

The entries were numbered. They didn't name the newspaper or reporter who wrote it, or mention whether the person was black or white. I won the award for the best series. The prize was awarded at the Page One Ball. Oh, I was so thrilled! And I was shocked, too, because I beat some people who had been perennial winners. One had won a Pulitzer Prize the year before and had entered a series. I said that if I don't win anything else again, I had won that.

When the *Courier* introduced a new magazine section in 1952, Garland was named associate editor. In preparation for this assignment, she took courses in magazine writing and

editing at the University of Pittsburgh. When the magazine section was phased out, she became woman's editor and in 1960 was named entertainment editor.

Over the years, Garland continued to write two separate versions of her ''Things to Talk About'' column, one for the local and another for the national edition of the *Courier,* but in 1955 she also began writing a weekly column about television, called ''Video Vignettes.'' Though she focused on programs featuring African Americans, she also wrote about significant productions of all types, interviewing black and white producers and performers when they came to town. She commented on the way blacks were portrayed on television and waged a personal protest when relevant programs were discontinued or black performers and newscasters dismissed. To make certain her points got through to those responsible, she would send copies of her column to network and station managers. She was the first African American journalist to initiate such a column and sustained it until a month before her death, making it one of the longest-running television columns in newspaper history.

By the mid-1960s the *Courier* was in the throes of serious financial problems due to high production costs, mistakes in management, and the mainstream press's incursion into coverage of black topics. The number of editions had been cut back and the lustre had faded from the *Courier*'s reputation. Paychecks began to bounce, but Garland held on. As she told Collins: ''I loved the *Courier*. It was everything to me. I had spent the greater part of my life there, so I wanted to work even if I didn't get paid. I thought maybe we could keep on and hold it together.''

Garland Named Editor-in-Chief

In 1966 John Sengstacke, publisher of the *Chicago Defender,* which had been the first black press giant, and owner of several other black newspapers, purchased the *Courier*'s assets and renamed it the *New Pittsburgh Courier.* At the time Garland held dual posts as women's and entertainment editor. Sengstacke broke with tradition by naming her city editor, a management-level post. Although harassed by a colleague, the *Courier*'s business manager, Garland persevered. In 1972 she became the paper's editor-in-chief. She worked day and night reorganizing the paper into sections, developing new beats, and emphasizing features. She changed the Women's section to the Leisure and Living section, including articles about men.

In 1974 Garland was named ''Editor of the Year'' by the National Newspaper Publisher's Association (NNPA). That year also she was named ''News Hen'' of the year by the Women's Press Club of Pittsburgh. In 1975 she received a National Headliner Award from Women in Communications, Inc., formerly Theta Sigma Phi, the national journalism society. The Women's American ORT, a Jewish women's group, honored her for ''bridging the gap between the races.'' A tireless civic worker, she belonged to several organizations and served on many boards. Eventually the walls of her home were covered with plaques and citations.

When Garland stepped down as editor-in-chief in late 1974 due to health problems, Sengstacke named her assistant to the publisher, relying on her advice. She continued to write her columns and played a major role in the paper's editorial operations. In 1976 the *Courier* won the NNPA's John Russwurm Award, which is given to the best black-oriented paper in the country. After she retired in 1977, Garland continued as editorial coordinator and consultant, writing her columns, contributing feature articles, and working one day a week in the office doing editing and layouts. In 1978 and 1979 she served as a juror for the Pulitzer Prize, journalism's highest honor. Garland worked up until three weeks before she died on April 5, 1988, of a heart attack following surgery for a cerebral aneurysm.

Frank Bolden, who worked for NBC after leaving the *Courier* and serves as consultant for the Western Pennsylvania Historical Society, assessed her overall impact:

> Without her, the *New Pittsburgh Courier* would have folded, in that period after Sengstacke came in. Under her, it became a better-prepared product. She didn't appreciate making mediocrity respectable. Hazel was one of the two top women in (black) journalism, the other being Ethel Payne of the *Chicago Defender.*

Garland received her last honor in 1988, shortly before her death, when *Renaissance Too,* a Pittsburgh magazine, established a scholarship fund for journalism students in her name and that of Mal Goode, a former *Pittsburgh Courier* staffer and the first black journalist in network television. Connie Portis, publisher of the magazine, credited the two of them with inspiring her to go into business for herself. Portis also named the structure where her offices are located the Garland and Goode Building, commemorating them with a plaque and portraits. As Portis said in an interview: "I just want black kids in this neighborhood to see a building that is named for people they can be proud of, people who will make them want to excel."

Perhaps it is as an example that Garland made one of her most significant contributions. Many women in journalism and related communications fields consider her their role model. Among them is her daughter, Phyllis (Phyl) Garland, an author, music critic, and educator who began her career at the *Pittsburgh Courier,* going on to become New York editor of *Ebony* magazine, then a professor at Columbia University's Graduate School of Journalism. When asked to advise the young, Hazel Garland would say: "We must always have the three D's: Desire, Determination and Dedication. We must not let anything turn us aside. And to be truly successful, we must always reach back and try to lift someone else as we climb."

REFERENCES:

Bolden, Frank E. Telephone interview with Phyl Garland, October 20, 1994.

Collins, Jean E. *She Was There: Stories of Pioneering Women Journalists.* New York: Julian Messner, 1980.

"Courier Editor/Journalist Hazel Garland Dead at 75." *New Pittsburgh Courier,* April 6, 1988.

Davis, Marianna W., ed. *Contributions of Black Women to America.* Vol. 1. Columbia, S.C.: Kenday Press, 1982.

"Former Courier Editor Hazel Garland Dies." *Pittsburgh Press,* April 6, 1988.

Garland, Phyl. "Blacks in Journalism." In *Encyclopedia of African-American Culture and History.* New York: Macmillan, 1995.

"Hazel Garland, Pioneer Journalist." *Pittsburgh Post-Gazette,* April 6, 1988.

"Journalist Hazel Garland, Former Courier Editor, Dies." *Jet* 74 (April 25, 1988): 59.

"Nationally Known Journalist, Civic Leader, Hazel Garland Dies at 75." *New York Daily News,* April 6, 1988.

Portis, Connie. Interview with Phyl Garland, July 22, 1993.

Phyl Garland

Zina Lynna Garrison

(1963-)

Tennis champion

With victories in the 1988 Olympics in Seoul, South Korea, Wimbledon, the United States Open, Australian Open, French Open, Canadian Open, Virginia Slims tournaments in European and American cities, and in the Tokyo Doubles, Zina Lynna Garrison is ranked among the top tennis players of the world. Aside from her athletic records, she is well known for her encouragement of inner city young people interested in careers in sports and other areas of endeavor.

Garrison was born on November 16, 1963, in Houston, Texas, the last of the seven children of Mary and Ulysses Garrison. To emphasize that she was their last child her parents chose the final letter of the alphabet to begin her name, Zina. Prior to her Zina's first birthday Ulysses Garrison, a letter carrier for the Houston post office, suffered a fatal stroke. In the same year, Zina's twenty-one-year-old brother, William, a catcher in the Milwaukee Braves minor league system, died after being struck by a baseball. Mary Garrison raised her children as a single parent while working as an aide in a nursing home. Because Zina was the baby of the family, born so many years after the other children, she received much attention from her mother and her brothers and sisters. But since the gaps of ten years and more made her interests and those of her siblings widely different, she grew up almost as an only child.

Garrison believes she has had the gift of clairvoyance from an early age. She reports that a dramatic demonstration

Zina Lynna Garrison

of this talent occurred in 1983 when she was in New Jersey, playing in the U. S. Open. Her siblings, not wanting to disturb her concentration in the games, withheld telling her their mother was seriously ill in Houston. But Garrison claimed intuitive knowledge of the exact instant her mother suffered an episode of cardiac arrest and interpreted that as the time of her death. She learned later that in actuality her mother lived two days longer.

Garrison's introduction to tennis came when she was ten years old and went with her brother Rodney to MacGregor Park, a tennis facility in what was formerly the well-to-do all-white Riverside section of Houston. She watched for an hour, fascinated by seeing John Wilkerson, the resident coach, give a lesson to a student. When Wilkerson saw this keen interest, he invited her to take a racket and try the game that would assume a dominant role in her life. Wilkerson became her coach, as well as friend and father figure, as he sharpened her skills. He stressed discipline and the basics of the game, once forcing Garrison to complete a practice game with the racket she had broken by throwing it to the ground in a fit of rage.

Garrison Becomes Top Ranked Tennis Player

Because Garrison was such a natural player, within two months Wilkerson entered her in local competitions. By the time she was fourteen years old, she was among the top players of her age group in the country; four years later she was rated number one of all the junior players. On the day of her graduation in 1982 from Ross S. Sterling High School in

Houston, she went directly to the French Open to compete in her first professional match. In 1983, the year she turned twenty, she was ranked among the top ten women tennis players in the United States.

At the same time that Wilkerson was teaching Garrison, he had another promising MacGregor protégée, Lori McNeil, who in 1986 was ranked number fourteen in the United States. Garrison and McNeil became a formidable doubles team and best friends. They played together until 1987 when problems arose that led to the dissolution of the partnership and a change of coach by Garrison. Garrison retained the services of Willis Thomas, who was well acquainted with her rise in the world of tennis. Garrison felt that although Wilkerson had given her the basis to develop as a professional and had contributed to her rapid advancement, the perfect relationship had begun to deteriorate; they had reached a standstill as a team.

The break with Wilkerson came at the time of two major disappointments in Garrison's life. She had been forced to miss both the French Open and Wimbledon because of a stress fracture in her right foot, and on a more traumatic level, she was still suffering from not having accepted the loss of her mother four years earlier. Garrison's mother had been her friend, her greatest booster and supporter, the person she could telephone to share successes and challenges. With her mother's help Garrison found it easier to adjust to the contrast between the modest African American section of Houston where she grew up and the affluence she was experiencing traveling as a professional athlete.

Denying her mother's death, Garrison went into a depression that manifested itself in her overeating. After suffering a bout with bulimia, she sought professional assistance and was finally able to understand her behavior and to reconcile herself to her loss. This restored order in her life, allowing her to refocus upon herself and her life as a professional athlete.

Star Wins Olympic Medals

In the 1988 Olympics in Seoul, South Korea, Garrison won a gold medal in doubles with Pam Shriver and a bronze medal in singles. Her overall ambition is to achieve a Grand Slam victory in the four greatest annual events in tennis: the Australian Open, the French Open, Wimbledon, and the United States Open. To date the goal has escaped her. She came close to winning one of the major tournaments, the 1990 Wimbledon, having defeated Monica Seles and Steffi Graf, but lost to Martina Navratilova in the finals. This was the first time a black woman had reached the finals in a Grand Slam competition since Althea Gibson was victorious at Wimbledon in 1957 and 1958.

Garrison has won numerous landmark matches, defeating such luminaries as Chris Evert for the first time in 1985 and again in an emotional meeting at the 1989 U. S. Open. She has won matches in singles, doubles, and mixed doubles in

U.S. cities such as Oklahoma City, Indianapolis, San Diego, Oakland, Chicago, Newport, Washington, D.C., Houston, San Francisco, New Orleans, and Boca Raton and Amelia Island, Florida. Outside of this country she has taken titles in Britain, Canada, Australia, Korea, and Japan.

Garrison Becomes Community Servant

Zina Garrison is well known for her community service work, more than most others in her field. She visits schools in cities where she plays to give clinics and talk to students to motivate them not only to pursue sports but to make commitments to serious study as well. After obtaining the 1988 Olympic medals, she appeared at Public School 125 in Harlem, in the midst of a blinding rain storm. The students were surprised that a person of her status would inconvenience herself to come to see them, especially in the unfavorable weather of that day. Her reward was a packet of individually written letters filled with expressions of appreciation for her interest in them and good wishes for her career.

Since 1988, Garrison has supported youth organizations, antidrug programs, and projects designed to improve the lot of the homeless through funding from the Zina Garrison Foundation. In the summer of 1992, she opened the Zina Garrison All-Court Tennis Academy, which provides opportunities for economically disadvantaged children to increase their self-confidence through tennis. Her mission is to encourage young people who may be potential tennis professionals, including African Americans and other minorities, to seek places to learn the game, even though they may have more access to sports such as football, basketball, and baseball. For example, she explains that, while women basketball players have limited opportunities after college, women can continue competing in tennis for years beyond graduation. Garrison's dream is to establish a shelter for the homeless and initiate additional junior tennis programs in Texas.

Zina Garrison often demonstrates an unusual degree of sportsmanship by applauding her opponent's spectacular plays. And she was among the small number of major representatives of the game to attend the funeral of Arthur Ashe, the respected African American tennis star who succumbed in 1993 to AIDS acquired through contaminated blood transfusions.

Garrison Weds Jackson

In December 1988, a family friend introduced Garrison to Willard Jackson, an executive in an environmental management firm. They were immediately attracted to each other and were married in September of the following year in a magnificent ceremony in Houston's Windsor United Methodist Church. The ten bridesmaids included Lori McNeil, the original doubles partner whose friendship Garrison had renewed; Katrina Adams, another doubles partner; actress Robin Givens; Cheryl Jones, tennis coach at the University of Southern California; and La Ronda Jackson, sister of the groom. The newlyweds left the church in a classic 1937 Rolls Royce,

leading a train of twelve limousines. For their honeymoon they went first to Tokyo, where Garrison was a member of the United States Federation Cup team, and then to West Germany.

Jackson has organized International Public Relations and Marketing for Athletes (IPMA), through which he serves as Garrison's manager. The combination of her intenseness and basic shyness with Jackson's ability to offer comfort and support at just the right moment has fueled Garrison's stream of successes on the court. They live in Houston and enjoy the company of their two dogs, Ace and Wimbley, and Garrison's collection of stuffed animals. Garrison finds pleasure entertaining her nieces and nephews, golfing, jogging, and playing tennis and softball with her brothers and sister.

Honors have come to Garrison in various forms. To celebrate her accomplishments in her sport, Washington, D.C. declared January 6, 1982, Zina Garrison Day. Illustrating her high regard in professional tennis circles, her picture was included in the Lipton/World Tennis Association calendar for 1987. She was national spokeswoman for the YWCA Tennis program in the summer of 1990. In honor of the Zina Garrison All-Court Tennis Academy, and Garrison's other community service work, *Family Circle* magazine chose her for its 1992 Player Who Makes a Difference Award. For this occasion the magazine and Hormel Foods each donated ten thousand dollars to her chosen charities. During 1990-91, Garrison was an alternate on the World Tennis Association Player Council, and from 1990 to 1992 she served on the board of directors of the association.

At first, Garrison was perceived as lacking the presence and personality to attract commercial contracts from large corporations. In spite of her disappointment she saw no racial prejudice involved, but considered it a reaction to her youthful looks and apparent lack of maturity. With the more sophisticated image she has developed under the direction of IPMA, she has been featured as a glamorous woman in *Essence* magazine and *Black Elegance,* has been a guest on the *Arsenio Hall Show* on two occasions, and has had much more success with endorsement contracts. Garrison has represented a fast food chain, Wilson rackets, Yonex rackets, and Reebok clothing and has appeared in a public service anti-litter announcement.

One of the top rated and highest paid tennis professionals in the world and the first black woman to reach the Wimbledon finals since Althea Gibson did so in the late 1950s, Zina Garrison can truly be classified as a trailblazer. Among the few black women to achieve success in a game dominated by whites, she appears not to be disturbed by her singular status. She believes it is her personal attributes—the talent and dedication she brings to the game—that are most important.

Even though Garrison is satisfied with the overall treatment she has received from the media, occasionally she gets questions from individual reporters that seem to indicate a lack of sensitivity and which make it difficult for her to completely ignore racial issues. She has learned to respond with understanding, in ways that set an example for other black people who are pioneers in sports.

Current Address: c/o Andrew P. Moran, 5625 Milart Street, Houston, TX 77021.

REFERENCES:

Faingold, Noma. "Strike a Pose: Glamour is Alive in Women's Tennis." *Inside Tennis* 11 (August 1991): 26.
"Garrison Has the Right Stuff." *Inside Women's Tennis* 13 (August 1989): 12-14.
Higdon, David, J. "Zina on Her Own." *Tennis* 24 (March 1989): 33-37
Hine, Darlene Clark, ed. *Black Women in America.* Brooklyn: Carlson Publishing, 1993.
"Little Steps, Giant Strides." *City Sports* 16 (October 1990): 31-35.
"Living a Dream." *Sports Illustrated* 71 (November 27, 1989): 71-76.
"Tennis Ace Zina Garrison Ties Houston Love Match." *Jet* 77 (October 23, 1989): 52.
Tracy, Steve. "On Center Court." *Spirit* (May 1988): 34-52.

Dona L. Irvin

Amy Jacques Garvey

Amy Jacques Garvey
(1895-1973)
Feminist, journalist, organization leader, activist

Amy Jacques Garvey, best known as the second wife of Marcus Mosiah Garvey, the founder and first president general of the Universal Negro Improvement Association (UNIA), is one of the foremost black feminist journalists of the twentieth century. As the editor of the women's page of the *Negro World,* the UNIA's official organ, from 1922 to 1928, she successfully promulgated a nationalist thought that embraced the doctrine of pan-Africanism, extolled the greatness of Africa, and promoted a politically informed community activism among black women. Garvey was a central force in keeping the UNIA together during her husband's indictment and trials for mail fraud (1923), perjury and income tax evasion (1924), and incarceration for alleged mail fraud (1925-1927). In her role as liaison between Marcus Garvey and UNIA officials and as secretary-treasurer of the Marcus Garvey Committee for Justice and the Marcus Garvey Freedom and Protection Fund, she traveled throughout the United States, speaking about Garvey and the UNIA. These activities and the publication of a two-volume book, *The Philosophy and Opinions of Marcus Garvey* (1923-25), which she compiled and edited, kept his name alive, promoted the UNIA, and created goodwill among some who had opposed Garvey. In 1963, Amy Garvey published *Garvey and Garveyism,* an important work tracing his life and philosophy. This book provides a great deal of insight into Amy Garvey's relationship with Marcus Garvey, the UNIA, and the Garvey philosophy.

The eldest child of George Samuel and Charlotte Jacques, Amy Jacques Garvey was born in Kingston, Jamaica, on December 31, 1896. The daughter of formally educated, middle-class parents, Garvey was raised in relative comfort and educated at Wolmer's Girls' School and Colment's Girls' School. Her values were firmly rooted in a middle-class ethic, but she gained wide exposure through books and other people. Garvey credited her father with providing her an invaluable education, which helped to cultivate her mind and a positive sense of self. Although her father had wanted a son, he concentrated his energies on the development of Amy's mind and personality, employing an approach generally reserved for male children. On Sundays they sat together reading international publications, and he would give her writing assignments designed to enhance her skills of analysis. It was in this manner that she developed her literary skills and a broad, general understanding of world affairs. Her management of the family farm and later employment for four years as a clerk and secretary in the office of her family attorney exposed her to business and organizational techniques and afforded her an opportunity to learn legal process. These experiences prepared Garvey for her later careers as journalist, administrator, and wife of Marcus Garvey.

Garvey arrived in New York City in the summer of 1919. Living in Harlem, she secured a job teaching night school at Public School Ninety-Six. As the roommate of Amy Ashwood, Marcus Garvey's first wife, Amy Garvey was introduced to the UNIA and exposed to the ideal of Garveyism. By December 1919 she was employed as the confidential secretary of Marcus Garvey, and she was a bridesmaid at Ashwood and Garvey's wedding. The marriage lasted only a few months, ending in divorce in 1922. Between 1920 and 1922, Amy Garvey and Marcus Garvey developed a very close relationship and they married in July 1922.

Cause of Nationalist Movement Embraced

The Garvey's union was not one made for love. By Garvey's own testimony, Marcus Garvey married her because he needed someone he could trust to preserve the UNIA and to carry forth the message of black nationalism should he be imprisoned or assassinated. Long after Marcus Garvey's death, she contended that "we were wedded to a cause. Even in death we are not divided." Whatever the relationship, it is evident that they developed an exceedingly strong bond built upon supreme trust and an unfailing commitment to the propagation of black nationalism. Garvey felt neither dominated nor overshadowed by Marcus; rather she felt that she was an equal partner in a movement that could bring about the liberation of Africans worldwide. Garvey, like her husband, believed in "Race First." This was the theme of her life and work. In 1960, in a letter to Lerone Bennett, she said that although her face was wrinkled from "years of tension, work and strain . . . I thank God for the opportunity to serve my people, by standing besideor[sic] behind him, and since his passing, by standing up for him."

For several months in 1923 and following Marcus Garvey's incarceration in 1925, Garvey became her husband's stand in, spokesperson and the foremost articulator of his philosophy. More than any other individual it was Amy Garvey who kept the organization functioning from 1925 to 1928. It was during this time that her sphere of influence was significantly enlarged. Transcending her role as personal secretary and editor of the women's page she became a central part of the UNIA leadership. Although Garvey held no official office in the UNIA, she was in fact the editor of the *Negro World* during this period. For Garvey running the UNIA was not a difficult task. Her literary, oratorical, and organizational skills, as well as her ability to deflect and withstand criticism, made her a superb administrator.

Assuming the tasks of raising funds for her husband's defense and the publication of the *Negro World,* Garvey succeeded in keeping the organization and Marcus Garvey's philosophy alive. From the beginning she had been a controversial figure in the UNIA: her position as confidential secretary, subsequent marriage to Garvey, elevation to UNIA office manager, and assumption of authority, without official recognition of the organization, made her the target of enmity and jealousy among some UNIA members. Moreover, for some of the males in the UNIA, her strident feminism and penchant for labeling black men sexist and unsupportive of black women was annoying and perceived as destructive to the organization. Undaunted by controversy and criticism, she successfully ran the national office, published *The Philosophy and Opinions,* supervised the publication of the *Negro World,* and raised the funds for Garvey's defense. Her constant

intonation that Garvey was being persecuted by the government, not prosecuted, won support for the UNIA. The organization's membership and visibility soared.

Public questioning and criticism of Amy Garvey's role in the UNIA surfaced in July 1923 in an editorial in the *Negro World* entitled "Look Out for Mud." Ostensibly in defense of Amy Garvey's character, T. Thomas Fortune, the paper's editor, suggested that she was being attacked by some for assuming power without authority. Claiming that Marcus Garvey, as president-general, had designated three male UNIA officers as the caretakers of the organization during his absence, he stated emphatically that Amy Garvey held no office and exercised no control in the organization, and that it was unconscionable "to attempt to drag the name of an innocent and helpless woman into an arena where she cannot properly defend herself." Garvey retorted in a letter to the editor that she was neither helpless nor innocent and certainly not ignorant of "the depths to which colored men can stoop to further their petty schemes even at the expense of a downtrodden race such as ours."

Jamaica and Beyond

Amy Garvey succeeded in keeping the UNIA in operation during Garvey's incarceration. Although she was confronted with controversy, and Marcus Garvey's enemies struggled to control and take over the organization, with an iron will she prevailed. Amy Garvey's role in the organization took a decisive turn in the fall of 1927. In November President Calvin Coolidge commuted Garvey's sentence and ordered him deported to Jamaica. On November 26, Marcus Garvey was released from prison and subsequently deported. During the initial months following his deportation, Garvey made efforts to go to Honduras, Yucatán, Venezuela, Brazil, and some other places where the UNIA had gained a following. Each of these countries rejected his application for entry. Once it was clear that Garvey was destined to spend the remainder of his life in Jamaica, Amy Garvey quietly departed from Harlem for that island. Many of her friends were astounded by her decision. Few could fathom why a talented young woman would abandon her career to follow her husband, particularly since Garvey had been so stigmatized.

In Jamaica, Amy Garvey worked unsuccessfully with Marcus Garvey to develop the movement there; scorned by the black middle class, whom Garvey had earlier castigated for their lack of race consciousness, slavish adherence to white values, and rejection of the black masses, their efforts were thwarted at every turn. The ensuing Depression, which had an impact upon the world economy, affected the UNIA and Garvey's personal livelihood. It was in the midst of his struggle and economic decline that the Garveys began their family. Marcus Garvey, Jr. was born in 1930 and Julius Winston Garvey was born in 1933. Although the Garveys were politically active in Jamaica, childrearing took a substantial portion of Garvey's time, and during the 1930s she wrote and published less. Marcus Garvey edited and published a newspaper, *The Black Man,* and founded The People's Political party. Found guilty of contempt of court for a libelous plank in the party's manifesto, Garvey was fined and imprisoned for three months. He was then sentenced to six months in prison on charges of seditious libel for articles published in *The Black Man* which attacked goverment repression. He won an appeal of this conviction but concluded that life in Jamaica would mean constant harassment. In 1935 Garvey went to London, England, where he set up headquarters and remained until his death in 1940. Although Amy Garvey and the children joined Garvey in England in June 1937, she determined that they must return to Jamaica because of her son Marcus's increasing health problems. In September 1938 she and the children made a hasty departure from England during Garvey's absence.

During the 1940s and 1950s Garvey managed to support herself and to raise and educate her children through lecturing, writing, and contributions from family and friends. Both of her sons graduated from college with top honors and professional degrees. Marcus, the recipient of a B.A. and a law degree from Oxford University in England, returned to Jamaica, where he attempted to establish a legal practice and later became a professor at the University of the West Indies; Julius received a M.D. degree from McGill University and became a surgeon.

Garvey was politically active throughout most of her life. However, her activity was much diminished in the years before 1960 when she was raising her children. In the 1960s she became involved with the Black Power movement in the United States. The publication of *Garvey and Garveyism* and a collection of essays, *Black Power in America* (1966), propelled her back into the limelight. In 1960 Garvey was the honored guest of the Ghanaian and Nigerian governments and was extremely impressed with the diplomatic reception and special treatment she was accorded by the heads of state in those countries.

Nationalist Feminist Philososphy Advanced

Garvey revered the black women leaders of her generation who had worked unceasingly on behalf of their race and gender—women like Lucy Laney, Mary McLeod Bethune, Nannie Helen Burroughs, and Jane Edna Hunter. A student of black history, she contended that "there is too much ignorance among us as to what our men and women have accomplished." She suggested that among the educators and writers worthy of admiration were Charlotte Forten Grimké, Fannie Jackson Coppin, Maria Baldwin, Phyllis Wheatley, Frances Ellen Watkins Harper, and Victoria Earle Matthews. Growing up when the black women's club movement was in its heyday, she was very aware of the leaders and of the work of the National Association of Colored Women (NACW). The influence of the leadership and the work of the black women's club movement on Garvey was considerable, and it is clearly visible in her writings and in the ways in which she pursued her goals. She was driven by their words and deeds to continue the tradition of service and commitment they espoused. She viewed herself as part of a historical tradition of black women working for the liberation of their people. She argued that

"the foremost women in every community, state or nation . . . [are] those who do [the] most for others." Carefully studying these women and their work, Garvey embraced feminist views and developed political strategies similar to those of the early black women activists.

Garvey was very successful at incorporating issues of race, gender, and class into her writings and activities and in forging a nationalist feminist philosophy. The historical response of black women to gender discrimination must be considered within the context of racial oppression. Many of the nineteenth-century black middle-class women active in the NACW articulated a sense of their equality with black males and white females. Because of the dual burden of race and gender they developed what was referred to as "Practical Feminism." Garvey embraced the doctrine of Practical Feminism which defines the philosophy and strategies historically used by black feminist leaders to address issues of race and gender, essential factors which circumscribed the lives of all black women. Its basic tenet was the utilization of gender as a vehicle to address racial problems, with the understanding that gender issues were of equal importance with racial issues. However, since America defined them as black first and women second, their political agenda had to reflect that reality. The use of gender as a vehicle to address racial problems does not render the NACW a conservative, semifeminist organization as some historians have suggested. It simply defines the function of Practical Feminism in the organizing efforts of black women.

Although Garvey greatly relied on the philosophy and tactics of the early black clubwomen, she developed a unique analysis of the plight of black people worldwide, fashioning a black nationalist ideology and speaking in a black feminist tone that was different and more compelling than that of anyone who preceded her. Through her writings, speeches, and advisory and administrative role in the UNIA, she was able to establish a feminist leadership that influenced a whole generation of women. Though the UNIA included representatives of the black elite, it appealed primarily to the black working class. In the 1920s and 1930s, Garvey, like other black female activists, including Nannie Helen Burroughs, appealed to the masses of black women to recognize sexism, but not be repressed by it in their pursuit of the liberation of their people.

Contrary to white and some black feminists who felt that women should be emancipated from the cult of domesticity, Garvey advocated a cultural nationalism that called for the efficiency of black women in the domestic environment. Arguing that black women could not abandon domesticity because of the importance of child rearing to achieving a black nationalist objective, she said, "Women worth while are those engaged in blazing the way for unborn generations." Garvey asserted that there was no conflict in women being "leaders nationally and racially," that "the doll-baby type of woman is a thing of the past and the wide-awake woman is forging ahead, prepared for all emergencies, and ready to answer any call, even if it be to face the cannons on the battlefields."

Garvey was forthright in stressing the importance of black women to the advancement of their race and to the success of the UNIA. She argued that it was "doubtful that the organization [UNIA] could have reached the high point of strength end [sic] effectiveness it has without them. To take woman and her sympathies and work out of the association would be like taking the wife out of the home of the husband."

Although she felt that black men devalued black women, she did not believe that women should dominate. Women as the equals of men possessed special talents. Women, because of the way they were socialized, could be a powerful force in humanizing society. Highlighting the activities of women in Europe and the Third World, she contended that women were taking charge of their lives, throwing off domesticity, and performing "manly" tasks.

A remarkable woman with a prophetic vision, she lived a long and successful life. Garvey's life came to an end on July 25, 1973. She left an important legacy that has been embraced by a new generation of African American women. In one of her last writings she spoke about "The Role of Women in Liberation Struggles" (1972). In this article Garvey reiterated the key tenets of her feminist philosophy and paid tribute to Sojourner Truth, Harriet Tubman, and Angela Davis as symbols of "noble Black women" who were integral in the historical struggle for black liberation. She intoned that "Black women are not traitors, they are not cowards, they are truly the 'better half' of Black men."

REFERENCES:

Bennett, Lerone Jr. "The Ghost of Marcus Garvey." *Ebony* 15 (March 1960): 53-61.

Garvey, Amy J. *Garvey and Garveyism.* Kingston, Jamaica: A. Jacques Garvey, 1963.

———."The Role of Women in Liberation Struggles." *The Massachusetts Review* 13 (Winter-Spring 1972): 109-12.

———, ed. *The Philosophy and Opinions of Marcus Garvey.* 2 vols. 1923-25. Reprint. New York: Atheneum, 1969.

Hill, Robert. *Marcus Garvey and the Universal Negro Improvement Association Papers.* 7 vols. Los Angeles: University of California Press, 1983-86.

Hine, Darlene Clark, ed. *Black Women in America.* Brooklyn: Carlson Publishing, 1993.

Lewis, Ida. "Mrs. Garvey Talks with Ida Lewis." *Encore* 2 (May 1973): 66-68.

Martin, Tony. *Race First: Ideological and Organizational Struggle of Marcus Garvey and the Universal Negro Improvement Association.* Westport, Conn.: Greenwood Press, 1976.

Negro World, 1922-28.

Reed, Beverley. "Amy Jacques Garvey: Black, Beautiful & Free." *Ebony* 26 (June 1971): 45-54.

Smith, Honor Ford. "Women and the Garvey Movement in Jamaica." In *Garvey: His Work and Impact,* edited by Rupert Lewis and Patrick Bryan. Trenton, N.J.: Africa World Press, 1991.

Taylor, Ula Yvette. "Black Women and Political Activism: Amy Jacques Garvey." Master's thesis, University of California—Santa Barbara, 1987.

COLLECTIONS:

Information on Amy Jacques Garvey and Marcus Garvey may be found in the Marcus Garvey Memorial Collection, Fisk University Library.

Bettye Collier-Thomas

Mercedes Gilbert
(1889-1952)
Actress, poet, songwriter, playwright, novelist

The face of Mercedes Gilbert is forever preserved in the annals of African American cultural history because of her roles in several race films of the silent era. Notably, she appeared in a supporting role in Oscar Micheaux's film *Body and Soul,* starring Paul Robeson. Gilbert's significant contributions to society, however, were not limited to acting in silent films. She was well known during the 1920s and 1930s for numerous appearances in Broadway plays and on radio and for her one-woman theatrical presentations. Gilbert wrote and published songs, poetry, plays, and an obscure but significant novel. Scholars have noted that like the writings of Zora Neale Hurston, Gilbert's fiction work *Aunt Sara's Wooden God* documents folk life in the rural South, providing an important commentary on African American social history.

Mercedes Gilbert was born in Jacksonville, Florida, in 1889. Her father, Daniel Marshall Gilbert, had a furniture business while her mother, Edna Earl Knott Gilbert, owned a dressmaking enterprise. Mercedes Gilbert's early life is recorded in a brief unpublished autobiography preserved at the Schomburg Center for Research in Black Culture of the New York Public Library. As a child, Mercedes was apparently taught by a nurse at home for her kindergarten and primary grades. She entered school for the first time in the fourth grade at Boylan Home, a girls' seminary in Jacksonville.

Gilbert started writing poetry when she was six years old and had many opportunities to publicly recite her poems because her mother was a dedicated volunteer at the African Methodist Episcopal church that the family attended. When the Gilberts moved to Tampa, Florida, Mercedes Gilbert was enrolled in a Catholic school for a time. She later attended the Orange Park Normal and Industrial School before entering college at Edward Waters College in Jacksonville. After graduating from college, Gilbert was a teacher in southern

Mercedes Gilbert

Florida for a brief while. She decided to pursue nursing and entered the Brewster Hospital Nurses Training School. Upon graduation from nursing school, Gilbert worked at Brewster as assistant superintendent for two years. While still in school, she wrote a book of poems, *Looking Backward,* as well as several plays.

Gilbert moved to New York City in 1916 with the intention of practicing nursing. Because the nursing training program that she had completed lacked the reputation of larger hospital training programs, Gilbert was required to complete an additional three-year training program at Lincoln Hospital in order to practice nursing in New York City. Discouraged, she decided not continue in the field.

After supporting herself as a private nurse for a short time, Gilbert began work with Chris Smith, a songwriter, who assisted her in putting her poetry to music. Their first effort, "They Also Ran the Blues," became a hit and was recorded by several record companies. Gilbert managed and wrote songs for a jazz group that consisted of eight instrumentalists and a blues singer. Among her compositions recorded by Arto Records were "The Decatur Street Blues" and "Got the World in a Jug."

Life as Performing Artist Begins

On July 19, 1922, Mercedes Gilbert married Arthur J. Stevenson. In addition to writing songs, she was contributing to the Associated Negro Press. Soon, she would expand her

horizons by beginning an acting career in vaudeville and motion pictures. Her Broadway debut came in 1927 in *The Lace Petticoat.* The cast of 150, which was mostly white, included Daniel Haynes, a group of black male singers, and Gilbert. She went on to appear in *Bamboola; Home Bound; Play, Genius Play;* and *Lula Belle.* One of Gilbert's most memorable stage portrayals began in 1930 when she played the part of Zipporah, Moses's wife, during the five-year Broadway run and tour of *Green Pastures.* Succeeding the famous actress Rose McClendon, Gilbert played the interesting role of Cora Lewis during the 1935-36 Broadway season of Langston Hughes's play *Mulatto.* She performed in all-black productions of *Lysistrata* and *Tobacco Road,* and, in 1937, *How Come, Lawd.* Gilbert went on tour with her one-woman dramatic presentations beginning in 1941. In addition to her drama tours, she lectured on black history at colleges across the country.

In 1931, Gilbert published a collection of her writings entitled *Selected Gems of Poetry, Comedy and Drama.* It includes monologues in the southern dialect, such as "Talk on Evolution," and lyric poems like "Dreams" and "Loneliness." The monologues in this publication were compiled from radio broadcasts that Gilbert had made over the years. Also within the volume is the play *Environment,* a domestic melodrama about a woman's problems with her runaway husband and unproductive son. Gilbert wrote two other plays, *In Greener Pastures* and *Ma Johnson's Harlem Rooming House.*

In his forward to Gilbert's novel *Aunt Sara's Wooden God,* Langston Hughes compares the work to *Jonah's Gourd Vine* by Zora Neale Hurston and to *Ollie Miss* by George W. Henderson. Hughes writes that Gilbert's novel is the everyday story of thousands of black families below the Mason-Dixon line who were "living their enclosed lives always in hope that someday some one of them may escape the family group and go on to higher things. Their tragedy is that there is so small a foundation on which to base such a hope." The story is about a mulatto country boy whose mother worships him, but who cannot live up to her faith in him because of his conceit and insecurities. Ironically, he remains Aunt Sara's hero even in death although he has hurt so many people.

In *Negro Voices in American Fiction,* critic Hugh M. Gloster classifies Gilbert's novel under "Negro Fiction of the Depression." *Aunt Sara's Wooden God* is described as folk realism that deals with "miscegenation and intraracial color prejudice."

Gilbert died in March of 1952 at Queens General Hospital in Jamaica, New York. Her last address was listed as 108-13 164th Street, Jamaica, New York. She was survived by her husband. Gilbert contributed much to African American cultural history as a poet, songwriter, actress, and novelist. Her acting is one of the early examples of blacks in American cinema; her stage career as well as performances for radio and television have been recognized. Most significantly, Americans are deeply indebted to Mercedes Gilbert for her portrayal of southern rural life and issues of intraracial prejudice in *Aunt Sara's Wooden God.*

REFERENCES:

Gilbert, Mercedes. *Aunt Sara's Wooden God.* Boston: Christopher Publishing House, 1938.

————. *Selected Gems of Poetry, Comedy and Drama.* Boston: Christopher Publishing House, 1931.

Gloster, Hugh M. *Negro Voices in American Fiction.* Chapel Hill: University of North Carolina Press, 1948.

Hatch, James V., and Omanii Abdullah, eds. *Black Playwrights 1823-1977.* New York: Bowker, 1977.

"Mercedes Gilbert, Stage, Radio Actress." Obituary. *New York Times,* March 6, 1952.

Roses, Lorraine, and Ruth Elizabeth Randolph. *Harlem Renaissance and Beyond.* Boston: G. K. Hall, 1990.

Rush, Theressa Gunnels, Carol Fairbanks Myers, and Esther Spring Arata. *Black American Writers Past and Present.* Vol. 1. Metuchen, N.J.: Scarecrow Press, 1975.

Dawn Cooper Barnes

Thelma Thurston Gorham

Thelma Thurston Gorham
(1913-1991)
Journalist, educator, editor, writer, administrator

"She never let any obstacle or barrier stand in her way. She was a drum major for journalists, when it was difficult and dangerous for black people to enter the field. She was journalism at FAMU," said Frederick Humphries, president of Florida Agricultural and Mechanical University, where Thelma Thurston Gorham taught. "There was no stopping her," Humphries continued in the January 8, 1992, *Tallahassee Democrat.* During a career that spanned over fifty years Gorham devoted herself to writing, primarily stories for newspapers and magazines, and teaching journalism. She was a key figure in publicizing the cultural contributions of blacks in the black press.

Thelma Thurston Gorham was born on February 21, 1913, in Kansas City, Missouri, to Frank Thurston and Bertha Pearl Smith Thurston. Reared in segregated Kansas City, she knew firsthand the prejudice and discrimination that blacks faced during the period. She attended the public schools in Kansas City designated for blacks. In 1925 she and her mother moved to Detroit. After school hours as a twelve-year-old, she worked as a domestic with her mother in Detroit. Gorham knew then that she did not want to be a maid for life. She was convinced she would attend college and obtain an education.

Gorham was denied admission to the University of Missouri because of her African American descent. She also considered the University of Kansas in Lawrence, but decided against the school because it did not allow black people to swim in the campus pool. She is quoted in the October 24, 1991, *Florida Flambeau* as saying, "They thought our skin color would come off." Gorham pursued an undergraduate degree in journalism at the University of Minnesota in Minneapolis. The only black woman in the journalism program, she experienced many inequities, but decided to remain in her chosen field of study. When she took a course in journalism, the instructor failed to arrange an internship for her, although he set one up for other members of the class. Gorham was one of three black women in the entire senior class of 1935. After graduating, she became the police beat reporter for the *Kansas City Call.* By 1938 she was editor of the Kansas City, Kansas, bureau of the *Call.* From 1935 to 1941 she was also the chief feature writer.

Married in 1939 to Richard Gorham, an army officer, she followed him from one army base to another during World War II. Although the moves interrupted her career, she always managed to find a job in her field and to be a good mother to her son, Daryl Theodore. The Gorhams divorced in 1961. At one point Gorham was the only female editor for the *Apache Sentinel,* an official U.S. army publication at Fort Huachuca, Arizona, where black troops and the Women's Army Auxiliary Corps trained during World War II. From 1942 to 1944 Gorham worked at this army base as an editor, teacher, and public relations person. From 1947 to 1951 she was a professor of journalism at Lincoln University in Jefferson City, Missouri, which was the state-supported college for black students. She then returned to the University of Minnesota for further study and received her master's degree in 1951. During the 1950s she was an accredited correspondent for the United Nations Conference of International Organizations. While in New York, she wrote articles on the development of

U.S. policies toward the Third World for eight different newspapers. In the 1950s Gorham also worked as managing editor for the *Oklahoma Black Dispatch* and the *Oklahoma Eagle.*

In the 1960s Gorham expanded her career by becoming director of the Opportunities Industrialization Center in Kansas City, Missouri. OIC provided vocational and academic programs for persons whose entrance into the labor market had been halted because of their lack of education or skills. Many of the programs the center offered to lower-income blacks were successful.

Journalism and Teaching Career Combined

Gorham also continued to teach in the 1960s. In 1962-63, she worked at Central Senior High School in Kansas City, Missouri. She later received an associate professorship at Florida Agricultural and Mechanical University, a historically black college. She returned to the University of Minnesota from 1968 to 1971 as an instructor in communications. Gorham went back to FAMU again in 1971. Along with her teaching career she was a reporter for *Jet* and *Ebony* magazines from 1954 to 1984.

From the 1940s to the 1990s Gorham was a popular teacher. Her students loved her and considered her a role model. Lore Tellone, a student in her feature writing class at FAMU, told the *Florida Flambeau,* October 24, 1991, "I believe in her brilliance, in her capability and in her as a valuable contributor to her field. She has led several generations into the field of journalism. The students respected her very much." One of her colleagues at FAMU, Gale Workman, stated in the same article, "What used to amaze us is that she would turn to her desk and effortlessly, in about half an hour, type out those incredible columns." She constantly recalled stories of famous people she had interviewed.

Before she retired from FAMU around 1991, Gorham's office contained over thirty plaques honoring her accomplishments. Tables and bookcases in her office were stacked with her papers, articles, and books. A prolific writer, she communicated with the public in every way possible—as an author of children's books, a public relations officer on an army base, a high school teacher, college professor, reporter, and political activist. She told the *Florida Flambeau,* October 24, 1991, "I am a survivor. And I will keep on punching to get where I'm going. I have a number of gigs. I have not played out."

In spite of her forceful personality, Gorham struggled to achieve in her field. As a black woman, she had to push hard to open doors of opportunity. Victimized by sexism and racism, her ascent in journalism was difficult. Although she was initiated into Theta Sigma Phi, an honorary sorority for women, she was later dismissed from the group because she was considered an aggressive black. To be sure, she failed to obtain several positions because of her color and her feisty manner. Notwithstanding these difficulties, Gorham maintained an optimistic attitude and a determined spirit as she set her goals in life. She told the *Florida Flambeau,* October 24, 1991,

I guess my being a woman and of African-American ethnicity has caused some doors to be closed, but I'm not concerned. I feel that when one of those doors closes, another is opened somewhere.

Gorham was not motivated by the feminist movement or black militancy, but by the need to accomplish something personally. "I dictate my own standards and am in competition only with myself," she said in the February 8, 1976, issue of the *Tallahassee Democrat.*

Gorham loved teaching, for teaching was the means by which she could repay the help she had been given in past years. She recalled that Scottie P. Davis, her English teacher in high school, taught and encouraged her to write. Now it was her turn to teach others and pay her dues. She further stated in the *Tallahassee Democrat,* "What you put into the lives of other people, they in turn put into other people. It has a domino effect." Despite the length of time she had been a teacher, she was constantly amazed by the number of college students who lacked skills in reading and writing. She tried to educate the total person even though the student was in a journalism class.

Gorham's concern for the student did not go unnoticed. Boy Ruggles, chairman of FAMU's School of Journalism, commented on Gorham in the same *Tallahassee Democrat* article:

She doesn't put up with any foolishness from her students. She makes them produce and tow the line. They have to do things right and on time because that is how it is done on the outside.

The students nicknamed her T. T. (for Thelma Thurston) and constantly spoke of her dedication to them. Her maternal quality and love for her students encouraged them to seek her counsel on personal matters. She said in the *Tallahassee Democrat* piece, "After all, a university is an alma mater. It has to serve that function."

Writes on Black Themes

Gorham's reporting always revealed her interest in black life and history. She said during an interview for the *Tallahassee Democrat,* February 8, 1976, "Blacks made so many contributions to different cultures that were never publicized until recently." Hence, Gorham decided that during her lifetime she would report the untold stories about black accomplishments. As a child the only news stories she read about black people in the major newspapers concerned murderers, juvenile delinquents, or robbers. Only Joe Louis, the boxer, received favorable treatment in the press. Unless they appeared in stories in the black press, black accomplishments were ignored. She decided as a youth that if she became a journalist, she would write about the positive actions of blacks.

Gorham found racism in the newsroom. To avoid it, she wrote numerous free-lance articles, searching for authentic black experiences. For example, she wrote about the character and spirit of Thurgood Marshall, the first black justice on the U.S. Supreme Court. Up until the early 1980s she was the most exciting black female journalist in the country. She arranged interviews with black scholars, actors, writers, musicians, dancers, political leaders, and athletes. Gorham strove to portray her subjects honestly; to her, fidelity to her material was an art.

Gorham was firm in her beliefs and had an opinion on everything, according to those who knew her. "Politics is a mess and Reagan and Bush should have been impeached," she said in the January 9, 1992, *Florida Flambeau.* "What we have in Washington are a bunch of lawyers and everyone else playing footsie with the corporate structure," she continued. She had already decided not to pursue politics after running for the Kansas City Board of Education in the early 1960s. One of the men on the board tried to bribe her not to run. She felt that both white men and black men in Kansas City had sexist attitudes toward her.

As a serious black professional, Gorham tried to do well in her job. Many managers of newspapers believed that blacks generally were not viewed by the public as full-fledged journalists but as African Americans who offered valuable black point of view. Such complaints can still be heard from managers in newsrooms across the U.S. Since Gorham wrote for black magazines and newspapers, her morale never plunged too low, but she constantly lamented the fact that opportunities for minorities were limited in the field of journalism. Many of the larger news organizations in the U.S. provided internships to bring blacks into the journalism business, but few managed to enter.

Gorham was a pioneer in the field of journalism. At the beginning of her career in the 1930s she was the first black female reporter in the United States. By the early 1980s she was still listed as one of only fifteen black women to finish from major universities belonging to the American Association of Schools and Departments of Journalism.

Gorham participated in several organizations, including Alpha Kappa Alpha Sorority, Drifters, Urban League Guild, and Sigma Delta Chi Society of Professional Journalists. She is listed in *Who's Who and Why of Successful Florida Women.* Gorham was a member of the collective bargaining team for the United Faculties of Florida National Education Association. She was also a member of the civilian/nonmilitary Service Command Unit 1922 and served as editor of the post newspaper. She was selected as a Kellogg Fellow in Mass Communications, 1977-78. In 1986 the Tallahassee chapter of the National Association of Black Journalists designated her recipient of the First Black Communicator Hall of Fame Award.

In 1954, Gorham became an adherent of Baha'i, a religious movement that originated in Iran in the nineteenth century. Although she had been familiar with the religion, she accepted the faith because she wanted her son to have a religious base as he matured. Baha'i was the philosophy that guided her constantly. "One concern of Baha'i is to flow into a pattern of serving others. So whenever I feel there is a way I can serve I do," she said in the February 8, 1976, *Tallahassee Democrat.*

Gorham died of natural causes in her home in Tallahassee, Florida, on January 7, 1992. Funeral services were held at the Bethel Missionary Baptist Church and she was buried at Southside Cemetery. Her death marked the end of five decades of struggle to remove racial barriers in the journalism trade, both in the newsroom and in the classroom where her students trained for the field.

REFERENCES:

Brennan, Beth. *Who's Who and Why of Successful Florida Women.* Vol. 1. Winter Park, Fla.: Currier, Davis Publishing, 1985.
Duckworth, Erika. "Journalism Professor Irreplaceable." *Capitol Outlook* 18 (January 16-22, 1992): 1.
"Gorham Remembered As Real Force At FAMU." *Tallahassee Democrat,* January 8, 1992.
"Gorham's Life Offered Lessons of Lasting Value." *Atlanta Journal/Atlanta Constitution,* January 9, 1992.
"Legacy of A Pioneer." *The Famuan,* January 16, 1991.
"Pioneer Journalist Isn't Finished Yet." *Florida Flambeau,* October 24, 1991.
"Thelma Gorham is Quiet Black Leader." *Tallahassee Democrat,* February 8, 1976.
"Thelma Gorham Popular FAMU Professor." *Florida Flambeau,* January 9, 1992.
"A Warrior's Light Goes Out." *Tallahassee Democrat,* January 11, 1992.

Joan C. Elliott

Rosa L. Gragg
(1904-1989)
Educator, school founder, clubwoman, civic worker, church worker

Rosa Gragg devoted her life to uplifting the community, first in rural Georgia where she was a teacher and school principal and later in Detroit, Michigan, where she founded the Slade-Gragg Academy of Practical Arts. As the sixteenth president of the National Association of Colored Women, she guided the organization through many important accomplishments, including getting the Frederick Douglass Home in Anacostia, Virginia, listed on the National Register

Rosa L. Gragg

of Historic Sites. Gragg's involvement in civic activities extended beyond her women's club work. By presidential appointment, she sat on several federal committees that addressed, among other topics, issues of race and gender. She was also very active in civic affairs in Detroit, helping, for example, to plan the city's 250th anniversary celebration and participating in local historic preservation efforts.

Born April 30, 1904, in Hampton, Georgia, Rosa L. Slade Gragg was the daughter of Willis O. Slade, a minister, and Sarah V. Haynes Slade. After receiving her elementary and secondary education in Georgia, she graduated from Morris Brown College, Atlanta, Georgia, with a bachelor of arts degree summa cum laude. She did further study at Tuskegee Institute (now University) in Alabama, Wayne State University in Detroit, and the University of Michigan Rackham Extension in Detroit.

On June 10, 1926, she married James Robert Gragg, a Detroit businessman, who died on December 16, 1956. Their only child, James R. Gragg, Jr., graduated from Howard University, Washington, D.C., in 1957 and received his law degree from Wayne State Law School in 1962. He became a practicing attorney in Detroit and the state of Michigan and a judge.

Rosa Gragg began her career as a teacher in Eatonton, Georgia, where she eventually became principal of Eatonton High School. Later she was principal of Acworth (Georgia) High School. Acworth was one of many educational institutions founded in the South by the Julius Rosenwald Foundation. She led a drive to finance and construct a home econo-

mics and manual training facility for the Rosenwald school building in Acworth. She was also head of the department of English at Central Park College in Savannah, Georgia. In 1946 she founded the Slade-Gragg Academy of Practical Arts in Detroit, known as the Tuskegee of the North. The school closed in 1952.

Active as Clubwoman

Gragg's friendship with Mary McLeod Bethune, founder of the National Council of Negro Women, led to her work as organizer and founder of clubs and groups for black women. Long active with the National Association of Colored Women's Clubs (NACW), in 1941 Gragg led the Detroit Association of Women's Clubs in the purchase of a building—its meeting site—at the cost of twenty-one thousand dollars. The mortgage was paid in full by 1945. She became first vice-president of the national organization in 1957 and was national president from 1958 to 1964, the sixteenth woman to hold the position. In 1959 she began the first midwinter planning conference of the NACW, held at the association's headquarters in Washington, D.C., to launch the Enlistment Campaign for fund-raising and to address the need for membership in the association. It was during the thirty-second biennial convention held in New York City in 1960, over which she presided, that the NACW commissioned historian Charles H. Wesley to write the new history of the NACW. His work, *The History of the National Association of Colored Women's Clubs: A Legacy of Service,* was published in 1984.

Gragg helped to extend the NACW's long interest in the restoration and preservation of the Frederick Douglass home in the Anacostia section of Washington, D.C. In 1961 she launched the restoration program at a ceremony in the District of Columbia where leading educators and politicians were present, along with Joseph K. Douglass, the adopted grandson of Frederick Douglass. Congress passed Senate Bill 2399 in August 1962, which made the home a part of the National Capital Park and Recreation Service. Legislation was signed into law by President John F. Kennedy on September 5, 1962, making the home a national historic site. That year Gragg presented to the White House in memory of Douglass a portrait of Abraham Lincoln that had been in Douglass's library. This was the first time a black organization had presented a gift to the White House. The portrait was to hang in the Lincoln Room.

In 1962, still under Gragg's leadership, the NACW opened, in the District of Columbia, the Women's Health and Guidance Center, an information center that provided health instruction and advice to twenty thousand women who lived in a low-income area where high disease and mortality rates prevailed. The pilot program led to the establishment of two prenatal clinics, a testing program for tuberculosis, health screenings, and massive distribution of public health literature. Under Gragg's administration, the mortgage on the national headquarters building at 1601 R Street, N.W., was paid in full. In 1964 she was unanimously elected president emeritus.

Civic and Church Worker

In addition to the community service she provided through the NACW, Gragg worked through other civic, fraternal, and federal committees to address national and local needs. She was appointed to committees by three U.S. presidents. In 1941 President Franklin D. Roosevelt selected Gragg for the National Volunteers Participation Committee, Office of Civilian Defense. In 1960 President John F. Kennedy named her to the National Women's Advisory Committee of the Treasury Department and the next year to the President's Commission on the Status of Women. President Lyndon B. Johnson chose Gragg to be a member of the National Citizens Committee for Community Relations in 1964. In Michigan, Governor Van Wagoner appointed her advisor on race relations to the Michigan Office of Civil Defense in 1943 and Mayor Van Antwert of Detroit appointed her to the Commission of the Detroit Department of Public Welfare in 1949.

Other examples of her affiliations include the Ghandi Society for Human Rights, Advisory Council of the International Movement for the Atlantic Union, treasurer of the steering committee of the National Women's Committee on Civil Rights, Defense Advisory Committee on Women in the Services, Board of Supervisors of Detroit and Wayne County, and Women's Committee for Detroit Automotive Jubilee. She was a board member of the Women's Division of the Detroit Round Table and of the Women's Association of Goodwill Industries. Active in planning for celebrations in the city of Detroit, Gragg served on the Women's Committee for the 250th anniversary of Detroit, the Detroit Bicentennial Committee, the Detroit Historic Sites Committee, and the Detroit Historic Preservation Committee.

Gragg was active in the National Council of Negro Women, League of Women Voters, Women's International League for Peace and Freedom, the United Negro College Fund, and the Detroit Council of Churches. She was a life member of the NAACP and a member of the March of Dimes United Foundation, the Association for the Study of Afro-American Life and History, and Sigma Gamma Rho Sorority. She was also an honorary member of the Detroit Urban League Guild and of Lambda Kappa Nu and Tau Gamma Delta sororities. Additionally, Gragg served as a member of the board of trustees of Palmer Memorial Institute, Sedalia, North Carolina, and Wilberforce University, Xenia, Ohio.

For her outstanding civic work, Rosa L. Gragg was widely recognized. In 1942 *Crisis* magazine named her one of the first ladies of "Colored America," and in 1946 the *Detroit News* included her in its "Who's Who." In 1972 she was honored by the mayor and city council of Detroit with Rosa L. Gragg Day, and in 1975 the Detroit Public Library's Tribute to Black America honored her as one of twelve Black Detroit Leaders. Other awards received during her career include: recognition for outstanding service to the city by the Detroit

Commission of Public Welfare; outstanding graduate by Morris Brown College Alumni Association; outstanding service to the community by the Detroit Council of Negro Women; Richard Allen Award from the city of Philadelphia; leadership recognition, National Association of Colored Girl's Clubs; the Allen Anvil Award, AME Church; and the March of Dimes Service Award. Gragg received honorary doctorates from Paul Quinn College, then in Waco, Texas (1950), and Monrovia College, Liberia (1955).

A member of Bethel African Methodist Episcopal Church in Detroit, she was the editor of the *AME Recorder,* secretary of the AME's Michigan Conference, superintendent of the Sunday school, and president of the Christian Endeavor League. Also a playwright, she wrote and directed two religious pageants: *The Spirit of Bethel* and *Up on This Rock,* the latter dealing with the history of blacks in Detroit.

After a lengthy illness, Rosa L. Gragg died on Sunday, February 19, 1989, at the age of eighty-six. She was survived by her son, James Robert Gragg, Jr., two granddaughters, and a daughter-in-law, LaBarbara Gragg, superintendent of the Pontiac (Michigan) Public Schools. Services were held at Bethel AME Church, where she had been active. The *Michigan Chronicle,* February 25, 1989, quoted a number of her associates who spoke highly of her work. The minister of her church, Reverend Osborne, said, "Her passing is a great loss to the nation, our community and certainly, Bethel Church." Her longtime friend and business associate, Mary Watson Stewart, called her "a true friend, an open and loyal person whom people could depend on." Vila Payne, then the oldest member of the Women's Association, described her friend and colleague of over fifty years as "the epitome of greatness, a fine worker, a marvelous person." Rosa L. Gragg is remembered most for her concern for the struggles and aspirations of black women but also for her work in her church and the Detroit community.

REFERENCES:

Gragg, Rosa L. Questionnaire. Fisk University Library, September 26, 1966.

"Matriarch of Women's Clubs Distinguished Herself in Career." *Michigan Chronicle,* February 25, 1989.

Rosa L. Slade Gragg. Resume. Fisk University Library.

Wesley, Charles Harris. *The History of the National Association of Colored Women's Clubs.* Washington, D.C.: NACW, 1984.

Who's Who of American Women. 4th ed. Chicago: A. N. Marquis, 1965.

COLLECTIONS:

The papers and memorabilia of Rosa L. Gragg are in the Burton Historical Collection, Detroit Public Library.

Jessie Carney Smith

Micki Grant

Actress, singer, composer-lyricist

Micki Grant stated "Art is the best and most human form of communication." As an actress, singer, and composer-lyricist, she communicates with both children and adults. And her best-known work, the play *Don't Bother Me, I Can't Cope,* in which she starred and for which she composed the music and lyrics, relays a universal message transcending race and class divisions. Not only has Grant made award-winning contributions to the genre of musical theater, she has achieved success as a dramatic actress on both television and the stage and as a composer of advertising jingles.

Micki Grant was born Minnie Perkins in Chicago. In a letter to the author dated December 8, 1994, she described Micki Grant as a "professional name." She says, "Everyone, including my family, felt it suited me." She stated in a June 15, 1994, interview that the commonly published year of her birth, 1941, is incorrect. She said, "I don't reveal my age because of the ageism in the entertainment industry." Her father, Oscar Perkins, was a barber. Her mother, Gussie Perkins, a homemaker, still resides in Chicago. Her sister, Hattie L. Murphy, a retired administrator of the YMCA, also resides in Chicago. Grant spent a happy childhood within a close-knit family. She fondly recalls the visits of her mother's southern relatives.

Grant always knew that she would be in a creative field, and her parents and teachers were supportive of her interests. In a February 1973 *Ebony* article, Grant stated: "My father loved movies and used to sneak my sister and me to the movies, even on Sundays. Since this was a no-no in my religious family, we were told not to tell our mother. . . . That was the beginning."

Grant's first acting performance occurred at age six, when she played the Spirit of Spring in a community center production. By the time she was eight she was reading and writing poetry, and her mother gladly took her to functions that provided opportunities for her to recite poetry publicly. Susan Porche Lawson, her first drama teacher and a lifelong friend, gave her free private drama lessons. Grant got her start in music with free lessons on the double bass, which were given to her by Lucille Davis at McCosh Elementary School. Minnie Rose, a teacher at Englewood High School, encouraged her to write. Grant at one time entertained the idea of becoming a journalist.

After graduating from Englewood High School, Grant attended the Chicago School of Music and the University of Illinois. An accomplished musician on the bass, violin, and piano, Grant played in the orchestra of every school she attended.

Grant left the University of Illinois after three years to pursue her dramatic career in New York. During the 1960s, through a combination of talent, hard work, and luck, she appeared in a number of New York productions, including

Micki Grant

The Blacks, Funnyhouse of a Negro, and *To Be Young, Gifted, and Black.* In 1966 she married Ray McCutcheon, a news film editor at NBC. This marriage lasted twelve years. From 1966 to 1973 Grant played the attorney Peggy Nolan on the television daytime drama *Another World.* This role was the first story line in a daytime drama written for an African American.

Grant Becomes Award-Winning Composer and Lyricist

In 1970 Grant joined the Urban Arts Corps (UAC) in New York as artist-in-residence. Thus began her long and fruitful collaboration with Vinnette Carroll, who had created the UAC as a pilot program of the New York State Council on the Arts. Carroll conceived and directed the hit musical *Don't Bother Me, I Can't Cope,* while Grant was the composer and lyricist of its twenty-one songs and its leading lady. The two-act musical features songs and dances inspired by gospel, jazz, rock, and calypso music, as well as by the blues and traditional ballads. One important result of Grant's involvement with *Don't Bother Me, I Can't Cope* was that she regained her identity as Micki Grant. It indeed felt great to have someone ask her if she was Micki Grant instead of Peggy Nolan.

In the February 1973 *Ebony* article Grant explained the source of the play's universal appeal.

> [The play] attempts to say coping is a basic commitment of a mature, purposeful, involved human being, that we sometimes laugh to keep from crying, that life is not necessarily fair, that happiness is

a by-product, not an end product and that the ways in which we are similar are far greater than the ways in which we are different.

Don't Bother Me, I Can't Cope was first presented by small theaters around New York and elsewhere during the 1970-71 season. Its world premier occurred on September 15, 1971, at Ford's Theater in Washington, D.C., where it ran for thirty-two performances. In *Ebony* Grant stated, "To be truthful, we weren't aiming for Broadway then, but once we got on the road and saw what we had, that became our goal." The musical opened on Broadway in a slightly revised version on April 19, 1972. Unfortunately, Grant's father, whom she describes in an *Ebony* article as a "dreamer to whom nothing was impossible," died just one day before the play's preview showing in New York. The play closed on Broadway October 23, 1973, after 1,065 performances, with most of the original cast. Subsequently it was produced in Los Angeles, Chicago, again in Washington, D.C., and in San Francisco.

After their resounding success with *Don't Bother Me, I Can't Cope,* Grant and Carroll continued their collaboration, which lasted until 1985. Some of Grant and Carroll's productions are *Croesus and the Witch* (1971), based on a fable; *Step Lively Boy* (1972), adapted from an antiwar play by Irwin Shaw; and *The Ups and Downs of Theophilus Maitland* (1974), adapted from a West Indian folktale. Grant also provided some of the music for the Tony-nominated gospel musical *Your Arms Too Short to Box with God* (1975).

In a piece of personal correspondence dated June 15, 1994, Grant said, "I am especially proud of my contribution to the Broadway musical *Working,*" which was adapted by Stephen Schwartz from the book by Studs Terkel. Its score was nominated for a Tony Award in 1978, and it remains popular all around the country.

Diverse Creative Activities

Grant's creative and dramatic talents continue to be used in other ways. Writing commercials, for instance, has been a favorite sideline: she has found composing the lyrics and music to advertise well-known products both fun and profitable. For a short period she hosted the CBS children's show *Around the Corner,* and from 1982 to 1984, she was a cast member of the Emmy Award-winning daytime drama *Guiding Light.*

In 1985 Grant had a dramatic role in *Charlotte Forten's Mission,* a movie aired on public television, and in 1988 acted in *Anchor Man* and *Good Little Girls.* In 1988 she wrote the English lyrics for *Jacques Brel's Blues,* which opened in Paris. Her most recently completed project is *Carver (Don't Underestimate a Nut),* a play about the life of George Washington Carver, for which she wrote the book, music, and lyrics. The play was created for the Emmy Gifford Children's Theater. Presently she is writing a screenplay about a young woman inspired by the life of Bessie Coleman, an African American stunt and exhibition aviator.

Grant is an associate artist at Crossroad Theater Company in New Brunswick, New Jersey. Her next project for

Crossroads is a musical piece about a vibrant, talented singer who has to remind "the youngsters" that she is not ready to be put out to pasture.

Grant has been honored for her achievements on a number of occasions. She received numerous awards for *Don't Bother Me, I Can't Cope,* including the NAACP Image Award, two Drama Desk awards, an Obie Award, and two Outer Circle Critics' awards. In 1990 borough president Howard Golden issued the fourth proclamation for a "Micki Grant Day" in Brooklyn. And a similar proclamation was issued in 1993 by Mayor Sharpe James for the city of Newark, New Jersey.

Grant enjoys her work so much that she has developed few hobbies. She is energized by working on more than one project at a time. Fulfilling a long-deferred goal of completing her college education, she graduated summa cum laude with a B.A. degree in humanities from Herbert Lehman College of the City University of New York. She keeps physically active by walking in her Upper West Side Manhattan neighborhood.

Religion and family are still very important in her life. She attends her family reunion every two years, and she is active with the Canaan Baptist Church in Harlem.

When asked in a June 15, 1994, interview what advice she would give to any young person considering a show business career, Grant said, "Be sure you love it [show business] so much you can't do anything else." Her creative drive has resulted in works of very wide appeal, indicating that she indeed loves what she does. Grant exudes a well-being that suggests she is happy with her accomplishments, her present projects, and her many creative plans for the future.

Current Address: 250 West 94th Street, Apartment 6, New York, NY 10025.

REFERENCES:

Directory of Blacks in the Performing Arts. 2nd ed. Metuchen, N.J.: Scarecrow Press, 1990.
Grant, Micki. Letters to Phiefer L. Browne, June 15, 1994; December 8, 1994.
———. Telephone interview with Browne, June 15, 1994.
"Micki Grant: She Can Cope." *Ebony* 4 (February 1973): 100-09.

Phiefer L. Browne

Gray, Ida
See Nelson Rollins, Ida Gray

Eloise Greenfield
(1929-)
Children's author

Eloise Greenfield, one of the most popular and prolific writers of children's literature, said in *Something about the Author:* "Writing is my work. It is work that is in harmony with me; it sustains me. I want, through my work, to help sustain children."

Greenfield was born May 17, 1929, in Parmele, North Carolina, the second child of Weston W. and Lessie Jones Little. Her older brother was Wilbur. Parmele had very few permanent jobs available, so her father worked at many seasonal jobs on farms and in tobacco warehouses. When Greenfield was three months old, her father went north to Washington, D.C., to find a job and a place for them to live. A few weeks later, he sent for his family. After a series of temporary jobs, he finally found a permanent job with People's Drug Store, making deliveries on a bicycle and cleaning the store.

By the time Greenfield was eight years old, she had moved five times and had attended three schools. Rent was very high so her family had always lived with relatives and friends and shared the rent. Her parents' dream was to be able to rent a place for just their family. This dream finally came true when they were selected to be one of 274 families to live in Langston Terrace, a new low-rent housing project in northeast Washington. Young Eloise loved Langston Terrace, especially the playground that was the center of the complex. Another added attraction was the library, which was less than five minutes from her home. It was a good place to grow up, with caring neighbors, family and friends. Greenfield's life was that of a typical teenager, with music (studying piano and singing with groups), dancing, church, and school.

The greatest of all problems she faced was racism. The schools were segregated and though black people could sit anywhere on the streetcars, they were not allowed to sit down at drugstore soda fountains. Though Washington had its racial problems, Greenfield learned more about racism on visits to her grandparents in Norfolk, Virginia, and Parmele, North Carolina. She saw the chain gangs on the roadside and felt the racial prejudice when she—a child of twelve years—was told to go to the back of a very crowded bus in Norfolk. This was something she had never had to do before.

The beginning of World War II brought more changes. Being a teenager had its own way of keeping the seriousness of war out of Greenfield's life. However, when a neighbor's husband was killed, her screams into the night brought the grim reality of war into Greenfield's consciousness. Later, another neighbor, Bobby Greenfield, was drafted into the war. They had known each other since she was thirteen and each had told friends that they liked each other, but they had never told each other. That night they promised to write each other. Their letters were long and friendly, but not necessarily romantic. Meanwhile, Greenfield's life continued in a normal way. She graduated from high school at seventeen and attended Miner's Teacher's College (now the University of the District of Columbia) from 1947 to 1949, at which time she dropped out and took a clerk-typist job at the U.S. Patent Office. On April 29, 1950, five years after they promised to write each other, she married Robert Greenfield, who was now a procurement specialist. They later had two children, Steven and Monica.

Writing Career Begins

Greenfield's writing career began while she was still working at the U.S. Patent Office, but when three short stories were rejected, she gave it up, supposedly forever. However, in 1963 she published her poem, "To a Violin," in the *Hartford Times*. After this, she joined the District of Columbia Black Writers Workshop and seriously began developing her writing career. Throughout the 1970s and 1980s Greenfield published about two children's books a year, all with much success.

In *Something about the Author,* Greenfield says the following of herself as a writer:

> I want to be one of those who can choose and order words that children will want to celebrate. I want to make them shout and laugh and blink back tears and care about themselves. They are our future. They are beautiful. They are for loving.

Greenfield's books have often focused on the more difficult issues children encounter in their lives. In *Talk about a Family,* Greenfield tells the story of Genny, a little girl facing the painful breaking up and rearranging of her family unit. In both *Alesia* and *Darlene,* Greenfield tells the stories of handicapped children. In *Sister,* Doretha learns to use the good times as stepping stones, as bridges for the bad times. Greenfield has also written biographies of Rosa Parks, Paul Robeson, and Mary McLeod Bethune. She told *Something about the Author* that her goal in writing these books was "to make children aware of the people who have contributed to the struggle for black liberation."

A look at Greenfield's career shows how greatly successful she has been. She was writer-in-residence for the District of Columbia Commission on the Arts and Humanities in 1973 and again from 1985 to 1987. She was participant in numerous school and library programs and workshops for children and adults; member of the District of Columbia Black Writer' Workshop (co-director of adult fiction, 1971-73, director of children's literature, 1973-74); and a member of the African American Writers Guild and Authors Guild. She has been a contributor to numerous publications, including *World Book Encyclopedia, Black World, Cricket, Ebony, Jr., Horn Book, Negro Digest, Interracial Books for Children Bulletins, Ms., Negro History Bulletin, Scholastic Scope, Washington Post,* and numerous anthologies.

Greenfield has received a multitude of awards and honors recognizing her writing. These include the Carter G. Woodson Book Award from the National Council for Social

Studies, 1974, for *Rosa Parks* and the Irma Simonton Black Award from Bank Street College of Education, 1974, for *She Come Bringing Me That Little Baby Girl. Sister* was selected one of *New York Times* Outstanding Books of the Year in 1974.

In 1976 she was awarded the Women's International League for Peace and Freedom Award, and Coretta Scott King Award Honor Book citation from the American Library Association, both for *Paul Robeson.* She has also received the Coretta Scott King Award, 1978, for *African Dream. Childtimes* was named a *Boston Globe-Horn Book* Award Nonfiction Honor Book and one of the New York Public Library's Books for the Teen Age in 1980 and 1981. For the body of her work she won the National Black Child Development Institute Award in 1981 and the Mills College Award in 1983. She was recipient of the Jane Addams Children's Book Award from the Jane Addams Peace Association; Greenfield received the Washington, D.C., Mayor's Art Award in Literature in 1983.

Eloise Greenfield has accomplished her goals and in doing so she has created a notable legacy. Her writings will sustain and entertain the children of today and tomorrow as well as continue to enrich their lives.

Current Address: P.O. Box 29077, Washington, DC 20017.

REFERENCES:

Something about the Author. Vol. 61. Detroit: Gale Research, 1993.
Who's Who among Black Americans, 1994-95. 8th ed. Detroit: Gale Research, 1994.

COLLECTIONS:

Eloise Greenfield's literary works are in the Kerlan Collection at the University of Minnesota.

Phyllis Wood

Pam Grier
(1949-)
Actress

A former switchboard operator, Pam Grier became one of the busiest actresses in Hollywood in the 1970s and the queen of blaxploitation films. The character type she established and became identified with—the beautiful and sexy black woman who was at the same time fiercely aggressive, resilient, jubilant, and raunchy—led her to become a pinup girl for black college males and a fresh, welcome image for white women in the liberation movement. By pioneering a

Pam Grier

new role for black women in film, she made an important contribution to black film history.

Pamela Suzette Grier was born in Winston-Salem, North Carolina, on May 26, 1949. The second of three children, she has a sister and a brother. She grew up on one military base after another, as her father, an airplane mechanic in the U.S. Air Force, was shipped about. Her mother was a registered nurse. The family moved to Swindon, England, when Grier was five years old. They lived on military bases until she was fourteen. She especially appreciated the teachers and the education she received during her stay abroad. While the family had little money, Grier's parents believed strongly in education and reading. They were able to purchase a set of encyclopedias for their children to use in the home. The Grier children were only to shop for clothing at Goodwill stores or through Sears and Roebuck catalogs. Sometimes older relatives would send clothing they no longer used to the Grier children and Pam "wore them proudly, very proudly," she told Louie Robinson for *Ebony* magazine, June 1974. She also enjoyed the clothes she received from Goodwill because they were practically new, sometimes the discards of rich people.

When Grier was fourteen, the family returned to the United States and settled in Denver. She learned the "mean streets" of the rough Denver neighborhood where her family lived and shed her British accent so that she would blend in better with the local culture. Her European experiences probably made her appear to be a snob to her peers. She told Patrick Salvo for *Sepia,* February 1976, "I spoke English with an accent and liked having tea at four o'clock in the afternoon." Life on military bases had been sheltered and relatively noncompetitive, while in Denver Grier had to fight for survival: for example, she either struggled to keep her lunch money or pretended that she had none.

When she was a teenager, Grier's parents separated. Although she had known that the marriage was not harmonious, the actual breakup, which occurred without her parents offering the children an explanation, was so disturbing to her that she tried to punish them by not speaking for a week. However, the split did not disturb her sense of family or cause Grier to abandon the set of house rules that her mother had set. Education was still paramount, and Grier remained an A student. Grier recalls one teacher in Denver who questioned the intellectual ability and potential of black people and led her to grow up thinking she was basically stupid. Her family also contributed to her insecurity and confusion about herself. While telling her one day that she was beautiful, the next day the family might warn her that she was "nothing special." Consequently, she was uncertain about both her intellectual ability and her appeal.

After graduating from high school, Grier enrolled in Denver's Metropolitan State College with plans to become a pathologist. For a time she was a cheerleader for the Denver Broncos. Despite her conflicting feelings about her beauty and talent, Grier became second runner-up in the Colorado state competition for the Miss Universe Beauty Pageant. She entered a second beauty contest in Colorado Springs. Luckily for Grier, the contest was held at the hotel where comics Dan Rowan and Dick Martin were staying; their agent, Dave Baumgarten, witnessed the activity and invited her to move to Hollywood. The demand for black performers was high at the time, yet Grier expressed no interest in an acting career. Later, however, when Grier spent a vacation in Los Angeles, her mother, who had an unfulfilled desire to be an actress and singer, encouraged Grier to accept Baumgarten's offer. A dinner meeting with Baumgarten and his staff apparently helped convince her to move to Los Angeles. She left school and moved in 1968 to Los Angeles, where she lived with her cousin, Roosevelt (Rosey) Grier, a professional football player and later actor.

Film Career of Superstar Begins

Grier accepted a job as a switchboard operator with American International Pictures (AIP) and at the same time studied acting. While at AIP she carefully examined the story boards in the projection room, learned some technical aspects of filmmaking, and absorbed as much information about the inside workings of the business as possible. She listened in on calls while working the switchboard and learned that a producer was casting for a new film, a grade B movie entitled *The Big Bird Cage.* She landed a bit part in the film—her first—in 1969, when she was twenty years old. Grier's career progressed from there as she played various roles throughout the next decade in blaxploitation movies: a genre of films popular in the 1970s that featured predominantly black casts. She had lead roles in the films *Beyond the Valley of the Dolls* (1969) and *The Big Doll House* (1971). Her first big break came in 1972 when she played the leading role in *Coffy.* The film,

which cost $700,000 to make and grossed $8.5 million, made Grier a recognized star, launching a series of films and a multipicture contract for her with American International. That year she also played in *Women in Cages* and *Scream, Blacula, Scream* and appeared in a starring role in *Black Mama, White Mama* (based on the novel *The Defiant Ones*). She also had a brief, five-minute part in *Cool Breeze* and a major role as a pornography queen in *Hit Man.* She had the title role in *Foxy Brown* (1974). The next year she played a title role again, this time in *Friday Foster,* and also appeared in *The Arena* and *Bucktown.* Grier was the panther woman in *Twilight People* and played in *Drum* as well as *Greased Lightning,* all in 1977. Her other films are *Sheba Baby* (1975); *Fort Apache, the Bronx* (1981); *Something Wicked This Way Comes* (1983); and *Above the Law* (1988).

Grier played a variety of roles in her films, and she set precedents as a black actress. When her films ran in Chicago she was featured in quadruple bill that highlighted her ability to depict a range of personality types. A sexy godmother in *Coffy* and a flapper in *Foxy Brown,* she retained more of her natural look in *Sheba Baby,* then was demure and glamorous in *Friday Foster.* It was at this time that sources called her movies the only ones to show women who triumphed over men. While she was sometimes called "the black Raquel Welch" and her films earned her a number of questionable accolades, such as "Mocha Mogel" and "Super Sass," she told *Sepia,* February 1976, "I'm not at all like the way I am in my pictures." In reality, she felt she was an ordinary black woman who did not match the images she portrayed on film.

In *Blacks in American Films and Television,* Donald Bogle calls her "a sex symbol and the queen of B movies." She had started out in low-budget action and exploitation films and then moved on to rowdy, gaudy, cheap movies that earned big money at the box office. Bogle summarized the image in which she was cast: "A sexy, foul-mouthed, gun-totin' woman of action, who, if necessary, could bomb, burn, beat, shoot, or even castrate her way through any trying situation."

Since she had also posed nude in the black magazine *Players,* disrobed in some of her films, and had not played respectable roles, Bogle said that she enjoyed a lopsided stardom. However, not only was she a pinup girl for college men, but other groups came to view her image as socially significant for the time. Indeed, with her independent and forceful persona, she set a precedent for all black women in film and her work is important in black film history. She called herself an actress, not a sex object; she never felt exploited or that she exploited anyone. That the public could think she deliberately demeaned black women disturbed her intensely. She stated in the January 1979 issue of *Essence:*

> I make no apologies for the women I created. Actually I recreated. When I grew up I knew a certain kind of Black woman who was the sole support of her family and who would, if you disrepected her, beat you into the cement. She was the glue that held her family together, got them through. I admired her greatly. I still do. And she

still exists. I brought that lady to the screen—played her to the bone!

I created a new kind of screen woman. Physically strong and active, she was able to look after herself and others. If you think about it, you'll see she was the prototype for the more recent and very popular white Bionic and Wonder Women.

Life After Movie Stardom

After blaxploitation films became unpopular, about 1978, Grier dropped out of public view for a time, refused interviews, and would not reveal her activities. Concerned about her image, she became very selective in the roles she accepted. Grier now insisted that her name as an actress be changed to Pamela, which is, of course, her legal name, and greatly resisted the typecasting she had become accustomed to.

Education was still important to Grier, now as a means of strengthening her directing and producing skills so that she might enhance her position as an actress, especially in making films for AIP, and to learn the technical side of the business. In 1979 she studied at the University of California, Los Angeles, under director Roman Polanski. She formed her own production company, Brown Sun Productions, which incorporated the pet name her mother gave her when she was a child. Although her image turned around in the 1980s, she has not made a film since 1988. She still lives in Los Angeles.

Early in her career Grier had a close and satisfying relationship with Kareem Abdul-Jabbar, basketball star with the Los Angeles Lakers and a staunch Muslim. However, when she weighed her own background and profession against the requirements of being the wife of a Muslim, she chose to concentrate on her career, which would give her the economic means to support her family. "I wanted to do something for them," she stated in *Ebony,* June 1974. "But he was the most wonderful person in the world that you could ever spend time with." She also had a relationship with actor Richard Pryor but their engagement ended and apparently the two remained friends. "I liked him, I liked his honesty. And his strength. You have to be some kind of strong to be Richard's kind of honest," she said in *Essence* in January 1979.

Grier has been seen on television and she also tested her ability as a stage actress. She appeared on *Midday Live,* the *Mike Douglas Show,* and *Celebrity Sweepstakes* (1975); the *Tonight Show* (1975 and 1976); the *Merv Griffin Show* and *Hollywood Squares* (1976); *Roots: The Next Generation* (1979); *Love Boat* (1980); the *Today Show* (1981); *PBS Latenight, Essence,* and *Tough Enough* (1983); *Badge of the Assassin* and *Miami Vice* (1985); and *Night Court* and *Crime Story* (1986). Her one theater appearance was in *Fool for Love,* which played in Los Angeles in 1985.

Grier has been active in charities, particularly those that address drug abuse, and she has worked for Winnebelle Homes for Retarded Children in Los Angeles. She has also been a sponsor to a number of children all over the world, to whom she sends money for clothing and education. The five-foot-eight-inch-tall actress always gives the illusion of being much taller. By Hollywood standards she might not be beautiful: she has a space between her two front teeth and her nose is almost hooked, which early on led her schoolmates to nickname her "Hawk." But she was still a striking woman in all of her appearances. To keep fit, Grier has long been a jogger and a tennis player.

Though her image on film was controversial at the time, Pam Grier reshaped the movie industry by portraying black women as she had seen them in real life in order to show their strength, not to stereotype them. Her heroines were concerned with the terrifying social conditions in their communities. In her movies women triumphed over men, and she paved the way for new roles for white women. Because of Grier, it became acceptable for women to be strong and gutsy, prompting movie and television executives to bring forth more forceful female characters as positive role models for their audiences.

REFERENCES:

Boyle, Donald. *Brown Sugar.* New York: Harmony Books, 1980.

———. *Blacks in American Films and Television.* New York: Garland Publishing, 1988.

Egbert, Alan. "Pam Grier: Coming into Focus." *Essence* 9 (January 1979): 43, 104, 107-8.

Horton, Lucy. "The Battle among the Beauties." *Ebony* 29 (November 1973): 144-50.

"How to Survive in Hollywood between Gigs." *Ebony* 33 (October 1978): 40.

Mapp, Edward. *Directory of Blacks in the Performing Arts.* 2d ed. Metuchen, N.J.: Scarecrow Press, 1990.

Robinson, Louie. "Pam Grier: More Than Just a Sex Symbol." *Ebony* 31 (June 1974): 33-42.

Salvo, Patrick. "Pam Grier: The Movie Super-Sex Goddess Who's Fed Up with Sex and Violence." *Sepia* 25 (February 1976): 48-56.

Jessie Carney Smith

Lani Guinier

(1950-)

Lawyer, educator

A leading civil rights lawyer, Lani Guinier gained national attention when President Bill Clinton nominated her to head the U.S. Justice Department's civil rights division in April 1993. Although Guinier was considered exceptionally qualified for such a job by many people, Clinton later withdrew the nomination amidst controversy over her legal writings, which raise questions about race and political power in America. Responding to her critics, Guinier stated in an

Lani Guinier

interview, "We may aspire to a race-blind, or color-blind constitution, but we shouldn't confuse ourselves into thinking we live in a race-blind political reality." She further commented, "We have to stop thinking that when black people get some political power, that means white people lose political power."

Carol Lani Guinier was born on April 19, 1950, in New York City. Her grandfather was a Cambridge-trained barrister, and her father, Ewart Guinier, was an attorney and a history professor at Harvard who served as the first chair of the Department of Afro-American Studies. He died in 1990. Her mother, Genii Guinier, is Jewish. Lani Guinier has two sisters. According to a *Ms.* magazine article by Karen Branan, Guinier's mother was keen on teaching her daughters how to get along with others. Although they were raised in a black world, she took them to Jewish family cultural events and informed them that they should see themselves as "bridge people." Dale Russakoff noted in the *Washington Post* that for Lani Guinier, her mother helped her "to see the other person's side, not to internalize rejection, and to be able to fight back." In 1986, she married Nolan A. Bowie, a Philadelphia artist, and they have one son, Nikolas.

Guinier attended public school, graduating third in her high school class of 1,447. Guinier was an editor of her high school newspaper. She received a tuition scholarship to attend Radcliffe that was given by the National Merit Corporation and the *New York Times.* Guinier graduated from Radcliffe College in 1971 and received her law degree from Yale in 1975. Bill Clinton and Hillary Rodham Clinton were among her classmates at Yale. Between 1974 and 1976, she clerked

for Judge Damon Keith of the Sixth Circuit Court of Appeals of Detroit. From 1976 to 1977, Guinier worked as a referee for Wayne County Juvenile Court in Michigan. During the administration of Jimmy Carter, she worked for the civil rights division of the U.S. Department of Justice as an assistant to civil rights division head Drew Days. Between 1981 and 1988, Lani Guinier worked for the NAACP Legal Defense and Education Fund (LDF), the premier civil rights organization in the country. She was chief litigator on voting rights cases. In 1988 she joined the faculty at the University of Pennsylvania Law School.

Guinier's controversial legal articles raise questions about political equality for minorities. They include "No Two Seats: The Elusive Quest for Political Equality," *Virginia Law Review,* November 1991; "Keeping the Faith: Black Voters in the Post-Reagan Era," *Harvard Civil Rights-Civil Liberties Law Review,* 1989; and "The Triumph of Tokenism: The Voting Rights Act and the Theory of Black Electoral Success," *Michigan Law Review,* March 1991. In the latter article, quoted in the *Congressional Quarterly,* she argues, "For those at the bottom, a system that gives everyone an equal chance of having their political preferences physically represented is inadequate. A fair system of political representation would provide mechanisms to ensure that disadvantaged and stigmatized minority groups also have a fair chance to have their policy preferences satisfied."

Following her nomination to head the civil rights division of the U.S. Department of Justice, many of Guinier's critics, in analyzing her writings, suggested that she is an advocate of quotas and does not believe in majority rule. In response to the first accusation, as quoted from the same source, Guinier countered, "I do not believe in quotas. I have never advocated quotas." In fact, Guinier learned from her father the danger of quotas. In 1929, at Harvard College, he was the victim of a racial quota because he was denied financial aid on the grounds that one black student had already been granted a full scholarship. He was also barred from living in the dorms. As a result of his inability to secure financial resources, Ewart Guinier was forced to drop out of Harvard and work as an elevator operator. He later received his law degree from New York University.

In reply to the accusation that she does not believe in majority rule, in an interview on ABC's *Nightline* on June 2, 1993, cited in the *Congressional Quarterly,* Guinier noted:

> I don't have a quarrel with majority rule. And in fact, I believe that the majority should rule. I think that's the essence of democracy. But I would say ... consistent ... with what the Bush and even Reagan administration have said, that in some instances we have to worry, and this was certainly Madison's concern when he talked about the tyranny of a fixed majority. In some instances we also have to worry about protecting the rights of minorities where you have a local majority that may be acting in a prejudiced way to rig or corrupt or abuse the democratic process.

Clinton Withdraws Nomination

On June 3, 1993, President Clinton withdrew the nomination of Guinier, noting that her writings "clearly lend themselves to interpretations that do not represent the views that I expressed on civil rights during my campaign," according to the transcript of his announcement in the *New York Times,* June 4, 1993. In response to the withdrawal, Guinier stated that she felt that the president and many others had misinterpreted her writings. What perhaps disappointed Guinier and her supporters the most was the fact that Clinton refused to allow her to defend her writings before the Senate Judiciary Committee. Following the withdrawal of the nomination, the members of the Congressional Black Caucus were so infuriated that they refused to meet with the president. Leaders of the civil rights community and women's groups were also enraged.

Although the White House admitted that it mishandled the Guinier nomination, many seemed to view the vicious attack on the nominee by conservative elements as their way of getting revenge against those who blocked Robert Bork, one of Ronald Reagan's nominees for the U.S. Supreme Court, from being confirmed. Bork did, however, have an opportunity to defend himself before the Senate Judiciary Committee.

The controversy over the Guinier nomination pushed to the forefront the sensitive debate about race relations in America. As a result of her views, many people have come to see Guinier as a symbol of the ongoing struggle for racial equality. This was most evident at the July 1993 meeting of the NAACP, where she was the recipient of the Torch of Courage award by the association's magazine, *Crisis.*

As a national spokesperson for race relations, Guinier receives numerous speaking invitations. She has published a book on her views entitled *The Tyranny of the Majority* (1994) and has called on President Clinton to convene a summit on race relations. She continues to teach at the University of Pennsylvania Law School.

Current Address: School of Law, University of Pennsylvania, 3400 Chestnut Street, Philadelphia, PA 19104.

REFERENCES:

Branan, Karen. "Lani Guinier: The Anatomy of a Betrayal." *Ms.* IV (September/October 1993): 51.
Garrow, David. Interview with Lani Guinier. *The Progressive* 57 (September 1993): 28.
Idelson, Holly. "Withdrawing Guinier Nomination a No-Win Situation for Clinton." *Congressional Quarterly,* June 5, 1993: 1426.
Russakoff, Dale. "Lani Guinier, in Person: Who She Is and What She Believes in Got Lost in the Furor of Her Nomination." *Washington Post National Weekly Edition,* December 20-26, 1993: 6-9.
"Transcript of President Clinton's Announcement." *New York Times,* June 4, 1993.

Wickman, DeWayne. "Black and White, Can We Talk to Each Other?" *USA Today,* August 2, 1993.

Margaret C. Lee

Bonnie Guiton
(1941-)
Administrator, government official

Throughout her career, Bonnie Guiton has been in positions that show concern for the welfare of people of various cultural and socioeconomic backgrounds; she has worked to improve conditions for staff and students of public schools and colleges and has supported the education of adults and the rights of consumers. In addition to having had a California state appointment, she has worked in assignments with two U.S. presidents and with officials of other countries here and abroad. After an absence of sixteen years, she returned to the field of education in 1992 in the capacity of dean of the McIntire School of Commerce of the University of Virginia in Charlottesville.

Born in 1941 in Springfield, Illinois, as Henrietta Brazelton, Bonnie Guiton's family and friends called her Bunny. Because she disliked having unkind schoolmates transform that nickname into Bunny Rabbit and Peter Cottontail, she informally changed her name to Bonnie, which was much more to her liking. In the late 1980s, she made her adopted nickname her legal first name. Only a few longstanding personal friends and relatives know her as anything other than Bonnie.

Guiton's father, Henry Frank Brazelton, was unprepared to assume the role of husband and parent, so he left her mother, Zola Elizabeth Newman Brazelton, when Guiton was an infant. He had entered into the marriage only at the insistence of her maternal grandfather that he accept responsibility for the fatherhood of his unborn child, who never had the opportunity to know him. In Springfield, Zola Brazelton raised her only child to the best of her ability with the help of her parents. Guiton remembers the loving care of her maternal grandparents, at whose home she and her mother lived for a while, and the company of her aunt, Bernadine Wheatley (Aunt Dean), cousins, and, to a lesser extent, her paternal grandparents.

Guiton's mother, a domestic worker, struggled with alcoholism until she died in 1985, but Guiton knew her mother loved her and wanted her to have a more successful life than hers had been. Guiton and her mother were frequently at odds—they often silently disagreed and there were times when Zola Brazelton took her frustrations out on Bonnie. But during periods of sobriety, Zola offered her daughter encouragement and showed tenderness and an interest in her development. Guiton's mother, a stately, well-spoken wom-

Bonnie Guiton

an, made sure her child received a good, solid foundation in verbal and mathematical skills and that she got early religious training at Saint John Methodist Church in Springfield. When they moved to Oakland, California, Guiton took an active part in Saint John Baptist Church, at one time working in the church office.

Guiton and her mother moved to Oakland in 1954. When her grades began to suffer while attending McClymonds High School she knew it was not due to any lack of ability, but to a feeling that the subject matter had no relevance to her; she was only interested in vocational classes—typing, filing, and office procedures—that were clearly related to the working world she was preparing to enter.

Pursues Education and Career

After she graduated from McClymonds in 1959 and had found her first job, Guiton made a major investment in her personal appearance; regarding herself as homely, she took a course in self-improvement at a modeling school. She boosted her self-confidence by studying the basics of dress and carriage and learning how to choose clothes that brought out the best of her natural beauty. This was the genesis of today's Bonnie Guiton—poised, self-confident, and well-dressed.

In 1966, Bonnie Guiton married Harvey Guiton Jr. They ended the marriage eighteen years later. Their first child, Greg Anthony, born in 1968, lived only four days because of the prenatal effects of the radiation treatment Guiton was undergoing during pregnancy. Their daughter, Nichele Monique, born the following year, is a graduate of the University of

Virginia, now living in Alexandria, Virginia. She is a successful businesswoman, a director of sales for a French company that markets skin care products. Since both Guiton and her daughter live in Virginia, they visit often and enjoy a very close relationship.

Guiton decided to further her education when her daughter was a child, knowing that was the only path to significant career advancement. She made the personal sacrifices to begin the grueling schedule of simultaneous college study, full-time employment, and family responsibilities, including the care of her ill husband. She earned a bachelor's degree in 1974 from Mills College, a master's from California State University, Hayward, in 1975, and finally an Ed.D. degree from the University of California, Berkeley, in 1985.

Guiton's career began at Mills College in Oakland, where she was employed as a student secretary. Immediately after graduating from Mills in 1974 she started up the career ladder, first as assistant dean of students at Mills and then as interim director of the ethnic studies department and lecturer. Two years later, in 1976, she became the first executive director of the newly created Marcus A. Foster Educational Institute, an organization that provides motivational support to local school staff and students.

She remained with the institute until 1979, when she was employed as vice-president of the Kaiser Center, a subsidiary of Kaiser Aluminum and Chemical Corporation. Two factors led to this opportunity: first the high visibility of her position at Marcus Foster Institute brought her excellent performance to the attention of the board of directors, the majority of whom were corporate executives; secondly, the business climate of the period was one of increased interest in minority participation at the administrative level. While other organizations had indicated they wanted her services, Kaiser went a step further. They assembled a team of managers to determine where her experiences and abilities would be of greatest value to the corporation, rather than leaving it to the routine consideration of the personnel office. She worked at Kaiser from 1979 to 1984.

For eight years, Guiton was part of the national government in Washington, D.C., and of the government of the State of California in Sacramento. From 1984 to 1989, she served in the administration of President Ronald Reagan as vice-chair of the United States Postal Rate Commission and as assistant secretary of the United States Department of Education. In 1989 and 1990, she was special advisor to President George Bush in the United States Office of Consumer Affairs and assistant secretary in the vocational and adult section of the United States Department of Education. Governor Pete Wilson selected Guiton to be secretary of the California State Consumer Services Agency in 1991. She left in July 1992 to accept the deanship of the University of Virginia's McIntire School of Commerce.

One of the high points in Guiton's government service came in 1989 when she headed the United States delegation to the Organization on Economic Cooperation and Development's Committee on Consumer Policy. At the organization's international meeting in Paris, Guiton hosted a luncheon for leaders from twenty-six industrialized countries as they met to coordinate activities, discuss mutual concerns, and set policies and procedures for such issues as education, trade, and the protection of the environment.

When she began her career Guiton did not have a plan for progress. She believes that the previous struggles of individuals and organizations to increase employment chances for women and minorities made it easier for her to have broad career possibilities, but she is strongly convinced that it was left to her to be fully prepared for the opportunities and to be willing to devote long hours to her work. She recognizes her obligation to keep the door open for those who will follow by maintaining high standards in the workplace. Guiton feels that if she fails to do well, it will be more difficult for other minorities or other women to be taken seriously. She once said that it is important to "maintain a sense of humility and a sense of obligation and responsibility to put back into my community."

Administrator Sees Success, Challenges, and Frustrations

Guiton has welcomed the challenges she has faced because they have enabled her to make a difference in the lives of other people. But frustrations have come from knowing she was unable to do enough because of conditions beyond her control. During an interview given when she was assistant secretary for Vocational and Adult Education, Guiton gave an example of having tried to address on a national level the need for vocational education classes to train young students in basic skills. She developed a paper on the subject, made many recommendations, and gave numerous speeches on the need to train the more than 50 percent of high school graduates who do not go to college and who should be ready for employment in skilled positions. While some of her recommendations were taken up, she was frustrated to see that too little attention was given to the young people who would benefit from that kind of preparation.

When she was director of the Office of Consumer Affairs, Guiton was unhappy to learn that in many instances minority and poor people were forced to pay more for goods and services. She felt that wider dissemination of information about their rights as consumers and ways they can protect themselves from fraudulent practices of manufacturers and merchants would decrease the chances of their rights being violated.

The McIntire School of Commerce of the University of Virginia where Guiton is now dean is designed for third-year students who have completed two years of liberal arts studies and are on the way to undergraduate or graduate degrees in one of the several areas of the business school offers. When students finish the extensive course of study they are well qualified for lucrative jobs, and many have already been placed before they graduate. Guiton describes the school as an exciting place to work. She spends a portion of her time trying to further diversify the faculty and student body by increasing non-white and female representation.

In spite of frustrations and disappointments that have arisen from time to time, Guiton feels that her career has been successful to date. She had made career moves that were based upon the degree and type of fulfillment she anticipated. She thinks of herself as a "generalist," having been in a variety of positions—an educator and an administrator in academia, government, and the corporate world. Content where she is now, Guiton would like to continue making contributions she has been recognized for by direct contact with students at McIntire, individually and through student organizations and student activities, by speaking to community groups and involvement with community organizations, and through membership on corporate boards of directors. She shares her enthusiasm with students and faculty alike and is an inspiration on campus.

Before Guiton left California for McIntire College, she met Walter Hill, Jr., an executive who runs an advertising, promotions, and marketing operation. Their friendship of several months led to the couple's June 1993 wedding, which took place at a Baptist church in Alexandria, Virginia. Hill is a Virginian who maintains offices in several states including California.

Many honors have been bestowed upon Bonnie Guiton, all very special to her. When pressed to name those she considers particularly important she mentions the National Women's Economic Alliance Foundation 1992 Directors Choice Award, the YWCA's Tribute to Women in International Industry Award, the Candace Award of the National Coalition of 100 Black Women, and the Outstanding Community Leader and Humanitarian Award of the NAACP. She puts in a class by themselves the "recognitions from home," a citation from the Marcus Foster Educational Institute, and distinguished alumnus awards from McClymonds High School and the Peralta Community College District.

Guiton serves on several boards of directors, including Niagara Mohawk Power Corporation, Real Estate Investment Trust, Mills College, National Environmental Education and Training Foundation, Louisiana Pacific, and Hershey Foods Corporation.

Guiton's optimism comes from the knowledge that countless people like herself care enough about the future of the youth of America to continue their commitment to invest in their welfare. She is heartened to see concerned men and women giving time, energy, thought, and financial resources to undertakings that have objectives similar to those of her own.

According to Bonnie Guiton, the success of her career in education, the corporate world, and government is proof that "you can take a little black girl out of the streets of Oakland and find that she can successfully move in circles at all levels, including the White House and in diplomatic circles in other countries, as a result of much support from friends and family."

Current Address: McIntire School of Commerce, University of Virginia, Charlottesville, VA 22906.

REFERENCES:

Guernsey, Lisa. "Learning the Hard Way, Inspirational University of Virginia Dean Bonnie Guiton Scales Academia's Heights." *Albemarle Magazine* (February/March 1993): 22-31.

Guiton, Bonnie. Interview with Dona L. Irvin. March 15, 1993.

Dona L. Irvin

Jessie P. Guzman

Jessie P. Guzman

(1898-)

Researcher, writer, educator, school administrator

Through her research and publications on black themes, Jessie Guzman has helped to identify and preserve an important element in American culture. Overshadowed for a time by Monroe Nathan Work, noted bibliographer and director of records and research at Tuskegee Institute, she would come into her own, head the department, and for a brief period edit the important *Negro Year Book,* a detailed record of people, places, and events compiled by the department. She is an example of black women in the United States who were pioneer researchers and writers of history and culture.

Jessie Parkhurst Guzman was born in Savannah, Georgia, on December 1, 1898, the daughter of David C. and Ella Roberts Parkhurst. From early childhood she lived in the home of her godparents, the John P. Wraggs, who provided her with inspiration in her youth. John Wragg, a minister in Atlanta, was prominent in the religious life of Georgia for many years. The Wraggs were interested in activities that promoted the welfare and rights of black people. John Wragg established the New York-based American Bible Society's Agency for Colored People in the South, later to become national in scope and be renamed the William Ingraham Haven Agency.

Guzman completed high school work at Atlanta's Clark University in 1915. She attended Howard University in Washington, D.C., and was class historian. She graduated from Howard in 1919 with an A.B. degree and from Columbia University in New York in 1929 with an A.M. degree. From 1935 to 1936 she undertook additional study at the University of Chicago and later she studied at American University in Washington, D.C. Her work experience began when she became private secretary to John Wragg. She taught history at

New Orleans College (now Dillard University) in Louisiana from 1922 to 1923. From 1923 to 1929 she was research assistant at Tuskegee Institute in Alabama, then moved to Alabama State Teachers' College in Montgomery, where she taught history during the 1929-30 school year. Returning to Tuskegee in 1930, she held a variety of positions there, giving thirty-five uninterrupted years of service as research assistant and teacher of sociology, 1930-38; dean of women, 1938-44; and director of the Department of Research and Records from 1944 until her retirement in 1965. She married Ignacio L. Guzman, of Bayamon, Puerto Rico, a member of Tuskegee's faculty, in 1940.

Research Activities Begin

Guzman is best known for her activities in the Department of Research and Records at Tuskegee, first under the leadership of Monroe Nathan Work and then as director of the department. Work joined the Tuskegee staff in 1908 as a researcher. Tuskegee's president, Booker T. Washington, was being challenged and attacked by people throughout the country for inaccuracies in his writings and speeches. Since his public appearances and activities at the institution and elsewhere were so demanding, he had no time to carefully check the details in every statement he made. Errors were beginning to appear, and dates, names, places, and figures were sometimes inaccurate. Washington and the school's trustees were advised that Monroe Nathan Work, a competent educator then at George State Industrial College (now Savannah State College), should be hired for the job.

Work established the Department of Records and Research in 1908; it became the medium through which he and the institute could influence black life and race relations. The department kept a daily record of events in black life from every possible source, both private and governmental. In time, the materials collected consisted of thousands of books related to race, race relations, and social problems; countless bulletins, pamphlets, brochures, official documents, letters, and manuscripts; and thousands of clippings from newspapers and magazines arranged by topic and event. The department's major published works were *A Bibliography of the Negro in Africa and America* and nine editions of the *Negro Year Book,* both essential sources for early information on blacks throughout the world. First published in 1912, the yearbook brought together for the first time in a condensed form pertinent information on blacks and was a new and valuable attempt to register the progress of a race. Among the data the department and the yearbook provided were detailed statistics on lynchings, helping to publicize this particular activity wherever it occurred.

Guzman joined Work as a research assistant and worked closely with him in compiling and editing the *Negro Year Book* from 1923 to 1929. Drawing upon her expertise as a researcher and scholar, she edited the yearbook in 1947 and again in 1952 and wrote and signed a number of articles in the yearbooks. She contributed to black women's biography with her article "The Social Contributions of the Negro Woman Since 1940." In the article she called black women "the most disadvantaged group in America" and said that "sex disabilities in addition to all the liabilities of our race have left them unprotected victims of our social system." While her review of black women's work showed how black women had reached out into the community and affected the entire black race, the American people, and the world, she said in conclusion, "that larger group of unsung women who are carrying their share of the weight of the world's work, whose accomplishments as individuals will never be known, should not be forgotten."

Guzman has written pamphlets and other articles, including "The Role of the Black Mammy in the Plantation Household," *Journal of Negro History,* 1938; "Some Recent Literature By and About Negroes," *Service Magazine,* 1947; and "Contributions To Negro Life: Establishing and Directing the Department of Records and Research at Tuskegee Institute," *Journal of Negro History,* 1949. Guzman also wrote *Some Achievements of the Negro through Education* and *Civil Rights and the Negro—A List of References Relating to Present Day Discussions,* both research pamphlets that

were published by her department. Other articles were published in *Quarterly Review of Higher Education among Negroes, Vital Speeches, Journal of Educational Sociology,* and *Bulletin of Bibliography.*

Her professional affiliations and memberships include the Society of American Archivists, Southern Sociological Society, American Historical Association, Association for the Study of Afro-American Life and History, American Teachers Association, Alabama Teachers Association, Southern Conference Educational Fund (which she served as secretary), and National Achievement Clubs of the Southern Regional Council. Guzman also has a number of social and civic affiliations, including the Tuskegee Civic Association; the NAACP; the Women's International League for Peace and Freedom; and the Alpha Kappa Alpha Sorority. Guzman is a Methodist and a Democrat.

Guzman has received several awards and honors, including the Frederick Bancroft History Award, which she received in 1949 for her article in the *Journal of Negro History.* She was named Tuskegee Woman of the Year in 1950. She tried her hand at politics in 1954 when she became the first black to run for office in Macon County, Alabama.

Jessie Guzman played a significant role in preserving the history and culture of blacks in the U.S. and elsewhere through her research and published accounts of her findings. Although she is frequently referred to in passing, no in-depth attention has been given to her life and work. She now lives in a health care facility in Alabama.

REFERENCES:

Guzman, Jessie P. "Contributions to Negro Life: Establishing and Directing the Department of Records and Research at Tuskegee Institute." *Journal of Negro History* 34 (October 1949): 436-61.

———. "The Social Contributions of the Negro Woman Since 1940." *Negro History Bulletin* 11 (January 1948): 86-94.

Ploski, Harry A., and James Williams. *The Negro Almanac.* 5th ed. Detroit: Gale Research, 1989.

Troup, Cornelius V. *Distinguished Negro Georgians.* Dallas: Royal Publishing Co., 1902.

Who's Who in Colored America. 7th ed. Yonkers-on-Hudson, N.Y.: Christian E. Burckel, 1950.

Jessie Carney Smith

Mabel Dole Haden

Lawyer, organization leader, educator

In the May 1992 issue of *Class* magazine, Mabel Haden addressed the need for blacks to acquire self-respect and self-confidence, saying, "No one steps on a cobra, no one steps on a rattlesnake, but they will step on a worm." Long recognized as a feisty, hardworking, proud, and brilliant lawyer, Haden is best known as the current president of the National Association of Black Women Attorneys, an organization founded in 1972 by her colleague Wilhelmina Rolark. Having come through the organizational ranks as charter member, workshop speaker, chair of the Scholarship Committee (1978), and originator of the annual Red Dress Ball/scholarship fund-raiser, Haden now focuses her leadership energies on the areas of recruiting members, securing scholarships and internships for worthy women law students, encouraging networking among members, and keeping the NABWA financially solvent. It is safe to say that no one will be stepping on Mabel Haden.

Mabel Dole Haden, a practicing attorney in Washington, D.C., was elected president of the National Association of Black Women Attorneys (NABWA) in 1985. Her ascension to that position was largely due to her ingenuity and farsightedness as chair of the Scholarship Committee, which awarded its first scholarship at the 1978 NABWA convention. For an organization that had existed for only six years and had a membership of less than one hundred at the time of its first convention in 1974, this was a laudable accomplishment. The 1978 scholarship recipient was Bernice Smith, a student at St. John's School of Law. After the first NABWA scholarship was awarded, Haden was more determined than ever to maintain a scholarship fund. To this end, she devised the idea of the Red Dress Ball. The idea for this event sprang from a private party Haden attended, where all the women wore red formal gowns at the suggestion of a friend of Haden's. The scene was so pretty that it occurred to Haden that the red dresses would look pretty at a Red Dress Ball. The ball is a yearly fund-raiser, the proceeds of which are allocated to scholarships. The first ball took place in 1978. Sponsored by Congresswoman Shirley Chisholm (D-NY), the reception and dance were held in the Caucus Room of the Cannon House Office Building in Washington, D.C.

Although the NABWA is most closely associated with Wilhelmina Rolark, founder and president-emeritus, it is Mabel Haden who has been the impetus for enlarging the scope and visibility of the organization beyond the geographical confines of the nation's capital. This "fireball" attorney,

Mabel Dole Haden

who does not disclose the year of her birth, was the last child born to Mary Elizabeth Haden, who married at the age of fourteen and bore eleven children. Haden refers to herself as a "country bumpkin" in allusion to her upbringing in a rural area. Her family lived on thirteen acres of land where she and her sisters and friends roamed around the woods, climbed trees, and had the free rein of a spacious land area. In a 1993 interview, Haden said that two of her sisters were in boarding school when she was born. In fact, Haden and all of her sisters were sent to boarding school at the Allen Home School for Girls in Asheville, North Carolina. After graduating, all her older sisters taught school and mailed money back home to enable their mother, "Molly," to send the younger girls who would be coming after them. In the interview, Haden credited her mother with being her role model. As a young, single parent in Lynchburg, Virginia, her major goal was to see all her children receive an education. Haden, in further reminiscing about her mother, remembered that her hands were always rough and calloused due to constant hard work. The one time Haden noticed her mother's hands being soft was when she was bedridden with cancer.

Haden attended elementary school at Agenda Elementary in Lynch Station, Virginia. It was the school all the local black children attended due to segregation. The town was infamously known as the site where the first black was hanged in the United States. Haden first came to Washington, D.C., after graduating from Allen Home School to attend Howard University. While in college she worked at a job that paid twenty-five cents an hour. During her senior year, a lack of funds caused her to transfer to Virginia State College, where she earned a B.S. degree in education. After teaching in Fairfax County, Virginia, for fifty dollars a month, Haden returned to Washington in 1941 and taught school there until 1950. Haden's early teaching career was distinguished by her efforts to go beyond the confines of the classroom in meeting the needs of her students. In addition to attending to the intellectual needs of her students, Haden saw to it that their cultural and social outlooks were broadened by exposing them to art exhibits from foreign embassy collections. She upgraded her skills as a teacher by attending Morgan State College in Baltimore during summer vacations. In time, Haden decided to pursue her dreams of becoming a lawyer; when she discovered that Howard University Law School offered night courses, she enrolled.

Haden maintained her full-time teaching job while she attended night classes, and her first-year law school grades were good enough to warrant a scholarship. In an interview Haden noted that she was a student during the tenure of William Hastie as law school dean. Hastie, holder of a doctorate from Harvard Law School, later became governor of the Virgin Islands and Chief Judge of the U.S. Court of Appeals for the Third Circuit. After graduating from Howard University School of Law in 1948, Haden earned a master of laws degree from Georgetown University. Haden was one of only three Howard Law School graduates admitted to the District of Columbia bar in 1956. She was teaching full-time when she passed the Washington, D.C., bar examination at the first sitting. Haden then entered the private practice of law in the Washington metropolitan area.

In the June 1, 1988, issue of the *ABA Journal,* Haden was quoted as calling racial discrimination in the legal profession "apartheid in the courthouse." Haden first noticed the discrimination shortly after graduating from law school. She repeatedly saw young, white male lawyers get the prime business referrals while black lawyers got the less lucrative business, usually involving black clients. Haden said in the journal that she "represented prostitutes and construction workers for years at $50 a case." When she opened her own private practice in 1956, Haden had to slowly build up a clientele. To keep busy and augment her income, she became a real estate broker, which enabled her to better serve clients of her law practice who needed assistance with financing and interpreting contracts.

Heads Black Women Lawyer's Association

Haden is best known for her tenure as president of the NABWA. In a 1993 interview, she said that the national office is a two-woman operation and that a major focus is on keeping the NABWA financially solvent. To this end, she has encouraged potential donors to name the NABWA as beneficiary in their wills and she has solicited support from such luminaries as Shirley Chisholm, former Democratic presidential candidate, and Lionel Hampton, noted musician and longtime Republican. Haden's recruitment efforts have extended to nonpractitioners of law because she believes that all women can benefit from what the NABWA has to offer. The prime force behind the scholarship committee, Haden explained in the interview how scholarships are awarded. First- or second-year law students write papers and trial briefs from cases they work out, and the winner receives a prize of five thousand dollars. Many other students are assisted with internships or are recommended to leading law firms.

Haden has published professional articles in *Case and Comment Lawyers,* the *Washington Post, ABA Journal, Black Monitor, Legal Times,* and *District Lawyer.* In 1977 she was honored by Iota Phi Lambda Sorority (Gamma chapter) and cited in *Who's Who in American Law.* In 1992, Haden was presented with the National Bar Association (NBA) Greater Washington Area chapter's Charlotte Ray Award and inducted into the NBA Hall of Fame. She was also awarded the Generous Heart Award from the Jack H. Olender Foundation in 1992. She also received the Ollie May Cooper Award in October 1993 and in 1994 shared the Rape Crisis Award with Jocelyn Elders and a number of Hollywood personalities.

Haden has been married for 37 years to Russell George Smith, a native of England and World War II veteran who works as her accountant. She and her husband have no children but have always helped young people. Two of her special interests have been working to support Sharon Pratt Kelly, recently ousted mayor of Washington, D.C., long before other women and fellow attorneys did so, and lending assistance to Dorothy Height of the National Council of Negro Women; they are contemporaries in age and length of public service.

One of Haden's favorite avocational interests is poetry. Her love of poetry was fostered during her childhood. Her mother often recited poetry from memory and sang spirituals. Haden was amazed at the scope of her mother's memory. Like her mother, Haden memorized poetry, especially the works of Paul Lawrence Dunbar and Langston Hughes. After her last surviving sister died, Haden began to write poetry; she has submitted twenty-seven original poems to a publisher for a forthcoming book. Her poem "Black Hands" (1986) is printed on the back of the official NABWA T-shirt. She also enjoys listening to music, particularly the songs of Johnny Mathis.

Although she has been described as a "globetrotting idealist," Haden's values remain rooted in her Virginia upbringing. She never forgets the influence of her mother, who determined that no struggle was too great if it got her closer to her goal of educating all of her children. Haden always credits her mother with inspiring her habit of helping others. Photographs of Haden depict a stately, proud, immaculately coiffed, and tastefully groomed woman who most assuredly has fulfilled her mother's dreams. *NBA Magazine* reported in 1988 that Haden, never a self-promoter, advocates sisterhood and praises black women as "the backbone of our families . . . [and] . . . the smartest women in the world."

REFERENCES:

Burleigh, Nina. "Black Women Lawyers—Coping with Dual Discrimination." *ABA Journal* 74 (June 1, 1988): 64-68.

Carrolly, Denolyn. "Balancing the Scales—Black Women Attorneys." *Class* 14 (May 1992): 40-41.

Haden, Mabel. Telephone interviews with Dolores Nicholson, June 21, 1993; September 9, 1993; January 30, 1995.

Murray, Pauli. *The Autobiography of a Black Activist, Feminist, Lawyer, Priest, and Poet.* Knoxville: University of Tennessee Press, 1987.

The National Association of Black Women Attorneys, Inc., History. Washington, D.C.: NABWA, n.d.

Weatherford, Carole Boston. "Profile—Mabel D. Haden: Advocating Sisterhood." *NBA Magazine* 7 (January-March 1988): 6-7.

Dolores Nicholson

Helen Eugenia Hagan

Helen Eugenia Hagan
(1893-1964)
Pianist, educator

A talented concert pianist and private instructor, Helen Hagan began to demonstrate her skill during her college years. After studying in France, she returned to impress audiences throughout the United States. She was the first black to teach music in Chicago's downtown district and the first black pianist to give a solo recital in a New York concert hall. In recognition of her skill, she was sent to France to entertain black troops during World War I. Later unable to book shows because she was black, she turned to teaching and shared her expertise with students in black colleges.

Helen Eugenia Hagan was born in Portsmouth, New Hampshire, in January 1893, the daughter of John A. and Mary Estella Neal Hagan. The Hagans were a musical family: her mother was a pianist and her father a baritone singer. As a child she studied piano under her mother's instruction. Later the family moved to New Haven, Connecticut, where she obtained musical education in the public schools. By age nine, she was organist for the Dixwell Congregational Church in New Haven.

Hagan attended Yale University, where her prescribed curriculum included harmony, counterpoint, history of music, composition, and conducting. In 1910 she received Yale's certificate of proficiency in the theory of music. The next year she received the Julia Abigail Lockwood Scholarship, which was given to students who studied pianoforte in the School of Music and who performed best in an examination. She graduated from Yale University School of Music with a bachelor of music degree in 1912, having studied under Stanley Knight. She gave a performance of her own Piano Concerto in C Minor with the New Haven Symphony Orchestra at her commencement. According to Sylvia Dannett in *Profiles of Negro Womanhood,* she was cited for her "marked ability to conceive and execute musical ideas of much charm and no little originality." For this she was awarded the Samuel Simmons Stanford Fellowship, which enabled her to study abroad for two years. The award, given every other year to a member of the Yale music school, is awarded for proficiency in composition and piano. She studied in Paris, France, with Blanche Selva and Vincent D'Indy and in 1914 graduated with honors from the Schola Cantorum. When World War I began, she returned to the United States, later earning an M.A. degree from Teachers' College, Columbia University.

Concert Tours Successful

Hagan toured the United States as a concert pianist from 1914 to 1918. When the All-Colored Composers' Concert, promoted by William Hackney, was presented in Chicago's

Orchestra Hall on April 25, 1915, she performed her own Piano Concerto in C Minor. Her performance, as well as that of another black woman, a Miss Leon James, was cited as noteworthy. In 1918 the YWCA invited Hagan to entertain black servicemen in France with a group that included singer Jushua Blanton and Hugh Henry Proctor, a minister who led folk sings in camps.

Returning to the United States in 1919, Hagan settled in Chicago. She gave a recital at Sprague Memorial Hall at Yale University that has been called one of the most exciting concerts of her career. The press gave the concert good advance publicity as well as positive reviews afterward. According to Sylvia Dannett, "She played with ease and grace, received generous applause, and was recalled for many encores."

In 1920 Hagan married John Taylor Williams of Morristown, New Jersey, where she had once operated a piano studio. Williams had been a chemistry and physics teacher in Tallahassee, Florida, and in 1910 graduated from the Milwaukee Medical College. In Chicago, Hagan conducted a music studio in the Mendelssohn Conservatory of Music, which made her the first black to teach music in Chicago's downtown district. She gave her New York debut in October 1921 at Aeolian Hall, becoming the first black pianist to give a solo recital in a New York concert hall. She received critical acclaim for her performance and encouragement to continue her career.

Hagan had performed in concerts throughout the country and became known as a superior musician and an exceptionally fine pianist. She knew the problems black pianists faced when they sought bookings by agents who rarely, if ever, supported them. She discontinued her efforts to achieve greater fame and chose a teaching career instead. Beginning in the 1930s she joined the music faculties at Tennessee Agricultural and Industrial State College (now University) in Nashville and Bishop College in Marshall, Texas (now closed), and also gave private piano lessons. During her teaching years she guided and inspired many young black students. Returning to New York in 1935, she established the Helen Hagan Music Studio. In addition to teaching and coaching professional singers, the talented organist and choir director served churches in New Haven, Morristown, Chicago, and Marshall, Texas. In New York City she served Grace Congregational Church and as late as 1937 gave recitals. There she had attracted talented singers, many of whom became prominent in concert, oratorio, and opera.

Hagan was a charter member of the National Association of Negro Musicians and the Associated Music Teachers League. She was also a member of the Business and Professional Women's Clubs and the Alpha Kappa Alpha Sorority. She suffered from a lingering illness, then died on March 6, 1964, in New York City. Funeral services were held in Grace Congregational Church. Helen Hagan was a talented black artist who had some professional success, but due to the difficulties blacks faced in receiving bookings by agents, decided to turn to the black colleges to teach and inspire young black students.

REFERENCES:

Dannett, Sylvia G. L. *Profiles of Negro Womanhood.* Vol. 2. Yonkers, N.Y.: Educational Heritage, 1966.

Guzman, Jessie Parkhurst. *Negro Yearbook: A Review Affecting Negro Life, 1941-1946.* Tuskegee, Ala.: Tuskegee Institute, 1947.

Southern, Eileen. *Biographical Dictionary of Afro-American and African Musicians.* Westport, Conn.: Greenwood Press, 1982.

Jessie Carney Smith

Julia West Hamilton
(1866-1958)
Civic leader, church leader, clubwoman

Julia West Hamilton was a leader in church and civic organizations in Washington, D.C., for over sixty years. Her death notice in the *Washington Sunday Star,* February 23, 1958, quoted her as stating that she believed "we are mere servants of Christ working together toward one common end." Hamilton was a member of a number of organizations. She worked with army relief agencies, was president for over twenty-five years of the Phillis Wheatley YWCA in Washington, D.C., and was very involved in her local parent-teacher association, acting for ten years as president. She was perhaps best known, however, for her work in the black women's club movement. She was president for twenty-one years of the Washington and Vicinity Federation of Women's Clubs and served as treasurer of the National Association of Colored Women.

Julia West Hamilton was the daughter of former slaves from Charleston, South Carolina. Her father, Thomas W. West, was taught to read by his master's daughter over the objection of his master. After he met his future wife, Martha A., they had to get the consent of their owners to marry; permission was granted, but they were required to live apart in the homes of their respective masters.

Thomas West ran away to join the Union navy during the Civil War. After the war, he rejoined his wife in Charleston. Their daughter Julia was born the year after the war ended. During Reconstruction Thomas West worked for Peter Hains and the West family moved to Washington, D.C., in the early 1880s when Hains, a colonel, was assigned engineering duties in the city.

Hamilton attended the Avery Institute in Charleston, South Carolina, but her formal education ended when her family moved to Washington when she was twelve years old.

Julia West Hamilton

Her parents were ardent Christians. Her father was a member of Metropolitan AME Church, and her mother was a member of the Nineteenth Street Baptist Church. For over seventy years, Hamilton was a very active member of Metropolitan's board of trustees.

A few years after moving to Washington, D.C., Hamilton married John Alexander Hamilton of Petersburg, Virginia. John Hamilton was a social worker and missionary who served as president of the Baptist Sunday School Union. Julia West Hamilton established her own business as a dressmaker to help supplement the family income. She charged five dollars per outfit, complete with workmanship and material. She was so successful that she was able to hire workers to help her. She also worked at the Bureau of Engraving as a printer's assistant, earning $1.25 a day. She later worked for thirty-one years in the registrar's office of the Treasury Department until her retirement in 1933.

Lengthy Devotion to Women's Club Activities

A group of women met at the old Wage Earner's Building in Washington, D.C., and joined forces to establish the Washington and Vicinity Federation of Women's Clubs in 1920. And on November 9, 1924, Mary McLeod Bethune, Julia West Hamilton, Nannie Helen Burroughs, Lucie R. Pollard, Sue Sanders, Marion Butler, Margaret K. Kelson, and Alma J. Scott met in the Rose Room of the Phillis Wheatley YWCA at 901 Rhode Island Avenue to organize. They chose as their motto, "Aiming High and Building."

The federation grew out of the City Federation of Women's Clubs of Washington, D.C., which was established in 1920 at the request of Hallie Quinn Brown, seventh president of the National Association of Colored Women's Clubs (NACW). The City Federation joined with other women's clubs and thus was born the Washington and Vicinity Federation of Women's Clubs. The federation was organized at the suggestion of Mary McLeod Bethune, eighth president of the NACW. Julia West Hamilton was elected the first president of the club and served for twenty-one years until she was succeeded in 1945 by Isadora Letcher.

One of the first projects of the federation was to assist in establishing the national headquarters in 1928 at 1114 O. Street, N.W. The federation raised six hundred dollars for the new headquarters. Part of this building was used as a training center for domestics. The President's Room was also furnished and a piano, books, and bookcases were purchased.

Several other projects were undertaken during Hamilton's presidency. During World War II the federation aided in relief work, purchased war bonds and stamps, and worked in government and community centers. The federation assisted the NACW in caring for the Frederick Douglass Home in Anacostia, Virginia. The landscaping of the home gave jobs to many young people. This was made possible through the efforts of Mary McLeod Bethune, National Youth Administration director, and Julia West Hamilton, chair of the local Advisory Committee of the National Youth Administration.

The federation continued to grow, and by 1939 Hamilton reported that it consisted of twenty-one clubs in Washington, D.C., with a membership of about five hundred women engaged in many phases of educational, religious, and social work. As president of the Washington federation, Julia West Hamilton was a delegate at the biennial meeting of the NACW in Oakland, California, in 1926. She extended an invitation for the NACW to meet in Washington in 1928. The national organization had not met in the District of Columbia in thirty-two years and the Washington federation hosted a very successful convention.

Mary McLeod Bethune, president of the NACW, presided at the sixteenth biennial meeting in 1928. The convention was held from July 27 to August 3, beginning with a mass meeting at the Nineteenth Street Baptist Church on Sunday evening. The original meeting of the NACW in 1896 was held in this same church. Church pastor Walter H. Brooks welcomed the group, and Nannie Helen Burroughs directed a pageant depicting dramatic episodes in the history of the NACW. The day sessions were held at the Armstrong High School, and an evening session was held at the Metropolitan AME Church with Hamilton presiding. The presidential address by Bethune emphasized the value of having a national headquarters in Washington, D.C., and on July 31, 1928, a dedication service was held outside the headquarters at 12th and O. Streets, N.W.

It was at this 1928 NACW convention that Hamilton was elected national treasurer, receiving 480 out of 500 votes. Her financial report to the July 1930 NACW conference at Hot Springs, Arkansas, was voted the finest and most complete financial report ever presented and she was unanimously reelected national treasurer.

In her tribute to the NACW, Julia West Hamilton noted in her 1937 biennial financial report that "the background and tradition of the National Association is a rich heritage, which every colored Woman should be proud of and as we go on looking forward we might well remember the work of the splendid pioneer women who 'were forgetful of self and thoughtful of others.'"

In 1930 Hamilton was elected president of the Phillis Wheatley YWCA, having been a member since its organization on May 5, 1905. With the assistance of Harriet E. King, who served as industrial secretary of the YWCA, she organized its Industrial Department and served as chair of that department for eight years. As president, Hamilton attended many conferences and conventions representing the women of Washington, D.C.

In 1955 the Phillis Wheatley YWCA celebrated two anniversaries: the one hundredth anniversary of the worldwide YWCA and the twenty-fifth anniversary of Hamilton's presidency at Phillis Wheatley. A banquet was held in Howard University's Baldwin Hall with Mordecai Johnson, the school's president, as guest speaker. This branch of the Y had grown from two rooms on Maryland Avenue, S.W., to a building at 901 Rhode Island Avenue, N.W., with an annex at 1719 Thirteenth Street, N.W., and a summer camp at Highland Beach, Maryland.

Hamilton Extends Work to the Community

Julia West Hamilton's achievements were many. She was a member of the National Council of Negro Women; president of the Ladies' Banneker Aid Association and the Ladies' Crispus Attucks Association (each having over four hundred members); a national officer of the Interdenominational Ministers' Wives Association; and organizer and first president of the auxiliary of the James E. Walker American Legion Post. She also acted for a time as treasurer of the Women's Relief Corps, Auxiliary of the Grand Army of the Republic. With regard to this position, Hamilton stated in *The Parent-Teacher Journal,* October-November 1930: "It has been a labor of love to aid the Union veterans in their declining years in appreciation of their great service to the race and the preservation of the union."

Hamilton was also a trustee of the Washington Community Chest, a member of the Executive Board of the Public School Association of the District of Columbia and the Prince Hall chapter of the Order of Eastern Star, and a board member of the Ladies Cliff Rock Association. As president for over ten years of the Slater-Langston Parent-Teacher Association, Hamilton headed one of the most progressive and best attended parent-teacher groups in Washington. She also held honorary memberships in the Zeta Phi Beta Sorority and the

Howard University Alumni Association. As the first woman chairperson of the NAACP membership drive, Hamilton coordinated a successful entertainment program at the Washington Auditorium sponsored by Oscar DePriest.

The Julia West Hamilton League was formed in 1938. Its motto, "The only gift is a portion of thyself," was a constant reminder of the exemplary life of Julia West Hamilton. The league developed out of a group of ten women and was organized by Mrs. Ellen V. Johns Britain. The name of the league was chosen to honor Hamilton, who gave unsparingly of her time and love to the cause of humanity. Hamilton was a participating member of the league until her death. The league's purpose was to promote benevolence and interest in the cultural and educational life of the community; to help others develop skills for achieving better self-understanding, which in turn would lead to more sensitive and honest interactions among people; to encourage youth to aim early in life to achieve a good education, develop good character, and find a useful place in society; and to establish a monetary prize known as the Julia West Hamilton Award to be given to each of thirteen high schools and a four-year Julia West Hamilton Scholarship to be awarded to a high school senior every four years. The league also gave yearly contributions to the Hospital for Sick Children.

In 1948 Julia West Hamilton received a Citizen's Award for fifty years of Christian leadership in the Washington community. Over two thousand people attended the celebration, and Mordecai Johnson addressed the group as Hamilton received a citation, a purse, and a bound volume of letters from well wishers.

On Wednesday, May 14, 1969, the Julia West Hamilton Junior High School was dedicated. Located at Sixth and Brentwood Parkway in Northeast Washington, D.C., the school had twenty-eight classrooms, with a capacity for 1,498 students. The school cost $2,845,445. At the May 14 ceremony, Benetta Washington, director of the Women's Center Job Corps, gave a tribute to Hamilton. Hamilton's son, West Hamilton, a colonel, presented a portrait of her to the school. The Zeta Phi Beta Sorority made a presentation and awards were given by the Julia West Hamilton League and the Julia West Hamilton Memorial Membership Committee.

Julia West Hamilton died of pneumonia on Saturday, February 22, 1958, in Freedmen's Hospital, Washington, D.C. Her funeral was held on Wednesday, February 26, 1958, at the Metropolitan AME Church. The pastor, G. Dewey Robinson, officiated and read the eulogy. Resolutions were offered by Gertrude Rivers of the YWCA and Estelle Webster of Metropolitan AME Church. Remarks were given by Howard University president Mordecai Johnson, and Eastern Star services were given by the Prince Hall chapter. Burial was at Lincoln Memorial Cemetery. She was survived by three of her five children: two sons, West A. Hamilton, former member of the District of Columbia School Board, and Percival Y. Hamilton, both of Washington; and one daughter, Josephine Hamilton Pettie, a former District of Columbia school teacher now living in New York. She was also survived by three grandchildren and five great-grandchildren.

Hamilton's death brought an end to sixty years of selfless devotion to women's club work and civic activity. Fortunately, the community took notice of her outstanding contributions.

REFERENCES:

Hamilton, Julia West. *Biennial Financial Report to the Nineteenth Biennial Convention of the National Association of Colored Women, Inc.* Cleveland, Ohio, 1935.

———. *Biennial Financial Report to the Twentieth Biennial Convention of the National Association of Colored Women, Inc.* Fort Worth, Tex.: July 1937.

Julia West Hamilton Junior High School Dedication Ceremony. Washington, D.C., May 14, 1969.

"Mrs. Hamilton; Civic Leader." *Washington Post,* February 24, 1958.

"Mrs. Hamilton Dies at 91, Leader of D.C. Negroes." *Washington Sunday Star,* February 23, 1958.

"Mrs. Julia Hamilton Gets Citizens' Award." *Washington Evening Star,* October 16, 1948.

Records of the National Association of Colored Women's Clubs, 1895-1992. Part 1: Minutes of National Conventions, Publications, and President's Office Correspondence. Microfilm. Bethesda, Md.: University Publications of America, 1993.

Taliaferro, Clara S. "Julia West Hamilton." *The Parent-Teacher Journal* 1 (October-November 1930): 9.

Wesley, Charles H. *The History of the National Association of Colored Women's Clubs.* Washington, D.C.: NACW, 1984.

"Wheatley Y Plans Two Anniversaries." *Washington Post,* May 24, 1955.

COLLECTIONS:

Vertical file materials on Julia West Hamilton are in the Reference Department, Moorland-Spingarn Research Center, Howard University, Washington, D.C. Photographs are in the Prints and Photographs Collection, Moorland-Spingarn Research Center, Howard University.

Janet Sims-Wood

Gladys Riddle Hampton
(c. 1910-1971)
Business manager, record company executive, road manager, singer, modiste

Gladys Hampton was a partner in one of the most notable musical enterprises of this century—and she did not even play a musical instrument. Best known as the wife of band leader and vibraphonist Lionel Hampton, she was in many ways the foundation of his success, allowing him to concentrate on his music while she concentrated on business. She was ahead of her time as a businesswoman—the only woman in America to manage a big band orchestra and a record company. And she and Lionel Hampton were ahead of their time as a couple. As Lionel Hampton writes in *Hamp: An Autobiography,* they functioned as a team, "the perfect team for what we did. She was the businesswoman and I was the musician. She was the boss offstage, I was the boss onstage." She said in the August 1949 *Ebony,* "When it comes to bookings, transportation, taxes, payroll for thirty-four men, contracts, union problems and a thousand and one other things that the audience out front never sees or hears about, Lionel just walks away from everybody with a smile and tells them to 'see Mrs. Hampton.'"

Very little information is available about Gladys Riddle Hampton's life before her marriage to Lionel Hampton. Despite the fact that most sources give Hampton's birthdate as 1918, the exact date is unknown, and 1910 is a more accurate estimation. Part Native American, she was born on a reservation in Lehigh, Oklahoma. Nothing is known of her father, but her mother, Agnes Riddle, was an integral part of her and Lionel Hampton's lives. The Hamptons lived with her whenever they were in Los Angeles and eventually inherited the house. She also mothered Lionel after the grandmother who raised him died. Hampton was very quiet about a first marriage to a man identified only by his last name, Neal, who was both physically and mentally abusive. After living with Lionel Hampton in Los Angeles for several years, Gladys married him on November 11, 1936, in Yuma, Arizona. They had no children. She died of a heart attack on April 30, 1971, in her office in New York and was buried in Los Angeles, California, at Rosemont Cemetery.

Nothing is known of Hampton's father; he appears to have been absent during her childhood. When she was very young, her mother, Agnes Riddle, married a miner from Texas, and Hampton grew up in Dennison, Texas, with Mr. Riddle as a father figure. She attended Fisk University in Nashville, Tennessee, and then moved to Los Angeles, where her mother was running a boarding house, predominantly for railroad men. At some point in her early life, Hampton had become an accomplished seamstress. By 1929, she was a well-established modiste for MGM in Hollywood, counting among her clients Marion Davies, Randolph Hearst, Norma Shearer, Lord Mountbatten, and Joan Crawford, who remained her good friend for years. Despite her own success, in the January-February 1951 issue of *Color* she modestly described herself before meeting Lionel as "just a little dressmaker." Hampton was prominent in the black middle-class social scene in Los Angeles and frequently attended society dances and club functions.

It was at a dance of the Antique Art Club, where the then unknown Lionel Hampton was playing with the Quality Serenaders, that Gladys Riddle and Lionel Hampton first met. Lionel describes her in *Hamp* as "a beautiful girl—tall, light complected, carried herself well." He also describes her as confident and sure of herself. Having only recently arrived in Los Angeles, Lionel Hampton was looking for a new and more permanent place to live. Hampton told him that her mother ran a boarding house, gave him the address, and arranged for him to move in the next day. He writes in *Hamp* of that first meeting, "I didn't even know the girl's name and already she'd made a major decision for me. That was Gladys. It was 1929, and from that day until she died, she made all my major decisions."

With Lionel Hampton, Gladys Hampton's talents as a businesswoman were fully realized. Lionel Hampton cared little and knew even less about the business side of music, and soon after they met, Gladys took over business responsibilities from him. She began acting as an unofficial manager for him and negotiated his contracts with clubs in the Los Angeles area, including Frank Sebastian's Cotton Club. Other musicians were so impressed with the deals she negotiated for Lionel Hampton that they began to ask her to represent them as well.

Hamptons Struggle on the Road to Success

Gladys Hampton's dreams for Lionel, however, went beyond the Los Angeles clubs. She encouraged him to form a band and go out on the road because she believed that he needed to make a name for himself outside California. As a black American woman in the early 1930s, however, she realized that she could not serve as contract negotiator with white clubs outside Los Angeles. The band hired a white front man to get bookings and negotiate contracts because, as Lionel Hampton notes in *Hamp*, the fact that "Gladys was self-assured and businesslike . . . didn't take away from the fact that she was 'colored.'" Lionel continues, pointing out that at the time, "being a wom[a]n wasn't the problem so much as being black."

The early touring days were very difficult. Their front man, always one location ahead of them arranging performances, often neglected to leave money for them, and the band members frequently slept in the two cars in which they were traveling and ate bologna sandwiches or rice with ketchup. Lionel Hampton sings his wife's praises in *Hamp* for her endurance during those early years:

> She could have been back in L.A., living in comfort and making good money at her job with MGM. But Gladys believed in me. She had quit her job . . . and there she was sleeping in a cramped car and eating rice and ketchup when she could have been attending Antique Art Club balls. She believed in me, and she was convinced that we could make big money.

Her sacrifices went beyond that of simply enduring hardships. At one point, she even mortgaged her mother's house in Los Angeles in order to keep the band together. She also had to perform as a singer one night when the band had no money to hire one. Without any training or practice as a singer, she sang "Sophisticated Lady," the only song she

knew, over and over during the show, changing keys all the while and requiring the musicians to chase her up and down the scale. Later, she did sing on Hampton recordings, including "Sad Feeling," "Everybody's Somebody's Fool," and "Hey-Ba-Ba-Re-Bop." Road life became difficult for Gladys and Lionel Hampton, who by that time had financial difficulties. They returned to Los Angeles, where she very successfully resumed her designing business while Lionel Hampton continued improving his skills and headlining at well-known clubs.

In 1936, Benny Goodman called and negotiated a one-year contract with Gladys Hampton for Lionel Hampton to join the Benny Goodman Orchestra for $550 a week. According to James Collier, Lionel refused to go to New York without Gladys, and it "cost her a career to come east." Gladys Hampton, however, saw the move as a great opportunity and agreed to go. Gladys and Lionel were not yet married although they had been living together for years. Gladys's mother would not allow them to go unless they got married and sent her back the marriage certificate. Lionel Hampton says in *Hamp*, "We acted like we were married. In fact, a lot of people thought we were. . . . But we'd never gotten around to that formality." So they married on the cross-country drive, stopping in Arizona where they could be married in a matter of minutes, and immediately mailed the certificate to Agnes Riddle. Gladys Hampton's control of business interests was quickly established upon their arrival in New York. She had to instruct Benny Goodman to never again give any money to Lionel because, after receiving a two-week salary advance from Goodman, Lionel returned to their apartment in Harlem following an afternoon of shopping with only thirteen dollars in his pocket.

Astute Businesswoman Manages Lionel Hampton Orchestra

For four years, while Lionel played with the Benny Goodman Orchestra, Gladys Hampton learned about the music business in the process of traveling with the band. She believed in autonomy, so when she felt the time was right, she persuaded Lionel to go out on his own. He formed the Lionel Hampton Orchestra, and she managed it for the next thirty-one years. During the early years of the orchestra, Hampton was extremely frugal with money. She received much criticism from the musicians who joined the band for her firm business tactics, but she was also admired for her fairness.

By the mid-1940s the band was doing very well, with a gross income of one million dollars annually, and Hampton began branching out in her business enterprises by buying real estate in Los Angeles and New York. In 1949, she pursued other business interests within the music industry by forming a music publishing company, Swing and Tempo Music, which primarily published Lionel Hampton's compositions. She also started and headed a record label, Hampton Records, which was followed later by Glad-Hamp Records. Lionel Hampton believes that her only bad business decision was her unwillingness to join a partnership in the founding of Atlantic

Records. Believing that they were better off concentrating on their own label, she refused to invest the money to help start the new company.

It was also in 1949 that she was named Most Outstanding Woman of 1948 by Mary McLeod Bethune, commander-in-chief of the Woman's Army of National Defense. According to Lionel Hampton, "She was honored 'as an example of the leadership among women which is coming more and more into its own' and 'for unusual proficiency exhibited in business and managerial capacities as the only woman manager of a band in America.'"

By 1953, small musical groups were becoming very popular in America, and big bands were no longer as desirable. Big bands, however, were extremely popular in Europe because of the introduction of big band music by American soldiers in World War II. Seeing an opportunity in a new market, Hampton organized a European tour for the band, which took place in the fall of 1953. Although it was not financially successful, she believed it garnered considerable prestige for Lionel and his orchestra. Subsequent European tours proved to be more financially successful, and the band continued touring abroad periodically for many years, with officially sponsored trips to Israel, Ghana, and Nigeria as well.

Gladys Hampton was very stylish and was consistently named one of America's best dressed women. Her focus on style manifested itself in a concern for the band's appearance and showmanship and in a compulsion for shoes, furs, and jewelry. Lionel Hampton likens her shoe habit to that of former Phillipines first lady Imelda Marcos and describes recording sessions during which she had shoes sent up from the department stores to the studio for her to try on. When she died, she had a half million dollars worth of jewelry and thirteen fur coats, plus a room full of shoes.

Always aware of their good fortune, Gladys and Lionel Hampton were actively involved in helping others throughout their careers. They participated in and planned charity functions, serving such causes as church organizations, schools, and developing countries. They were most happy, however, to help their own community. With funding from the New York Urban Development Corporation, they planned the Lionel Hampton Houses in Harlem, which were begun in December of 1971. Ten years later, that complex was joined by another—the Gladys Hampton Houses, with 205 low-income units. In a fitting tribute to her, Lionel Hampton had a special inscription placed on the cornerstone: "God gave me the talent, but Gladys gave the inspiration."

REFERENCES:

Collier, James Lincoln. *Benny Goodman and the Swing Era.* New York: Oxford University Press, 1989.

Hampton, Lionel, with James Haskins. *Hamp: An Autobiography.* New York: Warner Books, 1989.

"The High Mark of the Lionel Hamptons." *Color* 7 (January-February 1951): 31-34.

"Lionel Hampton's Million Dollar Band Business." *Ebony* 4 (August 1949): 20-24.

Lisa Boyd

D. Antoinette Handy
(1930-)
Flutist, educator, administrator, radio host, writer

An accomplished and celebrated flutist, D. Antoinette Handy has preformed with numerous symphonies both in the United States and abroad. She is also an experienced music educator who has taught college courses and private lessons throughout most of her career. In 1990 Handy was appointed director of the National Endowment for the Arts' Music Program, after having served as acting director and assistant program director. The Music Program is one of the Endowment's largest operations, and before her retirement in 1993, Handy had administered the distribution of between eleven million and fifteen million dollars, money that provided backing for up-and-coming musicians and support for the creation of new music and for musical performances, organizations, and training institutions. At the height of her professional career when she joined the National Endowment for the Arts, Handy brought to the job a wealth of experience, skill, confidence, and intuition. Handy has also written numerous articles and three full-length studies on the history and characteristics of African American music.

Born October 29, 1930, in New Orleans, Dorothy Antoinette Handy is the great-granddaughter of Emmanuel Handy, a Mississippi legislator during Reconstruction, and the daughter of William Talbot Handy, Sr., a minister and respected leader in the New Orleans African American community for nearly sixty years. Handy received her musical foundation at home in her native New Orleans. Her mother, Darthney Pauline Pleasant Handy, gave her (and Handy's three siblings) piano and violin lessons starting at the ages of five and six, respectively. Her parents were natives of Hazlehurst, Mississippi, a town thirty-five miles from Jackson, where Handy now lives in retirement.

Between the ages of eleven and thirteen, Handy studied the trumpet. The family was then living in Dallas, Texas, where Handy took private music lessons from the high school band director, Stephen A. Jackson III. It was Jackson who introduced her to the flute, the instrument on which she was to focus. She became interested in the orchestral sound at a very early age, listening to the radio and recordings. She recalls that her mother took her to the concerts of the New Orleans Philharmonic Orchestra and that they had to sit in the "buzzard gallery," the designated section for African Americans.

D. Antoinette Handy

In a July 1, 1994, letter to Jessie Carney Smith, Handy wrote, "Acoustically, these were some of the best seats in the house."

Handy returned with her family to New Orleans and studied with Frank Ribitsch and Justus Gelfius, both members of the New Orleans Philharmonic, during her final two years of high school. She attended Spelman College in Atlanta for two and a half years, but went on to earn her bachelor of music degree from the New England Conservatory of Music in Boston in 1952 and her master of music degree from Northwestern University School of Music in Evanston, Illinois, in 1953. She was recognized as an Outstanding Alumni by both institutions in 1992. Handy also earned a diploma from the Paris National Conservatory in Paris, France, in 1955 and was awarded an honorary doctorate of music from the Cleveland Institute of Music in 1993. While attending Spelman, she met her future husband, Calvin Montgomery Miller, then a student at Morehouse College in Atlanta and later a political scientist and university professor. Married in 1959, together they have reared three children and become grandparents of four.

An African American woman's chances of securing a job as an orchestra musician in the early 1950s were nonexistent. Therefore, after finishing her master of music degree, Handy taught for a brief period at Florida Agricultural and Mechanical University, where she remained for only one semester. She wrote in her letter to Jessie Carney Smith,

> My goal was to be an orchestral flutist. I loved teaching, but found myself having to constantly bulk the system. Performing outlets did not exist.

For the good of all (except perhaps the students), I felt it best that I resign and continue pursuing my dream.

Flutist Becomes Symphony Musician

In late 1954, Handy went to France to study at the Paris National Conservatory. Following an unexpected audition, she was designated first flutist by the conductor of the Orchestre International, an orchestra supported by the French government that toured Germany in the interest of better foreign relations. She told Matthew Sigman for *Symphony,* September-October 1991, "It was some of the best orchestral playing I did in my life, merely because someone believed in me." This is another example of the all-too-familiar scenario of an African American musician having to gain recognition in Europe before being embraced by his or her own country. Before leaving France in 1955, she toured nine German cities as a soloist and chamber flutist with a pianist and cellist, under the auspices of the United States Information Services (USIS).

Handy spent more than twenty-five years as a symphony musician. Her achievements include performing as principal flutist with the Orchestre Internationale and the Musica Viva Orchestra in Geneva, Switzerland. In 1952 and 1953, she performed with the Chicago Civic Orchestra—a training orchestra of the Chicago Symphony—for which she is currently a consultant. Also in this country, from 1966 to 1976, she performed with a number of orchestras and symphonies, including the Symphony of the Air, under the conductorship of Leonard Bernstein; the Orchestra of America; the Radio City Music Hall Orchestra; the Bach Festival Orchestra in Carmel, California; and the Richmond (Virginia) Symphony.

Handy has had solo performances with the New Orleans Philharmonic in 1953 and 1965, the Orchestre Internationale and Orchestra Musica Viva in 1955, and at the Twentieth Annual Bach Festival in 1957. More recent solo performances include those with the Baltimore Symphony in 1973, the Performing Arts Society of Philadelphia (Master Soloist) in 1974, and the Richmond (Virginia) Sinfonia in 1980.

When Handy returned to the United States in 1955, her first goal was to become a member of the New York musicians' union. Though she had worked as a free-lance flutist while playing with the Chicago Civic Orchestra and earning her master's degree at Northwestern University (1952-53), she did not have union membership. The Chicago union was split along racial lines (as were most other musicians' unions in the country) and she was uninterested in the jobs that came through the black union. Following a verbal appeal before the New York union's executive committee, she was admitted without having to fulfill the customary residency requirement.

A Commitment to Teaching

After becoming a union member, Handy had many performance engagements, but like many other musicians, she supported herself with day jobs. Between 1956 and 1963 she worked as a travel agent for the country's first black-owned and operated travel agency. Working in a managerial capacity, she had the freedom to fulfill all her professional music assignments. She also held several teaching positions— at New York College of Music (1956-57), Metropolitan Music School (1956-63), Harlem YMCA (1957-59), and Henry Street Settlement (1960-61). From 1959 to 1961 she worked in the area of music therapy for the Alfred Alder Mental Hygiene Clinic and Music Rehabilitation Center.

When the civil rights movement was at its height in the 1960s, Handy and her husband returned to the South and become a part of the crusade. They returned to teach at Tuskegee Institute, a historically black college. Since then, Handy has shared her talent, scholarship, and insight with various young musicians across the country. Her primary teaching areas were music history, music theory, arranging, and instrumental coaching of various ensembles. She has served on the faculties of the following universities: Tuskegee (1963-64), Jackson State (1964-66), Virginia State (1966-71), Virginia Union (1979-80), and Southern University, New Orleans (1983). In addition, she was artist-in-residence in the Richmond, Virginia, public schools (1976-80) and resource teacher in the New Orleans public schools (1982-83), and she taught private flute, piano, and recorder lessons from 1952 to 1985.

Handy was organizer, manager, and flutist for the chamber ensemble Trio Pro Viva, which specializes in performing music composed by African Americans. She commissioned many compositions and a two-record album, *Contemporary Black Images in Music for the Flute,* which was released in 1972. Trio Pro Viva began performing in 1965 and appeared at American colleges and universities throughout the South and East as well as at the Kennedy Center for the Performing Arts; the Virginia Museum of Fine Art; the Renolda House, Winston-Salem; the Baltimore Museum of Art; and the Smithsonian Institution. Handy stopped performing with the trio in 1987; however, she continues to be their consultant.

In the early 1970s Handy went through what she refers to as a period of "de-conservatizing." She began to further explore the history of African American music and musicians in the U.S., from Mahalia Jackson to Jessye Norman and Dizzy Gillespie and from the Negro spiritual to nationalistic and electronic music. She conducted in-depth research during her tenure as a 1971 Ford Foundation Humanities Fellow at the University of North Carolina and Duke University. The results of this ongoing research include many lectures and various articles and reviews in journals such as *Black Perspectives in Music, American Music, Notes, Symphony Magazine, The Western Journal of Black Studies, Jazz Educators' Journal,* and *Arts Review.* She wrote three books based on her research: *Black Women in American Bands and Orchestras* (1981), *The International Sweethearts of Rhythm* (1983), and *Black Conductors* (1994), all published by Scarecrow Press. Between September 1972 and November 1973 she was a music journalist for the *Richmond Afro-American* newspaper. Thirty-three of her articles were self-published in 1974 under the title *Black Music: Opinions and Reviews.*

Following her research residency in North Carolina in 1971, she returned to Virginia State University to direct the Office of Education's Student Special Services program and to coordinate the Trio Student Special Services Program, which also included Upward Bound and Talent Search. Handy wrote to Jessie Carney Smith,

> I was able to do more to ensure fine art awareness and receptiveness through these programs than I was able to accomplish as a member of the university music faculty. I also worked in the area of career counseling and directed a cooperative program with Massachusetts Institute of Technology, involving Virginia State, Tennessee State, and Southern universities.

After elaborating on some of the things that can be accomplished through student services, she added:

> One of my most rewarding experiences was when I served as host and producer of a weekly broadcast for radio station WRFK-FM in Richmond, Virginia, (1979-80). "Black Virginia" was a public affairs interview program that allowed me to begin and end each program with the music of a black composer or that featured a black performer. I used every means possible to convey the message that "black music" is all-inclusive. This is a label that I did not create, but have learned to live with.

For her leadership and achievement in the arts, Handy has received recognition in the form of scholarships, honors, and awards. Among these are the Distinguished Contribution Award from the National Association of Negro Musicians; the National Music Achievement Award from the National Black Music Caucus; and the National Endowment for the Arts Performance and Distinguished Service award. Handy was one of twelve people selected for Aetna Life Insurance Company's 1994 Calendar of African American History.

Becomes Director for the National Endowment for the Arts

After a music career combining performance, teaching, administration, and scholarship, Handy was very well qualified for her job at the National Endowment for the Arts. Because there have been so many changes in the music profession over the last few decades, Handy always counsels students to think about options other than performances and private teaching. For example, courses and internships in music-related businesses provide a wider range of practical experience for some students. She is particularly proud of the young black women who worked under her supervision as fellows at the National Endowment for the Arts. She also feels that it is a good idea to combine performance with teaching as a university professor. In *Notes,* Spring 1992, she warned students, "One has to be prepared to do more than one thing." Observing the diversity of her career, she certainly has practiced what she preaches.

During Handy's tenure at the National Endowment for the Arts' Music Program, she was engaged in an ongoing dialogue with other administrators concerning the need to transform some aspects of the program. Under her leadership, several changes were made. For example, she saw to it that grants were more equitably distributed by means of a more diversified grant selection panel. Race, gender, and geography are now more fairly represented on the panel, resulting in more diverse grant awardees. Additionally, jazz has a higher profile.

Handy was instrumental in the Endowment's establishment of the National Jazz Service Organization, which, along with other groups, administers the National Jazz Network. The American Jazz Masters Program flourished under Handy's leadership. This program honors living jazz legends who have made significant contributions in the African American tradition to the art form. Furthermore, there is greater sensitivity to the status of minorities and a broadening of listening habits of music panelists.

Music panelists have said that Handy never hesitated to ensure that fairness reigned and that only the application was the basis for evaluation. Artistic excellence was never sacrificed. Such administrative skills were recognized by the major music service organizations served by the program: the American Symphony Orchestra League, the International Association of Jazz Educators, the National Jazz Service Organization, and Chamber Music America.

Handy retired from the National Endowment for the Arts in the summer of 1993. On the occasion of her retirement, two congressmen and one senator addressed the U.S. Congress in order to recognize and congratulate her. Statements of representatives William Jefferson (Louisiana) and Sidney Yates (Illinois) and Senator Claiborne Pell (Rhode Island) were entered into the *Proceedings and Debates of the 103rd Congressional Record, First Session* (July 27 and 28, 1993). Following her final presentation at the National Council of the Arts meeting in May 1993, she received kudos from the entire council and was serenaded by council member Roberta Peters of the concert stage and the Metropolitan Opera.

Handy is an African American woman pioneer whose hard-won accomplishments have benefitted other women of color. Each major step that she took throughout her career, including those that were not acknowledged, opened the door a little further, allowing an increasing number of women to enter. D. Antoinette Handy has been an unassuming, determined fighter all her life because she believes in excellence and fairness. She made a big difference and even now, in retirement, continues to do so.

Current Address: 2240 Queensroad Avenue, Jackson, MS 39213.

REFERENCES:

"Antoinette Handy: NEC Was the Foundation." *Notes: New England Conservatory* 18 (Spring 1992): 13.

Handy, D. Antoinette. Interview with Joyce Marie Jackson. Washington, D.C., December 6, 1992.

————. Telephone conversation with Jackson, October 15, 1993.

————. Letter to Jessie Carney Smith, July 1, 1994.

"Panel Calls for Decision on NEA Job." *Washington Post,* May 15, 1993.

Proceedings and Debates of the 103rd Congressional Record, First Session, July 27, 1993 and July 28, 1993.

Sigman, Matthew. "A Talent for Change." *Symphony* 42 (September-October 1991): 41-42.

Southern, Eileen. *Biographical Dictionary of Afro-American and African Musicians.* Westport, Conn.: Greenwood Press, 1982.

Who's Who among Black Americans, 1994-95. 8th ed. Detroit: Gale Research, 1994.

Joyce Marie Jackson

Ruth Wright Hayre

(1911-)

School superintendent, educator, philanthropist

Ruth Wright Hayre continued the commitment to education established by her forebears in the African Methodist Episcopal Church and was a pioneering black woman in the public school system of Philadelphia. She became the first black woman secondary school teacher, secondary school principal, and district superintendent in Philadelphia. She and her father share the distinction of being the first black father/daughter pair to earn doctorates from the University of Pennsylvania. Her leadership culminated in service as the first woman president of the Philadelphia Board of Education.

In 1988 Hayre created a vision of hope for 119 sixth graders and their parents at the Richard R. Wright and Kenderton public schools in north Philadelphia. She surprised them at graduation with an announcement that she had made provisions to pay for their college educations through her establishment of the "Tell Them We Are Rising Fund," provided they did their part by getting accepted to any accredited institution of their choice. She chose Richard R. Wright elementary school because it was named after her paternal grandfather, who went from being a slave to becoming a bank president and a college president. Kenderton Elementary was chosen because of its good academic reputation and the fact that nearly every member of the sixth grade was reading at grade level or above. Khalil Abdullah provides Hayre's reflections on her announcement at Richard R. Wright and Kenderton Schools:

> What I do hope and pray for is that all of my 119 children stay in school for the next six years, graduate from high school with a meaningful and functional education . . . with clearly defined goals

Ruth Wright Hayre

for life after high school and the necessary preparation to attain those goals.

Foundation in the AME Church

Ruth Wright Hayre, the granddaughter and daughter of ministers in the African Methodist Episcopal Church (AME), inherited a rich and valuable legacy. The AME Church was founded in Philadelphia in 1794 by Richard Allen, who was a slave for almost twenty years before he bought his freedom. After a religious conversion, Allen had concluded that one could not serve God honestly in bondage and oppressed circumstances. By 1816, several AME churches existed, and Allen served as the spiritual leader, or bishop, of a group of these. The AME Church greatly contributed to the development of independence and self-sufficiency in the black community. Recognizing the value and significance of having their own churches, blacks were inspired to develop their own educational and social institutions.

The AME Church leaders stressed education and created Wilberforce University in Ohio in 1856, the first higher education institution founded by black people in the United States. Bishop Daniel Payne, who was instrumental in the founding of Wilberforce, developed a group of courses that were required for all AME ministers, which served as an alternative to seminary study. The AME Church established more than a dozen academic institutions. These include, in addition to Wilberforce University, Morris Brown in Atlanta, Georgia, founded in 1881 and Shorter Junior College in North Little Rock, Arkansas, founded in 1886.

The oldest of five children born to Charlotte Crogman Wright and Richard R. Wright, Jr., a minister, Ruth Hayre grew up in Philadelphia. Hayre recalls in her unpublished autobiography,

> I was born in the home of my maternal grandfather (William H. Crogman) on the campus of Clark College in which he was professor of classical languages and at one time president. My mother was a graduate of Clark and had taught Latin and Greek there for eight years before her marriage— after a long courtship—to my father.

Raising five children and being a minister's spouse meant that Charlotte Crogman Wright was a role model for her family and others in their community. During the time that Bishop Wright worked in southern Africa for the AME Church, she contributed several articles to magazines and newspapers in Africa. She tells of her advocacy of education for women and her experiences living in Africa in her book entitled *Beneath the Southern Cross: The Story of an American Bishop's Wife in South Africa.* Hayre's father was a bishop in the African Methodist Episcopal Church, a realtor, and an editor of the *Christian Recorder,* the official document of the AME Church. He later became president of Wilberforce University in Ohio. Hayre inherited a tradition of community service and of helping those less fortunate through the examples her parents set, particularly her father, who attempted to help southern migrant blacks buy homes rather than rent them.

Ruth Hayre grew up in an upper-middle-class home that valued education. Her father studied abroad in Leipzig, Germany, and at the University of Berlin and earned a master's degree from the University of Chicago. He also received a doctorate in 1911 from the University of Pennsylvania. He was one of a handful of black men in the nation to earn such a degree from a prestigious white university. So it is not surprising that daughter Ruth attended predominantly white public schools, which were within easy walking distance of their middle-class home. At the time that Hayre was growing up in Philadelphia most blacks attended neighborhood de facto segregated elementary schools, which were staffed by black teachers only. Although there was no law prohibiting black students from attending predominantly white schools, very few black children attended schools outside of the black community. Hayre went to predominantly white Newton Elementary School. Since she lived in relatively close proximity to West Philadelphia High School for Girls, she went there, although it was a predominantly white high school. The West Philadelphia High School for Girls offered a college preparatory program, which made Hayre, who was always an outstanding student, academically ready for college. When Hayre entered the University of Pennsylvania, at the age of fifteen, she had won a city and a state scholarship. She was permitted to skip several grades at the elementary level and was only nineteen years old when she completed a degree in education at the University of Pennsylvania. She recalls in her unpublished autobiography,

> During college I concentrated mostly on my studies, participating in few campus activities. I lived at

home in order to save the cost of dormitory living, I was very active in programs of the Christian Association and also served as president of the Alpha Kappa Alpha Sorority undergraduate chapter. Also, during my years as a graduate student I edited the poems of Phillis Wheatley, a famous black poet of revolutionary days. This slender volume was published by the A.M.E. Book Concern, a publishing and printing business carried on by the African Methodist Episcopal Church, under the management of my father. I also had the opportunity to work in the offices of this firm serving as editorial assistant and proof reader for the *Christian Recorder,* one of the oldest black newspapers in the country.

Hayre believed that teaching would provide her with a promising future and said in an interview, "I really wanted to be a teacher. I felt that this was a profession where I would have a chance." At the time she attended the University of Pennsylvania women were allowed to major only in education. The sexism of the time meant that it was assumed that women, regardless of color, would be teachers at the elementary school and high school levels, leaving other academic pursuits to men.

Hayre earned her master's degree in English literature in 1931 from the University of Pennsylvania. She then moved to Arkansas to teach English, French, and Latin at a high school that was established under the auspices of the all-black Arkansas State College. She went to Arkansas because blacks were not allowed to teach in the Philadelphia secondary schools. In 1989, in an article in the *Philadelphia Tribune,* she reflected on her Arkansas experience with mixed emotions:

> I had a wonderful time in Arkansas. But I had no business being there, no matter how beneficial it was I should have been here, teaching high school here. Every one of my white high school classmates got jobs. My marks were higher than theirs, plus, I had a masters degree. They were appointed with just a bachelors.

Hayre left Arkansas in 1933 to teach at Dayton High School in Ohio, where she remained until 1936. She then moved to Washington, D.C., where she taught at the all-black Armstrong Industrial High School. It was during this time that she met and married Talmadge Hayre. In 1939, Hayre moved back to Philadelphia, where her husband received a job offer to teach chemistry at Cheney State University. Though she was pregnant at the time, Hayre taught in Sulzberger Junior High School and started work on her doctorate at the University of Pennsylvania. In 1949 she received a doctorate in English literature and languages. She has also taken graduate courses in administration at Temple and Columbia universities. The number of black students was always very small at the colleges Hayre attended, but racism existed.

While still in graduate school, Hayre decided to take Philadelphia's secondary school teacher examination. Though racism had prevented any blacks from passing it, she was not discouraged. She passed the written examination, but failed the oral part due to the color of her skin rather than her lack of knowledge. She recalls, "When I got called for the oral I'll never forget it. I came face to face with a panel of five old gray-haired white high school principals." She was not stopped by the panel's negative decision and, with the help of Floyd Logan of the Education Equity League, challenged the results. Hayre was also supported by Alexander Stoddard, school superintendent, who agreed that the first panel of testers had treated her unfairly. After being retested by a racially mixed group of educators, she passed the oral part of the examination and became the second black to be appointed to teach on the junior high school level in the Philadelphia school system. She taught English at Sulzberger Junior High School.

Hayre Achieves in Education

In 1946 Hayre became the first black high school teacher in Philadelphia when she was appointed to William Penn, a racially integrated girls school. In 1952 she became the vice principal of the school. Four years later she was promoted to principal. Hayre said in an interview:

> I was ahead of my time in some of my attitudes about public education, the now popular word "accountability" had never been used with regard to schools. Yet, as principal, I felt a school's program would be weak and ineffective if it did not produce memorable results. My staff and I developed the first motivational program in the Philadelphia schools (later imitated in other schools), known as the project Wings. Its objectives were clear-cut—to improve student attendance, to raise reading scores on standardized tests, to improve pupil attitudes and behavior (as shown by reduction of the number of disciplinary incidents), to improve the holding power of the school and reduce the alarming number of dropouts, to increase the number of students going on to college or other post high school institutions, to increase the number of job placements for students graduating from the commercial and home economics courses, to induce an overall tone of hope and inspiration among the student body (frequently referred to as "deprived") and their parents and community.

Hayre made reforms in what was known as an academically weak, restricted-learning school. She established the "Wings" program in an effort to prepare more students for college by motivating them and weaving college preparatory classes into the regular curriculum. Hayre feels that receiving the promotion to vice principal and being able to preside over students at their graduation in her first year of the position were the most memorable moments of her administrative career.

In 1963 Hayre left William Penn to become superintendent of district four in north Philadelphia. She continued to be an agent for change, as she was when she was principal, but this time on a larger scale, affecting more children. Recalling her superintendency, Hayre said: "I feel that there was never anything quite so thrilling as taking a school and turning it around and really making a classy educational institution out of it.''

In 1978 Hayre retired and began to devote her time to traveling, reading, and helping others. Not one to ever be idle, she became a lecturer on urban studies and administration at the Graduate School of Education at the University of Pennsylvania. Then in 1985 she began to serve a six-year term as a member of the Board of Education in Philadelphia. She served as president from 1990 to 1992, the first time a woman had held the position in the 184 years of the board's existence. She continues to work in the educational system because she wants education to become a priority that is achieved in part through the efforts of dedicated teachers who want to teach children to succeed.

"Tell Them We Are Rising" Program Founded

Hayre named the fund that she created to send children to college "Tell Them We Are Rising" because of an event in the childhood of her grandfather, Richard R. Wright, who revered education. Richard R. Wright attended Harvard and was president of Georgia State College and founder of the Citizens and Southern Bank, one of the first black banks in Philadelphia. The Wright family history tells of Richard R. Wright, a boy of ten at the time of the Civil War, meeting a Union army general who asked the black children he encountered what message he should take back with him. Hayre's grandfather replied, "Tell them we are rising."

Hayre was also inspired to establish the fund by multimillionaire Eugene Lang. After hearing that he had promised to pay for sixty students in an East Harlem school to go to college, she considered it a "great gesture" that she wished to accomplish.

Hayre does not disclose the amount her program costs. She told Roxanne Brown in *Ebony* magazine that her husband left her a "tidy sum" when he died and that she has invested her money wisely. "Tuition costs for half of the one hundred and nineteen students are in a trust account at Temple University, which coordinated the program, absorbs most of the operational costs, and provides tutors and program evaluation. If half of them go, it will be a tremendous success, because normally only a 10th would be expected to go." The "Tell Them We Are Rising" students are matched with mentors who serve as role models, advisors, and people who understand the college system.

Hayre is a dedicated teacher and concerned citizen who is a beacon of hope for a group of children in the Philadelphia school system whose chances of receiving a college education were virtually nonexistent until she came along with her "Tell Them We Are Rising" fund. She has certainly lived up to the legacy she inherited from her family.

Ruth Hayre is described by her daughter, Sylvia. E. Hayre Harrison, as "down-to-earth, levelheaded, generous, feisty, abounding in common sense and nurturing." In 1975 her colleagues honored her exceptional contributions to education and the Philadelphia community by creating the Ruth Wright Hayre Scholarship Fund. Between 1976 and 1989,

766 scholarships with a total value of seven hundred thousand dollars were awarded. Recipients are selected annually from classes of graduating seniors from Philadelphia's district four, which Hayre formerly served as superintendent. Philadelphia's school superintendent, Constance E. Clayton, describes Hayre as a person who influenced her. Clayton said, "It is because of her contributions that made it possible for a woman, for a black person to be your superintendent today."

Ruth Hayre currently resides in Philadelphia. She has a daughter and two grandchildren and a host of friends, colleagues, and admirers who cite her as a role model. She enjoys traveling, and although she is officially retired from Philadelphia's school system, she is an advocate of quality education for all young people.

Current Address: Artistic Director, DancEllington, P.O. Box 20346, Park West Finance Station, New York 10025.

REFERENCES:

Abdullah, Khalil. "To Give or Not to Give: Is There a Question?" *National Council of Negro Women* (Summer Supplement 1989): 1.

"A Bequest for Graduates." *Philadelphia Inquirer,* June 25, 1988.

Brown, Roxanne. "Two Women Send 146 Kids to College." *Ebony* 44 (April 1989): 76.

"College Bound." *Daily News,* June 25, 1988.

"Dr. Ruth Wright Hayre." *Philadelphia Tribune,* February 10, 1989.

"From a Pioneer, a Gift of Hope." *Philadelphia Inquirer,* July 17, 1988.

Hayre, Ruth Wright. Unpublished autobiography. 1975.

———. Interview. June 28, 1993.

"His Granddaughter Offers Today's Children a Chance." *Philadelphia Inquirer,* July 15, 1988.

Lincoln, Eric C., and Lawrence H. Mamiya. *The Black Church in the African American Experience.* Durham, N.C.: Duke University Press, 1990.

"The Man Rose from Slavery." *Philadelphia Inquirer,* July 15, 1988.

Rose, Clare. "Women's Sex Role Attitudes: A Historical Perspective." *New Directions for Higher Education* 44 (Autumn 1975): 4.

"Temple Alumni to Honor Hayre." *Philadelphia Tribune,* April 7, 1989.

Thompson, Darlene A. *The Sociopolitical Context of Philadelphia Public Schools, 1912 to 1972: Viewed in Retrospect by Ruth Wright Hayre.* Ph.D. diss., Temple University, 1990.

"A Tribute to an Outstanding Educator." *Sandford Herald,* August 21, 1988.

Who's Who among Black Americans, 1992-93. 8th ed. Detroit: Gale Research, 1994.

Young, Henry J. *Major Black Religious Leaders: 1755-1940.* Nashville: Abingdon, 1977.

Audrey Williams and Alyson Myers

Jessie Mae Hemphill
(1932-)
Blues singer, musician

Every blues performer reaches into the past and takes the form forward. This is especially true of those who live in the Mississippi Delta or have strong roots there. Jessie Mae Hemphill has lived and performed in the Delta for most of her life, and she is an important and well-known figure at blues festivals. The roots of her music run very deep, clearly reaching to Africa, as evidenced by basic instrumental styles, some of the instruments themselves, and the fundamental grounding of her music in drum rhythms. As an instrumentalist, Hemphill is known for her drumming (mostly bass drum) and tambourine playing. As a singer, she uses electric guitar for accompaniment. Her singing and accompanying style are tied to the soil in fundamental ways. Her themes are rural: the blues she sings relate to the country, to work, love, and a life that is not easy; when there is humor, it has an earthy flavor. Hemphill's heritage in music and the instruments she plays reach back at least three generations within her own family. Her grandfather, Sid Hemphill, a performer much in demand in Panola County, Mississippi, had a particularly strong influence on Jessie. Her importance for blues history is therefore twofold. First, she carries on a family tradition in music; second, she has developed and expanded that tradition into her own unique performing style.

Jessie Mae Hemphill was born on October 18, 1932, in Panola County, near her present home in Como, Mississippi. Her father was James Graham, a blues pianist, and her mother was Virgie Lee Graham, also a musician, who learned guitar, drums, and various stringed instruments from her father, Sid Hemphill. The Hemphills were a well-known family musical group in the area, and Jessie Hemphill used the family name from her earliest musical involvements, winning prizes as a youth for tambourine playing, as well as several local competitions in singing, drumming, and dancing. She began playing in family musical groups very early, probably before she was eight years old. She is the living reminder of her aunt Rosa Lee's statement that all of the members of the Hemphill family were musicians, including various aunts, uncles, and cousins, dating back at least as far as Jessie's great-grandfather, a well-known fiddler.

A Personal Blues Style with African Influences

As a singer, Hemphill's voice is light and melodious, with an occasional hint of vocal tremolo; her guitar styling often evokes the strong rhythms of fife and drum music. Her guitar sometimes "speaks" in the typical Delta blues style, using call-and-response interchanges between the guitar and voice in imitation of the song and speech rhythms. These are all clear African heritage elements. Two other musical instruments crucial to Hemphill's style are the quills and the diddley bow. The quills are a set of cane flutes bound or taped together

Jessie Mae Hemphill

like the panpipes; the instrument has African antecedents and was often used by the Hemphill family and other local musicians. Hemphill plays the diddley bow on her *She Wolf* album, in the song "Take Me Home and Put Me in Your Big Brass Bed." The diddley bow is a plucked one-string instrument with an African heritage that may be traceable to the Yoruba of Nigeria (as discussed in detail in Alan Lomax's *Land Where the Blues Began*). Hemphill's drumming displays a strong African element in its driving rhythms; this element can also be heard in her guitar playing and perhaps has its origins in the bass drum instruction she received from her grandfather.

In an August 1993 interview, Hemphill said that she learned a variety of instruments from her grandfather and from just living among her family. Eventually she learned to play drums, tambourine, fife, flute, guitar, trombone, saxophone, diddley bow, mouth harp (harmonica), Jew's harp, organ, and piano. The instruments she came to know and play regularly as a performer were drums, especially bass drum, tambourine, and electric guitar. She credits her aunt Rosa Lee with helping her develop her guitar technique. Occasions for music were family, church, and group picnics. In *Land Where the Blues Began,* Lomax names Hemphill as a drummer and quotes her comments on music and on women musicians. She refers to women players as very competent, often filling in for male performers who were farming or otherwise occupied.

The people of Panola, Tate, and Tunica counties have long been famous for their music and their picnics, which can be major local music and dance events. Jessie Hemphill's grandfather, Sid Hemphill, led a band and played in others that included fife and drum music as well as the usual string complement of violin, mandolin, banjo, and guitar; quills, harmonica, tambourine, and drums were also used. Sid Hemphill was recorded as early as 1942 by Alan Lomax for the Library of Congress; many of these recordings were later released on the Library of Congress's *Afro-American Folk Music from Tate and Panola Counties, Mississippi,* and some of these recordings were subsequently released on Atlantic Records' *Roots of the Blues* series.

Evolving Musical Career

Hemphill married J. D. Brooks of Memphis when she was a teenager, and she then performed as Jessie Mae Brooks. According to Hemphill, at that point her activities in music included socials, club dates, local fairs and festivals, and other outings in northern Mississippi and the Memphis area. She and Brooks subsequently separated. When she decided to pursue a career and preserve her family's name in music, she changed her name back to Jessie Mae Hemphill. Her musical career accelerated from about 1979 onward, taking her to engagements in states other than Mississippi. According to D. Antoinette Handy in *Black Women in American Bands and Orchestras,* she appeared in 1979 at the Delta Blues Festival in Greenville, Mississippi. She also appeared at the Beale Street Festival and in "Blues Alley" in Memphis as a singer and as a member of the Napoleon Strickland Fife and Drum Band and the Beale Street Jug Band. In 1980 she appeared in Richmond, Virginia, and Washington, D.C., for the Folklore Society of Greater Washington.

Since then, her performance engagements have taken her to Canada and nine European cities, including Vienna (1987) and Nantes, France (1991). She has recently performed at a blues concert in Pittsburgh (1990), the Smithsonian Institution's Folklife Festival in Washington, D.C. (1991), the Blues Festival in Des Moines, Iowa (1992), and many local festivals and engagements in the Memphis and northern Mississippi area, including an engagement at the annual Blues Festival in Clarksdale, Mississippi, on August 7, 1993. Hemphill's recordings appear on the Australian Au Go Go and French Black and Blue labels, and her song "Train, Train" appears on the Smithsonian Institution's recently released CD *Roots of Rhythm and Blues.* Her album *She Wolf* was released by the French Vogue label, and her album *Feelin Good* by the United States label High Water. She won W. C. Handy awards for best female traditional blues artist in 1987 and 1988, and *Feelin Good* won the Handy Award for best country blues album of the year in 1991.

Jessie Mae Hemphill personifies the blues in many ways. She began early as an apprentice in her grandfather's musical groups and has developed into a blues stylist with a national reputation and international concert credits. As all blues enthusiasts know, there is something very special about the Delta blues. It has a characteristic repertoire, chord structure, use of instruments, and song form; allusions to rural themes and plots; an undercurrent of African influence; and an overall earthy tone projected in its dialect, humor, and attitude toward life's twists and turns. As a present-day exponent of the Delta

blues, Hemphill brings a rich and deep family tradition to the music as well as broad experience, which manifests itself in her own personal style of expression. The deep roots of Hemphill's music will remain and the flowers will continue to blossom as her style develops over time.

Current Address: Box 975, Senatobia, MS 38668.

REFERENCES:

Dahl, Linda. *Stormy Weather.* New York: Pantheon, 1984.
"Deep in the Blues." *Nashville Tennessean,* July 18, 1993.
Evans, David. "Jessie Mae Hemphill." *Living Blues* (March-April 1985): 35-36.
Handy, D. Antoinette. *Black Women in American Bands and Orchestras.* Metuchen, N.J.: Scarecrow Press, 1981.
Hemphill, Jessie Mae, Interview with Darius L. Thieme. August 5, 1993.
Hine, Darlene Clark, ed. *Black Women in America.* Brooklyn: Carlson Publishing, 1993.
Lomax, Alan. *Land Where the Blues Began.* New York: Pantheon, 1993.
Mitchell, George. *Blow My Blues Away.* Baton Rouge: Louisiana State University Press, 1971.
Scott, Frank. *Down Home Guide to the Blues.* Chicago: Down Home Music, 1991.

Darius L. Thieme

Freddye Scarborough Henderson
(1917-)
Entrepreneur, travel agent, fashion designer, writer, educator

Freddye Scarborough Henderson is one of the most widely traveled African Americans in the world. Starting with an impressive career in fashion design, Henderson owned a dress boutique, wrote a weekly fashion column, and was the first black women in the United States to receive an M.A. in fashion merchandising. Henderson changed directions in the mid-1950s, opening one of the first black travel agencies in the country and becoming renowned for organizing tour packages, particularly to Africa. Henderson arranged and accompanied Martin Luther King, Jr. on his trip to Norway to accept the Nobel Peace Prize. She stepped dauntlessly into the China travel market after Richard Nixon made his trip to China in 1972. In 1973, at the invitation of Ethiopia's Emperor Haile Selassie, Henderson was invited on an inaugural air flight to China. Henderson is the co-owner of Henderson Travel Service, one of America's trailblazing black travel agencies.

Freddye Scarborough Henderson

Freddye Scarborough Henderson was born in Franklinton, Louisiana, on February 18, 1917. She grew up in Franklinton and graduated from Booker T. Washington High School as class valedictorian. Young Scarborough remained in her native state and acquired a B.S. degree cum laude in home economics from Southern University in 1937. Scarborough married Jacob Robert Henderson in 1941; Jacob Henderson was a public housing administrator in Atlanta, Georgia. She later attended the McDowell School of Costume Design in 1944, and the Traphagen School of Fashion Design in 1949. In 1950, Henderson received an M.S. degree in merchandising—the first black woman to receive this particular degree from the New York University School of Retailing.

From 1944 to 1950, Henderson managed her own fashion design and custom dress design boutique in Atlanta, Georgia. She discovered that "nobody was ready for a black with a masters in fashion merchandising. They thought I was charming and dynamic, but they weren't ready." So in 1950, she joined the faculty of Spelman College as an associate professor of applied art and clothing and also became an instructor for the Atlanta University summer school—she kept these two appointments until 1961. From 1950 to 1955, she was a fashion editor for the Associated Negro Press and wrote a syndicated column "Fashion Trends," published weekly in all the nations's leading black newspapers. From 1950 to 1954, Henderson was president of the National Association of Fashion and Accessory Designers. In 1952, she began work as a radio commentator and was featured on a program entitled "Freddye's Fashion Forum" on WERD radio station in Atlanta. Additionally, Henderson became a

celebrated fashion show commentator and lecturer and an authority on fashion, charm, and "international know-how." She lectured at black colleges around the South, such as Southern, Langston, Dillard, Morehouse, Morris Brown, South Carolina State, and Clark.

Despite Henderson's imposing credentials, as a black woman she was unable to break into fashion merchandising in Atlanta in the 1950s. However, she did not give up her aspirations. In 1951, as president of the National Association of Fashion and Accessory Designers, Henderson organized the first fashion show program ever sponsored by a black group in New York's Waldorf Astoria Hotel and focused national attention on black fashions. Paradoxically, it was her promotion of fashion that led to her change of career.

In 1954, Henderson directed the first Fashion Tour Group to visit the major fashion houses of Paris, Rome, and London. The all-black group was composed of afficianatos of haute couture who annually visited the fashion houses of Europe. In Paris, members of the group were personal guests of the House of Dior for a luncheon and fashion shows. The group also observed the International Press fashion show, and Henderson was the first black fashion writer to cover these shows.

What affected Henderson most about the trip was not the fashions, but rather the arrangements that had been made prior to their arrival: the admirable accommodations and the smoothness with which the trip was handled. She was overwhelmed with the group's cordial reception and with how well blacks were treated abroad in contrast to their treatment in America. With encouragement from her husband, Jacob, who had become a technical assistance officer with the United States Department of Commerce, Henderson grew intent on becoming a travel agent who would make it possible for black people to travel around the world in elegance.

Travel Agency Founded

In 1955, Rosa Parks refused to give up her seat on a Montgomery bus in Alabama. Henderson watched the turmoil that followed on television and came up with an idea. She decided to establish a travel agency that would open the world to other blacks. Henderson was sponsored by Pan American Airlines and SAS Airlines. Hers was the first black travel agency in Atlanta and only the fifth in the nation. To offset blacks' apprehension of travel, which resulted from restrictions on their travel in the United States, Henderson Travel concentrated on the convention market, taking black groups on tours and becoming nationally known.

In the late 1950s, many groups were going to east Africa, but west Africa was virtually overlooked by tourists because of its lack of airport and hotel facilities. Henderson, seventeen years before the surge of interest stimulated by Alex Haley and his *Roots* phenomena, inaugurated a specialty in African visits for African Americans. Henderson took the first large tour to west Africa—a group of women college graduates in a professional sorority—after chartering a DC-6 out of Paris for a tour that included Senegal, Nigeria, Kenya, and Morocco. By 1969, when Pan American Airlines instituted flights to west Africa, Henderson Travel was the only travel agency with expertise in west African travel, and it was chosen to establish Pan Am's tours. Henderson's business increased to the point where the agency wholesaled west African tours and became the only black-owned travel tour wholesaler in the country. This meant tour packages were produced for sale by other companies arranging tours. Africa emerged as the agency's distinctive trademark. More than 50 percent of its tours were Africa-bound, and Henderson gained renown as the foremost expert on travel to Africa.

In 1972, Henderson received the African Trophy. This award is given annually at the World Travel Congress Convention for the American Society of Travel Agents (ASTA) to the United States or Canadian travel agency that has done the most to promote travel to Africa south of the Sahara. Henderson is also the only black agent to be designated a certified travel counselor by the Institute of Certified Travel Agents. It is the industry's highest designation for proficiency and excellence in the operation of a travel agency and quite a feat for a women who before 1954 had never traveled outside of the United States. Henderson served as travel editor from 1957 to 1960 for the *Pittsburgh Courier,* a nationally circulated black newspaper, and received in 1959 and 1964 the KLM Royal Dutch Airlines Production Award. In 1964, Henderson was appointed to serve a two-year term as a member of the Travel Advisory Committee to the United States Travel Service by Secretary of Commerce Luther Hodges. She received an award from the Association of Travel Executives for consistent excellence in travel in 1972.

Henderson Meets World Leaders

Perhaps the most widely traveled black woman in America, Henderson has traveled extensively throughout the world. She has had some startling successes. In 1964, she organized one of her most interesting travel experiences: Martin Luther King, Jr.'s trip to Oslo to accept the Nobel Peace Prize. She has met leaders such as Premier Chou En Lai of China, Jomo Kenyatta of Kenya, and Emperor Haile Selassie of Ethiopia. In 1969, Freddye Henderson escorted Coretta Scott King when the widow of the martyred Martin Luther King, Jr. spoke in London's Saint Paul Cathedral.

As her travel agency developed, Henderson generated new markets and stepped bravely into the Chinese tourism market after former President Richard M. Nixon made his epochal trip to China in 1972. In 1973, Henderson was invited on an inaugural flight to China with a delegation led by the granddaughter of Ethiopia's Emperor Haile Selassie. Although she was dealing with a white market, Henderson had an edge because no other travel groups had been to China, and she was designated as agent by the Chinese.

The business branched out into other areas including trade missions, such as Andrew Young's trip to Jamaica and Trinidad, and promotions, such as the closed-circuit broadcast of Muhammed Ali's fights and the sale of beef and poultry in African markets.

Since her first trip to Paris, Henderson had become a world traveler visiting more than 150 countries and being entertained by royalty. And she reared four children, Carol Tyson, Jacob R., Jr., Gaynelle, and Shirley. All of the children have advanced degrees and are fluent in foreign languages; Henderson herself still only speaks English.

When her children were growing up, Henderson believed that blacks received a very poor education in Atlanta's public schools. The Henderson children were sent to private schools, aided by tuition grants for outstanding minority students, and were able to enter excellent colleges. Henderson told the *Atlanta Constitution* in 1983, "Between us, including my husband and me and our children, we have among us fourteen degrees and nobody has any money."

Henderson was very involved in civic affiars and was recognized by the *Atlanta Daily World* as the World Mother of 1951. In 1954, she was selected by Iota Phi Lambda Sorority as Woman of the Year in the Arts. Henderson received a special award from the National Association of Fashion and Accessory Designers in 1959. She was honored by her alma mater on the 1960 Alumni Day at Southern University. In 1968, she received the Zeta Phi Beta Sorority Outstanding Woman's Award, and in 1969 she received the Lola M. Parker Achievement Award from the Iota Phi Lambda Sorority. Henderson was named the 1982 recipient of the Joseph W. Rosenbluth Award for outstanding contributions to the professional status of the travel agency business spanning a twenty-seven-year career. She was also active in a number of civic organizations, including the YWCA, the World Fellowship Committee, and the Atlanta Council for International Visitors.

Current Address: 1691 Simpson Road, N.W., Atlanta, GA.

REFERENCES:

"Atlantan Was Pioneer in Black Tourist Travel." *Atlanta Constitution,* July 11, 1983.

Ebony Success Library. Vol. 1. Nashville: Southwestern Publishing Co., 1973.

Kalamu ya Salaam. "Don't Forget Your Ticket." *The Black Collegian* (January/February 1978): 30.

Ledlie, Joe. "Back to Africa Freddye Henderson Style." A release published by the (United States Information Agency) for distribution in Africa, n.d.

"Marketing the World for Fun and Profit." *Black Enterprise* 5 (January 1975): 21.

"New 'Gateway to the World' Swings Open on Hunter Street." *Atlanta Daily World,* November 16, 1955.

"1982 Rosenbluth Award Received by Henderson." *Travel Trade News Edition,* October 18, 1982.

"Out of Conflict Ideas Are Born." *Travel Agent* (July 25, 1980): 54.

"Travel Agency Has Record of Success." *Atlanta Constitution,* October 12, 1977.

"Travel Executive Rates China Trip Second Best." *Atlanta Daily World,* April 6, 1973.

Weiser, Morton. "Seek Nationwide Agency Chain to Tap Negro Market." *Travel Weekly* 28 (July 11, 1969): 1.

Casper L. Jordan

Alexis M. Herman

Alexis M. Herman

(1947-)

Government official, political organizer, management expert, entrepreneur, civic and social worker, women's rights advocate

Alexis Herman said in the November 1977 issue of *Essence*, "It's important that we set high goals for ourselves. It never occurred to me that I couldn't be anything I wanted to be." During her career, Herman has worked in politics, public relations, and with social service and women's rights groups. She has indeed achieved success in high level—and highly visible—positions. At the age of twenty-nine, she was sworn in as director of the Women's Bureau of the U.S. Department of Labor, thus becoming the youngest person ever to serve in that capacity. Now Herman serves as an assistant to President Bill Clinton and director of the White House Office of the Public Liaison—the department responsible for building public support for presidential priorities. She, along with Maggie Williams, the first black chief of staff to a first lady, play important roles in creating support for the Democratic political agenda.

Alexis Margaret Herman was born July 16, 1947, in Mobile, Alabama, to Alex Herman and Gloria Caponis Herman. She graduated from the Heart of Mary High School in Mobile (1965); attended Edgewood College in Madison, Wisconsin (1965-67) and Spring Hill College in Mobile (1967); received her B.S. degree in 1969 from Xavier University in New Orleans, Louisiana; and did graduate work at the University of South Alabama in Mobile (1970-72).

Herman began her professional career at the local level. Between 1969 and 1972, she was a community worker for Interfaith in Mobile, a social worker for Catholic Social Services, also in Mobile, and an outreach worker for the Recruitment and Training Program in Pascagoula, Mississippi.

In 1972, when Atlanta's Southern Regional Council wanted to determine whether a recruitment and training program designed to get blacks into the construction trades could be adapted to obtain white collar jobs for minority women, Herman moved to Atlanta to develop the program. Two years later, this project, known as the Minority Women Employment Program (MWEP), went national with Herman as its director. Through this pioneering initiative, several hundred women of color were placed in nontraditional private sector jobs.

Gains National Prominence

From 1977 to 1981, Herman was director of the Women's Bureau, Office of the Secretary, U.S. Department of Labor. Named to the position by President Jimmy Carter, Herman advised both Carter and labor secretary Ray Marshall on economic and social concerns of women in the workplace and directed the department's program for small, developing, and disadvantaged businesses. At the time of her appointment, not only did she become the senior black woman Labor Department official, she became the youngest director ever to serve in the history of the Women's Bureau.

The Women's Bureau has traditionally been responsible for formulating policies and implementing programs that address the concerns of many diverse women's groups. Among these groups are minority women (including black, Hispanic, native American, and Asian American), mature women (midlife), and women reentering the work force, as well as displaced homemakers, battered women, women who have been charged with crimes, low-income women, rural women, and women business owners. As director of the Women's Bureau, Herman became acquainted with the many problems that affect women in the workplace, and she worked hard to address the questions women asked about their plight. Her goal was to push the Women's Bureau into the forefront of issues concerning women, to get directly involved in existing programs, and to develop model programs for various groups of women who needed specialized help.

As Herman noted, major issues facing working women in the 1970s were job discrimination based on gender, age, or race; limited marketable job skills, particularly in nontraditional career fields; rigid work schedules; and child care. These issues continue to be major problems in the 1990s. Writing about the prospects for advancement for black women within the labor market in an article published in the May/June 1979 *Black Collegian,* Herman stated:

> Black women must be qualified to fill some of the better paying jobs in the areas where skills will be in demand. It calls for more women to move into the nontraditional, higher paying jobs. And it calls for more affirmative action efforts to ensure that Black women do indeed have equal opportunity for training and education, and for consideration in recruitment. It calls for increased numbers of Black women among those being hired, and among those being promoted on the job. Only then will we begin to see a drastic change in where Black women now stand in the labor force.

Herman noted further in another article she wrote for the *Black Collegian* (April/May 1980) that black women must also keep in mind that simply being qualified for a particular position is only part of the process of realizing job opportunities. Women, particularly those of color and those moving into nontraditional jobs, must be conscious of the fact that their constant vigilance is needed to ensure that equal employment opportunity and affirmative action policies are being properly enforced. Herman's other published articles on issues confronting women in the workplace include: "Minority Women, Professional Work" (*Manpower,* July 1975); "Black Women in the Workplace: Are Their Options Really Open?" (*Ivy Leaf, AKA Journal,* Fall 1977); "Equal Access to Equal Jobs for Workers" (*Operating Engineer,* December 1979); and "If She Were A Carpenter: Nontraditional Apprenticeships for Women in Prison" (*Corrections Today,* November-December 1979).

Herman's position with the Women's Bureau was a stepping stone to other jobs at the national level. In 1991, the Democratic National Committee (DNC) chair, Ron Brown, appointed Herman deputy chair of the DNC. She also served as chief of staff for the DNC beginning in 1989. In 1991 Herman was named chief executive officer of the 1992 Democratic National Convention Committee, with responsibilities for overall strategic management and production of the convention.

Starts Marketing and Management Firm

Recognized as an expert in the field of multiculturalism and diversity management as it relates to mergers and acquisitions, Herman has traveled extensively in the United States and abroad speaking on workplace issues. She is founder and president of the Washington-based marketing and management firm of A. M. Herman and Associates, which specializes in targeted marketing strategies, organizational analysis, and human resource management. She has demonstrated her ability to compete successfully in both the public and private sectors.

Herman has served in the capacities of leader, board member, and spokesperson for various service, professional, and religious organizations. She is a former chair of the National Commission on Working Women. She is a founding member of the National Consumer Cooperative Bank and has served on the boards of the Adams National Bank, the National Council of Negro Women, the National Democratic Institute, and the District of Columbia Economic Development Finance Corporation. During her tenure with the U.S. Labor Department, Herman was White House Representative to the Organization of Economic Cooperation and Development. She later cochaired the President's task force to establish a Women's Business Ownership Initiative for the federal government.

Herman has been involved with the United States Catholic Bishops Conference, the United States Catholic Conference on Social Justice, and the World Peace Commission; she also served on the board of the Campaign for Human Development (1972-75), the Catholic Church's national education and action program to combat poverty and injustice in the United States. As a member of Delta Sigma Theta Sorority, she has functioned in a wide array of leadership and group-service capacities.

Herman has received numerous awards and accolades. These include the Dorothy I. Height Award, Recruitment and Training Program; Outstanding Young Person of Atlanta (1974); First Woman Award, Negro Business and Professional Women's Clubs of Atlanta (1976); Outstanding Young Woman of the Year, District of Columbia; National Black Women's Political Leadership Caucus, Woman of the Year (1977); Award of Excellence, Non-Partisan Voters League (1977); Outstanding Young Woman of America (1978); Scroll of Distinction, National Association of Negro Business and Professional Woman's Clubs; Award for Affirmative Action in the Workplace, The Coalition of Labor Union Women (1978); Equal Opportunity Award, The Mexican-American Opportunity Foundation (1978); *Ebony* magazine's "50 Future Leaders" (1979); and Outstanding Young Woman of the Future, *Ladies Home Journal* (1980).

A determined, creative, personable, and compassionate woman, Alexis Herman has used her intelligence and political savvy to make a steady climb from local community organizer to her current position as assistant to the President and Director of the Office of Public Liaison. Her tireless work toward equality and social justice has broadened employment opportunities not only for black women, but also for many other traditionally underrepresented groups.

Current Address: Assistant to the President and Director of Public Liaison, Office of the Public Liaison, Old Executive Building, Room 122, Washington, DC 20500.

REFERENCES:

Alexis M. Herman. Biographical information. White House. 1994.

"Blacks Held Top Posts at Democratic Confab." *Jet* 82 (August 3, 1992): 10-11.

Dobrzynski, Judith. "Essence Women: Alexis Herman." *Essence* 8 (November 1977): 6.

Herman, Alexis. "Black Women in the Labor Force." *Black Collegian* 9 (May/June 1979).

―――. "Employment Opportunities for Black Women in the 1980's." *Black Collegian* 10 (April/May 1980): 96-99.

Moreman, Grace E., and Pearl G. Spindler. "Women in the Labor Movement and Organizations." In *The Women's Book of World Records.* Edited by Lois D. O'Neill. Garden City, N.Y.: Anchor Press/Doubleday, 1979.

Who's Who in American Politics. 13th ed. New Providence, N.J.: R. R. Bowker Database Publishing Group, 1992.

"Women in Government: A Slim Past, but a Strong Future." *Ebony* 32 (August 1977): 89-98.

"Women's Job Activist." *Washington Star,* April 1, 1977.

Marva L. Rudolph

Anita Hill

Anita Hill

(1956-)

Lawyer, educator

Anita Hill was catapulted into the limelight in the fall of 1991 when she testified before the U.S. Senate during the confirmation hearings for Clarence Thomas, who had been nominated by President George Bush for the U.S. Supreme Court seat recently vacated by Justice Thurgood Marshall. Hill charged that Thomas had sexually harassed her when she worked for him at the U.S. Department of Education and at the Equal Employment Opportunity Commission. Because of these allegations, the publicity surrounding the hearings was enormous. The Senate debate pitted the Republican party against the Democratic party and public opinion was split along racial and gender lines. Never before had the issue of sexual harassment—its defining characteristics and the implications of such behavior—received such widespread attention.

Born July 30, 1956, in a farming community six miles east of Morris, Oklahoma, Anita Faye Hill was the youngest of thirteen children. Her parents, Albert and Erma Hill, raised them as Baptists. Anita, called Faye by family and friends, was one of four siblings to become valedictorian of Morris High School. She continued her high scholastic achievement during her college years. In 1977 she graduated with honors from Oklahoma State University with a B.S. in psychology.

Since her graduation in 1980 from Yale University Law School, which she attended on an NAACP scholarship, Hill has actively pursued a career in the legal field. Her first position was at the law firm of Wald, Hardraker and Ross in Washington, D.C., where she worked from 1980 to 1981. After this, she became an assistant to Clarence Thomas, assistant secretary at the U.S. Department of Education. Thomas, a black man, was a Yale University Law School graduate. Before his position at the Department of Education, he had worked as an assistant attorney general for the state of Missouri and as legislative assistant to Senator John Danforth. What began as a positive working relationship between Thomas and Hill deteriorated after three months, according to Hill, when Thomas began asking her for dates and wanting to discuss sex, overtures that she refused. Nine months later, Thomas was tapped to chair the Equal Employment Opportunity Commission (EEOC). Thomas chose Hill to be his special assistant, a position she left in 1983. The Winter 1991/Spring 1992 *Black Scholar* quotes Hill's testimony at the Senate hearings, during which she said that "the work itself was interesting, and at that time it appeared that the sexual overtures which had so troubled me had ended."

An opportunity to teach law in her home state drew Hill to Oral Roberts University in 1983. She met the dean of the Oral Roberts University Law School when she visited the campus with her boss, Clarence Thomas, who had been invited to give a speech there. After Hill attended an afternoon seminar at the law school, the dean, Charles A. Kothe, told her he wanted to hire her. According to the *Black Scholar,* she said during her opening statement before the Senate on October 11, 1991, "I agreed to take the job, in large part because of my desire to escape the pressures I felt at the EEOC due to Judge Thomas." After teaching at Oral Roberts, she moved on to the University of Oklahoma College of Law at Norman, where she is currently a commercial law professor.

Hill Testifies against Clarence Thomas

In August 1991 an aide to Ohio Democrat Senator Howard Metzenbaum, a member of the Judiciary Committee, received a tip that Clarence Thomas sexually harassed Anita Hill during her employment with him in the early 1980s. After agreeing to testify before the committee, Hill decided in September to prepare a personal statement about the allegations, which she was assured would be kept confidential. This statement and an FBI report were circulated to the committee members. Thomas, when informed, vehemently denied the charges.

The Judiciary Committee sent Thomas's nomination to the floor of the Senate with no recommendation, having split their vote seven to seven. During the subsequent full Senate debate, Hill's name and a portion of the FBI report were leaked to *Newsday* and National Public Radio. On October 6, 1991, both news agencies made public Hill's allegations of sexual harassment against Clarence Thomas. Senate and public pressure to investigate these charges further pushed the Senate to reopen the hearings, which were carried live on the ABC, CBS, NBC, and C-SPAN networks.

From October 11 to October 13, 1991, all media were focused on what would become a national and international debate: What is sexual harassment and what are its consequences? Anita Hill became a household name as her allegations became the central issue that would determine whether Clarence Thomas was competent to be a Supreme Court justice. Her elderly parents flew to Washington, D.C., to demonstrate their support of their youngest child. According to the *Black Scholar,* during these open hearings, Hill told the senators, "It is only after a great deal of agonizing consideration that I am able to talk of these unpleasant matters to anyone except my closest friends."

The public was divided over who was telling the truth: was it Anita Hill or Clarence Thomas? Since the allegations referred to incidents that had occurred almost ten years before, Hill's credibility was decidedly in question. Why did she wait so long to air her grievances? Public opinion seemed to favor Clarence Thomas, though the various polls reflected racial and/or gender bias.

Many members of the African American community debated whether a black woman should bring such charges against a black man since, in their opinion, prejudice against blacks was already a major factor threatening their employment prospects. Jill Nelson, author of *Voluntary Slavery,* noted in *Essence* magazine, December 1991, that "clearly the Black community is not monolithic. There was diversity of opinion on every aspect of the hearings."

After intense debate, the Senate, by a vote of 52-48, confirmed Clarence Thomas as an associate justice of the Supreme Court on October 16, 1991, making him the second black appointed to the Supreme Court.

Aftermath of the Hearings

In a show of support along gender and racial lines, 1,603 black women issued a historic statement that appeared in the November 18, 1991, issue of the *New York Times.* Entitled "African American Women in Defense of Ourselves," the article conveyed their objection to the Thomas appointment and the Hill-Thomas hearings. In *Black Scholar* Winter 1991/ Spring 1992, Earl Lewis, director of the Center for Afroamerican and African Studies and associate professor of history at the University of Michigan, argued that the conservative image of blacks, such as that marketed to confirm Thomas, is what sells. He concluded, "Therefore, the hearings about Thomas were mostly about Hill, and the need to destroy her credibility as a believable product in the minds of the public. And by and large the strategy worked."

After the hearings, Hill returned to her duties as a law professor but began another career as an advocate against sexual harassment, speaking primarily before women's groups and corporate and government agencies concerned about sexual harassment in the workplace. When a staff writer from *Glamour* magazine, which had named Anita Hill one of its ten Women of the Year in 1991, visited Hill in Norman, she found the law professor inundated with letters from Americans reacting to the hearings. Of the 24,377 letters and cards the writer perused, fully 98 percent expressed their support of Hill. June Jordan, poet and professor of African American Studies and Women's Studies at the University of California at Berkeley, stated flatly in *The Progressive,* December 1991,

> Anita Hill was tricked. She was set up. She had been minding her business at the University of Oklahoma Law School when the senators asked her to describe her relationship with Clarence Thomas. . . . And with this televised victimization of Anita Hill, the American war of violence against women moved from the streets, moved from hip-hop, moved from multimillion-dollar movies into the highest chambers of the U.S. Government.

However, a *U.S. News and World Report* poll in 1992 indicated that the public was evenly divided (38 percent for Hill and 38 percent for Thomas) in their opinion about the credibility of the two, while during the hearings 60 percent of those polled believed Thomas and only 20 percent believed Hill.

While the weekly news magazines *People, Time, Newsweek,* and *U.S. News and World Report* reported on the hearings in successive issues in October, the *Black Scholar* devoted the entire Winter 1991/Spring 1992 issue to the debate about sexual harassment. Orlando Patterson, professor of sociology at Harvard University, stated in that issue,

> I am convinced that Professor Hill perfectly understood the psycho-cultural context in which Judge Thomas allegedly regaled her with his Rabelaisian humor (possibly as a way of affirming their common origins), which is precisely why she never filed a complaint against him. Raising the issue 10 years later was unfair and disingenuous.

Gloria Hull, professor of women's studies and literature at the University of California at Santa Cruz, remarked in the same journal, "In the final analysis, I think I have been forced to conclude that being a nice, good girl got Anita Hill what all 'nice girls' usually get: nothing—but further abuse." Julianne Malveaux, economist and writer, expressed still another sentiment when she concluded that "we [black women] have been taught silence, and Anita Hill's lifted voice is evidence that she finally found the Sojourner within her."

Heightened Awareness of Sexual Harassment

The January 1992 issue of *Essence* magazine includes an article entitled "A House Divided," which contains a sampling of other opinions about Hill that reveals the differing views of African Americans. Shahrazad Ali, author of *The Blackman's Guide to Understanding the Blackwoman,* accuses Hill of "vocational prostitution" for not confronting Thomas at the time of the alleged harassment. Donna Brazile, chief aide to Congresswoman Eleanor Holmes Norton, states,

> Hill's plight was facing an institution that is not only hostile to the needs of Blacks, but hostile and insensitive to the needs of women. I've heard people say, "How could she?" We Black women have always been supportive of Black men. . . . Being supportive does not mean you have to support every single Black man, regardless.

Haki Madhubuti, poet and professor, commented in *Essence* on what he saw as a positive outcome of the hearings:

> The fallout from this has heightened Black men's and women's awareness of sexual harassment. I hope that—as a result of this spectacle—Black men will be more conscientious about how they treat women in the workplace as well as in the home. I would also hope that women would be strong enough in the future to confront such harassment early rather than let it live in them as horror stories. I hope this event will enable us [black men] to grow and realize that our manhood does not depend on taking advantage of Black women.

For the American public in general, the hearings made sexual harassment an important issue. *Time* magazine reported in the October 19, 1992, issue that "most women continue to fear that if they cry harassment, they will be ignored, stigmatized, even fired." The article reported that 60 percent of all individuals who complained to the EEOC were told that "they had 'no cause' to proceed," and the commission filed only a small fraction of those complaints as sexual harassment cases. Yet, according to *People,* "Corporations across the nation are stepping up their efforts to educate employees about sexual harassment, and at the Equal Employment Opportunity Commission . . . calls requesting information on the definition of harassment have increased a hundredfold." A survey of women faculty reported in the *Chronicle of Higher Education* found that "most faculty women have said that they found Ms. Hill very credible."

Nobel Prize-winning author Toni Morrison edited a collection of essays entitled *Race-ing Justice, En-gendering Power: Essays on Anita Hill, Clarence Thomas, and the Construction of Social Reality.* Morrison stated in her introduction,

> In matters of race and gender, it is now possible and necessary, as it seemed never to have been before, to speak about these matters without the barriers, the silences, the embarrassing gaps in discourse. It is clear to the most reductionist intellect that Black people think differently from one another; it is also clear that the time for undiscriminating racial unity has passed.

As stated in the October 14, 1992, issue of *Chronicle of Higher Education,* the Senate hearings made Anita Hill a "national icon" for the issue of sexual harassment. Though Thomas's nomination was confirmed, her testimony inspired needed discussion on the hotly contested topic of sexual harassment. Even though some people believe that Hill's testimony was fabricated and that she did more to hurt than to help the cause of women in the workplace, Hill remains steadfast in her conviction that she did the right thing by testifying.

In 1992 Anita Hill took a sabbatical from teaching to explore the possibility of founding an institute for research on racism and sexism. The following year the University of Oklahoma Board of Regents approved a proposal to name a professorship after Hill that would be devoted to the study of discrimination in the workplace.

Current Address: Laguna Beach, CA.

REFERENCES:

"Anita Hill." *People* 36 (December 30, 1991-January 6, 1992): 46-47.

Brock, David. *The Real Anita Hill: The Untold Story.* New York: Free Press, 1993.

Garment, Suzanne. "Why Anita Hill Lost." *Commentary* 93 (January 1992): 26-35.

Guy-Sheftall, Beverly. "Breaking the Silence: A Black Feminist Response to the Thomas/Hill Hearings (for Audre Lorde)." *Black Scholar* 22 (Winter 1991/Spring 1992): 35-37.

Hill, Anita. "Opening Statement before the Senate Judiciary Committee, October 11, 1991." *Black Scholar* 22 (Winter 1991/Spring 1992): 8-11.

"Hill Resigning As Law Professor." *Nashville Tennessean,* March 17, 1995.

"A House Divided." *Essence* 22 (January 1992): 58-59, 92-93.

Hull, Gloria T. "Girls Will Be Girls, and Boys Will . . . Flex Their Muscles." *Black Scholar* 22 (Winter 1991/Spring 1992): 47-48.

Jordan, June. "Can I Get a Witness?" *The Progressive* 55 (December 1991): 12-13.

Leatherman, Courtney. "Once a Little-Known Law Professor, Anita Hill Now Is a 'National Icon.'" *Chronicle of Higher Education* 39 (October 14, 1992): 18A.

Lewis, Earl. "Race as Commodity: Hill and Thomas as Consumer Product." *Black Scholar* 22 (Winter 1991/Spring 1992): 66-68.

Malveaux, Julianne. "No Peace in a Sisterly Space." *Black Scholar* 22 (Winter 1991/Spring 1992): 68-71.

Morrison, Toni. *Race-ing Justice, En-gendering Power: Essays on Anita Hill, Clarence Thomas, and the Construction of Social Reality*. New York: Pantheon, 1992.

Nelson, Jill. "Hill versus Thomas." *Essence* 22 (December 1991): 134.

Patterson, Orlando. "Race, Gender and Liberal Fallacies." *Black Scholar* 22 (Winter 1991/Spring 1992): 77-80.

Sedman, Susan. "Mail Call in Norman, Oklahoma." *Glamour* 90 (March 1992): 30.

"She Could Not Keep Silent." *People* 36 (October 28, 1991): 11-13.

Smolowe, Jill. "Anita Hill's Legacy." *Time* 140 (October 19, 1992): 56-57.

Spencer, Cembalo. "The Chronology of the Clarence Thomas Confirmation." *Black Scholar* 22 (Winter 1991/Spring 1992): 1-3.

Sullivan, Kathleen M. "The Hill-Thomas Mystery." *New York Review of Books* 40 (August 12, 1993): 12-16.

Who's Who among Black Americans, 1994-95. 8th ed. Detroit: Gale Research, 1994.

Winternitz, Helen. "Anita Hill: One Year Later." *Working Woman* 17 (September 1992): 21.

Jacqueline Brice-Finch

Ann Hobson-Pilot

(1943-)

Harpist

As principal harpist in the Boston Symphony Orchestra, Ann Hobson-Pilot holds one of the most important positions for a harpist in the world of music. Joining the Boston Symphony—one of the nation's "Big Three"—as associate principal harpist in 1969, she was appointed principal harpist in 1980. She currently holds the Willona Henderson Sinclair Chair. When first auditioning for the Boston Symphony, Hobson-Pilot competed against thirty other harpists for the position of second harpist. She was the undisputed winner, and if she accepted the position, she would also be principal harpist in the Boston Pops. But she had a hard decision to make. She was then principal harpist in the National Symphony in Washington, D.C.; was second in the higher-ranked Boston Symphony sufficient justification to make the move? To make her decision easier, Boston upgraded the position from second harpist to associate principal

Ann Hobson-Pilot

harpist. The twenty-six-year-old's talent definitely warranted this additional effort on the part of the Boston Symphony.

Born November 6, 1943, in Philadelphia, Pennsylvania, Ann Stevens Hobson was the younger of two girls born to Grace Stevens Hobson and Harrison D. Hobson. Her mother, a pianist, taught in the Philadelphia public schools until 1971. She was for many years a concert pianist who frequently performed two-piano concerts with Leota Palmer Henderson, mother of the late African American concert pianist Natalie Hinderas. Hobson-Pilot's father, Harrison D. Hobson, now deceased, was a social worker.

Hobson-Pilot began studying the piano at age six, with her mother. The family's three-and-a-half year stay in Germany while Harrison Hobson fulfilled a military assignment provided the young Ann with constant exposure to new cultural experiences and enabled her to receive private piano instruction from German tutors. Back in the States, piano instruction continued. In an interview on September 16, 1975, Hobson-Pilot recalled that her piano practices at home were frequently interrupted with directives from her perfectionist mother—"E flat, not E natural," "Watch the pedal," "Check your key signature." Such orders were not always welcomed by the young music student. As she told D. Antoinette Handy in a 1975 interview:

> The thought occurred to me to take up an instrument that my mother could not tell me what I was doing wrong. Philadelphia's Girls High School had a strong music program. I approached the music chairman about participating. My first choice was

the flute, but there were already too many. The chairman suggested that I consider the harp, in view of my strong piano background.

From the time she took up the new instrument at age fourteen, harp and Hobson-Pilot seemed to mesh perfectly. As she explained to art journalist Robert Merritt for the January 23, 1978, *Richmond Times Dispatch,*

> I went to a school where they just happened to have a harp, and I decided almost immediately that it was worth all the trouble. First of all, I loved it, took to it immediately, and all the blisters, having to keep my nails cut short and lugging it around, that never bothered me. I knew it was what I wanted to do.

She soon became a member of Philadelphia's All-City High School Orchestra and played with various pick-up orchestras, including the all-black Philadelphia Concert Orchestra.

Early in Hobson-Pilot's senior year of high school, Philadelphia Symphony harpist Marilyn Costello, who also taught harp in the city's schools, indicated that the young harpist was of concert caliber. But the question in Hobson-Pilot's mind was, "What does the world want with a black harpist?" as she related in her interview with Handy. Women were fully accepted as harpists in symphonic circles, but blacks of either gender were not. Her parents shared this concern; nevertheless, they supported her decision to enroll at a conservatory. They insisted that she follow a music education program, however, to provide an alternative career in the case that she did not succeed as a performer.

Pursues Music Career

For post-secondary study, Hobson-Pilot enrolled at the Philadelphia Musical Academy. Beginning in 1962, she spent the first of several summers at the Maine Harp Colony—now known as the Salzedo Harp Colony—in Camden, Maine. It was at this colony that Hobson-Pilot encountered the noted harpist and teacher Alice Chalifoux, a member of the Cleveland Institute of Music faculty and the Cleveland Symphony. Hobson-Pilot entered the institute at the beginning of her junior year.

Earlier, in about 1960, Marilyn Costello had scheduled an audition for Hobson-Pilot with the Maine Harp Colony's founder and director, Carlos Salzedo. Costello was aware of the unwritten ban on black students at the music colony, but hoped that Salzedo would be so overwhelmed with Hobson-Pilot's talent that the rule would be suspended. Though very impressed, the master harpist pointed out that participants lived in Camden homes, and he did not believe the townspeople would accept a black. Hobson-Pilot recalled in the September 16, 1975, interview,

> This was hard for me to accept. This place was like a summer camp. You paid your money and you enrolled, even if you couldn't play. I was rejected only because of race.

With the death of Salzedo in August 1961, the walls of segregation began to collapse at the harp colony.

Hobson-Pilot graduated from the Cleveland Institute of Music in 1966. During her senior year, she was substitute second harpist with the Pittsburgh Symphony. But a rare opportunity presented itself when, shortly after her graduation, the National Symphony Orchestra's principal harpist injured a finger. With insufficient time for advertising and auditioning, a master harpist was needed at once to fill a one-year assignment. The orchestra's management contacted harp authority Alice Chalifoux, who in turn contacted her star pupil, Hobson-Pilot.

Appointed Principal Harpist with Boston Symphony

Hobson-Pilot's move to the Boston Symphony took place in 1969 when she accepted the positions of associate principal harpist with the Boston Symphony and principal harpist with the Boston Pops. She would soon join the harp faculty of the prestigious New England Conservatory of Music. In 1980, she became the principal harpist with the Boston Symphony. Also in 1980, she married R. Prentice Pilot, a freelance string bassist, teacher in the Boston public schools, and regular performer with the Boston Pops Esplanade Orchestra.

In addition to her membership in the Boston Symphony, Hobson-Pilot made solo appearances with other orchestras. She always received laudatory press response when she performed Argentinian composer Alberto Ginastera's Concerto for Harp and Orchestra. Following an appearance with the Richmond (Virginia) Symphony, the *Richmond Times Dispatch* reported, "Ms. Hobson-Pilot's mastery of her instrument showed in very certain terms. She swept, with ethereal expression, over the harp's entire range.... Ms. Hobson-Pilot's work was extraordinary." Of the same appearance, the *Richmond News Leader* wrote, "Ms. Hobson-Pilot and the orchestra were fully in command of the material.... [She] exhibited considerable skill, poise and style in bringing the various musical textures to the audience."

The *Wichita (Kansas) Eagle* wrote after a solo performance,

> Miss Hobson-Pilot is an incredible technician, but more, she is able to tear the harp out of its traditional raiment and give it new and vital voices. Certainly, one will be convinced after hearing her, that she not only knows as a musician what the harp is capable of with its present limited repertoire, but also what it may be required to explore in the future. If so, she is the artist to take us into that future.

Hobson-Pilot organized the New England Harp Trio in 1971. Composed of three members of the Boston Symphony Orchestra (flutist, cellist, and harpist), the trio performs chamber and solo works dating from the baroque period up to current times. Hobson-Pilot participated at the Marlboro and Newport Music festivals and is a member of the contemporary music ensemble Collage. She has performed with the Boston Symphony Chamber Players and has recorded with them on the Deutsche Grammaphon Label. Hobson-Pilot has also been featured soloist with the Springfield (Massachusetts) Symphony and the St. Trinity Orchestra of Port-Au-Prince, Haiti.

As the publication *Symphonium* indicated in its Fall 1992 issue, "When Boston Symphony Harpist Ann Hobson-Pilot writes her memoirs, the year 1992 will figure prominently." In 1992 she received enthusiastic reviews following the release of her first solo compact disc, which was issued by Boston Records Classical Corporation; she was honored at a concert and reception in celebration of her twenty-three years with the Boston Symphony; and she gave three performances of the Ginastera Harp Concerto with the Boston Pops Orchestra. The April 14, 1992, concert and reception was a part of the Boston Symphony Orchestra Committee on Cultural Diversity's efforts at diversifying the orchestra's audience, staff, and programming.

Music critic Richard Dyer commented in the *Boston Globe* on Hobson-Pilot's June 1992 solo appearances with the Boston Pops with African American Isaiah Jackson, as quoted in *Symphonium,* Fall 1992:

> The piece [Ginastera] is full of brilliant coloristic effects and strongly masked rhythms, both folkloric in origin. At one point the soloist drums on the soundboard; at another, she runs her hands along the strings instead of plucking them. The concerto requires sensitivity as well as strength; both qualities mark the long and imaginative cadenza that bridges the slow movement and the finale. Pilot has both strength and sensitivity; her playing was full of personality, her own, and Ginastera's.

Works Recorded

Recording became an active part of Hobson-Pilot's life beginning in 1991. This was the year that she recorded works by African American composer William Grant Still (1895-1978) for New World Records. She was assisted by violist George Taylor, bassist Prentice Pilot, and baritone Robert Honeysucker, all African Americans. Shortly afterward, she showcased her virtuosity on the solo compact disc issued by Boston Records Classical Corporation, recording works by Bach, Debussy, Hindemith, Salzedo, Faure, Ravel, Pierne, and Malotte. Proceeds from the sale of each compact disc are donated to the United Negro College Fund. The recording was done at the African Meeting House in Boston, the oldest surviving African American church in the country.

Concerning her solo album's cover design, Hobson-Pilot wrote in personal correspondence on January 24, 1994,

> I believe in role models. When I was growing up I never saw a black doing what I'm doing. That's the main reason I decided to put my face on the cover of my recording. I don't want to be anonymous. I want people to know that I'm a black musician.

Hobson-Pilot's 1993 recordings include the Harp Concerto by Norman Dello Joio, with the New Zealand Symphony; harp concertos by Ginastera and William Mathias; and Mathias's *Santa Fe Suite* for Solo Harp, with the English Chamber Orchestra in London, on the Koch International label.

Since 1988, Hobson-Pilot and her husband have conducted a concert series on the Caribbean Island of St. Maarten featuring African American musicians and composers in programs combining classical and jazz genres. During the 1993-94 season, concerts on the island of St. Croix were added.

Hobson-Pilot's talents and accomplishments have been acknowledged by the Pro Arte Society of Philadelphia, the Boston chapter of Girls Friends, and Sigma Alpha Iota, an international music fraternity that awarded her the 1991 Distinguished Woman of the Year Award. Philadelphia College of Performing Arts (formerly the Philadelphia Musical Academy) granted her the 1992 School of Music's Alumni Achievement Award, and the Cleveland Institute of Music bestowed the same honor upon her in 1993. In 1988 she received an honorary doctor of music degree from Bridgewater State College.

Despite her many artistic accomplishments, Hobson-Pilot has not forgotten those less privileged than herself. During the spring of 1993, Hobson-Pilot was the featured performer in a concert benefiting Boston's String Training and Educational Program (STEP) for minority students, a project sponsored by the Boston Symphony Orchestra, Boston University, the New England Conservatory, and the Greater Boston Youth Symphony Orchestra. She was assisted by her husband, Prentice Pilot, and the Boston Symphony's newest black member, cellist Owen Young. Hobson-Pilot is a member of the Boston Symphony Orchestra's Cultural Diversity Committee and the board of trustees of the Longy School of Music. She and her husband are co-directors of a music program in the Boston public schools, and she teaches troubadour harp at one of the city's middle schools.

Ann Hobson-Pilot has had a significant impact on the music world, not just through her symphony performances and recordings but also through her work as a teacher. Formerly a private instructor at the Philadelphia Musical Academy and Temple University Music Festival at Ambler, she currently teaches at the New England Conservatory and the Tanglewood Music Center. She often conducts clinics for young harp students, recalling that it was in the public schools that she got her start.

Current Address: Boston Symphony Orchestra, Symphony Hall, 301 Massachusetts Avenue, Boston, MA 02115.

REFERENCES:

"Capacity Crowd Cheers Chamber Music on St. Maarten." *Symphonium* 2 (Fall 1990): 2.
"Delightful New CD by Harpist Pilot." *Symphonium* 4 (Winter 1992): 1.
Handy, D. Antoinette. *Black Women in American Bands and Orchestras.* Metuchen, N.J.: Scarecrow Press, 1981.
"Harpist Pilot Enjoys Banner Year." *Symphonium* (Fall 1992): 1, 8.

"Harpist Says Her Profession Worth Trouble." *Richmond Times Dispatch,* January 23, 1978.

Hobson-Pilot, Ann. Interview with D. Antoniette Handy. Brookline, Mass., September 16, 1975.

———. Letters to Handy, May 17, 1979; January 20, 1980; January 24, 1994.

———. Telephone conversation with Handy, January 20, 1994.

Row, Steve. "2nd Serenade Is Fiery." *Richmond News Leader,* January 23, 1978.

Southern, Eileen. *Biographical Dictionary of Afro-American and African Musicians.* Westport, Conn.: Greenwood Press, 1982.

D. Antoinette Handy

Josephine Groves Holloway

Josephine Groves Holloway
(1898-1988)
Organization executive, college registrar, social worker

Called a pioneer, a lamplighter, and a hidden heroine, Josephine Holloway saw scouting as a vital extracurricular experience for young black girls and established the first black Girl Scout troop in Nashville. Later she became the first black Girl Scout executive in middle Tennessee. For thirty years she maintained a passionate, loyal, and single-minded devotion to scouting and found a place for blacks who were denied admittance to the white Girl Scouts. Her work built a foundation for the integration of Girl Scout troops in Nashville.

Josephine Amanda Groves Holloway was born on March 10, 1898, in a Methodist parsonage in Cowpens, South Carolina, the seventh child and second girl of ten children in the family of John Wesley Groves and Emma Gray Groves. Only three boys and two girls in the family lived to adulthood. Since John Groves was a Methodist minister, as was his father, it was not uncommon for the family to move often. When he realized that the frequent moves adversely affected his children's educations, John Groves settled the family in Greenwood, South Carolina. Holloway entered Fisk University the next year, about 1920. She was stricken with influenza during her second year at Fisk and was unable to continue her studies until the second quarter of 1921. On reentering college, she earned money to pay for her education by repairing tablecloths, winding clocks in the music practice room, and working in the school's dining hall. A sociology major, she graduated in June 1923 with an A.B. degree.

Holloway's service to humanity began in the summer of 1923 when she worked as a recreational and community staff member to upgrade the quality of life for blacks in her hometown. Meanwhile, she sent out job applications in search

of work. As quoted in Harriette Allen Insignares's biographical sketch of Holloway in *Leaders of Afro-American Nashville,* Holloway said, "The job that appealed to me most was Girls Worker at Bethlehem Center [in Nashville]. In this I could imagine using all of my skills and at the same time have a hand in reforming the world." She wanted most of all to reform the world for black girls, and in September 1923, she became "girls' worker" at the Bethlehem Center. In a questionnaire for the minority American women's project at Fisk University, Holloway wrote that she became a commissioned Girl Scout captain in the fall of 1924 and that she organized the first black Girl Scout troop in Nashville.

Brings Scouting to Nashville

Holloway learned of scouting from the files of the Bethlehem Center. Apparently there had been some attempts to institute scouting at the Blue Triangle YWCA—the black branch—but there was no other information on scouting in Nashville available locally. After appealing to the national Girl Scout office, Holloway got some of her questions answered. Juliette Gordon Lowe, a wealthy white widow from Savannah, Georgia, had introduced Girl Scouts in the United States, patterning it after a British program founded in the early 1900s. Lowe had formed a troop of "Guides" in England, then in 1912 founded the first troop in the U.S. The first troop in Nashville, founded in 1917, was for white girls only and had fallen into decline by 1923. Nonetheless, Holloway was determined to found a program for Nashville's black girls. She completed a training session with Lowe offered by the Southern Education Conference on Scouting, which was held in January 1924 at the George Peabody College for Teachers in Nashville. She was the only black allowed to attend, and at the end of the course she was commissioned captain. Girl scouting in Nashville was revived.

Girl scouting then became an essential part of the Bethlehem Center's program. Holloway wrote in her questionnaire for Fisk University that the troop of 150 to 160 girls became a registered platoon in 1924, after the scouting conference had ended. Holloway's position at the Bethlehem Center came to an abrupt end in the fall of 1925. On June 30 that year, she married Guerney Holloway, a former schoolmate and co-worker, and the "boys' worker" at the center. They were to have three daughters: Nareda Wenefred, Josephine Alzilee, and Weslia Juanita. The center's director, Mathee Nutt, forced Holloway's resignation, claiming that a married woman would not have enough time for her work. Holloway continued in the questionnaire for Fisk University,

> This was the beginning of the end of Negro Girl Scouts. No other captain was ever commissioned. My commission expired when I resigned. Girls' Worker carried on [the] program without commission or registering [the girls].

In time, her replacement allowed the troop to fold.

Holloway spent the months immediately following her resignation studying at Tennessee Agricultural and Industrial College (now Tennessee State University) in Nashville and received a second bachelor's degree in 1926. From 1927 to 1936 she was assistant registrar at Fisk University; she then took a job with the State Department of Public Instruction, where she remained until 1943.

In the meantime, her interest in Girl Scouts continued. Although the Girl Scout Council came into being in 1927, there were still no recognized black troops. Holloway established another troop on her own sometime between 1926 and 1933 and encouraged other blacks to do so as well. She had been rejected when she tried to register her unofficial troop in 1933, but continued her efforts anyway. Meanwhile, Guerney Holloway, who during that time studied at the University of Chicago, purchased for her the Girl Scout handbooks that the local council had denied her. She used the manuals to organize brownie, intermediate, and senior troops and taught the girls Girl Scout laws and all that they needed to know to become official members. Holloway's girls wore gingham uniforms but wanted to be "real Girl Scouts."

However, racism in the Nashville Girl Scouts continued. On October 4, 1938, the Girl Scouts' honorary president, Eleanor Roosevelt, came to Nashville to lecture at the request of the Nashville council. She was to speak before a group of whites at Ryman Auditorium, where the Grand Ole Opry was held, and then give a separate lecture before a "colored" audience. Roosevelt refused to give two speeches and insisted on a single presentation before a mixed audience. During her lecture and the performance of the Fisk Jubilee Singers, who were also on the program, all blacks were required to sit in the gallery section away from the whites.

Council Approves First Black Girl Scout Troop in Nashville

Holloway worked as a Girl Scout volunteer between 1940 and 1943 and organized twenty-five Girl Scout troops. She attempted to register her troops with the Girl Scout Council on October 11, 1942. It was not until May 1943 that the first troop was approved and the status made retroactive to the 1942 date, thus officially reestablishing scouting for black girls in Nashville. When Troop 200 became a reality, the Holloways's three daughters were members. Josephine resigned her position with the state in 1943 and became the first black professional Girl Scout worker in Nashville. From July 1, 1943, until she retired on July 1, 1963, she was organizer and field advisor to the Girl Scout Council. In addition, she was district director and a camp director, establishing the first day camp in 1944.

By 1945 the Girl Scout Council had learned to appreciate Holloway's work and, according to Elisabeth Israels Perry, complimented her for her "humble, gracious manner" when she referred to scouting as "the very best influence for girls." When the Nashville council hosted the annual meeting of the "Dixie" region of Girl Scouts in 1946, the sessions were to be biracial. Although black guests were denied living accommodations and access to social functions in local hotels, Holloway assured the council that "her people" would accommodate them in their own homes. From then on, the sessions were held in the War Memorial Building or the YWCA, where the meetings and social events were open to all guests.

After a wide search for land for the black troops, Holloway found some in Robertson County, near Nashville. She wrote in her questionnaire: "In the course of my work, I was instrumental in locating, buying, and setting up an approved (by Camping Assoc.) camp for Negro Girl Scouts. This did not exist in this area at the time. It was named Camp Holloway in my honor." Camp Holloway was dedicated in 1951. In 1984, Holloway and her husband donated forty acres of land adjacent to the camp to the Cumberland Valley Girl Scouts.

During her career, Holloway was a member of the American Camping Association, the National Association of Social Workers, Zeta Phi Beta Sorority, the Optimistic Study Club, Crisis Call, and the Parent-Teachers Association of various schools. After retiring, she became organizer and director of the first tuition-free volunteer tutoring school for dropouts and students below their achievement level in the Nashville area. Later the program was integrated into the public school system.

Before she died in December 1988 at age 90, Holloway had been widely recognized in Nashville for her contributions to the community. She was the first Woman of the Year named by the local chapter of Zeta Phi Beta Sorority, in May 1957. On June 19, 1976, the Cumberland Valley Girl Scout Council held a "Hall of Heroines" program to salute women in middle Tennessee and southern Kentucky who had made a vital contribution to their communities but who had not been properly recognized for their efforts; Holloway was called a "Hidden Heroine." In 1978 the Nashville branch of the National Association of Negro Business and Professional Women's Clubs presented her with the Sojourner Truth

Award. When the local Girl Scout council dedicated its new Girl Scout Center in Nashville on October 5, 1991, it honored Holloway again by naming its historic collection and gallery in her honor. A drive to raise fifty thousand dollars for the collection and gallery had begun at First Baptist Church in Nashville on May 21, 1990. At the dedication the city paid homage to Holloway in song, prayer, and story. Her life-size portrait hangs in the facility. A few of "Mrs. Holloway's girls" told personal stories and gave oral sketches of her life.

Josephine Holloway is one among other African American women who addressed the needs of black girls through scouting and who helped to break down the racial barriers that existed in the scouting organization. A strong-willed and caring risk taker, she was inflexible in her determination to bring girl scouting to Nashville's African American community. She always saw scouting as "the very best influence for girls."

REFERENCES:

"Girl Scouts Pay Tribute to Their 'Hidden Heroine.'" *Sunday Tennessean,* May 20, 1990.

Insignares, Harriette Allen. "Josephine Groves Holloway." In *Leaders of Afro-American Nashville.* Nashville: 1991.

Perry, Elisabeth Israels. "'The Very Best Influence': Josephine Holloway and Girl Scouting in Nashville's African-American Community." *Tennessee Historical Quarterly* 52 (Summer 1993): 73-85.

COLLECTIONS:

Biographical materials and other information on Josephine Holloway can be found in the Josephine G. Holloway Historical Collection and Gallery, Cumberland Valley Girl Scout Council, P.O. Box 40466, Nashville, TN 37204. A file on Holloway, which consists of a questionnaire, news clippings, fliers, and miscellaneous items, is in the Fisk University Library in Nashville.

Jessie Carney Smith

Bell Hooks

(1952-)

Feminist, critic, social activist, educator, writer

B ell Hooks has been praised as one of the few African American scholars whose writings acknowledge the effects of racism and sexism in the lives of African American women. Hooks, a college professor, has written several books and essays outlining her ideas on feminist politics and contemporary culture. She views the representation of many African Americans in films and books as exploitive, and she

Bell Hooks

calls for the liberation of black women, men and children through the elimination of the prevailing "capitalist-patriarchal system" in this country. Widely read in both academic and nonacademic circles, she now basks in the limelight as a writer, scholar, sought-after lecturer, and internationally known cultural critic.

Bell Hooks was born Gloria Jean Watkins on September 25, 1952, in Hopkinsville, Kentucky. In the 1970s, when she began her writing career, she adopted the pseudonym Bell Hooks, which was the name of her maternal great-grandmother. Hooks was one of seven children—six girls and a boy—born to Rosa Bell Watkins, a domestic worker, and Veodis Watkins, a janitor. Like many other writers, as a child she used books as an escape from her everyday world. Her particular love was poetry; in her autobiographical essay, "Black Is a Woman's Color," she says discovering the romantic poets was like losing a part of herself and recovering it. Walt Whitman was another favorite poet. She says Whitman showed her that "language, like the human spirit, need not be trapped in conventional form or traditions." She memorized poems and recited them to herself while ironing or washing dishes. Her family gladly turned off the television set to listen to her favorite poems. She wrote her own poetry in secret, and in her dedication to her collection of essays entitled *Ain't I a Woman: Black Women and Feminism,* she states, "My mother . . . told me when I was a child that she had once written poems—that I had inherited my love of reading and my longing to write from her."

It is not surprising that Hooks loved music as well as poetry. She sang in the church choir, and her father, an aficionado of John Coltrane, passed on to her his love of jazz. She liked the music of Louis Armstrong because of the pleasure it brought her father. For the girls in the family, the weekly program of soul music on the radio accompanied the Saturday morning routine of housecleaning. In between the household chores, they showed each other the latest dance steps.

As one of six girls in the family, Hooks fondly remembers the weekly ritual of waiting her turn in the kitchen to get her hair pressed. In "Black Is a Woman's Color," she recalls:

> For each of us, getting our hair pressed is an important ritual. It is not a sign of our longing to be white. . . . It is a gesture that says we are approaching womanhood. It is a rite of passage. . . . We are women together. This is our ritual and our time. It is a time without men. It is a time when we work to meet each other's needs, to make each other beautiful in whatever way we can.

In "Black Is a Woman's Color," Hooks shows that, despite her large family, she came "to understand the meaning of exile and loss." Although her family enjoyed her poetry recitations, her efforts to express her own opinions were construed as "talking back." Her family's reaction to her precocity was to tell her that she was an old woman reborn in the body of a child. In the thick book of fairy tales they gave her, she identified with the old women and the witches.

Within the Watkins family, the male and female roles reflected the patriarchal values of the dominant society. This became clear one frightening night at home. As she stood by helplessly, her father threatened her mother with a gun during a violent quarrel and told her to pack her bags and leave. Hooks was stunned by her mother's refusal to fight back and her refusal of her daughter's help. Hooks reflects in "Black Is a Woman's Color":

> For the mother is not simple. She is always torn. She works hard to fulfill his needs, our needs. When they are not the same she must maneuver, manipulate, choose. She has chosen. She has decided in his favor. She is a religious woman. She has been told that a man should obey God, that a woman should obey man, that children should obey their fathers and mothers, particularly their mothers. I will not obey.

This patriarchy at home had its counterpart in what she was taught about U.S. history in school. As she explains in *Ain't I a Woman,* she was confronted with both "sexual imperialism in the form of patriarchy" and "racial imperialism in the form of white supremacy." Although she attended all-black public schools and grew up under a system of racial segregation, her education in the "politics of race" differed little from that of her white contemporaries. Her female, African American sixth-grade teacher taught her to love and to be loyal to a government that was practicing segregation. She comments in *Ain't I a Woman,*

> Unknowingly [this teacher] implanted in our psyches a seed of the racial imperialism that would keep us forever in bondage. For how does one overthrow, change, or even challenge a system that you have been taught to admire, to love, to believe in?

Hooks first experienced an integrated environment when she went to Stanford University for her undergraduate studies, which she completed in 1973. She states in *Ain't I a Woman* that her undergraduate education neither questioned the existing relationship between blacks and whites nor led to a greater understanding of "racism as a political ideology." Instead it condoned white supremacy and male patriarchy. She encountered a subtle form of racism in the attitudes of some of the undergraduate professors, who ignored their students of color. Although she was an eager participant in the women's movement on campus, study of African American women was conspicuously absent, even in women's studies classes.

Groundbreaking Work on Black Feminism Published

At the age of nineteen, Hooks began researching *Ain't I a Woman: Black Women and Feminism,* while pursuing full-time studies at Stanford University. She spent six years writing and revising the book, which was finally published in 1981. The reputation of the original Bell Hooks as sharp-tongued fit the persona of her great-granddaughter, the writer Bell Hooks, who, unlike the genteel southern girl Gloria Jean Watkins, was quite outspoken. Hooks's inspiration to write *Ain't I a Woman* came from a few different sources. As an undergraduate, she often returned home from campus libraries angry because of the paucity of books on African American women. Seeing how upset she was, one of her male companions encouraged her to write the book. She also received encouragement and support from the African American women who worked at the Berkeley telephone office, where she was employed as an operator in 1973 and 1974.

Ain't I a Woman is a fiery polemic in which Hooks presents the thesis that racism and sexism have been powerful conjoined influences in the lives of African American women. Taking a feminist perspective on African American women's history from the period of slavery through the 1970s, she makes the controversial assertion that nineteenth-century African American women had a stronger feminist consciousness than their twentieth-century counterparts. She castigates both the contemporary, mostly middle- and upper-class white women's liberation movement and the contemporary black liberation movement as ignoring African American women.

In *Ain't I a Woman* Hooks describes herself as having been in the forefront of the feminist movement for ten years. She strongly condemns what she sees as the opportunism of many contemporary feminists.

> I became disillusioned as I saw the various groups of women appropriating feminism to serve their own opportunistic ends. Whether it was women university professors crying sexist oppression . . . to attract attention to their efforts to gain promotion; or women using feminism to mask their sexist attitudes; or women writers superficially exploring

feminist themes to advance their own careers, it was evident that eliminating sexist oppression was not the primary concern. While their rallying cry was sexist oppression, they showed little concern about the status of women as a collective group in our society. They were primarily interested in making feminism a forum for the expression of their own self-centered needs and desires.

According to Hooks, the goal of the feminist movement should not just be equality with men, which women have achieved in some measure, but an overthrow of the entire "capitalist-patriarchal system."

Not surprisingly, feminist presses did not rush to publish her manuscript. Nevertheless, while giving a talk at a feminist bookstore, Hooks made contacts that led her to South End Press, the publisher of *Ain't I a Woman* and all her subsequent books. *Ain't I a Woman* received harsh criticism from the academic community, but readers in other circles responded to it favorably.

Pursues Academic Career

Hooks decided to pursue a career as a teacher at the college level, thinking that it would provide both personal fulfillment and a forum for disseminating her ideas. To that end, she obtained an M.A. from the University of Wisconsin in 1976 and a Ph.D. in English from the University of California at Santa Cruz in 1983. The title of her dissertation is "Toni Morrison's Fiction: Keeping a Hold on Life." While obtaining her doctorate and shortly thereafter, she held a number of lectureships at various California universities. In 1985 she became an assistant professor of African American studies and English literature at Yale University, and in 1988 an associate professor of American literature and women's studies at Oberlin College. At Oberlin her courses in African American women's fiction and the politics of sexuality have been consistently filled with the maximum number of students. In 1993-94 she took a leave of absence from Oberlin to teach at the City College of New York.

In 1984 Hooks published *Feminist Theory from Margin to Center.* The premise of the book is an idea propounded in *Ain't I a Woman:* that the feminist theory of white, middle-class women "at the center" rarely takes into account the experiences of either men or women "at the margin." She criticizes the feminist perspective of such writers as Betty Friedan, author of *The Feminine Mystique,* a classic of the women's movement. According to Hooks, Friedan's disparagement of the housewife role is limited to the feminist perspective of the college-educated white woman.

Since 1989 Hooks has produced several books, including *Yearning: Race, Gender, and Cultural Politics* (1990), which won the Before Columbus Foundation's American Book Award. According to Lisa Jones in her essay "Rebel without a Pause," this book "solidified her reputation as an interrogator of postmodernism and cinema." *Breaking Bread: Insurgent Black Intellectual Life* (1991) is a compilation of lively dialogues with the scholar and social activist Cornel

West. And her *Black Looks: Race and Representation* (1992) is a collection of essays on cultural criticism. This book further established Hooks as an important film critic.

In her interview with Lisa Jones, Hooks discusses the representation of race in film. She views the preoccupation of African American filmmakers with entertaining characters considered degrading to the black race just twenty years ago as a sad commentary on the progress of African Americans toward equality with whites. She comments: "And it's important to note that these representations aren't just made by white people.... But what we're seeing is black people reproducing the prevailing "exploitive" images to create work that sells." She also laments the one-dimensionality of African American women in film.

The portrayal of African American women in the works of contemporary African American female writers also disheartens Hooks. She sees author Terry McMillan's book *Waiting to Exhale* as furthering the stereotype of the African American woman as the "bitchified, take-no-prisoners black." She considers Alice Walker's Tashi-Evelyn Johnson in *Possessing the Secret of Joy* and Sophia in *The Color Purple* as feeding the stereotype of the African American woman as victim. Hooks continues in her interview with Lisa Jones, "Part of what I want to turn my life into is a testimony to the fact that we don't have to be punished. That we don't have to sacrifice our lives when we invent and realize our complex selves."

Due to the breadth of her scholarly concerns as a feminist and cultural critic, Hooks has become one of the foremost contemporary African American intellectuals. *Publishers Weekly* ranks her *Ain't I a Woman* as one of the "20 most influential women's books of the last 20 years." She easily communicates with both academics and nonacademics. In popular periodicals such as *Essence,* she continues to hammer home the idea of the dire need of a feminist revolution in black society. She states in a July 1992, article in *Essence* called "Feminism—It's a Black Thang!" that many black people have misconceptions of feminism as representing the desire of white women to have equality with white men, but "in reality, feminism is a movement to end *all* sexism and sexist oppression." Through her scholarship, teaching, and activism, Bell Hooks works toward the vital goal of eliminating oppression.

Current Address: c/o South End Press, 116 Botolph Street, Boston, MA 02115.

REFERENCES:

Black Writers. 2d ed. Detroit: Gale Research, 1994.
Hooks, Bell. *Ain't I a Woman: Black Women and Feminism.* Boston: South End Press, 1981.
———. "Black Is a Woman's Color." In *Bearing Witness: Selections from African American Autobiography in the Twentieth Century.* Edited by Henry Louis Gates. New York: Pantheon, 1991.
———. "Feminism—It's a Black Thang!" *Essence* 23 (July 1992): 124.

———. *Feminist Theory from Margin to Center.* Boston: South End Press, 1984.

Jones, Lisa. ''Rebel without a Pause.'' *Village Voice Literary Supplement* (October 1992): 10.

Phiefer L. Browne

Shirley Horn
(1934-)
Jazz singer, musician

An outstanding singer, a sensitive interpreter of lyrics, and an expert pianist and accompanist, Shirley Horn justly deserves the fame and recognition she has attained as a jazz musician. Her artistic career has had its ups and downs over a period of more than forty years. In the early 1960s, aided by Miles Davis's avid interest in her, Horn's career blossomed. Then in the 1970s she performed and recorded less often and seemed to withdraw a bit from the musical scene. The 1980s saw a renewal of interest in Horn's music which has continued into the 1990s. She has performed and recorded both nationally and internationally and is widely known as a talented and exacting musician with a unique gift for using tempo to engage both fellow musicians and audiences in her songs.

Born on May 1, 1934, Shirley Horn is a native of Washington, D.C. Her father was a government worker for the General Accounting Office, and her mother was a homemaker. Horn's husband, Shep Deering, works for the Metro Transit Authority. Her early roots in music began with piano lessons when she was four years old; she was encouraged by her loving mother, who admired classical music. Horn accompanied a choir, played at Sunday school, and soon formed her own trio. At the age of thirteen, she won a citywide talent contest and earned a thirteen-week radio show engagement. She then was awarded a scholarship to Juilliard School of Music in New York. Financial considerations, however, prevented her from going to Juilliard, and she subsequently enrolled at Howard University in Washington, D.C., as a music major.

Musical Abilities Gain Notice

Horn acquired a taste for jazz early, and Billy Holiday's interpretations and vocal style were an important influence, along with artists Peggy Lee, Erroll Garner, Ahmad Jamal, and Oscar Peterson. She was able to obtain jobs while at college, playing at Olivia's Patio Lounge and later at other clubs in the nation's capital. Her first album, *Embers and Ashes* (Hi-Life, 1961), although not a major seller, caught the attention of Miles Davis, and he invited her to New York to share the stage with him at the Village Vanguard in 1962.

Horn fondly remembers this turning point in her career. As reported by John Leland in *Newsweek,* Miles Davis phoned when she was visiting her mother-in-law, and ''there were buttermilk biscuits and red-eye gravy on the table.'' The call, about which she had feelings of disbelief, led her to go to Davis's house in New York, where his children sang the album's songs for her. The opening with Miles Davis at the Vanguard awed her: Charlie Mingus, Sidney Poitier, and Lena Horne were there, and they became some of the biggest followers of her career. Musically, Horn appreciated Miles Davis's economy of expression. She stated in the same *Newsweek* article, ''I listened to a pianist who played a lot of notes, but it just left me cold. Then I heard Miles Davis play one note, and it made all the difference in the world.'' This same quality, an economy of means, is one of the key strengths of her own approach to jazz interpretation.

The Village Vanguard performances were a great success. The audience, with its sprinkling of stars and jazz musicians as well as the New York critics, was very appreciative of her talents. A Mercury recording contract followed, but after making two initial recordings she tired of the musical concept of a singer backed up with a big-band arrangement. For this reason, she sat out the remainder of the contract, choosing not to record in this setting. Nevertheless, she acquiesced when Quincy Jones subsequently invited her to sing lead songs in two movies, *A Dandy in Aspic* and *For Love of Joy.* However, being backed up by a big band was not her style. She tended to favor small groups, most often a trio with piano/voice, drums, and bass. This arrangement has since become her standard grouping.

Out of the Musical Spotlight

At this point, in the 1970s, Horn's career took something of a backseat to her role as a mother and homemaker. She felt the need to devote more time to raising her daughter through her teens, and therefore resisted travel, restricting her performances to local venues and limiting her recording sessions. Richard Lee, in a biographical portrait of Horn in *The Washingtonian,* suggests that another reason she slowed down her career may have been the emergence of rock and roll groups like The Beatles on the musical scene. Despite the urging of friends, she declined to change her singing style to accommodate this emerging musical genre.

During this hiatus, she nevertheless remained very active and, to her mind, never left the musical scene. She developed a considerable reputation as a jazz club performer and worked virtually all the major clubs in the Washington, D.C., area. Ironically, however, it took her signing a New York club date at Michael's Pub in May 1980 for her finally to be welcomed for an engagement at the prestigious Charlie's Georgetown in Washington, D.C., which, to that point, claimed not to engage ''local talent.''

Horn's Career Flourishes Again

When Horn returned to the national and international concert scene in the 1980s, it was clear that her friends, fans, and fellow musicians had not forgotten her, and she played to full concert halls. The Michael's Pub date earned her praise from the prestigious New York music critics. An appreciative Whitney Balliett, writing in the *New Yorker,* compared her approach to accompanying to the ''effortless, brilliant way Nat Cole played for himself,'' and considered her singing style rich, subtle, and flavored with widely varied dynamics. Rex Reed of the *New York Daily News* and John S. Wilson of the *New York Times* also wrote very favorable reviews.

Viewed historically, Horn's recent album *You Won't Forget Me* (Verve, 1990) is the culmination of her return to prominence as an artist. It was greeted favorably by several jazz critics and rose to first place on the Billboard charts. Neil Tesser, in his *Playboy* review, asserts that the album ''makes good on its title, with one indelible performance after another,'' each song filled ''with an appropriate blend of fragile resilience.'' Reviewing *You Won't Forget Me* in *Stereo Review,* Phyl Garland praises her ''mastery of form, sound and texture'' and ranks her ''among the finest of vocal interpreters.'' He also calls her a superb pianist whose ''chord progressions are rich, lush, and surprising in their beauty. She sustains a mood of grace, moving with ease from delicate balladry to buoyant swinging without ever breaking her spell. A master of phrasing, she can make time seem to stand still.''

Shirley Horn has recorded numerous albums both here and abroad, and has appeared in major clubs in New York, Washington, D.C., and elsewhere in the United States, as well as in London and Paris. She also performed at the North Sea Jazz Festival in The Hague in 1991. Besides Quincy Jones and Miles Davis, she has appeared with Richard Rodney Bennett, Wynton and Branford Marsalis, Toots Thielmans, Kenny Burrell, and others. Noted arranger Johnny Mandel prepared string and wind orchestrations on her recent album *Here's to Life* (Verve, 1992), and she has a well-deserved reputation among major performers as a demanding and excellent musician.

As a performer, Horn has a number of remarkable qualities. She is known as exacting, demanding, thorough, and self-critical. A number of critics and musicians have commented on her delicacy and subtle use of tempo, in particular her gift of imbuing a song with a sense of space. Tommy Cecil, a Washington, D.C., bass player who has worked with her, reports in Richard Lee's article in *The Washingtonian* that she has a ''crystal concept of what the music should sound like. Her timing is scary, it swings so deep. . . . She likes to use a lot of space. When there's as much space as she allows, you have to be confident of your own thing. She really tests you harmonically and rhythmically.''

Similarly, John Leland comments in *Newsweek* that on the recording ''Don't Let the Sun Catch You Cryin''' with Wynton Marsalis, ''she slows the tempo until each note becomes a statement, each line a surprise.'' In *Time* magazine Jay Cocks states his belief that this quality stems from a certain openness and a heart that's ''eager to share.'' Cocks quotes Horn's own explanation for her musical timing: ''It's just the way I feel about a song. They call me the slowest

singer in the world, but I don't talk fast either. You're trying to tell a story, to paint a picture.''

Horn's strengths as a musician bespeak a strength of character as well. Strong and independent, she has maintained a focus on her domestic life while at the same time pursuing a very public career as a performer. In addition to shifting her energies towards motherhood at a point in time when she and her daughter needed each other, there are other aspects to her life as a homemaker. She has remodeling skills and has done major work on her home on several occasions, renovating her kitchen and adding a back porch and den.

Shirley Horn is at her best as a singer when she is providing her own accompaniment. This approach works equally well in her personal appearances and on her recordings. She divides her repertoire between standards and less well-known songs, with a balance between uptempo numbers and ballads, showing, however, a preference for slower tempos. Her performing style features resilience, sensitivity, and a sense of intimacy. Among her biggest fans she can name such famous performers as Lena Horne, Sidney Poitier, Richard Rodney Bennett, Duke Ellington, Miles Davis, Quincy Jones, and Charles Mingus.

Horn is often described as a demanding musician who will not compromise her tastes upon demand. As she put it in *The Washingtonian,* ''I'll never play bad music—no way. I'm back to housework. I put another room on.'' She has been known to walk off a set upon occasion, to leave an inattentive audience and take a long break, and to take her time and sing in a manner demanding the full attention of both audience and musicians. On occasion this may have caused some difficulty with bookings, but this has not deterred her. She has persevered and preserved her unique approach to music, her dual abilities and sensitivities as pianist/accompanist and singer, and the overall love and zest she imparts to her jazz renditions, her audiences, and her fellow musicians.

Current Address: c/o Joel E. Siegel, Georgetown University, Washington D.C.

REFERENCES:

Albertson, Chris. ''Shirley Horn with Strings.'' *Stereo Review* 57 (July 1992): 76.
Balliett, Whitney. ''Jazz; Good Tidings.'' *New Yorker* 58 (June 19, 1982): 115-16.
Claghorn, Charles E. *Biographical Dictionary of American Music.* West Nyack, N.Y.: Parker Brothers, 1973.
Clark, Donald, ed. *The Penguin Encyclopedia of Popular Music.* New York: Viking Press, 1989.
Cocks, Jay. ''Taking Her Own Time.'' *Time* 137 (March 25, 1991): 66-67.
Garland, Phyl. ''You Won't Forget Me.'' *Stereo Review* 56 (April 1991): 84-85.
Review of *Here's to Life. Entertainment Weekly* (June 19, 1992): 73.
Review of *Here's to Life. Time* 139 (May 18, 1992): 81.

Kernfield, Barry, ed. *New Grove Dictionary of Jazz.* Vol. 1.
 New York: Macmillan, 1988.

Lee, Richard. "Shirley, Shirley." *The Washingtonian* 18
 (November 1982): 93-105.

Leland, John. "The Ballads of Shirley Horn." *Newsweek* 117
 (April 29, 1991): 60.

Leymaire, Isabelle. "For My Lady." *Unesco Courier* 44
 (July-August 1992): 80.

Tesser, Neil. Review of *You Won't Forget Me. Playboy* 38
 (April 1991): 22.

Darius L. Thieme

Cora Catherine Calhoun Horne

Cora Catherine Calhoun Horne

(1865-1932)

Suffragist, clubwoman, organization worker, social worker

Some women of the late nineteenth and early twentieth century allowed society to define their role; others defined it themselves. Cora Catherine Calhoun Horne accepted society's definition of motherhood but had her own view of the role of women. She was an activist for black and women's rights and found solace in ecumenicalism. In the view of some, she defied the conventional. She set her own goals and put morals, high standards, refinement, and intellect at the forefront. Her earnestness was admirable and at the same time forbidding. She was as unyielding in her fight for black and women's causes as she was in some of her interpersonal relationships. She found both lower-class blacks and white people in general intolerable. Because of her stance on black and women's rights, particularly her devotion to securing for women the right to vote, her influence continued to be felt long after her death. She was an inspiration to later activists who worked on behalf of blacks and women.

Cora Catherine Calhoun Horne was born in Atlanta, Georgia, in November 1865, the oldest of two daughters born to Moses and Atlanta Mary Fernando Calhoun. Her father was born a slave in 1829, and her mother was probably a free black—a Louisiana Creole of possibly African extraction. They were married in early 1865. Moses Calhoun became a retail grocer in Atlanta and later opened a small restaurant with a fruit stand on Decatur Street. In the 1880s he also owned a boarding house. He became a landowner and a prominent member of Atlanta's black bourgeoisie. Cora Calhoun and her sister, Lena, attended the new Storrs Elementary School located at Houston and Cortland streets. The American Missionary Association (AMA) had established the school in 1867, along with thousands of academic and industrial schools for a small number of children of the black middle class. Storrs was one of the AMA's strongest secondary schools in the South.

The family attended the First Congregational Church, often called "First Church" or "Big Church," which the AMA also established in 1867 for the new black middle class. It had close ties to Storrs School and to Atlanta University. By mid-1880 the family had moved twice, perhaps to better housing each time. Growing up in Atlanta, Cora and Lena Calhoun were belles of the black South and attended fashionable parties, picnics, and soirees. They were also known for their beauty. Cora was slim, pretty, elegant, and proud, yet Lena was the acknowledged family beauty. Their elite status was underscored by the colleges where they studied: Cora at Atlanta University and Lena at Fisk in Nashville—both founded by the AMA. At Fisk Lena Calhoun and W. E. B. Du Bois, whom her classmates called a "stuffed shirt," became romantically involved; however, she married a man named Frank Smith on Christmas Day, 1888, at Cora's home in Chattanooga. Du Bois later became a very prominent educator and writer.

A Prominent Society Figure

At Atlanta University Cora Calhoun Horne trained to be a teacher and finished in the school's fourth graduating class in 1881. Its academic program was said to be difficult and its student body relatively prosperous. Horne and many of her classmates became lifelong friends. One of them, Adella Hunt (Logan), descended from a family of free blacks in Georgia. Cora, Adella, and young women of their standing in the community centered their lives on the home, church, club activities, and cultural pursuits. Horne, who was well traveled, met Edwin Horn (then spelled without an 'e'), who was born in Tennessee in 1859. He grew up in Evansville, Indiana, and became a journalist, teacher, and poet. Cora and Edwin Horne were married on October 26, 1887, in Birmingham, Alabama, in the Calhoun home, where the family had moved a year earlier. According to Gail Lumet Buckley's history of the family, *The Hornes,* the press described the bride as "a lady of great taste and refinement, having figured very largely as the belle of Atlanta society."

The Hornes moved to Chattanooga, where Edwin Horne taught at the Gilmer Street School. He also was an owner of the lucrative Perry and Company—"The People's Drug Store"—and editor of the *Chattanooga Justice.* Later he purchased ten twenty-five dollar shares in Chattanooga's Penny Savings Bank. By 1889 their first son, Errol Stanley Horne, was born and Cora Horne's father, Moses, had died. Their second son, Edwin "Teddy" Fletcher Horne, was born in 1893. In 1896, as the Hornes' hope for a new South died and the South became entrenched in segregation, they decided to move to New York.

The Hornes settled briefly in the West Fifties, or the "Black Bohemia" section of New York City, also known as the best part of the Tenderloin section. Among their neighbors were poet James Weldon Johnson, novelist Charles W. Chesnutt, performer Bert Williams, and poet Paul Laurence Dunbar. Although the Hornes enjoyed the culture of the area, they were concerned that the Tenderloin section had by now become raw and dangerous. They moved to their dream home, a brownstone at 189 Chauncey Street in Brooklyn, and their sons became friends with Brooklyn's black bourgeoisie.

Edwin Horne was a teacher in New York City's public schools. He sued the city and won when a white teacher with less seniority was promoted over him. He was still denied the position, however, and had difficulty with the Board of Education because of the suit. In 1897 he changed his political party affiliation from Republican to Democrat and became secretary general of the United Colored Democracy. Around this time he also began to spell his last name with an 'e.' He and his friends, journalist T. Thomas Fortune and politician Ferdinand Q. Morton, were well rewarded for their work with Tammany Hall, the New York Democratic County Committee. On August 11, 1899, Edwin Horne was appointed assistant inspector in the Combustible Division of the New York Fire Department, an assignment that resulted from his political patronage.

A New Activist Emerges

The Hornes' third son, Frank Smith Horne, was born in August 1899. Cora Horne valued motherhood and placed it above all else; however, she started to become a new woman. Intellectual and free spirited, she needed other outlets. Thus, she became a founding member of the National Association of Colored Women. As a child she had been baptized Catholic but attended a Congregational church in Atlanta. On May 1, 1904, she received the sacrament of confirmation at Saint Benedict the Moor's Roman Catholic church in the Tenderloin district. The next year the Hornes' fourth son, John Burke Horne, was born.

Edwin Horne made an unsuccessful bid for a seat on the city council in 1910 when he ran on the Tammany ticket. His party aroused deep anti-Republicanism, and by 1911 some of the group's demands were met: the first black police officer was appointed in Harlem and Harlem's own 369th National Guard Regiment was established. The Hornes supported the work of the NAACP, which had been founded in 1909, and became members early.

Cora Horne expanded her volunteer and community activities and throughout 1913 she organized and directed a YWCA Red Cross unit. As her sons matured, she had more time to pursue interests beyond the home. She did not find housework, cooking, and babysitting suitable challenges. When she was at home, which by now was rare, she was usually resting, sipping tea, or reading, and she often ate alone in her sitting room. Meals for young John Burke Horne and housekeeping chores were left to Edwin Horne and the laundrywoman. The strain on the marriage was evident. Edwin Horne, who had been a man-about-town, whose complexion allowed him to be black or white to suit the occasion, and who loved the theater and fine restaurants, was different from Cora. By now they lived on separate floors and greeted each other formally as Mr. or Mrs. Horne.

Their son Teddy had married Edna Scottron, of a prominent Brooklyn family, and they now lived with the Hornes. The young couple's daughter, Lena Mary Calhoun Horne, who was to become a famous entertainer, was born on June 30, 1917. Edna Horne and her mother-in-law became adversaries, with Cora the dominant one.

Active in NAACP

Cora Horne was an activist with the NAACP. Her devotion to the organization inspired her to enroll her granddaughter, Lena, in the NAACP when she was two years old. (A photograph of Lena Horne as an NAACP member is printed in the October 1919 issue of the NAACP's *Branch Bulletin.*) After the East Saint Louis race riot in July 1917, in which nearly forty blacks were killed and the homes of many others burned, the NAACP defended ten blacks on murder charges. The NAACP Silent Protest Parade against lynching took place on July 28. Ten thousand people were present; women and children dressed in white and men with black arm bands marched down Fifth Avenue in total silence. All black middle-class clubs and primary organizations participated. Cora Horne was one of the marchers. The next year the Hornes' son Errol, who had been a lieutenant in the all-black Tenth Calvary and was later attached to a French unit, died of influenza. Cora Horne mourned his death by wearing only black, white, or gray from then on.

In the early 1920s Teddy and Edna divorced and Lena essentially became Cora Horne's last child and only daughter. Lena Horne attended the Ethical Culture School, a private school where Cora had established an ethical culture scholarship in her granddaughter's name. Cora Horne had become deeply immersed in ethical culture and showed little interest in the Catholic church. Late in the 1920s she became a disciple in the Baha'i faith.

Cora Horne's concern that people put their time to good use extended beyond the home and into the community, and she was not hesitant in making her views known there. In her autobiography, Lena Horne tells of a conversation she had years later with actor and singer Paul Robeson. Robeson said that Cora Horne helped him receive a scholarship to Rutgers University and that his childhood memories of her were vivid: she lectured to gangs of boys who loitered on Harlem's streets and ordered them to separate and ''be about something useful.'' The boys respected Cora Horne and at the same time were wary of her; they called her ''Tiny Terror.'' Lena Horne told Helen Arstein and Carlton Moss that Cora Horne and Robeson had mutual admiration for each other: Cora Horne considered him one of her many ''adopted sons'' and Robeson said she was like a mother to him when he needed it most. ''He often spoke of my grandmother and always with deep affection and respect,'' she said.

Still a small, thin, and mercurial woman, Cora, who had fair skin, now had streaked gray hair and a thin mouth and through the years continued to wear her traditional round, steel-rimmed glasses. She was known for the beautiful shoes she wore on her small, perfectly shaped feet, of which she was quite proud. But she was not a woman of warmth and never embraced or kissed young Lena. It was her grandfather's warm embraces, laughter, and playful games that young Lena found more appealing and that gave her a sense of family.

A member of the Brooklyn board of directors of the Big Brother and Big Sister Organization, Cora Horne represented the federation at a meeting in 1921 in Washington, D.C., where she met President Warren G. Harding.

Cora Horne and her good friend Minta Trotman, also an activist with the NAACP, sailed for Europe in autumn 1929, leaving Lena with another friend, Laura Rollock. Nothing is known about Cora Horne's activities from this time until her death in September 1932, except that she was a full-time social worker in Harlem. Her obituary identified several organizations that she served either as an officer or member, including the National Urban League, the Big Brother and Big Sister organization, Brooklyn Bureau of Charities, Katy Ferguson-John Hegeman (Sunday school) Houses, New York Branch of the Women's International League of Peace, and the Foreign Policy Association of the International Council of Women of the Darker Races. She had been one of the women from Africa, America, Haiti, the West Indies, and Ceylon who convened in Washington, D.C., in 1922 to establish the latter organization. She also still held membership in the National Association of Colored Women.

Cora Calhoun Horne set high standards for herself and for the African American race. She would not compromise her positions, particularly on suffrage and on the rights of women and her race, and she fought valiantly to achieve these rights. She was an important activist for these causes.

REFERENCES:

Buckley, Gail Lumet. *The Hornes: An American Family*. New York: Knopf, 1986.

Haskins, James. *Lena: A Personal and Professional Biography of Lena Horne*. New York: Stein and Day Publishers, 1984.

Horne, Lena. *In Person: Lena Horne. As Told to Helen Austein and Carlton Moss*. New York: Greenberg, 1950.

Horne, Lena, and Richard Schickel. *Lena*. Garden City, N.Y.: Doubleday, 1965.

Lewis, David Levering. *When Harlem Was in Vogue*. New York: Knopf, 1981.

Jessie Carney Smith

Whitney Houston
(1963-)
Singer, model

Whitney Houston will perhaps go down in history as one of black America's most highly acclaimed and successful musical performers. Houston's career has been meteoric, characterized by great success as a fashion model and as a singer whose work is popular in concert tours, videotapes, compact discs, record singles and albums, and movie soundtracks. Beginning with her debut album, *Whitney Houston,* in 1985, Houston has released a number of chart-topping songs which have garnered her a host of Grammy Awards, among other honors.

Whitney Houston was born on August 9, 1963, in Newark, New Jersey, and grew up in East Orange, New Jersey. Her parents are John R. Houston and Emily Drinkard Houston, and Whitney has two brothers, Michael and Gary. Houston's father is president and chief executive officer of her management company, Nippy, which was named for Whitney, using her childhood nickname. Her mother, better known as Cissy, is a long-time performer; she sang with the Sweet Inspirations—a soul group that toured and did record backup for such artists as Elvis Presley and Aretha Franklin. Cissy Houston was also featured in the gospel group the Drinkard Sisters, which included Dionne and Dee Dee Warwick, her nieces and Whitney's cousins. Houston's brother Michael is her road manager, and her brother Gary is one of her backup singers. In July 1992 Whitney Houston married Bobbi Brown, another award-winning singer, and in March 1993 she gave birth to her first child, a daughter.

In 1981 Houston graduated from Mount Saint Dominic Academy, a Catholic all-girls school in Caldwell, New Jersey. She left with a B-plus average, which was quite

Whitney Houston

remarkable because she maintained a modeling career and spent much of her time away from home from the age of sixteen. She holds an honorary doctor of humanities degree from Grambling State University in Louisiana.

Although Houston's formal music career did not begin until she finished high school, she became familiar with the world of entertainment early in life, which eased her entry into show business. As a child, she benefited on the one hand by singing in her church choir, and on the other hand by having a mother who could help train her and find suitable venues for her to display her talent. At the age of nine, Houston began singing in the choir of her church, New Hope Baptist Church, where she performed her first solo at the age of eleven; her mother was the choir director and had long shown an interest in developing Whitney's voice by coaching her. Houston first sang before a secular audience at the age of fifteen, performing with Cissy Houston at Carnegie Hall at a United Negro College Fund benefit concert. She also sang with Cissy Houston at area nightclubs and did background vocals for such singers as Chaka Khan and Lou Rawls.

While Houston's formal entry into show business did not begin with these early performances, they did, nevertheless, broaden her scope; it was her engagement at Carnegie Hall about 1978 that got her started in a career in fashion modeling. At the Carnegie Hall show, the exceptionally attractive, five-foot, eight-inch-tall Houston was spotted by a photographer who suggested she contact the Click modeling agency. She began with Click and later modeled with Wilhelmina. She appeared in such popular magazines as *Vogue, Cosmopolitan, Glamour, Seventeen, Essence,* and *Harper's Bazaar.*

Singer Achieves Superstardom

Given Houston's seriousness about singing and her obvious artistic ability, her parents sought to launch her formal career immediately upon her graduation from high school in 1981. They selected a management company for her, Tara Productions, with whom she signed. Through Tara Productions, Houston came into contact with her current personal manager, Gene Harvey, who participated in a promotions campaign for her. She worked with well-known performers, singing backup vocals; she also sang advertisement jingles. According to *Current Biography Yearbook, 1986,* she "was heard on albums by the Neville Brothers and the funk band Materials, and made an attention-getting contribution to the LP *Paul Jabara and Friends* (Columbia, 1983), on which she sang 'Eternal Love,' written by Jabara and Jay Asher." This exposure culminated in Houston's first major step toward becoming a superstar. With the release of *Paul Jabara and Friends,* Harvey and Tara Productions arranged a series of private club performances for Houston, open only to the media and recording executives. At one such club, Clive Davis, founder of Arista Records, recognized Houston's potential, and he subsequently assumed charge of her career, launching a two-year promotions campaign at a cost of a quarter million dollars. He ushered her into stardom, molding her persona and systematically positioning her within the world of popular music.

For Houston, Davis put together a media blitz. According to *Current Biography,* he had total involvement in developing her career, "grooming Miss Houston, preparing her debut album, and warming up the industry and the public for [her first] album." She appeared on television, was heard on the radio, and was featured in special showcases and in duets with the well-known singers Jermaine Jackson and Teddy Pendergrass. She had her own team of producers and songwriters, and she offered a taste of the power of her award-winning initial album with a highly successful singles promotion tour in Europe, in which she presented, among other songs, "All at Once."

When in 1985 her first album, *Whitney Houston,* was released to the public, her name became a household word. The album achieved unprecedented success, becoming the best-selling debut album for any solo artist ever. The LP prompted the release of several singles, including "How Will I Know?" "Greatest Love of All," "All at Once," and "You Give Good Love," and also resulted in videotapes of Houston singing and television performances. Further promotion included Houston's national concert tour, during which her performances frequently sold out, as was the case with her Carnegie Hall appearance in November of 1985.

Whitney Houston sold thirteen million copies. It won a Grammy Award and two National Music awards. It remained in the top ten longer than any previous album. Certain singles on the album were enormously successful in their own right. "How Will I Know?" was produced as a video, was a dance chart hit, and was widely shown on MTV. Her more socially conscious "Greatest Love of All" was also produced as a videotape and featured her mother, Cissy Houston; this video aired on nationwide television for the hundred-year celebration of the Statue of Liberty in 1986.

Since the meteoric success of Houston's debut album in 1985, she has been an untiring performer. Her second album, *Whitney,* was released in 1987, after being held in the wings for six months in order to accommodate the continued success of album number one. The second LP was no less dynamic, and it instantly made number one on album charts. It too contained outstanding singles; the song "Where Do Broken Hearts Go?" broke the previous record by becoming her seventh consecutive number-one hit. With this album, Houston had in her brief career won two Grammy awards, two Emmy awards, People's Choice awards, and twelve American Music awards. Her third album, *I'm Your Baby Tonight* (1990), went double-platinum. Her fourth album accompanied her acting debut in the movie *The Bodyguard* (1992), in which she starred opposite Kevin Costner. Houston's music career greatly benefited from her recording of the movie's featured song, "I Will Always Love You," written by country and western star Dolly Parton. By March 1993 the song had become rock music's longest running number-one hit ever; during the seventh annual Soul Train Music Awards ceremony, it won first place in the category Female Rhythm and Blues Single, and it won a People's Choice video award. On March 1, 1994, Houston picked up three Grammys for her *Bodyguard* soundtrack. "I Will Always Love You" was named Best Record of the Year; *Bodyguard* was named Album of the Year; and Houston was named Best Pop Vocal Performer (Female). Dolly Parton presented her the latter award. On March 15, 1994, at the eighth annual Soul Train Music Awards, the ballad was named best single of the year. Houston also earned the Sammy Davis, Jr. Award at the ceremony for the year's top entertainer.

Critical and Popular Reception Mixed

Despite Houston's phenomenal success, she is not without her critics, ranging from African Americans who claim that her work is not expressive enough of the black perspective to music critics who decry her choice of genre as beneath her artistic potential. With the release of her first album, there were some groans that she was too commercialized and perhaps not as socially conscious as she might have been, along with complaints that she aimed less at African American audiences than at other groups. For the most part, Houston's repertoire consists of ballads and dance tunes, yet there were complaints early in her career that her performances were not soulful enough because of their lack of the rhythm and dance showmanship. Houston responded to charges that her music was not "black" enough in the December 1990 issue of *Essence:*

> Black? Black—that bothers me.... What's Black? I've been trying to figure this out since I've been in the business.... I don't know how to sing Black—and I don't know how to sing white, either. I know how to sing. Music is not a color to me. It's an art.

Houston's third album, *I'm Your Baby Tonight,* was said to be more responsive to the black audience's expectation of showmanship and soulfulness. Although she continued to express more interest in song than in dance, she appeared to accept her fans' relish for dance tunes. She stated in *Ebony,* May 1991, "Dancing is fun, and if that's what people want, then cool, I can give that portion of myself to them, I have no problem with that. I'm a public servant in that sense."

As a performer and businesswoman, Houston gives back to the world much of what it showers upon her. She has contributed her time and money to a number of charitable causes. In 1988, for example, she contributed a quarter million dollars to the United Negro College Fund; she considers its 1990 award to her one of her most prized honors. She established the Whitney Houston Foundation for Children in the hopes of combatting illiteracy at a fundamental level; her mother heads this organization, and at the time of her wedding, Houston and her husband requested that all gifts be in the form of donations to the foundation. During the Desert Storm crisis, Houston's Super Bowl performance of "The Star-Spangled Banner" generated hefty compact disk and video proceeds that were directed to the Red Cross. In addition, Houston has invested in affordable housing for Newark citizens and has contributed money toward AIDS research and rehabilitation programs. In her first public appearance following the birth of her daughter, she sang "I Will Always Love You" at a benefit concert that raised a million dollars for the Saint Jude Children's Research Hospital, located in Memphis, Tennessee, and founded by the late Danny Thomas.

A deeply religious person, Houston is on very good terms with her family, with whom she works closely in her businesses. She is a warm, spirited, and compassionate individual who has not allowed fame to go to her head. Her beauty and talent are matched by her generous heart.

Current Address: c/o Arista Records, 6 West 57th Street, New York, NY 10019.

REFERENCES:

Ansen, David. "*The Bodyguard.*" *Newsweek* 120 (November 30, 1992): 80.

Cain, Joy Duckett. "The Soul of Whitney Houston." *Essence* 20 (December 1990): 54-56.

Chappelle, Tony. "The Three Faces of Whitney Houston." *The Black Collegian* 21 (November/December 1991): 128-30.

Current Biography Yearbook, 1986. New York: H. W. Wilson Co., 1986.

"Grammy's High Notes." *Nashville Tennessean,* March 2, 1994.

Jones, James T. IV. "Houston, Boyz II Men Ride 'Soul Train.'" *Nashville Tennessean,* March 10, 1993.

Nashville Tennessean, March 5, 1993; June 6, 1993.

Norment, Lynn. "The Wedding of the Decade." *Ebony* 48 (September 1992): 124-35.

Oermann, Robert K. "Is Whitney Houston Too Perfect?" *Tennessean Showcase,* June 16, 1991: 3.

Sports Illustrated 72 (March 11, 1991): 66.

Time 141 (July 27, 1992): 27; (December 14, 1992): 75.

Turner, Renee D. "How Celebrities Will Celebrate Christmas." *Ebony* 45 (December 1989): 31.

"Whitney Houston: 'Forever Daddy's Girl.'" *Ebony* 45
  (June 1990): 13-38.

"Whitney Houston Talks About the Men in Her Life." *Ebony*
  46 (May 1991): 110-18.

"Whitney, Toni Top 'Soul Train Awards.'" *Nashville
  Tennessean,* March 16, 1994.

Laura C. Jarmon

J. Imogene Howard

J. Imogene Howard
(1851-19??)
Educator, principal

J. Imogene Howard was one of a group of highly respected black women teachers in the New York public schools during the second half of the nineteenth century and the early part of the twentieth who deserve recognition as important historical figures. As New York prepared for the Columbian Exposition to be held in Chicago in 1893, her membership on the Board of Women Managers of the State of New York enabled her to promote the display of the work of black people at the fair.

Joan Imogene Howard was born in 1851 to Edwin Frederick Howard and Joan Louise Turpin Howard, who lived in a well-kept four-story brick house on Popular Street, situated in the aristocratic section of Boston's old West End. During the early part of the nineteenth century the Howard family of Boston figured prominently in the antislavery movement, along with their friends and fellow abolitionists William Lloyd Garrison, Lydia Maria Child, Charles C. Sumner, and Thomas Wentworth Higginson. J. Imogene's paternal grandparents had several sons, including Edwin Frederick, who married Joan Louise Turpin of New York and brought her into the family home. They had three children: Adeline Turpin Howard, the eldest, was born in New York; Joan Imogene Howard and a son, Edwin Clarence Joseph Turpin Howard, were born in Boston. The children were taught science and the finest literature, which shaped the careers they would later choose.

J. Imogene's brother Edwin Clarence Howard spent five years of his early life in Africa, there showing an interest in medicine. He also spent a year visiting hospitals and institutions in England and France as an observer and student. When Harvard Medical School revised its policy prohibiting blacks, Edwin Clarence Howard was admitted. In 1869 he graduated from the medical school, becoming its first black graduate. Altogether, Harvard graduated three blacks that year—Howard, George L. Ruffin in law, and Robert Tanner Freeman in dentistry. At some point Howard moved to Philadelphia and set up practice as a throat specialist. The handsome, convivial bachelor became a valued and prominent member of the Philadelphia County Medical Society, the Pennsylvania Medical Society, and the American Medical Association, frequently serving on behalf of the county society as delegate to state and national meetings. He was elected a member of the Philadelphia Board of Education in 1888 and served for eleven years.

Adeline Turpin Howard was a teacher in the Freedmen's schools, serving in Virginia, the remote country hamlets in Maryland, and along the banks of the Red River of Louisiana. Later she was principal and teacher in the Wormley Building in west Washington, D.C., where she was in charge of over six hundred students.

In 1865, when she was fourteen years old, J. Imogene Howard, as she was known, graduated from Wells Grammar School on Blossom Street in Boston, one of ten honor students who received silver medals. After taking an entrance examination, she enrolled at Girls High and Normal School in Boston, becoming its first black student. She completed her studies in three years, and in 1868 she became the school's first black graduate. She accepted a position as an assistant teacher in New York City's Colored Grammar School No. 4—later changed to Grammar School No. 81—on West 17th Street under the principalship of Sarah Thompkins Garnet.

Chooses Teaching Career

Mrs. N. F. [Gertrude] Mossell wrote in *The Work of the Afro-American Woman* that while Howard was teaching, she enrolled in a Methods of Instruction class held on Saturdays at the Normal College of New York, graduating with a diploma, master of arts, in 1877. According to Monroe A. Majors in *Noted Negro Women,* however, she received the master of arts degree from the College of the City of New York in 1879. Despite this confusion, it is known that she continued her studies, completing a three-year course at the University of the City of New York, where she had received a scholarship. The only black in her class, she received a master of pedagogy degree in 1892. Other black women graduates of the school include Mary Eato and sisters Florence T. Ray and H. Cordelia Ray, all of whom graduated in 1891; Eato and Florence Ray became prominent educators, as did Cordelia Ray, who was also a noted poet.

Noted Negro Women calls Howard "a bright and interesting talker" who "expresses her thoughts with a forcefulness that carries conviction to the hearer." Of the students in Colored Grammar School No. 4 where she taught, Howard said in the same source, "We have much to contend with that others have not," referring to the children with poor parents and with unsatisfactory role models in the home. These handicaps notwithstanding, Howard noted,

> I think it will be impossible to find a lot of children who exhibit more actual aptitude and acuteness. Their little intellects often seem to have been sharpened by even their short contact with an unsympathetic world, and as long as we are able to direct this precocity into the proper channels they will become good and useful men and women.

Sarah Thompkins Garnet (1831-1911) had been appointed principal of the school in 1863. The group of teachers who worked under her included several black women who took a prominent place in history: Mary Eato, Rosetta Wright, Florence T. Ray, Fannie Murray, Susan Elizabeth Frazier (who in 1869 became the first black appointed to a white-staffed school in New York), and Maritcha R. Lyons, as well as Howard.

When Garnet began teaching in New York City, the city maintained separate schools even though the state allowed but did not require separate school systems to be established by local communities. The board of education in 1883 proposed closing three of the "colored" schools, and since black teachers were not assigned to white schools, several of the black teachers would then lose their positions. In the meantime, the distinction of color was removed from the designation for schools and all schools in the system were numbered in regular, consecutive order and open to children regardless of race and nationality. In practice, however, the schools remained segregated, as did staffing. The law governing racially segregated staffs was changed in 1900, the year of Garnet's retirement. Howard then became principal, a position she held for eight years. In addition to teaching day school, for a period of time Howard was principal of the "colored" night school offered in the same building.

At some point during her tenure at the school, when 350 children were enrolled, the student body was predominantly female, a trend that seemed to prevail in all public schools. This was due to the fact that even though black children were enrolling in high schools more than ever before, many young men left school at an early age to find employment to meet family obligations. Monroe A. Majors quoted Howard in *Noted Negro Women* as stating, "The influence of one educated woman is certainly very great, but we try to educate both sexes."

In June 1900 Howard became a finalist in the New York Telegram Office's sixteen-month contest, "Trip to Paris." When the five winners were announced, her name was third, which entitled her to a trip to France and Belgium. Although sources say nothing more about the contest, Howard considered this the crowning event in her career.

Howard Joins Columbian Exposition

On June 3, 1892, the governor of New York appointed Howard to the five-member Committee on Education of the Board of Women Managers of the State of New York for the World's Columbian Exposition to be held in Chicago in 1893. The appointment was made public on June 7 at a meeting held in Albany and received wide press coverage. Howard was the first black woman in New York appointed to such a position. In addition to being a noted educator, Howard was committed to the black struggle. Since childhood she had felt that her mission in life was to improve the condition of the black race. She had taught, watched, and advised, and now she could help guide the world's view of black progress. According to Majors, "She feels that her people, who have made such grand strides in intelligence, industry and importance during the past decade, are entitled to recognition in Chicago's great Fair." She felt qualified and competent in her role.

Howard's responsibilities included representing the achievements of women in the field of education in the state of New York at the fair. She worked untiringly and painstakingly on an executive subcommittee that collected statistics on women's contributions and compiled information on the abolitionist Lydia Maria Child. Works collected became part of the rare book exhibition in the Woman's Building at the Chicago fair, and afterward the "Distinguished Work of the Colored Women of America" became an exhibit at the capitol in Albany, New York.

Apparently Howard was highly motivated to work and study and the school was extremely successful as result of her efforts. She had taught every grade required in the grammar department. However, the task may have taken its toll. According to Pauline Hopkins in an article for the July 1902 *Colored American Magazine,* "an indisposition of a serious nature compelled her to resign" in about 1908. Majors suggests in *Noted Negro Women* that Howard's friends encouraged her to resign because they feared the mental strain of the work would impair her health. She moved to Philadelphia, where she became a companion to an aunt, a Mrs. Bowers, the sister of her deceased mother, and to her brother, Edwin Clarence Howard. She presumably died there. Willard B.

Gatewood in *Aristocrats of Color* refers to J. Imogene and Edwin Clarence Howard as "among the late arrivals" readily accepted in the city's upper echelon of blacks. They brought with them a family heritage steeped in Boston's cultural and social life of the antebellum era.

J. Imogene Howard was an important early black teacher whose life should be examined in greater detail. Of particular importance to the history of blacks in the field of education is the work of a group of women—Sarah Garnet, Mary E. Eato, Susan Elizabeth Frazier, and others—who, along with Howard, taught young blacks in New York's schools during the late 1800s and early 1900s.

REFERENCES:

Gatewood, Willard B. *Aristocrats of Color.* Bloomington: Indiana University Press, 1990.

Hopkins, Pauline. "Famous Women of the Negro Race." *Colored American Magazine* 5 (July 1902): 206-14.

Lane, Roger. *William Dorsey's Philadelphia and Ours.* New York: Oxford University Press, 1991.

Majors, Monroe A. *Noted Negro Women.* Chicago: Donohue and Henneberry, 1893.

Mossell, Mrs. N. F. [Gertrude]. *The Work of the Afro-American Woman.* 1894. Reprint. New York: Books for Libraries, 1971.

Smith, Jessie Carney, ed. *Notable Black American Women.* Detroit: Gale Research, 1992.

Sollors, Werner, Caldwell Titcomb, and Thomas A. Underwood, eds. *Blacks at Harvard.* New York: New York University Press, 1993.

Jessie Carney Smith

Helen Humes

Helen Humes
(1913-1981)
Singer

Louisville, Kentucky, can be justly proud of Helen Humes, a jazz and blues singer who got her start in that community and went on to achieve fame in a career spanning some fifty years. In the late 1930s and early 1940s, Humes sang with the bands of Harry James and Count Basie. Later, she moved to the West Coast, where she recorded several hit rhythm and blues records and also became involved in films, appearing in some and dubbing vocals for others. Humes quit singing professionally for a while during the late 1960s and early 1970s, but she reemerged on the music scene at the 1973 Newport Jazz Festival. Afterwards, her career took off again, and she had regular engagements at popular New York

nightclubs and toured internationally. Although highly regarded as an outstanding interpreter of the blues, Humes disliked being labeled a blues singer, saying that she preferred ballads and torch songs. In truth, her singing style spanned several categories, and she was also praised for her jazzy improvisation as well as for her light, smooth, sensitive approach to lyrics.

Humes was born on June 23, 1913. Her mother, Emma Johnson Humes, was a schoolteacher, and her father, John Henry Humes, was one of the first black lawyers in Louisville. Humes was married from 1952 until about 1960 to a serviceman in the U.S. Navy. She continued to use her family name thereafter.

When she was growing up, music was an important part of Humes's home life; there was a piano in their home, and her mother and father sometimes sang duets. Although she had not had voice lessons, she sang and played piano and organ in her church. Humes's music career began early. As she said in the February 23, 1975, issue of the *Louisville Courier-Journal,* Bessie Allen, a local teacher, ran "a little Sunday School room and would teach us different instruments." The musicians from this Sunday school band then formed a dance band. It was Louisville's first black band, called the Booker T. Washington Community Centre Band. The members included Jonah Jones and Dickie Wells. The band played at local clubs, theaters, and dance halls. Humes first recorded at fourteen years of age, for Okeh Records, in St. Louis. She was recommended by Sylvester Weaver, a guitarist and singer in the local Louisville band. Her mother accompanied her to the session, where she recorded "A Worried Man Blues," "If

Papa Has Outside Lovin','' ''Do What You Did Last Night,'' ''Everybody Does It Now,'' and ''Million Dollar Secret.''

Although friends urged her to go to New York following her first recording session, Humes's mother insisted she finish her schooling first. After graduating from Central High School she went to Buffalo, New York, for a short visit. It turned into a two-year stay, during which she entered the performance world in earnest, earning thirty-five dollars a week at one nightclub and considering this all the money in the world.

Upon her return to Louisville, Humes began singing with the Al Sears band, including an engagement at the Cotton Club in Cincinnati in 1937. Count Basie's band came to Louisville and, after he heard her sing, he asked her to join his band at a salary of thirty-five dollars a week. She refused, saying that she could earn that much without leaving her present job. At about the same time, John Hammond heard her sing in New York and in 1936 arranged for her to record with Harry James. In Hammond's opinion, she was the best vocalist James had ever worked with. These recordings were very well received, but she never traveled with James; a black singer traveling and performing on stage with a white band was not yet customary.

Hammond's recognition of Humes established a pattern. Throughout her life major producers and critics of the day influenced her career: John Hammond set up her work with Harry James and Count Basie and her recordings with Columbia Records; Stanley Dance invited her to the Newport Jazz Festival of 1973; Norman Granz invited her to Jazz at the Philharmonic; and Leonard Feather, the well-known jazz critic, praised her in print and prepared an orchestration for her.

Career Blossoms with Count Basie

In 1938 Hammond arranged a session for Humes with Count Basie in New York. At that point Basie had Billie Holiday and James Rushing as his principal singers, but then Holiday left. Hammond convinced Humes to join Basie, who hired her to replace Holiday. She sang with Basie from 1938 to 1942 and then worked independently.

The character of her singing with the Basie Band varied: she sang standard popular songs of the day, special arrangements, ballads, and up-tempo numbers, but few blues tunes, as Rushing was the principal blues singer. One might think that she and Rushing would have developed a rivalry, but this was not the case; they formed a long-lasting friendship and shared a camaraderie both on stage and off. She added versatility to the Basie Band's repertoire and sang and recorded such songs as ''If I Could Be with You,'' ''Sing for Your Supper,'' ''My Heart Belongs to Daddy,'' and ''Between the Devil and the Deep Blue Sea.''

In 1945 Humes was working on the West Coast when she recorded ''Be-Ba-Ba-Le-Ba,'' a major hit that was followed by other hit rhythm and blues records such as ''Million Dollar Secret'' (1950). Also in the late 1940s and 1950s, she took on

some film work, performing with Dizzy Gillespie in *Jivin' in Bebop* and *Ee Baba Leba*. She dubbed vocals for movies, including Betty Grable's lead song in *My Blue Heaven*. Her association with Red Norvo in the 1950s took her on a tour to Australia in 1956 and 1957. Other engagements included performances at Cafe Society (1942, and also later); in Hawaii (1951); at the French Lick, Indiana, Jazz Festival (July 1959); and at Shelly's Manne Hole in Hollywood (1967). She returned to Australia in 1962 and again in 1964. ''The Rhythm & Blues Revue USA'' tour took her to Europe in 1962 and 1963. Also, there were other early 1960s concerts in Europe.

After an initial steep climb up the professional ladder and a period at the top stretching through the mid-1950s, Humes's career declined somewhat. She was virtually inactive musically from 1967 to 1972. She returned to Louisville to take care of her sick mother in 1967 and found employment in other fields. Her mother died in 1967, and she cared for her father until he died in 1975.

The Comeback

In the early 1970s a dramatic turn occurred in her career. Producer Stanley Dance came to Louisville in 1973 to persuade her to return to the stage for the Newport Jazz Festival being held in New York that year. Her professional singing career recommenced at the festival, where she sang at the July 3 Count Basie reunion concert as well as at the July 4 Louis Armstrong tribute concert.

Although Humes at first pleaded that she had almost forgotten how to sing, the response of her colleagues and the press attested to the fact that she certainly remembered. She earned accolades from the press and her peers for her performances at the Newport Jazz Festival and at the New York nightclub engagements that ensued. Humes sang at The Cookery and The Half Note in New York in 1974 and the Village Vanguard in 1975. Several subsequent engagements at The Cookery followed. She sang in London and France in 1973, 1974, and 1975, including engagements at the Nice Jazz Festival (France), and in Spain and Switzerland in 1975. She received the Music Industry of France Award in 1973 and the key to the City of Louisville in 1975.

Humes always believed in ''paying her dues'' by singing for charitable causes, and during this period she continually helped the elderly and aided with community concerns. She participated, for example, in concerts in 1975 for Louisville and Jeffersonville, Indiana, senior citizens' association projects and offered care, friendship and transportation to the elderly in her Louisville community.

Humes's recordings from the 1970s show her voice to have mellowed and darkened, and her approach sounds more mature. One hears her gift for improvisation somewhat balanced by introspection and a sense of reserve in her interpretations. The joy is there, of course, but often so is a calm, more patient approach. Her later work is represented on *Talk of the Town*, produced by John Hammond in 1975.

Humes was short but well built, with bright eyes and an endearing smile. She was perhaps a little portly upon her return to performing, leading Whitney Balliett to comment in *American Singers* that "extra pounds are to singers what nimble feet are to boxers: they add depth and range to the attack." Humes had a certain motherly quality that was projected into her interpretations, even when singing blues lyrics with racy double meanings.

Humes's voice quality was pure, smooth, and of somewhat high pitch and timbre. She had very good diction. Her sound was at the opposite end of the color spectrum from Ma Rainey and Bessie Smith; their style was darkened with moaning and shouting, but Humes's approach was smooth, lighter, and gentle. According to the *Louisville Courier-Journal*, July 23, 1978, Humes had the jazz singer's typical ability to improvise around a given melody and could vary her improvisations at will. Reviewing her *Talk of the Town* album, Leonard Feather commented in the *Louisville Times,* June 22, 1975, that she had "a way of making the blues sound ladylike, without destroying one whit of passion or authenticity." He added, "As a jazz singer, she imparts a joyful, swinging sweetness reflective of her warm personality."

Reportedly, Humes had no major musical influences and developed her own style. Rather than listen to records, she used the piano and sang the way she felt about the melody and lyrics right from the beginning. Whitney Balliett in *American Singers* likened her sound to that of Ethel Waters and commented on the instrumental flavor of her interpretations, her light vocal quality, and her ability to vary rhythm, tempo, and dynamics from a whisper to almost a shout.

In the opinion of many critics, Humes was an outstanding interpreter of the blues, rendering its various nuances from her particular perspective. Yet Humes complained that people often tried to type her as a blues singer, whereas she, as quoted by Balliett, preferred "pretty songs, torch songs," songs with meaningful lyrics. In reality, her style cut across categories. She sang blues songs with a jazz inflection, her popular songs and ballads were flavored with melodic embellishments and jazzy improvisation, and her jazzy rhythmic numbers were filled with joyful abandon. According to her obituary in the *New York Times,* September 14, 1981, she once said, "Bessie Smith and Ma Rainey were too bluesy for me." She liked ballads such as "I Got It Bad, and That Ain't Good" and "My Old Flame." Understandably, then, she listed George Gershwin, Fats Waller, and Hoagy Carmichael as her favorite composers. She had the reputation of being a happy singer. It was said that she could sing a sad blues tune and make the listener smile or feel content. Barney Josephson, owner of The Cookery in New York, reported in the *Louisville Courier-Journal,* June 23, 1978, that couples who were quarreling or arguing heatedly would often leave holding hands and feeling happy after hearing her sing.

Helen Humes's last singing engagement was in June, 1981, at the Hollywood Bowl's Playboy International Jazz Festival. She had hoped to work again at the Cookery in the fall of 1981, but illness forced her to cancel. After fifty years of work as a singer, she died of cancer on September 13, 1981, at the age of sixty-eight, in a nursing home in Santa Monica, California.

REFERENCES:

Balliett, Whitney. *American Singers.* New York: Oxford University Press, 1988.

"Basie Reunion Is a New Budding." *New York Times,* July 8, 1973.

Bogle, Donald. *Brown Sugar.* New York: Harmony Books, 1980.

Chilton, John. *Who's Who of Jazz.* Philadelphia: Chilton Book Co., 1972.

"Comeback . . . Louisville Singer Helen Humes Begins Three-Week Tour in Europe." *Louisville Courier-Journal,* February 27, 1974.

"A 'Complete Original,' Jazz Singer Helen Humes, Dies." *Louisville Courier-Journal,* September 14, 1981.

"Concerts to Benefit Senior Citizens." *Louisville Courier-Journal,* February 19, 1975.

Dahl, Linda. *Stormy Weather.* New York: Pantheon, 1984.

Feather, Leonard. Review of *The Talk of the Town. Louisville Times,* June 22, 1975.

Feather, Leonard, and Ira Gitler. *Encyclopedia of Jazz in the '70's.* New York: Horizon, 1976.

"Festival's Added Starter Stars." *Louisville Courier-Journal,* August 1, 1959.

"For Helen Humes, Another Charitable Trip Home." *Louisville Courier-Journal,* February 23, 1975.

Harris, Sheldon. *Blues Who's Who.* New Rochelle, N.Y.: Arlington House, 1979.

"Helen Humes and All That Jazz." *Louisville Courier-Journal,* July 23, 1978.

"Helen Humes 'Found' as Top Blues Singer." *Louisville Times,* December 24, 1959.

"Helen Humes Makes Hit in Jazz Festival." *Louisville Times,* August 1, 1959.

"Helen Humes: She Made the Blues a Happy Sound." *Louisville Times,* September 15, 1981.

"Helen Humes, Singer of Ballads and Blues." *New York Times,* September 14, 1981.

"Jazz Vocalist Helen Humes Dies at 68." *Louisville Times,* September 14, 1981.

"Local Jazz Singer May Make Big Time." *Louisville Times,* July 25, 1959.

"Louisville-born Singer, Helen Humes, on Comeback Trail, Wows Audiences." *Louisville Courier-Journal,* March 3, 1975.

"Louisville's Helen Humes 'Starting Over' on Vocal Career." *Louisville Courier-Journal,* June 30, 1973.

Mapp, Edward. *Directory of Blacks in the Performing Arts.* Metuchen, N.J.: Scarecrow Press, 1990.

The New Grove Dictionary of Jazz. 2 vols. London: Macmillan, 1988.

Placksin, Sally. *American Women in Jazz.* New York: Seaview Books, 1982.

Southern, Eileen. *Biographical Dictionary of African and African-American Musicians.* Westport, Conn.: Greenwood Press, 1982.

Darius L. Thieme

Ida Alexander Gibbs Hunt
(1862-1957)
Educator, Pan-Africanist, writer

Ida Gibbs Hunt, one of the early black women college graduates in the United States, was a teacher, social and civic activist, and author of journal and newspaper articles. Her concern was with advancing humanity and social justice. She was involved in three Pan-African congresses, serving variously as lecturer, planner, and conference participant. She was a product of the middle-class black society of the 1800s and 1900s that prepared its children to make a difference in black America.

Born on November 16, 1862, in Victoria, British Columbia, Ida Alexander Gibbs Hunt was one of five children born to Mifflin Wistar Gibbs (1823-1915), a Philadelphia native, and Maria Ann Alexander Gibbs (d. 1904), a Kentuckian. The other Gibbs children were Horace E. (b. 1864), Donald F., and Harriet Aletha Gibbs Marshall (1868-1941). Harriet became known as an educator, concert pianist, writer, and the founder of the Washington Conservatory of Music. A fifth child died before reaching adolescence.

Mifflin Gibbs travelled with abolitionist Frederick Douglass but left Douglass's camp in 1850. He became successful first in California as the co-owner of a boot and shoe firm, Lester and Gibbs. He was also owner and editor of the *Mirror of the Times,* an abolitionist newspaper and California's first black newspaper, founded in 1855. In 1866 Gibbs, who had moved to Canada and established a retail trade with miners and prospectors, was elected to the Common Council of Victoria, British Columbia; he was later reelected for the succeeding term. Around this time he read English common law with one Mr. Ring, an English barrister.

Although he remained in Canada for a while, in the late 1860s Gibbs sent his family to Oberlin, Ohio, because he felt schools were better there. Since conditions for blacks had improved after the Civil War, bringing about the changes he had struggled to achieve earlier, he was determined to make the United States his permanent home. By 1869 he joined his family in Oberlin where he studied in a local business college. Maria Gibbs and the other Gibbs children studied at Oberlin College. In 1872 the family moved to Little Rock, Arkansas, where Mifflin Gibbs joined Lloyd G. Wheeler and established a successful law firm, Wheeler and Gibbs. The next year Mifflin Gibbs became the first black elected municipal court

Ida Alexander Gibbs Hunt

judge. Later he held several offices in the federal government, including that of U.S. consul in Madagascar in 1897.

One of First Black Women to Receive Bachelor's Degree

Ida Hunt studied in the Oberlin Conservatory of Music from 1872 to 1876, then in the local public schools from 1876 to about 1879. In 1878 she joined the First Congregational Church in Oberlin. She completed her senior year of high school in Oberlin's Preparatory Department and became a boarding student at Oberlin. Hunt received a bachelor of arts in English in the 1884 graduating class, which included three black women who were among the early African American women to earn bachelor's degrees from an American college. Mary Eliza Church (later Terrell) and Hunt were friends before they entered Oberlin, classmates in the preparatory department, and dormitory roommates during their freshman and senior years in college. The third black woman to graduate with them was Anna Julia Cooper. These women became successful and were well known for their work as educators, leaders, and civil rights activists. Around 1885 Hunt reentered the Conservatory of Music to further develop her musical talent.

That same year Hunt joined her family in Little Rock for a while and became a missionary. Although the dates of her work during this period are unknown, for two years she taught Latin and mathematics in the State Normal School (now Alabama Agricultural and Mechanical College), in Huntsville, Alabama. Illness compelled her to return to Oberlin in 1889. Between 1889 and 1892 she studied at Oberlin, receiving an

M.A. degree in 1892. Roland Baumann, who wrote Hunt's biography for Dorothy Salem's *African-American Women,* notes that between 1892 and 1895 Hunt apparently was principal of the Preparatory Department in the State Normal School (now Florida Agricultural and Mechanical University) in Tallahassee, Florida. There she had a family connection. Her cousin, Thomas Van Rensselaer Gibbs (d. 1898), secretary of state in Florida in the late 1860s and by the 1890s a member of the Florida legislature, sponsored the bill that established the school, and was an administrator there when Hunt taught English in the higher level.

In 1895 Hunt joined her Oberlin classmates Terrell and Cooper at the M Street High School (later Dunbar Senior High School) in Washington, D.C., where the women had been invited to teach. Hunt taught English, a position she held until 1904 when she married William Henry Hunt (1869-1951). William Hunt had been secretary to Mifflin Gibbs while Gibbs was U.S. consul to Madagascar at Tamatave. When Gibbs resigned in 1901 due to advanced age, Hunt was appointed to the position. Because William Hunt received various assignments as U.S. consul, the Hunts spent the next twenty-seven years abroad. William Hunt's work took him to Tamatave (1904-06); St. Étienne, France (1906-26); Guadeloupe, in the West Indies (1927-28); St. Michaels, in the Azores (1929); and Monrovia, Liberia (1931-32). In late 1932 the Hunts resettled in Washington when William Hunt was reassigned to the State Department for a brief period. He retired from public service in 1932 and died on December 19, 1951.

Pursues Literary and Civil Interests

Hunt was a woman of many interests and talents and devoted her energies to organizations, especially international ones, that supported peace, women's suffrage, civil rights, and human and social justice in general. She joined Coralie Franklin Cook, Rosetta E. Lawson, Josephine Beall Bruce, and other black women in founding the first YWCA in the District of Columbia, which was incorporated on June 30, 1905. Later she was a board member of the Phyllis Wheatley YWCA. While the extent of her involvement is unknown, she figured in the Niagara Movement, the forerunner of the NAACP. Her presence in France between 1906 and 1926 put her in convenient position to become active in the Pan-African congresses held in Paris. Hunt was assistant secretary of the first congress held in 1919 and a participant in the second held in 1921. She and W. E. B. Du Bois cochaired the committee that planned the third conference held in London in 1923, when she presented a paper titled "The Coloured Race and the League of Nations."

Hunt was active with the Red Cross in France and in the United States as well. She was also a member of the Femmes de France, the Club Franco-Etranger, the Book Lovers Club, the Bethel Literary Society, the NAACP, the Washington Welfare Association, and the Women's International League for Peace and Freedom.

In addition to her lectures to teacher's associations and other organizations and audiences, Hunt published several articles in the *Journal of Negro History,* the *Negro History Bulletin,* and in newspapers in the United States and abroad. Her articles included "The Price of Peace" (1938), "Civilization and the Darker Races" (n.d.), and "Recollections of Frederick Douglass" (1953). For the most part, her lectures and writings enabled her to present the ideas of racial progress and reform she had gleaned from her experiences on the three continents where she had lived.

Nearly seventy years after graduating from Oberlin, classmates Hunt, Mary Church Terrell (1863-1954), and Anna Julia Cooper (1858-1964) came together for a reunion at Cooper's home in Washington, D.C., to reflect on their experiences as college graduates. They had graduated at a time when few women, particularly African Americans, received college degrees. According to the April 4, 1952, issue of the *Washington Post,* "the difficulties they encountered as mere female members of a recently-freed race only made their triumphs sweeter."

Hunt died at her home, 1215 Ingraham Street, N.W., Washington, D.C., on December 19, 1957. Although she was a member of Plymouth Congregational Church in the city, final services were held at the McGuire funeral home with Daniel G. Hill, dean of the Howard University School of Religion, officiating. She was buried in Lincoln Memorial Cemetery. The Hunts had no children.

Ida Gibbs Hunt served the community well. Her work demonstrated her concern for education, cultural development, and civil and women's rights. Her views are preserved in the articles she published on these issues.

REFERENCES:

Gibbs, Mifflin Wistar. *Shadow and Light.* Washington, D.C.: N.p., 1902.

Hutchinson, Louise Daniel. *Anna J. Cooper: A Voice from the South.* Washington, D.C.: Smithsonian Institution Press, 1981.

Logan, Rayford W. and Michael R. Winston, eds., *Dictionary of American Negro Biography.* New York: Norton, 1982.

"Mrs. Hunt, 96, Consul Widow." *Washington Star,* December 22, 1957.

"Mrs. Ida G. Hunt, 96, Judge's Daughter, Buried." *Baltimore Afro-American,* January 4, 1958.

"Reunited Trio Blazed a Trail." *Washington Post,* April 4, 1952.

Salem, Dorothy C. *African American Women: A Biographical Dictionary.* New York: Garland Publishing, 1993.

Woodson, Carter G. "The Gibbs Family." *Negro History Bulletin* 11 (October 1947): 3-12, 22.

COLLECTIONS:

Biographical information as well as school and alumni records of Ida Gibbs Hunt are in the Alumni and Development Office Records, Oberlin College. The Hunt Papers, Moorland-

Spingarn Research Center, Howard University, contain information on Ida and William Hunt.

Jessie Carney Smith

Kristin Hunter
(1931-)
Novelist, short story writer, educator, journalist

Kristin Hunter

Kristin Hunter is a prolific writer of short stories and novels for both adults and juveniles that have won critical acclaim for their realistic portrayal of the black urban experience. An important satirist of the 1960s and 1970s, Hunter believes that satire and humor are effective means of making social commentary. She says in Claudia Tate's *Black Women Writers at Work,*

> I'm interested in the enormous and varied adaptations of black people to the distorting, terrifying restrictions of society. Maybe that's why there is cheer and humor in my books. I marvel at the many ways we, as black people, bend but do not break in order to survive. This astonishes me, and what excites me I write about. Everyone of us is a wonder. Everyone of us has a story.

In 1981, Hunter became an adjunct associate professor of creative writing at the University of Pennsylvania; she has taught English there since the early 1970s.

Kristin Hunter was born September 12, 1931, in Philadelphia, the only child of George Lorenzo Eggleston, an elementary school principal, and Mabel Manigault Eggleston, a school teacher. A precocious child, she was a voracious reader by the age of four and before the age of twelve had read Isadora Duncan's *My Life* and *Don Quixote.* During her teen years she read Virginia Woolf, Henry Miller, Kant, and Schopenhauer, authors she said in the *Top of the News* that she's now "too lazy or too opinionated to tackle."

From Journalist to Novelist

Hunter's writing career began at age fourteen when, through the good offices of a columnist aunt, Myrtle Stratton, she started writing a youth column that was printed in the Philadelphia edition of the *Pittsburgh Courier.* Hunter's column appeared for six years. Hunter received positive encouragement to write from her aunt; her parents, however, gave her only a negative motivation. Their philosophy that "children should be seen and not heard" inspired her to read voraciously, to indulge in fantasizing, and to write as a mode of self-expression.

Hunter graduated from high school in 1947 and entered the University of Pennsylvania as an education major, her

parents having insisted that she become a teacher. After receiving her B.S. in 1951, she accepted a position as a third grade teacher but resigned before the end of the school term to pursue a writing career. Subsequently, she worked as an advertising copywriter and as an information officer for the city of Philadelphia. These positions entailed a great deal of writing and were important because they proved that she did not have to teach elementary school in order to earn her living. In 1952, she married Joseph Hunter, a writer and journalist. The course of their ten-year marriage (they were divorced in 1962) was marked by fierce competition between them as writers.

In 1955 Hunter won first place in a competition sponsored by CBS for her documentary *Minority of One.* In 1964, her first novel, *God Bless the Child,* was published. It recounts the story of Rosalie Fleming, who, in an attempt to escape from her ghetto surroundings, sets up as a petty numbers banker, thereby earning the enmity of the white males who control the illegal but lucrative numbers racket in the poverty-stricken black community. According to D. L. Patrick's 1986 edition of *Contemporary Novelists,* this novel "parodies the tale of the enterprising but low-born youngster who, since the origins of middle-class fiction, has set out to achieve a place in society by the application of nerve and energy." The novel portrays three generations of black women headed by Lourinda Baxter "Granny" Huggs, Rosalie's class- and color-conscious grandmother. Granny had worked for forty years as a domestic in the home of a wealthy white family, and Rosalie dies in an attempt to give her a ten-room house once belonging to a wealthy white woman. In doing so she had hoped to keep her grandmother in the elegant surroundings to which she had become accustomed as a domestic. Trudier Harris, in *From Mammies to Militants,* discusses Granny as a mammy character who "judges her family by standards and values she encounters in the white world." She says the novel explores these questions: "How can the attitudes which perpetuate self-destruction in black communities be killed? How can addiction to standards of beauty and lifestyles inappropriate to the black community be rooted out of the community? Perhaps Hunter sees no viable answer."

Hunter's second novel, *The Landlord,* was her most commercially successful. She says the situation for the novel presented itself to her one day when a rich white acquaintance, who had bought an apartment house, showed her some rent receipt books and described some of his tenants. She recalled in *Black Women Writers at Work,* "I never saw any of the characters in his house, but I could tell from what he was saying and from the names that they were inner city blacks, and everybody was running a game on him. I just knew this rich white boy was about to be taken." In *The Landlord,* a comic novel of maturation, Elgar Enders, a thirty-year-old white male, buys a dilapidated ghetto apartment building in order to prove himself to his millionaire father. This apartment building and the novel are peopled by an odd assortment of eccentrics, including Copee, who, though black, thinks he's Indian and harangues whoever will listen about the theft of the Indians' land; Copee's wife, Fanny, whose pastime is a succession of frivolous lawsuits; and DuBois, a homosexual professor without credentials whose unaccredited college periodically has a fire sale on degrees. At the end of the novel all the characters get what they want—or at least what they need. Copee is institutionalized, Fanny gets a beauty shop as a gift from Enders and becomes a successful businesswoman, DuBois gets to run a bona fide college, and Enders gets the love of his black tenants. Enders is transformed into a humanitarian: instead of extorting exorbitant rents from his tenants as a conventional slumlord would, he beautifies their surroundings. According to Thadious Davis and Trudier Harris's edition of *Afro-American Fiction Writers after 1955,* "Enders' financial reciprocity angered Hunter's critics, for they felt such reciprocity seldom, if ever, happens in real life." Hunter says in *Black Women Writers at Work,* "The point of the novel is that an immature white boy, by being pushed into contact with this bunch, is forced to grow up, to be responsible, to see reality. White men are allowed to remain boys until great ages because they're protected."

Becomes Successful Writer of Juvenile Fiction

The awareness, fed by civil rights struggles, that not enough books featured black children and the simplicity of Hunter's style led Hunter's publisher, Scribner's, to see her as a potentially successful writer of children's literature. From 1968 to 1973 she produced five works of juvenile fiction: *The Soul Brothers and Sister Lou, Boss Cat, The Pool Table War, Uncle Daniel and the Raccoon,* and *Guests in the Promised Land: Stories.* In the *Top of the News* she said of her books for young adults, "I hope they're peopled with three-dimensional characters, not just blackface Dick and Janes." As noted in

a *Contemporary Authors New Revision Series* (CANR) interview, Hunter finds writing for juveniles no more difficult than writing for adults except that she has had to overcome what Hunter describes as her own prejudice that "children's books are not as important or serious as adult books are, not high literature. . . . It helps that I'm not fully grown up yet!" As she explained in the *Top of the News,* she writes for older rather than for younger children "to avoid succumbing to the temptation to write down and be overly cute or condescending, therefore false. Older children can be addressed on an adult or near adult level."

Hunter's first novel for young adults, *The Soul Brothers and Sister Lou,* sold one million copies, was translated into several languages, and won several important awards, including the 1968 Council on Interracial Books for Children Prize. The heroine of this novel, Louretta Hawkins, joins a street gang along with four male friends. One of the gang members is killed by a policeman, who mistook an epileptic seizure for an attempted assault. Instead of having the customary violent reaction to their friend's death, the remaining gang members, at the instigation of Sister Lou, form a singing group, cut a record, and become immediately successful. Hunter says in *CANR,*

> [In *The Soul Brothers and Sister Lou*] I have tried to show some of the positive values existing in the so-called ghetto—the closeness and warmth of family life, the willingness to extend help to strangers in trouble . . . the natural acceptance of life's problems and joys—and there is a great deal of joy in the ghetto—and the strong tradition of religious faith. All of these attitudes have combined to create the quality called "soul" which is the central theme of the book.

Hunter's collection of short stories for children, *Guests in the Promised Land,* won the *Chicago Tribune* Book World Prize for the most outstanding juvenile literature of 1973. Hunter says in *Black Women Writers at Work,* "I'll tell you a secret: juvenile books pay better, not initially but over the long haul. You see there's always another crop of children for whom schools must buy books; libraries, parents, aunts and uncles continue to buy books."

Takes Academic Post

This period of great productivity for Hunter was marked by positive developments in her personal life. In 1968 she married journalistic photographer John I. Lattany, Sr., becoming the stepmother of John Lattany, Jr. and Andrew Lattany. In 1972 she became a lecturer in creative writing at the University of Pennsylvania.

In *The Survivors* (1975) Hunter explores in the unfolding relationship between B. J., a thirteen-year-old street hustler, and Miss Lena, a prosperous middle-aged seamstress, the possibilities of interclass and intergenerational harmony in the black community. Miss Lena was modeled in part on Hunter's grandmother, Lena Anderson Manigault, who also was a dressmaker. She becomes a surrogate mother to the motherless B. J., and he in turn teaches her about the complexities of street life.

Hunter developed the idea for her next novel, *The Lakestown Rebellion* (1978), from first-hand experience, growing up in the all-black community of Lawnside, New Jersey, and seeing it cut in two for the construction of a highway. The novel dramatizes how the black community, from preachers to prostitutes, comes together to sabotage the building of an interstate highway through their community. According to *Contemporary Novelists,* ''This story . . . renews the tradition of folk tricksters. A range of ingenious, zany, and simply unusual characters play the entire repertory of stereotypical roles popularly assumed to be black in order to stop the encroachment of 'progress' upon their lives.''

In 1981, Hunter published *Lou in the Limelight,* another novel for young adults and the sequel to *The Soul Brothers and Sister Lou.* In *CANR,* Hunter says,

In fact, I did this sequel, *Lou in the Limelight,* because over the years there was a continuous inflow of mail from young readers who wanted to know what had happened to the characters in *The Soul Brothers and Sister Lou.* It was really moving to see their belief in these characters as real people.

In *Lou in the Limelight,* the quartet of singers is exploited by the Mafia and succumbs to drugs and gambling. But like its predecessor, *The Soul Brothers and Sister Lou,* the novel ends on an upbeat note. Lou's Aunt Jerutha helps the singers to pay off their gambling debts, and they get ready to launch a new tour.

Since 1983 Hunter has been a senior lecturer in English at the University of Pennsylvania. In her *CANR* interview, Hunter states that her advice to would-be writers is ''not to write autobiographically'' and ''not get caught up in the hope of quick money.'' In the interview she describes her students as thinking ''they can write a bestseller about (and with) computers over the summer.'' Her advice is, ''Read all you can till you're 20, live all you can till you're 30, and write all you can after that. And fight all your life against regimentation, automation and standardization—all the forms of the Machine which want to make you obsolete.'' Hunter cites Colette as her literary idol because, as she explained in her *CANR* interview, she ''was not afraid to shock people, to show life as she saw it'' and because she wrote ''simple, limpid prose.''

Hunter is in the tradition of writers such as James Baldwin and Richard Wright who realistically describe the urban black experience, but her works have an optimistic, often satiric tone. She comments in *Contemporary Novelists:*

The bulk of my work has dealt—imaginatively, I hope—with relations between the white and black races in America. My early work was 'objective,' that is, sympathetic to both whites and blacks and seeing members of both groups from a perspective of irony and humor against the wider backdrop of human experience as a whole. Since about 1968 my subjective anger has been emerging, along with my grasp of the real situation in this society, though my sense of humor and my basic optimism keep cropping up like uncontrollable weeds.

Hunter was one of the few black writers of the 1960s who produced a work in tune with the integrationist spirit of the time. *The Landlord*'s relevance to the time was emphasized when it was made into a feature-length movie by a major company. Hunter is an important transitional figure between such women writers of the Harlem Renaissance as Zora Neale Hurston and Jesse Faucett and such contemporary black women writers as Toni Morrison and Alice Walker.

Current Address: 721 Warwick Road, Magnolia, NJ 08049.

REFERENCES:

Davis, Thadious M., and Trudier Harris, eds. *Dictionary of Literary Biography.* Vol. 33: *Afro-American Fiction Writers after 1955.* Detroit: Gale Research, 1984.

Harris, Trudier. *From Mammies to Militants: Domestics in Black American Literature.* Philadelphia: Temple University Press, 1982.

Hine, Darlene Clark, ed. *Black Women in America.* Brooklyn: Carlson Publishing, 1993.

Kilpatrick, D. L., ed. *Contemporary Novelists.* New York: St. Martin's Press, 1986.

''Kristin Hunter—Profile of an Author.'' *Top of the News* 26 (January 1970): 149-151.

Tate, Claudia. *Black Women Writers at Work.* New York: Continuum, 1983.

Wiloch, Thomas. Article on Kristen Hunter, including interview with Hunter by Jean Ross. In *Contemporary Authors, New Revision Series,* Vol. 13. Detroit: Gale Research, 1984.

Phiefer L. Browne

E. Belle Mitchell Jackson
(1848-1942)
Educator, entrepreneur, religious worker, reformer

E. Belle Mitchell Jackson

One of the earliest African American teachers in Kentucky to be researched and discussed, E. Belle Mitchell Jackson was also active in the black women's club movement. In the 1890s she led a small group of African American women in the foundation of the Colored Orphan Industrial Home in Lexington, Kentucky. This facility continues to exist as a community-service agency.

Eliza Belle Mitchell Jackson was born in Danville, Kentucky, on December 31, 1848, to Mary and Monroe Mitchell. Her father had earned enough money by working as a carpenter to buy his freedom and that of his wife. They used their limited resources to send their daughter to private schools for African Americans, first in Danville and then later in Xenia, Ohio. Jackson's upbringing in the Methodist Church and the example set by her parents instilled in her a strong sense of Christian duty and a desire to help those less fortunate than herself.

Civil Rights Encounter Stirs Controversy

In the fall of 1865, Jackson received considerable attention because of her association with a white abolitionist preacher, John G. Fee, who later became a founder of Berea College. Fee was superintendent of Camp Nelson, a union military installation in Kentucky. In Kentucky, African Americans were not free until the Thirteenth Amendment was ratified in December 1865. During and following the war, blacks gathered at Camp Nelson for protection by the missionaries and troops. The camp was operated by the army with support from the U.S. Sanitary Commission and the Freedmen's Bureau. Employed by the American Missionary Association (AMA), Fee was responsible for educating the African American soldiers who arrived at the camp hoping to earn their freedom by enlisting in the army. Most of the women and children who accompanied the men also desired educations. The teachers were all white missionaries provided by the AMA.

Fee, however, believed that an African American teacher would serve as the best role model for the black soldiers and their families. After encountering Jackson while visiting her church, which was not far from Camp Nelson, Fee was struck by her demeanor and appearance. After meeting with her and her parents, Fee became convinced that she was ideal for his work at Camp Nelson and asked her to teach at the camp. Recognizing this as a good opportunity, but aware that her assignment at the camp might cause racial tension, Jackson accompanied him.

Fee's attempt at integration did not go as he desired. He had failed to anticipate the strong racist reactions of the missionaries. Jackson rooming and eating in the same building as her white coworkers created considerable commotion. Most people present on Jackson's first day at Camp Nelson felt obliged to inform the AMA of their displeasure. The following account comes from Fee's autobiography:

> I gave to her in the common dining-hall a chair and place at the table at which I presided. The presence of this young lady at one of the several tables in the common dining-hall, produced a sensation. A chaplain to one of the regiments, whose home was down in Maine, together with some army officials also boarding at the hall, protested against this young woman's eating in the common boarding-hall. All the lady teachers (white) sent there by the American Missionary Association and the Freed-

man's Aid Society, refused, with two exceptions, to come to the first tables whilst the young woman was eating. She was, in person, tidy, modest, comely. . . . A major, whose home was in Illinois, and the steward, whose home was in the same State, came to me and suggested that I remove the young woman. I saw the moment for decision had come, and in a quiet manner I said, "I will suffer my right arm torn from my body before I will remove the young woman." And that they might see that I was not arbitrary in my decision, I said, "The young woman is fitted for her position; she is modest and discreet; she is a Christian, and as such Christ's representative: What I do to her I do to him."

Despite Fee's support, Jackson's stay at Camp Nelson was short-lived. Within a few days of her arrival, a petition was circulated in opposition to her sharing the same privileges as the white teachers and demanding her dismissal. According to a letter sent by W. W. Wheeler to George W. Whipple, both members of the AMA, the white teachers were not opposed to Jackson teaching in the camp, but they refused to eat and live in the same area as "a woman of Color." Shortly after Jackson arrived at Camp Nelson, Fee left to attend to personal business in Berea. It was then that the camp commander asked Jackson to leave.

Though just seventeen and immersed in a hostile environment, Jackson showed strength and character when she was asked to leave. She indicated she could not leave then—on Saturday—as her wash was already out and she did not desire to travel on the Sabbath; consequently, she left the following Monday. When Fee returned to the camp, Jackson had been dismissed and he had been demoted. By January 1866, Fee had left Camp Nelson to continue his work at Berea, for which he became well known.

Despite Jackson's dismissal, the "Belle Mitchell Incident," as it has become known, secured a civil rights victory for African Americans. When the AMA was pressed to respond, it sent a committee to Camp Nelson and, as noted by Richard Sears in *Practical Recognition of the Brotherhood of Man,* required all the teachers "to sign a paper declaring they would not make complexion a condition of association among teachers." It is unclear what, if any, impact this incident had on the decision to close Camp Nelson a short while later.

Refuses to be Defeated by Prejudice

Jackson did not allow her experience at Camp Nelson to hinder her commitment to racial uplift. After leaving the camp, she returned to Danville, but remained there only a short time before the AMA invited her to teach in a free school for African American children in Lexington. The Missionary Free School of Color opened in August 1865, and grew to over fifty students by November of the same year. During this time, neither the city of Lexington nor the state provided funds for the education of African Americans. Private, social, philanthropic, and religious groups operated the segregated schools that existed. In addition to teaching in Lexington,

Jackson taught at schools in Frankfort, Louisville, Nicholasville, and Richmond.

Jackson left teaching in 1867 to continue her education. She entered Berea College but left before earning her diploma to marry Jordan Carlisle Jackson, whom she had met while teaching in Lexington. This marriage united two courageous individuals in an untiring struggle for the human rights of African Americans. E. Belle and Jordan Jackson worked as a team, making a lasting impact on the social, educational, religious, and political life of African Americans not just in Lexington but throughout the state of Kentucky.

Jordan Jackson was a businessman, banker, politician, newspaper editor, author, and advocate for education. Born a slave in Fayette County on February 28, 1848, he had no formal education, but he taught himself to read and write. His respect for education eventually led to his being elected a trustee at Wilberforce University in Ohio and at Berea College in Kentucky. He also served on the committee that presented a bill to the Kentucky General Assembly that resulted in the establishment of the State Normal School for Negroes, which is now Kentucky State University. Jordan Jackson's brother John, the first African American to graduate from Berea College, became this school's first president in 1887. Jordan Jackson's other political activities included his service as chairman of a group organized to protest the passage of the Separate Coach Law. In 1892, the Republican party elected Jackson a delegate from the state-at-large to the National Republican Convention in Minneapolis. Jackson was perhaps best known for his business activities. He operated the first African American undertaking business in Lexington, Porter and Jackson, and expanded it to include a livery stable. Jordan Jackson became a friend of Booker T. Washington, who described Jackson's funeral home and livery stable in *The Negro in Business* as "the finest in Central Kentucky." Jackson also served on the executive committee of the National Negro Business League, which was established by Washington.

E. Belle Jackson supported Jordan Jackson in all his professional endeavors. Jordan Jackson was once quoted as saying that E. Belle was the best investment he ever made and that he owed much of his success to her. In addition to moral support, she provided financial support: at one point she gave him her life earnings so he could continue a political campaign.

However, E. Belle Jackson was not content with merely assisting Jordan in his numerous business enterprises. Along with a friend, she operated a millinery business in downtown Lexington, "the only colored milliners in Lexington," according to R. C. O. Benjamin in *Negro Business Directory Fair Souvenir for Lexington, Kentucky.*

The Jacksons were active members of St. Paul African Methodist Episcopal (AME) Church. They raised two children, Minnie and Henry Mitchell, and involved them in church activities. Their granddaughter, Sadie Yancey, made her name as a prominent educator. After earning a doctorate from Columbia University, Yancey served in several administrative positions at historically black colleges, including dean of women at Florida Agricultural and Mechanical University and at Howard University.

Even though Jackson would have been considered among the black middle class of Lexington, she recognized that most African American women faced the triple threat of racism, sexism, and poverty. This compelled her to work in numerous civic and service organizations. She became active in the black women's club movement, and her life exemplified her commitment to its principles, particularly its emphasis on racial uplift. She served as president of the Kentucky Association of Colored Women and later was instrumental in helping to establish the Phyllis Wheatley branch of the YWCA in Lexington. As president of the Kentucky state chapter of the Association of Colored Women, she followed the dictates of the president of the National Association of Colored Women, Mary Church Terrell, who is quoted by Paula Giddings in *When and Where I Enter* as stating "Self-preservation demands that [black women] go among the lowly, illiterate and even the vicious, to whom they are bound by ties of race and sex . . . to reclaim them."

Founds Home for Orphans

Jackson's most significant contribution was the founding of the Colored Orphan Industrial Home in Lexington in 1892. The history of the home is truly a story of remarkable achievements despite almost insurmountable obstacles. The board of managers, headed by Jackson, proved to be quite resourceful in acquiring the necessary funding for the home. Money was extremely limited within the African American community, which was only one generation away from slavery. The managers labored in numerous ways to raise funds. Concerts, plays, lectures, neighborhood fairs, and tea parties were given, and donations were solicited from churches, schools, other social and civic organizations, and individuals. The managers solicited funds from the city and county governments long before social service programs were supported by local governments. The fund-raising efforts of the managers took them beyond the local community to seek money from philanthropists in the northern and eastern United States; they even travelled to London, England. They employed a professional philanthropist, the only white person associated with the home, who solicited support from some of the era's most renowned individuals.

The home's educational program, which included religious and common school instruction and industrial training, served as the vehicle for racial uplift. The children's religious education stressed Christian principles. Each child was required to have a common school education, which included basic instruction in reading, writing, and mathematics. In fact, once admitted, no child could leave the home unless he or she was able to read and write. The educational program was tailored to the individual needs of the children, and some were sent to private schools. Other children were sent to schools outside the city, such as the Red Cross Hospital in Louisville, the Frankfort Normal School, and Tuskegee Institute in Alabama.

The industrial training program merged all the aims of the educational program—teaching religious principles, habits of industry, and the work ethic—while simultaneously insuring the institution's maintenance. The home modeled its industrial training program after the philosophy of Hampton Institute and Tuskegee Institute. Every child was required to learn a trade. The instruction focused on blacksmithing, sewing, chair-caning, cooking, carpentry, painting, gardening, and laundry work.

The managers accomplished their goal of racial uplift through the industrial training program. Children residing in the home were prepared to be self-sufficient. In addition to preparing the children for future usefulness as workers, the industrial training program fostered such character traits such as responsibility and thriftiness.

Jackson served on the Board of Managers of the Colored Orphan Industrial Home for almost fifty years. In addition to helping children, the home provided food, shelter, clothes, and medical care for destitute elderly women. The home responded to community needs by functioning as a bank, church, school, and community center whenever the need existed. Though the home ceased to provide residential care for children in the 1980s, the facility continues to function today as the Robert H. Williams Cultural Center, still providing community services over one hundred years after being founded by Jackson.

As an educator, religious worker, businesswoman, and reformer, E. Belle Jackson lived a long life in service to the community. She is best remembered for her efforts to improve the lives of homeless and destitute women and children. She died in 1942 at the home of her daughter and is buried in Greenwood Cemetery, Lexington, Kentucky, beside her husband.

REFERENCES:

Benjamin, R. C. O. *Negro Business Directory Fair Souvenir for Lexington, Kentucky.* Lexington, 1899.

Burnside, Jacqueline G. "Black Symbols: Extraordinary Achievements by Ordinary Women." *Appalachian Heritage* 15 (Summer 1987): 11-16.

———. "Philanthropists and Politicians: A Sociological Profile of Berea College, 1855-1908. Ph.D. diss., Yale University, 1988.

Byars, Lauretta F. "Lexington's Colored Orphan Industrial Home, 1892-1913." *Kentucky Register* 89 (Spring 1991): 147-78.

Dunnigan, Alice Allison. *The Fascinating Story of Black Kentuckians: Their Heritage and Traditions.* Washington, D.C.: Associated Publishers, 1982.

Fee, John G. *Autobiography of John G. Fee, Berea, Kentucky.* Chicago: National Christian Association, 1891.

Fouse, W. H. "Educational History of Negroes of Lexington, Kentucky." Masters thesis, University of Cincinnati, 1937.

Giddings, Paula. *When and Where I Enter.* New York: William Morrow and Co., 1984.

Harris, Lawrence. *The Negro Population of Lexington in the Professions, Business, Education and Religion.* Lexington: n.p. 1907.

Johnson, W. D. *Biographical Sketches of Prominent Negro Men and Women in Kentucky.* Lexington: Standard Printing, 1897.

Mitchell, Myrtle Y. Interview with Lauretta Flynn Byars, March, 1991.

Sears, Richard. *Practical Recognition of the Brotherhood of Man.* Berea, Ky.: Berea College Press, 1986.

Washington, Booker T. *The Negro in Business.* Boston: Hertel, Jenkins and Co., 1907.

Wheeler, W. W. Letter to George W. Whipple, August 31, 1865. American Missionary Society Archives 44187. Amistad Research Center, Tulane University.

COLLECTIONS:

Minutes and Annual reports of the Colored Orphan Industrial Home Boards of Managers and Trustees are available in Special Collections and Archives, University of Kentucky Library. A copy of the oral history interview with Myrtle Y. Mitchell is available in the Oral History Collection, University of Kentucky Library.

Lauretta Flynn Byars

Ida L. Jackson

Ida L. Jackson

(1902-)

Educator, humanitarian

Highly honored as the first African American woman to graduate from the University of California, Berkeley, and the first black teacher in the public schools in Oakland, California, Ida L. Jackson is equally esteemed as the founder of a summer institute for rural teachers in Mississippi and a health project for people in the area. She is today a nonagenarian who displays a continued interest in current issues.

Ida L. Jackson, who was born on October 12, 1902, in Vicksburg, Mississippi, comes from a rich ethnic heritage of African, American Indian, French, and Irish roots. Both paternal grandparents were from Nigeria; her maternal grandmother was born in the United States, while her maternal grandfather was a native of Marseille, France. Jackson's mother, Nellie Portier, a homemaker, was born on Canal Street in New Orleans. Her father, Pompey Jackson, a minister, farmer, and carpenter, was born in Anniston, Alabama, in 1855.

About ten years before Jackson's birth, a kind white woman warned her father of a lynch mob that was determined to take his life for having proven in a court of law that he, and not a white man, owned a plot of land. He fled Monroe, Louisiana, by wagon with his wife and three sons, who were all less than four years old. After arriving in Vicksburg, Jackson's father built a one-room house and added to it until it had the needed bedrooms for his growing family, which eventually included six children. Being the youngest child and the only girl gave Jackson a favored position within the closely-knit family, where she was protected and lovingly referred to as "the baby" long after she reached adulthood. She tagged along after her brothers Alonzo, James, Samuel, William Edward, and Emmett Lee.

Encouraged by their father to allow the young child to build on her early ability to read well and to express herself fluently, Jackson's brothers let her look over their shoulders as they did their homework. One day she followed the boys to school. Learning that the preschooler could read and recite the multiplication tables, the teacher invited Jackson to tutor the older students. This was the genesis of her interest in teaching and using her talents to make life better for others. It was strengthened by her parents' emphasis on the value of higher education as a way of escaping the segregation and discrimination they continually experienced in their lives.

With the death of her father when Jackson was ten, her mother and brothers renewed their commitment to see that she received the proper education to develop to her highest potential. She graduated from Cherry Street High School in Vicksburg in 1914, a few months prior to her twelfth birthday.

After high school, Jackson first studied at Rust College in Holly Springs, Mississippi, and then transferred to New Orleans University and entered its Peck School of Domestic Science and Art. Here she came under the wing of the school's matron, Mrs. Fisher, a white woman who took a personal interest in the young student and relieved her of the dull, menial duties required of the other students. After leaving Peck School, Jackson was admitted to the senior class at the Normal School of New Orleans University and graduated with a teaching diploma and a certificate in domestic science. With diploma and certificate in hand Jackson accepted the offer to teach sewing at Peck School and at the same time continued to study at New Orleans University (which later merged with Strait College to become Dillard University). She remained there until she and her mother left to join her brothers in Oakland, California, in 1918.

Jackson's brothers had given glowing accounts of the freedom from racial prejudice in California and had assured their sister she could get a far superior education at the University of California. They knew that with a degree from the university and a California teaching credential she would have no difficulty getting a teaching position. Such were Jackson's expectations when she reached Oakland in 1918.

Challenges Racial Barriers in California

Once in Oakland, Jackson and her mother first occupied a room in the home of a woman in West Oakland. Then Jackson's mother rented a small house behind the spacious home of Mrs. Sarah Ridgeway, a motherly, warm-hearted woman. Mrs. Ridgeway appreciated the care Jackson's mother took of the little house and the garden she had planted, and after three months offered to sell the larger home on the front part of the lot to the Jackson family. Thus the large three-story home at 623 Fifty-eighth Street became the Jackson home.

As a very young woman, Jackson's ambition was to be a foreign missionary, but her five protective brothers, acting in place of the deceased father, discouraged a career that would take their only sister into another land. In later years her thoughts turned towards law. But the lack of opportunities for African American attorneys, coupled with the satisfaction of the first experience of teaching at Peck School and the memory of the very early time when she helped older students with reading and arithmetic, tipped the balance towards a career in teaching. Hers was not an overwhelming desire to become a teacher; however, having a teaching diploma and a year's experience in the classroom made the school system a logical place to enter the job market.

When Jackson told a friend about her intention to apply to the Oakland public schools, she was ridiculed for even thinking that a black person could obtain a job teaching in Oakland. Nonetheless she went to the office of the county

superintendent to request an employment application. The superintendent provided the application, but suggested she enroll at the University of California to complete course work for the full California teaching credential. On her way out of the building she saw notices for civil service examinations for post office jobs. Soon she was taking the ferry from Oakland to San Francisco to work at the San Francisco post office. Since this occurred at the end of World War I, all of the women at the post office were dismissed within six months to accommodate the returning male veterans.

Prejudice Seen on University Campus

Despondent over the loss of the post office position, Jackson went to the University of California to inquire about registration. Although it was six weeks into the semester, she was able to register for ten units of class work. With great pride in being part of such a famous institution and strong determination to master her studies, she received an A.B. in 1922 and an M.A. the following year. She had survived the overwhelming feeling of isolation and lack of recognition that were major parts of her experience as a student at Berkeley.

Jackson was the force behind the creation of the Rho Chapter of Alpha Kappa Alpha Sorority, chartered at Berkeley on August 21, 1921. Probably the biggest disappointment of her time at Berkeley was President David P. Barrows's support of the *Blue and Gold,* the campus newspaper, in its failure to fulfill a commitment to print the Rho Chapter's membership picture. His defense was that the women of the sorority were not representative of the university.

It was not easy for Jackson to secure approval for her master's thesis, "The Development of Negro Children in Relation to Education," in which she rebutted the United States Army's findings that blacks are incapable of progressing beyond the intelligence of a fifteen year old. When her committee withheld approval, the Graduate Council voted to grant her degree. This incident was a determining factor in her decision to discontinue study at the University of California and to pursue the doctorate she had begun at Columbia University.

Ultimately Jackson recovered from the isolation, slights, and frustrations that troubled her at Berkeley. Her feelings toward the university softened, largely because the institution has honored her on several occasions. In what she describes as a high point in her life, she was invited to march in the academic procession of the 1968 Centennial Celebration and was selected as one of the thirty-nine alumni to write their biographies for *There Was Light, Autobiography of a University, Berkeley: 1868-1968* recognized her as a valued alumna with citations, introductions, and special presentations. One year she was Berkeley's official representative at the inauguration of a new president of Dillard University.

California's First Black High School Teacher Appointed

After leaving the university in 1923 Jackson became the first black woman to teach in a high school in California, in the Imperial Valley town of El Centro. She taught English, cooking, and sewing at East Side High School, a segregated school for Mexican American and African American students. In El Centro, Jackson formed her first meaningful teacher-student relationship, a friendship with a Mexican American girl that continued into the years the student lived in Jackson's Oakland home while she attended the university.

Never abandoning her desire to teach in Oakland, Jackson faithfully renewed her application. It took action by the northern California branch of the NAACP and sympathetic whites before Jackson was offered a long-term substitute teaching position at Prescott School in West Oakland, starting in 1924.

Jackson came to Prescott fully intending to succeed, and she was prepared to face the disadvantages of being the only black teacher in the city. But it was an uphill fight for acceptance from the first moment when the principal, who had not been informed about the ethnicity of the new teacher, was unprepared to greet her. He restructured her classes so that she taught an ungraded group of students—those who could not read, or were discipline problems. The brightest spot in the first day came at noontime when two Italian girls handed her a bouquet of flowers in a display of affection.

Jackson feels that as a pioneer she was never allowed to progress as she should have in Oakland schools. However, as with the University of California, the passage of years brought extensive acknowledgment of her contributions. Starting when she was a university student and into her career, Jackson was active in the NAACP and in women's and community organizations. She also sponsored a series of black history and black culture programs, and she used the talents of young people for musical recitals and operettas at the Fifteenth Street African Methodist Episcopal (AME) Church, now the First AME Church.

Alpha Kappa Alpha's Humanitarian Projects Begin in Mississippi

In 1933 Jackson heard Arenia C. Mallory, director of the Saints Industrial School in Lexington, Mississippi, speak of the abject poverty in that state. The description moved Jackson to organize Alpha Kappa Alpha's Summer School for Rural Teachers, staffed by members of the sorority on a volunteer basis. The school was designed to improve the quality of teaching for black children. Here she would be a missionary, not in Africa, but in the South of her own country.

After two years it was apparent that health care was the most pressing need in Mississippi's Holmes and Bolivar counties, and Jackson instituted a health clinic that continued its operations for an additional eight summers. Sorority sisters who were health practitioners drove to Mississippi to give nutritional advice, health care instruction, inoculations against diphtheria and small pox, and general dental care. As it became more and more difficult for people to come to a school or to a church to consult the physicians and dentists, Jackson

converted the project into a unique mobile service, long before this was an accepted way to reach isolated citizens. In the course of her activities Jackson met Eleanor Roosevelt and elicited her support for the health clinic.

In 1926 Jackson met Mary McLeod Bethune, president of the National Association of Colored Women. In that year Bethune presided over the association's fifteenth biennial session, held in Oakland. Through Bethune's influence, Jackson was one of the three African American women privileged to observe the United Nations in session in its early years in the 1940s.

Jackson took a leave of absence from teaching in 1936 to study for a doctorate at Columbia University in counseling and guidance. When she was ready to write her dissertation she encountered difficulties similar to those she faced attempting to get her master's at Berkeley. She opted not to pursue it further and put her energy into her work and into community service. Before Jackson returned to Oakland she worked for a year as dean of women at Tuskegee, where she became friends with scientist George Washington Carver.

Jackson never married, not from an absence of suitors, but due to the demands of her many activities. She remembers the fatherly attitude of her brothers as they screened any young man who indicated an interest in their sister.

With her brother Emmett, Jackson purchased a twelve-hundred-acre ranch along the scenic coast of Mendocino County in northern California in 1945. When he died less than five years later, Jackson operated the ranch alone for a while, living in the house that she had built there and raising wild turkeys and exotic peacocks. Having lived on the ranch since she retired from teaching in 1953, she sold the property in 1965 and returned to Oakland. Later she purchased a three-story Victorian house in East Oakland, where she now lives. The home, called "Wrestacres," was originally built for Walter Butler, president of the northern California NAACP, the organization that brought pressure on the school board to hire her as its first black teacher. She vividly recalls conversations with W. E. B. Du Bois when she was a young woman and he was a guest of the Butler family in that same house.

Current Address: 10 Excelsior Avenue, Oakland, CA 94610.

REFERENCES:

Bornor, Nellie. "She Lit a Candle." *Negro Digest.* 18. (November 1968): 43-46.
"Ida Louise Jackson: Overcoming Barriers in Education." An Interview Conducted by Gabrielle Morris, 1984, 1985. The University of California Black Alumni Series. Bancroft Library. University of California, Berkeley, 1990.
Jackson, Ida Louise. "Ida L. Jackson." In *There Was Light: Autobiography of a University, Berkeley: 1868-1968.* Edited by Irving Stone. Garden City, N.Y.: Doubleday, 1970.

———. Interview with Dona L. Irvin. March 9, 1993.

———. Interviews with Vera Griffin. Oakland Museum Cultural and Ethnic Affairs Guild Black Pioneers Oral History Project, December 14, 1971; January 19, 1972.

                                                                             Dona L. Irvin

Janet Jackson

Janet Jackson
(1966-)
Singer, actress

Janet Jackson is the only member of her family to emerge fully from the shadow of her enormously famous brother, singer Michael Jackson, and become a major star in her own right. Her albums and videos enjoy tremendous popularity, and she is the winner of a Grammy and several American Music awards. While her attempt to make a name for herself as a movie actress was not successful, she continues to be a major recording artist, having the same number of gold singles to her credit as Aretha Franklin.

Janet Demeta Jackson was the tenth child born to Joseph and Katherine Scruse Jackson. She was born in Gary, Indiana, on May 16, 1966. Joseph Walter Jackson, born on July 26, 1929, in Fountain Hill, Arkansas, was the son of Samuel Jackson, a high school teacher, and Chrystal King Jackson, a former student of his. There were five children in Joseph Jackson's family, one of whom, a sister, died at the age of seven. Samuel Jackson was a distant father and a harsh disciplinarian with his children, behavior traits that also characterized his son Joseph when he became an adult. Samuel and Chrystal divorced; Joseph lived with his father until Samuel married for a third time, at which point he joined Chrystal and the other children in East Chicago. Joseph became an amateur boxer and dropped out of school in the eleventh grade. Katherine Jackson was born Kattie B. Scruse on May 4, 1930. She had a younger sister, Hattie. Her parents were Prince Albert Scruse, a railway worker and tenant cotton farmer, and Martha Upshaw Scruse. When Katherine was one and a half years old, she contracted polio, which left her with a limp. Her parents moved to East Chicago in 1934, and Prince Scruse found work as a Pullman porter. Prince and Martha Scruse divorced in 1935. Katherine Scruse was a shy girl who did not finish high school. Joseph Jackson had already been married and divorced before he wed Katherine, although he had met her prior to his first marriage. After a six-month engagement, Joseph and Katherine married on November 5, 1949. They settled in a small two-bedroom house in Gary, Indiana, where Joseph had a job as a crane operator in a steel mill.

Jackson's older siblings are Maureen (Rebbie, pronounced Reebie), born May 29, 1950; Sigmund Esco (Jackie), born

May 4, 1951; Tariano Adaryl (Tito), born October 15, 1953; Jermaine LaJuane, born December 11, 1954; LaToya Yvonne, born May 29, 1956; Marlon David and Brandon, born March 12, 1957 (the twins were premature and Brandon died within twenty-four hours); Michael Joseph, born August 29, 1958; and Stephen Randall (Randy), born October 29, 1961. There is also a younger half-sister, Joh' Vonnie, born to Joseph Jackson and Cheryl Terrell on August 30, 1974. The family did not learn of this child's existence until about 1980.

By the time Jackson was born, many changes had taken place within the family. Internally, probably the most important change was that Katherine Jackson was baptized as a Jehovah's Witness in 1963. Although Joseph Jackson did not follow her into the faith, he did not interfere with her efforts to raise the children in this quite puritanical denomination, and it seems that Michael, LaToya, and Rebbie became the most committed. Externally, the older Jackson brothers, pushed by their father, were close to making a breakthrough in show business. On July 23, 1968, the Jacksons auditioned for Motown in Detroit, and developments in their career led Joseph and the boys to move to Los Angeles in the fall of 1969. In December 1969 Katherine Jackson, her daughters, and her youngest son joined the rest of the family on the West Coast.

Childhood in Limelight

Jackson grew up amidst the affluence surrounding a successful show business family. This meant that she would have the lessons of public relations built into her education. A primary lesson was the very loose connection between image and truth. Michael Jackson had to learn this lesson at the age of ten. Accustomed to telling the truth, he nonetheless was instructed to tell interviewers that he was eight years old and that Diana Ross discovered him, both untrue statements. J. Randy Taraborrelli, in his biography of Michael, quotes him as saying at a later date: "I figured out at an early age that if someone said something about me that wasn't true, it was a lie. But if someone said something about my *image* that wasn't true, then it was okay. Because then it wasn't a lie, it was public relations."

This poses a problem in any attempt to depict Janet Jackson's early life. For example, in September 1993, Lynn Norment wrote in *Ebony*,

> Jackson says that she grew up in a loving home and that her parents, Joseph and Katherine Jackson, were strict disciplinarians. But she denies that they were abusive, as was alleged by sister LaToya Jackson in her book. "That's just a bunch of crap," Janet says of LaToya's charges that their father sexually and physically abused her.

LaToya Jackson's account of a dysfunctional family in her autobiography is much nearer the mark than the rosy accounts given for public relations purposes over the years. Unfortunately, her mixture of fact and what appears by most accounts to be fiction makes it difficult to lend credence to any otherwise unattested statement in her memoir. As a girl and the youngest child, Janet Jackson may also have had a somewhat different experience than her older siblings; indeed, some observers see her as the least scarred child and the most well-adjusted adult. The charges of sexual abuse of the girls by Joseph Jackson are quite unsubstantiated. What does seem to be true is that Joseph Jackson was a man who was unable to express his love and who did beat his children severely, especially his sons. It also appears to be true that he and, eventually, the older sons abused the younger sons by engaging in inappropriate sexual behavior in their presence.

Randy and Janet Jackson were also probably older than Michael when they learned about their father's constant infidelities, so most likely the shock was less for them. Janet was not touring with her father and thus was not as often a direct witness to the parade of women entering his hotel room. However, in 1980, when she was fourteen, she was apparently involved in a scene in which her mother, for once, exploded and attacked a woman she presumed was one of Joseph Jackson's mistresses. Gina Sprague, the alleged mistress, worked at Joe Jackson Productions, and she admits to having a close relationship with Joe Jackson but is adamant in denying any intimacy. On October 16, 1980, according to the police report filed by Sprague and documents filed in her suit against Joseph, Katherine, Randy, and Janet Jackson, Katherine appeared in the office with Randy and Janet and attacked Sprague with the assistance of her two children. The attack did in fact take place, and other witnesses cited in Taraborrelli's Michael Jackson biography concur in saying that Janet was there. However, if LaToya Jackson's eyewitness account is to be believed, the young woman involved was not Janet but Randy's girlfriend Julie.

There were also severe tensions involving other interfamilial relationships, especially as it became clear that Michael Jackson was going to become a superstar on his own. Children, however, tend to accept their families as normal, and not all was bleak. Katherine Jackson was a loving woman who did her best for her children even if she was unable to shield them from their father's rage. Also, unlike her older siblings, Jackson appears to have had the experience of dealing with children outside the family. While part of her education was conducted by private tutors, she did attend public schools in Encino for some time and then switched to Valley Professional School, a private school from which she graduated in 1984.

Jackson Begins Professional Career

Jackson first appeared on stage in April 1974, when she was seven. She and her brother Randy sang and did impressions of such stars as Sonny and Cher in the family's Las Vegas act. She also joined the other members of the family in 1976 on *The Jacksons,* a thirty-minute, four-episode summer replacement program. She again played in comedy bits, including one in which she did an excellent imitation of Mae West. She proved to be quick to learn lines, and her good sense of timing seemed even better when set against her siblings' floundering attempts at dialogue. She attracted the attention of Norman Lear, who was looking for someone to play Penny Gordon Woods, an abused child, on the television comedy *Good Times*. This initiated a series of television roles. Jackson was on *Good Times* for two seasons, 1977-79. She then appeared in *A New Kind of Family* from December 1979 to January 1980 in a short-lived effort to revive this show, which had been a flop. In 1981-82 she played Charlene DuPrey on *Different Strokes* and then in 1984-85 she was Cleo Hewitt on *Fame.*

Fame involved location work in New York, and the eighteen-year-old Jackson escaped for a while from family supervision, discovering many aspects of life from which she had been sheltered. She also made another break with the family. While the Jacksons were on the Victory Tour, she married, eloping on September 7, 1984, with James DeBarge, a musician in the group Debarge, which recorded for Motown. She had known DeBarge for some time—he would ungallantly claim that they had first had sex when she was fifteen after they met on the set of *Soul Train.* The Jackson family disapproved of Janet's marriage. DeBarge was aggressive, immature, and undependable. In addition, he was an addict. There was a very difficult month while Debarge, Janet Jackson, and Joseph Jackson lived together in the Encino home. The couple moved out, and Jackson had a very trying time. Her brother Michael finally persuaded her that ending the marriage was the only solution. She left DeBarge on January 7, 1985, and applied for an annulment, which was granted on November 18, 1985. While it may possibly be true that Jackson was pregnant before the marriage and had an abortion as DeBarge claims, there is apparently no truth to the rumor that she gave birth to a child who is secretly being raised in Europe.

Janet Jackson is reported to be close to Michael, and it is to him that she looked when she began her recording career. She not only followed his advice about the importance of persistence and hard work, she was the only sibling to come and watch him work on his videos. Her first album, *Janet Jackson* (1982), reached number 84 on the pop chart and had three hit singles, including "Young Love" and "Give Your Love to Me." *Dream Street* (1984), which brothers Michael, Marlon, Tito, and Jackie contributed to, reached 187 on the chart. Sales were about 250,000 for both. It was at this point that Jackson really began to work and to change musical direction.

First Major Hit

In 1986 Jackson had her first very successful album, *Control,* recorded for the A&M label. She worked on the album with John McClain, who helped make her into a star. McClain shaped her body through diet and exercise, sent her to a vocal coach, and hired Paula Abdul to work on her videos. Joseph Jackson, who was still trying to be her manager, did not like this close relationship with McClain, did not want her to work with the writing-producing team of Jimmy Jam (James Harris III) and Terry Lewis, and did not like the album the first time he heard it. Since *Control* sold eight million copies worldwide and one of its songs, "What Have You Done for Me Lately," was a major hit, Jackson was only further convinced that she and her siblings were justified in their low opinion of their father's management ability. "Control" and "What Have You Done for Me Lately" were both number-one singles. Nominated for three Grammies and nine American Music awards, the album won two American Music awards in 1987. Making her mark through her stage presence and her dancing, which some place on a par with Michael's, Janet Jackson has only one defect as a performer—a limited vocal range. Her svelte and attractive appearance, resulting from diet, exercise, and plastic surgery, showed that she had shed the reason for Michael's nickname for her, Dunk (based on Donkey). *Ebony* named her one of the ten most beautiful black women in America in 1987.

Jackson decided to address social issues in her next album, *Janet Jackson's Rhythm Nation 1814* (1989). (The number 1814 was meant to be mysterious, but Francis Scott Key wrote the words to "The Star Spangled Banner" in 1814.) The album was again produced by Jam and Lewis, who wrote nearly half the songs; Jackson wrote only one completely by herself, "Black Cat," which was one of the three most successful singles on the album, along with "Miss You Much" and "Escapades." Again the album sold some eight million copies worldwide. In conjunction with the album, Jackson undertook her first tour, beginning in Miami, Florida, on March 1, 1990, and ending in Japan on November 16 of the same year.

Jackson's status as a major star was confirmed by the release of *Janet Jackson's Rhythm Nation 1814* in 1990. She was the first artist to have seven top-five singles from a single

album. For this album she won three American Music awards in January 1991, MTV's 1990 Video Vanguard Award, and, for the "Alright" video from it, an award from *Soul Train.*

When Jackson Records was formed as part of a new deal between CBS Records and Michael Jackson, it was expected that Jackson, who often asked her brother for advice, would be the first singer to sign with the new label. However, she went to Virgin Records. The contract for an estimated thirty-two million dollars was signed in March 1991 and was the largest recording contract in history. (Michael Jackson held off completing his "billion"-dollar contract until after Janet signed so as not to reduce the publicity she received.)

As Jackson consolidated her recording status, she was reordering her private life. She bought a home in San Diego and later a beach house in Malibu. She is no longer managed by her father. Unmarried, she maintains an open relationship with former choreographer René Elizondo, with no expectation—on her part at least—of marriage at any time. It is reported that she maintains a close relationship with her mother but concentrates on keeping her distance from the family in order to avoid getting involved in their problems. She continues to make contributions to such charities as the United Negro College Fund and the Make-A-Wish Program. The foundation supporting this program for terminally ill children gave her its Humanitarian of the Year Award in March 1991.

Jackson tried to expand her options in show business by appearing in a film. Her choice of project seemed wise, since she worked with John Singleton, the young black director who had received Oscar nominations for best director and best original screenplay for his first film, *Boyz N the Hood. Poetic Justice* appeared in the summer of 1993. It was on the whole poorly received by reviewers, as was Jackson's performance. Richard Schickel said in *Time,* July 26, 1993, "[Singleton] doesn't know how to coax a performance out of Jackson, who relates to the camera lens as if it were a mirror." Anthony Lane said in the *New Yorker,* August 2, 1993, "*Justice* provides the first starring role for Janet Jackson. If it should prove to be the last, I doubt whether Hollywood would mourn; she struggles hard, but can't do much with the absurd demands placed upon her by the movie." The movie was a top box office draw during its first week but died in the second due to bad reviews and bad word of mouth.

Continuing Success

Jackson's latest album, called simply *janet.,* also appeared in the summer of 1993. The *New Yorker* reviewer was far more positive about it than about the movie, saying, "After listening to Jackson's latest album "janet.," I decided that there was a stronger pulse of sexual determination in a single chorus of "This Time" than in the whole of her debut movie." Lynn Norment said in her record review column in *Ebony,* September 1993, that the songs on the album "explore love, sensuality, the power of sisterhood and Jackson's own evolving self-identity." This album was again produced by Jimmy Jam and Terry Lewis, and it sold more than six million copies. Jackson undertook a major world tour to promote it in

1993-94. In 1994, when "Any Time, Any Place" gave Jackson her fourteenth gold single, she tied Aretha Franklin as female solo singer with the most gold singles.

Part of her current quest is to project the image of adult sexuality. "If" is very suggestive. As quoted in the *Nashville Tennessean* of July 31, 1994, the producer Jimmy Jam said, "The lyrics to 'If' are not explicit lyrics—they leave you to use your imagination and fill in the blanks. The blanks aren't very big blanks, but they're blanks nonetheless." The video of "If" shows Jackson grabbing the crotch of dancer Omar Lopez, and in her stage show she even feigns caressing the crotches of members of the audience.

Janet Jackson has not yet achieved on tour the scale of success achieved by Michael, but she is definitely a major star. Recent awards include a Grammy in 1994 for the best rhythm and blues song, "That's the Way Love Goes." She received an Oscar nomination for her song "Again" from *Poetic Justice.* She also received an unprecedented ninth Soul Train Award. A hard working professional who strives to please her audiences, Jackson seems destined for continued success as a singer.

Current Address: c/o Virgin Records, 338 North Foothill Rd., Beverly Hills, CA 90210.

REFERENCES:

Andrews, Bart. *Out of the Madness.* New York: Harper Paperbacks and Rose Books, 1994.

Brooks, Tim, and Earle Marsh. *The Complete Directory to Prime Time Network Shows 1946-Present.* 5th ed. New York: Ballantine, 1992.

"Confidence No Problem for 'Suggestive' Jackson." *Nashville Tennessean, Showcase,* July 31, 1994.

Current Biography. New York: H. W. Wilson, 1991.

Givens, Ron. "Janet Jackson: *janet.*" *Stereo Review* 58 (September 1993): 96.

"Jackson, Company Deliver Drama, Funk at Starwood." *Nashville Tennessean,* August 1, 1994.

Jackson, LaToya. *LaToya.* New York: Signet, 1992.

"Jackson Stages Sensual Riot of Dance, Dazzling Theatrics." *Nashville Banner,* August 1, 1994.

"Janet Jackson Ties Aretha Franklin for Most Gold Singles." *Jet* 86 (August 29, 1994): 36.

Johnson, Robert E. "Janet Jackson." *Jet* 86 (August 8, 1994): 52-59.

Lane, Anthony. "Blank Verse." *New Yorker* 69 (August 2, 1993): 76-78.

Norment, Lynn. "Grown-up Janet Jackson Talks about Racism, Sensuality and the Jackson Family." *Ebony* 48 (September 1993): 36-42.

Ritz, David. "Janet's Passions." *Essence* 24 (May 1993): 84-86, 140-42.

———. "Sound Off." *Ebony* 48 (August 1993): 25.

Schickel, Richard. "Love N the Hood." *Time* 142 (July 26, 1993) 67-68.

Taraborrelli, J. Randy. *Michael Jackson.* New York: Ballantine, 1992.

Robert L. Johns

Caterina Jarboro
(c. 1898-1986)
Opera singer

Caterina Jarboro is known as the first African American singer to sing a principal role with an all-white opera company, the Hippodrome Theater in New York. She successfully pursued a career as an opera and concert singer at a time when there were few opportunities open in these fields to people of her race. In addition to the very few operas she had a chance to perform in this country, she appears to have enjoyed at least moderate success in the opera houses of Europe for a number of years before World War II, although her European career can only be sketched. Her concert performance career in the United States is likewise not well documented, nor are many details of her life, especially during the later part.

Jarboro herself is at least partly responsible for some of the confusion in accounts of her life. On February 29, 1972, she gave an interview to James V. Hatch and his black drama class at City College of New York. Some of the statements in this interview, however, seem to owe more to her sense of the dramatic than to the realm of fact. This state of affairs is unfortunate since the interview is a major source of current knowledge of the singer.

According to the 1972 interview, Caterina Jarboro was born in Wilmington, North Carolina. An orphan, she was brought up in Catholic convents and orphanages. Other sources, including the Wilmington newspapers and Maude Cuney-Hare in *Negro Musicians and their Music,* give a different account. These sources state that she was born Katherine Yarborough, changing her name to Catarina Jarboro when she became an entertainer. Her father was John Wesley Yarborough (1850-1924), a barber with a shop at 212 N. Front Street in Wilmington. Her mother was (Ann?) Elizabeth Harris Yarborough (1864-1913). There is some confusion about her mother's first name—the *Wilmington Star* gives it as Ann in a July 8, 1987, article while other sources cite it as Elizabeth. Since one of the Yarborough's daughters was named Anna Eliza, Ann may have been an unused first name. Elizabeth Harris is credited by one source with playing the organ at St. Thomas Catholic Church, and others say that she sang in the church choir. Local tradition also says that Katherine Yarborough pumped the bellows of the church organ.

The Yarborough family was Catholic and produced six children, all born at the family home, 214 Church Street: Josephine S., Douglas, John Wesley Jr., Anna Eliza, Katherine, and Joseph S. According to the *Wilmington Star,* Kathe-

Caterina Jarboro

rine Yarborough was born on July 21, 1898, five years earlier than the birth date she used in later years. At the time of her death in Manhattan on August 13, 1986, she was survived by a sister—Anna Gayle of Palmetto, Florida—and a brother—Joseph Yarborough of Philadelphia. She was buried on Staten Island.

Yarborough was educated in the Catholic schools of Wilmington and at Gregory Normal School. At the age of thirteen she moved to Brooklyn, New York, to live with an aunt and continue her education. She returned to see her family in her childhood home for a last time when her mother died in 1913. There is no other information about her activities during the decade between her leaving home in 1911 and her appearance in the musical *Shuffle Along* in 1921.

In the 1972 interview, Jarboro downplays her involvement in the *Shuffle Along* production. She says that she was kept mostly backstage because she was too young and her skin too dark for a regular position in the chorus, yet she also says that she understudied a principal and appeared on stage several times before she left for Europe in 1921. This account may not be entirely true. She was twenty-three at the time, and while it is very difficult to judge a complexion accurately in black and white photos, she was a strikingly handsome woman with light skin. A desire to minimize her connections with popular music may also be evident in her failure in the interview with Hatch and his class to mention her work in *Runnin' Wild* of 1923. She implies that she left for Europe to study almost immediately after *Shuffle Along* rather than some five years later in 1926, as other sources have indicated. It is also possible, despite her statement that she never

married, that there was a marriage during this period. Langston Hughes and Milton Meltzer wrote in *Black Magic*, "Marrying a man who sympathized with her ambitions, she persuaded him to send her to Europe." This is the only reference to any marriage and may be no more than a bit of unfounded gossip. Hannah Block, who restored the Yarborough house in Wilmington, was quoted in the *Wilmington Star* in August 1986 as saying, "The convent sisters here discovered she had such a magnificent voice. They arranged to have her sent to New York for lessons when she was 13 years old, and they arranged for her to go to Milan, Italy."

Singer Makes Opera Debut

It is a credit to her courage and determination to pursue a career in classical music that Jarboro did go to Europe to study and pursue her dream. She said in the Hatch interview, "When you want something so very badly, you'll get it, but you have to want it yourself."

Jarboro went to Paris in 1926 to further her education in music; there she found work as a soloist in French churches. With the aim of securing training in singing opera, she went to Italy in 1928 and became the pupil of Nino Campinno. On May 21, 1930, she made her debut at the Puccini Opera House in Milan, where she sang *Aida*, a role she repeated some twelve times. She also gave two performances of *L'Africaine* in Italian. She then secured engagements in Belgium in Gounod's *La Reine de Saba* and Meyerbeer's *L'Africaine*. When Jarboro returned to the United States in early 1932, she had a contract with the San Carlo Opera in Milan, and she had sung in Naples, Toulouse, Nice, Monte Carlo, Lyons, Narbonne, St. Moritz, and Biarritz. Contracts in Madrid and Barcelona had to be canceled due to the outbreak of the Spanish Civil War.

Initially, Jarboro intended to stay a short time in the United States but prolonged her return to explore career possibilities in this country, in particular with the newly formed Chicago Opera Company. There was talk of her singing *Aida* at a summer performance in Ravinia, just outside Chicago, and also of her singing the lead role in Clarence Cameron White's opera *Ouanga*, which was not premiered until 1956 by the National Negro Opera Company at the Metropolitan Opera House. She filled her time with a successful series of concerts. In December 1933 Jarboro went back to Wilmington to give a benefit concert at Thalian Hall for the Colored Empty Stocking Fund. She accepted an offer from the Chicago Opera Company, which Alfredo Salmaggi was trying to build up as a popular price company in the midst of a depression that saw the old Chicago Civic Opera Company close and the Metropolitan Opera Company in dire financial straits. On July 22, 1933, she sang *Aida* at the Hippodrome Theater in New York, becoming the first black American to sing with an all-white opera company. The engagement was so important to African American society in Harlem that blacks filled half the seats in the theater. Maude Cuney-Hare quotes the music editor of the *New York Times* as writing,

> The young soprano brought to its presentation last
> night some admirable attributes—a vivid dramatic

sense that kept her impersonation vital without overacting, an Italian diction remarkably pure and distinct, a musical feeling for phrase and line and voice whose characteristically racial timbre, husky and darkly rich, endowed the music with an individual effectiveness.

Her success was such that she repeated the role two days later, this time with the celebrated African American baritone Jules Bledsoe in the role of Amnistro, her father, another black first. In September there was another performance at Ebbetts Field, and she opened the Hippodrome season that fall, again in *Aida.* However, there were no offers from any other opera companies in the United States, due to racism and also to the financial difficulties the Depression caused for all the performing arts. In addition, it would be many years before opera management would disregard racial identity in casting, so Jarboro would be considered only for roles of darker-skinned heroines like Aida.

In the face of these circumstances, Jarboro returned to Europe, making her headquarters in Brussels and continuing her career in European opera houses, including those in Russia, Latvia, and Lithuania. She said in the 1972 interview that she was in Russia when the outbreak of the World War II forced her to return to the United States. She then worked for the army as an interpreter and was wounded in a convoy in Italy, which caused her to return home.

Between the outbreak of World War II and her official retirement in 1955, little is known about the musical activities of Jarboro, although she seems to have settled in New York. There were two town hall concerts, of which she was very proud, on April 19, 1943, and February 6, 1944. She sang a second time in Wilmington, this time at a benefit concert for the Community Boys Club in the Wilmington Industrial High School Auditorium on January 28, 1951.

Wilmington remembered its daughter. In 1982 she attended the first Saint Thomas Celebration of the Arts, which was dedicated to her. In conjunction with the celebration, a plaque was placed on her childhood home on February 28, 1982.

Enough is known about Jarboro to recognize the importance of her career. It is unfortunate that the present state of knowledge about her life does not allow a fuller presentation. She overcame tremendous obstacles in pursuing a singing career and her success argues for a considerable measure of talent as well as willingness to run risks in pursuit of her ambition. Hannah Block remembered for the *Wilmington Star* of July 8, 1987, that on the day in 1982 when the plaque on her childhood home was dedicated, Jarboro began to cry as she visited the interior of the house she had not seen since 1913. When Jarboro was reminded that people would be out front soon, Block said, "She just threw her shoulders back and her head went up. It was just like she was going on stage. She just took control." Block summed up her impressions: "She was a diva if there ever was one. All she had to do was walk into a room, and everyone would turn and look at her. She was smart as a whip."

REFERENCES:

"Caterina Jarboro." Obituary. *New York Times,* August 16, 1986.
"Caterina Jarboro." Reproduction of concert program cover. Newspaper clipping. New Hanover County Public Library.
"Catherine Jarboro to Sing *Aida* with the Chicago Opera Company." *New York Age,* July 22, 1933.
"Catherine Yarborough Back; May Appear in Chicago Opera." *Chicago Defender,* March 12, 1932.
Cuney-Hare, Maude. *Negro Musicians and Their Music.* Washington, D.C.: Associated Publishers, 1936.
"First to Sing in Metropolitan Opera House." *Wilmington Journal,* March 19, 1981.
"Friends Mourn Caterina Jarboro, Opera Star and Pioneer." *Wilmington Star,* August 23, 1986.
Hughes, Langston, and Milton Meltzer. *Black Magic.* Englewood Cliffs, N.J.: Prentice-Hall, 1967.
Jarboro, Caterina. Interview with James V. Hatch and his black drama class. City College of New York, February 29, 1972. Hatch-Billops Collection, New York City.
Kellner, Bruce, ed. *The Harlem Renaissance: A Historical Dictionary for the Era.* New York: Methuen, 1984.
Mapp, Edward. *Directory of Blacks in the Performing Arts.* 2d ed. Metuchen, N.J.: 1990.
"The Queen of Sheba." *Chicago Defender,* July 18, 1936.
Saint Thomas Celebration of the Arts, Wilmington, N.C. Program dedication page. 1982.
"Singer Caterina Jarboro of Wilmington: 'She Was a Diva if There Ever Was One.'" *Wilmington Star,* July 8, 1987.
Southern, Eileen. *Biographical Dictionary of Afro-American and African Musicians.* Westport, Conn.: Greenwood Press, 1982.
Story, Rosalyn M. *And So I Sing.* New York: Warner Books, 1990.
"Yarborough Home Plaque." *Wilmington Journal,* February 25, 1982.

Robert L. Johns

Louise E. Jefferson
(1908-)
Calligrapher, illustrator, art director, cartographer, photographer

Louise E. Jefferson is a professional commercial artist and was formerly the art director for a publishing house, one of the first women ever to hold such a position. Her work has reached many people who may well have paid little attention to her name. For example, book designs, book

Louise E. Jefferson

jackets, and book illustrations are seldom roads to fame in large circles, and posters are more often destroyed than saved. Nevertheless, she has built a fine body of work in the field of graphic arts and in her secondary field of photography.

Louise E. Jefferson was born in 1908 in Washington, D.C., to Paul and Louise Jefferson. Her father was a calligrapher for the U.S. Treasury. She came from a musical family and had an exceptional knowledge of music: her parents were pianists, her grandmother a notable soprano, and her grandfather an organist at a church in the District of Columbia. She attended public schools in Washington, D.C., and Howard University. She took private lessons in fine and commercial art and learned calligraphy from her father. Jefferson emphasized the versatility needed in a career such as hers when she explained in *Opportunity* magazine, Spring 1947, why she began early to follow her parents' advice: "Learn more than one thing well—learn many things."

> Everything dovetails, you know. You have no idea how many kinds of information, picked up one place or another, will come in handy.... A commercial artist must have an encyclopaedic mind— for you can never tell what you will be called upon to depict or interpret.

Although she was urged to study music, she chose the graphic arts and moved to New York City to pursue her vocation. There she studied at the School of Fine Arts at Hunter College, Columbia University, and with Ralph Pearson and Riva Helford. She also came into contact with many artists and writers of the Harlem Renaissance.

Free-Lance Artist Becomes Art Director

In 1935 she was a founding member of the Harlem Artist's Guild, a WPA project in which she was associated with sculptor Augusta Savage and poet Gwendolyn Bennett. For a time, beginning in 1931, she roomed with the multitalented Pauli Murray in Harlem, when both were poor and struggling. Murray would later become a noted lawyer, author, educator, and civil rights and women's movement activist. One source of Jefferson's income were posters she did for the YWCA for seventy-five cents each—enough for the two women roommates to have the dinner special at the luncheonette across the street and to leave a nickel tip. Jefferson's work led to freelance jobs for the Friendship Press, which was the publishing agent of the National Council of Churches, and in 1942 she was hired full time by the press. She eventually became art director, a job she held until 1968. Jefferson does not remember racism as an obstacle at her job, but she did not always escape the sexism of her male superiors. In her perception, she retired just before she would have been let go by men who had recently taken over the press and who were systematically firing women regardless of their experience or knowledge.

Jefferson's work with the Friendship Press allowed her to take on many other free-lance jobs for New York publishing houses, like Doubleday and Viking. Her activities were financially rewarding enough that she was able to purchase a cooperative apartment in Morningside Heights, where Thurgood Marshall was her neighbor, and also to purchase property in Connecticut in the 1950s.

Jefferson's work covers a wide range, from match covers to book design. An early commission, about 1937, was sixty posters for the federal government for the Texas Centennial Exposition. Her first book design achieved instant notoriety; her illustrations for *We Sing America,* a 1936 songbook, depicted black and white children playing together and incurred the wrath of Georgia governor Eugene Talmadge, who ordered the book banned and burned. Besides designing and illustrating books, Jefferson did numerous political and cultural maps and pictograms, such as those for *20th Century Americans of Negro Lineage* (1969). Other work included covers for the magazines *Crisis* and *Opportunity.* For forty years she designed all of the NAACP holiday seals, and for twenty years she created the program covers for the National Urban League's Beaux Arts Ball.

Jefferson's interest in graphic arts extended to photography, although she considers this work a sideline. She developed the habit of always carrying a camera and even today there is one on a shelf by her front door. Her files contain well over five thousand photographs, including many taken of celebrated African Americans such as Charles Drew, Lena Horne, Martin Luther King, Jr., and Thurgood Marshall. She points out that free-lance work is not always continuously remunerative and recalls once having to sell two cameras to pay heating bills.

In 1960 Jefferson began a series of five trips to Africa over a ten-year period, two of them supported by grants from the Ford Foundation. These trips were the background for her book *The Decorative Arts of Africa,* published in 1973. She created almost all of the some three hundred photos and drawings in the work.

A Busy "Retirement"

Upon her retirement from the Friendship Press, Jefferson set up base at a studio in her secluded East Litchfield, Connecticut, home. There she continued to work and pursue her hobbies of gardening and small carpentry. She had to give up the home in the early 1980s when her friends insisted that she was too frail to live alone. She then moved to an apartment in New Jersey, which was burglarized soon after—fortunately, her photographic equipment was overlooked. This incident, combined with a noise level that interfered with her work, led her to establish herself in a cottage in Litchfield near the town common.

Jefferson's work has been exhibited at the Schomburg Center for Research in Black Culture (New York City), the Baltimore Museum of Art, the Oliver Wolcott Library (Connecticut), the Austin Arts Center at Trinity College (Connecticut), and the CRT Craftery Gallery in Hartford, Connecticut. She is especially proud of an exhibit on Matthew Henson, the first man to plant a flag at the North Pole, which she did for the New York Bank for Savings. Jefferson is a member of the American Institute of Graphic Arts, the Photographic Society of America, and Alpha Kappa Alpha sorority.

Louise Jefferson is a sports enthusiast, loving especially tennis and swimming. This reflects her determination to overcome a childhood case of infantile paralysis. Pauli Murray in *Song in a Weary Throat* characterized her as "one of the most agile persons I ever knew." In her younger years she taught swimming for the YWCA, including several summers as swimming instructor and crafts counselor at a YWCA camp. This physical energy continues to be manifest and many people observe that her "retirement" activities resemble the full-time work activities of other people. In her meticulously organized home she maintains extensive records of her long and productive career.

Current Address: 86 West Street, Litchfield, CT, 06759-0464.

REFERENCES:

Badger, T. A. "Louise Jefferson Pursues Many Goals—Illustrator—Photographer." *Torrington and Winsted, Connecticut, Register Citizen*, June 10, 1983.

Banks, T. J. "Artist Honors African Crafts." *Hartford Advocate*, March 7, 1984.

Begnal, Martin. "Portrait of a Unique Lady." *Torrington and Winsted, Connecticut, Register Citizen*, September 30, 1993.

Black Women of Connecticut: Achievement against the Odds. Hartford, Conn.: Connecticut Historical Society, [1993].

Granger, Lester B. "The Credit Line is Lou's." *Opportunity* 25 (Spring 1947): 91-92.

Humphrey, Elizabeth. "Litchfield Artist Knows No Bounds." *Litchfield, Connecticut, Enquirer*, April 2, 1986.

Jefferson, Louise E. Letter to Jessie Carney Smith, July 18, 1994.

Moutoussamy-Ashe, Jeanne. *Viewfinders: Black Women Photographers*. New York: Dodd Mead, 1985.

Murray, Pauli. *Song in a Weary Throat*. New York: Harper and Row, 1987.

Robert L. Johns

Elaine B. Jenkins
(1916-)
Entrepreneur, consultant firm founder, educator

After breaking down racial barriers to become the first black teacher in the Denver public schools and having a successful career as an educator and educational administrator in Washington, D.C., Elaine Jenkins founded One America, Inc., a national and later international business consultant firm. Her company became one of the nation's top one hundred black businesses in 1973.

Born April 2, 1916, in Butte, Montana, Elaine B. Jenkins is the daughter of Russell S. Brown, Sr., who was a prominent clergyman in Washington, D.C., and Floy Smith Brown. She married Howard Jenkins on June 24, 1940; he later became a lawyer and a member of the National Labor Relations Board. Elaine Jenkins received her B.A. degree from Denver University and her M.A. degree from Ohio State University. She also studied at Catholic University, American University, and Georgetown University, all in Washington, D.C.

Beginning her career in Denver, Jenkins became the first black teacher in the public schools there. Sometime later she moved to Washington, D.C., and continued her work as a public school teacher. For a time she was assistant superintendent of the National Training School for Girls, which had been founded in 1909 by the Woman's Convention Auxiliary of the National Baptist Convention. In 1964 the school was renamed the Nannie Helen Burroughs School to honor its first president. Jenkins was also a consultant in the Headstart Training Program for Teachers in Integration.

After a twenty-year career as a teacher, Jenkins saw a need to work in a different manner with the black community, aspiring to guide men and women in business development. Perhaps she was influenced by the history of her own family, which was business oriented. Her grandfather, Charles S. Smith, founded the first black business school at Wilberforce University in Ohio.

In 1970, when she was fifty-four years old, Jenkins used the entire family savings to found the consultant firm One America, Inc., in the District of Columbia. The firm offers services in affirmative action planning, rehabilitation coun-

Elaine B. Jenkins

seling and placement, program design and evaluation, technical and management assistance, data processing, and training. The family-run business operated with Jenkins as president and her three children in key positions: Judith E. Jenkins as vice-president; one son, Larry, a financial officer with the firm; and her other son, Howard III, a project marketing officer. Speaking of his mother's devotion to the company's purpose, Larry Jenkins said in a July 9, 1985, *Washington Post* article, "She has incorporated 20 years of teaching school into the business realm. Despite the fact that she often travels in circles of people with money she is very much committed to helping people."

Jenkins has long been committed to the belief that "the root of black entrepreneurship is in the black community," the article continues. She criticizes black leadership for its failure to direct blacks toward greater economic development. Jenkins states in this article that the opportunities for black business development are present but unexplored in a number of areas. "Blacks could develop sound businesses in criminal justice, geriatrics, and horticulture." According to Jenkins, they need to learn how to make money as well.

The lack of dialogue between affluent and poor blacks also concerns Jenkins. "Black businesses need to hire and encourage more blacks to participate in the real world of business," she is quoted as saying. She asserts that funds for black business development could be raised within the black community. She notes that federal and local government grants are other sources of capital, adding that some black millionaires have been willing to invest in potential black entrepreneurs. She states in the *Washington Post* article,

Once we as a race learn to utilize and help each other and develop creative business plans then we will learn what it feels like to be competitive. . . . [I]f we won't have money to spend, then that's where we need to begin.

Black Women Challenged as Entrepreneurs

Jenkins has a special interest in seeing that more black women become business leaders. They should "get on board for business opportunities in the 90's," she says in the *Washington Post* article. She notes that while women have succeeded as teachers, social workers, and other professionals, they could use their acquired skills to establish sound businesses. This worked well for Jenkins herself, who left teaching to become an entrepreneur. She told Carol A. Morton for *Ebony* magazine, November 1975, that black women were already attracted to business leadership and that "a black woman dreams of having all the opportunities that a white man or woman would have because she knows that she is just as capable." Jenkins also revealed that she was influenced by the success of families in business, citing the work of the Kennedys and Rockefellers.

A member of Delta Sigma Theta Sorority, Jenkins worked through the organization at its conventions to help black businesswomen develop plans for beginning or strengthening businesses. Writing in *Delta* in November 1972, Jenkins noted the great challenges black women face and called on them to maintain their identities as "capable people in the flooding tide of women power and at the same time keep a stance of support for our black men." She expressed a special hope for stronger families, a more positive image of black men, and increased opportunities for bright black women.

Writing about her life as mother, business leader, and guide whose experiences may well serve to influence women, blacks, and other minorities, Jenkins said in the *Washingtonian,* October 1982,

I was a black "Jewish mother"—strong-willed. If I said do it, do it. . . . I couldn't afford to make mistakes. From the anxieties of a black family reared in a white world, I was aware of the need to be educated, to have certain rules of conduct, to have good speech, and to develop whatever tools you need to cope.

One America One of Top 100 Black Businesses

One America enjoyed immediate and tremendous success. In 1973, after only three years of operation, the firm had become one of the nation's Top 100 Black Businesses as defined in *Black Enterprise.* By 1975, One America had grown to a staff of twenty-two in Washington, D.C., and thirteen in the Houston office. By 1985 it had expanded to become an international consultant firm for countries in Africa, Asia, and the Near East. Jenkins subsequently retired and her daughter took over the firm's operations.

While her career as a teacher and entrepreneur blossomed, Jenkins stayed active in a number of civic and service organizations and activities. President Richard M. Nixon appointed her to the Nelson Commission to study the efficiency of the District of Columbia. In the early 1970s the Secretary of the Department of State appointed her to the Citizen's Advisory Council on European Affairs. In 1974 she received a presidential appointment to the National Advisory Council on Education of Disadvantaged Children. She was appointed a citizen representative to the White House Task Force on Recruitment in 1986. Later, the secretary of defense selected her for the forty-fifth annual Joint Civil Orientation Conference. She has been a member of the Urban League, United Givers Fund, Washington D.C., and Alpha Wives (which she founded), and she served as president of the Howard University Faculty Wives. Jenkins was national cochair of Delta Sigma Theta Sorority, national vice-president of the Women's Black Political Caucus, a trustee of the District of Columbia Institute on Mental Health, a panel member for Health, Education, and Welfare Fellows, a member of the City Council Advisory Committee on Industrial and Commercial Development, and regional vice-president as well as first black corporate vice-president of the Association of United States Army. Active in politics as well, she was chair of the Council of 100 Black Republicans and director of the Foundation for the Preservation of the Two-Party System. In June 1986, *Jet* called her "boss lady in GOP strategy" and one of the "ten most fabulous Black women in the nation's capital." At that time she was vice-president of the powerful District of Columbia Republican Committee.

In recognition of her achievements, Jenkins has received numerous awards, including the Community Appreciation Award, Tri-Schools of Southwest Washington, D.C., 1970; Community Service Award, University of Denver, 1988; Eartha M. M. White Award and the Woman of the Year Award, National Business League; and Lifetime Achievement Award, Small Business Association. In 1985 *Dollars and Sense* magazine named her Woman of the Year.

Elaine Jenkins has been a strong proponent of black business development, especially for black women. Her life has been a successful mix of family, career, business, politics, and community service. She deserves great recognition for her work, particularly in the area of black economic development.

REFERENCES:

Booker, Simeon. "Ticker Tape USA." *Jet* 63 (November 15, 1982): 13; 70 (June 16, 1986): 8.

"Elaine Jenkins Is the Key to One America's Success." *Washington Post,* July 9, 1985.

Jenkins, Elaine B. "Promises to Ourselves as Black Women." *Delta* 60 (November 1972): 29.

Morton, Carol A. "Black Women in Corporate America." *Ebony* 31 (November 1975): 106-14.

"Mothers and Daughters." *The Washingtonian* 18 (October 1982).

Who's Who among Black Americans, 1994-95. 8th ed. Detroit: Gale Research, 1994.

Helena Carney Lambeth

Sebetha Lee Jenkins
(1939-)
Educator, college president, administrator

In a 1993 interview, Sebetha Jenkins expressed the sentiments of a modern-day pioneer and a leader in the emerging vanguard of the new black American woman when she said:

> Somehow strong support systems begin with black women. Whether it's social, economical, racial, church, home, or friendships, the meaningful support systems emanate from the "sisters." I think it goes back to our ancestors who taught generations of sisters to give birth to a race and to "be wind beneath the wings."

As president of Jarvis Christian College in Hawkins, Texas, Jenkins speaks with authority on the value of education and strong support systems.

Sebetha Lee Jenkins was born in Learned, Hinds County, a rural town in Mississippi. She is the daughter of Thomas Lee and Eunice Nelson Lee. Her mother was an elementary school principal for forty-two years, a community activist and leader, church pianist, local seamstress, and counselor. She devoted her life and talents to her family and to her community. Jenkins married in 1962. Now divorced, she has one child, a daughter, Jennifer, who is not only a fashion and beauty consultant but also a doctoral student in biology at the University of Kentucky and an associate professor of biology at Kentucky State University. Jenkins also claims as her children countless numbers of young people who, during her thirty-three-year career, were her students.

Jenkins explained in a 1993 interview with Edward B. McDonald the origin of her unique forename, which is pronounced "See-beth-thuh," in this way: "I am named from grandmother Seretha and her sister Elbetha. The two names combined, Seretha plus Elbetha, equals Sebetha. It is strictly a homemade name!" In addition to a wonderful sense of humor, Jenkins can certainly count among her personality traits a strong sense of activism, which seems to be hereditary. In all of her personal reminiscences, whether of her grandparents, mother, herself, or her daughter, she continually speaks of service, of contributing and giving back to community and family. From early on in her life, the young Sebetha dreamed of being a "doer." She said in the same interview, "I have vivid memories of early career dreams, playing school house and being the person in charge, going to see Marian Anderson when I was nine or ten years old and then deciding I would be a world-famous contralto singer, and living on my grandparents' farm where I learned to work but declined the offer to be a farmer." She also credits her grandfather, Andrew Stamps, with helping to instill in her many fine qualities:

> My grandfather taught me how to assume responsibility, achieve my goals, and remain steadfast. He also loved, encouraged, and believed in me. Subse-

Sebetha Lee Jenkins

quently, I have never expected any less from my uncles, boyfriends, mentors, co-workers, and male employees, and friends. Generally, they have given to me no less.

Jenkins enrolled at Jackson State University in Jackson, Mississippi, in 1956 and received her bachelor's degree in English and French in 1960. During this time she took a course on the Bible as literature taught by poet Margaret Walker. The class left an indelible impression on her, inspiring her to write a collection of her own poems. Among her favorite poems are her own "Ode to Miss Sadie" and Walker's renowned "For My People."

Jenkins began her teaching career in 1960 when she taught high school English and French in Clarksdale, Mississippi, where she remained until 1962. She then taught in Madison County (1962-64) and Hinds County (1964-66). She received fellowships to participate in the National Defense Education Act Institute Scholar's Program at North Carolina State in 1962 and at Loyola University of Chicago in 1964. She worked for one year, 1966, as a program analyst for Coahoma Opportunities in Clarksdale. From 1967 to 1975 she was an English instructor at the Coahoma Junior College, distinguishing herself as department head from 1973 to 1975.

Earns Graduate Degrees

While employed in Clarksdale, Jenkins entered Delta State University in Cleveland, Mississippi, and received a master of education degree in English in 1970. She was named a National Endowment for the Humanities Fellow to the

University of Massachusetts in 1973. In 1975 she entered Mississippi State University in University, Mississippi, to pursue a doctorate in educational administration and community college education. From 1975 to 1978, while working on her doctorate, she was employed as a field staff specialist for Title IX and Sex Equality at the Mississippi Educational Services Center at Mississippi State. After completing her dissertation, "The Perceptions of Selected Administrators and Faculty toward Faculty Inservice Training Programs in Junior Colleges of Mississippi," Jenkins was coordinator of Title III Programs, Institutional Research and Affirmative Action, at Coahoma Junior College from 1978 to 1979.

From 1979 to 1986, Jenkins assumed several positions at Mississippi State. She was assistant to the vice-president and director of minority affairs from 1979 to 1985. She was also an assistant professor in educational administration and community college education at Mississippi State from 1985 to 1986. Later she was promoted to the position of assistant to the president of the university. The school recognized her dynamic talents by presenting her with Outstanding Leadership Awards in 1982 and 1984. Mississippi State also honored her with the Most Outstanding Administrative Professional Woman Award from the President's Commission on the Status of Women, the Outstanding Services Award, the Outstanding Achievements in Advising Award, and the Most Outstanding Educational Leader Award for 1985-86.

From 1986 to 1990, Jenkins was assistant to the president and director of minority affairs at the University of Akron in Ohio. While in Akron, her impressive abilities did not go unnoticed. The Upward Bound Program at the university presented her with an Outstanding Support of Educational Opportunity Award in 1987. The Akron-Canton Alumnae of Delta Sigma Theta Sorority honored her with a Founder's Day Award in 1987. The Alpha Tau chapter of Alpha Phi Alpha Fraternity at the University of Akron presented her with a Hard Work and Accomplishment Award in the same year. In addition, Jenkins received various community service awards from such groups as the Akron branch NAACP, the Akron YWCA, the Southern Christian Leadership Conference, the U.S. Postal Service, the Black Law Students Association, and Jack and Jill of America. She is a charter member of the Clarksdale-Marks chapter and the Mississippi Golden Triangle chapter of Delta Sigma Theta Sorority and a charter member of the Organization for Professional Women's Development of Starkville, Mississippi. She served as president and vice-president of the Board of Big Brothers/Big Sisters of the Golden Triangle Area from 1979 to 1986 and holds memberships on numerous other boards.

Heads Texas College

Jenkins is now president of Jarvis Christian College, which is located just outside Hawkins, Texas. The school is affiliated with the Christian Church (Disciples of Christ), one of the denominations that emerged from the Restoration movement among Protestants in Kentucky at the start of the nineteenth century. The denomination is distinguished by making the Bible the only basis for faith and practice and by performing baptism by immersion. Although predominantly white, it has always had black members and has long maintained work among African Americans. At the start of the twentieth century, the educational program was transferred to the denomination's Christian Woman's Board of Missions. The first visible result of the new structuring was the formation of Jarvis College in 1912.

Jenkins succeeded Charles Berry as president of the school in 1990. She is a dynamic and eloquent speaker who continues to uplift many people with her sense of optimism and hope. In October 1993, she was keynote speaker at the Founder's Convocation at her alma mater, Jackson State. Jenkins has come full circle. But she remembers her childhood: through the support of her community, she developed an insatiable desire to receive and to impart education. She said in the 1993 interview:

> Education has always been envisioned by our foreparents as the passage from slavery, discrimination, and second-class citizenry into equality, justice, and the comforts of life. This vision only can be realized when we bring back to the classroom and to the home a combined sense of racial, cultural, and educational importance for this new generation.

Jenkins maintains that support systems for black Americans emanate from three undeniably important foundations:

> As black Americans, we own three institutions that absolutely must survive: the strength of our family, the eternal hope of our church, and the impact of our black private colleges, the three cornerstones of black history and the firmest support systems for black children.

She also believes that the future holds much promise for black Americans, whom she calls "the most enduring race of people."

> We have an innate ability to remain steadfast and unmovable in our quest for equality and justice. And yet sometimes we feel that only the dream is possible; the attainment of equality and social, political, and economic fairness seem always just beyond our grasp. But, of course, we continue to endure.

Jenkins appears well equipped to face the challenge of leading one of the nation's historically black colleges and educating its students for leadership positions in society. Already highly recognized as an educational leader, she has contributed much to the advancement of her race and is herself determined to be a "support system" for black Americans in the future.

REFERENCES:

Jenkins, Sebetha. Interview with Edward B. McDonald, December 20, 1993.

———. Resume, 1993.

Murphy, Larry G., J. Gordon Melton, and Gary L. Ward, eds. *Encyclopedia of African American Religions.* New York: Garland Publishing, 1993.

Edward B. McDonald

Patricia Prattis Jennings
(1941-)
Keyboardist, composer, songwriter, editor

Patricia Prattis Jennings is one of the finest symphony keyboardists in the United States. As a highly acclaimed solo and chamber music performer, as well as a prize-winning songwriter and the founder and editor of a newsletter that highlights the accomplishments of African American symphony musicians, Jennings seems assured a significant place in American music history.

Jennings was the first black woman (and fifth black) to join the roster of a major symphony orchestra. Her contract with the Pittsburgh Symphony began with the 1964-65 season, as the orchestra started on an eleven-week State Department-sponsored tour of Europe and the Middle East. Because of this affiliation, Jennings was obligated to join the white musicians union, Local 60, rather than the all-black Local 471. This was a first for Local 60, since it was 1965 before the two local unions merged. As principal keyboardist for the orchestra for nearly three decades—covering the piano, organ, harpsichord, and celesta—she has for a number of years held the Mr. and Mrs. Benjamin F. Jones III Endowed Chair. And as she has remarked in conversation, "I've been lucky to have been able to make such a good musical life for myself in my hometown." Those familiar with her work will certify that more than luck has made possible the events of the last thirty years.

Jennings is also the founder and editor of *Symphonium,* a publication "For and About the Professional African-American Symphony Musician." Established in 1988, this newsletter serves as a unifying force for those African Americans currently involved in the professional orchestral business, offers encouragement and motivation for those with aspirations toward a symphony career, and alerts mainstream fans to the activities and accomplishments of players, conductors, composers, and administrators of major, regional, and metropolitan symphony orchestras.

Born July 16, 1941, in Pittsburgh, Pennsylvania, Jennings is the only child of pioneer journalist Percival Leroy Prattis and Helen Marie Sands Prattis. Percival Prattis, a Hampton Institute (now University) graduate, was for many years the editor of the *Pittsburgh Courier* and was the first black journalist admitted to the periodical press galleries in the U.S. Congress. Jennings shared the following with the *Pittsburgh*

Patricia Prattis Jennings

Post-Gazette's Mark Kanny: "My father listened to classical music on records. . . . He had lots of 78s and would shave in the morning, while listening to either classical music or [NBC newsman] Martin Agronsky. He was, after all, a newsman."

Helen Prattis, a native of Pittsburgh, attended Cheney State University. She and daughter Patricia often played the piano together until Patricia surpassed her in proficiency. But it was Helen Prattis who monitored her daughter's practice sessions with a buzzing timer. The initial schedule called for an uninterrupted fifteen minutes, then thirty minutes, and so on. It is Helen Prattis, a poet with over three hundred poems published under the title *Everyday Verse,* who maintains the many scrapbooks cataloging Jennings's personal and career highlights, and who until recently made many of Jennings's gowns.

Both parents were very supportive of their musically talented daughter. As Helen Prattis stated in the September 3, 1989, *Pittsburgh Press* (Sunday Magazine), shortly following Jennings's silver anniversary with the Pittsburgh Symphony,

[T]hough we encouraged Pat to be her best, we didn't aspire or think she would go on to things like this. You don't dream that far. . . . Pat's the kind of person who would succeed at anything she set her mind to. But it is not something we'd let ourselves count on happening.

Jennings began studying the piano at age six and the violin at age eight. She was always performing for an audience, imaginary or real. Initially the audience consisted of her dolls, which lined the top of her spinet piano. Her first

Steinway grand piano was purchased with money she earned from her *Pittsburgh Courier* paper route.

Violin study lasted for only four years, during which time Jennings acquired enough skill to become concert mistress of the Westinghouse High School Orchestra. She was also violinist with Pittsburgh's All-City Orchestra, the Pittsburgh Symphony's junior program, and the Carnegie-Mellon Orchestra. Jennings was selected to join the Pittsburgh Symphony Orchestra's junior program, which paired high school students with the senior orchestra in concert, at age thirteen. She made her first appearance as piano soloist with the Pittsburgh Symphony at the age of fourteen, performing Mozart's *Coronation* concerto under the direction of William Steinberg. By this time, she was convinced that her musical future rested with the piano rather than the violin.

Jennings received a bachelor of fine arts and a master of fine arts from Carnegie-Mellon University (then Carnegie Tech) in 1962 and 1963, respectively, and took additional courses at Indiana University. At Carnegie-Mellon she studied with Harry Franklin; at Indiana University, she studied with Sidney Foster. Other instructors and coaches included Americo Caramuta, Sheila Paige, and the black concert pianist Natalie Hinderas.

When Boston Pops conductor Arthur Fiedler sought a pianist for his short-lived World Symphony Orchestra in 1971, his choice was Jennings. Appearing at three sites—Walt Disney World, Orlando, Florida; Philharmonic Hall, New York City; and John F. Kennedy Center for the Performing Arts, Washington, D.C.—she was one of fifty-two American musicians, among whom there were five blacks, including three women.

Solo and Chamber Music Performed

Through the years, keyboardist Jennings has distinguished herself as a solo and chamber music performer as well. She was a founding member of the Pittsburgh Chamber Soloists, participated in the famed Marlboro Festival at Marlboro, Vermont, and appeared in the Pittsburgh Symphony's Chamber Music at Heinz Hall Series. She has also performed solo and chamber works for radio programs. She was featured on "Artists in Concert" on WQXR in New York City and "Music from Pittsburgh" on WQED-FM in Pittsburgh.

In addition to solo appearances with the Pittsburgh Symphony and the Pittsburgh Youth Orchestra, Jennings has soloed with the Baltimore, Houston, and Pacific (California) orchestras, among others. During the 1976-77 season Jennings joined with the Pittsburgh Symphony music director, Andre Previn, to perform four-hand Mozart sonatas on the Emmy-nominated PBS television series *Previn and the Pittsburgh.* The following season she and Previn again shared the spotlight in a televised performance of Mozart's *Concerto for Two Pianos.*

In 1977 she was invited by clarinetist Benny Goodman to perform George Gershwin's "Rhapsody in Blue" in the original jazz version at Avery Fisher Hall with a jazz band specifically assembled for the occasion and conducted by Morton Gould. There were additional performances at the Concord and Dorothy Chandler pavilions in California and at the Wolf Trap Performing Arts Center in Virginia. The latter performance was later aired on WCEV-PBS.

Jennings was soloist for nine concerts in the Pittsburgh Symphony's thirteen-concert tour of the Far East and at the Edinburgh Festival in 1987, at which she performed Gershwin's Piano Concerto in F. When in 1989 Jennings performed Gershwin's "Rhapsody in Blue" with the Pacific Symphony Orchestra of Santa Ana, California, under the direction of Jorge Mester, the local *Orange County Register,* July 6, wrote,

> [I]nspired, unusually spontaneous . . . few [pianists] bring the improvisational freedom, the rhythmic verve and the sheer musical conviction that Jennings brings to the work. Hearing her play Gershwin was like hearing the music for the first time. . . . [She] heightens the music's tension by momentarily frustrating the melody's tendency toward resolution. In the hands of a less sensitive artist, such a device could easily sound affected, but Jennings made it sound completely natural.

Jennings was one of the featured pianists on the highly acclaimed Pittsburgh Symphony recording of Camille Saint-Saens's *Carnival of Animals.* Along with the Pittsburgh Symphony's principal cellist, Anne Martindale Williams, she recorded Leonardo Balada's *Three Transparencies of a Bach Prelude.*

During the course of one of Mary Pat Flaherty's interviews with Jennings for the September 3, 1989, *Pittsburgh Press,* Jennings stated:

> Getting up there on stage and playing, that's showing off. It pleases me to know I bring pleasure and enjoyment to people who listen, but it's not useful. . . . I'm a pianist but I want to sample other interesting things that life has to offer. I don't want my life to be dominated by music. . . . I'm an incredible celebrity to the one half of one percent of the people who go to the symphony. . . . I've signed some autographs and I'm always flattered at being asked, but I realize that most humans have no connection whatsoever with classical music.

Jennings Founds Newsletter

Jennings's decision to create the newsletter *Symphonium* in 1988 followed her participation in a three-day conference at Harriman, New York, sponsored by the Music Assistance Fund of the New York Philharmonic. Entitled "Toward Greater Participation of Black Americans in Symphony Orchestras," the conference brought together around one hundred orchestral musicians, administrators, and educators, primarily black. As Jennings explained in the September 1991 issue of *about . . . time,*

It was an amazing weekend. I didn't feel there would be, ever again in my lifetime, that large a group of black, classical orchestra players gathered in one place at the same time. I thought it would be a shame if we lost track of each other after that conference was over, so that's how *Symphonium* was born.

Chances are that a childhood interest was being revived as well. She had grown up with a love of words and reading and had worked summers in varying capacities for the *Pittsburgh Courier.* Her most enjoyable experience, even then, was that of editing. Her job for *Symphonium,* which is published three times a year, is primarily to edit articles by others and occasionally to offer an editorial. Jennings's second husband, Charles H. Johnson, whom she married in 1984, has been very supportive of the publication and, since his retirement as director of consumer services for Hornes Department Store, has assisted in its distribution.

Without foundation support, and devoid of grants by choice, the newsletter is paid for by voluntary contributions. But Jennings is certain that the publication is filling a gap. Well aware that the career of a symphony musician can be relatively brief, particularly if he or she insists on performing at an optimum level, Jennings told Mary Pat Flaherty during the course of one of her interviews for the September 3, 1989, *Pittsburgh Press,*

> I'm not going to play forever. So I think about leaving a mark after I'm done performing. I think writing may be what does that for me. I'm good at that and I think I can be useful that way.

Other extremely successful ventures, but of limited duration, were Jennings's cheesecake business and artistic directorship of a solo and chamber concert series. She made cheesecakes for a few months and sold them to small restaurants. This experiment ended when, following a Pittsburgh Symphony tour, there was an urgent demand for eleven cheesecakes within the next twenty-four hours. The cheesecakes were delivered, but Jennings quit the business afterward. She said in *about . . . time,* September 1991, "I told the restaurants that I just had to stop; it was too much work. It was hard to do that and practice."

Jennings's commitment to exposing black excellence in the area of classical music led her to accept the position of artistic director of the Virtuoso Series for Pittsburgh's Manchester Craftsmen's Guild. Underwritten by the Duquesne Light Utility Company, solo and chamber concerts were presented in the guild's acoustically magnificent 350-seat K. Leroy Irvis Concert Hall. The concept of corporate and social communities working in partnership in Pittsburgh was something Jennings had long hoped to bring to reality. During the course of two seasons, 1989 to 1991, Pittsburgh audiences were introduced to such solo artists as Ann Hobson Pilot (harpist, Boston Symphony), Darwin Apple (violinist, St. Louis Symphony), Marcus Thompson (solo violinist and faculty member of the New England Conservatory and Massachusetts Institute of Technology), Hubert Laws (flutist/recording artist), Owen Young (then cellist with the Pittsburgh Symphony, now a member of the Boston Symphony), Wilfred Delphin and Edwin Romain (duo pianists), and the Uptown String Quartet.

Talent as Composer and Songwriter Demonstrated

Not to be overlooked are Jennings's skills as a composer and songwriter. Her Christmas song "Gifts of Love," composed in 1980 with lyricist Linda Marcus, sold seventeen thousand copies in its first year. Premiered in December 1981 by the Cleveland Orchestra and the Cleveland Orchestra Children's Chorus, the work has since become a staple in the Christmas repertoires of school and community choral groups throughout the United States and Mexico. Her mid-1970s "Jesus Is All I Need," written for the choir at Wesley Center African Methodist Episcopal (AME) Zion Church, where she was the organist, was a semifinal winner in the 1977 American Song Festival Contest. Also, Jennings composed the signature music for *In Celebration of Women* for WQED-TV and performs her own set of cadenzas for Mozart's Concerto in C Major, K. 467.

It should be noted that Jennings shared her musical talent with Wesley Center AME Zion Church beginning at a young age when her feet barely reached the pedals. She later assumed the role of church organist and director of music, remaining in these positions for more than two decades—long after she had joined the roster of the Pittsburgh Symphony.

Many people have benefited from Jennings's experience and understanding of the world of music. Whenever the subject of minority participation in symphony orchestras is discussed, Jennings's opinions and advice are solicited. She serves on the boards of the Pittsburgh Literary Council, the Steinway Society, and the Project String Training and Educational Program—Pittsburgh (Project STEP—Pittsburgh). Project STEP—Pittsburgh is an offshoot of the Boston-based STEP organization, which first sought out promising African American youngsters to become professional classical musicians. Project STEP—Pittsburgh is based at Duquesne University.

In recognition of her contributions to the field of music and her many other accomplishments, the weekly publication *In Pittsburgh* voted Jennings Best Instrumental Performer, 1988. In September 1991 she was inducted into the international music fraternal organization for women, Sigma Alpha Iota (Pittsburgh Alumnae Chapter), as a national honorary member.

Patricia Prattis Jennings is determined to be useful, both now and when her days of performing are over. The options are many—writer, editor, arts consultant, artistic director, or some activity not yet considered. Whatever her decision, it is likely the responsibility will be met with style, sophistication, and a wealth of skill. As the title of the *Pittsburgh Press's* September 3, 1989, article on Jennings indicated, "Success Is Just an Overture."

Current Address: 1349 North Sherilan Avenue, Pittsburgh, PA 15206-1759.

REFERENCES:

Handy, D. Antoinette. *Black Women in American Bands and Orchestras.* Metuchen, N.J.: Scarecrow Press, 1981.
Jennings, Patricia Prattis. Interview with D. Antoinette Handy. Pittsburgh, Penn., February 2, 1977.
———. Letters to D. Antoinette Handy, March 29, 1977; March 9, 1978; September 19, 1988; September 30, 1988; October 17, 1988; December 30, 1988; September 4, 1989; April 9, 1990; April 26, 1990; March 10, 1993; January 4, 1994; February 2, 1994; March 21, 1994.
McDaniel, Sharon. "Patricia Prattis Jennings/Words and Music." *about . . . time* (September 1991): 18-20.
"Pat Jennings, Baltimore Symphony Guest, Draws Enthusiastic Response." *Pittsburgh Courier,* July 3, 1976.
"Previn Returns to City, Energy Crisis Dims Hall." *Pittsburgh Post-Gazette,* February 11, 1978.
"PSO Experiment with Visual Performance." *Pittsburgh Tribune-Review,* January 8, 1994.
"A Spirited Pacific Symphony Finally Goes Forth on Its Own." *Orange County Register,* July 6, 1989.
"Success Is Just an Overture." *Pittsburgh Press* (Sunday Magazine), September 3, 1989.

D. Antoinette Handy

Amelia E. Johnson
(1858-1922)
Poet, editor, novelist, educator

Amelia E. Johnson, known as Mrs. A. E. Johnson, was a late nineteenth- and early twentieth-century novelist, poet, editor, and teacher. With her first novel, *Clarence and Corinne; or, God's Way,* she made important contributions to African American literature. The novel was the only the second published by an African American in the United States and the first Sunday school book produced by an African American woman. In addition, Johnson was the first woman and the first African American to be published by the American Baptist Publication Society, one of the largest publishing houses in the country.

Amelia Etta Hall Johnson was born in Toronto, Canada, in 1858, to parents who were natives of Baltimore, Maryland. She was educated in Montreal but in 1874 moved to Baltimore, where she found work as a teacher. On April 17, 1877, she married Harvey Johnson of Virginia. A successful Baptist minister and a writer, Harvey Johnson championed civil rights for African Americans. The couple had three children. On March 29, 1922, after a two-day illness, Amelia E. Johnson

Amelia E. Johnson

died. Her obituary in the April 7, 1922, *Afro-American* commended her "Christian character" and her "attainments"; she was survived by her husband and her children, Mrs. N. A. M. Shaw, Prentiss Johnson, and Harvey Johnson, Jr. She was interred in Laurel Cemetery in Baltimore, Maryland.

Literary Career Begins

Johnson began writing poetry at an early age, but it was not until after her marriage that she was published. Her writing grew out of her concern for the moral well-being of African Americans; thus, it is didactic in tone and content. Her early poems and stories appeared in various African American periodicals, including the *Baptist Messenger, Our Women and Children,* and the *American Baptist.* In his *Noted Negro Women,* Monroe A. Majors stated, "Her writings are varied; she having a clear conception of what a poet means, she is reserved in her compositions, and so deep is her thought that her productions ward off the minnows in search for those who inhabit deep water."

It was Johnson's concern about her race that led her to become aware of the need for a literary journal for young people that would also provide a forum for African American women writers. Therefore, in 1887 she established the *Joy,* an eight-page, monthly paper that contained original stories, poems, and interesting items solicited for the publication. The *Joy* was well received by the public. The *Baltimore Baptist,* the weekly journal of the white Baptists of Baltimore, praised the paper as original and creditable. As noted in I. Garland Penn's *The Afro-American Press and Its Editors,* there was

also praise for the editor for having "done a good work, and shown the way for some others to follow." The *National Baptist,* one of the country's most widely circulated white denominational journals, also favorably reviewed the *Joy.* Johnson's story "Nettie Ray's Thanksgiving-day" appeared on the Family Page of the *National Baptist,* and the journal periodically published her poetry as well. She created the Children's Corner in the *Baltimore Sower and Reaper,* in which she sometimes included her own original work. Two such pieces were "The Animal Convention" and "The Mignotte's Mission." Johnson also began another publication, the *Ivy,* which was designed to encourage African American youths to read and to promote knowledge of African American history.

Johnson Publishes First Novel

Johnson's history-making novel, *Clarence and Corinne; or, God's Way,* was published on April 20, 1890. The novel was acclaimed by both African American and white religious journals. Penn described Johnson as a "fine writer," "a talent worthy of her husband," and "a silent agent at work to break down unreasonable prejudice, which is a hinderance to the race." The book was praised for its "healthy tone" and appropriateness for "Sunday-school readers," as "encouraging to young and old," as being "carried on in a natural, graphic, pathetic, and deeply interesting way," as a novel that "ought to be in every home" and that children should read "until they make the principles set forth by the writer the rule of their life."

Clarence and Corinne does not deal with the issue of race. There is no indication that the book is either written by an African American or about African Americans; in fact, the illustrations portray white characters. Rather, Johnson is mainly concerned about proper moral education. The novel is didactic and attempts to show the goodness of God and the Christian way of life. In the story, Clarence Burton, a twelve-year-old boy, and his nine-year-old sister, Corinne, are extremely poor. Their father is an abusive drunkard, and their mother is resigned to her lot in life. The mother soon dies, the father disappears, and, after the funeral, the children are separated and cast out into the world. The remainder of the novel shows the children being influenced by both good and evil individuals and encountering many problems, such as illness and false accusations, which serve to move them toward salvation and reunion.

One of the issues addressed in the story is the evil of alcohol. Mr. Burton's excessive drinking has a devastating effect on his family. He abuses his wife and fails to provide financially for his family, forcing the children to drop out of school. Their mother, Mrs. Burton, who is not a Christian, is without hope. After her death, Clarence sums up the situation:

He's made us miserable—no, it wasn't him, either;
it was that dreadful, dreadful stuff whiskey. Yes,
drink ruined our father, and now it's killed our
mother; and nobody cares for us because we're the
children of a drunkard. People don't even want to

give me work because of it; and they call me "old drunken Burton's boy."

The story teaches that many things are good in moderation. Through the people the children encounter, Johnson points out good Christian behavior. Miss Rachel Penrose, who takes Corinne in for a time, uses the Bible in a hypocritical way. The true Christian way of life is shown by contrasting her behavior with that of the sisters Helen and Mary Gray, who also take Corinne in. Corinne finds new hope and happiness and laments Clarence's ignorance of the things that could bring him contentment. He eventually comes into contact with a decent Christian woman who leads him to a knowledge of the need for repentance. Finally, Clarence and Corinne are reunited, and both understand that the trials and tribulations they have experienced have been for the best because, through them, they have learned to live "God's ways." "God's ways are not our ways," Johnson counsels; "our ways would often lead us into doubtful places." The book ends with an exhortation to the reader:

Blind unbelief is sure to err,
and scan his work in vain.
God is his own interpreter,
And he will make it plain.
Thus, God's way has been made clear.

Uplifting Messages

In 1894 Johnson's second novel, *The Hazeley Family,* was published by the American Baptist Publication Society. Like her first novel, it was designed to teach ethical behavior and to be used as Sunday school literature. Both books emphasize that things happen for the best and that people must accept their situations cheerfully and live decently and honestly. As in *Clarence and Corinne,* this book does not address or concern any specific race of people. *The Hazeley Family* focuses on responsibility and duty. The family of the title consists of a father who works on the railroad; a mother who is lackadaisical about her home and family; and daughter Flora and her brothers, Harry and Alec, who lack any direction in life and border on being shiftless. Just as in *Clarence and Corinne,* there are separations and reunions and a happy ending.

Flora is sent to stay with her aunts Bertha Fraham and Sarah Martin to learn domestic skills, but they mistreat her. She returns home, only to become depressed by the conditions she finds there. A neighbor reminds her of her responsibilities to her family, a message that is underscored by a minister, who says, "Whatsoever thy hand findeth to do, do it with thy might." The minister emphasizes the difference between "house-work"—cleaning and cooking—and "home-work"—keeping members of the household healthy and happy. Flora takes the message of the sermon to heart and begins working to make her home a bright and cheerful place. As a result, the members of her family begin to change their ways by staying at home and avoiding the streets. In addition, the mother's attitude changes and the young who come in contact with her begin to imitate her homemaking, her caring,

and her godlike ways. When Mr. Hazeley dies, Harry, the oldest son, begins to drink and gamble but finally learns the error of his ways through a friend named Joel Piper, who has suffered in the same way as Harry. Piper has accepted Christ and is able to convert Harry.

Precepts designed to foster the reader's moral development include, "You should always be polite to an old person," "True worth will always receive its proper recognition," and "too late" is a phrase that is only true of earthly desires. For the most part, the fathers in this novel are shadowy figures. However, they are still the breadwinners and of prime importance for that reason. For instance, even though Mr. Hazeley has only been present sporadically, it is his death that catapults Harry into a life of debauchery. By the end of the novel, all the characters who display immoral attitudes have either died, left the scene, or repented, and all is bliss.

Johnson's 1901 novel, *Martina Meridan; or, What Is My Motive?,* is also a book that was geared for use as Sunday school literature. It, too, deals with family life, and, as Ann Allen Shockley states in *Afro-American Women Writers, 1746-1933,* it teaches lessons "on truth, obedience, right and wrong, and love for the Heavenly Father."

Although she did not specifically write about blacks, through her work, Mrs. A. E. Johnson strove to morally uplift the African American race. Penn says that she wrote "from affection for the race, and loyalty to it." She desired "to help demonstrate the fact that the colored people have thoughts of their own, and only need suitable opportunities to give them utterance." Johnson believed that other African Americans would follow her lead and far exceed her talents as a novelist. Thus, she hoped to educate her race not just by precept but also by example.

REFERENCES:

Johnson, A. E. *Clarence and Corinne; or, God's Way.* 1890. Reprint. New York: Oxford University Press, 1988.
———. *The Hazeley Family.* 1894. Reprint. New York: Oxford University Press, 1988.
Majors, Monroe A. *Noted Negro Women: Their Triumphs and Activities.* Chicago: Donohue and Henneberry, 1893.
Penn, I. Garland. *The Afro-American Press and Its Editors.* 1891. Reprint. New York: Arno Press and the New York Times, 1969.
Peques, A. W. *Our Baptist Ministers and Schools.* 1892. Reprint. New York: Johnson Reprint Corporation, 1970.
Scruggs, Lawson Andrew. *Women of Distinction: Remarkable in Works and Invincible in Character.* Raleigh, N.C.: L. A. Scruggs, 1893.
Shockley, Ann Allen. *Afro-American Women Writers, 1746-1933: An Anthology and Critical Guide.* Boston, Mass.: G. K. Hall, 1988.
Simmons, William J. *Men of Mark: Eminent, Progressive and Rising.* Cleveland, Ohio: George M. Rewell, 1887.

Helen R. Houston

Eddie Bernice Johnson
(1934-)
Politician, consultant firm founder, nurse

Eddie Johnson is the first black woman to represent Texas in Congress since Barbara Jordan. The Dallas district from which she was elected came into being in part because of her skills in Texas state politics, particularly her effective use of her state senate position as chair of the Redistricting Committee during the 1991 redrawing of congressional districts, which was mandated by the U.S. census. She also had a successful career as a nurse, serving as chief psychiatric nurse at Dallas's Veterans Administration Hospital from 1967 to 1972. In addition, she achieved success as a business consultant, establishing her own firm in 1981. Her success in politics began with her election to the Texas legislature in 1972, continued with her 1986 election to the Texas state senate, and culminated in her 1992 election to the U.S. Congress, where she now represents the Thirtieth Congressional District of Texas.

Eddie Bernice Johnson was born in Waco, Texas, on December 3, 1934, to Edward Johnson and Lillie Mae White Johnson. She attended school in Waco, and after graduating, she attended a variety of educational institutions. In 1955, she graduated with a certificate in nursing from Holy Cross Central School of Nursing in South Bend, Indiana; she also studied at St. Mary's College of the University of Notre Dame. In 1967, she earned her bachelor of science degree in nursing from Texas Christian University (TCU). Her undergraduate nursing education at TCU was sponsored through a National Institute of Mental Health grant. In 1976, she received her master of public administration degree from Southern Methodist University.

That Johnson firmly believes in the importance of education is indisputable. In addition to the educational training already mentioned, she has studied at Texas Woman's University and has taken several other courses. In 1978 she participated in the Conflict Resolution Training Program at the Wharton School, University of Pennsylvania. Also during 1978, she attended a four-week course sponsored by the American Management Association.

For five years, from 1967 to 1972, Johnson was the chief psychiatric nurse at Dallas's Veterans Administration Hospital. In 1972, Johnson's nursing career came to a close, and her illustrious political career began. She had been active in Dallas politics since the 1960s. In 1972 she decided to run for office to fill the need she saw for greater representation of the black community. In that year she won a landslide victory in her bid for a seat in the Texas House of Representatives, representing District 33-D, in the Dallas area. She became the first black woman elected to the Texas House of Representatives from Dallas County since 1935. She served in the Texas legislature from 1972 to 1977. As a member of the Texas

Eddie Bernice Johnson

House of Representatives, Johnson worked on the Labor and Constitutional Amendments committees. In 1972, she was a member of the National Democratic Credentials' Committee as well as a member of the Texas State Democratic Executive Committee. From 1976 to 1978, she served on the Democratic National Committee, and between 1972 and 1976 she was a Texas state delegate on the committee. For twelve years, Johnson was vice-chairman of the state Democratic Convention. During her second legislative term, she made history by becoming the first woman in Texas to chair a major house committee, the House Labor Committee.

Johnson's political achievements extend beyond the state and local levels. In 1977, President Carter appointed Johnson regional director of the Department of Health, Education and Welfare. She served in this position until 1980.

Johnson also has expertise as a businesswoman. From 1979 to 1981, she served as a consultant to Sammons Corporation, a multibusiness conglomerate that manages over forty companies. In 1981 she established Eddie Bernice Johnson and Associates, a consulting firm that reviews and analyzes business and financial plans for businesses interested in servicing the Dallas-Fort Worth area. Since 1988, she has maintained a concession business, one of only eleven minority- and woman-owned businesses in the Dallas-Fort Worth International Airport complex.

In 1986, after a nine-year hiatus from elective office, Johnson made a bid for the upper house of the Texas legislature and won a senate seat, representing District Twenty-three. She held this office for six years.

Johnson Elected to Congress

In 1991, Johnson, who was chair of the senate Redistricting Committee, presented a plan for the establishment of a black majority district in downtown Dallas. After succeeding in her efforts to create District Thirty, she was elected to represent it in the U.S. Congress in 1992, receiving 74 percent of the vote in the general election. This new political victory makes Johnson the first African American to represent the state of Texas in Congress since Barbara Jordan. She serves on the Public Works and Transportation Committee as well as the Science, Space and Technology Committee. Also a member of the historically important Black Caucus, Johnson was recently elected by that body to serve as whip. In her capacity as a representative to the lower house of the U.S. Congress, Johnson has pledged to make the economy, health care, education, jobs, the environment, and the expansion of employment opportunities for minorities her legislative priorities.

As a result of her significant contributions as a public servant, Johnson has received three honorary doctoral degrees from some of Texas's finest colleges, including Bishop College, Dallas, Texas (1979); Jarvis Christian College, Hawkins, Texas (1979); and Texas College, Tyler, Texas (1989). She holds memberships in numerous local and national organizations, including the American and Dallas Group Psychotherapy societies, the Behavioral and Social Science Association, the Urban League, the NAACP, the Black Chamber of Commerce, and the National Council of Negro Women. Johnson remains very active in Texas Democratic party politics.

Johnson's numerous honors include the Hospital Sustained Superior Performance Award (1971); the Holmes School Outstanding Service Award (1971); and Greyhound Corporation's Woman of the Year Award (1971). In 1993 the National Black Nurse Foundation honored her with a banquet and a plaque. In addition to her active social and political life, Johnson, who is a Baptist, has served on a number of religious boards, including the Texas Christian Education Board. She is married to Lacey Kirk Johnson and is the mother of a son, Dawrence Kirk.

Current Address: 2515 McKinney Avenue, Suite 1565, Dallas, TX 75201.

REFERENCES:

Who's Who among Black Americans, 1975-76. Northbrook, Ill.: Who's Who among Black Americans Publishing Co., 1976.

Who's Who in American Politics, 1989-88. 11th ed. New York: Bowker, 1987.

Who's Who in Government, 1975-76. 2d ed. Chicago: Marquis, 1975.

Women in Public Office. 2d ed. Metuchen, N.J.: Center for American Women and Politics, 1978.

Yvette Alex-Assensoh

Virginia Johnson
(1950-)
Dancer

Virginia Johnson had the extraordinary goal of becoming a classical dancer. This is a career open to few persons of any race and to almost no blacks. She was fortunate, however, in that she came into contact with Arthur Mitchell and the Dance Theatre of Harlem, which Mitchell had founded with the aim of giving African Americans the opportunity to develop and display their skills in ballet. Johnson was dancing with the company when it officially opened on January 8, 1971. Despite her mastery of classical technique—she was the best in the company—Lydia Abarca outshone her for a few years, but Johnson grew as a dancer over the years to become an acclaimed star.

Virginia Alma Fairfax Johnson was born on January 25, 1950, in Washington, D.C. Her father, James Lee Johnson, was a naval architect, and her mother, Madeline Murray Johnson, taught physical education at Howard University. Johnson has an older sister, Suzanne, who worked in marketing for Calvin Klein during the 1980s, and a younger brother, Kurt, a banker.

Joins Dance Theater of Harlem

Johnson attended public school in Washington, D.C. When she was thirteen, Johnson began to study dance on a scholarship at the Washington School of Ballet under the tutelage of Mary Day, co-founder of the school and a noted choreographer and teacher. As a teenager, Johnson's aspirations in the field of dance were increased by seeing Mary Hinkson, a soloist with the Martha Graham Company—the first black dancer she had ever seen with a major company. After her graduation from high school, she enrolled in the School of Arts of New York University as a university scholar. Given the paucity of openings for blacks in ballet performances, Johnson felt her only career choice was to become a teacher. In addition, there was not enough of an emphasis on ballet in the overall program for Johnson's taste. Learning of Arthur Mitchell's classes in Harlem, she began to work with him on Saturdays. By the time the Dance Theatre of Harlem had become a reality and was ready to open officially, she had progressed to the point that she danced the lead in three world premiere roles choreographed by Mitchell for the opening performance.

For the next few years Johnson appeared in almost all of the works in the company's repertory. She displayed an impressive technique and she showed a special affinity for works choreographed by Mitchell, like *Holberg Suite.* However, technique alone is not enough for a great dancer, and she lacked the ability of her colleague Lydia Abarca to pull audiences into her performances. In the late seventies, she worked hard on growing as a dancer. She accepted guest engagements with other companies and experimented with

Virginia Johnson

choreography, devising a solo for George Crumb's television film *Ancient Voices of Children* and a program for her first one-woman concert in 1978 at Marymount College in New York City. She also took on a succession of new and challenging roles for the Dance Theatre of Harlem. These included both character roles and the more abstract roles associated with the choreography of George Balanchine. Her unusual height and her long arms and legs made her an ideal Balanchine ballerina. She excelled in Balanchine's *Allegro Brillante* and in the rhythmic complexities of the second movement of *Agon.*

Explores Dramatic Dance Roles

As she grew as a dancer, Johnson developed the ability to find dramatic nuance even in abstract ballets, and she welcomed the introduction of more dance dramas into the repertory of the Dance Theatre of Harlem. She transcended the limitations of the choreography to win a personal triumph in the role of Blanche Dubois in *A Streetcar Named Desire* in 1982. A vast American public had the chance to see this ballet when it was presented on PBS in February 1986. Coached by choreographer Agnes DeMille and Sallie Wilson, one of the great interpreters of the role of Lizzie Borden, she triumphed again in 1983 in *Fall River Legend. Current Biography* quotes Anna Kisselgoff's tribute in the *New York Times:* "From the start she's frail rather than strong, stricken in the heart when her hopes for happiness are killed. It is not only Miss Johnson's excellent acting that one should praise but the quality of her dancing, its broken quality of despair, its

desperate intensity." She also won high praise from Agnes DeMille.

Johnson continued to interpret new dramatic dances while not neglecting works featuring pure dance. In 1984 she had the chance to dance in the full-length production of *Giselle.* Dating from 1841, it is the oldest ballet in the classical repertory and the quintessence of romanticism. Mitchell transposed the setting from a German village to a Louisiana plantation without sacrificing any of the romantic atmosphere. Mounting the ballet is a major challenge for any company, and dancing it exposes the dancers to comparisons with a myriad of stellar performers. Johnson's performance in the London premiere in July 1984 won great praise, which was echoed by New York critics and audiences after the United States premiere two months later. Johnson has also danced the role with the Ballet de Cuba and the Royal Ballet. The Dance Theatre of Harlem's production was broadcast on NBC television. On June 21, 1989, she danced *Giselle* for the twentieth anniversary of the company. Anna Kisselgoff wrote of this performance for the *New York Times* two days later, "She is a lovely, frail Giselle, with her long neck extending the stemlike curve of her body, a human version of the lilies at her grave."

The life of a classical dancer is not easy. Twenty years is a long time in the life of a ballet company and in the life of a dancer. By the spring of 1990, the Dance Theatre of Harlem was facing a major financial crisis and shut down for six months. Johnson said that she would use the time to work on a bachelor's degree in history. She was not sure that she would be able to continue at New York University and was investigating cheaper schools. Fortunately, major grants from the American Express Travel Related Services Company and from the Lila Wallace-Reader's Digest Fund helped reduce the debt of the Dance Theatre of Harlem and stabilize its finances.

Johnson is still dancing solos with the company. She says of her success in Dance Theatre of Harlem program notes for 1994,

> There are three reasons. . . . Being a member of a new company allowed me to grow and mature, in tandem with the company. Secondly, I credit patience and discipline—it takes 10 years to become a dancer and then 10 more years to become an "artist." Finally I never lost the excitement of doing exactly what I've always dreamed of doing.

Johnson has received a number of recognitions for her achievements. She has been honored with a Young Achiever Award; she was named an Outstanding Young Woman of America from the National Council of Women in 1985; and in 1991 she was presented with the *Dance Magazine* Award. During Dance Theatre of Harlem's South African tour in 1992, she served as community outreach instructor.

Virginia Johnson overcame the obstacles that stood in the way of her career in classical dancing and in so doing helped the Dance Theatre of Harlem achieve longevity as a ballet company. A great performance artist, her achievements will long linger in the minds of those fortunate enough to have seen her.

Current Address: c/o Dance Theatre of Harlem, 466 West 152nd Street, New York, NY 10031-1896.

REFERENCES:

"Birthday Party for the Harlem Troupe." *New York Times,* June 23, 1989.

Current Biography. New York: H. W. Wilson, 1985.

"The Dance: *Giselle.*" *New York Times,* March 14, 1987.

"Dance: Harlem Troupe in *Fall River Legend.*" *New York Times,* April 7, 1986.

"Dance Theater of Harlem Gets a 2d Million-Dollar Grant." *New York Times,* June 19, 1990.

Dance Theatre of Harlem. Program Notes. 1994.

"Dance Theatre of Harlem in *A Streetcar Named Desire.*" Press Release. Public Broadcasting Service, 1986.

"DTH Bounds into a Beautiful 20th Year." *New York Post,* June 23, 1989.

"Harlem Dance Back on Its Feet." *Washington Post,* March 29, 1991.

"The Human Side of Harlem Troupe's Crisis." *New York Times,* April 10, 1990.

Ribowsky, Mark. "The Black Invasion of Ballet." *Sepia* 25 (April 1976): 68-74.

"Solemn, Giddy, Dazzling: Nijinska." *New York Times,* June 29, 1989.

"The Very Hard Times of Harlem's Dance Theater." *New York Times,* July 25, 1991.

Robert L. Johns

Claudia Jones

United States in the hopes of finding greater economic opportunity. Jones and her family arrived on Ellis Island in February 1924 and made their home in Harlem. She was married for a brief period during the 1930s to a man named Jones. Claudia Jones died on December 25, 1964, in London, England, and as noted by Buzz Johnson, author of *I Think of My Mother,* a biographical work on Jones, she quite appropriately is buried in Highgate Cemetery next to the grave of Karl Marx.

The mass migration of persons of African descent from the southern United States and the West Indies to Harlem filled the community with the collective problems and prospects of newly arrived people. Those arriving were confronted with segregation, low paying jobs, unemployment, crowded living conditions, and racially restricted opportunities for social and educational advancement. The Cumberbatch clan struggled to survive the harsh realities of Harlem life. Jones's mother, a worker in New York's garment district, faced a grueling schedule of long hours and overwork and died when Claudia was only twelve years of age. Despite her father's determined efforts as a single parent to provide for his family, there was never enough money and young Claudia had to leave school and find work. The family was so financially strapped that Jones could not even participate in her junior high school graduation ceremony because they could not afford a new dress.

The termination of Jones's formal education did not signal, however, the end of her intellectual and social growth. A teenager during the dismal years of the Depression, she witnessed social unrest as the poor and underprivileged in society struggled against the forces of racism, sexism, and

Claudia Jones
(1915-1964)
Political activist, black nationalist, feminist, journalist

A communist her entire adult life, Claudia Jones was in the vanguard in the twentieth-century struggle for African American liberation, socialism, women's rights, world peace, and West Indian and colonial independence. Her legacy looms large on the landscape of history.

One of four children, Claudia Cumberbatch Jones was born on February 21, 1915, in Port-of-Spain, Trinidad, which was then a British colony. The overwhelming conditions of poverty in Trinidad compelled her parents to migrate to the class exploitation. According to Johnson, Jones experienced a deepening social awareness that, in her own words, incited her "to develop an understanding of the suffering of my people and my class and look for a way forward to end them."

Joins Young Communist League

In 1931 nine young African American men ranging in age from twelve to nineteen were tried and convicted of raping two white women in Scottsboro, Alabama. The evidence in the case clearly indicated that the charges were false. The steadfast action of the Communist party, and particularly its mass rallies in defense of the "Scottsboro Boys," convinced Jones at the age of eighteen to become a member of the Young Communist League (YCL). An excellent writer, she became a journalist for the YCL and was editor of its journal, *Weekly Review*. In the YCL, she displayed her intelligence and sharpened her leadership skills. Fully committed to the Communist cause, she turned down an attractive drama scholarship and instead served on the staff of the Communist party newspaper, *Daily World.*

An able organizer, Jones effectively communicated with black working people and assumed several positions of leadership in the YCL, including chairperson of the National Council of the Education Office of New York State. In 1941 she became national director of the Young Communist League. Jones viewed her involvement in the Communist movement as the logical outcome of her life experiences. She explains in Johnson's book:

> It was out of my Jim Crow experiences as a young Negro woman, experiences likewise born of working class poverty that led me to join the Young Communist League and to choose the philosophy of my life, the science of Marxism-Leninism—that philosophy that not only rejects racist ideas, but is the antithesis of them.

As a Marxist-Leninist, Jones linked the fight against racism with the battle against sexism, national oppression, and imperialism, all of which found their bedrock in class struggle. With the outbreak of World War II, she initially opposed the participation of the United States. Jones did not want to see a repetition of World War I, which, in her view, was an imperialist struggle that brought a tide of racist violence against blacks in its aftermath. In 1940 she wrote a booklet in opposition to World War II, *Jim Crow in Uniform.* Jones recounted in the booklet how an African American soldier, Jesse Clipper, gave his life in battle like so many others, yet after the war the shadow of Jim Crow still loomed large over the lives of African Americans. She pointed out that colonialism had not lessened its grip on the people of the Caribbean and Africa and that the burden of a war economy was carried on the backs of the working class.

But with Germany's attack on the Soviet Union, she changed her position. Her allegiance to the war effort arose from the perspective of antifascism; for Jones, the defeat of fascism was part and parcel of the democratic fight against national oppression, racism, sexism, and colonialism.

In articles she wrote during the war, Jones daringly called for the admission of women into the armed forces and their use in combat duty. She demanded an end to segregation and the disfranchisement of African Americans and additionally sought a lowering of the age requirement for the vote.

Emerges as Outspoken Leader in the Communist Party

As a Marxist-Leninist, Jones resolutely held to the doctrine of democratic centralism, the Leninist principle that while the party's central leadership is responsible for formulating policies and directives, the rank-and-file membership has the right to engage in debate and criticism—democratic exchange—concerning the policies and actions of the party. When the Communist Party of the United States of America (CPUSA), under the leadership of Earl Browder, decided to abandon its policy of national self-determination for African Americans in the black belt South, Jones initiated the party debate over this change in the CPUSA organ, *Political Affairs.* In her "Discussion Article" she castigated Browder's stance as "based on a pious hope that the struggle for full economic, social and political equality for the Negro people would be legislated and somehow brought into being through reform from on top."

In her article Jones gave a political analysis of national self-determination, viewing it as "a scientific principle that derives from an objective condition and upon this basis, expresses the fundamental demands (land, equality and freedom) of the oppressed Negro people."

Her opposition inspired even veteran black Communists, such as Harry Haywood, to enter the debate within the party ranks. Jones's leadership was also an inspiration to women in the party. She was an ardent foe of sexist and racist practices against black women both inside and outside the party.

Neglect of Black Women Cited

Jones's most quoted written work is probably the article "An End To the Neglect of the Problems of Negro Women," which first appeared in *Political Affairs* in June 1949. Keenly aware of the growing militancy of black women in the black liberation movement, Jones chided progressives and especially Communists for "the gross neglect of the special problems of Negro Women." Citing the fact that black women experienced triple discrimination—as workers, as blacks, and as women—she declared, that black women "are the most oppressed stratum of the whole population." Jones gave special attention to the "white supremacist" assault on black women and the legal case of a black woman named Rosa Lee Ingram, who had been incarcerated along with two of her sons for killing a white man as she "defended her life and dignity." Jones went on to state in the same article: "The Bourgeoisie is fearful of the militancy of the Negro woman, and for good reason. The capitalist knows, far better than many progressives seem to know, that once Negro women undertake action, the militancy of the whole Negro people and thus of the anti-imperialist coalition, is greatly enhanced."

The neglect of black women's problems by progressives and particularly the Communist party resulted in the virtual nonexistence of black women leaders in the black liberation movement. Even where they were present in great numbers, as, for example, in the rank and file of certain trade unions, black women leaders were exceptions to the rule. Yet the few exceptions proved to be shining examples of Jones's claim. Tobacco trade unionists Moranda Smith and Velma Hopkins in Winston-Salem, North Carolina, led successful strikes and their actions accelerated the democratic gains of all workers.

Jones's commentary was particularly pointed with regard to the plight of black women domestic workers. The relegation of black women to domestic status tended to cultivate white chauvinism among white men and women. And the poison of white chauvinism also entered into the domain of the Communist party. The social relationship of "madam-maid" caused black women to be viewed as inferiors. Whites often referred to black women, regardless of age, as "girls," and some Communists were guilty of perpetuating the exploitation of black domestic workers by not employing domestics through the Domestic Workers Union (DWU). Others in the party withheld support for the DWU by not helping to strengthen or build it.

Jones's article on the neglect of black women also condemned male Communist party members for their social interactions with black women. Jones questioned their resistance to dating black women and to intermarriage, choices they considered personal rather than political.

As a proponent of women's rights, Jones served as secretary to the party's National Commission on Women. While deeply committed to the special interests of women and especially black women, Jones was not blind to the broader forces at work. She consistently explained the issues relating to gender in terms of their connection to class struggle, anti-imperialism, and the battle for peace. Thus she wrote such articles as "For the Unity of Women in the Cause of Peace" and "Foster's Political and Theoretical Guide to Our Work among Women."

Faces Government Repression

During World War II, the U.S. government and the Soviet Union became allies in the international fight to rid the world of fascism. But with the Cold War, those persons in the United States thought to be sympathetic to the Soviet Union, including radical trade unionists, socialists, Marxist intellectuals, and members (or those thought to be members) of the Communist party, came under attack. During the Truman administration, loyalty boards were established to uncover federal government employees whose loyalty to the United States was questionable. And the infamous political witch hunt of Senator Joseph McCarthy of Wisconsin occurred in the early 1950s.

Black activists, among the most famous of whom were Paul Robeson, W. E. B. Du Bois, Ben Davis, and Henry Winston, were also targeted for attack. Black women activists were also investigated: Eslanda Goode Robeson, Louise Thompson Patterson, Maude White Katz, and Claudia Jones were just a few. Organizations fighting for black democratic interests, from the Civil Rights Congress to the Council on African Affairs, were hounded.

Jones's advocacy of action against exploitation and oppression, socialism, and world peace did not go unnoticed by the government. In 1948 she was arrested and faced deportation to Trinidad. Though she had been applying for U.S. citizenship since 1940, her applications had been denied. After being held in jail for six months, she was released on bail and immediately began to speak out against the government's repression. While out on bail and fighting her case in court, she was again arrested under the McCarren-Walter Act of 1952, which tightened controls on aliens and immigrants. Jones was again released on bail while her deportation was under review. Ultimately the government prevailed, and she began a prison term in January 1955. Jones and her close comrade, Elizabeth Gurley Flynn, were sent to the federal prison at Alderson, West Virginia. Despite Jones's deteriorating health, prison officials refused to improve her dietary and medical care. The pressure brought to bear on her behalf by a defense committee on the outside finally forced some changes. Jones's diet was somewhat improved, and she was transferred from a segregated area.

In prison, Jones fought against the institution's segregation and began teaching and organizing her fellow inmates. Health problems did not deter her from displaying her well-honed leadership skills or from showing compassion for the women she came to know in prison. Many of the inmates sought her counsel, and she was more than willing to oblige. Even the black women who acted as security officers in the prison encountered discrimination and segregation. Jones inspired them to fight against the indignities they faced.

Appeals for Jones's release reached international scope and on October 23, 1955, she left Alderson. Despite the efforts to block her deportation, she was forced to depart for England in December 1955. Many people from around the country sent messages showing their support, and a substantial group gathered at the Hotel Theresa to send her off and to show their respect and love.

Campaign Launched for Caribbean and Colonial People

When Jones arrived in London, she did not retire from the battleground for liberation. Despite her poor health, she put all her energies in the struggle to liberate the Caribbean people and to end imperialism. Jones's agenda included actively organizing in black communities in London, engaging in international struggles to end colonialism, and advocating world peace. She became active in the Caribbean Labor Congress, the Communist party of Great Britain, and the West Indian Workers and Student Association. Not unlike the residents of Harlem, London's black population confronted racism in every sector of life. In 1958 racist thugs attacked black people in London's Notting Hill area, and job discrimination was rampant.

Jones put her journalistic and organizational experience to work and in 1958 founded the *West Indian Gazette,* which became the primary organ for the interests of black people in London. The paper, officially named the *West Indian Gazette and Afro-Asian-Caribbean News,* defended black people against racist violence and explored the issues of colonialism in the Caribbean and Africa. In 1962 she joined a hunger strike outside the South African Embassy to protest the imprisonment of Nelson Mandela. Jones was an ardent anti-imperialist and socialist to her final days. Her many editorials in *The Gazette* covered a wide range of topics, from the defense of Cuba and the dangers of atomic war to Martin Luther King, who was the subject of her last editorial.

Claudia Jones's contributions as a political theorist and activist have left their mark in United States society. In Washington, D.C., a progressive bookstore was named in her honor, and many activists, from Angela Davis to the late Walter Rodney, are direct beneficiaries of her legacy. The words inscribed on Jones's tombstone best summarize her life: "Valiant fighter against racism and imperialism who dedicated her life to the progress of socialism and the liberation of her own Black People."

REFERENCES:

Allen, Robert L. *The Reluctant Reformers.* Washington, D.C.: Howard University Press, 1974.

"Claudia Jones, February 21, 1915-December 25, 1964." *Political Affairs* 44 (February 1965): 63-64.

Davis, Angela Y. *Women, Race and Class.* New York: Random House, 1981.

"A Fighting Caribbean-American Leader." *Peoples' Daily World,* February 10, 1989.

Flynn, Elizabeth Gurley. *The Alderson Story.* New York: International Publishers, 1963.

Haywood, Harry. *Black Bolshevik: Autobiography of an Afro-American Communist.* Chicago: Liberator Press, 1978.

Hine, Darlene Clark, ed. *Black Women in America.* Brooklyn: Carlson Publishing, 1993.

Horne, Gerald. *Communist Front.* Cranbury, N.J.: Associated Universities Press, 1988.

Johnson, Buzz. *I Think of My Mother: Notes on the Life and Time of Claudia Jones.* London: Karia Press, 1985.

Jones, Claudia. *Ben Davis, Fighter for Freedom.* New York: New Century Publishers, 1954.

———. "The Caribbean Community in Britain." *Freedomways* 4 (Summer 1964): 341-57.

———. "Discussion Article by Claudia Jones." *Political Affairs* 25 (August 1945): 67-77.

———. "An End to the Neglect of the Problems of Negro Women." *Political Affairs* 28 (June 1949): 51-67.

———. "For the Unity of Women in the Cause of Peace." *Political Affairs* 30 (February 1951): 151-68.

———. "Foster's Political and Theoretical Guide to Our Work among Women." *Political Affairs* 30 (March 1951): 68-78.

———. *Jim Crow in Uniform.* New York: New Age Publishers, 1940.

———. "The Struggle for Peace in the United States." *Political Affairs* 31 (February 1952): 1-20.

Thomas, Elean. "Remembering Claudia Jones." *World Marxist Review* 30 (March 1987): 67-69.

John McClendon, III

Edith Irby Jones
(1927-)
Physician, educator, organization leader

Edith Irby Jones is known as a trailblazer in the medical field. In 1948 she was the first African American student to be admitted to a southern medical school. As the first black student and woman to attend and graduate from the University of Arkansas School of Medicine, Jones made national headlines. Drawing attention to her pioneering role in overcoming racial barriers, *Life* magazine, January 31, 1949, reported that Jones was "the only Negro in the University of Arkansas Medical School—or, for that matter, in any white medical school in the whole South." Praising Jones for breaking new ground for blacks in southern medical schools, H. Clay Chenault, the vice-president of the University of Arkansas School of Medicine, promised that she would be treated no differently in the classroom than other students in her class. *Ebony,* January 1949, likewise underscored her historical breakthrough: "22-year-old Edith Mae Irby is the first Negro to attend mixed classes in a Dixie university since Reconstruction Days."

Edith Irby Jones was born in Conway, Arkansas, on December 23, 1927. The daughter of Robert and Mattie Buice Irby, she was raised in Hot Springs, Arkansas, by her mother, who supported the family by working as a cook after her husband died when Edith was eight years old. A commitment to medicine was instilled in Edith at an early age. As a teenager growing up in Hot Springs, she lost a brother and sister to typhoid fever; in addition, reports *Ebony,* January 1949, she saw "many suffering people come to regain their health" in the mineral waters of Hot Springs. "It was then, while I was still in high school, that I made up my mind to become a doctor," she said. "By studying pediatrics it is possible that I can learn to prevent sickness that occurs in later life. If we can build strong children, we will have healthy men and women."

First Black to Attend Medical School at the University of Arkansas

Jones's passion for medicine inspired her to become a high achiever. Educated in the public schools in Hot Springs,

Edith Irby Jones

she graduated as an honor student from Langston High School in 1944, then attended Knoxville College, Knoxville, Tennessee, where she received a bachelor of science degree in 1948. That summer she studied clinical psychology at Northwestern University in Chicago, Illinois. Having placed twenty-eighth out of 239 applicants on the Association of American Medical Colleges aptitude test, Jones applied and was accepted at the University of Arkansas School of Medicine. Her education was financed by a black newspaper in Little Rock, the *State Press,* and by proud alumni of Langston High School, reported *Life* on January 31, 1949. Determined to succeed in spite of discrimination and enforced isolation—the school's segregationist policies remained in place, she experienced racial affronts, and she was not allowed to eat in the cafeteria with her classmates or use the same restrooms—Jones ranked in the top half of her class when she graduated with a doctorate of medicine in 1952. Whitaker notes in *Ebony,* June 1986:

> She has a tradition of breaking new ground—quietly obliterating racial and sexual barriers. As the first Black student to attend and graduate from the University of Arkansas School of Medicine, she . . . helped signal the dawn of a new era for Blacks in southern medical schools.

Assessing her pioneering spirit, Jones said in the same article, "My way of fighting is to go in and be the best I can. That's how I cope. I don't think about the difficulty."

Jones graduated from medical school in 1952 and in the ensuing years she continued to break down racial and sexual barriers. In 1975 she became a major influence in the history

of the National Medical Association (NMA) as the first woman to chair the Council on Scientific Assembly, and in 1985 Jones was elected the first woman president of the NMA. Charles Whitaker explains in the June 1986 issue of *Ebony* the significance of her accomplishment: "Not only was Dr. Jones's installation as president historic, it also marked the beginning of a new more visible era for the NMA. . . . Her high profile has been instrumental in heightening public awareness of such long standing concerns as the need for more Black doctors and improved health care for the poor and elderly."

After serving her internship at the University Hospital in Little Rock, Arkansas, Jones operated a private general practice in Hot Springs from 1953 until 1959. She did a residency in internal medicine at Baylor Affiliated Hospital in Houston, Texas, from 1959 to 1962; she was the first African American in the program. Jones studied at the West Virginia College of Medicine in 1965 and Cook County Graduate School in 1966; she has also taken graduate courses in Houston.

Since 1962, Jones has been a clinical professor of medicine at Baylor College of Medicine and at the University of Texas. In 1962 she also became chief of cardiology at St. Elizabeth's Hospital and associate chief of medicine at Riverside General Hospital, both in Houston. In addition to teaching and maintaining a successful private practice, Jones has held appointments at several Texas hospitals, including Hermann Hospital, Methodist Hospital, Town Park, St. Anthony Center, St. Joseph, Montrose Care Center, St. Thomas Convalescent Center, and Mercy Hospital.

Trailblazer Heads National Medical Association

Since her childhood, Jones's first priority has been to help others: "I've always wanted to render a service. . . . I feel that serving people is what I was put here to do and I'm going to keep doing it as long as I can," she said in *Ebony,* June 1986. Jones has made good on that commitment. Not only has she paid the medical school tuition for selected deserving students as her "debt to society," but her leadership in the medical field has made her one of the most honored women in the nation. During her one-year tenure in 1985 as the first woman president of the NMA, a black organization with approximately fifteen thousand members, Jones traveled extensively throughout the nation promoting the NMA and its programs. A charismatic woman, her speeches and public appearances are very appealing to audiences.

Jones has displayed her commitment to service in numerous other leadership positions: chair of the board of trustees of Knoxville College, her alma mater; chair of the Utilization Committee, Methodist Hospital; president of the Arkansas Medical, Dental, and Pharmaceutical Association; chair, Internal Medicine Commission, St. Elizabeth Hospital; board of directors and chair, Committee for Homemakers Family Service; chair, Board of Delta Research and Education Foundation; board, Third National Bank Control Group; board of directors, Sudan Corporation; board of directors,

Afro-American Book Distributors; and Medical Advisory Board, Planned Parenthood of Houston. Other business, civic, and professional memberships include Delta Sigma Theta Sorority, Links, NAACP, National Council of Negro Women, Top Ladies of Distinction, Girl Friends, Women of Achievement, Order Eastern Star, PTA, and YMCA.

Jones contends that black doctors are more likely to become attached to black patients on a personal level than white doctors treating white patients. She said in a January 27, 1986, *Jet* article that black doctors "are concerned about their patients' financial problems, housing problems, and other worries, so it becomes a very personal thing." Jones emphasized in *Jet* that it is important for doctors to attend patients' funeral services to lend support to the families: "I certainly feel the responsibility does not end with the death of a patient. There is a responsibility to help the family before and after death, depending on how the physician relates to the family."

Jones has been cited by many groups for her outstanding contributions. She received an award in 1965 from the Houston Medical Forum for Outstanding Achievement in Religious/Civic Affairs and Scientific Literature; President Richard Nixon's award for exemplary medical service; and the President's Distinguished Service Award, Knoxville College, National Alumni Association, 1979. She was named Woman of the Year by the Charmetters, 1965, and was honored with an Edith Irby Jones Award Day, State of Arkansas, 1979. She has also been recognized for her achievements by the Jack Yates Federal Girls Club, 1969, and Kato Models, 1974.

Jones and her husband, James B. Jones, who is now deceased, had three children—Gary, Myra, and Keith. She is now a grandmother. During an illustrious career as a doctor that has lasted over forty years, Edith Irby Jones has made significant contributions to the medical field as well as major inroads for black women. Because of her dedication and commitment to service, she is one of the most respected internists in the country.

Current Address: 3402 South Parkwood Drive, Houston, Texas 77021.

REFERENCES:

"Arkansas Medical School Opens Its Doors." *Ebony* 4 (January 1949): 13-17.

"Attending Patients' Rites a Good Idea for Doctors." *Jet* 18 (January 27, 1986): 16.

"Edith Irby Goes to School." *Life* 26 (January 31, 1949): 33.

"Edith Irby Revisited." *Ebony* 18 (July 1963): 58.

"Open Door." *Time* 52 (September 6, 1948): 40.

Whitaker, Charles. "Breakthroughs Are Her Business." *Ebony* 41 (June 1986): 90-96.

Who's Who among Black Americans, 1994-95. 8th ed. Detroit: Gale Research, 1994.

Jacquelyn L. Jackson

Elaine R. Jones

(1944-)

Organization executive, lawyer, civil rights activist

"From early childhood I have always known that the struggle for equality would be my life," Elaine R. Jones told Lynn Norment for *Ebony* magazine. Jones's law training and focus on civil rights led her to a position of influence early in life; she became the first woman director-counsel of the NAACP Legal Defense and Educational Fund. In this role she addresses problems relating to civil rights, hate crimes, discrimination, health care, education, and voting rights.

Elaine R. Jones was born March 2, 1944, in Norfolk, Virginia, the only daughter of a pullman porter and a schoolteacher. Family discussions at mealtime centered on a variety of topics and provided Jones a healthy perspective on worldly matters and a strength that she could draw on in later life. "Ours was a family of words and ideas," she said in *Black Enterprise.* In 1965 she received a bachelor's degree with honors from Howard University, Washington, D.C. She was the first black woman admitted to the School of Law at the University of Virginia, receiving her law degree in 1970.

While Jones was offered a position with the Wall Street law firm, Mudge, Rose, Guthrie & Alexander, she joined the NAACP Legal Defense and Educational Fund (LDF) instead. "I always wanted to work with my own people," she said in *Black Enterprise.* "I thought I'd go back to Norfolk, hang out my shingle, and handle anything what walked in the door." Her law school dean, Jack Greenberg, well known in the LDF, urged her to join the LDF, where she became one of three lawyers who traveled the South arguing death penalty cases. In 1973 Jones was named managing attorney in the LDF's New York office.

From 1975 to 1977 Jones left the LDF to work as special assistant to the U.S. Secretary of Transportation, William T. Coleman Jr. She returned to the LDF, helped establish and manage the Washington, D.C. office, and became its first official legislative advocate on Capitol Hill. In 1988 she was promoted to deputy director-counsel of the LDF, making her second in command behind Julius Chambers. Jones handled her previous duties and in addition took on the overflow of work from Chambers's office. Besides supervising a battalion of private lawyers who donated their time and effort to the LDF cases, Jones also made speeches and participated in other public and private affairs on behalf of Chambers and the LDF.

One of Jones's primary responsibilities was to monitor federal judicial appointments and civil rights initiatives of the House and Senate Judiciary Committees. Evidence of her work can be seen in the scores of briefs written in support of or against nominations made by Presidents Reagan and Bush, including a 1987 brief against the appointment of Robert H.

Elaine R. Jones

Bork to the Supreme Court. In 1989 Jones petitioned against the appointment of William Lucas, a black Michigan lawyer, who was nominated as Assistant Attorney General for Civil Rights, on the grounds that he was unqualified for the position. "We do not fight to do a job simply because we're black. It is demeaning," she said in *Black Enterprise*. The nomination was denied. Jones received public attention again in 1991 during the confirmation hearings of Supreme Court nominee Clarence Thomas when she consistently spoke against the appointment on *The MacNeil-Lehrer NewsHour* and elsewhere.

First Woman to Head Legal Defense Fund

Until 1993 Julius L. Chambers headed the LDF. Thurgood Marshall, later Associate Supreme Justice of the Supreme Court, founded the LDF in 1940 and was its first director-counsel. Both Marshall and the fund became widely known for Marshall's hallmark case, *Brown v. Board of Education*. Once an arm of the NAACP, the LDF split from the organization in 1957 for tax purposes, and the two organizations had a continuing relationship in name only. The LDF had had only three leaders—Marshall, Jack Greenberg and Julius L. Chambers. When Chambers resigned in 1993, Jones became the board's choice from among the thirty candidates from inside and outside the organization. She had already set a fine record as a dedicated and competent manager, litigator, and strategist as well as a tireless and outspoken advocate for civil rights. *Black Enterprise* said that she was diligent, persuasive, and had a "unique ability to build coalitions among competing factions." She was known as a political mastermind whom

Joseph Lowery, president of the Southern Christian Leadership Conference, called "informed, brilliant and practical," as quoted in the same article.

Jones and the LDF have fought relentlessly to uphold equal education and voting rights legislation. She told Lynn Norment in *Ebony,* "We have to be, as we have been, the best there is in civil rights litigation. We are good at what we do, and we work hard at it." The LDF has also challenged the system of electing state court judges, particularly in the South, calling the practices discriminatory. The LDF opposes the death penalty, taking the stand that the practice is biased against the poor, minorities, and the disabled. Jones believes that the LDF must broaden its vision to address issues such as the causes of poverty in minority communities, funding for schools, toxic waste in black communities, health care in inner-city neighborhoods, and the enhancement of minority businesses. Above all, the LDF sees its main responsibility as ensuring that civil rights victories are not eroded.

Jones's effectiveness is enhanced by her relations with well-placed persons. The friendship between Jones and Hillary Rodham Clinton began in the 1980s when they worked on an American Bar Association project on women in law. Both lawyers envision greater progress on civil rights issues and more blacks appointed to federal benches. Her friendship with Clinton and other people in high places, including Attorney General Janet Reno and John F. Kennedy Jr., have never distracted Jones nor led her to depart from values set in childhood or to forget what life was like growing up in the segregated South.

When she can find time for matters beyond the LDF responsibilities, Jones devotes some time to her membership in the National Bar Association, Old Dominion Bar Association, Virginia Trial Lawyer's Association, the International Federation of Women Lawyers, and the Delta Sigma Theta Sorority. She has served on the panel of arbitration of the American Stock Exchange. Her honors and awards include the Recognition Award for outstanding legal service to the community, Black American Law Students' Association, 1974; and Special Achievement Award, National Association of Black Women Attorneys, 1975.

Jones is upbeat and enthusiastic about life and her career. *Black Enterprise* called her a woman with "a common touch that in no way undermines her lightening quick intellect." Jones said in the journal, "Whatever I tell you is what I think. That honesty has worked for me. And when times are the worst, that's when honesty serves us best." Her life is focused on civil rights and career, not marriage and motherhood. "I have not done a good job of balancing my job and my life," she told Lynn Norment. Except for the many dinners, luncheons, and receptions she must attend as a part of her job, social life generally does not exist for Jones. She finds some time to read, especially her favorite mystery novels, and to work out on her treadmill. She shuttles between New York and Washington, D.C., to handle the affairs of her two offices.

Elaine Jones has followed through with her childhood goal to help others in the role of a lawyer. She has had a lifetime commitment to civil rights and has been able to address civil rights issues through her leadership in the NAACP Legal Defense Fund.

Current Address: NAACP Legal Defense and Educational Fund, 1275 K Street, NW, Suite 301, Washington, DC 20005.

REFERENCES:

Clarke, Caroline V., and Jonathan Sapers. "Jones for the Defense." *Black Enterprise* 24 (August 1993): 64-67.
Contemporary Black Biography. Vol. 7. Detroit: Gale Research, 1994.
Norment, Lynn. "Introducing: Elaine R. Jones. Nation's Top Civil Rights Lawyer." *Ebony* 48 (June 1993): 66-67.
"Prize Partnership." *Vogue* 183 (June 1993): 178-81.
Weatherford, Carole Boston. "Elaine Jones: Fighting for Our Civil Rights." *Essence* 24 (December 1993): 52.
Who's Who among Black Americans, 1994-95. 8th ed. Detroit: Gale Research, 1994.

Jessie Carney Smith

Elayne Jones

Elayne Jones
(1928-)
Percussionist, timpanist

Timpanist and percussionist Elayne Jones has been "a different drummer" in routinely forbidden musical territory. She attracted national attention in 1949 when she joined the New York City Opera and Ballet Company orchestras, representing a first for a black American. Her talent and preparation made her one of New York City's most sought-after freelance musicians throughout the 1950s, 1960s, and early 1970s. In 1965, National Education Television released a half-hour special for national viewing, *A Day in the Life of a Musician,* that featured Jones. She attracted international attention in 1972 when she emerged victorious in a competition with forty other musicians for the position of timpanist with the San Francisco Symphony Orchestra. Jones then became the first black to hold a principal position in a major symphony orchestra in the United States. Throughout her life, Jones has fought to break down the racial and sexual barriers that have stalled the careers of many female black musicians. Her fight against discrimination came to national attention in 1974, when she was denied tenure with the San Francisco Symphony Orchestra. Though she lost her battle with the symphony, Jones continues to be remembered for her efforts to open doors for blacks and women in the world of music.

"Joshua with the Kettle Drums," as one journalist referred to Jones, was born on January 30, 1928, in New York

City. She is the daughter of Cecil C. Jones and Ometa Winfield Jones, both of whom migrated to the United States from Barbados. They came in search of opportunity, which neither found. Jones's mother had studied piano in Barbados with Jones's paternal grandfather, who was a church organist. Instead of enjoying the opportunity to pursue a career as a concert pianist in the United States, Ometa Jones was forced to become a domestic in order to help support the family. Jones's father came to the U.S. in pursuit of a career as an artist. Instead, he spent his life working as a Brooklyn-Manhattan Transit subway towerman. He died shortly after retiring, while preparing to establish a greeting card business. Jones's parents invested all of their dreams in their only child, Elayne.

Ometa Winfield Jones did manage to continue offering some piano instruction. Her star pupil was her daughter, whom she started teaching at age six. The teacher/student relationship lasted for about a year, at which time Elayne switched to another instructor. Jones wrote in a letter dated January 9, 1994, that both her mother and father were strict disciplinarians, offering "an exposure that prepared me for the rigors of the symphony orchestra. Practice and school-work were mandatory."

Jones successfully auditioned on piano for entrance into the select senior High School of Music and Art in New York, which she began attending in 1942. Jones's first choice of instrument was the violin, for which she was told that she was too skinny. She then considered a brass instrument, but was told that she had insufficient lung power. She was then handed a pair of drum sticks. She had some prior percussion experience from her participation in the Girl Scouts' drum and bugle corps. Jones said in an interview on September 10, 1975,

> I guess they thought I wouldn't stick with it. Also, there may have been a link with the mistaken notion that all black folks have rhythm. As luck would have it, I took to drums like a duck takes to water. As much as I enjoyed the piano, the experience of playing with other people in an orchestra was so profound and beautiful. Drums are more sociable than piano.

Having graduated from the drum and bugle corps, she participated in the All-City High School Orchestra and the All-City High School Band, as well as various instrumental ensembles at the High School of Music and Art.

Wins Ellington Scholarship to Juilliard

Just prior to graduating from Music and Art in 1945, Jones learned of a citywide competition offering three outstanding students scholarships to the Juilliard School of Music, scholarships sponsored by Edward Kennedy ("Duke") Ellington. One of the three winners, Jones was an Ellington Scholarship recipient for three years and her fourth and final year at Juilliard was covered by the institution. At Juilliard she studied with the New York Philharmonic's timpanist, Saul Goodman. In a 1952 interview with Alan Siegler of the *Daily Compass*, Jones remembered:

> He [Goodman] was a proud teacher who used to run down the halls of Juilliard and drag people out of neighboring classrooms to see my crossbeats, i.e., a turning of rapidly moving sticks one over the other across the set of drums in a blur of movement and sound.

While enrolled at Juilliard, Jones took advantage of all opportunities to perform. She played with the American Youth Orchestra under the direction of the outstanding African American conductor Dean Dixon for two years and with the National Orchestral Association from 1945 through 1951. Athletically as well as musically gifted, she played baseball and tennis, developing strength and stamina. In a September 10, 1975, interview, she characterized the Juilliard experience as a very enjoyable one, "except for occasional jabs from fellow male students."

Percussionist Joins New York City Opera and Ballet

Jones left Juilliard with a professional diploma and a post-graduate diploma. The summer following her graduation, she attended the Berkshire Music Festival at Tanglewood, Lenox, Massachusetts, on a scholarship from the Boston Symphony Orchestra. Shortly before her graduation, she learned that the New York City Opera and Ballet would soon be needing a percussionist. But "they were not exactly eager to have a girl on drums," she noted in the June 2, 1961, *New York Mirror*. The organization sought a recommendation from the Philharmonic's Saul Goodman, who convinced "the powers that be" that Jones was the person for the job. She was

accepted and began her New York City Opera and Ballet affiliation with the 1949-50 season. Jones's hiring received national attention because it reflected an issue that was becoming important across the country. Jones remained with the ballet until 1952 and the opera until 1961. "I left because of my husband's demands that I be a wife and mother," she wrote in a January 9, 1994, letter.

Jones had married George Kaufman, a Jewish doctor, in 1953. Following a series of conversations between Jones and Robert E. Lesoine in 1972, Lesoine wrote in *Cultural Living Magazine,* "She had met a man who treated her like a person . . . made her feel like something important . . . something more than an object and she married him. . . . But somehow the communication broke down." Elayne and George Kaufman were divorced in 1964, following the birth of three children— a son and two daughters (1954, 1956, and 1959).

Jones recalled in a January 9, 1994, letter,

> I have never missed a performance or rehearsal since I started playing professionally in 1948. That includes even during the times my children were born. I planned them, so I would have them at a time that I was on a break. With the help of a physician husband, the children were born during the slow months.

She continued, stating, "My husband said that the priorities in my life were in this order—my career, my children, and lastly, him."

Jones left the New York City Opera primarily because she wanted to attempt to save her marriage. However, when the world renowned maestro Leopold Stokowski formed his American Symphony Orchestra in 1962, he asked Jones to join. As Jones recalled in an interview on September 10, 1975, "Stokowski chose me to play with his orchestra without an audition. I had played several recordings with him and he had guest conducted the New York City Opera. He was familiar with my playing." Jones played with the orchestra for ten years and Stokowski remained one of her greatest fans for the remainder of his life. In the January 1972 issue of *Music and Artists* he wrote,

> Elayne Jones . . . is a very great artist. I know the timpani-players in other countries and some of them are very great; but she is equally great. She is one of the greatest in the whole world for her instrument, for technique, but particularly for imagination.

Her own success notwithstanding, Jones continuously worked on behalf of other talented African American musicians. In 1956, Jones and two other black musicians called at the office of *New York Times* critic Howard Taubman to state the case for black instrumentalists. Taubman subsequently wrote in the *New York Times,* April 22, 1956, "There are a number of capable Negro musicians worthy of consideration by our major musical organizations. . . . Music, which knows no barriers of language, should lead the way in striking down those based on color."

Jones was most active in drawing up, soliciting support for, and gaining the successful passage of an antidiscriminatory clause included in the bylaws of Local 802-American Federation of Musicians in the early 1960s. She was one of the founding members of New York City's fully integrated Symphony of the New World, organized in 1965 ("to right the wrongs in hiring practices in major symphony orchestras"), and served as the ensemble's first president. She was a frequent radio and television panelist when the topic was the integration of American orchestras.

Controversy Emerges with San Francisco Symphony

In 1972 Jones won a competition for the position of timpanist with the San Francisco Symphony Orchestra. She would also be timpanist with the San Francisco Opera Orchestra. Approaching the end of her first season, Jones stated in an interview with journalist Duston Harvey that appeared in the *Afro-American* on March 24, 1973:

> It's been a long struggle against two prejudices and it isn't over yet.... [B]eing black is worse than being a woman in everything except baseball, football and basketball.... I had to prove that music could be played by anyone who loves it. And I never let anything stand in my way. It's been a terrible burden because I always felt I had to do better; that I wouldn't be allowed the lapses other musicians have.

As noted in D. Antoinette Handy's *Black Women in American Bands and Orchestras,* the press routinely singled out Jones for praise following San Francisco Symphony concerts. Examples of such endorsements, dating from 1972 to 1974, include: "If the world has a finer timpanist, I have not heard one"; "Special note should be given Elayne Jones in her unbeatable reading of the solo tympani part"; "Orchestra as a whole is sounding better than ever"; "Elayne Jones, sure the best timpanist in the business today"; "A musician first, a percussion virtuoso second. Clear articulation, fine intonation and technical savvy"; and "We have a drummer who can phrase like a lieder singer."

But as reported in the nation's leading newspapers and summarized in *Newsweek,* June 17, 1974,

> Jones, the only black, and Nakagawa, the only native Japanese in the orchestra, have been fired. In San Francisco, players are hired by open auditions (they play behind screens) for a two-year probation and then come up for tenure before a seven-member players' committee elected by the orchestra. Disapproval by the committee is tantamount to dismissal from the orchestra. In May 1974, six out of eight applicants for tenure, all of them white, were approved by the committee; Jones and Nakagawa were not. Why?

Lengthy articles continued to appear in major publications throughout the country, all deploring the action of the players' committee.

The establishment of a players' committee was the outgrowth of long-standing disputes in the San Francisco Symphony between the orchestra's musical directors and orchestra personnel. Throughout the Jones/Nakagawa dispute, Japanese conductor Seiji Ozawa was at the helm. His only public statement during the controversy indicated that he believed both musicians should have been granted tenure.

Shortly after her dismissal, Jones asked the U.S. District Court to order the San Francisco Symphony and Musicians Union, Local 6, to grant her tenure. Her suit also demanded fifty thousand dollars in damages for emotional distress and anguish. She charged the tenure committee members (all white, all male) with "racism, sexism, and jealousy."

Jones and bassoonist Ryohei Nakagawa were offered—and they accepted—employment with the orchestra for the following season. Jones dropped her lawsuit when, in August 1975, she was granted another audition before a new players' committee with a court monitor. After again being denied tenure, she filed a $1.5 million damage suit in August 1976. Following the 1976 reauditioning, Ozawa lined up with the players' committee. He subsequently resigned from the San Francisco Symphony to take up full-time leadership of the Boston Symphony.

A "Support Committee for Elayne Jones, Timpanist" was formed, which included such well-established individuals as singers Leontyne Price, Shirley Verrett, and George Shirley; singer/actor Harry Belafonte; composers William Dawson and Hale Smith; conductors Leopold Stokowski, Leonard DePaur, and Everett Lee; pianists Don Shirley and Billy Taylor; journalist Nat Hentoff; congressman Ronald Dellums; and publisher Carlton Goodlett.

On December 20, 1977, Jones wrote the following to her friends and sponsors: "This is probably the most painful letter I have ever had to write.... My endeavor to expose racism has been thwarted. Summary judgment has been granted; the case was dismissed." As *New York Times* music journalist Donal Henahan had written on September 7, 1975, "The cause of orchestral democracy, while still breathing strongly, has felt the heavy hand of 'I'm All Right, Jack' unionism pressing against its windpipe. Bad show, all around."

Jones remained in San Francisco, where she continues to play with the San Francisco Opera. For a brief period, she was a faculty member at San Francisco Conservatory. She also does some private teaching.

Jones has also kept herself occupied by spending many hours on the tennis courts (acquiring numerous trophies in competitions) and by performing lecture-demonstration concerts for children and adults in schools, community centers, and other gathering places. Her objective is to bring people into the world of symphonic music and to make the music come alive for those who have a mistaken perception of what classical music is and who plays it. For this activity, she has been commended by the Youth Juvenile Hall and Mercy High School in San Francisco. Though her controversy with the San Francisco Symphony is still spoken of in musical circles, the issue is closed, and unfortunately, Jones, the timpanist and percussionist, is almost completely ignored by the music establishment.

As Jones contemplates her future, she has the satisfaction of recalling a career that has spanned close to half a century: she has played under the leading conductors of our time, including Leonard Bernstein, Pierre Monteux, Fritz Reiner, Bruno Walter, Arthur Fiedler, James Levine, Edo de Waart, Henry Lewis, Dean Dixon, Mstislas Rostropovich, Kurt Adler, and Dimitri Mitropoulas; she has played most operas in the standard repertoire and most of the standard orchestral literature; she has received the LaGuardia Memorial Award (1965), the High School of Music and Art's Outstanding Alumna Award (1965), and the National Association of Negro Musicians's Distinguishcd Service Award (1993); and she was for many years one of the most respected professionals in the business.

On January 9, 1994, as Elayne Jones prepared for a vacation in Barbados, she wrote in a letter, "I am not physically or emotionally ready to retire. So I have taken a one year leave of absence [from the opera company] to investigate how I can best use my years of experience to benefit young African American people."

Current Address: 130 Amber Drive, San Francisco, CA 94131.

REFERENCES:

"About That Timpanist Who Got Drummed Out." *New York Times,* September 7, 1975.

"Elayne Jones, Who Knocks Down Walls with 'Kettles.'" *Daily Compass,* June 12, 1952.

"An Even Break." *New York Times,* April 22, 1956.

"The First Lady of Tympany." *New York Mirror,* June 2, 1961.

Handy, D. Antoinette. *Black Women in American Bands and Orchestras.* Metuchen, N.J.: Scarecrow Press, 1981.

Harvey, Duston. "What It's Like Being a Black Drummer in a Major Orchestra." *Afro-American,* March 24, 1973.

Jones, Elayne Kaufman. Interview with D. Antoinette Handy. San Francisco, September 10, 1975.

———. Letters to Handy, October 11, 1975; November 14, 1975; January 3, 1976; March 22, 1976; April 15, 1977; December 20, 1977; February 27, 1979; January 9, 1994.

———. Telephone conversation with Handy, January 10, 1994.

Lesoine, Robert E. "The Groovy Timpanist." *Cultural Living Magazine* (August 30, 1972).

Stokowski, Leopold. "Leopold Stokowski Speaks." *Music and Artists* (January 1972): 12.

"Talented Symphony Additions." *San Francisco Examiner,* January 23, 1973.

"Votes vs. Notes." *Newsweek* 83 (June 17, 1974): 109.

D. Antoinette Handy

Grace Jones
(1952-)
Entertainer, dancer, model, singer, actress

Of all the popular stars on the current entertainment scene, Grace Jones is perhaps the most difficult to label. A singer, dancer, actress, and fashion model, she alternately presents herself as extremely feminine, very masculine, or androgynous. In fact, it is Jones's enigmatic approach to performing that constitutes her special appeal. She is at her most feminine singing "I Want a Man" or dressed in a fine fur at a theater opening or a club soiree, her most androgynous as the demonic seductress/vampire of *The Vamp,* her most masculine as a leather-dressed motorcyclist on her Honda. She has modeled haute couture for Yves St. Laurent and Givenchy. She is recognized as a shaping force in the experimental use of all types of visual imagery in today's performance media. The visual statement she makes dominates her stage presence. She has taken strikingly different roles as a movie actress: a barbarian warrior in *Conan the Destroyer* with Arnold Schwarzenegger and a smoothly alluring villainess in James Bond's *A View to a Kill* with Roger Moore. Appearing on her record jackets in a multiple-image chorus line, in a sailor suit, in a white-veiled wedding dress, as an athlete skipping rope, or as a snarling leopard in a cage, she seems to strive always for a different point of view, a new theme, a bold and controversial statement.

Grace Jones was born on May 18, 1952, in Spanishtown, Jamaica, to Robert and Marjorie P. Jones. Hers was a large family, including six brothers and sisters. Grace Jones's mother was a seamstress and often made her own clothes, modeled after the latest Parisian fashions. Grace credits her mother with helping her acquire a taste for chic clothes and the latest styles. Grace Jones's father, a Pentecostal minister, and her mother moved to Syracuse, New York, when Grace was young, leaving the children in the care of relatives. Grace joined her parents in Syracuse in 1964, continuing her schooling there and entering Syracuse University in 1968, where she intended to prepare for a teaching career as a French language instructor. She acquired some tutelage and experience in drama at Syracuse and left after a year to begin her performing career in Philadelphia and New York in local theaters and nightclubs.

Following her early experiences in Philadelphia and New York, Grace Jones's career began in earnest in Paris in the early 1970s. In a December 1977 interview in *After Dark,* she characterized this period as her "campaign" for attention. Stories abound concerning her escapades with fellow models Jerry Hall and Grace Cleveland—dancing on tables in clubs, wearing shocking costumes, and generally behaving audaciously. *Current Biography Yearbook* reports, "One night she danced in public with only a baseball cap, satin running shorts and body glitter for a costume. 'We'd go dancing and end up on the floor. And before you knew it, *Elle* magazine picked me off the street and did a story on me.'"

Grace Jones

The campaign succeeded. Excellent modeling engagements followed with major European magazines, advertisers, and fashion designers. Her pictures appeared in *Elle, der Stern, Vogue,* and *Pravda,* she was featured at major fashion shows for Yves St. Laurent and others, and she was photographed by prominent European photographers, including Helmut Newton and Guy Bourdin. A chance demonstration of her possibilities as a singer in a Paris club led to a recording contract with Island Records, yielding two major hits, "La Vie en Rose" and "I Need A Man," released in 1977. The latter song zoomed to number one on charts in the United States, and Jones was ready for a triumphal return to New York. She was a smash hit from the start, opening in 1977 at Les Mouches, a popular large disco bar favored by the New York gay set, with whom she has been a special favorite.

Grace Jones's disco act was molded and developed during her relationship with Jean Paul Goode, a Parisian artist and photographer who moved to New York and became art editor of *Esquire* magazine in 1969. Their relationship began in 1977, and he is the father of her son, Paulo, born in 1980. Goode produced a number of Jones's videos and stage reviews, designed costumes for her, and styled her hair. Jones's disco act was extremely popular and provocative, taking her on tours in five continents, including Canada and the United States, and earning for her the sobriquets "Disco Diva" and "Disco Queen." She appeared at times as a caged panther, as a boxer, as a singer with an accordion, as Marlene Dietrich, and as an androgynous model. Always looking for a different challenge, Jones and Goode moved on to devise their new concept of living theater, or *tableaux vivants:* static scenes in which Jones exploits many facets of visual imagery. This new form of nightclub act centered primarily on costume, lighting, and setting. Changes in Jones's act included portraying a mood or theme through a static presentation, akin to a living portrait, and using strong and evocative visual statements accentuated by makeup (she is her own makeup artist), music, and costumes.

Film and Video Career Launched

While Jones's modeling career and live performances continued, new professional opportunities opened up. She was able to launch a film and video career. Again, her roles varied widely, from the barbarian warrior of *Conan the Destroyer,* to the alluring villainess of *A View to a Kill,* to the outlandish vampire in *The Vamp.* A number of videos and recordings have subsequently been produced, and in the process, her singing has improved to a more musical contralto. Sometimes she belts out her lyrics, sometimes she sings with gentleness; sometimes her movements are sharp and angular, sometimes more flowing. Her album covers use art thoughtfully: sometimes a portrait, sometimes a montage, sometimes a multiple image, but always one sees the strong desire to make a statement—often a controversial one. As an artist, Jones thrives on controversy, and she constantly moves to new challenges.

Jones has had a number of male companions over the years, including a restaurateur, a hair stylist, an artist, and, most recently, kick-boxer Hans Lundgren and his body builder/actor twin brother, Dolph (seen in a major role opposite Sly Stallone in *Rocky IV*). Perhaps the most important and influential of her partners to her career was Jean Paul Goode. Jones now lives in a spacious Greenwich Village apartment, and she frequents the New York nightclub and theater scene, constantly exploring new ventures. She recently opened a restaurant called La Vie en Rose.

A cover story in *Interview* magazine discusses several facets of Jones's career and reveals interesting aspects of her personality: her appeal to the gay set, her love of furs and finery, her inner nature—at times male, at times female, at times neither or both, at times playful, at times forceful. In the story, arranged in dialogue form between Jones and authors Andy Warhol and Andre Leon Talley, she discusses artistic ideals and themes in her work and mentions her fashion career, with its dramatic beginnings in Paris in the early 1970s, naming designers Yves St. Laurent, Givenchy, and LouLou De la Falaise as important influences. She also discusses the issue of sex and changing roles, alluding to her belief that her particular male and female traits stem from her childhood. The *Interview* article includes the famous Mapplethorpe photograph of her in body paint by artist Keith Haring.

Grace Jones attributes the strength she projects to the strong women in her family, particularly her mother. Additional contributing factors are her strict upbringing and her large family, in which she had to assert herself or face the consequences. Her flair for the dramatic can also be traced to her youth, when she wore copies of designer clothes to school, arranged dramatic skits, and cultivated the ambition of becoming a movie star and singer. The family was musical; her mother sings and Grace received piano lessons at home. Always close to her family, she visits her parents and her relatives in Jamaica, and her mother is often in New York with her. Her record albums include *Portfolio, Warm Leatherette, Nightclubbing, Living My Life, Island Life,* and *Slave to The Rhythm.* Her videos include *A One Man Show* and *A State of Grace.*

Current Address: c/o John Carmen, 148 West 23rd Street, New York, NY 10011.

REFERENCES:

Bogle, Donald. *Brown Sugar.* New York: Harmony Books, 1980.

Current Biography Yearbook, 1987. New York: H. W. Wilson, 1987.

Durgnat, Raymond. "Amazing Grace." *American Film* 7 (January-February 1986): 31-34.

"Grace Jones." Interview. *After Dark* 10 (December 1977): 73-78.

Haddad, M. George. "Grace Jones." *Black Stars* 28 (February 1979): 52-56.

Hitchcock, H. Wiley, and Stanley Sadie, eds. *New Grove Dictionary of American Music.* 2 vols. New York: Macmillan, 1985.

Jordan, Pat. "Amazing Grace Jones." *Mademoiselle* 88 (November 1982): 46-60.

Norment, Lynn. "The Outrageous Grace Jones." *Ebony* 34 (July 1979): 84-94.

Seideman, Tony. "Grace Jones: *State of Grace.*" *Rolling Stone* 22 (April 24, 1986): 62.

Warhol, Andy, and Andre Leon Talley. "Grace Jones." *Interview* 22 (November 1984): 54-61.

Wohlfert, Lee. "Couples." *People* 22 (April 23, 1979): 104-6.

Darius L. Thieme

Grace Morris Allen Jones
(c. 1876-1928)
Educator, school founder, fund-raiser, postmaster, clubwoman, reformer, writer

After founding integrated vocational training schools in Iowa and working as financial agent for two other schools, Grace Allen Jones was instrumental in ensuring the survival of Piney Woods Country Life School in Mississippi,

Grace Morris Allen Jones

an institution that virtually introduced education to the area. In addition to teaching academic and vocational subjects, she worked with mothers in rural communities to help them uplift themselves and their families. According to sources, she founded The Cotton Blossoms singing group, which raised funds nationwide to support Piney Woods. Working through the Mississippi Federation of Women's Clubs, she was instrumental in the establishment of a school for blind black students and a facility for delinquent black youth.

The daughter of James Addison Morris and Mary Ellen Pyles Morris, Grace Morris Allen Jones was born on January 7, 1876 (some sources say 1879), in the Mississippi River town of Keokuk, Iowa. Later the family moved to Burlington, Iowa, forty-three miles upriver, where Grace was educated in the public schools. She studied at the Burlington, Iowa, high school, from 1891 to 1894, where she completed a course of studies in English. From 1894 to 1895 she was a student at Burlington City Normal School. At the end of that school year Jones took an examination, received a teacher's certificate, and was appointed to teach at a school in Bethel, Missouri, where she remained for one year. From 1896 to 1898 she was assistant teacher of "colored" schools in Slater, Missouri. Her whereabouts after leaving this position are unclear. Since it is known that she married Laurence Jones in 1912 and that Allen is a part of her name, it is possible that she married and relocated during these years.

Although the date is not documented, it is known that Jones returned to Burlington and completed a course at Elliott's Business College. It appears she profited greatly from this course because she went on to found—singlehandedly—the Grace M. Allen Industrial School in Burlington in 1902 and also to establish other vocational training schools in the city. In its first year of operation Allen Industrial School employed a faculty of five and had a student body of fifty-five. Faculty and students were integrated since the school was so successful that white families had asked permission to send their children there. After public funds were used to strengthen education in the area, Jones closed the school in 1906. Then she traveled as fund-raiser for Ambidexter Institute of Springfield, Illinois, and also served as financial agent for the Eckstein-Norton Normal and Industrial Institute at Cane Springs, Kentucky. She took a summer course at an unnamed institution in 1909. Eckstein-Norton awarded her an honorary master's degree in 1910 for her work in helping the school to survive. For two years, 1910 through 1912, she took a course in public speaking and elocution at Chicago's Ziegfield Musical College.

Meets Future Husband

Although she had had a rich and full existence to this point, Jones's life was to take a new and equally rewarding course. While she was in Iowa City raising funds for Eckstan-Norton, she met Laurence Clifton Jones, a junior at the University of Iowa, who spoke at a downtown church in Iowa City at the request of the First Baptist Church Missionary Society. Laurence Jones had read extensively on the condition of blacks in the South and knew well the work and views of Booker T. Washington, W. E. B. Du Bois, and others. Since Grace Jones was familiar with the condition of blacks in Kentucky, he asked her to contribute something from her experience. The speech of the articulate, vigorous, bright-eyed young woman stirred and inspired him. He immediately considered her the most enthusiastic black woman he had ever met and privately determined that they would meet again when he had advanced in his career.

Laurence Jones, son of John Q. and Lydia Foster Jones, attended public schools in St. Joseph, Missouri, and graduated from high school in Marshalltown, Iowa, and from Iowa Central Business College in 1893. He received a bachelor's in philosophy from the State University of Iowa in 1907. Laurence Jones and Booker T. Washington had corresponded, and Jones was in line for a position at Tuskegee. However, he decided instead to go to a little industrial school in Hinds County, Mississippi, that had been founded on the self-help concept of Tuskegee. Two years later he left Hinds and set out for a tiny place called Piney Woods, twenty-one miles southeast of Jackson, Mississippi, determined to found a school with a similar orientation. He noted in *Piney Woods and Its Story* that his people were "in the darkness of ignorance with all its superstition and fears, and how they needed light, and how the light was sure to come." In 1910 Laurence Jones founded Piney Woods Country Life School. According to Rudolph P. Byrd in *Generations in Black and White,* Charles Duane Van Vechten of Cedar Rapids, Iowa, father of Harlem Renaissance benefactor Carl Van Vechten, was a co-founder of the school. Certainly he was a benefactor for many years. Writing about the school in *Black Women in*

American Bands and Orchestras, D. Antoinette Handy said that it was "open to the materially impoverished, the social misfits, the lame and the blind, as well as the more affluent applicant."

Piney Woods and Its Story

Since the time Laurence Jones and Grace Jones met, the two had corresponded, and she continued to occupy a special place in his mind. She was about five years older and at first seemed much more experienced than he. Now, however, he had become the founder and principal of a school, and he had status in the community. When they met again, Jones was fascinated with the young principal's success but not with his long hair and bushy mustache. According to Beth Day in *The Little Professor of Piney Woods,* she questioned, "What on earth made you do that! . . . I can't even see you for all that foliage." He grinned and responded, "There wasn't any other way to make the people listen." She thought this was his way of attracting people's attention and continued, "And I remembered you as a rather handsome young man."

On June 29, 1912, in Des Moines, Iowa, Grace Allen married Laurence Clifton Jones. They honeymooned briefly in Minnesota. Grace Jones lived with his mother for a time in Marshalltown while Laurence went back to his job of fund-raising. They had two sons, Turner Harris, born May 6, 1914, and Laurence Clifton, Jr., born December 10, 1917. When the school opened for its third year on October 12, 1912, Laurence Jones introduced Grace as his bride. According to Beth Day in *The Little Professor of Piney Woods,* the unpretentious country folks whispered curiously about what the "little 'Fesser," as they called him, had "done fo' hisself." She was immediately his partner in the life of the school. Filled with an abundance of energy, she taught English, sewing, and handicrafts. As an efficient officer worker and an expert fund-raiser, Jones would help the school survive.

At that moment, however, the school's survival was at risk. When the Joneses met with faculty, students, and parents on the opening day of the 1912-13 school year, a bleak picture of the school's future dominated. Parents reported that, for the third year in succession, the boll weevil and heavy rains had caused the farmers' crops to fail and left them with no money for their children's tuition. But the young men reported on their work in the fields and the application of new techniques the school had taught them. The young men and women students had taught younger children how to read, write, and cook, and had organized Sunday school classes. Some had managed to save a few pennies to start a school band. After the faculty, students, and parents had spoken and received congratulations and encouragement from the principal, according to Beth Day, Grace Jones rose, bowed to a warm reception, and continued with a message of hope and encouragement that "went right to the hearts of her listeners." She launched into her plans for the school with heartening enthusiasm. She was immediately accepted.

That opening day students poured into the school. One widow, the mother of twelve, walked twelve miles to see if her oldest daughter could enter without having her tuition paid. Beth Day's description of the entering crowd is touching:

> Children, children, children. Orphans, half-orphans, children of slaves, children of broken homes, children who had never seen a railroad or a train. Children on foot, in wagons, children with their parents, and children alone.

When they could, the parents paid their bills with a load of hay, jars of fruit, or live geese—or they left them unpaid.

Finds Life's Work at Piney Woods

Jones had found her niche. She made notes of what she saw and the stories the students told her. She talked with one girl whose mother had died and left her with five younger children to raise. At home only on weekends, she would cook and clean for the week ahead, walk seven miles to the school where she lived with relatives, and walk seven miles to return home on Fridays and begin the routine again. That year the school would accommodate eighty-five boarders and all of the day students who applied, for it was too heartbreaking to turn students away. According to Beth Day, Jones told her husband, "I suppose I knew from what you had told me that it would be heartbreaking. But somehow I didn't quite realize there would be so many and so pitifully poor." She asked her husband how many children there were in the area who had access to education only at Piney Woods, and he told her there were 11,250 potential students. "If you had hunted the world over, you couldn't have picked a spot where a job was more needed. . . . What a place to dedicate your life," Grace Jones concluded.

When classes began, Jones taught most of the English classes and, as she was director of girls' industrial studies, she supervised and directed handicrafts as well. She became executive secretary of the school that year. The Joneses agreed that more buildings were needed and that they would work all summer to raise the money. Grace Jones headed this fund-raising work. The children would not be denied access to an education as long as the Joneses had the physical strength to help.

The teachers worked to strengthen the community during the year, and the Joneses developed questionnaires and distributed them throughout the area to solicit information that would help them evaluate the school's work and guide them in programming school activities. They wanted to determine what home improvements had been made and what had been done to improve the children's minds. In addition to teaching classes, Grace Jones formed mothers' clubs, went into the community to work with local women, organized sewing, cooking, and canning groups, and gave home and group instruction in these activities. These are examples of the mothers' clubs that had earlier been prevalent throughout the black South. She also helped Laurence Jones hold farmers' conferences. Both types of groups were well attended. Local men and women were invited to the campus, where they would attend classes. These classes were often crowded,

sometimes reaching sixty members in size, and added to the Joneses' already heavy workload.

The work of the Joneses and Piney Woods was threatening to whites in the segregated community. But Grace Jones realized early on that they had to live in a white world and that prejudices were deeply imbedded in the community. She shared her husband's appreciation and love for the whole human race and expressed it by acts of kindness and neighborliness.

Despite years of poverty at the school, it was clear that Piney Woods would continue, but the school still needed a board of trustees and a state charter. On May 17, 1913, the charter was drawn, signed, and submitted to the governor of Mississippi. Piney Woods Country Life School, located in the Braxton community—the hill country of Rankin County—legally and formally came into existence. Its purpose, as cited in Jones's book, was "to establish, maintain, and develop a country-life school" where educators would "train the head, heart, and hands of colored boys and girls for a life of Christianity, character, and service." Tuition would be low, for the school made every reasonable effort to educate the poor people of the Black Belt South.

The following summer Laurence and Grace Jones signed up for the Redpath Chautauqua Circuit, a public speaking tour that would enable them to take the school's story north and earn money to help the school that fall. As they traveled, they were exposed to the usual prejudices and humiliations and denied access to restrooms, food, and hotel service. According to Beth Day in *The Little Professor of Piney Woods,* on one occasion Grace Jones, unable to find sleeping accommodations, had been forced to spend the night with a "woman of questionable reputation." They soon built up a circle of acquaintances who shared their homes with them.

When the United States entered World War I, family and school responsibilities prevented Laurence Jones from entering officers' training camp at Des Moines, Iowa. He satisfied his patriotic impulses by serving as the county and state speaker for Liberty Loans, chairperson of the black Red Cross for Rankin and Simpson counties, and assistant director of the Armenian Relief Campaign in the state. He was also the only black executive of the First United War Work Drive in Mississippi.

The school's first class, made up of six students, graduated in 1918. From then on, Laurence and Grace Jones and the other teachers saw the fruits of their labor reflected in the successes of their students. For example, Georgia Lee Myers, a 1919 graduate, went on to build three rural schools with the help of the Julius Rosenwald Fund. Then she returned to Piney Woods to head the elementary department.

The school still struggled, and in 1919 Laurence and Grace Jones decided to go north again to raise funds. Jones was torn between leaving her two small boys behind and soliciting funds to save the school. According to Beth Day, she told another teacher, a Miss James, "I don't feel that I have the right to let my two stand in the way of two or three hundred who so need what I can do for them." On a whirlwind campaign, the Joneses spoke as many as four times daily and coaxed, begged, and cajoled people to support the school. Between lectures, Grace Jones went from store to store picking up a dime here, a quarter there, from those who listened. Within a few days they had enough money to send bank drafts back to the school to rebuild the boys' dormitory, which had burned that year. Almost everyone at Piney Woods worked on the building, and by commencement Dulany Hall had been completed. It was decided that it would become a girls' dormitory and the boys would occupy the girls' old facility. After her first year at the school, Miss James, so moved by the work of the Joneses, said, "To have known, and worked with, such people, is to have tasted life's honey."

The Cotton Blossoms Organized

Jones was a multitalented woman. She recognized that many of the students had innate musical ability and she wanted to organize the singers at Piney Woods into a formal group that could help raise money for the school by performing. Laurence Jones had similar feelings about their talent; nevertheless, the singing group had been originally organized as a way for the students to make friends and to advertise the school—raising funds was not its primary purpose. In 1921, when a white visitor asked about the number of students who came to the school untrained yet sang naturally without instruction, according to Day, Laurence Jones commented, "Any four colored boys are a quartet."

Grace Jones decided to take a group of singers with her that summer on her fund-raising tour, thinking that not only would it be a way to raise more money but that it would also be a good opportunity for the students to see the country and meet people. If the group was successful, she would continue the singing engagements during the school year. The school purchased a seven-passenger touring car and Grace Jones's newly organized quartet, The Cotton Blossoms, set out with a repertoire of Negro spirituals. Headed for the North, they would sing as they never had before. Eula Kelly, a young student who moved in with the Joneses as a part of the household, went along to care for the two Jones boys. As the little band rested and Eula watched the boys, Jones drove into the next town to arrange bookings for the day. They would sing up to six performances a day in churches, before civic groups, for private parties, in hotels, or elsewhere. Jones soon learned that they profited more when the group appeared without charge and then, after a stirring performance, she told the school's story and asked for contributions.

The group, often on meager rations, was invited for hot meals with the church folk where they performed. Their tour of Iowa was especially pleasant, since Jones knew people there who would shelter the group from the wet and cold. But as they faced bad weather elsewhere, Jones pleaded for access to church basements, railroad stations, or any dry shelter, or they simply stacked up in the car until they could travel on.

The summer was a success. Jones's personal contacts and the emotional appeal of the singers enabled her to raise far more money than expected. Those who expressed an interest in the group were added to a mailing list to receive the

school's news publication, *The Pine Torch*. With the funds that Laurence Jones had raised on his own successful campaign added to those that Grace and the singers earned, the school could now afford a second new building, Goodwin Hall.

The Cotton Blossoms actually were comprised of groups of five, six, or seven singers. The groups were all male, all female, or mixed and eventually some groups were comprised exclusively of blind students. Jones had predicted with accuracy the impact of the groups on fund-raising, and they kept a steady flow of money and other gifts coming to the school. This was reminiscent of what the Fisk Jubilee Singers and the Hampton Singers had done for their institutions as musical messengers of goodwill. Where all of the groups were concerned, people in sections of the East thought of the singers as minstrels. By 1927 the big touring car was replaced by "house cars" that took The Cotton Blossoms on tour. According to John Lovell in *Black Song,* Laurence Jones equipped the cars with the comforts of home. Since this antedated the modern trailer, Lovell continued, Laurence Jones "should probably have applied for a patent." Grace Jones took the singers on an eighteen-month tour that ranged from California to New England. They raised thousands of dollars. After Grace Jones died, Eula Kelly, who had finished a business course in Iowa, supervised the singers, and Laurence Jones came to rely heavily upon the various groups, sometimes as many as a dozen at a time, to raise money and to promote interracial goodwill.

Work with Women's Clubs

Despite her involvement with the Piney Woods school and the African Methodist Episcopal church, Jones saw a need for greater community participation. When she was not away with The Cotton Blossoms on singing tours, speaking, or making contacts for tours, she devoted her energy to agitating for prison reforms in Mississippi. Now that World War I was over, there was renewed interest in club work. Jones was president of the Mississippi State Federation of Colored Women from 1920 to 1924, the fifth woman to serve in this position. During her tenure she traveled throughout Mississippi and reorganized the state group, originally formed in 1903, by encouraging existing clubs to grow stronger and establishing new ones as well. During her term of office the women succeeded in their efforts to establish a state commission for blind black residents. Later the commission appropriated three thousand dollars to support efforts already underway at Piney Woods to educate blind youth.

Jones was also active in the National Association of Colored Women's Clubs, of which she was elected statistician in 1925. She joined two other members on a committee to present a petition for a home for delinquents and a probation officer. Among other recommendations, the committee also called for the establishment of a home for delinquent blacks, a colony for the feebleminded, and a school for the blind. Her leadership eventually led to state appropriations in 1940 to build Oakley Training School, a reform school in Mississippi established to keep black youth from the jails and prisons where hardened criminals lived. The school opened in 1943. Despite these numerous activities, Jones still had time to serve as postmistress of Piney Woods in 1924. She also liked to write, and while little is known of her writings or where they were published, it is recorded that she wrote an article entitled "What the Women of Mississippi Are Doing."

Grace Jones showed exhaustion in 1927 after a long tour with The Cotton Blossoms to California and New England. The diagnosis was pneumonia. She died in 1928 in Braxton and was buried at Piney Woods school by an old cedar tree. Laurence Jones fully recognized the importance of Grace Morris Allen Jones to the life of Piney Woods school. He ended his book on Piney Woods with the acknowledgment that, while she was barely mentioned in the book, she had a vital part in the school: "To record . . . [her worth] would make a book itself and then it would be half-told, for it is too great to be fashioned into words. Only the lives of those she has helped express it."

REFERENCES:

Byrd, Rudolph P., ed. *Generations in Black and White.* Athens: University of Georgia Press, 1993.

Davis, Elizabeth Lindsay. *Lifting as They Climb.* Washington, D.C.: National Association of Colored Women, 1933.

Day, Beth. *The Little Professor of Piney Woods.* New York: Julian Messner, 1955.

Handy, D. Antoinette. *Black Women in American Bands and Orchestras.* Metuchen, N.J.: Scarecrow Press, 1981.

Jones, Laurence C. *Piney Woods and Its Story.* New York: Fleming H. Revell, 1922.

Lovell, John, Jr. *Black Song: The Forge and the Flame.* New York: Macmillan, 1972.

Mather, Frank Lincoln, ed. *Who's Who of the Colored Race.* Vol. 1. Chicago: Frank Mather, 1915.

Wesley, Charles Harris. *The History of the National Association of Colored Women's Clubs.* Washington, D.C.: NACW, 1984.

Who's Who in Colored America. New York: Who's Who in Colored America Corporation, 1927.

Who's Who in Colored America. New York: Who's Who in Colored America Corporation, 1929.

Jessie Carney Smith

Sarah Gibson Jones
(c. 1843-1938)
Educator, school founder, journalist, poet, lecturer, clubwoman

A multitalented woman, Sarah Jones was well-respected as a school teacher, poet, lecturer, and leader in the black women's club movement in Ohio. In recognition of her poetry, the Ohio State Federation of the National Association of Colored Women's Clubs named her poet laureate.

Sarah Emily Gibson Jones was born in Alexandria, Virginia, on April 13, 1843 or 1845, the third of eleven children born to Daniel and Mary Gibson. Although little information about her parents is available, it is known that her father was an intellectual who read widely in English literature. Monroe Majors wrote in his *Noted Negro Women* that her mother was "a quiet and practical woman, gentle, firm and efficient." Since education was important to them, in 1849 Jones's parents moved to Cincinnati, where they expected the schools would offer their children a better education than they would have received in Alexandria. Sarah Jones began her studies in a private school; she was taught first by a Mrs. Hallam and later by a Mrs. Corbin, who came from an old white Cincinnati family. Her parents paid twenty-five cents per week for her education. Later on she attended free public schools.

Jones became a teacher in Newton, Ohio, in 1860, then later took a position as a governess for a family who lived near Oxford. Following that experience, she opened a private school in her home. In September 1863, after receiving a teaching appointment in the Cincinnati schools, she closed her school.

Two years later, in 1865, she married M. P. H. Jones, twenty years her senior and the younger son of Samuel Jones, a pioneer Baptist minister in Ohio. Her husband, whom Majors called "a gentleman of fine literary attainments," was a clerk on the "colored" school board. He died on October 3, 1891, after a lingering illness. Two of their three children died in infancy, and their surviving son, Joseph Lawrence, became a talented businessman in Cincinnati.

Sarah Gibson Jones

Sarah Jones continued teaching, working in Cincinnati's Eastern District School for five years, in Mt. Health for two years, and then in Walnut Hills, near Columbus, Ohio, until 1875. In that year she returned to Cincinnati and taught in Douglass School, where she would remain for thirty-six consecutive years. When she retired in 1911, she ended a forty-eight-year teaching career. In Ruth Neely's book *Women of Ohio,* it is stated that she "ranked among the best educators in the state, not alone because of her ability as an instructor but also through the example she set for youth." She was also the first black teacher to participate in the state's teacher's pension plan.

Publishes Writings

Not only was Jones a talented teacher, she had excellent writing skills as well. In 1862 she worked with J. P. Sampson, editor of the *Colored Citizen,* and wrote a number of articles on various topics. She also contributed to the *Christian Recorder* and the *Indianapolis World.* She was a woman who appreciated fine literary works. When Julia Ringwood Coston founded *Ringwood's Afro-American Journal of Fashion* in 1891, which, according to Lawson Scruggs in *Women of Distinction,* aimed "to satisfy the common desire among us for an illustrated journal of our own ladies," a number of readers and subscribers wrote to give their evaluation of the magazine. In *Noted Negro Women,* Majors published Jones's March 1, 1892, letter to Coston indicating that she was pleased with the publication and hoped it would be successful. A subscriber who then lived in Walnut Hills, Ohio, Jones was

particularly concerned about the talented members of the black race whose work and reputation had received only local notice.

> We have among us here and there women and men of considerable literary ability and sterling moral worth, of whom we may be proud, who have . . . led lives of such seclusion that they are not known beyond the locality in which they reside by name, yet whose influence has been wielded for good, and who should not be encouraged to remain in obscurity.

The talented Jones, known for her public readings, was often sought out by churches, literary societies, and other groups to give presentations. After writing a lecture in 1883, she set out on a lecture circuit that included appearances before sizeable audiences in such cities as Dayton, Zanesville, Cincinnati, and Walnut Hills. Her lecture schedule, however, became too time-consuming for one already fully employed as a teacher, and she decided to discontinue touring.

Jones Named Poet Laureate

The Ohio State Federation of the National Association of Colored Women's Clubs (NACW) was officially recognized in July 1901 at the NACW annual convention held in Buffalo, New York. Carrie W. Clifford was the founding president of the Ohio organization. Clifford also founded a newspaper known as the *Queens Garden,* financing it herself for a while. When the state convention met later that year, the delegates voted to assume publication of *Queens Garden* as the official organ of the state federation. In 1906, at the state convention held in Lima, Jones was honored for her literary work and named poet laureate for the Ohio federation—an honor she held until her death. She had written most of the songs used in the Ohio federation's meetings, and many poems for the paper and for other occasions as well. In *Women of Ohio* she was called "a poet of rare ability." Hallie Q. Brown, in *Homespun Heroines,* published "Ode to Woman," a poem of Jones's that celebrates women.

> All to Woman! the mother of man,
> Whose worth can never be measured.
> Her moral and mental and physical life
> As mother, or sister, or sweetheart or wife,
> And oft, too, as friend, is e'er treasured.

When the seventh annual convention of the Ohio federation was held in Toledo in 1907, Jones was named first vice president. She was among the original group of clubwomen who organized the Home for Aged Colored Women.

Apparently Jones had a full life; although she stopped her public lectures while she was teaching, she still had time for community service. In 1884 she was appointed a "lady manager" of the Colored Orphan Asylum, a position that she held for a number of years. During World War I she was president of the Soldiers Comfort Club. Among other activities, the club members sent sweaters and other provisions to soldiers in Hamilton County. She was also president of the Progress Club of Cincinnati.

An active member of Union Baptist Church since her youth, Jones taught Sunday school, sang in the choir, and served in other capacities. She was very religious and believed that the world should have "one faith and one baptism." After a nine-year illness, Jones died on October 21, 1938. Though often called a "noble woman," she apparently was misunderstood at times by those who knew her and was the target of malicious gossip for an undisclosed cause. She is known in Ohio history for her contributions as a teacher, poet, journalist, lecturer, and community servant.

REFERENCES:

Alexander, Charles. "The Ohio Federation at Dayton." *Alexander's Magazine* 1 (August 15, 1905): 7-21.

Alexander, F. M. W. "Conventions Held by Our Women." *Alexander's Magazine* 4 (September 15, 1907): 269-73.

Brown, Hallie Q., ed. *Homespun Heroines and Other Women of Distinction.* Xenia, Ohio: Aldine Publishing Co., 1926.

Majors, Monroe. *Noted Negro Women.* Chicago: Donohue and Henneberry, 1893.

Neely, Ruth, ed. *Women of Ohio: A Record of Their Achievements in the History of the State.* Vol. 1. Chicago: S. J. Clarke, c. 1939.

Scruggs, Lawson. *Women of Distinction.* Raleigh, N.C.: Lawson Scruggs, 1893.

Wesley, Charles Harris. *The History of the National Association of Colored Women's Clubs.* Washington, D.C.: NACW, 1984.

Jessie Carney Smith

Star Jones

(1962-)

Lawyer, television correspondent, television host

Star Jones has come a long way from the very small town of Badin, North Carolina, where she was christened with the name Starlet. According to Jones, her mother gave her the unique name because of the twinkle in her eyes. In a March 9, 1992, *New York* magazine interview, Jones said:

> My mother swears that when I was born I had very, very black eyes and little tiny sparkles in them, and she said, "She's my little star." . . . Can you imagine this is a lawyer's name? It sounds like a stripper's name.

But Shirley Jones Byard was right, for her little Starlet did grow up to become a bona fide star, first as a commentator on *Court TV* then as an NBC legal correspondent, and now as the host of her own show, *Jones and Jury,* a cable-channel program that films actual court cases.

A feature story in the April 13, 1992, *People Weekly* magazine traced the career of Star Jones, a young lawyer who burst onto the national television scene in 1991. Born in 1962, she lived in Badin until her mother graduated from college and took Star and her sister, Sheila, from their grandmother's home to begin a new life in Trenton, New Jersey. Jones's mother, Shirley, married James Byard, chief of security for the city of Trenton. Jones holds her stepfather in high regard and said in the *People Weekly* interview, "I'm 100 percent closer to my stepfather. . . . My mother has given me my personality, but my stepfather has given me my heart."

The sacrifices that Shirley Byard made by leaving her daughters in North Carolina were worth it because she was able to secure a well-paying job as a municipal human services administrator and could afford to send the girls to parochial schools. In 1979 Jones enrolled at the American University in Washington, D.C., and she is a 1986 graduate of the University of Houston Law Center. Jones enjoyed her undergraduate years, as she made herself over and worked on her transition from starlet to star. In the *People Weekly* interview, she said, "[I] shortened [my] name to Star and buffed [my] image." She also gained enough clout among her sorority sisters to be elected national vice-president of undergraduate affairs of Alpha Kappa Alpha Sorority.

In 1986 Jones began working in the Brooklyn district attorney's office as a prosecutor and later as an assistant district attorney. The courtroom was a tailor-made environment for Jones's charismatic personality. She was successful as a prosecutor. Many consider this job to be extremely stressful, but Jones found it very exciting. She has described herself as an expert in the field of one-witness violent crimes, where the jury has no evidence to go on other than the testimony of the one witness, who is the key to the case. Whereas most prosecutors end their involvement in these cases once the verdict is rendered, Jones kept in contact with witnesses afterward and maintained a personal interest in their lives. As a lawyer, she was best known for her high level of commitment to her job and her sensitivity towards the oppressed. But her charisma was what brought her to the attention of the television program *Court TV,* for which she was first a guest and then a studio commentator during the William Kennedy Smith rape trial. In February 1992 NBC offered Jones a six-figure contract to become the network's legal correspondent. During the rape case against boxer Mike Tyson and the Rodney King police brutality trial in Los Angeles, Jones was highly visible on the *Today Show* and the *NBC Nightly News* broadcasts as the major interpreter of court proceedings.

Although it seemed that Jones focused on the high-profile celebrity cases, she defended her assignments as crucial to providing viewers with the information they wanted to know. She told Degen Pener for a March 9, 1992, *New York* magazine interview,

> I think people are watching trials because they want to know, Is there fairness in our criminal justice

system? Do you have to have money to get off? Is there racial prejudice? Does a woman's word carry as much weight as a man's word?

Responding to her detractors, who labeled her the next Oprah Winfrey, Jones told the same interviewer, "I've actually had my hands in it. I'm not a talking head."

Jones and Jury Show Begins

On September 12, 1994, Jones's syndicated show, *Jones and Jury,* premiered on cable television channels across the nation. The show is similar to *The People's Court,* but Jones notes a major difference: on her program there is an actual jury. On *Jones and Jury,* members of the audience are sworn in as the jury and their verdict is the final legal decision. She firmly believes that her show will not only serve the public but also educate viewers. Because the 120-member audience is really the legal jury, the participants bringing their grievances to her small-claims court must abide by the jury's rulings.

One of Jones's major goals is to improve the image of the legal profession and, to that end, she employs procedures designed to influence the way viewers perceive lawyers. For example, Jones translates the language of the law into her version of common everyday language, which she calls "Starspeak." The jurors are allowed to ask questions of litigants and witnesses after hearing Jones's cross-examinations. Another goal is to ensure that her show enables viewers to learn how the law can serve them as average citizens. The cases that are litigated are ones to which ordinary people can relate, such as a suit against a termite company for causing the death of the family dog and a case in which an Alzheimer's victim was being sued by her daughter.

Jones also participates in professional activities that are not related to the field of law. During the summer of 1994, she served as a panelist for the UNITY '94 convention in Atlanta, Georgia. The week-long event was attended by over six thousand minority journalists from four minority journalist organizations: the Asian American Journalists Organization, the National Association of Black Journalists, the Native American Journalists, and the National Association of Hispanic Journalists. Jones's panel dealt with the issue of racial insensitivity, with emphasis on the furor created by *Time* magazine's distortion of the cover photograph of O. J. Simpson. Her fellow panelists were Jesse Jackson (minister and politician, representing the Rainbow Coalition), James Gaines (*Time* magazine), and Donna Britt (*Washington Post*).

Jones described herself in the April 13, 1992, issue of *People* as being "more comfortable talking than doing anything else." When she moved to NBC, the issue of how she would handle her new fame arose. She assured a reporter for *People* that her family would keep her in line. In the same article, while admitting that her mother thought her to be "the best thing since swinging doors," Jones confessed that her sister was not all that impressed with her since she had not made the cover of the *National Enquirer* for some highly implausible reason. Photographs of Jones show a full-figured woman with flawless brown skin and a well-coiffed hairstyle,

wearing high-fashion, tailored suits adorned by flamboyant jewelry. She has admitted a fondness for frequenting New York's Zabar's delicatessen—as well as a desire to lose weight. Jones has presumably found a substitute for Zabar's since she has relocated to Los Angeles, California, where her new show is taped. She still enjoys listening to jazz, a lifelong passion, and has been transformed into a genuine "Angeleno" since she now has a pool where she and her friends hang out. Nonetheless, it will most likely be those sparkling eyes that earned her the name Starlet that *Jones and Jury* viewers will keep foremost in their minds. One of her former colleagues said of Jones: "She walks into a room and lights it up." Unquestionably, Jones is charismatic. But not only does she entertain viewers, she educates them and defends the legal profession and its practitioners. A lawyer and experienced legal correspondent, Star Jones is not just a "talking head."

REFERENCES:

Allis, Tim, and Sabrina McFarland. "Star Quality: Ex-Prosecutor Star Jones Soars as NBC's Legal Eagle." *People Weekly* 37 (April 13, 1992): 91-92.
"Go Channel Surfing for Fall's Syndicated Shows." *Nashville Tennessean,* September 5, 1994.
Gregory, Deborah. "Star Jones." *Essence* 25 (January 1995): 42.
"Minority Journalists Meet for First Time to Gain Fairness and Power in Media." *Jet* 86 (August 15, 1994): 14-17.
Ozemhoya, Carol U. "Look Who's Talking." *Upscale* 6 (August 1994): 62-65.
Pener, Degen. "Star Power for NBC." *New York* 25 (March 9, 1992): 22.
"Star Jones, in Defense of Lawyers." *USA Today,* September 2, 1994.
"Who's News." *USA Weekend/Nashville Tennessean,* September 9-11, 1994.

Dolores Nicholson

Florence Griffith Joyner
(1959-)
Athlete

Florence Griffith Joyner's contribution to the world of sports is unique. Dubbed Flojo, the fastest running woman in the world brought glamour and pizzazz to track and field events. In the 1988 Summer Olympics her record-breaking speed won her three gold medals. But she also captured the attention of sports reporters and fans alike when she appeared in see-through body suits, one-legged leotards and bikini briefs. Her make-up was glamorous down to her fingertips, which were manicured and exotically polished. For

Florence Griffith Joyner

this woman athlete to look good is to run well, and to feel like a winner she has to do both.

Joyner was born Delorez Florence Griffith in Los Angeles, California, on December 21, 1959, the seventh of eleven children. Her mother, Florence Griffith, was a seamstress, and her father, Robert Griffith, an electronics technician. Her parents divorced in 1963 when Joyner was four years old. Mrs. Griffith moved from the Mohave Desert to Los Angeles, where she settled with her family in the Jordan Downs housing project in Watts.

To avoid being confused with her mother, throughout her childhood Florence was called DeeDee. Close friends and family still call her that today. Life for the Griffith family was difficult. In an August 1, 1988, *Newsweek* article Joyner recalled days when they ate "oatmeal for breakfast, lunch, and dinner" but added that there were no days when they were without food. Her mother always seemed able to overcome obstacles, to make a way out of no way.

One way Florence Griffith worked out her family problems was in church. A deeply religious woman, when she moved to Los Angeles and faced life as a single parent of eleven children, she joined St. James African Methodist Episcopal (AME) Church. Here she brought her children for their religious training and here she found spiritual and community support to sustain her. Prayer and daily Bible reading was the custom in the Griffith household.

Joyner began school at the Ninety-second Street Elementary, where she started running track in second grade at age seven. She chose running for a sport because it was free,

no special equipment was needed, and, as she said in the *Chicago Tribune,* July 18, 1988, she could just "get in the wind." She also chose this sport because it was one in which only one of her siblings participated. Joyner often practiced running when she visited her father in the Mohave Desert. Chasing jack rabbits prepared her to win the 50- and 70-meter dashes at Ninety-second Street and at Markham Junior High School.

As a member of the Sugar Ray Robinson Youth Foundation, Joyner was encouraged by Anne Hall, the Watts youth director, to focus on her running style. Joyner excelled in all her races, beating both girls and boys. Sugar Ray was an organization for disadvantaged youth in Los Angeles. Joyner spent weekend outings with the group and once met Sugar Ray Robinson in person but was too shy to "ever look him in the eye," as she recalled in the July 25, 1988, *Sports Illustrated.*

The quiet but poverty-stricken ghetto of Watts changed drastically in the mid- to late-1960s. In August 1965, Watts was the scene of the first of several urban riots that occurred during the 1960s. Riots shook the area again in 1968, following the assassination of Martin Luther King, Jr. What once was a poor but cohesive community became a ticking time bomb of frustrated, angry, unemployed people who had lost hope in civil rights and black power. Their despair produced a breeding ground for drugs and violence. A dramatic rise in crime and gang membership characterized the 1970s Watts neighborhood where Joyner grew up.

Develops Diverse Interests

While she was in high school, Joyner's many interests and her family, which included her maternal grandmother, Gertrude Scott, a beautician, kept her too busy to get into trouble. She learned to crochet, knit, style hair, and manicure nails. When she was not running she was doing someone's hair, and when she was not occupied as a hairdresser, she read poetry and kept a diary. On Wednesday nights the family held its weekly powwows. Each member of the family was expected to read from the Bible and to confess her or his wrongdoings over the past week. Joyner often sought escape from these disciplinary sessions but was usually captured by a sibling and brought to center circle.

Florence Griffith supported all of her daughter's interests except watching television. She encouraged her daughter to be herself, no matter how eccentric that might be. One example of Joyner's nonconformist nature is that instead of the family dog, she wanted a boa constrictor for a pet. While household rules were strict—no television during the week and lights out by ten o'clock—Joyner was allowed her choice of a pet. Her boa, named Brandy, often frightened her high school friends and offered as much protection as any canine companion.

Joyner views her upbringing as strict, but she said in *Newsweek,* "Everybody in the family survived. Nobody does drugs, nobody got shot at. [I]t was because we were afraid of Mama's voice. We didn't know how poor we were. We were rich as a family."

Track Star Sets New Records

In 1974, Joyner won her track competition in the annual Jesse Owens National Youth Games, which allowed her an all-expense-paid trip to a track meet in San Francisco. She won again in 1975. Following her second victory, Jesse Owens, the 1936 Olympic track gold medalist known as "the Ebony Antelope" congratulated her in person. But he was also the one to tell her she could not attend the track meet for the regional competition in Texas because she had won the previous year. Joyner, never having traveled outside of California, was terribly disappointed and recalls disliking Jesse Owens until she found out later he was the winner of four gold medals.

Joyner excelled in track and field events through high school, setting school records in the sprints and long jump. In June 1978 she graduated from David Starr Jordan High School. That fall she enrolled at California State College, Northridge. She completed her freshman year but could not afford to return in the fall of 1979. She worked as a bank teller and hoped to be able to save enough money to return to school the following year. Fortunately a young sprint coach at Northridge, Bobby Kersee, was interested in her as a potential member of his team. He sought her out and helped her apply for financial aid. She returned to Cal State, Northridge, and majored in business. Performing well academically, she earned a 3.25 grade point average. But when Kersee accepted the job of assistant coach at UCLA, Joyner was forced to make a choice. UCLA did not offer business as a major. However, she decided that Kersee was the best coach for her and that working with him would improve her running. Joyner admits in *Sports Illustrated,* "I chose athletics over academics."

In 1980, Joyner reluctantly followed Kersee to UCLA. She changed her major to psychology. The move was good for her track career because it placed her in competition with the best runners in the United States. Joyner decided to compete for the Olympics. She set her goal for the 1980 Summer Olympics and narrowly missed making the Olympic team, placing fourth in the 200-meter event at the Olympic trials. Valerie Brisco came in third. Brisco and Joyner were rivals from their days in high school. As things turned out, the United States boycotted the 1980 Olympics because of the Soviet invasion of Afghanistan.

Looking back, Joyner is glad she joined Kersee's World Class Track Club at UCLA. She recalled in *Sports Illustrated,* "The team at UCLA was so much fun. We'd get together for Bobby's birthday. We'd pitch in to buy him a suit, to make him presentable for the indoor season." But some of her teammates thought *her* unpresentable. They described her extremely long fingernails as talons, and one teammate even said to her, "We all know you are different. Why do you have to show it?" But Joyner was unfazed by the remarks. She had always created her own style and what other people thought mattered little. She has described herself as shy and usually quiet, but at the same time she is bold in her nonconformity. She remembers how shy she was in elementary school but also recalls how she used to braid her hair in one braid that stood straight up on top of her head. The children laughed at her and she laughed too but never changed her hairdo.

In 1981 Joyner was a member of the U.S. 400-meter relay team for the World Cup. The team established an American record of 42.82 seconds. In 1982 Joyner won the NCAA 200-meter, but in 1983, Merlene Ottey defeated her in the NCAA 200-meter championship. That year, however, Joyner won the NCAA 400-meter in 50.96 seconds. This was the fastest time for an American woman at that time.

On a warm June day in 1983, the Griffith clan gathered in Westwood to watch DeeDee receive her bachelor of arts degree in psychology from the University of California at Los Angeles. Armed with a college degree that she thought enabled her to do nothing but go to graduate school, Griffith realized she had come to a crossroads in her life. Her interests did not lie in the field of psychology; therefore, she decided not pursue a graduate degree. Multitalented and energetic, Joyner tried to do too many things at the same time. She trained for the 1984 Olympics and worked styling people's hair, designing clothes, and writing.

Joyner placed second in the 200-meter at the Summer Olympic Games in Los Angeles, behind teammate Valerie Brisco-Hooks. Joyner was ranked second worldwide among women track stars by *Track and Field News* in 1984 and 1985. Second place did not feel good to her. The news media made it worse by always comparing Brisco-Hooks and Joyner.

Joyner Deals with Defeat

Even though Joyner won a silver medal for sprinting the 200-meter in 22.04 seconds, she was almost a fourth of a second behind Brisco-Hooks's time of 21.81 seconds, as the media constantly reminded her. Emotionally, Joyner was more than disappointed. Joyner wanted to beat her long-time rival, but more than that she wanted to be number one. Her number two placing depressed her and lessened her ability to focus. Joyner seemed caught in a holding pattern.

Following the 1984 Olympics, Joyner took a job as a customer service representative with the Union Bank Company of Los Angeles. She worked nights braiding people's hair. Joyner was engaged to marry Greg Foster, an Olympic hurdler, but found herself thinking less about marriage and her fiancé than a woman in love normally would. Therefore, in 1986, she broke her engagement to Foster. She was practically in retirement. Her training was sporadic and she gained an excessive amount of weight.

At the Crossroads: Choosing the Way

By 1987, Joyner had managed to work through some of her anger and disappointment at placing second in the 1984 Olympics. She told Craig Masback for *Ms.* magazine, October 1988, "When you've been second-best for so long, you can either accept it, or try to become the best. I made the decision to try and be the best in 1988." Another issue for Joyner was her desire to pursue her other interests. She wanted to try her talents at acting, writing books, and designing fashions; in addition, she liked creating elaborate hairstyles, and she wanted to have children. How, she wondered, could she do all of this and still make the sacrifice in time and effort to become number one? She knew, however, that if she did not try, she would never be satisfied with any of her other interests. She had to win the gold in order to free herself to do other things. She had to be number one in order to get on with the rest of her life.

Clearly resolved to win, she approached her old friend and coach Bob Kersee and asked him to help her train for the 1988 Olympic trials. Willing to help, Kersee insisted that she would have to dig deep and bring forth all she had inside. She would have to adhere to a rigorous regime. Joyner promised to make training her top priority.

About this time, Al Joyner, the 1984 Olympic triple jump gold medalist and older brother of Jacqueline Joyner-Kersee, heptathlon world record holder, began his all-out campaign to win Joyner's heart. She told Kenny Moore in *Sports Illustrated,* "He devoted so much time to me I was overwhelmed. He's so positive. He's the guy I dreamed about."

With Kersee's expert coaching and Al Joyner's moral support Joyner placed second to Silke Gladisch of East Germany in the 1987 World Championship 200 in Rome. Joyner's special diet of vitamins, amino acids, and water gave her strength. All summer Al helped her to train, and in July he asked her to marry him. She knew he was honest and patient, and her family, which included thirty nieces and nephews, thought he was wonderful, yet she hesitated and would not give him an answer. Al felt she was testing him, so he patiently waited.

The answer came one Sunday afternoon. After church she and Joyner took Khalisha, her niece, and Larry, her nephew, to Chuck E. Cheese's Pizza Place. Ten-year-old Khalisha kept urging her aunt to tell Joyner she would accept his marriage proposal. Khalisha knew he had asked her aunt because she had engineered that too. But Al was easier to coach than her aunt. Larry Wiggs, Khalisha's eight-year-old brother, won a prize playing skee-ball, a little rubber key chain spelling out the word "yes." Khalisha grabbed the prize from him and rushed to where the two adults sat. Pushing the little yellow rubber prize into her aunt's hand she told her it was the perfect answer. The bright yellow and unique style of the "yes" was Joyner's style and Khalisha knew it. Joyner took Al's hand and wrapped his fingers around the rubber charm. When he opened his hand and saw the "yes" he was both happy and relieved.

Delorez Florence Griffith and Alfredrick Alphonzo Joyner married in Las Vegas on October 10, 1987. The couple moved to an apartment in Van Nuys, California. One room was filled with wedding pictures and photo albums that held the memories of October 10. Another room contained toys, in unopened boxes, and baby clothes, both boys' and girls', for the family they intended to have when she slowed down.

Joyner continued to train and her husband paced her. The day came when Al could no longer beat Joyner in the 100 yards. A typical day for Joyner included four hours of work at Anheuser-Busch, where she performed clerical duties in the employee relations department; a four-hour workout, usually supervised by her husband instead of Kersee, including one and a half hours in the weight room; rushing home to prepare dinner; and perhaps a braiding job in the evening, which could take anywhere from three hours to seven and could earn her from seventy-five to two-hundred dollars. When she was not braiding hair, she was designing clothes. She ended each day with another workout, either running or doing leg curls on the hamstring-leg extension machine that takes the place of her kitchen table.

FloJo Goes for the Gold

In July 1988 at the Olympic trials in Indianapolis, Joyner's rigorous training and mental focus paid off. In a stunning lacy outfit she called an "athletic negligee," she broke Evelyn Ashford's world record of 10.76 for the 100-meter by running it in 10.49. Her time was amazing. But, according to Moore in *Sports Illustrated,* what was even more surprising to those who watched her was the idea that "a beautiful woman in lingerie can run as fast as all but a handful of men." Joyner believes her one-legged suits and flashy colors actually enable her to run better. She said in the July 25, 1988, *Sports Illustrated* article, "Colors excite me. Sprinting is excitement."

At the 1988 Summer Olympics in Seoul, South Korea, Joyner could not wear her energizing bodysuits. Olympic rules require every participant to wear the standard-issue uniform. During the 100-meter quarterfinals Joyner finished with a record-breaking time of 10.62 seconds. In the semifinal she beat her closest competitor, Heike Drechsler, who sprinted in at 10.91. Joyner came in at 10.70 seconds. Her husband was so excited by her speed he jumped up to chase her, leaving their belongings unprotected. When he returned someone had stolen their camera.

Refusing to be uniform, Joyner came to the final with her long nails sparkling in the sun. One was painted with the Olympic gold rings on a red background, one said "U.S.A.," one was polka dots, and one said "gold" on a blue background. The race began and Joyner chased down a twenty-year dream. At 70 meters she knew she had caught the dream that had eluded her in 1984. She ran the 100-meter in 10.54 seconds. But the time was not recorded as an official Olympic record. A tail wind of three meters per second disqualified the time, so her 10.62 time from the quarterfinals would be used. Joyner won the gold for the 100-meter race.

In the 200-meter Joyner set a world record and won the gold with a time of 21.34 seconds. She won another gold medal in the 400-meter relay. Finally she took a silver medal for the 1600-meter relay. In four days she had broken four records. Joyner won more medals than any American woman track athlete ever had. The Associated Press named Joyner Female Athlete of the Year for 1988, and she also received the Sullivan Award, given annually to an American amateur athlete who by performance, example, and good influence promotes the ideal of good sportsmanship. Joyner has been harassed by rumors that her remarkable performance was due to the use of steroids. The charges, however, were never substantiated, and Joyner vigorously denies them.

On February 25, 1989, having reached her goal of being number one and at the height of her career, Joyner announced her retirement from track and field. She was now free to pursue her many other interests. The Joyners' first child, Mary Ruth, was born in 1990. President Bill Clinton appointed Joyner chair of the President's Council on Physical Fitness in 1993.

Current Address: 11444 West Olympic Blvd., Los Angeles, CA 90064.

REFERENCES:

Axthelm, Pete. "The Fastest Woman Ever: Florence Griffith Joyner Sets the Trials on Fire." *Newsweek* 112 (August 1, 1988): 61.

Current Biography Yearbook, Vol. 48. New York: H. W. Wilson Co., 1989.

Masback, Craig A. "Siren of Speed." *Ms.* 17 (October 1988): 34.

Moore, Kenny. "Get Up and Go Flo, Go." *Sports Illustrated* 69 (July 25, 1988): 160.

———. "Heart and Seoul." *Sports Illustrated* 69 (August 1, 1988): 16-23.

———. "Very Fast, Very Fast." *Sports Illustrated* 69 (September 14, 1988): 158-62.

Smith, Jessie Carney, ed. *Epic Lives: One Hundred Black Women Who Made a Difference.* Detroit: Visible Ink Press, 1992.

"Time Bandits Make the Team: Sprinters Eke Out Split Seconds Wherever They Can." *Chicago Tribune,* July 18, 1988.

Who's Who among Black Americans, 1994-95. 8th ed. Detroit: Gale, 1994.

Nagueyalti Warren

Marjorie Stewart Joyner
(1896-1994)
Entrepreneur, educator, philanthropist

A woman who packed achievements from a half-dozen different careers into a lifetime stretching for nearly a century, Marjorie Stewart Joyner fully deserved her reputation as a legendary figure in the city of Chicago. Joyner's multidimensional achievements have stretched from her early and influential business leadership in the field of black beauty culture to her success as an inventor of new machines and processes in that industry. Through her associations with Madame C. J. Walker and Mary McLeod Bethune, she

Marjorie Stewart Joyner

became nationally recognized as an educator and lecturer, advocating the development of black business and the support of historically black colleges and universities. In Chicago she remains a cherished figure as the symbol of the annual Bud Billiken Parade, the largest African American parade in the United States. That she is known simultaneously as "The Grande Dame of Black Beauty Culture," the "Godmother of Bethune-Cookman College," and the "Matriarch of the Bud Billiken Parade" underscores the diversity of her contributions and the ease with which she moved in both inner-city life and high society.

The daughter of George Emmanuel Stewart and Annie Dougherty Stewart, Joyner was born Marjorie Stewart on October 24, 1896, near Monterey, Virginia, high in the Blue Ridge Mountains. Her father was an itinerant school teacher in Highland County, Virginia, who had worked for a time with Booker T. Washington. Her mother was a housewife who had married her father when she was only fourteen years old and a student in his classroom. Her maternal grandmother, Fannie Allegheny, was a slave of William A. Dougherty, a Highland County landowner; Dougherty was reputed to be Joyner's grandfather. Life in poverty and mountain isolation was difficult for the Stewarts. Of thirteen children born to the couple, only four lived past infancy: Bessie, Mary, Marjorie, and Lucretia.

In 1904 the couple left Monterey for Dayton, Ohio, where George Stewart obtained a position as a teacher at a white preparatory school. Shortly after their arrival in Dayton, the Stewarts separated; they later divorced. Annie Stewart moved to Chicago, and an Ohio court awarded custody of

Marjorie to her father. For the next several years, until 1912, Joyner lived in various places: with an aunt, a grandmother, and the German-Jewish family who ran the school at which her father taught.

In 1912, the same year the Miami River flooded Dayton, Joyner was sent to Chicago to live with her mother. Attempting to finish eighth grade at the Johnstown elementary school, she was regularly interrupted in her studies by having to take temporary jobs: waiting tables, cleaning, and caring for children. She later attended Englewood High School, but did not graduate. During this period she met her future husband, Robert S. Joyner, while roller skating in front of her home. They were married on April 4, 1916, and remained a close couple for fifty-seven years until his death in 1973. Born in Memphis, Tennessee, Robert S. Joyner became a podiatrist and was active in southside Chicago religious and civic circles. The couple had two daughters: Anne Joyner Fook and Barbara Joyner Powell, both educators.

After her marriage, Joyner enrolled in the white-owned A. B. Molar Beauty School, and in 1916 became its first black graduate. She opened her first beauty shop several weeks later at 5448 South State Street, in a mixed black and white neighborhood. Her initial customers were white. A request from her mother-in-law soon changed the direction of her life. As Joyner recalled:

> One day my mother-in-law asked me to do her hair. When I got through with her hair she looked like an accident going somewhere to happen. She said you can't do anything with my hair [but] there is a woman coming to town; her name is Madame Walker. I am going to give you money to go down to her class; she is teaching how to do black hair.

Joyner Collaborates with Madame C. J. Walker

Joyner paid seventeen dollars and fifty cents for a training course with Madame C. J. Walker, a steel comb, and a bag of preparations. She received a certificate as a "Walker agent." For the next three years, until Madame C. J. Walker died in 1919, the two worked closely together on developing the network of Walker agents, beauty schools, and shops in Chicago and across the Midwest.

Within months, Joyner became Madame Walker's chief spokesperson and organizer in Chicago and one of her most trusted aides. Joyner's three years with Madame Walker, her swift ascent to the heights of the developing black beauty culture industry, and the network of friends and associates she made as a result shaped the remainder of her life. By 1919, she became national supervisor for more than two hundred Madame C. J. Walker beauty colleges; she was later named a vice-president of the company and chief instructor of its fifteen thousand Walker agents. She was to remain with the Walker Company for more than fifty years.

Her organizational skills proved phenomenal. According to the Illinois Writers Project's "Negro in Illinois" study, at the height of the Depression the Chicago school had an "average attendance of over 200 students." Joyner demon-

strated "Walker products in a trailer, which she used for travel throughout the country." In 1924 she was one of three women who helped write the first Illinois law governing beauty culture and regulating its schools and salons. Two years later, Joyner became the first black woman to receive her license as a beauty culturist. In later years, she frequently contended that the study of hair had given her "a creative mind" and led her to find "new solutions to problems."

Along with her skills as an entrepreneur and public speaker, she now became known as an inventor. Her dissatisfaction with the length of time it took to complete a permanent wave with the method Madame Walker had taught her spurred Joyner to invent a permanent wave machine in 1928. The accepted method treated the hair piece by small piece. In a recent article in the *Reader* she said:

> I naturally saw a need for something that would hasten the procedure. . . . If you could wrap the hair in six or eight sections and apply heat at one time, inside of ten minutes you would have what you would have had if you stood there for over an hour using her method.

Joyner sought and received a patent on her machine, based on drawings submitted by her cousin, a teacher at Chicago Normal School. Joyner and close associates continued to use the machine, although it was never placed on the market due to lack of capital. In 1987, the Smithsonian Institution, as part of its exhibit on black migration, displayed Joyner's permanent wave machine and a complete replica of her original 1916 salon. According to an article in *Beauty Classic,* the display contained many original items, including "two operator's chairs, a beauty shop sign, beauty products, photographs, a diploma, and artifacts of hair styling implements. These tools beautified the locks of many noted personalities, such as Marian Anderson, Dinah Washington, Billie Holliday, and many more."

Over the next twenty-five years, Joyner developed a stream of new products for the Walker Company. Her most popular, "Satin Tress," the predecessor of today's relaxers or permanents, was trumpeted by *Ebony* in 1949: "Madame Walker Has New Hairdressing Treatment. Oldest beauty culture firm claims its Satin Tress will revolutionize industry."

Beginning in 1932, Joyner sought to participate in contests sponsored by the white-controlled beauty associations. In an interview, Joyner said that each year her applications were rejected on technicalities, until finally she was told: "'You have to be an American to participate.' I said, I am; all my people were born here. They said, 'Oh, no, you have to be white to be an American.' That's when I decided we needed our own organization."

Joyner Founds Beauty Culture Organizations

Joyner founded two intertwined organizations in 1945: the United Beauty School Owners and Teachers Association and the Alpha Chi Pi Omega sorority and fraternity. These two grew to become the primary organizational expressions of the black beauty culture industry.

With white beauty schools admitting only a token number of black beauticians to learn new techniques, Joyner, at the urging of Mary McLeod Bethune, organized a 1954 trip by 195 cosmetologists to Paris to learn the latest methods. "I vowed," she said in *Ebony* in 1954, "to take the biggest group of Negro beauticians in all of history overseas to learn from the masters themselves." The trip, widely reported in the press both in Europe and the United States, was a public relations dream, bringing deepened professional respect to the black beauticians' organizations. Jill Nelson in *Essence* magazine noted that Paris was not Joyner's only destination: "I traveled for Madame Walker to all the West Indian islands, plus Paris, London, Rome, West Africa and the Holy Land. . . . There was an open market in these countries because no one there, at that time, was dressing colored people's hair.

Although she had not been able to finish high school before her career began, in later years Joyner sought to broaden her own education. In 1924 she became one of the first black graduates of the Chicago Musical College, earning a certificate in dramatic art and expression. By 1935 she attained a diploma from Chicago Christian High School; she took college courses at Northwestern University and the Illinois Institute of Technology before earning her B.S. in 1973, at the age of seventy-seven, from Bethune-Cookman College.

Joyner's association with Mary McLeod Bethune began while Madame C. J. Walker was still alive. Bethune met Joyner on a trip to Chicago and recognized her speaking abilities. Joyner said in an interview that later, when Walker and Bethune were talking, Walker told Bethune:

> "Marjorie is on my payroll. Any time you want her to help you, it won't cost you anything." That's how I became a speaker and fundraiser for Bethune-Cookman College. Dr. Bethune was trying to reach black people for education; I was trying to reach black people for beauty culture, for Mme. Walker. There were few places for a black person to get higher education then. . . . Everything you were trying to do, you had to think up ways to beat this color line, this Jim Crow.

She became one of Bethune-Cookman College's leading fundraisers and advocates, working closely with Eleanor Roosevelt and Nelson Rockefeller to expand the school. The United Beauty School Owners and Teachers donated hundreds of thousands of dollars to the college. In the 1970s, a residence hall there was named for Joyner. According to *Ebony* magazine in 1954, at the end of her life, Bethune wrote to Joyner: "My dear, dear Marjorie. If I had you with me every day . . . we could turn half the world over."

In Dayton Beach, Florida, located in the Jim Crow South, even the elimination of segregated seating at Bethune-Cookman choir concerts became a tension-filled event. One concert attended by Eleanor Roosevelt and Joyner was threatened by the Ku Klux Klan. It is reported that the black men on campus got together and said: "Let the KKK come. They'll never remember getting out."

It was far from Joyner's only experience with Jim Crow in the South. On one trip to speak at a sorority convention in Texas, she was ordered out of the "white" cars as the train prepared to leave Cairo, Illinois. Accustomed to being shuttled to the "colored" car, she was told this time that she would have to leave the train entirely, since no "colored" car was available. Anxious not to miss her speaking engagement, she offered to ride anywhere else, and was sent to the baggage car. She recalled: "I stretched my feet out on a box, and I rode all night in that baggage car. The next morning I found out it was a coffin that I had been leaning against. Even Rosa Parks didn't have to ride with a coffin."

Civil and Political Organizations Attract Joyner

Joyner's association with Bethune and other school benefactors led to her involvement with civil rights and political organizations. When Bethune organized the National Council of Negro Women in 1935, Joyner was one of its founding members. During World War II, Eleanor Roosevelt asked Joyner to help lead the Women's Division of the Democratic National Committee.

By the mid-1930s, in line with a national trend among black voters, Joyner had become closely associated with the Democratic party in Chicago. Mayor Edward Kelly turned to Joyner in 1943 for help in opening a servicemen's center on the south side of the city for black servicemen who were excluded from the white USO clubs. Joyner then opened Servicemen's Center Number 3 and provided top entertainers, including Lena Horne and Duke Ellington. She sold war bonds and drew black churches, politicians, and civic organizations into the work. Her behind-the-scenes efforts to challenge USO segregation, however, failed.

Politically, Joyner remained allied with Congressman William L. Dawson, and later with Chicago mayor Richard J. Daley, breaking stride with the Daley family only when Harold Washington became the city's first black mayor in 1983. Much of her considerable political influence drew on her close association with the *Chicago Defender,* its founder Robert S. Abbott, and his successors. The attorney for the Walker Company, S. B. Ransom, had advised Madame Walker and her daughter, A'Lelia, to work more closely with the newspapers in the black community. By 1920 Ransom asked Joyner to develop a working relationship with Abbott. The relationship developed into one of great mutual trust. In later years, when Abbott's nephew, John Sengstacke (the current president of the *Defender*), graduated from high school, Abbott asked Joyner and Bethune to bring the young man from Savannah, Georgia, to Chicago. Shepherding the nervous Sengstacke into a Pullman car, the two women spent the train journey to Chicago giving him lectures about education and politics.

From its inception in 1929, Joyner headed the *Defender*-sponsored Bud Billiken Parade, often called the largest annual African American parade in the United States. The parade, begun by Abbott as a way to thank *Defender* newsboys, blossomed under Joyner's leadership into a massive community event, complete with floats and invited celebrities. By 1945 she was also named chairwoman of Chicago Defender Charities, the philanthropic arm of the newspaper. In this capacity, she led food and clothing drives and a self-help program in a blighted housing project, and she coordinated flood relief fundraising efforts for the American Red Cross.

Throughout her life, Joyner was active in the affairs of her church. When the AME bishop presiding in Chicago removed a minister she respected, Marjorie Joyner and Robert Joyner assisted the majority of the congregation of Old Saint Mary's AME Church in splitting away to form a new church, Cosmopolitan Community Church. At first, the new congregation met in their dining room. But after Mary G. Evans assumed leadership of the church in 1932 as its pastor, it rapidly expanded, eventually becoming one of the most influential churches in the south side black community. It was rare in the 1930s for a black woman to lead a large congregation. Evans, operating outside denominational controls, was able to build a community house with a gymnasium, day-care facilities and a senior citizens' home. Joyner, a deeply religious woman, always took an active role in Cosmopolitan Community Church. Joyner considered Evans, along with Walker, Bethune, and Abbott, one of the major influences on her life and perspectives.

In her long life, states the *Reader,* Joyner was "almost everywhere and met almost everyone." Her trips to New York for the Walker company regularly brought her into contact with such notables as Adam Clayton Powell, Sr., Father Divine, and Duke Ellington. She met Marcus Garvey, the founder and first president of the Universal Negro Improvement Association, in New York and later traveled to Jamaica to meet with him while demonstrating Walker products in the Caribbean. The Chicago Renaissance of the 1930s and 1940s brought Joyner into close contact with entrepreneurs like Jesse Binga and Anthony Overton; writers like Arna Bontemps, William Attaway, and Roi Ottley; and entertainers of every description. Her many associates have included Ida B. Wells Barnett, Carter G. Woodson, and Jane Addams, as well as presidents Franklin D. Roosevelt, John F. Kennedy, and Jimmy Carter.

Many honors have been bestowed upon Joyner. She was awarded an honorary doctor of humanities degree from Bethune-Cookman College in 1961. The National Council of Negro Women named her one of five outstanding achievers in 1990. That same year Mayor Richard M. Daley declared her birthday "Dr. Marjorie Stewart Joyner Day" in Chicago. Awards, plaques, and photographs from her life covered the walls of her home and were donated to an archive. Her birthday celebration has been a major annual event on Chicago's calendar. In addition to the exhibit on her cosmetology work at the Smithsonian, Joyner has been the subject of major museum exhibits in Chicago at the DuSable Museum, the University of Illinois, and the Chicago Public Library and of television shows on the work of senior citizens.

Joyner was a slight, bent figure who walked with difficulty, but she nevertheless knew how to seize and captivate an audience. When asked to stand and be recognized at a social, political, or educational function, she invariably took the microphone and the opportunity to share anecdotes and advice with those present. "It is always the same story," she said in an interview, "about getting before the public with your message and getting with people."

At age ninety-eight Joyner went to work at the *Chicago Defender* every day, busy with the arrangements for the Bud Billiken Parade and with Defender Charities and responding to the many requests for information about her life. Every Sunday, she attended Cosmopolitan Community Church and actively participated in its affairs. A "renaissance woman" who was truly a pathbreaker in several different fields and a legendary achiever for nearly a full century, Joyner considered her life to be still unfolding. She died of heart failure at her home on South Wabash Avenue in Chicago on December 27, 1994. Her funeral was held at Fellowship Baptist Church on December 31. She was survived by a daughter, Barbara Powell, and several grandchildren and great-grandchildren.

REFERENCES:

"Beauty Pilgrimage." *Ebony* 9 (August 1954): 38-44.

"Bethune-Cookman Honors Dr. Marjorie S. Joyner." *Chicago Defender,* May 15, 1976.

Brown, Michael. "Dr. Joyner To Be Honored on 94th Birthday Today." *Chicago Defender,* October 28, 1990.

Bundles, A'lelia P. *Madame C. J. Walker.* New York: Chelsea House, 1991.

Calloway, Earl. "DuSable Exhibits the Legend of Dr. Marjorie Stewart Joyner." *Chicago Defender,* December 11, 1986.

Carey, Malanna. "The Smithsonian Salutes a Real Pioneer." *Beauty Classic* 4 (January 1987): 30-31, 52.

Colin, Mattie Smith. "Honor Mrs. Joyner, 32 Seniors." *Chicago Defender,* June 5, 1976.

Costonie, Toni. "Memories of an Early Salon." *Shoptalk* 3 (Spring 1984): 88-89.

———. "Renaissance Woman: Marjorie Stewart Joyner." *Renaissance* 1 (November-December 1990): 5-8.

"Council of Negro Women Salutes Achievers." *Jet* 77 (January 15, 1990): 26.

"Integration Comes to the Beauty Business." *Ebony* 21 (August 1966): 140-42.

"Joyner Legend Exhibit Feature." *At Chicago* 3 (January 30, 1985): 1, 8.

Joyner, Marjorie Stewart. Interview with the author. Chicago, Vivian G. Harsh Research Collection of Afro-American History and Literature, May 4, 1993.

Langer, Adam. "You Know, I'm 95 and I Know What I'm Talking About." *Reader* (September 11, 1992): 9, 22-25.

Locke, Henry. "Hail Joyner on 90th." *Chicago Defender,* October 28, 1986.

Macdonald, Anne L. *Feminine Ingenuity: Women and Invention in America.* New York: Ballantine Books, 1992.

"Madame Walker Has New Hairdressing Treatment." *Ebony* 4 (January 1949): 62-64.

"Marjorie Stewart Joyner, 98, Business Leader, Activist, Philanthropist, Dies in Chicago." *Jet* 87 (January 16, 1995): 54.

Nelson, Jill. "The Fortune That Madame Built." *Essence* 14 (June 1983): 84-86, 154-55.

Nichols, J. L., and William H. Crogman, eds. *Progress of a Race or the Remarkable Advancement of the American Negro.* Naperville, Ill.: J.L. Nichols and Co., 1929.

Ortiz, Lou. "Black Cosmetology Pioneer Is a Role Model for Success." *Chicago Sun-Times,* November 18, 1991.

"So This Is Washington. . . ." *Chicago Defender,* May 24, 1958.

Watson, Cordie. "Profiles of a Legend: Exhibit on Dr. Joyner Opens." *Chicago Defender,* February 9, 1985.

Who's Who among Black Americans, 1992-93. Detroit: Gale Research, 1992.

COLLECTIONS:

The Marjorie Stewart Joyner Papers, which include correspondence, photographs, clippings, scrapbooks, and oral history interviews with Joyner, are located in the Vivian G. Harsh Research Collection of Afro-American History and Literature, Chicago Public Library. See also Illinois Writers Project/"Negro in Illinois Papers," also located in the Vivian G. Harsh Research Collection. A replica of Joyner's original 1916 salon and other artifacts and photographs from her work as a cosmetologist are located in the National Museum of American History, Smithsonian Institution.

Michael Flug

Jacqueline Joyner-Kersee
(1962-)
Athlete

Jacqueline Joyner-Kersee is the "First Lady of Sports." When Joyner-Kersee was born, her grandmother took one look at her dark-eyed granddaughter and read the future she saw reflected in the infant's eyes. According to *Sports Illustrated,* August 11, 1986, she predicted, "someday this girl will be the first lady of something [great]" and insisted that her granddaughter be named for Jacqueline Kennedy. At the age of thirty, Jacqueline Joyner-Kersee became the first woman in Olympic history ever to win back-to-back gold medals in the heptathlon—making her the world's greatest woman athlete and superwoman of seven events.

Jacqueline Joyner-Kersee was born on March 3, 1962, in East St. Louis, Illinois. Joyner-Kersee's mother, Mary Joyner, who was seventeen years old when Jacqueline was born, had married Alfred Joyner in 1959, when she was fourteen and he was sixteen. They had four children: one son, Alfred, Jr., and three daughters, Jacqueline, Angela, and Deborah. Jacqueline is the oldest daughter.

Mary Joyner worked as a practical nurse and Alfred Joyner as a construction worker on crews that frequently moved to other cities. He was never able to find permanent work in their hometown. When he quit construction, he became a railroad switch operator but had to work in Springfield, Illinois. The two-hour drive from East St. Louis allowed him to come home only on the weekends.

East St. Louis, even in the early sixties, was a deteriorating, crime-ridden, economically depressed industrial town—a frightening place to live for many of its residents. When Joyner-Kersee was eleven years old she witnessed a murder right in front of her house. The house where she grew up, according to a September 12, 1988, *Maclean's* article, "was little more than wall paper and sticks," with water pipes that froze in winter, forcing the Joyners to heat their bath water on the kitchen stove. In spite of the area where they lived, the Joyners were not a spiritually impoverished family. The children's home training was solid, consisting of a strong work ethic and traditional values, including a strict adherence to conventional gender roles.

The best thing about the East St. Louis neighborhood where the Joyners lived was the Mayor Brown Center, a sports and recreation park directly across the street from their house. Joyner-Kersee's mother insisted that she and her sisters behave in a polite and ladylike way that was thought to be pleasingly feminine. Mary Joyner enrolled her girls in art and dancing classes offered at the Mayor Brown Center, but Joyner-Kersee found these activities neither interesting nor challenging. So while her mother sent her to the center to become a lady, she became an athlete. It was at the center that she discovered competitive sports. Both parents initially disapproved of her interest in track and field; her mother, not surprisingly, found it too masculine for her daughter. But Joyner-Kersee was not to be dissuaded. When she was nine years old she entered her first track competition. She finished last. Her father advised her to quit but she persisted.

Joyner-Kersee believed she would improve, and she did. At her second track meet, she placed second, third, and fourth in separate events. Then, in another meet, she won three seconds. The day finally arrived when she was able to come home and tell her parents she had won five first places. Her parents' attitudes changed. They did everything they could to support her efforts, yet her mother never failed to stress the importance of education. Joyner-Kersee believes she inherited her love for sports from her father, who was a hurdler and a football player in high school. By the time Joyner-Kersee was twelve years old she could leap more than seventeen feet in the long jump. Her ability was so phenomenal she was an inspiration to her older brother, Al, who started competing in track and field events himself.

Joyner-Kersee, as a teenager, thought her mother was extremely old-fashioned. For example, she prohibited her

Jacqueline Joyner-Kersee

daughter from dating until she was eighteen years old. Joyner-Kersee, in fact, thought her mother's rules were not only old-fashioned, but unfair and shortsighted. Actually, Mary Joyner saw for her daughter a kind of existence she herself could never have and determined not to let the distraction of the opposite sex prevent Jacqueline from enjoying a bright and promising future free from too many taxing responsibilities. Joyner-Kersee did not understand her mother's reasoning, but fortunately she did not rebel after her initial resistance. Instead she focused all her energies on athletic and scholastic achievement. When a coach at the Mayor Brown Center informed Joyner-Kersee that the quickest way to the Olympics was through mastery of a variety of specialties, she started training for the five-event pentathlon.

Called Finest Female Athlete in the State

At fourteen Joyner-Kersee entered Lincoln High School and continued to participate in track and field events. She won four consecutive National Junior Pentathlon Championships her first year in high school. She also set a high school record of 20 feet, 7 1/2 inches in the long jump in her junior year of high school. She played volleyball and was a member of the Lincoln High School girl's basketball team. Joyner-Kersee often led the basketball team to victory over its opponents with her average of 52.8 points per game. She became known as the greatest female athlete in the state of Illinois.

In 1980 Joyner-Kersee graduated in the top 10 percent of her class. Because of her grades and athletic ability she received a number of scholarships for basketball and for the pentathlon. Since her favorite sport was basketball, she chose the basketball scholarship offered by the University of California at Los Angeles.

The summer following her high school graduation, Joyner-Kersee competed in the United States Olympic trials and made the team. She improved her record in the long jump by leaping 20 feet, 9 3/4 inches. However, this was the year that the Soviet Union invaded Afghanistan and the United States boycotted the games. Joyner-Kersee's disappointment was eased somewhat by her excitement over attending college in Los Angeles in the fall.

As September finally approached both Joyner-Kersee and her brother, who was returning to Arkansas State University, prepared to leave home. An excited family and an especially proud mother wished them well. In only a few weeks Joyner-Kersee was performing as a star forward for the UCLA Lady Bruins. She maintained a solid B average and decided to major in history and minor in communications.

Pain Used for Gain

In January 1981, just as Joyner-Kersee began her second semester at UCLA in Los Angeles, she received news of her mother's sudden death. Mary Joyner, only in her late 30s, was stricken by a severe attack of spinal meningitis and died. Her mother's death was a crushing blow for the eighteen-year-old. Fortunately, a young assistant coach at UCLA understood what she was experiencing; he too had lost his mother when he was an eighteen-year-old freshman.

With comfort and encouragement from coach Bob Kersee, Joyner-Kersee found she was able to use her grief to gain "a clearer sense of reality," according to the *Maclean's* article. She was just beginning to understand and to appreciate her mother's determination. Now she found that she too had her mother's determined spirit and she would use it to continue with her life. Coach Kersee urged Joyner-Kersee to not allow her multi-event skills to deteriorate. But Joyner-Kersee insisted on concentrating on basketball and the long jump. Kersee not only saw this as a waste of her talents but also knew that the busier he kept the young student-athlete the less likely she would be to succumb to depression over her mother's death.

Kersee took it upon himself to personally coach Joyner-Kersee. He totaled up her best performance in the heptathlon, which includes the 200-meter dash, 100-meter hurdles, 800-meter run, high jump, shot put, long jump, and javelin throw. Her performance in these events showed that without any special training, she was within four hundred points of Jane Fredrick, the United States' 1981 heptathlete. Joyner-Kersee agreed to train for the heptathlon, although she continued to worry that she might spread herself too thin.

Both Joyner-Kersee and her brother, Al, were selected to represent the United States at the track and field world championships in Helsinki, Finland, in 1983. For the first time in her years of competition Joyner-Kersee suffered an injury serious enough to prevent her from competing. She pulled a hamstring muscle, the first of many such injuries. Joyner-Kersee recalled in the February 1987 *Track and Field News,* "The Helsinki meet was the first time I ever encountered an injury . . . that was so bad I couldn't compete. I always felt before that I could overcome any physical problem, but Helsinki was the first time I felt my legs just couldn't go anymore. That blew me away mentally because I never had experienced anything like that before"—even with her asthma she had always been able to manage. From this experience Joyner-Kersee was to learn that there is more to life than setting and accomplishing personal goals, knowledge that enabled her to grow as a person. She came to accept herself as a vulnerable body, not as an athletic machine. And she learned to experience joy in the accomplishments of others, even when missing out on her own.

Athlete Has Moments to Remember

Joyner-Kersee graduated from UCLA in the spring of 1984 with a bachelor of arts in history and a mass communications minor. Her only regret on commencement day was the fact that her mother was not alive to see her walk across the stage and receive her degree. Joyner-Kersee maintained her B average throughout her undergraduate years. Along with earning her degree, she qualified for the United States team selected to compete in the 1984 Olympics. Her brother also qualified.

When the sister-brother team arrived in Los Angeles, Joyner-Kersee was favored to win a gold medal in the heptathlon but her brother Al was not expected to place. However, another hamstring injury sustained a few weeks prior to the Olympic events hampered her performance. Ironically, Joyner-Kersee placed second while her brother won the gold medal in the triple jump. Yet she recalls the 1984 Olympics with great happiness. She told *Ebony* magazine,

> The happiest moment for me was the day my brother, Al, and I both won Olympic medals in Los Angeles in 1984. We were one of the few brother-sister Olympic teams. We both wanted to go, and we both wanted to win gold medals. I won a silver medal for the heptathlon and he won the gold medal for the triple jump. I was much happier to see him win. It was disappointing to lose the gold, but it meant a lot more to me that my brother won the gold medal. There is more to life than personal goals.

Following the Olympics Joyner-Kersee continued to train under the watchful eye of her mentor and coach, Bob Kersee, and on January 11, 1986, after a long friendship, she and Kersee, who is eight years her senior, married. They made their home in a three-bedroom bungalow in Long Beach, California. It is often referred to as the "prison" by the members of Kersee's World Class women's track club, who claim that once inside the house there is no escaping the rigorous routine required of those in training.

For Joyner-Kersee a typical day begins at 7:30 A.M. She exercises by running, has breakfast, and then drives the freeway from Long Beach to UCLA's campus in Westwood, about an hour away. She trains for three or four hours, which includes weight training. Normally she consumes at least sixteen glasses of water a day. By the time her workout is complete it is late afternoon. Joyner-Kersee then drives to her daily appointment with her physical therapist, who works on any sore or strained muscles. By the time she arrives home, Kersee has beat her there and it's 7:30 or 8:00 P.M. Kersee has dinner, which usually consists of steamed fresh vegetables, pasta, and grilled chicken or fish, waiting for her. Most evenings are spent with teammates. In the "prison" they watch videos of their performances and discuss techniques for improvement.

When Bob Kersee first observed Joyner-Kersee run, she impressed him with her raw speed. Her problem, however, was the hurdles. Determined to overcome her weakness, Joyner-Kersee gave up basketball and restructured her training to eliminate the hamstring injuries. At the 1986 Goodwill Games in Moscow, Joyner-Kersee cleared her hurdles. She set both American and world records. She completed the 100-meter hurdles in 12.85 seconds; set a heptathlon record of 23 feet in the long jump; ran the 200-meter dash in 23 seconds; and completed a 62-inch high jump and a shot put of 48 feet, 5 1/4 inches—all on the first day. On the second day Joyner-Kersee threw the javelin 163 feet, 4 inches and set the world record by two hundred points. Joyner-Kersee was the first American woman to hold a world record in a multi-event since Mildred "Babe" Didrikson set a triathlon mark fifty years before.

Leaving Moscow, Joyner-Kersee and her husband/coach headed for the United States Olympic Festival in Houston, Texas. While Joyner-Kersee was clearly focused on setting new records, her husband/coach was struggling with inner conflicts. Knowing she was tired and sore from the competition in Moscow, her husband wanted simply to take her home. But as her coach, he knew she was healthy and in good shape to go for more records. In Houston she set the record for the 800-meter run with a time of 2:09:69. This performance clinched for her the 1986 Sullivan Award for Most Outstanding Amateur Athlete. Joyner-Kersee also was named Athlete of the Year by *Track and Field News* and received the Jesse Owens Award for 1986.

Athlete Goes for the Gold

The momentum Joyner-Kersee reached in 1986 continued into the new year of 1987. She won the women's points-standing of the Mobile Grand Prix track and field indoor series. This was an amazing feat because in each event she competed against a specialist, as there was no heptathlon in the meet. In the August Pan American Games in Indianapolis, she tied the world record in the long jump competition held by Heike Drechsler of East Germany. From the Rome World championships, Joyner-Kersee brought home two gold medals, in the heptathlon and the open long jump.

All these wins were leading up to one event. The five-foot ten-inch, 150-pound athlete intended to capture Olympic gold at the 1988 games in Seoul, Korea. At the summer games she did indeed win the gold medal in the heptathlon. The win felt good and was addicting. She definitely planned to do it again.

The 1992 Olympic games in Barcelona, Spain, offered the challenge Joyner-Kersee longed for. At the age of thirty, she became the first woman in Olympic history ever to win back-to-back gold medals in the heptathlon. Moments after her 1992 triumph she posed a question, captured in the *Washington Post,* "Wouldn't it be great to complete my career back on American soil, in Atlanta in 1996?" Only seven times in the history of the Olympic games has a woman scored over seven thousand points in an event in the heptathlon. All but one of those times, the woman was Jackie Joyner-Kersee. Of her seven-event sport, Joyner-Kersee said in the

1987 *Current Biography Yearbook,* "I like the heptathlon because it shows you what you're made of." What she is made of is amazing grace and determination. She has shown the world there is more to come from East St. Louis than crime.

Joyner-Kersee continues to set records, a true measure of her greatness. At the 1993 World Track and Field Championships held in Stuttgart, Germany, Joyner-Kersee, still the reigning champion in the heptathlon, overcame illness to win her fourth world title. "I definitely believe this is my greatest triumph," she told *Jet* in September 1993, referring to the close competition in the week-long event. In 1994 she jumped 24 feet, 7 inches at the New York Games and set a new U.S. record. She topped her 1987 record by one and a half inches and was just slightly off the world record of 24 feet, 8 1/4 inches.

Joyner-Kersee exemplifies the best in an athlete, regardless of gender. Her greatest contribution to the world is her life example. She has shown that the American dream of rags to riches success is a reality toward which children can aspire if they are willing to work very hard and not be sidetracked by frivolous pursuits.

Current Address: P.O. Box 21053, Long Beach, CA 90801.

REFERENCES:

"After Four Events, It's Joyner-Kersee in the Heptathlon." *New York Times,* August 2, 1992.
"Blacks Take Gold at World Track and Field Championships." *Jet* 84 (September 6, 1993): 52, 54.
Current Biography Yearbook. New York: H. W. Wilson Co., 1987.
"Death of Namesake Jackie O. Inspires Jackie Joyner-Kersee to New U.S. Long Jump Record." *Jet* 86 (June 6, 1994): 56.
Dolphin, Ric. "Ghetto Goddess." *Maclean's* 101 (September 12, 1988): 66.
Hendershott, Jon. "Jackie Joyner, the Ubiquitous One." *Track and Field News* 40 (February 1987): 6-7, 42.
Jordan, Pat. "Wonder Woman: No One Is a Better Bet Than Jackie Joyner-Kersee." *Life* 11 (October 1988): 89.
"Joyner-Kersee Alone atop Olympus." *Washington Post,* August 3, 1992.
Kort, Michele. "Go, Jackie, Go." *Ms.* 17 (October 1988): 30.
Moore, Kenny. "Proving Her Point." *Sports Illustrated* 69 (October 3, 1988): 28.
———. "Quest for New Conquests: Jackie Joyner-Kersee Triumphantly Took on the 400 Hurdles." *Sports Illustrated* 70 (June 5, 1989): 80-82.
"A Successful Test for Joyner-Kersee." *New York Times,* August 18, 1993.
Turner, Renee D. "My Happiest Moment." *Ebony* 43 (March 1988): 86.

Nagueyalti Warren

Amalya Lyle Kearse

(1937-)

Judge, lawyer, writer

A trial lawyer who earned an outstanding reputation in the courts as a gifted legal scholar, first-rate legal writer, and shrewd analyst, Amalya Kearse was the first black woman partner in a major Wall Street law firm and the first woman ever to sit on the federal appeals court in Manhattan. For bridge aficionados, she is equally brilliant as a tournament bridge player and author, editor, and translator of books and articles on the game.

Born in Vauxhall, New Jersey, on June 11, 1937, Amalya Lyle Kearse is the daughter of Robert Freeman Kearse, a former postmaster, and Myra Lyle Smith Kearse, who first practiced medicine then became an antipoverty official. "My father always wanted to be a lawyer," Amalya Kearse recalled in the June 25, 1979, *New York Times,* "but the Depression had a lot to do with why he didn't. I got a lot of encouragement." Amalya Kearse studied at Wellesley, where she majored in philosophy. While a student there she decided her future. "I decided I wanted to be a litigator," she said in the same article. "I can trace that back to a course in international law at Wellesley. There was a moot court, and I found that very enjoyable." She graduated from Wellesley College with a B.A. degree in philosophy in 1959 and received the J.D. degree cum laude, near the top of her class, from the University of Michigan in 1962. While at Michigan she was research assistant to legal scholars John W. Reed, Samuel D. Estep, and Alan N. Polasky and a member of the Order of the Coif, an honor society in law. As the school's *Law Review* editor, she was responsible for articles and comments on commercial law, property law, and civil procedures. In recognition of her legal expertise and performance on the Law Review Editorial Board, she was awarded the Jason L. Honigman prize.

Kearse was admitted to the New York Bar in 1963. In 1967 she was admitted to practice before the U.S. Supreme Court. From 1962 to 1979 she was in private practice as a trial lawyer with the Wall Street firm of Hughes, Hubbard, and Reed. Although she was the first black woman partner in a major Wall Street firm, Kearse at the time was barely known in Manhattan's legal community. Orville Schell, a senior partner in the Hughes, Hubbard, and Reed firm, said in the June 25, 1979, *New York Times:* "She became a partner here not because she is a woman, not because she is a black, but because she is so damned good—no question about it." She

Amalya Lyle Kearse

was an adjunct lecturer at New York University Law School from 1968 to 1969.

Named Appellate Judge

On June 21, 1979, President Jimmy Carter appointed Kearse to the U.S. Court of Appeals, Second Circuit, in New York City, which hears cases in the Federal Court House in Manhattan. The appointment was part of a package of 152 federal appeals and trial judgeships that the Omnibus Judgeship Act created and President Carter signed into law in October 1978. Her appointment came after a widely publicized presidential search to locate blacks and women for judgeships. When she began her legal career in 1962, her race and gender were not necessarily to her advantage, nor had she particularly identified with championing the causes of women or blacks. According to the May 3, 1979, issue of the *New York Times,*

> Those were two bad things to be. . . . Kearse had fought a double prejudice in becoming one of the first women and first black lawyers to become a partner in a leading Wall Street law firm. . . . She had to be better, and she was.

By this time the two traits, coupled with her qualifications, made her especially appealing.

Kearse was the first woman and second black to serve in the Second Circuit, New York City; the first black was Thurgood Marshall, who by 1979 was a Supreme Court judge. Kearse, then forty-one years old, was also one of the youngest judges ever to sit on the court of appeals. She had decided against applying for an opening on Manhattan's federal district court, where trials were held, choosing instead to pursue the appellate opening because, as she said in the June 25, 1979, issue of the *New York Times,* "I've always liked to write and engage in legal analysis." A colleague at Hughes, Hubbard, and Reed said of her appointment in the May 3, 1979, *New York Times,* "She'll make a terrific judge. She is a brilliant legal scholar, a good writer, and an excellent analyst—the kinds of things you need to be a good appellate judge."

At the time of her appointment, Kearse had set an excellent record in the courts. On the appellate court she wrote the opinion that barred police from observing a suspect through a telescope without a warrant. She joined a court majority in permitting television networks to broadcast the Abscam tapes. She supported another majority upholding a New York State ban on school prayers. Kearse helped overturn a lower court's ruling that Vietnam veterans damaged by Agent Orange could sue the manufacturers.

Kearse's outstanding reputation as a lawyer and judge continues to be widely recognized. On two separate occasions during President Bill Clinton's administration her name has surfaced as a possible candidate for a high federal position, the most recent time being in May 1994 when the president acknowledged the difficulty of his task in choosing a Supreme Court nominee to replace retiring justice Harry A. Blackmun. He considered expanding the court's ethnic diversity by naming either a Hispanic, Jose A. Cabranes, or a black, Amalya Kearse. Neither was named.

Judge Is Expert Bridge Player

Described in the June 25, 1979, *New York Times* as a woman with "a slightly glacial exterior," she is known also as a delightful person. She works almost nonstop. "You get involved in lawsuits, and things happen," Kearse said in the *New York Times* article. "You work a lot, almost all of the time, every weekend and evening," she continued. "Working days are 12 and 15 hours long. Literally, there is no time for anything else." However, this woman with many sides to her personality found time to play on the softball team for Hughes, Hubbard, and Reed and was an agile forward on its women's basketball team.

The *New York Times,* May 3, 1979, called Kearse "a person of apparent contradictions":

She loves physical activity, yet has chosen the contemplative path. Strangers are struck by her reserved demeanor, but those who know her well speak of her warmth. She is enthusiastic about her avocations and is a tournament bridge player, yet her work weeks stretch to 100 hours, leaving her little time for diversion.

Highly regarded as one of the most talented bridge players in the country when she was quite young, Kearse wrote *Bridge Conventions Complete,* first published in 1975 and with a third edition in 1990. She became furious with Hart Publishing Company for its editorial work on her 1980 book, *Bridge at Your Fingertips,* claiming that sections were omitted. She won a temporary order restraining the publisher from printing and distributing additional copies of the book until the case was adjudicated. In 1976 she edited the third and most recent edition of the *Official Encyclopedia of Bridge.* In 1979 she translated and edited *Bridge Analysis.* For a while her preoccupation with her bridge books took time away from playing the game. She had already won two major national titles in 1971 and again in 1972 when Kearse and her partner, Jacqui Mitchell, a full-time player, won the Women's Pair Championship in Miami Beach in 1986, her first success at the world level and Mitchell's fourth world title. Kearse was also National Women's Team Bridge Champion in 1987.

Kearse has been widely active in organizations and the community. She served on the executive committee of the Lawyers Committee for Civil Rights under Law, from 1970 to 1979. From 1976 to 1979 Kearse was a trustee of the YWCA in New York City. Since 1977 she has been a member of the American Law Institute and since 1979 a fellow of the American College of Trial Lawyers. From 1977 to 1979 she was a member of the President's Committee for Selection of Judges. She has served on the Committee of Visitors of the University of Michigan Law School. She is a member of the American Bar Association and the Association of the Bar of the City of New York. Kearse was a member of the board of directors of the NAACP's Legal Defense and Education Fund from 1977 to 1979 and of the National Urban League from 1978 to 1979. She has been active also with Big Sisters. Since 1975 she has been a member of the American Contract Bridge League National Laws Committee.

A woman of reserved demeanor in public, yet congenial among friends and firm in her beliefs, Amalya Kearse overcame the double prejudice of gender and race to become a federal appellate judge. She believes in hard work that stretches over many hours and enjoys writing, whether legal opinions or books on bridge. Though fully committed to her profession, she finds time for an equally rewarding avocation.

Current Address: U.S. Court of Appeals, Foley Square, Room 1006, New York, NY 10007.

REFERENCES:

The African-American Almanac. 6th ed. Detroit: Gale Research, 1994.
"Amalya Lyle Kearse." *New York Times,* June 25, 1979.
Davis, Marianna W., ed. *Contributions of Black Women to America.* Vol. 1. Columbia, S.C.: Kenday Press, 1982.

"Federal Judge Is a Winner of World Bridge Pair Title."
    Unidentified article, Special Collections, Fisk University
    Library, Nashville, Tenn.
"Judge Kearse Hires Lawyer." *New York Post,* March 6,
    1980.
"New York Black Picked as One of Three U.S. Judges." *New
    York Times,* May 3, 1979.
"Sketches of Three Judges." *New York Times,* September 10,
    1981.
"Wall Street Lawyer and a U.S. Judge in Line for Federal
    Appeals Bench." *New York Times,* March 13, 1979.
"Week of Tumult over Court Brings Victory to Breyer." *New
    York Times,* May 15, 1994.
Who's Who among Black Americans, 1994-95. 8th ed.
    Detroit: Gale Research, 1994.
Who's Who in America. 46th ed. Wilmette, Ill.: Marquis
    Who's Who, 1991.

Jessie Carney Smith

Maida Springer Kemp

(1910-)

**Labor leader and consultant, women's and civil
rights activist**

Maida Springer Kemp raised the standard of living and
quality of life for thousands of black women garment
workers in the United States through her work with unions,
including the well-known International Ladies Garment
Workers' Union. Well acquainted by personal experience
with the unfair treatment women garment workers received,
she carefully studied union training courses and became
highly knowledgeable about union rules, regulations, and
agreements. She went on to become a highly influential union
leader and was known internationally for her work.

In 1917 Adina Forrest Stewart (Carrington) left the
Republic of Panama to journey to New York City. She
brought with her seven-year-old daughter, Maida, born May
12, 1910. The two were part of the great migration of West
Indians, who would eventually comprise over 20 percent of
Harlem's black population. In the urban ghetto of Harlem the
West Indians vied with a black exodus from the rural South of
largely unskilled and poorly educated Americans for housing,
jobs, and resources. The West Indians adamantly adhered to
many of their native customs, especially those concerning
food selection and preparation, family life, social relations,
religion, and politics. They were ambitious workers, and
many were skilled tradesmen and professionals who pioneered in opposing labor discrimination, opening the way for
blacks in new fields of employment. All of these factors
contributed to ethnic clashes between the West Indian immigrants and black Harlemites.

Maida Kemp and her mother were representative of the
West Indians pouring into Harlem. Adina Stewart was very
ambitious and would soon be practicing a trade—she became
a licensed beautician—that would enable her to support her
family. Most importantly, she and her daughter were literate
and in full command of the English language. Unlike many of
their southern black comrades, they knew how to survive in a
harsh new climate.

Maida Kemp's father, Harold Stewart, was a West
Indian canal foreman who had migrated to Panama after being
educated in England. Her mother greatly admired the leading
black intellectuals of that era and was an ardent supporter of
Marcus Garvey, an early black Nationalist and separatist who
espoused racial consciousness and pride in the early 1900s.
Kemp and her mother came to America at the peak of the
Garvey movement's hypnotic hold on black Americans, and
Adina Stewart was a member of Garvey's Universal Negro
Improvement Association (UNIA), a stockholder in the Terry
Holding Association (a self-help agency affiliated with the
Garvey movement), and a Black Cross nurse.

Kemp attended public school in New York and then a
black boarding school in New Jersey for four years. Although
it was an industrial school, the black teachers were very well
educated and probably overqualified for the positions they
held. William H. Hastie, later governor of the Virgin Islands
and U.S. federal judge, was Kemp's science teacher, and
Lester Granger, future executive director of the Urban League,
was the school commandant. Notable black Americans such
as W. E. B. Du Bois and Paul Robeson were regular assembly
speakers.

After graduating from high school, Kemp studied at the
Malone School of Beauty Culture and became a licensed
beautician. Despite this training, she disliked "doing hair," as
her work was called in the black community, and became a
receptionist at Poro College and Malone School, sister institutions. During this time she met her first husband, Owen
Springer, a clerk and dental mechanic for an international
dental firm. A native Barbadian, Springer was renowned for
his expertise at repairing dental instruments, although his
being black never failed to shock his clients initially. After
their 1928 marriage, the Springers, Owen Springer's parents,
and other relatives all lived in the same apartment building. In
1929 Maida gave birth to a son, Eric. Owen Springer's salary
was drastically reduced due to the Great Depression, and the
young mother had to find a job to help support her family.

Explores World of Labor Unions

In 1932, as a twenty-two-year-old mother of a three-
year-old son, Kemp found work as a finisher in a nonunion
garment shop whose owners required overtime work without
pay, denied lunch breaks, and demanded that workers repair
garments without receiving compensation. By 1933, Kemp
had joined the International Ladies Garment Workers' Union
(ILGWU), despite its weak reputation, and became a member
of the Strike Committee that spearheaded the 1933 strike
against the code that set the standard wage for garment
workers at fifteen dollars a week. The union wanted a program

to upgrade worker skills and better working conditions. After the strike, Kemp began to attract the attention of union officials, and she enrolled in a nine-month series of courses that taught new workers about communication skills, parliamentary procedure, and union rules, regulations, and agreements. As a neophyte union lobbyist, Kemp sought minimum wages for workers who were receiving only thirty-seven cents an hour.

For many years, Kemp was affiliated with ILGWU Local 22, formerly a local for a single language group. By the time she became a member, it was composed of thirty-two nationalities, but did not include Italians. Despite her pride in the advances made by labor unions, Kemp was quite aware that they were still guilty of racial and gender discrimination. She also knew that black women would fare better as union workers than as domestic day workers in the suburbs.

Kemp realized that the key to improving conditions would be worker education. But first, she would need to further her own education. The ILGWU sent her to its own facility, the Educational Department of the ILGWU, as well as the Hudson Shore Labor School and the Rand School of Social Services. As an executive board member of Local 22, Kemp received first aid training and became captain and the business agent of the Women's Health Brigade. In 1942, Kemp was the education director of Local 132, the Plastic Button and Novelty Workers' Union, in charge of familiarizing new workers with the organization. Because the war effort had seriously depleted the male work force, the incoming worker pool was mainly composed of women new to the mass worker environment, refugees from war-torn countries, newly released prisoners, and southerners, all of whom were despised by the more experienced workers. Kemp had to design a program with the primary goals of forging a common bond among workers and changing attitudes about racial, ethnic, geographic, and gender stereotypes. Her educational program focused on areas that all workers agreed were in need of improvement: wages, work hours, work conditions, and safety measures. Solidarity was also effected by means of the structure of the educational program. Weekend Institutes were social affairs as well as places of learning.

Kemp was also instrumental in starting the Unity House, a leisure activity facility for union workers. From 1945 to 1947, she worked in the Complaints Department of Local 22-Dressmaker's Union and mastered the mechanics of contractual affairs. By 1947, Kemp had been promoted to business agent for Local 22 and served a thirteen-year tenure as the first black so chosen. She later became an executive board member and chair of the education committee; she also served as shop representative to settle price disputes.

Kemp Forges Labor Alliances

Kemp was influenced by the talents and skills of many women role models whose assertiveness caused them to be very visible in the higher echelons of union leadership. These included Rose Schneiderman, who headed the Women's Trade Union League; Fannia Cohns, who supervised education activities and the pamphlet and book department for the

ILGWU and was also ILGWU historian; and Charlotte Adelman, who organized the Laundry Workers' Joint Board.

By the end of World War II, Kemp was not only being recognized locally but also nationally. In 1945 the American Federation of Labor (AFL) selected her to represent the American labor movement in England during a two-month tour. She was the delegate to the United States Division of Psychological Warfare, sent to observe the effects of the war on English children. In 1951 she studied worker education in Sweden and Denmark as an American-Scandinavian Foundation Scholar. During that same year, Kemp was awarded an Urban League scholarship to study in England at Ruskin College, Oxford University. She formed pivotal relationships there as she met African students who were labor officials in their countries. In 1955 she was the AFL representative to the International Confederation of Free Trade Unions' three-week seminar in Africa.

In 1956 Kemp originated a program to bring African students to Harvard University, and she went to Africa to develop it. With headquarters in Tanganyika, she faced much opposition from the British labor hierarchy and from many American labor officials. Her supporters were those African students she had befriended in England while studying at Ruskin College. As trade unionists, they were the rising political leaders with connections to the current black political leaders, whose support and official blessings Kemp needed to succeed. By the 1970s, Kemp had established a firm reputation as an international expert in labor education. She was the consultant to the 1978 Nairobi Seminar of Women Workers, a meeting that attracted women from fourteen African countries. Kemp's alliances with such African leaders as Julius Nyerere, president of the Tanganyika African National Union and later president of his country, and labor official Tom Mboya prompted her appointment to the ILGWU international staff in the 1980s and led to her being named a consultant for the African Labor History Center.

Kemp has also used her organizational skills in arenas other than organized labor. She has enjoyed a long membership in the National Council of Negro Women. As vice president, she helped organize the council's International Women's Year meeting in Mexico. Afterwards she was in the twenty-seven-member delegation that returned to America and investigated rural development and day-care centers in Mississippi, then went to Florida to celebrate the centennial birthday of Mary McLeod Bethune, founder of Bethune-Cookman College in Daytona Beach.

Influential Work with A. Philip Randolph and Pauli Murray

Kemp had a long association with A. Philip Randolph, leader of the Sleeping Car Pullman Porters Union. In the 1930s she and her son marched in the parade to commemorate the awarding of a union contract to the Pullman Porters. Through the years, she kept abreast of Randolph's notable successes in forcing changes in federal laws dealing with discrimination in the workplace. In 1942, the year after the threatened March on Washington, Randolph was engaged in a bitter struggle to win a stay of execution for a black Virginia sharecropper sentenced to die in the electric chair for shooting his white landlord. When Randolph decided to stage a silent parade to protest the unfair execution of Odell Waller, there was no structure, no plan, no money for the demonstration. So, Kemp, along with Dollie Lowther, of the Laundry Workers' Union, Bessie Bearden, of the Housewives' League, Layle Lane, Anna Hedgeman, and Harlem youth groups, assisted Pauli Murray, a leading black civil and women's rights activist, with organizing the parade.

In 1945 Kemp and Murray were selected as two of twelve Outstanding Women in American Life by the National Council of Negro Women. At that time they lived in Brooklyn on neighboring streets, and Murray was a frequent visitor to the Kemp home. Kemp lived with her husband, son, and mother in a four-story brownstone house that was always home to union activists, visiting diplomats, African nationalists, and fellow Panamanians. In 1949 Murray ran for the city council from Brooklyn's Tenth Senatorial District, and Kemp served as her campaign manager, utilizing the experience she had gained some years before in an unsuccessful run for a New York State Assembly seat on the same labor-liberal ticket.

In late March of 1951 a ceremony was held by the Executive Committee of the Women's Division of Christian Service, Board of Missions of the Methodist Church to present "first copies" of Murray's book *State's Laws on Race and Color* to representatives of the United Nations, the government, the clergy, and American Libraries. Because Murray was hospitalized at the time, it was Kemp who first notified Murray's elderly aunts of the honor and escorted them to the presentation ceremony. Kemp's extensive contacts enabled her to assist Murray in relocating to Ghana in the late 1950s to teach at the Ghana School of Law. After a six-year stay in Africa, Murray returned to America and, while working as an administrator at Benedict College in South Carolina, she went with Kemp to Georgia to investigate a self-help project funded by the National Council of Negro Women. When Kemp's mother, Adina, was dying, Murray rushed to comfort the woman who had served as a surrogate mother to her. At the funeral, Murray functioned as both friend and clergywoman. When she wrote her family history, *Proud Shoes,* she acknowledged Kemp, her son, and her mother for their love and support.

In the 1970s Kemp served as the Chicago Conference hostess for the A. Philip Randolph Institute; she had earlier organized the institute's Midwestern Regional office. Through her continued involvement in labor activities, she met her second husband, James Kemp, a native Chicagoan to whom she was married in the mid-1960s. He was president of the local union of Building Service Employees, a longtime member of the Illinois Fair Employment Practices Commission, and a member of the Regional Transit Authority Board. Maida Kemp's son, Eric Springer, graduated from Rutgers University and the New York University School of Law. He has served as a law professor, Equal Employment Opportunity Commission (EEOC) compliance director, corporate officer, and principal in a Pittsburgh law firm.

Kemp has also been a faithful servant of the NAACP for many years. In 1978 she represented the organization as a task force member in a group that toured five South African cities. She, her son and his family, and her husband are all life members of the NAACP. Kemp has been a board member of Chicago's DuSable History Museum, the Urban League, and the National Organization for Women. A published author, her articles appear in Hudson Shore Labor School publications and *Opportunity* and *Justice* magazines.

Kemp is a serious collector of cookbooks that give historical and political vignettes as well as recipes. An excellent cook, she has long harbored the desire to be a chef or a dietitian. She is fluent in French, Spanish, and Swahili and has always been interested in other cultures. She continues to maintain her affiliation with the Episcopal Church.

When Maida Springer Kemp came to America as a seven-year-old girl, a casual onlooker might have dismissed her as another black child with three strikes against her: her race, her gender, and her status as an immigrant. But Kemp had a strong, self-sufficient mother who guided her life. According to Marianna Davis in *Contributions of Black Women to America,* "Her mother's involvement in the Garvey movement, the black church, and the boarding school prepared her for labor activism." Maida Kemp learned from Garvey that "Black is beautiful," from the church that all people are made in God's image, and from the New Jersey boarding school she attended that one gains pride through accomplishment. But through it all, her primary role model was a black woman—her mother.

REFERENCES:

Anderson, Jervis. *This Was Harlem: A Cultural Portrait, 1900-1950.* New York: Farrar, Strauss, Giroux, 1982.

Davis, Marianna W., ed. *Contributions of Black Women to America.* Vol. 2. Columbia, S.C.: Kenday Press, 1982.

Hill, Ruth Edmonds, ed. *Women of Courage.* Based on the Black Women Oral History Project. Cambridge: Radcliffe College, 1984.

Hine, Darlene Clark, ed. *Black Women in America.* Brooklyn: Carlson Publishing, 1993.

Jacobson, Julius, ed. *The Negro and the American Labor Movement.* Garden City, N.Y.: Anchor Books, 1968.

Kemp, Maida Springer. Interview. Black Women Oral History Project, Schlesinger Library, Radcliffe College, 1978.

Lerner, Gerda. *Black Women in White America.* New York: Vintage Books, 1973.

Murray, Pauli. *Proud Shoes.* New York: Harper and Row, 1978.

———. *The Autobiography of a Black Activist, Feminist, Lawyer, Priest, and Poet.* Knoxville: University of Tennessee Press, 1987.

"Negroes Now Get Non-Racial Jobs." *Ebony* 11 (September 1956): 27.

Ploski, Harry A., and James Williams, eds. *Negro Almanac.* 5th ed. Detroit: Gale Research, 1989.

Salem, Dorothy, ed. *African American Women: A Biographical Dictionary.* New York: Garland Publishing, 1993.

Who's Who among Black Americans, 1990-91. 6th ed. Detroit: Gale Research, 1991.

"Women's Clubs: They Turn from Social Circles to Social Service." *Ebony* 32 (July 1977): 71-80.

COLLECTIONS:

The papers of Maida Springer Kemp are in the Schlesinger Library, Radcliffe College, Cambridge, Massachusetts.

Dolores Nicholson

Yvonne Kennedy

(1945-)

Educator, state representative, college president

Yvonne Kennedy

Adistinguished and committed educator—a woman known for her ability to get the job done—Yvonne Kennedy is the president of Bishop State Community College in Mobile, Alabama. She was also the first African American woman elected to the Alabama House of Representatives from Mobile County. She now serves on the powerful Ways and Means Committee and was chair of the Alabama Legislative Black Caucus. She is the only African American woman ever to be named First Lady of Mobile.

Yvonne Kennedy was born on January 8, 1945, the eleventh of twelve children born to Thelma McMillian Kennedy and Leroy Kennedy, Sr. The Kennedys as well as the McMillians represent several generations of native Mobilians. Kennedy's paternal grandparents were two of the founders of Stewart Memorial Christian Methodist Episcopal (CME) Church, where she received her religious education and where her family worshiped regularly. Both parents were employed at Brookley Air Force Base in Mobile.

Kennedy recalls that her mother, who died in 1985, was a visionary woman of great strength, blessed with a generous amount of mother wit. She taught her daughter best by example, and her kindness was expressed in everything she did. With twelve children, a husband, and a full-time job, she did it all. In a family of eight brothers and three sisters, Kennedy enjoyed an active childhood. Her father was a devoutly Christian, strong-willed man. He died in 1978.

Throughout her life Kennedy has participated in many aspects of the church. Growing up, she performed in church programs. Later, she represented the church at annual CME conferences and taught Sunday school. Finally, she served on the Board of Christian Education and the Board of Trustees at Stewart Memorial Church. In 1978 Stewart Memorial CME Church honored Kennedy by naming their largest community outreach effort the Yvonne Kennedy Educational Center.

Kennedy began her formal secular education in the public schools of Mobile County, which were segregated at the time she entered. School in the Kennedy household represented the opportunity for the kind of freedom and security her parents had never known. Thelma Kennedy inspired her daughter to always "put her best foot forward." In the classroom as in the Sunday school room, Kennedy distinguished herself. In 1962 when Kennedy graduated from Central High School, she ranked in the top 10 percent of her class.

The sit-in movement, which started February 1, 1960, and the freedom rides that followed in the spring of 1961 created a political climate Kennedy would not soon forget. She entered college the year that the civil rights movement took a decided turn toward confrontation in Alabama and was met with increased violence. The riots, demonstrations, jailing of Martin Luther King, Jr., in Birmingham on Easter Sunday 1963, and finally the assassination of Medgar Evers in Mississippi in June 1963 seemed to indicate her family's decision to have Kennedy live at home while attending college was a sound one.

Kennedy enrolled at Bishop State Junior College (formerly Alabama State College, Mobile Center). In addition to being able to save money by living at home and commuting to class, Kennedy reports that her family environment was indeed sheltered, meaning her parents were not ready for her to leave home. In 1964 Kennedy earned the associate in arts degree from Bishop and transferred to Alabama State University in Montgomery. In her second year at Bishop and again in 1966 at Alabama State, Kennedy received the President's Award for academic excellence.

Leadership Qualities Emerge

During the fall of 1964 Kennedy entered Alabama State as a junior and immediately involved herself in the social, political, and academic life of the campus. She pledged Delta Sigma Theta Sorority and quickly assumed a leadership role, becoming president of the Pyramid Club and then president of the Beta Eta chapter of Delta Sigma Theta Sorority. Currently she is national first vice-president of the organization. Kennedy was also secretary of Alpha Kappa Mu National Honor Society, was elected to Who's Who among Students in American Colleges and Universities, joined the Bridge Club, and worked on the yearbook staff, becoming its editor-in-chief.

In 1965 Kennedy won the coveted title Miss Alabama State University. But she remembers 1965 for another, quite different reason. Politically the South was heating up as the summer arrived. On March 7, 1965, just prior to spring break at the college, a group of civil rights workers attempted to march in a demonstration from Selma to Montgomery to protest the denial of voting rights to African Americans. The marchers were stopped by Dallas County sheriff's deputies and Alabama state troopers who violently attacked their ranks, sending seventeen African Americans to the hospital and injuring sixty-seven others.

College students at Alabama State were outraged. Kennedy, however, was not ruled by her anger. As a member of the Student Government Association, she organized the students and encouraged them to write home for permission from their parents to join the march when it was rescheduled. When Kennedy learned that Martin Luther King, Jr. would lead the march from Selma, beginning March 21, 1965, she and the group of students from Alabama State University planned to meet the marchers at the Montgomery county line and march with them to the state capitol. Kennedy recalls her excitement as she participated in this history-making event. At the foot of the Alabama State Capitol thousands of African Americans were gathered to demand justice as citizens of the United States. She was inspired by this black show of nonviolent force and by the speech delivered by King from the steps of the capitol.

Although deeply touched by the civil rights movement, Kennedy's focus was education, not politics. She graduated in 1966, having earned a bachelor of science degree with a major in English and social science. She continued her education in the fall at Morgan State University in Baltimore, Maryland, where she received a two-year graduate assistantship. An active graduate student, she served as advisor to the Alpha Gamma chapter of Delta Sigma Theta Sorority and worked as a research assistant in the Department of English, where she was pursuing her degree. In 1968, she gained membership in Lambda Iota Tau Literary Society. Kennedy graduated in 1968 with a master of arts degree in English.

After graduation Kennedy returned to Mobile as instructor of English at Bishop State Junior College, where she had been a student scarcely seven years earlier. Kennedy was employed to teach Introduction to Literature, English and American literature, and courses in freshman composition. But she was also requested to assume a leadership role as one of two chairpersons to head the self-study for accreditation. Under her leadership, in 1970 the college gained full accreditation by the Southern Association of Colleges and Schools. Also during her tenure as an instructor, Kennedy was elected president of the Bishop State Faculty Organization.

In 1971 Kennedy was asked to coordinate the Higher Education Achievement Program (HEAP), a federally-funded program targeted for minority students at Bishop. Even though she enjoyed classroom teaching, she accepted the position hoping she would be capable of making a difference in the lives of young people. As coordinator of HEAP, Kennedy supervised a staff of eight people, including instructors, counselors, and support staff. One hundred students were enrolled in the program. She designed the curriculum, which consisted of English, mathematics, and counseling sessions. The success of HEAP led to another job offer.

The Southern Association of Colleges and Schools offered Kennedy the position of associate director for its Cooperative Programs, Education Improvement Program (EPI). Kennedy requested a leave-of-absence from Bishop State and accepted the position, moving to Atlanta, Georgia, in September 1974. As associate director, Kennedy was responsible for editing a newsletter entitled "EPI Communique." She supervised twenty to twenty-five colleges, both public and private, two-year and four-year, throughout the eleven-state southern region.

In April 1976, Kennedy's two-year leave ended and she returned to Bishop State as coordinator of the federal government program known as Title III. In this role, she prepared and monitored grant applications. By now administration clearly was Kennedy's niche. In her position as Title III coordinator she reported directly to the president. Kennedy's decision to remain in administration led her back to school. She enrolled at the University of Alabama and received a doctor of philosophy degree in higher education administration in 1979.

A group of concerned citizens approached Kennedy and urged her to run for state office in 1979. At first she refused, thinking they were not serious. Then others urged her to consider it. She decided to run. In 1979, she became the first African American woman from Mobile County to win an election to the Alabama House of Representatives, House District 103. Currently Kennedy is in her fourth term as a state representative.

First African American Woman To Head Alabama State College

In 1981 Kennedy was appointed president of Bishop State Junior College, becoming the first African American woman to head a state college in Alabama. As president of

Bishop State, Kennedy's dynamic leadership has been without equal. She expanded the junior college into a much larger community college by consolidating the three public two-year colleges in Mobile. Bishop State Community College is the second largest institution of higher education in Mobile. It offers a comprehensive curriculum consisting of more than one hundred academic, technical, and occupational areas, including allied health sciences. Kennedy instituted the college's first capital campaign; no other Alabama public two-year college had ever conducted a capital campaign, and she exceeded her goal of one million dollars. Kennedy led the college in establishing an endowment. The college has grown in student population as well as expanded to include the multimillion dollar state-of-the art O. H. Delchamps Jr. Student Life Center and Conference Complex, and the historic Central High School building was acquired and has undergone extensive renovations.

An active life is all Kennedy has ever known. She has been designated the majority floor leader in the Alabama House and served two consecutive terms as chairperson of the Alabama Legislative Black Caucus. She was also elected party leader by the Alabama Caucus of House Democrats. In 1988 her peers honored her with the Outstanding Legislator Award. Her professional activity seems never to cease, but when it slows down she finds time for an equally active social life.

During the Seventy-fifth Diamond Jubilee Convention of Delta Sigma Theta Sorority in 1988, Kennedy was unanimously elected national president for a two-year term; she was unanimously reelected in 1990. Kennedy's election marked the first time a Delta Southern Regional resident was elected to lead the national organization. As chief executive officer of Delta Sigma Theta Sorority, Kennedy held sway over a membership of 175,000 college-educated women. She took her charge seriously, and during her tenure she directed the multimillion dollar renovation of the National Headquarters Office and established the New Delta Membership Intake Program, the School America Program, the Delta Great Teachers Program, and the Summit III Program: Preparing Our Sons for Manhood.

Kennedy is an avid bridge player, and to relax she often makes time for tennis. The recipient of numerous honors and awards, she was named in 1989 and 1992 one of *Ebony* magazine's "100 Most Influential Black Americans." She was named Citizen of the Year by Kappa Alpha Psi Fraternity, Mobile Alumni chapter in 1980, and by Omega Psi Phi Fraternity, Mobile Alumni chapter in 1984. In 1982, Kennedy was named Outstanding Career Woman by Gayfers and Educator of the Year by Palestine Temple Number 18.

Kennedy's honorary degrees include Doctor of Humane Letters from the Alabama Interdenominational Seminary (1986), Doctor of Humane Letters from Lane College, Jackson, Tennessee (1988), and Doctor of Laws from Alabama State University (1988). Kennedy's board memberships are numerous. She is a member of the Lay Board of Directors of First Southern Federal Savings and Loan Association; board of directors for the Mobile Area Chamber of Commerce, the

Symphony Concerts of Mobile, and Mobile chapter of the American Red Cross; advisory board member for the Salvation Army; member of the Alabama Women's Commission; District member, State of Alabama Senior Citizen Hall of Fame Commission; Board of Trustees, Mobile Bay Area Partnership for Youth; and Board of Trustees at Miles College.

Kennedy's theory of success is based on the idea of excellence. Taught to put her best foot forward at all times, she teaches this philosophy to others. She has benefitted from this teaching, becoming a noted state educator, politician, and community leader.

Current Address: 351 North Broad Street, Mobile, AL 36690.

REFERENCES:

Kennedy, Yvonne. Telephone interview with Nagueyalti Warren. February 21, 1994.

Phelps, Shirelle. "Black Women College Presidents." *Ebony* 41 (February 1986): 108.

Who's Who in Black America, 1994-95. 8th ed. Detroit: Gale Research, 1994.

Nagueyalti Warren

Jayne Harrison Kennedy-Overton

(1951-)

Actress, model, dancer, spokesperson, television host, producer

One of the more recognizable faces in the United States in the 1970s and 1980s was that of Jayne Kennedy-Overton, model, spokeswoman, actress, and television sports anchor. Although she appeared in a variety of television shows and numerous print and television advertisements, she is perhaps best remembered as the co-host of the CBS sports program *NFL Today*. Kennedy-Overton made history as the first black woman ever to anchor a network sports show. Today, Kennedy-Overton, along with her husband, owns a production company that produces full-length films, television shows, videos, and plays. They have also established a company for the purpose of showcasing the work of black artists.

Jayne Harrison Kennedy-Overton was born in Washington, D.C., in 1951. Shortly after her birth, the family moved to

Jayne Harrison Kennedy-Overton

the suburban town of Wickliffe, Ohio, which is near Cleveland. Even though she was raised with four brothers and sisters, she stood out.

At the age of eighteen, Kennedy-Overton won the title of Miss Ohio and later participated in the Miss USA beauty contest. With her natural good looks she quickly gained attention. Shortly after the contest she settled into the job of legal receptionist. However, this job only lasted two weeks before she had her first big break. Having previously appeared in three Bob Hope specials, she became a regular on the popular television show *Laugh-In*. Her next move was to the Dean Martin show. There she worked with the "Ding-a-Ling Sisters" and began dancing two shows a night.

Her beauty did not escape the eye of Leon Isaac Kennedy. Popularly known as Leon "the Lover" for his work in movies and radio, Leon Kennedy was on his way to becoming a well-known actor and producer. In 1971, two months after their first meeting, Leon proposed, and nine months later the two married in Detroit. Leon quickly became Jayne's producer; thus, the two not only had a personal relationship, but a business relationship as well.

With her five-foot-ten-inch frame, beautiful face, and warm voice, Jayne Kennedy-Overton became very popular as a model and spokeswoman, and she quickly found work in television commercials and magazine advertisements. She did promotions for Jovan Musk and products manufactured by Adidas, Revlon, and the Coca Cola Company (Tab soft drinks). She also began doing episodic television work; her first part was in the show *MacMillan and Wife*.

First Black Woman to Anchor Sports Show

Jayne Kennedy-Overton's best-known role, however, was in the sports world. The first black woman to anchor a network sports show, Kennedy-Overton co-hosted the popular CBS program *NFL Today*. This was a natural career move for Kennedy-Overton since she had long had an interest in sports; she was a cheerleader in high school. Although she only stayed with the program for two years (1978-80), it made her a nationally known figure not only for her beauty, but for her brains as well.

Kennedy-Overton continued to work in television and guest starred on dozens of shows, including *Love Boat, Benson,* and *Entertainment Tonight.* In 1981, she hosted the Rose Bowl Parade and won an Emmy Award for her work.

Her work in films included two features, which her husband Leon produced and acted in. *Penitentiary* and *Body and Soul* were popular movies in the late 1970s and early 1980s. *Body and Soul* featured Leon Kennedy as a boxer and Jayne as a newswoman who writes a story on him and ends up falling in love. As a promotion for the movie, Kennedy-Overton appeared on the cover of the men's magazine *Playboy.* The magazine contained shots from the love scenes of *Body and Soul.* Despite her popularity, Kennedy-Overton was criticized by both black men and women who were outraged with her decision to pose. Even though the *Playboy* photographs generated public disapproval, Kennedy-Overton remains proud of her work and contends the entire experience brought her closer to God. After the film's release, her work in it earned her the NAACP Image Award for best actress. Shortly after making the film, Kennedy-Overton created an advanced exercise album called *Love Your Body and More.*

In 1982, after ten years of marriage, Leon Kennedy and Jayne Kennedy-Overton surprised friends and family with the announcement that they were divorcing. Many people had thought theirs was a storybook marriage, yet after several separate projects and a great deal of time apart, they made a mutual decision to divorce, and they parted amiably.

Now in her early thirties, Kennedy-Overton renewed her relationship with longtime friend Bill Overton, an actor and businessman who had once done a photo shoot with her. During their long courtship, Kennedy-Overton became aware of a physical ailment. She was suffering from endometriosis—a painful disorder in which the same type of mucous membrane that lines the uterus is found growing in other areas of the pelvic region. One possible cure for this condition is pregnancy. Jayne had decided at a young age that she wanted children, so after discussing it with Bill, she became pregnant. In May 1985, Jayne wed Bill Overton on a Bermuda beach with both of their parents present. Then on November 20, 1985, she gave birth to their first child, Savannah Re. She is still happily married and told *Jet* magazine, May 9, 1988, "Bill has brought me nothing but joy and contentment."

In the late 1980s Kennedy-Overton was still considered one of the most popular figures in the United States. In 1987 she was voted one of the Ten Most Beautiful Black Women in

America in *Ebony's* July issue. Another wish came true in 1989 when she gave birth to a second daughter, Kopper.

Kennedy Seen as Role Model

Currently, Bill Overton and Jayne Kennedy-Overton live on a farm in West Paris, Oxford County, Maine, with their two daughters and Bill's daughter from a previous marriage, Cheyenne. Kennedy-Overton and her family spend eight months of the year in Maine and four months in Los Angeles, California, but Kennedy-Overton says she prefers Maine. In Maine she and her husband formed Marathon Real Estate and Development at Lake Christopher in order to build condominiums.

Kennedy-Overton and her husband also formed the production company Enleyetning Concepts, which has produced feature films, television shows, and a children's home video. In addition, the two worked with the Maine Film Commission on a family-oriented feature film called *Jughead.*

In 1990 the couple produced a play by Cepheus Jaxon entitled *The African American.* It completed a thirty-week run at the Inglewood Civic Theater in suburban Los Angeles. The play recounts the four-hundred-year history of African Americans in words, song, and dance. In the fall of 1990 *The African American* made a five-city tour and Kennedy-Overton found a new love in producing. She told Aldore Collier for *Jet,* September 24, 1990, "I like being able to control my own destiny.... For me personally, I don't necessarily have to be a star on stage or screen. Being a star has never been my motivation. Doing what I like has always been what's kept me involved in this business and I love what I'm doing now."

Kennedy-Overton plays an active role in her community and is seen by many as a role model. She is a devout born-again Christian and participates in soul-saving crusades. Her willingness to help others keeps her busy with many organizations. She does charity work for the National Lung Association, the Sickle Cell Anemia Foundation, and the National Endometriosis Foundation. She is a national spokeswoman for the National Council of Negro Women, which holds seminars and clinics for the black community. She is on the board of the Efficacy Institute, which offers a program that teaches motivation to college-bound students. Despite her active participation in many groups, she and her family still find time to host a group of New England inner-city youths on their farm every summer.

Recently Kennedy-Overton and her husband formed a new company called Positively Beautiful Images. The purpose of their new company is to print, distribute, and showcase inspirational work from black artists, photographers, and authors.

At a young age, Kennedy-Overton had already had a very full career. As a model, dancer, actress, and television host, her face was widely recognized. Today, as a mother and a businesswoman, she is recognized for her work with charitable organizations and for her community service. As a black woman, Kennedy-Overton has helped to break down racial barriers in every field in which she has worked. She continues to fight these barriers through her active involvement in the community and the projects sponsored by her companies.

REFERENCES:

Collier, Aldore. "Jayne Kennedy Tells of Producing New Play, Wants to Have Boys." *Jet* 78 (September 24, 1990): 34-36.

Coultas, Carol A. "Hollywood Actress Finds the Good Life in Maine." *Lewiston-Auburn (Maine) Sun-Journal,* September 27, 1987.

"Jayne Kennedy-Overton Reveals What She Wants Most for Her Daughter." *Jet* 74 (May 9, 1988): 56-57.

"Life after Leon and *NFL Today.*" *San Francisco Examiner,* November 9, 1988.

Randolph, Laura B. "Portrait of a Woman Who Lost Her Husband and Found Herself." *Ebony* 38 (July 1983): 107-9.

————. "The New Jayne Kennedy—Wife, Mother, Woman." *Ebony* 41 (March 1986): 132.

————. "Jayne Kennedy-Overton: 'I Was 200 Pounds, Devastated, and Embarrassed.'" *Ebony* 47 (October 1992): 66-70.

Nicole D. Elliott

Yolanda Denise King
(1955-)
Actress, producer, director

Commitment, dedication, and a willingness to accept the responsibility of the King legacy constitute the fabric of Yolanda King's life. Growing up in an environment where struggle for human dignity was not just talked about but fully lived, the eldest daughter of civil rights leader Martin Luther King, Jr. continues in her own way the unfinished work of her father. As founding director of cultural affairs at the King Center in Atlanta, Yolanda King has a unique artistic vision that encompasses her father's dream but projects her own reality. As she explained in an interview: "While it is imperative to actively challenge the forces that deny human beings their right to a decent life . . . one must also stimulate and alter the hearts and minds of both the privileged as well as those who have been too long denied."

Yolanda Denise King was born on November 17, 1955, in Montgomery, Alabama, the first child of Coretta Scott King and Martin Luther King, Jr. Her birth occurred just two weeks prior to the historic day Rosa Parks refused to give up her seat on the bus, thus triggering the Montgomery bus boycott that ultimately changed the nation and the South where Yolanda would grow up. Her father, then minister of Montgomery's Dexter Avenue Baptist Church, was one of the organizers of

Yolanda Denise King

the boycott. Her mother, a young, classically trained singer-musician and activist from her college days, was intent on being a good minister's wife and mother. Yolanda King was two months old on January 30, 1956, when their house was bombed while her father attended a mass meeting for the bus boycott, which was entering its second month. On this night Martin Luther King, Jr. became known as an advocate for nonviolent protest. A crowd of angry African Americans had surrounded King's house because they were aware that his wife's and infant daughter's lives were threatened. But King insisted that they remain peaceful. The calmness and correctness of King's decision surprised even him. Coretta King, who found that she could not retire from the battle front even to relax with her new baby, was to recommit herself to a struggle that encompassed more than being a good wife and mother. She told Brian Lanker for his book *I Dream a World* of her reaction to the Montgomery bombing, ''I realized then that I could be killed and that it was important to make this my struggle also.'' Thus the decisions of both of Yolanda King's parents shaped her life.

As a little girl King was the center of her parents' attention. Totally unaware of the sacrifices her mother and father had decided to make and unaffected by the bus boycott, she enjoyed her only-child status. Two events occurred in 1958, one that altered her life and one that foreshadowed her future struggles. Martin Luther King III was born in 1958, bringing an end to Yolanda's existence as a solitary child. Her brother, affectionately called Marty, became her close companion. While this event was joyous but life altering, the next event was frightening and potentially life shattering. Just ten

years before his actual assassination, Yolanda's father narrowly escaped death when an African American woman stabbed him in the chest while he was autographing books at a store in Harlem. But for the most part, Yolanda and her siblings, Martin, Dexter Scott, and Bernice, lived sheltered lives, oblivious to the dangers their parents faced to secure the future of their freedom. Her parents knew the importance of childhood havens undisturbed by adult worries. As a result of the nurturing environment provided by her parents and grandparents, church, and community, King developed as a bright, expressive, confident, and talented child.

In 1960 the King family moved from Montgomery to Atlanta, where Yolanda King began school. Because she was born after October 15, she was required to wait until she was almost seven years old before she could enter school. Rather than wait, her parents enrolled King in Hanley, a small private school situated in northeast Atlanta where she spent less than a month before being skipped to the second grade. In the third grade she attended Oglethorpe Elementary School, which is near the Atlanta University Center where James Weldon Johnson and countless other African Americans had been educated in segregated Atlanta.

At ten King began to develop a social consciousness and awareness of the outside world. She, her brother Martin, and the Ralph Abernathy children integrated Spring Street Elementary school in midtown Atlanta. Of this time she recalls some wonderful teachers who were welcoming and tried to make them comfortable, but she also has memories of another kind. Her first racial confrontation occurred at Spring Street school when a white child called her a ''nigger.'' King held fast to her home training and responded nonviolently. For her, this encounter was just the beginning of trying times—times when she would come to question the value of nonviolence.

Talent Surfaces Early

King wrote and produced her first play, ''Riches and Royalty,'' when she was eight years old. Although written during the early sixties, the play's theme remains pertinent. ''Riches and Royalty'' was written in church during one of her father's sermons. The play was based on a queen (played by King) who invited people from around the world to visit her and explain their culture. Thus, her first dramatic effort was multicultural (not a buzz word at the time) and educational. When asked how she selected her theme, King replied that she must have been influenced by something she was studying in school.

King's mother, herself an artist who contributed to the struggle for freedom by creating a freedom concert that portrayed the civil rights movement, incorporating hymns, spirituals, and freedom songs and narrating the story of the nonviolent struggle from Montgomery forward, recognized her daughter's budding talent. Coretta King enrolled nine-year-old Yolanda in The Actor's and Writer's Workshop, a theater school in Atlanta. The school provided direction and focus to King's longings, enabling her to decide what she wanted to do with her life. Like her mother, King wanted to educate people and give them new ways of seeing life through creative arts.

The first twelve years of King's life were normal and relatively uneventful. Of that time she recalled in an interview:

> Daddy was the one who played with us. We did not have a lot of time together but the time we did have was fun. He taught me to swim and played a lot of games with us. He never whipped or spanked us. He didn't believe in it. He taught us by example how to live a good life . . . a life that would contribute to society. Daddy was my first buddy, and above all else I knew that he loved me. I was tremendously loved.

Awareness of her parents as people special to herself and her brothers and sister, to the world, and especially to the African American community began when King was about nine years old. When she was nine she joined her father on a voter registration drive. Of course she heard rumors about her father's activities and heard and watched news flash across the television screen announcing her father's arrests. In the beginning she had a hard time because the schoolchildren teased her when her father was jailed. As she told Ellen Hopkins in *Rolling Stone,* however, as she matured and became more aware of the struggle, she resolved, "Since all our friends were in the Movement, I thought what daddy did was natural. Everybody went to jail, right?"

King often learned about her father's activities on news reports as she watched television. On April 4, 1968, while watching the evening news, she was shocked by a news bulletin that transformed her life. News of her father's assassination stunned then horrified the twelve-year-old. Poised on the threshold of adolescence, King was struck a tragic blow.

The Road to Memphis: A Life of Service

After hearing the announcement of her father's murder, King recalled screaming and running to her room where she fell on her knees in prayer. Then she remembered going to her mother's room to help her pack. The calmness of disbelief enabled her to function and not cry. On April 8, 1968, King and her two brothers accompanied their mother to Memphis City Hall where Coretta King announced to the grief-stricken crowd that the children had come because they wanted to. For Yolanda King, Memphis, like the ancient Egyptian city, represented a religious and political self-centering. She now understood her father's message and his sacrifice.

Perhaps the most difficult challenge for her was coming to terms with her grief and managing the accompanying anger that challenged her strength to love. She realized that the healing had begun when schoolmates asked her if she didn't want to hurt or to kill James Earl Ray, the man convicted of her father's murder, and she could honestly say no because nothing she could do to Ray would bring her father back. But no sooner than she recognized her approaching recovery than another tragedy struck the King family.

On July 21, 1969, Yolanda King's uncle A. D. King, a minister, her father's only brother, was found dead in the swimming pool of his southwest Atlanta home. A. D. King's wife and youngest children, Esther Darlene, thirteen, and her brother Vernon, eight, were vacationing in Jamaica with Yolanda and her family when they heard the news of his accidental drowning.

Recalling the words of her father, King had to believe suffering was redemptive or she would not have survived the loss of her father and then her uncle and gone on to succeed in high school, where she was president of her sophomore and junior classes and vice-president of her senior class. Her extracurricular activities centered on acting. Working closely with acting coach Walter Roberts, Julia Roberts's father, King perfected her skills. At fifteen she was cast opposite a white male student as the prostitute, Doris Waverly, in *The Owl and the Pussycat.* Her decision to play the part of a depraved character sent shock waves throughout Atlanta's African American community. Many of those who disapproved voiced their objections to her grandfather, Martin Luther (Daddy) King, Sr. When he seemed unable to alter his granddaughter's decision, they threatened to leave his church. Other objections came from those who in 1971 were outraged to see an African American woman cast opposite a white man.

The external pressure was so overwhelming that Daddy King announced that he would not attend her performance. However, Yolanda King's mother stood firm, indicating she would stand by her daughter's decision. Her mother understood her daughter's need and right to chart her own path in life. Daddy King attended her performance after all and recognized his granddaughter's talent—her ability to engage people with moving enactments of different life situations.

The Road North: College and Beyond

In 1972, King graduated from Atlanta's Henry Grady High School. She ranked in the top 10 percent of her class. King had planned to attend Antioch College, her mother's alma mater and one of the few colleges that offered a cooperative program that enabled students to work in their chosen areas while pursuing a degree. She knew that experience would count the most, especially in the theater. With her mind made up, it was quite unsettling when on a visit to the Antioch campus she changed her mind. She had only applied to three other schools—Smith, because a high school friend went there, a school in Minnesota, which she decided was too cold a place to live, and Spelman, which she claimed she could not attend if she ever wanted to grow up. Always one to chart her own path, she would find it exceedingly difficult to do so at Spelman, where Jennie C. Parks, her paternal great-grandmother, graduated in 1898, where her grandmother, Alberta Williams King, graduated in 1924, and where her aunt, Christine King Farris, graduated in 1948 and was on the faculty.

King entered Smith College in the fall of 1972, almost by default. She was sixteen years old. As a young coed, King found herself personally challenged about her father's philosophy. She was shocked to realize that she had not read any of his books. She had also not read the Bible. She thought she did not need to since she was in church "eight days a week." So, she read works by Malcom X and Franz Fanon and all of her father's works as well as the Bible. When she questioned her father's belief in nonviolence, her reading revealed that she also believed it to be correct. She believed it took more courage and strength and certainly more intelligence to resolve problems nonviolently.

Had it not been for the cooperative college arrangement at Smith, King doubts she could have survived the isolation and difficulty she faced as an African American theater arts major. African American women were cast in demeaning roles, and it was difficult for her to get on-stage training. However, because of the collective that included Amherst College, Hampshire College, Mount Holyoke, and the University of Massachusetts, Amherst, King was able to take classes at the University of Massachusetts's Kirby Theater, which enabled her to play major roles, take courses in black theater, and direct dramatic productions. Although there were few African American students at Smith, there were enough in the area to form the Black Theater Workshop, which King helped to organize. This group put on its own productions. King co-directed several student productions, including *Contributions* by Ted Shine and Sister Sonjii. She acted in *Stormy Monday* and *Five on the Black Hand Side,* and she was Sister Moore in James Baldwin's *The Amen Corner.*

Despite her family's fear that going to Northampton, Massachusetts, would isolate her from the African American intellectual tradition that had nurtured her grandmothers and aunt at Spelman, and her grandfather, father, and uncle at Morehouse, King was fortunate to find African American mentors willing to guide her at Smith. At Smith she took classes from Johnnella Butler and Manning Marable, and at the University of Massachusetts she studied under Johnetta B. Cole. Able to express herself through the arts and affirming her identity with an African American studies and theater arts double major, King was satisfied with her choice for a college. She completed her sophomore year and returned home to work for the summer.

On June 30, 1974, in an incident more shocking than the assassination of her father or the death of her uncle, the entire congregation of Ebenezer Baptist Church watched as a madman fired the gun that killed Yolanda's grandmother, Alberta Williams King. Once again sorrow and suffering that did not appear redemptive sent Yolanda King to reread her favorite book, *The Strength to Love.* As noted in the October 1974 issue of *Ebony,* perhaps she also recalled her grandmother's own words uttered during times of suffering and grief: "We are not so special that nothing difficult shouldn't come to us. You must prepare yourself to meet it and live with it."

Founds Theater Companies

King earned her bachelor of arts degree in theater and African American studies from Smith College in 1976. That fall she enrolled in New York University, where she received an M.F.A. in theater. Following her graduation from NYU,

she toured the country with the Christian Theater Artist Company, which she helped to found.

In 1979 King met Attallah Shabazz, the eldest child of Betty Shabazz and Malcolm X. Together they seemed to discover the common ground their fathers were moving toward. They shared the pain, disbelief, emptiness, and sorrow one experiences with the loss of a parent. Both sought catharsis through the dramatic arts. Both women, daughters of slain leaders, were working to carry forward the ideas of their fathers. With identical goals and similar dreams, King and Shabazz formed NUCLEUS, a company of performing artists dedicated to expressing positive energy through the arts. Their play *Stepping into Tomorrow* is a collaborative effort to speak to young people and enable them to feel good about themselves. The play is performed by NUCLEUS in more than fifty cities a year, in churches, schools, community centers, and local theaters.

King, in spite of the sometimes burdensome family legacy she must assume, has managed to focus her vision and her efforts and to say no to unrealistic demands people try to force on her because of her willingness to serve and her family's legacy of sacrifice. In *Tracks,* a one-woman show, King successfully portrays the philosophy of her father and celebrates his life. She plays sixteen roles in this multimedia theatrical production. For her, acting is liberating; her role model and inspiration as an artist is Maya Angelou. *For Colored Girls Who Have Considered Suicide When the Rainbow is Enuf* is one of her favorite plays, and she especially liked the Broadway production of *Dream Girls* and the movie *The Color Purple.* King appreciates woman-centered art, embraces vibrant colors—her favorite color is purple or fuchsia—and is politically correct enough to say her favorite foods are fresh fruits and vegetables but honest enough to reveal that what she really enjoys is a good pound cake or a chocolate layer cake.

King's film credits include featured roles in *Hopscotch* and the NBC production of *King,* in which she was cast as Rosa Parks. Although she loves acting she sees herself moving toward producing and directing for these are the areas where actual control of images begins. Through her production company, Higher Ground, she intends to produce a documentary film about her mother.

King holds lifetime membership in the NAACP and is a member of the Southern Christian Leadership Conference, Fellowship of Reconciliation, Women's International League for Peace and Freedom, and Habitat for Humanity. She is also a member of Ebenezer Baptist Church in Atlanta. She serves on the board of directors of the Martin Luther King, Jr. Center for Nonviolent Social Change and is founding director of the King Center's Cultural Affairs Program.

An actor, producer, and director, Yolanda King has established her own way of promoting her father's legacy of nonviolent social change. Through a unique and inspiring artistic vision, particularly in her one-woman show *Tracks,* she has established her position in the world of struggle.

Current Address: King Center for Nonviolent Social Change, 449 Auburn Avenue, N. E. Atlanta, GA 30312-1590.

REFERENCES:

Assensoh, A. B., and Y. M. Alex. "Keeping Faith with the Dream." *African World* 1 (November-December 1993): 20-23.

Bims, Hamilton. "He Never Gives Us More Than We Can Bear." *Ebony* 29 (October 1974): 37.

Hopkins, Ellen. "Their Fathers' Daughters." *Rolling Stone* (November 30, 1989): 76-84, 120, 123-24.

King, Yolanda. Telephone interview with Nagueyalti Warren. February 10, 1994.

Lanker, Brian. *I Dream a World.* New York: Stewart, Tabori and Chang, 1989.

"Reverend A. D. King Drowns in Pool." *Atlanta Constitution,* July 22, 1969.

Smith, Jessie Carney, ed. *Epic Lives.* Detroit: Visible Ink Press, 1992.

Nagueyalti Warren

Gladys Knight

Gladys Knight
(1944-)
Singer, business executive, television producer, actress

With her distinctive and versatile "gospel-flavored" contralto, Gladys Knight, the driving force behind Gladys Knight and the Pips, led the singing group to the top of the music charts for more than three decades. Scoring a string of hit gold albums and top-ten singles over their thirty-seven years together, Gladys Knight and the Pips—composed of her brother Merald "Bubbah" Knight, Jr., and cousins William Guest and Edward Patten—captured an international audience and gained recognition as one of the most successful and enduring family singing groups in show business. Often called one of the greatest female soul singers of our time, Knight was propelled to superstardom with her electrifying performances on such hit ballads as "If I Were Your Woman" (1970), "Make Me the Woman That You Go Home To" (1971), "Midnight Train to Georgia" (1973), "Help Me Make It through the Night" (1974), "Neither One of Us" (1974), and "Best Thing That Ever Happened to Me" (1974). She continued to cut hits with the group in the 1980s and as a solo performer in the early 1990s. Despite a number of personal and professional crises and contract disputes, Gladys Knight and the Pips stayed together for almost forty years. Knight offered an explanation for the group's longevity in *Jet,* May 8, 1989, stating, "Not only are we family, but we realize that each person is an individual."

A native of Atlanta, Georgia, Gladys Knight was born on May 28, 1944, into a musical family. Her parents, Merald Knight, Sr. and Elizabeth Woods Knight, were members of the Wings Over Jordan Gospel Choir and performed at local churches throughout the city. Gladys Knight's parents separated in the early 1950s, and she and her three siblings were raised by her mother, who encouraged Gladys's talent. Knight made her singing debut at age four, appearing on the southern gospel circuit with the Mount Moriah Baptist Church Choir, the Wings Over Jordan Choir, and the Morris Brown [College] Choir. By the age of seven, Knight was a veteran child star of television, talent competitions, and local concerts. She won three successive competitions on the Ted Mack *Amateur Hour* in 1952, singing "Because of You," Brahms's "Lullaby," and "Too Young."

Origins of the Group

Later that year, the Pips made their first group appearance as a quintet at a family birthday celebration; the original group was composed of Gladys, her brother and sister, Merald Knight, Jr. and Brenda Knight, and cousins William and Eleanor Guest. In honor of their cousin and first manager, James "Pip" Woods, the group called themselves the Pips—later they understood the name to stand for Perfection in Performance. When Knight was twelve, they teamed up with Supersonic Productions and played at small, local clubs. On their first national tour in 1956, the Pips opened for R&B greats Sam Cooke and Jackie Wilson. The result was their first record, "Whistle My Love."

In the late 1950s and early 1960s, the Pips performed regularly at major theaters and auditoriums on the R&B circuit and achieved widespread popularity. At this point, Eleanor Guest and Brenda Knight left the group and were replaced by Edward Patten and Langston George. Signed by the Huntom label, the Pips released their first national hit in 1961, "Every Beat Of My Heart"—a recording leased to Vee Jay and re-recorded by the Fury label simultaneously—followed by a second top-five hit in 1962 also on Fury records, "Letter Full of Tears." After Langston George left the group in 1961, the lineup of Gladys Knight, Merald "Bubbah" Knight, William Guest, and Edward Patten became "something of an institution with their flashy stage show and tight choreography," according to *Who's Who in Rock.* Both hits helped to establish the now well-known format of Gladys Knight and the Pips, featuring the versatile lead of Knight with the Pips as backup.

In 1965 the group signed with Soul records, a subsidiary of the Motown label, and stayed with them for several years. They won acclaim with numerous hit singles, including "Take Me in Your Arms and Love Me" (1967), their enormously popular "I Heard It Through the Grapevine" (1967); "It Should Have Been Me"(1968); and "Nitty Gritty" and "Friendship Train" (1969). Although they enjoyed a crossover and captured a worldwide audience touring with the Motown revue, the group was dissatisfied at Motown and felt that they were given second-rate material. According to *Ebony,* June 1973, "Within the company's rigid caste system, they felt under appreciated." That year, the group moved to Buddha Records. In the same *Ebony* article, Knight revealed why they chose to move to another record company: "It was time to push on up. . . . There are too many political doings, like a rostrum of who's selling the most hits or who's in good with the president. They play favorites and nurture one group to the detriment of another, despite the fact ten artists can earn ten times as much money as one. If you're not part of the in-crowd, forget it. We've put too much agony into our work to break down and beg for bones." In the late 1970s, a legal dispute ensued with Motown over the royalties to several unreleased recordings that the group left behind.

Recording Team Attracts Wider Audience

After their departure from Motown, Gladys Knight and the Pips started their own campaign for wider audience appeal with television appearances on several major shows: *In Concert, Midnight Special, Soul Train, American Bandstand, The Tonight Show,* and *Mike Douglass;* in England, they were seen on *The Old Grey Whistle Test* and *Top of the Pops.* In addition, they made appearances at college campuses and popular spots in Boston, Chicago, New York, Las Vegas, and Europe.

Gladys Knight and the Pips entered a period of unprecedented success after switching to Buddha Records. They recorded the number-one hit LP *Imagination,* which featured three hit singles, "Midnight Train to Georgia," "Where Peaceful Waters Flow," and "Best Thing That Ever Happened to Me." Further chart blockbusters followed, bringing

them international honors and acclaim: "The Way We Were/ Try to Remember," "On and On," and "I've Got to Use My Imagination." Steve Bloom said in *Rolling Stone,* June 30, 1988:

> It was there [Buddha Records] that the distinctive call-and-response sound of Gladys Knight and the Pips blossomed. Though songs like "Midnight Train To Georgia" and "Best Thing That Ever Happened to Me" flirted with the middle of the road, Knight's heavy-throated, heartfelt vocals, backed by the Pips' almost comical repeats, touched a chord with black and white audiences alike. And when she challenged Barbara Streisand with a gutsy version of "The Way We Were" in 1975, Knight figured she would never have to look back.

By the mid-1970s Gladys Knight and the Pips were ranked the number-one vocal group in the United States, and Knight's spectacular performances were commanding widespread attention. While her voice was not considered outstanding by some, it had blossomed and matured. She could match Etta James and Aretha Franklin or be as blue as Janis Joplin. The Pips added a time-honed harmony that had not been known since the fifties, observed *Rolling Stone.*

Gladys Knight and the Pips won trophies in two categories during the 1974 Grammy awards ceremony: Best Pop Vocal Performance by a Duo, Group, or Chorus for the single "Neither One of Us" and Best R&B Vocal Performance by a Duo, Group, or Chorus for "Midnight Train to Georgia." During the summer of 1975, the group hosted their own weekly NBC variety show.

In 1976, Knight's career moved into high gear as she made her acting debut in the half-hour sitcom *Pipe Dreams,* directed by D. Stephen Verona. Her husband at the time, Barry Hankerson, Jr., co-produced and co-starred in the show. The show, about a woman who journeys to Alaska to win back her husband, was a ratings failure and lasted only one season. At the end of the 1970s, she and the Pips broke up briefly because of legal entanglements with Buddha, complicated by continuing legal difficulties with Motown; for three years Gladys Knight and the Pips recorded separately.

Reunited in 1980, Gladys Knight and the Pips teamed up with Columbia, debuting with a new album, *About Love,* composed and produced by Nick Ashford and Valerie Simpson. While their first two Columbia releases in the early 1980s were only marginally successful, in 1983 the group recorded the gold album *Visions,* which yielded a modest hit single, "Save the Overtime for Me." There followed a succession of hits, such as "Taste of Bitter Love" and "Bourgie, Bourgie," followed by a final album for Columbia, *Life.* Later, the group recorded the title song for the movie *The Buddy System.*

Moving to MCA records in 1986, Gladys Knight and the Pips continued to make hit records. In 1988 they released the smash hit *All Our Love,* their twenty-fifth album, containing the top twenty hits "Love Over Board" and "Living Next to Nothing." Charles Whitaker observed in *Ebony,* September 1988,

The group came out with *All Our Love,* their first release in more than two years. It accomplishes the remarkable feat of blending both the contemporary and nostalgic aspects of the group's sound, laying their blues and gospel-drenched vocals over pulsating 1980s-style rhythm tracks. The album also restores the group to pop music prominence.

But in 1989 the members of the group disbanded to pursue separate interests. Knight explained that the members of the Pips had their own personal and business enterprises, and they needed the freedom to devote the proper time to them.

Knight Achieves Solo Stardom

Knight had her own reasons for wanting the group to disband for she had already begun experimenting on her own. In 1985-86, she costarred with Flip Wilson in the CBS sitcom *Charlie and Company,* which was later canceled. That same year, Knight joined Dionne Warwick, Stevie Wonder, and Elton John on the gold single "That's What Friends Are For" (Arista) and also recorded the original version of "Wind beneath My Wings." She teamed with Bill Medley in 1988 on "Love on Borrowed Time," the theme song for the movie *Cobra,* and sang another theme song for the James Bond movie *License to Kill.* Her decision to concentrate on a solo career was based on her need to grow as an artist. She told *Jet,* May 8, 1989, "You need to keep finding those avenues if you plan to keep competing. You just can't keep giving people a show, show, show and record, record, record. You need to do some other things creatively that are unexpected, but still on the same quality level."

Making her solo debut at Bally's Grand Hotel-Casino in Las Vegas in 1991, Knight was supported by a host of superstars: Patti LaBelle, the O'Jays, Barbara Mandrell, Dionne Warwick, and the Platters, reported *Jet.* Since then she has released a new solo album, *Good Woman,* a work in which she attempts to express herself, to reach a younger audience, and to be contemporary. The October 1991 issue of *Essence* called the album "vintage Knight: smooth yet earthy, timeless yet just right for now." Future plans are to produce a second episode of the weekly television drama *Sisters* and to continue performing. Knight recognizes that music changes constantly, and, as she stated in *Jet,* she believes that singers must be able to change while "maintaining your base."

In addition to being a fabulous entertainer, Knight is a businesswoman. She is president and CEO of Knight Nutritional Hair Supplements and Shakeji, a family-run management firm that includes a public relations firm, a merchandising company, and a production company. Shakeji is managed by her son Jimmy Newman, vice-president, and daughter, Kenya Love, executive administrator. Knight also has a fifteen-year-old son, Shanga Ali Hankerson.

With a strong belief in family and in God, it seems Knight will always remain close to the Pips: "I miss them. I'm a harmony person and I still have it, and I enjoyed working with the guys," she told *Essence* in October 1991. Assessing her career in show business, the personable song stylist pointed to her strong faith as the source of her success in the same *Essence* article: "I just go inside, inside. I pray a lot. It's just kind of natural. . . . We're supposed to relate to Him on a daily basis, and I try to do that." *Essence* stated in May 1992 that her longevity came from "her 'sturdy power base'—the wide audience of black and white, young and not-so-young, and urban and southern fans she has satisfied for nearly four decades."

Among her many awards as both soloist and member of Gladys Knight and the Pips are four Grammy awards, an honorary doctor of humane letters from Morris Brown College, the NAACP Image Award, and a Special Award for Inspiration to Youth by the Washington, D.C., City Council.

The twice-divorced mother of three and grandmother of three announced in April 1993 that she would marry Les Brown, the highly acclaimed Fortune 500 motivational speaker, on Thanksgiving Day, 1993. Since then the wedding date has been put on hold because of the couple's various professional obligations. Knight has been one of the most popular and enduring forces in the music world for over four decades. Today, she continues to entertain and excite her audiences. Through her self-confidence, deep faith, ability to work with others, and drive to succeed, Gladys Knight has achieved superstardom.

Current Address: c/o Shakeji Inc., Golden Arrow Drive, Las Vegas, NV 89109.

REFERENCES:

Bloom, Steve. "Gladys Knight in No Man's Land." *Rolling Stone* (June 30, 1988): 23.

"The Fifth Essence Awards." *Essence* 23 (May 1992): 66.

Fong-Torres, Ben. "Gladys Knight and the Pips." *Rolling Stone* (June 6, 1974): 53.

"Gladys Knight Goes Solo and Tells Why." *Jet* (May 8, 1989): 5-59.

Little, Benilde. "Just Gladys." *Essence* 22 (October 1991): 52-55.

Mack, Lonnie, ed. *Encyclopedia of Rock.* New York: Schirmer Books, 1988.

Mason, B. J. "Gladys Knight and the Pips: It's a Family Affair." *Ebony* 28 (June 1973): 173.

Stambler, Irvin, ed. *The Encyclopedia of Pop, Rock and Soul.* Rev. ed. New York: St. Martin's Press, 1989.

Whitaker, Charles. "Gladys Knight and the Pips Mark 36 Years of Making Music." *Ebony* 43 (September 1988): 72-80.

Who's Who among Black Americans, 1994-95. 8th ed. Detroit: Gale Research, 1994.

Who's Who in Rock. New York: Facts on File, 1981.

Jacquelyn L. Jackson

Patti LaBelle

(1944-)

Singer, actress

Patti LaBelle has been a star for thirty years and recognized as a superstar for at least ten. She began her singing career in one of the many doo-wop girl groups of the 1960s. In the 1970s the group, which was then a trio named Labelle, changed its image, giving audacious and spectacular performances and moving in the direction of hard rock. The three women managed to keep black audiences while making a breakthrough to specialized white audiences. In the process they achieved notable success on records. When the group broke up in 1976, LaBelle undertook a solo career that led to even greater heights. Her appeal broadened to the point that by the mid-1980s she was a genuine superstar. While she has added acting to her repertoire of skills, she is still known primarily as a singer and recording artist.

Patti LaBelle was born Patricia Louise Holte on May 24, 1944, in Philadelphia. One of five children, she had three sisters and a brother. Her father, Henry Holte, was a railroad worker. Her parents separated when LaBelle was twelve, but her father kept in touch with the family. He and LaBelle remained close. Henry Holte died in 1989 from emphysema; he was also suffering from Alzheimer's disease. Her mother died of heart disease in 1985. In fact, the entire decade of the eighties was marked by family tragedy. LaBelle's three sisters, Vivian Rogers (1936-82), Barbera Purifoy (1940-84), and Jacqueline Padgett (1946-89), all died of cancer.

As a child, LaBelle was so shy that her mother offered her money to play with other children. LaBelle refused, preferring instead to stay inside and sing in front of the mirror. This shyness has persisted in her private life, and LaBelle says that she finds it difficult to express anger openly. In performance, of course, LaBelle is quite different. She told *New York Times* reporter Stephen Holden in a February 23, 1986, article, "When I get on stage, all the feelings I've kept bottled up come out." In the *Encyclopedia of Pop, Rock & Soul,* Irwin Stambler quotes another interview in which she said that on stage she felt like someone different and "that somebody wasn't afraid like my normal self was." In a March 1976 *Sepia* interview with Patrick Salvo, she phrased her response to her audience even more provocatively, "It's like being naked and having sex with your music . . . having orgasms with something you love."

The wildness of the performer contrasts with a solid devotion to her family. LaBelle married Armstead Edwards in

Patti LaBelle

1969; she had known him for many years and proposed when she realized that her brief engagement to another performer was headed toward a potentially disastrous marriage. Edwards, a former high school administrator, is now her business manager. They have one son, Zuri (Swahili for beautiful), born on July 17, 1973. In addition there are two grown sons in the family, Stanley and Dodd, whom LaBelle and Edwards adopted when their mother, a neighbor, died. LaBelle and her husband reside in Wynnewood, an affluent suburb of Philadelphia. Despite her regrets at missing important moments in family life because of career commitments, LaBelle is realistic in her self-evaluation, recognizing that her choice to become a performer is one that she would make again.

Bluebells Singing Group Formed

Patti LaBelle began her singing in the Beulah Baptist Church choir, where she acquired her grounding in gospel music, which is the foundation of her later performing styles. When she was in her teens, she joined a group called the Ordettes that performed in the city parks in Philadelphia. In 1961 the manager of the Ordettes brought LaBelle and Cindy Birdsong from the Ordettes together with Nona Hendryx and

Sarah Dash to form the Blue Belles. The Blue Belles' first single, "I Sold My Heart to the Junkman," went gold in 1962 and reached fifteen on the charts. The group was renamed Patti LaBelle and the Bluebells in that year, and their recordings "Down the Aisle" (1963) and "You'll Never Walk Alone" (1964) enjoyed modest success, reaching the top forty.

In 1965 the Bluebells moved to Atlantic Records, where they made two albums, *All or Nothing* (1965) and *Take Me for a While* (1966), both of which have a gospel-based soul sound. In addition to recording, the group became popular on the rhythm and blues circuit and toured abroad. Due to apparent mismanagement, this success did not translate into money for the women. In 1967 Cindy Birdsong left to join the Supremes, and the group continued as a trio. While their popularity in performance remained high, their recording success diminished and morale dropped.

In 1970 Vicki Wickham, a British television producer, took over management of the group, which was renamed Labelle. The singers spent six months in England working on a new sound and a new look. Their music became a kind called "progressive black," which contained elements of funky soul, pop, and hard rock, with a political stance added. Especially in the songs Nona Hendryx began writing, the women sang and their performances demonstrated a theme of personal freedom, which appealed not only to blacks but to other groups seeking to escape from oppression, especially in the sexual sphere. The sleek "doo-wop" grooming gave way to costumes and theatrics designed to amaze and even shock the more conventional audience—a trend labeled glitter rock. The move was a success. Labelle reached new audiences and at the same time retained black audiences who had been indifferent when Jimi Hendrix had moved toward hard rock.

In 1971 Labelle opened for the rock band The Who on their tour of the United States; the same year they made their debut album, *Labelle*. The two succeeding albums featured many songs by Nona Hendryx. She wrote six of the nine on *Moonshadow* (1972) and seven of the nine on *Pressure Cookin'* (1973). One song that Hendryx did not write on *Pressure Cookin'* was the political song "Something in the Air / The Revolution Will Not Be Televised," a militant poem by the young black poet Gil Scott-Heron set to music. Labelle was very active in New York City, where the group built up large audiences. Beginning by opening for Bette Midler at the Continental Baths, a homosexual venue, they moved on to headline at top rock nightclubs, like the Bottom Line in Greenwich Village, and eventually played at Town Hall and Carnegie Hall.

Labelle's first albums were produced for Warner Bros. and RCA. In 1974 the group moved to Columbia's Epic label and recorded *Nightbirds,* which went gold. "Lady Marmalade" from that album became a number one single in 1975 and became an icon of disco music. The sales of the song were not hurt by the public uproar caused by its sexual content, and the album rode the initial vogue of disco to success. Unfortunately, disco soon became an uninteresting formula, and

LaBelle felt that the group's attempts to do further disco numbers were failures.

LaBelle's road tour, in conjunction with the release of *Nightbirds,* continued to feature extravagant stage effects: at one point LaBelle descended to the stage on an invisible wire flapping her arms with a fur and feather train twenty feet long. It was also on this tour that Labelle became the first pop group to perform on the stage of the Metropolitan Opera House in Manhattan. They drew very mixed audiences, including blacks, gays, political activists, feminists, and jet-setters. Their audiences included people as extravagantly costumed as the performers, like the person described by Patrick Salvo in the March 1976 *Sepia* article as "clad in black tights, thick red garter belts, a see-through chiffon scarf, and gold spiked-heel shoes." The three singers' costumes projected different images. Hendryx, whose stage accessories included a whip and handcuffs, told Salvo, "Breaking it down, I think I get all the rapists! Patti gets the guys looking for a sexy mama, and Sarah gets the boyfriend types who want to wine and dine her."

It was difficult for the group to translate the excitement of performance to records, however, and the women frightened or alienated large sections of the wider public. The last two albums for Epic, *Phoenix* (1975) and *Chameleon* (1976), did not sell well. Then, in late 1976 during a tour, the group broke up. According to one version of this event, the women wished to move in different musical directions. Nona Hendryx wanted to move closer to rock and Sarah Dash leaned toward disco while LaBelle wanted to do more ballads. Other varied—and sometimes lurid—accounts of the events surrounding the breakup receive no support from any of the principals. The group's last concert together was on December 16, 1976.

LaBelle Goes Solo

All three women suffered from the breakup of a close-knit group that had worked together for nearly sixteen years, and they had to struggle to adjust to a major change in their lives. According to *Essence,* February 1978, LaBelle was the one most dissatisfied with the touring. She was torn between the road and her deep feelings for her husband and home. She was also upset with the ungrounded rumors of lesbian relationships among the women and the possible effect they might have on her relationship with her husband. After the split LaBelle was so upset and so frightened of going solo that she and her husband spent time seeing a psychiatrist and rebuilding a solid relationship before she felt capable of performing on her own for an audience. She also took greater charge of her own career. Her husband came to her support later by giving up his high school administrative post and becoming her manager. The two managed to place their financial affairs on a sound footing.

LaBelle's first solo album, named simply *Patti LaBelle,* appeared in 1977, and she retained her live audiences. LaBelle remained with CBS and recorded several more albums. A personal business milestone in 1983 was the opening of a clothing boutique, LaBelle Ami, on Philadelphia's South Side.

Beginning with her first solo tour LaBelle gradually began toning down the more extravagant aspects of her costumes in order to reintroduce elegance. She continued to tour with great success, spending about eight months on the road. If possible, she travels on the crew's bus since she dislikes flying.

While her success in performance continued, LaBelle's recording career seemed to be slowing down in the early 1980s. However, by the time the decade reached the halfway point, her recording success had reached new peaks and she was often on the charts. The album *I'm in Love Again* (1983) went gold and two singles from it, ''If Only You Knew'' and ''Love, Need, and Want You,'' were her first to reach the top of both the pop and R&B charts. In 1984 a duet with Bobby Womack, ''Love Has Finally Come at Last,'' made its mark. Her very elaborately produced album *Winner in You* (1986), which cost a million dollars to make, was a major success and went platinum. It was restrained compared to her earlier albums—though not when compared to many other singers' work. This album finally confirmed her superstar status in the eyes of the entire world. In that same year ''On My Own,'' a duet with Michael McDonald, was a huge hit.

With the slowdown in recording success in the early 1980s, LaBelle began to act. Her debut was on a PBS production of Stud Terkel's *Working* in 1981. She appeared in the 1981-82 tour of Vinnette Carroll's *Your Arms Too Short to Box with God* and in the September 1982 Broadway revival. She remained with the show's post-Broadway tour, which ended in June 1983. Other movie credits are *A Soldier's Story* (1985), *Beverly Hills Cop* (1985), and an NBC television movie, *Unnatural Causes* (1986).

LaBelle's song from the soundtrack of *Beverly Hills Cop*, ''New Attitude,'' was a big hit and another song, ''Stir It Up,'' was popular that year as well. Also in 1985, she made memorable appearances on television in *Motown Returns to the Apollo* and the *Live Aid* benefit concert, as well as on her own special broadcast on Thanksgiving. The following year she appeared with Gladys Knight and Dionne Warwick on an HBO special *Sisters in the Name of Love*. In 1991 she appeared as a recurring character on the weekly show *A Different World*. In 1992 LaBelle appeared in the short-lived sitcom *Out All Night* for NBC.

A common word used in descriptions of the soft-spoken, private Patti LaBelle is warmth, a quality expressed in her love of cooking for those around her. She is small, only five feet three inches tall, but great in spirit. Her concern for other people is reflected in her charity work in East Coast cities, including her hometown of Philadelphia. On a national level she has worked for a number of years for Big Sisters of America, One to One, and the United Negro College Fund. Her work has been recognized in the form of a Key to the City from Philadelphia, a medallion from the Congressional Black Caucus, the NAACP Image Award, an Ebony Achievement Award, and the Essence Award.

Patti LaBelle remains a very popular singer and performer, more popular now than ever. Her greatest triumphs in recording came nearly a quarter of a century after her first hit record. After several nominations, LaBelle won a Grammy in 1991 for Best Rhythm and Blues Vocalist for *Burnin'*. (She tied with Lisa Fischer.) On March 3, 1993, LaBelle was awarded a star on the Hollywood Walk of Fame. In a presentation that showed symbolically how her appeal transcends generational lines, the young singing group Boyz II Men was on hand to serenade her with ''End of the Road.'' For Patti LaBelle, that occasion was clearly not the end of the road but only a pause along the way.

REFERENCES:

Current Biography. New York: H. W. Wilson, 1986.

Ebert, Alan. ''After 16 Years a Group Breaks Up—LaBelle—A Whodunit.'' *Essence* 8 (February 1978): 72-87.

———. ''Girlfriend! Patti LaBelle.'' *Essence* 21 (March 1991): 68-70, 104-7.

''Essence Awards.'' *Essence* 21 (October 1990): 55-68.

Hardy, Phil, and Dave Lang. *Encyclopedia of Rock.* New York: Schirmer, 1987.

Heywood, Richette. ''Patti LaBelle Says 'Forget My Hair and Costumes Because My Voice Is the Real Me.''' *Jet* 76 (June 26, 1989): 24-27.

Hine, Darlene Clark, ed. *Black Women in America.* Brooklyn: Carlson, 1993.

Holden, Stephen. ''Patti LaBelle: A Pop Diva Takes Off.'' *New York Times,* February 23, 1986.

Larkin, Colin, ed. *The Guinness Encyclopedia of Popular Music.* Chester, Conn.: New England Press Associates, 1992.

''Patti LaBelle Gets a Star on Hollywood Walk of Fame.'' *Jet* 83 (March 22, 1993): 61.

''Patti LaBelle Starts New Career on *A Different World.*'' *Jet* 79 (January 21, 1991): 58-60.

''Patti LaBelle Tells How Death of Three Sisters Gives Her a New Attitude.'' *Jet* 78 (July 16, 1990): 56-58.

Randolph, Laura B. ''The Other Patti LaBelle: Wife, Mother, and Cook.'' *Ebony* 41 (April 1986): 31-36.

Salvo, Patrick. ''The Sexiest Singers in Show Business.'' *Sepia* 25 (March 1976): 44-53.

Sanders, Charles L. ''Patti LaBelle: On Her Own and Doing Great.'' *Ebony* 33 (September 1978): 162-70.

Southern, Eileen. *Biographical Dictionary of Afro-American and African Musicians.* Westport, Conn.: Greenwood Press, 1982.

Stambler, Irwin. *Encyclopedia of Pop, Rock & Soul.* Rev. ed. New York: St. Martin's Press, 1989.

Weston, Martin. ''Labelle.'' *Ebony* 31 (May 1970): 100-109.

Who's Who among Black Americans, 1994-95. 8th ed. Detroit: Gale, 1994.

Robert L. Johns

Queen Latifah
(1970-)
Rap artist, actress, business executive

Queen Latifah is one of the few women to make a mark in the male-dominated field of rap music, and she has done so by not simply imitating the men. She has established a reputation as rap's first feminist. As a result, she is the first person in the field to have made a breakthrough into the over twenty-four-year-old market. Not content with just making records and videos, she has formed a record and management company specializing in rap artists. Endowed with a striking appearance, she has also acted in movies and in a television series.

Dana Owens, born in 1970 in Newark, New Jersey, was the second child of Lance and Rita Owens. Rita Owens was eighteen years old when she gave birth to Dana. Her father was a policeman who sympathized with the Black Panthers. In a December 3, 1990, *New York* magazine article, Queen Latifah said, "He was a supporter of self-defense and lifting the race." The marriage of her parents was troubled, and the couple parted for good in 1978; Lance Owens, Sr. did, however, stay in touch with his children. Queen Latifah's brother, Lance, Jr., was older than his sister by a year; a policeman, he died in a motorcycle accident on April 26, 1992, an event which devastated her.

Rita Owens and the children moved to the High Court project in East Newark. A strong woman, Rita Owens set two goals for herself: to get the children out of the project and to attend college. With a full-time job and a part-time job combined with study at Kean Community College, she accomplished her goals in two years. In 1980 she became an art teacher at Irvington High School.

Queen Latifah was classed as intellectually gifted when she was in the second grade, and her mother managed to scrape together the tuition to give her child a better education at a parochial school. Dana Owens became Latifah when she was about eight. A Muslim cousin gave her the nickname, which means "delicate" and "sensitive" in Arabic. Queen was Latifah's own addition later.

The family established itself on Littleton Avenue in Newark. Queen Latifah sang in the choir of the Shiloh Baptist Church in Bloomfield, New Jersey. She had her first public singing triumph when she sang a version of "Home" as one of the two Dorothys in a production of *The Wiz* at Saint Anne's parochial school. She had the voice, but not the look for the role since she was already tall.

This height was an advantage when Queen Latifah entered Irvington High School, where her mother taught. She became a power forward on the basketball team, and during the time she was there the team won two state championships. Overall she made her mark in high school. She was the only senior to win four awards: Most Popular, Best All Round, Most Comical, and Best Dancer. The fall after her graduation,

Queen Latifah

she entered the Borough of Manhattan Community College. She was considering a career in broadcast journalism, but her college plans were sidelined because of the other developments in her life.

In her first year of high school—as a sophomore—Queen Latifah began informal singing and rapping in the restrooms and locker rooms. In her junior year she formed a rap group, Ladies Fresh, with her friends Tangy B and Landy D in response to the formation of another young women's group. Queen Latifah wrote her first rap to "take out" this other group at an Irvington High School talent show. Soon the group was making appearances wherever they could. Rita Owens was a catalyst; she was in touch with the students and the music. She invited Mark James, a local disk jockey known as D.J. Mark the 45 King, to appear at a school dance. The basement of James's parents' house in East Orange, which was equipped with electronic and recording equipment, became the hangout of Queen Latifah and her friends. They began to call themselves the Flavor Unit.

James was beginning a career as a producer and made a demo record of Queen Latifah's rap "Princess of the Posse." He gave the demo to Fred Braithwaite, "Fab 5 Freddy," host of *Yo! MTV Raps,* who played it for Dante Ross, who worked for Tommy Boy Music at that time. Tommy Boy signed Queen Latifah and in 1988 issued her first single, "Wrath of My Madness" and "Princess of the Posse," and then her second, "Dance for Me" and "Inside Out." Both sold about 40,000 copies without the support of a video. In the spring of 1989 Queen Latifah made her first European tour and her first appearance at the Apollo, which was quite successful. Her first video, "Dance for Me," was made in June 1989. In October 1989 the album *All Hail the Queen* appeared, most of which was produced by Mark James. Dinitia Smith said of it in *New York* magazine, December 3, 1990: "A novel blend of hip-hop, house reggae, and jazz, it touches on themes of poverty, apartheid, homelessness, and women. Latifah raps *and* sings on the album, unusual for a rap artist." The album led the New Music Seminar of Manhattan to give her the award of Best New Artist of 1990, and the album reached sales of over a million.

Even as Queen Latifah was beginning to earn money, she displayed interest in investment, putting money into a delicatessen and a video store on the ground floor of the apartment in which she was living. (She currently owns a video store that makes home deliveries.) She came to realize that there was an opening for her in record production. While she was making her own deals and making money in the process, many of her fellow rap artists were making disadvantageous recording arrangements. She organized and became chief executive officer of Flavor Unit Records and Management Company headquartered in Jersey City. By late 1993 the company had signed seventeen rap groups, including the very successful Naughty by Nature. Distribution of Flavor Unit's records was being handled by Motown, which was pressing her to move the operation to Los Angeles.

Latifah Becomes Actress

Queen Latifah's own career was flourishing as her third album, *Black Reign,* came out in 1993 following the 1991 major hit album *Nature of a Sista'*. Her fame and presence translated into film appearances, including roles in *Juice, Jungle Fever,* and *House Party 2,* and television appearances on such shows as *Fresh Prince of Bel-Air.* In these early efforts she almost always wore her trademark home-made crown, which she has now given up, and the parts hewed closely to her public image. In the 1994 film *My Life,* however, she played nurse to a patient dying of cancer. In addition, she was taking on a role in a sitcom, *Living Single.* This program went on the air in the fall 1993 season on the Fox network and demonstrated her flair for comedy. The program has strong ratings.

Despite the necessity of living in Los Angeles because of her television work, Queen Latifah feels that her base is still in New Jersey, where her mother lives, and she has a home in Wayne. Her mother, Rita Owens, is still a definite influence in her life. In addition to her teaching job, Owens serves as art director of her daughter's company. Eight years ago she also founded her high school's nonprofit antidrug organization, SAC (Students Against Crack). It is because of her mother's influence that Queen Latifah avoids strong language. The

major area of difference between the two women concerns smoking. Owens disapproves, and Queen Latifah is allowed to smoke only in her bedroom of the New Jersey home.

As a woman in the mostly male world of rap, Queen Latifah became celebrated by feminists. Initially she was not too happy with the label. In the *New York* magazine piece she said:

> I have a fear of feminism. To me, feminists were usually white women who hated men. A lot seemed to be gay. They were always fightin'. I didn't want to be that. . . . I don't want to be classified with them. What I have is common sense. I don't want chivalry to be dead. I want to have a man who will pull the chair out for me. I want to grow old with somebody.

She then said that she believes in "womanism—feminism for black women, to be natural, to have her sisterhood." She also found more common ground than she had first thought as she actually met some feminists. Her position as a defender of women against the slurs common in rap came under challenge when she produced Apache's "Gangsta Bitch." She recognized its potential to be a hit but did not foresee the controversy the lyrics would cause. In an October 1993 *Essence* article she defended herself by saying, "I wish people would leave rappers alone. We aren't the problem. We simply reflect what is going on in our society. Plus, if I believe in an artist and I sign them, [then] I don't feel it's my place to tell them how to make their music."

Queen Latifah is still young, but she has emerged as the major feminine voice in rap, become a businesswoman, and demonstrated potential as an actress. She has already shown a talent, intelligence, and drive that augur her continued success.

Current Address: c/o Motown Record Company, 6255 Sunset Boulevard, Los Angeles, CA 90028.

REFERENCES:

Collier, Aldore. "Queen Latifah Reigns On and Off TV." *Ebony* 49 (December 1933): 118-24.

Gregory, Deborah. "The Queen Rules." *Essence* 24 (October 1993): 56-58, 114-15, 118.

———. "The Queen Mother." *Essence* 24 (October 1993): 58, 121.

Pond, Steve. "Hail to the Queen." *TV Guide* 41 (October 16, 1993): 23-25.

Smith, Dinitia. "The Queen of Rap." *New York* 23 (December 3, 1990): 124-32, 138-46.

Robert L. Johns

Jennifer Lawson

(1946-)

Television and film company executive, film producer and editor, writer, educator, civil rights activist

Jennifer Lawson

J ennifer Lawson was the first black executive vice-president of programming and promotional services for the Public Broadcasting Service (PBS) in Washington, D.C., and the highest ranking woman to serve in public television. She took the position in 1989, when PBS faced a 12 percent drop in viewership due largely to the emergence of cable channels offering comparable programming. PBS was also the victim of what Richard Zoglin in *Time* called a "byzantine bureaucracy," caused by local station control and decentralization of series selection and scheduling, as well as funding. When the PBS board of directors began planning for a complete overhaul of its organizational structure, board president Bruce Christiansen stressed the need to hire a person who was capable of implementing the new structure. He was later quoted in the December 10, 1990, issue of *Time* magazine as saying that what the board wanted was "a Solomon . . . someone with extraordinary political skills as well as program judgement. And someone who [is] willing to take the heat." That person was Lawson, who made her mark on public television by meeting head on the challenges mandated by the PBS board of directors in 1989.

On June 8, 1946, Jennifer Karen Lawson was born in Fairfield, Alabama, a suburb of Birmingham. Her father, William DeLeon Lawson, owned a repair shop, and her mother, Velma Foster Lawson, was a teacher. Lawson credits her parents with being the most influential people in her life because of the many skills they encouraged her to acquire. Unlike most girls of her era, Lawson learned to repair cars because her father believed that a woman who could fix a car transmission could always find a job. Willie Lawson was not only a mechanic and businessman, he was also an inventor especially interested in rocketry. Both parents encouraged their daughter's creative talents in art and the sciences.

Joins Civil Rights Movement

Lawson was rewarded for her love of learning in 1963, when Tuskegee Institute granted her a full science scholarship. As a premedical major, she interned at the Sloan-Kettering Cancer Research Center in New York during the summer of 1964. Despite her interest in studying science, Lawson was drawn to the civil rights cause in Alabama, a major arena of political activism during her college years. She began working for the Student Nonviolent Coordinating Committee (SNCC) as a volunteer artist and eventually dropped out of college at the age of nineteen to become a civil rights activist. As a SNCC staffer and field organizer, Lawson worked in rural Alabama on black voter registration drives and adult literacy programs. During her three-year stint as a civil rights worker, Lawson's interest turned from science to communications as she gained a new sense of maturity and an awareness of the effects of empowering formerly illiterate and disenfranchised rural blacks. In a December 18, 1989, *Jet* article, she cited the Civil Rights movement as the turning point in her life:

> I began to see that there was a larger ill . . . [and] it required more courage to try to address that ill than it did to deal with the individual sick person. I felt the time was ripe for us to change this society and eradicate institutionalized racism.

After leaving Tuskegee in 1965 or 1966 (sources vary), Lawson worked as an illustrator and then as coordinator for the National Council of Negro Women in Washington, D.C. She moved to Mississippi to direct an adult education program before returning to Washington as art director of *Drum and Spear* magazine. Still seeking to put her proven talents in the communications field to better use, Lawson went to Tanzania to work on a government publishing project. The objective was to work with illiterate people and form a coalition of Africans and black Americans with a common interest in the arts. In this environment, Lawson's interest in the visual arts became keener as she sought ways to work with a largely illiterate population. She found it quite ironic that the project utilized print materials in a society better known for its oral tradition, with a target group largely comprised of nonreaders. It was in Tanzania that Lawson realized that film and television would soon rival the print medium as educational tools with the greatest potential for effective worldwide use.

In 1972, Lawson returned to the United States and began formally to prepare herself for a career in communications. She enrolled in graduate school at Columbia University and in 1974 received a master of fine arts degree in film studies. During the next six years, Lawson worked in New York as an associate producer at William Greaves Productions, as an assistant professor of film studies at Brooklyn College, and as an executive director of the Film Fund. She freelanced as a film editor and screenwriter while at the same time producing documentaries. Personal achievements included the publication of her first short story and having her first screenplay made into a movie. Lawson's Film Fund experiences provided entry to the world of filmmaking, as this agency issued grants to independent filmmakers who met the main criterion of addressing social issues. These positions prepared Lawson to move to the next level of her steady progress up the corporate ladder.

In 1980 she became the program coordinator at the Corporation for Public Broadcasting (CPB). Within three years, she was promoted to associate director for drama and arts programs. Other promotions followed. She was named administrator of the CPB Program Challenge Fund, and in 1988 she was appointed director of the Television Program Fund. Gene Kaat, the CPB vice-president of programming, described Lawson's meteoric rise in the October 1, 1990, issue of *Broadcasting:* "She's home grown having come into CPB and flowered here."

As the senior programming executive, Lawson was responsible for a forty-two-million-dollar budget, and she allotted funds for shows covering a wide spectrum of audience interest. *Alive from Off-Center,* an avant-garde show, and *The Mahabharata,* referred to as "a bizarre miniseries" by Sandra Salmans in *Savvy Woman,* were two of the most controversial programs aired during the time she was director of the Television Program Fund. Lawson's nine-year tenure at CPB put the finishing touches on her administrative, accounting, political, and creative skills.

Enters the Corporate World of PBS

The Public Broadcasting Service was chartered by Congress in 1978 as an alternative to commercial television. At the time, there were only three television networks from which to choose and, according to Kurt Andersen in the July 26, 1993, issue of *Time,* "You could watch *Gomer Pyle* or *Land of the Giants* or *Lawrence Welk*." This indictment of commercial television was matched by perceptions of public television as elitist. When the decision was made to hire Lawson as a top corporate executive, the board at PBS knew that this image had to be dispelled if PBS was to be attractive to a broader range of viewers. But the executive board faced other problems as well. As outlined in the October 20, 1989, *New York Times,* the most crucial issues were congressional pressure to offer more alternative programming, the need to devise more consistent standards for financing programs, and stiff competition from commercial cable networks. Speaking on the need for public television in general and PBS in particular, Andersen commented in the July 26, 1993, *Time*

article, "In a world of CNN, C-SPAN, A&E, The Discovery Channel, public TV begins to seem redundant."

A problem of more immediate concern was the network's internal structure. Described by Richard Zoglin in the December 10, 1990, issue of *Time* as "an unwieldy, multiheaded beast," PBS was at a disadvantage due to three major factors: the majority of PBS series were under the domain of individual stations as far as initiating and producing programs; scheduling was controlled by local program directors; and funding was provided by public and corporate sources, with the largest sums of money coming from local pledge week fund drives during which affiliates aired shows preferred by their own local markets. In 1987 the PBS board of directors had devised a comprehensive plan that defined new programming and financing strategies. Once Lawson came on board, some two years later, the plan then had to be presented to Congress and ratified by the three hundred plus public television affiliates.

On October 19, 1989, Lawson became the first black executive vice-president of national programming and promotion services for PBS and the top programming executive in public television in the country. Her major responsibilities were identifying, financing, distributing, and promoting a national schedule of programs. She reported directly to Bruce L. Christiansen, president and chief executive of PBS, and had two vice-presidents reporting directly to her. Her job called for her to determine what would be available for audiences to watch on public television. With the board-approved call for more centralized leadership in programming came expected resistance from the network of over three hundred local PBS stations still empowered to schedule programs as they desired. The local stations were mostly concerned about the one hundred million dollars placed at Lawson's disposal for program funding. This centralization of funding limited them to one funding source, as opposed to the former practice of seeking funding from both PBS and CPB.

Increases Diversity on PBS

Lawson was very clear and decisive in publicizing her priorities: to offer more cultural diversity, to improve and expand children's programming, and to increase the PBS audience through improved promotion. In *Savvy Woman,* March 1990, she vowed to "update the look and style of PBS . . . [and be] willing to take risks to expand the notion of what TV can be." She was astute enough to understand that PBS affiliates would have to accede to her plans. She resorted to her own brand of shuttle diplomacy to effect that result. The first strategy was traveling to the offices of program executives and listening to their concerns before explaining her vision for PBS. The next move in her strategy was to zone in on the Alexandria, Virginia, corporate headquarters, where she replaced the departmental system of operation, which she considered narrow in focus and limited by the rigidity of the structure, with a task-oriented team system. Finally, Lawson practiced the "honesty is the best policy" rule in responding to the viewing public's concerns and misperceptions about programming changes, especially as reported in the media.

She actually answered every letter sent by angry viewers, explaining her vision for PBS as well as addressing their fears.

PBS viewers have indeed benefitted from Lawson's vision. In September 1990, the *Civil War* series was scheduled to run for five consecutive nights rather than one night per week for five consecutive weeks. Lawson always makes clear that she did not develop the series but did make the scheduling decision in addition to planning the strategy to advertise the series on the three commercial networks. The payoff was tremendous: *The Civil War* became the highest ranked series and most-watched show in the history of public television, drawing over fifty million viewers. The A. C. Neilsen ratings were 9.0 with a thirteen share for all five nights. With each rating point equal to 931,000 households and each share representing the percentage of televisions across the country tuned in to the show, the final figures translated to fourteen million viewers nightly. In late 1990, Lawson publicized her own programming plans for the future: a children's game show, a Soviet family situation comedy, a showcase for pop music, and a dramatic series about human relationships. In mid-1991, the most talked about upcoming PBS project was a seven-part series entitled *Columbus and the Age of Discovery.*

An example of Lawson implementing her plans to display more diversity in programming was her decision to fund two projects by Henry Hampton, founder and president of Blackslide, Inc. This independent documentary filmmaker is best known as the producer of the 1987 TV series *Eyes on the Prize: America's Civil Rights Years,* which won more than forty prestigious awards. His most recent productions have been *The Great Depression,* which aired on PBS in October 1993, and *Malcolm X: Make It Plain,* which aired in January 1994. Lawson supported Hampton when he became seriously ill while completing production on the projects she had approved. She praised him for his dedication to meeting deadlines and for not letting his illness deter him from meeting his goals. When Lawson was in the process of taming the PBS bureaucracy, it was Hampton who complimented her diplomatic strategies. He told *Time* magazine for the December 10, 1990, article, "In some ways Jennifer is the only person who could have done this. . . . (She really does listen.)" Nevertheless, there are detractors and doubters who fear that Lawson's vision may be too extreme. Some contend that PBS may end up duplicating commercial television programming; others believe that PBS serves a privileged few; still others fear that their favorite shows will be axed. A former employee complained in the July 26, 1993, issue of *Time* that "anything apart from the norm won't be allowed. . . . (They aren't really interested in innovation.)"

Decisions Challenged

In 1994 a devastating attack on PBS came from Charlayne Hunter-Gault, featured reporter on the *McNeil/Lehrer NewsHour* and the first black woman to attend the University of Georgia. Hunter-Gault joined the show in 1978 as a correspondent and backup anchor and has received positive reviews from her co-anchor, Jim Lehrer, who, according to the *Los Angeles Times/Calendar,* July 31, 1994, credits her

with having "a special skill . . . the ability to sit down with somebody and get them to talk. . . . She's terrific at it." Hunter-Gault's main complaint, cited in the same source, was that PBS's principal programs, aired during prime hours, are anchored by white males. Lawson answered the charge by responding that her major goal of committing PBS to diversity has indeed been met, as exemplified by the presence of Hunter-Gault on the *McNeil/Lehrer NewsHour* as well as by the appearance of other minorities in highly visible positions on popular programs. Hunter-Gault's next complaint concerned her own series, *Rights & Wrongs,* a half-hour show produced by Globalvision, a New York-based independent production company, that was rejected for national distribution by PBS in 1993. Her executive co-producers, Danny Schechter and Rory O'Connor, question the rejection because of Hunter-Gault's national reputation for quality news reporting. Lawson replied to this charge by criticizing Hunter-Gault's show for its human rights emphasis and its execution, claiming that "the McNeil/Lehrer program covers the same ground with more flexibility." Hunter-Gault also complained that she was not featured often enough on the McNeil/Lehrer program, a charge refuted by the executive producer, who cited her frequent appearances when she was in South Africa. Lawson regrets that Hunter-Gault saw the entire matter as a racial issue.

In early 1995, Lawson's career with PBS came to an end when she resigned her post as programming chief. Reorganization of PBS in January of that year had left Lawson with a greatly reduced role, and as she told *Jet,* "I began to consider whether this is the best way to make a contribution."

Lawson's first marriage ended in divorce in 1980, and she subsequently married Anthony Gittens on May 29, 1982. Gittens is the executive director of the Washington, D.C., International Film Festival and the Black Film Institute. He and Lawson are the parents of two sons. In 1990, Lawson was named one of the "101 Most Influential People in Entertainment Today" by *Entertainment Weekly.*

In the foreword to the 1994/95 edition of *Who's Who among Black Americans,* Lawson addresses the impact of new technologies on contemporary society and says that African Americans must meet new challenges in a more technologically advanced society. She also urges African American leadership to assist the disenfranchised in seeing the positive side of the new opportunities that are opening up, rather than viewing change as a threat, and to encourage them to have a vision of promise and possibilities and to pursue their dreams. Lawson certainly has practiced the advice she has given to other black leaders, for she influenced the lives of millions of Americans through her work in public television.

REFERENCES:

Andersen, Kurt. "How Necessary Is PBS?" *Time* 142 (July 26, 1993): 75.
Baskerville, Dawn M., Sheryl Hilliard-Tucker, and Donna Whittingham-Barnes. "21 Women of Power and Influ-

ence in Corporate America.'' *Black Enterprise* 22 (August 1991): 68.

''Black Broadcasting '91: 30 Who Stand Out.'' *Broadcasting* 121 (September 9, 1991): 54.

''Civil Rights Movement Led Lawson to Her PBS Career.'' *Jet* 77 (December 18, 1989): 38.

Contemporary Black Biography. Vol. 1. Detroit: Gale Research, 1992.

Ferguson, Andrew. ''PBS: The Yanni State.'' *National Review* 46 (May 2, 1994): 72.

''How I Did It.'' *Working Woman* 16 (April 1991): 57-58, 60.

''Jennifer Lawson Leads PBS to Best Ratings Ever with *The Civil War* Series.'' *Jet* 79 (October 22, 1990): 34.

''Jennifer Lawson: Teaching and Delighting.'' *Broadcasting* 119 (October 1, 1990): 95.

Norment, Lynn. ''Women at the Top in the Entertainment Industry.'' *Ebony* 48 (March 1993): 106-14.

Norris, K. Anthony. ''Blackslide's Henry Hampton: Telling and Selling the Truth.'' *American Visions* 9 (February/March 1994): 46-47.

Norris, Michele L. ''Jennifer Lawson—Programming Chief.'' *Essence* 21 (April 1991): 32.

''PBS: Appoints New Programming Chief.'' *New York Times,* October 20, 1989.

''PBS Programming Chief Jennifer Lawson Resigns.'' *Jet* 87 (March 6, 1995): 7.

''Public TV Is Seeking to Centralize Programs.'' *New York Times,* June 21, 1990.

Robins, J. Max. ''Hunter-Gault Hits the Ceiling.'' *Variety* 27 (August 8-14, 1994): 32.

Rosenberg, Howard. ''Time to Fine-Tune the Picture.'' *Los Angeles Times/Calendar,* July 31, 1994: 5, 76, 78, 82.

Salmans, Sandra. ''Channeling Her Energy.'' *Savvy Woman* 11 (March 1990): 16.

Who's Who among Black Americans, 1994-95. 8th ed. Detroit: Gale Research, 1994.

Who's Who of American Women, 1993-94. 18th ed. New Providence, N.J.: Marquis Who's Who, 1993.

Zoglin, Richard. ''The Wisdom of Ms. Solomon.'' *Time* 136 (December 10, 1990): 76.

Dolores Nicholson

Rosetta E. Coakley Lawson

Rosetta E. Coakley Lawson

(c. 1854-1936)

Educator, religious worker, reformer, club leader, temperence leader

Rosetta E. Coakley Lawson was totally committed to the elevation of black people as witnessed through her work as educator, national temperance organizer and lecturer, and leader in black women's organizations. She is an example of a dedicated black woman who effectively met the people's educational and community needs as well as developing and supporting her own family life.

Lawson was born in King George County, Virginia, around 1854. Young Rosetta and her mother, a free black woman, moved to Washington, D.C., in 1862. Her father, a slave, had fled for freedom when she was two years old. She attended private schools and the District of Columbia's public high school. During the summer of 1872 she volunteered in the office of George F. T. Cook, the superintendent of ''colored schools'' in Washington and nearby Georgetown. In this position she reviewed teacher records for the year to verify the accuracy of statistics. Only the best teachers were assigned as examiners. Cook observed her accuracy, thoroughness, efficiency, and fondness for the assignment which she was given. When the new term opened in 1873, Cook persuaded the Board of Trustees to assign Lawson indefinitely for clerical work in his office. She was so successful in this position that she became assistant superintendent when Horace W. Parke resigned one year later. Lawson's new position immensely broadened her experiences. She visited all schools above the fifth grade and, along with the superintendent, held oral examinations of all students in arithmetic, penmanship, map drawing, and word analysis. She met distinguished educators from a variety of states and countries who were interested in the current trend of educating black people, many of whom were former slaves. She remained in the position for twelve years, until June 1885.

During this period Lawson maintained a home for her aged mother and grandmother. She agonized over her limited funds, the impending cost of additional education, and whether or not she should leave her position to continue her studies.

Lawson was then attracted to the idea of public education through Chautauqua, a lecture circuit. She organized a large circle of teachers in the district, and from 1880 to the end of 1884, she and a group of women known as The Irrepressibles pursued a course specifically organized for the Chautauqua Literary and Scientific Circle. In 1884, the Irrepressibles went to Chautauqua, New York, where they completed the course and received a diploma. In the same year, Rosetta E. Coakley married Jesse Lawson, of Plainfield, New Jersey.

The Lawsons had four children: James F., a major in the armed services; Josephine L. (Harley), a graduate of Oberlin, and later an English specialist at Dunbar High School in Washington, D.C.; Edward H., an educator at Shaw Junior High School, also in Washington; and Lieutenant Wilfred W. Lawson, who became registrar at Tennessee Agricultural and Industrial State College in Nashville and director of agriculture for the state of Tennessee.

Characteristic of women of her time, Rosetta Lawson felt strongly that women should guide their children in the use of appropriate language. In an interview, James Lawson, her grandson, of Boyd, Maryland, remembered a story that was repeated often about Lawson: "She was coming up Vermont Avenue (where she lived) one day and heard a child's voice—using vulgar language. 'Now that's what you hear when mothers are not at home with their children,' she said to her companion. When she got to the corner the voice said, 'Hi, Mom.' It was her son."

Lawson Becomes Temperance and Club Leader

For thirty years, Rosetta Lawson was national organizer and lecturer for the Women's Christian Temperance Union (WCTU). The Washington, D.C., chapter recognized her long tenure and made her a life member of the national organization. Later, she became national organizer emeritus. Lawson's temperance activities took her to nearly every state and to foreign cities such as Toronto, Canada; Edinburgh, Scotland; and London and Liverpool, England. She attended the world WCTU conference held in Paris in 1900.

Lawson's interests extended beyond temperance into many areas of community life, especially women's issues. Her husband had been appointed commissioner of the Northwestern Territory for the Cotton States and International Exposition of 1895 in Atlanta, Georgia. He encouraged Rosetta, then secretary of the Ladies Auxiliary of the exposition in Washington, and Josephine Beall Bruce, the auxiliary's president, to assemble a national conference in the city, the Atlanta Congress of Colored Women. The auxiliary already focused on themes of national concern—social purity, improvement of the home, and child culture—and aimed to establish more clubs, including some for children.

The Atlanta conference was the second national conference held for black women; the first was the National Federation of Afro-American Women held in Boston earlier in 1895. Representatives from twenty-six states and the District of

Columbia attended the Atlanta meeting held in December of that year. In Josephine Bruce's absence, Rosetta Lawson organized the meeting. Although Frances E. W. Harper, Victoria Earle Matthews, and Margaret Murray Washington urged Lawson to run for president of the Atlanta Congress of Colored Women, she declined in favor of Lucy Thurman. Thurman had just been appointed national superintendent of WCTU work among black people, and Lawson argued that, with Thurman as president, the cause that was equally dear to both of them might be more effectively served.

When the Atlanta Congress of Colored Women held its second meeting in Nashville, Tennessee, in 1897, during the Tennessee centennial, the women decided that the race was not strong enough to support an additional black women's organization. The Congress was dissolved in Nashville that year. The same concerns had been raised the previous year, when the members of the National Federation of Afro-American Women and the National League of Colored Women felt threatened by a proliferation of organizations called "national." Supporting the unified efforts of black women, the two groups merged at their national conventions, held in Washington in July 1896, to form the National Association of Colored Women (NACW). Lawson was hostess at the final meeting of the National Federation of Afro-American Women in Washington in 1896.

Organizes YWCA for African Americans

Continuing her work for black women's causes, Lawson, in 1905, served as president of the Booklover's Club. The idea of a Young Women's Christian Association for black women in Washington, D.C., also seemed appealing. Lawson attended a meeting held by a representative of the Chicago YWCA and led the Booklover's Club members in organizing the Colored Young Women's Christian Association, later known as the Phillis Wheatley YWCA. She sent invitations to club members to attend a meeting on April 5, 1905, to consider the feasibility of organizing the Y. The meeting focused on need for suitable housing for girls and women seeking work in Washington. The group met again on May 5, 1905, and formally organized the YWCA, which was incorporated in the District of Columbia on June 30 of that year and was housed in the old Minor Institution Building. The incorporators included Coralie Franklin Cook, Mamie E. Hilyer, Josephine Beall Bruce, Marian P. Shadd, and Ida Gibbs Hunt. Lawson headed the executive committee.

In 1909, Lawson became president of the Home for Friendless Girls in the District of Columbia, an organization which Caroline Taylor, a leading spirit among area black women, had founded in 1866. Many teachers and community leaders in the area volunteered their services there.

Jesse and Rosetta Lawson devoted their lives to the cause of inspiring black people through education. They held a meeting at their residence in late April 1906, in which Mifflin Wister Gibbs, United States consul to Madagascar, Kelly Miller of Howard University, Judson W. Lyons, register of the treasury, and other influential leaders organized a branch of the Bible Educational Association at the nation's capital. Jesse Lawson became president of the Inter-Denominational Bible College, which was established to provide a socially and morally uplifting education to Washington's black working class, many of whom had come from the South. On February 17, 1917, the college became Frelinghuysen University.

Rosetta Lawson graduated from the School of Chiropractic and Allied Sciences at Frelinghuysen University; she then taught anatomy and allied sciences at the institution. Originally located in the Lawson's home, Frelinghuysen University eventually relocated to 601 M Street, N.W. Jesse Lawson died November 8, 1927, and on June 15, 1930, Anna Julia Cooper, educator, scholar, writer, feminist, and activist, was inaugurated as the second president of the institution. Rosetta Lawson continued to support the school. She was also active in Sunday school and other aspects of the church. She worked in Bands of Mercy for children, and for sixteen years she was financial agent for Stoddard Baptist Church Old Folk's home.

Nothing is known about her later life. James Lawson said in his interview that she was ill for six to eight months before she died. According to James McGuire, her death records at McGuire Funeral home in the District of Columbia show that she died of chronic nephritis on April 19, 1936, when she was about eighty-two years old. Her funeral was held at Nineteenth Avenue Baptist Church on April 22, and she was buried in Washington's Woodlawn Cemetery. Lawson is important for her devotion to the education and cultural and social uplift of black people. An active member of black women's organizations and a participant in numerous social and charitable groups, Lawson has left a notable example for later generations of black American women.

REFERENCES:

Davis, Elizabeth Lindsay. *Lifting as They Climb*. Washington, D.C.: National Association of Colored Women, 1933.

Hine, Darlene Clark, ed. *Black Women in America*. Brooklyn: Carlson Publishing, 1993.

Hutchinson, Louise Daniel. *Anna J. Cooper, A Voice from the South*. Prepared in conjunction with an exhibit at the Anacostia Neighborhood Museum, Washington, D.C., 1981.

———. Telephone interviews with Jessie Carney Smith, March 28, 1995; March 31, 1995.

Lawson, James. Telephone interview with Jessie Carney Smith, March 28, 1995.

McGuire, James. Telephone interview with Jessie Carney Smith, March 30, 1995.

Pendleton, Lelia Amos. *A Narrative of the Negro*. Washington, D.C.: Press of R. L. Pendleton, 1912.

Scruggs, Lawson. *Women of Distinction*. Raleigh, N.C.: L. A. Scruggs, 1893.

Helena Carney Lambeth

Maria Coles Perkins Lawton
(1864-1946)
Clubwoman, educator, political activist, lecturer, columnist

The life of Maria (pronounced Mo-ri-ah) C. Lawton—educator, political worker, club leader, reformer, newspaper reporter, and lecturer—was the quintessential embodiment of the motto of the National Association of Colored Women's Clubs, "Lifting as We Climb." Much of her life's work was dedicated to forming organizations for the purpose of improving not just the lot of African American women but of all African Americans. Her career as a noted public speaker on issues of race and gender began in 1897. In the 1920s, she became involved in Republican party politics and the labor movement.

Maria Coles Perkins Lawton was born in Lynchburg, Virginia, on April 30, 1864. Her parents were Robert Alexander Perkins and Mildred Booker Cabell Perkins. There is little record of her early childhood. Her secondary education was completed at Lynchburg High School. After graduation, she attended the Richmond Institute, Richmond, Virginia, and Howard University in Washington, D. C.

Lawton returned to Lynchburg to teach in the public school system after completing her education at Howard University. She married William Rufus Lawton on May 7, 1886. He was a minister and a mathematics professor in Lynchburg. He later became a high school principal in Beaufort, South Carolina, and a professor of history and civil policy in Jefferson City, Missouri. The Lawtons had seven children—Ethel, Irene, Eunice, Cuthbert, Frank, Harry, and Robert—who were born between the years 1887 and 1906.

In 1892, Lawton and her family moved to Brooklyn, New York, where her husband had been appointed to pastor Siloam Presbyterian Church. He went on to pastor several Presbyterian churches in the New York City and New Jersey areas. William Lawton was one of the first African American civil servants in the New York City area. He worked at the Kings County district attorney's office and the marriage license bureau. In New York, Maria Lawson did not continue her teaching career; instead, she began a new career as a newspaper reporter for the *Standard Union,* a daily newspaper in Brooklyn. She would work there twenty years, making her one of the small number of African American women in Brooklyn with professional careers. The Lawtons were among Brooklyn's prominent African American residents. They both were very active in laying the foundations for a thriving African American community in Brooklyn, which around the turn of the twentieth century rivaled the Manhattan African American community in prominence.

Lawton's speaking career began in 1897, as she became increasingly involved in the women's club movement as well as in Brooklyn and New York State politics. Her speaking career caused her to travel extensively throughout New York

Maria Coles Perkins Lawton

State and New England. She was most noted for her lectures on issues of race, gender inequity—especially in the labor force—and children's education.

Foundation Built for an Improved Black Community in Brooklyn

African American women in Brooklyn were instrumental in the establishment of effective community-based improvement organizations that were designed to care for the needs of the aged, the orphaned, the poor and destitute, and the children of working mothers. By the turn of the twentieth century, several such community organizations had emerged, with the general mission of improving the urban living conditions of African Americans. Lawton and many of her contemporaries in the community—including Verina Harris Morton Jones; Mary Angela Dixon, wife of the prominent Brooklyn minister William T. Dixon; and Ella Crowder—founded numerous local organizations. Some of these organizations were the Silver Lock Club of Concord Church (1901), the Brooklyn NAACP, Big Sister organizations, branches of the YWCA and YMCA (1902), and the Brooklyn branch of the National Urban League (1910). The successful Lincoln Settlement House, which provided youth counseling and day care for the children of working mothers, was established in 1908. Far ahead of their time, the women of Brooklyn established a free kindergarten in the Siloam Presbyterian Church, where Lawton's husband pastored.

The church also became the site for Lawton's senior citizen's center project. She originally began the seniors program in 1939 on Bridge Street in downtown Brooklyn. The program moved to the YMCA on Third Avenue, then later to St. Phillips Parish, and eventually it came to be located at Siloam Presbyterian Church. The seniors program continues to this day. It is located on Hart Street in Brooklyn, and bears the name Maria Lawton Senior Center. The program provides senior citizens with a full range of social services, meals, and recreational activities.

These organizations were interdependent and worked cooperatively. Local leaders like Lawton were firm believers in community organization as a means of improving living conditions, providing needed services, and confronting the forces of racism. In addition to her involvement in local community improvement organizations, she became an active member of the Brooklyn chapter of the NAACP. The chapter sponsored an antilynching meeting which featured such noted speakers as Walter White and James Weldon Johnson.

Lawton and other members of the Brooklyn NAACP initiated protests against racial discrimination in Brooklyn, and as with most local chapters of the organization, they added their voices to protest racial discrimination throughout the nation. As a reporter for the *Brooklyn Daily Standard Union,* she was aware of the damage done to black communities by the negative images of African Americans portrayed in the press. She was instrumental in the organization of NAACP protests against the use of the term ''darkies'' by a local Brooklyn newspaper, compelling them to issue an apology to the community. The organization helped combat the discriminatory practices of local movie theaters and led protests against police brutality in the African American community.

Lawton Becomes Key Figure in Women's Club Movement

Lawton is most remembered for her contributions to the women's club movement. She became one of the most active African American women of her day in the National Association of Colored Women's Clubs (NACW) at the local, state, and national levels.

The third state organization to affiliate with the North Eastern Region of the NACW was the Empire State Federation. Founders of the federation were influenced by the overall mission of the NACW as it had been established by Josephine Pierre Ruffin. The clubs that initially affiliated with the Empire State Federation were mainly located in and around New York City and Buffalo. Lawton was appointed state organizer in 1912. Under her effective leadership, clubs from the Hudson River region and the central part of New York joined the federation. By the early 1920s there were 103 clubs affiliated with the state federation.

According to Charles Wesley, the mission of the NACW was ''to foster and promote the education of women and girls; raise the standard of the home; work for moral, economic, social, and religious welfare of women and children; endeavor to protect the rights of women and children who work; secure and use its influence for the guarantee of human rights.''

Lawton was a brilliant organizer. Like her notable contemporary Mary Church Terrell, she believed in the necessity of organizations in the movement to uplift the lives of African Americans in general and African American women in particular. In 1915 Lawton was instrumental in the founding of the New Jersey State Federation of Colored Women's Clubs. She was a featured speaker during the closing session of that club's founding ceremonies. The theme of the meeting was "The Necessity of Organization."

Lawton's club membership and work was not limited to the Empire State Federation. Her other club memberships included the Woman's Loyal Union, the Woman's Club, the Queen Ester Circle, and the Urban Neighborhood Club. In addition to her role as state organizer for the Empire State Federation, she served as the federation president from 1916 to 1929, and as national chairperson of the NACW Program and Literature Committee from 1926 to 1929.

As testimony to her success as a clubwoman, the M. C. Lawton Club was founded in 1919 as an affiliate of the Albany region of the Empire State Federation. The club was established to promote civic and cultural activities primarily for black people in the community. A second club named after Lawton was established in 1937 in the New York City area.

Political Activities Parallel Club Work

Lawton combined her club work with political activities. Her most notable political involvements began in the 1920s, after the passage of the Nineteenth Amendment, which granted women the right to vote; however, her organizational skills had earlier been recognized by New York's political leaders. In 1914, Lawton was designated by Governor Martin H. Glynn of New York, a Democrat, to represent the state at the National Negro Educational Congress in Oklahoma City, Oklahoma. She was also the New York representative to the meeting of the congress in Saint Louis, Missouri.

After the passage of the Nineteenth Amendment, Lawton became an active member of the New York Republican party. Her husband was one of the local organizers and presidents of the Kings County Colored Republican Organization. Lawton and her husband frequently held teas and luncheons in their home on Willoughby Street for local and state leaders and members of the Republican Party. During this period in American politics, the Republican party was viewed by many blacks as the best hope for African Americans because it lacked the divisions between northern and southern members evident in the Democratic party.

Many members of the NACW's affiliate organizations were also members of the Republican party, and in 1924 the League of Republican Colored Women was organized. It included four hundred representatives from forty-one states of the union. The club was one of the first national political organizations for African American women. Although there is no official documentation of Lawton's association with the league, it is clear that she was influenced by the political attitudes that prevailed in the African American community.

After the National Republican Committee began to include women in its official family, a number of African American women were elected as committeewomen to represent the African American community. On April 17, 1924, at the New York Republican State Convention, Louise M. Fairweather became the first African American woman to be elected a delegate-at-large. That year, Lawton was appointed director of the eastern division of the Republican National Convention and endorsed the nomination and election of Calvin Coolidge.

Following the lead of Mary Church Terrell, who channeled her efforts towards the unionization of African American female workers in the 1920s, Lawton became active in the labor movement. As a working woman, she understood the need for labor organization among African American women. Lawton was a representative of the state of New York at the Labor Conference of Women held in Washington, D.C., in 1924. According to Paula Giddings, organized efforts were a means of obtaining justice in the work world for African American women: justice in the form of equal pay for equal work, inclusion in areas reserved for men, a forty-four-hour work week, social insurance (worker's compensation and pensions), maternity benefits, and job training.

Lawton's memory is kept alive through her grandchildren, Frank Lawton, Jr. and Dorothy Bowen—the children of her son, Frank Lawton—who still live in Brooklyn. She has a great-grandaughter, Yvonne Halyard, and a great-great-granddaughter, Tonora Tanya Smalls. Other family members have not been located despite the efforts of Lawton's granddaughter, Dorothy Bowen. In a recent interview, Bowen fondly remembered Lawton as "the most wonderful grandmother that anyone could ever have," as well as a fervent advocate of racial equality. According to Bowen, Lawton became relatively inactive during the later years of her life—from 1940 until her death. She spent most of that time reading and calling her 'political' friends in order to stay informed of political events. Her husband died in 1944, and the last two years of her life were spent in loneliness, mourning the loss of her husband and battling cancer. She died in 1946.

Maria C. Lawton was a woman of courage and tireless commitment. Her efforts to better the lives of African Americans in the Brooklyn community and the state of New York through her involvement in women's clubs, the NAACP, political groups, and labor organizations were significant. Her skills as an organizer helped to propel the movement to improve the lives of African Americans to new heights during the late nineteenth and early twentieth centuries.

REFERENCES:

Black Women in Brooklyn. Brooklyn: Brooklyn Historical Society, 1985.

Bowen, Dorothy. Telephone interview with Walton Brown, January 12, 1995.

"Carry the Fight to Cleveland." *New York Times,* June 2, 1924.

Connolly, Harry X. *Blacks in Brooklyn from 1900 to 1960.* Ph.D. dissertation, New York University, 1972.

Davis, Elizabeth Lindsay. *Lifting As We Climb.* Chicago: National Association of Colored Women's Clubs, 1933.

Giddings, Paula. *Where and When I Enter: The Impact of Black Women in Race and Sex in America.* New York: Morrow, 1984.

Mather, Frank Lincoln. *Who's Who of the Colored Race.* Chicago: N.p., 1915.

"Negroes Seek Coolidge." *New York Times,* June 20, 1924.

Welty, William. *Black Shepherded, a Study of the Leading Negro Clergymen in New York City, 1900-1940.* Ph.D. dissertation, New York University, 1969.

Wesley, Charles Harris. *The History of the National Association of Colored Women's Clubs.* Washington, D.C.: NACW, 1984.

Walton L. Brown

S. Willie Layten

S. Willie Layten
(1863-1950)
Feminist, organization leader, educator, clubwoman, political worker

For many years S. Willie Layten headed the Women's Convention of the National Baptist Convention, and through it she fought unceasingly for women's rights in the church. Outside the organization, she was an agitator for black political power. She was an early leader in the National League for the Protection of Colored Women (NLPCW), a forerunner of the National Urban League. She was the first black woman field secretary of the league. Layten supervised the collaboration of the NLPCW, the National Association of Colored Women, and the Women's Convention. The three organizations worked together to protect the rights of female migrant workers in the North. Their particular concern was black women but they did not exclude other women from the benefits of their services.

Sarah Willie Layten, generally known by the name she called herself, S. Willie Layten, was born in Granada, Mississippi, in 1863. She was the daughter of William H. Phillips, a minister; sources do not give her mother's name. Layten grew up in a family that advocated racial self-determination. Her father, a staunch supporter of a trained black ministry, was part of a movement for black denominational hegemony. In 1881 Layten graduated from LeMoyne College in Memphis and much later took graduate courses in sociology at Temple University in Philadelphia and extension courses in social work at the University of Pennsylvania. She moved with her parents from Memphis to Fort Smith, Arkansas, where her father became pastor of a local church. For a while, Layten taught in the public schools. She married in 1882 and moved to Los Angeles, where her only child, Madalene, was born.

According to Evelyn Brooks Higginbotham in *Righteous Discontent: The Women's Movement in the Black Baptist Church, 1800-1920,* "By her own testimony, Layten had championed rights for blacks and women when she was a young girl." She had become well acquainted with the racial and gender concerns of black Baptist women, who began to address such issues during the late 1800s. Now she could begin her own activism by serving as a leader of women's religious and secular organizations in California: she became president of the Western Baptist Association of California, she was part of an unsuccessful 1890 drive to establish a national women's foreign mission convention, and she was also a founder of the California Federation of Colored Women's Clubs.

Layten moved to Philadelphia in 1894, joining her parents, who had settled there when her father became pastor of Shiloh Baptist Church. She was to spend the rest of her life in Philadelphia. Nothing is known about what happened to Layten's husband. According to Higginbotham, Layten's husband's name is never mentioned in her speeches and writings, her father's writings, or in biographical accounts. By the time she moved to Philadelphia, she was in effect a single mother with a young daughter, and she became nationally known on her own.

Heads Women's Convention

Layten continued her work in religious clubs. When the Women's Convention, the auxiliary to the National Baptist Convention, was organized in Richmond, Virginia, in 1900, she was elected president. She held the position forty-nine years, retiring in September 1948 due to failing health, and was elected president-emeritus. Other officers who were elected in 1900 also became well-known leaders in the convention and the black community, including Nannie Helen Burroughs of Kentucky and Washington, D.C., corresponding secretary, and Virginia E. Broughton of Tennessee, recording secretary. They, too, held their positions for many years. Burroughs succeeded Layten as president.

Though highly regarded by her Baptist sisters, Layten's advice was not always heeded. The Women's Convention held its annual conferences simultaneously with the National Baptist Convention. When the women held their second annual conference in 1901, Elias Camp Morris, president of the National Baptist Convention, urged the women to operate as a board under the larger male parent organization and report annually to the male-controlled convention. Layten agreed and recommended the change during her address to the group. The women refused, however, and kept their own identity.

Without doubt, Layten was an advocate for cooperation among women's groups and interracial understanding. She represented the Women's Convention before the Woman's Missionary Union, a southern white Baptist organization, at its annual meeting in Nashville, Tennessee, in 1904. The delegates from the union attended a citywide conference on black Baptist women. Layten commented on the cooperative spirit between the groups and called the 1904 meeting the greatest achievement for women that year, although she knew that the International Conference of Women was meeting in Berlin, the National Association of Colored Women was assembled in St. Louis, and the Women's Temperance Union was scheduled to meet later that year. She argued that the joint meeting of the black and white women was highly significant because it set a precedent for interracial cooperation and was a crucial step toward greater racial understanding in the South.

Layten was concerned with the tendency of society to hold black women accountable for the behavior of the race as a whole. According to the *Journal of the Fifth Annual Assembly of the Women's Convention,* held in 1904, Layten urged black women to react:

> Mothers be stern, be firm and yet you can be kind and sympathetic. As a race we cannot afford to contribute ONE single life to the bad, though the individuals force it upon us. We are impoverished, unfortunately the minority of bad Negroes have given the race a questionable reputation; these degenerates are responsible for every discrimination we suffer.

Association to Protect Women Formed

Perhaps as much through her work as president of the Women's Convention as from her own childhood background, Layten had a keen interest in social reform. The black Baptists in the women's convention movement were also the educated elite of the community and became leaders in secular organizations as well. The convention embraced secular reform activity, which complemented and gave meaning to their church work. Church and secular organizations worked together.

Frances Kellor, a white social worker, and Layten, president of the Women's Convention, worked closely in the National League for the Protection of Colored Women (NLPCW). According to Layten's article "The Servant Problem," an account of her work with migrant women published in *Colored American Magazine* in January 1907, the NLPCW grew out of the Household Research Association, an intermunicipal organization that studied conditions affecting domestic service. The NLPCW identified unscrupulous employment agencies in the North that imported large numbers of blacks from the South and detailed the demoralizing conditions for blacks once they arrived in the larger cities. The league worked to improve the moral and financial condition of women employed in domestic service. Kellor founded protective associations in New York and Philadelphia as early as 1905.

During her address before the 1905 Women's Convention, Layten reported on these early activities of the two-month-old NLPCW and its rescue home for migrant women. This may have been the Mary S. Tribbett Home for Girls, which Layten was instrumental in founding. The convention and the protective associations worked to protect migrant women who moved North from excessive travel costs and other exploitive practices. Blacks and whites in employment agencies, lodging houses, churches, and working girls' homes formed support groups to aid the migrants. In addition, churches in the North and South were intermediaries between Layten and women who wished to migrate North. According to Higginbotham, women who wanted to migrate worked through their churches and, in turn, the churches contacted Layten, who gave them directions and other pertinent information. The churches also facilitated Layten's work by encouraging only those who seemed well able to travel to migrate and by sending representatives to meet the ships and trains that carried the new arrivals. They also helped the migrants find lodging and suitable employment.

The NLPCW officially established branches in Philadelphia and New York in 1906. To reach migrant women at key arrival points, other branches were added in Boston, Memphis, and Baltimore between 1906 and 1910. The work would not be complete until branches in Richmond, Charleston, Savannah, Jacksonville, and New Orleans were added. Layten replaced Kellor as general secretary of the NLPCW in 1910. Her article "The Servant Problem" appeared when she headed the Philadelphia association. In it she wrote:

> We are seriously concerned about the large number of women of our race whose existence is lived among tubs, scrub brushes, pans, pots, and who by their skill in their places of service, and by their upright lives, are contributing much toward laying the foundation for the era when nothing shall be considered menial that is well done.

The NLPCW promoted better servants, better service, and increased numbers of employers who would offer better working conditions. Layten called for help:

We appeal to our "race pride" people to become interested in this work, believing it to be one of the most helpful ways of solving the so called race problem, North as well as South. Few of us recognize the possible power of our people in domestic service—while our brilliant orators plead eloquently the Negroes' rights, their voices are seldom heard by the powers that be, but while those who serve acceptably and well, filling helpful positions or trust as domestics, are capable of creating a sentiment favorable to the Negro in his struggle for opportunity and a just verdict.

In the year before it was formally organized, the Philadelphia association aided over one thousand young women. In the four months after it was officially established, it aided over 450 black women and girls and 16 white women and girls in its work at the docks. Since many new arrivals who came by train did not know that hundreds of trains ran to Philadelphia daily or that there were several railroad stations, they were bewildered when friends and families whom they expected to meet were not there. Their confusion made them easy prey for thieves and confidence tricksters. The NLPCW alleviated this problem by meeting arriving women at their trains.

Formation of the National Urban League

In 1911 the NLPCW merged with the Committee on Urban Conditions and the Committee for Improving the Industrial Conditions of Negroes in New York to become the National Urban League. Layten became one of its first field secretaries and the only woman in this role. The other secretaries appointed at the time were Victor Flinn and Eugene Kinckle Jones. When George Edmund Haynes of the National Urban League, along with Ida Wells Barnett, spoke to the annual meeting of the Women's Convention in 1918, he praised the Baptist women and Layten for their work in social reform.

Through her speeches before the annual Baptist women's conventions from 1905 on, Layten kept the Baptist women informed about the activities of the protective association. Calling for "practical Christianity," she spoke of the social and economic needs of blacks. In 1910 the Women's Convention's Committee on Recommendations praised the NLPCW for its work and, according to Higginbotham, thanked Layten for "placing our Baptist women in charge of a work that is destined to reach, rescue, and save girls as no other agency now operating." The women also pledged financial assistance to the league. In her annual address of 1912, after the formation of the National Urban League, Layten reported about her position with the league, addressed the status of urban migration of women, and called for women's groups to monitor the problem and work with the women in their area.

Layten was aware of the great work of the Baptist women thus far. Commenting on their contributions during the convention's first two decades, president Layten remarked in her annual address before the Women's Convention in 1915:

We have extended . . . membership to every State and territory in the Union; we have found quiet and obscure women, who knew not their talents, and we have brought them forth, given them inspiration and work, and developed them into some of the strongest and most resourceful women of the age. . . . The Convention is in reality—an institute—our effort is to teach and prepare women for service.

The problem of black women migrants still had not eased by 1915. Layten said the predicament was "alarmingly undermining our moral and industrial systems." Black women were still being neglected and were still "victim[s] of men of all races." The courts ignored their concerns; as Layten stated it, the unsuspecting black girl from the South "is often a joke to justice." Problems surrounding the women abounded: few positions other than domestic service were available, prostitution had increased, and the migrants, often from southern rural districts, went to cities where "graft and political corruption . . . seared men's consciences." Even a woman's black brothers could not protect her for fear of retaliation by whites. Layten called on missionary societies, fraternal organizations, women's auxiliaries, and mothers' clubs to work with the young women, investigate their new surroundings, and help locate decent homes for them.

In this speech Layten also addressed the social service responsibility of the church and asked the church to "reduce preaching to teaching" in order to facilitate the protection of homes, women, and children. She continued, "Bring education closer to religion, relate it to health needs, industrial life, character building, work in prisons, reform among men, collect and organize social facts."

Supports National Association of Colored Women

Since early in the twentieth century Layten had been active in the National Association of Colored Women (NACW). She spoke at the tenth biennial meeting of the NACW in September 1918, presenting a paper on black women migrants. During World War I, she called for cooperation between the NACW and the Baptist women, urging the Baptist women to work with the NACW in its study of black women in the national war effort. She asked the women to help win the war by conserving food and fuel, buying Liberty Bonds and war stamps, and planting liberty gardens. Immediately after the war, she encouraged blacks to use the Great Migration to their political advantage. She urged women, who themselves could not vote, to educate black migrant men about their political rights; she prevailed upon northern urban churches to assist in these efforts, calling churches the most logical institutions to develop a voter education program.

Layten's work in the community extended to numerous other areas as well. Her position with the Baptist women led to her membership on the executive board of the World Baptist Alliance. She represented the Baptist Women's Convention in Stockholm, Sweden, in 1922 and again in Toronto, Canada, in 1929. She was a principal speaker at the Alliance meeting in Atlanta, Georgia, in 1939. She continued to organize women's groups wherever she traveled. One of the organizations of which she was most proud was the Women's Auxiliary to the Bahamas Baptist Convention.

Layten's political stance did not go unnoticed. In the 1920s, recognizing her great organizational skills, the National Republican Committee of Pennsylvania appointed her to organize black women in the state. She was also a member of the Temporary Commission to Study the Life of the Urban Population, as well as the first woman of any race to work with the Travellers Aid Society. Founder of what became the Southwest-Belmont YWCA, Layten donated the first dollar for the Y movement. Through her efforts a building was secured for the operation of the Mary S. Tribbitt Home for Girls, located at 1510 Catherine Street in Philadelphia. Although for a number of years Layten held a salaried position as a probation officer in the municipal court, she was not paid for her other community service.

A complete record of Layten's honors does not exist, but it is known that State University in Louisville, Kentucky, conferred on her the degree of master of arts. Later, after delivering a commencement address at Selma University, she was awarded an honorary doctor of laws from the school.

After a four-year illness, S. Willie Layten died at her home in Philadelphia, located at 764 South Twenty-third Street, on Saturday morning, January 14, 1950. Funeral services were held the following Thursday at Shiloh Baptist Church, where her father had pastored and she held membership. She was buried in the family lot in Merion Cemetery. She was survived by her daughter, Madalene Tillman.

Layten was an influential black woman leader who devoted her entire life to fighting for the rights of blacks and women. She realized the importance of black women in the development of a wholesome life for black people. As noted in the _Philadelphia Tribune,_ January 17, 1950, she "gave unsparingly of her time and resources to rescue unfortunate girls, feed, shelter and clothe them, and place them in gainful employment."

REFERENCES:

"Deaths: 1947-1951." In _Negro Yearbook,_ 1952. Edited by Jessie Parkhurst Guzman. New York: William H. Wise, 1952.

Higginbotham, Evelyn Brooks. _Righteous Discontent: The Women's Movement in the Black Baptist Church, 1800-1920._ Cambridge, Mass.: Harvard University Press, 1993.

Journal of the Second Annual Session of the Women's Convention Auxiliary to the National Baptist Convention. Second Annual Session, Cincinnati, Ohio, September 11-16, 1901. Third Annual Session, Birmingham, Ala., September 17-22, 1902; Fourth Annual Assembly, Philadelphia, Penn., 1903; Fifth Annual Assembly, Austin, Tex., September 14-19, 1904; Sixth Annual Assembly, Chicago, Ill., 1905; Tenth Annual Session, New Orleans, La., 1910; Twelfth Annual Session, Houston, Tex., 1912; Eleventh Annual Session, Chicago, Ill., 1915; Nineteenth Annual Session, Newark, N.J., September 10-15, 1919; Twentieth Annual Session, Indianapolis, Ind., 1920. (Sessions numbered as printed.)

Layten, S. W. "The Servant Problem." _Colored American Magazine_ 12 (January 1907): 13-15.

"Mrs. S. W. Layten, National Baptist Figure, Dead Here." _Philadelphia Tribune,_ January 17, 1950.

Rhodes, E. M. "The Protection of Girls Who Travel: A National Movement." _Colored American Magazine_ 13 (August 1907): 114-15.

Jessie Carney Smith

Mollie Huston Lee
(1907-1982)
Librarian, civic leader, organization leader

Mollie Huston Lee became one of the most distinguished African American librarians during the segregation era. Through her determination, strength, and exceptional qualifications, she became a respected authority in her profession on the local, regional, and national level. Challenged by the need to expand cultural horizons for African Americans, Lee succeeded in making worthy contributions to public libraries by establishing a library for the black community in Raleigh, North Carolina, and by creating a premiere collection of books by and about African Americans.

Mollie Huston Lee was born in Columbus, Ohio, January 18, 1907, to Corrina Smith Huston and Rolla Solomon Huston. She married James S. Lee in 1935 and was the mother of one son, James S. Lee Jr.

Lee's first library experience came at Howard University where she served as a student library assistant. She completed her undergraduate degree at Howard in 1929 and received a bachelor of library science degree from Columbia University in 1935. From 1930 to 1935, she was librarian at Shaw University in Raleigh, North Carolina, having studied at Columbia while she was employed at Shaw. At Shaw, she saw the need among African Americans in the surrounding geographical areas for a special African American literary collection. She felt this need could best be met through the services of a public library.

Founds First Library in Raleigh for Blacks

At the time, there were no public library facilities available to African Americans in Raleigh. In 1935, Lee and a group of citizens met to establish a public library for the African American population. A library site was selected and

Mollie Huston Lee

equipment was purchased. Resources included 890 books, Lee's enthusiasm, and the support of many friends.

The library was a storefront room with big show windows, located on crowded East Hargett Street. When patrons were unable to come to the library, Lee went to them with market basket in hand; she regularly took library books to various offices and businesses near the library. With this philosophy of community outreach, she promoted the use of the library and its resources and encouraged people to borrow books. In spite of poor economic conditions, Lee's sheer force, hard work, and the concern of friends resulted in the growth of the library's resources.

Lee's leadership and the demand for services enabled the library to progress. By July 1948, sufficient funds had been raised through contributions, gifts, and financial promotions to purchase a large house. This public library facility for African Americans was eventually named as a memorial for stage actor Richard B. Harrison. For almost twenty years, the Richard B. Harrison Public Library made its second home on South Blount Street. The library was noted regionally and nationally for providing special services and programs geared to the needs of the aged, blind, disadvantaged, and illiterate. Existing libraries in many southern localities are direct outgrowths of Lee's influence and patient persuasion in teaching users and patrons about the resources and facilities of libraries.

The Harrison Library's collections of books and other materials by and about Americans of African descent placed it in a category of its own in the Southeast. The collection's high

ranking among public libraries was no accident. With painstaking efforts, Lee assembled a comprehensive and high quality collection. During the early period of her collecting, the life span of publications about African Americans was short—usually they were out of print within two years. It was advantageous for the collector to purchase books as soon as possible upon publication. Through the years, Lee watched the lists of those who published or sold African American books. She found the University Place Book Shop in New York City to be an excellent source of rare items. Lee would go to University Place Book Shop for two and three days at a time to select books.

In this way, the collection at the Harrison public library grew over a period of thirty-eight years. It was literally a book-by-book growth, because the library lacked the benefit of substantial donations of either books or money. The most assistance for a period of twelve years was an annual appropriation by the North Carolina State Library. This aid gave recognition to the value of the collection and made it accessible to the public libraries of North Carolina through the State Library's Interlibrary Loan Services. The primary reason for the existence of the Negro Collection—which was officially designated the Mollie Huston Lee Collection of Black Literature in 1972—was Lee's dedication to the African American populations of Raleigh, Wake County, and North Carolina and her desire for them to know about and be proud of their heritage.

Not only did Lee aspire to develop a program of library service in the South for African Americans, she also accepted the responsibility to train personnel to serve African American libraries. As early as 1942, the Harrison library was used as a practical laboratory to provide training experiences for students in library science from the schools of Atlanta University, North Carolina Central University, and the University of North Carolina at Chapel Hill. As opportunities for library education and training increased, Lee actively sought and obtained scholarships for students and counseled them in their search for careers in the library profession. From 1946 to 1953, Lee served as the supervisor of Negro School Libraries in North Carolina. She has been appropriately referred to by Ray Nichols Moore in the *Wilson Library Bulletin* as a "librarian's librarian."

Vision Leads to Library Association

Lee thought there should be a professional organization to encourage and stimulate North Carolina's black librarians. In 1934 the North Carolina Negro Library Association (NCNLA) was founded, becoming the professional organization for those who supported her efforts. The North Carolina Negro Library Association had an impressive record of professional activities for twenty years. It gave young black librarians the privilege of participating fully in the program of the profession. It also gave African American librarians opportunities to take on leadership roles. In 1943, the NCNLA became the first library association controlled by African Americans admitted as a chapter of the American Library Association (ALA). The association held its last annual meeting in 1954. The NCNLA was dissolved because the ALA and the North Carolina Library Association finally opened membership to librarians of African descent.

Lee was involved in many community organizations and activities. She received numerous awards and other forms of public recognition for her dedicated and distinguished service to public librarianship and public education. Lee was an active member over the years in professional organizations such as ALA and NCNLA. She was the second African American elected at-large to the ALA Council, serving for the years 1950 to 1954. She also served as a consultant at ALA meetings. In 1971, she represented ALA at the White House Conference on Aging. After Lee's official retirement in 1972, she remained actively involved in her profession, continuing her activities of consulting and lecturing at library schools.

Lee's activities as a citizen of the state of North Carolina were significant and noteworthy. She was appointed by the governor of the state to serve on the State Library Commission. For her many professional and civic contributions to the state, Lee in 1971 was the first African American woman elected ''Tar Heel of the Week.''

An important African American bibliographer, a pioneer in community outreach, and an accomplished leader in her field, Lee is remembered with esteem by her living peers and former students. Her work as the librarian at Shaw University, supervisor of Negro School Libraries in North Carolina, and librarian at Richard B. Harrison Public Library in Raleigh ensured that her community had access to a public library and the services of well-trained librarians.

REFERENCES:

Browning, George-Stradley. ''The Service of Richard B. Harrison Public Library, Raleigh, North Carolina.'' Master's thesis, University of North Carolina, Chapel Hill, 1962.

Lee, Mollie Huston. ''North Carolina Negro Library Association, 1935-54.'' *Library Service Review* 2 (October 1955): 10-32.

Moore, Ray Nichols. ''Mollie Huston Lee: A Profile.'' *Wilson Library Bulletin* 49 (February 1975): 432-39.

Speller, Benjamin F. Jr., and James R. Jarrell. ''Profiles of Pioneers: Selected North Carolina Black Librarians.'' In *The Black Librarian in the Southeast: Reminiscences, Activities, Challenges,* edited by Annette L. Phinazee. Durham: North Carolina Central University Alumni Association, 1980.

COLLECTIONS:

Correspondence, papers, and other documents that comprise the Mollie Huston Lee Collection are located in the Black Librarians Research Collection, School of Library and Information Sciences, North Carolina Central University, Durham, North Carolina.

Benjamin F. Speller Jr.

Shirley A. R. Lewis
(1937-)
College president, educator, religious fund director

Whether in the area of academic affairs, linguistic pluralism, African studies, English, or literacy, Shirley A. R. Lewis has fulfilled her long-established goal of improving the lives of African American young people. Now as the first woman president of Paine College in Augusta, Georgia, she has moved into a key position which gives her a wider arena for uplifting young lives.

Shirley Ann Redd Lewis was born on June 11, 1937, in Winding Gulf, West Virginia, the daughter of Robert F. Redd, a school teacher, and Thelma Danese Biggers Redd. Although they divorced when Lewis was young, both her parents were very supportive and provided a rich background which continued to shape her life as she developed. When Lewis was five years old, she became distressed that two of her cousins who began school had learned to read when she could not. Her father taught her to read from the cousins' books, which she says set the stage for her abiding appreciation for the feeling of empowerment brought on by access to education and to literacy.

After her parents divorced, Lewis alternately lived with each parent in various parts of the country, as her mother sought employment and as her father helped augment his teacher's salary through summer work. Lewis consequently lived in Beckley, West Virginia; Harlem, New York; Cambridge, Massachusetts; and other cities in the East, finally settling in Berkeley, California, where her mother acquired a position as a children's nurse. Lewis said in an interview that she is very proud of the fact that her parents maintained civil relations with each other and were both very nurturing to her. As she grew up in California, her father kept in close touch by mail and reviewed her school progress each report card period. Her mother provided support for her development and made it possible for her interest in reading to grow by providing books in their home library. When Lewis was twelve years old, she had read works for mature readers such as *The Street* by Ann Petry and Richard Wright's *Native Son,* along with children's literature. Lewis's mother also read and recited poetry to her, introduced her to opera and the theater, and influenced her interest in music through her own interest in jazz, blues, and classical music.

Lewis became interested in politics early on. As she moved about the country with one or the other of her parents, she continually ran for class office. She says that based on her parents' expectations, it seemed the thing to do. Her first elected position was as vice president of her fourth grade class at Russell School in Cambridge, Massachusetts. In Berkeley, California, she attended Garfield Junior High School where, due to gerrymandering, she was the only black student in the school. Lewis was elected vice president of the student body

Shirley A. R. Lewis

and was elected a class officer throughout her public school career.

Upon graduation from Berkeley High School, Lewis entered the University of California at Berkeley, graduating in 1960 with a B.A. in Spanish and speech. She did graduate work in education at California State University at San Francisco and at Hayward and received her general secondary teacher's credential from the latter.

Lewis has had wide experience in the field of education. She was a Spanish teacher in the Ravenswood City School District, East Palo Alto, California, 1962-63; reading teacher at Sagamore Hills Children's Inpatient Psychiatric Hospital, Northfield, Ohio, 1963-64; and mathematics teacher at Junior High School #2, New York City, 1965-66.

An Intellectual Exploration of Africa

In 1963 she married Ronald Lewis, a psychiatric social worker. When they lived in New York the Lewises were active in the arts, black heritage, and African and African American affairs. Inspired by the presence of many African leaders and by their associates in the city of New York, they decided to visit West Africa to learn more about African culture and customs. The Lewises made the first of three trips to Ghana in 1966. They also visited Liberia, Senegal, Nigeria, and the Ivory Coast. They returned to Ghana in 1968 through the Forum for African Studies and pursued courses of study at the University of London and the University of Ghana at Legon. In the summer of 1968 Lewis and her husband received certificates of African studies by participating in a

joint program of the University of London and the University of Ghana. In Ghana she received intensive training in African culture, focusing on African carryovers in African American life. She has maintained an intellectual and cultural relationship with Ghana, and since then has shared her learning with numerous students and community members in the United States.

Lewis reentered the University of California at Berkeley in 1968 to pursue a master's degree in social work. In 1970 she received an M.S.W. degree with a specialty in community organization. In the process, she worked with welfare rights organizations and community-based schools where she formed programs to help alienated black students learn to read. In 1971 Lewis and her husband served as staff for the Forum for African Studies. In that capacity they coordinated field studies for program participants.

Continuing to establish a diverse educational record, Shirley Lewis became educational development training officer at the Lawrence Berkeley Laboratory, Berkeley, 1971-72. There she was responsible for training blacks and other employees for job upgrading. When she entered Stanford University, she served as reading and composition instructor at Nairobi College, East Palo Alto, California, 1972-75; and instructor in linguistics and English at Foothills Community College, Los Altos, California.

All of Lewis's subsequent academic experiences have been at the college or professional school level. As a graduate student she was a supervisor of the Stanford Teacher Education Program, 1972-74, then held positions in the Stanford School of Education's Program on Cultural and Linguistic Pluralism, 1974-79. The research position afforded Lewis the opportunity to train teachers of black students in school districts across the United States. Working with Stanford professor Robert L. Politzer and researcher Mary Rhodes Hoover, Lewis coauthored research memoranda, linguistically fair student tests, and other teacher training materials. The primary outcomes of this work were that black students could achieve and learn to read regardless of their linguistic or socioeconomic status and that teacher knowledge of and attitudes toward black students correlated with student achievement.

In 1979 Lewis was awarded a doctorate in education from Stanford University. Her doctoral studies focused on language acquisition and literacy for bidialectal and bilingual students. Her doctoral thesis investigated the effects of speech variety dominance and cultural heritage attitudes on reading comprehension. A significant but serendipitous finding was that many black children dominant in vernacular black English with positive attitudes toward their heritage and culture outperformed other black students as well as the white student control group on seven out of eight tests. For Lewis, this finding underscored the need to maintain and enhance personal and cultural self-esteem among black children.

In 1979, after completing her doctorate, Lewis moved to Nashville, Tennessee, with her family where she held a part-time position as adjunct assistant professor of education in the Department of Teaching and Learning at George Peabody

College of Vanderbilt University, 1979-80. Lewis then moved to Meharry Medical College in Nashville where she worked as educational specialist for the Department of Family Medicine and special assistant to the vice president for academic affairs, 1981-84. Her work focused on faculty development and student achievement. In 1984 she was appointed the associate dean for academic affairs, becoming the first woman associate dean in the School of Medicine at Meharry.

Heads Black College Fund

Her broad background and experience in college administration prepared Lewis for important management positions with the United Methodist Church. She was executive director of its Black College Fund from 1986 to 1991, and in 1992 her position was elevated to that of assistant general secretary. Her responsibilities for the Black College Fund were wide and demanding. Lewis administered, promoted, and distributed the United Methodist Church's Black College Fund, an annual fund of more than $7 million which supports a consortium of eleven Methodist-related historically black colleges. Her work involved coordinating proposal reviews in amounts ranging from $250,000 to $1 million for academic, capital, and program awards. She conceptualized and participated in regional and national projects related to fund management, educational policy, and institutional accreditation. She interacted with higher educational constituencies, including the United Methodist University Senate, the United Negro College Fund, institutional boards of trustees, and other college and university constituencies.

Lewis created the Ambassador Scholars Program within the Black College Fund, which enabled students to travel the country to promote historically black colleges and universities and the Black College Fund. She did public relations work with churches, national organizations, and colleges and universities involving public speaking, conducting workshops, and conceptualizing and creating promotional reports, articles, and resources. She gained extensive fund-raising experience while in office. She was one of the eleven members of the College of Education Plenary Committee for the new United Methodist-supported Africa University, in Old Mutare, Zimbabwe, which opened officially on April 24, 1994. This experience enabled her to extend her goal of providing education for youth to communities in Africa. These activities put Lewis in a highly visible position in the church and in black higher education.

Elected First Woman President of Paine

A news release from Paine College, Augusta, Georgia, announced on April 23, 1994, that the college had made history by electing its first woman president, Shirley A. R. Lewis. She became one of only four women presidents in the forty-one schools in the United Negro College Fund system. The thirteenth president of Paine was elected during the Board of Trustees' annual spring meeting. She replaced long-time president Julius S. Scott Jr., who was retiring from the 112-year-old historically black liberal arts college. Paine was one of the institutions in the Black College Fund that Lewis had administered earlier; the school also receives support from the Christian Methodist Episcopal Church and the United Negro College Fund.

Lewis knew that accepting the new position would have an impact on her immediate family; therefore, the offer required a family decision. Her husband, Ronald, who, until he retired in 1994, directed school social work and attendance in the Metropolitan Nashville Public Schools, and her daughter Mendi, a senior at Spelman College in Atlanta, gave her their full encouragement and support. On accepting the appointment Lewis told the Board of Trustees that she had adopted her mother's philosophy and applied it to all black children. When her mother asked her earlier if she wanted the position at Paine and Lewis said yes, she repeated what she had told her since Lewis was a child: "I think if you want to do it, you can do it." At Paine Lewis plans to help students become what they want to be. According to the *Augusta Chronicle* for April 24, 1994, she called fund-raising her top priority. She sees recruitment and retention of students at Paine her greatest challenge and wants to build a national reputation for the school. "It is my hope to take Paine College, the wonderful things it has done, the tradition, and to cast that image nationwide," she said. Lewis also expressed concern for African American males, many of whom are at greater risk now than others had been before. In her November 7, 1994, letter, she said, "Paine College can and should be a place for the sustenance of African American males. Somehow education is frequently perceived as being uncorrelated with being African American." Lewis also plans to build a strong liberal arts tradition based in the humanities, and perhaps develop a program in international business.

Lewis speaks often at educational conferences, colleges, and universities. She has given commencement addresses at such schools as Philander Smith College, Claflin College, and Rust College. She has held consulting positions with Bennett College, Clark Atlanta University, Dillard University, Meharry Medical College, Wiley College, and other black institutions; with the Formative Evaluation Research Associates at the University of Michigan; with the National Institute of Education; and with a number of school districts in California, New Jersey, New York, and Tennessee.

Lewis is also a scholarly writer whose contributions have been primarily in the area of linguistics and English. She collaborated with R. L. Politzer and M. R. Hoover to write "A Semi-Foreign Language Approach to Teaching English to Bidialectal Students," in *Applied Linguistics* (Center for Applied Linguistics, 1980). She also wrote "Practical Aspects of Teaching Composition to Bidialectal Students: The Nairobi Method," in *Issues in Composition* (Lawrence Ehlbaum, 1982); and "Humanistic Research: A Tool for Literacy," in *Successful Schools* (Onyx Press, 1983). In addition, she has published important works on black colleges, including "The Future of Black Institutions: The Black Family, the Black Church, and the Black College," *Position Papers* (Cincinnati, Ohio, National Meeting of Black Methodist for Church Renewal, March 19, 1993); "Historically

Black Colleges Enjoy a Renaissance,'' *Black Issues in Higher Education* (August 27, 1992); and ''A Shared Dream,'' *The Interpreter* (February-March 1988).

Numerous community groups have benefitted from Lewis's expertise and generosity toward volunteer groups. In Nashville she served on the executive committee of the YWCA board of directors and she has also been active with the Girl Scouts of America, the United Way Appropriations Committee, the Mental Health Society, the Black Cultural Alliance, the Center for Black Family Life, and numerous other groups. Her affiliations with black women's groups include the Links and the Alpha Kappa Alpha Sorority. Her keen interest in black and African heritage led her to become involved in a number of Kwanzaa activities in Nashville, including the Kwanzaa Committee, which she and her husband founded. She was a chief early promoter of Kwanzaa. She has been liturgist and greeter at Clark Memorial United Methodist Church in Nashville. In 1990 *Dollars and Sense* magazine named her one of America's Best and Brightest for her professional commitment and dedication.

Lewis is at once impressive, confident, unpretentious, poised, and gracious. She has a warm and contagious smile. Together the Lewis family exudes maturity, confidence, love, and a strong sense of belonging. They are especially devoted to the Methodist Church and to African culture and heritage.

Lewis credits her success not only to the love and support of her parents, but also to the influence of a number of black professional women in Berkeley: women from the Links, the Alpha Kappa Alpha Sorority, the National Association of Negro Business and Professional Women, and women of the St. Augustine Episcopal Church where she grew up. ''They watched and nurtured me. They invited me to give speeches and to attend their teas. They told me to aim high,'' she said in an interview. In her life and work, Lewis has in turn passed this optimistic advice on to others. Her concern with the uplift of young people is apparent in her unswerving dedication to education and in the broad and meaningful experiences that have made Shirley Lewis exceptionally well-prepared to lead Paine College, its students, and faculty to new heights.

Current Address: Office of the President, Paine College, 1235 Fifteenth Street, Augusta, GA 30901.

REFERENCES:

''Committee Nominates Woman to Head Paine College.'' *Augusta Chronicle,* 1994. Undated article.

''Dr. Shirley A. R. Lewis Elected President of Paine College.'' *Chamber Vision* 21 (June 1994): 5.

Lewis, Shirley A. Curriculum Vitae. N.d.

————. Letter to Jessie Carney Smith. November 7, 1994.

————. Telephone interview with Jessie Carney Smith. September 11, 1994.

''Paine Makes History: Elects First Female President.'' News release. Office of Public Relations, Paine College, April 23, 1994.

''Paine Picks First Lady President.'' *Augusta Metro Courier,* April 27-May 4, 1994.

''President: Fund-raising Will Be Top Priority.'' *Augusta Chronicle,* April 24, 1994.

COLLECTIONS:

Files of Lewis's work with the Black College Fund of the United Methodist Church are located at 1001 Nineteenth Avenue, South, Nashville, Tennessee. Files from her presidency of Paine College are located in her office at the college.

Jessie Carney Smith

Charlotte E. Linden
(1859-1919)
Poet, laundress, clubwoman

Charlotte E. Linden, who wrote under the name Mrs. Henry Linden, is primarily known for the poems she published shortly after the turn of the century. While not an accomplished poet, Linden is a rare example of a late nineteenth-century manual worker turned businesswoman. When the opportunity arose, Linden also became very involved in club work and the women's movement. In her life, she is an exemplar of her generation's hopes to improve conditions by hard work and collective action. This is demonstrated in the lines she wrote, ''To better the condition of humanity, / For the Cultivation of the mind, / To tear down the walls of ignorance / Then we are lifting as we climb.''

''[Queen Victoria's] kingdom saved my father and gave him freedom sweet, / And I was born her subject, a Canadian complete.'' While neither her parents' names nor her exact birthplace are known, it is documented that Linden was born in Canada on September 22, 1859. Her father fled slavery in Kentucky as a boy, and in Canada he married a well-educated Canadian schoolteacher, although he remained illiterate. Around 1867 the family returned to Campbell County, Kentucky, her father's home county, located on the Ohio River just upstream from Cincinnati. There her mother worked as a schoolteacher. According to Linden's autobiography, although ordered to leave Cambell County by ''rebels,'' her father refused: ''as slavery was over and he was free he thought that he had a right to live where he pleased.'' The discovery that the group of malcontents was preparing to burn them out and that powder had already been placed under the house apparently changed his mind, and the family left to live near Richmond, Ohio, for about two years. Linden's father secured a responsible job as a foreman for two real estate men, but ''he lost his mind, becoming melancholy; he was perfectly harmless, but could do no business.''

Learns Laundry Business

Linden was not yet twelve years old when she had to stop school and go to work, starting as a nurse but becoming a cook by the time she was thirteen. For a while, her father was able to do some farm work, but he then had a relapse, so the family moved to Delaware, Ohio, in the hope that the spring water there might help him. There Linden found work in a newly established Chinese laundry for a dollar a day. Her fellow workers were white, but she was the only one determined to learn the secrets of the trade. "[The Chinese] will pretend to teach you, but if you are not pretty sharp you will never learn," she stated in her autobiography. She succeeded in learning, but her fellows did not.

In her view a woman is "always helping, / Too, to carry the burden of those she chances to meet, / Or her husband if she is a wife." Linden's first two marriages were disasters. At the age of seventeen, she married over the objections of her parents. Her husband, moreover, was abusive and a gambler and sold her clothes and the furniture while she was out working. After two years, she was genuinely frightened for her life and ended the marriage by divorce. She said that her former husband "went from bad to worse until he died, but before his death he married a white woman and she grew as tired of him as I did." She met her second husband, a railroad detective, while she was cooking in Florida. They seem to have settled in Springfield, Ohio. This second husband was a spendthrift who died after a lengthy illness, leaving her with three-year-old and six-month-old sons, Walter and Robert, and with five hundred dollars left to pay on her home.

Business Acumen Leads to Success

Considering these adverse circumstances, Linden was justifiably proud of her business acumen. She opened a laundry while her second husband was alive and to this business she added dry-cleaning. She states in her autobiography:

Of these two trades I have made a success in life. After I learned my trade as a cleaner I had just fifty cents to start my business with, but in six years that fifty cents made me four thousand dollars that I could see. My work was altogether for actresses and transient trade at the hotels, so the hotels and theatres have proved a blessing to me. Today I am worth several thousand dollars, living well and doing a first-class business. This is told to help some one else who may have my experience or one just as hard.

Fortunately, Linden's third husband was very good to her. Old enough to be her father, Henry Linden was born a slave and fought in the Civil War. Although he was in fairly bad financial condition at the time of their marriage, his business recovered and "he d[id] the largest transfer business in Springfield." He had raised a "credible family of children" and was a very good stepfather. Linden also credits him with being the inventor of a piano-moving truck, a hose union, and window curtain rollers, all in use although he had

to sell the patent rights. It was apparently a very happy marriage.

Linden had been a member of various clubs for about ten years before she found the leisure to become active in them around 1901. She threw herself into the club movement with the same energy she displayed in her business endeavors. In 1910, she was a member of the Phyllis Wheatley Club, the Friday Afternoon Study Club, the Wednesday Afternoon Club, the Wheel of Progress, the Sisters of Ruth (Oddfellows), and the Dames of Pythias. She was president of the first two. The clubs did charitable work and offered opportunities for self-improvement. The Phyllis Wheatley Club had adopted an orphan, and the Friday Club was working on developing a day nursery and kindergarten. It was in the Wednesday Afternoon Club that Linden took up needlework about 1905, and with characteristic energy, she completed nearly 250 pieces of needlework in about five years.

Launches into Poetry

Club work inspired her interest in poetry, which she approached in the spirit of all her other enterprises. She wrote her first poem in January 1905. She took her first fifteen poems, printed them as a pamphlet under the title "Scraps of Time," and sold over five hundred copies in four months at twenty-five cents apiece. She then expanded her market by contributing her poems to magazines and newspapers, including the *Daily News,* the paper with the largest circulation in Springfield. Linden's poems are moral and religious exhortations, presenting the qualities she believed accounted for her own successes in life. Even the event on which her poem "The Riot in Springfield, Ohio, February 26, 1906" was based did not dent her faith in progress and uplift, although it called forth her indignation. The subject of the poem was apparently one of a series of antiblack riots.

The collection *Autobiography and Poems* (c. 1910) is the principal source of information about Linden's life. Both her claim and achievement as a poet can be judged from these lines:

Everybody has a gift,
If they did but know it,
And if you cultivate some taste
Your study soon will show it.

I studied the art of needlework,
And soon adopted to it;
And as I studied farther on
I discovered that I was a poet.

I then and there began to write
And I am still sticking to it,
And some of the best critics in the land
Have indorsed me as a poet.

Linden was more than a local figure. For a number of years she was treasurer of the Ohio Federation of Colored Women's Clubs and attended both state and national conventions. She worked for women's suffrage and was very active in the Woman's Christian Temperance Union (WCTU), even serving as delegate to the national and international convention in Brooklyn. She was an active member of her African Methodist Episcopal (AME) Church.

Linden died of pneumonia on April 13, 1919. Her husband had died three months earlier. She was survived by her two sons, Walter and Robert Williams, as well as other members of her family, including her mother. She was buried in or near Springfield, Ohio, in Ferncliff Cemetery. Linden's philosophy toward her life and works is summarized in her *Autobiography and Poems:*

> It is worthwhile to do something. What need you care for the would-be critics that are doing nothing and criticize your efforts? Take new courage and "pull for the shore." My efforts were criticized, but what did I care for that. I started with that expectation, but with God as my leader I expected to win the fight in the end.

> Dare to be true, dare to do the right,
> With Christ as your leader
> You will win the fight.

REFERENCES:

Linden, Mrs. Henry. *Autobiography and Poems.* Springfield, Ohio: Mrs. Henry Linden, c. 1910. Reprinted in *Collected Black Women's Poetry.* Edited by Joan R. Sherman. Vol. 4. New York: Oxford University Press, 1988.

"Mrs. Henry Linden Dies of Pneumonia." Newspaper clipping provided by Clark County Public Library.

Robert L. Johns

Melba Liston
(1926-)
Musician, arranger

Melba Liston appears in an *Ebony* illustration, June 1977, playing a "stand-up" solo on her trombone, standing next to Dizzie Gillespie in his famous big band of the early 1950s. She is the only woman in this all-male group, and she was chosen, as were most of the members of this fine aggregate of musicians, by Gillespie himself. Gillespie's choice of Liston to play in the impressive company of the big band he assembled, and to appear as a featured soloist, demonstrates her stature in what has long been a "man's world," the world of the professional band musician. Liston has had a truly full career as a jazz musician, arranger, composer, band leader, and teacher.

Melba Liston was born on January 13, 1926, in Kansas City, Kansas. Her mother and father, Lucille and Frank Liston, enjoyed music, and there was a piano in the home. Her father played stringed instruments. On Melba's insistence, her

mother purchased a trombone for her when she was seven. Her grandfather encouraged her as she taught herself to play by sounding out familiar tunes on the instrument on her back porch. Not everyone in the family approved, and her grandmother warned her of the seamier side of life in the music world. She later mused that although her grandmother apparently only knew personally about music in the church, her early warnings were right on target.

The family moved to Los Angeles in 1937, and at this point Liston's musical education moved swiftly forward. From a very early age she had been teaching herself to sing songs she heard and liked by her own number system. As she progressed on trombone, she played and sang in school groups and learned some music theory. Liston's chief inspiration, however, came from a musical group sponsored by the Parks and Recreation Department and taught by Alma Hightower. Hightower was an accomplished musician who played saxophone, drums, and piano. She taught the group to act, dance, sing, and recite poetry as well as to play musical instruments. They performed for various dances, public functions, openings, and other occasions. Hightower's tutelage and personal commitment to youth made a permanent impression on Liston. She developed a strong desire to succeed in what was obviously a man's world, as well as to one day teach students and motivate young people herself.

At sixteen, Liston reached a personal goal. She joined the musician's union, together with some school friends, and began to work in a pit band for the Lincoln Theatre playing for vaudeville acts. In 1943 the theater closed, and she joined Gerald Wilson's band. Wilson, a composer and arranger as well as a bandleader, employed her as a copyist and taught her the rudiments of scoring and arranging. Soon she was not only performing but was very active in helping prepare charts for the band as well. As a section musician, she learned a great deal by listening and developed a desire to write interesting melodic lines for the various parts of an ensemble.

Liston played with Wilson until 1948 and through him she was able to meet many of the jazz luminaries of the period and feel welcome in their company: these included Billie Holiday, Dizzy Gillespie, Count Basie, Duke Ellington, Dexter Gordon, and Fletcher Henderson. In the forties she was invited to her first recording session by Dexter Gordon, whom she knew from her school days. At that point, she was shy and uncomfortable as a soloist. She really did not want to go to recording sessions, but she was encouraged by her friends. She overcame her fears, and her musical talent showed through even at that early date. Many subsequent invitations to "sit in" on sessions followed.

Singled out by Dizzie Gillespie

When the Wilson group disbanded, Liston played briefly with Count Basie, and then she was invited to join Dizzy Gillespie's big band. Gillespie called her in California and asked her to bring two arrangements with her. Wilson took her to New York to join the group, which included, among others, John Coltrane, Jimmy Heath, and John Lewis. This was, of course, a distinct honor for her, but it apparently caused a stir among the band members because of their general resentment and their gender prejudice, which Gillespie unceremoniously quashed. After reading her charts, she was accepted as a musician and member of the group, acquiring the nickname "Mama." The other band members were also no doubt more inclined to accept Liston once they heard their leader threaten them with an open door should they reject her. Following this engagement, she helped put together a group to work with Billie Holiday on a southern tour in 1949.

After the Billie Holiday tour, which did not enjoy the success it merited, Liston became somewhat disenchanted with the sexism, competitiveness, and constant travel of the music business. Perhaps she also saw a few of the things her grandmother had warned her about when she was a child. Consequently, with her family's encouragement, she applied for and took a job with the Los Angeles Board of Education, leaving professional musicianship for a time. She also got married—the first of three marriages that unfortunately failed for her. After a hiatus of several years, however, her desire to be active musically returned, and she took up her instrument to play again.

From this point on, her career progressed swiftly once more. Gillespie invited her to join a new band he was assembling for a State Department tour of the Middle East in 1956. Another Gillespie tour, to South America, followed in 1957. For these tours she prepared several outstanding arrangements, including "My Reverie," "Stella by Starlight," and "Annie's Dance." She worked on a tour of Europe in 1959, led by Quincy Jones and featuring Harold Arlen's folk opera *Free and Easy,* with a subsequent concert tour of the European jazz scene.

In the sixties, Liston's work as an arranger took on added importance. She came to the forefront, arranging works for Charles Mingus's memorable Town Hall concert in 1962 and Duke Ellington's Jazz Society Orchestra concert in 1963. In addition, she served as Eddie Fisher's music director in 1964. She began a lengthy association with jazz pianist Randy Weston, arranging pieces for and contributing ideas to his albums *African Suite, Little Niles, High Life,* and *Blues to Africa,* on through the 1992 release of his *The Spirits of Our Ancestors.* Continuing her work as an instrumentalist, she appeared as trombonist in concerts with Budd Johnson at Lincoln Center and in "Instant Jazz," at Town Hall in 1965. Her work for orchestra included a symphonic arrangement for the Buffalo Symphony, featuring Clark Terry, and an arrangement of Randy Weston's "Three African Queens" for the Boston Pops Orchestra with Weston.

Liston has been interviewed several times over the years (see, especially, Handy, Dahl, Hine, and Placksin) and seems to have a very positive attitude towards jazz and her fellow musicians. This is reflected in the joy she imparts to her compositions and arrangements. Although she was at first frightened of doing solos and unsure of her ability to improvise at sessions, she was warmly welcomed and sought after almost from the start. She has been much in demand, first as a performer and later as an arranger, throughout her career of about fifty years. One can hear her grow musically by

comparing her first sessions with Dexter Gordon in the 1940s to her later work with Dizzy Gillespie, and that with her own groups in the 1980s. Youthful verve and a cool melodic approach in the 1940s and 1950s mature to a more introspective and musically advanced style in the 1980s. Her skill as an arranger has stood the test of time, as is certainly attested to by her span of more than thirty years of work with Randy Weston.

Perhaps remembering her own experiences as a youth, and the outgoing commitment of Alma Hightower when she was growing up, Liston made very important contributions to youth groups in New York and elsewhere during the late 1960s and early 1970s. She taught at the Pratt Institute in Brooklyn, New York, establishing the Pratt Institute Jazz-in-Action Orchestra, worked for The Jazz Mobile, and formed the Harlem Back Street Tour Orchestra. She established the Pittsburgh Jazz Orchestra in 1964 and worked with youth jazz groups in Watts, California, in the early 1970s.

Jazz Bands Formed

Liston's next assignment was very challenging and acknowledged her success with young people. She visited Jamaica in 1970 and in 1973 was asked to return there and direct the Department of Afro-American Music at the Jamaica School of Music. She worked there until 1979, inviting many guest musicians to come and work with her students. Among those who came were Elvin Jones, Frank Foster, and Lester Bowie. Enrollment increased dramatically; she instituted courses in theory, jazz history, improvisation, and musical instruments; a new building was built; and performing activity blossomed for her band and jazz choir.

Once again the United States concert world beckoned. In 1979 two entrepreneurs in Kansas City, Carol Comer and Dianne Gregg, conceived the idea of having a Women's Jazz Festival in Kansas City and of inviting Liston back home to headline the event. It took some very serious persuading to induce her to leave her work in Jamaica and come back to Kansas City. They succeeded, and the festival was a great success. She agreed with interviewer Linda Dahl that the Kansas City experience changed her life and drew her out of retirement. She received very tempting offers for engagements to follow, but wanted to form her own women's jazz group, to play her own music. This all meant that she had to go back to Jamaica to pack and "tidy things up," so that she could start on the concert circuit again. She then settled in New York and formed her group.

Liston first tried her concept of an all-women's group in 1957 for a four-week engagement in Bermuda. She put together a five-piece group that was warmly received and had their tour extended. As she later told Linda Dahl, "They'd never seen women play. We were cookin'." The membership of that particular group changed somewhat to include men, and they played some more concerts in the United States (Detroit, Pittsburgh, and the East Coast) and then disbanded. In 1980, however, Liston wanted to form a new group, relying on her own arrangements and demanding sensitive musicianship. The new group had seven members and was named

Melba Liston and Company. They toured the European festivals that summer, followed by an Asian tour in the fall. As drummer Dottie Dodgion tells it in Dahl's *Stormy Weather,* "We were in Fiji and out-of-the-way places. . . . And they were delighted—they were in awe! They don't see very much jazz, let alone *ladies.* I was big in Fiji!" The players liked Liston's arrangements, said the music was "fun to play," and compared her work to Duke Ellington's.

Liston suffered a stroke in the mid-1980s and had a lengthy convalescence. She moved back to Los Angeles in 1989 and resumed writing and arranging. She wrote arrangements for the Dexter Gordon tribute concert in New York in 1991 and arranged charts for Randy Weston's African Rhythm Orchestra concert entitled "Blues to Africa," which opened the 1991 edition of Jazz at Lincoln Center on September 13, 1991. Randy Weston's 1992 release, *The Spirits of Our Ancestors,* features her arrangements. A joint collaboration from Liston and Weston, *Volcano Blues,* appeared in 1993. Both were issued by Antilles Records.

Liston's compositions include "Just Waiting," "All Deliberate Speed," and "Melba's Blues." Among the artists she has arranged for are Dizzy Gillespie, Tony Bennett, Eddie Fisher, Billie Holiday, Duke Ellington, Abbey Lincoln, Diana Ross, Charles Mingus, Aretha Franklin, Quincy Jones, Ray Charles, and Billie Eckstine. Her recordings include *White Gardenia,* an album by Johnny Griffin recorded as a tribute to Billie Holiday; "Mischievous Lady" and "Lullaby to Rhythm," with Dexter Gordon, for Dial Records in 1947; *Dizzy Gillespie at Newport,* Verve Records, 1957; and numerous appearances as arranger or musician on albums by Randy Weston, Quincy Jones, Mary Lou Williams, the Metronomes, Elvin Jones, and many others.

Among her awards are a Grammy Award nomination; the Universal Jazz Coalition Award for Outstanding Contributions to Jazz, Fifth Annual Women's Jazz Festival, June 1982; the annual Black Music Conferences Distinguished Achievement Award, April 1984; the Triple Talent Award as arranger/composer/musician at Freddie Jetts Pied Piper, 1971; and the Conductor/Christian Achievement Award for Outstanding Service.

Chris Abersold, who reviewed the *Volcano Blues* album, reported in *Stereo Review* in December 1993 that Liston has "retired her trombone." It is difficult to contemplate Liston in retirement, even from playing trombone, which she has often said saved her from many periods of near depression. Certainly she is still active as an arranger. Perhaps she is one of those rare individuals who has to set aside time in order to retire. In any case, Melba Liston has had a very full career, contributing much to the profession as a musician.

Current Address: c/o Verve/Antilles Records, 825 8th Avenue, New York, NY 10019.

REFERENCES:

Abersold, Chris. "Randy Weston/Melba Liston, *Volcano Blues.*" *Stereo Review* 58 (December 1993): 122.

Dahl, Linda. *Stormy Weather.* New York: Pantheon Books, 1984.

Feather, Leonard. *The Encyclopedia of Jazz in the Seventies.* New York: Horizon Press, 1976.

———. *The Encyclopedia of Jazz in the Sixties.* New York: Bonanza Books, 1966.

Gillespie, Dizzy, with Al Fraser. *To Be, or Not . . . to Bop.* Garden City, N.Y.: Doubleday, 1979.

Hadley, Frank-John. "Randy Weston/Melba Liston, *Volcano Blues.*" *Down Beat* 60 (November 1993): 82.

Handy, D. Antoinette. *Black Women in American Bands and Orchestras.* Metuchen, N.Y.: Scarecrow Press, 1987.

———. "Conversations with Mary Lou Williams." *Black Perspective in Music* 8 (Fall 1980): 204, 207.

Hine, Darlene Clark, ed. *Black Women in America.* Brooklyn: Carlson Publishing, 1993.

Kernfeld, Barry, ed. *New Grove Dictionary of Jazz.* London: Macmillan, 1988.

Palmer, Robert. "*The Spirits of Our Ancestors.*" *Rolling Stone* (May 14, 1992): 108.

Petrie, Phil W. "Melba Liston: The Woman, the Horn, the Dream." *Essence* 12 (October 1981): 13.

Placksin, Sally. *American Women in Jazz.* New York: Seaview Press, 1982.

Southern, Eileen. *Biographical Dictionary of Afro-American and African Musicians.* Westport, Conn.: Greenwood Press, 1982.

"Whatever Happened to Melba Liston." *Ebony* 32 (June 1977): 122.

Whitehead, Kevin. "Randy Weston, Lincoln Center, New York." *Down Beat* 58 (December 1991): 72-73.

Darius L. Thieme

Eleanor Young Love
(1922-)
University administrator, educator, counselor, librarian

Eleanor Young Love became the first black administrator at the University of Louisville when she was named assistant dean in 1969. Remaining at that institution until 1993, she also became the first black to receive the university's twenty-five year award. Love continues to serve the needs of African Americans as the president of the Lincoln Institute Foundation Board, which helps gifted, underprivileged high school students by providing them with college scholarships. Thoroughly involved in the education of young people, she has served as a principal, librarian, and counselor. The most significant contribution that she personally feels she has made has been as a role model to students, both black and white. As the first black administrator at the second largest state school in Kentucky, she feels especially proud to know

Eleanor Young Love

that through her interaction with the students, she was breaking down some of the stereotypical images that many of the white students held about African Americans. She changed their racial attitudes and enriched their lives by teaching them that all people are equal and worthy of respect.

Born at Lincoln Institute, in Lincoln Ridge, Kentucky, on October 10, 1922, Eleanor Young Love was destined to become an educator. Her father, Whitney M. Young Sr., was the first black president of Lincoln Institute, a small private high school for blacks in rural central Kentucky. Her mother, Laura Ray Young, was the first black postmaster in Kentucky and the second in the United States. Eleanor Love and her older siblings, Arnita and Whitney, obtained their college degrees from Kentucky State College, and all became prominent in their fields.

Her sister, Arnita Young Boswell, who is now a retired professor from the University of Chicago, founded the National Hook-Up of Black Women, which implements projects to aid African American youth. Whitney M. Young Jr. became nationally known for his work as the head of the National Urban League. Two educational programs in Kentucky have been named in his honor. The Whitney M. Young Jr. College of Leadership Studies at Kentucky State University, his alma mater, is an honors program which strives to develop leadership abilities in its students through a comprehensive liberal arts curriculum. The other program, administered by Eleanor Love through the Lincoln Institute, provides educational enrichment programs and funds college scholarships for talented underprivileged high school students. Elea-

nor Love, who is now divorced, has two children, David Whitney Love and Laura Young Love.

Growing up in a campus environment, Love was strongly influenced by her father's work as president of Lincoln Institute, and she decided to become an educator as well. She graduated as salutatorian and received the Best All Around Girls Award from the Institute in 1940. She then enrolled in Kentucky State College (now University) following in the footsteps of her brother and sister. At Kentucky State she participated in a number of extracurricular activities including the Drama Club, Alpha Kappa Sorority, and cheerleading. To pay the costs of her education, Love worked in the college library. In 1944, after completing her A.B. in English, she accepted a scholarship from Atlanta University to attend its library school.

With her newly acquired B.L.S., in 1946 she began work as a librarian at Florida Agricultural and Mechanical University, where she stayed until 1951. She then became the head librarian at Fairleigh Dickinson's Bergen Junior College Campus. In 1953, when her father informed her that he needed a librarian to keep his school accredited, she returned home to work at Lincoln Institute for the next fourteen years. During that period she also served as the principal and counselor for the boarding school.

Love, a lifetime learner, continuously took classes while working in these positions, earning a master's in education and an A.C.E.D. from the University of Louisville and a doctorate in education from the University of Illinois in 1970. About her education she said in an interview, "Every time that Daddy needed something in his institution, I went back to school and got another degree." Then she would assume the required role at the Institute to assist her father.

Becomes School's First Black Dean

In 1967 Love began her tenure at the University of Louisville as director of the Upward Bound Program. She served as the administrative assistant and director of student personnel before completing her doctorate. In 1969 she became the school's first black assistant dean. After twenty-five years with the university, having reached the rank of full professor in 1978, she retired in 1993 from the Educational Psychology Department.

Retirement from the University of Louisville gives Love more time to devote to the many other occupations that she continues to pursue. Since 1987 she has served as a counselor for the Human Development Company, an employee assistance program. She counsels employees in the areas of family, drug and alcohol abuse, and marital relations. Those who need Love's assistance will agree that her office hours never seem to end, and she is also willing to talk with people who stop by her home in need of an understanding ear and helpful advice.

As president of the Lincoln Foundation Board, Love maintains her involvement with African American young adults in grades seven through twelve. Through the foundation's endowment from the Whitney M. Young Scholars Program, she funds full four-year college scholarships for gifted, impoverished youths who would not otherwise attend college. Love has always maintained an active role in programs that assist and support persons less fortunate than herself, especially African American youth. About her work with the scholars program for middle and high school students, she said in an interview, "My Daddy once told me, look for the good in every child and I think all my life, I've kept to that. In fact I've passed that along to my own children."

One of Love's community activities is serving as the chairperson of the Human Relations Commission for Louisville and Jefferson County. She is very active in the Westwood Presbyterian Church. She lectures in workshops, churches, and colleges on many topics including diversity and the importance of an education. She is also a member of the Louisville Public Library task force.

As a result of her involvement in the community, Love has received two Governor's Appreciation Citations and been named a Kentucky Colonel (the state's highest honor) by two governors. She has received the Urban League's Equality Award, the NAACP Worthington Award twice, the University of Louisville Minority Affairs Award twice, the YMCA Black Achievers Award, the Kentucky State University Outstanding Alumni Award, and numerous other honors.

Current Address: 1926 Goldsmith Lane, Unit No. 99, Louisville, KY 40218.

REFERENCES:

Dunnigan, Alice A. *The Fascinating Story of Black Kentuckians: Their Heritage and Tradition.* Washington, D.C.: Associated Publishers, 1982.

Horton, John Benjamin. *Profiles of Contemporary Black Achievers of Kentucky.* Louisville: J. Benjamin Horton and Associates, 1982.

Love, Eleanor Young. Telephone interview with Karen Cotton McDaniel, September 15, 1994.

Outstanding Alumni: Centennial Booklet. Frankfort: Kentucky State University, 1986.

Who's Who among Black Americans. Detroit: Gale Research, 1992.

Karen Cotton McDaniel

Maritcha R. Lyons
(1848-1929)
Educator, writer, lecturer

Maritcha Lyons made a career in the Brooklyn schools, where she taught for forty-eight years, eventually becoming an assistant principal and a teacher trainer. She was active in the woman's club movement, was a writer, principal-

Maritcha R. Lyons

ly of nonfiction, and developed a reputation as a public speaker. She was a member of the pre-Civil War free black elite in the North and of the post-war black elites of Brooklyn and New York. Her unpublished memoirs offer insight into her life as well as anecdotes about such persons as various members of the Remond family, Alexander Crummell, Frederick Douglass, Mary E. Eato, and Ida Wells Barnett. The eight biographical sketches she contributed to Hallie Q. Brown's *Homespun Heroines and Other Women of Distinction* (1926), which are considered her most important published works, cover figures from Sarah H. Fayerweather (1802-1868) to Agnes J. Adams (1858-1923).

Maritcha Remond Lyons was born on May 23, 1848, in a house owned by her maternal grandmother at 144 Centre Street in New York City and died on January 28, 1929, in her nephew's home on Stuyvesant Avenue in Brooklyn. She was the third daughter of Albro Lyons (1814-1895) and Mary Marshall Lyons (1814-1894). Her paternal grandparents were George Lyons (1783-?) and Lucinda Lewis Lyons (1790-?). George Lyons, the second to bear this name, was directly descended from an enslaved African who married a Shinnecock Indian on Long Island. The children of this marriage automatically shared their mother's free status. Lucinda Lewis Lyons was a light-haired, blue-eyed woman of mixed Dutch and Indian extraction.

Maritcha Lyons's maternal grandmother was Elizabeth Hewlett Marshall (c. 1779-1861), whose brother James Hewlett was an actor connected with the first attempt to establish a black theatrical organization, the African Players, from 1821 to 1823. She married young and was a widow by the age of twenty. She next married Joseph Bray and became a member of the Abyssinian Baptist Church. Bray died after a few years. Her third marriage was to Joseph Marshall (?-c. 1828), a native of Maracaibo, Venezuela, who fled to New York rather than comply with his family's wish that he become a Catholic priest. In New York he joined the African Methodist Episcopal (AME) Zion Church. In this marriage between a Methodist and a Baptist, the children were brought up as Episcopalians. The choice was perhaps dictated by the proximity of a flourishing parochial school at Saint Phillip's Protestant Episcopal Church. Of the twelve children of this marriage only four survived infancy, and three of those died as young adults. Only Mary Marshall, Maritcha Lyons's mother, lived to old age. Joseph Marshall, Mary Marshall's father, was a house painter who prospered and built a house on Collect (now Centre) Street directly opposite the site of the original Saint Phillip's Protestant Episcopal Church. Upon Joseph Marshall's death, Elizabeth Marshall built a house at the rear of the lot and established a bakery in the basement of the original building. Proceeds from this property provided some income for Elizabeth Marshall in her old age, when she was living with her daughter's family.

Maritcha Lyons's parents, Albro Lyons and Mary Joseph Marshall, were married by Peter Williams, Jr. at Saint Phillip's in 1840. (Peter Williams, Jr. was a leader in founding Saint Phillip's, and as pastor of the church he became the first black Episcopalian priest in the United States.) The new family first established itself in the Centre Street house, where Maritcha Lyons and two older sisters were born; they moved to Pearl Street about 1849 and shortly thereafter to Oliver Street. Her father prospered, becoming the proprietor of a seaman's home on Vandewater Street and of a seaman's outfitting store on Roosevelt Street. Thus his children grew up in relative affluence and comfort. They also learned at an early age crucial lessons about conditions among less fortunate blacks. Since it was completely natural in his profession for black strangers to enter and leave his premises, Albro Lyons became an effective agent in the Underground Railroad, and the children became accustomed to the vital importance of saying nothing about these matters. Albro Lyons estimated that he and his wife directly helped a thousand fugitives.

The Lyons family had five children: Mary Marshall, who was born in 1843 and died before the birth of the second child, Therese (1847-1923); Maritcha (1848-1929); Pauline (Mary Elizabeth Pauline) (1850-1894); and Albro, Jr., born in 1853. Therese married a printer from Providence, Rhode Island, Charles H. Burrill. The family moved to Nashville, Tennessee, where Charles was one of the founders of the *Nashville Globe* and a proofreader for the National Baptist Publishing Company; they had one child, George Willis, who worked in the electrical section of the Long Island Railroad Company. Maritcha Lyons was living with this nephew and his family at the time of her death. Pauline married twice; both marriages were brief, cut short by the deaths of her husbands. Her first marriage, to William Edward Williamson, produced one son, Henry Albro (1875-1965), who became a devoted Mason and the author of several books on the organization. The second marriage produced another son, James Lyons Kingsland, and

Pauline also became responsible for Leon, a stepson from an earlier marriage of her husband. Maritcha Lyons never married, and it also appears that Albro, Jr. never married.

Navigating Educational Opportunities for African Americans

Albro Lyons and Mary Marshall Lyons had the difficult task of finding an adequate means of educating their children among the limited options available to blacks at the time. They first tried sending Maritcha Lyons and her older sister, Therese, to the segregated school open to them in New York City. When this choice proved unsatisfactory, the parents had the girls establish legal residence in Williamsburg (now part of Brooklyn), where they attended Public School No. 19. It is possible that at least Therese Lyons, who completed school there, came in contact with Sarah Tompkins Garnet (1831-1911) and Georgiana F. Putnam (1839-1914)—it is known that the two teachers worked in the Williamsburg school early in their careers. Both of these women were notable teachers in the New York school system and important role models for many black girls. Garnet became principal of a public school in Manhattan, and Putnam became principal of an independent primary school. Maritcha Lyons would later write biographical sketches of both women.

Soon after she began her schooling, Lyons developed a physical disability that kept her out of school until after her thirteenth birthday. The only detail known about the disability is that she had to wear mechanical devices to support her spine. She was under the care of Dr. James McCune Smith, the best man at her parents' wedding, her godfather, and the first American black to earn an M.D. (University of Glasgow, Scotland, 1837). Smith also had a pharmacy, the back room of which became an informal clubroom for the black intellectual elite of New York. He was thus eminently fitted to help the family keep the young girl's interest in learning alive even as formal lessons were suspended. The family's affluence at this time is shown by their ability to buy a piano and pay for lessons for Lyons, who became quite proficient. She was eager to go back to school.

As soon as her health permitted, Lyons attended Colored School No. 3 at Broadway and Thirty-seventh Street, an elementary school then under the direction of Charles L. Reason, one of the first blacks to earn a college degree and also one of the first to teach mixed-race college classes, both at the abolitionist Central College in New York State. Reason had firmly established Philadelphia's Institute for Colored Youth as a preeminent educational institution before moving to New York, where he became one of the most respected and beloved teachers of his generation. Lyons displayed considerable determination both in making up for the years she had lost and in making the trip from her home to school. She often had to make the trip of several miles on foot since drivers on the Broadway stage line would ignore her signal to stop and even jeered at her on occasion. Under the direction of Reason and his assistants, Helen Appo Cook and Mary Anderson, Lyons made remarkable progress and graduated in the early spring of 1864, although she had to wait a few weeks until after her sixteenth birthday at the end of May to receive her diploma.

Before the date of her graduation, the Draft Riots of July 1863 caused a drastic change in the family fortune. Albro Lyons's businesses were ruined, and on the third day of the riots, after repeated alarms, the family's house was ransacked and nearly burnt out. The two children still living at home had previously been removed to safety on the first day of the riots. When the mob entered the house, Albro Lyons escaped over the back fence to the police station, and Mary Lyons took refuge with a German neighbor, who had taken the precaution of loosening boards in the intervening fences in order to make her escape possible. After police inspected the badly damaged house and extinguished the fire, they conveyed Mary Lyons to the Williamsburg ferry, where steamboats were assembled to protect blacks either by taking them away or by pulling out into the middle of the river. Mary Lyons collected the children, who were probably staying in Brooklyn, traveled the length of Long Island, crossed the Long Island Sound, and eventually took refuge with the Remond family in Salem, Massachusetts. Abro remained behind.

Mary Lyons's connection with the Remonds was close. The father, James Remond—invariably addressed by the family as Sir—ran businesses in Salem, Massachusetts, and Newport, Rhode Island. Before her marriage, Mary Lyons had worked as a clerk in his Newport confectionery store during the season when elite families stayed in the area and had then been employed to teach the Remond daughters how to work with hair, a skill she had learned from a French hairdresser. Maritcha Remond was a bridesmaid at Mary Lyons's wedding. All of the Remond daughters were successful businesswomen, with the exception of the youngest, Sarah, who poured her energies into abolition, becoming a noted speaker and worker in the movement—her efforts reflected the whole family's staunch devotion to the cause. Susan Remond followed her mother's profession and became a fancy cake maker. Cecelia, Maritcha, and Caroline ran hairdressing establishments and the largest wig factory in the state of Massachusetts.

The Lyons family reluctantly returned to New York in the late fall. Since Albro Lyons's New York businesses were ruined and he could not reestablish them, the family eventually decided to move to Providence, Rhode Island, in 1864. One factor in the decision was the good reputation of the city's schools. There, Albro became an ice cream maker, and his wife resumed the hairdressing work she had given up twenty-five years earlier at the time of her marriage.

When Mary Lyons tried to place her three youngest children in the public schools—Therese had already completed her education—two were refused admission to the elementary school because of the existence of a separate colored school, and Maritcha Lyons could not enter high school because a state law forbade the admission of blacks. The attempt to break the color barrier lasted several months during which time Lyons was allowed to address the state legislature in support of her cause. Finally, she won, but as a graduate of a "caste" school, she had to officially enter the elementary

school as a first grader and pass an examination before she could obtain the certificate allowing her to enter the high school. This formality was quickly accomplished. On May 5, 1869, Lyons became the first black high school graduate from the Providence High School. She was an excellent student but had to face the difficulty of being the first and only black student. She was sustained by her scholastic success, her proficiency on the piano—which she would consent to play on special occasions—and her own determination to succeed in a school to which her white fellow students had entry as a matter of course.

Lyons Teaches Nearly Fifty Years

The family discussed sending Lyons to Oberlin College, but the idea was rejected, in part because of her own desire to begin working. Since the high school diploma was a sufficient credential at the time, she began to teach in a Brooklyn school in October 1869. In 1918, after teaching for forty-eight years in the Brooklyn schools, Lyons retired; she had served twenty years as an assistant principal. She began at Colored School No. 1, later Public School No. 67. There she was at first under the direction of principal Charles L. Dorsey, a member of the Philadelphia Dorsey family. He was an inspiration to young teachers, as was his former pupil and later assistant, Mary E. Eato. Lyons unhesitatingly placed Eato alongside Fanny Jackson Coppin of Philadelphia's Institute for Colored Youth, Maria Baldwin of the Agassiz School of Charleston, Massachusetts, and Charlotte Forten Grimké as one of the four greatest teachers she had ever known. When the last vestiges of the separate school system were abolished, Lyons transferred to Public School No. 83 as an assistant principal. She had taught all grades for ten years, and for the final twenty years before her retirement, she supervised the first three grades, a responsibility that included overseeing from six to nine hundred students and supervising the practice teaching of candidates from the training school. She thus became the second African American to train teachers in the New York Public School System. A testimonial to the effectiveness of her work and the affection with which she was regarded by her former students was the naming of an organization of former students of Public School No. 67 the Maritcha R. Lyons Association.

Brooklyn offered Lyons many ways to satisfy her craving for further education, ranging from private classes taught by fellow teachers to classes at Brooklyn Institute, where she studied languages and music for ten years. She early established a regime of devoting four or five evenings a week to her studies and was justly proud of her ability to keep up with the ongoing pedagogical revolution and to pass the examination for assistant principal without any formal training. Also important was her involvement in club work, which she undertook seriously and with devotion to a high ideal of service. Her initial involvement was as a founding member of the Women's Loyal League of New York and Brooklyn.

Lyons was no stranger to family responsibilities. In 1888, she and her brother, Albro, Jr., were joined in keeping house by their parents. In semiretirement, Albro, Sr. had become sexton of a white church in Plainfield, New Jersey, but he and his wife spent their final years with the children. Mary Lyons was eighty at the time of her death in 1894, and Albro, Sr. was just short of his eighty-second birthday at the time of his death in 1895. Pauline Lyons died in 1894, further adding to the family responsibilities of Albro, Jr. and Maritcha, who took charge of their two nephews and stepnephew. Towards the end of her life Maritcha Lyons lived with Sarah Fayerweather, a fellow clubwoman, and after Fayerweather's death she stayed with her nephew George Willis Burrill.

Makes Important Contributions to Biography

The most important currently known efforts of Lyons as a writer date from the last years of her life. She wrote eight important biographical sketches for Hallie Q. Brown's *Homespun Heroines and Other Women of Distinction* (1926), making her the second largest contributor to the volume after Brown herself. An important source of information about Lyons's own life and about her sketches and appraisals of some of her contemporaries is the ninety-one page typescript of her unpublished autobiography, *Memories of Yesterdays: All of Which I Saw and Part of Which I Was.* There is further material to investigate in the Williamson archive at the Shomburg Center for Research in Black Culture in New York, ranging from her high school graduation essay, ''Which Furnishes the Better Subject for Art, Mythology or Christianity?'' to letters to the editor written in the last years of her life.

As she developed as a teacher, Lyons also became a notable public speaker. In 1870 at a large Brooklyn meeting to celebrate the ratification of the Fifteenth Amendment to the Constitution with Hiram G. Revels, the first black United States senator, as a main attraction, Lyons was asked to read a poem, and she revealed one of the assets that was to win for her a reputation as an effective public speaker: a voice that was audible throughout a large hall. This was a rare quality for a woman at the time—proper ladies were taught to speak softly and to be completely inaudible at the distance of a few feet.

She spoke often and well—some of her friends thought she was too willing to speak on any occasion, even on very short notice. It appears she undertook only one lecture tour, giving a talk on ''Manhood Suffrage'' in Brooklyn; New Haven, Connecticut; Providence, Rhode Island; and Portland, Maine. Only once was there a question of remuneration beyond travel expenses and hospitality, and this was for a speech at Wilberforce University to celebrate the anniversary of the university chaplain, Thomas G. Steward, the husband of Susan Maria McKinney Steward, a pioneering woman physician, sister of Sarah Tompkins Garnet, and a close personal friend of Lyons. Unfortunately, though she prepared her speech, Lyons missed the occasion because of an attack of pneumonia.

At one point, Lyons won a debate with the young Ida Wells Barnett, who was just beginning her career as a speaker. She then coached the young woman in the art of extempore speaking. Lyons's characteristic modesty did allow her to mention a tribute from a family member in her autobiography.

A niece persuaded her to buy a special new outfit for an important speaking engagement. The niece confessed afterwards that Lyons's eloquence was so stirring that any extraordinary attention to dress was superfluous.

Contributions to Battle for Racial Equality

It was in connection with her public speaking that Lyons characterized herself as a race woman. Her response to racism was not passive or accommodationist. She was not naive; she clearly saw large social forces at work, such as those that made it more difficult for African Americans to gain a modest prosperity in New York City in the later half of the nineteenth century compared to the first half. She knew that concentration of businesses and capitalism had narrowed the range of opportunities open to blacks. Still she insisted on the importance of continued efforts by blacks to take charge of their own destiny. Toward the end of her life she wrote in *Memories of Yesterdays:*

> We are yet in shackles. Venality, a want of race solidarity, of race consciousness; a lack of organization, of breadth of vision, a shrinking from the assumption of responsibility and a distaste of self sacrifice of the patriotic sort, these combine to weigh us down and hinder us from either recognizing or utilizing our possibilities as an important group in the great American cosmopolite makeup. In civil and political affairs we are a negligible quantity, instead of a determining factor. In a certain way we make Jim Crowism, convict leasing, debt encumbrance, even lynching possible by our indifference, apathy, and the dereliction of continued protest. [Lapses in spelling and punctuation corrected by writer.]

In the presence of the troubles of this world, Maritcha Lyons was sustained by her religious faith. She remained deeply attached to Saint Phillip's Church, even when circumstance and conviction led her to worship elsewhere. She ended her days in the high church or Anglo Catholic branch of the Episcopalian Church. As her life drew to a close, she could look back on it and face death with equanimity. She wrote in her autobiography:

> I now find myself practically a ''shut-in.'' Am I content? Yes, with everything except myself. My work was accomplished, not perhaps as well as it might have been done by another, but as well as I with my limitations could do it. My opportunities have been numerous, and valuable; my friends have formed a tower of strength; my life has been crowned with mercies and rich with compensations. With never a doubt as to a proper choice of a vocation, with no great problems to confront me, no exceptional sacrifices demanded of me, the experience of life has not disheartened me and the discipline of life has, I humbly trust, been aiding in consuming the dross and refining the gold accumulated while I have been nearing four score years.

REFERENCES:

Brown, Hallie Q., ed. *Homespun Heroines and Other Women of Distinction.* Xenia, Ohio: Aldine Publishing Co., 1926.

Logan, Rayford W., and Michael R. Winston, eds. *Dictionary of American Negro Autobiography.* New York: Norton, 1982.

Lyons, Maritcha Remond. *Memories of Yesterdays: All of Which I Saw and Part of Which I Was.* Unpublished autobiography. New York: Shomburg Center for Research in Black Culture.

Smith, Jessie Carney, ed. *Black Firsts.* Detroit: Gale, 1994.

———, ed. *Notable Black American Women.* Detroit: Gale, 1992.

Sterling, Dorothy, ed. *We Are Your Sisters.* New York: Norton, 1984.

COLLECTIONS:

Henry Albro Williamson Collection. New York: Shomburg Center for Research in Black Culture. Reel 1 contains material dealing with Maritcha Remond Lyons and her family.

Robert L. Johns

Hulda Margaret Lyttle

Hulda Margaret Lyttle
(1889-1983)
Nurse, hospital and school administrator

Hulda Margaret Lyttle was held in high esteem by her medical colleagues as a leader in the nursing profession and a hospital and nursing school administrator. Her career spanned more than four decades, of which she rendered almost thirty years of service to the George W. Hubbard Hospital and Meharry Medical College in Nashville, Tennessee. During her tenure at Meharry, Lyttle was an assertive and progressive catalyst for change in the nursing profession.

Hulda Margaret Lyttle was born in 1889 in Nashville, Tennessee, to David and Rebecca Lyttle. Biographical information pertaining to her parents is scarce; however, it is known that her mother worked for Smiley Blanton, a Nashville physician, caring for his ailing stepmother. While the names of the schools where Lyttle received her primary and secondary education are not known, sources agree that in September 1910 she entered the first class of the George W. Hubbard Hospital Training School for Nurses.

Lyttle was one of twelve members to enter the first class. In an interview with Evelyn Tomes, former professor and chair, Division of Nursing, School of Graduate Studies of Meharry Medical College, Lyttle spoke of her experiences and duties as a student enrolled in the hospital's training school for nurses. She told of "wearing a hobble skirt with a tight band at the bottom and how an upper-class student planned to make the freshmen 'hobble around here,' and [of her] being placed with a junior nurse." In addition to attending classes and acquiring the theoretical knowledge of nursing, Lyttle gained practical experience through various assignments. She and other students were taught how to make a patient's bed properly. For six weeks she was assigned to the Diet Kitchen and later was given duty on numerous wards. Because there was no housekeeping personnel, Lyttle and other trainees were responsible for scrubbing and mopping ward floors. The cleaning of floors and making of beds were done in the early morning, prior to the doctors' rounds.

Three months after entering the professional nursing program Lyttle began her clinical experience, which entailed rotating twelve-hour shifts of duty. The young student nurse gained recognition as a bright scholar who was capable of giving the necessary and proper care to patients. A person of compassion, the aspiring nurse preferred ward assignments, which enabled her to work with the less fortunate or charity patients. She told Evelyn Tomes it was her belief that "they needed the most and best attention available." As she progressed in her studies, Lyttle became proficient in operating-room procedures and techniques. She became known for her ability to effectively dress wounds with dispatch, and attending physicians rewarded her for her talent by requesting her assistance in the operating room. In 1914 Lyttle, Lula Woolfolk, and Rhoda Pugh, a transfer student from Nashville's J. T. Wilson Hospital School of Nursing, were the first graduates of the George W. Hubbard Hospital Training School for Nurses.

Because Smiley Blanton was extremely satisfied with the quality of care given to his stepmother by Rebecca Lyttle, he promised that her daughter would be given the opportunity to continue her nursing education. After Lyttle completed Hubbard's professional course of study, she became the beneficiary of Blanton's promise. He recommended Lyttle to the superintendent of nurses at New York's Lincoln Hospital School of Nursing, a health-care facility with which he had been formerly affiliated and one of the few schools in New York City that accepted African Americans. The Hubbard alumna was admitted to Lincoln Hospital School of Nursing. Lyttle successfully increased her clinical knowledge and experience, and in 1914 she received her six-month certificate.

After completing her studies at Lincoln Hospital School of Nursing, Lyttle was asked by Charmian Hunt, her former teacher and Hubbard's superintendent of nurses, to substitute for her at Southern University's School of Nursing until her contract with Hubbard terminated. In 1915, after her work at Southern University ended, Lyttle returned to Nashville from Baton Rouge and passed the state nursing examination required for licensing.

Association with Hubbard Hospital and Meharry Medical College

Upon her return to Nashville, Lyttle's professional and academic proficiency earned her recommendations for the position of head nurse at Hubbard Hospital from George W. Hubbard, president of Meharry Medical College, and Josie Wells, superintendent of the hospital. Hunt, who was proud of her student's accomplishments, also recommended Lyttle for the position. Lyttle's appointment at Hubbard Hospital was the beginning of thirty years of professional service rendered to the hospital and the medical college.

Upon assuming her duties as head nurse, Lyttle immediately set about the task of evaluating the nursing program. After careful analysis, she instituted four administrative changes: the adoption of a set date for entrance to the nursing school; the establishment of regular class schedules; improvement in the quality of instructional courses; and a stop to placing beginning nursing students on hospital night duty.

In 1921 John J. Mullowney became president of Meharry Medical College, and in April of that year, following the death of Josie W. Wells, Paul H. Dietrich became superintendent of Hubbard Hospital. Dietrich was impressed with the changes initiated by Lyttle in the hospital's nurse-training program, and it was not long before he appointed her assistant superintendent. In 1922 Dietrich put several significant changes into effect, including modification of the nursing curriculum based upon recommendations from the National League of Nursing Education. Admission required high-school graduation or its equivalent, the number of faculty members was increased, volunteer educators from George Peabody College conducted classes in public health and dietetics, and an alliance was formed with the Nashville Council of Public Health Nursing. This affiliation allowed Hubbard's third-year nursing stu-

dents to gain three months of practical experience in public-health nursing. In addition to these changes, student nurses were not allowed to miss classes except due to illness, and former graduates were given the opportunity to take continuing education courses taught by Dietrich and instructors from George Peabody College.

Lyttle's conscientiousness and administrative abilities were rewarded when she was named director of the School of Nursing. She performed her new responsibilities while also carrying out her duties as assistant superintendent. After Dietrich's departure in 1923, Lyttle was appointed superintendent of Hubbard Hospital. She said in an interview, "They said that I was conscientious . . . knew the work and they could depend on me." Her duties included the supervision of nurses' training, hospital housekeeping, and record keeping. During her three-year tenure Lyttle implemented the employment of maids and orderlies, the equipment of the central supply room, the rotation of supervisors and head nurses, and the placement of graduate nurses on night duty.

In an eight-year period, Lyttle ascended the administrative ladders of Meharry Medical College and Hubbard Hospital. Given the fact that both the medical school and the hospital were under the leadership of white executives who, for the most part, had paternalistic attitudes toward black education and were generally adhering to the governing racist and sexist ideas of the era, this was a significant accomplishment.

In 1925, ill health forced Lyttle to request a leave of absence from her responsibilities at the hospital and nursing school. In the January 1926 issue of the *Meharry News,* it was announced that the officers of the hospital and the college accepted her request for a one-year leave of absence with great regret. Within a short period of time, Lyttle regained her health and returned to Hubbard Hospital and Meharry Medical College. Upon her return, Lyttle continued her campaign to upgrade the quality of nursing care and education at the Nashville medical institution.

Significant Improvements Initiated

Lyttle and the administration improved the nursing curriculum and initiated a program to further enhance the academic standing of the existing staff. During the late summer of 1926, Mary C. Wheeler, general secretary of the Michigan Graduate Nurses Association, was invited to give a series of lectures in nursing education at Meharry Medical College. A few weeks later, after Wheeler returned to Michigan, she contributed a box of books to the nursing school. This was the foundation upon which Meharry's first nursing library was built. Under Lyttle's progressive leadership, the nursing school's teaching staff was supplemented by faculty from Meharry's medical school and adjunct professors from Peabody College for Teachers, Fisk University, and Riverside Sanitarium.

With funds appropriated by the Rockefeller Foundation, the Julius Rosenwald Fund, the Edward Harkness Foundation, and George Eastman of the Kodak Corporation, in 1931

Meharry Medical College and Hubbard Hospital moved from South Nashville to a new six-acre site in North Nashville. Located across the street from Fisk University, the new facility consisted of three buildings, including a dormitory for student nurses.

By the early 1930s, Lyttle and the administration had brought about many significant changes in the nursing program of Meharry. All students who entered the nursing school held high school diplomas and many had undertaken postsecondary study. The accepted scientific courses were augmented with such courses as Modern Health and Social Movements, Public Health and Nursing, and History of Nursing and Medicine. Beginning in 1936, the School of Nursing offered summer graduate courses conducted by Phoebe M. Kendel, professor of nursing education at Colorado State Teachers College. Meharry's graduate extension program was attended by students from cities across the United States.

In 1938 Meharry changed the name of its nursing education program from Training School for Nurses to School of Nursing. Applicants were required to have at least one year of college work. Because of Lyttle's accomplishments as a nursing educator and school and hospital administrator, she was named dean of the School of Nursing. Working in close association with Edward Lewis Turner, who was elected president of Meharry Medical College by the Meharry board of trustees, Lyttle expanded the course of clinical instruction. They made provisions for students in their senior year to study endemic maladies for a two-month period at the Isolation Hospital in St. Louise. In August 1938 the New York Board of Regents informed Meharry officials that its School of Nursing was accredited by the State University of New York. The changes in the nursing course resulted in an increase in the number of students who passed the comprehensive nursing examination administered by the State Board of Nurse Examiners.

A proponent of continuing education for nurses, Lyttle set an example for both her student nurses and the nursing faculty. During the summers of 1933, 1935, and 1936 she took extension courses at the University of Colorado. In 1938 she received a bachelor of science degree from Tennessee Agricultural and Industrial State College, and in 1939 she received a fellowship from the General Education Board of the Rockefeller Foundation to study nursing school organization and administration at the University of Toronto School of Nursing. A year later she completed the course.

Lyttle was an active participant in professional nursing organizations. In 1929, during the twenty-second annual convention of the National Association for Colored Graduate Nurses (NACGN), held in New York, Lyttle addressed the convention's hospital session. Seven years later, in 1936, she was elected first vice president of the NACGN and in 1939 she was elected president of the NACGN's southern region. During her presidency, Lyttle traveled throughout the South and her trips were narrated in *National News Bulletin.* At the Southern Conference meeting held March 17-18, 1939, she was the special honoree at the conference banquet.

Retires from Hubbard Hospital and Meharry

Lyttle retired in 1943 after giving almost thirty years of dedicated service to Meharry Medical College and Hubbard Hospital. According to a feature story by Evelyn Tomes in the 1976 *Commemorative Journal of Meharry Nursing,* her colleagues and students said in an issue of the *Meharrian:* "Because of her indomitable will and constant blazing of paths in the nursing profession, she has made this one of the most outstanding schools for Negroes."

Subsequent to her retirement from Meharry Medical College, Lyttle worked in various health-care positions around the country. For almost a year, she provided her services and expertise in the United Services Organization (USO) in North Carolina. Later, she moved to Houston, Texas, where she was to manage a recently inaugurated school of nursing. However, because the school's organizational and operational standards were inadequate to meet the academic needs of prospective student nurses, Lyttle, with assistance from the state board, closed the school. She then moved to California and for a while worked as a private-duty nurse. In 1948 Lyttle accepted a position with the University of California as administrator of the School Health Programs. Later, she took the position of superintendent of the National Baptist Bath House Hospital in Hot Springs, Arkansas. There she met S. M. Frazier, to whom she was married in May 1954. Subsequently, they moved to Miami, Florida. Even as a sexagenarian, she retained her continuing desire for education. In 1958 she received a vocational certificate from Florida's State Department of Education, and in 1959 she took extension courses at Florida Agricultural and Mechanical University. In addition to holding a teaching certificate from the state of Tennessee, Lyttle received a teaching certificate from the state of Florida in 1961.

Lyttle was considered one of the most outstanding graduates of Meharry Medical College's School of Nursing. Three years after her retirement, on June 23, 1946, the student nurses' residence was named Hulda Margaret Lyttle Hall. Fourteen years after she was so honored, in September 1960, the Meharry board of trustees voted to close the nursing school due to mounting debt and the loss of its senior nurses, who also held teaching positions in the nursing school. Soon after becoming cognizant of the board's actions, Lyttle mounted an aggressive fund-raising campaign to secure a plaque listing all of the nursing school's graduates. Successful in her efforts, a commemorative bronze plaque was placed in the lobby of Hubbard Hospital.

After moving to Miami, Lyttle continued to be an active participant in the community. She was a member of the Miami Chapter of Links, the Alpha Kappa Alpha Sorority, and the Church of the Open Door. Perhaps because of her lifelong career, Lyttle was ever aware of human mortality. According to her obituary, "She planned her Home Going while in the prime of her life and made her complete funeral arrangements."

On Sunday, August 7, 1983, at Cedars of Lebanon Medical Center in Miami, Hulda Margaret Lyttle's life ended at 94 years of age. Her funeral was held on August 10 at the Church of the Open Door, and she was interred in Lincoln Memorial Park, Miami. According to *The Commemorative Journal of Meharry Nursing,* Lyttle was "never too busy or tired to hear the problems of nurses, or to give them advice from her rich store of experience." She is remembered for her lasting contribution to the African American community as a nursing educator, a hospital and school administrator, and a counselor to her students.

REFERENCES:

"Dedication of Hulda Lyttle Hall." *Meharry Bulletin* 13 (August 1946).

"In Memoriam—Hulda Margaret Lyttle-Frazier: 1889-1983." *Meharrian Year Book.* Nashville: Meharry Medical College, 1984.

Lyttle, Hulda M. "A School for Negro Nurses at the George W. Hubbard Hospital and Meharry Medical College: Nashville, Tennessee." *American Journal of Nursing* 39 (February 1939): 133-38.

The Meharry News, January 1926; October 1930.

National Association for Colored Graduate Nurses Program. Twenty-ninth annual convention, New York, N.Y., August 18-21, 1936.

National News Bulletin, February 1939.

———. Tennessee Newsreel Section, September 1939.

Roman, Charles Victor. *Meharry Medical College, A History.* Nashville: Sunday School Publishing Board of the National Baptist Convention, 1934.

Sloan, Patricia E. "Early Black Nursing Schools and Responses of Black Nurses to Their Education." In *Black Women in United States History,* edited by Darlene Clark Hine. Brooklyn: Carlson Publishers, 1990.

Summerville, James. *Educating Black Doctors: A History of Meharry Medical College.* Tuscaloosa: University of Alabama Press, 1983.

Tomes, Evelyn. "Hulda Margaret Lyttle Frazier." In *The Commemorative Journal of Meharry Nursing.* Vol. I, 1901-1976. Nashville: Meharry Medical College, 1976.

Wynn, Linda T. "Hulda Margaret Lyttle Frazier: 1889-1983." *Leaders of Afro-American Nashville.* Nashville: Local Conference on Afro-American Culture and History, 1994.

COLLECTIONS:

The Meharry Medical College Archives contain Hulda M. Lyttle's personal papers. The Evelyn Tomes Black Nursing Collection at Meharry contains an unpublished "Biographical Sketch of Hulda M. Lyttle" by Tomes and oral history interviews that Tomes held with Lyttle.

Linda T. Wynn

Julianne Malveaux

(1953-)

Economist, television host, writer, columnist, activist

With her combined careers as journalist, academician, and television host, Julianne Malveaux has become a successful and highly visible figure of national reputation. Since her teenage years she has been committed to women's rights, civil rights, and the African American struggle, working continuously through a variety of channels to bring about change.

Julianne Marie Malveaux was born September 22, 1953, in San Francisco, the oldest of five children—her siblings are James Paul, Marianne, Mariette, and Antoinette. While both parents were educators, her father, Paul Warren Malveaux, was also a realtor, and her mother, Protcone Alexandria Malveaux, a social worker.

Malveaux studied economics at Boston College, graduating magna cum laude in 1974 with a bachelor's degree and completing a master's degree in 1975. Continuing her studies in that field, she graduated from Massachusetts Institute of Technology in 1980 with a doctor of philosophy degree.

An academic scholar from 1980 through 1991, Malveaux was most recently a visiting faculty member in the African American Studies Department at the University of California, Berkeley (1987-91). She has been a staff member of the Council of Economic Advisors (1977-78), the Rockefeller Foundation (1978-80), the New School for Social Research (1980-81), and San Francisco State University (1981-85). In addition, from 1987 to 1989 she was affiliated with Stanford University's Institute for Study of Research on Women and Gender.

Her talent as a writer was noticed early on. Malveaux first published in the late 1960s when she was teenager, contributing a poem to the *Journal of Black Poetry*. Between her high school and college years, Malveaux published again, this time a review of the book *Blake, or the Huts of America,* by Martin Delany, in the *Black Scholar*. While in college she won an *Essence* magazine contest with her poem "Black love is a bitter / sweetness" and her work was published again in a later issue of the magazine. Her popular and academic writings have appeared in other magazines, newspapers, and professional journals.

Now a syndicated columnist, Malveaux's weekly column has appeared since 1990 nationally in about twenty

Julianne Malveaux

newspapers throughout the King Features Syndicate. She has written the "Left Coast" column for *Emerge* as well as the column "Economics and You," published in *Essence* magazine. Writing on a variety of themes such as women's issues, racism, and reading, and prominent topics in the media such as U.S. intervention in Haiti, the crime bill supported by President Bill Clinton, and gender-based exclusion within the NAACP, she has contributed regularly to *Ms.* magazine and *USA Today* and weekly to the *San Francisco Sun Reporter.* In her feature "Women's Silence Is Indefensible," a King Feature Syndicate release for August 11, 1994, Malveaux examined the disintegration of the NAACP as a result of the activities of former executive Benjamin Chavis and charges of sexual harassment against him. A member of the organization most of her life and an officer in the San Francisco branch, the internal turmoil troubled Malveaux. For Malveaux, the circumstances involve both a civil rights organization and the matter of women's rights—areas of her longstanding concern. Although women comprise the majority of the NAACP membership, the elected board is heavily populated with male members. She wrote, "Part of the problem is the absence of women's voices at the leadership level. This whole situation has become a 'men's thing' with few women weighing in on executive decisions.'' She noted further the NAACP's problematic record on women's leadership, which dates back to 1983. In that year former board chairwoman Margaret Bush Wilson risked her leadership role when she challenged former executive director Benjamin Hooks and lost her position.

Radio and Television Appearances

In addition to her writings, Malveaux is a regular commentator on sociopolitical issues on radio and television, especially on CNN's *CNN and Company.* She was a panelist on the PBS show *To the Contrary* and occasionally served as fill-in talk show host on San Francisco's news-talk station KGO. She left San Francisco in September 1994 for a new program, ''Malveaux in the Morning,'' which is aired on station WPFW-FM, 89.3, in Washington, D.C.

Malveaux frequently serves as a consultant to institutions and organizations. She has consulted for numerous women's and civil rights organizations, including the National Organization of Women's Legal Defense and Education Fund and the National Coalition of 100 Black Women. Her academic publications include *Slipping through the Cracks: The Status of Black Women,* which she coedited with Margaret Simms (1986). She has completed a manuscript on the status of black women in the labor market. She also published a collection of her newspaper columns under the title, *Sex Lies and Stereotypes: Perspectives of a Mad Economist* (1994). Her ongoing research focuses on the labor market and public policy and the impact of such policy on women and minorities.

Malveaux believes she is a born activist. Certainly her involvement as an activist was demonstrated by the time she was a teenager and as she entered college. Her college years began at the time campuses across the nation were settling down from the protests of the sixties. Malveaux has been involved in community work in San Francisco, California. She tried her hand in the political arena for a while, and in 1984 ran an unsuccessful campaign for a seat on the San Francisco Board of Supervisors. That same year she sponsored the ballot initiative called Proposition J that divested over $300 million of city pension funds from companies doing business with South Africa. She worked in 1986 to keep local playgrounds open.

Malveaux's memberships and organizational affiliations are numerous and she has held or currently holds leadership positions in civic, civil rights, political, and women's organizations. She was president of the San Francisco Business and Professional Women's Club, 1987-89, and the local Black Leadership Forum, 1989-90. She has served as vice president of the San Francisco NAACP. On the national scene, Malveaux is vice president of the National Child Labor Committee and a board member of the Center for Policy Alternatives. Currently, she is first national vice president of the National Association of Negro Business and Professional Women's Clubs.

Malveaux said in an August 30, 1994, interview, ''I can't be categorized,'' which suggests the diversity of her interests and activities. At times Malveaux's devotion to activism caused her to be ''looked on as an oddball,'' she said. Many of her black sisters are career women, a position she endorses, and Malveaux's contention is that ''struggle and career go together.'' As an activist, her longstanding commitment has been to women's rights, civil rights, and the African American struggle.

Current Address: WPFW-FM, 702 H Street, NW, Washington, DC 20001.

REFERENCES:

Malveaux, Julianne. Biographical statement sent to Jessie Carney Smith. March 1994.
———. Telephone interview with Jessie Carney Smith, August 30, 1994.

COLLECTIONS:

Copies of Julianne Malveaux's various news articles are on file in her possession.

Jessie Carney Smith

Grace A. Mapps
(?-c. 1891)
Educator, administrator, poet

Grace A. Mapps, who attended New York Central College in McGrawville in the nineteenth century, became the first African American woman to acquire a college degree from a four-year program despite the societal forces that militated against such an accomplishment. She was a woman going to college in an era when education for women was deemed unnecessary. She was black in a country which deemed most blacks intellectually inferior to whites and therefore unfit for higher education. Even in the North she would have faced racism or color prejudice. And though she reportedly inherited property from her father's estate, a college education was costly.

Mapps also earned recognition for her accomplishments as a teacher, administrator, and poet. However, her contributions to black American culture have gone largely unnoted in the twentieth century. This is so for a variety of reasons, including the scarcity of reliable biographical information on Mapps, the conflicting nature of accounts of her achievements, and the fact that at the time of her death, Mapps's poems, which frequently appeared in African American periodicals, were left uncollected and have not—with one exception—yet been located.

It is difficult to compile a sketch about Mapps's life that is both complete and known to be accurate because the data available rests primarily upon biographical snippets or notes from contemporary sources. Moreover, Mapps's achievements have unfortunately become confused with those of Sarah Mapps Douglass and Grace Douglass, family members who were also socially prominent abolitionists, civic activists, and education advocates. The place and date of her birth, her parentage, and the place and date of her death have never been positively established. In all likelihood, however, Grace A. Mapps was born in New Jersey. A biographical note by Fanny Jackson Coppin in her *Reminiscences of School Life, and Hints on Teaching* (1913) states that Mapps was a "native of Burlington, New Jersey," and that she "died there several years ago."

Nineteenth-century sources report that in 1852 Mapps became the first black woman to graduate from a four-year college, taking a degree from New York Central College in McGrawville, New York. Mapps taught at the Institute for Colored Youth (ICY), Philadelphia's Quaker-sponsored private school for African Americans, and was the first woman to head what has been variously called the Female Department, the Girls' Department, or the Girls' High School Division at the institute. Gertrude Mossell, a contemporary of Mapps and a journalist and chronicler of women's issues and the cultural events of the day, described Mapps in *The Work of the Afro-American Woman* as belonging to a "family noted for its acquirements in music, literature, and art."

Mapps was evidently a respected poet whose contemporaries thought her work "rank[ed] well with that of other black writers in her time and with the poetry appearing at the close of the nineteenth century," as noted by Mosell. Mapps, however, never published a collected volume of verse and neither the anthologists of her day or those of the present have located, collected, or republished any of her poetry barring the single poem, "Lines," which appeared in the November 1859 *Anglo-African Magazine*. In an April 1936 article discussing African Americans and Quakers published in the *Journal of Negro History,* Henry J. Cadbury notes Mapp's death in Burlington and indicates that the year was 1891. According to Cadbury, Mapps resigned from the ICY in 1864 and moved to Burlington to care for her mother.

Cadbury devotes some attention to the man Grace A. Mapps knew as her father, David Mapps, and his wife, Grace, who became members of the Society of Friends in Little Egg Harbor, New Jersey. David and Grace Mapps lived first in Green Bank and then Tuckerton, New Jersey. David Mapps, a staunch Quaker, had been both a riverboat trader, with his own boat and crew, and a farmer; he was evidently quite successful in these occupations and highly regarded by those who knew him as a man "possessed of good talents, . . . considerable property, and much business." He had also served on the School Committee of his community. The couple frequently entertained traveling Friends. Cadbury states that Grace Mapps died in 1833; David remarried in 1835. His second wife, Anna Douglass Mapps, was a teacher. Intriguingly, David and Grace Mapps were reported to have no children. Cadbury cites an 1820 diary entry by Charles Osborn, a Quaker and antislavery editor who visited the Mapps family. Osborn wrote of David Mapps:

He and his wife are respectable members of our society. They are well settled, and are in the way of entertaining Friends travelling in truths's service. They have no children of their own, yet have several in family, children and laborers, all people of color, and who appeared to be well ordered.

Possibly, then, Grace A. Mapps was either a foster child or an adopted child of the Mapps. Yet Cadbury thought that David Mapps had "both a son and a daughter" and that these children, along with his second wife, Anna Douglass Mapps, inherited substantial property. Regardless of whether Anna Douglass Mapps was her stepmother or foster mother and David Mapps her biological or foster father, Grace A. Mapps made her family proud.

Mapps Becomes First Black Woman College Graduate

In the face of tremendous pressures due to her race and gender Grace A. Mapps acquired a college education and became recognized as the first African American woman to graduate from a four-year program in the United States. By November 1852 Mapps had graduated from the college in McGrawville and was hired by Philadelphia's Institute for Colored Youth to head the Girls' Department, just two months after a former McGrawville classmate and fellow poet, Charles L. Reason, went to ICY to head the Boys' Department and to lead the new high school as its principal.

The ICY was established with a bequest from Richard Humphries, a West Indian former slaveholder who provided ten thousand dollars in his will to educate African American children in Philadelphia. When the institute opened in 1837, it was intended to serve as an agricultural, mechanical, and trade school with some small attention given to teacher training. Reason and Mapps were the first two teachers hired after the ICY was fully reorganized as a normal school, with its curriculum redesigned to emphasize a classic education and teacher training. Subjects offered included reading, writing, mathematics, bookkeeping, grammar, composition, geography, philosophy, physiology, science, hygiene, public speaking or elocution, logic, and phrenology. Along with her other courses, Mapps may have also taught Greek.

Mapps remained at the institute for approximately twelve years. During that period, although the ICY's status as an educational institution was adversely affected by its cramped quarters and the poor economic conditions of the surrounding neighborhood, the school saw significant change and development. Graduates from ICY were welcomed as teachers and productive community members wherever they went. The teaching staff expanded and its members were recognized as pillars of the community, active in churches, civic organizations, and politics. Among the first to join Mapps and Reason was Sarah Mapps Douglass, Grace A. Mapps's cousin. Douglass merged her small private school into the larger institute, becoming head of the school's Preparatory Department; she worked at the school for fifty years. However successfully Grace A. Mapps performed her job as head of the Girls' Department during the 1850s, in the mid-1860s, ostensibly because of "ineffective" leadership, she was replaced by Fanny Jackson, later to become Fanny Jackson Coppin. Mapps subsequently left Philadelphia and returned to New Jersey, her home state.

Mapps the Poet

Although Fanny Jackson Coppin said in *Reminiscences of School Life* that Mapps was a "frequent contributor to several periodicals prior to the Civil War" and had "a literary rating of high order," "Lines," which appeared in the *Anglo-African Magazine* in 1859, is the only extant example of her poetry. Mossell reprinted the poem in her essay "The Afro-American Woman in Verse," included in her volume *The Work of the Afro-American Woman,* along with another poem from the *Anglo-African Magazine,* by the now celebrated Frances E. W. Harper. Mossell argued that the poems compared favorably to some of the best poetry being produced by blacks at the turn of the century. For Mossell, the poems represented just two "blossom[s]" from one "garden of poesy," and there were other, as yet undiscovered, "gardens of beauty."

"Lines" reveals Mapps's education and gentility. Rather than reflect on any political or racial issue of the day, Mapps chose as her subject death and immortality. The poem is cast in a conventional mode, utilizing the eight-line or octave stanza form. The diction of the poem is elevated and its sentiments are suitably refined. Its contemplative mood reflects the somber subject and Mapps adheres to traditional notions of Christian piety.

> A solemn strain, the organ blending,
> Like a priest's voice, its glorious chord,
> Is on the charmed air ascending;
> "Come, let us sing unto the Lord."

Mapps presents a careful picture of nature as the poem's speaker reflects on the beauty of an autumn day. Maple trees toss their "silvery leaves up to the sky," there is a "harvest sun, serenely shining," and the speaker hears "sweet voices" present in the wind. The evocative sights and sounds of late summer force the speaker to reflect upon the absent "friends of [her] youth" and she wonders whether or not to weep for them. But the certainty of the changing seasons reminds the speaker of "God's most holy love," and from this observation she derives comfort and solace. The speaker concludes that she "may not walk the earth alone, / Nor sorrow for departed days." In the poem's final stanza Mapps demonstrates the power of faith to comfort the grieving:

> I know the friends I loved so well,
> Through the years of their life-long race,
> Lifted sweet eyes of faith to God,
> And now they see his blessed face.
> Thou, Lord forever be my song,
> And I'll not weep for days gone by;
> But give Thee back each hallowed hour,
> A seed of immortality.

As the first black woman to earn a college degree, a respected teacher and a leader in education, and a poet who

contributed to the leading African American journals of her day, Grace A. Mapps won the regard and admiration of her peers. She was indeed a notable figure whose contributions to African American culture merit further study and recognition.

REFERENCES:

Cadbury, Henry J. "Negro Membership in the Society of Friends." *Journal of Negro History* 21 (April 1936): 179-213.

Coppin, Fanny Jackson. *Reminiscences of School Life, and Hints on Teaching.* 1913. Reprint. New York: Garland Publishing, 1987.

Lane, Roger. *William Dorsey's Philadelphia and Ours.* New York: Oxford University Press, 1991.

Mossell, Mrs. N. F. [Gertrude]. *The Work of the Afro-American Woman.* 1894. Reprint. New York: Oxford University Press, 1988.

Perkins, Linda Marie. "Quaker Beneficence and Black Control: The Institute for Colored Youth, 1852-1903." In *New Perspectives on Black Educational History.* Edited by Vincent P. Franklin and James D. Anderson. Boston: G. K. Hall, 1978.

Sterling, Dorothy, ed. *We Are Your Sisters: Black Women in the Nineteenth Century.* New York: Norton, 1984.

Yellin, Jean Fagan. *The Pen Is Ours: A Listing of Writings by and about African-American Women before 1910.* New York: Oxford University Press, 1991.

Sandra Y. Govan

Vivian Osborne Marsh
(1897-1986)
Community activist, clubwoman, government official

People who knew Vivian Osborne Marsh remember her involvement in a variety of community activities, and they continue to honor her as one of the most influential African American residents of the San Francisco East Bay Area. She held offices in women's clubs and in several fraternal organizations, notably the Order of the Eastern Star, and founded many chapters of Delta Sigma Theta Sorority on the West coast. She was a staunch member of the Republican party and the first African American to sit on the Planning Commission and the Board of Adjustments of Berkeley, California.

Marsh was born in Houston, Texas, on September 5, 1897, the youngest of the four children of Benjamin Osborne

Vivian Osborne Marsh

and Alice Estes Osborne. Alice Osborne, having become a widow in 1910, moved to Berkeley with her two daughters, Vivian and Bessie, in 1913, when Marsh was sixteen. It is known that Bessie was later involved with her well-known sister in some community activities, but there is no further information about Vivian's other two siblings.

When Marsh first came to Berkeley as a high school student, there were few African Americans in attendance. She and her friends visited in each other's homes and walked to school and church together. They enjoyed a social life built around house parties and going to the well-chaperoned annual picnics sponsored by St. Augustine Church or the West Indian Association, usually held at Shellmound Park in Emeryville. Idora Amusement Park on Telegraph Avenue in Oakland, with its bright lights, tempting foods, attractive souvenirs, and thrilling rides, was a popular place for the young people on weekends.

After Marsh graduated from Berkeley High School in 1914, she sent an admission application to the University of California, Berkeley, accompanied by records from her two secondary schools, Berkeley High and Houston High School. In spite of her excellent grades in both schools, the university required her to take four entrance examinations. However, after she successfully passed the first two, she was exempted from the remainder and approved for admission. She learned later that her experience helped in discontinuing the policy of automatically reviewing applicants from Southern schools more rigorously than other admission candidates. Marsh received a bachelor's degree in anthropology in 1920 and a master's in the same subject two years later with a thesis

entitled "Types and Distribution of Negro Folklore in America."

Marsh's life was filled with important firsts as an African American. She was the first black woman to major in anthropology at Berkeley, and she and Belinda Davison Mabson of San Francisco were the first to obtain master's degrees from there. There were additional impressive trailblazing accomplishments in the years that followed.

Vivian Osborne married Leon F. Marsh, Sr., originally from Houston, Texas, on October 1, 1921. This was a second marriage for Leon, Sr. He had served in the Philippines in the U.S. Army from 1897 to 1900 and was discharged in San Francisco. He lived in that city until 1905, when he moved to Berkeley and bought the house at 2838 Grant Street where he and his bride made their home. In World War I Leon, Sr. reenlisted, served in France, and was again discharged, this time as a first lieutenant. After Leon, Sr. died in September 1968, Vivian Marsh continued to live on Grant Street until her death in 1986.

The Marshes had two sons: Roy Curtin Osborne and Leon F. Marsh, Jr. Leon, Jr., the first African American firefighter in Berkeley, died in 1956. He had been named Outstanding Young Man of the Year by the East Bay Council of Business and Professional Women for his participation in civic affairs. When Marsh died she was survived by Roy Curtin Osborne and a stepson, Gerald Marsh; two daughters-in-law, Dorothy T. Marsh and Mavis O. Osborne; two grandsons; four granddaughters; and twelve great-grandchildren.

Sorority Founded at Berkeley

In 1920 when Dean of Women at the University of California Lucy Stebbins told Marsh about Delta Sigma Theta Sorority's interest in the black women of the school, Marsh set the wheels in motion for the formation of that sorority on the Berkeley campus. Intrigued by Delta's overall program and its demand for high scholastic achievement, she contacted her fellow African American women students and sought their response. Shortly after she graduated with a bachelor's degree, Marsh founded the undergraduate Kappa Chapter, the first black sorority on a college campus in the western part of the country. Despite their pride in the occasion, the charter members who met in Wheeler Hall on February 13, 1921, resented the choice of words in a front page article in the campus newspaper, the *Daily Cal*, when it told readers about the new "Negress" sorority.

Eight years later, in 1929, Marsh organized Omega Sigma Alumna Chapter so that Bay Area women could continue their involvement in Delta after leaving college, and she subsequently founded chapters at other universities in the West. She served her sorority as the first president of both Kappa and Omega Sigma chapters, Far West regional director, and national president. With her sister, Bessie Osborne, she initiated the Patroness Club in 1948, in the San Francisco East Bay Area. This was a vehicle for mothers of pledges living in the vicinity—and other women available to act as substitute mothers for girls away from their families—to participate in the sorority's activities and support the younger women's efforts.

In 1972 Marsh celebrated fifty years of uninterrupted active membership in Delta Sigma Theta. She was most proud of two projects during her tenure as national president, the Traveling Library and the Teen Lift. The library supplied books to rural districts in Georgia, and the Teen Lift provided transportation for adolescents to visit people and places beyond their immediate environment and to attend events such as symphonies and operas.

Involvement in Fraternal Organizations Widens

The husband and wife team of Vivian and Leon Marsh, Sr. was widely respected for the exceptional contributions they made to fraternal groups in California. In 1916 Leon Marsh, Sr. organized Adonis Lodge No. 25, Free and Accepted Masons of the Prince Hall Family, one of the largest lodges in the California jurisdiction, and served as its first master. Also, he was Worthy Joshua of Loyalty Court Number 28, Heroines of Jericho; Worthy Patron of Queen Esther Chapter Number 4, Order of the Eastern Star of the Prince Hall Family; Grand Worthy Patron of the Golden State Grand Chapter, Order of the Eastern Star; and Grand Chancellor of the Knights of Phythias. Adonis Lodge honored him, a thirty-third-degree Mason, with a testimonial dinner less than a year before he died.

Within the time of her service to lodges Marsh held many positions of honor: Worthy Matron of Queen Esther Chapter Number 340; Most Ancient Matron of Heroines of Jericho; Worthy Counsellor of the Order of Calanthe; and Grand Worthy Counsellor of the Order of Calanthe for California. In the Heroines of Jericho, Marsh organized Loyalty Court Number 28 in Berkeley; St. Francis Court in San Francisco; Xavier Court in Fresno; and other courts in San Jose and Sacramento. Marsh established nine chapters in the Eastern Stars, and, as Grand Worthy Matron, she presided over the founding of chapters in Tulare and Los Angeles. She held the official positions until she became fatally ill.

Marsh's lodges participated in projects that made a difference in the community. There were scholarship grants to students; donations of food, clothing, and money to people in need; visits to shut-ins; and sick and burial benefits to members. She gave credit to her mother for teaching her the value of sharing her finances, time, and talents with those whose lives had not been as fortunate as hers.

Marsh Contributes to Women's Clubs

The Phillis Wheatley Club was Marsh's first exposure to African American women's clubs. In 1916, before she graduated from college, she joined Phillis Wheatley, made up of younger women but part of the California State Association of Colored Women. In 1941 she was elected state president of the association, becoming the first executive officer to come

up the ranks from the youth group. A dispute within the state organization resulted in the formation of four sections: Southern, San Diego, Central, and Northern, of which Marsh was a member. The four sections formed the California State Association, which was, in turn, part of the National Association of Colored Women. The Northern Federation adopted as its project the establishment of the Fannie Wall Children's Home and Day Nursery in Oakland.

On a broader level, Marsh was an officer of the National Council of Negro Women. The council, whose objective was to disseminate information nationwide about all matters that affected the lives of black Americans, had been organized by Mary McLeod Bethune, with headquarters in Washington, D.C. When Marsh became regional director, she formed an East Bay Council and councils in Richmond, Fresno, and Sacramento. Because of her admiration for the quality of Marsh's work, Bethune arranged for her to be the state supervisor of the National Youth Administration, an agency that found jobs for young people during the Depression of the 1930s.

Political Activities Bring Clout

As with Delta Sigma Theta Sorority and the lodges, Marsh participated in the affairs of African American women's clubs until she became sick, traveling over the country in official capacities. At the same time, she was serving the larger community in a variety of political roles. Politically she was in the unique position of being a Republican in a locality where the great majority of black people belonged to the Democratic party. However, this did not seem to cause significant conflicts in her interactions with representatives from differing political ideologies, or with organized labor.

Marsh was the first black woman in her area to share in the influence and power of the white-dominated political machinery. Men and women with different ethnic backgrounds, educational levels, incomes, and political convictions came to her door seeking help in solving dilemmas having to do with employment, housing, education, or dealing with the establishment. They knew that because she sat on the County Central Republican Committee and the State Republican Legislative Council and had ties to government officials, Marsh could secure considerations that would be out of their reach if they were unassisted. Senator Joseph Knowland, Republican, held neighborhood voter meetings at her home and State Senator Nicholas Petris, Democrat, sought her advice in making decisions having to do with black people. In 1959, at the urging of well-wishers, Marsh ran for a seat on Berkeley's city council, but she was defeated.

In the 1950s the city council of Berkeley appointed Marsh to the Planning Commission, the group that drew up the master plan for the city. As a member of the commission and chair of the Board of Adjustments, she was involved in monitoring adherence to the master plan and reviewing applications for variances.

The people of the East Bay Area have paid tribute to Marsh on many occasions, first in 1947 when Zeta Phi Beta

Sorority named her its first Woman of the Year. In September 1970 she was honored at a banquet sponsored jointly by Acacia Lodge Number 7, Free and Accepted Masons, and Queen Esther Chapter Number 4, Order of Eastern Star. This was followed by Order of Calanthe's breakfast in honor of their Grand Worthy Counsellor in 1978. And Delta Sigma Theta Sorority celebrated the sixtieth anniversary of its initiation on the Berkeley campus with a tribute to Marsh, the founder of Kappa Chapter. Berkeley mayor Eugene ''Gus'' Newport proclaimed the date February 21, 1981, ''Vivian Osborne Marsh Day.''

In further recognition of her standing in the community, military officials chose Marsh to launch a World War II U. S. Navy cargo ship, the *S.S. Ocean Telegraph,* at Moore's shipyard in Oakland. Her other community activities included committee work with the YWCA, YMCA, and the Community Chest. She was a member of Taylor Memorial Methodist Church, where she attended Sunday services whenever her travel schedule permitted.

The illness that led to Marsh's death struck when she was attending a convention of the Court of Calanthe in El Centro, California. After a strenuous day of meetings she sent some of the younger people to get fish dinners and went upstairs to rest in a bedroom of Mable Rash's home. When they called to her that the food was ready, they found that she had passed out. She had suffered a severe stroke from which she never regained full consciousness. After initial treatment in El Centro, the Supreme Court of Calanthe and Delta Sigma Theta Sorority shared the twenty-six hundred dollar cost of an air ambulance to Berkeley, for a stay of less than a month in Herrick Hospital. From Herrick she went to Shields Convalescent Home in El Cerrito, where she died about three months later, in March 1986.

Marsh's home, a two-story house at 2838 Grant Street in Berkeley, still stands, but is no longer occupied by her survivors. In her lifetime it was always a welcome place for visitors to come and share its warmth and the home cooked food—especially the monkey bread that Marsh loved to bake—or to play the piano and sing. The dining room table was invariably full of working papers, but they were readily pushed aside to make room for eating. There were shelves around the walls of the living room and dining room to display the commemorative plates that she had collected when she traveled or had been given to her by distinguished people, fellow club members, sorority sisters, and other admirers.

Having freely shared her wealth with people in need, as well as her time and talents, Marsh was not an affluent person in her later years, and the medical expenses of the last months of her life added to the strain on her finances. After she died, auctioneers bought her valuable furnishings, clothing, sheet music, jewels, and watches. But she had achieved her goal of making a significant difference in the lives of people in her community and of setting an example for younger women.

REFERENCES:

Boswell, Vallie. Interview with Dona L. Irvin. June 23, 1993.

Delta Sigma Theta Sorority. Berkeley Bay Area Alumnae Chapter. *Working Together for the Common Good.* Berkeley, n.d.

Giddings, Paula. *In Search of Sisterhood: Delta Sigma Theta and the Challenge of the Black Sorority Movement.* New York: Morrow, 1988.

Lee, Samantha. Interview with Dona L. Irvin. June 19 and 30, 1993.

Marsh, Vivian Osborne. Interview with Mary Hubbard Jones. Oakland Museum Cultural and Ethnic Affairs Guild Black Pioneers Oral History Project, January 19, 1972.

Maybuce, Euradee. Interview with Dona L. Irvin. June 22 and 30, 1993.

Roberts, Eleanor. ''Miriam Matthews.'' In the *Black Women Oral History Project.* Edited by Ruth Edmonds Hill. Vol. 7. London: Meckler, 1991.

Williams, Delmar. Interview with Dona L. Irvin. June 10, 1993.

Williams, Mary T. Interview with Dona L. Irvin. June 22, 1993.

Dona L. Irvin

Harriet Gibbs Marshall
(1868-1941)
Pianist, educator, school founder

Harriet Gibbs Marshall had a dream. She wanted to open a music conservatory for African Americans that would not only inspire and train new black artists, but also uplift the community by preserving the rich African American musical heritage and by increasing the number of performances by professional musicians open to black audiences. Marshall's dream became a reality in 1890 when she founded a music conservatory at Eckstein-Norton University in Kentucky. She was also the founder of the Washington Conservatory of Music and School of Expression in Washington, D.C., in 1903.

Harriet (Aletha) Gibbs Marshall was born on February 18, 1868, in Victoria, British Columbia, to Mifflin Wistar Gibbs and Maria Ann Alexander Gibbs of Kentucky. She had two siblings, Ida Gibbs and Horace E. Gibbs. Marshall's father was a high achiever. A successful businessman and lawyer, he was elected a municipal court judge in Little Rock, Arkansas, in 1873. His political career included being elected to the Common Council of Victoria for two terms, and in 1879 President William McKinley appointed him United States Consul at Tamatave, Madagascar. When he was a young man, Mifflin Gibbs traveled with the famous abolitionist Frederick Douglass on lecture tours, and he had early associations with the Underground Railroad. Besides the inspiration Marshall

Harriet Gibbs Marshall

undoubtedly received from her father, she also received strong support from her husband, Napoleon Bonaparte Marshall, an attorney and Harvard graduate who practiced law in Massachusetts and New York.

Music Conservatories Founded

Marshall began her early piano studies in Oberlin, Ohio. She later attended Oberlin College and in 1889 became the first African American to complete the entire course at Oberlin's Conservatory of Music. According to Oberlin College records, she did not receive her Mus.B. degree until 1906, however, because Oberlin did not grant degrees in music at the time she attended. She pursued a postgraduate education, studying music in, among other places, Boston, Chicago, and Paris, France, where Moskowski was her piano instructor. After returning to the United States, she gave successful piano recitals throughout the country. In 1890 Marshall founded a music conservatory at Eckstein-Norton University in Cane Spring, Kentucky. According to Rayford Logan and Michael Winston in their *Dictionary of American Negro Biography,* "Her aim was to help preserve the rich heritage of Negro music and to develop the musical talent of Negroes." This is where Harriet Marshall started living her dream.

In 1900 Marshall was appointed director of music for the "colored public schools" of Washington, D.C. Doris McGinty wrote in *The Black Perspective in Music,* Spring 1979, "Although Miss Gibbs had a staff of seven, she exercised no control over the official position of the system or its written statements, for all official documents were written by a white supervisor, who expressed exclusively the point of view of white pupils." In 1903, while working in this post, Marshall founded the Washington Conservatory of Music and School of Expression. McGinty also stated,

> Remembering her ideal of establishing a music conservatory and no doubt frustrated in her position with the public schools, Miss Gibbs called together a small group of capable music teachers, all of them graduates of recognized universities and conservatories of America. They agreed upon the need for a conservatory in the city, organized a board of management, and opened the doors of the Washington Conservatory of Music.

The conservatory was located at 902 T Street, Northwest, and the building where it was housed was a gift from her father. The conservatory was a landmark facility for the development and promotion of black talent and for the preservation of African American music. According to McGinty, it filled a void in the community:

> The state of music in the black community of Washington, D.C., was such as to make it especially responsive to the opening of the new school of music and to the music events which the school would later sponsor. Professional performances were limited in the white community, both in number and quality; and blacks were excluded from attending the performances. The black community, however, cultivated its own musical interests. As in the white community, there was no formal concert season. But there was the usual complement of church services, memorial services, meetings, receptions, graduation exercises, dances, sings, parties, and excursions through which music played a vital role in the black community.

The conservatory, then, provided an outlet that did not exist at the time for African American musicians.

Harriet Gibbs married Napoleon Bonaparte Marshall in 1906. He taught music history at the conservatory and also handled many of the school's business arrangements. The conservatory graduated eleven students at its first commencement exercise, held at the Metropolitan African Methodist Episcopal (AME) Church. Although the sizeable auditorium could seat eighteen hundred people, McGinty reported that the room was completely filled and hundreds of people were turned away.

New Life in Haiti

Marshall left the conservatory for a period of time when her husband's career began to take a different direction after his service as an infantry captain in World War I was over. In 1922 Napoleon Marshall obtained a position with the U.S. legation in Haiti, which he believed would evolve into a diplomatic post; however, he was appointed only as a clerk. He and Harriet Marshall spent six years in Haiti and were devoted to improving living conditions for the Haitians. They joined others who advocated the removal of U.S. Marines from Haiti. In 1926 Harriet Marshall cofounded the Jean Joseph Industrial School in Port-au-Prince and in 1930 published a book entitled *The Story of Haiti,* which, according to McGinty, received positive reviews when it was published in the United States.

Marshall returned to the Washington Conservatory of Music full time after her husband's death in 1933. In 1937 she expanded the conservatory and created the National Negro Music Center. Logan and Winston noted that "the new center featured a library and departments specializing in research, creative work, and teaching young people." Not only was her dream expanding, but the conservatory was well respected and deemed by many a prestigious institution.

Marshall died suddenly on February 25, 1941. The conservatory remained open for a while under the supervision of her niece, Josephine V. Muse. After Muse's death, the conservatory doors were closed and all of its assets auctioned. The monies raised were presented to Howard University in Washington, D.C., to establish the Gibbs-Muse Scholarship Fund for music students.

Harriet Gibbs Marshall set her goals early on and seized the opportunity to help create a better future for African Americans. With vision, dedication, and commitment, she achieved what she set out to do: she established a facility where black musicians could cultivate their talent, and she helped earn black music and musicians well-deserved respect. Fortunately for her—and for many musicians and music lovers—she was able to see her dream come true.

REFERENCES:

Logan, Rayford W., and Michael R. Winston, eds. *Dictionary of American Negro Biography.* New York: Norton, 1982.

McGinty, Doris E. "The Washington Conservatory of Music and School of Expression." *The Black Perspective in Music* 7 (Spring 1979): 59-71.

Washington Tribune, March 1, 1941.

Dhyana Ziegler

Constance Hill Marteena
(1903-1976)
Librarian, educator, writer, organization leader

Constance Marteena played an important role in the library profession through participating in the development of the North Carolina Negro Library Association as a professional organization for African American librarians and

Constance Hill Marteena

in guiding its merger in 1954 with the North Carolina Library Association. She also distinguished herself in library administration and education in North Carolina. She was director of the Thomas F. Holgate Library at Bennett College in Greensboro and an instructor in the college's teacher-librarian certification program. She is less well known for her important research work to identify notable African American women and her development of a library collection on African American women at Bennett.

Constance Hill Marteena was born in 1903 in Richmond, Virginia, to Irene Robinson Hill and Reuben T. Hill. She prepared herself for a professional career by attending Hartshorn Memorial College in Richmond (now Virginia Union University) and received a bachelor of science degree from Hampton Institute (now Hampton University) in Hampton, Virginia, in 1933. She studied librarianship at the Graduate Library School, the University of Chicago, and was awarded a master of arts degree in 1946. She wrote her master's thesis on "Afro-American Women prior to the 20th Century." She also completed postgraduate work at the Catholic University of America in Washington, D.C.

Marteena's work experience included employment as director of public information at North Carolina Agricultural and Technical State University from 1929 to 1937, secretary to the president and director of public information at Bennett College from 1937 to 1939, and librarian and instructor at Bennett College from 1939 to 1967. Marteena conducted library science courses and in-service summer training sessions at Bennett College for persons holding teacher-librarian positions in North Carolina. Many students entered the library profession because of her inspiration and guidance. She was also a consultant for the Accreditation Committee of the Southern Association of Colleges and Schools.

Marteena was elected president of the North Carolina Negro Library Association at its eighteenth annual conference in 1952 and held the position until 1954. According to Mollie Huston Lee in *Library Review,* October 1955, her administration was marked by her ability to obtain prompt cooperation from the operational agencies of the association. She called executive committee meetings often and saw to it that the programs of the association were carefully planned and implemented. Her frequent communications to the association's members seeking their suggestions for a better conference gave them the feeling of being an integral part of the program. Under Marteena's leadership the merger of the North Carolina Negro Library Association and the North Carolina Library Association was completed, thus ending segregation of professional library organizations in North Carolina.

Marteena's literary skills were commendable and her contributions to professional journals were many. She published articles in *Library Review,* the official journal of the North Carolina Library Association. She also wrote articles for the *New York Times* and the *Greensboro News and Record.* In addition, Marteena wrote *The Lengthening Shadow of Women: The Biography of Charlotte Hawkins Brown,* who was president of Palmer Memorial Institute in nearby Sedalia, North Carolina. Among her other writings is *Afro-American Women in Art: Their Achievements in Sculpture and Painting,* compiled by the Negro Heritage Committee, Beta Iota Omega chapter of Alpha Kappa Alpha Sorority. She initiated the publication of *Who's Who among Black Librarians* in the 1950s. She was compiler for the publication *Who's Who among Black Women,* which was written for the Greensboro chapter of Alpha Kappa Alpha Sorority.

Marteena's research and publications on African American women were important in identifying and recording the achievements of black women and came at a time when little attention was given to their work. While she produced works that have since been used by other scholars to develop research projects, Marteena's contributions have not received the attention they deserve. The fruits of her labor are evident at Bennett College, where she developed a library collection on African American women.

On December 29, 1978, Constance Hill Marteena died at her home in Greensboro and was survived by her husband, Gerald F. Marteena, four nephews, and several nieces. Gerald Marteena had been an educator, engineer, and dean of the School of Engineering at North Carolina Agricultural and Technical State University.

Constance Marteena made a permanent difference. She helped to racially integrate the library profession in North Carolina, strengthened libraries by providing education to employees, and preserved the culture and accomplishments of African American women through her publications and development of a library collection devoted to them.

REFERENCES:

Lee, Mollie Huston. "North Carolina Negro Library Association, 1935-54." *Library Review* 2 (October 1955): 10-32.

North Carolina Negro Library Association, Research Committee. *Who's Who in North Carolina Negro Libraries.* Salisbury, N.C.: Carnegie Library, Livingstone College, 1954.

Speller, Benjamin F., Jr., and James R. Jarrell. "Profiles of Pioneers: Selected North Carolina Black Librarians." In *The Black Librarian in the Southeast: Reminiscences, Activities, Challenges.* Edited by Annette L. Phinazee. Durham, N.C.: North Carolina Central University Alumni Association, 1980.

COLLECTIONS:

Correspondence, papers, and other documents relating to Constance Hill Marteena are located in the Holgate Library, Bennett College, Greensboro, North Carolina.

Benjamin F. Speller, Jr.

Roberta Martin
(1907-1969)
Gospel singer, composer, arranger

A seemingly inauspicious event in 1931 led to a major new musical movement, the birth of modern gospel as it is now known. In that year, gospel pioneers Thomas A. Dorsey and Theodore R. Frye appointed Roberta Martin as their accompanist for a newly formed youth gospel choir at Ebenezer Baptist Church in Chicago. Martin's role in this new movement cannot be minimized; she was at once composer, arranger, publisher, soloist, inspirational group leader, and recruiter. Her contributions grew out of the accomplishments of her predecessors, who included Dorsey and Frye, and a chain of composers, singers, and worshippers stretching back at least to the eighteenth century, all of whom participated in a spiritual and hymn-singing tradition with musical roots in Africa. The movement begun by Martin, which was basically evangelical in nature, spread throughout the world and left a wealth of printed and recorded compositions. The longevity and vitality of this music has had a profound and pervasive influence on the music world.

Roberta Evelyn Martin was born in Helena, Arkansas, on February 12, 1907. Her family moved to Cairo, Illinois, when she was eight and then to Chicago when she was ten. She went to the public schools and graduated from Wendell Phillips High School in Chicago, having studied piano with the choral director, Mildred B. Jones. Her musical studies began when she was six, studying piano with an aunt and subsequently playing piano for Sunday school and various choirs. After high school she continued her musical studies at Northwestern University, with the ambition of preparing for a career as a concert pianist. Thus Frye and Dorsey made a propitious choice: she was a talented and well-trained young person who could sing, accompany, arrange, and direct.

Martin's knowledge of the gospel music genre was slight at first, but she learned quickly, adapted and improved upon the accompanying styles then prevalent, developed rapidly as a dynamic leader, composer and singer, and began rapidly to spread the "good news" of her gospel ministry.

An important early influence on Martin's growth as a gospel musician was the visit of the Bertha Wise quartet group, which visited and performed at Ebenezer Baptist Church in 1933. Their visit inspired Theodore Frye and Roberta Martin to organize a male quartet group with Martin as accompanist and occasional soloist. Especially influential were Wise's strong piano stylings, her dominating contralto voice, and the close male quartet harmonies. The Frye-Martin Quartet enjoyed a good reception and soon became the Roberta Martin Singers. Originally, the group had four male singers: Norsalus McKissick, Robert Anderson, Willie Webb and Eugene Smith. Later, women were added to the group. These included Bessie Folk, Delois Barrett Campbell, Myrtle Scott, and Lucy Smith Collier; later female members were Myrtle Jackson, Gloria Griffin, Romance Watson, Archie Dennis, and Louise McCord. Each individual had particular musical qualities that added to the effectiveness of the group, for example, McKissick's tone and delivery, Campbell's broad range, and Collier's stylings as pianist and organist.

Martin Influences Modern Gospel

As composer, arranger, and accompanist, Martin's range was broad and her influence is felt among today's gospel luminaries. Her accompanying style drew upon various strains within the genre, which were then adapted, innovated, improvised, and given a special flavor all her own. She featured a strong bass, fundamental chords strongly reinforced, a somewhat syncopated but vigorously pulsating, rocking beat, innovative chord substitutions, and overall a kind of tension between melody and accompaniment that undergirded the message of the words. As a composer, her form favored a hymn construction, with repeating choruses and a straightforward diatonic melody with few embellishments. Her choral style drew upon the strengths of her ensemble, and favored a melodic lead supported by close harmonies often using substitute chords at cadences. She apparently liked a wide-ranging soprano part, a high baritone and a lyrical tenor. Above all, however, the word movement was direct, and not hidden by counterpoint. Thus, again, the focus came to the message delivered by the words.

A view of Martin's compositional process as well as her musical preferences is provided by Horace Clarence Boyer in an article in *We'll Understand It Better By and By*. The sample of music selected for study by Boyer includes fifty-two songs, selected by Martin and representing her musical tastes. It includes songs composed by Martin, James Cleveland, and twenty-two other gospel song composers. Significantly, he points to an African heritage, as exhibited in the melodic construction, comparatively narrow range, small intervals, and pentatonic or gapped scales used in the songs studied. One might also point to a modal cast to some of the melodies and a soft syncopated flavor as additional qualities pointing to African influences. He finds the European heritage principally represented in the harmonies and formal construction. In summary, one finds a heterogeneous group of songs that are unified in their style and content, reflecting a continuing tradition of composition, arrangements, and performance values reaching back to African roots and forward to modern innovations.

As a performer, composer and arranger, the reservoir from which Martin drew her strength flows from several currents. There is the emotional aspect, as expressed in soul-stirring words that reach inside the listener: words such as "mercy," "joy," "peace," "sin," and "grace." There is the tradition of the hymn itself, a congregational and participatory sharing of sentiments through music. This tradition, of course, extends back to the historic compilation of hymns published in 1801 by Richard Allen, *A Collection of Spiritual Songs and Hymns from Various Authors,* and extends forward to *The New National Baptist Hymnal of 1977*. There is also the spiritual, revised, transformed, and in a new setting. In *Black Song: The Forge and the Flame,* John Lovell points to several songs, including Martin's setting of "Didn't It Rain," as retaining gospel's close kinship to the spiritual. While acknowledging the shift in preferences from the traditional spiritual to the gospel, John Work III points out in a 1949 *Journal of American Folklore* article that this was merely a transition of style to something new, exciting and striking.

A similar shift occurred in the role of the accompanist. Work acknowledges this, having observed this new role of both pianist and choir in about 1937 at Zema T. Hill's church in Nashville, Tennessee: the rhythmic piano, pulsating rhythms, and striking participatory elements popular among the youth, and their absorption of these new musical values. With Martin, the role of the pianist reached added prominence, and many attribute to her the origin of the modern gospel pianistic style. According to Horace Boyer, in *We'll Understand It Better By and By,* "Roberta Martin played piano with the nuances of a Horowitz, the inventions of an Ellington, and the power of an Erroll Garner, all the while playing 'straight from the church.'"

Finally, in Martin's music the role of the soloist became more pronounced. She acknowledged this in her continual search for strong solo voices within her ensemble and then by featuring them prominently once they were a part of the group. Solos drew strongly on improvisation, rhythmic alterations, vamps (short, repeated choral strains), and the close relationship between soloist and audience/congregation that are the hallmark of gospel. All of the above values were incorporated in her compositions. In addition, she encouraged other composers by performing their new songs and publishing their output through her company.

A Gifted Leader and Mentor

With her group Martin was always in demand and kept to an intensive schedule of concerts. The group's performance schedule took them to all regions of the United States and to Europe. The highlight of Martin's 1963 European tour was a performance at the Spoletto Festival in Italy. Despite the demanding schedule, the major concerts, and the recording sessions, she did not hesitate to visit storefront churches and to offer her support to other choirs and soloists. It was during such a mission, visiting a small church in Bessemer, Alabama, that she discovered a young choir director named Alex Bradford. With Martin's support and tutelage, he went on to achieve success and fame. She published the compositions of many rising gospel musicians, including James Cleveland, featuring his compositions with her group.

Martin's output, including that of the Roberta Martin Singers, was some one hundred recorded compositions, performed and issued over a period of about forty years. She recorded mostly on the Savoy record label and earned three gold records. Through the Roberta Martin publishing company, she published two hundred and eighty gospel songs, including compositions by herself, James Cleveland, Alex Bradford, and several others. Among her most popular songs are "Try Jesus, He Satisfies," "If You Pray," "Just Jesus and Me," and "God is Still on the Throne." Her many arrangements include "Everybody Won't Get There," "I Heard the Voice of Jesus Say," "Amazing Grace," and "Didn't It Rain."

The interviews with former members of her Roberta Martin Singers published in *We'll Understand It Better By and By* paint a picture of Martin as a gifted leader and musician and a deeply spiritual person. She continually prayed with her singers, individually and as a group, taught Bible classes, and had great faith in the power of prayer up to the time of her death, when she refused strong medication. She continually offered a helping hand to others, including the elderly and infirm; on one occasion while on tour she drove an elderly citizen to the hospital in her car. She loaned money, offered clothing, taught and counseled, and all the time was busy composing new songs to support the gospel ministry. She was a strict musician and taskmaster, striving always for a better performance. In the words of Archie Dennis in *We'll Understand It Better By and By,* "she taught us that God will endeavor to make the song and the singer one. . . . the message was greater than we were."

Martin and the singers carried the gospel message far and near and left a legacy long to be remembered. Roberta Martin married James Austin in 1947 and they had one son, Leonard Austin. Her brilliant career, and that of her ensemble, contin-

ued into the late 1960s and brought her the love of those she touched with her music. She was particularly admired by gospel musicians, singers and supporters throughout the country, especially in her hometown of Chicago. When she became ill at the end of her life, she was visited often by members of her group, who prayed with her during her final illness. She died in Chicago on January 18, 1969. Following her death, at perhaps the largest funeral in Chicago's history, an estimated 50,000 persons visited Mount Pisgah Baptist Church to pay homage to this great lady of gospel music.

REFERENCES:

Bontemps, Arna, "Rock, Church! Rock." In *International Library of Negro Life and History; The Negro in Music and Art,* edited by Lindsay Patterson. New York: Publishers Co., 1967.

Boyer, Horace Clarence. "Black Gospel Music." In *The New Grove Dictionary of American Music,* edited by W. Wiley Hitchcock. Vol. 2. London: Macmillan, 1986.

———. "Roberta Martin." In *The New Grove Dictionary of American Music,* edited by W. Wiley Hitchcock. Vol. 4. London: Macmillan, 1986.

———. "Roberta Martin; Innovator of Modern Gospel Music." In *We'll Understand It Better By and By,* edited by Bernice Johnson Reagon. Washington, D.C.: Smithsonian Institution Press, 1992.

Broughton, Viv. *Black Gospel, An Illustrated History.* Poole, Dorset, England: Blandford Press, 1985.

Burnim, Mellonee. "Functional Dimensions of Gospel Music Performance." *Western Journal of Black Studies* 12 (Summer 1988): 112-21.

Dorsey, Thomas A. "Ministry of Music in the Church." In *Improving the Music in the Church,* by Kenneth Morris. Chicago: Martin and Morris, 1949.

Goodrich, Robert, and Robert M. W. Dixon. *Blues and Gospel Records: 1902-1942.* London: Storyville Publications and Co., 1982.

Hannah, Clayton L. "The Best of the Roberta Martin Singers." Record album notes. Savoy Records, 1979.

Heilbut, Tony. *The Gospel Sound.* New York: Simon and Schuster, 1971.

———. "The Roberta Martin Singers, The Old Ship of Zion." Record album notes. Kenwood Records, 1973.

Hine, Darlene Clark, ed. *Black Women in America.* Brooklyn: Carlson Publishing, 1993.

Lovell, John, Jr. *Black Song: The Forge and the Flame.* New York: Macmillan, 1972.

Reagon, Bernice Johnson, ed. *We'll Understand It Better By and By.* Washington, D.C.: Smithsonian Institution Press, 1992.

Roach, Hildred. *Black American Music: Past and Present.* 2nd ed. Malabar, Fla.: Krieger Publishing Co., 1992.

Salvo, Patrick, and Barbara Salvo. "45 Years of Gospel Music." *Sepia* 74 (April 1974): 60-64.

Southern, Eileen, ed. *Biographical Dictionary of Afro-American and African Musicians.* Westport, Conn.: Greenwood Press, 1982.

———. *The Music of Black Americans.* 2nd ed. New York: W. W. Norton, 1983.

Williams-Jones, Pearl, and Bernice Johnson Reagon. "Afro-American Gospel: A Crystallization of the Black Aesthetic." *Ethnomusicology* 19 (September 1975): 373-84.

Williams-Jones, Pearl, and Bernice Johnson Reagon, eds. "Conversations; Roberta Martin Singers Roundtable." In *We'll Understand it Better By and By,* edited by Bernice Johnson Reagon. Washington, D.C.: Smithsonian Institution Press, 1992.

Work, John W., III. "Changing Patterns in Negro Folk Songs." *Journal of American Folklore* 62 (April-June 1949): 136-44.

Darius Thieme

Ruby Grant Martin

Ruby Grant Martin
(1933-)
Government official, lawyer

Gracious, charming, and quick to smile, Ruby Grant Martin is an extraordinarily intelligent and talented woman who uses her energies for the advancement of society's disadvantaged. Throughout her career as a federal and state attorney and administrator, she has been fierce in her dedication to improved economic and educational opportunities for blacks, courageous in her efforts to assure legal protection for minorities and the poor, and tenacious in her determination to exact better lives for women and children. According to a biographical sketch on Martin, "All of her life has been spent, either directly or indirectly, engaged in some activity designed to help minorities, poor people, children at risk, the less fortunate, those whom the system has failed or have fallen through the cracks in the system."

Martin was born on February 18, 1933, in the small rural town of Lake Village in southeastern Arkansas. When she was nine, the family moved to Cleveland, Ohio. It was there, in the predominately white city educational system, that she attended elementary and secondary schools. Her classmates were most often the children of Jewish, Russian, and Ukrainian immigrant workers. Her biographical sketch notes that "Ruby is fond of saying that her father insisted that she get better grades than her classmates because he spoke sterling English, whereas, most of their parents did not speak English at all." She maintained her ties with the rural South, however, by spending most of her summers in the Arkansas home of her grandmother and aunt. Moving to the urban Midwest did not insulate Martin from the effects of racism. She lost a high school class election and is convinced her minority status caused the defeat.

Martin's early education was acquired in mostly white schools but her undergraduate and professional degrees were obtained at historically black institutions. She received a B.A. from Fisk University in 1956 and an LL.B. from Howard University School of Law in 1959, ranking number one in her law class.

Her college experiences gave her much insight into racial inequality. She clearly remembered those days in "Reinventing Race Relations," a speech she gave on December 8, 1992, at the Richmond Urban Forum: "As a colored college student in Nashville, the capitol of Tennessee, . . . I was subjected to all of the officially imposed racial separation and sanctions, as well as all of the instances of abuse and the indignation that were heaped upon me and my fellow classmates, simply because we were colored in a city of the deep south." She recalls being forced to ride in the back of the bus and being barred from the fitting rooms in stores downtown. She also recalls those "survival" techniques she employed, such as bringing her blond, blue-eyed Fisk roommate to try on clothes for her.

Attending law school in Washington, D.C., Martin encountered racism often. She continued in "Reinventing Race Relations": "What made the situation in the nation's capitol so much more heartbreaking was that persons from the international community, even those whose skin was blacker than mine and whose hair was more kinky than mine, were allowed to dine in restaurants and patron theaters whose doors I could not even darken, no pun intended." Not to be outdone, however, the law students simply borrowed native wear from the African students and went wherever they liked. "So, once again we were able to foil the system that tried to dehumanize us by making fun of it," she said. Incidents such as these, she contends, were the beginnings of her personal encounter with and analysis of American race relations. She determined to put her legal education to work to right the wrongs American blacks were experiencing.

Civil Rights Act of 1964 Drafted

Martin's career began in Washington, D.C. From July 1960 to May 1965, she was staff attorney for the U.S. Commission on Civil Rights. Established in 1957, this fact-finding agency was created to discern the status of minority groups in the country; much of the information gathered and the recommendations made by the commission provided the basis for the federal civil rights legislation passed during the 1960s. As a federal government lawyer, Martin helped draft and implement as law the Civil Rights Act of 1964. During this time, she also served as staff investigator for the Cleveland Community Relations Board, an agency that is part of the city's civil rights division.

From May 1965 to May 1967, Martin's activities were varied. During this period she was confidential assistant to the assistant to the Secretary of the Department of Health, Education, and Welfare (HEW); all of these positions were connected with civil rights programs. Through its civil rights programs HEW worked to enforce federal legislation and followed executive orders to ensure that discrimination on the basis of race, color, or national origin was eliminated.

May 1, 1967, brought an important appointment for Martin. She was named director of the Office of Civil Rights for the Secretary of Health, Education, and Welfare. The responsibilities of the office included investigation, negotiation, and compliance activities. As an advisor to the secretary, the director determined the policies for the civil rights program and was an advocate for their controversial aspects. In March 1969, Martin became codirector of the Washington Research Project. This public-interest law firm was devoted to securing legal protection for poor people and minorities. To that end, it engaged in litigation and monitored selected federal administrative agency programs.

Four years later, Martin left the Washington Research Project and began her tenure as associate counsel for the House Committee on the District of Columbia. Two years later, she was appointed general counsel. This D.C. committee is a standing committee of the House of Representatives. During this time, Martin helped write the Home Rule Bill for the District of Columbia and was instrumental in establishing the University of the District of Columbia.

In 1978 she left Washington and carried her expertise to Richmond, Virginia. There, her private practice never veered from the arena of public issues. She served as a consultant to various foundations and as president of Partin and Rosi—a public-interest law firm that assists foundations and corpora-

tions in developing youth employment programs, corporate social responsibility, and other programs relating to social issues.

Serves as Commonwealth Secretary

From January of 1990 to December of 1993, Martin served the Commonwealth of Virginia as secretary of the administration. Selected for this post by her Howard classmate and the first elected African American governor, L. Douglas Wilder, Martin held one of eight state cabinet positions. She assisted the governor in conducting general administrative duties, coordinated twelve state agencies, and became the most important cabinet official in issues involving Africa.

The remarkable career of Martin is a testament to her intelligence and perseverance. She attributes much of her sense of justice and self-determination to her beloved father. Among her most treasured possessions is a sepia photograph of him, standing straight and proud in the post office section of his small store, where he was a postmaster. A man who possessed a sense of "rightness," he believed that a better day would come; he firmly instilled in his daughter the belief and confidence that she could help that day arrive. It is with affection and pride that Martin often speaks of her father. In a speech given at an NAACP dinner on October 23, 1991, she said: "My wonderful, departed father . . . was my inspiration; he made me enthusiastic about life, he made me achieve, he gave me a sense of responsibility and a feeling that I had to do things 'for the public good.'" She also credits him with creating in her a healthy value system, one that has been the foundation of her career and that guided her toward public service. On November 17, 1992, in remarks addressed to a group of professional secretaries, she said:

> While my father instilled me with pride, enthusiasm, and self-confidence, perhaps the most important thing he did for me was to tell me that I was smart, that I could be anything that I wanted to be, and that I have to be something important. . . . He said that because I was so smart and competent that I had a special gift and that gift carried with it a special responsibility—that responsibility was to make a difference, and to leave a legacy of achievements and successes so that people would know that I had been there.

To this end, Martin chose government service as the primary vehicle for implementing her father's vision. In accepting the NAACP Freedom Fund Award in 1991, she admitted that in many ways, state government has been one of her most difficult challenges. She then elaborated on her personal views of the challenge of public service. Her statements evidence an idealism that underlies her whole life's work:

> I never thought of what I have done through the years as prize worthy or award winning, and I guess

that is another reason why this award is so special to me. I just always thought that I was simply doing my job—doing my part—pushing and shoving to help make this Nation, this State, and this Community, a better, more humane, more responsible and most responsive place for people who can't always help themselves.

Public service is indeed a well-chosen way for Martin to pursue her commitment to making a better world. She believes firmly that those who enter the political arena or who work in the nonprofit sector must always be mindful of their responsibility, must always be accountable in their decisions, and must always "wear . . . integrity and . . . commitment like a badge of honor," she said on June 9, 1993, in an address delivered at the Leadership Metro Richmond graduation ceremony. Responsibility for social improvement, however, does not rest solely in the hands of a few; Martin is adamant that the task must be shared. She repeatedly calls for the partnership of public and private forces to address the issues confronting society and to jointly seek solutions. She also often includes in her speeches a call for individual accountability; she made this challenge an integral part of her address to the Leadership Metro Richmond graduates: "The diploma that you are going to get means that all of you must assume some special responsibility for our society and for making our society better, no matter where you are and no matter what you are doing."

Martin has very definite ideas about the philosophical basis of the racism she has fought so long and so hard to eradicate. In "Reinventing Race Relations," she explained how her initial outrage at the perpetrators of racism evolved into an understanding that the real forces behind this social evil are unseen:

> The hidden villains are faceless, nameless, elusive and evolving. They are people, they are policies, and they are procedures that pit people against each other, promote homogeneity and discourage diversity. These hidden villains are constantly changing—they are active, passive, up front, and undercover. But, there is one constant theme that dominates these hidden villains of progressive race relations in America. . . . And, the constant is economics, money and power.

Repeatedly, Martin has called upon corporate America to confront social realities, to deal with injustices, and to assume leadership for improving the welfare of all citizens. She quite simply asks others to be as accountable as she has been.

Professional Recognition and Affiliations

The distinguished career of Martin has brought her much recognition. In 1967, she was listed in *Outstanding Women in America*. In 1968, she was the youngest woman ever to receive the Distinguished Federal Women's Award. This annual award is given by the U.S. Civil Service Commission to six federally employed women. In that year, she also received the Distinguished Service Award from the Department of Health, Education, and Welfare and the Outstanding Negro Woman of the Year Award from the Women's Auxiliary of the National Dental Association. More recently, Martin has been the recipient of the NAACP's Freedom Fund Award, 1991; Howard University's Distinguished Alumni Award for Post Graduate Achievement in Law and Public Administration, 1991; and the NAACP's Public Service Award, 1992. In 1969, she received an honorary doctor of laws from Western College of Women (now Miami University of Ohio, Oxford, Ohio); in 1993, she received another honorary doctorate from Virginia Union University.

Her professional affiliations include membership in four bar associations: the Ohio Bar, admitted in 1960; the District of Columbia Bar, admitted in 1978; the Virginia Bar, admitted in 1979; and the National Bar Association.

Martin's other professional activities through the years have been numerous. She was a member and the treasurer of Women Executives in State Government. She has also been on the board of directors of several organizations: the Children's Defense Fund; the Southern Regional Council; the Carpenter Center, Richmond, Virginia; and R-TEC, also in Richmond. She is a former consultant to the Rand Corporation for Special Projects in Education in Los Angeles and was chairperson of the Port of Richmond Commission. Other memberships include Xavier University of Louisiana's Public Policy Advisory Committee, Virginia State Council of Higher Education, the Vestry of St. Paul's Episcopal Church, and the Executive Committee of Spottswood Civic Association.

Ruby Grant Martin is married to Henry S. Martin, a dentist who at one time directed the dental health program of Washington, D.C. They have two sons, one daughter, and three grandchildren.

Martin has certainly lived by her father's admonition: "Ruby, make sure that people know that you have been there." She has declared that she truly enjoys being both black and female. She said in her November 17, 1992, speech at the international meeting of professional secretaries, "I am a positive woman and positively a black woman. . . . I adore being both." The walls of her office are graced with large, framed portraits of African American women who have made contributions to all aspects of life for the past two hundred years. It is a record of heroic achievement. She sits surrounded by these portraits, which comprise a roster of African American women who have helped shape the destiny of the nation. She sits among them not merely physically but also spiritually—for she too is a significant part of this country's history.

REFERENCES:

Gilliam, Annette. "Ruby Martin: The People's Advocate." *Essence* 3 (July 1972): 42-43.

Martin, Ruby G. Remarks of Ruby G. Martin. Fourth Annual Aquaculture Field Day at Virginia State University, Petersburg, Virginia, November 9, 1990.

————. Remarks of Ruby G. Martin. Rotary Club of Emporia, Virginia, December 11, 1990.

————. Acceptance Remarks of Ruby G. Martin. NAACP Dinner, Richmond Center, Richmond, Virginia, October 23, 1991.

————. NAACP Membership Speech of Ruby G. Martin. Richmond, Virginia, June 4, 1992.

————. Remarks of Ruby G. Martin. Professional Secretaries International Meeting, Richmond, Virginia, November 17, 1992.

————. ''Reinventing Race Relations.'' Address given at the Richmond Urban Forum, Richmond, Virginia, December 8, 1992.

————. Address by Ruby G. Martin. Leadership Metro Richmond Graduation Program, Richmond, Virginia, June 9, 1993.

————. Interview with Margaret Duckworth. Richmond, Virginia, August 4, 1993.

Margaret Duckworth

Ernestine McClendon

Ernestine McClendon
(1918-)
Actress, talent agent, educator

Unable to find sufficient employment as an actress or roles she considered demanding enough, Ernestine McClendon became a successful talent agent in New York and California. She was the driving force behind the campaign to get the television industry to reverse their ban on hiring blacks for commercials, and she arranged the contracts for some of the first blacks who appeared in television promotion spots. Her firm, McClendon Enterprises, was the first black talent agency in the East. McClendon was also the first in her field to be franchised by all unions as a theatrical agent.

Born Ernestine Epps on August 17, 1918 (some sources say 1924), in Norfolk, Virginia, Ernestine McClendon studied at a historically black institution, Virginia State College, Petersburg, Virginia. From 1935 to 1936 she studied acting with Michael Howard at Columbia University in New York City. McClendon married George Wiltshire and they adopted a daughter, Phyllis. It is not known how or when she obtained the name McClendon.

McClendon's eighteen-year acting career dates back to 1950, when she obtained her first television role, as Clementine in the Celanese Theatre's *No Time for Comedy*. That same year she appeared in the Schlitz Playhouse's *Lady with a Will.* Other television performances were in the Lights Out production *The Skeptic* and the Philco Television Playhouse production *The Mother.* She also appeared with black comedian Pigmeat Markham on the *Ed Sullivan Show.*

McClendon's film career began in 1957, with a part in *A Face in the Crowd.* Other films in which she appeared are *The Apartment* and *The Rat Race* in 1960 and *The Young Doctors, The World by Night,* and *The Young Savages* in 1961.

During this period McClendon was active in the theater as well. In 1958 she played Liz in *Time Out for Ginger* at the Woodstock Playhouse. In 1959 she played Bella in *Deep Are the Roots* at the New Jersey Playhouse, and she appeared in *Allen of the Sunset* for O. B. Playhouse. In 1959-60 she was Berenice in *The Member of the Wedding,* E. L. T. Playhouse. Also in 1960 she played in another O. B. production, *The Goose.* She was Lena Younger in *A Raisin in the Sun* and finally, in 1960-61, McClendon was Catherine Creek in *The Grass Harp* at the E. L. T. Playhouse.

In spite of what appeared to be a rather successful acting career in films, television, and the theater, McClendon found no comfort in acting as a profession. She told *Ebony* in March 1969, ''There just wasn't enough work and what little there was involved the stereotyped roles of maids and other servant types. I'd do good, demanding roles in summer stock, then return to New York and find nothing worthwhile.''

Now known on Broadway as Ernie, she faced constant artistic frustration as a result of being denied acting jobs when she had already demonstrated her considerable acting ability. Whites were in demand, not blacks—a situation that caused her to shed tears at night. She could find nothing more than occasional part-time employment.

McClendon Establishes Talent Agency

It was the shocking discovery by her daughter, Phyllis, of a black man in a television commercial that propelled McClendon into action and led to an important breakthrough for African Americans. She began a letter-writing campaign demanding that television use more blacks in commercials. She sent approximately one hundred letters to advertising agencies on Madison Avenue in New York City as well as to manufacturers of the products advertised on television. While some recipients of the letters refused to respond, others attempted to justify the absence of blacks: "Our sponsors don't want Negroes" was a typical response.

Dissatisfied with the responses she did receive and annoyed with those who refused to answer, McClendon mailed some four hundred additional letters. She left the part-time job that she held in a store and for six months concentrated on her one-woman campaign to find black talent and present it to the industry for use in promotions. Through letter writing she had finally broken down some of the manufacturers' resistance, particularly as she described to them the economic impact of blacks who bought their products. To satisfy the advertising agencies' requests for blacks that had now begun, she would have to make certain that the talent was available. This was the beginning of her work as a theatrical agent, in about 1960.

In 1963 she opened what was to become a top Broadway talent agency, McClendon Enterprises, located in the heart of New York City on Forty-fifth Street. Her clients were white as well as black; however, she knew that white agencies tried to win over her white clients. Her husband gave her advice and assisted with telephone calls when he could. McClendon was largely responsible for the appearance of blacks in television commercials. She concentrated on television commercials because, as she told *Ebony* in March 1969, "They are where the money's at. If it hadn't been for commercials, I couldn't have maintained my office." McClendon came to this conclusion after considering the monetary rewards of a network commercial that ran then for thirteen-week cycles with financial benefits from each run and rerun. For example, in 1969 a Nabisco commercial, that used seven of her clients who were children, had run for over two and one-half years, was still being aired, and had earned each child over ten thousand dollars in residuals, from which McClendon received a 10 percent fee from each client. In late 1968, McClendon had fifteen clients performing off Broadway, several others with key roles in upcoming films, two acting as regulars on television soap operas, and eighteen in commercials.

McClendon, who located for her clients positions in the theater, movies, television, radio, and nightclubs, was the first woman in her field to be franchised by all unions as a theatrical agent. Her union franchises were with the American Guild of Variety Artists, the American Federation of Television and Radio Artists, Actors Equity, and the Screen Actors Guild. In addition to paying a fee for the franchises, she was examined carefully as an agent because she was a woman and she was black.

At some point while she lived in New York the multitalented agent founded and taught at the Harlem Theatrical Workshop. She was also a drama coach, writer, and producer.

Injured in an automobile accident in 1971 that left her with a rod in her leg and constant pain, McClendon relocated her business to California because of the better weather conditions. She opened a West Coast office in Los Angeles while her husband continued to operate the New York office. When Wiltshire became ill shortly afterward, McClendon sold the New York agency and concentrated on establishing clients in California. She advertised in two Hollywood trade journals and ran an open letter to producers advising them that she would not "pay money under the table" so that her clients could work. The responses were positive and McClendon Enterprises began to flourish in California. In time she represented hundreds of well-known television, movie, stage, and radio actors, writers, directors, and variety acts. Among those who had become successful through her agency either in New York or California were Raymond St. Jacques, Gloria Foster, Gail Fisher, and Morgan Freeman. Virtually nothing is known about McClendon's life in recent years. However, the 1994-95 *Who's Who among Black Americans* reports that she no longer owns the agency.

In partial recognition of her work, McClendon received the Woman's Award in 1969 and in 1970 she was named one of Two Thousand Women of Achievement. In the March 1969 *Ebony* article, the magazine called her "warm, emotional, considerate, impulsive, calculating and demonstrative, catty at times." These traits, coupled with her determination and perseverance, enabled McClendon to become a successful businesswoman.

McClendon was a champion for the involvement of blacks in the entertainment industry in general and in television in particular. She achieved in spite of the racial bias that kept her from pursuing her own career as an actress and became a giant in a field that benefited hundreds of black performers.

REFERENCES:

Davis, Marianna W., ed. *Contributions of Black Women to America.* Vol. 1. Columbia, S.C.: Kenday Press, 1982.

"Ernestine McClendon Becomes Top Broadway Talent Agent." *Ebony* 24 (March 1969): 82-88.

"How Liberal Is Show Business?" *Sepia* 12 (March 1963): 40-42.

Mapp, Edward. *Directory of Blacks in the Performing Arts.* 2d ed. Metuchen, N.J.: Scarecrow Press, 1990.

Morton, Carol A. "Black Women in Corporate America." *Ebony* 31 (November 1975): 106-10.

Ploski, Harry A., and James Williams. *The Negro Almanac.* 5th ed. Detroit: Gale Research, 1989.

Who's Who among Black Americans, 1994-95. Detroit: Gale Research, 1994.

"Woman on a Cracking Line." *Sepia* 12 (January 1963): 40-44.

Jessie Carney Smith

Gay Johnson McDougall

Gay Johnson McDougall
(1947-)
Lawyer, social activist, administrator

When the National Coalition of 100 Black Women presented the 1990 Candace Awards to ten outstanding black Americans, the names of some awardees were familiar. But other awardees, equally deserving, were largely unknown to the general public; one such award recipient was Gay Johnson McDougall, director of the Southern Africa Project of the Lawyers Committee for Civil Rights under Law and founder and director of the Commission on Independence for Namibia. With worldwide attention focused on recent changes in South Africa—the ascendancy of Nelson Mandela and blacks being given the right to vote and participate in the governance of their country, McDougall is now being recognized as a major player on the international scene. Her expertise as a leading authority on international law led to her selection as one of five non-South Africans and the lone American on the sixteen-member Independent Electoral Commission (IEC). The group was assigned the task of monitoring the implementation of the democratic process in South Africa, specifically, the first elections held in the country that were open to all races. Leading publications featured articles on some of the black Americans who were selected as members of official delegations assigned to watch the voting, but it was McDougall, largely unknown and apparently content to remain so, who was the only American empowered to run the presidential election and certify the results. The irony of this turn of events was not lost on McDougall, who, upon receiving notification of her IEC confirmation, told the *Washington Post* of April 26, 1994: "My God, you mean for nearly 15 years I'm denied a visa to the country, and now I'm going to run the election!"

Gay Johnson McDougall is a native Georgian who grew up in Dixie Hills, a northwest Atlanta neighborhood. She was born on August 13, 1947, to Louis Johnson, a hospital cook, and Inez Gay Johnson, a high school mathematics teacher.

Her sister Marcia Johnson Alston and mother still reside in Atlanta. McDougall attended English Avenue and Anderson Park elementary schools and in 1965 graduated from Booker T. Washington High School. She cites her mother and aunts as primary influences during her younger years. Inez Johnson earned a master's degree in mathematics from Atlanta University and taught at Booker T. Washington High School for some forty years; she was also sponsor of the Einsteiners Club. A longtime member of St. Mark's African Methodist Episcopal (AME) Church, Inez Johnson was a faithful church worker and Sunday school superintendent. McDougall's aunts were social workers who, along with their sister, were well known for their compassion for the needy.

In a *Washington Post* Style column dated April 26, 1994, McDougall explained the origin of her name, Gay, which is her mother's maiden name and the name of a Georgia town. McDougall's ancestors were enslaved in Gay, a place she described as "a sort of Faulkneresque Southern white town that had their, you know, 'colored people.'" In a July 29, 1994, interview, McDougall recounted the life of her great-grandfather, who lived in the town of Gay. A circuit-riding AME minister and presiding elder, the Reverend Jordan Reese Gay had earned a seminary degree from Morris Brown College in Atlanta. McDougall laughingly recalled her family's many stories about his two wives and dominant personality.

McDougall was faced with a formidable challenge in the spring of 1965. Out of all the black female high school graduates in Atlanta, she alone was admitted to Agnes Scott College, an all-white women's college in Decatur, Georgia. In the July 29, 1994, interview, McDougall explained that for some years, it had been a pro forma act to submit the application of a qualified black female just to test the admissions office. Much to her surprise, since she really hadn't even considered it as a viable possibility, she was accepted. McDougall's days at Agnes Scott were very stressful, largely because of three factors: the ordinary stress of any high school graduate making the transition to college; being in an all-white situation with adjustments to be made on both sides; and the environment itself, a school where former plantation owners sent their daughters for a finishing school education as a prerequisite to becoming a proper southern wife of refinement and gentility.

Practice of Law

After two years, McDougall transferred to Bennington College in Vermont. McDougall described it as "an avant garde, free-floating place that was ideal for self-starters and one where I could be comfortable and set my own agenda." She remembered her satisfaction with the winter work term, a requirement for all students; she had assignments at the *Boston Globe* as a city room reporter and in Washington, D.C., at the U.S. Commission on Civil Rights General Counsel Office. McDougall received a bachelor of arts degree from Bennington in 1969. She gravitated towards a career in law, having worked in voter registration drives and civil rights campaigns. In 1972, she graduated from Yale Law School with a doctor of jurisprudence degree and was hired by a New York corporate law firm. In an interview for the *Washington Post,* April 26, 1994, she discussed her reasons for joining Debevore, Plimpton, Lyons and Gates:

> I was really there to learn to be the best professional that I could be . . . because I thought that the issues I cared about deserve that. Our side ought to be as good as their side. My thought was to go to their side and get trained. So that's what I did. And after a little over two years, I decided I had gotten as much as I could from them at that time.

McDougall had also gained experience as a legal clerk at Cravath, Swaine and Moore, another New York law firm while still in law school. In 1975 she began a one-year stint as an unpaid general counsel with the National Conference of Black Lawyers (NCBL). This position enabled McDougall to use her professional talents to advance her African interests. She began to focus on African liberation movements and was the United Nation's representative for the NCBL. McDougall's next position was as a staff attorney for the Minimum Standards Unit of the New York City Board of Corrections. This unit was one important outcome of the 1971 Attica prison riot, and in 1977 it was still dealing with the need to legislate basic human rights for prisoners. According to McDougall in the *Washington Post* interview, these rights included:

> the right to have a shower every day, with soap . . . to get at least one hour of exercise a day . . . to have sunlight in the place where they are kept. . . . I think that tells you a lot about what the conditions were that led to Attica.

In 1977, McDougall enrolled in the London School of Economics and Political Science. She completed her studies in 1978 and earned a master of laws degree with a concentration in public international law. This environment provided McDougall with what she needed to set her own agenda. She had the best of both worlds: future African leaders from Zimbabwe, Namibia, and South Africa were in London formulating plans to gain control of their respective countries, and, at the same time, she was studying at a school known as a testing ground for political activists interested in social justice issues. McDougall described this time in her life as a heady experience. She associated with people who, as she stated in the *Washington Post,* "inspired . . . centered . . . helped me find . . . what I had always been searching for, a way to deal with the issues we were dealing with in the '60's and the '50's in the South." McDougall was becoming more able to refine and expand the Georgia brand of social activism practiced by her mother and aunts during her formative years.

McDougall Becomes Active in African Affairs

In 1979 McDougall worked for a year as associate counsel in the New York City office of the deputy mayor for criminal justice. In 1980 she assumed the directorship of the Southern Africa Project of the Lawyer's Committee for Civil Rights under Law, the position that led to her selection as one of the key overseers of the 1994 South Africa elections. McDougall provided the leadership that enabled the project to increase both its budget and the number of pro bono lawyers who represented political prisoners and took on court proceedings dealing with the effects of apartheid. The impetus for the founding of the Southern Africa Project was the 1967 Terrorism Act, passed by the South African Parliament, which gave police the right to detain political activists without access to a trial or legal representation and to torture suspects during interrogation. The project began on a small scale, with staffing by corporate lawyers who were able to take sabbaticals. McDougall's arrival coincided with worldwide publicity about the horrible effects of apartheid in South Africa. Speaking about the effectiveness of the project, McDougall told the *Washington Post* interviewer:

> I would say we have been responsible for getting literally thousands of people out of jail. We helped to mount cases that challenged a lot of apartheid laws and caused many of them to be overturned. . . . We helped communities who were being forcibly removed to get legal counsel to resist, and a lot of them won.

The Washington, D.C.-based Lawyers' Committee for Civil Rights under Law (LCCRUL) was founded in 1963 and now has 165 members, seven local groups, and an operating budget of two million dollars. It publishes quarterly committee reports and an annual report detailing activities carried out by local committees of private lawyers in eight major American cities. These activities include assisting poor and minority groups residing in urban centers. The focus of the national office is on reform efforts aimed at employment, voting, and housing discrimination. As director of the Southern Africa

Project, McDougall testified before Congress and the United Nations; raised over a million dollars annually to finance South-African trials and other expenses; organized and financed the defense preparations of political prisoners in South Africa and Namibia; organized six international conferences in South Africa that focused on governance after apartheid; produced an annual series of briefing papers and publications on the state of affairs in South Africa and Namibia; recruited and coordinated pro bono services of lawyers in major corporate law firms; and lectured on South-African issues across the country and in the media.

The most ambitious project undertaken by McDougall was establishing the Commission on Independence for Namibia, a bipartisan group of thirty-one Americans who monitored the United Nations-supervised, year-long process leading to elections in Namibia. She was highly involved in critical procedures that led to Namibia's becoming Africa's fifty-second nation on March 21, 1990. She was responsible for arranging trips for commissioners to monitor the country, publishing and distributing internationally the only weekly reports on the transition process, and reporting to the United Nations secretary general. In 1984, McDougall served as consultant to the United Nations Council for Namibia.

McDougall Becomes Part of History

In early 1994, McDougall was notified that she had been named to the sixteen-member Independent Electoral Commission (IEC) in South Africa; she was one of only five non-South Africans selected and the only American. Designed by South African political leaders, this agency was charged by Parliament with running South Africa's first all-race elections and overseeing the implementation of a new South African democracy. McDougall's place was well earned. According to a *USA Today* report, March 31, 1994, "McDougall's reputation for fairness and thoroughness in constitution-writing seminars she ran for South Africa's political parties won her a spot on the electoral commission."

McDougall's selection was tinged with irony; she recalled having been spied upon by South African officials who had a full dossier on her legal and antiapartheid activities. Specific IEC election duties of McDougall included: organizing the election by training some four hundred American citizens to serve as official election observers, overseeing the printing of election ballots, setting up polling stations, issuing voter identification cards, and certifying the final vote tallies for the three major political parties that ran candidates.

There were some South Africans who reacted negatively to McDougall's high visibility. As she told the *Washington Post,* she was criticized as being "abrasive in her passion to achieve goals." McDougall took the comment not as a personal affront but as being applicable to Americans in general, who are often perceived as being "blunt compared to South Africans. We tend to press points more." Her tenacity, forcefulness, and insistence on accuracy were characteristics of her response to any assignment, but all the more crucial in this situation since she knew that there was widespread speculation that ballots were being tampered with. McDougall's

important role in the South Africa elections was attested by the August 1994 *Ebony* Special Issue, which features a photograph of Nelson Mandela casting his first ballot with McDougall standing at his side.

McDougall has been admitted to practice law before the U.S. District Court of the Southern District of New York (1977), the U.S. Supreme Court (1979), and the Court of Appeals of the State of New York (1984). She is the author of numerous articles dealing with apartheid, U.S. policy proposals, Namibian independence, and international law issues, which have appeared in leading newspapers and law journals. McDougall serves on the board of directors of CARE, Africa Watch, the International Human Rights Law Group, and the Robert F. Kennedy Memorial Foundation; she is an advisory board member of the Africa Society of International and Comparative Law. She holds memberships in the Council on Foreign Relations, American Society of International Law, and TransAfrica Forum Scholars Council. In September 1994 McDougall became executive director of the International Human Rights Group, a Washington, D.C.-based organization that deals with human rights projects abroad, especially in Cambodia, Romania, Africa, and Latin America.

McDougall has been married since 1991 to John Payton; a first marriage ended in divorce in 1978. Payton is a partner in the law firm of Wilmer, Cutler and Pickering and a litigator who has argued civil rights cases before the U.S. Supreme Court. He is a graduate of Claremont College and Harvard Law School. In support of his wife, he accompanied her to South Africa, where he served as an observer in the northern part of the country during the elections. Payton was considered for the position Lani Guinier was denied, that of Assistant Attorney General for Civil Rights. It is surmised that his purported erratic voting record was one reason his nomination was scuttled. McDougall described her husband to the *Washington Post* interviewer: "I have met one hell of a lot of incredible people in my work in all these years and I don't think I've met anybody who is more committed to equal rights and social justice and issues of that sort than John Payton."

McDougall is a physically imposing woman who exudes an air of calm, poised sophistication. Mary Ann French says in the April 26, 1994, *Washington Post:* "Her face is elegant. Her bearing is noble, with only an occasional hint of haughtiness. Her skin is flawless. Her eyes are pools of amber.... Her dimpled smile comes easily."

McDougall has very little leisure time, but she does make time to enjoy the company of friends, movies, and beach holidays. During the July 29, 1994, interview, McDougall was queried about the relatively little publicity she received when she was monitoring the South Africa elections as compared to other election observers. She expressed some curiosity about it but noted that she had never sought publicity. While admitting that everybody likes their work to be recognized, she stated: "I'm not willing to push just to get it." In reviewing her life and accomplishments, it is quite clear that McDougall has never expended her energies on superfluous matters. She has used her talents to achieve the same goals she ascribed to her mother and aunts in the *Washington Post* interview: "Caring about the way people [live] . . . trying to find a way to reorder the world so that everybody lives a decent life."

Current Address: International Human Rights Law Group, 1601 Connecticut Avenue, NW, Suite 700, Washington, DC 20009.

REFERENCES:

Bennett, Lerone, Jr. "15 Days That Shook the World." *Ebony* 49 (August 1994): 60-81.

Brown, Frank Dexter. "Under Specter of Pretoria, Namibia Moves to Freedom." *Black Enterprise* 19 (June 1989): 52.

"Candace Awards Presented to 10 Outstanding Blacks during New York Ceremony." *Jet* 78 (August 6, 1990): 15.

"The Election Onlookers Ogling as History Happens." *Washington Post,* April 26, 1994.

"Farce in Namibia." *The Nation* 249 (August 21-28, 1989): 191-92.

Floyd, Patricia A. Telephone interview with Dolores Nicholson, July 25, 1994.

Johnson, Bill. "Cover Story I—South Africa". *Destiny Magazine* (June 1994): 20-27.

Massaquoi, Hans J. "Namibia: Free at Last." *Ebony* 45 (June 1990): 124-28.

McDougall, Gay J. Professional Resume.

———. Telephone interview with Dolores Nicholson, July 29, 1994.

McKinney, Gwen. "Namibia: On the Road to Freedom." *Essence* 21 (October 1990): 111-14.

Smith, Darren L., ed. *Black Americans Information Directory.* 1st ed. Detroit: Gale Research, 1991.

"South African Odyssey." *Washington Post,* April 26, 1994.

"Speaking of People." *Ebony* 49 (August 1994): 6-7.

"U.S. Expert: Boycott Won't Stop S. Africa Vote." *USA Today,* March 31, 1994.

Dolores Nicholson

Viola Harris McFerren

Viola Harris McFerren

(1931-)

Civil rights and social activist

In 1960 Viola Harris McFerren and others made history with a direct action protest against the restrictive racial policy of American apartheid that was exploiting and excluding African Americans living in Fayette County, Tennessee. An unrelenting champion of the right of African Americans to exercise their freedom to vote, McFerren was one of the organizers of Fayette County's "Tent City," a makeshift community that was formed when hundreds of black tenant farmers who had recently registered to vote were thrown off the land by white property owners. Tent City attracted national attention, and by the end of 1960 the U.S. Department of Justice stepped in to ensure that the civil rights of African Americans in Fayette County were not violated. Eleven years after the 1954 *Brown v. Board of Education* decision, McFerren, along with other parents, filed suit against the school system to compel compliance with the school desegregation mandated by *Brown.* Instrumental in bringing antipoverty funds to the county, McFerren later served as a member of the National Advisory Committee of the U.S. Office of Economic Opportunity. Because members of her race endured unequal protection under the law and contemptuous attitudes from white business owners, she assisted in orchestrating a refusal-to-buy campaign against local white merchants. Although at times fearful for the safety of her family, McFerren staunchly sought racial equality for African Americans in rural southwestern Tennessee.

The eleventh of twelve children, Viola Harris McFerren was born to Joseph Thomas Harris and Rose Etta Webb Harris on October 19, 1931, in Michigan City, Mississippi. Her father, a farmer, was born in Conway, Arkansas, on March 23, 1888, and died on July 23, 1972. Her mother, engaged full-time as a homemaker, was born near LaGrange, in Fayette County, Tennessee, on December 22, 1890, and died on August 23, 1972. Both parents were interred in the Moore family cemetery in Michigan City.

McFerren was reared in the economically depressed cotton community of Benton County, Mississippi. She received her elementary education at an all-black, one-room, one-teacher school with approximately sixty-five other students. Because Benton County made no provisions for the secondary education of people of African descent, when McFerren completed the eighth grade, she attended high school in Fayette County, Tennessee, near the Mississippi state line. To receive her secondary education, McFerren walked five miles, boarded a makeshift bus with no heat, and rode about thirty-five miles one way to the segregated Fayette County Training School in Somerville. Just before her graduation from the Somerville school, on December 13, 1950, she married John McFerren (from whom she divorced in 1980), and they became the parents of five children (fraternal twins, John, Jr. and Jacqueline, born August 28, 1958; Claudia, born February 28, 1960; Daphene, born November 22, 1961; and Harris, born November 4, 1963). The quest for an education had brought Viola McFerren to Somerville and, although blacks endured many inequities in the rural southwestern Tennessee county of Fayette, she settled there.

After establishing permanent residence in one of the country's most poverty-stricken counties, McFerren became a registered cosmetologist. Like many of their ancestors, John and Viola McFerren cultivated the land. For almost a decade, they lived modestly and quietly, rearing their children, farming eight acres of cotton and corn, and trying to make ends meet.

People of African descent have been a part of the Fayette County area since the opening of the territory in the early 1800s. Numerous pioneers who migrated to the locality brought black slaves with them. According to the U.S. census of 1830, slaves numbered 3,193 out of a total population of 8,652. Thirty years later, African Americans outnumbered European Americans by a ratio of two to one. This ratio remained constant until 1980, when the census report revealed an African American population of 51 percent and a white population of 49 percent. Based on 1990 census data, African Americans constituted 44 percent of Fayette County's populace, as compared to its white populace of 56 percent.

Although blacks had outnumbered whites in Fayette County since the mid-1800s, it was not until 1883 that an African American, David Foote Rivers, was elected to the state legislature; he served until 1887. Monroe Gooden, whose term of office lasted from 1887 until 1889, was the last person of African American heritage from Fayette County to serve in the Tennessee General Assembly. Beginning with the passage of suffrage restrictions in 1889-90, few African Americans voted and almost none were allowed to register in the county.

Two circumstances brought the prospect for a change in traditional southern ways to the fore in the 1950s. There was direct nonviolent protest by blacks, symbolized by Rosa Parks's refusal to yield her seat on a bus in 1955, and the passage of a new civil rights bill. On September 9, 1957, the 85th United States Congress enacted the first civil rights bill since 1875. According to Albert P. Blaustein and Robert Zangrando, the 1957 Civil Rights Act "was not a far-reaching measure in substance, but it was a clear indication that the legislative branch was undertaking responsibilities that had previously been left to the executive and judiciary." This civil rights legislation, among other things, empowered the U.S. government to initiate civil suits in federal courts, where any individual or group was prohibited from or threatened for exercising their right to vote. Additionally, the act established the Civil Rights Commission which had the authority to gather evidence of voting violations. Most of the litigation on Negro voting rights involved legislation designed to prohibit people of African descent from voting in party primaries. Two years later, John and Viola McFerren led a black voter registration drive in Fayette County.

Torch Carried for Civil Rights

Viola McFerren's interest in the civil rights struggle began in 1959 when her husband led a voter registration drive in Fayette County. The McFerrens' concern was sparked by the absence of black jurors for the Burton Dodson trial. Dodson, an African American farmer, was on trial for the alleged murder of a white man in 1941. Because African Americans were denied the right to participate in the electoral process, they were omitted from the pool of potential jurors. John McFerren and others formed The Original Fayette County Civic and Welfare League, Inc. (TOFCC&WL). With assistance from J. F. Estes, an African American attorney from Memphis representing Dodson, they filed a charter of incorporation in Nashville with the purpose of promoting "civil and political and economic welfare for the community progress of Fayette County." The first project undertaken by the league was a voter registration drive.

TOFCC&WL was formed in the spring of 1959 and in June and July managed to persuade a number of African Americans to register to vote. However, when the Democratic primary was held in August, registered African Americans were not allowed to cast their ballots. Members of the league filed a federal suit against the local Democratic party, and in 1960 the court gave the blacks of Fayette County their first taste of victory. On April 20, 1960, the court issued a restraining order against the Fayette County Democratic Committee. The ruling prohibited the committee from obstructing African Americans' right of franchise. "In the past [B]lacks were prevented from voting because of a state or local law, county custom, or political practice," said the ruling judge. "This will no longer be an excuse for white primaries." According to a statement by a U.S. Justice Department official published in the November 17, 1959, edition of the *Memphis Commercial Appeal,* this was the first legal action filed against a political party for unfair primary practices under the Civil Rights Act of 1957.

When John McFerren first became involved in the movement to secure African American voting rights, Viola McFerren attempted to dissuade his active involvement. She said in an interview, "I'll have to be frank and say I was just scared to death, and I did everything . . . I could to discourage him, because I was absolutely afraid. . . . But nothing I said to him stopped him."

Realizing John McFerren's resolve to continue in the movement, Viola McFerren turned her debilitating fear over to a power greater than herself.

I decided I would just pray about the situation and just leave it completely up to our Eternal Father. Finally, all of that fear left. I didn't feel tired, worried, and dragged out. . . . It was at this time, I decided to work in the Movement. I knew that regardless of what other people feel or say, that this struggle is right . . . if our lives is [sic] going to make it better for all of the thousands of Black lives in Fayette County, then what is it to lose five little lives?

With that resoluteness and steadfast determination, Viola McFerren became an unremitting torchbearer for justice.

As African Americans pursued their constitutional rights to participate in the electoral process, Fayette County's white residents began using their economic dominance to try to make blacks "stay in their place." Many lost employment, credit, and insurance policies. Whites refused to sell them goods and services. Some white doctors withheld medical treatment from their patients of African descent. The ultimate act of oppressive racial intimidation came when, without notice in the winter of 1960, white property owners evicted hundreds of recently registered black tenant farmers. However, the leadership of the league did not surrender. Without hesitation and with the support of Shephard Towles, an African American property owner, they formed a makeshift community known as "Tent City." Surplus army tents were erected and homeless families prepared themselves to face the bitter winds of winter. The settlement became an emblematic statement against white oppression.

Although gripped by fear and encumbered with domestic responsibilities, Viola McFerren was an active participant in the movement from its beginning. The league's office was maintained in the McFerrens' home, and Viola worked assiduously serving the needs of the its members.

McFerren said in an October 1993 interview, "I could see all of what was happening to people, all of this wrongdoing that was being brought upon black folks. . . . I don't care what happens to me as long as I am trying to do what I feel is right and something that is necessary to be done." With that conviction, she was determined to give of herself and assist in advancing the cause of civil rights in Fayette County.

By the end of 1960, the situation in Fayette County attracted national attention. An exposé by Ted Poston in the *New York Post* brought the activities of the league before the citizens of the entire country. On December 14, the U. S. Justice Department filed suit against forty-five landowners, twenty-four merchants, and one financial institution for violating the civil rights of African Americans. On July 26, 1962, the "landowners were permanently enjoined from 'engaging in any acts . . . for the purpose of interfering with the right of any person to register to vote and to vote for candidates for public office.'"

Although the racist policies of whites did not subside for several years, McFerren refused to let them become a stumbling block on the road to equal rights. Through the efforts of the TOFCC&WL and those of people like the McFerrens, federal agencies assisted the black people of Fayette County in attempting to eliminate white oppression.

Community Uplift Programs Sought

After reading a newspaper article in 1964 regarding the Head Start program, a plan sponsored by the U.S. government that provides the preschool children of poor families educational training, meals, medicine, and school services, McFerren immediately went to work to secure the program for the children of Fayette County. She sought assistance in drafting the proposal, which was approved by officials in Washington. Although she intended the benefits of the program to accrue to all children in the county, the local board of education approved the implementation of Head Start for African American children only. McFerren was also in the forefront of bringing federally-sponsored kindergarten and adult basic education programs to the county. President Lyndon B. Johnson's War on Poverty brought other federal programs into the county, such as the Neighborhood Youth Corps, the Job Corps, and Upward Bound.

In 1965, McFerren was a plaintiff in the Fayette County school desegregation case filed on behalf of her son, John McFerren, Jr. The suit was filed in order to compel local school officials to comply with the desegregation of schools which was enunciated in the 1954 U.S. Supreme Court decision of *Brown v Board of Education*. Legal counsel for the plaintiffs was provided by the noted Nashville civil rights attorney Avon N. Williams, Jr. One year later, the case was successfully adjudicated and the board of education was ordered to desegregate its school system. McFerren and the other plaintiffs in the school desegregation case intervened in 1970 in a federal court case instigated by thirteen African American teachers who had been dismissed by the Fayette County Board of Education. The federal court ordered that schools in Fayette County be desegregated. The "separate but [un]equal" schools were consolidated under the name of Fayette-Ware High School; the Fayette board of education was mandated to maintain a 60 percent black and 40 percent white ratio in the schools; blacks began to serve on the board of education; and new school facilities were constructed.

Ten years after McFerren began her struggle, many of the formal racial barriers had crumbled. However, African Americans still encountered racist attitudes and behaviors, ranging from police brutality to insulting treatment from white businesses. Because of this, in the 1960s she assisted in organizing a refusal-to-purchase offensive against local white merchants. McFerren not only worked to bring about civil and social changes in Fayette County, but she also traveled outside county lines to expose the county's callous, cruel, and unfair treatment of its African American residents.

In 1966 Viola McFerren was appointed by President Lyndon B. Johnson to serve as a member of the National Advisory Committee of the U.S. Office of Economic Opportunity. She was a charter member of the Fayette County Economic Development Commission and of the reinstituted Fayette County chapter of the NAACP. She currently serves as president of TOFCC&WL.

A member of Sims Chapel Missionary Baptist Church in Michigan City, Mississippi, Viola McFerren was invited by President Johnson to attend the White House conference called "To Fulfill These Rights." She was awarded a Certificate of Commendation by President Richard M. Nixon, and in 1989 she was one of fifty West Tennessee volunteers honored by President George Bush. For her role as a "fearless leader of voter register, desegregation and equal housing in Fayette County," McFerren was accorded in 1992 the Women of Achievement Award for Heroism.

Phoenix Rising

Two things remain constant in Viola McFerren's life: her faith in God and her belief in education. When asked in an interview for Robert Hamburger's oral history entitled *Our Portion of Hell, Fayette County, Tennessee* if she was influenced by her former husband to join the Fayette County movement, McFerren replied:

> I don't believe this is something the individual decides to do. I think there must be some power beyond us that somehow permitted us to become involved. . . . I feel that God [had] a stronger hand in it. . . . I [was] just a tool that [was] being used and I [didn't] really have full control of myself. . . . I want to feel that the things I [did] are things my Eternal Father wanted me to do.

To satisfy her thirst for learning, McFerren furthered her education by taking courses at Jackson State Community College and Memphis State University (now the University of Memphis). A promoter of education, she diligently encourages civic and social organizations and churches to provide scholarships to young, needy students in Fayette County.

Because of the efforts of Viola McFerren and TOFCC&WL, the Tennessee Historical Commission erected a historical marker commemorating Tent City and the challenge encountered by its residents. McFerren, who has served as executive director of the Fayette County Commission on Aging for the past fifteen years, said in an October 1993 interview, "It is so rewarding to be able to lend a helping hand to point a person into a direction that benefits them." Because her parents involved her in community activities when she was young, she credits them for her participation in community affairs and for her dedication to serving the civil and social needs of the people of Fayette County.

Effective in the movement for African American equality, Viola McFerren was a torchbearer in Tennessee's campaign for human rights during the early days of the modern civil rights era. She and other African Americans in Fayette County refused to sit back calmly and endure racist practices until organized assistance came from the outside to foster social change. With determined, collective initiative, they began the process of social change themselves.

REFERENCES:

Bass, Jack, and Thomas E. Terrill. *The American South Comes of Age.* New York: McGraw-Hill, 1986.

"Black List of Registered Voters." *Ebony* 15 (September 1960): 34.

Blaustein, Albert P., and Robert Zangrando, eds. *Civil Rights and the African-American.* Evanston, Ill.: Northwestern University Press, 1991.

"Cold War in Fayette County: A White Minority Uses Harsh Economic Power in Desperate Attempt to Drive Out Militant Negro Leaders." *Ebony* 15 (September 1960): 27-29.

"Fayette Inquiry Preceded Suit: Report of Civil Rights Panel Alleged Prejudices against Negroes." *Memphis Commercial Appeal,* November 17, 1959.

"The Fight for the Right to Vote, Historical and Memorial Calendar." Somerville, Tenn.: The Original Fayette County Civic and Welfare League, 1991.

Foner, Eric. *Freedom's Lawmakers: A Directory of Black Officeholders during Reconstruction.* New York: Oxford University Press, 1993.

Hamburger, Robert. *Our Portion of Hell, Fayette County, Tennessee: An Oral History of the Struggle for Civil Rights.* New York: Links Books, 1973.

Humphrey, Hubert L. Letter to Viola McFerren, December 19, 1966.

Lamon, Lester. *Blacks in Tennessee: 1791-1970.* Knoxville: University of Tennessee Press, 1981.

McFerren, Viola H. Interviews with Linda T. Wynn. October 4 and 6, 1993.

Morton, Dorothy Rich. *Fayette County:* Tennessee County History Series. Vol. 24. Edited by Charles W. Crawford. Memphis: Memphis State University Press, 1980.

"Mrs. McFerren in Washington for Major Meetings." *Fayette Falcon,* June 9, 1966.

"Negroes Plan Counterattack: Both Sides in County Intend 'To See End.'" *Ebony* 15 (September 1960): 30-34.

"Negroes Tell of Struggle: Voting Pushed Them off Plantation, They Charge." *Chicago Daily News,* January 13, 1961.

"7 Women of Achievement." *Memphis Commercial Appeal,* March 30, 1992.

"Struggle for Civil Rights Recalled by Participants." *Fayette County Review,* September 7, 1988.

"Suit Is First under New Act." *Memphis Commercial Appeal,* November 17, 1959.

Tent City. . ."Home of the Brave" (pamphlet). Industrial Union Department, AFL-CIO, 1961.

"Tent City Shooting Incident Solved: White Youth Admit Firing Blanks." *Memphis Press-Scimitar,* January 3, 1961.

"U.S. Fayette Landowners End Suits." *Memphis Commercial Appeal,* July 27, 1962.

Vickers, Betty B., ed. *Tennessee Statistical Abstract, 1992/ 93.* Knoxville: University of Tennessee, Center for Business and Economic Research, 1993.

"Viola McFerren: Lending a Helping Hand." *Fayette County Review,* July 28, 1983.

"West Tennesseans Sparkle amid Bush's 1000 Points of
   Light." *Jackson Sun,* November 17, 1989.
Wynn, Linda T. "The Dawning of a New Day: The Nashville
   Sit-Ins, February 13-May 10, 1950." *Tennessee Histori-*
   cal Quarterly 50 (Spring 1991): 45.
———. "List of Tennessee African-American State Legis-
   lators, 1873-Present." N.p., 1993.

COLLECTIONS:

Tent City Historical Marker File. On file in the offices of the
Tennessee Historical Commission, Nashville, Tennessee.

Linda T. Wynn

Doris Evans McGinty

Doris Evans McGinty

(1925-)

Musician, educator, writer

In 1947 Doris Evans McGinty became the first American
woman to earn a doctorate in musicology from Oxford
University in England. As a teacher, she has influenced an
entire generation of musicians, and as a scholar, her important
research has revealed much about the rich musical life among
blacks in Washington, D.C.

McGinty was born on August 2, 1925, in Washington,
D.C., the daughter of Vallean Richardson Evans and Charlie
Evans. She was married on September 6, 1956, to Milton
Oliver McGinty and has three children: Derek Gordon McGinty,
Dana Winston McGinty, and Lisa Megan McGinty.

McGinty received her early education in the public
schools of Washington, D.C. She began piano lessons at the
age of seven and was encouraged to pursue music by her
mother, who was a pianist. Additional music instruction
occurred at school and in the Junior Preparatory Department
of Howard University, where she studied with Andres
Wheatley. While still quite young, McGinty played for the
Sunday school at the Metropolitan African Methodist Episcopal Church in Washington. She gave her first public recital at
age twelve. McGinty remained at Howard for her undergraduate work, completing a bachelor of music degree in 1945 and a
bachelor of arts in 1946. Her major teacher was the well-
known pedagogue Warner Lawson. McGinty left Washington
to pursue graduate studies, earning a master of arts at Radcliffe
College in Cambridge, Massachusetts, in 1947. She returned
to Washington after completing her master's degree to accept
a position as assistant professor of music history at Howard
University.

McGinty entered Oxford University in England as a
Fulbright fellow in 1951. Studying with two of the world's
foremost musicologists, John Westrup and Egon Wellesz,
McGinty began work towards a Ph.D. The following year, her
Fulbright Fellowship was renewed, and she was also awarded
a General Education Board grant. Westrup, then head of the
Department of Musicology, supervised McGinty's research in
opera and medieval music. She studied Byzantine and early
church music with Wellesz, who referred to McGinty, according to an article in the *Washington Afro American,* as "one of
the most brilliant pupils in the department's history." Wellesz
held McGinty's thesis, "Music of the Middle Ages," in high
regard and recommended the manuscript for publication in
England. In a letter to Warner Lawson at Howard University,
Wellesz wrote that McGinty's work represented "one of the
most significant contributions to music in recent years."
McGinty completed her doctorate in 1954. She later wrote, "I
never published the dissertation. Interest in Medieval Music
was submerged as I began teaching and found such a need for
research and writing on the subject of African American
music."

After returning from England, McGinty resumed her
teaching and scholarly activities at Howard University. She
occasionally accepted brief teaching assignments elsewhere,
such as an appointment as visiting professor during the
summer of 1956 at Texas Southern University. In 1974 she
was a Phelps-Stokes Caribbean exchange scholar, and she
was honored with Outstanding Teacher awards in 1963 and
1974. During the period from 1977 to 1985, McGinty served
as chair of the Department of Musicology at Howard.

Scholar Promotes African American Music

McGinty's numerous publications focus almost entirely on African American music and musicians. Her writing style is engaging, yet direct, especially when the subject is her native Washington. She wrote in *More Than Dancing,* "The Black community of Washington, D.C., has always placed great importance upon its music. Although today the musical profile of this community is vastly different from that of earlier times, the emphasis on music has remained constant." McGinty's scholarly reputation is international in scope, and she has written an article for the revision of the prestigious German reference work *Musik in Geschichte und Gegenwart,* as well as articles published in *Schulfunk Westdeutscher Rundfunk.* She has made significant contributions to the historical literature on African American women musicians, especially those active in the Washington, D.C., area during the nineteenth and early twentieth centuries. Her biographical essays on major black musicians have appeared in *The New Grove Dictionary of American Music* and *Dictionary of Negro Biography.* She was a contributing editor and compiler of the "New Books List" for *The Black Perspective in Music* from 1975 until 1991. She now serves as a member of the Editorial Advisory Board for the journal *American Music* and reviews books for such publications as *Journal of Negro Education, Journal of Negro History, Music Educators Journal,* and *Fontes Artis Musicae.* She has also contributed articles to the *Journal of Human Relations* and the *Black Music Research Journal.*

McGinty retired from full-time teaching in 1991 and now holds the esteemed rank of professor emerita. She remains active as a scholar, author, and guest speaker. Of her current activities, McGinty stated,

> I have continued my interest in writing about the music of black Americans (mainly in Washington, D.C.), the contributions of black women, and related matters. In the area of music among blacks in Washington, my writings have broken new ground as the information has been buried in archival sources as has been the case with so much material relating to the black experience. There is yet much to be done, and I hope to accomplish some of it.

Of her tenure as a music educator, she continued,

> I hope that during my years as a teacher I have contributed to the education of the next generation of scholars (and others also, of course) through my work at Howard University as well as through other contacts with students and that I have directed some of their interest toward the study of blacks in music. I can say with pride that there is a cadre of students whom I have taught and who are now dotted about the United States, teaching, and writing in a few instances. It is exhilarating to hear from them and to know of their work; they encourage me to believe that my years spent in teaching have borne fruit.

McGinty holds memberships and has held offices in the American Musicological Society, the Association for the Study of Afro-American Life and History, the College Music Society, the Music Library Association, and the Sonneck Society for American Music. McGinty continues to be the preeminent scholar currently researching the activities of black musicians in the Washington, D.C., area.

Current Address: Department of Music, Howard University, Washington, D.C. 20059.

REFERENCES:

"Howard Professor Gets Ph.D. at Oxford." *Washington Afro American,* March 6, 1954.

McGinty, Doris Evans. "The Black Presence in the Music of Washington, D.C.: 1843-1904." In *More Than Dancing: Essays on Afro-American Music and Musicians.* Edited by Irene V. Jackson. Westport, Conn.: Greenwood Press, 1982.

——. Letter to Juanita Karpf, October 25, 1993.

Southern, Eileen. *Biographical Dictionary of Afro-American and African Musicians.* Westport, Conn.: Greenwood Press, 1982.

Who's Who among Black Americans, 1993-94. Detroit: Gale Research, 1994.

Juanita Karpf

Leatrice B. McKissack
(1930-)
Business executive, educator

Leatrice Buchanan McKissack, the chief executive officer of Nashville, Tennessee's McKissack & McKissack, Architects & Engineers, Inc., the oldest African American architectural firm in the United States, is characterized throughout the business community as a spirited and take-charge administrator. Although iron willed and a perspicacious negotiator, McKissack is a genteel woman who projects the savoir faire she developed during her academically and culturally enriched rearing on the campus of Fisk University. She serves as a role model for women in business.

Leatrice McKissack was born to Archie Buchanan and Catherine Brummell Buchanan in Keytesville, Missouri, on July 27, 1930. She was the second child and only girl of five children born to her parents. Her brothers are Harold, John, Donald (now deceased), and Ted Buchanan. Their father was a farmer and a native of Keytesville and their mother, a schoolteacher, was born in Trenton, Missouri. McKissack began her primary education in the school system of Marceline, Missouri. When her father died in 1937, her mother moved to Nashville and later married Alrutheus A. Taylor, a noted African American historian and educator. Taylor received his

Leatrice B. McKissack

Ph.D. degree from Harvard University and later was the dean of Fisk University's College of Liberal Arts. As McKissack grew up on the historic campus of Fisk University, her life was enriched by her exposure to renowned luminaries of the Harlem Renaissance. These included such notables as Charles S. Johnson, the distinguished sociologist, writer, founder and editor of the Urban League's *Opportunity* magazine, and the first African American to serve as president of Fisk University; Langston Hughes, a rebel poet and the most prolific writer of the Harlem Renaissance; Aaron Douglas, the preeminent graphic artist of the Harlem Renaissance, who refused ''to compromise and see blacks as anything less than a proud and majestic people''; Arna Bontemps, a two-time recipient of *Opportunity* magazine's Alexander Pushkin Award for poetry, who was one of the Harlem Renaissance's most productive contributors and later librarian of Fisk University; and John W. Work III, director of the Fisk Jubilee Singers, multifarious composer, ethnomusicologist, educator, and author.

After leaving Missouri, McKissack continued her primary and secondary education in Nashville public schools. While a student at Pearl High School, she was the recipient of the Harris Medal, which was awarded to the student-scholar with the highest grade point average over a three-year period in biology, chemistry, and physics. In 1947, she graduated from Pearl High School and entered Fisk University, where she majored in mathematics and minored in chemistry. Two years after entering Fisk, in October of 1949, she married William DeBerry McKissack, one of six sons born to Moses McKissack III and Miranda P. Winter McKissack. William's father was a Nashville architect and founder of the McKissack

and McKissack architectural firm. Marriage and domesticity did not hinder Leatrice from completing the necessary requirements for college graduation. William and Leatrice became the parents of three daughters: Andrea, born June 12, 1950, and twins Cheryl and Deryl, born May 15, 1961. In 1951, Leatrice McKissack graduated from Fisk University with a baccalaureate degree in mathematics.

Teaching Career

A year later, Leatrice McKissack began her teaching career in the segregated Nashville Public School System. She was assigned to the all-black Meigs Junior High School in East Nashville. There she taught elementary grades for nine years, was a Girl Scout leader, and participated in extracurricular activities. Five years after she began teaching, McKissack earned a master's degree in psychology from Tennessee Agricultural and Industrial State University (now Tennessee State University). Beginning with the 1961-62 school year, she was assigned to North Nashville's Wharton Junior High School. At Wharton, she was instrumental in developing and writing a proposal calling for the team-teaching approach to education. The Nashville Board of Education approved the concept and its implementation in the city's educational program. Until ill health forced her to retire in 1969 from the teaching profession, McKissack team-taught mathematics and science to Wharton's fifth-grade students.

It was during her period of recuperation that McKissack became actively involved in the community. She was appointed to the Amistead II Art Advisory Board. Serving on Amistead's advisory board stimulated her interest in collecting works by black artists. She gathered an extensive collection of pieces produced by blacks, including some by Aaron Douglas, a close family friend. In addition to her interest in art, McKissack became a charter member of the American Institute of Architects (AIA) Auxiliary; a life member of the Nashville Symphony Guild, for which she served as treasurer; and a member of Meharry Medical College's Mental Health Board. She was also involved in managing the family-owned 216-unit College Hill Apartments. It has been said that at the time of its construction, the McKissack-owned College Hill Apartments was the only privately owned African American housing complex in the country. Although she was busy with parenting, active in community affairs, and involved in the management of the family's College Hill Realty Company, according to a November 1990 article in *Nashville Business and Lifestyles,* Leatrice McKissack was ''living the life of Riley—traveling, going to the spa, and just having a good time.'' In 1983, without warning, the sprightly former mathematics and science teacher found herself going from ''doing almost nothing to being president of a company. And I mean overnight,'' said McKissack in the same article. ''I didn't sleep for three months.''

Architectural Tradition

The McKissack and McKissack architectural tradition dates back to the first Moses McKissack, of the Ashanti tribe of West Africa, who was sold into bondage to William McKissack of North Carolina. In 1822 he married a Cherokee Indian named Mirian; the couple had fourteen children. As a slave, he used a hammer, chisel, and square and became a master builder. He passed these skills on to his ninth child, Gabriel Moses McKissack, who moved to Pulaski, Tennessee, after the Civil War and continued in the building trade. When Moses II began his business in Pulaski, builders were often responsible for designing their structures. He, like his father before him, taught these skills to his son, Moses McKissack III (1879-1952), who initially worked with his father. In 1890, Moses III worked for an architect in Pulaski, drawing, designing, and assisting with building construction. He acquired an excellent building reputation in Pulaski, and from 1903 to 1905 McKissack built houses in Athens and Decatur, Alabama, as well as in Mount Pleasant and Pulaski, Tennessee.

In 1905, Moses III moved to Nashville, Tennessee, to start a construction business of his own. McKissack's first major commission in Nashville was the Carnegie Library (now Academic Building) on the Fisk University campus. He officially began to advertise as an architect in 1909; the *Nashville City Directory* listed him as a "colored architect" along with eighteen other architects in the city. By 1920 McKissack was designing buildings for clients in all sections of Nashville, and his reputation spread throughout the state. Moses III was assisted in most of his pursuits by his younger brother, Calvin Lunsford McKissack (1890-1968), who worked with Moses as a general contractor during the summers of his college years. The McKissacks offered contracting services, with a number of masons, carpenters, and laborers on staff. In 1921, when the Tennessee professional registration law was codified, the McKissacks were among the first registered architects in the state. A year later, Calvin joined Moses III on a full-time basis as a partner in the firm and their architectural expertise grew. Moses and Calvin McKissack composed Tennessee's first professional African American architectural firm. They were very successful across the southern states, and their most notable buildings were African American educational institutions and churches.

In 1942, the firm of McKissack and McKissack received national recognition when they secured a $5.7 million government contract for the Ninety-ninth Pursuit Squadron Air Base in Tuskegee, Alabama. This was the largest contract ever given at that time by the U.S. government to African Americans. In the same year, Moses and Calvin received a Spaulding Medal for operating the most outstanding Negro business firm in the United States.

In recognition of Gabriel McKissack's contributions to the architectural heritage of Tennessee, the Tennessee Historical Commission approved the erection of a historical marker at the intersection of Childers and Grigsby streets in Pulaski, near the house where Gabriel McKissack reared his family. The Giles County Historical Society was responsible for suggesting that Gabriel McKissack be honored in this way.

Between the years 1973 and 1985, the National Park Service of the U.S. Department of the Interior recognized the contributions of McKissack and McKissack to the historic building heritage of the country when it listed four McKissack buildings in the National Register of Historic Places. The four buildings are: the Fisk Carnegie Library, constructed in the classic revival style in 1908; the George W. Hubbard residence, built in 1920 in colonial revival style for the president of Meharry Medical College; the Morris Memorial Building, constructed in the neoclassic style in 1924 for the National Baptist Convention U.S.A.; and the neoclassic Capers C.M.E. Church, completed in 1925. All four buildings are located in Nashville. In addition to state and national recognition, the city of Nashville paid homage to Moses McKissack III when it named McKissack Middle School and McKissack Park in his honor.

Moses McKissack III died at age seventy-three in December 1952, after having been in the architectural business for forty-seven years. Following Moses's death, his brother Calvin L. McKissack ran the firm, becoming president and general manager. After his Uncle Calvin's 1968 demise, William DeBerry McKissack, the son of Moses III, picked up the reins of company leadership. William continued the family tradition until illness forced him to retire in 1983. It was into this three-quarters-of-a-century-rich architectural tradition that Leatrice McKissack entered when she became the chief administrator of McKissack & McKissack, Architects and Engineers.

McKissack Heads Architectural and Engineering Firm

While in Washington, D.C., to attend the 1983 graduation exercises of her daughters Cheryl and Deryl McKissack from Howard University, Leatrice McKissack learned of her husband's sudden stroke. Two days after William DeBerry McKissack became impaired, Leatrice McKissack assumed the leadership of her husband's company. She convened a stockholders' meeting, enlarged the board of directors, and brought in an outside consultant team of architects and engineers to advise the firm. Buttressed by the counsel she received from the team of consultants, the former schoolteacher-turned-chief executive officer resolutely went about the mission of directing the architectural firm of McKissack and McKissack.

Fourteen years of retirement and the suddenness with which she was propelled into the forefront of the seventy-eight-year-old company made jumping into the corporate environment difficult, the new CEO said. She was quoted in the December 7, 1990, issue of the *Nashville Banner* on her new leadership position: "When I took over . . . all I knew about architecture was how to spell it. . . . The hardest part of coming into the business was the uncertainty of not knowing what the heck I was doing. I was thrust into a business where I knew none of the people and nothing about architecture." As McKissack lurched through the labyrinth of technical language, she found herself "trying to find order in a sea of chaos," she said. "It was hard just to understand architectural contracts." McKissack overcame her lack of technical knowledge by surrounding herself with talented architects and engineers. When asked how she was received by the firm's employees, the corporate executive responded, ''Many were resentful . . . so I had to deal with that. Basically, they left or I ended up firing all but one of them.'' With each passing day McKissack grew more confident in her role as the company's chief administrator. In addition to coping with her husband's illness and managing the architectural firm, McKissack also was the chief overseer of McKissack Contracting Company, the College Hill Realty Company, and Devonal, an apartment complex. She later sold all these family-owned businesses.

After being at the company's helm for a year, McKissack had mastered the ins and outs of the business world. In 1984, she sued the city of Nashville to obtain city contracts for the firm. ''Where did this feisty woman come from?'' asked one municipal official quoted in the April 22, 1992, *Washington Post.* ''Her husband was nice.'' McKissack and McKissack architects have designed plans for buildings and renovations on the campuses of Fisk University, Tennessee State University, and Meharry Medical College. The firm also has been awarded contracts outside of Nashville, including a fifty-million-dollar renovation project for dormitories on the campus of Howard University in Washington, D.C.

Well known for its design of educational and religious facilities, the firm was also acknowledged for its diversity when the Tennessee State Building Commission awarded it the design contract for the National Civil Rights Museum located in Memphis, Tennessee, at the site of the Lorraine Motel, where Martin Luther King, Jr. was assassinated. According to the July 14, 1991, *Nashville Banner,* McKissack considers this her most outstanding project. ''It was an honor to be chosen as an architect for a museum to honor Dr. King. . . . I don't think we . . . ever had a project this difficult. . . . It was one of the most challenging projects.''

In August of 1993, McKissack & McKissack, Architects & Engineers received its first contract with the Tennessee Valley Authority when the firm was chosen to design a crew maintenance facility in Corinth, Mississippi, and an in-processing facility at the Sequoyah Nuclear Plant in Chattanooga, Tennessee.

On February 28, 1988, approximately one year after the McKissack firm was selected by the state of Tennessee to do design work for the National Civil Rights Museum, McKissack's husband died in Washington, D.C. It was shortly after his death that she asked her daughters, all professional engineers, to join the family's architectural firm. ''I didn't have any fears about bringing my daughters into the firm. I just decided that this was family. It was a legacy,'' McKissack stated. Today, Cheryl McKissack Hosten operates the McKissack and McKissack branch office in New York and her twin sister, Deryl McKissack Cappell, runs the firm's Washington, D.C., office.

Leatrice McKissack draws upon her past experience as a classroom teacher to achieve her goal of keeping McKissack and McKissack a prospering enterprise. As in the classroom, McKissack leads by example. The quintessential staff motivator communicates with and gains input from her employees

at every level. McKissack is responsive to her clients' needs. To provide first-rate service and a high-quality end product, she is always available to her clients. The assertive McKissack frequently relies on her own firsthand experiences when speaking to women's groups, telling them that they have to ''keep fighting . . . keep knocking down the walls.''

Recognition and Honors

Beginning in 1988, after five years' hard work, McKissack accrued a number of local, state, and national honors. She was accorded the Business Woman of the Year Award by the Tennessee Department of Economic and Community Development, Office of Minority Business Enterprises (1988 and 1990); Women Owned Business Award, Nashville (1990); NAACP award for more than fifty years in business (1990); Small Business of the Year Award by the United States Small Business Administration (1990); Minority Regional Entrepreneur (1990); National Female Entrepreneur of the Year Award (1990, presented by President George Bush); Business Award of the Year by the Tennessee Black Caucus of State Legislators (1990); Distinguished Alumni Award by the National Association for Economic Opportunity (1991); National Honoree, School of Business, Howard University (1992); and Premiere Black Woman of Courage Award from the National Federation of Black Business Owners (1993).

When McKissack won the National Female Entrepreneur of the Year Award, she was selected from a national pool of 105 nominees. McKissack and McKissack's CEO was chosen because of the firm's sound financial health, its growth, the number of jobs it created, and the difficulties it surmounted. Under her leadership, the firm opened three satellite offices—in Memphis, Washington, D.C., and New York City—and personnel increased from ten to twenty-eight employees. Since 1983, the firm has been awarded contracts in the tens of millions of dollars, including the fifty-million-dollar contract with Howard University.

McKissack is a member of Caper's Memorial Christian Methodist Episcopal Church, where she serves as a trustee. In addition to her church work, she serves on numerous boards, committees, councils, and commissions, including the Federal Reserve Bank Board Advisory Council of Atlanta, Georgia; American Federation of Art Board; Bennett College Board of Visitors; State of Tennessee Employment Security Advisory Council; the Tennessee Women's Forum; the Nashville Area Chamber of Commerce; Metro Planning Commission; Metropolitan Arts Commission; Cheekwood Fine Arts Center and Botanical Gardens; and the United Way Robertson Association Advisory Committee. She is a life member of the Fisk University General Alumni Association, the NAACP, and the National Conference of Christians and Jews. In 1983, as a part of the Nashville-Metropolitan public schools' Adopt-A-School Program, McKissack & McKissack, Architects & Engineers adopted McKissack Middle School.

In 1991 the McKissack women, with eyes ever toward the future, formed the McKissack Development Corporation. This McKissack company was established for the purpose of meeting the great need for affordable housing across the country. Built on the historic foundation established by its male leadership, with its structure reinforced in the present by its strong, assertive female leadership, McKissack and McKissack's bright future seems assured.

Although the firm's matriarch is not an architect nor an engineer by training, she is an astute entrepreneur. Her magnetic personality and her determination are assets as she goes about the mission of leading McKissack and McKissack. As CEO, one of her responsibilities is to secure contracts for the company. She spends a great deal of her time traveling to meet prospective clients. "I basically bring in the work," McKissack says. "I'm just out there talking and meeting folks all the time." Over the years the firm has designed approximately five thousand structures and McKissack is adamant that the nearly century-old company will continue into the twenty-first century.

Current Address: McKissack & McKissack, Architects and Engineers, 2014 Broadway, Suite 260, Nashville, TN 37203.

REFERENCES:

"Architect McKissack: Keep Knocking down the Walls." *Washington Post,* April 22, 1992.

"Architecture Firm CEO, Ex-Teacher began at Square 1." *Nashville Banner,* December 7, 1990.

Gite, Lloyd. "The New Entrepreneur: Like Mothers, Like Daughters." *Black Enterprise* 22 (August 1991): 93-96.

"Leatrice McKissack: Enterprising Entrepreneur." *Nashville Business and Lifestyles,* November 1990.

McKissack, Leatrice B. Letter to Linda T. Wynn. August 10, 1993.

———. Interview with Linda T. Wynn. August 20, 1993.

"McKissack Receives Honor in Salute to Blacks in Business." *Metropolitan Times,* March 22, 1992.

"McKissack, Top Minority Female Entrepreneur, Runyon Advocate." *Metropolitan Times,* September 16, 1992.

Nashville City Directory. Vol. 45. Nashville: Marshall-Bruce Polk Co., 1909.

"Rights Museum Tough Project for Architect." *Nashville Tennessean,* July 14, 1991.

Smith, Maxine. "Leatrice McKissack: Building Business." *Essence* 21 (March 1991): 36.

"Sons of Gabriel McKissack." *Giles County Journal,* July 25, 1989.

Weathers, Diane. "Master Builders from the Past Fight for the Future." *Black Enterprise* 8 (March 1978): 39-42.

Who's Who among Black Americans, 1994-1995. Detroit: Gale Research, 1994.

Wynn, Linda T. "Building Tennessee: The Story of the McKissacks." *The Courier* 16, no. 1. Nashville: Tennessee Historical Commission, 1977.

———. "McKissack and McKissack." Leaders of Afro-American Nashville Series. Nashville: Nashville Conference on Afro-American Culture and History, 1985.

COLLECTIONS:

Papers of the McKissack and McKissack architectural firm dating from 1921 to 1972 are in Special Collections, Martha M. Brown-Lois H. Daniel Library, Tennessee State University. Other business papers and an interview with William DeBerry McKissack are in Special Collections, Fisk University Library. More information is located in the Gabriel Moses McKissack Historical File, which is on file in the offices of the Tennessee Historical Commission, Nashville, Tennessee. The offices of the commission also contain "McKissack and McKissack Buildings in Nashville (1909-1930) Thematic Resources," U.S. Department of the Interior, National Park Service, National Register of Historic Places Nomination Form. See also Board of Architectural and Engineers Records, 1922, Box 1(2820A) and Box 4(2324G), located in the Tennessee State Library and Archives.

Linda T. Wynn

Patricia Carwell McKissack
(1944-)
Children's author, educator, consultant, storyteller

Patricia McKissack is a prolific writer of books for children and young adults, primarily historical fiction and biography. The approximately one hundred works she has published address a wide range of subjects and are known for their clarity and appeal to readers. She writes to build bridges of understanding through books. Her childhood experiences listening to storytelling in the family spurred her to become a successful storyteller as well.

Patricia McKissack, who prefers to be called "Pat," was born August 9, 1944, in Smyrna, Tennessee, a small town near Nashville, to Robert and Erma Carwell, who were civil servants. When she was three years old, her family moved to St. Louis. Her parents divorced later and her mother, her brother Robert Nolan Carwell, and her sister Sarah Frances Carwell (now Stuart) relocated to Nashville. Pat McKissack remained with her paternal grandparents in St. Louis for several years then joined her mother and maternal grandparents in Tennessee. She attended Tennessee State University in Nashville, graduating with a B.A. degree in English in 1964. In 1975 she received her M.A. in early childhood literature and media programming from Webster University in St. Louis.

At Tennessee State University, McKissack became reacquainted with Fredrick McKissack, who had started his college career after a three-year stay in the Marine Corps. In her statement in *Something about the Author,* she wrote:

Patricia Carwell McKissack

I had known him practically all my life. We grew up in the same town, where every family knew every other family, but [Fred] was five years older and you just didn't date boys who were five years older than you. When I was fifteen and he was twenty dating was forbidden. But when I was twenty and he twenty-five it was perfectly okay.

Fred McKissack proposed to Pat Carwell on their second date, and she accepted. Four months later, on December 12, 1964, they were married. She remembers that both families and friends felt they had made a foolish mistake. However, they knew they were right for each other. Their decision was a good one, because they have reared three sons, Fredrick Lemuel and Robert and John (twins), coauthored many books, and built successful businesses together.

McKissack's love for reading developed when she was about seven years old. She also had an early interest in writing. She said in the flyer *Patricia C. McKissack and Fredrick L. McKissack,* "I began writing at an early age. I had pen pals in three countries. I remember writing a poem in third grade. My teacher liked it and told me it was well written. That thrilled me." After she had married and had children, she began to spend more time in the library and found it her "lifesaver," she said in a flyer published by Random House. In the quiet, peaceful atmosphere of the library she identified reading interest levels in literature from beginning readers to adult books. To expand her knowledge of children's materials, she read publisher's catalogs, writer's magazines, and book reviews and attended workshops and seminars. Although she did not publish during this time, she honed her

skills as a writer and at the same time helped her sons to become excellent readers and writers.

While working on her master's degree at Webster University, McKissack wrote for the preschool series "L Is for Listening," broadcast by KWMU-Radio from 1975 to 1977 and also wrote radio and television scripts. In addition, she has contributed articles and short stories to such magazines as *Friend, Happy Times,* and *Evangelizing Today's Child.* McKissack also taught English at a junior high school in Kirkwood, Missouri, from 1969 to 1975 and at Forest Park College, St. Louis, and a course "Writing for Children" at the University of Missouri from 1976 to 1982. She served as children's book editor at Concordia Publishing House, a publishing arm of the Lutheran Church-Missouri Synod, from 1976 to 1981. She left to become a freelance writer, editor, and teacher of writing. Today Pat McKissack is co-owner with her husband Fredrick L. McKissack, Sr. of All-Writing Services. Together they conduct educational workshops, lecture at universities, and speak at educational meetings and seminars on the subject of minority literature for children. In addition to works bearing her name, Pat McKissack has published a number of works—now out of print—under the name L'Ann Carwell.

McKissack is also active in the storytelling community and was elected in 1992 board member of the National Storytelling Association. "Long before I became a writer," she said in a flyer from Random House, "I was a listener and an observer." Her relatives were "dynamic and skilled storytellers." She remembered in the flyer:

On hot summer evenings our family would sit on the porch and listen to my grandmother tell a hair-raising ghost story, or my mother would recite Dunbar poems or Bible stories. Sometimes we'd get a real treat when my grandfather would dramatize an episode from his childhood, told in the rich and colorful dialect of the Deep South. I can still hear him beginning a yarn, saying: "It was back in nineteen and twenty-seven. I disremember the exact day, but it was long 'bout July, 'cause the skeeters was bitin' whole chunks outta my arms."

Writing Fills Void in Literature

McKissack's writing career began in Kirkwood, Missouri, where she was teaching English to eighth graders in 1971. She wanted to introduce her students to Paul Laurence Dunbar, a well-known African American poet. When she found no juvenile biography of Dunbar in the library, she decided to write one herself. "I spent the whole summer working on the Dunbar manuscript," she told Jessie Carney Smith on February 20, 1995, "It was the first time I had disciplined myself to write a book—beginning, middle, and end. The idea of sharing it with real readers was scary, too." But she did share her first efforts, and her eighth graders were brutally honest. They said the manuscript was boring! McKissack continued:

At first I was embarrassed and hurt. But when I re-read the manuscript from a young reader's point of view, I realized my students weren't wrong. The book was boring. I rewrote the Dunbar manuscript at least five times before my students' responses to it changed for the better.

After having written nearly one hundred successful books, McKissack is still concerned about the readability of her material, especially her nonfiction. "My students taught me a lesson that has been the cornerstone of my career as a writer," she said in the same interview. "Keep the material interesting, fast-moving, and up-beat; keep the reader involved and tell a good story, and kids won't have time to be bored."

When asked in the interview what she found interesting as a young reader, McKissack answered without hesitation. "Everything!" But, fairy tales, myths, legends, ghost stories, and science fiction are among her favorites. Clearly, among the many things the McKissacks have in common, one is definitely their love of books and reading. "Fred is the only person I know who read his math book," she said laughingly. Their personal bookshelves are crowded with over fifteen hundred books.

Another influence in the lives of the McKissacks was the civil rights movement of the 1960s. She said in a telephone interview with Jessie Carney Smith, "Martin Luther King, Jr. was—and still is—my hero. He helped change a system that was politically and morally corrupt without violence." The McKissacks also found the Vietnam War and the television coverage of American soldiers in combat very disturbing. She continued in the interview:

I grew up during a time when the country was at war in Vietnam and going through a social and political revolution here at home. In 1960, when a group of students held a sit-in at a Greensboro, North Carolina, five-and-dime store, I was a junior in high school. When man first walked on the moon in 1969, I was married and the mother of three sons. I remember my prom, pledging Alpha Kappa Alpha, graduating from college, my first teaching job in Lebanon, Tennessee, and my wedding. But I also remember where I was and what I was doing the day Dr. King was killed. It was a season of sorrow.

Explaining to today's children just how difficult—but yet how exciting—those times were motivated the McKissacks to write *The Civil Rights Movement in America from 1865 to Present.* During an interview for *Something about the Author,* Fred McKissack, who participated in the Nashville sit-ins, said, "The reason we write for children is to tell them about these things and to get them to internalize the information, to feel just a little of the hurt, the tremendous hurt and sadness that racism and discrimination cause for all people, regardless of race."

The McKissacks' nonfiction works help fill a void in literature about African and African American contributions and their struggles for freedom and justice for readers in kindergarten through high school. But McKissack also writes fiction because she feels it fills yet another void in literature for children. She wrote to Jessie Carney Smith: "When children don't see themselves in books, they aren't motivated to read. If children don't read often they usually don't read well. And soon that translates into failure. I don't want that to happen, so I try to create characters children enjoy reading about. The hope is they will then read more and thus read better."

Several of her fictional characters are warmly recognized by school children all over the country. *Flossie and the Fox, Mirandy and Brother Wind, Messy Bessey,* and *Nettie Jo's Friends* are on required reading lists in school districts all over the country. In her workshops, she wrote to Jessie Carney Smith, she tells participants that "The little girls in my books are my daughters. Since I had three sons, I had the joy of creating my own daughters without the headaches that usually go along with raising them."

These books have received many positive reviews, especially *Flossie and the Fox.* According to McKissack's biographical statement for 1995, *Kirkus Book Review* called the work "a perfect book."

Pat and Fred McKissack encourage other African Americans to write. "Writing is a kind of freedom," Pat McKissack said in *Something about the Author.* "Writing allows us to reach far more children than ever imagined. We try to enlighten, to change attitudes, to set goals—to build bridges with books." She continued: "It's a big world and we are just two writers. We cannot possibly represent 30 million African American experiences. We shouldn't have to either. There's room for many points of view."

Their hope for more African Americans to accept the challenge of writing was realized when their oldest son, Fredrick McKissack, Jr., became a journalist. He began his career as a sports writer and in February 1995 joined the staff of *The Progressive Magazine,* located in Madison, Wisconsin. He wrote *World Myths and Legends II* with Ellen Dolan, and in 1994 coauthored *Black Diamond, The Story of the Negro Baseball Leagues* with his mother, Pat McKissack.

McKissack's writings have brought her wide recognition. Her awards and honors include the Helen Keating Ott Award, National Church and Synagogue Librarians Association, 1980, for editorial work at Concordia Publishing House and the C.S. Lewis Silver Medal which awards outstanding contributions in the area of religious books for children, Christian Educators Association, 1985, for *It's the Truth, Christopher,* and *Abram, Abram, Where Are We Going?* In 1989 *Mirandy and Brother Wind,* illustrated by Jerry Pinkney, received a Caldecott Honor Award as well as the American Library Association's Coretta Scott King Award for illustration. *Parenting Magazine* selected *Nettie Jo's Friends* as a Best Book of 1989 for Text and a Parent's Choice Award for Text. McKissack received the Jane Addams Children's Book Award, Women's International League for Peace and Freedom, and Coretta Scott King Award, both in 1990 for *A Long Hard Journey: The Story of the Pullman Porter;* Newbery Honor Award and Coretta Scott King Author Award, both in

1993 for *The Dark-Thirty: Southern Tales of the Supernatural* and again in 1995 for *Christmas in the Big House-Christmas in the Quarters;* Coretta Scott King Honor Award as well as the Boston Globe-Horn Book Award for Nonfiction, 1993, for *Sojourner Truth: Ain't I a Woman?;* and another Coretta Scott King Honor Award in 1995 for *Black Diamond, The Story of the Negro Baseball Leagues.* Pat and Fred McKissack have also received an Image Award from the NAACP for their work in children's literature. In 1993 they were named Tennessee Authors of the Year by the *Nashville Banner,* receiving the honor for their research and writing. They were jointly honored again in 1994 when they received an honorary doctorate degree from the University of Missouri, St. Louis.

To highlight some of their work, Pat and Fred McKissack contributed to *The World in 1492,* edited by Jean Fritz, 1992, and collaborated on beginning readers series, both for Children's Press and Milliken. McKissack collaborated with author Mavis Jukes and wrote her first movie script in 1991. The movie, produced by Disney Educational Productions under the title *Who Owns the Sun,* won several major film awards.

McKissack spends her free time relaxing in her old renovated home near St. Louis, working in the family garden, or "junking," which she defines as visiting antique shops. The McKissacks enjoy plays and films, particularly art films. With their friends, she and her husband enjoy horseback riding, boating, and outdoor activities. McKissack's devotion to writing children's books and to freelance writing leaves little time for anything else. She has in progress two picture books, a biography of playwright Lorraine Hansberry, and a book about the Tuskegee Airmen of World War II.

Well known for her work as children's author, editor, consultant, and storyteller, Pat McKissack has enriched the lives of thousands of young people and their mentors across the nation. While she has been rewarded for her work with many honors and awards, the compelling stories she writes and tells have been equally rewarding to young readers and listeners. She and her husband Fredrick McKissack have become ambassadors of understanding and good will.

Current Address: All-Writing Services, 225 South Meramec, Suite 206, Clayton, MO 63105.

REFERENCES:

Children's Literature Review. Vol. 23. Detroit: Gale Research, 1991.
Contemporary Authors. Vol. 118. Detroit: Gale Research, 1986.
McKissack, Patricia. Letter to Jessie Carney Smith, February 20, 1995.
———. Telephone interviews with Jessie Carney Smith, February 17 and 22, 1995.
McKissack, Patricia, and Fredrick McKissack, Jr. *Black Diamond: The Story of the Negro Baseball Leagues.* Book jacket. New York: Scholastic Press, 1994.
"Patricia C. McKissack." Flyer. New York: Random House, n.d.
"Patricia C. McKissack & Fredrick L. McKissack." Flyer. New York: Scholastic Inc., n.d.
Something about the Author. Vol. 73. Detroit: Gale Research, 1993.

Jessie Carney Smith and Phyllis Wood

Terry L. McMillan
(1951-)
Writer, educator, editor

A relative newcomer to the list of best-selling authors, Terry McMillan is an exciting and vibrant novelist who examines African American life and, more specifically, relationships. Her novels are realistic stories about the African American experience. When asked in a 1992 conversation with Quincy Troupe, which appeared in *Emerge* magazine, about a place for works like hers, McMillan responded by saying that, although her work from the beginning used imagery in a rather pedestrian way, this quality ensured a direct communication with readers that she valued.

The oldest of Edward Lewis McMillan and Madeline Washington Tillman's five children, Terry L. McMillan was born on October 18, 1951, in Port Huron, Michigan, a factory town approximately sixty miles northeast of Detroit. Her mother worked at auto plants and, at one time, a pickle factory, and her father was a blue-collar worker. McMillan characterized these as normal jobs when later considering whether or not she had what it took to make a good writer—good enough to make a decent living at it. Her father was an alcoholic who beat his wife frequently, and as a result her mother divorced him in 1964; three years later he died.

The only books available to McMillan in her home were the Bible and the required reading for school. It was not until she acquired a job shelving books in a local library at age sixteen that she began to read for pleasure. Upon discovering a book by James Baldwin, McMillan felt embarrassment and fear because she had not "a clue that if we did have anything important to say that somebody would actually publish it," according to her introduction to *Breaking Ice: An Anthology of Contemporary African-American Fiction.* African American authors were not included in any textbooks McMillan used in Literature 101 in high school, and she had never questioned the omission of such, but quite frankly she had never heard of any. The people she knew hardly read any books. Thus, she was embarrassed by her ignorance of African American writers, but she also seemed equally embarrassed or ashamed of being black. All that she had ever been made aware of were the inferiorities of African American people, not their strengths; but as she became aware of notable

Terry L. McMillan

figures through reading Alex Haley's biography of Malcolm X, she realized that African Americans had a history, and a proud history it was.

McMillan later immersed herself in classic African American literature when she enrolled in a class at Los Angeles City College. She explains in the introduction to *Breaking Ice:*

> I couldn't believe the rush I felt over and over once I discovered Countee Cullen, Langston Hughes, Ann Petry, Zora Neale Hurston, Ralph Ellison, Jean Toomer, Richard Wright, and rediscovered and read James Baldwin, to name just a few. I'm surprised I didn't need glasses by the end of the semester. My world opened up.

McMillan's writing career began with a poem she wrote in reaction to getting her heart broken in a love affair at age twenty. She did not intend to write a poem but like magic it appeared on the page, lightening and lessening the pain. Later a friend discovered the poem on her kitchen table and asked to publish it in a new black literary magazine he had just started at the college. Writing then became an outlet for her dissatisfactions and her way of trying to make sense of what she saw happening around her. It became a way of trying to fix what she thought was broken, to explore personally what she didn't understand. Ultimately, she came to write about people, particularly African American people, instead of about ideas.

At age twenty-two, upon transferring to the University of California, Berkeley, McMillan thought first of becoming a social worker but decided instead to major in journalism, in which she received her B.A. degree. She then left California

for New York City, enrolling in a master's degree program at Columbia University, where she studied screenwriting. She dropped out, attributing her decision to discontinue her studies to the racism she faced at the school. McMillan says in *Breaking Ice,* "I never could stop writing, which ultimately forced me to stop fighting it. It took me even longer to realize that writing was not something you aspire to, it was something you did because you had to."

After dropping out of Columbia University, McMillan took a word processing job in a law firm in Manhattan. Her personal life then took a turn for the worse. Living with a boyfriend, Leonard Welch, who had lost his job and turned to dealing cocaine to support himself, McMillan began drinking and using drugs. In the early 1980s, states the February 1993 issue of *Current Biography,* "she recognized in herself the seeds of the alcoholism that had consumed her father and resolved to overcome her addiction. Since then she has been drug-free and sober." McMillan's relationship with Welch lasted three years and produced a son, Solomon, born in 1984.

McMillan likes the genre of the short story. Her first short story, "The End," was published in 1976 while she was a student at the University of California, Berkeley, by Ishmael Reed, novelist and founder of the Before Columbus Foundation. She submitted a collection of short stories to Houghton Mifflin, the publishing firm; while rejecting the stories, the publisher did show an interest in the novel she mentioned in her letter to them.

McMillan Publishes First Novel

McMillan's first novel was begun when she was told by the Harlem Writer's Guild that her short story "Mama" should be a novel. She spent four weeks at the MacDowell artists' colony and two weeks at the Yaddo colony expanding the story into a novel of over four hundred pages, *Mama,* which Houghton Mifflin accepted for publication. It appeared in 1987.

McMillan found it necessary to promote the novel herself, as her publishers limited its exposure to press releases and galleys. She sent out over three thousand letters to chain bookstores, independent booksellers, universities, and colleges, which gained her several reading engagements by the end of the summer of 1987. In an interview with Wendy Smith that appeared in *Publisher's Weekly,* May 11, 1992, McMillan stated that she told her publisher, "I've never been passive, and I'm not going to start now!" Launching her own publicity campaign and scheduling her own book tour, she generated thousands of sales even before the official publication date of *Mama.* She told Smith, "My editors called and said, 'Terry, we don't think this would have happened if you had not done all this.'"

Mama earned McMillan critical praise as an important contemporary novelist. This first novel, said Valerie Sayers in the August 5, 1989, *New York Times Book Review,* "was original in concept and style, a runaway narrative pulling a crowded cast of funny, earthy characters." It recounts the story of Mildred Peacock's struggle to raise her five children and defend herself against an abusive, alcoholic husband, Crook. Living in a "ragged" house in Point Haven, Michigan, a "deadbeat town," Mildred would have left Crook had it not been for their five children. Mildred Peacock is not an exemplar of the black women's experience but rather, in the words of Michael Awkward in the summer 1988 issue of *Callaloo,* "an alcoholic, nerve-pill popping, frequently self-centered character whose strength is manifested in her ability to survive (sometimes barely) the difficulties which fate—and her own, often thoughtless, actions—brings about her way." Mildred is not always likable, but regardless of her weaknesses and failures, she does love her family and finds in them a source of strength—and she is unforgettable.

Disappearing Acts Explores Relationships

In 1987 McMillan accepted a teaching position at the University of Wyoming in Laramie, and in 1988, she was awarded a National Endowment for the Arts fellowship. She has also received awards from PEN American Center, the Author's League, the Carnegie Fund, and the New York Foundation for the Arts. By 1989 McMillan had moved with her son to Tucson, Arizona, to begin teaching at the University of Arizona.

McMillan's affection for her characters and identification with them continues in her second novel, *Disappearing Acts,* published in 1989 by Viking. With her three-year association with Welch serving as inspiration for this story, McMillan writes about the deteriorating relationships between African American men and women, particularly the "doomed relationship of Zora Banks, an aspiring songwriter and Franklin Swift, an often unemployed contractor." The two fall in love, but although both have sworn off any future relationships, their prospects for lasting togetherness are thwarted by their past love affairs, and even more by their differences in backgrounds. The story is narrated from the alternating points of view of the two main characters: Franklin, frustrated by his previous relationships, his inability to hold a job, his limited educational background, his troubled family and lack of support from them, his uncooperative spirit, and his hot temper; and Zora, troubled by her failed relationships with men and a desire to feel needed and loved, her three abortions, her struggle to stop concentrating so hard on what's missing in her life and to be grateful for what she does have, and her fear of being in a world where she does not make a difference. Their voices are authentic and realistic, despite the distaste some readers have for the profanity. The novel is lively, sparking with electricity, and yet at the same time McMillan shows great sympathy for her characters, creating in the reader compassion for what they went through in their lives.

The success and appeal of the novel gained McMillan an offer from MGM to make it into a movie. After having bought the rights to the book, MGM commissioned McMillan to write the screenplay. As *Disappearing Acts* was selling several thousand copies and McMillan enjoyed the well-deserved success of her novel, a defamation of character suit was filed by Leonard Welch, her former lover and the father of her

child, charging that McMillan had divulged the intimacies of their relationship, using him as a model for her leading male character, Franklin. He claimed that the novel was written out of malice and revenge. The New York Supreme Court ruled in McMillan's favor, however, in April 1991, the judge declaring that Welch appeared not to be any of the things Franklin was: lazy, emotionally disturbed, alcohol and drug dependent, and physically abusive to his girlfriend.

As McMillan read anthologies for her students to use, she realized that African American writers were rarely included. This led her to compile *Breaking Ice: An Anthology of African-American Fiction.* As she continued to examine her bookshelves, she decided to include in her anthology of contemporary African American fiction not just well-established authors but also writers who had not yet been published, as well as writers with one story or novel published who had not yet been recognized. She received nearly three hundred submissions, fifty-seven of which appear in the anthology, which includes seasoned, emerging, and unpublished writers. Many of the stories are excerpts from novels, and all reflect the varied and distinct voices of a new generation of African American writers.

Waiting to Exhale Hits Best-Seller List

Shortly after *Disappearing Acts* was published, McMillan already had an idea for her third novel. According to Audrey Edwards in the October 1992 issue of *Essence* magazine, she revealed plans for her next book to her editor at Viking, stating it would "be about some black women who were having trouble finding men. They were educated, smart, attractive—and they were alone." *Waiting to Exhale* appeared in 1992, reaching the *New York Times* best-seller list at the same time as the works of two of America's most renowned African American female writers, Toni Morrison and Alice Walker; neither of the two acknowledged her work or its tremendous success. McMillan said in the October 1992 issue of *Essence,* "I've dropped them notes over the years congratulating them when their books have come out, and it hurts that they've never done the same for me."

Nonetheless, it was McMillan who received $2.64 million for paperback rights to *Waiting to Exhale,* which sold over 700,000 hardcover copies by the end of 1992, outselling Walker's *Possessing the Secret Joy* and Morrison's *Jazz* by three to one, according to Faye Childs of Blackboard African American Best-Sellers List, Inc. Readers of McMillan's novel were not only African Americans but persons of varied ethnicity, attesting to the fact that her stories were realistic enough to reach far beyond the boundaries of race and class.

The four main characters are Savannah Jackson, a smart and successful television producer; Robin Stokes, an insurance company executive hooked on a "lying, sneaky, whorish Pisces"; Bernadine Harrison, Savannah's college roommate, who, after eleven years of marriage to a successful businessman, is betrayed and must start all over after divorcing him; and Gloria Matthews, a hair salon owner who is overweight and afraid to get involved with a man. The women discuss honestly and candidly all the "knots" (issues) in their lives and in their relationships. McMillan shows how these characters develop strength as they seek satisfying relationships, deciding to appreciate what they do have and live their lives in spite of the presence or absence of a man. They determine not to give men authority over their lives and seek to become empowered by their own inner resources and beauty.

Having earned millions of dollars has bought her substantial security. She lives in a five-bedroom, southwestern-style home in Danville, California, in the San Francisco Bay Area. McMillan, however, is ever mindful that her celebrity status is transient and realizes that as quickly as fame is achieved, it can pass away. Today she exhibits much of the sass and style displayed by the characters she creates. Responding to critics who objected to her heavy use of profanity and male-bashing, McMillan retorted in *Publisher's Weekly,* May 11, 1992, "That's the way we talk. And I want to know why I've never read a review where they complain about the language that male writers use!" Despite the frequent use of profanity in both her novels and interviews, McMillan comes off as an honest, sincere, down-to-earth home girl with a mission to write about the real world in the language and tone that real people use when they are not trying to impress or stand as role models for their race.

Current Address: Free at Last, P. O. Box 2408, Danville, CA 94526; (agent) c/o Molly Friedrich, Aaron Priest Literary Agency, 122 East Forty-second St., Suite 3902, New York, NY 10168.

REFERENCES:

Akward, Michael. "Chronicling Everyday Travails and Triumphs." *Callaloo* 1 (Summer 1988): 649-50.

Bates, Karen Grigsby. "Possessing the Secrets of Success." *Emerge* 4 (October 1992): 47-49.

Contemporary Authors. Vol. 140. Detroit: Gale Research, 1993.

Contemporary Literary Criticism. Vol. 50. Detroit: Gale Research, 1988.

Contemporary Literary Criticism. Vol. 61. Detroit: Gale Research, 1990.

Current Biography 54 (February 1993): 36-39.

Edwards, Audrey. "Terry McMillan: Waiting to Exhale." *Essence* 23 (October 1992): 77-78, 82, 118.

Freely, Maureen. "Croaking with Hideous Voices." *The Observer* (May 10, 1987): 20.

McMillan, Terry, ed. *Breaking Ice: An Anthology of African-American Fiction.* New York: Viking Penguin, 1990.

"Profile of a First Novelist: Terry McMillan and *Mama.*" *Writer's Digest* 67 (October 1987): 58.

Sayers, Valerie. "Someone to Walk Over Me." *New York Times Book Review,* August 5, 1989.

Smith, Wendy. "Terry McMillan: The Novelist Explores African American Life from the Point of View of a New Generation." *Publishers Weekly* 239 (May 11, 1992): 50.

Troupe, Quincy. "A Conversation with Terry McMillan." *Emerge* 4 (October 1992): 51-52, 56.

Brenda Robinson Shaw

Georgia L. McMurray
(1934-1992)
Civic worker, child care advocate

Georgia L. McMurray, one of the five 1992 *Essence* Award winners, was described in *Essence* magazine in this manner: "Like many black women who commit their lives to service, Dr. Georgia L. McMurray falls into what she calls the "triple A" categories of advocate, activist, and academician." McMurray's chief concern was in providing for New York City's underserved population of poor children, youth, and families. Realizing that no social group could be served well on a need-by-need basis, she planned, implemented, and oversaw interlocking and interrelated service programs that provided for the multiple needs of the poor. When a changing political scene and her own declining health caused her to leave public administration, McMurray turned her energies to private administrative and management activities that helped agencies and organizations implement programs designed to aid the city's needy. The "advocate, activist, and academician" left a legacy that stands as a model for designing methods to service society's impoverished children, youth, and families.

Georgia L. McMurray was born on March 18, 1934, to Daisy Gatewood McMurray Fullen (her mother remarried) and George McMurray. She and her two sisters, Caroline Johnson and Marvine Fullen, were born in Philadelphia, Pennsylvania. George McMurray, a Tennessee native, was a self-employed barber and Daisy McMurray, a Wadesboro, North Carolina, native, was a cafeteria worker and garment industry worker who also helped organize the Philadelphia Garment Workers' Union. McMurray graduated from Girls' High School in Philadelphia and, because of her outstanding musical talent, was awarded a Marian Anderson Scholarship to college. As a high school student, McMurray was one of the original members of Singing City, a group of local students that performed throughout the state of Pennsylvania. She was also a member of the New Bethlehem Baptist Church choir. In 1959 McMurray received a bachelor's degree in sociology from Temple University and in 1962 a master's degree in social work from Bryn Mawr College.

Becomes Advocate for Children, Youth, and Families

McMurray spent her entire career planning and implementing services for New York City children and youths. She first gained attention in the late 1960s as the founder of Project Teen Aid, a program for pregnant adolescents that still exists. The problem of teenage pregnancy was always foremost on McMurray's agenda because pregnant teenagers were once routinely expelled from public schools due to the belief that they were "bad" girls who would negatively influence the "good" girls. McMurray was especially concerned about the effects that little or no education would have on poor black and Latino pregnant girls; she cited as causal factors of teen pregnancy the existence of little, if any, female-specific education and the lack of high expectations for young people.

McMurray's work was recognized by the administration of Mayor John Lindsay, and she was hired in 1969 to direct an Early Childhood Task Force that would develop services for young children and families. This job led directly to her next position as the first commissioner of the New York City Agency for Child Development, which oversaw the city's child-care and preschool programs not handled by the Board of Education. In 1971, the year the agency opened and McMurray became its first commissioner, the agency's annual budget was $101.2 million, and it had a staff of 450 employees. The agency's main purpose was to promote opportunities for the city's 825,000 preschool children, a group that included 250,000 poor children. When McMurray became commissioner, there were around 260 day-care centers in New York City, with a service population of 15,000 children. Within three years, more than 300 day-care centers had opened and over 45,000 children were being served.

A major priority set by McMurray was planning for round-the-clock centers to provide not only day care and night care, but also adolescent services for youths needing to escape negative home environments. Other innovative plans generated by McMurray were: using female neighbors to care for the children of working mothers; expanding the number of Family Day Care programs, known as Mom and Pop centers, to continue as licensed sites for the placement of young children; increasing day-care program spatial allocations to accommodate latch-key children who needed to be off the streets and out of empty apartments; meeting the needs of children ineligible for or not enrolled in Head Start programs; establishing citywide counseling resource centers for parents; and setting up federally funded centers for middle-class families who could afford to pay operating costs. McMurray knew what New York City parents wanted because she visited day-care centers and attended community meetings on a regular basis. In an interview with Virginia Lee Warren, McMurray said: "I've found that in many neighborhoods the first generation immigrants don't understand about day care centers. . . .[g]oing out and meeting parents is the best part of my job."

Few administrators, whether at the local, state, regional, or national level, systematically visit their constituents with such frequency; this is a task usually delegated to an employee well below the top level. That is why McMurray was so demeaned when her capabilities and competence were seriously questioned when she was being considered for reappointment as commissioner in the mid-1970s.

McMurray Triumphs Over Adversity

Although her pioneering efforts had gained her the support of some important government officials, McMurray had detractors and political enemies, too, probably as the result of her effort to centralize resources formerly spread among varied city agencies dealing with public day-care services. The issue of whether McMurray was capable of continuing to administer an agency known to be among the most effective in New York City arose because of malicious rumors about her failing physical health. She had long suffered from a congenital degenerative illness known as Charcot-Marie-Tooth disease, which causes muscular atrophy in the legs and accompanying bone damage. Caroline Johnson, McMurray's sister, said in an interview that, as a child, McMurray could not participate in strenuous outdoor activities with her sisters and friends; she stayed indoors and read or entertained herself with music, both favorite pastimes. As a graduate student, she refused to undergo an operation that would have required her to be in traction for nine months. In the 1970s, McMurray underwent two artificial hip replacement operations and began using metal crutches. Just as the earlier threat of an operation did not prevent her from pursuing her career goals, the later operations did not impede her progress as commissioner. When Mayor Edward Koch, the successor to Mayor John V. Lindsay, took office, all agency administrators tendered their resignations, a standard professional courtesy. However, McMurray's resignation, unlike many others, was accepted by the new mayor because of political pressure against her reappointment. Her sister related that McMurray knew she wouldn't enjoy the same level of professional respect and camaraderie in the new administration as she had in the old, and she was prepared for what occurred. She refused to protest the rumors spread by her detractors and accepted another position that was, in reality, a promotion. This was a position as deputy general director with the Community Service Society, which she held from 1978 to 1986. At this agency, McMurray concentrated on research, policy planning, and lobbying on a wide range of issues.

Due to the progression of the rare and relentless muscle-wasting disease, McMurray became totally paralyzed. To compensate for the loss of muscular ability, she learned to operate a computer with a mouthpiece and to maintain mobility with the use of a motorized wheelchair. Her physical limitations did nothing to diminish her advocacy of poor children and their families or her intellectual pursuits. From her home, she functioned as administrator of the GLM Group, a human services, management, and research organization. From this new base, the agency provided research, training, technical assistance, and a wide array of management services to government and nonprofit organizations with programs for children and families. McMurray produced reports on the homeless, the demographics of urban poverty, and model programs for children and youth. McMurray also functioned as distinguished professor of social policy in the Graduate School of Social Service at Fordham University both before and after her condition worsened.

Recognition Given to Pioneer

In recognition of her pioneering and tireless efforts to upgrade the quality of life for children and families, as well as her determination to maintain the quality of life she desired as a person and as a professional, McMurray has been singled out for prestigious honors and awards. She was one of five 1992 *Essence* Award winners. She was cited for proving that ''a physical challenge of any kind—whether an early pregnancy or a rare disease—need not be a limitation to excellence.'' Also in 1992, McMurray was cited for distinguished service by the Children's Aid Society. That this woman could accomplish so much despite the most adverse conditions seems amazing to most people. To her sister, Caroline, it is not at all amazing. With pride, she relates how their parents had always been role models. They had stressed that the McMurray girls could be whatever they wanted to be and that nothing could keep them from reaching their goals. Caroline is now the primary care giver for her mother, now eighty-seven years old and totally disabled as a result of diabetes.

After the announcement of McMurray's death, she was eulogized by such respected organizations and agencies as the Associated Black Charities, the Family Day Care Program of the New York Foundling Hospital, the Harlem Dowling West Side Center for Children and Family Services, the Women's Forum of New York, the Public Education Association, the New York Urban League, the New York City Chapter-National Association of Social Workers (of which she was once president), and the Community Service Society of New York. In an article in the magazine *Working Woman* entitled ''Against the Odds,'' which focuses on the employment of disabled women, Andrea Fooner had this to say about McMurray: ''Even an exceptionally strong and adaptive personality is not immune to the complexities of pursuing a career while handicapped. . . . Clearly her disability made her more vulnerable to attack at a critical point in her career, yet McMurray maintained her professionalism and made a career advance.'' David R. Jones and David W. Smith, president and chair, respectively, of the Community Service Society of New York eulogized McMurray in the *New York Times:*

> Her compassion, intelligence, warmth, and professionalism helped design programs for N.Y.'s indigent when federal neglect of cities and popular indifference to the poor threatened low-income New Yorkers. In a life dedicated to public service, she accomplished much. She will not be forgotten.

In a wheelchair, operating a computer with a mouthpiece to overcome limitations imposed by limbs still and lifeless, one woman believed what her parents had told her during her childhood when those limbs functioned. As a result, hundreds of thousands of New York children and families have been enabled in their efforts to have at least a piece of the ''American Dream.'' Pregnant teenagers are no longer ostracized and excluded from the education they will need to support their children; and millions of American citizens have benefitted from the research generated by a woman who continued to contribute to society even after losing much of her physical abilities.

REFERENCES:

''Dr. Georgia L. McMurray.'' *Essence* 23 (July 1992): 76-78.

Fooner, Andrea. ''Against the Odds.'' *Working Woman* 8 (October 1983): 140-43.

Johnson, Caroline. Interview with Dolores Nicholson. July 17, 1993.

Saxon, Wolfgang. ''Georgia L. McMurray, 58, Leader in Services for New York Children.'' *New York Times,* December 19, 1992.

Warren, Virginia Lee. ''An Interview with Georgia McMurray, New York City's Commissioner for Children Development.'' *Children Today.* Vol. 1, No. 1 (January/February 1972).

Dolores Nicholson

Barbara McNair
(193?-)
Singer, actress, entertainer

Since her career began in the 1950s, Barbara McNair has starred in Broadway theater productions and films, appeared in numerous television shows, hosted her own syndicated television variety show, and sung in nightclubs both nationally and internationally. Although her personal life has not always been carefree, she told *Newsweek* magazine in 1966, ''nobody is ever going to cry listening to me sing.'' She entered the American entertainment industry at a time when racial integration was taking place across the United States, including the world of show business.

McNair was born and raised in Racine, Wisconsin. Sources vary in recording her date of birth, ranging from 1934 to 1939. Her father, Horace McNair, was a factory foreman. Early in her career, McNair said in a 1958 *Ebony* magazine interview, ''Mom is my biggest booster. She encouraged me and saw that I got good instructions. I consider her my Number 1 fan.'' She has two brothers and two sisters. Her half-sister Juanita Moseley has been a valued companion throughout her career. McNair's first marriage in 1955 to a childhood sweetheart, Earl Wright, ended in divorce. Her second marriage to white club owner and public relations agent Jack Rafferty also ended in divorce. She then married white businessman Rick Manzie, who was found shot to death in December 1976 in their Las Vegas home. In 1979 McNair married white architect Ben Strahan.

McNair first sang at church and school in Wisconsin. When she was in the sixth grade, her performance of the song ''Deep River'' at school confirmed her desire to be a singer.

Barbara McNair

She said in the 1966 *Newsweek* interview, "When I was a girl in Racine, I always had what I needed—but not what I wanted. The important thing in life is to know the big from the little, and the big is 'I.'" On completing high school, she attended the Racine Conservatory of Music with money her mother had saved from the family budget. In 1953 she attended one year of college at the University of California, Los Angeles, because she had heard that one of her idols, Dorothy Dandridge, had been discovered there. She then moved to New York in 1954, where she worked as a typist at the New York Federation of Settlements. Her first break in the entertainment industry came when she sang at the Village Vanguard, which led to a string of singing engagements that brought her to the attention of gossip columnist and news commentator Walter Winchell and producer Richard Kollmar. Kollmar gave McNair her first role on Broadway in 1958 when she starred in the theatrical production *The Body Beautiful.*

McNair was the first black to appear on the "Ten Most Beautiful" list. Donald Bogle in *Brown Sugar* describes the young McNair as "a wholesome looking, demure young woman with magnetic dark eyes and a warm, lush smile." Bogle likens McNair to singer and actress Diahann Carroll, whom he describes as a "light-skinned beauty" with a "bourgeois image." Petite at five feet four inches, McNair was described in *Ebony* in 1964 as having the following attributes: "a good figure (34-24-35) that flatters curve-hugging gowns, reddish brown skin that glows under a spotlight, a 'commercial' voice that shifts easily from Broadway to the blues." In 1972 Prentice-Hall published McNair's *The Complete Book of Beauty for Black Women.*

McNair Becomes Rising Star

The Body Beautiful, McNair's first theater experience, concerns an amateur college boxer who turns professional. In 1980, she told Bob Lucas of *Jet* magazine, "I remember my first Broadway show, *The Body Beautiful.* It was three years from when I was first asked to opening night. Then the darn show closed in three months. But I love the stage." Although the play did not enjoy a particularly successful run, critic Brooks Atkinson noted that McNair sang well and that she, with a co-star, "set off a few highly necessary Roman candles when the plot stops long enough in the first act to give them an opportunity." At this time she also had a record, *Bobby,* in the top ten.

McNair received much attention when she took over the role Diahann Carroll left in the Broadway production of *No Strings* in 1962. The play achieved some notoriety for its plot, which focuses on the love affair in Paris between a white American novelist and a black high fashion model. In *Brown Sugar,* Donald Bogle writes of the play, "In Black America, . . . *No Strings* may have had good intentions, but it had come too late in the day. In this era of sit-ins, protests, and of an evolving black nationalism, the idea that a black woman might have an affair with a white man was viewed as being politically treasonous." Even though McNair's own romantic attachments mirrored this discredited social role, her relationship with the black community did not seem to suffer, as Bogle points out with reference to articles of the time in *Jet* and *Ebony.*

In 1962 McNair also had a small role in the film *Spencer's Mountain,* starring Henry Fonda and Maureen O'Hara, where she is listed in the credits as the "graduation singer." She continued her nightclub singing career, and the 1966 *Newsweek* article "I'm Gonna Make It," noted that "the spirited songs that Barbara sings mirror the girl herself. With a big grin and diction that makes every word count, she lets the audience know, in the nicest possible ways, about her driving ambition." The same source quotes her as saying, "I want what I haven't had yet; a smash record, a movie, a starring role in a successful Broadway musical."

In 1968 McNair appeared in the film *If He Hollers, Let Him Go* as the lost love of a black man, played by Raymond St. Jacques, who has been wrongly sent to prison for the murder of a white woman. When he escapes from jail, a white man attempts to hire him to kill his rich wife. Instead, St. Jacques's character rescues the wife and tries to clear himself. McNair's character assists him, even though she married his brother while he was in prison. In 1969 McNair took a part in the movie *Stiletto,* an adaptation of Harold Robbins's novel about a Mafia assassin that starred Britt Ekland.

Throughout the 1960s McNair made numerous appearances on a wide variety of television shows. She was featured on Arthur Godfrey's *Talent Scouts,* the *Ed Sullivan Show,* the *Danny Kaye Show,* the *Dean Martin Show,* and *The Most in Music.* She guest starred in such series as *Dr. Kildare, Mission: Impossible, I Spy,* and *Hogan's Heroes.* In 1969 McNair reached the apogee of her television career when she hosted her own syndicated entertainment variety show, *The*

Barbara McNair Show. The sixty-minute show ran for approximately one year and featured such famous performers as Bob Hope, Rich Little, and the musical group The Turtles. She thus joined the few black entertainers who had their own television shows at the time—Bill Cosby, Leslie Uggams, and Diahann Carroll.

McNair Meets Success and Hardship

In the 1970s McNair continued her work in nightclubs, film, and television. Her film *Venus in Furs* was released in 1970. An Italian/British/German production that was an adaptation of a novelette by Leopold von Sacher-Masoch, it also featured James Darren and Klaus Kinski. The film attempts to show the mental processes of a musician as he seemingly witnesses a series of sexual encounters that end in murder. McNair sang the title song, which was written by Robert and Richard Sherman. She also had a part in the 1970 film *They Call Me Mister Tibbs,* the sequel to *In The Heat of the Night,* starring Sidney Poitier. The film, in which she played Tibbs's wife, Valerie, received less favorable reviews than its predecessor.

In the early seventies, McNair had guest roles in *McMillan and Wife, To Rome with Love,* and *Mod Squad.* She appeared on the *Jack Paar Show,* the *Mike Douglas Show,* and the *Merv Griffin Show.* She also appeared on such celebrity shows as *All Stars, The Match Game, Celebrity Tennis,* and *The Gong Show.* In 1972 her career was threatened, however, when she was arrested for allegedly possessing heroin, charges that were later dropped. She told William Earl Berry in *Jet* magazine, "I do not use narcotics of any kind. I've never taken drugs, never had any need for them. With my kind of life, you can't function if you take drugs." Although many of her engagements were cancelled because of her arrest, in 1973 she starred in a racially integrated Broadway revival of *The Pajama Game.* McNair played a grievance committeewoman to Hal Linden's white factory foreman. Walter Kerr in reviewing the production wrote in the *New York Times* that "one of the few moments of interest is provided by the black and white mix."

In December 1976, while she was singing in Chicago, McNair's third husband, Rick Manzie, was found murdered in their Las Vegas home. McNair found it difficult to continue performing after this tragedy. She told Bob Lucas in *Jet,* "For months I just couldn't do anything. People kept telling me I had to get back to work for my good. Finally, gradually, I started working. But for a year there was no joy in it." Within the year death again visited McNair when Manzie's mother died from a heart attack while staying with her. She also was summoned to be a witness in legal proceedings against her former financial advisor, Harry Margolis. According to *Jet,* she testified that she believed her financial assets were five hundred thousand dollars but that Margolis "said it was in the nature of $50,000, which was a shock to me."

In 1978 McNair, who had begun working again, met white architect and businessman Ben Strahan, to whom she was married in Las Vegas in December 1979. Along with her career as a performer, she was to head the entertainment division of one of Strahan's businesses, B and B Industries. McNair continued her work in television in the late 1970s and 1980s, appearing on such shows as *Police Woman, Vega$, Gong Show, $1.98 Beauty Show, Over Easy,* the *Mike Douglas Show, The Jeffersons,* the *Redd Foxx Show,* and *Beauty and the Beast.*

A member of the American Guild of Variety Artists, Stage Artists Guild, American Federation of Television and Radio Artists, and Actors Equity Guild, McNair's contribution to the entertainment industry has been varied. *Newsweek* characterized her singing style as "radiating good cheer and bouncy optimism . . . with a big, polished, sultry voice, happy and warm as a midsummer's day." In her theatrical and film roles she often portrayed glamorous black women. She said in the same *Newsweek* article, "Show business is made for dreaming. I don't have dreams. I have desires." Her television appearances span more than three decades. The earliest of these, in the 1960s, demonstrate the lifting of the color bar in American popular culture, as do the careers of other black performers of the time. In the 1980 *Jet* interview with Bob Lucas, McNair repeated the advice given to her by Sidney Poitier: "If you want to be an actress, you have to do what I did. I went up for every part that came along. I didn't wait for them to say we want a Black man for this part. Sometimes you have to convince the producer, and that way you can create parts for yourself."

Although McNair's assimilation into white American culture was out of step with the search for a black ethnic and cultural identity, she heightened the visibility of blacks in the American entertainment industry. Her career as a singer, actress, and entertainer has lasted for more than thirty years. The wide range of her public appearances—in nightclubs, television, film, and theater—attests to her appeal as a performer.

Current Address: c/o Moss Agency Ltd., 113 North San Vincente Boulevard, Beverly Hills, CA 90211.

REFERENCES:

Atkinson, Brooks. Review of *The Body Beautiful. New York Times,* January 24, 1958.

Bagar, Robert. "Beggar's Holiday a Brilliant Musical." *New York Theatre Critic's Reviews* 7 (1946): 204.

"Barbara McNair—Twelve Years to Broadway." *Ebony* 13 (May 1958): 69-74.

Berry, William Earl. "What Dope Arrest Is Doing to Career of Barbara McNair." *Jet* 43 (December 7, 1972): 54-57.

Bogle, Donald. *Brown Sugar: Eighty Years of America's Black Female Superstars.* New York: Harmony Books, 1980.

Canby, Vincent. Review of *They Call Me Mister Tibbs. New York Times,* July 9, 1970.

"I'm Gonna Make It." *Newsweek* 67 (January 10, 1960): 64.

Kerr, Walter. Review of *The Pajama Game. New York Times,* December 16, 1973.

Lucas, Bob. "Barbara McNair Starts New Life after Trage-dies." *Jet* 57 (February 7, 1980): 46-50.
"'No Strings' for Barbara." *Ebony* 19 (January 1964): 43-50.

                                        Kathleen T. Flanagan

Claudia McNeil

Claudia McNeil
(1917-1993)
Actress, singer

Claudia McNeil was one of the most active and critically acclaimed actresses of the twentieth century. Most noted as an actress who brought new depth to the role of the powerful matriarch, McNeil is best remembered for her portrayal of Lena Younger ("Mama"), the poor black widow who tries to keep her family together in Lorraine Hansberry's *A Raisin in the Sun.*

Claudia McNeil was born in Baltimore, Maryland, on August 13, 1917, two months after her parents had divorced. She never knew her father, Marvin Spencer McNeil, and her mother raised her alone. Annie Mae Anderson McNeil, an Apache Indian, moved her family to New York City after having asked her husband to leave. There she owned a grocery store and ran the household. Claudia spent most of her life in New York City.

When Claudia was twelve, Annie Mae McNeil became ill and Claudia was put up for adoption. She went to work for the Heckscher Foundation as a mother's helper. Through this position she met a Jewish couple, the Toppers, who later adopted her. She grew up in their household and became fluent in Yiddish.

McNeil's singing career began while she was still a teenager. She debuted at a Greenwich Village supper club, The Black Cat, in 1933 at the age of sixteen. This job earned her only $13.50 a week. Even though her interest in entertainment began as a teenager, she graduated from Wadley High School in New York City and became a licensed librarian before her career expanded into theater.

At age nineteen, McNeil married her first husband, whom she once described as a "very wonderful man." She had two sons, but lost her husband in World War II. Both her sons were killed in the Korean War. Years later she commented in an interview with Carol Morton that was published in *Ebony,* "I don't have anything else to give to the United States now except my taxes."

With five hundred dollars from the Toppers, Claudia McNeil, at age twenty, went to find her place as a professional singer. She performed at such nightclubs as The Famous Door, The Onyx, and The Greenwich Village Inn, all in New York City. Her nightclub act centered on the songs of Ethel Waters. She also performed in vaudeville theaters and on the radio.

McNeil's work in radio, which was short-lived, began in 1951. During a two-year period she was program coordinator and entertainer for the Jamaican Broadcasting Company in Kingston, Jamaica.

When she was in her thirties, McNeil returned to the United States, where her career expanded. She began acting on the advice of Ethel Waters and made her first stage appearance at the Duxbury Playhouse in Massachusetts where she spent several seasons. This was followed by appearances at the Ann Arbor Drama Festival in Michigan and a South American tour as a vocal soloist with the Katherine Dunham Dance Company.

Makes Stage Debut

It was not until 1953, at age thirty-six, that McNeil made her legitimate New York City stage debut. Her first Broadway role was as a replacement for Tituba in Arthur Miller's *The Crucible.* The next role she auditioned for was at the request of Langston Hughes. Hughes asked her to play the part of Mamie in the stage production of *Simply Heavenly,* based on Hughes's *Simple Takes a Wife* and his other *Simple* stories. The premiere on May 20, 1957, at the Eighty-fifth Street Playhouse (off-Broadway) won her critical acclaim.

McNeil's next appearance in a play was in 1958 in the role of Mary in the National Theatre production of *Winesburg, Ohio.* She also made several television appearances that year on shows such as the *Molly Goldberg Show, Camera Three, Personal Story,* and *Spotlight.* In an NBC Dupont Show of the Month, McNeil performed another matriarchal role when she played the wise Berenice Sadie Brown in Carson McCullers's *Member of the Wedding.*

The performance that McNeil is most noted for is her portrayal of Lena Younger, "Mama," in Lorraine Hansberry's groundbreaking play, *A Raisin in the Sun.* The play opened on March 11, 1959, at the Ethel Barrymore Theater, and McNeil played for 531 performances. She drew critical and popular acclaim as a black widow who desperately tries to keep her family together as they endure the hardships of being black and living in South-side Chicago in the 1950s. McNeil received glowing notices as a powerful, God-fearing matriarch and, according to the *New York Times* in November 1993, critics found that McNeil "imbued that simple character with nobility of spirit."

Being consistently cast as a powerful mother figure brought comparisons with other actresses who filled such roles, particularly Hattie McDaniel, who played Mammy in *Gone with the Wind.* Lindsay Patterson, editor of *Black Films & Film-makers,* pronounced that "her [McNeil's] matriarchal exchanges with Beneatha in 'A Raisin in the Sun' are not too unlike Mammy's strong words with Scarlet in *Gone with the Wind.*" Donald Bogle also commented that "McNeil seems grossly like the Mammy of Hattie McDaniel vintage, but without her humor and spontaneity and her work was most effective when she was hooting, yelling, and reprimanding." It was McNeil's performance in this role that brought more depth to the character of Mama by showing a serious woman.

Expands Career with Film Roles

The year 1959 was also important for Claudia McNeil because she made her film debut in Columbia's release *The Last Angry Man.* The film was widely noted at the time. According to Bogle, it remains of interest not only as "an old-style sentimental picture about a kindly white doctor (Paul Muni), but also because it introduced many new black performers along with Claudia McNeil—Cicely Tyson, Godfrey Cambridge, and Billy Dee Williams also went on to pursue noteworthy careers." Later on in the year she repeated her role as Mamie in Langston Hughes's *Simply Heavenly* in a television play.

McNeil went on to do other films after *The Last Angry Man* but none so important or popular as the film version of *A Raisin in the Sun.* She reprised her role as Mama and starred with the original cast from the play—a cast that included such greats as Sidney Poitier, Ruby Dee, and Diana Sands. Critics again praised this outstanding cast of the film directed by Daniel Petrie. On screen, said the *New York Times* in November 1993, McNeil was "stolid, voluminous, and serene as a mother trying to control her son and wanting to buy her family a respectable home."

Honored with Nominations

In 1962, McNeil remarried, but the marriage ended in divorce after only two years and she never married again. This same year she returned to the stage to play the role of Mama in Peter S. Feibleman's *Tiger, Tiger Burning Bright,* a play based on his novel *A Place without Twilight.* She received widespread praise and her performance earned her a Tony nomination.

McNeil's abilities were noticed not only on the stage. When she returned to television in 1963 for the episode "Express Stop from Lenox Avenue" in the CBS series *The Nurses,* her performance resulted in an Emmy nomination. The following year she returned to the theater to repeat her role as Berenice in a touring production of *Member of the Wedding* and also starred in the CBS television production of *Look Up and Live.* McNeil was featured on the television show *Profiles in Courage* (NBC), and she traveled abroad in a U.S. State Department tour. Her performance as Sister Margaret in James Baldwin's *The Amen Corner* took her to Israel, Switzerland, Austria, France, Germany, Scotland, and England. While in England, she received the London Critics Poll Award for best actress.

Between 1967 and 1974 McNeil starred in several television and theater productions. In 1967, she was able to use her Yiddish in her role as Sarah Goldfine, a Jewish mother, in Carl Reiner's comedy *Something Different.* Also in 1967, she performed in the CBS production of *Do Not Go Gentle into That Good Night.* After this project she played Ftatateeta in the stage production of *Her First Roman,* a musical based on George Bernard Shaw's *Caesar and Cleopatra.* The production also starred newcomers Leslie Uggams and Richard Kiley, but unfortunately, it failed to draw any favorable criticism. Her next role, also on stage, was as Mrs. Devereux in *The Wrong-Way Light Bulb.* In 1970 she starred in two of three one-act plays in Ted Shine's *Contributions.* Her roles included Martha in *Plantation,* and Mrs. Love in the title play. She also managed to find time to do the film *There Was a Crooked Man.*

During the 1970s McNeil could frequently be found on television. She did episodes for popular television shows such as *Mod Squad, Cry Panic,* and *Kup's Show.* She also did several television productions. *Incident in San Francisco,* the NET Playhouse production of Lorraine Hansberry's *To Be Young, Gifted and Black,* and *Moon and the Wolf* both featured Claudia McNeil.

In 1972 she was once again called to fill the role of matriarch. The Cinerama film *Black Girl,* directed by Ossie Davis, deals with matriarchal black family life. In it Lindsay Patterson reports she was called a "powerhouse."

The year 1975 was an important one for McNeil because it brought her back to the performance she loved best. After a twelve-year self-imposed absence, McNeil returned in her stage role as Lena Younger in *A Raisin in the Sun.* McNeil had put this role aside to expand her career, but she also hesitated to work on this project because of the deaths of some of the original cast. Lorraine Hansberry died at a very young age, and Diana Sands, who played Beneatha, had also passed away. Another factor that critics brought up when she decided to reprise her role was the way she looked. In the original production, McNeil had weighed almost 300 pounds; she now had reduced her weight to 159 pounds. Despite her fears and those who questioned her ability to deliver because of her physical appearance, McNeil came back to give a commanding performance. According to Carol Morton in *Ebony*, McNeil noted, ''There was a time when I acted the role, now I live it.'' Morton stated that ''every person in the audience seemed drawn into the very center of the magnificent performance on stage.'' McNeil felt so strongly about the play she commented to Morton, ''There are some plays you have to live and *A Raisin in the Sun* is one of them. You have to live it. I carry the burden so heavily that I'm still under the influence.''

After 1975, McNeil continued to work in theater but slowed down her work pace. She was featured in the television production of *American Women: Portraits in Courage* in 1976. And in 1978 she made her first singing appearance in twenty-one years at Michael's Pub in Manhattan. It was the first time she had made a singing performance since her role in the 1957 production of *Simply Heavenly*. Her last stage performance was in 1981 in the Equity Library Theater production of *Raisin,* a musical based on the Hansberry play. Once again she was praised for having a commanding presence.

McNeil retired in 1983 and moved into the Actors' Fund Nursing Home in Englewood, New Jersey, in 1985. She lived there for nine years. After a lifetime on stage and screen, Claudia McNeil died Thursday, November 25, 1993, at age seventy-seven due to complications of diabetes.

Claudia McNeil had an impressive and noteworthy career as an actress, singer, and entertainer. She was a devout Catholic who was known to say a prayer before every performance. She had a variety of interests that ranged from interior decorating to collecting milk glasses, antiques, and rare books. A serious dramatic actress, McNeil was continuously noted for her impressive and invigorating performances. At a time when roles for black actresses were few, Claudia McNeil brought depth and presence to every role she took. Although not nearly recognized enough, McNeil was a true grande dame of the theatrical world.

REFERENCES:

Bogle, Donald. *Toms, Coons, Mulattoes, Mammies, and Bucks.* New York: Viking Press, 1973.
———. *Brown Sugar.* New York: Harmony Books, 1980.
''Claudia McNeil, 77, an Actress Best Known for 'A Raisin in the Sun.''' *New York Times,* November 29, 1993.
Hine, Darlene Clark, ed. *Black Women in America.* Brooklyn: Carlson Publishing, 1993.
Mapp, Edward. *Directory of Blacks in the Performing Arts.* Metuchen, N.J.: Scarecrow Press, 1978.
Morton, Carol. ''Claudia McNeil—136 Pounds Lighter.'' *Ebony* 30 (September 1975): 70-75.
Notable Names in the American Theater. Clifton, N.J.: James T. White and Co., 1976.
Patterson, Lindsay, ed. *Black Films and Film-makers.* New York: Dodd, Mead, 1975.

Nicole D. Elliott

Carrie Meek
(1926-)
U.S. representative, educator, administrator

Carrie Meek, the first black lawmaker elected to represent Florida in the U.S. Congress, speaks in a soft, southern drawl. But underneath the gentle tone, she is full of spirit and commitment and rage at the injustices suffered by the poor. This sixty-seven-year-old grandmother from the ghetto in Miami, Florida, is in the 103rd Congress to represent the have-nots and the powerless. ''Most people my age are happy to go home and rock their grandchildren, but I am not ready for that,'' states the oldest freshman member in the U.S. House of Representatives. ''I am neither a political neophyte nor an outsider. I didn't run against congress. I ran to make congress look good,'' she said in the May 12, 1993, *Orlando News/Sun Sentinel.*

Born on April 29, 1926, in Tallahassee, Florida, Carrie Meek is the granddaughter of a slave named ''Miss Mandy,'' from Lilly, Georgia. Meek, the twelfth and youngest child of Carrie and Willie Pittman, was a premature baby who outlived her infant twin brother. Because of her petite size, the family nicknamed her ''Tot.'' Notwithstanding their indigent circumstances, Meek enjoyed her family life. While her father worked as a sharecropper and a caretaker of a large farm and collected rents, her mother worked as a domestic and laundress.

Growing up in a poor Tallahassee neighborhood called Black Bottom, Meek was well acquainted with segregation and poverty. During the 1930s and 1940s, blacks enjoyed few civil rights. She told the *Washington Post,* December 16, 1992,

> When I look and see what I endured, there's no wonder that I have some scars, even though I don't see them. When things happened, my rage can come up quickly and that rage, I'm sure, is buried within me from all those years, all those years of living under the worst kind of segregation.

During the era of segregation Meek experienced many indignities and cruelties. At that time she could not try on shoes, hats, and other clothing in the stores. If she ventured downtown, she found few rest rooms for ''colored.'' If thirsty, she had to search for a ''colored'' water fountain. Like all blacks, she was humiliated on the segregated transit system. While white children played in parks with baseball diamonds, play equipment, and swimming pools, she and her playmates were restricted to vacant lots.

Carrie Meek

Fortunately, Meek's education was not limited to inadequate schooling and dilapidated buildings. Florida Agricultural and Mechanical College (now University), a black college in Tallahassee, began a laboratory elementary school in which Meek enrolled. "Few black kids today get the same kind of education I was fortunate to receive," she told the *Washington Post*. Black teachers encouraged her and provided a curriculum that included black history. As a child, Meek became familiar with the writings of Richard Wright. She remembers attending a lecture on the peanut by George Washington Carver and also heard a lecture on race by W. E. B. Du Bois. She was always a tomboy, so it surprised no one when she showed a great interest in sports. In high school and college she ran anchor in the 440-yard relay. Although only five-feet five-inches tall, she became an avid basketball player and was known for her long shot.

After graduating as valedictorian from Florida A. and M. High School, Meek attended college there on campus. Limited finances prevented her from pursuing her dream of becoming a doctor. Instead, Meek decided to become a teacher, which was the main option for black women in a segregated labor market. After graduating from Florida A. and M. University with a major in physical education in 1946, she enrolled at the University of Michigan, where she received a master's degree in public health in 1948. She recalls leaving for Ann Arbor in 1946 on a segregated train with $150 wrapped in a handkerchief hidden in her bosom. At this time blacks were barred from attending graduate school at white colleges and universities in Florida. As compensation, the state of Florida paid the tuition and transportation costs for a few black students to attend predominantly white universities outside the South.

Armed with her master's degree, Meek taught first at Bethune-Cookman, a black college in Daytona Beach, Florida, and then at Florida A. and M. in Tallahassee. Eventually she was offered a position teaching physical education and health at the newly opened Miami-Dade Community College. The community college had two campuses: one for whites and one for blacks. In 1963, Miami-Dade Community College merged its two campuses; Meek was one of the people who agitated for integration. For thirty-one years, she taught at the college and was director of community service and continuing education. In 1979 she attended Florida Atlantic University for further study.

Meek Moves from Ghetto to Congress

Gradually Meek became involved in politics. Liberty City, the impoverished ghetto in Miami, became her power base. While most middle-class blacks moved away from the area, some still lived there who had good jobs and maintained average incomes. Meek was one of those who refused to leave. There were (and still are) many very poor persons living in Liberty City. According to Meek, one does not need to visit Somalia or Haiti to see poverty in its extreme. Outraged by the needs of the people, she decided to get involved in politics.

Meek said that her earlier experiences in college sports prepared her for politics. From sports she developed a competitive spirit and learned the give and take of games and the meaning of winning and losing. After participating in political rallies, meetings, and conventions, Meek finally decided to run for a seat in the Florida House of Representatives. She was elected in 1979 and served until 1983. In 1983 she was elected to the Florida Senate and served there until her election to the U.S. House of Representatives in 1992. During her career in Florida politics, Meek became known for her commitment to the poor, the blacks, and the elderly. From 1979 to 1992 Meek thrived in the rough-and-tumble world of Florida politics, in spite of the fact that white males ruled the capitol.

After winning the Democratic primary for the U.S. House of Representatives in September 1992 with 83 percent of the vote, Meek faced no Republican challenger in the general election. She had the honor of being the first black person to represent Florida in the U.S. Congress in the twentieth century. She said in the *Congressional Quarterly,* January 16, 1993, that the honor was a dubious one, since blacks from Florida should have had representation in the U.S. Congress decades ago.

Meek represents the Seventeenth Congressional District of Florida in the U.S. House of Representatives. The Seventeenth District has the state's largest number of black citizens and the most loyal Democratic constituents. Meek's district is predominantly black, yet she represents not only American-born blacks, Haitians, Jamaicans, Bahamians, and Dominicans, but also Arabs, Koreans, and whites. Meek arrived in Washington in January 1993 and has been on the go since then. She was the only freshman elected to the House in November 1992 who landed a place on the powerful Appropriations Committee. Traditionally, a position on this committee was earned by voting with the leadership, diligently performing committee work, and stroking people in high places. However, the House Speaker, Thomas S. Foley, added a freshman to the committee because there were so many newcomers.

Foley did not assign Meek to the Appropriations Committee just because she was a freshman legislator, however. Meek desired the position, and immediately after her election in November 1992, she went to Washington to approach members of the Congressional Black Caucus and influential women members of Congress in order to make her name known. She also sought support from the Florida delegation, which lost seats on the Appropriations Committee with the retirements of Democrats William Lehman and Lawrence J. Smith. She emphasized to the members of the House that she was a veteran legislator who had served on the Florida Appropriations Committee and that she did not run against congress but was there to work with them. Also to her advantage was the fact that the House leadership desired diversity among committee members. Meek, a female and black, obtained the appointment. On the Appropriations Committee she worked on two subcommittees—Military Construction and Energy and Water.

Problems of Haitian Refugees Addressed

Meek is as concerned about the Haitian refugees as she is with black Americans' problems. She is working to alter the government detention programs and to allow more Haitians to enter the country. A number of Haitian refugees have been maintained as prisoners on Guantanamo Bay because of their HIV-positive status. She has lobbied President Clinton on behalf of the Haitians. She said in *USA Today,* June 14, 1993, "It is a disgrace that we who pride ourselves on justice, compassion and freedom should turn away persons who have demonstrated a credible fear of persecution merely because they are ill." Meek believes that blacks will never find opportunities in America until they develop their own businesses and banks as the Cubans did. She feels that more state and federal programs, along with private investments, are necessary for blacks to secure financial power. She has seen many federal programs designed to help the poor that have had little or no effect. She recalls how white companies came in and took the money and left when the programs were over. Black administrators were equally guilty.

Meek has experienced racial rebellions in Florida, including the public turbulence in 1980 when eighteen people lost their lives and four hundred were wounded in three days of street violence. The violence erupted when Arthur McDuffie, a black insurance salesman, was killed by white police officers. As a result of McDuffie's death, the city was literally set afire. It looked like a war zone. Meek was on the scene as various speakers demanded justice. She told the *Washington Post,* December 16, 1992, "Things were done, they were done because people felt the rage. The rage in all of us comes out. Even in peaceful people like me."

Friends and foes claim her name is not indicative of her true temperament. On the surface Meek may appear calm, but underneath she has a fighting spirit that cannot be subdued. Meek has never thrown a brick at police officers, but she feels the anger of her constituents toward law enforcement officials. While she never joined the Black Panthers, she identified with their cause.

Jack Gordon, one of the leading liberals in the Florida Senate, knows Meek as a determined, knowledgeable, and professional person. He sees her as a hard worker who understands the issues she faces. Smart, humorous, and likeable, Meek does not let people control her. With her forceful personality, she is not overlooked. Gordon said that "she doesn't hesitate to speak up for what she considers black issues." Defending her, he said in the same article that she does not "mau-mau" anybody (that is, she does not constantly refer to whites as racist). On the other hand, Richard Langley, a conservative Florida state senator, respected her perseverance, although he found her politics loathsome. According to the *Washington Post,* he said that Meek "is a nice, well-meaning Christian lady. But she's another tax and spend liberal, and she's got tunnel vision as far as race is concerned." Langley described Meek as a motor mouth and a grandstander who saw everything in black and white. Speaking on her own behalf she said in the same article, "I didn't go into politics with a chip on my shoulder. But I let people up there know I expected to get the same results as anybody else."

Meek's admirers claim that she has the know-how to communicate the aspirations, hopes, and dreams of the downtrodden, working-class black Americans who are in need of health reform, better jobs, higher average incomes, and better housing for themselves and their children. Some of her legislative achievements include funding for fair housing enforcement and initiating Dade County's Model Surtax Housing Bill, which provides $12 million per year for low and moderate cost housing.

A divorcee, Meek is the mother of three children, who are now grown. In addition to her daughter Sheila, Meek has another daughter and one son, Kendrick. Sheila Davis remembers her mother as a hard-working single parent. Davis told the *Washington Post* that Meek "was the total and sole breadwinner. Some people do get alimony and child support; my mother did not. She had all the pressure of a high-profile career, but there wasn't a high-profile salary to go with it." Davis speaks of her mother's determined personality: "I think people should understand this is not someone you want to cross. My mother is funny and warm and friendly, but she is very tough. She had to be." Her daughter stated that her mother has been a politician as long as she can remember. As children, she and her sister and brother were taken from one political rally, convention, or meeting to another. Meek's two former husbands, both of whom she divorced, are dead.

Meek still owns her modest home with hedges and burglar bars on the edge of Liberty City, the Miami ghetto. When in Miami she attends the Union Grave Missionary Baptist Church. But wherever she is, Carrie Meek, a newcomer in the U.S. Congress, carries with her a concern for the urban poor, regardless of race.

Current Address: 404 Cannon House Office Building, Independence Ave, Washington, DC 20515-0917.

REFERENCES:

Congressional Quarterly 51, suppl. no. 3, January 16, 1993, 71.
"D.C. Welcomes Woman to Congress." *San Francisco Examiner,* December 2, 1992.
"Haitians Arrive Today." *USA Today,* June 14, 1993.
"Meek Hath Inherited." *Scottsdale (Arizona) Press,* December 1992.
"Meek: Making History at Age 66." *Miami Herald,* January 5, 1993.
"Piece of Cake." *Orlando News/Sun Sentinel,* May 12, 1993.
"Tardy Arrival Fails to Dim Spirits of Meek's Fans." *Miami Herald,* January 5, 1993.
"The Woman from Liberty City." *Washington Post,* December 16, 1992.

Joan C. Elliott

Mabel Mercer

Mabel Mercer
(1900-1984)
Singer

Mabel Mercer's influence and impact as a singer extended far beyond those for whom she performed, even though her public was vast and very appreciative. Yet, she stressed intimacy, both in delivery and in terms of the small audiences of the cabarets and clubs she favored as performance sites. Fans came from Europe and the West Coast to hear her perform in the St. Regis Room in New York in 1975 and at her concert in Town Hall with Bobby Short in 1968. Her influence on others of her profession was profound, and her singing affected the styles of more than a dozen major performing artists. As a performer, she was the quintessential cabaret singer of the old school. Her style was personalized and intimate, and she focused directly on her individual listeners. She was a superior interpreter of lyrics, projecting feelings and text outward. At its best, Mercer's music was wrapped in warm emotion and vibrant feeling. She imbued her songs with the innuendo and cadences of speech, so that the art of singing was deemphasized and words and music blended into a poetic whole.

Mabel Mercer was born in Burton-on-Trent, Staffordshire, England, on February 3, 1900. Her mother was an English vaudeville entertainer, and her father was a black American jazz musician. Her father died before she was born. Her mother later remarried. Mercer learned to sing and dance early and, after leaving school at age fourteen, joined her aunt's vaudeville troupe. She later toured England with a singing group and was invited on a tour of the Continent. She settled in Paris in the 1920s, meeting Ada "Bricktop" Smith and performing at several venues before beginning a lengthy engagement (1931-38) at Bricktop's Cafe. At this time Bricktop's was an important Paris cabaret, frequented by a very famous international clientele including Ernest Hemingway, the Duke and Duchess of Windsor, F. Scott Fitzgerald, Gertrude Stein, Cole Porter, and many others.

Mercer left Paris at the outbreak of World War II, going first to New York in 1938, then to the Bahamas, where she married Kelsey Pharr, a noted American jazz musician. She returned to New York in 1941. Her marriage to Pharr subsequently ended in divorce and she did not remarry. Her residence remained in New York, where her career centered around several clubs and cabarets, notably Le Ruban Bleu, Tony's, the Byline Room, and the St. Regis Room. She purchased a farm in Chatham, New York, in the 1950s. At first this was her retreat between performances, but gradually it became her primary residence. She performed well into the final years of her life in the 1980s, presenting her public with a career of some seventy years on stage and more than fifty years as an honored major artist.

Develops an Influential Personal Style

Mercer's importance and influence as an artist cannot be overstated. As a singer, she stressed interpretation and projection of feeling over vocal expression. She sang more than a thousand songs in her lengthy career and reported having at least one hundred "at the ready" at a given time. Her repertoire featured the songs of Alec Wilder and Cole Porter. Wilder is particularly noted for his sensitive texts and for adapting or matching melodic and poetic nuances. Perhaps for these reasons Wilder's approach made his works favorites among the cabaret set in post-World War I London and Paris. Certainly, they suited Mercer's style. As for Cole Porter, sensitive melodies are his strong point, and Mercer reported singing his songs to him while seated at his table at Bricktop's Cafe in the 1930s.

Mercer credits her famous style, which emphasizes diction, lyrics, and projection, to her mother's early tutelage. At an early age, she would ask Mabel to sing to an empty theater from the stage while she sat in the balcony. Her mother stressed from the outset that her diction must be clear and sharp and that the listener must be able to understand every word. So it remained throughout her career, as is amply testified by her critics and fans alike. Composers and writers, particularly, praised her attention to conveying the message of the lyrics.

Her voice is not her strong point; rather, her delivery and presentation define her style. According to her obituary in the April 21, 1984, issue of the *New York Times,* Alec Wilder referred to her delivery as a graceful parlando, and, speaking about her interpretations, called her "the guardian of the tenuous dreams created by the writers of songs." Perhaps because of their internal lyricism, some songs remained favorites of hers throughout her career, especially "The End of a Love Affair," by Bud Redding, "While We Were Young," by Alec Wilder, and "Fly Me to the Moon," by Bart Howard. Other songs she often featured included Dorothy Fields and Jerome Kern's "Remind Me," Cy Coleman's "The Riviera," and Richard Rodgers and Lorenz Hart's "Little Boy Blue," which she championed faithfully for ten years before Frank Sinatra, Lena Horne, and Margaret Whiting also began to sing the song.

Another aspect of her performance, her tendency to sing seated, also developed early. As she tells it, in Paris she was sometimes requested to sit down and sing a song next to a customer. She developed an impersonal way of doing this, and then decided to take this approach onto the stage, singing from a chair. This added a note of intimacy to her stage manner. It became a hallmark of her stage presence, together with her formal attire and regal bearing. It was this well-known image that her friends celebrated by placing a Queen Anne chair atop her birthday cake at her seventy-fifth birthday party at the St. Regis Roof in New York on February 3, 1975.

Singer Focuses on Clubs and Cabarets

After Mercer launched her career in Paris in the 1930s she came to the United States, where she focused on performing in major clubs and cabarets, mostly in New York. Like many other cabaret singers, she preferred staying at one congenial site for a relatively long engagement. Thus, in some

fifty years as a cabaret singer and artist, she performed engagements of some seven years each at Bricktop's in Paris and Tony's and the Byline Room in New York. She averaged six months at several other sites, including the St. Regis Room, the Cafe Carlyle, and Downstairs at the Upstairs. She also had Stints at Cleo's, The Playboy Club in London, and The Mocambo in San Francisco.

Her television credits include a 1972 PBS special, *An Evening with Mabel Mercer and Bobby Short and Friends,* and a five-part BBC special entitled *Miss Mercer in Mayfair,* celebrating her return to London to perform after an absence of forty years. Her concert engagements included a Town Hall concert with Bobby Short in 1968, repeated in 1969, and concerts at Alice Tully Hall in New York and the Dorothy Chandler Pavilion in Los Angeles.

Perhaps Mercer's greatest legacy may be witnessed in the impact she has had on the many major artists who have listened very closely to her singing and become professionally indebted to her in elements of style and manner of presentation. Those she influenced include Frank Sinatra, Bobby Short, Margaret Whiting, Billie Holiday, Mary Lou Williams, Eileen Farrell, Nat King Cole, Barbara Cook, Hugh Shannon, Peggy Lee, Lena Horne, Tony Bennett, Johnny Mercer, Johnny Mathis, Leontyne Price, and Barbara Streisand. Frank Sinatra termed her his best music teacher, stating that "she taught me everything I know"; Bobby Short termed her the guiding light of his career and praised her determination and strength; Margaret Whiting said that her whole world of music and singing changed when she heard Mercer perform; Billie Holiday listened to her regularly while Mercer was performing at Tony's on Fifty-second Street in New York in the 1940s—so much so that Holiday almost lost her job at a club across the street, so the story goes; working in another medium, Mary Lou Williams, jazz pianist and a lifelong friend of Mercer's, stated that she applied Mercer's way of shaping a musical line to her piano phrasing. Eileen Farrell and Mercer performed together in concert in 1982.

Mercer is well represented on records. Atlantic Records, commemorating her seventy-fifth birthday in 1975, issued a four-record boxed set, *A Tribute to Mabel Mercer,* which summarized her long and impressive career. Stanyan Records reissued a previously issued Decca album, *Mabel Mercer for Always* in 1975. Also available at that time were Atlantic's three-disc set, *The Art of Mabel Mercer, Mabel Mercer and Bobby Short at Town Hall* (two discs), and her *Mabel Mercer Sings Cole Porter* (available separately on Atlantic and also included in the four-record seventy-fifth birthday set). Some of these recordings are still available on cassette or CD. In addition, a video, *Mabel Mercer, Forever and Always,* was released in 1990 by VIEW Video, recorded at a late career engagement at Cleo's supper club.

During the 1960s and 1970s writers often commented on Mercer's diminished vocal range, particularly in the upper register. Mercer herself agreed, in the February 26, 1970 *Washington Post* she termed her range a "basso profundo," with a "strange, gravelly middle register." Nevertheless, she stated that her prime emphasis was always on the clarity of the lyrics and "telling a story." She made the point to Hallie I. West for the *Washington Post* that sadness, to her, is the strongest emotion. She cautioned, however, "I'm not a sad-hearted person. I have a healthy detachment about my songs." Her aim, she said, was not to sing about her own personal feelings, but about those of the listener, making the song come alive for her audience.

Triumphant Final Performances

For a while, in the 1970s, she became selective with regard to her appearances, choosing them sparingly. Towards the end of her career, however, Mercer returned to full activity. In 1977 she appeared full-voiced at a Carnegie Hall concert. She traveled to London for the first time in forty years, performing at the Playboy Club and appearing in the five-part BBC-TV special, *Miss Mercer in Mayfair*. In 1978 she appeared at the Mocambo in San Francisco and at the Dorothy Chandler Pavilion in Los Angeles. In 1981 she was honored by eighteen composers and performers at the Whitney Museum in New York, at an evening entitled "The American Cabaret." She gave two performances in 1982 at the Kool Jazz Festival in New York. She also gave a concert of Alec Wilder songs in Alice Tully Hall in 1982, as well as a duo concert with Eileen Farrell, finishing the evening with two dramatic readings.

Mercer was feted at a gala seventy-fifth birthday party at the St. Regis Roof, attended by about four hundred of her friends and admirers. She sat with Roy Wilkins, and those present included Bobby Short, Cy Coleman, Alexis Smith, Helen Merrill, Greta Keller, Julius Monk, Jimmy Daniels, Ada "Bricktop" Smith, Margaret Whiting, *New York Times* critic John W. Wilson, *New Yorker* critic Whitney Balliett, Jimmy Daniels, Sylvia Sims, Mary Lou Williams, Ruth Warwick, and Hugh Shannon.

Stereo Review magazine presented its first Award of Merit to Mercer in 1974 and later renamed the award the Mabel Mercer Award, given for outstanding contributions to the quality of American musical life. Recent recipients of the award include Frank Sinatra in 1984 and Isaac Stern in 1985. Additional awards she has received include an honorary doctorate of music from Berkeley College of Music in 1975, the Whitney Museum Award in 1981, and the Presidential Medal of Freedom, presented to her by President Ronald Reagan in 1983.

A *Life* magazine portrait article in 1965 celebrates her fifty years on stage and captures her relaxing at her farm in Chatham, New York, still at the peak of her lengthy career. Whitney Balliett, for his September 6, 1982, *New Yorker* article, also visited her farm, describing graceful, comfortable living in a homey atmosphere. Her friends often visited, and she was close to nature, loved animals and flowers, and kept many pets. Congenial with her neighbors, she was a graceful hostess and an excellent cook whose recipes were frequently published. Alec Wilder gave her a hickory tree on her seventy-fifth birthday, and he was a frequent visitor to her farm, taking pleasure in the rejuvenating qualities of the place and its setting. The farm gradually became a full-time residence

where she could enjoy the relaxing comfort of country life and the company of her friends. Following her concert activity in the fall of 1983, she suffered coronary illness and died in Pittsfield (Massachusetts) Hospital of respiratory arrest on April 20, 1984.

After Mercer's death, a foundation was established in her name to promote and revitalize cabaret singing as an art form. Donald Smith directs the Mabel Mercer Foundation and is a strong advocate of cabaret singing, as well as being the leading publicist and promoter in this country of this once-thriving art form.

To her public, Mabel Mercer left a legacy of more than fifty years as a solo performer. She is remembered for her unique approach to the presentation of a song: intimate, focused on the audience, with crisp pronunciation and tasteful attention to emotional nuances. Her lyricism and precise diction set a standard for many major singers who openly stated their indebtedness to her artistic treatment of the poetic aspects of the text. Her contribution reached singers from Sinatra to Streisand, Short to Minelli, and echoes of her style will continue to be heard on the concert stage and on recordings for years to come.

REFERENCES:

"Awards and Premiers." *Black Perspective in Music* 9 (Fall 1981): 243.

Balliett, Whitney. *American Singers*. New York: Oxford University Press, 1979.

———. "Our Footloose Correspondents in the Country." *New Yorker* 58 (September 6, 1982): 40-49.

Bogle, Donald. *Brown Sugar*. New York: Harmony Books, 1980.

Clark, Donald, ed. *Penguin Encyclopedia of Popular Music*. London: Penguin Group, 1989.

Current Biography. New York: H. W. Wilson, 1973.

Dahl, Linda. *Stormy Weather*. New York: Pantheon Books, 1984.

Hemming, Ron. "The New Erteguns' New York—New York Cabaret Music." *Stereo Review* 54 (February 1989): 150-51.

Hentoff, Nat. "Mabel Mercer Sings Cole Porter." *The Progressive* 49 (November 1985): 41.

Hine, Darlene Clark, ed. *Black Women in America*. Brooklyn: Carlson Publishing, 1993.

Hitchcock, H. Wiley, ed. *New Grove Dictionary of American Music*. London: Macmillan, 1986.

"Inner Sorrow." *Washington Post,* February 26, 1970.

Kupferberg, Herbert. "Isaac Stern, This Year's Recipient of the Mabel Mercer Award Is Truly a Fiddler to the World." *Stereo Review* 50 (February 1985): 45-49.

"Mabel Mercer." Obituary. *Time* 23 (April 30, 1984): 68.

"Mabel Mercer's 50th Year on Stage." *Life* 59 (October 15, 1965): 123-25.

"Mabel Mercer, Phraser of Songs, Dies." Obituary. *New York Times,* April 21, 1984.

"Mabel Mercer, the Queenly Piper of Song." *New York Times,* February 23, 1975.

"Mabel Mercer, Storyteller in Song, Hailed at 75." *New York Times,* February 4, 1975.

Mandel, Howard. "Mabel Mercer." Record review. *Down Beat* 57 (August 1990): 61.

Mapp, Edward. *Directory of Blacks in the Performing Arts.* 2d ed. Metuchen, N.J.: Scarecrow Press, 1990.

Reilly, Peter. "Mabel Mercer Sings Cole Porter." *Stereo Review* 50 (November 1985): 116.

"Singer Mabel Mercer Dies at 84." Obituary. *Variety* (April 25, 1984): 87.

Slonimsky, Nicholas J., ed. *Baker's Biographical Dictionary of Music and Musicians.* 8th ed., rev. New York: Schirmer Books, 1992.

Southern, Eileen. *Biographical Dictionary of Afro-American and African Musicians.* Westport, Conn.: Greenwood Press, 1982.

Tyler, Ralph, "'Bare Bones' Cabaret in Danger of Becoming a Showbiz Fossil." *Variety* 336 (October 11-12, 1989): 198.

Who's Who in America, 1976-77. Chicago: Marquis Who's Who, 1977.

Who's Who of American Women, 1969-70. 6th ed. Chicago: A.N. Marquis, 1970.

Darius L. Thieme

Stephanie Mills

Stephanie Mills

(1957-)

Singer, actress, entertainer

Stephanie Mills, who went from child star to teen Grammy Award-winner to adult singing sensation, is one of the most dynamic, resilient, and versatile entertainers to grow up on the stage. She first entertained audiences as a toddler. In her teen years, she portrayed Dorothy in the Tony Award-winning show *The Wiz,* a black musical based on the classic children's tale *The Wonderful Wizard of Oz* by L. Frank Baum. It was Mills's captivating voice in that successful show that catapulted her to fame. On stage and off, Mills has demonstrated perseverance and determination. And, under the scrutiny of critics and fans alike, she has grown and matured in the challenging arenas of popular music and rhythm and blues. The "plain" young woman with a voice that almost seems too big for her has blossomed into a graceful, humble, and tenacious African American role model.

Stephanie Mills, born March 22, 1957, in Brooklyn, New York, to Joseph Mills and Christine Mills, is the second youngest of six siblings. In the family lineup, Stephanie Mills is the baby girl. Her sister Audrey is eight years older than Stephanie. Her older brother, Joey, is ten years her senior. Her other older sisters are Waliyyah Salaam and Judy, who is now an actress in Los Angeles. She has a younger brother, Allen.

Hers was not an entertainment family; Joseph Mills worked for the City of New York and Christine Mills worked as a hairdresser.

Yet early on, Mills loved music. As a youngster, she listened to the radio and sang and danced around the house as if she was a movie star. She was such a tiny thing that her doting siblings, especially her sisters, treated her like a baby doll, sometimes dressing her three times a day.

Later, everyplace became her stage and anyone who would pay attention became her audience. When she was three years old, while most kids her age were just learning to form sentences, Mills entertained her family with songs. When she grew older and started school, her voice became a familiar one at many school functions. By the time she turned seven, she was baptized and singing in the choir at the Cornerstone Baptist Church in Brooklyn. So impressive was the voice that erupted from this small child that her older siblings trotted her around Brooklyn from one talent show to another.

In recalling her childhood and its musical influences in a 1983 story in the *Chicago Tribune,* Mills talked about her early musical inclinations:

> Nobody pushed me into anything. . . . I just loved music. If I had to name one person that I consider an inspiration, it would be Diana Ross, but I like a lot of other people too—Barbara Streisand, Carly Simon, Dolly Parton. I always was listening to the radio, and I used to sing at home and in church. I always wanted to sing.

Age deepened her determination. When Mills was nine, she answered an advertisement in the *New York Post* calling for youngsters to audition for a Broadway show. Mills auditioned about three times, and her singing and dancing landed her a small role in the musical *Maggie Flynn,* starring Shirley Jones and Jack Cassidy. Others who shared the stage with her in the production included *Fame* star Irene Cara and Sharon Brown, who later starred in the Broadway hit *Dreamgirls.* Three months later, *Maggie Flynn* flopped. Far too ambitious to be discouraged, Mills kept busy. She moved on to the Negro Ensemble Company Workshop, an off-Broadway troupe. She performed at her sister's homecoming dance and continued to sing at the Cornerstone Baptist Church. At age eleven, the spunky girl with the grown-up voice mustered up the nerve to face the Amateur Hour audience at Harlem's legendary Apollo Theater. Mills thrilled the crowds for six weeks running. After each performance, she walked away as the first-place winner. Her exuberance and professionalism not only delighted the audiences, but also the theater owners, who offered Mills her first professional booking—a week's engagement as an opening act for the Isley Brothers.

Easing Down the Road to Stardom

Little came of Mills's 1974 debut single, *I Knew It Was Love.* However, Mills's record and her powerful mezzo-soprano caught the attention of Ken Harper, who was gearing up for an all-black Broadway musical. As she recalled in the October 2, 1983, *Chicago Tribune:*

He asked me to audition for him and after three auditions I got the part. I had seen the "Wizard of Oz" movie, starring Judy Garland, on television when I was a kid and I had always enjoyed the fantasy. I never thought about doing the role myself. And when I started playing Dorothy, I never tried to recreate what Judy Garland did. I couldn't touch that. That was her movie and she made her mark with it. What I had to do was to make Dorothy my role by bringing all of my emotions to the part and thinking about how a little black girl would react to finding herself in Kansas and meeting a scarecrow and a witch and all those other weird people.

From the opening night's dazzling performance until the close of the show, Mills was the Wiz kid in *The Wiz,* which ran from 1974 to 1979. During the show's run, Mills used her electrifying voice to turn "When I Think of Home" into a song that America associated as much with her as "Somewhere Over the Rainbow" had been associated with Judy Garland. Mills helped to make *The Wiz* one of Broadway's longest running plays. As she did, her popularity grew. She became a familiar face on television talk shows, sang for the president, and visited the White House as a guest.

After leaving the show, Mills toured as the opening act for Teddy Pendergrass, the Commodores, the O'Jays, and Neil Sedaka until she became a headline act. According to Craig W. Reid in *Sepia* magazine: "She performed to rave reviews, and from that point on, it became apparent that her bubble was not going to burst until super-stardom was achieved. You'd think that she would have gotten caught up in the "little brat" syndrome, but those who know her claim that her small feet remained planted to the ground."

From 1979 to 1981, Mills churned out gold and platinum albums. From her came such popular tunes as "What 'Cha Gonna . . . Do with My Loving," "Put Your Body In It," "Keep Away Girls," "How Come U Don't Call Me Anymore," "Sweet Sensation," "Never Knew Love Like This Before," and "The Medicine Song." According to *Billboard* magazine charts, in 1979 Mills's *What 'Cha Gonna Do . . . with My Loving* album was number twenty-two on the charts for nine weeks. The next year, her *Sweet Sensation* album, containing the hit "Never Knew Love Like This Before," burrowed in at number sixteen for twenty-two weeks.

Mills had made her mark. In 1980 "Never Knew Love Like This Before" became a million-selling pop single. That year songs such as "Feel the Fire" and "Take Me in Your Arms Tonight" won her a Grammy for Best Female R and B Vocalist. A year later, her vocal gift earned her an American Music Award, also in the category of Best Female R and B Vocalist. Critics raved about her shows. Craig W. Reid wrote in *Sepia* magazine:

Ms. Mills's show is as flawless as her album. Her throat defying voice and Broadway showmanship come together on stage and give her an awesome presence that has had a devastating effect on audiences from her native New York to San Francisco. It is no coincidence that her name is on the tips of more and more people's tongues when they talk about "the baddest lady on the music scene."

Mills Swept Up by the Cyclones

In 1978, ironically, the girl who created the role of Dorothy in the Broadway production of *The Wiz* was snubbed when plans were made for a movie version. The part went to Diana Ross. Mills was not even asked to audition for the part. Later, Mills would say that she was "hurt but not jealous."

According to Craig Reid, some people agreed that, if Stephanie Mills *was* jealous about the movie version, losing it to Diana Ross would have softened the disappointment because Mills had long idolized Ross. Reid also noted,

Ms. Mills seemed more disturbed by that fact that the motion picture was short of its self-proclaimed expectations than the fact that she was not part of it. Mills told *Sepia* "*The Wiz*" could have been the first black classic and it just wasn't that. The film was good for the way that it was done, but it could have been a whole lot better.

Up to this point, Mills lived with her family and led a very sheltered life. The siblings that cuddled her as an infant now became very protective. Mills was a superstar and her family wanted nothing to ruin what clearly had the markings of a promising career. With the money Mills earned from her success, she bought the family a twenty-seven-room house in Mount Vernon, New York.

A tightly knit group, little came between members of the Mills family. Yet at age twenty-three, the baby girl was lonely. She had sung incredible love songs, but now Mills longed for love and marriage for herself. So, when the opportunity presented itself in the form of a handsome, caring, charming young suitor, it was the most natural thing in the world for Mills to fall head over heels.

A mutual friend brought Mills and Jeffrey Daniel together, telling Mills that the two would be perfect for one another. For Mills, it was love at first sight. On June 13, 1980, Mills wed the tall, talented Jeffrey Daniel, then a singer with the soul group Shalamar. It should have been the most glorious and joyful time in her life, but her marriage dissolved before her eyes. After a turbulent period—helped along by disapproving, but well-intentioned family members and friends of both young singers—Mills filed for divorce in September 1981. The couple had no children. Mills commented on the breakup of her marriage in the February 1982 *Ebony:* "We needed time to let our marriage take root and grow, but time was something we didn't have enough of because of our careers. He was away from home a lot with Shalamar, and I was on the road, too. I think we both wanted the marriage to work, but it just didn't."

Meanwhile, her public popularity hit a slump. According to *Ebony* magazine: "Privately, insiders whispered the phrase that, in Hollywood could spell the end of a career: Stephanie Mills, they said, had peaked." Now Mills and her manager had "the seemingly impossible task of proving to an unbelieving industry that both Stephanie and her sound could regenerate the kind of excitement it took to sell millions of records and make it back to the top of the charts."

During this time, Mills recalled in *Ebony:*

I used to take everything, particularly the rejection, very personally. If a record didn't sell, I assumed it was because of me, my sound, because of something I did or didn't do. It took me a long while to understand just how large a part politics plays in this business, that many times it's not necessarily talent that determines if a record will sell or a role will be given, but whose money or marketing or power is behind you. Before that realization took hold, there were some pretty low days.

Rainbow Seen at End of Storm

Though adored by millions and idolized by black and white youth, in the early years Mills suffered from a poor self-image brought on mostly by the superficial standards that often made European features the beauty standard in the entertainment fields. Mills, with radiant brown skin and striking African features, did not recognize her beauty. She grew up being teased because of her small stature and her wide nose. She felt as if she were the classic ugly duckling. She told *Ebony* magazine in March of 1988: "I was always the shortest kid in the class, wore braces and the guys called

me 'Train Tracks.' I used to read fashion magazines and wish I could look like the models. It has only been recently that that feeling has gone away."

While entertainers such as Diana Ross, Donna Summer, and Jayne Kennedy were considered pretty girl stars, Mills was said to be plain. When producers rejected her for some singing and acting roles because she did not have the right look, Mills resorted to cosmetic surgery to make her nose less prominent.

Through the storms, Mills held her peace and concentrated on refueling her career and reexamining her personal life. More and more she turned to the things she had always been able to depend on—mostly family and God.

In 1981 her new album, *Stephanie,* landed at number thirty on the charts and remained there for five weeks. During the spring of 1983, Mills diversified and expanded her acting to television. She appeared in successive episodes of ABC's *Love Boat* and took a two-week stint as a singer on the NBC soap opera *Search for Tomorrow.*

Stephanie Mills Is Home Again

In late 1984, Mills returned to Broadway in *The Wiz.* The second time around, Mills was as captivating and believable a Dorothy as she had been a decade before. Her return to the stage was marked with the vigor and fervor she had exhibited ten years earlier. When the show ended, she again turned to recording.

A rejuvenated Mills produced five number one R and B hits between 1986 and 1992. They were: "I Have Learned to Respect the Power of Love," "I Feel Good All Over," "(You're Puttin') A Rush on Me," "Something in the Way You Make Me Feel," and "Home" (from *The Wiz*). In 1987 "If I Were Your Woman" catapulted the singer to number nine on the charts for nine weeks. In 1992 Mills released an album of Christmas classics and a new soul album titled *Something Real.* She returned to *The Wiz* for the third time and took the show on tour across the country. It did not matter that the show was now in its third revival; audiences greeted Mills with enthusiasm.

Offstage, Mills made a few changes in her personal life. After living in Los Angeles for about a decade, she traded the hustle and bustle of that city for the relative peace and quiet of North Carolina. All the triumphs and trials had brought her almost full circle. Instead of the insecure young entertainer who wandered into the limelight as an adolescent, Mills was a new woman with a new attitude about life, love, and work. In 1992 *Ebony* quoted her as saying:

I learned something from all the experiences that has made me the person I am today. I've undergone a spiritual renewal from 1990 to 1992. It has been very educational to me in learning myself, through my music and through therapy. I'm really getting to know what Stephanie wants to do. Before, I was just a puppet entertainer. Things were done for me and around me. Now, I control everything, and that's a good feeling.

The diminutive Mills is a size four and weighs about ninety-seven pounds. Her sculptured figure took three years to perfect and fits well with her sexy new image.

Over the years, Mills has remained close to her family and has learned that "when all of that other stuff—fame, money—is gone, your family will still be there." Several family members comprise part of her personal and business management organization, including Cassandra Mills, her sister-in-law and manager.

Mills married again in 1992. According to the *Charlotte Observer*, she married Michael Saunders, a program director for a Charlotte, North Carolina, radio station (WPEG 98-FM). Saunders is a native of Chester, South Carolina. The couple lived in Charlotte until late 1994 when they moved to Hollywood where Saunders took a job as band director and consultant with Lest Bank Management, which manages artists ranging from Luther Vandross and Tony! Toni! Tone! to Richard Marx and Meat Loaf. The company also manages Mills. Saunders said he would not be managing his wife.

Mills is a perfectionist and has learned to guard her privacy. Away from the stage and concert halls, she is a homebody and an avid reader. She loves movies, football games, basketball games, and wrestling. She also enjoys playing tennis. When she can get away, Mills loves to travel, especially "to Japan, 'cause it's the only place where all the clothes are my size," she joked during a 1987 interview with the *Chicago Tribune*. Mills stays fit and keeps her energy up with a diet of fish and chicken and no red meat. One of her favorite outlets is working with Hale House in New York, an organization that cares for abandoned babies and babies born to drug-addicted mothers, as well as the mothers of such children.

REFERENCES:

"Bringing Up Baby: Stephanie Mills in the Family Spotlight." *Washington Post,* May 19, 1980.

Campbell, Bebe Moore. "A Sassy New Stephanie." *Essence* 18 (January 1988): 60-62, 92.

Detroit Free Press, October 10, 1982.

Detroit Free Press, October 7, 1986.

"Detroit's in Love with Stephanie Mills." *Michigan Chronicle,* July 7-13, 1993.

"Dreamgirl's Voice Stirs Audience." *Detroit Free Press,* October 7, 1982.

"Grown Up but Still a 'Wiz' Kid at Heart." *Chicago Tribune,* October 2, 1983.

"Hot Buttons." *Charlotte Observer,* October 28, 1994.

"Mills Has 'Something Real.'" *Tennessean Showcase,* December 13, 1992.

"Musical Couple Heads West." *Charlotte Observer,* September 28, 1994.

Norment, Lynn. "The New Stephanie Mills." *Ebony* 68 (December 1992): 32, 38, 40, 134.

Reid, Craig W. "Stephanie Mills: 'The Wiz' Girl." *Sepia* 29 (April 1980): 56-61.

Sanders, Charles L. "Stephanie Mills: The Painful Education of a Young Superstar." *Ebony* 57 (February 1982): 36-38, 40.

"Sound Judgement." *Detroit Free Press,* October 10, 1982.

"Stephanie Mills: New Look, New Life, New Love." *Ebony* 63 (March 1988): 27-28, 32, 35.

"Stephanie Mills: The Wiz Kid becomes Quite a Lady." *Black Stars* 8 (July 1979): 24-26.

Whitburn, Joel. *The Billboard of Top 40 Albums.* Revised and enlarged ed. New York: Billboard Books, 1991.

Who's Who among Black Americans, 1993-1994. 8th ed. Detroit: Gale Research, 1994.

Who's Who in Entertainment, 1992-1993. 2d ed. Wilmette, Ill.: Marquis Who's Who, 1993.

"Wiz to Whiz: Fame Has an Apt Pupil in Stephanie Mills." *Chicago Tribune,* August 16, 1987.

Sandra D. Davis

Leona Mitchell
(1949-)
Opera singer

Since the mid-1970s Leona Mitchell has been regarded as a leading American lyric-spinto soprano—a lyric soprano with dramatic qualities. Mitchell herself dislikes such rigid categorization, preferring to call herself simply a soprano. She has appeared throughout the world in operas, concerts, and recitals. She has also distinguished herself on recordings and in television, and she made her film debut in the early 1980s, starring in *Yes Giorgio* with the famous tenor Luciano Pavarotti.

Mitchell made her debut with the Metropolitan Opera in 1975, in the role of Micaela in Georges Bizet's *Carmen,* a role that she sang when she made her professional debut in 1972 with the San Francisco Spring Opera. She made her European opera debut with the Geneva Opera in 1976. During the 1978-79 season, Mitchell sang twelve Micaelas at the Metropolitan, as well as Mademoiselle Lidoine in *Dialogues of the Carmelites* by Poulenc and Pamina and the Celestial Voice in *Don Carlo* by Verdi. She has sung at all of the major opera houses of the world. Critics continuously extol her outstanding vocal capabilities and musical instincts.

The tenth of fifteen children, Leona Pearl Mitchell was born on October 13, 1949. She was raised in the small town of Enid, Oklahoma. Her father, Hulon Mitchell, was a Church of God in Christ minister and her mother, Pearl Olive Leatherman Mitchell, was a nurse and piano teacher. Of her early years, Mitchell remembers that she realized how many children there were in the family when she was called on to wash the dishes. She further remembers that there was "every kind of musical instrument in the house. . . . [W]e all played by ear."

Leona Mitchell

All fifteen children sang in Hulon Mitchell's choir. The family formed the Musical Mitchells gospel group and traveled throughout Oklahoma, appearing in concert as well as on radio and television.

Mitchell's vocal talents were recognized when she was very young by members of her family, church, and school. Throughout high school, her favorite subjects were foreign languages and history and she had visions of becoming an ambassador. When one of her high school teachers encouraged her to listen to an opera recording, she remembered in the March 20, 1983, *New York Times,* it was quite an experience, "the most wonderful thing I had ever heard."

The recipient of the first full scholarship granted to a voice major by Oklahoma City University, Mitchell entered the school at age seventeen. During the course of an interview with Sarah Moore Hall for *People* magazine, September 3, 1979, Mitchell recounted her first experience with opera as a performer.

> It was a workshop production of something called "The Story of Ruth.". . . I had to be dragged into it. When you're from Enid, you've hardly ever heard of opera. I was a freshman and thought "Moon River" was serious music.

By college graduation in 1971, Mitchell had performed ten leading roles; studied ballet, modern dance, and foreign languages; and completed the necessary academic and music courses to complete her degree. Mitchell has never regretted her choice of school. She told Stephen Wadsworth for *Opera News,* February 10, 1979, "I had very good training there.

Now that I've seen a lot of other singers from other . . . schools, I'm grateful." In turn the state has been proud of her. As the first native of Oklahoma to sing with the Metropolitan Opera, she received an "Outstanding Oklahoman" citation in 1975, and the same year she was named "Ambassadress of Enid." Her alma mater awarded her an honorary doctorate of music in 1979 and her induction into the Oklahoma Hall of Fame took place in 1983.

Mitchell married in 1971, but became a widow in 1973 when her husband was killed in a car accident. In 1980, she married Elmer Bush III, whom she met in Los Angeles while performing the role of Bess in George Gershwin's folk-opera *Porgy and Bess.* Bush, then a teacher in the Los Angeles Public School System and a member of the Albert McNeil Jubilee Singers, later took a leave of absence from teaching in order to serve as Mitchell's road manager. During the course of a 1987 interview with Gary Schmidgall for *Opera News,* Mitchell said, "Elmer has a settling effect on my career. He's a calm individual, sees things logically and keeps an eye off into the future, which balances nicely the emotions and temperament of my world behind and on the stage."

Mitchell's first solo album, *Presenting Leona Mitchell with Kurt Herbert Adler: An Operatic Partnership,* was recorded in 1979 in Kingwall Hall, London, and was released by London and Decca Records in 1980. Mitchell and Adler recorded nine arias with the National Philharmonic Orchestra, and both described the experience as a "very special collaboration." The Mitchell/Adler collaboration and friendship began in 1971, shortly following Mitchell's graduation from college. She was a contestant in the San Francisco Opera Auditions and Adler, then general director of the San Francisco Opera, was a judge. Mitchell had already won over thirty vocal competitions.

Auditioning for the San Francisco competition with "Ernani, involami" from Guiseppe Verdi's *Ernani,* a very difficult selection, Mitchell garnered a marvelous ovation from the audience and won the first prize, the James H. Schwabacher Award. The prize carried with it the opportunity to study under Adler's supervision for ten weeks as a participant in the Merola Opera Program, with an apprenticeship in Santa Fe. It was in 1973 when Adler first engaged Mitchell to sing the Micaela role for the San Francisco Spring Opera and gave her two smaller parts, "suited to a fledgling," with the San Francisco Opera.

Singer Gains International Attention

Mitchell had attracted international attention in 1975 with her performance of Bess in London Records' complete recording of Gershwin's *Porgy and Bess.* The orchestra was the Cleveland, under the direction of Lorin Maezel. The same year she made her debut with the Metropolitan Opera, performing her San Francisco Micaela. Other leading roles followed. When she appeared with the San Francisco Opera in 1976 in Pietro Mascagni's *L'Amico Fritz,* one critic wrote, as quoted in the liner notes by Gerald Fitzgerald, "Her refulgent, expanding top voice hit 100 on the goose-pimple meter . . . a world class soprano." Mitchell made her debut with London's Royal Opera in 1979, during the company's tour of Japan and Korea.

The singer graced the cover of *Opera News* on February 10, 1979, announcing the cover story "Here to Sing," by Stephen Wadsworth. The article was subtitled "Soprano on the Rise. Leona Mitchell Comes into Her Own with No Less Than Five Roles at the Met This Season." When Wadsworth brought up the subject of racial prejudice, specifically the tendency of some opera directors to type-cast on the basis of race rather than ability, Mitchell responded:

> I don't like it. . . . I don't like any of it. I mean it's stupid. . . . [E]ven to use the terminology—Negro, black singers. . . . What about singers, period?. . . They just shouldn't be saying that somebody doesn't look the part.

Wadsworth also asked if she thought black voices had any special qualities. Mitchell answered,

> Yeah, I think there is a difference. I think there are some black sounds. . . . I think it's a certain quality blacks bring to music. . . . I think maybe what we're talking about is not so much a vocal thing as it is a music-making thing. There's something about black music-making that's . . . now it's my turn for a cliché—it's the soul of it.

Heidi Waleson captioned her March 20, 1983, *New York Times* feature article on Mitchell "A Lyric Soprano Ventures into Heavier Fare." That season she would undertake a new repertory, that of a dramatic soprano. Mitchell indicated that it was not an impromptu decision. Waleson stated that Mitchell considers herself an "Italianate-type" singer who is happiest in the "brilliant, top-to-bottom coloratura of Verdi" and the "gutsy, dramatic, legato singing of Puccini." Mitchell planned to keep balancing her heavy roles with the lighter ones, simply to keep her voice agile. "I want to mix these roles up. . . . I want to always keep my repertory varied. And that means longevity." She further remarked, "I'm a soprano, and I do what feels comfortable. I get very annoyed at being classified lyric or spinto."

In a 1987 interview with Gary Schmidgall, Mitchell summarized her goals:

> For me before, it was the excitement of singing with Placido [Domingo] or Marilyn [Horne] or Luciano [Pavarotti], debuting here and there. What thrills! But after all that, it really comes down to being an artist. Opening this festival or getting that new production is not so important now. Now I'm concerned with trying to do 100 percent—the impossible. Now it's paramount to be the best I can be.

The soprano was one of a select group of subjects considered in Rosalyn M. Story's book *And So I Sing: African-American Divas of Opera and Concert* (1990). Labeling Mitchell one of the "Voices of a New Generation," Story points out that Mitchell is one of the busiest singers in

the world and reminds readers that she represents the new group of young American singers who did not go to Europe for their training. She adds that Mitchell also "bypassed the usual rite of passage—the obligatory tour of duty in Europe's smaller houses."

Extremely popular with conductors and orchestras throughout the world, Mitchell has appeared with the major symphonies of New York, Boston, Chicago, Philadelphia, Cleveland, Los Angeles, Pittsburgh, San Francisco, London, Bologna, Israel, Scotland, and other places. Her highly acclaimed recitals have taken place at such venues as Lincoln Center (New York City), Kennedy Center (District of Columbia), Ambassador Auditorium (Pasadena, California), and the San Francisco Opera House. In addition to her annual appearances with the Australian Opera, recent tours have included a summer 1991 opera performance in Buenos Aires and recitals in Mexico City and the Far East (Japan and Hong Kong).

Mitchell has a successful career, many major accomplishments to her credit, a husband and family, and residences in New York City and Houston, Texas. As early as 1979, she speculated on her future to Stephen Wadsworth:

> A whole lot of singers make their mistake—they put their whole lives into just career. Well, I think as an individual and from my background I have so much to do. And if I ever retire I don't think I'll keep coming back, because I find such fulfillment in relationships, real relationships with people, and in life itself.

As for singing, she told Wadsworth she planned to work constantly "to make the voice more mellow, more round-toned, whatever—more expressive, that's it—to make the music better."

Current Address: c/o Kevin S. Hassler, Columbia Artists Management, 165 West 57th Street, New York, NY 10019.

REFERENCES:

Fitzgerald, Gerald. Liner notes. *Presenting Leona Mitchell with Kurt Herbert Adler: An Operatic Partnership.* Decca and London Records, 1980.

Hall, Sarah Moore. "Diva Leona Mitchell Also Cheers Up Tenors and Impresarios, but for Opera Fans, It's Love at First Bite." *People* 12 (September 3, 1979): 96-97.

"A Lyric Soprano Ventures into Heavier Fare." *New York Times,* March 20, 1983.

Rich, Maria F., ed. *Who's Who in Opera.* New York: Arno Press and the New York Times, 1976.

Schmidgall, Gary. "Puccini Heroine Leona Mitchell." *Opera News* 51 (January 31, 1987): 21-22.

Southern, Eileen. *Biographical Dictionary of Afro-American and African Musicians.* Westport, Conn.: Greenwood Press, 1982.

Story, Rosalyn M. *And So I Sing: African-American Divas of Opera and Concert.* New York: Warner Books, 1990.

Wadsworth, Stephen. "Here to Sing." *Opera News* 43 (February 10, 1979): 11-13.

                                        D. Antoinette Handy

Mildred R. Mitchell-Bateman

(1922-)

Psychiatrist, state mental health administrator

In the May 1969 issue of *Vogue* magazine, Mildred Mitchell-Bateman was described as an "ascetic, small, contained woman with a misleading modesty and a stubborn spine . . . [one who] speaks so softly that legislators must listen." This psychiatrist and mental health administrator has dedicated her professional life to the creation, management, and oversight of comprehensive services in the field of mental health. In 1962 she became the first woman in the United States hired to head a state department of mental health. She was also at one time the chair of the Department of Psychiatry at the Marshall University School of Medicine in Huntington, West Virginia. Mitchell-Bateman's work has been well characterized by her own terse, pithy *Vogue* quote: "I go at whatever I do."

Mildred R. Mitchell-Bateman is a native of Cordele, Georgia, who was born to S. Q. and Ella McLeod Mitchell on March 22, 1922. She attended Barber-Scotia College in Concord, North Carolina, and graduated from Johnson C. Smith University in Charlotte, North Carolina, in 1941. Five years later, she graduated from the Women's Medical College of Pennsylvania and then completed a one-year internship at Harlem Hospital in New York City. She served her psychiatric residency at Winter Veterans Administration Hospital as a fellow at the Menninger School of Psychiatry in Topeka, Kansas, from 1952 to 1955.

Improves Mental Health Care in West Virginia

In the late 1950s Mitchell-Bateman worked at Lakin State Hospital in West Virginia as physician, clinical director, and superintendent. In the early 1960s, she functioned as supervisor and acting director of the West Virginia State Department of Mental Health, and from 1962 to 1977 as the full-time director. This was the first time an American woman had assumed such a position. As a state administrator in a southern state with a mountainous, isolated, and extremely needy population, Mitchell-Bateman was challenged to find new and innovative ways of providing services to patients. She utilized the VISTA program and Federal Foster Grandparents Program as means of providing emergency services in isolated pockets of the state. In 1967 she received the Medical

Mildred R. Mitchell-Bateman

College of Pennsylvania National Board Award, an annual presentation made in recognition of the health care contributions of female physicians or medical scientists. The award also aims to encourage other women in the health care field.

Mitchell-Bateman has been prominently featured in leading publications as disparate as *Vogue* magazine and state textbooks. As director, her greatest accomplishments were increasing the number of local community mental health programs and federal spending for mental health in West Virginia. According to Stephanie Harrington in *Vogue* magazine, Mitchell-Bateman's administrative skills were widely recognized for changing the general public's perception about mental health by "transforming lock-up institutions . . . to comprehensive mental health centers that provide pre- and post-hospital care, rehabilitation, teacher training, programs for alcoholism, retardation, and prevention of mental handicapping in children." In 1969, *Vogue* published a series of "Passionate Rebels" as role models; Mitchell-Bateman was featured. In 1987, the West Virginia State Department of Education published a Title IX Project for social studies as a supplemental unit. Mitchell-Bateman is profiled in the second section, which covers contemporary women.

Because of her outstanding contributions in the field of mental health, she has also served as a member of the Defense Advisory Committee of Women in Services, medical advisor for the Commission on Rehabilitation Administration, a member of the board of directors of the National Association of Mental Health, and a trustee of the Menninger Foundation and Barber-Scotia College. She has been a member of the American Psychiatric Association, the American Medical

Association, the West Virginia Medical Association, the Cabell County Medical Society, and the American College of Psychiatry.

Mitchell-Bateman, a life-long Presbyterian, married William L. Bateman in 1947 on Christmas Day. She is the mother of two daughters. Stephanie Harrington, *Vogue* writer, said of her: "physician, wife, mother, Dr. Bateman [draws] on the discipline and devotion of her Presbyterian girlhood in curing social-medical-economic ills long neglected." Mitchell-Bateman currently lives in Huntington, West Virginia.

REFERENCES:

ABMS Compendium of Certified Medical Specialists, 1990-1991. 3d ed. Vol. 5. Evanston, Ill.: American Board of Medical Specialists, 1990.

Butler, Dee. *The Emergence of Women in West Virginia History: A Title IX Project for Social Studies.* Charleston: West Virginia State Department of Education, 1987.

Harrington, Stephanie. "The Passionate Rebels—Once You Start, You Finish." *Vogue* 153 (May 1969): 170.

"Kathleen Foley Named Recipient of the 1987 Medical College of Pennsylvania National Board Award." *Philadelphia PR Newswire,* April 13, 1987.

Ploski, Harry A., and James Williams, eds. *The Negro Almanac.* 4th ed. New York: John Wiley and Sons, 1983.

7,000 Successful Blacks. Vol. 1. Ebony Success Library. Nashville: Southwestern Publishing Co., 1973.

Who's Who in America 1984-1985. 43rd ed. Chicago: Marquis Who's Who, 1984.

Dolores Nicholson

Sybil Collins Mobley
(1925-)
Certified public accountant, educator, college administrator

Known in the corporate world for her talent in the field of business and in academia for her competence as a business school dean, Sybil C. Mobley has established one of the nation's outstanding schools of business and developed a mutually rewarding relationship between corporations and her employer, Florida Agricultural and Mechanical University. She is sought out for memberships on corporate boards—positions still widely inaccessible to significant numbers of black women.

Sybil Collins Mobley was born on October 14, 1925, in Shreveport, Louisiana. Her father, Melvin Collins, was first

Sybil Collins Mobley

an educator and then established the *Shreveport Sun,* the oldest weekly newspaper in Louisiana. Her mother, Cora Jones Collins, became an elementary school teacher in Bossier Parish, Louisiana. Sybil Collins married James Otis Mobley, now deceased, and is the mother of three children—James, Jr., Janet Yolanda Sermon, and Melvin Edward.

After graduating from high school, Mobley entered historically black Bishop College in Marshall, Texas, where she had a double major in sociology and economics and received a B.A. degree. (The college has since closed.) Her interest in the field of business was born there. She continued her studies at the Wharton School of Finance and Commerce at the University of Pennsylvania, majoring in accounting and minoring in economics, and she graduated in 1961 with an M.B.A. In 1964 she received her Ph.D. degree from the University of Illinois, Urbana, with a major in accounting and minor in economics. She became a certified public accountant in the state of Florida.

Mobley joined the faculty of Florida Agricultural and Mechanical College (now University), Tallahassee, in 1963 as a professor in the business department. Her academic and administrative abilities led to her promotion to department head in 1971, and she has been dean since 1974, when the department became the school of business. It is now called the School of Business and Industry.

A variety of summer appointments with leading businesses and financial institutions enriched Mobley's professional experience. She served with International Business Machines, Union Carbide Corporation, and Chase Manhattan

Bank, all in New York City, and Price Waterhouse in Los Angeles.

Business Dean Builds Successful Program

When Mobley joined the Florida A and M faculty in 1963, few companies recruited students from its business department. But she was successful in reversing that practice. *Florida Trend* published a special report on Florida's black managers in January 1987 and noted Mobley's success in leading the business school to national prominence. By then the school's student body of 1,150 had become racially mixed. The report said that the students "may well be the most sought-after raw business talent in the nation." Recruiters from 150 corporations had visited the school the previous fall, and up to twenty prospective employers courted each graduate.

Mobley earned a permanent place for the business school on the recruiting programs of Fortune 500 companies. "She keeps her finger on the corporate pulse and improves her students' job prospects," the Florida report said. The Florida A and M program was called one of the most unusual in the country. Not only were the students able to differentiate between a stock and a bond but they also knew how to dress for success and how to select an appropriate wine when dining with Wall Street's inner circle.

Mobley stresses "polishing the professional side" of her students. The professional development program that she originated broadened the typical student's experience significantly. Each student was to complete three internships with separate companies in three different geographical areas. Students also ran seven college-based corporations, five of which were dummy businesses. The others were real income-generating firms and included a life insurance company and a property management firm for a strip shopping center near the campus.

She told the *Florida Trend* that her program equipped students with what the business world wanted in new talent. "You get things done a lot faster when you're wired into the corporate community," she commented. To demonstrate the extent of her involvement in the corporate community, she has lined the entrance to the business school facility with bronze plaques identifying companies that have contributed $100,000 or more to the endowment, which was $6.2 million in 1987.

Grooms Students for Successful Corporate Careers

Mobley's success with companies required research. She determined what the companies disliked about new graduates: "The firms told us that most of the new hires were technically competent, but that they had a lot missing when it came to team skills, communication skills, social skills and assertiveness." Mobley took action to correct these deficiencies. She took an unusual step when she merged the business curriculum with the university's liberal arts program and

immediately received rave reviews from the Florida State University system. "Its student body comprises what is, in all probability, the largest pool of qualified black students in the USA," an external consulting team reported after visiting the business school in 1984. The chairman and chief executive officer of Champion International, Andrew Sigler, agreed. "Sybil Mobley delivers a hell of a product," he said during a visit to the campus. Champion has also employed graduates of the school.

Mobley has changed the School of Business and Industry from a program that enrolled almost exclusively Floridians to one that is attractive to students nationwide. In 1987, for example, more than 90 percent of its students were from out of state. Active recruits are those who have been considered by the National Merit Foundation. The successful applicant must score a minimum of one thousand on the Scholastic Aptitude Test as well as graduate in the top ten percent of his or her class. Persistent in her drive to maintain a top-level school, Mobley is rigorous in her efforts to lure the best and the brightest.

Mobley is highly respected in the business community and sought after for her expertise. In the corporate world she is a member of the board of directors of Anheuser-Busch Company, Champion International Corporation, Hershey Foods Corporation, Southwestern Bell Corporation, Premark International, Sears Roebuck (first black woman member), Southeast Banking Corporation, Southeast Bank (North America), and Dean Witter, Discover and Company. She has held a number of consultantships, including membership on the consultant panel to the Comptroller General of the United States and consultant to the Internal Revenue Service in Atlanta. Her expertise was acknowledged further when she was appointed special consultant and team leader to the United States Agency for International Development (USAID), providing consulting services for USAID to industrialists in Cameroon, the Ivory Coast, and Liberia.

Her organizational affiliations are numerous. She has served on the board of directors of College Placement Services, and in her professional associations she is on the board of directors of the American Assembly of Collegiate Schools of Business, the National Association of Accountants for Public Interest, and the Commission on Education for the Business Professions of the National Association of State Universities and Land Grant Colleges. She is currently a member of the board of governors of the Institute of Internal Auditors. Her commission memberships in Florida include the Energy Commission, the Human Relations Commission, the Constitutional Revision Commission (as an alternate), and the Tax Reform Commission. She served as president of the International Association of Black Business Educators, vice president of the American Accounting Association, and vice president of the American Institute of Certified Public Accountants. In recognition of her contributions and expertise, she has received honorary doctorate degrees from the Wharton School of Finance, Babson College, Bishop College, and Hamilton College. She also received the Robert Russa Moton Leadership Award from the National Business League. Mobley is a member of the Alpha Kappa Alpha Sorority.

Mobley's scholarship has earned her a membership on the editorial board of the *Accounting Review*. She also has published widely in prestigious journals of accounting and economic development.

Sybil Mobley has developed the business school at Florida A and M into a program of national prominence: its students are readily placed in the corporate world. In so doing, she has successfully mixed the corporate and academic worlds.

Current Address: School of Business and Industry, Florida Agricultural and Mechanical University, Tallahassee, FL 32307.

REFERENCES:

Davis, Marianna W., ed. *Contributions of Black Women to America.* Vol. 1. Columbia, S.C.: Kenday Press, 1982.

"Florida's Black Managers." *Florida Trend* (January 1987): 78.

Mobley, Sybil Collins. Resume. N.d.

Norment, Lynn. "Top Black Corporate Directors." *Ebony* 49 (October 1994): 36-38, 40-44.

Reynolds, Rhonda. "25 Black Women Who Have Made a Difference in Business." *Black Enterprise* 25 (August 1994): 76-78.

Who's Who among Black Americans, 1994-95. 8th ed. Detroit: Gale Research, 1994.

Jessie Carney Smith

Carol E. Moseley-Braun

Carol E. Moseley-Braun
(1947-)
Lawyer, politician, radio host

On March 17, 1992, at her campaign headquarters at Chicago's McCormick Center Hotel, Carol Moseley-Braun lifted her hands, swayed from side to side, and broke into her familiar infectious smile as she moved to the music of "Ain't No Stopping Us Now" and "We Are Family." Having just defeated longtime democratic senator Alan Dixon in the Illinois primary, she was on the most important path in her life: the one leading to the United States Senate. Running as a Democrat, Moseley-Braun won the senatorial election the following November. The first black woman in the U.S. Senate, Moseley-Braun, quoted in *Jet* magazine, told her cheering supporters: "We have won a great victory tonight. . . . You have made history. And as much to the point of history making you are showing the way for our entire country to the future." Prior to her election to the U.S. Senate,

Moseley-Braun had a successful career as a lawyer and as a member of the Illinois House of Representatives.

Carol E. Moseley-Braun was born on August 16, 1947, in Chicago, Illinois, the eldest child of Joseph Moseley, a policeman, and Edna A. Davie Moseley, a medical technician. The comfortable, middle-class setting of Moseley-Braun's early life was far from ideal, however, for her father, a frustrated musician from a musical New Orleans family, sometimes took out his personal disappointments on Moseley-Braun by beating her. A mature Moseley-Braun later commented on the family situation in a *Washington Post* article: "I had to grow up fast." Perhaps as a result of the stress of such domestic violence, Edna Moseley placed Moseley-Braun's two brothers and a sister in her care when she was eleven. The same article reports that, when she was sixteen, Moseley-Braun's parents divorced, her father moved to California, and she and her siblings, along with Edna Moseley, settled in with their maternal grandmother for two years, in a house "at 41st Street near Lake Michigan [in a neighborhood] called Bucket of Blood." This is the middle class Oakland section of Chicago today, but then her grandmother's domicile was, according to a March 6, 1992, *Chicago Reader* article, "an old house . . . a formidable slum. For the first time, Braun lived among very poor blacks on violent streets."

Moseley-Braun's exposure to the darker aspects of black life instilled in her a belief in public service, the *Washington Post* continues. Moseley-Braun states, "When you get a chance to see people who are really trapped and don't have options and you've got all these blessings, you've got to be a pretty ungrateful person not to want to do something." The blessings Moseley-Braun referred to included her education at the University of Illinois at Chicago, from which she graduated in 1967, and at the University of Chicago Law School, from which she obtained a J.D. degree in 1972. It was at the University of Chicago law school that she met Michael Braun, a white fellow student, whom she married in 1973; he is the father of her only child, Matthew.

Political Career Begins

Moseley-Braun's public life started with her work as an assistant U.S. attorney from 1974-77. Prior to this, she worked at a private firm. The U.S. Attorney position was pivotal to her career; as Moseley-Braun noted in the *Chicago Reader,* "It opened up for me the way [federal] government interfaces with local and state government, how policy is made, and what opportunities there are for changing things via the courts." In 1977, running as a Democrat, she won a seat in the Illinois House of Representatives, serving the Hyde Park area near the University of Chicago, which was and remains a liberal as well as racially integrated neighborhood.

Moseley-Braun displayed no perceptible timidity during her career in the Illinois legislature. According to the *Washington Post,* "Early on she successfully sued her own party's leader . . . Speaker Michael J. Madigan . . . to overturn a redistricting plan." Moseley-Braun's boldness and integrity gained her public notice and the respect of her colleagues, both of which were integral to her future career in Illinois politics. Moseley-Braun was a member of the Illinois House of Representatives until 1988. During these years she championed educational reform and redistricting for fairer legislative districts. In addition, she worked against investing in South Africa and discrimination by private clubs. She received the Best Legislator Award in 1980 and 1982 from the Independent Voters of Illinois and numerous other recognitions for her political contributions. A charter member of Illinois Women for Government, she was honored by major black organizations such as the National Association of Business and Professional Women's Clubs. Moseley-Braun also found time to write newspaper articles for the *Hyde Park Herald* and the *South Shore Scene.* In addition, she was a radio talk show host for WXOL in Chicago.

Chicago's first black mayor, Democrat Harold Washington, admired Moseley-Braun's energy and in 1983 designated her his floor leader in the House, even though she was not the senior legislator. Apparently her relationship with Washington was not without conflict, however. According to the *Washington Post,* he blocked her bid for the lieutenant governorship in 1986.

Nineteen eighty-six was a devastating year for Moseley-Braun for other reasons as well. Her mother was seriously ill and had a leg amputated, and one of her brothers died as a result of his drug and alcohol abuse. To add to this, Moseley-Braun and her husband divorced; according to *USA Today,* she said she had experienced "15 very good years and one very bad." When she ran for the U.S. Senate, however, Michael Braun worked on her campaign.

This low period in Moseley-Braun's life was brief. She successfully campaigned for the office of Recorder of Deeds and in 1988 became the first black elected to an executive office in the history of Cook County government. Managing a staff of three hundred people and a budget of eight million dollars, Moseley-Braun, according to the *Chicago Reader,* "dramatically reorganized" the recorder's office.

Moseley-Braun's personality and appearance have always been counted as pluses in her political career, contributing to her broad cross-racial and cross-economic appeal. *Essence* says of Moseley-Braun: "Part of Braun's appeal is her personal style. Pecan-colored, with a short, tousled haircut, she has a smile that engages her mouth and her eyes. Her look is professional hip." The *National Review,* however, said that Moseley-Braun liked to point out a sign in the restroom of her Chicago office that read, "I'm 51 per cent sweetheart, 49 per cent bitch. Don't push it." While running for the Senate, she described her style of politics in the *Chicago Sun-Times:* "Anybody who's ever worked with me knows . . . I don't like labels, never have. . . . So if I have a role in politics or government, it is to find the places where we can agree . . . to promote cooperation without in any way compromising my principles and my beliefs."

Although raised as a Roman Catholic, Moseley-Braun attended the Vernon Park Church of God and Christ until her election to the Senate in 1992. During her senatorial campaign Moseley-Braun described her religious preferences: "Born-again Christian—that would fit." Her religious background and deeply ingrained beliefs have led her to oppose abortion personally but to support a woman's right to choose.

Politician becomes Activist in U.S. Senate

Moseley-Braun was inspired to run for the U.S. Senate after watching Senator Alan Dixon vote to confirm Clarence Thomas as a Supreme Court justice in 1991. Thomas's confirmation hearings garnered an unusual amount of attention when a former colleague of the judge's, law professor Anita Hill, accused him of sexual harassment. Braun felt that Dixon's and the Senate's actions in the matter showed that the body was a group of elite white men who were out of touch with the American people. Defining herself in her Senate campaign as an agent of change, Moseley-Braun tapped into an anti-incumbent grassroots sentiment that ultimately carried her to victory. Moseley-Braun likes to point out her commitment to her constituents. The *Chicago Sun-Times* reported that she emphasized this at the height of her battle for the Senate seat by reminding people, "I have a record of accountability . . . and a record of keeping my word. I am prepared for (the senate) job."

In her tradition of fearlessness, Moseley-Braun became active in Congress immediately. In February 1993 she urged President Clinton to sign legislation sponsoring research on women's health issues. She made her position on health care clear from the start and was quoted in the *Chicago Reader* as saying, "I intend to be very active. . . . I will be a major advocate right off the bat for a universal, comprehensive, single-payer system."

Moseley-Brown gained national attention on July 22, 1993, when she caused the U.S. Senate to bow to her on an issue involving the symbol of the Confederacy. The United Daughters of the Confederacy (UDC) sought to renew a design patent for its insignia, which featured the original flag of the Confederacy encased in a wreath. Initially the Senate intended to approve the proposal, sponsored by Senator Jesse Helms, who called the UDC "delightful gentleladies," and supported by Senator Strom Thurman. The next day the *Washington Post* noted Moseley-Braun's protest, which caused the Senate to reverse itself. On the final vote, the eloquent and angry Moseley-Braun bristled with outrage and argued that the issue dealt with symbolism for descendants of slaves.

> The issue is whether or not Americans such as myself who believe in the promise of this country . . . will have to suffer the indignity of being reminded time and time again that one point in this country's history we were human chattel. We were property. We could be traded, bought, and sold. . . . This vote is about race . . . and the single most painful episode in American history. . . . [The Confederate flag] has no place in our modern time . . . no place in this body . . . no place in our society.

Moseley-Braun's record in two year's service in the Senate led to her appointment in January 1995 to the powerful Senate Finance Committee. She is the first woman appointed to a full term on the committee and the first Illinois senator in three decades to serve on the committee. She said in the January 23, 1995, issue of *Jet,* "I am aware of the historical significance of this appointment and I am extremely proud to be a part of that history."

Moseley-Brown declared in early 1994 that she will run for reelection to her senate seat in 1998. As she fought to determine her future in politics, she demonstrated a self-confidence which was lacking in 1992, replaced her chief of staff, reduced her campaign debt, and distanced herself from President Bill Clinton. Although her approval rating among some of her constituents in Illinois has declined, and the *Chicago Tribune* for February 12, 1995, reported that her "comeback is still a work in progress," she aims to defend her place in history.

REFERENCES:

"Carol Moseley Braun: First Black Woman Elected to U.S. Senate." *Jet* 83 (November 23, 1992): 8-14.

"Carol Moseley Braun Runs for the Senate." *Chicago Sun-Times,* January 1992. *Indigo* supplement.

Coyne, John R., Jr. "Woman of the Year?" *National Review* 14 (September 1992): 24-25.

Hine, Darlene Clark, ed. *Black Women in America.* Brooklyn: Carlson Publishing, 1993.

Levinsohn, Florence Hamlish. "Carol Moseley Braun." *Chicago Reader,* March 6, 1992.

"Moseley-Braun Seeks Women's Health Bill." *Chicago Defender,* February 18, 1993.

Nelson, Jill. "Carol Moseley Braun: Power Beneath Her Wings." *Essence* 23 (October 1992): 57-58, 120, 122, 124.

"Politician 'Can Take Adversity.'" *USA Today,* March 26, 1992.

"Senate Bows to Braun on Symbol of Confederacy." *Washington Post,* July 23, 1993.

"Senator Carol Moseley-Braun of Illinois Appointed to Senate Finance Committee." *Jet* 87 (January 23, 1995): 4.

"Voter Revolt: A Giant-Killer in Illinois." *Newsweek* (March 30, 1992): 38-39.

COLLECTIONS:

The Carter G. Woodson branch of the Chicago Public Library has a newspaper clippings file on Moseley-Braun. The Chicago Historical Society has a microfilm copy of the *Chicago Reader* article, which contains detailed information about Moseley-Braun's personal and political life.

Margaret Perry

Mary Ella Mossell
(1853-1886)
Missionary

Mary Ella Mossell added the role of missionary to Haiti to her traditional role as a nineteenth-century wife. She and her minister husband shared a joint success in Port au Prince made possible in large part because of her ability to establish contacts not only with the common people but also with the elite members of society. The Mossells' stay in Haiti was frightening at times due to disease and political unrest. After nursing her family through bouts of yellow fever and smallpox, Mossell dramatically saved her husband from being killed by rebels, but at the cost of her unborn daughter and her own health.

Mary Ella Forrester Mossell was born in Baltimore, Maryland, on May 22, 1853, and died in the same city on June 29, 1886. Her father was Perry Forrester, identified by George F. Bragg, Jr. in *Men of Maryland* as a businessman who was a "commissary in the army under Gen. B. F. Butler during the Civil War [and] killed at Richmond, Virginia." Little is known of her mother, except that she was a free person of color, as was her husband. Mossell's extensive education suggests that the family was at least modestly affluent, even after her father's death.

Mossell began school when she was five years old. In 1867, at the age of fourteen, she entered the Baltimore Normal

Mary Ella Mossell

School, from which she graduated in 1871. In addition to her school studies, which included some language training in Greek, Latin, and German, she took music lessons from childhood on. On October 29, 1874, she married Charles W. Mossell. A minister in the African Methodist Episcopal (AME) Church, Charles Mossell was a fellow native of Maryland. He was a graduate of Lincoln University in Pennsylvania and also of a theological seminary in New England.

Begins Missionary Work in Haiti

In 1877 Mossell and her husband went to Haiti as missionaries. They were to remain there for seven years. Mossell set out to acquire the necessary language skills, learning French, Haitian Creole, and Spanish. Her first contacts with the people came as she sat in plain sight on her porch working brightly colored yarns into a pattern. Curiosity won out among the women passing in the street, and they gradually overcame their suspicion of the foreign woman. She widened her circle of acquaintances and induced many women to come to the school and to join the church.

It was also difficult to reach the elite, but Mossell succeeded by drawing upon her musical abilities. Not only did she play the piano in cultured salons, she also composed pieces. There were pieces entitled "La grande marche," which was dedicated to President Solomon, "Le bouquet," dedicated to General Ligitime, and "La grande marche patriotique," as well as several songs in Creole. (Unfortunately, much of this music has been lost.) The combined efforts of husband and wife bore fruit in the form of five young Haitian

men who left to complete their educations at Lincoln University. All were dedicated workers for their denomination, and one, John Hurst, became a bishop of the Haitian AME Church.

The difficulties of missionary work were compounded by the dangers of disease. The whole Mossell family fell prey to yellow fever and a sister of Charles Mossell's, Alveretta, who had joined the missionary effort, died. In a subsequent outbreak of smallpox, Mary Mossell's nursing saved their only daughter, Mary M. Lee, who would later write an account of her mother for Hallie Q. Brown's *Homespun Heroines.*

The most dangerous events of Mossell's stay in Haiti occurred on September 22 and 23, 1883, during the Bazelias Revolution. Some ten acres of homes and shops in Port au Prince were destroyed. A small American flag displayed in front of the Mossell home offered no protection. The rebels forced their way into the house, killing or wounding many of the people who had taken refuge there. The buildings were set on fire, and her husband was hustled off to be killed. John Mercer Langston, who was U.S. minister in Port au Prince when the Mossells resided there, said in his eulogy for Mary Ella Mossell:

> Now came the supreme hour of Mrs. Mossell. She alone could, under the circumstances, and she alone did, by her courageous, heroic conduct, prevent the assassins' foul purpose on her husband's life. Her imploring words, her womanly, earnest efforts; her whole appearance and manner, so impressive and subduing, as, clinging to her husband, she was borne on as he, by the crowd, through the streets, pulled and hauled, and pushed under the direst threats and fearful manifestations of personal violence, could but draw to her and her husband, in such sore condition, at least a friend of two who would seek their succor and relief. So it happened, and they were saved.

The consequences for Mossell were dire. She gave premature birth to a daughter who did not survive. Her other daughter was missing for four days. Her health was ruined, and she lived only two more years. The family returned to Baltimore soon after these traumatic events, and Mossell died on June 29, 1886. She was buried in Laurel Cemetery, and a memorial service was held some weeks later in Trinity AME Church.

Mary Ella Forrester Mossell well deserved Langston's praise. She had the courage to enter a new and hazardous environment to undertake an active role as a missionary. Her qualities were equal to the challenges she met.

REFERENCES:

Bragg, George F., Jr. *Men of Maryland.* Baltimore: Church Advocate Press, 1925.

Brown, Hallie Q., ed. *Homespun Heroines and Other Women of Distinction.* Xenia, Ohio: Aldine Publishing Co., 1926.

Langston, John Mercer. *From the Virginia Plantation to the National Capitol.* Hartford: American Publishing Co., 1894.

Majors, Monroe A. *Noted Negro Women.* Chicago: Donohue and Henneberry, 1893.

Robert L. Johns

Jennie Dee Booth Moton
(1879-1942)
Educator, civic leader, clubwoman, government worker

Jennie Dee Booth Moton

Described in the *New York Age,* March 19, 1921, as "one who's a mother to all human kind," Jennie Booth Moton was the driving force behind her husband, Robert Russa Moton, the president of Tuskegee Institute. However, she is also of interest and importance in her own right. She devoted her life to serving the needs of others, primarily through her work with the black women's club movement. Additionally, toward the end of her life, she served with the U.S. Department of Agriculture as a field officer in the South.

Born February 24, 1879, in Roanes, Gloucester County, Virginia, Jennie Dee Booth Moton was the daughter of Ellen and Robert Booth. Her father's occupation was farming and oystering. Moton's parents were both of mixed racial heritage. Her father was mixed Indian, black, and white. Her mother was mixed black and white. She had six brothers and five sisters. Moton herself was the mother of five children: Catherine, Charlotte, Jennie, Robert R., and Allen W.

Student records show that Moton entered the Hampton Institute (now Hampton University) in Hampton, Virginia, on October 15 or 16, 1896, and graduated on March 8, 1900. After graduating, Moton taught for eight years in the grade school at the Whittier Training School at the Hampton Institute.

In 1906 or 1907 Jennie Booth Moton met Robert R. Moton, who had enrolled in Hampton in 1884. After his third year he began teaching in Cottontown, Cumberland County, Virginia. While he was teaching, Robert Moton also read law in the office of the Farmville superintendent of schools and received a license to practice as a lawyer. Returning to Hampton in 1899, Robert Moton completed his education and became assistant commandant in charge of the male student cadet corps. In 1891 he was appointed commandant with the title of "Major." He held this title throughout his life.

At 3:00 P.M. on Wednesday, July 1, 1908, Jennie Dee Booth married Major Robert R. Moton in a simple ceremony in Memorial Chapel on the campus of the Hampton Institute. She was attended by her sister, Mrs. A. A. Freeland, and he was attended by Allen Washington, a captain. The ceremony was performed by Hollis B. Frissell. The church was decorated with palms and ferns. After an informal reception in Cleveland Hall Chapel, the bridal couple left by train for a two-week trip to Robert Moton's home in Rices, Virginia, and later traveled to Gloucester County to visit the bride's parents. Around August 1, they returned to reside at the Normal School at Hampton Institute.

While at Hampton, Moton was not only a homemaker and mother, but also a member of various committees, including the reception committee. On June 18, 1909, she cosponsored a reception for the teachers in the Hampton Institute Summer School. In 1912, she hosted a tea for the Douglass Literary Society.

Tuskegee Years Bring Challenge

Robert Moton worked at Hampton until 1915 when he was appointed principal of Tuskegee Normal and Industrial Institute (now Tuskegee University) to replace Booker T. Washington. Moton's selection was no surprise, since he had worked closely with Washington to promote the Tuskegee-Hampton ideal of biracial cooperation and vocational education. Moton preached the same doctrine of hard work, self-improvement, and optimism as Washington did, and the two men also held joint fund-raising rallies throughout the northern states. Along with this new job came the responsibilities of unofficial advisor to the federal government on racial policies and the appointment of blacks to federal positions. Moton was also an advisor to philanthropic organizations that gave funds to black educational institutions.

The Motons were somewhat reluctant to leave Hampton as both had elderly parents in the area and Robert Moton's career at Hampton was well established. A farewell reception was held on Monday, May 8, 1916, in Marshall Hall at Hampton. Hollis B. Frissell spoke of the love all Hampton's staff had for the Motons and how sorry they were to see them leave even though they were proud that Robert Moton had been called to such an important position. The Motons received a grandfather clock that was to stand in the hall of their new home at Tuskegee.

Following Robert Moton's inauguration at Tuskegee, he and his wife established their home among very pleasant surroundings there where he, Jennie Moton, and their four children—two girls and two boys—grew to be just as happy as they had been at Hampton. Another child was born while they were at Tuskegee.

A quiet and unobtrusive woman, Jennie Moton was a persistent and untiring worker on behalf of Tuskegee Institute. She was also a community worker who helped those in distress. Although she held no official position on campus before 1925, she saw to the comfort and well being of both students and teachers at Tuskegee Institute.

On December 23, 1923, Moton displayed another of her talents. She directed a Channing Pollock play entitled *The Fool,* which displayed the dramatic reading abilities of Charles Winter Wood along with the Tuskegee Players. The play was staged at the Tuskegee Institute Chapel.

Margaret Murray Washington, Booker T. Washington's wife, and Moton were like sisters. They saw each other daily, devoted themselves to the Tuskegee Institute, and worked side by side in the local and national women's club movement. They traveled to conventions together and to meetings of the Commission on Interracial Cooperation. Eventually, Margaret Murray Washington's health began to fail, and Moton saw to her needs until her death.

When Margaret Murray Washington died on June 4, 1925, Moton became director of the Department of Women's Industries at Tuskegee and president of its women's club. After Washington's death the remodeled quarters of the Division of Domestic Science were renamed Margaret Washington Hall. The Department of Women's Industries offered both high school and college courses. On the high school level, training in academic subjects amounting to the fifteen units required for college entrance was combined with vocational courses. The college courses led to the bachelor of science degree and prepared graduates for employment in public and private schools, government service, commercial enterprises, and supervisory positions. Buildings and equipment for the department included Dorothy Hall, Margaret Murray Washington Hall, and the Practice Cottage. There was a staff of twenty teachers.

Women's Club Activities Begin

Moton was extremely active in the women's club movement on both the local and national levels. On July 19 and 20, 1920, the twelfth biennial session of the National Association of Colored Women (NACW) met at the Tuskegee Institute. Moton welcomed the women on behalf of the Tuskegee Women's Club. Mary Church Terrell paid tribute to Margaret Murray Washington, who was ill and unable to attend the meeting.

On October 6 and 7, 1920, a conference of one hundred white women from the Women's Division of the Commission on Interracial Cooperation met in Memphis, Tennessee, to discuss relations between black and white women. Formerly an all-white male organization, the Commission on Interracial Cooperation was founded in 1918, and females were added in 1920. These ladies were the heads of women's organizations of the Protestant churches and leaders in the Young Women's Christian Association. As a means of getting the viewpoint of cultured black women, they invited Margaret Murray Washington, Moton, Elizabeth Ross Haynes, and Charlotte Hawkins Brown to speak at the conference. At first there was some distance and mistrust among the women. Yet the black women spoke with frankness and without self-consciousness or embarrassment.

Most of these white women were northerners who had not known of the existence of these prominent black women. Through drafts written by Lugenia Burns Hope, Margaret Murray Washington, and Moton, the concerns of blacks, such as child welfare, education, suffrage, protection of black girls, and elimination of lynching, were addressed. The ladies pledged to work through their organizations in local communities to promote cooperation between black and white women. All in all, by 1925 some progress had been made to help eliminate a few of the problems of blacks in the South. At the 1924 Southern Interracial Committee meeting, Moton was elected to their executive committee.

In 1929 Moton was elected state president of the Alabama Association of Women's Clubs. This organization was founded in Montgomery on December 19, 1899. It was through the efforts of the women in this organization that such projects as the Mount Meigs Industrial School for Boys and Girls, the Parlow State School for the mentally retarded in Tuscaloosa, and the Searcy Hospital in Mount Vernon were established. Other projects included voter registration drives, youth programs, fund-raising for scholarships, and a war bond program.

During Moton's term as president of the Alabama Association of Women's Clubs (1929-36), she reorganized the state departments to coincide with those of the NACW. The junior club organization was also greatly improved during her presidency. The thirty-third convention of the Alabama Federation of Colored Women's Clubs (the name by which the Alabama Association of Women's Clubs was known at the time) met May 31 to June 2, 1934, on the campus of the Tuskegee Institute. Moton presided with dignity, handling difficult problems with wisdom and tact. The theme was "Woman's View of the New Deal." Day sessions were held in Margaret Murray Washington Hall.

Moton's idea of building portable cabins for tuberculosis patients was well-received. Through the cooperation of individual clubs, it was hoped that these cabins would be installed in every county of the state. The highlight of the convention was the stirring address by the prominent black educator, civil rights activist, and feminist Nannie Helen Burroughs, who stayed throughout and contributed to many sessions. Burroughs had served as the 1934 commencement speaker at Tuskegee Institute, making her the first woman to give this speech at the school.

Presides at National Meeting of NACW

Moton was the eleventh president of the NACW from 1937 to 1941. She presided over the twenty-first biennial convention in Boston, Massachusetts, July 21-29, 1939, and also the twenty-second biennial convention in Oklahoma City, Oklahoma, July 26-August 1, 1941. It was at the Oklahoma biennial that Moton announced her intention to complete all old projects prior to embarking upon new projects. She named a Committee on the Press and a Committee on Resolutions. At the Sunday, July 27, mass meeting held in conjunction with the biennial, Moton presented Mary McLeod Bethune, the honorary president of NACW, to the assembled audience. Bethune's address was entitled "Negro Women Facing Tomorrow."

During Bethune's visit to the Oklahoma biennial, she announced that President Franklin D. Roosevelt had issued an executive order for full participation in the defense program by all persons, regardless of race, creed, color, or national origin. This meant that Roosevelt was prohibiting discrimination against blacks in the defense industries. Bethune told the audience that this was the first formal declaration issued on behalf of blacks since Abraham Lincoln's Emancipation Proclamation.

On July 28, 1941, Moton introduced Frances Williams of the Consumer Division and Hallie Q. Brown, a women's and civil rights proponent active in the women's club movement, who spoke on the Student Loan Fund. Moton then presented E. A. Miller of the Southern Division of the Agricultural Adjustment Administration (AAA), who spoke of Moton's efforts to bring educational programs to women in the South.

At the close of the Oklahoma City convention, president Moton presented her biennial address. She urged the women not to accept the concept of birth control since children were the foundation of the home. This speech was widely applauded, and her presidency was considered extremely successful in general. Through the efforts of Mary McLeod Bethune and Moton, the NACW developed a close relationship with the leadership of the nation.

At the close of Moton's administration, the Committee on Resolutions read expressions of appreciation honoring Moton, Mary McLeod Bethune, and A. Philip Randolph for their assistance in getting President Roosevelt to issue the proclamation barring prejudice against blacks in the defense industries. After her tenure as president, a Hall of Fame was established in the state room of the Montgomery Federation of Women's club house, where pictures of all past state presidents of the Alabama Association of Women's Clubs were displayed. Included were the two prominent women who had served as presidents of both the Alabama Association of Women's Clubs and the NACW, Margaret Murray Washington and Moton, wives of the first two presidents of Tuskegee Institute. Moton also served as chairperson of the Board of Trustees of the Nannie Helen Burroughs Training School for Women and Girls.

At the fiftieth anniversary celebration of Tuskegee in 1931, Moton was hostess to trustees, alumni, and other visitors to the campus. Her office in Dorothy Hall was headquarters for all plans for the entertainment of the guests. The principal's reception was held in her home. In 1931, Bennett College in Greensboro, North Carolina, conferred an honorary degree of master of arts upon Moton. According to an article in the *Southern Workman,* January 1932, David D. Jones, the school's president, presented the award, calling her a "loyal daughter of Hampton; teacher and worker with girls; exemplar of womanhood; leader and helper of women of high degree and lowly estate; strong factor for interracial understanding and good will; staunch and intrepid helpmate amid threatening dangers; faithful and vigilant mother."

Moton Begins Government Service Activity

Starting in 1936, Moton served as a field officer for the Southern Division of the Agricultural Adjustment Administration (AAA), later the Agricultural Stabilization and Conservation Service, an agency of the U.S. Department of Agriculture. The AAA administered aid to farmers through parity payments and programs to conserve soil resources and stabilize prices of farm products. The field workers held conferences and meetings with black farmers. They also studied landlord-tenant issues and the effects of the agricultural conservation program on cooperating black farmers. Moton traveled throughout nine southern states working with black and white farmers to improve agricultural conditions.

According to the *Records of the National Association of Colored Women's Clubs, 1895-1992,* in an April 15, 1939, letter to W. W. Alexander, head of the Farm Security Administration, Moton wrote,

> I am especially interested in bringing about a better standard of living of the farms operated by Landlords, and have been given permission to do what I could, in this regard, in Alabama, Mississippi, Arkansas, and Louisiana. The idea is to solicit the cooperation of the Landlords, and get them to consent to have the Farm and Home Agents, teach their Live At Home Program, on their plantation. I believe, of course, we can change the attitude of the tenants, and the landlords, and bring about a better understanding between the two. This would result in improved housing conditions, the tenants having sufficient time to produce a year round garden, and to raise enough food and feed for his family and livestock. The matter of drinking water, and other essentials, necessary to good health, is also strongly emphasized.

After Robert Moton retired from Tuskegee Institute in 1935, the family returned to the Moton estate at Holly Knoll, Capahosic, Virginia, where Robert Moton died on May 31, 1940. He was buried at Hampton Institute. The Capahosic site became a meeting place for United Negro College Fund institutions later on.

Moton continued to be an active force in the community. She served as a member of the Margaret Murray Washington Memorial Foundation, and in October 1942 she was appointed a consultant in home nursing for the National Red Cross. She also served as a race relations advisor for the U.S. Division of Physical Fitness in Philadelphia, Pennsylvania.

Moton died on Wednesday, December 23, 1942, at Dixie Hospital in Virginia. She was sixty-two years old. She was buried alongside her husband at Hampton Institute after funeral rites in Memorial Chapel. Tributes were paid by E. A. Miller of the AAA and Nannie Helen Burroughs. Moton was survived by her five children: Catherine Patterson, wife of Frederick D. Patterson, then the president of Tuskegee Institute; Charlotte Moton of the Federal Security Agency in Washington, D.C.; Jennie Moton; Robert F. Moton of Tuskegee Institute; and Allen W. Moton, a member of the armed services. She also left behind a sister, two brothers, and three grandchildren.

The January 2, 1943, *Norfolk Journal and Guide* quotes a description of Jennie Moton's life by J. E. Wright, a Middlesex, Virginia, minister: "Mrs. Moton was not only a faithful, loyal effective worker, but her wise counsel, her courage and devotion to duty were a benefit to all of us. She was a person you could not help but love."

REFERENCES:

Burroughs, Nannie H. "The Challenge of the New Day." *Tuskegee Messenger* 10 (June 1934): 2, 11.
"Domestic Science Building Named Margaret Washington Hall." *Tuskegee Messenger* (May 9-23, 1931): 20.
"Farewell Reception." *Southern Workman* 45 (June 1916): 385.
Logan, Rayford, and Michael R. Winston, eds. *Dictionary of American Negro Biography*. New York: Norton, 1982.
"A Marriage Beautiful." *Fishermen's Net* (July 4, 1908).
Moton, Robert Russa. *Finding a Way Out: An Autobiography*. New York: Negro Universities Press, 1969.
"Mrs. Jennie Moton Buried at Hampton." *Norfolk Journal and Guide,* January 2, 1943.
"Mrs. Moton Honored." *Southern Workman* 61 (January 1932): 5.
"Mrs. Robert Moton, Widow of Educator." *New York Times,* December 27, 1942.
"Mrs. Robert R. Moton Surprised by Friends." *New York Age,* March 19, 1921.
"Mrs. Robert Russa Moton Elected to Interracial Board." *Tampa Bulletin,* July 1924.
Murray, Florence, ed. *The Negro Handbook*. New York: Current Reference Publications, 1944.
Neverdon-Morton, Cynthia. *Afro-American Women of the South and the Advancement of the Race, 1895-1925*. Knoxville: University of Tennessee Press, 1989.
Newman, Debra L. *Black History: A Guide to Civilian Records in the National Archives*. Washington, D.C.: National Archives. Trust Fund Board, 1984.
Records of the National Association of Colored Women's Clubs, 1895-1992. Part 1: Minutes of National Conventions, Publications, and President's Office Correspondence (Microfilm). Bethesda, Md.: University Publications of America, 1993.
"Southern Women and Race Relations." *Southern Workman* (December 1920): 537-38.
Wesley, Charles Harris. *The History of the National Association of Colored Women's Clubs*. Washington, D.C.: National Association of Colored Women's Clubs, 1984.
"Woman's View of the New Deal." *Tuskegee Messenger* 10 (July 1934): 1, 8.

COLLECTIONS:

Moton's student records, articles about her, and a photograph can be found at the Hampton University Archives, Hampton, Virginia. Other information can be found in the Robert R. Moton Papers in the Hollis Burke Frissell Library, Tuskegee University, Tuskegee, Alabama.

The Moton Family Papers are located at the Library of Congress, Washington, D.C. Records of the Agricultural Stabilization and Conservation Service (Record Group 145) are located at the National Archives, Washington, D.C.

Janet Sims-Wood

Jeanne Moutoussamy-Ashe
(1951-)
Photographer, writer, AIDS activist

Jeanne Moutoussamy-Ashe has made her mark on America through her photography and her work on behalf of AIDS victims. She has worked as a photojournalist and has published extensively in books and magazines. In addition, she has written a groundbreaking historical guide to black women photographers.

Jeanne Marie Moutoussamy-Ashe, the youngest of three children, was born in 1951 to John Warren and Elizabeth Rose (Hunt) Moutoussamy. She was the only girl in the family with two older brothers, John Warren and Claude Louis. She married tennis superstar, Arthur Ashe (1943-1993), and with Ashe had one daughter, Camera Elizabeth.

Moutoussamy-Ashe, a third generation African American, is of mixed heritage. Her paternal grandfather, who

Jeanne Moutoussamy-Ashe and daughter Camera.

originated in Saint François, Guadeloupe, came to America and married the daughter of a slave from Louisiana. The name Moutoussamy is the English version of his East Indian name "Moutou-swami." Her maternal grandfather was of Cherokee ancestry. Moutoussamy-Ashe's father was an architect and her mother was an interior designer in Chicago while Jeanne was growing up. Through her parents Moutoussamy-Ashe grew up in an atmosphere that emphasized the visual arts. With this constant exposure, it is not surprising that she developed a passion for a visual medium like photography. She began taking drawing and painting lessons at the age of eight at the Art Institute of Chicago. She continued to paint throughout her teen years. At one time she also modeled and appeared in a commercial for the product Mr. Clean.

Career as Photographer Begins

In 1971 Moutoussamy-Ashe enrolled in the College of New Rochelle, New York, where she took her first photography course. When she encountered the work of Roy DeCarava, a photographer of Harlem life, it stimulated an interest in photography as her life's work and changed her artistic focus. After one year in New Rochelle, she transferred to the prestigious Cooper Union School of Art in New York City. During her junior year she received a fellowship which allowed her to tour West Africa for a semester. She toured seven West African countries photographing the people, their lives, and their customs. From this experience, she produced three photographic studies. Armed with an impressive color portfolio and numerous hours of hands-on experience, she felt confident enough to seek a full time position with NBC as a television photojournalist. Moutoussamy-Ashe was immediately hired by NBC's art director. Juggling her job and school she continued her program of study, graduating with a B.F.A. in photography in 1975.

In 1976 Jeanne Moutoussamy met her future husband, Arthur Ashe. Even before they met, she jokingly told a friend that she was going to marry him. In his book *Days of Grace,* which includes photographs by Moutoussamy-Ashe, Ashe discussed her effect on him the moment he met her at a benefit for the United Negro College Fund on October 16, 1976. Ashe was one of the celebrities at the event to promote the scholarship program. Moutoussamy-Ashe was photographing the activities for NBC. Ashe said that, while she was photographing him, he "took a mental picture of her as maybe, just maybe, what my heart desired.'' The couple went on their first date a few days later and were married four months after that on February 20, 1977, by Andrew Young, who was then ambassador to the United Nations.

Moutoussamy-Ashe has always been an independent woman with a sense of self worth and purpose. She elected not to lose her identity and maintained her maiden name along with that of her husband's. In a 1981 interview with *Sepia* magazine, she said that the three most important experiences in her life were her marriage, her trip to West Africa while in art school, and her three trips to South Africa. Her first two trips were with her husband in his role of sports superstar and went very smoothly. However, on her third trip, she did not travel as an American celebrity wife. Instead, she went alone experiencing firsthand the apartheid that prevailed and was nearly arrested.

Being the wife of a superstar has afforded her the opportunity to not be in the business strictly for financial gain. She has had the freedom to develop her work based on her feelings and her inner spirit. Her work documents the overwhelming concern she holds for black people and their lives, whether in America, South Africa or elsewhere. This is evident in her photographic work on the culture of the people of Daufuskie Island off the coast of South Carolina published in 1982 as *Daufuskie Island: A Photographic Essay.* Her experiences as a black woman in the white male dominated field of photography led her to explore the history of African American women in the profession. The result of that research is her much acclaimed 1986 book, *Viewfinders: Black Women Photographers,* which documents the work and lives of black women photographers from 1839 to 1985.

Exhibitions

Moutoussamy-Ashe has had many individual and group exhibitions in major national and international cities including Chicago, New York City, Boston, Washington, D.C., Los Angeles, Detroit, Paris, London, and Florence. In 1978 she also participated in a traveling exhibit which toured the Soviet Union. Throughout her career she has also contributed photographs to numerous magazines and newspapers, including *Ebony, Black Enterprise,* the *New York Times, Essence, Life, Smithsonian, World Tennis, Self,* and *Sports Illustrated.* Moutoussamy-Ashe has also been a photo-commentator for the television show *PM Magazine.* In addition to her books previously mentioned, she has provided photographs for Arthur Ashe's book *Getting Started in Tennis* (1977) and *Songs of My People: African Americans, A Self Portrait,* edited by Erin Easter (1991).

Other professional accomplishments of Moutoussamy-Ashe's include being commissioned by President Jimmy Carter's Administration to provide official photo-portraits of U.S. Cabinet members, including Patricia Roberts Harris. Her work has become a part of the permanent collections of the Schomburg Center for Research in Black Culture, the Studio Museum in Harlem, the New York Public Library, and the Columbia Museum of Art and Science in Columbia, South Carolina.

In describing Moutoussamy-Ashe's work, art dealer and photographer Frank Stewart told Judith Wilson for the May 1986 *Essence* magazine that she uses a ''strong sense of people, especially black people with a classical simplicity of design to produce images that make powerfully direct visual statements.'' Her best friend, obstetrician Machelle Allen, described her to Laura B. Randolph for the October 1993 issue of *Ebony* as a ''woman of tremendous poise and internal strength.'' In a 1993 interview with *Ebony,* Moutoussamy-Ashe describes herself as ''very independent'' and says that Arthur Ashe ''taught me a greater love of myself. He brought out so many things in me that I didn't know I had inside.'' Arthur Ashe, in fact, helped her transform her ideas into books. His death inspired her book *Daddy and Me.* Arthur Ashe died February 6, 1993, of complications related to AIDS, which he had contracted from a tainted blood transfusion following a heart attack in 1979.

Moutoussamy-Ashe told Laura B. Randolph for *Ebony* that *Daddy and Me* is a family project designed ''to help other children understand you can live with illness and help people who are sick.'' The book contains Moutoussamy-Ashe's photographs of routine family activities during the last year of her husband's life. The text is written in their daughter Camera's words, making it easy for other young children to identify with and understand the situation.

In addition to her work as a photographer, Moutoussamy-Ashe remains busy with projects to help others in her community. She is one of the founders of the Black Family Cultural Exchange, which is comprised of African American women in New York City and Connecticut who provide a series of book fairs for black youth. The profits from these fairs provide scholarships and books for local community centers. Since her husband's death, Moutoussamy-Ashe has continued her work as photographer and has also become a spokesperson for AIDS education and research. She currently resides in New York City in an East 87th Street apartment with her daughter.

REFERENCES:

Ashe, Arthur, and Arnold Rampersad. *Days of Grace: A Memoir.* New York: Alfred Knopf, 1993.

Barboza, Steve. ''Faces of Africa: Through Jeanne Ashe's Eyes.'' *Sepia* 30 (December 1981): 38-41.

Contemporary Black Biography. Detroit: Gale Research, 1994.

Dowling, Claudia Glenn. ''Daddy and Me.'' *Life* 16 (November 1993): 61-69.

Hine, Darlene Clark, ed. *Black Women in America.* Brooklyn: Carlson Publishing, 1993.

Moutoussamy-Ashe, Jeanne. *Viewfinders: Black Women Photographers.* New York: Dodd Mead, 1986.

———. *Daufuskie Island: A Photographic Essay.* Columbia, S.C.: University of South Carolina Press, 1982.

Randolph, Laura B. ''Jeanne Moutoussamy-Ashe: On Love, Loss and Life after Arthur.'' *Ebony* 48 (October 1993): 27-34.

Willis-Thomas, Deborah. *An Illustrated Bio-Bibliography of Black Photographers, 1940-1988.* New York: Garland Publishing, 1989.

Wilson, Judith. "A Look at Three Contemporary Artists." *Essence* 17 (May 1986): 120-24.

Karen Cotton McDaniel

Anna Evans Murray

Anna Evans Murray

(1857-1955)

Kindergarten advocate, educator, clubwoman, civic leader

Anna Evans Murray, a prominent educator, dedicated her life to the establishment of free kindergarten education and the training of kindergarten teachers in the District of Columbia schools and to the development of the black child. She came to the district to teach music at Howard University and at Mott School. She also became active in civic affairs, always keeping in mind her mother's admonition that "education is a pearl of great price by which you will be able to set yourself free in your environment, wherever that may be."

Murray's mother, Henrietta Leary, was the daughter of a French woman, Juliette Anna Meimorial. Her maternal grandfather's mother descended from a Crotan Indian. Her father, Henry Evans, was a free man in North Carolina at the time of the Nat Turner insurrection of slaves in 1831. After the North Carolina state constitution of 1834 took away the right of suffrage from all African Americans, he traveled on horseback to Oberlin, Ohio, where he became a skilled artisan for the college. Evans' wife and family came to Oberlin from North Carolina by covered wagon, and Evans became a property owner. A cabinet-maker and undertaker, he gave his thirteen children the opportunity of an education at Oberlin College. Active in the underground railroad, Murray's father "was one of the famous Wellington rescuers of John Price, fugitive from his master, John G. Bacon." Her uncle, Lewis Sheridan Leary, was shot during the insurrection at Harper's Ferry, and her cousin, John Anthony Copeland, Jr., was hanged with John Brown.

Anna Evans Murray graduated from Oberlin in 1876 and in 1879 married Daniel Murray, assistant librarian at the Library of Congress and compiler of the unpublished work, "The Historical and Biographical Encyclopedia of the Colored Race Throughout the World." He died in 1925. Five of their seven children lived, graduating from college and becoming eminent in their fields. Daniel graduated from Oberlin and became a violinist in New York City. George Henry studied at Harvard and Howard; he became an instructor at the Cardozo Business High School and later taught at the Commercial High School. Nathaniel Ellison graduated from Cornell then taught biology at the Armstrong Manual Training School. Harold, an engineer in Brazil and later a paper manufacturer in Mexico, also studied at Cornell. A third Cornell graduate, Paul Evans, worked for the federal government.

Murray Becomes Civic Leader and Educator

Murray's first five years of teaching in the district at the Mott School convinced her of the necessity of free kindergartens and of the need to train teachers to direct the kindergartens. In 1895, as Education Committee chair of the National League of Colored Women (NLCW) in Washington, D.C., Murray devoted herself to the establishment of free kindergarten classes for black children. She managed a normal school established by the NLCW in October 1896, training kindergarten teachers for the six or seven free kindergartens established by the league. Seven of her teachers were appointed to teach in the district public schools. In 1898, she successfully lobbied for a twelve-thousand-dollar federal appropriation to establish kindergarten classes. She and Sara I. Fleetwood represented the Colored Women's League at the Congress of Mothers in 1898. Through contacts at the convention, Murray secured the patronage of Phoebe A. Hearst, wife of the senator from California, for the Kindergarten Training School for about five years. Through her efforts a second appropriation from the congress was made in 1906 for the inclusion of kindergarten teacher training courses at Miner Teachers College, then Miner Normal.

Murray joined other leaders in the NAACP in the early 1900s, seeking social improvement in the fight against prejudice and segregation. At the turn of the century, Murray, assisted by Lily Moore, directed the free kindergarten program at the Colored Settlement House in the District of Columbia. In 1934 Murray was part of the Citizens Advisory Committee on Hot Lunches for School Children in the District. Nearly eighty years old in 1937 and still interested in the continuation of the nursery schools as part of the public school system, Murray presented a plea at a congressional hearing for the establishment of a health center at First and Lawton Streets where the highest percentage of tuberculosis deaths occurred at the time. She also advocated the purchase of land in the vicinity of the Douglas and Simmons schools for playground facilities to lessen traffic accidents.

Murray was vice president of the Public School Association and an officer in the Association for Childhood Education, which honored her with a reception on her ninetieth birthday, March 2, 1947. Mary W. Holmes of the Washington Association for Childhood Education, retired kindergarten teacher, aided by fifteen other teachers, initiated the celebration of Murray's birthday and the recognition of her contribution to the education of younger children on her eighty-fifth birthday. The celebrations became large affairs, celebrated on or near her birthday, March 2, paying tribute every year to Murray and to other noted educators. Murray was also a member of the YWCA and of Saint Luke's Episcopal Church.

Throughout her life, adding to her husband's *Encyclopedia* became a favorite hobby for Murray. She also enjoyed collecting the Reconstruction Era cartoons by Thomas Nast which were published in *Harper's Weekly*. According to Jessie Fant Evans, among her prized possessions was a "tooled, leather-bound copy of Jefferson's Bible, with the text in parallel columns of Hebrew, Latin and English." She also says of Murray:

> She herself is the author of a published pamphlet, "Thomas Jefferson, the Abolitionist." Her story of Phoebe Fraunces of her own race, daughter of the colored New York tavern keeper, whose loyalty saved the life of George Washington upon the eve of attempted assassination, and to whom it is reported he said, "Your fidelity has saved my life, to what reserve the Almighty knows," has been dramatized and used widely as a school play in various colored high schools.

Murray also published "In Behalf of the Negro Woman" in the *Southern Workman* (1904), praising the efforts of black women to make their homes comfortable in spite of the unfavorable socioeconomic factors and criticizing the views expressed by Eleanor Tayleur in "Negro Woman" in *The Outlook* (1904). Murray states:

> The education of the Negro child should reach lower down, for long before he reaches the age of six years (the legal age for entrance to public schools) the work has been done which makes of him either a useful citizen or a worse than useless drag upon his community and his race. . . . Let the

kindergarten become the basis for all instruction, for it offers the only logically safe, sure, and natural means for the training of the individual and the re-creation and reproduction of the ideal life as it should exist in the home, the community, and the nation. Give us two generations of children trained under this system of education and we will change the present menacing aspect of the American race problem, whether within or without our borderland, to one of sympathy and harmony.

Murray died at the age of ninety-eight on May 5, 1955, at her home in the District of Columbia. Her sons George H., Nathaniel, and Harold, along with twelve grandchildren, survived her. She is remembered best as a staunch advocate of nursery schools, kindergarten education, the training of teachers for those purposes, and, in general, for the wholesome development of the child.

REFERENCES:

"Anna Murray Nears Her 80th Birthday Still Aiding Her Race." *Washington Star,* August 15, 1937.

Giddings, Paula. *When and Where I Enter: The Impact of Black Women on Race and Sex in America.* New York: Morrow, 1984.

Harris, Robert L., Jr., "Daniel Murray and *The Encyclopedia of the Colored Race.*" *Phylon* 37 (September 1976): 270-82.

Hine, Darlene Clark, ed. *Black Women in U.S. History.* Brooklyn: Carlson Publishing, 1990.

———. *Black Women in America, an Historical Encyclopedia.* 2 vols. Brooklyn: Carlson Publishing, 1993.

Hull, Gloria T. et. al, eds. *All the Women Are White, and All the Blacks Are Men, But Some of Us Are Brave: Black Women's Studies.* New York: Feminist Press, 1983.

Hutchinson, Louise Daniel. *Anna J. Cooper: A Voice from the South.* Washington, D.C.: Smithsonian Press, 1981.

"The Leary Family." *Negro History Bulletin* 10 (November 1946): 27-34, 47.

"Mother of D.C. Kindergartens Is Honored on Ninetieth Birthday." *Pittsburgh Courier* (Washington), March 15, 1947.

"Mrs. Anna Evans Murray, 98, Ex-Teacher and Civic Leader." *Washington Star,* May 6, 1955.

Murray, Anna Evans. "In Behalf of the Negro Woman." *The Southern Workman* 33 (April 1904): 232-34.

"The Observance of the Seventy-fifth Anniversary of Public Education for Negroes in the District of Columbia." *The Negro History Bulletin* 3 (December 1939): 37-40.

Tayleur, Eleanor. "Social and Moral Decadence." *The Outlook* 48 (January 30, 1904): 266-71.

Claire A. Taft

Gloria Naylor

(1950-)

Short story writer, novelist, playwright

To explore a range of characters united in their quest for wholeness, to seek a causal connection between desperation and violence, and to celebrate the endurance of the human spirit: these are the touchstones of Gloria Naylor's fiction. Her four novels—*The Women of Brewster Place* (1982), *Linden Hills* (1985), *Mama Day* (1988), and *Bailey's Cafe* (1992)—grapple with moral and emotional crises. In her short stories, novels, and plays, Naylor challenges the reader to respond to basic human needs and emerge with a better sense of self. Although many of her characters reside on the periphery of society, their relentless quest for dignity remains undiminished.

Gloria Naylor was born on January 25, 1950, to Roosevelt Naylor, a transit worker, and Alberta McAlpin Naylor, a telephone operator, in Robinsonville, Mississippi. Naylor's early years in the South would later provide fertile soil from which to mold a variety of her fictional characters. The Naylor family's eventual migration to the North was typical of African Americans in pursuit of economic stability as well as better educational opportunities for their children.

Before choosing writing as a primary career, Naylor worked as a Jehovah's Witness missionary, serving New York, North Carolina, and Florida from 1968 to 1975. Horrified by the assassination of Martin Luther King Jr. while she was in high school, Naylor believed that changing the world meant finding a "solution to the chaos" by evangelizing to the populace, according to the *Washington Post* on October 21, 1983.

Having become dissatisfied with the restrictiveness of the Jehovah's Witness organization, Naylor committed herself to completing her education. It was during a sophomore creative writing seminar at Brooklyn College that Naylor read Toni Morrison's *The Bluest Eye,* which gave her the courage to begin "gathering the authority within" to become a writer. In a conversation with Toni Morrison published in *Southern Review,* she remembers the dramatic moment well:

> It said to a young poet, struggling to break into prose, that the barriers were flexible; at the core of it all is language, and if you're skilled enough with that, you can create your own genre. And it said to a young black woman, struggling to find a mirror to her worth in this society, not only is your story

Gloria Naylor

worth telling but it can be told in words so painstakingly eloquent that it becomes a song.

For the first time, at the age of twenty-seven, Naylor recognized that there was more to literature than reading the works of Ralph Ellison, Jane Austen, Charles Dickens, James Baldwin, William Faulkner, and the Brontë sisters. Being either male or white, Naylor discovered, was not the necessary prerequisite for writing good literature. Moreover, the revelation that black women had penned great works opened a new world for Naylor, and she immersed herself in the writings of African Americans. Feeling most complete when "expressing [herself] through the written word," she said in the *Southern Review* article that her period of repressed silence was over, and she had stories to tell.

While an undergraduate at Brooklyn College, Naylor decided to test the waters by publishing her first short story in a 1980 issue of *Essence* magazine. The story, entitled "A Life on Beekman Place," was revised in the final draft as Lucielia Louise Turner's chapter in *The Women of Brewster Place,* published two years later. Naylor earned a bachelor's degree in English from Brooklyn College of the City of New York in 1981 and a master's degree in African American Studies from

Yale University in 1983. Since the early 1980s, she has taught and conducted workshops at George Washington University, New York University, Boston University, Princeton, the University of Pennsylvania, Brandeis University, and Cornell University.

Depicts Reality of Black American Women

Naylor's first novel, *The Women of Brewster Place* (1982), won the American Book Award for First Fiction in 1983, and it established her as an accomplished writer. She opens the work by showing how geography determines character. Through the clandestine deliberations of a white alderman and a realty company owner, Brewster Place becomes the ''bastard child'' of an urban ghetto, literally and figuratively cut off from the rest of the city. People who live there can live nowhere else. Seven strong-willed women—Mattie, Etta Mae, Kiswana, Ciel, Cora Lee, Lorraine, and Theresa—form a microcosm of diversity in terms of background, age, marital status, political persuasion, and sexual preference. Poor, disinherited, flawed, and vulnerable, all of these women single-handedly consolidate their strengths to form a vibrant community. Mattie Michael, resident matriarch and dream keeper of Brewster Place, becomes emblematic of what it is to be black and female in America. Miss Mattie's dream of a block party to fund improvements on Brewster Place unites the women. They dismantle the wall that ultimately isolates them from ''respectable folk.''

Washington Post reviewer Deirdre Donahue praised Naylor's accomplishment in *The Women of Brewster Place*, stating,

> Naylor is not afraid to grapple with life's big subjects: sex, birth, love, death, grief. Her women feel deeply, and she unflinchingly transcribes their emotions. . . . Naylor's potency wells up from her language. With prose as rich as poetry, a passage will suddenly take off and sing like a spiritual. . . . Vibrating with undisguised emotion, *The Women of Brewster Place* springs from the same roots that produced the blues. Like them, her book sings of sorrows proudly borne by black women in America.

In 1985, two years after receiving her M.A. degree from Yale, Naylor published her second novel, *Linden Hills*. This sequel to *The Women of Brewster Place* chronicles the Luther Needed family history through four generations and examines the promise of the American dream gone wrong in Linden Hills. Although successful, upper-middle-class blacks with material wealth, the Needed patriarchs oppress women. The Needed wives—Luwana Packerville, Evelyn Creton, Priscilla McGuire, and Willa Prescott—find their lives defined only in relation to their spouses. As babymakers who perpetuate the family name, the Needed wives become marginalized at the hands of both their spouses and offspring. Naylor inserts a womanist discourse in the narrative by allowing Willa Prescott to transcend adversity and give voice to the Needed wives.

African religious folk traditions serve as the context for Naylor's third novel, *Mama Day* (1988), written with the aid of a grant from the National Endowment for the Arts. Within the closed community of Willow Springs, located between Georgia and South Carolina, Naylor empowers another matriarch in the tradition of Mattie Michael and Willa Prescott Needed. A conjurer and a descendant of the island's mythic founder, Sapphira Wade, Mama (Miranda) Day awaits the opportunity to pass the family heritage to her great-niece, Ophelia.

The first half of the narrative focuses on Ophelia's return to Willow Springs from New York City with her new husband, George. However, the action reaches a climax when Ophelia, known as Cocoa on the island, becomes ill due to the ''hoodoo'' magic of Ruby, a jealous rival. A hurricane, characterized by Mama Day as a ''storm born in hell,'' destroys the only bridge to the mainland. The hurricane, which functions as an organizing principle for the concluding chapter, sets the stage for healing to occur.

Apprenticeship Ends

In her fourth novel, *Bailey's Cafe* (1992), Naylor continues her established tradition of female bonding and survival in a hostile urban environment as she did in *The Women of Brewster Place, Linden Hills,* and *Mama Day*. Naylor sets the tone by using the blues as a unifying metaphor in the epigraph:

> hush now can you hear it can't be far away/
> needing the blues to get there/ look and you
> can hear it/ look and you can hear/ the blues
> open/ a place never closing: Bailey's Cafe.

Bailey is the maestro who conducts a symphony of disharmonies referred to in more familiar terms as the blues. In the rhythmic prelude, Bailey explains that the customers ''don't come for the food and they don't come for the atmosphere,'' but they come to find answers within themselves. Like choral voices, the cafe patrons—Sadie, Eve, Sweet Esther, Mary, Jesse Bell, and Mariam—enter and inform the narrative with tales of everyday circumstances in song. In addition, the lives of less frequent visitors to Bailey's Cafe serve as variations from the melodic line of life, but they too are inextricably bound to play their roles in the symphony.

Similarly, double consciousness functions equally as part of Naylor's visionary company, and it informs her prose style in the tradition of Pulitzer Prize winners Toni Morrison and Alice Walker. To be a woman of color and female means relinquishing autonomy and following the prescribed dictates of a patriarchal society. By evoking the ritual of memory as a catalyst for action, Naylor involves the reader and the characters simultaneously. Together they creatively recreate the present and its impact on the future. Mattie, Willa, Miranda, and Eve break down traditional barriers of exclusion to empower themselves.

Essays and screenplays are part of Naylor's repertoire, but they receive less attention than her novels. A stage adaptation of Naylor's novel *Bailey's Cafe* awaits final revision. Best known for her novel *The Women of Brewster Place*, Naylor scripted both a mini- and weekly series about ghetto life in the 1960s. Although the mini-series garnered an audience of 40 million viewers in 1989, the weekly series based on *The Women of Brewster Place* did not fare as well. With strong financial backing from Oprah Winfrey's Harpo Productions, the future appeared bright in 1990. Winfrey portrayed Mattie Michael, and Olivia Cole appeared in the role of Miss Sophia. It was given one of ABC's best prime-time placements, coupled with a guarantee of thirteen episodes. At the same time, Naylor became the founder and president of One Way Productions, an independent film company, which was established to bring *Mama Day* and other projects to the screen. Although she has achieved success for her essays and has given some attention to writing screenplays, Gloria Naylor is better known for her novels and for the depth that her works have achieved in helping the reader to grapple with the experiences of life.

Current Address: c/o Viking Penguin, 375 Hudson Street, New York, NY 10014-3657.

REFERENCES:

Andrews, Larry R. "Black Sisterhood in Gloria Naylor's Novels." *CLA Journal* 33 (September 1989): 1-25.

Belenky, Mary Field, Blythe McVicker Clinchy, and Nancy Rule Goldberger. *Women's Ways of Knowing: The Development of Self, Voice, and Mind.* New York: Basic Books, 1986.

Christian, Barbara. "Gloria Naylor's Geography: Community, Class, and Patriarchy in *The Women of Brewster Place* and *Linden Hills.*" In *Reading Black, Reading Feminist,* edited by Henry Louis Gates Jr. New York: Meridian, 1990.

Donahue, Deirdre. Review of *The Women of Brewster Place. Washington Post,* October 21, 1983.

Holloway, Karla F. C. *Moorings and Metaphors: Figures of Culture and Gender in Black Women's Literature.* New Brunswick: Rutgers University Press, 1992.

Matus, Jill L. "Dream Deferral, and Closure in *The Women of Brewster Place.*" *Black American Literature Forum* 24 (Spring 1990): 49-64.

Naylor, Gloria. *The Women of Brewster Place.* New York: Viking Penguin, 1982.

———. *Linden Hills.* New York: Viking Penguin, 1985.

———. *Mama Day.* New York: Vintage, 1988.

———. *Bailey's Cafe.* New York: Harcourt, 1992.

Naylor, Gloria, and Toni Morrison. "A Conversation." *Southern Review* 21 (July 1985): 567-93.

Ward, Catherine C. "Gloria Naylor's *Linden Hills:* A Modern Inferno." *Contemporary Literature* 28 (Spring 1987): 67-81.

Sharynn Owens Etheridge

Ida Gray Nelson Rollins
(1867-1953)
Dentist

B orn in the early years of freedom from slavery, Ida Gray Nelson Rollins became the first black woman to earn a dental degree in the United States. She was not only a college graduate but also established herself in a profession that was growing in its scientific contributions to human health. From her graduation to the end of her life, she was often cited as an example of achievement and inspiration for others to follow.

Ida Gray Nelson Rollins was born March 4, 1867, in Clarksville, Tennessee. Her mother was Jennie Gray and her father was a white man. Jennie Gray never married and died while still in her teens. Family members arranged for Nelson Rollins to live with a relative, Caroline Gray, who had moved to Cincinnati, probably in 1867 or early 1868. Caroline Gray was born about 1833 in Clarksville, Tennessee. She was unable to read or write. In Cincinnati, she worked as a seamstress and also accepted foster children as boarders some of the time. Caroline Gray was the mother of three children. Howard, the oldest, was partially disabled and worked at various times as a stableman, porter, or night watchman. Susan, the second oldest, married James Barnett in 1880. Mary, the youngest, was the same age as Nelson Rollins. Nelson Rollins and the other children attended Cincinnati's racially segregated schools. Nelson Rollins graduated from Gaines High School in 1887 at the age of twenty.

Becomes a Dentist

By the early 1880s Nelson Rollins was working as a seamstress or dressmaker. At some point in the mid-1880s she went to work in the office of a dentist, Jonathan Taft, who had achieved distinction and prominence in his field. Taft was a cofounder and an early president of the American Dental Association, and he actively promoted opportunities for women to become dentists. About 1859 or 1860, Taft gave a short three-month apprenticeship to Lucy Hobbs (later Lucy Hobbs Taylor), which led to a longer apprenticeship with another dentist and enabled her to become an independent practicing dentist in 1861. She then sought admission to the Ohio College of Dentistry in Cincinnati, and after several years of effort, was admitted. She graduated in 1866, becoming the first white woman in the country to earn a dental degree.

In 1875, Taft, who was then dean of the Ohio College of Dentistry and editor of the *Dental Register,* was recruited to become the first dean of the Dental Department at the University of Michigan in Ann Arbor. Within three years, women were enrolling in the dental school almost every year. After assuming his duties in Ann Arbor, Taft maintained a private practice in a Cincinnati office with Dr. William Taft, probably working there in the spring and summer. Nelson Rollins worked either full time or part time in the office of Jonathan and William Taft for perhaps as long as three years. Her

Ida Gray Nelson Rollins

acquaintance with Jonathan Taft attracted her to the University of Michigan, and her office experience enabled her to pass the entrance examination given to all applicants to the dental school. She began her study in October 1887 and graduated in June 1890, making her the first African American woman to earn a degree in dentistry in the United States. In 1896 Mary Imogene Williams graduated from Howard University's dental school and became the second African American woman to hold a dental degree.

Returning to Cincinnati, Nelson Rollins opened an office on Ninth Street and practiced there from 1890 to 1895. In March 1895, she married James Sanford Nelson of Chicago. James Nelson was born in Canada in 1860, immigrated to the United States in 1870, and became a naturalized citizen in the 1880s. Nelson worked as an accountant for the city of Chicago for many years. In the 1890s he enrolled at the Chicago College of Law, receiving his degree and becoming a lawyer about 1897. He also was a captain and quartermaster with the Eighth Illinois National Guard Unit. In Chicago Ida Nelson Rollins established an office at Armour Avenue and 35th Street, but, for reasons of economy and convenience, by 1898 she had closed that office and opened one in her home at 3558 South State Street. By 1903 she had moved both her home and her office to South Wabash Avenue, her office on the first floor at 3654 Wabash and her home upstairs at 3652 Wabash. She continued to practice dentistry at that address until her retirement in the 1930s and lived there the rest of her life.

As a dentist, Nelson Rollins served all races, all ages, and both sexes. She was considered especially good with children and devoted a substantial portion of her practice to young-

sters. She inspired one of her patients, Olive M. Henderson (later Olive M. Officer), to attend and graduate from Northwestern University Dental School in Chicago. By 1912 she had opened an office in Chicago, becoming the second African American woman dentist in Chicago.

Publications highlighting the activities of black society in Chicago often mention Nelson Rollins as a prominent dentist, but give no additional details. She was vice president of the Professional Women's Club of Chicago, composed mostly of black women medical doctors and lawyers. It was organized in 1927 and had a membership of about twenty in the 1930s. From the mid-1920s until the early 1940s, Nelson Rollins maintained a summer cottage in Idlewild, Michigan, a resort area that attracted African American vacationers from throughout the Midwest. James Nelson died March 11, 1926, and Ida married William A. Rollins, a waiter, in February 1929. He died June 20, 1944, as a result of a hit-and-run automobile accident. Nelson Rollins, who never had children, died May 3, 1953, in Chicago. Her gravestone contains the inscription: "Dr. Ida Gray Nelson Rollins, 1st Negro Woman Dentist in America."

REFERENCES:

Aptheker, Bettina. "Quest for Dignity: Black Women in the Professions, 1865-1900." In *Women's Legacy: Essays on Race, Sex and Class in American History.* Amherst: University of Massachusetts Press, 1982.

Dannett, Sylvia G. L. *Profiles of Negro Womanhood.* Vol. 1. Yonkers, N.Y.: Educational Heritage, 1964.

Driskell, Claude Evans. *The History of Chicago Black Dental Professionals, 1850-1983.* Chicago: C. E. Driskell, 1983-84.

Dykes, De Witt S., Jr. "Ida Gray Nelson Rollins, D.D.S." In *Profile of the Negro in American Dentistry.* Edited by Foster Kidd. Washington, D.C.: Howard University Press, 1979.

General Catalogue of Officers and Students, 1837-1911. Ann Arbor: University of Michigan, 1912.

Kelsey, Charles. "Ida Gray: Class of 1890." *Alumni Bulletin.* Ann Arbor: University of Michigan School of Dentistry, 1977-78.

McCoo, F. A., Sr. *"Say It with Pictures": Achievements of the Negro in Chicago, Illinois the Past Twenty-Five Years.* Chicago: F. A. McCoo, 1933.

Ninth Census of the United States. Ohio. 1870.

Peckham, Howard H. *The Making of the University of Michigan, 1817-1967.* Ann Arbor: University of Michigan Press, 1967.

Robb, Frederic H. H., ed. *The Negro in Chicago, 1779 to 1929.* 2 vols. Chicago: Washington Intercollegiate Club of Chicago, 1929.

Tenth Census of the United States. Ohio. 1880.

Twelfth Census of the United States. Illinois. 1900.

Williams, Mack V. *Williams' Cincinnati Directory.* Cincinnati: Williams and Co., June 1868, June 1883, June 1885, June 1887.

De Witt S. Dykes, Jr.

Constance Berry Newman

(1935-)

Government official, entrepreneur

A career public servant, Constance Berry Newman has been employed by several federal government departments and agencies and has become known for her work in a number of areas, including consumer safety, housing, personnel management, and cultural programs. She worked both in the Bush-Quayle Presidential campaign and on the Presidential Transition Team after the 1988 election, thus becoming known in political circles as well. As under secretary of the Smithsonian Institution since 1992, she is the chief operating officer and the second ranking official at the world's largest museum and research complex.

Born July 8, 1935, in Chicago, Illinois, Constance Berry Newman is the daughter of Joseph Alonzo Berry and Ernestine Siggers Berry. She grew up in Tuskegee, Alabama, and graduated from Tuskegee Institute High School. Newman received an A.B. degree from Bates College, Lewiston, Maine, in 1956 and a bachelor of science in law from the University of Minnesota School of Law in 1959. She was married to Theodore Newman; they divorced in 1980.

Constance Berry Newman

Presidential Appointments

Newman's career as a public servant began in 1961 and continues to the present. Most of her work has been based in Washington, D.C. A Republican, she has received four presidential appointments with three Senate confirmations. Fresh out of law school, she began work in government in 1961 as a G-3 clerk typist in the Department of Interior. She never equated her low-level position with race or gender, remembering that "A lot of times . . . minorities make a mistake by crying in our beer," she told *Black Enterprise* in August 1974. But she felt challenged and stated in the same article that she thought she had become a little tougher because of it. "Having worked my way up through the bureaucracy gives me certain strengths. I know all the games people play at every level," she said.

Continuing her career with the government, Newman later became a research analyst on the National Commission on Civil Disorders (Kerner Commission), worked for the Migrant Division of the Office of Economic Opportunity in the Midwest, and from 1969 to 1971 served as special assistant to Secretary Elliot Richardson in the Department of Health, Education, and Welfare. She was director of VISTA (Volunteers in Service of America) from 1971 to 1973.

Appointed by President Richard M. Nixon, Newman was commissioner of the Consumer Product Safety Commission from 1973 to 1977 and vice-chair from 1975 to 1976—one of the top women in government then. The commission is watchdog for the safety and effectiveness of thousands of consumer products. Newman's most important responsibilities were to ensure that the problems of low-income people

were considered. She said in *Black Enterprise* that she viewed herself "as an equal opportunity employment officer" wherever she went. She felt that she had an important responsibility on the commission to see that the policies of the commission consider the problems of low-income people. "On a more personal level . . . I'm interested in proving that minorities are effective and efficient in the jobs they do," she added. In her position Newman was especially concerned with the millions of injuries as well as the permanent disabilities and deaths each year associated with consumer products. She said in the November 1974 *Black Enterprise,* "We have to convince the manufacturers they have an obligation to design products with safety in mind."

For one year, 1976-77, she was assistant secretary of the U.S. Department of Housing and Urban Development. In 1977, she cofounded the business firm Newman and Hermanson Company, in Washington, D.C. Newman and Hermanson was a policy research company that worked in international development, housing, transportation, and urban development. Newman remained its president until 1982 when the company was sold.

From 1982 to 1987 Newman worked as a consultant. Her clients included the Ministry of Interior of the Government of Lesotho in South Africa, which she served as Cooperative Housing Foundation consultant. In that capacity, she advised the Ministry of Interior on establishing a quasi-public housing organization to receive funding from the World Bank. She was also consultant for the firm Coopers and Lybrand, the U.S. Department of Labor, the Cooperative Housing Foundation, and the Equal Employment Opportunity Commission.

Newman became active in the Bush-Quayle campaign in 1988 and was deputy director of national voter coalitions. She was codirector of outreach for the Presidential Transition Team in 1988-89. For three years, June 1989 to June 1992, she was director of the U.S. Office of Personnel Management, the first black to hold that position.

Work at Smithsonian Institution

Since July 1, 1992, Newman has been under secretary of the Smithsonian Institution. She replaced her longtime friend, Carmen Turner, who died in April 1992. Robert M. Adams, secretary of the Smithsonian Institution, said in a letter announcing Newman's appointment:

> Constance Newman has . . . a distinguished record of achievement. . . . Mrs. Newman's wisdom and versatility as a policy maker and outstanding success as a high level manager in many different settings in the private and not-for-profit sectors as well as the Federal government, are a perfect fit for the complex and rewarding opportunities that I think she will find here. Her many other interests and activities in such fields as housing, minority and urban issues, in which she also has an impressive record of accomplishment, make her exactly the kind of individual that the Smithsonian is proud to bring into a position of leadership.

Newman responded to the appointment in the *Smithsonian Institution News* of May 14, 1992, saying:

> It has been an honor for me to serve for the last three years in the administration of President Bush and now I am excited and honored to have been appointed by Secretary Adams to work with him and the Smithsonian. I can think of no other institution at this time in our history that can serve to unify the nation through art, history, science, research and education.

The Smithsonian Institution operates fifteen museums and galleries, the National Zoological Park, and research facilities in eight states and the Republic of Panama. As under secretary, Newman is the chief operating officer and the second-ranking official at the Smithsonian, with responsibility for the day-to-day operations of the world's largest museum and research complex. Her comments on the museum's financial difficulties impressed the U.S. Congress, which had complained that the Smithsonian "has taken on too much." According to the May 15, 1992, *Washington Post,* Newman reported that for the previous three years she had dealt with budgetary constraints. "It requires all managers to evaluate their organizations and to set priorities. When you are in a tight situation, you cannot do everything." When asked if she saw any "leftward leanings" in the Smithsonian's exhibitions, Newman said in the same article, "My background is not art or history or anthropology and I'm not going to pretend that it is." She considered it unwise to discuss the exhibits then but necessary to acquaint herself with all the institution's operations.

Writing and Service on Boards

Although her work responsibilities have been demanding, Newman has still found time to engage in other activities such as teaching, writing, and serving on boards. She was a Woodrow Wilson Visiting Fellow from 1977 to 1985 and a member of the adjunct faculty at the John F. Kennedy School of Government, Harvard University, from 1979 to 1982. Her writings include: "The Consumer Product Safety Commission: Does It Can the Ash Report," which she coauthored with James A. Brodsky and Judith A. Hermanson and published in the *George Washington Law Review* (May 1975); "Research and Policy Making Under Uncertainty, A Case Study: Spray Adhesives," in *The Evaluation of Social Programs,* edited by Clark C. Abt (1976); and *Legal Impediments to Metrification,* U.S. Metric Board (1981).

Her past memberships and affiliations include member of the Administrative Conference of the United States; the Energy Council, American Standards Institute; Board of Overseers, Morehouse College School of Medicine; chairperson and member of the Executive Committee, Defense Advisory Committee on Women in the Services; member of the Presidential Rank Review Board; and director, Radio Free Europe, Radio Liberty. She is a founding member of Executive Women in Government and the Evaluation Research Society. She has been a member of the Board of Trustees, Community College of Baltimore since 1985. Beginning in 1986, she has served on the Board of Directors, U.S. Committee for the U. N. Fund For Women, Inc., and has been a member of the Women's Equity Action League and the Presidential Rank Review Board. Currently Newman is on the Board of Trustees of The Brookings Institution and the National Academy of Public Administration. She is also a member of the Board of Governors of the Center for Creative Leadership, vice-chairperson of the National Research Council's Board of Testing and Assessment, and a member of the NAACP.

For her outstanding work, Newman received the Secretary's Award for Excellence from the U.S. Department of Housing and Urban Development in 1977 and the Secretary of Defense Medal for Outstanding Public Service in 1985. She has received honorary doctor of laws degrees from Bates College (1962), Amherst College (1980), and Central State University in Ohio (1991). Since the 1970s Newman has lectured widely to the military, businesses, and academic and civic organizations. She continues to contribute to the nation's cultural affairs through her office as under secretary of the Smithsonian Institution.

Current Address: Under Secretary, Smithsonian Institution, 1000 Jefferson Drive, SW, Room 219, Washington, DC 20560.

REFERENCES:

Adams, Robert M. Letter to Smithsonian Institution E Mail Users, May 14, 1992.

"Constance Berry Newman." Biographical statement. Office of the Under Secretary, Smithsonian Institution, Washington, D.C.

Constance Berry Newman. Resumé. May 7, 1992.

"Constance Berry Newman, Director of Office of Personnel Management, Appointed Smithsonian Under Secretary." *Smithsonian Institution News,* May 14, 1992.

Cummings, Judith. "Black Women in Public Life." *Black Enterprise* 5 (August 1974): 33-35.

"An Interview with Constance B. Newman." *Black Enterprise* 5 (November 1974): 51-54.

"Newman Goes to Smithsonian." *Washington Post,* May 15, 1992.

Who's Who among Black Americans, 1993-94. 8th ed. Detroit: Gale Research, 1994.

Jessie Carney Smith

Jeanne Noble

Jeanne Noble

(1926-)

Educator, writer, consultant, college administrator, organization leader

As a young college student, Jeanne Noble knew that there was a wider world beyond her own. Aware of her own potential as well as what the world had to offer, she realized her dream of becoming an educator. More than that, she became a master teacher and a noted scholar in the field of education, known especially for her research on black women and her influential books *The Negro Woman College Graduate* and *Beautiful, Also, Are the Souls of My Black Sisters.* Noble has also found time to serve on a number of government panels; she was, in fact appointed to federal commissions by three U.S. presidents. Additionally, her board memberships have been numerous, and she has acted as a consultant to school systems and corporations as well.

Born in Albany, Georgia, on July 18, 1926, Jeanne Noble was the eldest of four children—one girl and three boys—born to Aurelia and Floyd Noble. Jeanne Noble's father disappeared when she was four or five years old, leaving the task of child rearing to her mother and grandmother, Maggie Brown, who taught first grade in the same classroom for fifty years. While Noble's mother envisioned a "good marriage" for her daughter, Noble's grandmother encouraged her to pursue a career so that she could provide for herself. Maggie Brown had a florist shop where she worked each day after teaching school. The florist shop was run by Noble's brother William. Noble said in a July 1993 interview that "there was a special chemistry between my grandmother and me," especially since Noble's mother was very young and "more like a sister." Not only was Maggie Brown the youngster's role model, but she managed to keep the family from experiencing poverty by stressing the importance of education as a way to avoid need and want.

In the interview Noble reflected on her childhood, especially her involvement in the Episcopal Church, in which her mother was very active. With some humor and regret, she recounted her childhood visit to a white camp in Sea Islands, Georgia. Since she had always attended black camps, she assumed that she was to take part in activities with the white children. However, she realized her mistake when she was sent home, being described as "too forward" by the camp leaders for having participated. This episode was traumatic for the youngster, who, bewildered by racism, abandoned the church for many years. Since she had always been a "goody two-shoes," to be sent home was devastating. Maturity and experience in the wider world, however, have brought her back to her religious roots, and she is now very active in the Episcopal church she attends in New York City.

Nobel's undergraduate days at Howard University, which granted her a B.A. degree in 1946, also contributed to her social maturation. She had always wanted to attend a black college—the only ones with which she was familiar. She described herself in the interview as a very "provincial" college student who refused to take classes from white professors. Instead, she sought out such illustrious teachers as E. Franklin Frazier (her advisor), Alain Locke, and Sterling Brown; all three contributed to the intense intellectual activity at Howard University at the time.

Much to Noble's surprise, her true intellectual powers were awakened when she enrolled in a humanities course taught by a white Quaker theologian. According to Noble, the Quaker saw her as a gifted student. Under his influence, Noble changed her attitude toward whites. In the interview she expressed regret that she had failed early on to adopt a "more gestalt attitude" toward the white world. She was only nineteen when she graduated from Howard.

Noble pursued a master's degree at Columbia University in New York City, graduating in 1948. After four years working as a teacher and dean, she returned to Columbia and was awarded her doctorate in educational psychology and counselling in 1955. Later she studied at the University of Birmingham in England.

After obtaining her master's degree, Noble decided to become a teacher when she met the president of historically black Albany State College, in Albany, Georgia, who asked her to teach summer school. According to Noble, "I fell in love with teaching and never left [the field]." She taught at Albany State College from 1948 to 1950.

In 1950 Noble reluctantly accepted the position of dean of women at Langston University, Langston, Oklahoma, another historically black school, where she worked from 1950 to 1952. When the president of Langston, Lamar Harrison, asked her to become dean, Noble had at first demurred, thinking that the job consisted only of being a disciplinarian and "sending home pregnant girls." As it turned out, Noble very much enjoyed her work at Langston, where she also sat on the administrative council. However, Noble knew that she needed a doctorate to obtain the respect she wanted.

In 1952 Noble left Langston to pursue higher education studies at Columbia University on a full-time basis. From there she went to New York University, where she taught in the Center for Human Relations in the Department of Educational Sociology. Noble notes that she was probably the first African American woman to move up the ranks to a tenured position—from assistant professor to full professor—at a major white institution of higher learning. Currently, she is professor of guidance and counseling at the graduate school of Brooklyn College of the City University of New York. During her career Noble also was a summer visiting professor at the University of Vermont and Tuskegee Institute (now University) in Alabama.

Works on Education and Women Published

Noble is the author or coauthor of several books that give evidence of her dedication to the field of education. In 1960 her *College Education as Personal Development* was published, cowritten with Margaret Fisher, then dean of South Florida University. Noble describes this book as "speaking to freshmen" in a freshman orientation course. She and Fisher wanted students to know the value of a liberal arts education. In 1970 *The Negro Woman College Graduate* was published. This book, which examines the education of four hundred black women who had four years or more of college education, won the Pi Lambda Theta Research Award. In the book, Nobel says, "College offers a student fresh opportunities to learn, to explore new ideas about himself, to modify those he

already has." *Beautiful, Also, Are the Souls of My Black Sisters* was published in 1976. The title paraphrases a Langston Hughes poem. The book grew out of research on African American women that Noble had been doing. In the July 1993 interview she described *Beautiful, Also,* as "a more psychosocial look at black women" than a history of black women. The book, Noble said, is a "montage" of black women, ranging from the single parent, to the singers, such as those in church choirs, who have told the story of black women through song, to the black woman writer. Noble added that at the time she was writing *Beautiful, Also,* African American writers like Alice Walker and Toni Morrison were gaining prominence, as were black women's organizations.

Also active in the media, Noble produced a record album, *Roses and Revolutions,* for Delta Sigma Theta Sorority in 1973. With Ruby Dee and Ossie Davis, she coproduced the video *75 Years in Retrospect* and a public service announcement on drug abuse featuring Natalie Cole. She was cohost of *Straight Talk,* a weekly television show that ran the summer of 1979, and a professor on *The Learning Experience,* a weekly educational show on WCBS television that aired in New York for five years and won a regional Emmy Award in 1977.

Busy Consultant, Board Member, and Committee Worker

Noble has held a number of consultantships. She was part of the Robert Havighurst Study of the Chicago School System and acted as consultant on school desegregation programs in Norwalk, Connecticut; Philadelphia; Miami; Seattle; Bridgeton and Teaneck, New Jersey; and Boston. She was also consultant for Fordham University's Program for the Development of Black and Puerto Rican Principals. In the corporate world, she has served as consultant to the Ford Foundation's Social and Economic Development Division on Special Projects; Exxon Corporation; and Mutual of New York Insurance Company's Affirmative Action Plans and Staff Training. She has also been a board member of the Federal Trust Bank.

In 1963 *Ebony* magazine commended Noble as "one of the 100 most influential Negroes of the Emancipation Year." Certainly her varied career in public service and education justifies such a commendation. She has served on various government commissions at the requests of U.S. presidents Lyndon B. Johnson, Richard Nixon, and Gerald Ford. For example, she worked on the National Education Professions Development Commission, the Commission on an All-Volunteer Armed Services, the National Advisory Commission on Selective Service, and the Commission of Presidential Scholars. Other government appointments include the UNESCO Commission, Bicentennial Commission, Advisory Panel on Essentials for Effective Minority Programming, and the Corporation for Public Broadcasting. Secretary of Agriculture Orville Freeman appointed her to the Joint Committee to Study the Extension Services of the Department of Agriculture, and she was later appointed to the Defense Advisory Committee on Women in the Services. In 1964 she accepted the invitation of Sargent Shriver, then director of the Peace

Corps and the Office of Economic Opportunity, to head a committee to develop plans for a Girls' Job Corps, a component of the federal antipoverty program. In 1967 she was director of training for the Harlem Domestic Peace Corps, on part-time loan from NYU. Outside the federal arena, she served on the American Council of Education's Commission on the College Student and chaired the National Association of Women Deans and Counselors's Research Committee.

Noble has been active with a number of other organizations. She has served as a member on the boards of the Urban League of Greater New York, the Haryou Act, and the International Center for Integrative Studies. She was a national board member of Girl Scouts of the USA and for twelve years served the scouts as a member of the Executive Committee, assistant secretary, and USA delegate to the World Assembly in Denmark. Noble has served on the board of trustees of Marymount Manhattan College in New York and of Lincoln University in Pennsylvania. For six years she served on the Board of Governors of Common Cause, and she has served as a member of the Alvin Ailey Dance Foundation. She joined the Women's Africa Committee and attended the Conference on Women of Africa and African Descent in Ghana as a delegate from the committee. A former national president of Delta Sigma Theta Sorority, Noble was the youngest person ever elected to that post. Later, she was first chair of the sorority's National Commission on Arts and Letters and worked with the commission as it conducted a study for the Corporation of Public Broadcasting designed to devise ways to increase black viewership of public broadcasting. She is also former national vice-president of the National Council of Negro Women.

In recognition of her outstanding accomplishments, Noble has received numerous awards, including the Bethune-Roosevelt Award for service in the field of education, 1965; Lifetime Achievement Award from the National Association of Black Women in Higher Education, 1989; and honorary doctor of humane letters from Bennett College, Greensboro, North Carolina, May 1991. In 1993 the Consortium of Doctors gave her its highest tribute, the Award of Perseverance.

An ardent sports aficionada, Noble is also a skilled tennis player and an excellent swimmer. She serves her church, the Episcopal Church of the Ascension in New York City, as a member of the vestry and a lay reader.

Noble's prestigious career as an educator and public figure has caused her to reflect on the status—past and present—of the African American. In general, Noble believes that present-day African Americans need to regain a sense of being an "organized community" by relying once again on such voluntary organizations as clubs and sororities whose good works are now only sporadic. She also sees the need for parents to take a more active part in their children's educations while presenting them with true heroes or heroines—African Americans "living life." The present younger generation, laments Noble, is attracted only to celebrities such as rap singers and sports stars. True champions of African American culture, such as author Toni Morrison, are hard to sell to the young.

In conversation Jeanne Noble demonstrates that she is forceful, candid, and persuasive. She radiates the self-confidence that has obviously propelled her throughout her distinguished career. She is in touch with the past and what it can teach as well as with the present and what it can offer. From a "provincial" youngster, she has matured into a shining example of what the African American can achieve in the United States.

Current Address: Graduate School, The City University of New York—Brooklyn College, City University of New York System, New York, NY 10021.

REFERENCES:

Noble, Jeanne. Curriculum Vitae. N.d.
———. Telephone interview with Grace E. Collins, July 1993.
"Organization to Honor Professor Jeanne Noble." *Savannah News-Press,* July 3, 1993.
Ploski, Harry A., and James Williams, eds. *The Negro Almanac.* 5th ed. Detroit: Gale Research, 1989.
Robinson, Wilhelmina. *Historical Negro Biographies.* New York: Publishers Co., 1968.
Shockley, Ann Allen, and Sue P. Chandler. *Living Black American Authors.* New York: Bowker, 1973.
"Speaking of People." *Ebony* 11 (June 1956): 4.
"Tribute to Dr. Jeanne L. Noble." Unidentified document in the author's possession.
Troupe, Cornelius V. *Distinguished Negro Georgians.* Dallas: Royal Publishing Co., 1962.

Grace E. Collins

Marita Bonner Occomy

(1899-1971)
Writer, educator

Although she has not been as widely recognized as some of her more well-known contemporaries identified with the Harlem Renaissance, Marita Bonner Occomy deserves attention as a highly innovative and versatile writer. In the 1920s and 1930s, she won many literary competitions sponsored by the magazines *Crisis* and *Opportunity,* the two major periodicals that published the works of promising young artists of the Harlem Renaissance period. Indeed, during her lifetime, Occomy's publications appeared exclusively in these two journals. Between 1925 and 1941, she published three short plays, two essays, a review of a volume of poetry, and seventeen short stories. Five short stories remained in manuscript at the time of her death. These stories are included in *Frye Street and Environs: The Collected Works of Marita Bonner* (1987), coedited by Occomy's daughter, Joyce Occomy Stricklin, and Joyce Flynn. Occomy's other major professional activity was teaching, a vocation she pursued during various periods of her life. After 1941, she devoted herself primarily to her family. She died after being injured in a fire in 1971.

Marita Bonner Occomy was born on June 16, 1899, in Boston, Massachusetts. Her parents were Joseph Andrew and Mary Anne Noel Bonner. The other Bonner children, Bernice, Joseph, and Andrew, did not survive beyond childhood. Occomy graduated from Brookline High School, where her courses included German and music. In 1918, she began studies at Radcliffe College. As a junior there, she gained distinction by being admitted to Professor Charles Townsend Copeland's course in writing. According to *Crisis,* the course was restricted to "the sixteen best writers, graduates and undergraduates in each college year.... [A sketch by Occomy,] 'Dandelion Season,' was selected to be read annually to Radcliffe classes." Before her graduation from Radcliffe in 1922, Occomy taught in a local high school. She subsequently taught in a Bluefield, West Virginia, high school and at Armstrong High School in Washington, D.C.

In Washington, she interacted with many writers of the Harlem Renaissance. The noted poet and playwright Georgia Douglas Johnson was a close friend. In 1930, Occomy married William Almy Occomy and moved to Chicago, the setting of her Frye Street stories. William Occomy, a Rhode Island native, graduated from Brown University. After her marriage, Occomy published her works under her full name,

Marita Bonner Occomy. The Occomys had three children: William Almy, Jr., Warwick Gale, and Marita Joyce.

Writings Address Race and Gender Issues

Occomy's first piece of published fiction, "The Hands—A Story," appeared in *Opportunity* in August 1925. The story's narrator, a physically unattractive loner, assumes the usual role of the author as he uses his imagination to fashion the life story of a complete stranger, a fellow bus rider. The stranger's hands are the key to the narrator's assumptions about the circumstances of the stranger's life, for they indicate a life of toil and struggle. The narrator muses on the concept of "Christ-in-all-men," and the story as a whole delineates the racial injustices blacks encountered in early twentieth-century American society, no matter how hard they worked. These themes recur in many of Occomy's later works.

Occomy's first work of published nonfiction, "On Being Young—a Woman—and Colored," has a clipped, imagistic style. It won the 1925 *Crisis* prize for best essay. In the first part of the piece, Occomy captures the exhilaration of youth and suggests that many opportunities are available to gifted young people:

> Somehow you feel like a kitten in a sunny catnip field that sees sleek, plump brown field mice and yellow baby chicks sitting coyly, side by side, under each leaf. Desire to dash three or four ways seizes you.

> That's Youth.

In discussing racial issues in this essay, and in her writings as a whole, Occomy does not present easy, romantic visions of solidarity between disadvantaged and more affluent blacks. In "On Being . . . Colored," she exposes the emptiness of the life of the black bourgeoisie, who spend their time playing cards and watching movies. She describes the two groups of blacks as "[m]illing around like live fish in a basket. Those on the bottom crushed into a sort of stupid apathy by the weight of those on top. Those on top leaping, leaping; leaping to scale the sides; to get out."

The larger society does not escape criticism either, for Occomy exposes the emptiness of what is "out" of the basket: the materialistic values of Western society. She writes that "[t]he Greeks had possessions, culture, . . . [but] [t]hey were lost because they lacked wisdom."

Also in this essay, Occomy identifies the impact of sexism not just on black women, but on women generally:

> For you know that—being a woman—you cannot twice a month or twice a year, for that matter, break

away to see or hear anything in a city that is supposed to see and hear too much.

That's being a woman. A woman of any color.

Occomy's other stories from the 1920s include "The Prison-Bound," "Nothing New," "One Boy's Story," and "Drab Rambles." "The Prison-Bound" depicts the "iron walls" of a failing marriage. Although the story emphasizes the wife's disappointments, the husband's point of view is represented as well. Both fail to directly communicate their deepest feelings to one another, a condition that itself indicates the depths of their imprisonment.

"Nothing New," set in Chicago, introduces Frye Street, which would become the setting for many of her stories. Prejudice is indeed nothing new in this story of interracial love. As a child, Denny, the story's black male protagonist, is literally driven back when he crosses a racially defined boundary. As a young man, he encounters prejudice again when he and Pauline, a white girl, fall in love. When told to "[s]tay on [his] own side"—the message he heard during his childhood transgression—Denny reacts violently, killing the man who has triggered the old memory. Denny is tried and executed by the state. Joyce Flynn points out that "Nothing New" presents a situation similar to the drowning of Eugene Williams in Chicago in 1919. Williams reportedly had crossed an unofficial but rigidly enforced racial boundary while swimming and drowned when he was too frightened to come ashore at the "white" beach.

In "One Boy's Story," Occomy draws on Greek and biblical stories in a painful and tragic tale of the American South. The narrator, the son of a black mother and a white father, kills his father with a sling shot. The boy then loses his ability to speak after injuring his tongue on the pin of his mother's brooch. Well-read, the boy himself makes connections with the stories of Oedipus, Orestes, and David. By adopting the pseudonym Joseph Maree Andrew to write this story, Occomy underscores its male point of view. And in using names taken from her immediate family in the pseudonym, she also pays tribute to her father and her deceased brothers.

Dramas Influence Writers of the Harlem Renaissance

Occomy is perhaps most innovative in her three dramas, all of which were published in the 1920s. The first was *The Pot-Maker (A Play To Be Read),* published in *Opportunity* in February 1927. In this work, Occomy concentrates on depicting the personal limitations of each character. A newly ordained minister, Elias Jackson, is willing to let his wife's lover, Lew, die. However, in his very eagerness to judge others, Elias is also flawed, or a "pot with a crack in it." Elias recognizes his error in condemning others, and he tries to save his wife Lucinda when she is in danger. However, the ending implies that he may have perished along with Lucinda and Lew.

The stage directions are an integral part of the play's message, as shown by the passage that introduces Lucinda:

You can see she is a woman who must have sat down in the mud. It has crept into her eyes. They are dirty. It has filtered through—filtered through her. Her speech is smudged. Every inch of her body, from the twitch of an eyebrow to the twitch of muscles lower down in her body, is soiled.

Occomy's second play, *The Purple Flower,* is perhaps the most experimental of the three. It won first place in the 1927 *Crisis* drama awards. In *Black Female Playwrights,* Kathy Perkins notes that in this play, Occomy is "possibly the first black woman to use surrealism." The play addresses racial injustice and the prospects for resolving the conflict between blacks and whites. Characters include the impatient "Young Us" and a wise "Old Man." "The Purple Flower" is the prize, life at its fullest at the top of the hill. The call for blood at the end suggests that violence must precede change unless whites heed the drama's warning to end their unfair treatment of blacks.

Violence is also a part of Occomy's third play, *Exit: An Illusion* (1929). Dot and Buddy are the only two speaking characters in the play. Dot, a light-skinned black, sees herself as doomed and speaks of her "date" with death allegorically. Buddy, her lover, misunderstands and accuses Dot of infidelity. In casting death as a silent white man ("Exit Mann" by name), Occomy shows the force of history on the minds and actions of black people. She effectively blends psychological realism and surreal allegory.

Elizabeth Brown-Guillory notes in *Wines in the Wilderness* that although Occomy's plays were not performed publicly during her lifetime, they "were read and savored during the Harlem Renaissance by some of its finest artists, including Georgia Douglas Johnson, May Miller, and Langston Hughes, who would go on to see their own plays produced." Occomy's interest in drama is also shown through her membership in Washington's Krigwa Players group. Krigwa theater groups were started in several cities throughout the country by W. E. B. Du Bois under the auspices of *Crisis.* Originally spelled Crigwa, the letters stood for the Crisis Guild of Writers and Artists.

Two short prose works complete Occomy's publications of the decade. She won another *Crisis* prize for the essay "The Young Blood Hungers" (1928). Like "On Being Young—a Woman—and Colored," the essay articulates the desires of a new generation; and like *The Purple Flower,* it portends violence if justice is thwarted. Occomy's review of *Autumn Love Cycle,* a book of poems by Georgia Douglas Johnson, was published in 1929. In it, Occomy uses a poetic, metaphoric style. She compares love to a fire and contrasts the "flame mad and consuming" of youthful passion with the smoldering fire of more mature emotion.

Stories Examine Effect of Environment on Characters

In 1933, Occomy's "A Possible Triad on Black Notes" received honorable mention in *Opportunity*'s literary contest. The foreword to "Triad" emphasizes the multiethnic character of Frye Street: "All the World is There." This world is also interconnected and fluid; pinning down one's ethnic identity is often difficult. In the first part of ''Triad,'' ''There Were Three,'' three characters are portrayed—a mother and her son and daughter. The young man dies from a fall from a hotel window, after discovering his mother is a prostitute. The mother loses her mind. Occomy does not tell the reader what happens to the daughter. The story concludes, ''Sometimes I wonder which door opened for that third.''

In the second story, ''Of Jimmy Harris,'' the title character is hardworking and unassuming. When Jimmy becomes critically ill, his materialistic, unsympathetic wife is already setting her sights on his doctor as her next suitor. Jimmy's death is clearly precipitated by the stresses of his essentially empty emotional life.

In ''Corner Store,'' the third story in the triad, the main characters are a Jewish family: Anton and Esther Steinberg and their daughter, Meta. The story shows how life in Frye Street is indeed ''interconnected and fluid.'' Esther learns that Anton has a black mistress and that Meta loves the mistress's nephew. Although the point of view is omniscient, the major frame of reference throughout is Esther's. In capturing and understanding Esther's sense of betrayal by her family, Occomy avoids stereotyping. In telling the story from Esther's point of view, Occomy demonstrates her firm grasp of many different cultural perspectives.

As is typical of Occomy's works, ''Triad'' makes clear that environmental forces underlie the problems the protagonists face. At the same time, she does not absolve her characters from wrongdoing or romanticize those who fall. Another example of negative environmental forces is the story of Jimmy Joe in ''Tin Can'' (1934). His promise and beauty are clear: ''There are no words in any language under the sun rich enough in color, movement and sound to make you see a young black boy lilting a slim seventeen-year-old body through a dance.'' But his character is formed even sooner: ''It's too late when fourteen years or more of haphazard, slap-dash, hit-or-miss, grab-bag living has snatched you through the lowly life of poor colored homes in black sections.'' Jimmy Joe ends up in the electric chair.

Several of Occomy's short stories show the impact of the lack of genuine communication or knowledge. In ''A Sealed Pod'' (1936), Viollette's murderer escapes and an innocent man is hanged for the crime. In ''The Whipping'' (1939), a white prison warden considers herself to be a kind person; however, she fails to comprehend the forces that have caused a black mother's incarceration. In ''One True Love,'' Nora, a domestic, attempts to become a lawyer, but the many disadvantages she has experienced cause her ambitions to be thwarted. And it is not until she is dying that ''buttercolored'' Nora fully appreciates the love of faithful, working-class, dark-skinned Sam. Nor does Sam ever know that Nora did indeed love him.

''Hate Is Nothing'' (1938) provides a significant exception to the stories in which intraracial snobbery and lack of communication prevail. In this story, a dark-skinned wife receives support from her husband when his color-conscious mother oversteps her bounds. Occomy published this story under a pseudonym and it may have autobiographical elements.

Both ''Hongry Fire'' and ''Patch Quilt'' have female protagonists who exact justice in response to the acts of family members. In ''Hongry Fire'' (1939), a mother who is terminally ill takes drastic action to save her family from the damaging influence of her daughter-in-law. The mother dies peacefully even though she has enacted judgment by taking a life. In ''Patch Quilt'' (1941), a wife is the last of the townspeople to discover her husband's infidelity. She wounds him with an ice pick, and his arm is useless thereafter. The two remain together in a loveless marriage. As pointed out by Joyce Flynn in *Dictionary of Literary Biography,* the completely rural, southern setting of ''Patch Quilt'' sets it apart from Occomy's other work; at the same time, the story's bleak look at relationships forestalls any simplistic romanticism about such a setting.

Works Published Posthumously

Some stories were not published until after Occomy's death, when they were collected in *Frye Street.* These include ''On the Altar'' (written 1937-40), ''High Stepper'' (1938-40), ''Stones for Bread'' (1940), ''Reap It as You Sow It'' (1940-41), and ''Light in Dark Places'' (1941). For the most part, these later works demonstrate a greater development of plot than the sketchier earlier works. The later stories also reveal a firm vision and a slight optimism, even if that optimism extends only to justly received retribution. Discussing those of Occomy's stories that were not published during her lifetime, Flynn reports in *Frye Street* that ''Occomy used her best handwriting and apparently glossed the hard-to read words for the readers she knew would one day find her.''

For the last thirty years of her life, Occomy turned more fully to her family and to pursuits other than writing. She became very interested in Christian Scientist philosophy; as a teacher, she last worked with mentally handicapped students. She died in Chicago on December 6, 1971, after being injured in an apartment fire.

In ''A Portrait of My Mother,'' published in *Frye Street,* Joyce Occomy Stricklin provides an illuminating, brief memoir. Stricklin describes her mother as having a ''gentle brown complexion'' and a stylistic flair: ''[Mother] always said it was the accessory or accent that moved anything beyond the ordinary.'' Stricklin notes that her mother's guidance was also memorable: ''She . . . steered us away from the disheartening blandness of living only for material goals. Yet she instilled a type of worldly poise.'' Thus, it is not surprising that her works expose the dangers of materialism and show the value of facing reality unflinchingly.

REFERENCES:

Brown-Guillory, Elizabeth, ed. *Wines in the Wilderness: Plays by African American Women from the Harlem Renaissance to the Present.* Westport, Conn.: Greenwood Press, 1990.

Flynn, Joyce. In *Dictionary of Literary Biography.* Vol. 51, *Afro-American Writers from the Harlem Renaissance to 1940.* Detroit: Gale Research, 1987.

Flynn, Joyce, and Joyce Occomy Stricklin, eds. *Frye Street and Environs: The Collected Works of Marita Bonner Occomy.* Boston: Beacon Press, 1987.

Hine, Darlene Clark, ed. *Black Women in America.* Brooklyn: Carlson Publishing, 1993.

Occomy, Marita Bonner. "The Hands—A Story." *Opportunity* 3 (August 1925): 235-37.

———. "On Being Young—a Woman—and Colored." *Crisis* 31 (December 1925): 63-65.

———. "The Prison-Bound." *Crisis* 32 (September 1926): 225-26.

———. "Nothing New." 33 *Crisis* (November 1926): 17-20.

———. *The Pot-Maker (A Play To Be Read). Opportunity* 5 (February 1927): 43-46.

———. "One Boy's Story." *Crisis* 34 (November 1927): 297-99, 316-20.

———. "Drab Rambles." *Crisis* 34 (December 1927): 335-36, 354-56.

———. "The Purple Flower." *Crisis* 35 (January 1928): 9-11.

———. "The Young Blood Hungers." *Crisis* 35 (May 1928): 151, 172.

———. Review of *Autumn Love-Cycle,* by Georgia Douglas Johnson. *Opportunity* 7 (April 1929): 130.

———. "Exit—An Illusion." *Crisis* 36 (October 1929): 335-36, 352.

———. "A Possible Triad on Black Notes, Part One: There Were Three." *Opportunity* 11 (July 1933): 205-207.

———. "A Possible Triad on Black Notes, Part Two: Of Jimmie Harris." *Opportunity* 11 (August 1933): 242-44.

———. "A Possible Triad on Black Notes, Part Three: Three Tales of Living: Corner Store." *Opportunity* 11 (September 1933): 269-71.

———. "Tin Can." *Opportunity* 12 (July 1934): 202-205; 12 (August 1934): 236-40.

———. "A Sealed Pod." *Opportunity* 14 (March 1936): 88-91.

———. "Black Fronts." *Opportunity* 16 (July 1938): 210-14.

[Joyce N. Reed, pseud.] "Hate Is Nothing." *Crisis* 45 (December 1938): 388-90, 394, 403-404.

———. "The Makin's." *Opportunity* 17 (January 1939): 18-21.

———. "Hongry Fire." *Crisis* 46 (December 1939): 360-62, 376-77.

———. "Patch Quilt." *Crisis* 47 (March 1940): 71-72, 92.

———. "One True Love." *Crisis* 48 (February 1941): 46-47, 58-59.

Perkins, Kathy A. *Black Female Playwrights: An Anthology of Plays before 1950.* Bloomington: Indiana University Press, 1989.

COLLECTIONS:

Manuscripts and related Occomy materials are in the Arthur and Elizabeth Schlesinger Library, Radcliffe College, Cambridge, Massachusetts.

Arlene Clift-Pellow

Hazel O'Leary
(1937-)
U.S. Secretary of Energy, government official, lawyer, business executive, consultant

The first woman to become U.S. Secretary of Energy, Hazel O'Leary is a confident and determined leader in President Bill Clinton's cabinet. She has seen many sides of the energy world, from industry to government, as a consultant, federal regulator, lobbyist, and corporate executive. She now heads the agency that determines the direction of energy development in this country, and she has emerged as one of the most powerful women in the world.

Hazel Rollins O'Leary was born on May 17, 1937, in Newport News, Virginia, the daughter of Russell E. Reid, a physician. O'Leary's birth mother, whose name is thus far unpublished, was also a physician. She and her sister, Edna Reid McCollum, of San Bernadino, California, who is older by fourteen months, were raised by their father and stepmother, Hazel Palleman Reid. O'Leary told Richette L. Haywood for *Ebony* magazine that her family stressed the importance of helping other people. She learned this lesson by observation at home as well as through her teachers at school. For example, her grandmother kept clean clothes arranged by size in a box on her back porch and distributed them to others as the need arose. Her grandmother was also a founder of the black public library in her community. "I grew up in a family and an environment where opening the doors for others and literally opening your front door to others was not only expected but was a practice," she said.

She spent the first eight years of her school life in the racially segregated public schools of Newport News. Edna McCollum told the *Washington Times,* February 4, 1993, that they led relatively sheltered lives and that their father drove them wherever they needed to go. According to the *Washington Post,* January 19, 1993, O'Leary's parents recognized her alertness, self-confidence, and ability "to do anything," and decided that they wanted the best for her. They sent their daughters to Essex County, New Jersey, where they lived with an aunt and attended Arts High School for artistically talented youth. In high school O'Leary studied voice and alto horn. She received a bachelor of arts degree cum laude from Fisk University, Nashville, Tennessee, in 1959, and on May 11,

Hazel O'Leary

1980, was elected an alumni member of Fisk's chapter of Phi Beta Kappa. Her alma mater also awarded her an honorary doctor of laws degree on April 30, 1994, after she delivered the commencement address. Although she was interested in pursuing a law degree after completing her undergraduate work, she postponed her goal and married Carl Rollins, a physician. They had one son, Carl G., now a practicing attorney in Washington, D.C. She received a J.D. degree from Rutgers University School of Law in 1966.

Broad Experience in Public Service

O'Leary has had a variety of experiences in law and public service. After passing the New Jersey Bar, she became assistant prosecutor in Essex County, New Jersey, in 1967. She was subsequently named assistant attorney general in the state. By now divorced, she moved to Washington, D.C., where she became a partner in the accounting firm of Coopers and Lybrand. O'Leary's work in public service and energy policy began during the Ford administration and continued under three presidents. She joined the Federal Energy Administration (FEA) during Ford's presidency and from 1974 to 1976 was director of the Office of Consumer Affairs/Special Impact. This office managed many of the antipoverty programs initiated during the Great Society years of the 1960s and O'Leary became known as an advocate for the poor. From 1976 to 1977 she was general counsel for the Community Services Administration. She was assistant administrator for conservation and environment with the FEA from May 1977 until the following October, when the FEA became part of the new Department of Energy (DOE). From 1978 to 1980,

during President Jimmy Carter's presidency, she was chief of the DOE's Economic Regulatory Administration. Under both the Ford and Carter administrations O'Leary was responsible for regulating the petroleum, natural gas, and electric industries and the federal government's conservation and environment programs. She supervised more than 2,000 lawyers, accountants, and engineers.

O'Leary received praise as well as criticism for her work. She was often called a fair administrator, and some environmentalists and energy executives cheered her innovative conservation programs, including underwriting the cost of insulating homes for low-income families. But critics attacked some of her policies, specifically the Fuel Use Act, which they said substituted energy friendly power supplies, such as nuclear power, coal, and oil, for the less friendly but cleaner natural gas.

John F. O'Leary, who was to become her husband in 1980, was deputy energy secretary under President Carter. Hazel O'Leary left the DOE when the couple set up their own energy consulting firm, with Hazel O'Leary as vice president and general counsel, a position she held from 1981 to 1989. Their company was an international energy, economics, and strategic planning firm located in Washington, D.C. The firm specialized in the preparation of expert testimony, project financing, and the development of independent power plants. It lobbied Congress and state legislatures on issues involving the energy industry and attracted foreign clients who needed help adjusting to this country's dramatic shifts in energy policy. General Public Utilities Company, owner of the Three Mile Island plant that is infamous for a partial core meltdown in 1979, hired John O'Leary as chairperson to salvage the company.

John O'Leary died in 1987. Two years later O'Leary closed their firm and became director of Applied Energy Services, an independent power producer traded on the American Stock Exchange, and director of NRG Energy, the major unregulated subsidiary of Northern States Power Company. She joined Minneapolis-based Northern States Power Company as executive vice president for public and environmental affairs and vice president for human resources. On January 1, 1993, she was promoted to president of the company. The company provides energy to parts of five contiguous states in the northern Midwest tier of the country. While the company generates much of its electricity from coal and nuclear reactors (anathema to the environmental community), it also invests heavily in wind power and energy conservation.

Under O'Leary's direction, the Northern States Power Company developed into a leading and progressive utilities company. But the company's treatment of nuclear waste concerned environmentalists. In 1989 when the company, owner of three nuclear power plants, needed more space, O'Leary helped plan for the temporary above ground storage of spent radioactive fuel at Northern States Power Company's Prairie Island Nuclear Plant in Minnesota, located in close proximity to homes on the Mdewakanton Sioux reservation. Many residents of the area said that Northern States Power acted tyrannically in its dealings with state agencies and the legislature. Later on the company stymied public debate about storage sites on television channels in Minneapolis.

First Woman Secretary of Energy Named

On December 21, 1992, President-elect Bill Clinton announced his intention to nominate O'Leary to serve as the seventh Secretary of Energy, which would give her control over what the *Dallas Morning News* called on December 18, 1992, "one of the largest and most troubled bureaucracies in the federal government." On January 20, 1993, President Clinton nominated her for the position. In spite of the cynicism of environmentalists, who were displeased with her past record, critics did not fight O'Leary's nomination as Secretary of Energy, and on January 21, 1993, she was confirmed by the U.S. Senate. She was sworn into office at a White House ceremony on January 22.

O'Leary's designation to President Clinton's cabinet pleased women's and black groups who wanted more representation in top government. President Clinton acknowledged that pressure to appoint more women to his cabinet was a consideration in selecting her but further stated that her background and qualifications were the deciding factor. Her selection for the position surprised Northern States Power Company as well as the power brokers in Washington, D.C. The press generally commented on her openmindedness, keen intellect, loyalty, honesty, and sure judgment, as well as her experience both as a regulator and as someone who had been employed by companies that themselves had been regulated.

Conservation vs. Traditional Energy Sources

During her statement and testimony at her confirmation hearings on January 19, 1993, published in the February 1993 issue of *DOE This Month,* O'Leary said "There is a new public awareness of the importance of energy policy." She was dismayed over the amount of foreign oil consumed in the United States and wanted to reduce the nation's reliance on it.

O'Leary called for reform in specific areas: the environment, natural gas, and cleanup. In terms of the environment, she said in her testimony at the confirmation hearing, "The health and quality of our environment and economic performance are linked to our energy policy decisions." She also saw a need to increase the use of natural gas, a cleaner fuel than other fossils. Regarding cleanup, she said the nation needs to increase its reliance on renewable energy and clean up contaminated waste sites. She called for a continuation of nuclear testing and modified production of armaments. Praising the national energy laboratories as "jewels," she stressed their contributions to national security in the form of new technology for industrial, medical, and communications communities.

During O'Leary's confirmation hearing she managed to present a balance between conservation and the use of traditional sources of energy. Nuclear cleanup is a major priority but it is not O'Leary's only concern. Her task is to develop an energy policy that will release the United States from its dependence on foreign oil in a cost effective and environmentally safe way. At the same time she has to withstand pressure from conservatives to leave the situation as it is. The department is pushed and pulled from many directions—by advocates of fossil fuel and the nuclear industry, and by representatives from states that produce natural gas, and by representatives from states with nuclear waste storage sites and nuclear reactors.

Releases Formerly Classified Documents

During the first months of O'Leary's tenure, President Clinton wrote in his *100 Day Report* on the DOE's accomplishments that she was "acting decisively . . . to help America create good jobs, compete in the global marketplace, protect the environment, and reinvent the government while maintaining national security." Noted for her policy of openness, O'Leary has gained widespread support as head of energy. Since assuming the position, the DOE has disclosed information about the federal government's human radiation experiments after World War II. These experiments primarily took place during the 1940s and early 1950s, but some have occurred as recently as the 1980s. Eleven thousand documents reviewed disclosed that in at least forty-eight experiments humans were given radioactive isotopes, generally without their consent, to determine the effects of radiation on the body. The DOE has made thousands of documents once kept secret available for public use. Of primary interest to the public was O'Leary's announcement in December 1993 that documents related to human radiation experiments and exposure to barium and strontium at government weapons laboratories across the country were to be released. Other DOE documents are to be released as the National Security Council approves.

O'Leary has been active in a number of organizations throughout her career. She has held memberships on the Advisory Committee of the Hubert H. Humphrey Institute of Public Affairs and on the boards of the Greater Minneapolis Red Cross, the University of Minnesota Foundation, and the Northwest Area Foundation. She served on the governor of Minnesota's Commission on Long Term Financial Planning and Management and has a seat on the Colorado think tank known as the Keystone Center. She was a trustee of the William Mitchell College of Law and the Saint Paul Minnesota Chamber Orchestra.

She belongs to the Executive Leadership Council, a forum for black corporate executives. In addition, she is a member of the Committee of 200, a businesswomen's group; Links, a black women's service organization; and the Business Council for a Sustainable Energy Future, a new group of industrialists and environmentalists whose goals are to encourage the use of natural gas.

O'Leary's professional life leaves little time now for a personal life. "I run my life so as not to have a life," she told Richette L. Haywood for *Ebony.* However, between meetings she manages to attend an exercise class at least twice a week.

Hazel O'Leary has demonstrated throughout her career that she is capable of making hard choices, whether or not her decisions are controversial. A pioneer, she has succeeded as an expert in a field where women are rarely found. During her tenure as energy secretary, she has gained the support of many people who initially questioned her commitment. She is fulfilling the Clinton administration's mandate and her own goal to create safe nuclear waste facilities, and she leads efforts to reduce the nation's dependency on oil and coal.

Current Address: U.S. Department of Energy, 1000 Independence Avenue, SW, Washington, DC 20585-0001.

REFERENCES:

"The Clinton Administration's 100 Day Report: Department of Energy Accomplishments." April 30, 1993.

"Clinton Picks Record Number of Blacks for His Cabinet." *Jet* 83 (January 11, 1993): 5.

Contemporary Black Biography. Vol. 6. Detroit: Gale Research, 1994.

Dallas Morning News, December 18, 1992.

"An Energetic Networker to Take Over Energy." *Washington Post,* January 19, 1993.

Haywood, Richette L. "Secretary Hazel O'Leary: Bright, Charming, Tough." *Ebony* 50 (February 1995): 94-100.

"Hazel O'Leary Is Appointed Secretary of Energy." *Ivy Leaf* 17 (Spring 1993): 39.

Healey, Jan. "Hazel R. O'Leary: A Profile." *Congressional Quarterly* 23 (January 1993): 177.

"More Exposure to Radiation Minus Consent Revealed." *Nashville Tennessean,* June 28, 1994.

"New Energy Chief Has Seen 2 Sides of Regulatory Fence." *New York Times,* December 22, 1992.

"Nominee Is a Veteran of Atomic-Waste Battle." *New York Times,* January 9, 1993.

O'Leary, Hazel. News conference. Little Rock, Arkansas, December 2, 1992.

"O'Leary Supports Military-Civilian N-Waste Solution." *USA Today,* August 13, 1993.

"A Plentiful Energy Source Burns Bright." *Washington Times* (national edition), February 4, 1993.

"Secretary O'Leary at Confirmation Hearing." *Doe This Month* 16 (February 1993): 3, 7-8.

Thompson, Garland L. "Four Black Cabinet Secretaries—Will It Make the Difference?" *Crisis* 100 (March 1993): 17-18.

COLLECTIONS:

Biographical information on Hazel O'Leary, as well as miscellaneous newspaper clippings and articles from the *DOE News* that describe her position on energy and that of the Clinton administration, are in the U.S. Department of Energy, Office of Public Affairs, Washington, D.C., and in the Fisk University Library.

Joan C. Elliott

Owens, Dana
  See Latifah, Queen

Lillian Adams Parks

(1932-)

School superintendent, social activist, civic leader

Lillian Parks has spent most of her life and career in the schools of East Saint Louis, Illinois, rising to the post of superintendent of schools. Rather than dismiss her native city as a hopeless case of urban decay, she has striven to address its problems and look toward the future. She has been a major force behind Project Speak, an attempt to teach black students the "standard English" that young people need to function well in the wider society. Her efforts in one school district have influenced the manner of teaching English to all African Americans in Illinois.

Lillian Adams Parks and her twin sister, Vivian, were born on November 8, 1932, in the predominantly black city of East Saint Louis, Illinois. Her parents, Horace Adams and Fairview Edna Dameron Adams, produced two other sets of twin girls and one boy. Parks has lived in East Saint Louis virtually all her life, and she and her family have all been actively involved in the educational, civic, cultural, and political affairs of the city. All of the Adams children are educators.

Parks's interest in education and social welfare can be traced in her heritage. Parks's grandfather, Walter Adams, was a prominent educator in Mississippi. Her mother was a teacher in Tennessee before moving to Illinois. In 1928, her father, a highly respected educator and civic leader, was the first African American man to seek a position on the Board of Education in the state of Illinois. He founded the powerful Paramount Democratic Organization, a political group that secured many opportunities for African Americans in the 1930s and 1940s.

Growing up in a family of educators and social activists, Parks was taught that through education, all of one's goals could be achieved. She was also taught that individuals must be a positive force in the community in which they live. These principles have guided Parks throughout her academic and professional careers.

After graduating from East Saint Louis's Lincoln High School, Parks earned a bachelor of arts degree in English education from the University of Illinois. In 1957, she received a master of arts degree in elementary education with highest honors from Washington University. Parks was awarded a doctor of philosophy degree in curriculum and administration with honors from Saint Louis University in 1976.

Lillian Adams Parks

Motivated by Civic Pride

An experience Parks had at the University of Illinois made an indelible impression on her. When she was asked as a new student to name her hometown, the other students snickered when she said that it was East Saint Louis; Parks was determined to make the students swallow their snickers. She committed herself to being the best in her class, the best in everything she did. She told Rube Yelvington of that experience: "What could have been a negative served as a positive for me. That was my attitude." That commitment to excellence has guided Parks throughout her career.

Parks began her teaching career in 1953 at Sumner High School in Kansas City, Kansas. The following year she became an elementary school teacher at Dunbar School in East Saint Louis. She taught at the elementary level for three years. Parks then became a high school English teacher. While teaching at Lincoln High School in East Saint Louis, she saw that many young African American students lacked language proficiency. She discussed this with her twin, Vivian, who initiated Project Speak, an oral language program devoted to helping young black people speak "standard English" and gain confidence in themselves. The program was designed for children so strongly under the influence of the special dialect of their culture that they failed to learn standard American English. The federally funded program, which was directed by Parks, was highly successful. Thousands of African American young people participated in the program. Many went on to college and graduate school and are now productive residents of the East Saint Louis community and other cities in the country. Several received scholarships in speech, and several have made their mark on television and the stage.

In 1976, as a result of her work with Project Speak and her other community involvements, Parks was selected as a *Saint Louis Globe-Democrat* Woman of Achievement for her contributions in the area of social welfare. Presenting the award to her, the publisher of the *Globe-Democrat* made the following comments:

> Dr. Lillian Parks has been called, aptly, the "need lady." In her home community of East St. Louis, whenever a human need arises, this mother, educator and civic leader is there to help meet that need. One important need she recognized . . . that of helping young black people gain self-confidence and a better chance for jobs by learning to speak what Dr. Parks calls "standard English." This was accomplished through Project Speak.

In an interview with Rube Yelvington after the announcement of her selection as a Woman of Achievement, Parks said: "I don't have any time to waste; the things I do have to have a need behind them. If you're going to give your time and talent, it must be upgrading something, going where there is a need for it."

Parks's sister Lee Annie Bonner was a *Globe-Democrat* Woman of Achievement for civic leadership in 1971. Her twin, Vivian, received the distinction for her work in education in 1980. That same year Parks was presented the Merit Award by the University of Illinois College of Education for achievement and leadership in education. She was the first African American to receive this award.

Linguistic Scholarship Encourages Black Success

In 1980 Parks codeveloped a program, "Identifying the Morphological and Synthetic Features of Black Dialect," with the United States Office of Education and Southern Illinois University. This program evolved from her work with Project Speak. The purpose of the program was to get more African Americans to recognize the value of standard language and to emphasize the interrelation of speech and success in the world. Books and teaching materials developed for the program aid teachers throughout the state of Illinois in teaching standard English to African Americans.

Although Parks's greatest commitment is to bringing excellence to the East Saint Louis school system, she has found time to provide leadership through her civic involvement. She is a past national president of Jack and Jill of America. Parks is the organizer and a past president of the Gateway Chapter of the Links. She is a member of the Board of Trustees of Ranken Technical College in Saint Louis. Parks was the first African American and the first woman to serve as president of the Saint Clair County School Administrators, an organization of principals, superintendents, and other administrators promoting excellence in education. For her work with this organization and her outstanding contributions to the field of education, Parks was honored by the State of Illinois Education Department with the Those Who Excel Award.

Like her father, who was a politician and civic leader, Parks is deeply concerned about the future of East Saint Louis, which can be described as a city fallen upon hard times. Rube Yelvington offers a quote from Parks that summarizes her dedication to reversing the plight of her city:

> It will take time to erase the stigma. We'll get dynamic, sensitive persons for leadership. But I don't run. I've always been that way. I'm hoping for a better day. I don't plan to go anywhere. Like Langston Hughes said, "Hold fast to your dream."

East Saint Louis Names First Woman School Superintendent

After serving as deputy superintendent of East Saint Louis School District 189 for ten years, Parks was appointed superintendent in 1990. She became the first woman to serve in that position. During her tenure as superintendent, many notable improvements were made in the school system. Parks considers her most significant accomplishment to be that of upgrading the academic achievements of students. Her four A's—Attendance, Atmosphere, Achievement, and Attitude— were evident during her tenure. Through her efforts, overall attendance rate rose from 85 percent to 97 percent in four years. Students achieved local, state, and national honors in academics, athletics, and the arts.

Lillian Parks is married to Alvin Parks, Sr., coordinator for athletics in East Saint Louis School District 189. They are the parents of two: a daughter, Lauren, who has followed in her parents' footsteps as an educational consultant, and a son, Alvin, Jr., who is in management at Procter and Gamble Company.

Parks retired from the East Saint Louis school system in 1993. She continues to work for excellence in public education as a consultant, locally and nationally.

Current Address: 1029 La Pleins Drive, East St. Louis, IL 62203.

REFERENCES:

Parks, Lillian. Interview with the author. June 1, 1993.
St. Louis Globe-Democrat, December 18, 1976; December 19, 1976; January 19, 1977.
Yelvington, Rube. *East St. Louis—The Way It Is, 1990.* Mascoutah, Ill.: Top's Books, 1990.

Janie Greenwood Harris

Lillian Rogers Parks

(1898-)

Servant, memoirist

Lillian Parks—through her vivid memoirs of her many years as a White House maid and her experiences as the daughter of the number one White House maid—throws open the back door of history and lets light fall onto some of the most powerful families in the world. Seamstress and light-duty maid at the White House for thirty years, Parks compiled her reminiscences of five First Families in *My Thirty Years Backstairs at the White House.* Published in 1961, the book offers candid glimpses into the behind-the-scenes lives of the Tafts, the Hoovers, the Roosevelts, the Trumans, and the Eisenhowers. Parks's forthright observations, counterbalanced by her sensitivity toward the people she writes about, captured the imagination of the public and propelled her book onto the best-seller list for twenty-six weeks. Excerpts from *My Thirty Years Backstairs at the White House* were published in one hundred newspapers in the United States and around the world. In January of 1979, the book was presented as a four-part miniseries on NBC, starring Leslie Uggams as Parks.

Lillian Rogers Parks was born in 1898 in Washington, D.C., to Maggie and Emmett Rogers, who were from Virginia. At the age of six, according to the *Washington Post,* January 29, 1979, she contracted polio from living in "mosquito-ridden Foggy Bottom." The disease put her on crutches for the remainder of her life, but it did not dim the spirit and energy of this feisty girl who would grow to all of four feet ten inches.

Starts at White House as "Helper"

Parks's White House adventures began in 1909 when her mother, Maggie Rogers, went to work as a White House maid for President William Howard Taft. At that time Maggie Rogers—now alone and the sole support of her twelve-year-old daughter, Lillian, and her ten-year-old son, Emmett—moved into the home of old family friends, the Arthur Jameses at 1824 L Street, in the northwest section of the city. They lived there for eight years. While Rogers tended to her duties at the White House (often working late into the evening), the Jameses (he was a mortician who conducted his trade in the house next door to his residence) lavished attention and affection on Lillian and Emmett. Under the watchful eyes of Maggie Rogers and the Jameses, who had no children of their own, Lillian and Emmett thrived. But Lillian's health became a matter of concern. Her chronic bouts of illness kept her away from school most of the time. To keep her daughter close at hand and to occupy the mind of this mentally alert child, Maggie Rogers frequently took Lillian—now on crutches—to the White House, where she could be a "helper" to her mother by performing light tasks such as turning down beds.

Maggie Rogers remained at the White House throughout the Taft, Wilson, Harding, Coolidge, and Hoover administra-

Lillian Rogers Parks

tions; she retired during Franklin Delano Roosevelt's term of office. Like her daughter, she wanted to write a book about her White House years and was even encouraged to do so by Eleanor Roosevelt. Although she had kept notes and discussed certain observations with her daughter, declining health prevented her from writing her book. Parks said in *It Was Fun Working at the White House* that it was her mother's dying request that she write a book. Thus, in actuality, *My Thirty Years Backstairs at the White House* embraces over a half century of the experiences and observations of both women. Parks acknowledged her mother's contribution in the book's dedication:

> To Maggie, My Mother,
> Who Urged Me to Complete The Backstairs Story
> of the White House,
> Which She Began So Long Ago
> When She Bore the Proud Title
> Of Number One White House Maid.

Although Parks did not attend school regularly as a child, she remembers fondly her year as a first grader at St. Ann's Catholic School, located in northwest Washington, calling it a place where "you could never be idle." According to Parks, the sisters at St. Ann's encouraged their young students to mend their own clothes. Every weekend, she says, the clothes were put on a table. Then the children had to look through the pile, find their own garments and mend them. "I always had a needle and thread in my hands. . . . Sewing got to be a part of me." After St. Ann's, Parks attended Thaddeus Stevens School on 21st Street, N.W., the first school for black children built with federal money. She stayed at Thaddeus Stevens for four years, graduating from the 8th grade. For a brief period, less than a year, she attended Phelps Business High School in the District, but because of poor health, she was sent home to rest.

No longer a student in the school system, Parks turned her attention to a vocation. She discovered that her inclination to sew was still strong. Directly across the street from the Rogers house, now at 1011 19th Street, N.W., were dressmaking shops set up by neighborhood women in their homes. Parks began training with a seamstress whom she remembers as Mrs. Taylor. But after one year, Parks left Taylor to go to work for a large bustling dressmaking shop owned by what she called a "society lady." Many "society" dressmaking shops, owned and operated by "women of means," flourished during the war years, Parks related in an interview. The proprietors would often hire as many as thirty young girls to sew and make hats. Parks remembers that the shop where she worked, called "Francis," on Connecticut and M Streets, employed as many as thirty-five young seamstresses at one time. "We would all be running up and down the steps with scissors in our hands, or we'd be ironing, and cutting out patterns." Parks stayed at "Francis" for four years. During this apprentice period, she maintained her connection with the White House through her mother, Maggie Rogers, and her own occasional visits. Aware of her sewing skills, the White House housekeeper grew to depend on her to repair torn and tattered linen, which was often sent to her by the White House chauffeur. Parks's employment at the White House as a member of the regular staff was virtually inevitable. Parks married in 1935 but was soon divorced. She had no children.

Goes to the White House

According to *My Thirty Years Backstairs at the White House,* in 1929, Lou Hoover, wife of President Herbert Hoover, invited Parks, "Maggie's little girl," to come to the White House "to sew and do light maid's work." She and her mother would be together as official White House employees. Parks remained throughout the Eisenhower years. Weather permitting, she typed out her book in the backyard of her home in the late afternoon. It was published at the dawn of the Kennedy presidency.

The day before the publication of *My Thirty Years Backstairs at the White House,* Jacqueline Kennedy demanded that her staff pledge never to write memoirs of their White House experiences. Had she read Parks's book, she would have noticed that the so-called revelations are guided by the author's own strict code of ethics: "I never revealed any bad things," said Parks. "My mother always told me to be a lady," she recounted in *People* magazine, January 29, 1979. In her book, Parks expresses her philosophy about the relationship between the household staff and the First Families:

> Living in the White House is like being on the stage, where tragedies and comedies play alternately. And we, the servants of the White House, are the supporting cast. . . . We bit players protected our stars, the President and the First Lady, and in no way did we embarrass any member of the cast.

Parks's book, for the most part, is filled with lighthearted, warm recollections of the First Families.

One of her earliest memories is that of President Howard Taft giving her a scoop of caramel-coated ice cream that Helen Taft had returned to the kitchen because of the president's weight problem. Parks recalled in *People* magazine that a special bathtub had to be installed in the White House because President Taft "would get stuck in a normal tub and it would take two men to pull him out."

The First Ladies

Throughout the book, Parks gives her personal assessments of the First Ladies. She admits a special fondness for Lou Hoover, confessing that on the day of Franklin D. Roosevelt's inauguration, she shed "a few private tears" at the loss of the "[kind] woman." Of Eleanor Roosevelt, Parks says that the White House staff knew immediately that she was going to be a different kind of First Lady when she "pitched right in and helped" the "speechless" moving men unpack books and carry furniture. Bess Truman set the "best example" for a First Lady as far as the help was concerned, remembers Parks, but she did require that a bar of soap be discarded after one use.

Mamie Eisenhower, according to Parks in *Jet* magazine, March 16, 1961, was the "most feminine" of all the First Ladies. Concerned with keeping a youthful appearance, she discouraged her grandchildren from calling her Grandma and avoided dresses that she felt made her look old. Parks recalls in *My Thirty Years Backstairs at the White House* that Mamie Eisenhower had a quick temper but was able to gain composure rapidly.

Parks defends her First Ladies against the harsh critical judgments of outsiders. For example, she protects Eleanor Roosevelt from the charge that she traveled excessively. One female White House visitor was overheard to say that "Eleanor should stay home and take care of her husband." But Parks divulges that when Mrs. Roosevelt invited the same lady on a trip with her, "she didn't hesitate for a moment to accept, leaving her husband behind!" Many women, says Parks, criticized Mamie Eisenhower's hair bangs in the White House powder room but would show up later wearing this very same style. In a more serious vein, Parks raises the issue of Mamie Eisenhower's rumored alcoholism. Parks dismisses the charges as fallacious and suggests that Mamie Eisenhower's affliction with an inner ear disturbance from childhood and a heart condition may have affected her equilibrium.

FDR Calls Parks "Little Girl"

Parks writes about the presidents too, confessing a "special kinship" with Franklin D. Roosevelt because they shared a physical disability—polio. According to *People,* Roosevelt always called her "Little Girl" and encouraged the tiny seamstress to use the presidential elevator to get between floors. President Dwight D. Eisenhower, recalls Parks in *Jet,* had a quick temper that caused his wife to fear that he would "bust out at the wrong time."

White House guests flow in and out of Parks's book, from American legends like the actor Tyrone Power and folk heroine Amelia Earhart to world leaders such as Winston Churchill, who, Parks says in *My Thirty Years Backstairs at the White House,* used to "parade down the hall to see the President [Roosevelt] wearing a towel." Even the White House ghosts have a part in Parks's vivid recollections.

In 1969, Parks published an illustrated version of her book for young readers, *It Was Fun Working at the White House.* And in 1981, she published *The Roosevelts: A Family in Turmoil.* This work focused on the complex personal difficulties that plagued the Roosevelt household, revealing specific details concerning the troubled marriage of Franklin and Eleanor, as well as the relationships that both had outside of the marriage.

Today, Parks lives in a house in northwest Washington, D.C., that is filled with White House memorabilia. When she retired from her service at the White House she expressed in her book a keen sadness about leaving: "No more living at the White House as if it were my home. No more sharing the lives, the laughter, the sicknesses, the sorrows and the secrets of the Presidential families. But she also wrote of starting a museum from the items that she and her mother had collected over their fifty-one years in service at the White House: Helen Taft's fans, the walking canes of FDR, a tray that Lou Hoover had fashioned entirely out of butterfly wings, a lock of hair from Amelia Earhart.

In the summer of 1992, the Smithsonian Institution's Festival of American Folk Life sponsored a program called "Workers at the White House," held to celebrate the two-hundredth anniversary of the White House. Lillian Rogers Parks was one of the featured speakers. She generously shared with all those in attendance some of the many stories of her White House years.

Current Address: 110 Van Buren Street, N.W., Washington, D.C. 20012.

REFERENCES:

"The Backstairs View of Lillian Parks: Warm, Kind and Peppery." *The Washington Post* (Style Section), January 29, 1979.

"Her Tales of White House Life Head for TV, but Lillian Parks Knows How to Keep a Secret." *People* 11 (January 29, 1979): 26-27.

Hunt, Marjorie. Telephone interview with Barbara J. Griffin. July 31, 1993.

"The Maid Who Wrote a Best Seller: White House Story Teller." *Negro Digest* 11 (May 1962): 29.

Parks, Lillian. Interview with Barbara J. Griffin, January 27, 1995.

———. *My Thirty Years Backstairs at the White House.* New York: Fleet Press Corporation, 1961.

———. *The Roosevelts: A Family in Turmoil.* Englewood Cliffs, N.J.: Prentice-Hall, 1981.

Parks, Lillian, in collaboration with Frances Spatz Leighton. *It Was Fun Working at the White House.* New York: Fleet Press Corporation, 1969.

"White House Maid Pens Book about Presidential Families." *Jet* 19 (March 16, 1961): 48-49.

Barbara J. Griffin

Lucy Parsons
(1853-1942)
Anarchist, socialist, communist, journalist, poet

A multidimensional pioneer, Lucy Parsons not only was one of the first black activists to associate openly with left radical social movements, she emerged as a leader in organizations primarily composed of white males. In her associations with anarchist, socialist, and communist organizations, Parsons took up the causes of workers, women, and minorities, as well as the homeless and unemployed.

Lucy Parsons's origins are shrouded in mystery. Much of the mystery is due to her own conflicting accounts of her place of birth, name, date of marriage, and national origins. The best record dating her birth indicates sometime in March 1853, and her birthplace was probably on a plantation in Hill County, Texas. She publicly denied her African ancestry and claimed only a Native American and Mexican mixed heritage. According to Carolyn Ashbaugh in *Lucy Parsons, American Revolutionary,* however, there is a very strong probability that she was born a slave, and there is historical evidence that she lived with a former slave of African descent, Oliver Gathing, before her union with Albert Parsons in 1871.

Albert Parsons, a confederate soldier in his youth, was a radical Republican and was the subject of violent mob attacks both as a result of his politics and his marriage to a woman of darker hue. (Albert Parsons was white.) Texas's hostile environment as a Ku Klux Klan stronghold made the couple's departure imperative, and in 1873 they took up residence in Chicago.

Albert and Lucy Parsons arrived in Chicago during a period stamped by an economic crisis and intense labor unrest. The clashes between workers, whose material conditions had eroded drastically, and capitalists, who had enlisted armed support, were daily public encounters. Albert Parsons was a printer by trade, and the couple made their home in a poor working class community. Living among Chicago's impoverished yet militant workers was the catalyst for the Parsons' political transformation from radical Republicanism to radical labor movement activism. The Parsons had two children: Albert Richard, born in 1879, and Lula Eda, born in 1881. Lula Eda died in 1889 from lympodenomia.

Lucy Parsons

Their initial association with the political left was through the Social Democratic Party and the First International, founded by Karl Marx and Frederick Engels. It was through this contact the Parsons became aware of the socialist ideology of Marxism. Their ties to these groups, however, were short-lived, since both organizations were disbanded in 1876, the year the Parsons became affiliated. In the wake of the dissolution of the Social Democratic Party and the First International, they joined the Workingmen's Party of the United States.

Black Socialists Emerge

The Chicago chapter of the Workingmen's Party (WPUSA) held many of its meetings in the Parsons' home. Albert, as a representative of the WPUSA, vied in the 1877 local elections for ward alderman. The year 1877 was a crucial turning point in the history of the United States. It marked the end of the Reconstruction era and the start of the first general strike ever witnessed in this country, the great railroad strike of 1877. While the WPUSA did not start the strike, it was the most active political party to lend organized support to it. It attempted to infuse the strike with socialist propaganda. Out of the strike and the political womb of the WPUSA were born the first black socialists in the United States, Lucy Parsons and Peter H. Clark. Clark had joined the Workingmen's Party in March 1877 and was affiliated with the Cincinnati branch.

While the party's work around the strike had considerably enhanced its visibility and membership roll, a political division resulted in the formation of a new party in December 1877, the Socialistic Labor Party. (In 1892, the name became

the Socialist Labor Party.) The SLP organ, the *Socialist,* became a means for Parsons to express her views on the struggles of the working class. In addition to poems, she penned articles denouncing the capitalist class and describing the plight of the workers. Parsons combined writing for the *Socialist,* speaking for the Working Women's Union, and motherhood. The Working Women's Union, founded some time in the mid-1870s, pressed women's issues before the SLP and demanded women's suffrage as a party platform item, as well as equal pay for men and women.

By the early 1880s, both Parsons and Peter H. Clark had left the SLP. Clark departed due to the neglect of a specific program addressing the issue of black people, while Parsons left to join the International Working People's Association. The IWPA was an anarchist organization; it called for the abolition of the state, cooperative production, and autonomy of workers through voluntary association. Parsons's personal denial of her African ancestry was politically reflected in her silence on the SLP's failure to give specific attention to the plight of black people. The foremost problem of the SLP, in Parsons's view, was its reformism; that is, its peaceful approach to transforming capitalist social relations.

Advocates Violent Overthrow of Capitalism

The IWPA was open to all methods which would lead to the overthrow of capitalism. Accorded to Carolyn Ashbaugh, she stated:

> Let every dirty, lousy tramp arm himself with a revolver or knife on the steps of the palace of the rich and stab or shoot their owners as they come out. Let us kill them without mercy, and let it be a war of extermination and without pity.

Parsons had no illusions about the peaceful transfer of power, nor any belief in the peaceful coexistence of capitalism and labor. However, she did cling to one of the SLP's illusions, that racism would immediately be eradicated in class struggle. The SLP believed further that the origin of racist violence was not in racism, but in the dependency of black people as workers. According to Philip S. Foner, in *American Socialism and Black Americans,* Parsons wrote an article in the April 3, 1886, *Alarm,* entitled "The Negro: Let Him Leave Politics to the Politician and Prayers to the Preacher," in which she argued against the idea that acts of violence toward black people were due to racial prejudice. She suggested that "It is because [the Negro] is poor. It is because he is dependent. Because he is poorer as a class than his white wage slave brother of the North."

Though Parsons belittled the complexity of the relationship of racism to capitalism, she, unlike most African American leaders in 1886, called for armed resistance by black people. According to Foner, she made the point, "You are not absolutely defenseless. For the torch of the incendiary, which has been known with impunity, cannot be wrested from you."

This statement is most revolutionary and radical, especially when placed in the context of African American political leadership. The year 1886 was the high tide of Booker T.

Washington's accommodationist posture. On May 1, 1886, Parsons was a key leader in the strike at Haymarket Square, Chicago, for an eight-hour work day. The strike ultimately resulted in a bombing and the arrest of Albert Parsons and seven other activists. Lucy Parsons attempted to rally a defense of the "Haymarket Eight" and made over forty speeches in a tour of seventeen states as part of this effort. In 1887, however, Albert Parsons was executed, along with three of his comrades.

Parsons Founds Newspaper

The added tragedy of the death of her daughter shortly following her husband's execution did not discourage Parsons's involvement in radical politics. In 1892 she started her own paper, *Freedom*, which covered such issues as lynching and peonage of black sharecroppers. By 1905, she became a founding member of the Industrial Workers of the World. The IWW's political line espoused the independence of trade unions and their control of the wealth and power. She worked closely with William "Big Bill" Haywood and Elizabeth "The Rebel Girl" Gurly Flynn, both of whom later joined the Communist Party.

Organizing the homeless and unemployed, Parsons led significant battles in San Francisco in 1914 and Chicago in 1915. The cause of political prisoners became a central focus for her in the 1920s and she joined the International Defense Fund. She was involved in the cases of Tom Mooney, the trade unionist, the "Scottsboro Boys," and Angelo Herndon. She was elected to serve on the national committee of the ILD in 1927. In 1939, she became a member of the Communist Party.

In 1942 Parsons died in a fire in her home, which was subsequently ransacked by government authorities. Papers, books, and other sources that captured the long life of a veteran of the political movements of the left were removed. Lucy Parsons's legacy was preserved, however, by the younger members of the Communist Party, for whom she had been a source of knowledge, experience, and political wisdom.

REFERENCES:

Ashbaugh, Carolyn. *Lucy Parsons, American Revolutionary.* Chicago: Charles H. Kerr Publishing Company, 1976.

Foner, Philip S. *American Socialism and Black Americans.* Westport, Conn.: Greenwood Press, 1977.

Hine, Darlene Clark, ed. *Black Women in America.* Brooklyn: Carlson Publishing, 1993.

Katz, William L. *The Black West.* Seattle: Open Hand Publishing, 1987.

Parsons, Lucy, ed. *Famous Speeches of the Eight Chicago Anarchists.* New York: Arno Press and the New York Times, 1969.

Salem, Dorothy, ed. *African American Women: A Biographical Dictionary.* New York: Garland, 1993.

John McClendon, III

Jennie R. Patrick
(1949-)
Chemical engineer, educator, motivational speaker

Jennie Patrick is the first African American female to earn a Ph.D. in chemical engineering in the United States. Prepared for anything life threw her way by the nurturing she received from her caring parents and the black teachers who instructed her during her early years of schooling, she had the emotional, mental, and academic freedom to choose a career freely, with no consideration given to gender or race. Her strong commitment to scientific excellence is joined by her equally strong commitment to positive social change for disadvantaged black youth in the United States.

The fourth of five children, Jennie R. Patrick was born in Gadsden, Alabama, on January 1, 1949. Patrick spent her early years in segregated schools in her hometown. Her parents, James and Elizabeth Patrick, had no education beyond the sixth grade; he worked as a janitor and she was a maid. However, they wanted very much for their children to be educated and to succeed, and they encouraged them to attain excellence in whatever they wished to accomplish. Their difficult life prompted Patrick's early obsession with independence. She told Marie Bradby for the Fall 1988 issue of *U.S. Black Engineer:* "As a child, the thing that struck me the most was the hardness of my parents' life. They always talked constantly about using the mind as a way out of poverty." In addition to her parents' teachings, Patrick learned much on her own. She revealed to Bradby:

> As a child, everything I was exposed to was through reading. I didn't have anything in particular. I would go to the library and thumb through things. I was exposed to the encyclopedia. We had two to three sets. I would sit and read those. You were able to go from one world where it was very limited to one that had everything through your imagination.

As a child, Patrick enjoyed a nurturing environment not only at home but also at school. During her early years of schooling, she had several helpful black teachers who made a lasting impression on her by challenging her to search for knowledge and use her own abilities to do whatever she wanted. In 1964 Patrick entered the newly integrated Gadsden High School. The academic setting there was different in many ways. She told Bradby, "The Black schools had very little equipment in their labs. The white schools had everything." It was at Gadsden High School that she faced her first real problems with being a part of a very small minority. It was also here that the love and nurturing she had received as a child began to stand her in good stead. Academic, emotional, psychological, and physical survival became her greatest challenge. She made a commitment to succeed. It was a difficult situation: violence was rampant and she was harassed by white students, but she would not take their abuse and met force with force. Although she was discouraged by her white

Jennie R. Patrick

teachers and counselors, her difficult beginnings at the school did not affect her academic performance: she graduated with honors.

Overcomes Obstacles to Earn Chemical Engineering Degree

Patrick's interest in science was born early. "As a kid, I wasn't sure what engineers did, but there seemed to be an awe about them. People admired them and considered them hardcore technical people," she told Bradby. She entered Tuskegee Institute (now Tuskegee University) in 1967, where she remained for three years. When the program in chemical engineering that she had selected for a major was discontinued at Tuskegee, she transferred to the University of California at Berkeley. She worked a year to obtain money for her education at Berkeley, then received her bachelor of science degree in chemical engineering in 1973. While in school, Patrick was an assistant engineer for Dow Chemical Company (1972) and an assistant engineer for Stouffer Chemical Company (1973).

In graduate school at the Massachusetts Institute of Technology (MIT), as at Berkeley, Patrick not only had the demanding schedule required of all students, but the greater challenge of overcoming racial prejudice. At MIT from 1973 to 1979, she concentrated in thermodynamics, homogeneous nucleation, and heat and mass transfer. She was a research assistant while pursuing a doctorate. In 1979 she earned her Ph.D. in chemical engineering, becoming the first black female in the United States to do so. Her dissertation was titled "Superheat-Limit Temperature for Nonideal-Liquid Mix-

tures and Pure Components." During her years at MIT, Patrick also worked as a Chevron research engineer and an Arthur D. Little engineer.

After obtaining her Ph.D. degree, Patrick first went to work for General Electric Research in Schenectady, New York, where she stayed for three and a half years. Here she developed a research program in supercritical fluid technology—an area then in its infancy. In 1983 she switched to Phillip Morris in Richmond, Virginia, where she designed a state-of-the-art research plot plant in super critical extraction. In 1985 she moved to Rohm and Haas Company Research Laboratory in Bristol, Pennsylvania, working in emulsion technology and polymer science as she supervised other employees. In 1990 she became assistant to the executive vice president of Southern Company Services. Patrick has now returned to Tuskegee to the Department of Chemical Engineering, which closed during her studies there but has been reestablished. She now serves there as 3-M Imminent Scholar and Professor of Chemical Engineering.

Science and Survival Promoted

Though she has received many honors and much other attention for her technical accomplishments, Patrick's recent emphasis has been on promoting the progress of young black people in U.S. society. She said in an autobiographical essay, published in the Fall 1989 issue of *Sage* magazine, that for the first six years after leaving MIT, she spoke to predominantly black audiences at colleges and schools across the country. Considering the restrictions on her time, she felt that if she wished to make a permanent and lasting impression on young people, she would need to develop a mass media approach to sharing her experiences and perspective.

I started devoting considerable thought to various approaches to this project. The focus will be to teach young African Americans survival tactics in hostile environments. However, these strategies are valuable to everyone. The desired outcome is to provide psychological, emotional, and mental tools that allow African Americans to establish values, goals, standards, independence, and awareness. These tools are essential if we are to have our destiny in our own hands. This project will focus on historical contributions of Blacks worldwide, as well as highlight the subtle but intentional psychological and mental weapons that are used against us daily. By using some of my personal experiences, I hope to provide insight on the power of an independent thought process which ensures survival accompanied by happiness and self-assurance.

In counseling students she advises:

Be very serious about taking the science courses, and math in particular. Math is the subject about which the statement has been made that Black people don't do very well. I firmly believe in the concept of you being who you think you are and if you accept something like that, then you really won't be able to do it well. And so the first thing is to instill a sense of "can do" in young Blacks, and to make them understand that they must not accept limitations put on them by others.

Although the experiences in her life have been rewarding, Patrick often reflects on her interaction with people and wonders "why didn't those before me share more of themselves with me." She wrote in a letter to Jessie Carney Smith on January 13, 1995, that many young people lack "the insight to use or appreciate the knowledge of time"; consequently, she shares herself with them extensively.

Fights for Health and Safety in the Workplace

Perhaps if others in her profession had been more forthcoming with Patrick, she could have avoided the unfortunate experiences that changed the course of her life. She continued in her letter:

> I would have never imagined that I could have selected a profession that would destroy the normality of my life by exposing me to thousands of industrial chemicals in the work place. In all professions there are probably health hazards. Depending on the profession these hazards will be greater or less. What we must understand as individuals is that our lives and health are our responsibility. Total hazard-free work environments are not the norm.

Patrick concentrates her current efforts on hazards in the workplace and community. Her description of her health problems and her warnings for young people deserve full attention. She continued:

> I have developed a health problem that most people will never understand or appreciate, known as "multiple chemical sensitivity." This condition has made me become extremely allergic to many, many common substances such as perfume, cologne, hair spray, and cleaning agents. This condition has taken away the normality of my life. I urge young people to recognize the importance of not viewing an employer as the protector of your health. Police the environments in which you work or live to make sure it is safe for you and your family.

Patrick is a member of the prestigious scientific organization Sigma Xi and the American Institute of Chemical Engineers. She has received several honors, including the National Organization of Black Chemists and Chemical Engineers Outstanding Women in Science and Engineering Award in 1980, and she was a subject in the Exceptional Black Scientists Poster Program in 1983.

Patrick is married to Benjamin Glover and they have no children. Physical fitness is a central part of her life—she jogs, and she walks three miles each day. She is also an avid flower and vegetable gardener.

She continues her work at Tuskegee and her efforts to instill in young African Americans the sense of history and the sense of self that she believes are necessary for them to reach their goals.

Current Address: Department of Chemical Engineering, Tuskegee University, Tuskegee, AL 36088.

REFERENCES:

Bradby, Marie. "Professional Profile: Dr. Jennie R. Patrick." *U.S. Black Engineer* (Fall 1988): 30-33.

Kazi-Ferrouillet, Kuumba. "Jennie R. Patrick: An Exceptional Black Scientist." *Black Collegian* 14 (January-February, 1984): 102.

Patrick, Jennie R. Letter to Jessie Carney Smith, January 13, 1995.

———. Telephone interview with Jessie Carney Smith, January 13, 1995.

———. "Trials, Tribulations, Triumphs." *Sage* 6 (Fall 1989): 53.

"Speaking of People." *Ebony* 36 (May 1981): 6.

Who's Who among Black Americans, 1994-95. 8th ed. Detroit: Gale Research, 1994.

Vivian O. Sammons and Jessie Carney Smith

Dorothy Smith Patterson
(1930-)
Nurse, teenage parent advocate, humanitarian

Dorothy Patterson has made notable contributions to the welfare of teenage parents and to the health and social well-being of the general population in this country and in such foreign locales as Nigeria and the South Pacific island of Ponape. She is a public health nurse and school nurse whose career includes widespread volunteer service. Patterson's interest in teenage pregnancy led her to form support groups for teenage parents, and she has also organized classes for teenagers offering instruction on such topics as birth control and sexually transmitted diseases. In addition, she has published articles dealing with women's reproductive health.

Dorothy Smith Patterson was born in Jackson, Georgia, on April 4, 1930. Cincinnati, Ohio, was the hometown of Patterson's parents, Avery Hasker Smith and Lois Virginia Bailey Smith, and their daughter, Earline, but Patterson was born in Jackson so her maternal grandmother could help care for her and her two-and-a-half-year-old sister.

Avery Smith, who was born in 1903 in Spartanburg, South Carolina, died of a heart condition in 1946 at age forty-three. As the oldest male of nine children, he withdrew from school before the twelfth grade when his father became ill. He held the family together by going to work immediately. After

Dorothy Smith Patterson

his marriage to Lois Bailey, he provided a comfortable living for his family through steady employment during the depression years of the 1930s. He was a skilled mechanic for the Cincinnati Milling Machine Company and held additional jobs making deliveries for a store and repairing automobiles. As head of his household he made the decisions and gave directions which he expected to be followed. He was also warm and nurturing, giving compliments to his daughters when he felt they had done well and bringing flowers and candy to his wife to celebrate special occasions.

Patterson's mother, Lois Smith, was born in Conyers, Georgia, in 1906. With encouragement from her father, a Methodist minister and a member of the board of directors of Paine College in Augusta, Georgia, she graduated from that school as a music major. She continued to study piano, organ, and voice at the Cincinnati Conservatory of Music. Lois Smith was the organist for her church and taught piano and voice lessons in her home until two days before she died in 1981 at age seventy-six.

In her youth Patterson took refuge in books and used her scholastic ability to compensate for her shyness. It was easier for her to develop a close relationship with her mother than with her father, who was more demanding of perfection. When she was fifteen years old, an incident occurred that changed Patterson's relationship with her father. It started when Avery Smith severely criticized his daughter for celebrating having received an A in an advanced class by skipping another class and going to the movies with schoolmates. For the first time, Patterson was able to express her anger at his lack of appreciation for her hard work in school, and her

feelings that she had earned the right to celebrate her achievement. To her surprise he accepted her reasoning. This incident, which happened close to the time of his death, made it possible for them to develop an improved understanding of each other and added to Patterson's loving memories of her father.

After her father died, Patterson, her sister, and her mother moved to Hawaii. Patterson studied at the University of Hawaii for two years and for one year at Spelman College in Atlanta. Then she joined her mother, who by that time had settled in Los Angeles.

At the University of California, Los Angeles, Patterson took a vocational assessment test that showed she had an aptitude for nursing. She entered a three-year program of course work and training at Los Angeles County General Hospital that included housing and a stipend in exchange for her help with patient care. After another year of classes at UCLA and a field placement, in 1956 she received a bachelor of science degree in nursing and public health, a public health credential, and school nurse certification. In 1975 she completed a master of arts in health education and secondary education at the University of San Francisco. Patterson chose the school site and the public health arena to escape the hierarchical situations in hospitals where nurses—mostly women—were relegated to second-class status in relation to physicians—usually men.

Patterson married Charles Watson in 1957, but they divorced in 1960. They had a son, Mark, who was born in 1959 and died unexpectedly in 1985. In 1962 she married Charles Patterson, then a graduate student at the University of California, Berkeley. He died in May 1994. Their daughter Tracy, born in 1965, is a graduate of Antioch College who aspires to begin advanced work in African American studies. For two years Tracy has been director of the summer program of Encampment for Citizenship, an organization designed to prepare young people for U.S. citizenship by offering discussions of politics, voting obligations, religion, labor unions, and race relations.

Patterson's career has been centered in northern California. Her sister, Earline Evans, now retired, lives with her family in Pomona, in southern California. The sisters maintain contact by regular telephone conversations and occasional visits.

Nursing Career Begins

In 1957 Patterson went to work for the Alameda County Health Department in the predominantly African American section of West Oakland. Here she dealt with the community's many social problems: poverty, unemployment, poor housing, lack of education in the adult population, high student drop out rates, and teenage pregnancy. She formed support groups for teenage parents to help them cope with the challenges related to parenting, infant and reproductive health, and finances. She taught them to puree foods for their babies and arranged for the young mothers to exchange baby clothes and call upon each other for child care during school hours.

She stressed the value of continued education, and her responses to requests for medical information about birth control and the prevention of sexually transmitted diseases included referrals to Planned Parenthood and other agencies. However, her supervisor did not agree with this approach to what Patterson viewed as the contemporary way of life for a large number of adolescents and gave orders to discontinue that part of the instruction.

Patterson next accepted a job in 1960 with the Berkeley Health Department, where public health nurses not only spent the afternoons in a clinic and made home visits but also saw children at school in the mornings. She started a support group for women whose husbands were involved as students or faculty members in the University of California's laboratories with the production of bombs and nuclear testing to help them deal with the marital conflicts that arose from the women's discomfort with this type of scientific pursuit. It was a strenuous schedule for Patterson, but one that was never devoid of excitement.

In 1962 Patterson went abroad with her husband as he conducted research for a doctoral dissertation. Charles Patterson studied the development of the African elite in London and African countries by interviewing Africans who attained leadership status through education in Western schools and those who rose through the tribal or village traditional system in their homelands. Patterson spent most of the two-year period in Nigeria, where she worked for the University of Ibadan's teaching hospital, becoming involved in a medical and nutritional research project in the village of Osegere. Her primary interest was the growth processes of Nigerian infants and toddlers. Supported by National Institute of Health funds, Nigerian government funds, and money from a British science foundation, she ran a well baby clinic, provided general health information to mothers, and instituted a birth and death registry for the village. She received a commendation from the Royal Society of Health for the registration system.

Patterson wept with joy when she first set foot upon African soil in Sierra Leone. She speaks with nostalgia about the food, the infectious drumming and dancing, and the excitement of seeing men and women who looked exactly like her relatives and friends at home. She was struck by the warmth of the Africans, which was apparent even in situations where there were language barriers. But she had to adjust to specific aspects of African culture. For example, it was not socially acceptable to sit in a chair that someone had vacated without allowing sufficient time for the soul of that person to depart.

Designs Health Care Programs

Starting in early 1966 Patterson was employed in Washington, D.C., by the United Planning Organization, an arm of the antipoverty program with responsibility for its health components. She planned and developed a health program for the nation's capital city. She was proud of the hearing and sight screening project designed for children in day-care programs and young men, mostly drop-outs from school, who were misdemeanor detainees in the county jail. The two

groups were selected because neither had yet had adequate testing. Hearing aids or glasses could make a difference in their interest in school and their performance in classes. Patterson was equally pleased with the clinic for older citizens, which, among other services, checked blood pressures and monitored seniors for the appearance of diabetes—benefits that helped to keep them healthy and functional.

When she returned to Berkeley in 1967, Patterson participated in the city's Collaborative Problem Solving Project. In preparation for school desegregation, the project sought to stimulate a dialogue between school personnel and parents from differing cultures and to help parents relate to people and agencies that made decisions affecting the education of their children. For three years Patterson worked in two elementary schools, overseeing the efforts of parents, teachers, and administrators to identify and achieve common goals.

Patterson took her next position in 1971, when she joined the School Health and Nutrition Service program (SHANS) in the Oakland school district. SHANS demonstrated that attention to the special physical and psychological needs of pupils could improve their classroom performance. One student, for example, experienced a significant increase in his self-confidence, evidenced by improvement in conduct and comprehension of the teacher's lessons, after Patterson referred him to a physician for correction of a tied tongue. When federal funds were exhausted in 1974, SHANS came to an end and Patterson transferred to Fremont High School in Oakland.

Confronts the Problem of Teenage Pregnancy

At Fremont, Patterson saw an appallingly high rate of teenage pregnancy: eighty girls in a student body of eight hundred in 1974 became mothers before graduating, with the majority of them not returning to classes after delivery. She formed an advisory committee of parents and school staff that devised a course, Human Relations Workshop, taught by a team composed of two counselors, the student activities director, the football coach, and Patterson, the school nurse. The workshop gave teenagers the opportunity, in a school environment, to talk about their values, how to make their behavior conform to their ideals, and how to cope with sexual pressures. The team advised the students about the available community resources for reproductive health information and care and Patterson developed a health provider directory for district-wide use.

When the team would no longer teach the workshop on a volunteer basis and the school district would not underwrite the salary for a teacher, the program was discontinued. But the records of Planned Parenthood and the venereal disease clinic near the school showed increased student use, and pregnancies at Fremont dropped from eighty to fifty-five by mid-1978 when the workshop came to an end.

After the Fremont High School experience, Patterson worked for a year as a perinatal health educator in the three cyesis centers of Oakland schools from 1978 to 1979, bringing health and personal counseling to pregnant students and young mothers returning to classes after the birth of their children. She then worked as a teacher on a special assignment that addressed a variety of needs having to do with student health, especially the health of pregnant teenagers. She compiled needs assessment data that resulted in grants from the state of California and private foundations which were used to underwrite programs for pregnant teens and teenage parents at three high schools, three child-care centers, one infant program, and two programs for toddlers where child development and parenting are taught. The combination of case management, academic programs, and support services—including a job preparation component—makes it easier for the young mothers to prepare to be independent. Before she retired in 1990 she had brought in over seven million dollars for the programs.

Patterson has offered her volunteer services in several foreign countries. During the summer of 1978 she designed an educational program for young women on the South Pacific island of Ponape that helped narrow the educational gap between men and women there. Patterson started the program with nine young women, three of whom are now health visitors, the equivalent of public health nurses in this country; others are teachers. Patterson has flown refugee missions to Kuala Lumpur, Hong Kong, and Saigon and has brought child victims of the civil war in Lebanon to Dallas for treatment. In Nigeria, she taught first aid to forest rangers.

The First Unitarian Church of San Francisco named Patterson and her husband joint recipients of its 1993 Conard Rheiner Award in recognition of their dedication to the community and to the church during more than thirty years of membership. Since 1993 she has been president of the Unitarian Universalist Service Committee, a nonprofit, nonsectarian group that supports programs here and overseas. Its objective is to foster improvement in living conditions for all people—especially women and children—through advancements in areas such as health care, education, and leadership development. This assignment requires her to travel all over the world.

Patterson chaired the Cultural and Ethnic Affairs Guild of the Oakland Museum when it founded the Black Filmmakers Hall of Fame. She has been on the board of directors of the American Civil Liberties Union, the East Bay Perinatal Council, the California Alliance Concerned with Adolescent Parents, and the Starr King Theological Seminary. She was appointed to Berkeley's first Police Review Commission, to the Alameda County Mental Health Commission, and to the Mayor's Committee on Excellence in Berkeley.

Among Patterson's numerous awards are those from the National Council of Negro Women, the Ponape Agricultural and Trade School, the NAACP Legal Defense and Education Fund, the Marcus Foster Educational Institute, Sister Clara Muhammad School, the Buffalo Soldiers, and the California State Assembly.

Throughout her career Patterson has published articles on women's reproductive health. Her writings help round out her life as a health professional who has been particularly concerned with women's health, teenage parents, and the well-being of people in this country and abroad.

Current Address: 1159 Miller Avenue, Berkeley, CA 94708.

REFERENCES:

Patterson, Dorothy Smith. Interview with Dona L. Irvin. June 4, 1993.

Dona L. Irvin

Sarah E. C. Dudley Pettey
(1868-1906)
Educator, school administrator, feminist, lecturer, columnist

A staunch advocate of equal rights for African Americans and women, Sarah Pettey devoted her short life to fighting racism and sexism. She played a significant role in the battle Southern blacks waged against white supremacy during Reconstruction, working as an educator, school administrator, newspaper columnist, lecturer, and church volunteer and leader. An extremely well-read, articulate woman, she gave voice to African Americans' desire for equal educational and economic opportunities.

The eldest of Edward Richard Dudley and Caroline E. Dudley's nine children, Sarah E. C. Dudley Pettey was born November 9, 1868, in New Bern, North Carolina. Her parents, both former slaves, raised Sarah and her siblings, two brothers and six sisters, in an atmosphere that emphasized community service and education. Her father spent over twenty years in public service, most notably as a member of the North Carolina House of Representatives, beginning the first of his two elected terms in 1870. While a slave, her mother learned to read and write. M. A. Majors in *Noted Negro Women* describes Caroline Dudley as having been a "pioneer heroine" in the movement to educate Southern blacks during the later days of the Civil War.

In 1889, Pettey married Charles Calvin Pettey, a bishop in the African Methodist Episcopal (AME) Zion Church. Born a slave in Wilkes County, North Carolina, in 1849, Bishop Pettey was a widower with two children at the time of his marriage to Sarah. The couple had five children of their own. Bishop Pettey died in 1900. In 1906, Sarah Pettey, still a young woman, died at the age of thirty-seven after a short illness.

Pettey received an excellent education, beginning with home tutoring under the instruction of her mother and grandmother, who first taught her how to read and write. She entered the New Bern graded school at the age of six, completed the three grades then available to African American children, and in 1881 went on to the State Normal School. There she studied under George H. White, the first African

Sarah E. C. Dudley Pettey

American to serve as a solicitor for the second judicial district of North Carolina. At the age of twelve she entered the Scotia Seminary in Concord, North Carolina, a highly progressive school that aimed to give African American women a classical education, including instruction in Latin and Greek. Among its alumnae is Mary McLeod Bethune, who entered Scotia four years after Pettey graduated with first honors.

After graduating from Scotia Seminary in 1883, Pettey returned to her native New Bern and embarked on a short but highly successful career as a teacher and school administrator. She spent a year as a second assistant at the New Bern graded school before being promoted to assistant principal. In addition, she also taught at the Craven County Teacher's Institute for two summers. D. W. Culp characterizes her in *Twentieth Century Negro Literature* as having been an "able, brilliant, and magnetic teacher." She gave up her teaching career when she married Charles Calvin Petty.

Racial and Gender Equality Sought

Marriage probably enabled Pettey to have a greater voice in the politics of her day then she would have had if she had remained single. Her husband proved an able, sympathetic, and supportive ally in her efforts to improve the situation of African Americans and women. According to Glenda Gilmore in *North Carolina Historical Review,* Bishop Pettey frequently shared his pulpit with his wife during his travels throughout his church district, giving her the opportunity to express her views on women's rights after he spoke to the congregations on matters pertaining to race and the church. Those who heard

her read the two papers she prepared for these occasions, "Woman the Equal of Man" and "Woman's Suffrage," often praised her powerful rhetoric and her speaking abilities.

Bishop Pettey apparently agreed with his wife regarding women's equality. On May 23, 1898, he made a highly controversial decision to ordain Mary Jane Small as the first woman elder in the AME Zion Church. The church, Sarah Pettey writes in an essay published in Culp's *Twentieth Century Negro Literature,* allowed women to become a "mighty power." Extremely involved in church activities herself, she served as an organist for various churches and as a national officer in the AME Zion Woman's Home and Foreign Missionary Society from 1892 to 1900. Perhaps her most lasting contribution is the column she began writing in 1896 for the AME Zion Church's weekly newspaper, *The Star of Zion.* Gilmore notes that Pettey used the "Woman's Column" to address a variety of issues, including religion, feminism, race, and politics.

Pettey clearly recognized that the African American struggle for equality could not be won without the help of women. In her 1902 essay published in Culp's collection, she describes women's importance to "the civilization and enlightenment of the Negro race." This essay stresses the crucial role women played as mothers. In this role, women were responsible for instilling essential moral values in their children, who would become the next generation of leaders. She writes, "Home is the bulwark and citadel of every race's moral life. The ruler of the home is mother. A faithful, virtuous, and intelligent motherhood will elevate any people." Mothers should, she writes in this essay, be intelligent and strive to educate themselves and their children. "When our homes become intelligent, we shall have intelligent statesman, ministers, and doctors; in fact the whole regime that leads would be intelligent." In this essay she issues an optimistic call for action from women, inviting them to emulate Frances Ellen Watkins Harper, Sojourner Truth, Phillis Wheatley, Ida Wells Barnett, and other "noble women" who labored on behalf of their race. She says:

> The role that the educated Negro woman must play in the elevation of her race is of vital importance. There is no sphere into which your activities do not go. Gather, then, your forces, elevate yourself to some lofty height where you can behold the needs of your race; adorn yourself with the habiliments of a successful warrior; raise your voice for God and justice; leave no stone unturned in your endeavor to route the forces of all opposition. There is no height so elevated but what your influence can climb, no depth so low but what your virtuous touch can purify. However dark and foreboding the cloud may be, the effulgent rays from our faithful and consecrated personality will dispel; and ere long Ethiopia's sons and daughters, led by pious, educated women, will be elevated among the enlightened races of the world.

Sarah Dudley Pettey lived a life consistent with the views she expresses in this essay and in her lectures and columns. She knew that the road to progress for African Americans had to be paved by men and women working side by side as equals, toiling to overcome economic and political oppression. She labored in a southern environment marred by Jim Crow laws and the growing forces of white supremacy. Discouraged by the success white supremacists began having at the turn of the century, Pettey moved north, never returning to the South. Now, almost one hundred years after her death, we can look back on the life of this exemplary woman and realize that she was, in many ways, a woman ahead of her time. Through her writings, she continues to be a teacher, demonstrating the importance of freedom and literacy to the ongoing struggle for racial and gender equality.

REFERENCES:

Culp, D. W., ed. *Twentieth Century Negro Literature or Cyclopedia of Thought by One Hundred of America's Greatest Negroes.* Napierville, Ill.: J. L. Nichols and Co., 1902.

Gilmore, Glenda Elizabeth. "Gender and Jim Crow: Sarah Dudley Pettey's Vision of the New South." *North Carolina Historical Review* 68 (July 1991): 261-85.

Hine, Darlene Clark, ed. *Black Women in America: An Historical Encyclopedia.* Brooklyn: Carlson Publishing, 1993.

Hood, J. W. "Mrs. Sarah E. C. Dudley Pettey." In *One Hundred Years of the African Methodist Episcopal Zion Church; or, The Centennial of African Methodism.* New York: AME Zion Book Concern, 1895.

Majors, Monroe A. *Noted Negro Women: Their Triumphs and Activities.* Chicago: Donohue and Henneberry, 1893.

Pettey, Sarah E. C. Dudley. "What Role Is the Educated Negro to Play in the Uplifting of Her Race?" In *Twentieth Century Negro Literature or Cyclopedia of Thought by One Hundred of America's Greatest Negroes.* Edited by D. W. Culp. Napierville, Ill.: J. L. Nichols and Co., 1902.

Candis LaPrade

Billie Goodson Pierce
(1907-1974)
Jazz and blues pianist and singer, dancer

Billie Goodson Pierce was a blues and jazz pianist, singer, and dancer who, with her trumpeter and cornetist husband, DeDe Pierce, led the New Orleans Preservation Hall Jazz Band during the 1960s. She is best known for her work with this band because it was during this time that both she and her husband gained national, as well as international, renown. In fact, the Pierce husband and wife duo can be

Billie Goodson Pierce

considered one of the primary contributors to the revival or "Second Coming" of New Orleans jazz in the 1960s. Their contribution comes mainly from the unique Creole flavor of their brand of blues, boogie-woogie piano, and jazz.

Pierce not only broke into, but also endured and flourished, in an almost completely male-dominated musical genre. Linda Dahl, who interviewed Pierce for her work *Stormy Weather: The Music and Lives of a Century of Jazzwomen,* notes that "a woman musician attempting to break into jazz needed more than musical talent; she needed great self-confidence, a tough, no-nonsense attitude and the skills of a diplomat." Pierce certainly possessed all of these qualities and regarded her beginnings as a professional musician as a welcome challenge. When asked about her start as a pianist in the 1920s, Linda Dahl reports that she replied, "I don't know if it was rough or not. I was rough along with it." With her charisma and self-confidence, it is easy to see how Pierce has become a role model for many young and hopeful women just starting in the world of music.

Wilhemina Goodson Pierce was born on June 8, 1907, in Marianna, Florida. She died in New Orleans, Louisiana, where she had lived most of her life, on September 29, 1974. She is buried at the Saint Louis Cemetery in New Orleans. She came from a large, music-loving family, in which she was one of seven children. Her parents, Madison H. Goodson and Sarah Jenkins Goodson, were both musicians, as were her six sisters—all of whom were pianists, like Pierce. Although Pierce was born in Marianna, her family soon moved to Pensacola, Florida, where she was raised from infancy. In 1935 she married jazz trumpeter "DeDe" Pierce (Joseph de

Lacrois, born February 18, 1904, in New Orleans). They were together until DeDe's death on November 23, 1973.

Pierce's musical career began at a very early age. She taught herself to play the piano when she was about seven years old. She was never formally trained and in fact never learned to read music—"she didn't have to," Dahl reports Pierce telling her. Instead, she acquired the basics from her Baptist parents, who were fond of singing hymns. In *Black Women in American Bands and Orchestras,* D. Antoinette Handy provides some of Pierce's memories of her childhood days:

> Most all of my days I've been playing music. I started playing the blues. My mother and father you know, were very religious people. Me and my sisters would get around the piano and have a good time playing ragtime and singing the blues. Somebody watched out for daddy and when he'd come, we'd break into, "What a Friend We Have in Jesus." He never knew the difference.

Not only was Pierce influenced by her family, she was also greatly affected by the music of the local bands in Pensacola, as well as by the many New Orleans groups that toured the South in the early 1900s. Dahl also offers some of Pierce's fond memories of her formative years:

> She and her sister Edna used to wait until their father went to bed and sneak out to hear the bands—often to find that another Goodson sister, Sadie, was holding down the piano chores. Billie recalled that "whenever a show at the Belmont Theater would get in a pinch for a piano player . . . the manager would send for a Goodson girl, not caring which one he got."

At fifteen years of age (some sources say ten), Pierce got her first big break when she was allowed to work temporarily as an accompanist for Bessie Smith—"Empress of the Blues"—who was to become not only a major influence on Pierce's musical career, but her favorite singer.

Show Business Career Begins

Pierce's show business career really took off in 1922 at the age of fifteen, when she left home to play professionally as a traveling performer. When Clarence Williams, Bessie Smith's regular accompanist, became ill, Pierce was offered the position and a chance to tour with Smith's show, working theaters throughout Florida. She gladly accepted the offer.

For nearly ten years she worked with various bands in her hometown state, as well as throughout the South. From 1922 to 1927, she toured the Gulf Coast with her sister Edna Goodson in the all-black Mighty Wiggle Carnival Show as a singer, dancer, and pianist. During the late 1920s, she played with Slim Hunter's Orchestra, the Douglas Orchestra, the Joe Jesse Orchestra, and the Nighthawks Orchestra in local clubs. The instrumentation of these bands was very similar to that of the New Orleans groups of the period: trumpet, trombone, banjo, drums, piano, and bass. During the early part of her career, Pierce also frequently worked as an accompanist for Gertrude "Ma" Rainey, Mary Mack, and Ida Cox. Along with Bessie Smith, Cox was a major influence on Pierce's music. Suddenly, Pierce was beginning to gain recognition as a blues pianist and singer.

New Orleans Offers Opportunity and Fame

In 1929, Pierce went to New Orleans as a temporary replacement for her older sister Sadie Goodson, a highly regarded professional musician who was then playing in Buddy Petit's legendary band, which was performing on the *SS Madison* on Lake Ponchartrain. Pierce immediately felt comfortable in the Crescent City. She decided to settle there in 1930.

Pierce spent the years of the Great Depression earning a dollar a night working in the rough waterfront taverns and honky-tonks along Decatur Street. She played with such groups as Mack's Merrymakers, Joe Peeple's Band, Armand Piron, Alphonse Picou, Kid Rena, Punch Miller and Billy, and George Lewis's Orchestra. While working with clarinetist George Lewis at one of these establishments, in a band that Billie herself put together, she met DeDe Pierce, who later joined the four-piece band. On March 28, 1935, having known each other for only three short weeks, Billie and DeDe were married. Thus began a lifetime partnership of marriage and music.

DeDe Pierce got his start in music when he received a hand-me-down trumpet from a cousin who played in an all-girl band. He began playing by ear. He later took a few lessons from Kid Rena and then learned to read music from Paul Chaligny, a veteran musician who was known as the leader of the old Onward Brass Band during the late 1800s. His first experience as a professional musician was his performance with the Arnold De Pass band. DeDe Pierce's New Orleans upbringing and Creole, French-speaking ancestry helped to enliven his repertoire, which included such famous blues tunes as "Sallee Dame" and "Eh La Bas."

After Billie and DeDe married, the couple worked primarily at the popular weekend club Luthjen's, a small neighborhood dance hall on Marais Street. During the late 1930s they also played, together or separately, in clubs along Decatur Street and in little French Quarter spots with typical New Orleans names such as Kingfish's, Pig Pen's, The Cat and The Fiddle, and Popeye's. They played with many of New Orleans' finest musicians, among them Alphonse Picou, Big Eye Louis, and Emile and Paul Barnes. It was not long before Billie and DeDe had themselves become big names in the city.

In 1951, the Pierces recorded for Bill Russell's American Music label and were included in an anthology compiled by Sam Charters. During the late 1950s, the Pierces were relatively inactive musically because both were plagued by ill health. DeDe was stricken with glaucoma, which caused him to go blind. Billie had a stroke which left her paralyzed for months. She was determined to recover so that she could devote herself to DeDe's care. Fortunately, both Billie and DeDe made splendid recoveries. DeDe adjusted to his disability and soon the couple was able to continue playing together.

Preservation Hall Career Begins

The 1960s, however, proved to be a much more successful decade: it was during this time that the Pierces staged a remarkable comeback, both physically and musically, and achieved international fame. Their success was due in part to the rebirth of New Orleans jazz and the founding of Preservation Hall in 1961 by Sandra and Allen Jaffrc. Thc Pierces became leading figures and principal attractions in the Preservation Hall Jazz Band, along with William Humphrey (clarinet), Cie Frazier (drums), Jim Robinson (trombone), and Allen Jaffre (tuba).

One of the reasons the duo became so renowned is precisely because they succeeded in combining the Billie's classic blues and ragtime jazz style with the Creole and folk influences of DeDe to form a unique blend of jazz that perfectly symbolized the South. In fact, the Jaffres opened Preservation Hall with the hunch that there was and would continue to be a growing interest and audience for this unique southern style of jazz—now commonly called Dixieland. The fact that Billie and DeDe quickly became known as the mainstay of the Hall during the 1960s and early 1970s proved that indeed the Jaffres were correct. The Pierce combination was a winning one.

The couple kept their classic blues style alive by combining tasteful and sensitive low-keyed variations. Billie Pierce was described as having a rough and earthy style, as well as being a moving singer. She wrote and sang songs such as "Get a Working Man," "Panama Rag," "Freight Train Moanin Blues," "Going Back to Florida," "Good Tonk Blues," "In the Racket," and "Billie's Gumbo Blues."

DeDe Pierce was influenced not only by his French Creole culture but also by the New Orleans marching brass bands. His trumpet playing was described as clear and syncopated. He was sang with or without Billie, although she was the primary vocalist of the two. He helped to make the song "Eh! La Bas" famous. Some of his other songs include "I Got Rhythm," "Yeah Man," and "Pork Chops."

The fame and recognition that resulted from the Pierces' involvement with the Preservation Hall Band led to work on many recording labels, among them Atlantic and Riverside. There were also a great number of touring opportunities. The duo spent many months on the road, playing at college jazz festivals, concert halls, and nightclubs.

Billie and DeDe made appearances on television and radio programs from coast to coast. Some of their most significant television appearances included those for *David Brinkley's Journal* (NBC), *New Orleans Jazz* (PBS), and *Anatomy of Pop: The Music Explosion* (ABC). In 1967 the Pierces toured Europe and the Orient with the Preservation Hall Jazz Band. In the late 1960s and early 1970s, the band also appeared at Philharmonic Hall in Lincoln Center. In addition, the Pierces toured with the Grateful Dead, Jefferson Airplane, and other rock groups.

The Pierces enjoyed their time in the limelight until 1973. It was during this year that DeDe fell seriously ill with cancer of the larynx and related problems. He died on November 23, 1973. Billie Pierce, inconsolable, virtually gave up music after the death of her husband. Less than a year after DeDe's death, Pierce entered Sara Mayo hospital, where she died of natural causes. She was 67 years old. According to Paige Van Vorst of *Downbeat* magazine, "DeDe's death . . . broke up a team of forty years' standing, and Billie never returned to full-time playing. Her death further reduces the number of authentic traditional jazz musicians."

Billie Pierce's life was one filled with adventure and excitement, as well as hardship and struggle. Although the rough life of the jazz musician is not one that many women chose, her choice has been applauded by jazz and blues enthusiasts all over the world.

REFERENCES:

The Black Perspective in Music 3 (Fall 1975): 345.

Borenstein, Larry, and Bill Russell. *Preservation Hall Portraits.* Baton Rouge: Louisiana State University Press, 1968.

Carr, Ian, Digby Fairweather, and Brian Priestly, eds. *Jazz: The Essential Companion.* London: Grafton Books, 1987.

Chilton, John. *Who's Who of Jazz.* New York: Macmillan, 1972.

Clark, William. *Preservation Hall: Music from the Heart.* New York: W. W. Norton & Co., 1991.

Dahl, Linda. *Stormy Weather: The Music and Lives of a Century of Jazzwomen.* New York: Pantheon Books, 1984.

Handy, D. Antoinette. *Black Women in American Bands and Orchestras.* Metuchen, N.J.: Scarecrow Press, 1981.

Harris, Sheldon, ed. *Blue's Who's Who.* New Rochelle, N.Y.: Arlington House Publishers, 1979.

Hine, Darlene Clark, ed. *Black Women in America.* Brooklyn: Carlson Publishing, 1993.

New York Times, October 3, 1974.

Placksin, Sally. *American Women in Jazz: 1900 to the Present.* New York: Seaview Books, 1982.

Southern, Eileen. *Biographical Dictionary of Afro-American and African Musicians.* Westport, Conn.: Greenwood Press, 1982.

The Times Picayune, October 4, 1974, section 1, 8.

Unterbrink, Mary. *Jazz Women at the Keyboard.* Jefferson, N.C.: McFarland, 1983.

Van Vorst, Paige. "Wilhelmina Goodson 'Billie' Pierce." *Downbeat* (November 21, 1974): 10.

Tanty R. Avant

Ponchitta Pierce

(1942-)

Television host and producer, magazine writer and editor

Through almost three decades as a magazine and television journalist, Ponchitta Pierce has earned such descriptions as "a terrific talker" and "a great interviewer." Cathleen Schine also described her in *Vogue,* April 1986, as "sharp and funny" and "modest and classy." When Pierce becomes the interviewee, the accuracy of these terms rings true. Her conversation focuses on the lessons she has learned and on contributions by many other Americans rather than on her own accomplishments.

Ponchitta Marie Anne Vincent Pierce was born in Chicago, Illinois, on August 5, 1942. Her parents are from New Orleans, Louisiana, which Pierce also calls home. Alfred Leonard Pierce was a plasterer and contractor, Nora Vincent Pierce a teacher. Ponchitta Pierce said in a June 6, 1993, interview that "everybody believes their parents are extraordinary," and she readily acknowledges that many of her own qualities are "a combination of both their influences." From her father she gained "a healthy dose of realism in terms of how to conduct business." Aside from his own work, he managed the family's rental property. From her mother's example, Pierce developed a desire to reach out to people and to work to improve life for others. She describes her mother as "extraordinary, especially in terms of her sensitivity to others. She has a unique capacity to reach out to all kinds of people."

Pierce also reminisces, "I was blessed to grow up in the South during my formative years as a black American with a large extended family." Through interactions with her many aunts, uncles, and cousins, she learned about family values and acquired a sense of self-esteem. "There's nothing quite so special as a large southern black family," she states.

When she was in the eighth grade, Pierce moved to a new home in Los Angeles, California. During her teen years there, she attended Bishop Conaty High School, a Catholic all-girls school. She still values the "very rigorous intellectual environment" and the "attitude toward learning and discipline and education" that the nuns established for their students. Pierce's lifelong "love of books" and her "comfort in the world of ideas" began to develop in this environment. The nuns also saw her interest in writing and—in spite of her difficulty with spelling—encouraged her to pursue a career in journalism.

At the University of Southern California, Pierce expanded her interest in communications by writing for the student newspaper and editing the yearbook. She majored in journalism and graduated cum laude with a bachelor of arts degree in 1964. Her college experience included a summer of study at England's Cambridge University in 1962. A testimony to her continuing interest in education occurred in 1986, when

Ponchitta Pierce

Franklin Pierce College in Rindge, New Hampshire, presented her an honorary doctorate of humane letters.

Pierce Named Editor

In 1964, Pierce received a letter from John Johnson of *Ebony* asking her to consider a position as assistant editor for *Ebony* and *Jet* magazines. She accepted the invitation. By 1965 she had become associate editor, and in 1967 she advanced to the dual position of New York editor for *Ebony* and New York bureau chief for its publisher, Johnson Publishing Company (JPC). She views this time at *Ebony* (1964-68) as "crucial in terms of the development of my career." In a special issue of *Ebony* (November 1992) celebrating its fiftieth anniversary, she states in the article "JPC Babies Born in 1942": "*Ebony* was the best thing that ever happened to me. . . . To be able to see and understand Black history in the '60s through the eyes of *Ebony* and *Jet* when the broader society did not have a great appreciation for it was a wonderful oasis. It gave me my center as a journalist and as a Black person."

Pierce went on to edit and write for other magazines. From 1971 to 1977 she served as a contributing editor for *McCall's.* In addition, she wrote for *Reader's Digest* from 1976 to 1977 and was roving editor for the magazine from 1977 to 1981. She describes her work with *Reader's Digest* as an invaluable experience that further developed her discipline as a writer: "It is a big gift to be able to write concisely but with impact." Pierce has also written for such magazines as *Ladies Home Journal, Parade, Family Circle,* and *Newsday,* and has served as an editorial consultant for the Phelps Stokes Fund (1971-78).

Attracted to Television Journalism

Pierce entered the world of television journalism in 1968 as a special correspondent for CBS News. Her responsibilities included reporting for the *CBS Evening News* and conducting interviews for the *CBS Morning News.* Pierce stayed in this position until 1971. In 1973, she joined the staff of WNBC-TV in New York. From 1973 to 1977 she cohosted *The Sunday Show,* a Sunday morning magazine program. Her next series, *The Prime of Your Life* (1977-80), was a public affairs program directed toward the concerns of older metropolitan residents. Then from 1982 to 1987 she served as host and coproducer for WNBC-TV's *Today in New York.* She has also hosted programs for New York's WNET, Channel 13.

Since 1987, Pierce has divided her time between free-lance writing and television production. She enjoys the opportunity that writing offers to be "more analytical, more creative," and to "explore a topic in depth." But she also enjoys exercising a different set of skills through live journalism— "the ability to think fast and respond on your feet." The television medium also offers "more immediacy" and the advantage of being "seen as you are."

When questioned about her accomplishments, Pierce comments directly only on her "ability to make enormous mistakes and survive them." That she works hard at her career is evidenced by her observation that she is not so much proud of her achievements as she is "amazed that one is able to do so many things in such limited time." She willingly shares some of the lessons she has learned. Early in life, she discovered that "you don't have to be perfect, you just have to be prepared." She emphasizes the value of developing "an inner compass" about your own endeavors, so that amidst undue criticism or effusive praise, you know when you have—or have not—given your best effort.

Because Pierce seeks to give her best, praise does come her way. In 1967 she became the first recipient of the annual Penney-Missouri Magazine Award. According to *Ebony,* November 1967, the J. C. Penney Company and the University of Missouri School of Journalism cosponsored the one-thousand-dollar prize "to honor excellence in women's interest journalism in national magazines." The article that won the competition, "The Mission of Marian Wright," appeared in the June 1966 issue of *Ebony.* Pierce quickly points out that she had "a unique subject" to write about and that the photographs were taken by Moneta Sleet, Jr., who eventually became the first black to win the Pulitzer Prize for photography.

Other awards followed. Steven Scheuer notes in *Who's Who in Television and Cable* that, in 1968, Pierce received the New York Urban League's John Russwurm Award "for sustained excellence in interpreting, analyzing, and reporting the news." In 1969 she won the Woman behind the News Award. In 1970 the National Theta Sigma Phi Sorority presented her the Headliner Award for "outstanding work in

the field of broadcasting." Then in 1974 she won the American-Italian Women of Achievement (AMITA) Award for distinguished achievement in the field of communications arts. During 1987 she received both the National Women's Political Caucus Exceptional Merit Media Award and the American Women in Radio and Television Commendation Award.

The style of broadcasting that evoked such honors is described by Cathleen Schine in her 1986 *Vogue* article about *Today in New York:* "The show moves along, zip, zip, zip, but it's never jumpy, and she [Ponchitta Pierce] is skeptical without turning skepticism into a religion the way the guys on *60 Minutes* do, or a titillating quest for gossip the way Barbara Walters does." She characterizes Pierce as "a white-gloved killer interviewer" and tells about a guest who thought so too. When the gentleman commented on her thoroughness as an interviewer, Schine says that Pierce "laughed and replied, 'I gotta tell you, we also have a great staff.'" Schine reflects, "I guess so, but how many times have you heard an anchor credit the research staff?"

That same spirit of genuine respect for the achievements of other people is evident when Pierce talks about her role in journalism. Instead of focusing on herself, she places her role within the larger context of contributions by many contemporaries. The successes of black journalists have made it much easier for all minorities to achieve. "It's wonderful," she says, "to look around and see people of my generation who are making a mark on the country." She mentions such people as Donna Shalala, secretary of Health and Human Services; Marian Wright Edelman, lawyer and children's rights activist; and Henry Cisneros, secretary of Housing and Urban Development. Then she adds, "We have grown up in a time when there is so much to do—and we're doing it—and that's a good feeling."

While Pierce recognizes that journalists today "now benefit from bridges crossed by my generation," she knows that there are heights yet to be conquered. She recommends to people considering a career in journalism that they work hard and that they be earnest about their profession. She emphasizes that journalists have "a serious responsibility to be committed to understanding what's important."

The topics covered in even a small sampling of Pierce's articles demonstrate the variety of her interests: "Crime in the Suburbs" (*Ebony,* August 1965), "Problems of the Negro Woman Intellectual" (*Ebony,* August 1966), "The Returning Vet" (*Ebony,* August 1968), "The Legacy of Martin Luther King" (*McCall's,* April 1974), "Three Steps to Self-Confidence" (*Reader's Digest,* June 1975), "The Prime Time of Her Life," about Diane Sawyer (*Ladies Home Journal,* October 1989), and "'Still Trying To Fight It,'" about racism (*Parade,* January 1993).

Experienced Moderator

Pierce has served as moderator for a number of discussions focusing on important issues. In 1985, she moderated

"Arms, Allies and the Search for Peace," a student town-hall meeting between former U.S. Secretary of State Alexander Haig, Jr. and students from New York City schools. Another town-hall meeting in 1986 gave Atlanta, Georgia, high school students the opportunity to talk with former President Jimmy Carter. The topic on that occasion was "How Foreign Policy Is Made: The Case of Central America." In 1991, she led a Foreign Policy Association study trip to Mexico City to discuss "Free Trade: What Will It Mean for Mexico and the United States" with President Carlos Salinas de Gortari, his cabinet, and other leaders. In August 1993, she moderated a symposium, "Women's Health: What Are We Going to Do About It?" for *Mirabella,* for which Hillary Rodham Clinton presented the keynote address.

This busy woman also makes time for many service organizations and professional associations. She is on the board of governors of the Foreign Policy Association and a member of the Council on Foreign Relations. She is on the board of directors of Upward, The Dance Theatre of Harlem; the Voice Foundation; the Third Street Music School Settlement; the Madison Square Boys and Girls Club, and Inner-City Scholarship Fund; and the International Women's Forum. In 1965, she served as a delegate to the first Asian-American Women Journalists Conference and wrote a report titled "The Status of American Women Journalists on Magazines." In 1973 she was a delegate to "Food, Health, and Development," an international symposium held at the World Health Organization in Geneva, Switzerland. She is a member of Women in Communications, American Women in Radio and Television, and the American Federation of Television and Radio Artists.

From conducting one-on-one interviews to moderating symposia, Pierce has come in touch with numerous people, individually and collectively. She feels particularly blessed to have "the opportunity to meet extraordinary people." She believes that "you become a summation of the people you know. They challenge you to think in different ways, and you find yourself growing more and more as an individual." As she has matured, she has found herself becoming "much more sensitive to consensus building," learning "how to incorporate different viewpoints—be objective." No doubt, Pierce has touched as many lives as have touched her own.

Current Address: 25 West 54th Street, New York, NY 10019.

REFERENCES:

"Backstage." *Ebony* 26 (November 1967): 26.
"McCall's World." *McCall's* 104 (June 1977): 12.
Pierce, Ponchitta. "JPC Babies Born in 1942: Leaders and Celebrities Grew Up with JPC Magazines." *Ebony* 48 (November 1992): 86.
———. Telephone interview with Marie Garrett. June 6, 1993.

Scheuer, Steven, H., ed. *Who's Who in Television and Cable.* New York: Facts on File, 1983.
Schine, Cathleen. "Thinking Heads Charlie Rose and Ponchitta Pierce: Under Cover of Night, TV Gets Smart." *Vogue* 176 (April 1986): 12.

Marie Garrett

Mary F. Pitts
(1860-1914)
Educator, clubwoman, organization worker, temperance worker

Mary F. Pitts's career demonstrates her devotion to the cause of advancing the black race. After teaching in several states, she became very involved in temperance activities and women's clubs and organizations, including the YWCA. She had a special concern for the well-being of black girls and women, working tirelessly in various efforts on their behalf.

Born September 19, 1860, in Liberty, Missouri, Mary Alice Ford Pitts was the daughter of Edith Jane and William A. Ford. She had two brothers, William Jackson and Charles, and one sister, Sarah Jane. When Pitts was very young, her father died, and after her mother married educator Jesse Newman, another brother, James Albert, was born.

Pitts was educated in Chicago, where the family moved while she was a child. She attended Jones School on Twelfth Street and Calumet School. At the age of fifteen, she graduated with highest honors from Douglass High School. Since at the time it was not necessary to have a college degree to teach school, Pitts was able to use her training to embark upon a career as an educator. She taught in Cairo, Illinois; Villa Ridge, Illinois; East Saint Louis, Illinois; Ziegler, Illinois; Davenport, Iowa; and St. Louis, Missouri.

Pitts's mother, Edith Jane Newman, died on August 31, 1881. The family soon moved to Davenport, Iowa. Four years later, on August 6, 1885, Mary Alice Ford married W. H. H. Pitts in Davenport. They had six children: Jesse A., Edith Jane, Sarah, Clyde, Albert, and Viola Napier. Only the last two children lived beyond infancy.

In the fall of 1887 the Pitts family moved to St. Louis. Having grown up in a religious environment, Mary Pitts still had her religious faith. She departed from her family's Episcopalian faith and joined St. Paul's AME Church, located then at Eleventh and Green streets. She was deeply involved in church work throughout her life and at various times held leadership positions in the churches to which she belonged. At

St. Paul's she was an officer of the trustee board, president of the missionary society, a Sunday school teacher, district superintendent of the Sunday school, and a worker in the Allen Christian Endeavor League.

Reaches Out to Troubled Black Girls

Pitts was especially concerned about the welfare of young black girls: she labored in many different ways to secure their well-being. She worked untiringly with a group of women to form a society to address this concern. Later, the Girls Rescue Home was established to assist girls who were abandoned, runaways, or who had disciplinary problems.

Active also in the Women's Christian Temperance Union (WCTU), Pitts was asked to organize a union among blacks. She responded by forming the Harper WCTU and was its first president. In October 1887 or 1888 the fifteen-member union opened a shelter for homeless children and supported it through donations, subscriptions, and by providing entertainment for the community. The children were housed until they were twelve years old, at which point they were placed out for adoption on a three-month trial basis. If the home was suitable and the arrangement proved mutually satisfactory, the stay became permanent by adoption. After Pitts's death, the group was renamed the Pitts-Harper WCTU in her honor. She was also city district superintendent and later state organizer of temperance work for blacks. As a result of her work, several local unions were organized in St. Louis and elsewhere in the state. Pitts's commitment to the temperance movement was all-encompassing, extending even to her church. Her fervent opposition to the use of wine for church sacrament led church officials to replace it with unfermented grape juice. It was said that she was never too occupied with other activities to respond to the call for temperance work.

Pitts's efforts on behalf of young girls and women led to the establishment of a black branch of the YWCA in St. Louis, the Wheatley branch. First the association met in various places, then found a temporary location at Garrison and Lawson avenues. Hearing that plans were underway to expand the quarters for the white YWCA, Pitts called on the secretary of the white branch. She spoke with the board of directors and several members and was successful in obtaining their existing facility, located at Garrison and Lucas avenues, as a permanent home for the black branch.

Pitts never lost sight of the neglected children of her race who lived in the St. Louis area. She was one of the organizers of the St. Louis Colored Orphans Home, a member of its executive board, and several times its president.

When the First National Conference of Colored Women of America was held in Boston, Massachusetts, in 1895, Pitts, a delegate, was appointed to the committee to establish the convention's platform. Pitts gave a brief history of the Harper branch of the WCTU, which she had founded. She also cited a need for an endowment to sustain the union's work. At the time she was president of the orphans home, and Pitts described the scope of the Orphanage's work. Her remarks are printed in *A History of the Club Movement among the Colored Women of the United States*. She said,

> We keep regularly employed a matron, nurse, and cook. While non-sectarian, it is emphatically a religious institution. While we try to meet the physical and mental wants of our children, we also give them religious instructions and a reverence and love for God's word.

Advocates Cooperation among Women

The next year the first annual convention of the National Federation of Afro-American Women was held in Nineteenth Street Baptist Church, Washington, D.C., with Margaret Murray Washington as president. Pitts spoke on "How Can the National Federation of Colored Women Be Made to Serve the Best Interests and Needs of Our Women," also published in *A History of the Club Movement*: "In uniting the women of the various sections into one great union, we entertain every difference of opinion and belief, we are orthodox and heterodox, suffragists and anti-suffragists, temperance and anti-temperance, Christians, agnostics and theosophists." The women needed to "rub down the rough edges of eccentricities" and respect each other's opinions, according to Pitts. She saw women in a highly visible position in the world, in an era of promise. The women should remain undaunted in the midst of calamity and stand "shoulder to shoulder, singly and together."

The movement to organize black women into the National Association of Colored Women's Clubs (NACW) reached St. Louis just after the turn of the century, and in 1904, four years after the state association was formed, the St. Louis City Association was organized. It was founded by Maria L. Harrison, with the assistance of Susan Paul Vashon and Pitts. The city association hosted the national group that same year, when Josephine Silone Yates was president.

After a seven-week illness, Mary Pitts died on Sunday, May 10, 1914. She had devoted a lifetime to the black community as a teacher, church and temperance worker, and promoter of the community-wide programs that the NACW encouraged. Her work deserves greater recognition.

REFERENCES:

Davis, Elizabeth Lindsay. *Lifting As They Climb*. Washington, D.C.: National Association of Colored Women, 1933.

A History of the Club Movement among the Colored Women of the United States. Washington, D.C.: National Association of Colored Women's Clubs, 1902.

Wesley, Charles Harris. *The History of the National Association of Colored Women's Clubs*. Washington, D.C.: NACW, 1984.

Jessie Carney Smith

Deborah Prothrow-Stith
(1954-)
Physician, educator, consultant, administrator

Deborah Prothrow-Stith, a nationally recognized public health leader, is a consultant to community clinics and centers, schools, and state government on violence and the prevention of violence among adolescents. In her view, violence is the most dangerous threat to the health of young people in the United States. Prothrow-Stith established the country's first violence prevention office at the state level and devotes her practice, research, publications, and public efforts to addressing the issue of violence among young people.

Deborah Prothrow-Stith was born on February 6, 1954, in Marshall, Texas, to middle-class parents, Mildred B. and Percy W. Prothrow, Jr. The family relocated to Atlanta when Percy Prothrow became manager of Atlanta Life Insurance Company. Prothrow-Stith's mother became a teacher in the public school system in Atlanta. Her parents stressed education and hard work and held high expectations for their two daughters. Lady Percy, Prothrow-Stith's sister, was seven years her senior. In Atlanta Prothrow-Stith attended Anderson Park and Collier Heights elementary schools. She started high school at Therell in Atlanta but graduated from Jack Yates High School in Houston, Texas.

Prothrow-Stith recalled in a telephone interview on May 18, 1994: "My parents were the persons who shaped my philosophy on life. Both parents taught me to work hard and to enjoy life and people." She continued, "My parents' basic philosophy on parenting stressed love, love, and more love. My sister and I went to church every Sunday. I was reared with a sense of responsibility for the world and what happens in it." Her life exemplifies the lessons she learned from them.

Prothrow-Stith was born during the year of the famous Supreme Court case *Brown v. Board of Education.* The court's decision on May 17, 1954, led to the desegregation of the public school systems in the South. She did not experience the effects of the decision until she reached high school. She recalled in the interview: "I was among the first black students to attend Therell High School in Atlanta. This was my first exposure to white teachers and students. I felt I was there to prove that I was as smart or smarter."

She always worked diligently on her studies and graduated with honors from high school. In high school she developed an interest in mathematics, and she chose the subject as her major when she entered Spelman College in Atlanta. However, she later shifted to premedicine. Upon graduating from Spelman magna cum laude in 1975, she attended Harvard University Medical School in Cambridge, Massachusetts. She graduated with a doctorate in medicine in 1979.

Recognizes the Scope of Violence in U.S. Society

In July 1979 Prothrow-Stith began her internship in internal medicine at Boston City Hospital. As an intern she

Deborah Prothrow-Stith

was horrified at the sight of so many young patients who were the victims of violence. Constantly seeing young teenagers dying or being stitched up and sent back out, she began to conceive strategies that might halt this social disease. She began to think of violence as a health issue, and it became her cause. She believed that it was time for the country to rid itself of this devastating problem.

After completing her training in internal medicine at Boston City Hospital, Prothrow-Stith was board certified with a Massachusetts license. From January 1982 to June 1982 she was a senior resident in charge of the Medical Surgical Unit at Boston City Hospital. During this time her interest in violence prevention was further stimulated.

Once her residency at Boston City Hospital was finished, Prothrow-Stith became the consulting physician at Libre Methadone Detoxification Clinic, where she worked from 1983 to 1986. Other professional experience includes her codirectorship of Boston's Health Promotion Center for Urban Youth, Department of Health and Hospitals, from 1985 to 1987. In addition, she was clinical chief of Harvard Street Neighborhood Health Center's Adolescent Clinic from July 1986 to September 1987. She was also a staff physician at Boston City Hospital.

In 1987 Prothrow-Stith became the first woman and youngest commissioner of public health in Massachusetts, having been appointed by the governor. As the state health officer she was responsible for policy and program development and day-to-day management of the commission. The chair of the Public Health Council, she was in charge of all state health policies. She handled a department with more than 4,500 employees and a budget of over $300 million. Her office operated seven public-health hospitals. While in office she expanded treatment programs for AIDS and drug rehabilitation—she doubled the treatment slots for intravenous drug users—and led the state on such health issues as environmental health, tuberculosis, and immunizations. She also set up criteria for utilization of new health-care technologies. Prothrow-Stith was instrumental in obtaining money for community health centers to support adolescent services. In addition, she established the country's first violence prevention office at a state health department.

In 1989 Prothrow-Stith became vice president of Community Care Systems in Massachusetts, a private hospital company that owned and managed seven psychiatric hospitals. She held one of the five senior management positions, with responsibility for medical affairs.

Sees Violence Prevention as Health Issue

The dean of the Harvard School of Public Health hired Prothrow-Stith in 1990 as assistant dean of government and community programs to bridge the gap between academic public health programs and public health practice. In the Office of Government and Community Programs, this young doctor serves as the liaison between the community, government officials, and the Harvard School of Public Health Research Program. She also develops community outreach programs and transfers successful programs to independent and community control. Since 1990 she has been director of the Violence Program at the Harvard Injury Control Center. She is also a lecturer in the department of Health Policy and Management, Harvard School of Public Health.

At the Harvard School of Public Health, Prothrow-Stith was for a time the principal investigator for research grants. She arranged funding for the Boston Program for High Risk Youth, the Boston Violence Prevention Program, and the New England Injury and Prevention and Research Center. An expert in violence prevention, she continues to submit proposals and find funding for projects that treat adolescent violence, attitudes and behavior, and peer pressure. Several of these funded projects include Care for Children Hospitalized for Violent Injury, Violence Counseling Project for Students, Violence Prevention Protocols for Health Care Providers, and the Community Based Violence Prevention Model. The latter project provides ideas for a community-based violence prevention model that can be utilized in a variety of health-clinic settings. This project also gives support to local efforts at violence prevention. As a consultant, Prothrow-Stith provides seminars all over the country to bring an understanding of violence to outreach workers and teachers and to help them learn how to address the issue. "Because violence is epidemic, we should treat it as a public health issue," says Prothrow-Stith in the 1991 publication *Deadly Consequences,* the first book on violence as a public health issue for a mass audience, which she coauthored with Michaele Weissman. In this work, seen by some people as the battle cry of the contemporary United States as the country faces a seemingly losing battle with violence, Prothrow-Stith and Weissman present an analysis of the problem of violence and offer solutions for the epidemic. "Every day more than 60 Americans die of homicides. That means 450 a week, 1900 a month, 23,000 a year. Violence should no longer be tolerated." She feels that violence should be treated as a public health issue, like child abuse or drunk driving.

> Doctors don't just treat the victims of child abuse, but they alert social workers to situations that need attention. They don't just treat the victims of car accidents, but lobby for seat-belts and stiffer penalties for driving drunk. So why not treat violence too, as "one piece of a larger picture?"

Prothrow-Stith argues in *Deadly Consequences* that stiffer sentences and more jails alone will not stop the violence; instead, a more preventative approach that seeks to change society's values is needed.

> Violence has no racial or geographic fence around it. Violence is learned behavior which popular culture glamorizes making it look easy, painless, guiltless and a way to solve problems. As a society we think it's justified. We need to prevent violence, not just treat the victims. We stitch them up and send them out for more.

Change Through Education

There is no consensus on the remedies, just as there is no consensus on the causes of urban violence. Prothrow-Stith sees the rise of street culture as a consequence of extreme poverty. To lessen the sources of violent anger, she explains in *Violence Prevention Curriculum for Adolescents,* negative peer pressure must become less enticing to youth. Prothrow-Stith designed a curriculum and began teaching adolescents that the use of violence is not an answer to life's troubles.

> When I teach I say from the very first cartoon, all the way through *Lethal Weapon,* you are taught violence is funny, entertaining and successful. It's the way heroes solve things. But it's painful and does not solve problems.

She tells her students to list all the things that make them angry. But she emphasizes that the best solution to getting angry is to try to stop angry behavior and to substitute another behavior. In each one of her seminars she stresses a behavior that is negative but then deals with it positively and nonviolently. During each lesson, the student is encouraged to overcome fear or anger. Prothrow-Stith's ability to articulate the need for alternate behavior has led many of the adolescents to adopt a new perspective concerning violence.

Examining violence as a social disease, Prothrow-Stith has developed public health strategies not only in *Violence Prevention Curriculum for Adolescents* and *Deadly Consequences,* but also in many papers for medical journals and other magazines. In the process of educating teachers and health-care workers, she has authored or coauthored thirty-four publications on medical and public-health issues. Her interest in the issue of violence has led to numerous television appearances. Prothrow-Stith appeared on *Good Morning America,* (ABC), February 1992; *Frontline,* (PBS), March 1992; *Dateline NBC,* April 1992; *Violence in America,* a Tom Brokaw special on NBC, May 1992; and *Life Choices,* (NBC), 1992. She is frequently a guest on national and local radio and television talk shows.

Prothrow-Stith has received three honorary degrees: doctor of public service from North Adams State College, North Adams, Massachusetts; doctor of education, Wheelok College in Boston, Massachusetts, in 1992; and doctor of humanities from Springfield College, Springfield, Massachusetts, in 1993. Other awards include the World Health Day Award, the American Association for World Health, 1993; Salem State College Criminal Justice Community Award, Criminal Justice Department, 1993; Hildrus A. Poindexter Distinguished Service Award for Outstanding Service in the Field of Health, Black Caucus of Health Workers of the American Public Health Association, 1993; Rebecca Lee Award, Massachusetts Department of Public Health, 1993; and the Secretary of Health and Human Services Award, 1989.

She has served on several national boards. She became a trustee of Spelman College in Atlanta in 1989, and from 1988 to 1991 she was a trustee of the Museum of Science, Boston, and a trustee of the Women's Educational and Industrial Union, Boston. Her committee memberships include the Department of Human Services's Blue Ribbon Panel on Youth Violence Prevention, Washington, D.C., and she is a member of the Centers for Disease Control in Atlanta. She is also a member of the Hyams Foundation in Boston and of the Board on Health Promotion and Disease Prevention, Institute of Medicine, Washington, D.C.

Concerned with the effects of violence on the fabric of society, Prothrow-Stith stated in the May 18, 1994, interview:

> I worry that we will not rid ourselves of the mean spirit that penetrates many aspects of our society. I worry less about our children, for in them I find hope, energy and the desire to get along. I worry most about the adults who make money off the industry of violence: selling guns, producing violent movies, more prison buildings, and accepting violence as a fact of life.

Prothrow-Stith is married to Charles Stith, a Methodist minister and activist for economic justice in Boston's South End. They are the parents of two children, a son, Percy, and a daughter, Mary. They live in Roxbury, a neighborhood in Boston that has the lowest per capita income and the highest homicide rate in the state of Massachusetts. Prothrow-Stith is conscious of the issue of violence as both a community member and a professional.

Prothrow-Stith, whose interest in violence prevention began while she was a medical intern at Boston City Hospital, is relentless in her efforts to combat violence among youth by developing programs to alter attitudes and behavior. Through her educational programs, publications, and media appearances, she has become widely known as a talented and conscientious black woman health professional who concentrates on a major health menace—violence among the young.

Current Address: Harvard School of Public Health, 677 Huntington Avenue, 718-E, Boston, MA 02115.

REFERENCES:

Prothrow-Stith, Deborah. "Interdisciplinary Interventions Applicable to Prevention of Interpersonal Violence and Homicide in Black Youth." In *Surgeon General's Workshop on Violence and Public Health.* Washington, D.C.: U. S. Department of Health and Human Services, 1986.

———. *Violence Prevention Curriculum for Adolescents.* Boston: Education Development Center, 1987.

———. "The Epidemic of Violence and Its Impact on the Health Care System." *Henry Ford Hospital Medical Journal* 38 (1990): 175-77.

———. "Can Physicians Help Curb Adolescent Violence?" *Hospital Practice* (June 15, 1992): 193-206.

———. Telephone interview with Joan C. Elliott, May 18, 1994.

Prothrow-Stith, Deborah, H. Spivak, and A. J. Hausman. "The Violence Prevention Project: A Public Health Approach." *Science, Technology, and Human Values* 12 (Summer/Fall 1987): 67-69.

Prothrow-Stith, Deborah, and Mark Rosenberg. "Changing Our Violent Ways." *Harvard Magazine* (September-October 1992): 14, 16.

Prothrow-Stith, Deborah, and Michaele Weissman. *Deadly Consequences: How Violence Is Destroying Our Teenage Population and a Plan to Begin Solving the Problem.* New York: Harper Collins, 1991.

Spivak, Howard, Deborah Prothrow-Stith, and Alice J. Hausman. "Dying Is No Accident." *Pediatric Clinics of North America* 35 (December 1988): 1339-47.

Who's Who among Black Americans, 1994-95. 8th ed. Detroit: Gale Research, 1994.

Joan C. Elliott

Georgiana Frances Putnam
(1832-1912)
Educator

Georgiana Frances Putnam was a master teacher who had a long career in the public schools of Brooklyn, New York. She knew the hopes of the African American community as emancipation occurred and also shared with them their disappointment as those hopes were dimmed. Her family was deeply rooted in Massachusetts, and her parents were prominent civil rights activists and supporters of the famous abolitionist William Lloyd Garrison. As interesting as Putnam is herself, her family connections also offer a fascinating illumination of the world of free blacks in New England.

Georgiana Frances Putnam was born in Boston, Massachusetts, probably in the family home at 16 Belknap Street, in 1832. Her father was George M. (possibly W.) Putnam (c. 1796-1861), a prosperous hairdresser who moved his business from 211 Washington to 2 Bromfield Street in the year of her birth. He was most likely born in Danvers, Massachusetts, the son of Asahet Putnam. George Putnam married Jane (originally Jenny) Clark (?-1874) of Hubbardston on July 3, 1825. The choice of a minister from the Second Universalist Society of Boston to perform the wedding ceremony may reflect George Putnam's religious affiliation. Jane Clark, the daughter of Peter Clark and Mitty Rhodes, could trace her ancestry to Anthony and Jennie Clark, who settled in Hubbardston in 1768. She had six brothers and three sisters, five of whom also moved to Boston. Anthony F. Clarke (his spelling), George Putnam's young brother-in-law, became a partner in the hairdressing establishment in 1837. George and Jane Putnam had six other children besides Georgiana: Joseph H. (1826-1859), Helen S. (1830-1907), Jane M. (1834-1899), Adelaide V. (1836-?), George (1843-1846), and Wendell Phillips (1846-1847).

Family of Abolitionists

George and Jane Putnam were prominent members of the black community in Boston. They allied themselves with William Lloyd Garrison. In 1831 George Putnam was one of two people to call for a meeting of blacks to discuss grievances, and Jane Putnam became president of the women's auxiliary of the group that was formed. It was in George Putnam's home that the black community presented Garrison with a silver cup in March 1833 in recognition of his antislavery efforts. Additionally, George Putnam's efforts to change conditions at the Smith Street Grammar School were to have a decided impact not only on the lives of his children but on the lives of other students at the school as well. Smith Street was the only school open to blacks in Boston at the time. Blacks were not happy with the school, and in 1844 they charged that the white principal, Abner Forbes, was an overly severe disciplinarian who was "incompetent to teach black students" because of his conviction that blacks were inferior to whites. The Putnams' son Joseph was a teaching assistant at the school, but George Putnam testified before the Boston School Committee. Although Abner Forbes was reappointed, many blacks began to boycott the school. George Putnam was one of the boycotters and also one of the eighty-five African Americans to sign a petition in 1846 to close the school.

To secure a better education for his children, in 1845 George Putnam moved his family to 9 Oak Street in Salem, Massachusetts; he retained his business in Boston. This was to be the address of the family until 1860, when George Putnam moved to Worcester, where he died on March 29, 1861. One of the major inducements to move to Salem, the quality of the unsegregated schools available, was also one of the main reasons for James Forten, Jr.'s decision to send his daughter Charlotte Forten Grimké to Salem to live with the noted black abolitionist family of Charles Lenox Remond and Amy Remond. Grimké would later become an acclaimed black poet and essayist. Her diaries bring the milieu of the Putnams and the Remonds to life. She was very close to certain members of the Putnam family. For example, Jane Putnam had opened a hair salon in Salem, and Charlotte Forten, as she was known then, records taking it over so that the older woman could go to Boston for a meeting. Unfortunately the diaries include little separate notice of Georgiana.

The Putnams and the Remonds were members of the small, educated black elite of the northern states, a group whose members were often personally acquainted, with ties reinforced by marriage. While the experiences of this group were widely different from those of the great mass of blacks, both in the North and in the South, they were intensely concerned with the cause of abolition. Nor did their privileged position shield them from the sting of prejudice. The Putnams shared the middle-class views and values of their white contemporaries with two exceptions, their fervent support of abolition and advocacy of women working outside the home. According to Maritcha Lyons, quoted in her biographical sketch in *Homespun Heroines,* the girls

> anticipated with enthusiasm a near future when they could attempt to be self-sustaining with the ultimate end of arriving at positions of confidence affording both dignity and competence. Animated by this spirit of independence each girl who reached maturity made her mark and became a vitalizing factor in the community where she settled.

Teaching Career Begins

Georgiana Putnam moved to Williamsburg, New York, in 1852 to become a teacher in the segregated school established there in 1844. There she became a colleague of Sarah Tompkins Garnet. In 1855 Williamsburg became part of Brooklyn. In 1863 when Sarah Tompkins Garnet became principal of a Manhattan school, Putnam became assistant principal of the Brooklyn school, which was now called Colored School No. 1 and later became Public School No. 67. Her mother, Jane Clark Putnam, came to live with her, and in 1869 they settled in a house at 37 Fort Greene Place. Jane Putnam died in 1874; Georgiana continued to live at that address. In 1891 Georgiana Putnam became principal of Public School No. 68, Colored School No. 2.

In September 1892 T. McCants Stewart, the only black member of the Brooklyn Board of Education, led a mass meeting to petition for the abolishment of segregated schools. Foreseeing that integration meant that she would probably lose her principalship, Putnam opposed the move. When the schools were integrated in March 1893, Putnam did indeed lose her position. She was demoted to assistant principal and assigned to another school. Three years later she retired and went to live in the family home in Worcester with her sister Helen. She died there on March 25, 1912, from arteriosclerosis. For the four years before her death she had been an invalid as a result of rheumatism. After a private funeral at home, her body was taken to Hubbardston for burial.

The friendship that began between Putnam and Sarah Tompkins Garnet in the Williamsburg school lasted until Garnet's death in 1911, despite their differences in temperament. Lyons leaves us wondering about the exact nature of their differences, however, with her statement, ''The points of likeness between the two were few, the points of contrast, many.'' Lyons moves on immediately to their common ground as teachers:

> Each had a deep interest in the general well being of a child; believed that a normal child should develop normally, and that the days of youth and adolescence should be the habit forming period and that it was the special duty of a teacher to supplement the parent's effort to see that a child acquired those habits recognized by all as forming the base of a life of usefulness and contentment.

Both women were to make the transition from the older pedagogical tradition to that of the professionally trained teacher. Lyons describes Putnam's activities as assistant principal of the large integrated school she worked in before her retirement:

> In this extended sphere of activity she knew just what to do and how to perform the responsible task of assimilating the diverse nationalities that comprise the rank and file in a cosmopolitan school. She was well prepared to help her teachers to help themselves to become familiarized with school routine and to catch the spirit underlying the effort; making it fruitful and vigorous. To the last day of her active service Miss Putnam kept in close touch with the multiplied affairs, administrative and executive, attached to the satisfactory oversight of hundreds of pupils. She particularly and practically demonstrated that scientific teaching discriminates between unity and uniformity; that a teacher should possess something above and beyond booklearning and a minimum of culture. Of a speculative, philosophic turn of mind, she weighed and tested all new departures in the work before indorsing them. . . . With her the result of education was the emphasis of progress in physical and mental alertness, in moral clarity of insight.

Lyons further provides a characterization of Putnam and a whole generation of African Americans, of which she herself was a member. Before emancipation they had looked forward to ''a future in which they could thrive and expand under the sanctity of law; be protected and sheltered in the exercise of those citizen rights upon the concession of which the fate of the republic had hinged.'' She continues:

> The gradual revelation of the true inwardness of the actual state of things dismayed many, disheartened not a few. Still the majority of thinking persons with tightening of lips and squaring of shoulders met the plain indecisions of deferred hope with a compo-

sure almost amounting to stoicism. These could discern a practical policy, that of aiming to stand erect under the most disabling conditions, that of attempting to advance in the face of apparently insuperable obstacles. They were sustained by the conviction that to live life faithfully, if not fully, lies within the power of every self-respecting individual. Georgiana Putnam was one who understood this and applied it and the life she developed during a lengthy series of busy fruitful years was right and enduring in its aspiration and its accomplishment.

REFERENCES:

Brown, Hallie Q. *Homespun Heroines and Other Women of Distinction*. Xenia, Ohio: Aldine Publishing Co., 1926.

''Georgiana F. Putnam.'' Death Notices. *Worcester Evening Gazette,* March 25, 1912; March 27, 1912.

''Georgiana F. Putnam.'' Death Notice. *Worcester Evening Post,* March 25, 1912.

Oden, Gloria. ''The Black Putnams of Charlotte Forten's Journal.'' *Essex Institute Historical Collections* 126 (October 1990): 237-53.

Stevenson, Brenda, ed. *The Journals of Charlotte Forten Grimké*. New York: Oxford University Press, 1988.

Robert L. Johns

Charlotta Gordon Pyles
(c. 1806-1880)
Abolitionist, lecturer

Charlotta Gordon Pyles had no formal education, yet her zealous quest for freedom for her family and other enslaved blacks impelled her to leave Iowa in 1854 to speak against slavery in Pennsylvania, New York, and the New England states. In Philadelphia, where she was welcomed and entertained by Quaker families, Pyles had the privilege of speaking in Independence Hall. Several times during the lecture tour she met with and confided in the great abolitionist and journalist Frederick Douglass. It is evident that he admired this woman's courage, for he honored her with a poem in the December 12, 1855, *Frederick Douglass Paper*. Although Douglass misspelled Pyles's name, entitling the poem ''Charlotte Piles,'' his description of her leaves no doubt who the subject of the poem is: ''A noble woman, now travelling in the free States, soliciting aid for the redemption of part of her family from Republican slavery.''

Little is known of the early life of Charlotta Gordon Pyles. She was born a slave around 1806 and was of mixed ancestry, having a father who was part German and part Negro

Charlotta Gordon Pyles

and a mother who was a full-blooded Seminole Indian. So it is not surprising that Pyles is described by Jones in *Palimpsest* as being "tall and straight as a pine, with high cheekbones, copper-colored hue, and straight, glossy black hair."

According to Mrs. Laurence C. Jones, a granddaughter of Pyles, social reformers, including Susan B. Anthony, John B. Gough, and Lucretia Mott, marveled at this unlettered woman of color and her resoluteness. They wrote letters of recommendation, thereby making it easier for her to have an audience during her travels. Jones said in her article "The Desire for Freedom," published in *Palimpsest* in May 1927, "The most precious heirlooms among her descendants today are the photos and letters of these men and women, given to Charlotta Pyles as personal reminders of their association with her in a noble cause."

Pyles fought against slavery not only on the lecture tour, but also from her home, which became a haven for runaway slaves. Many slaves from the state of Kentucky, where Pyles and her children had previously been enslaved, and some she met on her travels through Tennessee and Missouri made their way to her Keokuk, Iowa, home. There, Pyles and her white friends helped them escape to Canada.

Before ever being freed, Pyles had come to understand the complexities of slavery through her own experience. In Bardstown, Kentucky, she had been the slave of Frances Gordon, who inherited Pyles and her children from her father. The Gordons were Wesleyan Methodists and, on his death-bed, Mr. Gordon made his daughter Frances promise to free the Pyles family according to the Wesleyan Methodist rule for

the manumission of slaves. In 1853 Frances moved the slaves north and freed them.

It was a blessing that Frances Gordon, and not her brothers, inherited Pyles and her family; her brothers did not hold the same religious views about manumission. So envious were they of their sister's "possessions" that they kidnapped Benjamin Pyles, Charlotta's second oldest son, and sold him to a slave driver in Mississippi. This act caused Frances Gordon to take legal action to establish her possession of the Pyles so she could ensure the safety of the rest of the family. She moved the family to Springfield, Kentucky, and at one point had them jailed as a safety precaution.

In addition to Charlotta Pyles and Frances Gordon, the traveling group included Charlotta's husband, Harry MacHenry Pyles, and their children, Emily, Barney, Paulina, Sarah Ann, Mary Ellen, Henry, Charlotta, Elizabeth, and Mary Agnes. Also among the group was a daughter from Charlotta's previous marriage to a man named John McElroy, Julian McElroy Kendricks. Julian was accompanied by her children, Thermon and Louanne. Emily Pyles Walker, the eldest child from the second marriage, had three boys along with her— John Wesley, Daniel, and James Walker. Julian's husband, Joseph Kendricks, and Emily's husband, Catiline Walker, belonged to other masters and could not go with the family.

Purchases Freedom for Enslaved Relatives

Unlike his wife, Harry MacHenry Pyles was a free black, the son of William MacHenry, who was from Scotland, and his light-colored maid. With his blue eyes and fair complexion, Harry resembled his father. In order to feel less guilty about his mulatto son, William MacHenry declared Harry free, thus allowing Harry to travel where he wanted without being bothered. He could visit Charlotta and the children at any time although he could not have charge of his family. This was due to yet another complex rule of slavery that declared that children of a free Negro and a slave inherited the status of the mother. William also provided Harry training in harness and shoe mending and gave him a shop where he could ply his trade. The shop also allowed Harry to support his wife and eleven children in a comfortable way.

Since Harry MacHenry Pyles was a free black, he was able to travel with his wife and children and Frances Gordon. The party left Bardstown, Kentucky, in early fall 1853, and traveled by wagon to Louisville, Kentucky, where Gordon had to validate her right to remove her slaves from the state. To insure their safety from her brothers as well as from slave hunters, Frances Gordon hired a white minister, Reverend Claycome, to come from Ohio to Kentucky to accompany her and the Pyles family northward. Having completed the legal matters, the party took a steamboat to Saint Louis via Cincinnati. Once in Saint Louis, a white man named Nat Stone offered to guide them to Minnesota for a fee of one hundred dollars. A few days into the trip, Stone demanded another fifty dollars. Gordon was so afraid of what could happen to them in Missouri, a slave state, that she agreed to the additional fifty dollars. Gordon knew the advantage she, Stone, and Rev.

Claycome, as whites, provided, since the party had been stopped several times in Missouri, but had not been bothered.

Hallie Q. Brown records in *Homespun Heroines and Other Women of Distinction* that "after leaving St. Louis, the Pyles and Frances Gordon started overland in their schooner wagon, traveling in Woodford County, Saline County, across the Missouri River on the ferry to Howard County, then Shelby, then Monroe.... [T]hey finally crossed the Des Moines River and arrived at Keokuk." While the original destination was to be Minnesota, the cold winter of the Midwest forced the group to settle at Keokuk, a trading post with one small tavern on the river bank.

Lectures to Raise Money

After settling her family in Keokuk, Iowa, Pyles felt compelled to tour the East lecturing in order to raise $1500 for each of her enslaved sons-in-law. Taking care of their wives and children who were with her in Iowa had become too much of a burden. This lecture tour, a thousand miles away in strange territory, was a difficult task for a poor woman who had never had a day's schooling in her life. So well did she plead, however, that in six months she had raised three thousand dollars. She went back to Kentucky, where she bought the two men and returned them to their families in Iowa. Somehow word of her efforts reached the kidnapped Benjamin, who was still in Mississippi. He wrote asking that she pay fifteen hundred dollars to free him and only one of his brothers-in-law. Pyles replied that as he had neither a wife nor children he could find the wherewithal to free himself. According to Jones, Pyles's granddaughter, Benjamin was vexed by this answer and never again wrote to the family. The family did learn that he was later sold in Fayette County, Missouri, and was known as Benjamin Moore.

Jones states that Harry MacHenry Pyles and his oldest son, Barney, built a brick house on Johnson Street in Keokuk, Iowa, for Frances Gordon and the Pyles. The 1857 Keokuk *Directory,* however, lists their residence as Southside Bank, between Fourteenth and Fifteenth Streets. Regardless of where they lived, it is clear that, even after Frances Gordon freed the Pyles, they continued to live under one roof as one family. Gordon was like a doting grandmother to the children. Jones writes that her mother, Mary Ellen, the child of Charlotta and Harry Pyles, was Frances Gordon's favorite "and back in Kentucky had been the one chosen to live in the big house. Whenever Miss Gordon went to church or visiting, she took Mary Ellen with her. Her fair complexion, grey eyes and light hair frequently caused her be mistaken for a white child." According to Hallie Q. Brown in *Homespun Heroines,* "Miss Gordon thought so much of Mary Ellen that she never allowed her to be punished.... Miss Gordon [would] intervene and say, 'Let her go this time, Charlotta, and the next time she must be attended to.' "

Even if Mary Ellen was spoiled by Miss Gordon, she inherited her mother's courageous and industrious spirit.

According to *Homespun Heroines,* she was seventeen when the family arrived in Iowa and had never attended school, but once in Keokuk, she hired out to a Quaker family in Salem in exchange for room and board and a chance to go to school. Mary Ellen then encouraged her sister Mary Agnes to join her. After four terms of school, Mary Agnes returned home, but Mary Ellen stayed the full limit of time afforded her as a colored girl.

The Pyles were zealous in their quest for education. Charlotta Pyles's daughter Charlotta appealed in 1876 to the white school in Keokuk to admit her son Geroid Smith after he finished the eighth grade of the "very inadequate colored school." According to Hallie Q. Brown, when the white school did not admit her son, the younger Charlotta Pyles appealed to the "courts of Iowa and secured the decision of opening Keokuk High School to white and black; thus her son became one of the first colored high school graduates in the state of Iowa in 1880."

This passion for education was passed on to the grandchildren as well. The nine children of Mary Ellen and James Addison Morris were also educated in Iowa. Their youngest daughter and her husband, Laurence C. Jones, worked as educators at the Piney Woods School in Mississippi. Mary Ellen, in her later years, joined the Joneses and worked with them until her death at age ninety-one. In the words of Mrs. Laurence C. Jones, "And so the spirit of a noble woman, Charlotta Pyles, goes marching on in the efforts of her grandchildren to educate the negro [sic] race in the Southland."

When she died from heart disease on January 19, 1880, at the age of seventy-four, the same pallbearers from the First Baptist Church of Keokuk who had carried the remains of Frances Gordon carried those of Pyles. (Frances Gordon died in the early 1870s in the Pyleses' home.) She was so well liked and respected that two Iowa newspapers, the *Burlington Hawkeye* and the *Keokuk Daily,* carried notice of her death. Former slave, abolitionist, and lecturer, Charlotta Pyles possessed an indomitable spirit in her fight against slavery, and she taught her children and grandchildren that with faith and education they could overcome the evils of racism.

REFERENCES:

Brown, Hallie Q. *Homespun Heroines and Other Women of Distinction.* Xenia, Ohio: Aldine Publishing Co., 1926.

"Called Home." *Burlington Hawkeye,* January 20, 1880.

"Died." *Keokuk Daily,* January 21, 1880.

Douglas, Frederick. "Charlotte Piles: A Poem in Her Honor." *Frederick Douglass Paper,* December 12, 1855.

Jones, Mrs. Laurence C. "The Desire for Freedom." *Palimpsest* 8 (May 1927): 153-63.

Register of Deaths. Lee County, Iowa, 1867-1903.

Margaret Ann Reid

Florence Spearing Randolph
(1866-1951)
Evangelist, minister, missionary, suffragist, lecturer, club leader, temperance leader

Florence Spearing Randolph's achievements as an evangelist, minister, missionary, suffragist, lecturer, club leader, and temperance leader rank with those of some of the most celebrated Americans in history. Yet, as important as her contributions were and as well known as she was, less than a decade after her death she became an obscure figure. Unfortunately, this has been the plight of many African Americans, particularly females, whose papers remain uncollected and whose lives rarely are celebrated in the pages of history books.

Florence Spearing Randolph was born in Charleston, South Carolina, on August 9, 1866, the seventh child of John Spearing and Anna Smith Spearing. She was born into a family of privilege and culture, whose free black lineage stretched back almost two generations before the Civil War. As the daughter of a prosperous cabinet maker and a member of the black elite, she was expected to become educated and pursue a career in one of the few professions available to women of color. Her limited choices included teaching and dressmaking. She combined the two professions and became a dressmaker and an instructor at a dressmaking school.

Randolph attended local public schools and was a graduate of Avery Normal Institute in Charleston. Since most southern public schools for African Americans were limited in their offerings and usually covered only grades one through three, normal schools were established for students who desired additional training and who wished to teach. For many years a certificate from a normal school was considered an acceptable credential for teaching in most black public schools, particularly in the rural South. The majority of African Americans at this time, recently freed from slavery, were poor and uneducated and had few options beyond working in the fields or at the most menial and servile jobs. Large numbers of black girls of this class worked in domestic service or in the fields.

In 1885, at the age of nineteen, Randolph moved to New Jersey, taking up residence with an older sister in Jersey City. In Jersey City she could earn as much as $1.50 a day as a dressmaker, as compared to fifty cents a day in Charleston, and she could live and work in a freer environment. It was in Jersey City that she met and married Hugh Randolph of Richmond, Virginia, who worked on the railroad as a cook for

Florence Spearing Randolph

the dining car service of the Pullman Company. The Randolphs had one child, a daughter named Leah Viola, who was born in February 1887. Leah Viola later married J. Francis Johnson, a successful physician in Washington, D.C. Hugh Randolph died in 1913.

In 1886, Florence Spearing Randolph became a member of the Monmouth Street African Methodist Episcopal (AME) Zion Church, where she was appointed Sunday school teacher and class leader for the young people. As a child in Charleston, she had frequently accompanied her blind grandmother on house visits to pray with the sick and to explain the Scriptures. This experience left a deep impression on the young Randolph, who later was determined to pursue a career in the ministry. In the late 1880s, under the tutelage of a Greek and Hebrew scholar, she began studying the Bible. In 1925 she completed a "synthetic Bible course" offered by the Moody Bible Institute of Chicago, Illinois, known for its training of missionaries. In 1926, following her appointment as minister to Wallace Chapel in Summit, New Jersey, she enrolled in an advanced course at Madison and Drew Seminary, later known as Drew University. She was frequently referred to as a distinguished graduate of Drew Theological Seminary.

Begins Temperance and Church Work

Throughout the late 1880s and early 1890s, Randolph operated a flourishing dressmaking business from her home, located in downtown Jersey City. It was during this period that she began to exhort and became very active in temperance and church work. The term exhort, meaning to incite by argument or advice, was widely used in the nineteenth century. Lay ministers and other persons who were considered to be rousing speakers and made urgent appeals for support of causes or who gave strong warnings or advice were called exhorters. In biographical notes, Randolph speaks of the experiences that drew her to the ministry:

> For several year I conducted a very successful dressmaking business, with seven in my workroom beside myself. Two dressmakers and 5 apprentice girls. Then one day while sitting by my window trying to design a pattern this happened: ... A crowd gathered in front of a saloon just across from my house (for one had saloons those days on almost every corner). With the curiosity of a woman, I walked across to discover the trouble. It was there that I saw quite a young man whom I suppose was not accustomed to saloon drinking and perhaps gambling, become intoxicated and noisy. The Saloon Keeper disregarding his youth soon called the police and a patrol wagon had come to take him away, hence the crowd. Speaking aloud to myself, I said, "If I had my way I would close every saloon before night." A white woman standing near, a president of the WCTU [Women's Christian Temperance Union] told me if you feel that way come and join the WCTU and help us bring about prohibition. Finding the lady lived on the very next block to me I became a member of No. 1 WCTU of Jersey City, soon became one of the local members which marked the beginning of 14 years of real missionary work among those who suffer from strong drink and from poverty. Thus as a WCTU, Christian Endeavor, Kings Daughter and Sunday School Teacher I soon developed into a Bible student, discovering that one can do a real telling work for God and humanity.

Ministerial Work Causes Stir

During the unexpected illness of R. R. Baldwin, the pastor of the Jersey City AME Zion Church, Randolph was granted permission to start a meeting that turned out to be one of the greatest revivals in the history of the church. Many other meetings followed; Randolph's youth and gender attracted large crowds, which helped to increase the membership of her church and others in the vicinity. Local press coverage and word-of-mouth revelations about Randolph increased her visibility and popularity. Invitations to speak and conduct revivals came from small churches and missions, white and black. Because of her success she was made a class leader and an exhorter and finally a local preacher. Randolph said it was then that "the ball of criticism, fault finding, and

persecution began rolling. In 1897 I was granted head preacher. Not that I wanted honors, nor sought them but pressure was brought to bear by the pastor." In 1898 she was admitted to the New Jersey Conference of the AME Zion Church. Her licensing as a preacher followed a lengthy and somewhat bitter debate. The presiding bishop was opposed to Randolph's appointment, and this set the tone for disaffection among fellow ministers who were opposed to elevating women to positions of authority in the church. This was just the beginning of many years of struggle to be accepted and treated as an equal in the AME Zion ministry.

Having been admitted to the New Jersey Conference, Randolph became conference evangelist. At the May 1900 AME Zion Church conference meeting in Atlantic City she was ordained a deacon and in August of that year she was a delegate to the Ecumenical Conference meeting in London, England. During this trip she also traveled to Scotland, France, and Belgium, speaking and lecturing.

Between 1897 and 1901, the Reverend Florence Spearing Randolph pastored several churches in New York City, Newark, New Jersey, and Poughkeepsie, New York. During her career, she pastored five churches in New Jersey, working without salary for the first twelve years. The churches to which she was assigned were small, poor, and struggling. Once the churches became solvent, she would be reassigned to another problem church. Her last difficult experience in her ministerial career was at Wallace Chapel in Summit, New Jersey. She served as pastor of this church from 1925 to her retirement in 1946 and was pastor emeritus until her death in 1951.

Racism, Sexism, and Colonialism Attacked

Randolph's work with the WCTU as an organizer and lecturer who spoke against the liquor traffic influenced her ministerial thought and style. Working in these capacities for the WCTU until after the repeal of the Eighteenth Amendment in 1933, she reflected the fiery zeal of the WCTU reformers. Her lectures and speeches were frequently very direct in their attack on racism, colonialism, and sexism. Even though her public posture was forceful and she spoke and worked on behalf of women's suffrage, she was accepted and supported by a number of men because of her feminine demeanor. In 1905, one male writer stated that "her sermons, lectures and public addresses are all the more attractive and impressive because of the modest womanly manner in which they are delivered. In the pulpit, or on the platform she is always a woman, and when she speaks [she] has something to say." This public posture served her well throughout her career.

Very early in her career, Randolph became identified with educational and religious movements that were supportive of interests on the African continent. In 1921 and 1922 she traveled in Africa, working for a while as a missionary in Liberia and spending more than a year on the Gold Coast, lecturing, preaching, and studying conditions. She made seven trips into the interior, traveling by lorry, ox-cart, canoe, and native carriers. She became well known in Africa for her work on behalf of the Quittah AME Zion Mission Sunday School and Varick Christian Endeavor Society. Randolph served as a preacher and teacher during her thirteen-month stay in Africa without salary, paying her own traveling expenses. Returning to the United States, she conducted a series of lectures designed to educate Americans about conditions in Africa.

Randolph's concern for the cause of foreign missions led to her appointment in 1912 as AME Zion Secretary of the Bureau. In 1916 she was elected president of the Women's Home and Foreign Missionary Society of the AME Zion Church, a post she held for twenty-five years. In addition to missionary work in the United States and Africa, her work extended to the fields of South America. In those years, most of the fund-raising for missionary work was conducted by women. Randolph always led in the raising of missionary money.

Randolph's work in the AME Zion church was singular and distinguished. In many ways she was a pioneer who expanded opportunities for women in the church through her achievements. Licensed as a local preacher in 1897 and conferred a deacon in 1900, she was among the first black women to be ordained. She was the first woman to be made an elder in the New Jersey Conference and one of the first in the church. In 1933, Livingstone College in Salisbury, North Carolina, bestowed upon her the honorary degree of doctor of divinity. She was the first woman of the AME Zion denomination to receive this honor from the college.

Leadership Seen in Women's Club Activities

Randolph's work as a minister, missionary, and temperance worker never overshadowed her work as an organizer. Randolph organized the New Jersey Federation of Colored Women's Clubs in 1915. Like most of her endeavors, the founding of the federation was influenced by her temperance work. Specifically, the federation was an outgrowth of a conference of women of color representing thirty societies of the WCTU of New Jersey who met in October 1915 to develop plans for arousing greater interest in the temperance movement among African Americans in the state. Randolph served for a number of years as the state president of the Temperance Union League, whose members included white and black women.

The National Association of Colored Women (NACW), founded in 1896, represented a coalition of women's clubs. To systematize and organize its work more efficiently, by 1915 the NACW established state federations comprised of clubs within a state. Initially, the New Jersey federation was composed only of temperance societies; later missionary societies were represented, and by 1917 the federation included any women's clubs "doing work for human betterment, church, civic, literary, business or political." In 1917, eighty-five clubs were enrolled with a combined membership of 2,616, and the objectives of the federation expanded to meet the needs of its diverse membership. In 1924 the Federation

had fifty-six active clubs with a total membership of 3,500. There were thirty-six delegates at its eighth annual session convened in Atlantic City in October 1923. It is significant to note that, along with the businesswomen and wives of lawyers, physicians, college professors, and teachers who were present, there were a large number of club representatives who were domestics and some who were day workers, who did not consistently work for one employer.

Randolph's philosophy had a great impact on the work of the New Jersey Federation of Colored Women's Clubs in its early years. Randolph was founder and first president from 1915 to 1927, and in her later roles as president emeritus and as a member of the board of trustees, she continued to influence the organization's structure and policies. Moreover, her position as the national chaplain of the NACW and her extensive contacts and visibility provided her with leverage and clout in her continuing role of leadership. Commenting on Randolph's leadership ability, a writer covering the federation's convention in 1923 observed, "She possesses unusual ability, tact, and cleverness, with a keen sense of humor. The effects of eight years of convention manipulation and education of delegates were plainly evident as one sat through the three days' proceedings."

The tenets of Randolph's philosophy are well known and can be observed in the course taken by the New Jersey federation. First and foremost, she was an integrationist and a feminist. Having grown up in the stultifying racial climate of post-Civil War Charleston, South Carolina, she had witnessed segregation and discrimination during the years when southern society was attempting to define the new relationship between blacks and whites. Even though her family's class and status shielded her from some of the worst elements of racism, in her daily life she saw the evidence of abuse, neglect, and oppression of her people. One of the key themes of her life was the need to work for the elevation of the black race and to stamp out racism. The lynching of a close family friend, a postmaster in Charleston, during the late nineteenth century had convinced her that an all-out assault on lynching was necessary. Thus the federation was an ardent supporter of the antilynching campaign.

Randolph skillfully used politics to effect change. The New Jersey federation established contacts and made known its concerns to elected state and national officials. Through its legislative department it conducted studies of legislation pertinent to race and gender issues. Members were encouraged to seek appointments to key boards and commissions where they could influence policy-making. Letters and appeals articulating the federation's concerns were sent to key political figures, and the press was adeptly used to publicize its activities and causes. Understanding the power of interracial coalitions, the federation frequently invited white women to work with them on public issues.

In 1919 the New Jersey federation joined with an unspecified group of white women to present an appeal to President Woodrow Wilson to "personally interest himself in the adjustment of race differences in this country." The group told the president, "You have spent many months in France in an earnest effort for interracial harmony. We beg that you will give a like skillful attention to interracial harmony here." The appeal addressed specific concerns relating to the riots that occurred in cities throughout the nation as a result of charges being brought against some black men for assaulting and raping white women. In the appeal the federation told President Wilson that, while the excuse given for lynching black men was that they assault white women's honor, as a student of history he knew that the assaults made on black women's honor were "written on the faces of our race." The federation's white supporters called for equal justice for black men and women.

The New Jersey federation became involved in a number of other activities during Randolph's tenure. These included: fund-raising for scholarships for students who excelled at the New Jersey Manual Training and Industrial School for Colored Youth at Bordentown; developing health programs; establishing homes for underprivileged girls; demanding that the state and national press exercise more responsibility in reporting news about African Americans; appealing to Congress to enforce the Fourteenth and Fifteenth amendments; and making requests to the attorney general and department of justice for abolishing peonage.

Randolph Works for Women's Suffrage

Randolph's feminist leadership displayed itself in her work as a suffragist for the passage of the Nineteenth Amendment and in other diverse efforts to elevate the status of women, particularly African American women. For years she served as a member of the executive board of the New Jersey State Suffrage Association. A key player in securing ratification of the suffrage amendment, Randolph spoke before the state legislature on its behalf. Shortly after the passage of the Nineteenth Amendment, in 1920, she was invited by former New Jersey governor Edward C. Stokes, then chairman of the New Jersey Republican party, to assist Lillian Feichert, head of the Republican women's division, in organizing and leading the women of New Jersey in the Warren G. Harding presidential campaign. In the 1930s she became a candidate for nomination for assemblywoman on the Republican ticket.

An ardent believer in the importance of learning black history, Randolph joined the Negro History movement engendered by Carter G. Woodson and actively supported the Association for the Study of Negro Life and History. The New Jersey federation was among the first of the New Jersey organizations to argue the significance of African American history and to sponsor programs during Negro History Week. In 1924 the federation, under the auspices of its race history department, held a statewide meeting to organize state activities for the celebration of Negro History Week.

Outspoken in her beliefs about racism and sexism, and untiring in her efforts to help the needy, Florence Spearing Randolph greatly influenced the lives of blacks—and of all Americans—through her ministry as well as her other activities, particularly her involvement in the temperance and suffrage movements. She deserves to be better known.

REFERENCES:

Burstyn, Joan N., ed. *Past and Promise: Lives of New Jersey Women.* Metuchen, N.J.: Scarecrow Press, 1990.
"Dr. Florence Randolph." *Star of Zion,* October 10, 1935.
Nichols, James L. *The New Progress of a Race.* Naperville, Ill.: J. L. Nichols and Co., 1929.
"Not to be Ministered Unto, but to Minister." *Chicago Defender,* December 11, 1937.
"Rev. Florence Randolph Given Honorary Degree." *New York Age,* July 8, 1933.
Richardson, Clement. *The National Cyclopedia of the Colored Race.* Vol. 1. Montgomery, Ala.: National Publishing Co., 1919.
"Useful Life of the Reverend Mrs. Florence Randolph." *Baltimore Afro-American,* September 28, 1912.
Who's Who in Colored America. 5th ed. Brooklyn: Who's Who in Colored America, 1940.
"Woman Missionary Honored by Zion." *New York Age,* June 1, 1916.

COLLECTIONS:

The Reverend Florence Spearing Randolph's papers, sermons, and memorabilia are in the possession of Bettye Collier-Thomas.

Bettye Collier-Thomas

Emma S. Ransom
(?-1943)
Religious worker, clubwoman, civil rights activist

In September of 1949 Cecelia Cabaniss Saunders, executive secretary of the Harlem YWCA, received a letter from a young woman student at Wilberforce University, the African Methodist Episcopal (AME) Church school in Ohio, inquiring about the career of Saunders's friend and colleague Emma Ransom. In her response to Arrella Payne dated September 24, 1949, Saunders commented on Ransom's tremendous influence upon her:

> She is one of the few women with whom I have been associating who profoundly influenced my life—she gave me much—in turn I have felt my obligation to pass it on, knowing that as Emerson says, "In the order of nature, we cannot render benefits to those from whom we receive them, or very seldom. But the benefit we receive must be rendered again, line for line, deed for deed, cent for

Emma S. Ransom

cent, to somebody." This is Mrs. Emma S. Ransom's message to me and to other women.

Emma S. Ransom was born to Jackson and Beattie Conner, both of whom had been slaves in West Virginia. Although neither her date of birth nor information about her childhood is available, it seems likely that she was born shortly after the Civil War. It is known that her parents eventually moved their family to Selma, Ohio, where Emma grew up, went to school, and worked as a teacher. In 1886 she married Reverdy Cassius Ransom (1861-1959), a graduate of Wilberforce University, whom she met during his time as a student pastor at the local AME church in Selma. From this point on, Emma Ransom's work and commitment to a Christian-based activism became tied to Reverdy Ransom's career as a minister and later as a bishop in the AME Church. Over the years Reverdy Ransom's assignments included pastorates in Springfield, Ohio (1890-93), Cleveland (1893-96), Chicago (1896-1904), Boston (1904-07), and New York (1907-12), and a continued stay in New York as editor of the *Christian Recorder* until 1924.

During the last decade of the nineteenth century, Emma Ransom became nationally known primarily through her work in the AME Church. In 1895 she and Lida A. Lowry began publishing *Woman's Light and Love for Heathen Africa,* the only AME missionary journal edited and published by women. In addition, Ransom and Lowry organized the first Conference Branch Mite Missionary Convention of the AME Church. Through her work with the missionary society, Ransom made an important contribution to the ongoing missionary work of black churches and also helped to build an institutional structure through which women could exert influence in the church. The Ohio correspondent of the *Woman's Era,* a national newspaper published by Josephine St. Pierre Ruffin of the Boston Woman's Era Club, reported on a visit with Ransom in 1895. The notice read,

> Mrs. Emma S. Ransom of Cleveland, one of the editors of "Woman's Light and Love for Heathen Africa," one of our missionary periodicals, and the only one published by our women, spent a few days with us. Mrs. Ransom is but to be seen to be loved. Though young in years she is making the world know she is in it.

Another important development in Emma Ransom's career came when Reverdy Ransom became the pastor of Bethel Church in Chicago. Here the two began to experiment with new institutional structures designed to meet the needs of an urban black population that required more from the church than religious services. In his memoirs, *The Pilgrimage of Harriet Ransom's Son,* Reverdy Ransom wrote,

> My first vision of the need for social services came to me as my wife and I almost daily, went through the alleys and climbed the dark stairways of the wretched tenements, or walked out on the planks to the shanty boats where our people lived on the river. My wife gathered a considerable Sunday School from these sources. We were also able to turn many to aspire in changing their material conditions as well as in things of the spirit.

In 1900 Reverdy Ransom founded the Institutional Church and Social Settlement in Chicago in order to begin to address the many various needs of Chicago's black community, and Emma Ransom took charge of the day nursery and kindergarten, domestic science classes, the Women's Club, and the Girls' Club. With these responsibilities, Ransom began to gain experience in the area of settlement house work and the developing field of social work, both of which would remain important to her throughout her career. She was, no doubt, influenced by the example set by Jane Addams at Hull House in Chicago, and Addams proved to be an early and vocal supporter of the Ransoms' work. In Chicago Emma and Reverdy Ransom also came to know Ida B. Wells Barnett, the antilynching activist and journalist, and also counted her among the supporters of the Institutional Church.

Ransom and the National Club Movement

The end of the nineteenth century and the beginning of the twentieth saw the development of a national network of African American women's clubs as well as the rise of a significant group of national leaders, including Ida B. Wells Barnett, Josephine St. Pierre Ruffin, Mary Church Terrell, and Margaret Murray Washington. Ransom's work, along with the work of many other women, helped to ground the National Association of Colored Women (NACW), and although she could not personally attend its founding convention in 1895, she sent greetings on behalf of the Women's Mite Missionary Society of the AME Church. In 1904, upon

Reverdy Ransom's transfer to Charles Street Church in Boston, Emma Ransom became an active participant in the work of the Northeast Federation of Women's Clubs, a member organization of the national body.

One of Ransom's extant pieces of writing, "The Home-Made Girl," was presented as an address before the 1905 Boston convention of the Northeast Federation of Women's Clubs. In the address, Ransom iterates a theme common in the discourse of African American clubwomen of the era—that any progress that African Americans as a group will make depends, in large measure, on the efforts of women. Ransom wrote in "The Home-Made Girl,"

> The colored women of America have a domestic and weighty task more difficult than that of any other class of women. The generation they are to rear and train is, for the most part, without antecedents of education or wealth. Theirs is a task of producing a womanhood which shall be able to stand upon its feet and hold up its head in the face of this American nation.

In addition, Ransom underscored the need for cross-class cooperation among African American women and chastised those who left the community after obtaining an education or wealth, as well as those who used women's organizations merely as a power base. "No, give us rather the plain woman of sturdy virtues, of industry, of motherwit and good common sense, for these are the women who have made us what we are." In addition to highlighting Ransom's religious sensibilities, this address illuminates her commitment to organizing among African American women and to playing a role in the advancements made by African Americans after Reconstruction.

Ransom at the Harlem YWCA

When Reverdy Ransom became the pastor of Bethel AME Church in New York City in August 1907, Emma Ransom continued her activist work. The *New York Age* described her as an eloquent speaker, and she became much sought after by organizations such as the Equal Suffrage League and the city's African American Young Women's Christian Association. Her work with the YWCA led to her election, in January of 1909, as president of the African American branch's volunteer Committee of Management. Her tenure in this position lasted until 1924.

With Ransom's guidance and help, African American women achieved a number of significant goals in the New York City YWCA. First, she oversaw the development of a building fund in order to provide the organization with a permanent home. During the New York City YMCA and YWCA's capital campaign in 1917, Ransom struggled successfully to gain a commitment from the white women in control of the YWCA's board to appropriate $100,000 for the construction of new facilities in Harlem for African American women. The branch had moved to rented space in Harlem in 1913 and finally opened its own buildings at 137th Street and Lenox Avenue early in 1920. In addition to assisting in the process of opening the new buildings, Ransom also made her mark on the New York City YWCA by serving, from 1920 until 1924, as the first African American representative on the Metropolitan Board, the body responsible for directing the numerous branches making up the city's YWCA. Moreover, she distinguished herself as the first African American woman to hold such a position in any YWCA in the country. Her work here helped to set in motion a process through which the New York City YWCA—and the national YWCA—began to move from being a biracial, segregated association towards being an interracial organization. She was also among the first group of African American women to attend a national YWCA conference in 1920. The Harlem YWCA paid tribute to Ransom's pioneering work with the YWCA by naming its newly-constructed residence, opened in 1926, the Emma Ransom House.

Shortly after the Ransom family's move to New Jersey in 1924 and Reverdy Ransom's election as a bishop of the AME Church the same year, Emma Ransom resigned as the president of the Harlem YWCA's Committee of Management. When Reverdy Ransom was moved to Wilberforce, Ohio, Emma accompanied him and immersed herself once again in the work of the AME Church, focusing especially on missions. She nevertheless maintained her membership in the Harlem YWCA, continuing to offer guidance and remaining in frequent touch with Cecelia Cabaniss Saunders concerning developments in New York. After a slight stroke in 1942 Ransom was forced to curtail her activities. Although Richard R. Wright, Jr., in his *The Bishops of the A.M.E. Church,* marks Ransom's death in the year 1941, she died on May 15, 1943, and was buried in Wilberforce, Ohio. She lived to see her son, Reverdy C. Ransom, Jr., and grandson, Reverdy C. Ransom III, ordained as ministers in the AME Church.

Ransom's contributions to African American history and to the history of the United States in general lie in a range of areas. She was a significant figure in developing avenues for women's participation in the AME Church and was one of many women married to ministers and bishops who expanded the boundaries of the activities of the minister's wife. In addition to her religious work, Ransom also played a role in the rise of national organizations dedicated to the pursuit of African American civil rights. Alongside her activities in the black women's club movement, Ransom was also involved in the work of the NAACP, having been elected to its executive board in 1916. In all her work, Emma Ransom strove to be the kind of woman she called on young African American women to be, as noted in "The Home-Made Girl": "the architect who builds and shapes the character of a people, builds them into enduring strength to tread the path of progress without fear."

REFERENCES:

Ransom, Emma S. "The Home-Made Girl: An Address." Convention of the Northeast Federation of Women's Clubs, Boston, August 11, 1905.

Ransom, Reverdy C. *The Pilgrimage of Harriet Ransom's Son.* Nashville: AME Sunday School Union, n.d.

Saunders, Cecelia Cabaniss. Letter to Arrella Payne, September 24, 1949.

Wright, Bishop Richard R. *Centennial Encyclopedia of the AME Church.* Philadelphia: AME Book Concern, 1916.

———. *Who's Who in the General Conference.* Philadelphia: AME Book Concern, 1924.

———. *The Bishops of the A.M.E. Church.* Nashville: AME Sunday School Union, 1963.

COLLECTIONS:

Information on Emma S. Ransom is located in the Cecelia Cabaniss Saunders personal correspondence file, Laura Parsons Pratt Research Center, YWCA of the City of New York.

Judith Weisenfeld

Phylicia Ayers-Allen Rashad

Phylicia Ayers-Allen Rashad

(1948-)

Actress, singer, dancer

Phylicia Rashad is best known as Clair Huxtable, the character she portrayed from 1984 to 1992 on the *Cosby Show.* In this role, according to Mark Kram in *Contemporary Newmakers,* television critics agreed that "with quiet grace and self-confident ease, she embodie[d] the essence of the 1980s woman—someone who nurtures husband and children while still maintaining a strong sense of personal achievement." In addition, Rashad has won renown for her work as an actress, singer, and dancer in television films and in the theater.

The product of an unusually artistic family, Phylicia Ayers-Allen Rashad is the second oldest child in a family of four children. Born on June 19, 1948, in Houston, Texas, she is the daughter of Andrew A. "Tex" Allen, a dental surgeon, and Vivian Ayers Allen, an artist and writer. Rashad's younger sister, Debbie Allen, is a talented actress, television producer, singer, dancer, writer, and director. Her older brother is Andrew "Tex" Allen, Jr., a jazz composer and musician. Her younger brother, Hugh Allen, graduated from the University of Texas in the mid-1980s.

The Allen household was educationally and culturally oriented. Phylicia Rashad's father continued to study dentistry throughout his career. A writer and a painter, her mother has made her own mark in life. In 1953, her book of poetry, *Spice of Dawn,* was nominated for a Pulitzer Prize. Her talents go beyond the canvas and the printed page. She is also a concert pianist. Speaking about her mother, Rashad's sister,

Debbie Allen, told Sheryl Flatow for *McCall's,* July 1987: "She is a genuine scholar. She ran a museum in Texas for years. It would be hard to grow up in a house with a woman like that and not develop some talent." Vivian Ayers Allen cultivated in her children an appreciation—even a fascination—for the arts and taught them many things before they started school. In an interview with Kathy Henderson of *Redbook,* published in April 1986, Rashad acknowledged: "Artistic expression was as much a part of our childhood as making mud pies."

When Rashad was only seven years old, her parents separated. She does not view their separation as "traumatic." During an interview with Judith Regan of *Ladies Home Journal* that appeared in April 1986, she recalled: "What I remember is that I felt loved by both my parents. I don't view their divorce a tumultuous or difficult period." In this same article Regan emphasizes the enormous gratitude Rashad feels for her father, who remained a strong, supportive force in her life until his death in 1984. She and her sister have endowed a scholarship fund in his memory at Howard University, their alma mater as well as his.

Encouragement Leads to Scholastic Success

Education, encouragement, support, pride, independence, and love were the main ingredients in the Allen family's formula for success. Both parents always encouraged their children to continue their educations, and Andrew Allen sent both Phylicia Rashad and Debbie Allen to Howard University in Washington, D.C., where he had received his doctor of dental surgery (D.D.S.) degree in 1945. Vivian Ayers Allen is held in high esteem by her children, who credit her with instilling in them lasting values at an early age. The early training Rashad received served as the foundation for her successful academic performance and her enormous achievements in the entertainment field. All four children were taught to read music before they entered grade school. Playing a musical instrument, serving as a drum majorette, and singing in choruses were all part of growing up for Rashad and her sister. Rashad also attributes her love of the arts and her appreciation for exotic things to her mother. Television at home was discouraged and there was no rush to repair a broken set. Concerts and dance lessons filled much of the time that most children devote to watching television.

Both Rashad and Debbie Allen graduated with honors from Howard University. Rashad earned a bachelor of fine arts degree in 1970. She graduated magna cum laude, and in 1971 Debbie Allen graduated cum laude.

While she was a product of an exceptionally talented family, Rashad always knew that the road to stardom for young African American artists was paved with hard work and that she would have to have stamina and determination. Success in itself was not the goal. Until she signed on with the *Cosby Show*, she did not even have an agent. During the July 1987 *McCall's* interview, Rashad recalled:

> We had a family motto that if one of us makes it, we all make it. . . . For us, making it wasn't the goal. The goal was achieving excellence and living up to your inherent potential. Making it was side effect—something that happened.

In 1973, Phylicia married William Lancelot Bowles, Jr., a dentist in New York City. The couple had a son, William Lancelot Bowles III. The marriage ended in divorce in 1975. In 1978 Phylicia married Victor Willis, a former Village People lead singer. Two years later this marriage also ended in divorce.

On Thanksgiving Day, November 28, 1985, Ahmad Rashad, an NBC sportscaster, proposed to Phylicia during the national broadcast of the New York Jets-Detroit Lions football game. She accepted on the air, and the marriage took place on December 14, 1985. Before joining the staff of NBC Sports, where he won an Emmy Award, Ahmad Rashad was an all-pro football player with the Minnesota Vikings.

Phylicia and Ahmad are the parents of one daughter, Condola Phylea, who is named after Ahmad's mother. Together they have five children. At the end of 1993, in addition to five-year-old Condola Phylea, the Rashad family consisted of William Lancelot Bowles III, age 20, the son of Phylicia and her first husband, and Ahmad Rashad's three children from a previous marriage: Keva, age 22; Maiysha, age 17; and Ahmad, Jr., age 15.

Successful Acting Career Begins

Rashad's acting career began during the late 1960s while she was a student at Howard University. Like most young actresses, Rashad had her share of disappointments in auditioning for parts she lost. Her sister, Debbie Allen, encouraged Rashad to join her on the West Coast, but Rashad chose to stay in New York. She wanted to make it on her own—and make it on her own she did. She landed parts in theatrical productions, including *Ain't Supposed To Die a Natural Death* (1971). Created, written, and produced by Melvin Van Peebles, this play has 325 performances to its credit. In the 1975 production of *The Wiz*, Rashad played the part of a Munchkin. She landed a part as chorus girl and understudy in the Tony Award-winning *Dreamgirls* in 1981. From 1983 to 1984 she had a role on the ABC daytime series *One Life To Live*.

In 1984 Rashad rose to stardom as Clair Huxtable, the attorney wife of Dr. Cliff Huxtable, played by Bill Cosby, and mother of five children on the immensely popular *Cosby Show*, the most-watched television program in America from its debut in 1984 until it went off the air in 1992. Her role as a smart, sexy, and sassy attorney complemented Cosby's role as an obstetrician, and both won praise as parental role models.

Work on the Cosby show allowed time for other projects. In 1987, she appeared in the television film version of *Uncle Tom's Cabin*. "It was my mother who said I had to play Eliza," she recalled in a story for *Jet* in August 1987. "She said that I didn't understand what the book meant to her generation before. Perhaps this film will help today's generation understand," she concluded. Stephen Sondheim's Tony Award—winning musical *Into the Woods*, which opened on November 5, 1987, provided Rashad a starring role in 1988. "It was the first time I had a full, dramatic expression in a musical role, and it was a fantastic opportunity to be able to sing that fabulous score," she recalled in *Harpers Bazaar*, September 1988. In 1989, she played opposite Philip Michael Thomas in a suspense-filled television drama, *False Witness*. Her subsequent television films include *Polly* (1989), *Polly Coming Home* (1990), *Polly Once Again* (1990), and *Jailbirds* (1990). In addition to her work on stage and television, Rashad has one recording, *Josephine Superstar*, which consists of cover versions of songs made famous by Josephine Baker.

Rashad returned to Broadway during the summer of 1993, replacing an original cast member in another Tony Award-winning musical, *Jelly's Last Jam*. This time she performed with Ben Vereen and Brian Mitchell in the starring role of Sweet Anita, the independent, sensuous lover of Jelly Roll Morton, the self-proclaimed creator of jazz.

Spiritual Balance

Meditation plays an important role in Rashad's life. She speaks openly about her meditating and feels that meditation helped her land a leading role on the *Cosby Show* in 1984. She says:

> Before that I had a lot of work, understudying on Broadway in *The Wiz* and *Dreamgirls* and dramatic

parts with the Negro Ensemble Company.... I even had a recurring role on a daytime soap, *One Life to Live,* but it wasn't until I learned to focus myself that my career came into its own.

Next to her husband and children, meditation is the most important element in her existence. She meditates for an hour daily, preferably in the morning. She explained in the *Ladies Home Journal* article dated April 1986, "It's a very vital part of my life. It is as vital as breathing. I do it because I love it. I do it for my health." She gives Siddha meditation credit for her remarkable composure. In another *Ladies Home Journal* article, dated May 1992, she stated that this ancient spiritual practice focuses on finding "that within yourself that is still and quiet." When the day-to-day problems mount up and interfere with her performances, she finds meditation a great help.

In a fact sheet she filled out about herself for a production company, Rashad unequivocally attributed her success as an actress to disciplined living. She declared:

It is never too late to start putting discipline in your life and reaping its benefits.... Just the discipline of getting up every morning and saying "thank you." You would be surprised at how much is increased in your life if you just say "thank you" for what you have today.... Once discipline is started in the home, it just passes from one generation to another. Rising early, getting your work done and orderliness can help make life very beautiful.

Rashad finds time to share her disciplined and beautiful life in many ways, and these hours of dedicated service to others have not gone unnoticed. Her performance in the civic arena is noteworthy. Since 1990, she has served on the Board of Directors of Recruiting New Teachers; for two years she was a designated spokesperson for Save the Children (1989-91); and she served the Cancer Information Service as spokeswoman from 1990 to 1992.

Since her emergence as one of leading performers in the United States, Rashad has won several prestigious awards for her work in the entertainment world. For three consecutive seasons, 1985, 1986, and 1987, she received the NAACP Image Award for best actress in a comedy series. She also received two Emmy nominations for her role in the *Cosby Show.* She won a People's Choice Award, given to the most popular actress on network television. Her portrayal of Eliza in *Uncle Tom's Cabin* led to her being nominated for an Ace Award for best supporting actress in a television film in 1987. Another banner year was 1991, during which the Women in Film organization gave her the famous Outstanding Achievement Award, and she also received the Honoree of the Year Award from the Harvard Foundation for her contributions to American Arts and Intercultural Relations. In 1989 Rashad was honored by Barber Scotia College with an honorary doctorate of humanities degree and in 1991 she was given another by Providence College in Rhode Island.

Phylicia Rashad has graced the covers of many magazines. Her portrayal of a strong, warm, intelligent, and loving woman on the *Cosby Show* projected a tremendously influential image of the working mother. Most people know her only as Clair Huxtable, but she has extensive credits as an actress and talents that have made her successful in other areas of entertainment.

REFERENCES:

"America's Ten Most Beautiful Women Reveal Their Beauty Secrets." *Harpers Bazaar* 121 (September 1988): 188, 324-25.

Collier, Aldore. "Phylicia and Philip Are Lovers and Lawyers in Thriller, *False Witness.*" *Jet* 77 (October 30, 1989): 60-62.

Contemporary Newsmakers. 1987 cumulation. Detroit: Gale Research, 1988.

Current Biography, 1987. New York: H. W. Wilson Co., 1987.

Flatow, Sheryl. "Sisters: Debbie Allen and Phylicia Rashad." *McCall's* 114 (July 1987): 90-95.

Frederick, Monroe S. "Phylicia Ayers-Allen, Ahmad Rashad Exchange Wedding Vows in Church." *Jet* 69 (December 30, 1985-January 6, 1986): 62-64.

Hall, Jane. "TV's Reigning Mom, Phylicia Rashad, and Her Football Hero, Ahmad, Reveal a Match Made by Bill Cosby." *People Weekly* 28 (November 16, 1987): 95-98.

Henderson, Kathy. "Phylicia Ayers-Allen: Her TV Husband Married Her Off." *Redbook* 166 (April 1986): 80-82.

Mapp, Edward. *Directory of Blacks in the Performing Arts.* 2d ed. Metuchen, N.J.: Scarecrow Press, 1990.

Moses, Gavin. "Sportscaster Ahmad Rashad Scores with a Television Proposal to Cosby's Phylicia Ayers-Allen." *People Weekly* 24 (December 16, 1985): 64-65.

Norment, Lynn. "Phylicia and Ahmad Rashad: TV's Super Couple Juggle Careers and Family." *Ebony* 42 (May 1987): 148-50, 152-54.

———. "Ten Most Exciting Couples." *Ebony* 44 (February 1989): 164-66.

Parish, James Robert, and Vincent Terrace, eds. *The Complete Actors' Television Credits, 1948-1988.* 2d ed. Vol. 1. Metuchen, N.J.: Scarecrow Press, 1989.

"Phylicia Rashad Returns to Broadway in *Jelly's Last Jam.*" *Jet* 84 (August 16, 1993): 58-61.

Ransom, Lou. "Phylicia Rashad Tells Why She Plays Slave Role in *Uncle Tom's Cabin* Movie." *Jet* 72 (August 3, 1987): 24-25.

Rashad, Phylicia. Interview Fact Sheet. New York: White Girl Productions, 1992-93.

Regan, Judith. "Bill Cosby's Two Wives." *Ladies Home Journal* 103 (April 1986): 32-36, 162-64.

Rovin, Jeff. "'I'm Not the Perfect Mom.'" *Ladies Home Journal* 109 (May 1992): 80-82.

Who's Who among Black Americans, 1994-95. 8th ed. Detroit: Gale Research, 1994.

Felicia Harris Felder Hoehne

Della Reese

(1932-)

Singer, actress

Della Reese was one of the major black stars leading the breakout of black women musicians into the mainstream of pop music in the late 1950s. Her popularity led to numerous appearances on television, where she was the first black woman to host a variety show. Through her championship of gospel music in clubs, she played a part in bringing about the recognition of gospel by the general public. After her early recording success declined to some degree, she continued to be popular in clubs and on television.

Deloreese Patricia Early was born in Detroit, Michigan, to Richard and Nellie Early on July 6, 1932. She was the youngest of five girls and one boy. Her father was a factory worker and her mother, a domestic. She began to sing in the junior choir of the New Liberty Baptist Church when she was six. Because she could remember the words and carry a tune, she soon became a soloist. According to the account in *Current Biography,* when she was thirteen, Mahalia Jackson chose her to replace a singer who had become ill. This led to a position in Jackson's gospel choir, and Reese spent five summers touring with the group before she graduated from high school. She entered Wayne University in the fall of 1949 with the intention of majoring in psychology.

Due to her mother's death and her father's illness, Reese had to drop out of school after one year. She moved out of the family home and took a succession of jobs, including working as a taxicab driver. Initially she did not consider a career as a singer since gospel groups did not make much money and she felt it was inappropriate for a church member to sing in nightclubs. E. A. Rundless, pastor of New Liberty Baptist Church, helped her overcome this point of view when she was ready to try performing in clubs.

The accounts of her beginnings in show business are somewhat confused, even though all seem derived from interviews with her. The account given in *Current Biography* seems the most direct. It places her first major appearance in a nightclub at the Flame Showbar in Detroit in 1953. In this version, before she got her start as a professional singer, she appears to have remained in Detroit working at various jobs. Shortly after getting a job in a bowling alley-nightclub, she secured her first professional job by winning a contest that gave the winner a week's engagement at the Flame Showbar. By calling on the help of her friends, Reese managed to stay there for eighteen weeks. During her engagement at the Flame Showbar, New York theatrical agent Lee Magid heard her and found her a job in New York with Erskine Hawkins's orchestra in 1953.

Reese set down a somewhat different description of the beginning of her career in a June 1962 article for *Sepia.* There she says that she was singing in Detroit with a gospel group formed by her sister Marie and others called the Meditations

Della Reese

from about 1951 to 1952 while working at conventional jobs. She then decided in about 1953 to move to Chicago, where she joined Mahalia Jackson's gospel group and made her decision to enter the field of pop music. Her initial attempts to get a start in the pop field were rebuffed, and at least one person told her to go home and get married. She then returned to Detroit. Some support for this chronology occurs in a March 1960 article in *Ebony,* where it is stated that in early 1954 Reese was a switchboard operator and in late 1954 she recorded "In the Still of the Night" while she was working for the Erskine Hawkins band.

Regardless of the precise sequence of events, it was in the early 1950s that she adopted the name Reese. However, Pat Ferro was her first professional name. Ferro was a shortening of the name of her first husband, Vermont Adolphus Bon Taliaferro. A factory worker, Taliaferro was nineteen years older than Reese, and the marriage ended in divorce. After the marriage broke up she decided to split her first name and became Della Reese.

A second marriage followed. According to her own account in 1962, Reese believed that she was married to Leroy Basil Gray, an accountant, but then discovered that his divorce was not valid. The same situation appears to have occurred somewhat later. According to *Current Biography,* she told Jack Leahy of the New York *Sunday News* in 1963 that in 1961 she was briefly married to Mercer Ellington, the son of Duke Ellington, and the marriage was annulled when Ellington's previous Mexican divorce was ruled invalid. For many years Reese said that two failed marriages showed (in addition to the invalid Ellington marriage) that marriage was not for her. A late marriage proved more enduring, and she is now the wife of Franklin Thomas Lett, Jr. Reese adopted a daughter, Deloreese (c.1960-) in the summer of 1962. By this daughter she has a grandchild, Sean Ewing-Owens. Reese's marriage to Franklin Lett brought two children into the family, Dominique and Franklin Lett III.

Reese Becomes Singing Sensation

Whether the engagement with the Erskine Hawkins band occurred in 1953 or 1954, Reese is said to have earned sixty-five dollars a week during a nine-month stint but was restricted to singing three songs, which she learned to sing in different styles to overcome boredom. In 1954 Jubilee Records signed Reese, whose first release on the label, "In the Still of the Night," sold half a million records. Her first gold record was "And That Reminds Me" in 1957, which not only sold over a million copies but won her awards as the Most Promising Girl Singer of 1957 from *Billboard, Variety,* and *Cash Box.* Reese was one of the first female black singers to reach the popular charts at this time. Her success led to appearances on television and to a singing role in the film *Let's Rock* (1958). In 1959 Reese switched to the RCA Victor label and won her second gold record for "Don't You Know." This song was based on "Musetta's Waltz" from Puccini's opera *La Bohéme,* with music and lyrics adapted by Bobby Worth. The record reached the number two spot and was a best-seller for eighteen weeks. Reese's popularity and breakthrough status were recognized in 1960 when she was the first black singer to sing "The Star Spangled Banner" at professional baseball's All-Star Game.

In the 1960s Reese was appearing at the top clubs. She paid tribute to her religious roots by singing a spiritual in each set. In January 1962 she brought the Meditation Singers into her act at the Copacabana and began to tour with them the following month. The two-part performance was recorded by RCA Victor, and National Telefilm Associates filmed it for a television special. The first act introduced gospel singing and showed the development of the blues; the second demonstrated the influence of gospel and blues on contemporary popular music.

Current Biography described her singing style in 1971:

> Although her romantic ballads are well received by audiences, it is her exciting delivery of jump tunes, blues, and gospels that always brings down the house. Distinctive to her style is an unusually full-bodied voice of seemingly glass-shattering proportions and an eccentric manner of pronouncing lyrics through clenched teeth so that vowels become distorted and extra syllables are added. "Melancholy Baby" comes out "Melancholy Ba-aye-by" and "Put On a Happy Face" becomes "Put-uh On-uh a Happy-uh Face-uh."

Singer Hosts Variety Show

More than three hundred guest appearances on television both in the United States and abroad had by this time amply demonstrated Reese's appeal in that medium, and she became the first black woman to host a television variety show. The hour-long, syndicated program *Della* aired five days a week during the 1969-70 season in major northern cities and in nine southern cities. On the 250 taped programs, Reese sang and introduced two or three other entertainers. The program was not renewed for a second season, and she returned to the nightclub circuit. She also maintained her popularity as a recording artist.

In 1965 Reese changed to the ABC label, and then in 1969 to Avco Embassy Records. She sold more than a million copies of "It Was a Very Good Year," matching sales of her earlier "Bill Bailey" (1961). Her most popular albums before 1970 include *Amen* and *Story of the Blues* for Jubilee; *Classic Della, Moody,* and *Della by Starlight* for RCA; *I Like It Like Dat* and *Della Reese Live* on ABC; and *Della on Strings of Blue* and *Black Is Beautiful* on Avco Embassy.

By the early 1970s Reese's career was settling down. There were no more big record hits, but she still performed in clubs and continued to appear on television as both singer and actress. In that medium she enjoyed high recognition and acceptance by audiences. Between 1972 and 1986, Edward Mapp in *Directory of Blacks in the Performing Arts* lists nearly fifty shows on which she appeared, sometimes in a continuing or semi-continuing role. Her major work in the theater was on tours of *Ain't Misbehavin'* (1982) and *Blues in the Night* (1983). Her major recent film appearance was in *Harlem Nights* (1989).

This film led to a new television opportunity. While Reese and Redd Foxx were filming *Harlem Nights,* starring Eddie Murphy and Richard Pryor, they began teasing each other. The results were extremely funny to bystanders, and Eddie Murphy, seeing how well they played against each other, decided to become the producer of a situation comedy featuring the talents of the veteran performers. *The Royal Family* went on the air in the fall of 1991. Unfortunately, on October 11 while taping an episode of the series, Foxx had a massive heart attack and died. The attempt to salvage the show by the introduction of Jackee, former star on *Room 227,* was ultimately less successful than hoped.

Reese has had two close brushes with death. Around 1971—sources give different dates—she accidentally walked through a glass door in her California home, losing seven pints of blood and requiring a thousand stitches. As a result she had to turn down engagements for nearly a year and fell into arrears with the Internal Revenue Service. In 1975 she had to declare bankruptcy. She did not escape the debt to the IRS, which grew to $41,360, until after she signed on as a regular for the third season of the television series *Chico and the Man.* Then later while she was taping the *Tonight Show* in 1979, she had an aneurysm and had to have two brain operations in eleven days. Partially as a result of these experiences, she became a minister affiliated with the church alliance headed by Chicagoan Johnnie Colemon.

Della Reese sprang into prominence as a singer. She built on this foundation a long career in television both as a singer and an actress. CBS announced that she would star in a drama *Touched by an Angel* in fall 1994, another milestone for her on television. Her work was also recognized in 1994 by the award of a star on the Hollywood Walk of Fame.

Current Address: c/o William Morris Agency, 151 El Camino, Beverly Hills, CA 90212.

REFERENCES:

Collier, Aldore. "Della and Jackee Become TV Sisters in *Royal Family.*" *Jet* 81 (December 9, 1991): 58-62.
Current Biography. New York: H. W. Wilson, 1971.
"Della Reese." *Ebony* 15 (March 1960): 47-50.
"Della Reese's New Baby." *Sepia* 12 (January 1963): 20-23.
"Foxx Felled by a Heart Attack Taping TV Show; Calls for Wife and Dies." *Jet* 81 (October 28, 1991): 4-8, 57.
Gammond, Peter. *The Oxford Companion to Popular Music.* New York: Oxford University Press, 1991.
"Gospel to Pop to Gospel." *Ebony* 17 (July 1962): 107-12.
Kisner, Ron. "The Money Problems of the Stars." *Ebony* 32 (May 1977): 142-48.
Lewis, Shawn D. "Why I'm Not Married." *Ebony* 32 (September 1977): 124.
Mapp, Edward. *Directory of Blacks in the Performing Arts.* 2d ed. Metuchen, N.J.: Scarecrow Press, 1990.
Murrells, Joseph. *Million Selling Records from the 1900s to the 1980s.* New York: Arco Publishing, 1984.
"My Brush with Death." *Ebony* 44 (May 1989): 96-100.
Patsuris, Penelope. "The Invasion of the Angels." *TV Guide* 42 (August 13, 1994): 28-29.
"Redd Foxx and Della Reese Find Love Life Suffers in TV Series When Their Daughter Moves in with Kids." *Jet* 80 (September 23, 1991): 56-60.
Reese, Della, and Dave Hepburn. "I'll Be Single for a Long Time." *Sepia* 11 (June 1962): 23-26.
Who's Who among Black Americans, 1994-95. 8th ed. Detroit: Gale Research, 1994.

Robert L. Johns

Sylvia Lyons Render
(1913-1986)
Educator, researcher, manuscript curator

Sylvia Lyons Render was best known as a scholar of late nineteenth- and early twentieth-century writer Charles W. Chesnutt, and in her final years she was noted also for her work soliciting donations of manuscripts for preservation and use by researchers at the Library of Congress. She was the first African American to receive a Ph.D. degree from George Peabody College and the first to hold the position of manu-

Sylvia Lyons Render

script curator in Afro-American history at the Library of Congress.

Born June 8, 1913, in Atlanta, Georgia, Sylvia Lyons Render was the only child of Lewis Rudolph Lyons and Mamie Beatrice Foster Lyons. During her early years she lived in Atlanta; Tuscaloosa, Alabama; and Nashville, Tennessee. Although the Lyonses had little money, they were "very education conscious because education was seen as the way out," Render told Sara Williams for the *Alexander Gazette,* March 7, 1983. She graduated with high honors from Pearl High School in Nashville and later was valedictorian of her class when she received her diploma from Tennessee State University, Nashville, in 1934. For two quarters during the academic year 1934-35 she studied at the University of Chicago. She received a master of arts degree from Ohio State University in August 1952 and during the summers of 1954 and 1956 she studied at the University of Wisconsin, Madison. In August 1962 she became the first African American to receive a Ph.D. degree from George Peabody College for Teachers (now part of Vanderbilt University) in Nashville, Tennessee. Sylvia Lyons married Frank Wyatt Render on July 14, 1935, but was later divorced. They had one son, Frank Wyatt Render II, born on the first anniversary of their marriage.

Varied and Distinguished Employment History

From 1939 to 1950 Render held various clerical and professional positions with the state and federal government in Columbus, Ohio. She was cited for "meritorious service in manning essential war activities" while working as a member of the staff of the War Manpower Commission. Her employment experiences also reached into the field of journalism, and from 1948 to 1950 she was society editor and a columnist for the *Ohio State News* in Columbus.

Having grown up in a segregated community, Render admitted that her experiences in society helped her to develop a strong identity. She read widely and recognized her devotion to teaching and research. Pursuing her interest in education, from 1950 to 1951 Render was director of the Out-of-State Aid Program at Florida Agricultural and Mechanical College (now University) in Tallahassee, where she joined her former college dean, George W. Gore, Jr., who was the newly appointed president of the school. From 1952 to 1964 Render moved up in rank from instructor to assistant professor, associate professor, and then professor at the institution. She left Florida in 1964 and became professor of English at North Carolina Central University in Durham, where she remained until 1974. During her years in Durham, she was appointed visiting professor at George Peabody College for Teachers in the summer of 1970. She was also an adjunct faculty member at Duke University and George Washington University and served in the Black Executives Exchange Program of the National Urban League.

For many years the college classroom had been Render's main forum for presenting her ideas on human relations and the policies and practices that foster the survival and development of world civilization. Through the courses she taught in literature and history, particularly about African Americans, she was able to promote her ideas. In 1974 Render became manuscript historian and specialist in Afro-American history and culture in the Manuscript Division of the Library of Congress, Washington, D.C. She was the first African American to hold the newly created research position. She lived first in the District and then in Alexandria, Virginia. In her position she dealt with a wide range of little-known information about achievements of African Americans. She told Sara Williams for the March 7, 1983, *Alexander Gazette,* "Blacks have done so much and it is our responsibility to make these things known." She was one of seven staff members who assisted visiting researchers and correspondents from all over the world in locating information. Here she kept the same vision she had while teaching and, as she stated in a 1977 questionnaire for Fisk University, retained her belief in "the development of healthy self-concepts as well as acceptance of and empathy for others, especially those viewed as markedly different." Render wrote further in the questionnaire for Fisk University, "Now at our national library, I pursue the same goals, though more indirectly, while gathering, dispensing, and interpreting, here and abroad, largely factual information about Afro-American history and culture." She also told the *Alexander Gazette,* "After years of teaching, I thought working at the Library of Congress was the proper culmination for my career."

Render's primary responsibility was to solicit donations of manuscripts from private donors. She helped to acquire the records of the NAACP and the National Urban League. Her last successful solicitation was the papers of Samuel Lee Gravely Jr., the first black admiral in the Navy.

Render was best known as the primary authority on Charles W. Chesnutt, an African American essayist, short story writer, and novelist who published in the nineteenth and twentieth centuries, and she avidly pursued information about him in her research and wrote about him extensively. Among her publications reflecting her interest in Chesnutt are "Tarheelia in Chesnutt" in *CLA Journal* 9, September 1965; "North Carolina Dialect: Chesnutt Style" in *North Carolina Folklore Journal* 15, November 1967; and "Charles W. Chesnutt" in *Encyclopedia Britannica,* 1969, and later editions. In 1974 she edited and added an extensive introduction to *The Short Fiction of Charles W. Chesnutt.* She also wrote "The Black Presence in the Library of Congress" in *Library Lectures,* edited by Caroline Wire, 1975, and "Afro-American Women: The Outstanding and the Obscure" in *Quarterly Journal of the Library of Congress,* October 1975.

Devotion to Professional and Community Organizations

Although active as a teacher, researcher, and writer, Render was committed to professional and community service. She was a member of the National Council of Teachers of English, the Modern Language Association (also a member of the Delegate Assembly), the College Language Association, the South Atlantic Modern Language Association, the Association for the Study of Afro-American Life and History, the National Council of Teachers of English, the North Carolina Folklore Society, Phi Delta Kappa, Alpha Kappa Mu, and the Library of Congress Professional Association. Her devotion to scholarly research and discussions on African American themes led her to found and become first president of the Daniel A. P. Murray Afro-American Culture Association at the Library of Congress.

In the community she was active with the YMCA and YWCA both as a member and trustee. She was a life member of the NAACP. Render also served on the Urban League, was a volunteer with Boy Scouts of America, and participated in Gray Ladies, the American Red Cross, and the Human Relations Council. A member and "Golden Girl" of the Alpha Kappa Alpha Sorority, she served on the Panhellenic Council and was undergraduate chapter adviser to the sorority. A religious person, she was a charter and founding member of two church groups, serving at various times with one or the other group as trustee, historian, and secretary.

Honors and awards came early in Render's life and continued throughout her career. While in college she received the Anderson-Hilly Hale medal; she was also the ranking freshman and, later, valedictorian of her class. She was elected to Alpha Kappa Mu and Kappa Delta Pi honor societies. Render was the recipient of scholarships and fellowships from Alpha Kappa Alpha Sorority, the Peabody Fund, and the Southern Education Foundation. She received postdoctoral grants and awards from North Carolina Central University's Faculty Research Committee, the Ford Foundation, the American Philosophical Society, and the National Endowment for the Humanities. She was also a fellow in the Cooperative Program in Humanities at Duke University.

In 1981 the NAACP named Render Outstanding Woman of the Year and the next year Tennessee State University named her Outstanding Alumnae. Florida governor Bob Graham honored her in 1986 as one of Florida's outstanding black citizens. The recognition came during the state's official Martin Luther King Day commemoration in St. Augustine.

Soon after retiring, Render moved to St. Petersburg, Florida, where she died on Monday, February 3, 1986, at Tampa General Hospital. A memorial service and celebration of her life were held on Saturday, February 8, at First Baptist Institutional Church in the city. She was survived by her son, Frank W. Render II, three grandsons, one great-grandson, a daughter-in-law, and her stepmother.

Her statement on the questionnaire for Fisk University summarizes her devotion to the lives of those she touched in her work:

> I have observed adoption of the principles I have sought to inculcate by some of the individuals whose lives I have touched. A few have acknowledged my influence. That I have been able to contribute to the intellectual, aesthetic, and/or ethical growth of one or more human beings has been my most significant and satisfying accomplishment.

Sylvia M. Rhone

REFERENCES:

Render, Sylvia Lyons. Questionnaire. Fisk University Library, November 7, 1977.

"Researcher of Black History Retires after Fruitful Career." *Alexander Gazette,* March 7, 1983.

Shockley, Ann Allen, and Sue P. Chandler. *Living Black American Authors.* New York: Bowker, 1973.

Sylvia Lyons Render. Funeral Program. First Baptist Institutional Church, St. Petersburg, Florida, February 8, 1986.

Who's Who of American Women 1983-84. 13th ed. Chicago: Marquis Who's Who, 1983.

Jessie Carney Smith

Sylvia M. Rhone

(1952-)

Record company executive

The rigid dress code of Bankers Trust of New York prevented Sylvia Rhone from fulfilling her dream of becoming a financial high roller. Armed with a degree in economics from Wharton School of Finance and Commerce at the University of Pennsylvania, Rhone had no trouble securing a marketing specialist position at the firm but lasted only nine months because her preference for casual dress caused a problem. She told an interviewer for *Ebony,* November 1988, "I wore pants to work and all eyebrows turned up. No one actually said anything but they made it clear that what I'd done was unacceptable."

The trust company's position hastened Rhone's departure from the world of high finance and her entry into the field of commercial music, a move that seemed a reckless venture to many who knew Rhone. Taking a drastic pay cut, Rhone secured an entry-level position at a well-known record company. The position enabled her to get hands-on experience in the promotional end of the music business. From this lowly start, Rhone rapidly moved up the ladder, becoming a top administrator at three leading record companies.

The August 15, 1994, issue of *Jet* magazine featured a short article packed with headline news. Rhone, former chairperson and chief executive officer of EastWest Records America, had just been promoted to the position of chairperson of the new Elektra/EastWest Company. She now holds the distinction of being the first black woman to be appointed head of a major record label. The cover story of the August 1991 issue of *Black Enterprise* focused on twenty-one African American women corporate executives. At the time, only 3 percent of corporate management positions in the United States were held by black women, who comprised less than 1 percent of all women corporate officers in the country.

A native of Philadelphia, Sylvia M. Rhone was born on March 11, 1952, to James and Marie Christmas Rhone. While growing up in Harlem, she was an avid music fan who, as reported in *Ebony,* November 1988, "used to stand in the mirror and sing Aretha songs into [her] hairbrush." She graduated from college in 1974. After discovering that she did not want banking to be her life's work, Rhone made a career decision that seemed at the time to be taking her backward instead of forward. Realizing that she passionately loved music, she took a fifteen-thousand-dollar pay cut to start at the bottom of the record industry. Rhone accepted a secretarial position at Buddah Records, an independent company that once had distribution arrangements with such companies as Arista and Curtom. Buddah also once had recording contracts with a diverse group of artists, including the Edwin Hawkins Singers, Phyllis Hyman, Melba Moore, Gladys Knight and the Pips, the Isley Brothers, and, after the Motown shake-up, the gifted writer and musician team of Holland-Dozier-Holland. As a marketing specialist, Rhone could have secured a much higher-level job, but she decided that the experience would be worth it in the long run.

In an August 1991 *Black Enterprise* interview, Rhone said, "From the moment I sat in my new chair, I knew I was cut out for this business." Because she was attentive to the inner workings of the record company, Rhone was soon able to utilize her education in ways beneficial to Buddah and, within a year, she was elevated to the position of promotions coordinator, which led to a more prestigious job. She became the national promotions director for a small, independent label. Although the label soon folded, Rhone had gained valuable experience that enabled her to become a regional promoter for other independent labels. Her uncanny ability to discover and mold new black talent came to the notice of Atlantic Records. This company had once been a giant in the record industry with such stars as Aretha Franklin and Otis Redding under contract.

By the time Rhone's star was ascending, Atlantic's was on the wane, especially its Black Music division, which had been losing money for several years in a row. Furthermore, its once stellar roster of black stars was now just a sketchy reminder of better times. Despite many warnings from her industry peers, Rhone accepted the offer to become director of Atlantic's Black Music in 1985. The impetus for her decision was her memory of the company's heyday when, as a Harlem teenager, she was an Aretha "wannabe." Rhone told *Ebony,* November 1988, "I wanted to make us a star in Black music again." Those who doubted Rhone's ability to meet such a challenge were soon silenced when she succeeded in her quest to make Atlantic and black music once again synonymous. She began by changing the way the company marketed its acts and by developing new acts, among them LeVert, whose lead singer is the son of the legendary O'Jay's lead singer, Eddie Levert, and whose top-ten single went gold. In addition, other new acts she developed had top singles.

Within the year, Rhone became vice-president and general manager of Atlantic's black music operations and, shortly thereafter, senior vice-president of the company. Atlantic's chairman, Ahmet Ertegun, explained her rapid rise in the November 1988 *Ebony:* "Under her expert guidance,

our commitment to Black music has seen a revitalization marked by innovation, imagination and freshness. This is a well-deserved promotion for a most gifted woman."

Rhone became senior vice-president in 1986, and in 1987, Atlantic's Black Music division showed a profit. In 1988 the records of two of Rhone's protégés were number one: Gerald Albright saw his first LP, *So Amazing,* go to number one on the jazz charts and a new group called Troop saw its first single go to number one.

Rhone Heads Her Own Record Label

In 1991 Rhone's trailblazing achievements were rewarded when she was named co-president and chief executive officer of her own label under the auspices of Atlantic. At EastWest Records America she oversaw her label's recruitment, marketing, and promotion of recording artists with the assistance of a forty-seven-person staff. In *Black Enterprise,* August 1991, she described the new label as being "very similar to a boutique label . . . [where] we want to keep the register down to a manageable size of 25 to 30 releases per year." That same year Rhone became chairperson and chief executive officer of the newly formed Atco-EastWest label, which encompassed rock, pop, R&B, jazz, and rap, and also added forty acts, black and white, to her artist roster.

At the "Jack the Ripper" fifteenth annual convention and reunion, an August 1991 Atlanta event, Rhone was honored as one of four black heads of major record labels owned by America's leading record companies. The other award winners were men: Jheryl Busby (Motown), Ed Eckstine (Mercury), and Ernie Singleton (MCA). During her acceptance speech, quoted in the December 1991 *Black Enterprise,* she said: "It shows that African-Americans can not only create music, but control it as well. The world is watching us."

Rhone not only oversaw the development of artists who recorded for her label, she participated as well in corporate ventures designed to showcase the contributions of black musicians in new and innovative ways. Atlantic Records, EastWest Records, and the Warner Music Group initiated a lecture series entitled "Our Roots Run Deep" in honor of Black History Month. In the August 1994 premiere issue of *Tafrija,* a new entertainment magazine, Rhone and her cohorts Ed Eckstine (national president of Mercury Records) and Richard Nash (senior vice-president of Atlantic Records) are shown at the IMPACT convention in Atlantic City, New Jersey. There the lecture series sponsored Cornel West, director of the Afro-American Studies Program at Princeton University, who was a keynote convention speaker.

This innovative marketing scheme designed to highlight and publicize black music shows another facet of the genius of the forty-two-year-old Rhone, who was promoted again—to chairperson of Elektra/EastWest—during the summer of 1994. As the head of the new Elektra/EastWest Company, Rhone assumes sole responsibility for the recording businesses of Elektra, Asylum, EastWest, and their associated labels.

She has definitely lived up to a statement made in the December 1991 issue of *Black Enterprise* by Sharon Heyward, another black woman who has made great strides in upper-level management positions in the recording industry. Heyward explained that, although the recording industry is tough to break into, a person's potential is the key to a rapid rise. Speaking to the problem of blacks still having to be superior to their white counterparts, Heyward said, "Busby, Singleton, Eckstine, and Rhone are proving that we are as capable of running the entire entity as anyone else."

Rhone now heads a major corporation that has contracts with nearly two hundred acts and annual revenues reported to be in the hundreds of millions. In twenty years, she has made the astonishing transition from secretary to corporate executive officer. But, as Rhone recalled in *Rolling Stone,* October 6, 1994, it was not all champagne and roses:

> A glass ceiling definitely still exists, but I think it's being shattered everyday.... Those of us as minorities who break through the glass ceiling do get some scratches along the way . . . but I think there is definitely social change and headway being made. Some companies may hold out for a time, maintaining that archaic view of women as unsuitable executive material, but those old philosophies are changing drastically.

Current Address: Atco-EastWest, 75 Rockefeller Plaza, New York, NY 10019.

REFERENCES:

Ali, Lorraine. "Exiled in Guyville: A Report on How Women Are Faring in the Music Industry." *Rolling Stone* (October 6, 1994): 57-58.

Baskerville, Dawn, Sheryl Hilliard Tucker, and Donna Whittingham-Barnes. "21 Women of Power and Influence in Corporate America." *Black Enterprise* 22 (August 1991): 76.

Black Book: International Business and Entertainment Reference Guide. Chicago: National Publications Sales Agency, 1994.

Contemporary Black Biography. Vol. 2. Detroit: Gale Research, 1992.

Futrell, Jon, Chris Gill, Roger St. Pierre, and Clive Richardson. *The Illustrated Encyclopedia of Black Music.* New York: Harmony Books, 1982.

Norment, Lynn. "Women at the Top in the Entertainment Industry." *Ebony* 48 (March 1993): 106-14.

Randolph, Laura B. "Women in Dream Jobs." *Ebony* 44 (November 1988): 74-76.

"Shop Talk." *Tafrija—The Entertainment Magazine* 5 (August 1994): 73.

"Sylvia Rhone Named New Head of Elektra/EastWest." *Jet* 86 (August 15, 1994): 55.

Vaughn, Christopher. "Pumping Up the Jam for Profits." *Black Enterprise* 22 (December 1991): 51-56.

Who's Who among Black Americans, 1994-95. 8th ed. Detroit: Gale Research, 1994.

Dolores Nicholson

Condoleezza Rice
(1954-)
Educator, university administrator, Sovietologist

The childhood of Condoleezza Rice in segregation-era Birmingham, Alabama, has not prevented her from mastering the field of international relations to become a government official and a noted academician. She is the youngest person and the first black to serve as chief academic and budget officer at Stanford University. Highly respected in the predominantly male world of politics, nuclear weapons, and the arms race, she rose to international prominence as Sovietologist during the administration of President George Bush.

Condoleezza Rice was born November 14, 1954, the daughter of Angelena Ray and John Wesley Rice. Her father, who worked as a university administrator, often took the family on automobile expeditions. She remembers the family once driving north from Birmingham to Washington and not one hotel accepting them. On the same trip, her father took a picture of his nine-year-old Condoleezza in front of the White House, and, according to the *Washington Post,* she told him, "I'm standing in front of the White House now, but one day I'm going to be in it."

She described herself to the *Washington Post* as:

> A nice Southern girl who has . . . come a long way from Birmingham, from parents who cherished her dreams, the segregated school where her teachers chipped in to buy textbooks, and the restaurant that fell silent when her family entered one night to test the 1964 Civil Rights Act.

Rice's original interest was music. She also studied figure skating at one point. Until her junior year at the University of Denver, she was a music major intent on becoming a concert pianist. When her advisor told her that she would become a great musician some day, she suddenly realized that music was not her primary interest. She told the *Washington Post,* March 17, 1989, "I started looking around for a major and I needed one that I could finish quick. I like politics, I wasn't quite clear on what political science was, but it sounded interesting."

She received her B.A. degree from the University of Denver in 1974 at the age of nineteen. She graduated cum

Condoleezza Rice

laude and was a member of Phi Beta Kappa. She received her M.A. degree from the University of Notre Dame in 1975 and her Ph.D. in 1981 from the University of Denver's Graduate School of International Studies.

Rice was an intern with the U.S. Department of State in Washington, D.C., in 1977 and with the Rand Corporation in 1980. Her expertise and intellectual knowledge about the problems and realities of the Soviet Union and Eastern Europe were important elements for her immediate success. From 1981 to 1989, she taught political science at Stanford University, becoming an associate professor and serving as a member of the Center for International Security and Arms Control. Her performance earned her a teaching award in 1984. From 1985 to 1986, she was a fellow at the Hoover Institute, an internationally known think tank at Stanford. A one-year fellowship in 1987 gave her the opportunity to serve as special assistant to the director of the Joint Chiefs of Staff assigned to Strategic Nuclear Policy. In 1988, the U.S. ambassador to the Soviet Union invited her to speak on the arms control policy before Soviet officials and diplomats in Bulgaria.

Presidential Advisor

President George Bush selected Rice in 1989 to be his advisor on Soviet affairs. In that year, she also joined the National Security Council at the personal request of Brent Scowcroft, assistant to the president for National Security Affairs at that time. During this tenure, she was the highest ranking black woman on the council, advancing from her position of director to senior director of Soviet and Eastern European Affairs. She was President Bush's chief advisor during the summit meeting with Mikhail Gorbachev in Washington, D.C., and helped Bush prepare for the U.S.-Soviet superpower summit meetings on global peace.

Rice is a significant player in a predominantly male world of military strategy and international relations. Of her status, she told the *Washington Post:*

> This is still a very macho game. It's the last bastion—right?—military power. I don't mind the shock value at all. You walk into a room—you get it either here or in the Soviet Union—and people just don't understand, it doesn't compute somehow. But in the United States, people are getting more accustomed to it. There are more and more women out there on strategic policy issues today.

Rice was faced with gender and racial bias. An embarrassing public incident in 1990 brought Rice more attention than her prestigious and important position as a director of the National Security Council. While she accompanied a party of Soviet officials at the San Francisco airport, a secret service agent disregarded the White House identification that she wore and ordered her behind the security lines. Further ignoring her protest that she was a member of the group, he shoved her. The news media gave full coverage of the incident.

Rice returned to teaching at Stanford in 1991. On September 1, 1993, Rice became the youngest and first black chief academic and budget officer at Stanford University, making her second in command at the institution.

Rice, who is fluent in Russian, keeps herself current on issues in her field by reading *Pravda* and studying the Moscow press, including military journals. She has written *The Soviet Union and the Czechoslovak Army, 1948-1983* (1984) and *The Intermediate Nuclear Force Agreement: Implications for NATO Security: Proceedings of a Seminar for Members of Congress and Congressional Staff, December 10, 1987* (1988). With Alexander Dallin she also wrote *The Gorbachev Era* (1986). In addition, Rice has written numerous articles on Soviet and East European military policy in scholarly journals such as *Journal of International Affairs, Studies in Comparative Communism,* and *Current History.* She has also contributed articles to *Time,* the *Los Angeles Times,* and the *New York Times.*

Rice's expertise has been widely sought. In 1991, California Governor Pete Wilson selected her to serve on the bipartisan committee to draw new legislative and congressional districts in California. Also in that year she was elected to the twelve-member board of directors of Chevron and to the board of Transamerica Corporation.

Although Rice is an extraordinarily accomplished young woman, she does not seek the limelight. She avoids making headlines in the press and monitors the usage of the few photographs that she maintains in the news media. According to *Jet,* June 7, 1990, "A friend reported that she [Rice] is not in the business of compiling the most clippings. She takes more pride in a perfect record." Rice, a political expert who served in the Republican administration of President George Bush, represents what *Jet* magazine calls "the new breed of young Black conservatives."

Current Address: Office of the Provost, Stanford University, Palo Alto, CA 94305-2044.

REFERENCES:

"The Black Woman Russian Expert Who Advised President Bush at Washington Summit." *Jet* 78 (June 18, 1990): 4-7.
Contemporary Black Biography. Vol. 3. Detroit: Gale Research, 1993.
Randolph, Laura B. "Black Women in the White House." *Ebony* 45 (October 1990): 76-78, 90.
"Secret Weapon at the NSC." *Washington Post,* March 17, 1989.
Who's Who among Black Americans. 8th ed. Detroit: Gale Research, 1994.

Simmona E. Simmons-Hodo

Linda Johnson Rice

Linda Johnson Rice
(1958-)
Publishing company executive

L inda Johnson Rice is president and chief operating officer of Johnson Publishing Company in Chicago and one of the few black women publishing company executives in America. She has over twenty-five years experience with her father's thriving $294 million company, which is the parent corporation for such popular publications as *Ebony* and *Jet* magazines. She has expectations of adding new life to the company's magazines and of expanding the corporation's business in cosmetics and broadcasting. She wants to show America the first-rate character of the Chicago-based, family-owned Johnson Publishing Company. She has pursued that goal since age twenty-nine, when she was promoted to her present position. Today, at age thirty-six, she is preparing to take the fifty-three-old business well into the twenty-first century as its future chief executive officer.

Rice joined the Johnson family on March 22, 1958. Her father, John H. Johnson, started his company with an investment of $500 from mortgaging his mother's furniture in 1942 and published *Negro Digest.* According to Lois Therrien in "A Nice Graduation Present," he continued to thrive, building "an empire in publishing, broadcasting, cosmetics, hair care, and, in a separate company, life insurance." Her mother, Eunice W. Johnson, is *Ebony*'s fashion editor as well as director of their traveling fashion show, Ebony Fashion Fair.

Rice's older brother, John, died of sickle-cell anemia at age twenty-five, leaving his sister as sole heir to the Johnson empire. *Working Woman*'s Renee Edelman says that he was "never a rival for a role in the company" and preferred photography and sports to publishing. Linda Johnson Rice is married to André Rice, and they have one daughter, six-year-old Alexa Christina.

Rice entered the family business with enthusiasm instead of bowing to parental pressure. Her apprenticeship with the company began with frequent visits to the office from the time she was six years old. It was Eunice W. Johnson who took her daughter to fashion shows in Paris and continued to do so throughout Rice's teenage and college days. Rice worked as a summer intern during her undergraduate years and completed a bachelor's degree in journalism from the University of Southern California. At age twenty-three she went overseas to choose clothes for Ebony Fashion Fair, this time alone. She told Edelman in *Working Woman,* "That was a turning point. . . . I saw I could do it."

Becomes Publishing Company Executive

Rice's first full-time position with Johnson Publishing Company was vice-president and fashion coordinator. Later, as her title was changed to vice-president and assistant to the publisher, Rice was able to use and enhance skills that she had acquired as an intern. She learned directly from her CEO father and mentor and was involved in other aspects of his empire besides publishing, including Fashion Fair Cosmetics, advertising, and media. To enhance her hands-on experience in the office, she enrolled at Northwestern University's J. L. Kellogg Graduate School of Management. The MBA program taught her how to tackle business problems from an analytical point of view and to create innovative solutions for them. She graduated in 1987 and was promoted to president and chief operating officer of Johnson Publishing Company on June 20 of that year.

As president, one of Rice's favorite duties is attending editorial meetings. In an interview with Lynn Norment, she stated, "It is the creative process that I find stimulating, sitting down and letting the ideas flow among the different groups. I love the interaction with people. To me that's the best part. I'm a people-oriented person." She stresses the importance of bringing fresh young talent to the company and seeking new ideas for the business world, particularly for black-owned companies. She told Norment, "In regards to Black people, we have a treasure trove of information that nobody else really has. And we haven't really capitalized on that enough."

Rice has several good ideas of her own to modernize and expand the Johnson empire and to better serve the black community. The Fashion Fair Cosmetics line, for example, with its overseas offices in London and Paris, is a means to tap the international market of black women. Rice thinks the line will be "a major global player in the cosmetics field." Her frequent business trips to Europe with her mother gave Rice the ability to see such new horizons of untapped opportunity. Rice has also been instrumental in the development of Eboné Cosmetics for the mass market and "E-Style" Catalog, a joint venture with the Spiegel company.

Her work has attracted notice from the corporate boards of Bausch and Lomb, the Dial Corporation, and the Continental Bank of Illinois. Her interaction with other corporate leaders has helped her to see her own work in "a broader perspective." Her mother's advice, to have a sense of humor, has also helped Rice's work and image. She does not merely limit her work to the boardroom and executive offices of *Ebony* and *Jet,* two subsidiaries of the Johnson Publishing Company; she once worked behind the counter to promote Fashion Fair products. She told Lois Therrien that "sales skyrocketed during her one-hour stint at a Chicago store."

Rice's best friend and colleague is her husband André. They are mutually supportive, and each is extremely successful in the business world. She told Lynn Norment in an interview about her husband's influence on her work. "We have a great deal of respect for one another. . . . We agree to disagree." Rice's sense of humor, image, and positive relations with her husband and her father have helped her to develop into an even more effective executive leader.

Rice told Lynn Norment about her image-building activities:

> Every time I make an appearance somewhere, every time I make a speech, I'm selling the image of Johnson Publishing Co. I'm selling the image of Fashion Fair cosmetics, I'm selling the image of the Ebony Fashion Fair. I am constantly selling.

The "constant selling" has not been in vain. Lois Therrien called Rice a vibrant, energetic worker, who, influenced by European fashion, "eschews gray pinstripes for bright colors, polka dots, and slacks." She admits to being a "clothes horse," and her fashion sense reflects her management style: individual, creative and eye-catching. The future of Johnson Publishing Company is in more than capable hands.

Current Address: Johnson Publishing Company, 820 South Michigan Avenue, Chicago, IL 60605.

REFERENCES:

"Backstage." *Ebony* 42 (September 1987): 26.

Edelman, Renee. "When Little Sister Means Big Business." *Working Woman* 15 (February 1990): 82-86.

"Linda Johnson Rice." *Black Enterprise* 22 (June 1992): 318.

Norment, Lynn. "Ebony Interview with Linda Johnson Rice." *Ebony* 48 (November 1992): 208-15.

Therrien, Lois. "A Nice Graduation Present: Johnson Publishing." *Business Week* No. 3007 (July 1987): 40.

Erica L. Griffin

Helen Caldwell Day Riley
(1926-)
Religious worker, hospitality house founder, nurse, writer

Helen Caldwell Day Riley made her mark in the early 1950s at a young age with her social and religious work in the tradition of the Dorothy Day Catholic Worker movement and with her two autobiographical books, *Color Ebony* (1951) and *Not without Tears* (1954). She was the primary face behind the establishment of Blessed Martin House in Memphis, Tennessee, a house of hospitality intended to provide care and shelter for the poor, particularly women and their children. At the time, she could hardly have chosen a more difficult city than Memphis in which to try to build a religious organization that would transcend racial bounds, and in so doing, to attempt to live in accordance with the teachings of her church. Her life as she grew up in the South was marked not only by the omnipresent racism that oppressed all blacks, but also by her religious quest, which eventually led to her conversion to Roman Catholicism, a spiritual journey recounted in *Color Ebony*. About the time she married Jesse Riley in 1955, Blessed Martin House closed, and her life fell into a more outwardly conventional

Helen Caldwell Day Riley

pattern, but her religious beliefs and her service to others remained constant.

Riley was born in Marshall, Texas, to George and Velma Caldwell on December 31, 1926. Her father was then teaching music at Bishop College, one of a series of short-term positions he held at various black colleges and universities until he finally secured a stable post at Rust College in Holly Springs, Mississippi. Her mother was a kindergarten teacher at the time. When she was a child, Riley's family included an aunt, Big Helen, an older half-sister from her father's first marriage, Clara, an older brother, George, Jr., and a younger brother, William. Velma Caldwell possessed a genuine faith, which in time led her to became a Catholic, but George Caldwell was only marginally interested in religion. His real interests were music, psychology, and the natural sciences. The family's church affiliation depended upon the denominational affiliation of the particular college where he was teaching.

In addition to the various temporary appointments at black colleges George Caldwell held during his daughter's childhood, he also went to school for more training and occasionally worked as a pharmacist while she was growing up. The family was poor but never destitute. The Caldwells were living in Iowa City, Iowa, when Riley began school. She recalls experiencing little racial prejudice there, and so when the family first moved to Mississippi, the full southern system of segregation came as a traumatic shock. In spite of the family's efforts, they lived in poverty, even after George Caldwell obtained a continuing post at Rust College in about 1938. One low point occurred about 1935 when Riley was

nine. The family was living in Memphis and trying to make a go of running a restaurant. Velma Caldwell managed the restaurant while George Caldwell crossed the river to Arkansas to work on a farm. Money was short, and the middle-class values and religious beliefs of the family were difficult to maintain in a poverty-stricken slum. The children attended both public and private schools. They experienced being the poorest children in a school attended by the children of a black elite that may not have been much better off but that was able to maintain appearances. There were many other difficult moments. At one school where her father was teaching, her mother had to borrow butter, milk, sugar, and eggs to make Riley's birthday cake.

Another problem was apparently adding to Riley's unhappiness: her parents' marriage was under increasing strain. When George Caldwell went to Rust College with his children to take up a continuing appointment, Velma Caldwell remained in Memphis. The children spent the winter months with their father and the summer months with their mother; holidays were particularly difficult. After nearly a year, when Riley was eleven years old, she ran away from home. She went to Jonesboro, Arkansas, which was as far as her money would take her. There she was cared for by a family that found her. She stayed there two months, ran away again, and returned home. Back in Holly Springs, she felt the strain of being the subject of small-town gossip. Not only did the townspeople broadcast the story of her running away, but they also speculated on the oddity of a household without a wife. Her father further weakened the family's reputation in the town by not usually choosing his intimate friends from among the black elite and by not seeming to be interested in remarrying. Riley lived with her family in Holly Springs for seven years. It was not until she left home to go to nursing school that she was finally able to escape from the gossip. To compensate, there was a decided advantage to being the only woman in a male household: she participated almost as an equal in the conversations of her brothers and their friends, and her father encouraged intellectual discussion. He instilled in her a love of knowledge and a sense of racial pride, in part by elaborating upon the African American history she studied in school. Among the writers she studied at home, her favorite was Countee Cullen.

Riley's intellectual independence and her ability to question were being fostered; her religious thirst, however, was not being satisfied. As an adolescent she felt caught between a half-believing father and an unbelieving stepfather. Her mother had remarried, and her new husband was an embittered man who reviled Christianity as a hoax. Her mother retained her faith and stood up to the arguments of her new husband, whom Riley believed was caught in a self-defeating trap. In *Color Ebony* she wrote: "He really believes that, generally speaking, the Negro is inferior, and he hates himself for believing it and being one himself." He urged the children to succeed and make something of themselves yet discouraged them whenever they spoke of their dreams.

In 1943, at the age of sixteen, Riley entered Rust College. Her older brother, George, had been drafted, and she was attracted by the idea of becoming a nurse through the Cadet

Nurses program. Her decision to leave home to study nursing was reinforced by her father's sudden remarriage. In February 1945, just after her eighteenth birthday, she entered the Harlem Hospital nurse training program. She endured loneliness and had to learn to obey authority. She stated in *Color Ebony:* "I have never found it easy to give up my will." Nonetheless, she discovered a vocation in nursing, with its concern for birth, life, and death, and she and her schoolmates often discussed religion. After nine months she had to have her tonsils removed and spent three or four days mostly alone in a hospital room. This time gave her an opportunity to think through her religious convictions, and a chance encounter in her sickroom with a Catholic priest led her to begin instruction in the faith. She was capped as a nurse at the end of the first year, but continued her nursing education at various hospitals. Her religious instruction continued along with her nursing training, and after six months' study of the Catholic faith, Riley was baptized and entered the Catholic Church.

In the meantime she had met a young man named George Day, who was serving in the navy. Near the end of her second year in nursing school, Riley became pregnant. She took a job as a baby nurse in a small Catholic hospital, Misercordia, and awaited the birth of her son, MacDonald Francis (Butch). Contact with the nuns at the hospital deepened her faith, and conversations with both the nuns and the student nurses gave her a chance to interact with whites for the first time since her childhood. After a visit to Memphis, she left her son with her mother and returned to Misercordia while waiting to reenter nursing school. During her pregnancy she had become familiar with the Catholic Worker movement led by Dorothy Day and Peter Maurin. She now became a volunteer at the Mott Street house of hospitality, which was sponsored by the movement. It took some time before she could understand and share the religious and social ideas of the workers there. She had to learn to forgive again and again the alcoholics who sold the clothing given them to buy liquor instead. She wrote in *Color Ebony:*

> Very impractical, you think? People ought to be allowed to profit from their mistakes, not be encouraged in them. But bad people, careless, thoughtless, uncaring people also get hungry and cold. They also starve and freeze. They also belong to God. It takes great faith and charity to see that, and to go on forgiving and helping, to go on offering other chances even in the face of continued failure.

Other beliefs of the Catholic Worker movement, such as pacifism and nonviolent resistance, were particularly difficult for her, but her commitment grew. In *Color Ebony,* she quoted an essay by Peter Maurin: "People say I am crazy. They say I am crazy because I refuse to be crazy the way everybody else is crazy." She then added:

> All at once I knew I wanted to make people crazy his way too. When I made this decision, I think I began to clutch at the truth which will enable me to stand, that I might walk; the truth that admits God is not only our peace and salvation, but even our sanity. I was not crazy, nor were those others who

spent their lives in praising God or in trying to make the world a Christian world for His glory.

When she was a senior finishing her nursing program at Cumberland Hospital in Brooklyn, Riley received two pieces of shattering information. First, she was diagnosed with tuberculosis and placed in a sanitarium. The diagnosis was especially hard to accept at first because of events that had occurred earlier. It had been thought that she was tubercular at the beginning of her new training, but she was then cleared, with a period of rest suggested, and finally readmitted to the nursing program. It would be nineteen months after she entered the sanitarium before she was released. During this time she got the second piece of bad news: Butch was diagnosed with polio.

The last fifteen months of her hospitalization were spent at Stony Wold, where her ward of black and white women openly and candidly discussed race, religion, and politics. Riley wrote most of her autobiography, *Color Ebony,* at Stony Wold, a village in New York State, and also edited the hospital newsletter, *Sez,* in which she implicitly criticized the apparent reintroduction of a policy of segregated rooms and wards. She attributes the hospital administration's unease with her editorial stance for her transfer to another institution, from which she was discharged as an arrested case in a week. She was ordered to rest and to continue pneumothorax treatments, a procedure to collapse the lung. It would be a year before her doctors allowed her to work again.

Blessed Martin House Established

Riley returned south to a son who had almost completely recovered from his paralysis. In Memphis she continued to write, producing a column called "Looking Things Over" for the *Memphis World.* She wrote a letter to friends in New York about the time she was turned away from mass in Holly Springs at the now all-white church. She gave permission for the letter to be published in the *Catholic Worker,* and, as a result, she came into contact with other Catholics, both black and white, who were interested in establishing an interracial study group in Memphis. This group grew to a core membership of fifteen and eventually accepted the idea of opening a house of hospitality, which was Riley's mission from the beginning. After a year she also was able to begin work as a nurse at the city hospital—all the doctors were white, as was the administrative nursing staff, but the rest of the nursing staff was integrated. Riley who had come so close to completing her training to become a registered nurse, keenly felt her lower status as a registered practical nurse.

Establishing the house of hospitality meant that Riley would have to give up the security of a job. As she pressed for her own vision of the establishment, she met considerable opposition from both her own family and certain members of the study group. As Riley reported in *Not without Tears,* after the group had decided to set up the house, she was shaken by a series of anonymous letters from someone previously associated with the group accusing her of acting in "a selfish, individualist, arrogant, dishonorable and impetuous manner." The person added, "Do not pose yourself as a member of a community when you place yourself above community." The letters caused her great pain and despair, which was alleviated when she consulted the group's advisor, Father Coyne, a Josephite priest. He became angry and decisively rallied the group behind the project. Riley also followed his advice in asking for approval for the house from the bishop.

Bishop William Adrian gave his approval in 1950; he even made contributions from time to time. Blessed Martin House was opened on January 6, 1952, in an extremely dilapidated store in a slum area near Beale Street. In terms of volunteer workers it was an interracial venture. Riley and her son moved into a small back room. Care for children became Riley's first and major emphasis, and by spring Blessed Martin House was caring for fifteen to sixteen children on a regular basis and older children were also dropping in after school. Riley insisted that working mothers should volunteer to help out in return. This caused some problems—mothers were tired after a long day's work and some were very adept at making excuses. The house also became a shelter for women and children who were experiencing great difficulty. At times there was considerable strain on emotions, as well as on finances. In *Not without Tears* Riley told of one period when a woman and her children were occupying the one room normally used as a bedroom, Riley and her son were sharing a youth bed in the main room, and another woman and child also shared a small bed in the main room, along with another child in a crib. There was a nine-by-twelve-foot storeroom where the women kept their clothes, along with all the bedding for the house, leaving just enough room to reach the telephone, which was also in the storeroom. During the day there would be twenty-five or so day-care children in the main room.

Around 1954 the group decided to purchase a house because the original store building was becoming increasingly dilapidated. They found a duplex located on an alley. The building was sound, if in need of repair, and situated in the midst of the people they were trying to reach. With the help of volunteers, they repaired one side of the house when the tenant moved out and established themselves there.

The purchase of the house was made possible in part by Dorothy Day, who spoke in Memphis on behalf of the members of the group, raising their spirits immensely. The leader of the Catholic Worker movement saw that a check for four hundred dollars for a down payment arrived a few days later and printed an appeal in the *Catholic Worker* paper. Local volunteers and contributors also did their part.

Riley was in contact with other persons who worked at similar establishments. She communicated with staff at the twenty-five-year-old white Mary St. Onge of Nashville and the white organizers of the Caritas movement in New Orleans. Both St. Onge and Caritas, which recognized that their work would be more effective with an interracial staff, would have liked Riley to join them. Riley's name was starting to become known and she was invited to speak and participate in panels at places as far away as Bay Saint Louis, Mississippi, and Burnley, Virginia. In addition she was able to finish her second book, *Not without Tears,* in the nine months after

moving into the new house. The book's primary focus is Blessed Martin House and its work. As she wrote in *Not without Tears,*

> The work keeps growing and so does my own understanding of the problems of the people who are a part of it. Before I opened the house, and even after that, before we moved into the alley, I thought I knew something about poverty. I thought I had been poor. I have never been poor as these people are poor. I never knew about this kind of poverty.

Blessed Martin House did not stay open long after she wrote these lines. She married Jesse Riley in 1955, and they moved to California in 1957. 1956 is the last year she is listed in the city directory as Mrs. Helen Riley, Blessed Martin House, 218 S. Turley Street. The Rileys raised a family of five children, Butch, Richard, Paul, Margaret, and Monica Diane. While raising her family, Riley spent a considerable amount of time doing volunteer work for such youth activities as the Girl Scouts. Until 1975 she taught catechism to white, black, American Indian, and Mexican children and adults for St. Joseph's Church in Barstow; she also had a class for mentally handicapped children and adults. In 1965 she began working part-time for the San Bernardino County Library, where she became a permanent half-time worker about 1970. For about twenty years, she worked full-time as head of the Barstow Bookmobile of the county library. She is currently head of the Adelanto Branch Library, a position she has held for over two years. She still works with children, principally through storytelling. Her Black History Month programs are particularly popular.

As Riley's book *Not without Tears* confirms, she was a pioneer in trying to bring the teachings of her church into practice in the South. Her life, particularly her involvement in Blessed Martin House, has been a testimony to her faith.

Current Address: Adelanto Branch Library, 11744 Bartlett, Drawer J, Adelanto, CA 92301.

REFERENCES:

"Blessed Martin House Aids Negroes in Poorest District." Unidentified newspaper clipping, April 10, 1955. Memphis/Shelby County Public Library.

Blessed Martin House, Outer Circle Studies. Schedule, 1951-52. Memphis/Shelby County Public Library.

Davis, Cyprian. *The History of Black Catholics in the United States.* New York: Crossroad, 1991.

Day, Helen Caldwell. *Color Ebony.* New York: Sheed and Ward, 1951.

———. *Not without Tears.* New York: Sheed and Ward, 1954.

"House of Hospitality Opens Doors: Rests upon Foundation of Faith." Unidentified newspaper clipping, 1952. Memphis/Shelby County Public Library.

Notice. *The Colored Harvest* 64 (April 1952): 4.

"Reading, Rolling: County Bookmobile Racks Up 510 Miles a Week." *Victorville, California, Free Press,* July 1, 1991.

Riley, Helen. Letters to Robert L. Johns, June 24, 1994, and October 14, 1994.

"Spiritual Director Named for Blessed Martin's House." *(Nashville) Tennessee Register,* October 26, 1952.

"Storyteller Enchants Young Listeners." *Victorville (California) Free Press.* Undated press clipping.

Robert L. Johns

Kay George Roberts

(1950-)

Conductor, violinist, educator

K ay Roberts is one of a select group of black symphony orchestra conductors, and she ranks extremely high on the limited list of black women with this professional title. The first woman and second black to earn the doctor of musical arts degree in conducting from Yale University School of Music, Roberts is equally well-trained and experienced as a violinist. While her professional conducting assignments have increased, she has continued her responsibilities as professor of music and conductor of the University Orchestra at the University of Massachusetts at Lowell, a position she has held since 1978. Journalists have often written about her success against all odds. But as she explained to journalist Lorrie Grant in *Emerge* magazine,

> I feel confident enough that my background and my education and my skills, and what I bring to the performance, are accomplished; that I've earned it. . . . It's not usual to have a woman conducting. [But] I don't think about being in the minority; I just try to get my job done.

Kay George Roberts was born on September 16, 1950, in Nashville, Tennessee. Her father, S. Oliver Roberts, was a founder and chairperson of Fisk University's Department of Psychology and her mother, Marion Pearl Taylor Roberts, was a librarian at Tennessee State and Fisk universities. Kay Roberts is the youngest of three girls, recipients of advanced degrees in psychiatry, psychology, and music respectively. Her maternal grandfather, George C. Taylor, was the third president of Philander Smith College in Little Rock, Arkansas.

Roberts remembers always hearing music as a child. Her mother, Marion, played the piano, and Tennessee State and Fisk universities offered the community the best of music with their Lyceum Series. It was in the segregated Nashville elementary public schools that she encountered Robert Holmes, a public school teacher who convinced the Nashville Public

School Music Supervisor that black children deserved an opportunity to enjoy the experience of making music on string instruments, an experience readily available to children of other racial and ethnic groups. Since no string ensemble opportunities were available to black youngsters, Holmes organized the Cremona Strings for black youth in 1958. Violin study for Roberts began when she was in the fourth grade; she showed tremendous potential, and Holmes soon brought her into the ensemble. Holmes later remarked, "Kay . . . showed right away that she had a good ear. . . . Kay was always very serious. I saw her as a power player because she had a big beautiful tone.

With the arrival of Nashville Symphony music director Thor Johnson, the doors of the Nashville Youth Symphony were opened to blacks in 1964. Roberts's successful audition gained her admittance. In 1967 and 1968, during her senior year in high school at the Peabody Demonstration School of George Peabody College, now known as the University School of Nashville, she was invited to join the parent ensemble, the Nashville Symphony. She remained with this organization throughout her college years at Fisk University.

In 1971, maestro Arthur Fiedler of the Boston Pops Orchestra organized the World Symphony Orchestra, and Roberts represented the Nashville Symphony, upon the recommendation of Thor Johnson. There were participants from sixty nations, thirty-four states, and the District of Columbia. First violinist Roberts was one of five blacks, of whom three were women. While enrolled at Fisk University, the young violinist studied and performed in Colorado during the summer of 1969 at Rocky Ridge Music Center and was an associate fellow at Tanglewood in Lenox, Massachusetts, during the summer of 1970.

Subsequently, other engagements included the Little Symphony of Nashville, 1971-72; Yale Collegium Orchestra, 1972; Philaharmonia Orchestra of Yale, 1973-77; Institut des Hautes Etudes Musicales, Montreaux, Switzerland and Festival Orchestra of Two Worlds, Spoleto, Italy, summer 1974; Chamber Orchestra of New England, 1977-78; New Haven Symphony, 1972-80; Nashua Symphony Orchestra, 1980-84; and Indian Hill Chamber Orchestra, 1981-85.

From Violin to Conducting

Although she was a cum laude graduate in music from Fisk University in 1972, she minored in psychology, no doubt following a family tradition. It is worth noting that she entered Fisk as a mathematics major, changing to music only upon entering her junior year. In 1972, she entered the Yale University School of Music in pursuit of the master of music degree in violin performance, which she received in 1975. During her second year of residency, she enrolled in her first conducting class. As she recalled in *Emerge* magazine, "It was a final project and students who the instructor thought could handle themselves were given the opportunity to conduct the graduate school orchestra." She continued, "I guess he saw something. After that moment he made me a conducting major and it took off from there." This represented the beginning of a shift in Roberts's career choice.

Between the years 1973 and 1978, Roberts received the Charles H. Ditson Scholarship and the Bates Junior Fellowship from the Jonathan Edwards College of Yale. She was also a fellowship recipient of the National Fellowship Fund for Black Americans. In 1976, she received the master of musical arts in both conducting and violin performance. At Yale, the M.M.A. denotes completion of predoctoral studies required for the doctor of musical arts degree. This degree is awarded only after a candidate has demonstrated his or her qualifications through distinguished achievement in the profession.

Makes Conducting Debut

Conducting instructor Otto-Werner Mueller of Yale made a practice of taking a student along when he made guest conducting appearances, allowing his qualified students to share the rehearsal podium. During the 1975-76 season, Mueller gave Roberts the opportunity to rehearse both the Atlanta and Nashville symphony orchestras in Gustav Mahler's Symphony No. 1. The same season, Roberts made her professional conducting debut as guest conductor of her hometown orchestra, the Nashville Symphony. *Nashville Banner*'s Werner Zepernick wrote of the occasion, "Miss Roberts had the orchestra firmly in hand. She has a clear and steady beat and good understanding of the various styles."

Prior to receiving the D.M.A. in 1986, Roberts set out to further "demonstrate her qualifications through distinguished achievement." She became an active participant in conducting workshops and seminars and choral institutes, such as the Aspen (Colorado) Music Festival Conductors Program; Conductors Guild Workshop, West Virginia University; Conductors Seminar, Bershire Music Center, Tanglewood; and the American Symphony Orchestra League's (ASOL's) Conducting Workshop (San Francisco Symphony Youth Orchestra). She studied conducting with Murry Sidlin, Gustav Meier, and Margaret Hillis, and participated in master classes with Seiji Ozawa, Andre Previn, Leonard Bernstein, Edo de Waart, and the African American Denis de Coteau of the San Francisco Ballet. Meier, who worked with Roberts at Tanglewood, discussed his early impressions of the "qualifying" young baton-wielder in the *Chicgo Tribune* in 1992:

I was struck by the music involvement that was always evident in her conducting. . . . She's outgoing and knows how to get to the musicians, but the music is always first. It would be easy to get carried away and do your own thing. . . . She's got the right combination of humility and assertiveness.

Roberts accepted the position of assistant professor of music and conductor of the university orchestra at the University of Lowell (now the University of Massachusetts at Lowell) in 1978. During this time she was assistant conductor of the Mystic Valley Chamber Orchestra (1983-84) and the Greater Boston Youth Symphony Orchestra (1984-85), and appeared as guest conductor of the New England Women's Symphony (1979), Nashua Symphony Orchestra (1984), and the Nashville Symphony Orchestra (1982). In 1982, she assumed the leadership of the New Hampshire Philharmonic Orchestra, remaining at the helm until 1987. Utilizing her

administrative skills, she served as executive director of Boston's Project STEP ("String Training and Educational Program for Minority Students"), sponsored by the Boston Symphony Orchestra, Boston University, and the Greater Boston Youth Symphony Orchestra, from 1984 to 1985.

With the doctor of musical arts in hand in May 1986, Roberts's conducting activities accelerated, and she was promoted to full professor at Lowell in 1987. Roberts was selected for the position of music director and conductor of the Cape Ann (Massachusetts) Symphony in 1986 based on board members' observations of her skills in handling the New Hampshire Philharmonic. Both orchestras, being community organizations, presented tremendous challenges to their artistic leader. A local critic in the *Gloucester Daily Times* wrote of Roberts's debut appearance with the Cape Ann Symphony Orchestra:

A Sunday afternoon crowd . . . came to see Kay George Roberts. . . . The consensus was, she was super. . . . Roberts' conducting style is meticulous and demanding. From the moment she strides on stage, it is clear that this woman is in command. Her physical appearance . . . is striking. Her hand movements are precise and her facial expressions compelling.

Roberts remained at the helm of the Cape Ann Symphony through the 1987-88 season.

The *Boston Herald* published a feature story on Roberts when she received an invitation to conduct the Bangkok Symphony Orchestra in Thailand during the summer of 1986. The writer noted that Roberts was the first woman and first black to conduct the four-year-old Bangkok Symphony, consisting primarily of musicians from the Royal Thai Navy. Roberts was invited back to conduct the same organization in 1987. The concert honored His Majesty the King of Thailand on his sixtieth birthday. Entitled "From Classical Favorites to Jazz," the celebration was publicized as one of the most important cultural events of the year. The *Bangkok Press* commented: "The concert was one of the best of its kind in a long time and there was little doubt that conductor Kay George Roberts was behind the success, drawing life out of an orchestra not always known to perform with spirit."

In July 1987, Roberts made her New York City debut, conducting the New York City Housing Authority Symphony Orchestra for a concert in Damrosch Park. A professional orchestra formed in 1971, the sixty-member ensemble consists of members of minority groups and plays for those living in the city's housing projects at free summer concerts both in the projects and at city parks. She conducted the orchestra on several subsequent occasions, including performances at Alice Tully Hall, Lincoln Center in New York City, and Klein Memorial Hall in Bridgeport, Connecticut.

Conductor Reaches Early Fame

Roberts reached the big league when she conducted the Detroit Symphony in 1989 on the occasion of the orchestra's

"A Celebration of African-American Sacred Music" program. She returned to Detroit during the summer of 1989 to conduct the orchestra in a park concert. During the same year, Roberts conducted a chamber ensemble in a performance of Gloria Coates's "Voices of Women in Wartime" as a part of the American Women Composers Fourth Annual Marathon in Watertown, Massachusetts.

Roberts spent the 1989-90 academic year on sabbatical from Lowell in Germany, where she was appointed conductor of the Artemis Ensemble, an ensemble that performs and records works by women composers. She also received a grant from the German Academic Exchange Service to do research on German women composers and founded Ensemble Americana, a professional chamber group that performs and promotes contemporary American music in Germany. Composed of American and German professional musicians living in the Stuttgart area, the Ensemble Americana continues an ongoing relationship with Roberts.

The Black Music Repertory Ensemble, organized in 1988, was formed "to promote appreciation for the black musical heritage written between 1800 and the present" and made its New York City debut in September 1990. On the podium was Roberts. The following day, she appeared with the group on the "Today Show," on NBC television. She also led the group in a subsequent Chicago appearance.

Through the years, Roberts has been actively involved in the training of youth and has done residences with the Greater Dallas Youth Orchestra, the Greater Boston Youth Symphony Orchestra, the Rhode Island All-State High School Orchestra, Massachusetts's Southeast District and Western District Senior Orchestras, the Senior High School Orchestra Workshop at Sam Houston State University, the Texas All-State Philharmonic Orchestra, and the Cairo (Egypt) Conservatory Orchestra. The Texas All-State Philharmonic, under Roberts's leadership, appeared in February 1991, as a part of the Texas Music Educators Association meeting. Following the event, the association's orchestra chairperson felt obliged to write the following to its guest conductor, as Roberts related to D. Antoinette Handy: "I honestly feel it is the best performance by the Philharmonic Orchestra in the history of TMEA. You gave the students a positive and unforgettable experience. . . . I appreciated your professionalism and efficiency while still being friendly and warm."

Conducts Cleveland Symphony Orchestra

The year 1993 provided more opportunities and achievements for Roberts. She continued her work in Germany, and accepted another invitation to conduct the Nashville Symphony. She conducted a subscription concert with the Chattanooga (Tennessee) Symphony, as well as the Cleveland Symphony Orchestra in its Annual Martin Luther King, Jr. Concert in January 1993. According to Ronald Crutcher, vice president for academic affairs at the Cleveland Institute of Music and board member of the Cleveland Orchestra, "The electricity when she walked in the room proved she connected

with them [the audience]. They leaped to their feet with enthusiasm and the performance had not even begun." Recalled one veteran principal woodwind player, "Kay was a really clear thinker, had conceptualized the pieces, knew what she wanted and she was on top of everything." *The Cleveland Plain Dealer* critic lauded her "ability to communicate with the Cleveland Orchestra and singers of all races and creeds from 62 church choirs" and noted: "Roberts represents a triumph." This level of achievement is particularly notable because the Cleveland Orchestra is considered one of the premiere groups in the United States, according to a 1994 *Time* magazine article.

The measure of real success for a conductor is an invitation for a return visit, as was the case for Roberts's return to the Cleveland Orchestra's January 1994 Martin Luther King, Jr. Concert and a subscription concert in April 1994. Roberts's 1993 debut with the Cleveland Orchestra also led to an invitation for her to join the conducting roster of Shaw Concerts of New York City, the management agency that handles the career of international superstar soprano Jessye Norman. Between her January 1994 and April 1994 appearances with the Cleveland Orchestra, Roberts also conducted the orchestra at the Cleveland Institute of Music and the Savannah Symphony Orchestra.

Roberts is to be commended for her interest in contemporary music, as well as her special interest in the works of black and female composers. Roberts stated in the July 7, 1991, *Nashville Tennessean,* "I enjoy working with musicians and the challenge of making what's on the written page come alive. It [the orchestra] is like a single large instrument you get to play." She stated that she enjoys conducting premieres because she "enjoy[s] working with the composer."

Roberts has been the recipient of many awards and honors, including the Young Woman of Promise Recognition from *Good Housekeeping,* 1986; Distinguished Alumni of the Year Award from the National Association for Equal Opportunity in Higher Education; the Black Achievers Award of Greater Boston; Outstanding Woman in the Performing Arts from the League of Black Women in Chicago; the 1991 Distinguished Alumna Award from the University School of Nashville; a 1993 Music Achievement Award from the National Black Music Caucus of the Music Educators National Conference; and EM magazine's Woman of Distinction award in 1993.

It is often stated that a conductor's career does not really bloom until he or she reaches age forty. Having reached the magic number, and in view of her training, skills, and previous accomplishments, Roberts seems guaranteed greater achievements. It is an unwritten rule that the order of succession to the orchestral podium is European men, American white men, minority men, white women, and finally minority women. Roberts, "a minority within a minority," remains unphased by this imbalance. Though she is committed to the music of black and women composers, as well as contemporary American music, she is equally committed to the standard orchestral repertoire. Her guest conducting appearances are generally preceded by a focus on her racial and gender identity, but she seeks to be remembered simply as a qualified conductor who brings a new look to the podium and a different perspective to the music.

Current Address: c/o Hugh Kaylor, President, Shaw Concerts Inc., 1900 Broadway, 2nd Floor, New York, NY 10023.

REFERENCES:

"Breaking the Sound Barrier." *Nashville Tennessean,* July 7, 1991.

"Conductor Beats Odds with Her Baton." *Detroit Free Press,* February 19, 1992.

"Conductor: Black Woman Musician at U Lowell Succeeds in Field Dominated by Men." *Lowell Sun,* November 9, 1978.

"Good Conduct." *Chicago Tribune,* April 26, 1992.

Grant, Lorrie. "A Maestro with Quiet Confidence." *Emerge* (May 1993): 57, 58.

Handy, D. Antoinette. *Black Women in American Bands and Orchestras.* Metuchen, N.J.: Scarecrow Press, 1981.

———. *Black Conductors.* Metuchen, N.J.: Scarecrow Press, 1994.

Jennings, Patricia Prattis. "1993: A Significant Year for Conductor Kay George Roberts." *Symphonium* 5 (Fall 1993): 4.

"Kay George Roberts, Winida Treepoonpon Score with BSO." *Bangkok Press,* November 1, 1986.

"Kay Roberts Returns for Conducting Debut." *Nashville Tennessean,* May 28, 1976.

"Guest Conductor Inspires Young Dallas Musicians." *Dallas Morning News,* June 21, 1986.

"I Am a Minority within a Minority." *Stuttgarter Nachruchten-Kultur Magazine,* July 20, 1991.

"King Concert Reflects the Binding Power of Music." *Cleveland Plain Dealer,* January 13, 1993.

McDonald, Dianne H. "Conducting Becomes Her." *Newsweek on Campus* (April 1988): 38, 39.

"A Minority within a Minority." *Chattanooga News-Free Press,* February 18, 1993.

Munder, P. "Black Power." *Madame* (September 1989): 56, 107.

"Nashville Symphony Opens Summer Parks Concerts." *Nashville Banner,* May 31, 1976.

Roberts, Kay George. Letters to D. Antoinette Handy. July 28, 1976; March 21, 1986; May 26, 1988; September 7, 1989; December 13, 1989; May 9, 1990; July 10, 1991; July 29, 1991; February 24, 1994.

———. Interviews with D. Antoinette Handy, Washington, D.C., January 13 1986; January 15, 1986; Philadelphia, Pennsylvania, February 17, 1994.

"A Symphony of Firsts for Woman from Cambridge." *Boston Herald,* August 31, 1986.

D. Antoinette Handy

Jo Ann Gibson Robinson
(1912-?)
Civil rights activist, educator, writer

One of the most momentous events in the history of the United States, and especially in the history of the American civil rights movement, was the Montgomery Bus Boycott of 1955 and 1956. While this boycott is noted for bringing to national prominence a young Baptist minister named Martin Luther King, Jr., few people are aware of the very important role Montgomery's black women played in getting the boycott started and making it successful. One of those women was Jo Ann Robinson.

Jo Ann Gibson Robinson was born on April 17, 1912, near Culloden, Georgia. She was the youngest of twelve children born to Owen Boston Gibson and Dollie Webb Gibson. Her father died when she was only six. She was educated in the segregated public schools of Macon, located in an adjacent county, and graduated valedictorian of her high school class. After high school, she went to Fort Valley State College, and thus she became the first in her family ever to graduate from college. She taught in the Macon public schools after graduating. While in Macon, she was married briefly to Wilbur Robinson and had one child, who died in infancy. She never remarried.

After five years of teaching in Macon, Robinson moved by herself to Atlanta, where she earned her master's degree in English from Atlanta University. She later worked on her doctorate at Columbia University in New York City for one year. She spent one year at Mary Allen College in Crockett, Texas, teaching English and serving as chair of the English Department, before accepting a position as professor of English at Alabama State College in Montgomery in 1949.

Upon arriving in Montgomery, Robinson joined the Dexter Avenue Baptist Church and the Women's Political Council (WPC) of Montgomery. The WPC had been formed three years earlier by another Alabama State English professor, Mary Fair Burks. Both of these organizations were to play an important role in the bus boycott, and Robinson's position within each made her one of the most important figures in the boycott.

A Humiliating Bus Ride

Three months after starting her new job, Robinson had an experience that changed her forever. She wrote of this experience in her memoir, published in 1987 under the title *The Montgomery Bus Boycott and the Women Who Started It.* Just before Christmas, she prepared to take a trip to Cleveland, Ohio, for the holidays. She intended to take a public bus from the parking garage where she had left her car over to the house of a friend who had agreed to give her a ride to the airport. When she got on the bus, there were only two other passengers: a white woman in the third row and a black man near the back. Robinson sat in the fifth row of the nearly empty bus. At first she was unaware that the bus driver was speaking to her, but when she did notice, she realized he was saying, "If you can sit in the fifth row from the front of the other busses in Montgomery, suppose you get off and ride in one of them!" When she did not move, he came back and appeared ready to strike her while he repeated "Get up from there!" She quickly got up and ran to the front of the bus to exit, yet another violation of Montgomery's segregation practices, but the bus driver opened the door and let her off. With tears in her eyes, she walked back to the campus.

Over the next several years, a number of other incidents occurred on Montgomery's buses that served to infuriate the black community of the city. Each time, Montgomery's black leaders requested more courtesy from the city's bus drivers, but the response from city and bus officials was minimal. Due to her years in the North, living in New York and Cleveland, and her own experience with rude drivers, Robinson was more willing to fight than some of Montgomery's other black residents. For example, she wanted to organize a protest after the arrest of Claudette Colvin, a fifteen-year-old black student. After all the seats in the white section had been occupied, the bus driver ordered all blacks to stand to make their seats available to white riders. Colvin refused and had to be dragged from the bus kicking and screaming. E. D. Nixon, head of the Montgomery NAACP, decided Colvin's arrest would not provide a good test. Roberta Hughes Wright reports in *The Birth of the Montgomery Bus Boycott* that Nixon later recalled, "JoAnn Robinson liked to have had a fit. She jumped all over me."

Shortly after the Supreme Court ruled that segregation was unconstitutional, Robinson, who had succeeded Mary Fair Burks as the president of the WPC in 1950, threatened a boycott of the buses by blacks if abuse of blacks was not curtailed, but no significant changes were made.

Montgomery Bus Boycott Begins

Frustration was rising was within the black community; Robinson said in her memoir that "the straw that broke the camel's back" was the arrest of Rosa Parks on Thursday, December 1, 1955. Parks was a hardworking, forty-two-year-old seamstress who was well respected in the black community. On the day she was arrested, she boarded a bus after work and sat down in the front of the black section, just behind the section reserved for whites. Since it was rush hour, the white section quickly filled up, and the driver demanded that she give up her seat to a white man. She refused; she was tired from working and saw no reason why a woman should have to give up her seat to an able-bodied man. The driver then summoned the police and she was arrested. Later that night, Robinson got a call from Fred Gray, a local attorney and assistant pastor of the Holt Street Church of Christ. E. D. Nixon had asked Parks if he could use her case to test the constitutionality of the local bus ordinance and to rally community support around a day of protest. However, Parks was unsure about committing herself and said she did not know. Robinson and Gray agreed to call for a boycott the

following Monday, December 5, without waiting for Parks's consent.

For the next several hours, Robinson, John Cannon, chairman of the Business Department at Alabama State, and two senior students mimeographed approximately 52,500 leaflets. By four A.M. on Friday, December 2, they had the flyers completed, and they proceeded to distribute them during the day. Robinson eventually paid for the cost of thirty-five reams of paper out of her own pocket. Later that evening, a meeting was held at the Dexter Avenue Baptist Church to plan Monday's boycott and to schedule a follow-up meeting on Monday night at the Holt Street church.

The boycott was successfully staged that Monday, and six thousand people attended the meeting at the Holt Street church. It was there that the Montgomery Improvement Association (MIA) was organized, with Martin Luther King, Jr., pastor of the Dexter Avenue Baptist Church, chosen as president. Robinson did not assume an official position in the MIA since she was a state employee. She did not want to jeopardize her job or the status of the college by accepting a visible position. All those chosen to be officers were ministers, attorneys, or medical doctors who would not be subject to any type of governmental pressure. Robinson was, however, named to the MIA executive board because of her position as president of the WPC, and she attended meetings with city and bus officials in this new capacity. She even attended a meeting with Alabama Governor James Folsom along with Martin Luther King, Jr. and two other ministers. In addition to attending the executive board meetings every Monday night, King asked her to write a newsletter, which came to be called the *MIA Newsletter,* in order to keep participants and supporters of the boycott informed. Robinson attributed her selection to the fact that she was an English teacher and the publisher of a monthly campus newsletter. By the time the boycott ended, the weekly *MIA Newsletter* had grown to eight pages.

Menaced by Police

Despite her attempts to maintain a low profile, Robinson was too active and involved to remain invisible forever. In February 1956 she became the target of harassment for her work with the boycott. One night, while she was sitting in her living room with two friends, a police squad car drove up in front of her house. One of the policemen got out of the car and threw a large stone through her picture window. The friends who were with her that night boarded up her window (it stayed that way through the remainder of the boycott). They then went down to city hall with the license plate number of the squad car, along with the rock. The police refused to act.

Two weeks later, one of her neighbors spotted two men, both in police uniforms, pouring acid all over Robinson's car. It left several holes in the top, fenders, and hood. She kept the car until 1960 when she decided to move to California. Only after these attacks did Governor Folsom order state police to guard the homes of boycott leaders.

In mid-February, Judge Eugene Carter called a grand jury to investigate the bus boycott. Boycotts were illegal under Alabama state law although many felt at the time that the law was unconstitutional. The grand jury report and indictments were released on February 21. The boycott was judged to be illegal and 115 persons were named who were to be arrested the next day. One of those indicted was Robinson. She was fingerprinted, photographed (with number 7042), and processed. Her bail was set at three hundred dollars and bond was quickly provided by local businessmen. She was arraigned on February 24, but only King's trial date was set at the time. His trial was held in March, at which time he was found guilty.

In the meantime, the MIA's suit against Montgomery's city buses had been working its way through the federal courts. In mid-November, the U.S. Supreme Court ruled that the buses had to be integrated. This ruling was delivered by U.S. Marshals on December 20, 1956, and the boycott officially ended the next day. None of the others who were arrested and indicted, including Robinson, were ever taken to trial.

Several months after the boycott ended, Robinson, along with some other Alabama State professors, resigned. She decided to move to the English department at Grambling College in Louisiana. She remained there only one year before she moved once again, this time to Los Angeles, where she taught in the public schools. She also went back to graduate school for one year at the University of Southern California. She retired from active teaching in 1976.

After retiring, Robinson purchased six rental apartments and remained active in a host of civic and social groups, giving one day a week of free service to the city of Los Angeles and serving in the League of Women Voters, the Alpha Gamma Omega chapter of the Alpha Kappa Alpha Sorority, the Angel City chapter of the Links, the Black Women's Alliance, the Founders Church of Religious Science, and Women on Target. She also devoted time to a child-care center and to voter registration drives. In 1989, the Southern Association for Women Historians honored her for her 1987 autobiography, *The Montgomery Bus Boycott and the Women Who Started It,* but declining health prevented her from accepting it in person. Jo Ann Robinson's contributions to the civil rights movement, in the face of violent police intimidation, made her a notable and courageous figure in that historic struggle.

REFERENCES:

Branch, Taylor. *Parting the Waters: America in the King Years, 1954-63.* New York: Simon and Schuster, 1988.

Garrow, David J. *The Walking City: The Montgomery Bus Boycott, 1955-1956.* Brooklyn: Carlson Publishing, 1989.

Hine, Darlene Clark, ed. *Black Women in America.* Brooklyn: Carlson Publishing, 1993.

Parks, Rosa, with Jim Haskin. *My Story.* New York: Dial Books, 1992.

Robinson, Jo Ann Gibson. *The Montgomery Bus Boycott and the Women Who Started It: The Memoir of Jo Ann Gibson Robinson.* Edited by David J. Garrow. Knoxville: University of Tennessee Press, 1987.

Wright, Roberta Hughes. *The Birth of the Montgomery Bus Boycott.* Southfield, Mich.: Charro Press, 1991.

Derek Elliott

Carolyn Rodgers
(1942-)
Poet, critic, educator

Carolyn Rodgers, poet, critic, short story writer, and teacher, emerged as a distinctive poetic voice during the turbulent 1960s. She, along with other young Chicago artists like Haki Madhubuti and Johari Amini, symbolized a new breed of activist/writer. Rejecting an art-for-art's-sake philosophy and adopting a defiant stance, they demanded that creative works be a part of the struggle for black liberation. In her first two books of poetry, *Paper Soul* (1968) and *Two Love Raps* (1969), Rodgers reflects the spirit and principles of the Black Arts movement, often employing street language and a provocative tone calculated to shock the status quo. In subsequent volumes, such as *Songs of a Black Bird* (1969), *How I Got Ovah* (1975), *The Heart as Ever Green* (1978), *Morning Glory* (1989), and *We're Only Human* (1994), Rodgers, less influenced by black nationalism, explores other aspects of the human condition: feminism, relationships between men and women, loneliness, human frailty, spirituality, and the writer's role. She approaches these issues through her identity as an African American woman.

The youngest of four children—three girls and one boy—Carolyn Marie Rodgers was born to Bazella Cato Colding Rodgers and Clarence Rodgers on December 14, 1942, in a small segregated hospital on Chicago's South Side. She was the only child born in Chicago after the family migrated from Little Rock, Arkansas, to seek a better life in the North, and this earned her the title "city slicker" as she was growing up. Rodgers considered her parents' departure from Little Rock proof of their courage and integrity. She would draw inspiration from their example throughout her life. Rodgers's admiration for her mother as a God-fearing woman of strong character is clearly illuminated in poems such as "for muh' dear," "JESUS WAS CRUCIFIED, or It Must Be Deep," and "IT IS DEEP." According to the 1991 edition of *Contemporary Authors,* Rodgers calls her father "a hard worker" who provided an excellent model of "stability."

Rodgers remembers in *Contemporary Authors* that regular attendance at the nearby African Methodist Episcopal (AME) Church was compulsory in the Rodgers household: "Three or four times a week, my two sisters and brother and I were there when the church doors opened; and since we lived only two houses away from the church, we often opened the doors because we had been given the keys. . . . No if's and but's were acceptable, unless death was imminent." Rodgers's religious background provided the basis for her focus on spiritual themes in many of her autobiographical works, which reveal the artist's struggle to clarify her relationship with God and her mother in light of her 1960s black consciousness.

Rodgers attended Roosevelt University in Chicago but left one course short of graduation. However, in January 1981, she received her bachelor of arts degree in English from Chicago State University. In June 1984, she received her master's degree in English from Chicago State University.

Throughout her career, Rodgers has consistently combined writing and teaching. According to *Contemporary Authors,* shortly after leaving Roosevelt University, she became a language arts teacher at the YMCA, where she taught the works of James Baldwin, Richard Wright, and Gwendolyn Brooks to students who had often been neglected and abused. She also taught at Columbia College in Chicago (1969), and the University of Washington (summer 1970) and was a teacher and writer-in-residence at Chicago's Malcolm X City College (1971) and resident-poet at Albany State College (1971). She taught at Indiana University (summer 1973) and served as writer-in-residence at Roosevelt University (1983). In 1989 she returned to Columbia College. Rodgers has also reviewed books for the *Negro Digest,* the *Chicago Daily,* the *Chicago Sun-Times,* and the *Milwaukee Courier.*

In 1969, Rodgers won the first Conrad Kent Rivers Writing Award. In 1970, she won the Poet Laureate Award of the Society of Midland Authors for her collection *Songs of a Black Bird* (1969). And in the same year, she received a National Endowment for the Arts award for the poems in her first collection, *Paper Soul* (1968), and *Songs of a Black Bird* (1969).

Chicago Mentors Influence Work

According to Jean Davis in the *Dictionary of Literary Biography,* it was Rodgers's association with other Chicago artists and not her classroom experiences that led to her career as a poet. While working for the YMCA School Dropout Program, Rodgers became a founding member of the Organization of Black American Culture (OBAC) Writers Workshop, created and guided by Hoyt W. Fuller, editor of *Negro Digest.* Rodgers recalls in *Contemporary Authors* those early days at OBAC (pronounced Oh-Bah-See): "One night a week we came together to read our work to each other, to criticize and support each other, and to learn from our wonderful mentor, the late Hoyt W. Fuller."

Rodgers also joined Gwendolyn Brooks's writing workshop. Through these associations, Rodgers met other aspiring young artists, including Haki Madhubuti (Don L. Lee), Johari Amini (Jewel Latimore), and Cecil Brown. Rodgers, Madhubuti, and Amini cofounded Third World Press. Both Hoyt Fuller, who had previously published Rodgers's first works in the *Negro Digest*—a short story entitled "Blackbird in a Cage"

and a poem, "U. of C. Midway Blues"—and Gwendolyn Brooks, who encouraged her first collection of poems, *Paper Soul,* served as important mentors for Rodgers.

Shortly after joining OBAC, Rodgers published *Paper Soul.* In his introduction to the book, Hoyt Fuller places Rodgers among "the spiritual and cultural revolutionaries." Many of the poems reflect the tenets of the new Black Arts movement and, according to Betty Parker-Smith in *Black Women Writers (1950-1980),* established Rodgers as "an exemplar of the 'revolutionary poet.'" In theme and language—use of profanity, street idiom, and name calling—Rodgers's works represented a decisive challenge to the values of traditional culture. In "A NON POEM ABOUT VIETNAM or Try Black," Rodgers adopts a militant tone as she weighs the merits of black men participating in the war. Her verdict: "no black man (or negro) should fight the hunkie's war." Religion is also given a militant face. In "TESTIMONY" Rodgers makes Christianity more compatible with revolution. Christ is transformed into a "soldier" who can lift black folks off their knees and "shoot buckshot into their hearts." In subsequent collections, Rodgers sought a more personal relationship with Christ.

Despite the predominant tone of defiance in *Paper Soul,* Rodgers raises the issue of her own emotional frailty. In "ONE" she sadly observes, "People die from loneliness." Then, recounting her own struggle with illnesses and operations, beginning with the removal of her appendix at the age of fifteen, she declares life "an incurable disease" full of "sloppy dissections." Those who knew Rodgers often spoke of her vulnerability. In *Black Women Writers,* Betty Parker-Smith notes that Hoyt Fuller recalled his first impression of Rodgers as a "skinny and scared" young woman who "telegraphed a need to be stroked."

In 1969, Rodgers published her second book, *Two Love Raps.* This slim two-poem volume honors participants in the struggle for black liberation. "Black against the Muthafuckas," written in the style and language of the Black Arts movement, pays homage to the UMOJA Student Center in Chicago and those who participated in the Chicago Student March, in which students marched in solidarity against police aggression. Rodgers concludes on a note of black solidarity. In "Poems for Malcolm: Memorial '69," she creates a rhythmic "rapping" tempo as she pleads for creative tributes to Malcolm X, "the pimp who sold us ourselves." Throughout the poem, Rodgers repudiates the values of the established culture by ironically appropriating its derogatory labels to describe Malcolm X. She calls him a hustler whose life had impact on the people because he symbolized their reality.

After *Two Love Raps,* Rodgers published *Songs of a Black Bird.* This 1969 volume signifies another stage in the development of her themes. In this collection, she attempts to construct bridges between the past and the present as she now recognizes the unselfish nobility of an older generation of blacks who provided her generation with a standard for excellence. In "For H. W. Fuller," a poem Haki Madhubuti (Don L. Lee) calls "a hell of a tribute to a man," Rodgers respectfully admires the quiet persistence of her mentor, "standing in the shadows" and "chipping at the stones" of a cold society until it falls.

Bridging the Gap

In two companion poems in *Songs of a Black Bird,* "JESUS WAS CRUCIFIED, or It Must Be Deep" and "IT IS DEEP," Rodgers examines the complexity of the mother-daughter relationship and the generation gap. As noted in *Dictionary of Literary Biography,* the mother in "JESUS WAS CRUCIFIED, or It Must Be Deep," is one of "the staunch, old-fashioned [black] religious mothers who sacrifice for their children." She has come to the aid of her daughter who is ill. In the poem, the views of the older Christian traditionalist collide with those of the younger activist when the mother charges that the daughter's recent sickness is caused by her rage against society—"why it's somethin wrong wid yo mind girl / that's what it is." While the daughter rejects the mother's solution—redemption through prayer—with "I don't believe," Rodgers suggests a narrowing of the chasm between them as the daughter at the end of the poem inadvertently merges the identity of Christ with that of her mother: "catch you later on jesus, i mean motha!"

In the sequel, "IT IS DEEP," the daughter, experiencing a financial crisis, is again visited by her mother, who responds to her daughter's problem by pressing fifty dollars into her hand, saying, "you got folks who care about you." The daughter comes to realize that her mother, who is still "religiously girdled in her god" and who still fails to understand anything "relevant" or "Black," is "a sturdy Black bridge that [she] crossed over, on." According to Estella M. Sales in "Contradictions in Black Life," which appeared in the September 1981 *CLA Journal,* the religious tension lingering in these two poems is smoothed in the final sequence, "how I got ovah II/IT IS DEEP II."

The artistic dilemma of the black woman writer is introduced in *Songs of a Black Bird.* In Rodgers's "Breakthrough," Angelene Jamison, who contributed an essay on Rodgers to *Black Women Writers,* sees a manifestation of Rodgers's inner turmoil stemming from her battle to find her "own voice" amidst the demanding voices of her people—her own sense of self versus the Cause. Clearly committed to the plight of the black community, Rodgers internally struggles for a balance that will allow her to fulfill her own desires for artistic freedom without compromising her role as a writer and an activist.

How I Got Ovah, Rodgers's 1975 collection, continues the "bridging" process begun in *Songs of a Black Bird.* But she has brought to these poems a more seasoned perspective. The title comes from the Negro spiritual made famous by Mahalia Jackson. *How I Got Ovah* is about spiritual survival, about struggle and evolving, about crossing over what Estella Sales calls "the waters of confusion." Many of the poems are autobiographical and reflect the artist's search for inner peace. To get there, she must use bridges, "supportive structures," says Sales, that have been there all the while: her own inner voice, her ancestral support, and her deep religious beliefs.

Rodgers, the new-generation revolutionary, attempts to reclaim the past—her roots—in *How I Got Ovah,* beginning with her mother. In "Portrait" she marvels at her mother's frugality, which provided a way for her children to succeed: "mama spent pennies / in uh gallon milk jug / fuh four babies college educashuns." In "for muh' dear," the daughter, still conscious of a gap between her and her mother, now frames their differences affectionately and humorously: "told my sweet mama / to leave me alone / about my wild free knotty and nappy hair." As Parker-Smith has noted, the "sarcasm" of the earlier poems is gone. She seems to have come to terms with her mother. In the title poem, "how i got ovah," the poet acknowledges her ancestors as a bridge of love and support. Her links to their spirits (the cultural past) have enabled her to cross "the rivers of life."

A Tribute to Gwendolyn Brooks

Rodgers pays tribute to her spiritual mother, Gwendolyn Brooks, in "To GWEN." In "Breakforth. In Deed," a critical essay published in *Black World* in September 1970, a younger and more brash Rodgers claimed that Brooks's work—along with that of James Baldwin, Ralph Ellison, and Melvin Tolson—left "a nation of Blacks untouched." But now a mellowed Rodgers has come to appreciate Brooks's legacy to her generation. Mindful of the inability of language to convey proper tribute to her mentor, Rodgers simply calls Brooks, "mo luv and mo luv and mo luv and mo luv and mo luvvvvvvv."

A sense of spiritual unity is reached in *How I Got Ovah* as Rodgers makes peace with her Christian past—the religion of her mother. In "mama's God," she discovers that "mama's God never was no white man." And she achieves a reconciliation between Christianity and the revolution in "Jesus must of been some kind of dude" by conveying the story of Jesus's triumph in street language: "Jesus was cool and his rap was heavy. . . . Jesus was a militant dude sisters." In "how i got ovah II/ IT IS DEEP II," Rodgers completes the cycle begun in the earlier poems "JESUS WAS CRUCIFIED, or It Must Be Deep" and "IT IS DEEP," from *Songs of a Black Bird.* Rodgers, no longer left in a spiritual limbo, is "touched" by God in the presence of her mother.

In 1982 nationally acclaimed artists Ruby Dee and Ossie Davis staged in Dallas, Texas, a rousing tribute to Rogers's religious poetry, later broadcast on PBS. Backed by the entertainer Billy Preston, Dee and Davis transformed Rodgers's words into a dramatic expression of her spiritual joy and powerful vision. In 1993, Dee and Davis released a videotape of the production, entitled *Hands upon the Heart, Volume II.*

A Woman's Self-Esteem Explored

The sensitive issue of female self-esteem is explored in three poems from *How I Got Ovah:* "Slave Ritual," "Some Body Call," and "I Have Been Hungry." According to Jamison in *Black Women Writers,* in "Slave Ritual" and

"Some Body Call," Rodgers describes the plight of "Black women who suffer in silence . . . in deadlocked relationships." In "I Have Been Hungry," Rodgers exposes her own emotional scars, revealing that her father, who had three girls and one boy, wanted to reverse the equation to three boys and "one good for nothing / wanting needing love and approval seeking bleeding girl." His symbolic rejection left her emotionally starved and "craving the love [she] never got."

In the poem "For Women: Amazing Grace" from *How I Got Ovah,* Rodgers again focuses on the theme of female vulnerability. But it is the woman's communion with the Holy Spirit—her "shouting and moaning"—that provides her shelter against the "wild wind" of her man's fear of God and the power of her faith. Ironically, he is "saved" and "somewhat sanctified" because of her "amazing grace."

The spiritual force of *How I Got Ovah* climaxes in two poems: "The Poet's Vision" and "Living Water." In "The Poet's Vision," Rodgers considers her poetic talent a "divine" burden, "[seeing] . . . what people frantically try to hide." Calling herself a "piece fitter," she wonders if Jesus felt a similar burden. In "Living Water," Rodgers says that within her "there is a well," out from which the words of God "flow forever." It is these words that will take us over "the midst of hell" and "smack [us] all together into heaven."

Antar Mberi notes in his review of Rodgers's 1978 collection, *The Heart as Ever Green,* that the book reveals Rodgers's search for "truth, meaning, peace with equality, love and human compassion." The familiar themes are explored—troubled love, loneliness, spirituality, black consciousness, and feminism. For example, in "Feminism," she urges women to establish a sense of identity in their own right. "What is your claim to fame?" she asks, when there are "no husbands to be pillared upon." But according to Jean Davis in *Dictionary of Literary Biography,* the central theme of *The Heart as Ever Green,* symbolically represented in the title, is the determination to thrive and endure: images of growth and renewal abound throughout the book.

In "Earth Is Not the World, Nor All Its Beauty," she calls upon the reader to realize the potential riches that life holds in store. And in its sequel, "Earth Is Not the World, Nor All Its Beauty Poem II," she uses images from nature to celebrate the birth of hope "all golden," symbolized by the yellow forsythia, "a metaphor," writes Jean Davis, "for the process of annual renewal." The strength of her own will is captured eloquently in "The Black Heart As Ever Green," where Rodgers affirms that her own "Heart is ever green . . . like buds or shoots / determined to grow / determined to be."

Rodgers reserves her strongest expression of optimism for the human race in "Translation (thinking of Enoch) for Black People," the final poem in *The Heart as Ever Green.* Finding harmony and unity among nature, human beings, and African Americans' battle for freedom, she sees the possibility of a brighter tomorrow. Rodgers communicates this hope to humanity in general and to African Americans in particular when she writes, "I say / we will live / no death is a / singular unregenerating event."

Rodgers's 1989 collection, *Morning Glory,* continues her search for spirituality, love, and human compassion. Symbolizing both endurance and the freshness of youth, the morning glory becomes the central metaphor for what Rodgers sees as the fragility of the human condition. The idea of innocence corrupted by evil permeates the book. "Mother's Son, Mother's Sun" recounts the transformation of babies born pure "in their mother's souls" into the "thief, murderer, and junkie." "Darkness at Noon" evokes the haunting tragedy of innocence destroyed as Rodgers asks a sleeping woman sprawled on the church steps—steps defiled by blood and urine stains—"whose little girl did you used to be." But even while lamenting fallen innocence, Rodgers, in the title poem "Morning Glory," affirms the dignity of human life by evoking the glory that once was: "Where were we in the vase of time,/when we were young . . . in our morning glory."

But in "Angel Food," from Rodgers's 1994 publication, *We're Only Human,* the poet, now more somber, grieves for the children of Somalia, "angel food" to "Beelzebub's flies" that crawl in the out of their "defenseless open noses and mouths," while an indifferent world looks on with detachment. And in "This Brave New World," also included in *We're Only Human,* she admonishes television viewers who glare in numbed silence at pictures of "mutilated dead bodies in the bloody trenches of the streets" in "the Sudan, Bosnia, or South Africa." With chilling irony, Rodgers asks, "What do you expect?. . . We're only human." Rodgers articulates the reality of our world—its conflicts and contradictions. Her poetry is a truthful and powerful expression of the creative spirit.

Through her poetry, Carolyn Rodgers brings to the reader the breadth and depth of her complex vision. In her works she captures the rage of the black community, poignantly expresses the vulnerability of the lonely, and articulates the emotional dilemma of the woman—especially the black woman—struggling for meaningful existence in contemporary society. Along these lines, Rodgers examines her own place in the universe. But in her poetry, she also sees herself as mediator. She attempts to build bridges—bridges between the past and the present, between the old and the new, and between spiritual fragmentation and spiritual wholeness. Rodgers's poetry is a journey that reflects an evolving consciousness that brings to us a revelation of the human condition.

Current Address: P.O. Box 804271, Chicago, IL 60680.

REFERENCES:

Contemporary Authors Autobiography Series. Vol. 13. Detroit: Gale Research, 1991.

Hands upon the Heart, Volume II. Videocassette. Emmalyn II Productions, 1993.

Harris, Trudier, and Thadious M. Davis, eds. *Dictionary of Literary Biography.* Vol. 41: *Afro American Poets since 1955.* Detroit: Gale Research, 1985.

Jamison, Angelene. "Imagery in the Women Poems: The Art of Carolyn Rodgers." In *Black Women Writers (1950-*

1980). Edited by Mari Evans. New York: Anchor Books, 1984.

Lee, Don L. *Dynamite Voices 1: Black Poets of the 1960's.* Edited by James A. Emanuel. Detroit: Broadside Press, 1971.

Mberi, Antar S. Review of *The Heart as Ever Green. Freedomways* 20 (1980): 48-49.

Parker-Smith, Betty J. "Running Wild in Her Soul: The Poetry of Carolyn Rodgers." In *Black Women Writers, 1950-1980.* Edited by Mari Evans. New York: Anchor Books, 1984.

Rodgers, Carolyn M. *Paper Soul.* Introduction by Hoyt W. Fuller. Chicago: Third World Press, 1968.

———. "Breakforth. In Deed." *Black World* 19 (September 1970): 13-22.

———. *Morning Glory: Poems by Carolyn M. Rodgers.* Chicago: Eden Press, 1989.

———. *We're Only Human: Poems by Carolyn M. Rodgers.* Chicago: Eden Press, 1994.

Sales, Estella M. "Contradictions in Black Life: Recognized and Reconciled in *How I Got Ovah.*" *CLA Journal* 25 (September 1981): 74-81.

Barbara J. Griffin

Wilhelmina Jackson Rolark

Wilhelmina Jackson Rolark

19??-

Lawyer, politician, organization founder, researcher

In her dual role of attorney and local politician, Wilhelmina Rolark has improved the quality of life for residents in Ward Eight of the District of Columbia. And, as the primary force behind the establishment of the National Association of Black Women Attorneys (NABWA) and its founding president, she has helped to enhance the professional status of the black woman attorney. She has been a great inspiration to young black women who desire to become lawyers and, through her leadership in the NABWA, has provided them both financial assistance and guidance.

Wilhelmina Jackson Rolark was born in the early 1900s in Truxton, a suburb of Portsmouth, Virginia. Her father, John William Jackson, was a native of Washington, D.C., and one of only two black navy clerks at the Norfolk Navy Yard in Portsmouth. Rolark's mother, Margaret Boykin Jackson, was a Portsmouth native and a teacher prior to her marriage; afterwards, she worked as a substitute teacher and opened a nursery school in her home. In a July 2, 1993, interview, Rolark credited her mother with instilling in her a compassionate attitude toward those less fortunate than herself. During Rolark's childhood, it was common practice to keep retarded children hidden from public view, but the pioneering

Margaret Jackson enrolled such children in her nursery school. She patiently taught them the same curriculum as the other students while allowing for their slower and different ways of learning. Rolark's siblings, now deceased, were John H. Jackson, a Philadelphia-based Howard University School of Medicine graduate, and Gwendolyn Jackson Bowie, a Washington, D.C., teacher.

Rolark graduated from Truxton Elementary School and I. C. Norcum High School in Portsmouth. She received a bachelor's degree in 1936 and a master's degree in 1938, both in political science from Howard University. The magna cum laude graduate was privileged to have studied under eminent scholars in the field, including Ralph Bunche, E. Franklin Frazier, Eugene Holmes, and William Hansberry. In 1944 she earned a bachelor of laws degree from the Terrell Law School in Washington, D.C. This prestigious school was named in honor of Robert H. Terrell, a Howard law graduate and the first black judge of the District of Columbia Municipal Court.

In the July 2, 1993, interview, Rolark emphasized the advantages of attending night school law classes, which were taught by practicing lawyers, over day classes, taught by lawyers who were primarily theoreticians. This was probably one of the main reasons Rolark was able to pass the bar in October 1944, on her first attempt. In answer to an inquiry about her mentors and role models, Rolark remembered her high school history and English teachers, Mrs. Weaver and Mrs. Ewell, and Howard University history professor Harold Lewis. All were educators who were not only encouraging, but also highly qualified and widely respected in their fields. Rolark herself was fondly remembered by Jeannette Layton

Forrester, a longtime Nashville resident and Howard University (B.A., 1935) schoolmate. In a July 1, 1993, interview, Forrester said: "I remember Wilhelmina Jackson as being witty, brilliant, lots of fun, and a bookworm who didn't bother much with the boys or a social life. She had an excellent mind."

Rolark was married for thirty years to Calvin W. Rolark, a native of Texarkana, Texas, and a graduate of Prairie View Agricultural and Mechanical College. Calvin Rolark, who died in 1994, founded and was president of the United Black Fund and was editor and publisher of the *Washington Informer*. The Rolarks had two children, Denise Rolark Barnes and Calvin Rolark II.

Researcher for Landmark Study of Race Relations

Rolark participated in the preparation of the 1944 landmark publication *An American Dilemma,* written by the Swedish social economist and scholar Gunner Myrdal. She was hired as a research field worker to investigate the state of race relations in the South, particularly in the Carolinas and Florida. Rolark assisted in the drafting and use of questionnaires designed to elicit information from blacks about disenfranchisement methods employed by local and state voter registration boards. In the author's preface, her name is listed with other staff assistants and collaborators; in the footnotes, two of her 1939 interviews are cited.

Speaking about how she was personally affected by racial segregation while traveling to field-work assignment areas, Rolark related her pleasant experiences in North Carolina. She stayed in private homes due to state laws barring blacks from hotels and other public accommodations. In Salisbury, North Carolina, Rolark always stayed with Rose Douglass Aggrey, a local educator, state education official, and highly respected leader of black women's business and professional organizations. Rolark's mother and Aggrey were lifelong friends; therefore, the young, fledgling researcher was always welcome in the Aggrey home, an oasis in the segregated South.

Fight for the Rights of Black Women Attorneys Begins

One of the most notable achievements in the professional life of Rolark was the founding of the National Association of Black Women Attorneys in 1972. At a Miami meeting of the National Bar Association, Rolark began formulating plans for the organization because she sensed a general lack of interest in the professional needs of black women attorneys. In a June 21, 1993, interview, Mabel D. Haden, current NABWA president, spoke of the friction between Rolark supporters and those women who preferred to support the distaff branch of the National Bar Association. In spite of this opposition, Rolark proceeded with plans to organize black women attorneys. Joining her in this effort were three other attorneys: Barbara Sims, a law professor at SUNY-Buffalo; Gwendolyn Cherry, a practicing attorney and member of the Florida legislature; and Jean Capers, a Cleveland, Ohio, municipal court judge. Charter members, who received certificates of

recognition at the president's reception for the 1978 convention, were Rolark; judges Jean Capers, Norma H. Johnson, and Barbara Sims; and attorneys Mabel Haden, Lillian K. Chase, Sylvia Drew, Ruth H. Charity, Gwendolyn Cherry, Willie S. Glanton, Mary P. Hutchings, Inez V. Reid, Alice Rucker, and Lena P. Thurman.

The first areas of concentration for the new group were membership and a formal study of admission practices of law schools as they affected the status of black female applicants. Although the organization had fewer than one hundred members, NABWA's Executive Committee planned a national convention in Washington, D.C., just two years after it was founded; over three hundred black women attorneys, law students, and law-related career practitioners attended. A prototype agenda was set that featured a convention topic focusing on a pertinent issue, workshops dealing with issues affecting education and employment, speakers with leadership roles in diverse areas of government and public policy, and ceremonies honoring the notable achievements of black women attorneys. As the NABWA has grown, its agenda has also grown to include annual scholarships to black female law students; seminars; an awards luncheon; a mock trial; and the annual Red Dress Ball, which serves as the major scholarship fund-raiser.

Rolark, now the NABWA president emeritus, has assumed convention roles of high visibility. During the 1986 convention in Washington, D.C., a community meeting was held at Shiloh Baptist Church, where Rolark has long held membership. At the 1988 convention, she chaired the opening community forum. In 1989, she moderated a town meeting entitled "Uprooting Drugs from the Black Community"; panel members included government officials and representatives from area communities, churches, and schools. Rolark moderated public forums at the 1990 and 1991 conventions and, at the latter event, was one of five Sadie T. M. Alexander awardees at the Red Dress Ball. In 1992, at the nineteenth annual convention, Rolark convened the kick-off event, a town meeting. In 1984 the NABWA focused on its scholarship fund for needy black female law students and, instead of hosting its annual convention, held the first Red Dress Ball and sponsored a series of seminars on International Law and Women in Politics. Rolark's husband acted as master of ceremonies at the inaugural ball and Lionel Hampton served as honorary chairperson. Hampton, a longtime and current supporter, also provided his band for the evening's entertainment. Rolark's continued service to the NABWA is notable in that most founding presidents, upon retiring, reduce their participation in their organization's activities. Few leaders have the ability and temperament to serve as members under new leaders.

Politician Serves Needy Blacks

The NABWA has not been the sole focus of Rolark's professional life. She was elected District of Columbia Democratic councilwoman for Ward Eight in November 1976 and served four terms of four years each. Rolark was ousted in 1993 in favor of then-former Washington, D.C., mayor

Marion Barry. Barry was re-elected mayor on November 8, 1994.

Barry defeated Rolark on her own turf after sixteen years of service that had greatly benefitted Ward Eight. Interestingly, he chose to do battle with a seasoned politician who had supported him during his tenure as mayor. When the district polls closed and the votes were counted, middle-class Washingtonians were shocked; they never believed that the former mayor, who now had served a prison term, could defeat a four-term pillar of the community. Although Rolark was endorsed by current mayor Sharon Pratt Kelly and the thirteen council members, no council member came into Ward Eight to campaign publicly for fear of openly confronting Barry. Many people, in and out of the district, failed to understand that Barry's marital and drug-abuse problems, six-month prison stay, and loss of a councilman-at-large race were not deterrents in the eyes of the majority of Ward Eight voters. Barry was not a fallen hero to these voters, but a black man who had defied the white judicial, economic, social, and political systems. While Rolark relied on her stellar record of accomplishments, which indeed had improved the quality of life for Ward Eight constituents, Marion Barry walked the ward streets and went door-to-door shaking hands with the people who gave him the means to defeat Rolark by a three-to-one margin.

In the July 2, 1993, interview, Rolark described Ward Eight as "a microcosm of what is happening to blacks all over America . . . an area populated by some 74,000 people mostly on AFDC, with the lowest level of home ownership, the highest percentage of young people, and the highest percentage of single female heads of households." One reason Rolark initially sought office was her steadfast philosophical opposition to business interests and her strong belief in rent control and subsidized housing. As Ward Eight councilwoman, Rolark chaired the Judiciary Committee of the council for ten years (1982-92) and was a member of the Human Services, Housing, Labor, Self-Determination, and Economic Development committees. She was a cofounder of the annual Ward Eight Martin Luther King, Jr. Birthday Parade, sponsored by the Wilhelmina J. Rolark Constituent Committee. This event, which attracts thousands of participants and onlookers, was started as a means of improving the quality of life in the area. Honoring a black leader in a black neighborhood with black participants, this parade is unique to Ward Eight.

Ward Eight constituents were beneficiaries of Rolark's efforts in securing a new fire station and the Seventh District police headquarters; in finding funding and a location for a Ward Eight Senior Citizens Center; and in gaining council approval of a ward location for the Parole Supervision Office. As chair of the Judiciary Committee, Rolark took the lead in policy making in the area of corrections throughout the District of Columbia. Many current policies originated in her office and were passed into legislation, including the Youth Rehabilitation Act, the Juvenile Protection Act, the Good Time Credits Act, and the Medical and Geriatric Parole Law. In addition, innovative drug treatment programs were institut-

ed, and a Criminal Justice Improvement Commission was established. During her ten-year tenure as chair of the Judiciary Committee, Rolark conducted oversight hearings on AIDS in the prison system and initiated a program that made the District of Columbia's Department of Corrections Volunteer Program one of the largest and best in the nation.

As a councilwoman, Rolark was instrumental in the creation of the District of Columbia Energy Office and in the passage of such laws as the Bank Depository Act, the Penalties for PCP Protection Law, the District of Columbia Cable Television Law, the Pedestrian Protection Act, the Mandatory Seat Belt Law, the Guardianship, Protective Proceedings and Durable Power of Attorney Act, the Banking Superintendent Act, and more than two hundred other pieces of legislation.

Since 1947, in her private practice, Rolark has fought for fairness and lack of bias in the courtroom. Mabel Haden, in a June 21, 1993, interview, complimented Rolark for never having been afraid of white lawyers or judges and for always speaking her mind. Although Rolark once aspired to be a judge, she has remained a practicing attorney and an active member of the Washington, D.C., and National Bar associations, the American Bar Association, the Trial Lawyers Association, and the National Association of Black Women Attorneys.

She has served as a board member of both the Legal Aid Society and the Washington Organization of Women and as a member of the Early Childhood Development Center, the District of Columbia Board of Labor Relations, and the Shiloh Baptist Church at Ninth and P Streets. She serves in the church groups Naomi Circle and Frontiers, and she helped raise money to rebuild the church after a disastrous fire. Rolark is commissioner of the District of Columbia Human Rights Commission, general counsel for the United Black Fund, and vice president of the District of Columbia Bi-Centennial Assembly. In addition to recognition from professional affiliations, Rolark has received numerous other awards and commendations as public testimony to her untiring efforts to improve the quality of life throughout Ward Eight and the greater District of Columbia. Evidence of the high esteem in which both Rolark and her husband have long been held was a 1979 tribute dinner held in their honor at which they were praised for their community activism. The dinner was attended by over six hundred guests, and former mayor Walter Washington presented the couple with a picture of the first city council.

The long list of her other prestigious awards includes the National Child Support Enforcement Association's Legislator of the Year Award, the Senior Citizens Counseling and Delivery Service's Outstanding Service to Seniors Award, Shiloh Baptist Church's Woman of the Year Award, the District of Columbia Federation of Civic Associations Outstanding Service Award, and numerous others.

Mabel Haden characterized Rolark as she saw her:

She is modest and unpretentious. . . . She dresses well, yet nicely and neatly; she is a promoter of young women interested in law careers. . . . She is one who is not jealous of advancement opportunities for other blacks. . . . She is able to think on her own in an unbiased manner.

She added, ''She was born free! She is a great lady, not a great black lady, not a great Afro-American lady, but a great lady!''

REFERENCES:

''Barry Proclaims 'Spiritual' Renewal upon Release from Pennsylvania Prison.'' *Jet* 82 (May 11, 1992): 4.

''Community Action.'' *Jet* 55 (March 1, 1979): 40.

''Dr. Calvin Rolark, United Black Fund Founder, Dies in D.C.'' *Jet* 87 (November 14, 1994): 18.

''Ex-D.C. Mayor Barry Seeks City Council Seat.'' *Jet* 82 (July 6, 1992): 6.

Forrester, Jeannette Layton. Interview with Dolores Nicholson, July 1, 1993.

Haden, Mabel D. Telephone interview with Dolores Nicholson, June 21, 1993.

''Locals Present Gift of a $25,000 Chrysler to Ex-D.C. Mayor Marion Barry.'' *Jet* 79 (January 28, 1991): 9.

''Marion Barry Makes Political Comeback in D.C. Council Win.'' *Jet* 82 (October 5, 1992): 6-8.

Myrdal, Gunnar. *An American Dilemma: The Negro Problem and Modern Democracy*. New York: Harper & Brothers, 1944.

National Association of Black Women Attorneys. *History*. Washington, D.C.: NABWA, n.d.

Rolark, Wilhelmina J. Professional Resume.

———. Telephone interview with Dolores Nicholson, July 2, 1993.

Who's Who among Black Americans, 1994-1995. 8th ed. Detroit: Gale Research, 1994.

Dolores Nicholson

Esther Rolle
(1922-)
Actress

E sther Rolle has been an actress in live theater and on television since the 1960s. Her widest fame comes from her role as Florida Evans in two television series, first as a supporting character in *Maude* and then as a star of the very popular *Good Times*. She has continued to appear on television and in movies and make guest appearances since that time. In addition, she has striven to make black heritage better known through her work in educational videos and records

Esther Rolle

and through her one-person shows based on the lives of two historically important black women, Sojournor Truth and Mary McLeod Bethune.

Esther Rolle was born on November 8, 1922, in Pompano Beach, Florida. She was the ninth of eighteen children of Jonathan and Elizabeth Davis Rolle. The family came from the Bahamas, and Rolle's older sister, Estelle Evans (1905-85), also an actress, was born in Rolle Town, in the Bahamas. Their parents encouraged the older children to form a musical and dramatic group, which performed in local churches and lodges. The group had disbanded by the time Esther Rolle was old enough to join. She studied at Booker T. Washington High School in Miami and wanted at that time to become a journalist.

Rolle came north to Harlem to live with a sister and attend school. Life there was a decided cultural shock for Rolle, and she discovered that there were advantages to growing up in the South, most notably in being able to maintain a sense of identity. She told Bob Lucas for *Ebony* magazine, June 1974, ''Segregation allowed you to know yourself,'' pointing out the importance of the black history classes taught in school and the concerned adults who served as role models. She added, ''I found blacks were lost in a sea of white with no sense of belonging, no identity. . . . I was shocked when I arrived in New York and first saw Harlem. Not a black person owned a business on the 125th St. we'd heard so much about.''

From an early age Rolle seems to have been a rebel; she says that she stopped straightening her hair long before that became fashionable. She told Ted Stewart for *Sepia,* October 1974 that she saw herself

> as a militant who's going to keep right on your tail until you adhere to the letter of the Constitution. I've always considered myself a rebel. I don't go along with the crowd. If I don't believe in what you're saying, I don't have to go along. I don't have to join. I never lost a twig by being my individual self. In our country the way things are, anybody of worth is a rebel. If you are not, you are a nobody.

If this firmness of character was not present from her earliest years, it certainly developed and became a distinguishing trait of the adult woman.

Little is known in detail of Rolle's life before the early 1960s. It is said that she studied at Spelman College, Hunter College, and the New School for Social Work. She worked in the garment industry in New York and was married to a pants presser for seven years. This, her only marriage, ended in divorce. She has no children. According to Shawn Lewis in a May 1978 *Ebony* article, she was a principal dancer for the Asadata Dafora Dance Troupe in the 1950s. Asadata Dafora (1890-1965) is an important figure in black dance. He was born in Sierra Leone and came to the United States in 1929. He was active in dance in this country between 1934 and 1959. In the 1970s Rolle would join with Zebede Collins to organize revivals of his works by the Charles Moore Company. Rolle is also listed as a dancer with the Shogola Obola Dance Company. In her later years the focus of her career switched firmly to straight drama.

Extensive Work in the Theater

Rolle's credits in the theater include two undated off-Broadway productions, *Ballet behind the Bridge* and *Ride a Black Horse,* and also tours in *The Skin of Our Teeth* and *The Crucible.* In 1961 she appeared off-Broadway again in Jean Genet's *The Blacks.* She toured in *Purlie Victorious* in 1962, and in 1964 she made her Broadway debut in James Baldwin's *Blues for Mr. Charley.* This was followed by parts in *The Amen Corner* (1965) and *Happy Ending* (1968). Also in 1968 she made her London debut in *God Is a (Guess What?).* Rolle was a founding member of the Negro Ensemble Company, and between 1968 and 1971 she appeared in seven of the company's productions. She then played off-Broadway in *Rosalie Pritchett* in 1972. By this date she had appeared in television on the police series *N.Y.P.D.* and as Sadie Gray in the daytime drama *One Life to Live.* Rolle had also appeared in the film *Nothing but a Man,* with a second movie, *Cleopatra Jones,* to be released in 1973.

Launches Television Career

Rolle was starring in *Don't Play Us Cheap,* a musical by Melvin Van Peebles, and drawing a salary of $140 a week when she was asked in 1972 to join Norman Lear's television show *Maude* in the role of a sassy maid named Florida Evans. In spite of the money, she spurned the offer until she was assured that she would not be playing a stereotypical black maid and that she could provide her own input into the conception of the character. In *Maude* Rolle made such an impact on audiences that Lear developed the show *Good Times* to showcase her talent. The show was created by black writers Eric Monte, who had grown up in a Chicago project, and Mike Evans. Rolle insisted on and won the right to change lines she found objectionable.

Premiering in 1974, *Good Times* soon became one of the highest-rated shows on television. Since the series was a situation comedy featuring a black family living in a high-rise Chicago welfare project, it drew criticism as well as praise from black critics. It was accused of perpetuating black stereotypes. One critic quoted in *Sepia* in October 1974 called it "*Amos 'n' Andy* in the kitchen." Rolle responded in the same article, "Pooh, 98 to 99 per cent of it is reality. I couldn't participate fully if I didn't believe in it." However, she became more and more disgruntled as the show continued and left the program in 1977. She explained her departure in the May 1978 *Ebony* article: "Then the show got sillier and sillier and worse and worse, and I simply didn't want to do it anymore. Because of my values, and not being able to come to an understanding, I left." Rolle was persuaded to resume the role for the 1978-79 season.

In 1978 she began working on a one-person show about Sojourner Truth, *Ain't I a Woman.* She has toured widely in it with great success over the years. In 1990 she developed a similar one-person show based on the life of Mary McLeod Bethune. The one-person shows and a tour with *A Raisin in the Sun* in 1987 represent Rolle's major work in live theater since her departure from *Good Times.* She has also appeared in films, including *The Mighty Quinn* (1989) and *Driving Miss Daisy* (1990). The bulk of her work has been on television and in educational videos. She won an Emmy for her performance in the television movie *Summer of My German Soldier* in 1978, and in February 1989 she won rave notices for her role in a new television production of *A Raisin in the Sun.*

In addition to the Emmy, Rolle received an NAACP Image Award in 1975 for best actress in a television series and the AFT (AFL-CIO) Human Rights Award in 1983. In 1990 the NAACP honored her with its Leadership Award.

In 1991 Rolle received a much-appreciated honor when she was inducted into the Black Filmmakers Hall of Fame. She told Leisha Stewart for *Ebony,* June 1991, that "the honor was more 'emotionally impressive'" than any other she'd received. This was so, Rolle continued, "because it was from my own. I have never been given the chance I deserve in the mainstream industry. They never get beyond me as a maid. Black film, on the other hand, has seen something in me that mainstream didn't see or acknowledge."

In 1990 it seemed for a while that Rolle's career might come to an end. The car she was riding in rolled over on the interstate near the Nevada-California border, and she was seriously injured. Eleven of her ribs were shattered, and the orbit of her left eye was damaged. Thanks to skilled care and her indomitable spirit, she recovered. Esther Rolle remains active, touring with her one-person show and working on many other projects. Above all she continues to nurture the black pride that she herself so capably represents.

Current Address: c/o Traid Artist Inc., 10100 Santa Monica Boulevard, Los Angeles, CA 90067.

REFERENCES:

Haskins, James. *Black Dance in America*. New York: Harper Trophy, 1990.

Kisner, Ronald E. "New Comedy Brings Good Times to TV." *Jet* 46 (May 23, 1974): 58-60.

Klotman, Phyllis Rauch. *Frame by Frame—A Black Filmography*. Bloomington: Indiana University Press, 1979.

Lewis, Shawn. "Esther Rolle." *Ebony* 33 (May 1978): 91-96.

Lucas, Bob. "A 'Salt Pork and Collard Greens' TV Show." *Ebony* 29 (June 1974): 50-53.

Mapp, Edward. *Directory of Blacks in the Performing Arts*. 2d ed. Metuchen, N.J.: Scarecrow Press, 1990.

"'Raisin' Doesn't Typify Black Family Life: Rolle." *Jet* 72 (April 27, 1987): 59.

"Rolle in Fair Condition, Moved to UCLA Center." *Jet* 78 (September 10, 1990): 18.

Stewart, Leisha. "Esther Rolle: Good Times Continue for *Good Times* Star." *Ebony* 46 (June 1991): 64-66.

Stewart, Ted. "What's Happening to Black TV Stars." *Sepia* 23 (October 1974): 36-46.

Who's Who among Black Americans, 1994-95. 8th ed. Detroit: Gale Research, 1994.

                                                              Robert L. Johns

Rollins, Ida Nelson
See Nelson Rollins, Ida Gray

Lucille Mason Rose
(1918-1987)
Civic worker, political activist

Lucille Mason Rose, a longtime civil servant in New York City, was also a servant to humanity. She found training opportunities and jobs for unskilled workers. She served on numerous boards because, as she wrote in her own obituary published in the August 29, 1987, issue of the *New York Amsterdam News*, "she was committed to God and her fellow man."

Lucille Mason Rose

Lucille Mason Rose was born in Richmond, Virginia, on September 27, 1918. When she was seven years old, her family moved to the largely black Bedford-Stuyvesant section of Brooklyn, New York. There they opened a small restaurant, the Mason Dining Room. She attended Public School Number 3 and graduated from Girls High School in 1937. While a high school student, she became a member of the Brooklyn branch of the NAACP. After her father's death, she helped her mother in the restaurant, often leaving school during her lunch hour to serve the customers.

During World War II her husband, Peyton Rose, enlisted in the service. She became a welding trainee at the Brooklyn Navy Yard, where many of the largest warships were built. She worked on the battleship *Missouri*. She and her husband had one son, Cornelius. She received her B.A. degree from Brooklyn College in 1951 and later enrolled in the night program, receiving a degree in economics in 1963. She also held a master's degree in manpower planning and development from the New School for Social Research.

In her twenty-eight years working for the city of New York, Rose held many positions. Her first job, in 1949, was as a fiscal clerk in the Department of Social Services. According to the *New York Times,* in 1977 she said of the many jobs she had held, "I've gone step by step. They haven't let me skip a step." In 1963, under Mayor Robert Wagner, she became director of the Brooklyn Field Office of the New York City Department of Labor. The office was located in the Bedford-Stuyvesant area, a locale with many unskilled workers and people with little education. Soon after she went there, Rose developed various programs to upgrade skills and was soon making placements in the work force. The office was not an employment office, but the staff was engaged in helping young people learn about training programs and new and better job opportunities. According to the *Amsterdam News,* "she is charming, gracious, with tremendous know-how" and "was already making a vital contribution to the community when she was chosen for this challenging job. . . . [She] has a way of cutting through hindrances and getting things done."

In 1965, she received from the Sisterhood of Concord Baptist Church the Woman In Action Award for "outstanding service in grateful recognition for untiring services rendered to humanity." The award cited Rose for service as director of the Bedford-Stuyvesant Office of the New York City Department of Labor and for enabling employment of youth and adults. This service was called distinguished and invaluable, and despite the pressure of duties in both public and private endeavor, the award noted that she continued to work to improve the Brooklyn community.

Deputy Mayor Named

In 1966, Rose became the first director of the Bedford-Stuyvesant Manpower Center. In 1970, Mayor John Lindsay named her assistant commissioner, and later first deputy commissioner, for the city's Manpower and Career Development Agency. She remained there until 1972, when Mayor Abraham Beame named her commissioner of the New York City Department of Employment. The agency located job openings, placed people, and then trained them on the job. In 1977, Mayor Beame named her deputy mayor for Planning and Manpower. She was the first woman to be appointed a deputy mayor. Even with this high position, she still did menial tasks such as sweeping the sidewalk in front of her house and picking up the trash. After retirement, she continued as a manpower consultant part-time, with contracts from the federal government.

Also in 1977, the Brooklyn College Alumni Association honored her by naming her Alumna of the Year. This award is presented annually to recognize a "graduate who has achieved distinction in her field, has made a noteworthy contribution to the community and has reflected credit upon the college," reported the *New York Amsterdam News* on October 22, 1977.

Friends and associates called Rose the "Lady Dean of Black Women's Politics in Brooklyn." For many years, she was an active member of the NAACP. She served as New York State Program Chair and was an Executive Member of Social Service and a Golden Heritage Subscribing Member. In the 1960s, she was secretary and membership chair of the Brooklyn chapter of the NAACP. During that time, its membership grew to be the largest in the state, and it received several awards. She served on the National Democratic Executive Committee and was a member of the Democratic National Committee at the time of her death. In 1980, she was a delegate to the Democratic National Convention. She was a founding director of the Bedford-Stuyvesant Restoration Corporation. From 1983 until her death she served as vice-chair of the board. She volunteered her services to many organizations and received over one hundred awards for her work.

Among the local organizations she served were the Catholic Medical Center of Brooklyn and Queens, Central Brooklyn Coordinating Council, Community Planning Board 3, Key Women, Medgar Evers College, St. Francis College, St. Mary's Hospital, and the Salvation Army Brooklyn Advisory Council. Shortly before her death, she was elected president of the Bedford-Stuyvesant Brooklyn Chapter of the Lioness Club. In addition, she was active with the Coalition of One Hundred Black Women, the National Association of Negro Business and Professional Women, and the New York Urban Coalition.

From 1981 to 1985, Rose served as the first woman president of the Catholic Interracial Council. In 1985, the Council presented her with the John LaFarge Memorial award for interracial justice. She also served for many years on the board of the National Conference of Christians and Jews.

Rose converted to the Catholic faith in 1951 and attended Our Lady of Victory Church. She died August 15, 1987. She wrote her own order of service for the funeral, as well as her obituary. Her funeral was attended by approximately one thousand people, including Mayor Edward Koch of New York, three former mayors, and many high public officials, current and past, including former Congresswoman Shirley Chisholm, Manhattan Borough President David Dinkins, and former Manhattan Borough President Percy Sutton. Rose wrote in her obituary published in the August 29, 1987, issue of the *New York Amsterdam News:*

> Her church and her community were the center of her life for she was committed to God and her fellow man. She served on most of the boards of the organizations in the neighborhood, in the city, state and nation to help others, so her living was not in vain. She worked for the glory of God.

With the death of Lucille Mason Rose, the Bedford-Stuyvesant community lost a dedicated member of the community. Friends described Rose as a person of commitment, courage, concern and compassion for people of every race. She knew no color line.

REFERENCES:

Davis, Marianna W., ed. *Contributions of Black Women to America.* Vol. I. Columbia, S.C.: Kenday Press, 1982.

"Lucille Mason Rose, 67, First Woman Deputy Mayor." *Jet* 72 (September 24, 1987): 52.

New York Amsterdam News, April 23, 1966; October 22, 1977; August 22, 1987; August 29, 1987.

New York Times, August 18, 1987; August 19, 1987; August 20, 1987.

Ploski, Harry A., and Warren Marr II. *Negro Almanac.* 3rd ed. New York: Bellwether, 1976.

Who's Who in American Politics, 1985-86. 12th ed. New York: Bowker, 1985.

Ruth Edmonds Hill

Gertrude E. Durden Rush
(1880-1962)
Lawyer, educator, lecturer, organization founder, playwright, club leader

Gertrude E. Durden Rush was best known for her pioneering work in law: she was the first black woman admitted to the Iowa Bar and a cofounder of the National Bar Association. Until the 1950s she was the only black woman to practice law in Iowa. She held positions in national and local organizations in Des Moines and became known as well for her work with the Iowa Federation of Colored Women's Clubs and the National Baptist Women's Convention.

The daughter of Frank Durden, a Baptist minister, and Sarah E. Reinhardt Durden, Gertrude Elzora Durden Rush was born in Navasota, Texas, on August 5, 1880. The family moved to various locations in Kansas, then settled in Oskaloosa. Gertrude Rush studied at the Parsons, Kansas, high school from 1895 to 1898 and completed high school in Quincy, Illinois. Between 1898 and 1907 Rush appears to have been a teacher; however, the dates for her teaching career at different sites are unclear. She is said to have begun teaching with a high school diploma in Oswego, Kansas, where she remained for three years, and to have served in the Des Moines, Iowa, public schools. Some sources say that she taught in Des Moines from 1898 to 1905 while others say that she taught in government schools in the Indian Territory of Oklahoma for four years. She began the study of law in 1908 under James Buchanan Rush, whom she had married on December 23, 1907; she would work in his law office for a number of years.

James Buchanan Rush (1861-1918) was born near Peking, in Montgomery County, North Carolina, and later served as editor of *The People's Sentinel* in Greensboro. He attended Howard University School of Law and was admitted to the Indiana bar in 1892. He practiced law in Indianapolis from 1892 to 1894, in Fort Smith, Arkansas, from 1895 to 1898, and in Des Moines from 1898 to 1918. He was counsel for the North Star Temple Association, which was organized to purchase buildings in Des Moines for blacks who were starting businesses. He was also vice-president of the Des Moines Business League, a delegate to the Republican State Convention, and for two years campaign speaker for U.S. Senator Albert Cummins. J. Clay Smith wrote in *Emancipation* that one of James Rush's "most significant contributions was to the legal education of his wife, Gertrude Elzora Durden Rush."

Sources differ on the extent of Gertrude Rush's education after her graduation from high school. According to Frank L. Mather in *Who's Who of the Colored Race,* she also studied at the Westerman Music Conservatory of Des Moines. According to other sources, beginning in either 1908 or 1910 Rush studied at Des Moines College, receiving her A.B. degree in 1914. In 1919 Rush graduated from Quincy Business College. She completed her third year of law study in

Gertrude E. Durden Rush

1914 by correspondence at LaSalle Extension University of Chicago. She passed the bar examination and was admitted to the Iowa Bar in 1918, becoming the first black woman admitted to practice law in Iowa. Although another black woman, Beulah Wheeler, is known to have been admitted to the Iowa State Bar before 1945, some sources say she did not practice in the state. Thus, until 1950, Rush was the only black woman practicing attorney in Iowa. According to the article "To Celebrate Founder's Day" from an unidentified newspaper in the National Bar Association archives, Rush was "the first race woman to practice law in the middle west." (Violette Neatley Anderson passed the Illinois Bar in 1920.)

James Rush died before Gertrude Rush was admitted to the bar; afterward she took over his practice. She was elected president of the Iowa Colored Bar Association in 1921. J. Clay Smith called her the first woman in the nation to head a state bar group whose members included men and women. Commenting further on the importance of state and national bar groups founded by blacks, Smith said that black women lawyers "liberated themselves" at the group meetings. Reflecting on her life as a black and a woman lawyer, Rush once said that race had presented no particular problem, but early in her career clients let her know that they were bothered by her gender. In time, however, gender was not an issue.

Founds National Bar Association

After Rush was denied admission to the American Bar Association, in 1925 she and four black male lawyers—Joe Brown, James Morris, Charles Howard, Sr., and George

Woodson—founded the Negro Bar Association, which was later renamed the National Bar Association. Since blacks were ineligible for membership in white law associations because of their race, the NBA was clear in its purpose: to unite black lawyers for strength in any national emergency. Rush was also the only woman present at the NBA's first meeting. Although she was a cofounder, she is often called simply the first woman admitted to the National Bar Association. In 1982 the NBA established the Gertrude E. Rush Award, a trophy given annually during its Mid-Year Conference. According to Darren L. Smith's *Black Americans Information Directory,* the trophy was "to recognize individuals who have demonstrated leadership ability in the community within their profession; a pioneer spirit in the pursuit of civil and human rights; and excellence in legal education and perseverance in the law, public policy or social activism."

Rush was firm in her opinions regarding women's legal rights in estate cases. She contended in a probate case that a wife was entitled to receive her husband's earnings for three months prior to his death, exempt from all claims, and she was relieved when the Supreme Court concurred, forbidding an administrator from taking the money.

At some point Rush set up practice in Illinois, maintaining an office in that state and one in Des Moines, Iowa, at 907 Walnut Street. Gertrude Rush worked through a number of channels as she contributed to community uplift. The Iowa Association of Club Women, known first as the Iowa Federation of Afro-American Women's Clubs, was organized on May 27, 1902, in Ottumwa, Iowa. In 1910 the Iowa Federation affiliated with the National Association of Colored Women's Clubs (NACW) and was incorporated in 1913. From 1911 to 1915 Rush was state president and still later served as chairperson of the Mother's Department of the NACW. Her legal training led to her appointment as chairperson of the Legislature Department of the NACW. She remained active in the women's club movement until her death.

In 1912 Rush organized the Charity League, whose chief concern was with the welfare of black people in Des Moines. The organization was successful in having a black probation officer appointed in the Des Moines Juvenile Court. She guided the league in founding the Protection Home for Negro Girls, providing shelter for working girls at a nominal fee. The home operated until 1930. Rush's concern for the welfare of poor blacks in Des Moines led her to serve as a social case worker in the Associated Charities of the town.

In 1920 Rush became chairperson of the Citizenship Department of the Woman's Auxiliary to the National Baptist Convention. She was also elected attorney for the Woman's Auxiliary in 1924 and still held the position in 1950. In connection with her work with the auxiliary, she attended international Baptist conferences in Europe, Asia, and Africa. She also travelled widely in the United States. She often spoke to local groups, such as the Current Topic Study Club, drawing large audiences who came to hear the woman attorney discuss her travel experiences in the Holy Land and elsewhere. In 1950 she was vice-president of the board of the

National Baptist Convention's missionary training school in Nashville, Tennessee.

Although the extent of her work in suffrage is unknown, she was a member of the Colored Woman's Suffrage Club. Also active in other local organizations, Rush was a charter member of the Board of Directors of the Des Moines Health Center and the Dramatic Art Club and on the board of directors of the Des Moines Playground Association. From 1924 to 1926 she was secretary of the Des Moines Comfort Station Commission. Rush organized the Woman's Law and Political Study Club. She became a delegate to the Half-Century Exposition of Negro Emancipation held in Philadelphia and was a member of a committee to secure an appropriation for the Iowa Negro Exposition. She held membership in the Parliamentary Club of Des Moines and the Order of the Eastern Star. Rush was a charter member of the Blue Triangle YWCA and a member of the NAACP. She was an honorary member of Delta Sigma Theta Sorority.

Active in Research and Writing

By the 1950s Rush was as well known for her work in religion as she was in law. According to the article "Iowa's Only Negro Woman Lawyer Relies Firmly on the Golden Rule," from an unidentified newspaper in the Public Library of Des Moines, "a very worn Bible is almost as prominent as the well-thumbed Iowa code on the desk of Mrs. Gertrude E. Rush." Local court officials often called her the "Sunday school lawyer." She was well versed in the Bible and Biblical names and had read the Bible annually each year for ten years. Then active in research and writing, she began an exhaustive study of the 240 women of the Bible, completing stories on women of the Old Testament and beginning stories on those of the New Testament.

A woman of many talents and interests, Gertrude Rush became a playwright early in her life. The article "Iowa Colored Woman is Playwright," whose source and date are unknown, recognized her work as a new playwright and said that she had "written and staged one of the most beautiful sentimental dramas on the American stage." The reference was to "Royal or Shadowed Love," a love story filled with pathos and feeling from beginning to end. The article called Rush a woman with "literary ability of a high order." She staged *Paradise Lost* under the new title, *Satan's Revenge.* She wrote a number of pageants, including *Sermon on the Mount,* 1907; *Uncrowned Heroines,* 1912, and *Black Girls' Burden,* 1913. There is no known record of other plays by Rush until the late 1920s when she wrote patriotic works such as *Building the American Flag,* 1927; *Links in the American Union,* 1927; and *True Framers of the American Constitution,* 1928. Rush was also a songwriter. Her songs, all published by G. E. Durden, include "If You But Knew," 1905; "Jesus Loves Little Children," 1907; and "Christmas Day."

Rush was slowed by a stroke she suffered in 1958, causing her to partially retire from community service. She died of a stroke on Wednesday night, September 5, 1962, at Broadlawns Polk County Hospital in Des Moines. Funeral services were held at Corinthian Baptist Church, where she had been a longtime member and trustee. She was buried in Glendale Cemetery. Rush was survived by a brother, Albert O. Durden, who had relocated from Chicago to live with her in her residence at 1160 Thirteenth Street.

In 1991 a limestone sculpture honoring the founders of the NBA was unveiled at the Des Moines Public Library at 100 Locust Avenue, the location of the NBA's archives. A second monument in Rush's honor is located at St. Paul AME Church in Des Moines. In August 1994 Rush and three other women were inducted into the Iowa Women's Hall of Fame in a ceremony held in the State Historical Building Auditorium. In recognition of Rush's accomplishments, the Iowa Commission on the Status of Women wrote a tribute to her published in the September/October 1994 issue of *Iowa Woman*. Rush was a pioneer black woman lawyer who devoted more than forty years to legal activities. Her life balanced by work in civic, fraternal, legal, and religious affairs both in Des Moines and at the national level, Gertrude Durden Rush enhanced the educational and cultural life of her race.

REFERENCES:

"Attorney Gertrude E. Rush, 79, Passes." *Iowa Bystander,* September 13, 1962.

"First Race Woman Attorney of Iowa." *Chicago Defender,* November 14, 1925.

"Iowa Colored Woman is Playwright." Unidentified newspaper clipping, National Bar Association Archives, Public Library of Des Moines.

Iowa Commission on the Status of Women. [Biographical statement.] *Iowa Woman,* September/October, 1994.

"Iowa's Only Negro Woman Lawyer Relies Firmly on the Golden Rule." *Des Moines Register,* January 22, 1950.

Mather, Frank Lincoln, ed. *Who's Who of the Colored Race.* Chicago: n.p., 1915.

"Mrs. Rush Dies Here." *Des Moines Tribune,* September 6, 1962.

"Only Colored Woman Now Member State Bar." *Des Moines Tribune,* October 4, 1918.

"Parliamentary Club to Honor Rush." *Des Moines Register,* February 24, 1983.

"Pioneering Lives Are Remembered." *Des Moines Register,* August 23, 1994.

"Sculpture at Library to Be Unveiled Monday." *Des Moines Register,* July 11, 1991.

Smith, Darren, ed. *Black Americans Information Directory.* Detroit: Gale Research, 1990.

Smith, J. Clay, Jr. *Emancipation: The Making of the Black Lawyer 1844-1944.* Philadelphia: University of Pennsylvania Press, 1993.

"Study Club Presents Noted Woman Lawyer." Unidentified newspaper clipping, National Bar Association Archives, Public Library of Des Moines.

Wesley, Charles Harris. *The History of the National Association of Colored Women's Clubs.* Washington, D.C.: NACW, 1984.

Who's Who in Colored America. New York: Who's Who in Colored America Corp., 1927.

Who's Who in Colored America. 5th ed. Brooklyn: Thomas Yenser, 1940.

Who's Who in Colored America. 7th ed. Yonkers-on-Hudson, N.Y.: Christian E. Burckel, 1950.

Jessie Carney Smith

Patricia A. Russell-McCloud
(1946-)
Educator, lawyer, motivational speaker, entrepreneur

Russell-McCloud was a high-ranking attorney for the Federal Communications Commission when she started a second successful career as a professional orator. Her speech entitled "If Not You—Who? If Not Now—When?" first delivered at a breakfast in Cleveland, Ohio, for the National Association of Negro Business and Professional Women in April 1980, helped to launch her on her journey toward becoming a much sought after motivational speaker. She has her own corporation, Russell-McCloud and Associates, that provides speakers for a variety of audiences and offers training in the art of motivational speaking. She is regarded as one of the most dynamic speakers in America today, and her presentations have been described as brilliant and challenging. Commenting on her style in a publicity piece, Robert Wolgemuth insists that to say she is "an effective communicator would be akin to saying Renoir knew how to paint!"

Born in Indianapolis, Indiana, on September 14, 1946, Patricia Russell-McCloud was the last child and third daughter of Willie and Janniel Russell. Her parents were hardworking citizens. Her father did maintenance and custodial jobs and her mother was a domestic matron. While Willie and Janniel Russell faced limited opportunities, they had great expectations for their daughters, Barbara, Verdie, and Patricia. As in many African American families, the parents believed the church and the school were avenues for success. When she was a young child, it was common to see Patricia standing in a starched, ruffled dress with a crinoline slip reciting Bible verses and Easter speeches or a Christmas part in the local Baptist church her family attended regularly.

When in 1952 it was time for her to attend school, she held her teachers in the same high esteem as the preacher and her Sunday school teachers. By the time Russell-McCloud was eight years old, she had discovered the power of the human voice. She sang in church and in her school choirs, and she also took pride in giving welcome addresses and winning oratorical contests.

In high school Russell-McCloud's interest turned to history and political science. Given that her high school years

Patricia A. Russell-McCloud

occurred during the height of the civil rights movement—the Birmingham bombings, the March on Washington—this interest was natural and fed by evening news bulletins with Walter Cronkite announcing the number of blacks arrested for singing and praying for freedom or with flashes of black and white footage of demonstrators being attacked by water hoses and police dogs. Russell-McCloud was involved in the speech and drama club and the choir. When she graduated from Shortridge High School in June 1964, she planned to attend Kentucky State University and major in history and political science.

At Kentucky State Russell-McCloud continued to pursue her interest in public speaking, and her willingness to assist others made her a natural leader. At the end of her first year she was voted Outstanding Freshman. As a member of the Kentucky Players, a drama troupe, she often traveled to other campuses to perform. Also as a member of the concert choir, she sang alto; Russell-McCloud was frequently on stage. Of all her activities, the one she recalls most vividly was her experience pledging the black Alpha Kappa Alpha Sorority.

Her senior year, Russell-McCloud was faced with indecision relating to her choices for the future. Although she had prepared herself to teach—a safe, respectable profession—the outside world of the 1960s continued to intrude. On April 4, 1968, Russell-McCloud, shocked and saddened by the news of Martin Luther King's death, flirted with the idea of going to law school.

On Mother's Day weekend, 1968, Russell-McCloud received her bachelor of arts degree and, as a graduating

senior, was elected to Who's Who in American Colleges and Universities. Two opportunities presented themselves following her college graduation. The Detroit Public School System had offered her a job, and she had also been chosen by the Council on Legal Educational Opportunity (CLEO) to attend a special program at Harvard that would prepare her for law school. Because a steady income is so important for students from working-class backgrounds, Russell-McCloud signed the contract with the Detroit Public Schools. But she also attended Harvard during the summer of 1968.

Teacher and Lawyer

The Harvard program intensified her interest in law, but because she had signed a contract she felt compelled to honor it. Therefore, September found her at Foch Junior High School as a teacher instead of in law school as a student. She spent only one year at Foch, even though she enjoyed teaching and thought her students were wonderful and eager to learn. Detroit was too far from home. The next school year found Russell-McCloud at Arsenal Technical High School in Indianapolis. She preferred teaching high school to junior high school, but ultimately she knew the intellectual stretch she needed she would find in law school.

In the fall of 1970 Russell-McCloud entered Howard University Law School in Washington, D.C. Her experience there was intellectually stimulating and challenging. Russell-McCloud remembers Howard as a law school deeply committed to civil rights, and she was proud to be part of a tradition that produced such brilliant civil rights attorneys as Thurgood Marshall and those who preceded even him. But this tradition, which had been mostly male, was part of the challenge that she faced as a member of the first class consisting of more women than men. One incident in particular remains vivid in her memory. A young male first-year law student watched her take notes and commented: "You take notes so well, you should be a legal secretary."

Even though Russell-McCloud received a scholarship to attend law school, she still found it necessary to work in order to subsist and to buy books. From 1970 to 1973 she taught history at Federal City College (now known as the University of the District of Columbia) in Washington, D.C. In May 1973 Russell-McCloud graduated from Howard University Law School with the juris doctor degree. That summer she sat for and passed the Indiana Bar, and subsequently she was admitted to the District of Columbia Bar and the United States Supreme Court Bar Association.

Russell-McCloud's first job as a newly licensed attorney was with the Federal Communications Commission (FCC) in Washington, D.C. By 1975 she had risen to the highest level of employment within the commission. As chief of complaints, the Branch-Broadcast Bureau, FCC, she managed a staff of twenty-seven persons and had the power to recommend fines or revoke the licenses of 7500 broadcast stations.

In the eyes of her working-class family, Russell-McCloud had it all: education and a good government job! But she was bored. She began expending her energies on her avocation—

public speaking. Touring colleges, universities, and secondary schools, she talked to young people about fulfilling their dreams. On one of these speaking tours in Huntsville, Alabama, in 1982, she met Earl McCloud, Jr., an assistant professor of military science at Alabama Agricultural and Mechanical University and a minister.

Motivational Speakers Corporation Founded

On March 12, 1983, she married E. Earl McCloud, Jr., and moved to San Antonio, Texas. Leaving her high-pressure government job, Russell-McCloud decided to start her own business. Her husband encouraged her efforts, so in April 1983 she formed Russell-McCloud and Associates, a corporation of which she is president. Russell-McCloud and Associates is a motivational speaking and training organization that provides speakers for diverse audiences and has a mail order cassette and videotape service available for Russell-McCloud's most popular recorded speeches.

Russell-McCloud and her husband moved to Atlanta, Georgia, in 1985, where Earl McCloud completed a doctor of divinity degree at the Interdenominational Theological Center. Since her move to Atlanta, Russell-McCloud's business has flourished. From Atlanta, Russell-McCloud travels more than 400,000 miles a year and gives more than two hundred speeches to corporations, schools, colleges, universities, and government and civic organizations. She has made presentations throughout the United States, Great Britain, the Caribbean, and West Africa.

A typical day for Russell-McCloud begins with her going to the airport. She is a familiar face at Atlanta's Hartfield International Airport. Usually she catches the red eye, a 5:45 A.M. flight that enables her to be almost anywhere on the East Coast by nine or ten A.M. She then works all day and might be the keynote speaker at an evening banquet. If she spends the night in the city where she speaks, she catches a return red eye to Atlanta and is home by mid-morning. Highly energetic, she thrives on her busy schedule.

Russell-McCloud credits her mother for her success. Her mother's vision provided the inspiration she needed to believe in herself. "She was a noncollege-educated woman who always had a broader vision—a mind-set that encouraged one to believe that the sky is not the limit after all. I didn't think about obstacles and stumbling blocks, I just thought about the room at the top," Russell-McCloud recalled in a February 21, 1994, interview.

The most important results of her new career have been that she has fulfilled her dreams by owning her own business and that she enables others to find their true niches. As she stated in an interview, she has heard from many people who "felt they were caught in the clutch of circumstances by jobs, a marriage, or parenting" who have said, "You have made a difference in my life."

Russell-McCloud challenges those who listen to her to learn from her example and to take control of their own lives. "Whatever you want to be or do, it's your life, and you have a mandate to live it," she says. Russell-McCloud often ends her motivational speeches by telling her audience, "Good intentions do not make a success. You must move past neutral. You have to get in gear. Step out. Climb up. Get started. Go forth!"

The National Association of American Universities and Land Grant Colleges honored Russell-McCloud as outstanding alumna in 1981. She received the same honor from the National Association for Equal Opportunity in Higher Education. A participant in the Friendship Force, a goodwill tour of Mexico during the Carter administration, Russell-McCloud also holds keys to seventy-five American cities. She is an honorary member of the National Negro Business and Professional Women's Clubs. In 1982 she received the NAACP Education and Legal Defense Award. Honorary doctorate degrees have been awarded to Russell-McCloud by Bethune Cookman College, Kentucky State University, and North Carolina Central University. Russell-McCloud is a member of several boards, including the Links, the Links Foundation, and MINACT.

Recognized early in her life for her public speaking talent, Patricia Russell-McCloud has turned her skill as a motivational speaker into a service that inspires her audiences and demonstrates the multitalented capacity of America's black women. She has been recognized for her contributions and at the same time encourages others to recognize their own talent.

Current Address: Russell-McCloud and Associates, P.O. Box 2645, Peachtree City, GA 30269.

REFERENCES:

McCloud-Russell, Patricia. Telephone interview with Nagueyalti Warren, February 21, 1994.
"Testimonials, Patricia Russell-McCloud." Publicity piece. N.d.
Who's Who among Black Americans, 1980-1981. 3d ed. Northbrook, Ill.: Who's Who among Black Americans, Inc., 1981.

COLLECTIONS:

Robert D. Wolgemuth's *Testimonials,* 1984, are in the files of McCloud and Associates.

Nagueyalti Warren

S

Elizabeth Thorn Scott
(?-1867)
Educator, school founder, church worker

For establishing pioneer schools in both Sacramento and Oakland in the mid-1800s, Elizabeth Thorn Scott occupies an important place in the struggle to open up educational opportunities for African American children in California. Despite the significance of her contributions, the information available on Scott does not provide a full picture of her life.

Although the year of her birth is not documented, it is known that Elizabeth Thorn Scott was born in New Bedford, Massachusetts. During the Gold Rush—probably in the 1840s—she went to California, as a widow, and settled in Sacramento with her three children. In 1855 she married Isaac Flood, a man with many civic and social concerns. From the unclear records about his life, it appears that he was born in South Carolina in about 1815 and lived as a slave until he was freed in 1838 by his owner, William Brisbane. He then traveled with a son to California by ship in 1848, living for a while in El Dorado County. In about 1852 he moved to Brooklyn, California, a community near Lake Merritt that was annexed to the city of Oakland in 1872.

Elizabeth Thorn Scott

Schools for African American Children Established

Even though California was admitted to the Union as a nonslave state, the original public schools there operated on a segregated basis, first de facto and then from 1860 until 1872 under legislation that excluded black, Chinese, and Native American children. In response to the lack of educational opportunities for boys and girls of color, Scott established the first school in the state for these nonwhite children on May 29, 1854. It was a private school, and classes were held in the basement of Sacramento's St. Andrews Church, the first African Methodist Episcopal (AME) church on the Pacific coast. For her services as teacher she received fifty dollars a month—collected from the one dollar weekly tuition fees paid by the parents of the fourteen students.

The following year, after her marriage to Flood, Scott moved to her husband's home in Brooklyn, California, thus leaving the Sacramento school without a teacher. However, it reopened under the direction of Reverend Jeremiah B. Sanderson, a trailblazer in promoting education for African American students in San Francisco and Massachusetts. Some time later St. Andrews Church took responsibility for the school.

After settling in Brooklyn and becoming aware that there was no formal schooling available to the black children of the community, Scott solicited the cooperation of the children's parents to fill this need. In 1857, she opened another private school, this time in her home at 1334 East Fifteenth Street, near Fourteenth Avenue.

When the Board of Education of Oakland relocated the all-white Carpentier School to another site in 1864, the Shiloh AME Church purchased the building that was left vacant for the price of fifty dollars and transported it to the corner of Seventh and Market streets in West Oakland. This small, twenty-two by thirty-eight-foot one-room structure became the chapel of the church and the new site of Scott's school, where she continued to teach. When Scott died unexpectedly in 1867, the private school closed its doors, having survived for a decade after she founded it in Brooklyn.

Scott's school, along with the historic AME Mission that she and Isaac Flood helped to establish in 1858, are thought to be the first organizations for black people in Oakland and in Alameda County. The mission developed into the Shiloh AME Church, and then First AME, which still stands in North Oakland at the intersection of Telegraph Avenue and Thirty-seventh Street.

Isaac Flood worked as a paper hanger, laborer, steward, and whitewasher, as well as operating several small businesses. At one time he joined the search for gold in El Dorado County. He was part of the 1867 expedition of the *Petrel,* a schooner that sailed to Cocos Island, about 325 miles from Costa Rica, seeking buried treasure. There are no records to confirm the results of the crew's efforts. Flood returned to California in 1868, the year after Scott died, and worked actively for his church, for civil rights, and for the development of schools for black children. His presentations to the Oakland Board of Education had a decisive influence upon the opening of public schools to African American boys and girls. Flood was a well-known, well-respected citizen of Oakland until his death in about 1887.

Of the four children in Scott and Flood's family—Theodore, Horatio, George, and Lydia—the best known is Lydia Flood Jackson, born in 1862 in the home on East Fifteenth Street in Oakland where her mother had established a school. As an adult she was an effective speaker, well known for her ability to rally audiences to action for civil rights causes and issues having to do with women's rights.

Elizabeth Thorn Scott gave freely of her time and capabilities to her Methodist church, providing leadership in its involvement in the religious and social activities of the Oakland area during the nineteenth century. Her greatest contribution, however, was in the creation of educational opportunities for African American children, for whom there were no adequate schools.

REFERENCES:

Beasley, Delilah L. *Negro Trail Blazers of California.* 1911. Reprint. New York: Negro Universities Press, 1969.

Berkeley Interracial Committee. *Achievements of the Negro in California.* Chicago: Board of Education, City of Chicago, 1945.

Hausler, Donald. "Blacks in Early Oakland: 1852-1900." Unpublished manuscript.

———. "Elizabeth Flood's School: Oakland's First African American Institution." *Oakland Heritage Alliance News* 12 (Winter 1992-93): 3-4.

Jackson, George F. *Black Women Makers of History, A Portrait.* Windsor, Calif.: National Women's History Project, 1975.

Lapp, Rudolph M. *Blacks in Gold Rush California.* New Haven, Conn.: Yale University Press, 1977.

"Lydia Flood Jackson." *Oakland Tribune,* April 12, 1959.

COLLECTIONS:

Information on Elizabeth Thorn Scott can be found in the Northern California Center for Afro-American History and Life, Oakland, California.

Dona L. Irvin

Catherine Seal
(c. 1874-1930)
Religious leader

Catherine Seal (some sources say Seals), known to her followers as Mother Catherine, was the founder of her own Spiritualist Christian sect, which flourished during the 1920s in New Orleans and elevated her to the level of a living black deity, adored and revered by a multiracial following numbering in the thousands. Not since the days of her predecessor, voodoo priestess Marie Laveau, had the city paid such homage to a religious leader of color.

Some of the vital statistics of Catherine Seal's life are either unknown or open to question. Her will was written on October 11, 1929, at the request of white followers, who feared that after her death her estate would be taken over by the government. It gives her original name as Nanny and lists her father as Bill Cowans and her stepmother as Lue Cowans. Her birth mother is unidentified. It cites her place of birth as Hustonville, Kentucky, which is near Lexington. Her death certificate, dated August 1930, gives her age as forty-three, making her year of birth about 1887. However, her obituary in the *Pittsburgh Courier,* August 25, 1930, says that she was actually about sixty years old, and the *New Orleans Times-Picayune,* August 14, 1930, says she was fifty-six years old, which would give a birth year of about 1874. Research materials found in the Robert Tallant Papers at the New Orleans Public Library are especially useful sources of information on Seal. Tallant worked on the Louisiana Federal Writers' Project of the depression-era Work Projects Administration, which collected a great deal of firsthand testimony from contemporaries of Seal. Among the compilers involved were Tallant, Lyle Saxon, who was the head of the project, Hazel Breaux, and several black scholars, including Robert McKinney and Edmund Burke. Much of their data found its way into two books, the *New Orleans City Guide* (1938) and *Gumbo Ya-Ya* (1945). Independent of these efforts, two other researchers provided firsthand testimony of their meetings with Seal. The account of Edward Larocque Tinker, an expert on local history, first appeared in the *North American Review* in 1930. Pioneering African American cultural anthropologist and folklorist Zora Neale Hurston spent two weeks observing and interviewing Seal sometime during the spring of the same year, but her account did not reach print until a posthumously published anthology, *The Sanctified Church,* appeared in 1981.

Turned Away by Faith Healer

Seal came to New Orleans at the age of sixteen. She never went to school and was illiterate. Accordingly, it is unlikely that her teachings were based directly on the Bible. Her inspiration was said to have come from the Holy Spirit. Her calling to the ministry was precipitated by a stroke she suffered in 1922 after having been kicked in the stomach by

Catherine Seal

her unfaithful third husband. The stroke left her partially paralyzed on one side, with a drooping eye and mouth and a leg that dragged, causing her great discomfort. She learned that Brother Isaiah, an extremely popular old white preacher who had drifted down the Mississippi on a houseboat and set up practice on the Uptown docks, was apparently curing the sick and lame with prayer and a magic touch. Racked with pain, she made her way to the levee and braved a huge crowd for hours in the drizzling rain, awaiting her opportunity for the laying on of hands. However, according to Tinker, when she came face to face with him and held out her hands in silent supplication, Brother Isaiah merely shook his head and said, "I ain't healing no colored folks today." She staggered down the levee, fell to her knees in the mud, and resolved then and there to pray herself into a state of grace and good health: "Oh, Jehovia, hear me! Sweet Jesus, help me! Only give me the power to heal, and I'll help colored and white, just the same."

Seal later said that a spirit told her that her prayers would be answered and that she should find a religion of her own as soon as she was able. From that day on, her health began to improve, and people hearing of her cure came to ask advice about their own illnesses. Soon it was being said that she had healed many through, as Tinker says she put it, "revelation of the spirit of the Lord and by anointing of their innards" with castor oil or epsom salts. In 1922 she left her job as a cook to organize the Church of the Innocent Blood, the forerunner of many Spiritual churches in New Orleans.

Origins of Spiritual Church and Appeal of the Sect

Seal had a special purpose. She felt women had to be dissuaded from seeking abortions because each unborn child had the potential for being a holy saint. Pregnant women, both black and white, needed a refuge from men where they could be given help, at least until they had given birth. She eventually conceived the idea of her manger, a building big enough to serve as a hospital and refuge for unmarried pregnant women, which she built on land donated by one of her followers. It was her intent to prevent "the shedding of innocent blood" and to place unwanted children in orphanages. While she was still very young, Seal herself had lost her only two children when they were small. The emotional scar of that memory, coupled with the failure of her marriages, led to her exclusively matriarchal view of religion. Hurston comments in *The Sanctified Church:* "In the last analysis, only God and the mother counted, and childbirth was the most important element. Her Manger was dedicated to the birth of children, in or out-of-wedlock. She continually praised the bringing forth of new life. In her creed, there was no sinful birth."

During the eight years of Seal's ministry, she regarded all of her flock, white as well as black, as her children, and they eventually numbered in the thousands. She had so many white followers that Hurston believed the races to be equally represented. She quotes Seal: "I got all kinds of children but I am their mother. Some of them are convicts and jailbirds, some of them kills babies in their bodies; some of them walks the streets at night—but they's all my children. God got all kinds, how come I can't love all mine?"

The interracial nature of her ministry is reflected in this reference to Jesus, which Hurston selected from one of Seal's sermons: "He could have been born in the biggest White House in the world. But the reason He didn't is that He knowed a falling race was coming what couldn't get to no great White House, so he got born so my people could all reach." In 1940, when a worker for the Writers' Project Tallant Papers reminisced about Seal, she commented that "in a southern city traditionally ingrained with color prejudice and race distinction," the black and white men and women who followed Seal had "worked together in dignity and mutual respect."

Although Seal's charismatic appeal across the color line may have been remarkable, it was not unique—nor was her development of Spiritualist thought in general or her concept of "divine motherhood." These derived at least in part from her predecessor and mentor, Mother Leafy Anderson, a woman of African and Native American descent who arrived in New Orleans from Chicago in 1919. Like Seal, Anderson attracted a biracial following, and before her death in 1927 at the age of forty, she had established some dozen Spiritual churches in Chicago as well as New Orleans. In fact, most of the early Spiritual churches around New Orleans appear to have developed from, or been organized through, her efforts.

Seal attended Anderson's classes in praying, preaching, healing, and prophesying, all requisite skills for any Mother of a Spiritual church. A basic concept that Anderson developed was that of "spirit returning" or "spirit guides," the idea that people from the past, including a person's own loved ones, can come back in spirit form to guide the living. As one of her followers, quoted in Michael Proctor Smith's *Spirit World* (1984), put it, "It's like when you hear an inner voice telling you what to do. That's one of your spirit guides. You should listen to what your spirit guides tell you." Anderson taught that this communication with one's spirit guides could be established either through a medium or through prayer and that such communication put one in contact with the healing hand of God. According to the *Louisiana Weekly*, January 22, 1927, she demonstrated her intimacy with the spirit world in most extraordinary ways, as indicated by an advertisement that appeared in the last year of her life for a performance of the "spirit cantata" *A White Man's Sin and a Squaw's Revenge,* which promised that "the powerful Indian guide takes control of Mrs. Leafy Anderson, as the squaw."

Eventually, however, the two women, student and mentor, had a falling out. One of Anderson's flock, who is quoted in Smith, said that under her leadership, "we were all supposed to wear white in class. But Catherine came into class one day wearing a 'middy'-blouse with a red collar, which was against the laws, and they had a little misunderstanding." Not long after that, Seal went out on her own.

Building a Compound

Between 1923 and 1929, Seal preached and healed from a location on Jackson Avenue. However, the huge crowds that her services attracted were often harassed by the police. The noise and the tumult of the city made Seal nervous. As a result, she eventually moved to the property that had been donated by one of her disciples, which consisted of more than a city block near Flood Street below the Industrial Canal, a recently completed navigation channel at the eastern edge of town. The area was mostly undeveloped marshlands populated by many animals, some domesticated and some not. Large numbers of her followers lived there, some on the church property and many more in the neighborhood, which was some ten blocks all around. Although the compound was fifteen blocks from the nearest bus line and accessible only by a twisting and potholed earthen path that was impossible to navigate in the rainy season, the location had the advantage of being isolated and quiet. People remarked on how the winding route and the time and effort it took to traverse it kept one in constant suspense. It put visitors in the perfect frame of mind for whatever was to transpire once they reached the site.

Begun on November 4, 1929, and completed on January 4, 1930, the compound was comprised of a church building, three ramshackle houses where Seal permitted needy people of both races to live, and her signature structure, the imposing, tentlike manger, which was her personal domicile and sanctum. The entire compound was surrounded by a ten-foot fence of wooden boards, the construction of which she regarded as having been directed by God. However, she complained that instead of giving her the twelve-foot height specified in her vision, the contractors produced only a ten-foot fence. Each board in the fence was meant to represent a

nation, and the height of the fence was intended to keep strangers off the grounds.

Both a strong Roman Catholic influence (certainly not unusual for New Orleans) and an African one are evident in Hurston's description of the exterior of the compound and the interior of the chapel:

> A half-dozen flags fly bravely from eminences. A Greek cross tops the chapel. A large American flag flies from the huge tent. A marsh lies between Flood Street and that flag-flying enclosure, and one must walk. As one approaches, the personality of the place comes out to meet one. No ordinary person created this thing. . . . One does not go straight into the tent, into the presence of Mother Catherine (Mother Seal). One is conducted into the chapel to pray until the spirit tells her to send for you. A place of barbaric splendor, of banners of embroideries, of images bought and images created by Mother Catherine herself; of an altar glittering with polished brass and kerosene lamps. . . . The ceiling and floor in the room of the Sacred Heart are Striped in three colors and the walls are panelled. The panels contain a snake design. The African loves to depict the grace of reptiles.

The manger, with its red roof and sides of striped tenting partly open to the elements, was no less startling. In the middle was a raised platform where Seal held court. It contained a massive, ornate brass bed, which had been donated by a local Italian American family who owned a furniture store. She actually slept there, in full view of her congregation. There was also a piano, instruments for a ten-piece band, a huge coffee urn, a wood stove, and other furniture. The building was filled with backless benches. The whole structure was sixty feet long and fifty feet wide, and it could accommodate three hundred people. It was planned in detail by Seal herself, who had even made most of the pictures and statues that decorated the room, including a primitive looking five-foot clay statue that Tinker identifies as a black Jesus, others as Jehovia. The congregation viewed it as a fateful messenger to whom they must pray for forgiveness. A striking photograph of it is reproduced in *Gumbo Ya-Ya*.

Last Year and Characteristics of Ministry

Hurston paints a provocative profile of Seal as a magnetic religious leader. The reader can almost feel the awe that the folklorist experienced at the moment of their first meeting:

> Catherine of Russia could not have been more impressive upon her throne than was this black Catherine sitting upon an ordinary chair at the edge of the platform within the entrance to the tent. Her face and manner are impressive. There is nothing cheap and theatrical about her. She does things and arranges her dwelling as no occidental would. But it is not for effect it is for *feeling.* She might have been the matriarchal ruler of some nomad tribe as she sat there with the blue band about her head like a

coronet; a white robe and a gorgeous red cape falling away from her broad shoulders, and a box of shaker salt in her hand like a rod of office. And so it seemed perfectly natural for me to go to my knees upon the gravel floor, and when she signalled me to extend my right hand, palm up for the dab of blessed salt, I hurried to obey because she made me feel that way.

Services were held every night at 8:30, and Seal was assisted by a host of white-robed disciples whom she called her "Veils and Banners." Veils referred to the unbleached muslin headdresses that the women wore, and banners to the arm bands worn by the men. George Eagerson, an octogenarian and longtime resident of New Orleans, corroborates aspects of the published accounts. Himself a Catholic, he recalled in a July 23, 1993, interview that her women followers could be seen "all over town" dressed in their characteristic garb "just like nuns."

Seal's strongly feminist philosophy was reflected in the doctrine of her religion and the management of her church. Seal's experiences with men in her own life in the years before she received her calling are apparently what prompted her to handle the men in her congregation differently from the women. Women were encouraged to pray before the statue of Jehovia that their men would do the right things, but the men had to tell their troubles directly to Seal. She believed that everyone could be something good, but women had a special role: "It is right," she said to Hurston, "that a woman should lead. A womb was what God made in the beginning, and out of that womb was born Time, and all that fills up space."

Although Seal dictated strict codes of behavior and dress for her "children," she herself adopted no particular uniform. According to the *New Orleans City Guide,* her clothing was nothing less than original:

> The Lord told her what to wear, and it was usually spectacular. One of her favorite costumes was a voluminous white dress and white cap. A large key dangled from a blue cord tied around her waist. The members were permitted to kneel at her feet and make wishes as they kissed this key. Mother Catherine did not wear any shoes on her grotesquely large feet during the church services; she reminded her people that "the Lord went without shoes."

Although some eyewitness accounts mention rich purple garments instead of white, they almost all agree on the detail of the blue cord, which may be a holdover from the nineteenth century, when such an ornament was used in New Orleans to distinguish the dress of voodoo queens and kings.

Borrows from Many Traditions

For her services, Seal borrowed elements from any religion whose features appealed to her, but perhaps more so from Catholicism than any other. Visitors to the manger encountered a large holy water font, and Seal felt her own divinity to such an extent that she blessed the water in the hydrants at the homes of her followers without moving off her compound. For a small donation, the faithful could choose a votive candle or lamp and make a wish on it, although, to save money, they were never actually lighted. Not surprisingly, Seal, a former cook, made food and drink central to her rituals. There were several feast tables from which blessed lemonade in the summertime and blessed coffee in the wintertime were served. She healed principally through the laying on of hands, but suggestion and sympathetic magic were also employed. Her favorite remedy was a large dose of castor oil administered with a chaser of fresh-cut lemon to kill the taste of the oil. However, a supplicant did not actually have to be present, for she was said to have healed people who were great distances away without ever leaving her manger. She never asked for payment, but her congregation gave freely. "I will never forget the sight," said Hazel Breaux, a follower, in the Tallant Papers. "Mother Catherine was standing there after the service, and the people rushed up to her and started pinning dollar bills on her, and when they finished Mother Catherine's robe was just covered, from top to bottom, with them."

She always entered the church through a hole in the roof of a side room, symbolizing the idea that she had been sent down from heaven to preach the gospel. The men of the congregation helped her use a ladder to reach the top of the church. She always made a very solemn entrance, and the congregation remained quiet until she had blessed everyone. As she started preaching, her followers began to chant and stamp their feet rhythmically. For each one of her "amens" came a chorus of "yes" and "preach it." And preach it she did. Her sermons were poetic and touching, not merely exhortatory. This portion of one of Seal's sermons is printed in Hurston's *The Sanctified Church:*

> Good evening, Veils and Banners! God tells me to tell you (invariable opening) that He holds the world in the middle of His Hand. There is no hell beneath this earth. God wouldn't build a hell to burn His Breath. There is no heaven beyond that blue globe. There is a between-world between this brown earth and the blue above. So says the beautiful spirit. When we die, where does the breath go? Into trees and grass and animals. Your flesh goes back to mortal earth to fertilize it. So says the beautiful spirit.

Seal invited prominent people to dine at her manger, commenting that she liked to have "letter read" people around her, according to the *New Orleans City Guide.* She would sit at a table apart from her guests, explaining that, in the next world, she would be "high up in things," but that, in the things of this world, she knew her place. Nevertheless, she regarded herself as divine and was considered so by her followers. The grounds on which her church and manger were built were revered as hallowed. She never left the compound, but members of her congregation could be seen all over town carrying out her mission. Rumor had it that she was immortal, and she often preached about and predicted her own resurrection from the dead.

At times Seal appeared to have heart trouble. On several occasions, she suffered fainting spells during services, and a doctor had to be called. When her health greatly declined in the summer of 1930, she left New Orleans to visit her sister in Lexington, Kentucky. According to Mrs. LeGallais in the Tallant Papers, she told her followers, "I'm just a little tired; nothing's wrong. I'm just going home for a good rest—then I'll come back." She did not return. On Monday, August 11, only seven months after the manger was completed, she died in Lexington. Her last words, quoted in the Tallant Papers and the *New Orleans City Guide,* were said to have been "I's going to sleep a while, not die. The great God Jehovia, he's calling me. I wants to rest, but on the third day I's coming back to continue my good work with my people." Her death certificate gave the cause as "cardiac dilatation (dropsy)."

Memorable Funeral

Upon receiving the news of Seal's death, her followers arranged for her body to be returned by train to New Orleans, and they began to build a crude brick vault so that the remains could be buried within the church compound. Despite sweltering heat, hundreds of her followers, including a brass band, met the body at the station. Her body lay in state at the manger, where thousands filed past to pay their respects. As the undertakers arrived, two hours late, a sudden electrical storm broke. A downpour ensued, and the crowd panicked as lightning pierced the sky. It looked as if the funeral would have to be postponed until a black woman stepped forward and calmed the crowd, reminding them that Seal had been fearless and that she was present among them even then. She asked that they proceed quietly and fearlessly with the funeral. As the majority of mourners complied with the woman's request, the rain subsided to a steady mist, and the funeral procession began. City health officials had objected to her burial on the grounds, so Seal's remains, dressed in the purple regalia that she had often worn during her services, were carefully carried over the high board fence via a huge scaffold, placed in a hearse, and conveyed to St. Vincent de Paul Cemetery Number 2, where they are still located. To this day, Seal's burial site is an object of curiosity and, from time to time, even of devotion.

As it turned out, Seal's white followers proved to have been right when they insisted that she make out a will. The government did indeed seize her estate, which was valued at four thousand dollars. It was not returned to the congregation until 1933, when the legatees, who had lost their suit in lower court, won on appeal before the Louisiana Supreme Court. Seal's successor was her favorite assistant, Eliza Johnson, who had also left work as a cook for a family. A mother of fourteen children and by then about sixty-five years old, she was known as either Mother Rita or St. Albert, her spirit guide name. She had come from Baton Rouge to New Orleans, where, she said, Seal had cured her of lumbago merely by looking her in the face. After her leader's death, Johnson presided over what became known as the Church of the True Light.

Whether because of bad fortune, her advanced age, or her lack of the kind of charisma that Seal possessed, Johnson was unable to maintain the vitality of the original church.

Sometime before 1940, fire destroyed a house on the grounds of the compound, the original church building, and part of the manger. It was after the fire that Robert McKinney and Edmund Burke visited the compound for the Writers' Project. Both men found Johnson to be suspicious and not very forthcoming, and they reported that the church grounds had greatly deteriorated. All that was left, said Burke in the Tallant Papers, were "the remains of a once-great movement." "Mother Rita's program isn't clicking," said McKinney in the Tallant Papers. "You know," said Johnson, "ain't everybody who can bless castor oil and make it taste like Mother Catherine used to make it. I done tried that, you know." Thus came to an end what was once not only the largest religious cult in New Orleans but one of the largest in the nation. All that survives of the movement is the indelible memory of Seal herself. Whether prophet or pretender, schemer or saint, Catherine Seal possessed a powerful charisma that touched the lives of many. Perhaps more than any other religious leader of the South at the time, she transcended the earthly bonds of poverty and broke down barriers of race and social class with her personal vision of the spirit.

REFERENCES:

Eagerson, George. Interview with Edward B. McDonald, July 23, 1993.

Federal Writers' Project. *New Orleans City Guide.* Boston: Houghton, Mifflin, 1938.

Hurston, Zora Neale. *The Sanctified Church: The Folklore Writings of Zora Neale Hurston.* Berkeley: Turtle Island Foundation, 1981.

Kaslow, Andrew J., and Claude Jacobs. *Prophesy, Healing, and Power: The Afro-American Spiritual Churches of New Orleans.* New Orleans: National Park Service and University of New Orleans, 1981.

Louisiana Weekly, January 22, 1927; August 16, 1930; August 23, 1930; August 30, 1930; December 9, 1933.

Lynch, Hollis R. *The Black Urban Condition: A Documentary History, 1866-1971.* New York: Crowell, 1973.

New Orleans Times-Picayune, August 14, 1930.

Pittsburgh Courier, August 25, 1930.

Saxon, Lyle, Edward Dreyer, and Robert Tallant, comps. *Gumbo Ya-Ya: A Collection of Louisiana Folk Tales.* Baton Rouge: Louisiana Library Commission, 1945.

Smith, Michael Proctor. *Spirit World: Pattern in the Expressive Folk Culture of African-American New Orleans.* 1984. Reprint. Gretna, La.: Pelican Publishing, 1992.

Tinker, Edward Larocque. "Mother Catherine's Castor Oil: Visiting the High Priestess of a Negro Cult in New Orleans." *The North American Review* 230 (August 1930): 148-54.

COLLECTIONS:

The Robert Tallant Papers at the New Orleans Public Library contain interviews with Seal and her successor, Eliza Johnson (including the Robert McKinney interview, "Mother Catherine's Manager''), Mrs. LeGallais's account of Seal's funeral, copies of Seal's death certificate and will, and other materials.

Edward B. McDonald

Leah J. Sears-Collins
(1955-)
Lawyer, judge, state supreme court justice

Leah J. Sears-Collins is the youngest person and the first woman to sit on the Georgia Supreme Court. Also the first black woman trial lawyer in Georgia, she won election to the Fulton County Superior Court prior to her state supreme court appointment, making her the first black woman to win a statewide election in Georgia. She symbolizes the evolution of the Georgia Supreme Court, which historically has been conservative. The fair-minded, disciplined judge brings excellence and diversity to the court.

Born in Heidelberg, Germany, on June 13, 1955, to Onnye Jean Sears, an elementary school teacher, and army colonel Thomas Sears, Leah J. Sears-Collins was the second child in a family of three children, which included an older boy, Mike, and a younger boy, Tommy. Leah's father, a career military officer, was stationed in various places in the United States and around the world. There were frequent moves and the family lived in Germany, Japan, California, New York, and Washington, D.C. Eventually they settled in Savannah, Georgia, where her father was stationed when he retired.

Sears-Collins's mother, Onnye Jean Roundtree Sears, a Sand Springs, Oklahoma, native, graduated from Langston University in Langston, Oklahoma, in May 1951. She was an active member of Alpha Kappa Alpha Sorority and began her career as a teacher at age twenty-three in her home state of Oklahoma. Following her marriage to Thomas Sears she taught at whatever elementary school happened to be convenient to where she and her husband were stationed. Thomas Sears grew up in the Tidewater area of Virginia. He fought in both the Korean War and the Vietnam War, earning two Silver Stars as an aviator. In Savannah he ran for a seat on the school board, becoming its vice president, and was appointed to a position on the Model Cities Board. Thomas Sears died in November 1989.

Leah Sears-Collins lived in Germany and other foreign countries until she was four years old. The inequities in American society became apparent to her when the family returned to the United States. She toured New York City with her family and in a *National Law Journal* article remembered riding through Harlem and wondering, ''Why do the brown people here live so poorly?'' At four years old she suddenly was aware of her surroundings. She recalled in the *National Law Journal* profile, ''That was the moment I came to realize

there was such a problem with race in this world. That one scene has always replayed in my mind.''

At five years old Sears-Collins enrolled in the public school system of northern California. What she remembers about Monterey Elementary School is that in 1960 it was all white, as were most of the other schools she and her brothers attended. The one exception occurred when the family moved to Washington, D.C. She was a third grader and attended an all-black school because her parents wanted her to experience her own culture.

The Sears family moved to Savannah, Georgia, in 1968, when Leah was in eighth grade. She attended Bartlett Junior High School and later transferred to Wilder. Sears-Collins recalls no particularly unpleasant experiences at either of these schools even though they were mostly white, southern, and newly integrated. Because she was accepted, loved, and encouraged by her family, Sears-Collins had the self-confidence to expect success whatever the circumstances. This attitude led to her academic achievement and active participation in school activities.

In the high school she first attended, Beach High School, Sears-Collins participated in the Beta Club, a group of honor roll students, and the National Honor Society and became the first African American on the school's cheerleading squad. When Sears-Collins transferred to Savannah High School she continued her involvement in extracurricular activities and was the first African American cheerleader there as well. She recalls that her experiences in high school were difficult in ways she was then too young to comprehend. She said in *Savannah Magazine,* July 4, 1993, ''I didn't realize it at the time, but something like that does a lot to your self-esteem.'' The ''something like that'' to which she refers is the pressure of being the first African American to participate in a traditionally all-white activity, confronting racism without a critical mass of others to maintain her level of comfort. Even when all appeared well on the surface, there were subtle and unspoken challenges to her intelligence based on skin color. Despite these obstacles, she maintained excellent grades and graduated in May 1972.

When it was time for college, Sears-Collins confesses now that she wanted to spread her wings and go as far away from home as she possibly could. She applied to Cornell University in Ithaca, New York; to Syracuse, also in New York; to Radcliffe in Cambridge, Massachusetts; and to the University of Massachusetts at Amherst. Swayed by the full-tuition scholarship offered at Cornell, Sears-Collins headed north for four years of undergraduate education. At Cornell she was one of about fifteen hundred other African American students, which was not many given the student population at Cornell but was far more than she had been used to.

As a student Sears-Collins wrote poetry, became involved in the black and women's studies movements on campus, and decided to major in human development and family studies. Although her mother had been a member of Alpha Kappa Alpha Sorority, she refused to join the historically black sorority because at the time she thought Alpha Kappa Alpha was not black enough and that it was not politically correct to be "Greek." To please her mother, however, she later pledged a graduate chapter of the sorority.

The Return South: A New Life, A New Name

In June 1976, Sears-Collins graduated with honors from Cornell and on July 3 married Love Collins III, a young cadet she met at Cornell when he came to run track for West Point, where he was enrolled. They married in Butler Presbyterian Church in Savannah, Georgia. Leah and Love exchanged wedding vows and names, with her taking her husband's name and keeping her family's and him keeping his family name and adding hers to it. Love Sears-Collins was stationed in Columbus, Georgia. Leah Sears-Collins had been accepted at Duke University Law School. At the end of August she departed for law school in North Carolina. This time she found herself too far from home. After only five weeks at Duke, the newlywed dropped out and returned to Columbus to join her husband.

Sears-Collins became a feature writer for the *Columbus Ledger.* She stayed with this job only a year, during which time she applied to a law school closer to home. Entering Emory University Law School in Atlanta in August 1977, she was one of seven African Americans in her class. No African American professors and no African American administrators worked at the law school. She recalls that her experience at Emory University Law School was never pleasant. In addition to the long hours she spent studying, she was frustrated by the distance she and her husband had to commute to see each other as well as by the fact that they saw each other only on weekends. They made the sacrifice, however, because it was important for Sears-Collins to become a lawyer, something she had considered since 1963, when at the age of eight she had ordered catalogs from the law schools of Harvard, Yale, and the University of Michigan. However, at eight she had not counted on having a husband. Sears-Collins graduated from Emory University Law School in 1980. Admitted to practice law in Georgia in 1980, at the age of twenty-five, Sears-Collins faced a future full of promise.

Lawyer Becomes Superior Court Judge

Sears-Collins joined the large and prestigious Atlanta law firm of Alston and Bird in 1980, where she practiced business and intellectual-property law. But she had not yet found her niche. She was bored and frustrated. Summarizing her experience with the firm, she told Mark Curriden in *Barrister* magazine that it was "too much paperwork, not enough people work." In 1982, she quit this job in order to take a much lower-paying position as a traffic judge in Atlanta city court. While this position was far more interesting, it still was not her life's ambition to be a traffic judge.

For a while, however, Sears-Collins's energies were directed toward home. In June 1983, her son, Addison Sears-Collins, was born, and in December 1986, she gave birth to a daughter, Brennan, named for U.S. Supreme Court Justice William Brennan. By 1988, when Addison was five and ready

for school and Brennan was two, Sears-Collins decided to run for a seat on the Fulton County Superior Court. Campaigning as "A Superior Woman for a Superior Court," she was an outspoken opponent who would be tough to beat.

In a close three-way race, Sears-Collins emerged the winner, replacing a judge who had retired. She thus became the youngest person ever elected to a superior court judgeship in Georgia and the first African American woman in the history of the Georgia superior court. She was thirty-two. Sears-Collins related in a telephone interview that she established herself as an energetic, hardworking, scholarly, and caring judge who did not "flip-flop on issues just because of the political whims of the times." As a legal scholar, Sears-Collins hates legalese. Her own articles, which have appeared in the *National Law Journal, Court Review,* and the *Atlanta Lawyer,* are clear and concise. She wants to be understood and says lawyers have an obligation to be sure their clients understand legal documents. One way to insure this is to write the documents in clear English unencumbered by "whereases and wherefores." She believes judges must follow their own consciences and should not hold back from saying what they think on the bench or in written opinions.

Politically, Sears-Collins has been described as both moderate and conservative. The judge herself says in the *National Law Journal,* September 6, 1993, "I'm no liberal. I consider myself a moderate politically." Despite the fact that she supported the presidency of Ronald Reagan, she considers herself a Democrat. Not morally opposed to capital punishment, Sears-Collins is concerned about the apparent role race plays in the prosecutor's decision to seek the death penalty.

Governor's Call Leads to Supreme Court

On Monday morning, February 17, 1992, Sears-Collins was in her office at the superior court when she received a telephone call from Georgia's governor, Zell Miller. He announced that he was appointing her to the Georgia Supreme Court. At thirty-six, Sears-Collins was the youngest person and the first woman ever to sit on Georgia's highest court.

In a press release, Governor Miller said, "It was a strong and impressive field from which I had to choose. Each of the 10 candidates would make an outstanding appellate court judge and, in fact, someday may do just that. I have chosen Superior Court Judge Leah Sears-Collins, because she possesses in abundance the qualities an outstanding jurist should have: intellect, temperament and energy."

Sears-Collins brings diversity to the highest court in Georgia as an African American, a woman, and a young mother of two children. While these factors do not necessarily spell liberal, together they add up to a different perspective, one not previously represented. To those who claimed Sears-Collins was selected because of her race and or gender, implying she might not have been the most qualified for the job, Governor Miller responded in his press release: "I chose Leah Sears-Collins for this position because she is intelligent, scholarly, thoughtful, disciplined and fair minded. And I knew she would bring excellence to the court at the same time she was bringing diversity.'' Sears-Collins was sworn in on March 6, 1992.

With a career that demands she work hard and long hours, Sears-Collins's life as a judge, mother, and wife is one of juggling priorities and time schedules and relying on frozen foods. Not a superwoman, Sears-Collins claims to merely muddle along like most working women, attempting to get it all done. On holidays she is often in her chambers trying to catch up on paperwork. She arrives at work early, often stays late, comes in on weekends, and takes work home.

A typical day for Sears-Collins begins at 5:00 A.M. She has breakfast with her family and by 8:00 A.M. she is in her office. Most of her workday consists of reading and writing. She begins by reading opinions. Later she meets with staff, law clerks, and legal assistants to discuss a variety of issues. As cases cross her desk she rules on them and writes her opinions. Once a week justices meet to discuss cases. In her work Sears-Collins is disturbed by the American tendency to marginalize groups of people who lack power. She continued:

> I want my appointment to stand for what America should be. America is a wonderful combination of people from every race and every ethnic background, both genders, all moving ahead, working together, and I want this country to get over this separation; you know, being a woman is an alien kind of thing, as being black is.

Sears-Collins's mother believes that she should slow down, but the judge feels healthy and maintains a program of exercise, which includes cycling and rollerblading with her two children. In an interview, she described her philosophy for reduced stress and tension: ''Be kind to other people. It doesn't cost anything and it can mean so much to others and make life wonderful for you.''

In 1992 Sears-Collins received the ABA Brent Women Lawyers of Achievement Award. She also received the Community Service Award from the NAACP Atlanta chapter in 1988, the Distinguished Leadership Award for Outstanding Service in the Judiciary in 1988, and the Certificate of Appreciation from Fulton County in 1989. She was honored in a Salute to African American Business and Professional Women by *Dollars and Cents Magazine,* 1990, named Black Woman of Achievement by Southern Bell in 1990, and featured in the 1990-91 Calendar of Black History by Southern Bell. In 1989 she was named Outstanding Young Woman of America by the Atlanta Jaycees. She was awarded an honorary degree by Morehouse College in 1992.

Sears-Collins holds membership in numerous professional and civic organizations. She and her family are members of Ebenezer Baptist Church in Atlanta. Her hobbies include writing, and her favorite book is *Little House on the Prairie.*

Leah Sears-Collins's moderate political philosophy garners her support from a cross section of Georgia citizens. She is a leader with sound values and a clear vision. Although she may not want to be known as a black judge or a woman judge, but, rather, as a fair and hardworking judge, Sears-

Collins's statement in a March 4, 1992, interview that she has ''had to work harder, think faster, be more involved in bar issues, just to prove I belong on this court,'' reveals the extent to which her race and her gender have affected how she is perceived. Diligent and unbiased, this young Georgia Supreme Court judge can lead the high court into the twenty-first century.

Current Address: Supreme Court, 533 State Judicial Building, 244 Washington Street, SW, Atlanta, GA 30334.

REFERENCES:

Curriden, Mark. ''Rollerblading Justice.'' *Barrister Magazine* 20 (Summer 1993): 20.
———. ''A Jurist of First Impression.'' *National Law Journal* 16 (September 6, 1993): 27.
''The Female Factor: Influence of Women Growing on High Court.'' *Savannah Morning News,* July 6, 1993.
Norman, Tyler. ''Justifiably Honored: Savannah's Justice Leah Sears-Collins.'' *Savannah Magazine* (July 4, 1993): 20-23.
Reece, Chuck. Press Advisory. State of Georgia, Office of the Governor, February 17, 1992.
Sears-Collins, Leah. Telephone interview with Nagueyalti Warren, March 4, 1992.
Wooten, Jim. ''Justice Leah Sears-Collins Is, Indeed, Different.'' *The Atlanta Journal,* July 8, 1992.

Nagueyalti Warren

Lucy Stanton Day Sessions
(1831-1910)
Educator, abolitionist, writer, missionary, reformer

Lucy Stanton Day Sessions was the first African American woman to graduate from college. She finished Oberlin College in 1850, after completing the two-year Ladies Literary Course. The college, located in northeast Ohio, was well known for its abolitionist sentiment and activism and had the first collegiate program to grant enrollment without restrictions because of race or gender. Although twelve years later Mary Jane Patterson became the first black woman to receive a bachelor's degree, also from Oberlin, the literary program differed only in that there was no requirement for higher mathematics, Greek, or Latin. Since late in the nineteenth century, the college has recognized its Literary Course as the equivalent of the B.A. Though not much has been written on Sessions, it is known that during her lifetime she taught for both abolition and missionary societies. She was a member of the Women's Christian Temperance Union,

Lucy Stanton Day Sessions

she served as a church leader for the African Methodist Episcopal Church, and she fought for various other reforms through such associations as the Federation of Colored Women.

Lucy Stanton Day Sessions was born in Cleveland, Ohio, on October 16, 1831, the only child of Margaret and Samuel Stanton. The Stantons were recognized as mulattos, and, as noted in a 1910 *New Age* article, a contemporary described Sessions as "a beautiful mulatto maiden . . . with refined manners." Sessions died in Los Angeles on February 18, 1910, from complications of pneumonia and asthma. She is buried in the Rosedale Cemetery in Los Angeles.

Sessions's father, Samuel, was a free-born black who moved to Cleveland from the South during his youth and became a successful barber. Unfortunately, he died when Sessions was only eighteen months old. Family lore has it that he died just after walking with Sessions to a corner store to purchase a china pitcher. The pitcher became a family heirloom. Later, Martha Stanton married Samuel's business partner, John Brown, and bore four more children.

John Brown was well known in Cleveland for his antislave activism with the Underground Railroad network. He too was free-born and came to Cleveland from his native Virginia. He became the wealthiest African American in the city. According to Ellen N. Lawson in an article for *Western Reserve Magazine,* Sessions recalled that at times there were as many as thirteen runaway slaves in the home awaiting passage across Lake Erie into Canada. Thus, the children became acquainted firsthand with the cruel effects of slavery. They collected money from neighbors and acquaintances to support

the antislavery effort. From these experiences, according to the *New Age* article, Sessions as a youngster declared her dedication to "live to see slavery done away with, and [to] . . . go south to teach."

Education for black children was another area in which John Brown was very active. When Sessions was a child, Cleveland was a village of only about twelve hundred, with very few blacks. Although the family lived in a predominately white neighborhood, the children were barred from the city's schools because of a law passed in 1829 that prohibited blacks from attending state-supported schools. Brown, along with several other Clevelanders, organized the first school for African Americans in the city, based on a subscription system of monthly payments from the black citizens.

Embarks on Studies at Oberlin

After completing the courses available at the Cleveland Free School in 1846, Sessions enrolled in the Oberlin Collegiate Institute. While she was at Oberlin, she was very involved in student and college activities, and in her senior year she was elected president of the Ladies Literary Society, a very prestigious organization. She also joined the Oberlin Church, the first of many church affiliations during her lifetime.

Sessions was one of a number of students to present an address during the commencement ceremonies of 1850. Her essay, "A Plea for the Oppressed," made a passionate appeal for members of her class and the audience to become involved in the antislavery movement and other reform causes of the era. Stating that "truly this is the age of reform," she appealed to women to become more active in their homes and wherever they had influence. When she ended her speech, a man in the audience rose to remind the audience that only twenty years earlier, when the question of admission of blacks was before the trustees, some predicted that to do so would "ruin the institution." However, as noted in *The Oberlin Evangelist,* he continued, "The piece to which you have just listened shall decide upon the credibility of the prophecy." In spite of a long-standing tradition that prohibited applause during this solemn occasion, the audience "swept away every barrier" and responded enthusiastically. The essay was later chosen for publication in the school's newspaper and in Martin Delaney's *The Condition, Elevation, Emigration, and Destiny of the Colored People of the United States Politically Considered* (1852). (The essay may today be found in the Lawson-Merrill Collection, *The Three Sarahs,* Oberlin College Archives.)

After graduation Sessions began her career in education as principal of another "free" school in Columbus, Ohio. In 1852, she married William Howard Day, an Oberlin College graduate from the class of 1847. The couple moved to Cleveland, where he became a librarian at the Cleveland Library Association and in 1853 editor of Cleveland's first abolitionist newspaper, the *Alienated American.* In this newspaper in 1854, Sessions published a short story, "Charles and Clara Hayes," which authors Lawson and Merrill claim may be the "first instance of published fiction by a black woman." (The work was also published as "Lucy Stanton: Life on the

Cutting Edge,'' in *Western Reserve Magazine* 10, January-February 1983.) While they were in Cleveland, the couple had two children, William and Eliza, both of whom died in infancy.

Sessions and William Day moved across the lake to Ontario in 1856 to join a black Canadian community, Buxton. Little is known about her activities there, except that a child, Florence Nightingale, was born in 1858. In 1859, William left his wife and daughter in Buxton, ostensibly for a trip to England to solicit funds for the abolition effort. Sessions returned to Cleveland with a daughter to support and in 1864 applied for a teaching job with the American Missionary Association (AMA). Reverend James Thome, a former faculty member at Oberlin who knew the couple at college, told a Mr. Strieby of the AMA, as quoted in Lawson and Merrill, that William had "managed to run through with a handsome property belonging to his wife." In the same communication, Thome observed that William had abandoned Sessions some years before.

Although Sessions was rejected by the AMA for the teaching position because she was separated from William, and they preferred either single women, widows, or women in the company of their husbands, she was hired by a local abolition association to teach in Georgia in 1866.

Finally, in 1871, Sessions was accepted for a teaching position with the AMA in Fayette, Mississippi. One year later she divorced William. She remained in Fayette until 1884, when she moved to Chattanooga and taught there until 1903. She was married in 1878 to Levi Sessions, a Mississippian who worked odd jobs as a janitor, packer, and fireman.

While living in the South, Sessions was very active in the temperance movement, serving as president of the colored chapter of the Women's Christian Temperance Union. She was also grand matron of the Grand Order of the Eastern Star of the State of Tennessee, preceptress at the Normal Agricultural and Mechanical College in Normal, Alabama (1896-97), and an officer of the National Aide Women's Relief Corps. During this time she also continued to write and publish articles, primarily about religion in public schools, in local papers.

In 1903, Lucy Sessions and her husband moved to Los Angeles with her daughter. In Los Angeles she joined the African Methodist Episcopal Church, and in spite of advancing age, served in various leadership roles in the church, in the Women's Christian Temperance Union, and the city's affiliate of the Federation of Colored Women. At her death, the *New Age* newspaper described her as a "pioneer race leader."

REFERENCES:

Brown, Hallie Q. *Homespun Heroines and Other Women of Distinction.* Xenia, Ohio: Aldine Publishing Co., 1926.
City Directory, 1894-1903. Chattanooga, Tenn.
Lawson, Ellen Nackenzie. "Lucy Stanton: Life on the Cutting Edge." *Western Reserve Magazine* 10 (January-February 1983): 9-12.
Lawson, Ellen Nackenzie and Marlene Merrill. *The Three Sarahs: Documents of Antebellum Black College Women.* New York: Edwin Mellen Press, 1984.
Oberlin Evangelist 10 (December 17, 1850): 208.
"Pioneer Race Leader Called to Her Reward." *New Age,* 1910. Lawson Merrill Papers. Oberlin College Archives, Oberlin, Ohio.
Necrology Files. Oberlin College Archives, Oberlin, Ohio.

COLLECTIONS:

Documents pertaining to Lucy Sessions are located in the Lawson-Merrill Collection and the Oberlin College Alumni Records of the Oberlin College Archives, in Oberlin, Ohio.

Eiling Freeman, Umaimah Mahmud, and Adrienne Lash Jones

Betty Shabazz
(1936-)
Educator, nurse, community activist

Widow of the preeminent human rights fighter Malcolm X (El Hajji Malik Shabazz), Betty Shabazz was the mother of four girls and pregnant with two more when she witnessed the assassination of her husband on February 21, 1965, in the Audubon Ballroom in New York City. A remarkable woman who possesses great strength and determination, Shabazz successfully raised her six daughters while continuing her education. She received a Ph.D. degree in 1975. She has been instrumental in perpetuating the true legacy and memory of Malcolm X and an inspiration to the countless young people who want to carry on the struggle against the oppression of black people. She is a community activist and challenges herself and others to fight for a better quality of life in black and Hispanic communities.

Betty Shabazz was born in 1936. She was reared by foster parents who apparently adopted her, in Detroit, Michigan, where she attended Northern High School. Being the only child of adoptive parents, she very seldom thought about the outside world and her relationship to it. She told *Essence* magazine in 1992:

> I was not that exposed at the time I met Malcolm, nor did I have a lot of experience in the challenges that women face. Pick a week out of my life. If you understood that week, you understood my life. I went to school from Monday to Friday. On Friday I went to the movies. On Saturday I was at my parents' store. On Sunday I went to church. Sometimes on Saturday I would go with the young people from church to parties. . . . Detroit . . . [was] a Delta [Sigma Theta] town, so in high school I was a

Betty Shabazz

member of a (junior Delta) sorority called the Del Sprites.

Shabazz went to Tuskegee Institute in Alabama, which was her father's alma mater. She left Tuskegee Institute to go to nursing school in New York City after she switched her major from elementary education to nursing. She disliked Tuskegee because she experienced hostility in Alabama from whites, an issue her parents did not want to deal with; they thought her departure was her own fault. She first heard the word "racism" from Malcolm X, who introduced her to a whole new way of thinking, not only about herself, but also about the global condition of black people.

She met Malcolm X in her junior year when she was invited by a friend to attend a lecture at Temple Seven in Harlem. The first time Shabazz saw Malcolm X, she was immediately impressed with him. She thought he was clean-cut, no-nonsense, and focused. At the time, she felt that somehow she knew him. She told *Essence* magazine in 1992, "I felt that somewhere in life I had met this energy before."

Begins Work with Malcolm X at Temple Seven

Shabazz began to teach a women's class at Temple Seven, and Malcolm X advised her on what matters to stress. She typed and corrected papers for him. According to Shabazz in *Essence* magazine in 1992,

He would actively seek me out, ask me questions. He was different. He was refreshing, but I never

suspected that he thought of me in any way other than as a sister who was interested in the Movement. . . . There were too many people in line for his attention.

Shabazz eventually discovered that Malcolm X was very attracted to her. She later recollected, "I knew he loved me for my clear brown skin—it was very smooth. He liked my clear eyes. He liked my gleaming dark hair. I was very thin then, and he liked my Black beauty, my mind. He just liked me."

They had an unusual courtship; Shabazz, a Methodist, never "dated" Malcolm X, a Muslim, because at the time single men and women of the Muslim faith did not "fraternize," as they called it. Men and women always went out in groups. She went out to dinner with Malcolm X accompanied by another Muslim brother. Malcolm X called Shabazz from Detroit, their hometown, and proposed to her. While her parents liked Malcolm X and thought he was a nice young man, they objected to the marriage because he belonged to a different religion. She had grown up a Methodist and her parents did not want her to change. Besides, they thought Malcolm X was too old for her. Shabazz defied her parents and eloped with Malcolm X. At some point after her marriage, Shabazz converted to Islam.

In retrospect, Shabazz describes her seven years of marriage to Malcolm X as hectic, holistic, beautiful, and unforgettable. He was a good husband and father to their daughters. She told *Essence* magazine in 1992 that they had "the kind of life that one reads about, plans for or wishes for between a man and a woman. . . . I . . . think I was destined to be with Malcolm. And I think that Malcolm probably needed me more than I needed him—to support his life's mission."

Shabazz was unable to sleep for three weeks following the assassination of Malcolm X. Fortunately, she was invited to go to Mecca, where she sought solace and looked for meaning in her shattered life. She recalled in *Essence* magazine in 1992,

I really don't know where I'd be today if I had not gone to Mecca to make Hajj shortly after Malcolm was assassinated. . . . Going to Mecca, making Hajj, was very good for me because it made me think of all the people in the world who loved me and were for me, who prayed that I would get my life back together. I stopped focusing on the people who were trying to tear me and my family apart.

After she lost Malcolm X, Shabazz devoted virtually all of her time and energy to raising their six daughters (Attallah, Quibilah, Illyasah, Gamilah, Malaak, and Malikah) according to his principles and ideas. She gave them a well-rounded education and sought to instill in them a sense of ethnic responsibility for themselves, their people, and the broader society. For example, they studied Arabic and French and attended ballet classes in addition to taking black history courses. She raised them to be citizens of the global community. She encouraged them to travel so they could know more about Africa, the West Indies, and the Middle East.

Shabazz received an R.N. degree from the Brooklyn State Hospital School of Nursing, a B.A. in public health education from Jersey City State College, and became a certified school nurse. In 1975, she earned her Ph.D. in school administration and curriculum development from the University of Massachusetts at Amherst. She is now a professor of health administration at Medgar Evers College, Brooklyn, New York. She is also the director of institutional advancement and public relations at Medgar Evers.

Activist Becomes National Figure

Even though Shabazz is essentially a private person and considers herself a follower rather than a leader, she has become a national figure. She is in constant demand for speaking engagements across the country. She has received many honors, tributes, and prestigious awards, including the Congressional Record Award for her community service. She has hosted her own radio talk show on New York City's WBLS-FM. She has appeared on a number of radio and television shows and also works with Columbia Medical School on the Malcolm X Medical Scholarship Program for African American students.

Shabazz likes to travel because she believes it broadens her scope and sharpens her focus on life. She listens to classical music and likes jazz and rap as well. She told the *City Sun,* "I like rap because it's a creative art form that's developed by our young people."

Shabazz is an inspiration to young people as well as an advocate for their proper development. She challenges parents to be good role models for their children and to give them guidelines as to what they can and cannot do. She believes that parents should take chief responsibility for passing on the proud black cultural traditions to their children and for making them realize that it is their spiritual and moral duty to help oppressed people. Cathy Connors quotes Shabazz in the *Amsterdam News* from her speech before the National Urban League in 1990: Shabazz urged the audience to "sponsor our children . . . protect them . . . call newspapers and TV stations to complain about the way African-American children are portrayed. . . . We have to give them pride in their own culture, their roots, but we must make these decisions for children, not let them make too many careless ones on their own."

Shabazz has strong ideas and advice on raising children. She is constantly emphasizing to parents and educators the importance of teaching young people in such a way that they understand that the twenty-first century will be a century of self-sufficiency. In Shabazz's view, young people need to learn that they have to make things happen for themselves and that they must have purpose and an agenda. She told the *City Sun,* "Tasks and agendas are easier if you are focused. . . . We must use our brainpower, our energy, the essence of us as if it were money."

Like Malcolm X, Shabazz cares deeply about the struggle and plight of people of African descent in the United States. In a June 1993 interview in the *City Sun,* she revealed much of her philosophy of life and her views on a variety of topics. Here is what she had to say about African Americans:

> We're a very strong people. . . . We have a sense of our own responsibility and commitment. . . . We have been in this country so long and have made such a vast contribution, not only with our lives but in terms of development, invention and contributions. Other ethnic groups have come to America and are automatically treated as citizens with all rights and privileges, and somehow, African descendants still are struggling. Other ethnic groups can receive money for reparations, and yet, with our several hundred years of free labor and the additional years of unfair compensation for our labor, we have not received the rights and privileges of other ethnic groups. . . . However, I don't know of an ethnic group that is more powerful, that has made such contributions, that has been as tolerant and that still is willing to share and to do and to be. . . . We're a good people.

On black women in the United States, Shabazz told the *City Sun* in 1993,

> Given our resources and limited opportunities and options, Black women in America . . . are functioning at a remarkable high level, and compete on any level with women of the world . . . She tries very hard to be her own best friend and advise others to do the same. . . . Love yourself, appreciate yourself, see the good in you, see the God in you and respect yourself.

Shabazz feels very strongly that people must work in order to feel good about themselves. An extremely hard worker herself, Shabazz believes that working gives you a sense that you are a part of what is going on in the world. She recognizes the significance of a people having the opportunity to help shape lives and communities.

In this same interview, Shabazz shared her overall perspective on life: "I think I'm a realist. I see life as it is, but I also can vision it as I would like it to be." She feels that she is never alone because there is an energy of the universe that flows within her. She feels connected even when she is not with anyone. "And then, too, there's Malcolm's energy and his spirit."

> I don't feel sad. I feel fortunate. I feel very blessed spiritually. My soul is at peace. My heart is full of concern and love, and I understand the meaning of my own life and the lives of others. So, no, no, I'm never alone. I'm never cut off.

Betty Shabazz lives in Brooklyn, New York, and loves it. She told *Essence* magazine in 1992, "My life today is very peaceful. I'm a Sunni Muslim. . . . I don't eat pork. . . . I acknowledge the oneness of God. I pray. I contribute to charity. I fast. I work hard."

Current Address: Director of Communications, Medgar Evers College, 1650 Bedford Avenue, Brooklyn, NY 11225.

REFERENCES:

Cain, Joy Duckett. "Dr. Betty Shabazz Twenty Years after Malcolm X's Death, His Widow Speaks Out." *Essence* 15 (February 1985): 12.

Conners, Cathy. "Let's Sponsor Our Kids, Dr. Shabazz Tells Confab." *Amsterdam News,* August 4, 1990.

Ebony Success Library. Vol. 1. Nashville: Southwestern Publishing Co., 1973.

"Harlem Honors Dr. Betty Shabazz, Declares Malcolm X Blvd. Drug Free." *Amsterdam News,* March 30, 1991.

Knebel, Fletcher. "A Visit with the Widow of Malcolm X." *Look* 33 (March 4, 1969): 74-80.

Mandulor, Rhea. "Sharing Our Best with Others: An Interview with Dr. Betty Shabazz." *City Sun,* June 9-15, 1993.

Shabazz, Betty. "Legacy of My Husband, Malcolm X." *Ebony* 24 (June 1969): 172-82.

———. "Loving and Losing Malcolm." *Essence* 22 (February 1992): 50-54, 104, 107-9.

Bobbie T. Pollard

Patricia Walker Shaw

Patricia Walker Shaw
(1939-1985)
Business executive, organization leader, social worker

Universal Life Insurance Company in Memphis, Tennessee, named Patricia Shaw its first female president and chief executive officer, making her the first woman to head a major life insurance organization in the United States and placing her in one of the highest management positions held by a woman in the country. Progressing in seventeen years through a variety of positions within the company, Shaw moved into top-level management first as a vice president, and then, at age forty-three, as head of the company. She nurtured and expanded a family tradition of service to the black community. She also became the first female president of the National Insurance Association, an organization of minority insurance executives.

Lily Patricia Walker Shaw was the oldest of three children born to A. Maceo Walker and Harriet Ish Walker. She was born in Little Rock, Arkansas, on June 26, 1939, and grew up in Memphis, Tennessee. She came from a prominent family of high achievers, including her two grandfathers, who had been physicians. On her maternal side her great-grandfather, Jefferson Garfield Ish, was an educator for whom a school in Little Rock was named. Her great-grandmother

Marietta Ish was an artist. Her maternal grandfather, George Washington Stanley Ish, also of Little Rock, was a Yale-trained physician, and uncle Jeff G. Ish was a Yale graduate and an officer in Chicago's Supreme Life Insurance Company. Her paternal great-grandparents, Pat Hill Walker and George Walker, of Tillman, Mississippi, became farmers after being freed from slavery. Her paternal grandfather, Joseph Edison Walker, who was the first in the family to receive a formal education, graduated from Meharry Medical College in Nashville, Tennessee, founded Universal Life Insurance Company in Memphis in 1923, and, with his son, cofounded the Tri-State Bank. In 1952 Patricia Shaw's father, A. Maceo Walker, assumed the reins of the Universal Life Insurance company and led it for thirty-one years. In 1921 Joseph Walker, his wife, Lelia O'Neal Walker, and Roxy Crawford founded the Mississippi Boulevard Christian Church.

Shaw began her education at Hamilton Elementary School in Memphis and in 1956 graduated from Oakwood High School, a Quaker boarding school in Poughkeepsie, New York. She entered Fisk University, Nashville, Tennessee, that same year, graduating in 1961 with a bachelor of arts degree cum laude in business administration. On June 17, 1961, she married Harold R. Shaw, a Fisk schoolmate, and they moved to Chicago, where she became a social worker with the Illinois Department of Public Aid. She also studied briefly that year at the University of Chicago Graduate School of Business Administration. Shaw returned to Nashville and obtained a teacher's certificate from Tennessee State University in 1962. The Shaws moved to Memphis in 1966 when they went to work for Universal Life. That same year Patricia Shaw also enrolled in the Graduate School of Social Work at the University of Tennessee in Memphis, now known as the University of Memphis, and worked intermittently first as a social caseworker and then as a welfare worker.

Soon after graduating from Fisk in 1961, Shaw worked briefly for the family business, Universal Life Insurance Company, where she was a clerk in the underwriting department. She left her social work career and joined the company again in 1966, this time as a keypunch operator. The years that followed gave her broad experience and a great understanding of the operations of the company. In 1967 she was promoted to chief clerk in data processing. Afterward, she was named supervisor of the department and then later, supervisor and cashier in accounting.

Shaw moved into senior management in 1971, as an assistant vice president. Her promotions continued and she became vice president and associate controller in 1974, senior vice president and assistant secretary in 1980, and executive vice president in 1981. In the latter position Shaw was responsible for developing a new market thrust for the company and demonstrated her keen leadership and management abilities.

Heads Leading Insurance Company

In 1983 company president A. Maceo Walker, then seventy-three years old, announced his decision to step down from the position he had held since 1952. Determined to retain competent leadership for the firm, on February 11, 1983, the Board of Directors of Universal Life Insurance Company elected Shaw the new president and chief executive officer. An inaugural celebration for Shaw was held on Saturday, February 12, 1983, at the Hotel Peabody in Memphis. Her father, who held the majority of Universal's stock, would remain chairman of the board and of the Finance and Investment committee, where he would focus on one specific area of the company, investments. Shaw assumed control of the company's day-to-day operations. Then the country's fourth largest black-owned-and-operated insurance firm, Universal had assets exceeding sixty-one million dollars and business in force of more than a half billion dollars. It was also one of the largest minority-owned businesses in the mid-South, with 850 salaried employees on its staff. The company was licensed to operate in nine states and the District of Columbia. Thirty-six branch offices served policy holders across the country. The new position made Shaw the company's third president (all from the family dynasty) and first female head, and it elevated her to one of the highest management positions held by a woman in the country.

Shaw said in a press conference held at the time of her election to the presidency,

> Moving step-by-step through this company has been the most important learning experience of my life. I have become Universal Life's daughter, almost as much as I am Maceo Walker's daughter.

> The company has literally raised me as a businessperson . . . and they didn't spare the rod.

Pledges to Broaden Company's Customer Base

She saw the company's major challenge as the state of the economy, particularly rising inflation, and foresaw a future for the firm as a secure, full-service company that attended to the insurance needs of everyone, not just the economically disadvantaged customers who had been served in the past. In the press release she summarized her goals as company president: "I am convinced that by combining our traditional commitment to basic principles with our new and broader marketing profile, Universal Life will grow profitably in the years to come."

She had inherited her family's commitment to help the black race and, despite her broader vision for Universal Life, wanted the company to continue to be a bulwark of financial strength for black people. She told Lloyd Gite for *Essence,* June 1974:

> We believe we are the mother ship of Black economic development, and as the mother ship we have spawned all kinds of smaller ships in the Black community. We will continue to finance projects, through loans, that build Black businesses and Black churches, and we will continue to help Black Colleges survive.

Shaw and other new officers at Universal Life represented the "back to basics" economic philosophy adopted by many young black executives at that time. She said in *Mid-South Business,* February 28-March 4, 1983, "We're reclaiming our own. This brain drain and this dollar drain from our community needs to come to an end." Like many other black companies, Universal Life had supported black educational institutions and programs that increased social awareness among blacks, while at the same time much of the new black talent and money left the black community. She continued,

> We're not going to just give away thousands and thousands of dollars anymore [to colleges and universities] just because they wave minority in our faces. We want a return on our investment. . . . We want the counselors at the schools and the directors of the scholarship funds we've been giving our money to tell those students where this money is coming from.

Shaw's interests and abilities expanded into many areas, and she shared her time, talents, and resources with numerous institutions and organizations in Memphis and elsewhere. As early as 1973 she was named to the board of commissioners of Memphis Light, Gas and Water, and in 1981 she was elected vice chairperson. She was a member of the Memphis branch of the Federal Reserve Bank, later serving as chair of its board of directors. Tennessee Governor Lamar Alexander appointed Shaw to the State Commission of Minority Economic Development and to the Memphis/Shelby County Jobs Advisory

Council. Other board memberships included Stillman College and Tougaloo College (both in Alabama), the Economic Club of Memphis, Memphis Development Foundation, and the Memphis Plough Community Foundation.

Shaw was a member of Graduate Leadership Memphis in 1979, the LeMoyne-Owen College Advisory Council, the Business Advisory to Southwestern University, Operation Push (People United to Serve Humanity), the YWCA, the Panel of American Women, Delta Sigma Theta Sorority, and the Links. In 1983, after serving as treasurer and a member of the Board of Directors of the National Insurance Association, she was elected its president—the first woman to hold the position.

An exceptional and celebrated black woman, in 1974 the Alpha Kappa Alpha Sorority honored her for Meritorious Service in Business, and in 1980 Moolah Court No. 22, Daughters of Isis, selected her Outstanding Black Woman. She also received the Candace Award from the National Coalition of 100 Black Women, the J. E. Walker Minority Business Person of the Year Award from the Memphis National Business League, *Ebony* magazine's American Black Achievement Award, the Par Excellence Award from Operation PUSH, and the Outstanding Leadership Award from the Coca Cola and Dr. Pepper Bottling Company of Memphis. In 1983 she was honored by Memphis State University's Fogelman School of Business, and in that same year *Dollars and Sense* magazine named her one of the "Ten Outstanding Business and Professional People." Shaw was selected one of America's Top Black Business and Professional Women and in August 1985 she was jointly honored by *Dollars and Sense* and the national organization of Delta Sigma Theta Sorority.

Christianity and religion were a central part of Shaw's life. At an early age she was baptized in the Disciples of Christ church. Her deep religious feelings helped to sustain Shaw through an extended and unsuccessful battle with cancer. She died at 4:00 A.M. on Sunday, June 30, 1985. According to her funeral program, "She was a special person, with an exceptional, honest, positive, charming and beautiful character, and she left a special legacy." In addition to her husband, now vice president of claims at Universal Life, and her parents, Shaw's survivors include her son, Harold, Jr.; a brother, Antonio Maceo Walker; and a sister, Harriette Walker-Pruitt. A Service of Memory for Shaw was held at the family-founded Mississippi Boulevard Christian Church, where then-NAACP executive director Benjamin L. Hooks was among those who honored her with a tribute. She was interred at Elmwood Cemetery in Memphis. A. Maceo Walker, Sr. was reelected company president on July 19, 1985, serving until he retired a second time in February 1990. He died in 1994.

While Shaw benefitted from the business acumen of the men who preceded her as presidents of Universal Life, she acknowledged that her mother was one of the most positive influences in her life. Shaw was very rational, well organized, and secure about who she was. With her spiritual heritage and religious upbringing, added to her own ambition, preparation, and innate ability, Patricia Walker Shaw became one of the nation's outstanding black women business leaders.

REFERENCES:

Gite, Lloyd. "How I Made a Million." *Essence* 15 (June 1984): 70, 132, 135-36.
Ingham, John M., and Lynne B. Feldman. *African-American Business Leaders.* Westport, Conn.: Greenwood Press, 1994.
"New President at Universal." *Black Enterprise* 13 (June 1983): 36.
Norment, Lynn. "A Family Affair." *Ebony* 38 (May 1983): 75-76, 78.
Press Release. The Shaw Group, February 11, 1983.
"Universal Exec Aims for 'Back to Basics' in Marketplace." *Mid-South Business,* February 28-March 4, 1983.

COLLECTIONS:

Patricia Walker Shaw's papers, which include biographical data, family information, general correspondence, miscellaneous items on the Universal Life Insurance Company, and newspaper clippings (including a series of interviews with Shaw published in the *Memphis Commercial Appeal*), are in the Mississippi Valley Collection at the University of Memphis. The Memphis/Shelby County Public Library has a vertical file on Walker. Fisk University, in Nashville, Tennessee, maintains a biographical file on Walker that includes newspaper and journal articles, press releases, her funeral program, and other documents. Fisk also has a biographical file on her father, A. Maceo Walker, a former member of the board of trustees at the university.

Jessie Carney Smith

Susie Isabel Lankford Shorter
(1859-1912)
Religious worker, writer, clubwoman, educator

Susie Isabel Lankford Shorter combined the strenuous life of a nineteenth-century wife and mother with church and women's club work and a modest literary career. Although she kept house for her husband and large family—she bore eight children—domestic duties did not absorb all of her energies. She was extremely active in church and charity functions. She also found time to write. In addition to composing shorter pieces, she wrote a short book and undertook a magazine column. When she became very involved in the clubwomen's movement, she wrote the official song of the Ohio Federation of Colored Women's Clubs.

Susie Isabel Lankford Shorter was born in Terre Haute, Indiana, on January 4, 1859, to Whitten Strange Lankford, an African Methodist Episcopal (AME) minister, and Clarrisa Carter Lankford. Her father was born and educated in Indiana,

Susie Isabel Lankford Shorter

and he was recognized as a very able preacher. Daughter Susie was the eldest of five children. Accounts vary, but she seems to have attended school at Wilberforce in Ohio until about 1873 when her mother died; she was then fourteen, and she wrote a poem on the death. She returned home to keep house for her father and her siblings. The family moved to Baltimore, where her father was pastor of Bethel AME Church. Whitten Lankford soon remarried and Shorter was able to return to Wilberforce, where she studied for two more years. Her subjects included botany, rhetoric, French, music, algebra, and arithmetic.

Shorter's mathematics professor at Wilberforce was Joseph Proctor Shorter (1845-1910). Although she did not know of the incident for many years, she had already been recommended to the unmarried Joseph Shorter as a wife because of the excellence of her biscuits. T. H. Jackson, professor of theology at Wilberforce, had called on the family in Baltimore while she was keeping house and had consumed eleven of her biscuits. Jackson would officiate at her wedding to Shorter.

After completing her studies, Shorter began to teach, first at Rockville, Indiana, and then at Richmond, Indiana. In 1878, at Christmastime during her second year of teaching at Richmond, she married Joseph Shorter, who was the son of James L. Shorter (1817-87), ninth bishop of the AME church and a notable figure in the early history of the church. James Shorter had been a colleague of Daniel Payne in developing Wilberforce, for which he served as financial agent in 1866, raising about three thousand dollars. He was elected bishop in

1868 and is buried in Xenia, Ohio, very near the location of Wilberforce.

Joseph Shorter was born in Washington, D.C., on March 31, 1845. His early education took place in a private school in Baltimore, run by George Watkins. Seeking a better education for his children, James Shorter moved his family of six children to Wilberforce. Joseph Shorter entered the Primary Department and graduated from the Classical Department in 1871. After teaching with great success in Leavenworth, Kansas, for three years, he returned to Wilberforce as professor of mathematics in 1874, a post he held for twenty-three years. In 1896 he became superintendent of the combined Normal and Industrial Department. He was a noted teacher, an able administrator responsible for major new construction on the campus, and an active lay person in church affairs. Among his other duties, he was for twelve years recording secretary of the financial board of the General Conference of the AME Church. He died on March 25, 1910.

The marriage of Joseph Proctor Shorter and Susie Isabel Lankford Shorter produced eight children; three of them—Lee Jackson Shorter, Joseph Prattis Shorter, and Susie Pearl Shorter Smith—were still living in the mid-1920s. In addition to caring for a large family, Susie Lankford Shorter ran a small shop, later known as the College Inn, which catered to the needs of the Wilberforce students. She was also very active in church and club work. For a number of years she offered free kindergarten classes in her home for neighborhood children. Not only did she offer hospitality to large numbers of visitors, she also saw that sick college students got soup or a home-cooked meal to raise their spirits. For many years she was president of Wilberforce's Ladies' College Aid Society, an organization dedicated to helping students complete their studies. Her relations with the students were such that the Wilberforce chapter of the Young Men's Christian Association passed memorial resolutions upon the occasion of her death on February 23, 1912, at the age of fifty-three. Shorter had survived her husband by two years.

Shorter Writes for Publication

Shorter contributed a number of occasional papers to the *Christian Recorder* and also wrote pieces for the publication's "News Column." She wrote a paper on women in the AME church for the celebration of Bishop Daniel Payne's eightieth birthday in Jacksonville, Florida. This was published as a booklet in 1891 under the title *Heroines of African Methodism.* About 1892 she was connected with Julia Ringwood Costen's magazine, *Ringwood's Afro-American Journal of Fashion,* for which she wrote a column called "Plain Talk to Our Girls." It is not known whether she had any connection with a successor magazine, *Ringwood's Home Magazine* (c. 1893- c.1895). Since no copy of either magazine is known to survive, only excerpted pieces of Shorter's efforts remain.

Shorter fully shared the common nineteenth-century view of the woman as man's subordinate. She writes in *Heroines of African Methodism,*

It is a nice thing to be a *conversationalist,* a *musician,* fine *composer* or sweet *singer,* but if you want to live in peace and harmony with a *man* you must be able to sew buttons in the right place and have his meals well cooked on time (whether he is on time or not) and greet him, when he comes home, in a clean apron and with smooth locks. It is no *mean* thing to be a *good* cook, and surely detracts nothing from a highly polished woman. You must study, then, how you shall make *home attractive, make yourself so.*

The corollary of this position was that women could lay claim to a moral position superior to that of men. In this view, one of the major charges to women was to socialize their children properly, especially the males. Another outlet for women's energy were the efforts to reform and uplift society through religious revival, temperance, and raising moral standards. This spirit was also in large part present in the women's club movement, to which Shorter lent her support. Her most famous contribution is the Ohio Federation of Colored Women's Clubs' song, which was adopted by other state federations. Sung to the tune of ''The Battle Hymn of the Republic,'' the second and third stanzas run:

> We represent the women who were once denied a
> place,
> In the National Convention of the highly favored
> race,
> Nothing daunted we have struggled and we've
> made ourselves a place,
> Our motto, ''Deeds not words.''
>
> Chorus:
>
> Deeds not words shall be our motto,
> Deeds not words shall be our motto,
> Deeds not words shall be our motto,
> We're ''Lifting as we climb.''
>
> Our race must be enlightened, we must earn our
> daily bread,
> We must give our time and talent—and the hungry
> must be fed,
> We must root up sin and sadness, planting good and
> joy instead,
> Our motto, ''Deeds not words.''

Susie Isabel Lankford Shorter was an embodiment of the ideal of Christian womanhood held by many nineteenth-century men and women. Fulfilling her duties as a wife and mother, she engaged in the moral uplift of her people and her society. She worked for her church, engaged in club work, and wrote. Her endeavors were not unique to her alone, but her effective efforts brought her the recognition of her contemporaries.

REFERENCES:

Brown, Hallie Q., ed. *Homespun Heroines and Other Women of Distinction.* Xenia, Ohio: Aldine Publishing Co., 1926.
Majors, M. A. *Noted Negro Women: Their Triumphs and Activities.* Chicago: Donohue and Henneberry, 1893.
Scruggs, L. A. *Women of Distinction: Remarkable in Works and Invincible in Character.* Raleigh, N.C.: L. A. Scruggs, 1893.
Shorter, Susie I. *The Heroines of African Methodism.* Jacksonville, Fla.: Chew, Printer, 1891.
Smith, Jessie Carney, ed. *Notable Black American Women.* Detroit: Gale Research, 1992.
Wayman, Alexander W. *Cyclopaedia of African Methodism.* Baltimore: Methodist Episcopal Book Depository, 1882.
Wright, Richard R., Jr. *Centennial Encyclopedia of the African Methodist Episcopal Church.* Philadelphia: Book Concern of the A.M.E. Church, 1916.
———. *Encyclopedia of the African Methodist Episcopal Church.* 2d ed. Philadelphia: Book Concern of the A.M.E. Church, 1947.

Robert L. Johns

Jeanne C. Sinkford

(1933-)

Dentist, educator, college administrator, researcher, lecturer

Jeanne C. Sinkford, dean emeritus of the Howard University College of Dentistry, is a distinguished administrator, educator, researcher, lecturer, and clinician. She broke race and gender barriers in her rise to the top of her profession. The first woman dean of an American dental school, Sinkford graduated first in her class at Howard University. Committed to community service and social responsibility, Jeanne Sinkford has reached out and responded in full to the demands of her profession, striving to meet the needs of her patients and students as well as those of various dental research associations and government and community groups devoted to dental education and study. Sinkford has also been widely praised for her efforts to recruit women and minority students to the dental profession.

One of four daughters of Richard E. Craig and Geneva Jefferson Craig, Jeanne Frances Craig Sinkford was born on January 30, 1933, in Washington, D.C. Geneva Craig was born in Chesapeake Beach, Maryland, and moved to the Washington area around 1920. She worked for the U.S. Commerce Department for twenty years before retiring in 1964 as a classified documents printing supervisor. Prior to her death in 1989, Geneva Craig had been a member of Campbell African Methodist Episcopal Church in Washington, the Rosicrucians, and the Bridge to Freedom organization. Richard Craig, who had worked for St. Elizabeth's Hospital in Washington, died in 1964. Jeanne Craig married Stanley M. Sinkford on December 8, 1951. They had three children, Dianne Sylvia, Janet Lynn, and Stanley M.

Jeanne C. Sinkford

Education was very important to the Craig family. Geneva Craig was a school teacher before she became involved in government service. Jeanne Sinkford studied ballet and dance for eight years and was good enough to receive a scholarship offer for extended training in New York City. Her parents responded with a firm refusal when she told them of her plans to quit high school and leave for New York. At sixteen years of age, Jeanne Sinkford finished Washington's Dunbar High School. In an essay in *Legacy, the Dental Profession,* Sinkford noted:

> I grew up in a loving home where religion was synonymous with life. My beliefs, therefore, centered around strong relationships among family members that have formed the basis for loving and concerned actions throughout my life. Dreams are a part of my early existence. My dreams later became desires for achievement and actions which demanded a life of order and discipline. Being a minority and a woman required a strong work ethic, a sense of morality and decency, a willingness to ''turn the other cheek'' and a sincere motivation to help those who are less fortunate and underprivileged.

Sinkford's family was not financially well off, but all four daughters were encouraged to obtain as much education as possible, so they worked out a ''family plan'' whereby the older girl would help the next in line upon finishing college. However, Sinkford's education took eight years and her younger sister wound up helping her instead, even though Sinkford had scholarships all the way through Howard University and summer jobs to lighten the financial load. Among

the four daughters, Jeanne and Joyce went into medicine and Janet and Julia chose careers in education.

Sinkford majored in psychology and chemistry as a Phi Beta Kappa undergraduate at Howard University. When she was eighteen years old and a junior in college, she met and married a young medical student, Stanley M. Sinkford. Jeanne Sinkford initially spurned medical school, fearing that she would be forced to compete with her husband. The young couple wanted mutually compatible careers. She considered graduate work in psychology or dental hygiene, but her family dentist convinced her that she had the perfect background for pursuing a doctor of dental surgery degree.

Sinkford received her bachelor of science degree from Howard University in 1953 and her doctorate in dental surgery from the Howard University College of Dentistry in 1958, graduating first in her class. She stayed at Howard University and taught crown and bridge prosthodontics for two years before undertaking graduate study at Northwestern University in Chicago. Sinkford received the Louise C. Ball Graduate Fellowship Fund for Graduate Study in Dentistry, which supported her postdoctoral studies at Northwestern University. After her husband completed his military service in 1960, they moved to Chicago so she could begin her studies. Sinkford was seeking a good basic science foundation for the teaching and research that she always wanted to do. She wanted to correlate scientific and clinical research. She studied under Stanley C. Harris at Northwestern's dental school and completed a master of science degree in 1962 and a Ph.D. in physiology in 1963. Sinkford taught for one year at Northwestern while her husband was studying at the University of Chicago.

Few Women Seen in Dentistry

When Sinkford entered dental school, only 1.2 percent of dental students in the United States were women. However, the women's liberation movement helped to open doors for women in dentistry, and in the 1970s, more funds became available for all students, including women, and admission practices were liberalized. In an October 21, 1982, *Atlanta Daily World* article, Sinkford noted with pride that Howard University graduated a woman, Mary Wooten, in the dental school's first class in 1888: ''Howard has traditionally been one of the few U.S. dental schools to admit women on an equal basis as men.''

At the time of Sinkford's 1958 graduation, women made up 2 percent of dentists nationwide. There were five women in her class of fifty. Women were discouraged from dentistry and some faculty had prejudices against female students. Yet Sinkford was accepted by the male students because not only was she an excellent student, she was a leader as well and was elected class president. Sinkford believes that dentistry is a perfect career for women because of their sense of aesthetics and beauty, their ability to be sympathetic, and their small hands, which are helpful when working in delicate areas such as the mouth. In the 1976 publication *Profiles in Black: Biographical Sketches of 100 Living Black Unsung Heroes,* Sinkford recommended dentistry as a career for young women "without reservation because it affords a very useful, purposeful existence." Sinkford has actively recruited women and minorities to the profession. "Dr. Sinkford has been quite an inspiration," Renee McCoy-Collins, the first woman graduate from Howard's oral surgery program, emphasized in the *Atlanta Daily World* article. "The dean has been a perfect example of women's ability in dentistry."

Sinkford returned to Howard University in 1964 as chair of prosthodontics, the College of Dentistry's largest department. She was the first woman head of such a department in the country. Russell Dixon, dean of the College of Dentistry for thirty-five years, brought her into administration because of the leadership abilities he had seen in her. Sinkford moved from department chair to serve as associate dean from 1967 to 1974, with Dean Joseph L. Henry. At one time, Sinkford had a private practice in the evenings but gave it up to devote more time to her teaching career.

On August 24, 1972, Sinkford was named to a nine-member panel to study a U.S. Public Health Service experiment that began in 1932. In this experiment, four hundred African American men with syphilis went without medical aid for forty years in order to determine the effects of the disease on the human body. Known as the Tuskegee Syphilis Study, the panel had ninety days to report its findings and make recommendations. Sinkford has served on numerous other review boards and has frequently answered the community's call for her expertise and commitment.

Sinkford was inducted into the International College of Dentists on November 9, 1974, at the Shoreham-Americana Hotel in Washington, D.C. She was the first African American woman dentist inducted into the U.S.A. section of the college. She was also the first woman dentist inducted in Region IV, which includes Washington, D.C., Maryland, Delaware, Puerto Rico, and the Armed Services. At the time of her induction, Sinkford was on sabbatical leave pursuing a special program in pedodontics at Children's Hospital National Medical Center in Washington, D.C., where she worked on a patient-oriented treatment philosophy for the adolescent-age patient.

Becomes First Woman Dental School Dean

On July 1, 1975, the International Year of the Woman, Jeanne Sinkford was appointed dean of Howard University's College of Dentistry. Sinkford was the first woman to be appointed dean of any dental school in the nation. In a 1986 videotaped interview, *Chronicles of Outstanding Leaders in Dentistry: A Conversation with Jeanne Sinkford,* the doctor remarked, "If I had to work for the dean, I might as well be the dean." When questioned about reactions to her gender in the same interview, Sinkford stated,

> I tried very hard not to be a feminist, to be more of a humanist. That is, to make opportunities available to males and females. I have not tried to promote women per se. I tried to promote talent . . . whenever the individual has talent, move forward. I tried to keep mainstream our objectives and our goals. And

I am a tough administrator. I don't waste money and I don't fool around. It's a no nonsense thing, and I think individuals have grown to respect this.

The Washington, D.C. Democratic Women's Club honored Sinkford at an annual benefit fund-raiser dinner dance on January 19, 1979. The Winter 1978-79 issue of the *Howard University College of Dentistry Newsletter* congratulated its dean for the club's recognition of Sinkford for "her competence in a managerial and scientific position that was formerly dominated by men." Sinkford, in an April 1968 *Ebony* article, stated,

> It takes a lot for a woman to be in a top position, particularly in a male profession. You have to be better to be accepted as equal. Once your colleagues accept you as a competent person, they don't mind your being there. But men are resentful at first because they feel a woman has been selected for a position they might have taken.

Sinkford served sixteen years as dean at Howard University. During her tenure, she spoke and wrote about the crises and challenges of dental education. Four pages of Howard University's *Annual Report, 1986-1987, of the College of Dentistry* detail the activities of a very busy dean: service on some seventeen university committees, ten local committees, twenty national or international committees, participation in eighteen professional and scientific societies, several honors and awards, attendance at ten professional conferences, and publication of an article on trends on dental education in the twenty-first century.

Sinkford believes that dentistry must continue to evolve into a profession that includes education, research, and service as inseparable, essential components. Since July 1, 1991, she had been professor and dean emeritus of the Howard University College of Dentistry. She has since turned her attention to the needs of a growing segment of the population, geriatric dental patients. On November 4, 1991, she became director of the Office of Women and Minority Affairs, American Association of Dental Schools, Washington, D.C.

Sinkford has written a manual for fixed prosthodontics for undergraduate students. Her most significant contribution to dental education has been the nationally acclaimed background document for the Graduate Education Workshop, cosponsored by the American Dental Association and the American Association of Dental Schools. She is a contributing author to *Profile of the Negro in American Dentistry,* edited by Foster Kidd, and has written scores of professional articles.

The July 1975 *Journal of the National Medical Association* cites Sinkford's research experience as "broad, embracing caries activity tests, a study of sex chromatic in the buccal mucosa of rabbits, oral and dental characteristics of a tri-racial isolate, the effect of gingival retraction agents on human blood pressure, endodontic techniques and the processing of grant applications." Sinkford is a member of dozens of professional organizations and societies, including the American Prosthodontic Society, the International Association of

Dental Research, Omicron Kappa Upsilon, the Institute of Medicine of the National Academy of Sciences, and the National Medical Association. She has served on the Council of Dental Education of the American Prosthodontic Society and worked for the American Association for the Advancement of Science. Sinkford holds fellowships in the American College of Dentists and the International College of Dentists.

Sinkford shared these thoughts in *Legacy, the Dental Profession:*

> History has taught us that the great leaders of the world stirred the consciousness of men and thereby created monumental changes that the world would come to respect and to revere. I have been called a "black pioneer," a "renaissance woman," and a modern "Candace" for I have given many years of my life in dedication to the cause that social, cultural and educational inequities in our society can be overcome by forceful leadership and constant support for equal opportunity and civil liberty.

Sinkford's accolades are numerous. The Capital Press Club included her in its Thirty-first Anniversary Salute to Black Pioneers. Alpha Kappa Alpha cited her for exceptional professional achievement at the North Atlantic Regional Conference. She received alumni achievement awards from Northwestern University in 1970 and Howard University in 1976.

On Saturday, May 20, 1978, in the concert hall of the John F. Kennedy Center for the Performing Arts, Georgetown University School of Dentistry awarded Sinkford the doctor of science, honoris causa, degree. She was cited for her continuous efforts to recruit minority students and women to the profession of dentistry and for serving with great distinction as the first woman dean of an American dental school. In 1992, she received another honorary degree from the University of Medicine and Dentistry in New Jersey.

Jeanne Sinkford was one of the first Candace Award winners. The award is given by the National Coalition of 100 Black Women to recognize leadership achievements of black women in various fields of endeavor. Some black men have also won the award. Begun in 1982, the annual awards have had various corporate sponsors. The ebony and crystal award was presented to seventeen achievers on September 30, 1982, at the Metropolitan Museum of Art in New York.

In 1984 Sinkford was presented an award by the Family Life Center branch of the Boys and Girls Clubs of Greater Washington, D.C. She was honored for her achievements as a woman and her involvement in community affairs. That same year, she received an Award of Merit from the Board of Directors of the American Fund for Dental Health in recognition of her outstanding service and dedication to the ideals of the fund and contributions to the support of research, education, and service in dentistry. Sinkford served as a trustee advisor to the American Fund for Dental Health from 1975 through 1984. She has also been honored for her work with the United Negro College Fund.

Stanley M. Sinkford, her husband, is a pediatric cardiologist. He is the chief of pediatrics at D.C. General Hospital and professor of pediatrics at Howard University's College of Medicine. Jeanne Sinkford understood early on that she had to be organized and have support from her family to manage her work. She is active in Jack and Jill of America and with her children's activities. While she had to assume the responsibility for family and home life, Sinkford believes that a husband and wife must agree upon their goals. An active professional, parent, and spouse, Sinkford often worked fourteen-hour days. She acknowledges that it is not a lifestyle for everybody. Along with strong parental role models and professional mentors, Sinkford credits her husband for being very supportive and understanding, particularly about her time constraints. She has been able to have a successful marriage and a successful career.

Jeanne C. Sinkford combines her intellect and her humility in leading a dynamic life committed to her profession, community and society, her beliefs and ambitions, her family and friends. She does no less than her best effort at every turn. She concluded in *Legacy, the Dental Profession,*

> I believe in one supreme being, God, and I believe that man has been given free will which enables him to control his destiny. Life and death continue to be mysteries to us, for in the human life span, we occupy but a grain of sand on the beach of eternity. We are here but for a short period of time and the legacy that we leave must serve as a catalyst for the leaders of the future.

> We are very small particles but we are a part of the divine power of the universe. We will live again, for energy is neither created nor destroyed.

Current Address: 1765 Verbena Street, N.W., Washington, DC 20012.

REFERENCES:

Chronicles of Outstanding Leaders in Dentistry: A Conversation with Jeanne Sinkford. Videocassette. Washington, D.C.: International College of Dentists, U.S.A. Section, 1986.

Funnye, Doris Innis, and Juliana Wu, eds. *Profiles in Black: Biographical Sketches of 100 Living Black Unsung Heroes.* New York: CORE Publications, 1976.

"Howard's First Lady of Dentistry." *Ebony* 23 (April 1968): 103-8.

Kidd, Foster, ed. *The Profile of the Negro in American Dentistry.* Washington, D.C.: Howard University Press, 1979.

Sinkford, Jeanne C. "Current Status and Future Trends in Training Dental Practitioners and Dental Auxiliaries to Meet the Needs of the Black Community." *Journal of the National Medical Association* 68 (January 1976): 60-62.

———. "Modern Concepts and Trends in Dentistry." *Journal of the Baltimore College of Dental Surgery* 32 (July 1977): 2-9.

———. "Dental Education: Trends and Assumptions for the 21st Century." *Journal of the National Medical Association* 79 (February 1987): 227-31.

———. "Choose the High Road." In *Legacy, the Dental Profession: The Philosophies and Thoughts of Selected Dental Leaders Worldwide.* Compiled by Clifford F. Loader and Shigeo Ryan Kishi. Bakersfield, Calif.: Loader/Kisher, 1990.

———. "The Future of Dentistry: New Challenges, New Directions." *Journal of the National Medical Association* 82 (May 1990): 353-58.

———. Letter to Jessie Carney Smith, January 26, 1995.

Sinkford, Jeane C. and Joseph L. Henry. "Survival of Black Colleges from a Dental Perspective." *Journal of the National Medical Association* 73 (June 1981): 511-15.

"Two Dental Firsts." *Journal of the National Medical Association* 67 (July 1975): 326-27.

Who's Who of American Women, 1993-1994. Chicago: Marquis Who's Who, 1993.

"Women on the Rise in Dentistry." *Atlanta Daily World,* October 21, 1982.

Kathleen E. Bethel

Lucy Smith

Lucy Smith
(1875-1952)
Minister, healer, church founder

Elder Lucy Smith has been called the most successful and colorful black Holiness preacher and healer of the 1930s. Smith typified in background and motivation the founders of storefront churches on Chicago's South Side. She appealed to the emotionalism and traditional beliefs of substantial numbers of the southern black working class who moved to Chicago during the Great Migration of the 1910s through 1930s and who were alienated by the formality of the middle- and upper-class churches. She began holding prayer meetings in her home in 1916, becoming a "black puritan preaching holiness" and founding the interracial All Nations Pentecostal Church the same year. In the 1930s she moved the church to a modern building on a fashionable boulevard, where it became a landmark on the South Side. She fed and clothed the needy during the depression, and her work reached a wide radio audience. In thirty-eight years of preaching, she claimed to have healed over two hundred thousand believers.

Born on a Woodstock, Georgia, plantation on January 14, 1875, Lucy Smith was one of six children—four girls and two boys. She knew her mother but never saw her father. The children slept in the attic of the one-room log cabin where Lucy was born. The family sat on the floor as they ate their usual syrup and gravy, having a small piece of meat a few times a week. Their clothes were made from heavy mattress ticking. By age seven Lucy Smith had been neither to school nor inside a more conventional house. She started school at age thirteen, attending during the four months that school was open in that farm area—January, February, July, and August. She worked as a field hand on the land where the family lived.

Religious Interests Developed Early

Lucy married William Smith in 1896 and they had eleven children, nine of whom were born on the farm that they worked together. After they moved to Athens, Georgia, in 1908, William abandoned the family, thus placing the responsibility for family support solely on Lucy. In 1909 she and the children moved to Atlanta, where Lucy Smith sewed for a living. A Baptist since a childhood conversion at the age of twelve, Smith further developed her interest in religion in Atlanta, where she attended Springfield (Missionary) Baptist Church but did not join.

Lucy Smith continued to demonstrate an interest in religion after she moved to Chicago on May 1, 1910. First she joined Olivet Baptist Church, but she became dissatisfied and left in 1912 to join Ebenezer Baptist Church. Hearing that the white Pentecostals offered a satisfaction that the black Baptist churches did not provide, she began to attend Stone Church, a Pentecostal church with a white congregation. Two years later she was baptized in the Pentecostal faith and continued to attend Stone until she received her calling, which she defined as "divine healing" and which inspired her to begin her own religious career.

Spiritual Needs of Migrants Addressed

Lucy Smith, who had demonstrated a restlessness in her religious preferences, began to find solace only in her own efforts to provide religious fellowship to the city's socially disinherited. From 1916 to 1919, she held prayer meetings in the one-room house in which she lived—the beginning of her All Nations Pentecostal Church, which she founded in 1916. The movement was well timed: it coincided with the first wave of migrants from the South who sought to carry on the old-time shouting, uninhibited emotionalism, and "speaking in tongues" that they had known in their former communities and that many of the little store-front churches of Chicago offered. Her followers, who came for blessing, healing, and baptism, grew in number throughout the church's various moves and changes. This was a time when the sexist attitudes of major black denominations prompted black women to found independent Holiness and Pentecostal churches. Lucy Smith and Ida Robinson, a bishop and founder of the Mount Sinai Holy Church of Philadelphia in 1924, are two examples. But even within the Holiness movement Lucy Smith found herself the target of sexual discrimination. She told Herbert Morrisohn Smith, "They don't care for no woman leading a work, they think it's all right for her to help, but not to run things."

In 1926 Lucy Smith began construction of her first church building, located at 3716 Langley Avenue, at the cost of sixty-five thousand dollars. According to St. Clair Drake and Horace R. Cayton in *Black Metropolis,* she said, "My church is for all nations and my preachin' for all Christians." She told Herbert Morrisohn Smith:

> We has all kinds of people who comes here regularly. Swedes, Polish, Italians, just plain white folks, and Jews. I guess we has about five hundred members we kin count on regular. We has lots more that just comes and goes. Healing services is the foundation of this church.

Lucy Smith and her "Saints" offered special healing services three times a week. She told Smith: "I takes the blind, and the deaf, and the crippled, and all kinds of strokes, and lame of all kind on Wednesday afternoons. . . . The minor ones come Wednesday night. . . . Little things like headaches, pains about the body, and heart trouble, I handles them then."

Ministry Reaches Radio Audience

In about 1925 Lucy Smith said that "the Lord just spoke to me," and she called radio station WSBC and persuaded the station to broadcast her Sunday night services from 11:00 to 12:00. The program lasted ten months. Later her services were aired Sundays and Wednesdays on radio station WIND and reached audiences as far away as Alabama, Mississippi, Tennessee, Iowa, Nebraska, and Michigan. The *Chicago Defender* said that she was the first black religious leader to broadcast services on the air. At the time of her death, the *Chicago Defender* said that she was also the first Chicagoan "to broadcast the gospel on radio to Mexico and other distant points over station WGES."

Regardless of the class makeup of their members, black churches in Chicago during the Great Migration offered social and recreational programs for the community. Storefront churches as well as Lucy Smith's Pentecostal Church remained concerned with the new arrivals from the South and with those who were already members, for whom the churches' programs provided some spiritual comfort. In 1932 Lucy Smith and her church fed more than ninety people a day in the basement. Through her radio programs, Smith also was successful in her appeal for clothing for the needy.

To facilitate the building of a government project—possibly a housing project—Lucy Smith sold her first church for seventy-five thousand dollars and in 1937 began construction on a second structure, an eighty-thousand-dollar building located at 518 Oakwood Boulevard, which became her memorial. The value of her church's real estate was estimated at $143,000 at the time of her death. In 1950 *Ebony* magazine featured Lucy Smith as a successful faith healer who claimed to have cured two hundred thousand people in thirty-eight years of preaching the gospel in Chicago. She held nightly healing meetings. Her church boasted three thousand members. She reached one hundred thousand listeners in two weekly broadcasts over Chicago radio stations and claimed five thousand members in her radio club.

Elder Lucy Smith, as she was known, died in her Chicago home on Wednesday, June 18, 1952. Her funeral was historic for two reasons: it was the largest recorded in Chicago up to that time, and it ended a fourteen-day cemetery workers' strike that had caused two hundred bodies to remain unburied and stored in the city's churches. For nearly two days and nights, at least sixty thousand people gathered outside the All Nations Pentecostal Church, where she lay, to pay their respects. Four hundred law enforcement officers were assigned to keep crowds from storming the auditorium of the church. Choirs, gospel singer Mahalia Jackson, and others sang to over twenty-six hundred people at the funeral. Smith was carried from the church in a one-hundred-year-old handmade horse-drawn hearse, which led more than seventy-five cars, including three flower corteges and eleven buses. Lucy Smith's daughter, Adella, succeeded her as church leader. She was also survived by two sons, John and Henry.

Lucy Smith, whom Drake and Cayten called "the mother-image of the drifting black masses," was a large, heavyset woman with little education. She was friendly and approachable and demonstrated remarkable simplicity and deep human sympathies. She was calm and serene and driven by a great conviction that her mission was to serve the religious needs of the masses and to heal those who would believe.

REFERENCES:

Baer, Hans A., and Merrill Singer. *African-American Religion in the Twentieth Century: Varieties of Protest and Accommodation.* Knoxville: University of Tennessee Press, 1992.

Drake, St. Clair, and Horace R. Cayton. *Black Metropolis: A Study of Negro Life in a Northern City.* New York: Harcourt, Brace and Co., 1945.

Dupree, Shirley, ed. *Biographical Dictionary of African-American Holiness-Pentecostals, 1880-1990.* Washington, D.C.: Middle Atlantic Regional Press, 1989.

"Elder Lucy Smith, Famed Air Lane Pastor Buried." *Chicago Defender,* June 21, 1952.

"Faith Healer." *Ebony* 5 (January 1950): 37-39.

"50,000 at Last Rites for Elder Lucy Smith." *Chicago Defender,* June 28, 1952.

Foner, Eric, ed. *America's Black Past.* New York: Harper and Row, 1970.

Lincoln, C. Eric, and Lawrence H. Mamiya. *The Black Church in the African American Experience.* Durham, N.C.: Duke University Press, 1990.

Obituary. *Jet* 2 (July 3, 1952): 18.

Smith, Herbert Morrisohn. "Three Negro Preachers in Chicago: A Study in Religious Leadership." Master's thesis, University of Chicago, 1935.

Washington, Joseph R. *Black Sects and Cults.* Garden City, N.Y.: Doubleday, 1972.

COLLECTIONS:

Information on Lucy Smith is in the Illinois Writer's Project File, Vivian G. Harsh Research Collection, in Chicago.

Jessie Carney Smith

Lucy Harth Smith

Lucy Harth Smith
(1888-1955)
Educator, club leader, black history advocate

Dedicated to improving the conditions of blacks in Kentucky, Lucy Harth Smith made her mark in many arenas. Her chosen profession was education, but she also gained recognition as a national club leader for African American women, as an organizer of support groups for underprivileged black youth, and as a strong voice for advocating the inclusion of black history in schools in Kentucky and across the nation.

Lucy Cornelia Harth Smith was born in 1888 to Daniel W. and Rachel E. Brockington Harth in Roanoke, Virginia. Her marriage in 1910 to Paul Vernon Smith produced five children—Vernon C., Altha L., Paul V., Daniel E., and Edwin M.—all of whom attended college. Altha, the only daughter, died in 1934 from injuries sustained in a gymnastics exercise in college. Of Lucy Smith's four sons, two became dentists, one a college administrator, and one a minister.

Educated in the public schools of Roanoke, Virginia, Smith initially attended Hampton Institute before graduating magna cum laude from Kentucky State College in 1932. She later completed a master's degree at the University of Cincinnati. She taught in the Roanoke city school system from 1908 to 1910 before moving to Lexington, Kentucky, where she became an elementary school assistant principal at Booker T. Washington Elementary School. After seventeen years as assistant principal, she became principal in 1935 and remained in that position until her death in 1955.

Smith was active in many education associations during her lifetime and was the second woman president of the Kentucky Negro Education Association, a position she held from 1944 through 1946. When outlining the issues that she would concentrate on as KNEA president, she indicated that one of her recommendations would be to place black history in the school curriculum. Regarding this recommendation, Harvey C. Russell in *The Kentucky Negro Education Association* quotes Smith as saying in 1944: "Our pupils need respect for themselves as well as for others. We believe that literature telling of the achievements of Negroes should consistently confront the child in the classroom."

In this capacity she was instrumental in the adoption of two textbooks on African American life and history in the public school system of Kentucky. Her idea was that the teaching of black history would not only raise the self-esteem of black children but would also provide them with knowledge of the accomplishments of many who had gone before them. As one of the earliest members of the American Association for the Study of Negro Life and History, as it was known then, she promoted the study of black history in public schools across the country. Her dedication to this organization included serving as executive board member for thirty years, as national and state president, and as national parliamentarian.

Aids in Founding Health Camp

Always concerned about the total welfare of black youth, in 1942 Smith raised $2004.94 to establish The Colored Health Camp for underprivileged and undernourished black children. A black-owned farm was offered as the site for the camp in 1943. With the building supplies and lumber that her committee had solicited from lumber companies in Lexington, her husband and their youngest son, Edwin, built a 14 x 36-foot facility that provided a screened kitchen and seating for thirty children. During the camp's first year in operation, twenty girls attended the first two weeks and twenty boys attended the next two weeks without cost to their families. Later the camp was accepted as one of the agencies worthy of the support of the Community Chest of Lexington. With this new funding source, eighty-three children were helped the second year and one hundred and twenty the third year. During its existence the health camp served thousands of malnourished black children in Kentucky.

Smith was also one of the founders of the National Association of Colored Girls and served as the national supervisor of the organization for four years. A role model for young girls, she encouraged them to set high goals and equally high moral standards.

In a time of segregated schools and public facilities, she seized every opportunity to instill racial pride and high self-esteem in her students. "Lift Every Voice and Sing," known as the Negro national anthem, was sung before every event at her school. She also encouraged the girls at her school to ask for black dolls for Christmas. Following the Christmas break, she would hold a "doll beauty contest" in which only black dolls could enter.

When her school was scheduled to be enlarged, the architects designed the entrance to be on the side of the building facing an alley. Lucy Smith went to the Board of Education and argued that black children were already required to enter all buildings from either side or back doors, and it would be unfair to require the same thing of them at their own school. The entrance was subsequently changed to face a main street.

Actively involved in benevolent societies and charity organizations, Smith served on the administrative board and as parliamentarian for the National Association of Colored Women's Clubs. On the local level, she was president of the Kentucky Association of Colored Women's Clubs from 1943 through 1945. As president, she compiled and edited *The Pictorial Directory of the Kentucky Association of Colored Women*. This publication documents the purposes and accomplishments of the organization and gives names and addresses of officers and membership of each club, including photographs of members.

Smith's other activities include her service on the Lexington YMCA's Interracial Council, State Interracial Council, the Governor's Committee on Youth and Children, and the Women's Improvement Club. In 1939 she acted as representative for Kentucky at the California and New York World's Fair. She was named recipient of the Louisville Defender's Citation as an outstanding Kentuckian.

In August 1955, although she had been ill for about six months, she insisted on keeping a speaking engagement at the University of Southern California. Upon returning to Lexington, Kentucky, Smith, a diabetic, became seriously ill and never recovered. She was buried in Lexington. Sometime after her death, her personal papers, which included correspondence from Carter G. Woodson, Mary McLeod Bethune, Eleanor Roosevelt and other prominent personalities of her day, were accidently destroyed. Fortunately the autobiography that she had written a year earlier was not among those items. In Smith's honor, in 1974 the Kentucky Education Association established the Lucy Harth Smith-Atwood S. Wilson Award for Civil and Human Rights in Education. The first recipient of this award was Whitney M. Young Sr.

Smith has been described by those who loved her as a very pleasant, persuasive woman who was fairly large in stature and who could sometimes be domineering. She always knew what needed to be done and how to get the right people together to accomplish the tasks required. Smith recognized the many needs of Kentucky's black children and set out to find solutions to address these needs. She enhanced the quality of life of these children through efforts that led to improvements in their schools, raising their self-esteem, the inclusion of black history in schools, and other programs that she established or supported.

REFERENCES:

Dunnigan, Alice A. *The Fascinating Story of Black Kentuckians: Their Heritage and Tradition*. Washington, D.C.: Associated Publishers, 1982.

A Gallery of Great Black Kentuckians. Frankfort: Kentucky Commission on Human Rights, 1971.

"KEA Commission Announces New Award Program." *KEA News* 10 (February 7, 1974): 4.

Kentucky's Black Heritage. Frankfort: Kentucky Commission on Human Rights, 1971.

Russell, Harvey C. *The Kentucky Negro Education Association 1877-1946*. Norfolk: Guide Quality Press, 1946.

Smith, Camie. "Mrs. Lucy Cornelia Harth Smith." Unpublished manuscript. 1975.

———. Telephone interviews with Karen Cotton McDaniel, September 4, 1994; September 11, 1994.

Smith, Lucy Harth, comp., ed. *Pictorial Directory of the Kentucky Association of Colored Women*. Lexington: Kentucky Association of Colored Women, 1946.

Who's Who in Colored America. Yonkers, N.Y.: Christian E. Burckel, 1950.

COLLECTIONS:

The papers of Lucy Harth Smith including *The Paul Vernon Smith and Lucy Cornelia Harth Smith Family* (1954) and

Smith family photographs are in the possession of her son and daughter-in-law, Edwin and Camie Smith, Lexington, Kentucky.

Karen Cotton McDaniel

Mary Levi Smith

(1936-)

Educator, college president

Although American women continue to advance through the echelons of politics as mayors, governors, congresswomen, and senators as well as climb up the rungs of the economic ladder as chief executive officers of major corporations, women in academe have not experienced the same upward mobility as frequently. For example, relatively few state universities have women presidents. Rarer still are black women presidents of state universities. However, both women's and blacks' representation increased in 1991 when Mary Levi Smith became the eleventh president of Kentucky State University in Frankfort, a liberal studies, multicultural, racially balanced, land-grant institution.

Smith was born on January 30, 1936, in Hazelhurst, Mississippi, one of seven children born to William Levi, a Church of God in Christ minister, and Byneter Markham Levi. In a 1993 interview, Smith acknowledged the influence of both parents, stating that they "were extremely important and responsible for providing the foundation that enabled me to achieve my personal and professional goals."

Smith graduated from Jackson State University in 1957 with a bachelor of science degree. Her earliest association with higher education in Kentucky may be traced back to her days as a graduate student at the University of Kentucky, first in pursuit of the master of arts degree she received in 1964, and then the doctor of education degree in curriculum and instruction she received in 1980.

Smith's distinguished and varied career in education began in 1957. For the next seven years, she taught elementary grades in Mississippi and Tennessee public school systems. Then in 1964, Smith began teaching on the college level; during the next six years she served as the assistant director of the reading clinic at Tuskegee University and as a reading instructor there. Smith's professional association with Kentucky State University began in 1970 when she became the assistant coordinator of the In-Service Reading Program for Classroom Teachers of Kentucky. In 1974, Smith was appointed an assistant professor of education at Kentucky State, and later she was promoted to associate professor of education. In 1983 she was appointed professor of education.

Smith's graduate work and teaching experience have influenced her research activities. Her research has focused on

Mary Levi Smith

minority students, especially those interested in becoming teachers; factors that prohibit children from succeeding; and the ways children use language to learn to read. Smith's research, along with her teaching career, illustrates her commitment to young people. Smith said in her interview: "We have to invest in youth. If we don't, our future will be bleak. Nothing is more important than investing in our youth."

Appointed First Woman President of Kentucky State

Smith's career as an administrator at Kentucky State University began in 1981 when she became the acting chairperson of the Division of Education, Human Services and Technology; her administrative career advanced rapidly. In 1983, Smith was appointed dean of the College of Applied Sciences and later served as special assistant to the president. Then in 1988, Smith was appointed vice president for academic affairs, and one year later, she became the interim president. In October 1991 Smith assumed the presidency of Kentucky State University.

An outspoken advocate of education, Smith commented on the importance of a college education in a biographical sketch about herself: "I think that education is and should be a lifelong process. What we are doing at the University is helping prepare students for life, which means preparing them for learning throughout their lifetimes." Smith leads Kentucky State University as it heads into its second century of educating students. The university, with 2500 students and 130 faculty members, is a component of Kentucky's public higher educational system; its mission, as stated in the magazine of the National Association for Equal Opportunity in Higher Education (NAFEO), "is to excel as a small university with the system's lowest student faculty ratio."

Throughout the years, Smith has been active in many professional organizations, including the Kentucky Council on Teacher Education and Certification, the Kentucky Association of Colleges for Teacher Education, the Kentucky Association for Teacher Educators, the American Association of Colleges of Teacher Education, and the College Reading Conference. Smith remains a member of the National Board of Examiners for the National Council for the Accreditation of Teacher Education, and she continues to serve on various program evaluation teams for Kentucky's Department of Education. Smith's additional current professional activities include her roles as a member of the Commission of Colleges for the Southern Association of Colleges and Schools and as a member of the board of directors for the National Association for State Universities and Land Grant Colleges.

In addition to her many professional activities, Smith shares her considerable talents with the community. She is a member of the board of directors of United Way of Frankfort, the Frankfort and Franklin County Community Education Board, and the Governmental Services Center Board for the Commonwealth of Kentucky. Smith has also coordinated Little Miss Black Frankfort pageants and served on the board of directors for the Frankfort Arts Foundation. She has been active in community affairs for many years, and she demonstrated her understanding of the connection between learning and society in the 1993 interview when she stated, "Through higher education, you address the needs of the community." When asked how she finds time for her many professional and community activities, Smith continued, "You find time to do what is important."

Smith's efforts have been acknowledged by her professional colleagues and community associates. Kentucky State University cited her as an Outstanding Faculty Member in 1985. The National Association for Equal Opportunity in Higher Education bestowed on her the Outstanding Alumnus of Jackson State University in 1988. In 1989 the Pi Lambda Omega chapter of Alpha Kappa Alpha Sorority presented her with its Torchbearers and Trailblazers Education Award. In 1990 the Frankfort Alumnae chapter of Delta Sigma Theta Sorority gave her its Citizens Award, the Frankfort chapter of the NAACP presented her with its Woman of the Year Award, and the Lexington YWCA bestowed on Smith its Woman of Achievement Award.

Despite Smith's numerous professional and community obligations, she finds time to maintain an active family life. She is married to Leroy Smith, who teaches health and physical education courses at Kentucky State University and is a former head football coach. The Smiths have two sons and one daughter: Daneé, who is in the navy; Darryl, who is a dentist; and Angela Williams, who works for Ford Motor Company. The Smiths have three granddaughters and one grandson. Smith's campus, community, and family continue to receive the many benefits that her intellect, careful thought,

administrative skills, organizational strengths, and love bring to them.

Current Address: Office of the President, Kentucky State University, Hume Hall, Room 201, Frankfort, KY 40601.

REFERENCES:

"Biographical Sketch of Mary Levi Smith." N.p., n.d.
"Paths to Success: Institutional and Presidential Profiles of the Nation's Historically and Predominantly Black Colleges and Universities." *NAFEO* 14 (March/April 1993): 22.
Smith, Mary L. Telephone interview with Linda M. Carter. June 25, 1993.
Who's Who among Black Americans, 1992-93. 7th ed. Detroit: Gale Research, 1992.

Linda M. Carter

Mary Perry Smith
(1926-)
Educator, organization executive

Since 1953 Mary Perry Smith has made singular contributions to the quality of life for African Americans in the San Francisco East Bay Area. As a classroom teacher, she motivated young people to learn and, through the Mathematics, Engineering, Science Achievement Program, initiated by Smith at Oakland Technical High School and now a part of the curriculum in schools in ten other states, she has helped to increase the number of minority students who pursue degrees in mathematics and science-based subjects. She has also had an important influence on the formation and success of the Black Filmmakers Hall of Fame, which honors African Americans in Hollywood and encourages those who aspire to careers in the film industry.

Smith was born on May 29, 1926, in Evansville, Indiana, the fourth of six children of Henry Allen Perry, a minister, and Anna Whittaker Perry. Her family history is rich in examples of newly freed slaves who became successful, and it displays a strong tradition of emphasis on education, community service, and the ministry.

Both of Smith's paternal grandparents and her maternal grandfather were born into slavery. She has fond memories of sitting on the lap of her maternal grandfather, John William Whittaker, who was born in Atlanta, Georgia, in 1860. He graduated from Atlanta University in 1884, completed studies at Hartford Theological Seminary in 1887, and was then ordained a Congregational minister. Following his marriage to Anna Jeanette Connover in 1888, he was chosen by Booker

Mary Perry Smith

T. Washington to be the first chaplain of Tuskegee Institute. He served Tuskegee for thirty-seven years as chaplain, dean, and mathematics teacher. When he died in 1936, he was well known as a chaplain and pastor and was also recognized for his service to other organizations including the YMCA and YWCA. Rev. Whittaker is buried in the cemetery of Tuskegee University on the grounds of the chapel, in the company of Booker T. Washington and others important to that institution. His picture occupies a place of honor inside the chapel.

Smith's paternal grandfather, David Andrew Perry, born in Georgia in 1840, was among the newly freed slaves who were being taken by railroad box car from Georgia to the western part of the country, where work was said to be available. He left the group he was traveling with in Alabama, where he settled, making a prosperous living for his family on a five-hundred-acre farm and providing work for other freedmen. After becoming an African Methodist Episcopal minister he built a church and a school, and sent each of his nine children to Tuskegee. His wife, Emfield Walker Perry, was born in 1847.

Henry Allen Perry, Smith's father, was born on a farm near Union Springs, Alabama, in about 1885. When Perry graduated from Tuskegee as valedictorian of the class of 1915, Booker T. Washington gave him a ten-dollar gold piece as a reward for his scholarship. The value of that gold piece to Smith's family is greatly enhanced by the fact that this was the last graduating class before Washington's death. Perry attended Drake University and Indiana State University, then obtained a master's degree from Ball State Teacher's College. One summer when he was enrolled in an astronomy course at

the University of Chicago he brought home a telescope and treated the children to views of the stars.

Smith's father became an African Methodist Episcopal minister and a school teacher. He moved his residence many times due to his changing assignments with the church, but he was in Kokomo, Indiana, for more than twenty-five years, as teacher and pastor, father confessor, and counselor for entire families. He died in 1967.

Anna Whittaker, Smith's mother, was born in New Orleans, in 1895, into a family of nine children. Her father was pastor of the First Congregational Church in that city. She graduated from Tuskegee Institute and then did further study at Hampton Institute. Prior to her marriage she was an elementary school teacher.

When she was very young Smith heard her father talk at the dinner table about the accomplishments of great African Americans such as Frederick Douglass, Booker T. Washington, and his own father. Often she overheard discussions between him and visitors who came to their home—friends, other ministers, the bishop of the church—in which they explored their views of the day's happenings and their hopes for the future. From these conversations and regular reading of the *Chicago Defender* and the *Pittsburgh Courier,* she was informed about things that concerned the welfare of black people.

After Smith graduated with honors from high school in 1944 she went to Ball State University in Indiana where she completed the requirements for a bachelor's degree in three years by attending classes year round. She graduated in 1947 with majors in mathematics and chemistry. The next year, 1948, she received master's degrees in counseling and guidance and biochemistry from Purdue University. Subsequently, she did additional graduate study at the University of California, Berkeley, and at the University of San Francisco.

Smith began teaching mathematics at Texas Southern University in Houston, Texas, in 1948. There she met Norvel Smith, who taught business at the same institution. They were married in March 1951 and soon afterwards left Houston for Berkeley because each wanted to pursue a doctorate at the University of California. Smith completed the course work for a Ph.D. in educational psychology and then decided to return to teaching. She took a job as a teacher of mathematics and science in the San Francisco Unified School District in 1953. Eight years later, in 1961, she accepted a position in the mathematics department of Oakland Technical High School, where she remained until 1978.

Establishes Mathematics, Engineering, Science Program

Smith was enthusiastic when her principal asked her to take part in the evolvement of the Mathematics, Engineering, Science Achievement Program (MESA) at Technical High School. This was her chance to do something to change the direction of the education of African American and other minority students.

MESA came into being largely because of the foresight of Wilbur (Bill) Somerton, professor in the school of engineering at the University of California, Berkeley, and Bill Somerville, director of the university's Education Opportunity Program. Somerton wanted to add nonwhite students to the pool of graduates he offered to industries when they came seeking applicants for employment, and Somerville was eager to use his skills in program development to help launch the new venture to train more African Americans, Mexican Americans, Puerto Ricans, and Native Americans for mathematics- and science-based employment. Somerton and Somerville selected Technical High School as the initial setting to implement the model designed by Beth McNeil, director of the Morabito Fund, a San Francisco-based philanthropic organization and volunteer worker in Somerville's office. They chose Smith to develop the on-site relations with the students and to be the liaison with the university staff. Having performed extensive groundwork during the 1969 school year, Smith was ready to accept the first MESA students in September 1970. She continued to fine tune the program before it was extended into other school districts.

The MESA experience showed Smith that once students have the proper support, they will respond and work well. MESA is a comprehensive program that begins with the appropriate counseling to direct students into the more challenging classes and follows with instruction about the value of courses such as trigonometry, biology, physics, and chemistry in preparing for employment in technical fields. MESA also offers tutoring and arranges field trips to industrial sites, where students are warmly greeted and invited to sit in boardrooms and engage in conversation with employees who have prepared themselves through serious study. The program is rounded out by an award system, summer job placements, and opportunities for parental involvement. MESA is presently in operation in ten other states. Its graduates, many the first in their families to finish secondary school, have obtained degrees in engineering and other mathematics- or science-related subjects and are working in these fields all over the country.

Smith left teaching in 1978, but remained involved with MESA until she took full retirement in 1982. She still holds a seat on MESA's statewide board. She knows that MESA's effects will be long lasting, evidenced not only in the students' career records, but also in their success as parents who motivate their children to make thoughtful study choices.

Black Filmmakers Hall of Fame

While Smith was working with MESA, she was giving many hours of volunteer service to another project that was equally as demanding of her time and expertise. She was one of the founders of the Black Filmmakers Hall of Fame (BFHF), which was sponsored by the Oakland Museum's Cultural and Ethnic Affairs Guild. The planners of the museum had ignored the nonwhite population of the city, but after an effective boycott of its highly heralded opening in 1970, Ben Hazzard, an African American artist, was hired as curator of special exhibits and education to make the museum representative of Oakland's many ethnic groups. Hazzard formed the guild to help him prepare programs depicting the history and culture of Oakland's diverse ethnic groups, including African Americans, Asian Americans, Latinos, Native Americans, and Puerto Ricans.

At the urging of Morrie Turner, a syndicated comic strip cartoonist, and Harry Morrison, professor of physics at the University of California, and with the promise of help from Sonny Buxton, who was affiliated with a San Francisco television station, the guild became interested in finding a vehicle to promote recognition of African Americans in Hollywood. A group, including Roy Thomas of the Afro-American Studies Department of the University of California, Ruth Beckford, Sonny Buxton, Donald Therence, and Smith, began a series of meetings at her home, planning what was envisioned as a history of blacks in films.

The project began to take shape. The group accepted Sonny Buxton's idea that instead of a simple history, they should design a hall of fame, which would broaden the scope of the project and attract more Hollywood personalities. Hazzard approved the plans, and the guild president, Dorothy Patterson, brought its members into action. Teola Sanders suggested a gala "Dinner with the Stars" as a fund-raiser to underwrite costs; the management of the Paramount Theater on Broadway in downtown Oakland agreed to their use of that newly refurbished facility for induction ceremonies with the understanding that the payment of rent would depend upon ticket sales.

In 1974 the BFHF held its first award ceremony at the Paramount Theater. Among the inductees were Paul Robeson, Ossie Davis, Katherine Dunham, Bea Richards, and Sammy Davis Jr., along with such old-timers as Lincoln Theodore Perry (Stepin Fetchit), Eugene Jackson, Clarence Muse, and Lorenzo Tucker. The ceremony was warmly welcomed by the people of the Bay Area, who were happy to see these talented black performers recognized for their artistry, but the event was not a financial success. However, with funding from the city as well as from foundations, industries, and individuals, the BFHF has continued into its twentieth year. Its activities have been expanded to include a symposium at the university, where the public can hear the inductees talk about their careers in an informal setting, a lecture series on the history of black people in films, competitions in filmmaking and screenplay writing, and screening opportunities for independent producers who have no other outlets.

Smith is now president of the board of the BFHF and acting executive director. She is still strongly committed to the organization and is proud of its list of awardees, which is a complete who's who of black Americans in the movie industry. She also takes pride in the encouragement the BFHF gives to aspiring filmmakers.

Smith has served on the board of directors of many California organizations, including the Oakland Museum Association Board; the Oakland Museum Women's Board; the Management Center, San Francisco; Oakland Potluck; Statewide MESA; and Black Filmmakers Hall of Fame. She has received several honors, such as the Community Service Award from the Northern California Council of Black Professional Engineers for contributions to MESA; the Community

Service Award from the Department of Special Exhibits and Education, The Museum of Oakland, California; the William Elmer Keeton Award, presented by the Northern California Center for Afro-American History and Life; and the Civic Contribution Award from the League of Women Voters of Oakland. The Mary Perry Smith Award, established by the statewide office of MESA, is given annually to an outstanding MESA advisor.

Smith has published handbooks for advisors and for students in MESA, as well as a procedures handbook for directors. In addition she contributed to the 1985 publication *Early Identification and Support: The University of California, Berkeley's MESA Program.*

Current Address: 7006 Colton Boulevard, Oakland, CA 94611.

REFERENCES:

Smith, Mary Perry. Interviews with Dona L. Irvin. April 1, 1993; June 15, 1993.

Dona L. Irvin

Jane Morrow Spaulding

Jane Morrow Spaulding

(?-1965)

Clubwoman, social worker, community activist, political organizer, government official

Pioneering, influential, multifaceted in interests and abilities, Jane Morrow Spaulding was appointed in 1953 as assistant to Oveta Culp Hobby, Secretary of Health, Education, and Welfare. The first African American woman to hold such a high government position, Spaulding brought to her duties more than twenty years of experience in social services. Indeed, her work in women's organizations and in a full range of social, political, and community action programs clearly identified her as a model of energetic leadership, integrity, and wise counsel.

Sources give no information on Jane Esther Morrow Spaulding's year of birth, her parents, or whether she had any siblings. It is clear, however, that she was born in Kentucky and, while still an infant, moved with her parents to Nashville, Tennessee. She completed her elementary and secondary education in Nashville and then entered Fisk University, where she was greatly admired by her peers as beautiful, poised, and representative of the best in African American womanhood. One Fisk alumnus remembers her as mesmerizing, describing her effect on him as "dust" in his eyes.

On February 7, 1918, Jane Esther Morrow married Albert Lee Spaulding, a physician and assistant health com-

missioner in Charleston, West Virginia. Upon settling down in Charleston in the fall of 1918, she became active in community programs, speaking frequently at meetings and serving on interracial committees. Later she worked with the Congress of Industrial Organizations, the American Federation of Labor, and the United Mine Workers. Nothing more is known of her work with labor unions. Jane Spaulding also became the mother of one son, Albert Lee Spaulding, Jr., who followed in his father's footsteps, establishing a medical practice in Chicago, Illinois. Albert Spaulding, Jr. later married Chicagoan Marva Trotter Louis, former wife of heavyweight champion Joe Louis.

Becomes Active in Women's Clubs and Social Work

In addition to her domestic duties and labor union activities, Spaulding enjoyed her role as a member of the Charleston Woman's Improvement League. Cited as the oldest club for African American women in West Virginia, the league supported cultural activities, scholarships for deserving students, and youth organizations. A member for over fifteen years and president in 1940, Spaulding played an important role in establishing the Day Nursery, a permanent home for numerous black children as well as a day-care facility for others. In addition, the Washington Street Club House was acquired in 1940 when she was the league president.

Continuing the efforts of her predecessors in the office of local president, Spaulding also organized many activities designed to assist local women and girls, to provide wider educational opportunities, and to encourage a more responsible and productive African American community. Moreover, she concentrated on the national Women's Improvement League, reminding state officers and members of the advantages to be gained by working closely with the parent organization. She reorganized the local agenda to match that of the national program, targeting public health, child welfare, education, citizenship, and better homes. Further, she supported efforts to purchase a national headquarters building, to erect a memorial to Booker T. Washington, and to restore the Frederick Douglass Home in Anacostia, Virginia. She was a living demonstration of the league's motto, "Lifting as We Climb."

When the "Negro Division" of the West Virginia Relief Administration was created during President Franklin D. Roosevelt's first term in office, Spaulding was named its director. She worked for four years in this position, making certain that African American citizens were included in all relief programs established by both state and federal government agencies. Thomas E. Posey describes the West Virginia Relief Administration as a comprehensive effort supporting rural rehabilitation, homestead subsistence, vocational training centers, self-help and cooperative enterprises, improved housing, and several work projects for men and women, such as road building, food preservation, and sewing. Spaulding and community volunteers distributed information on the varied relief programs, matched local needs with rehabilitation efforts, and coordinated activities. In a special initiative, five graduates of West Virginia State College were awarded federal government scholarships to study at the Atlanta School of Social Work. Upon completion of their degrees, these students were expected to return to West Virginia to organize and maintain social welfare programs in African American communities. Spaulding was characterized in Posey's *The Negro Citizen of West Virginia,* published in 1934, as "the most prominent person in the field of social service . . . [whose] past achievements, especially in . . . social work, have made her the logical choice for this important position." Posey writes that Spaulding was widely known for having done an "unusually fine job for Negroes in the state." Moreover, for fifteen years, she had been identified with the West Virginia State Federation of Women's Clubs, the organization that, according to Posey, many people considered the "most constructive force" among private charities serving African Americans in that state.

In her position as director, Spaulding saw as one of her first tasks the compiling of information to be used in establishing a comprehensive educational, economic, and social program for West Virginia's African Americans. With the cooperation of numerous local organizations, she conducted a survey among the state's African Americans, a manageable task because Spaulding's local, regional, and national associates considered participation a way of showing their respect for her as an outstanding social worker engaged in important programs. Also significant is the fact that, while Spaulding's numerous contacts and varied experiences aided her in completing specific goals, they also provided her with a broad perspective, alternative strategies, and valuable insight into individual and group problems and their solutions.

While filling leadership volunteer positions at the local and state levels, by July 1934 Spaulding also held a regional office, having been elected second vice-president of the Central Association of Colored Women's Clubs during the fourth biennial session at Louisville, Kentucky. Her dedicated leadership on local, state, and regional levels was in accord with her commitment to organized efforts for aid and development.

On August 16, 1936, when the fifth biennial session opened in Charleston, West Virginia, Spaulding presided as state president and conducted a public mass meeting in the state capitol. In addition, during a meeting held in Oklahoma City from July 26 to August 1, 1941, Spaulding was chairperson of the Women in Industry Committee, a group through which she combined her interest in labor activities with her work for African American women. According to Charles Harris Wesley in *The History of the National Association of Colored Women's Clubs,* she emphasized her belief that "the National Association of Colored Women should assist women in industry in conjunction with various government bodies." Spaulding's sentiments were echoed by the featured speaker, Mary V. Robinson, director of the Division of Public Information of the Women's Bureau, whose topic was "The Negro Woman Worker in Our Democracy Today." Noting that two million women were in the labor force and that one of every five was colored, Robinson commended such outstanding black women as singer Marian Anderson, educator and activist Mary McLeod Bethune, and Willa Brown, the commercial pilot, for their contributions to the betterment of female African Americans. Mary V. Robinson might also have commended Spaulding for her support of that labor force because, in addition to her volunteer work in women's clubs, she had been active in welfare work, labor union activities, and programs for women in industry.

Spaulding Is Rewarded for Her Social Work

Spaulding's national reputation as an outstanding social worker, together with her active participation in national women's associations, brought her well-deserved recognition and reward. In 1951, she represented the U.S. Council of Women at the triennial conference of the International Council of Women in Athens, Greece. Also in 1951, she participated in the Human Rights Commission of the United Nations, which met in Geneva, Switzerland. In 1953, she was presented with the Woman of the Year Award by Philadelphia's branch of the National Council of Negro Women, and on February 26, 1954, she was honored, along with television host and columnist Ed Sullivan and Professor Auguste Hoggman of the University of Berlin, at the twentieth anniversary celebration of the National Council of Negro Women for "furthering the principles of brotherhood." According to the *New York Times* for February 27, 1954, Eleanor Roosevelt, speaker for this occasion, called for action in the cause of brotherhood, reminding the audience of a principle that guided Jane Spaulding's entire life: "It is not enough to have a brotherhood week . . . not enough to make fine speeches, to hold fine dinners and meetings. It is the actual practice which must follow the promises." The honors Spaulding received were just one indication of the extent to which she was identified with humanitarian causes.

In May 1955, Spaulding gained recognition of a different sort. In its third annual nationwide poll, reported by *Ebony* magazine, the National Association of Fashion and Accessory Designers (NAFAD) named her one of America's ten best-dressed women. Representing, according to the association, "the quintessence of good clothes sense," she and nine others were cited as having "achieved the ultimate aim of women the world over: that effortless look of quiet elegance." *Ebony* identified Spaulding as a "high government [Foreign Operations Administration] consultant," and further described her as "constantly speaking, traveling." On a personal note, she was portrayed as tall (5 feet, 9 inches) with a special fondness for "good hats, shoes, bags ... find[ing] Dior fashions suitable, but favor[ing] simplicity for daytime dress." Accompanying the article is a portrait of Spaulding, "sartorially prepared to meet the King and Queen of Greece four years before NAFAD caught up with the busy civic worker...." Indeed, she was a woman whose impeccable outer appearance matched her sterling inner qualities.

Spaulding caught the attention not only of fashion designers' associations but of individuals in influential government positions. One of the first African American women to support General Dwight D. Eisenhower for president, Spaulding was appointed in 1952 as special assistant to Mrs. Oswald B. Lord, cochair of Citizens for Eisenhower. Spaulding drew upon her considerable organizational and management skills and proved to be very effective in gaining black supporters throughout the United States. She was especially effective at informing African American voters about the Republican civil rights platform, which pledged improved citizenship and employment opportunities for minorities, including appointments for "qualified persons, without distinction of race, religion, or national origin, to responsible positions in the Government," as noted in *Congressional Quarterly's Guide to U.S. Elections*. The Republican party kept its promise in at least one instance by offering Spaulding an important position.

Spaulding becomes Government Appointee

On the recommendation of Mrs. J. Cheever Cowdin of New York, Henry Cabot Lodge, Jr., U.S. delegate to the United Nations, supported Spaulding for a government post. Then, in April 1953, when the Department of Health, Education, and Welfare [HEW] was established with Oveta Culp Hobby as its first secretary, Spaulding was appointed her assistant. The April 15, 1953, issue of the *New York Times* carried the headline "Welfare Worker Named Hobby Aide" and printed a photograph of the two women seated together in conference. Further evidence of the respect with which Spaulding was regarded upon her appointment can be seen in the outline of her duties: "As assistant to the Secretary, Mrs. Spaulding will have general staff assignments in the fields of education, social security, child welfare and health. As one example of the type of assignment that might come her way, her predecessor [Mrs. Anna A. Hedgeman] acted in a liaison capacity between the Federal Security Agency [forerunner to

HEW] and the Mid-Century Conference of Children and Youth." The clear inference that Spaulding's duties would be comparable to those that Anna Hedgeman had been assigned must have held great significance for Spaulding, who had long lobbied for equal treatment for African Americans.

Unfortunately, the apparent good will and evenhanded treatment that characterized Spaulding's appointment was short-lived. After only nine months as Oveta Culp Hobby's aide, Spaulding was reassigned. On January 22, 1954, HEW released to the press the entire text of Jane Spaulding's resignation along with the report that she had "accepted" a position with the War Claims Commission. Interestingly, her resignation from HEW on January 21, 1954, was accepted not by Oveta Hobby but by Nelson A. Rockefeller, acting secretary of the department. Moreover, according to the December 24, 1954, issue of the *New York Times,* there were charges by Clarence Mitchell, director of the Washington bureau of the NAACP, that Spaulding's job "had been abolished ... in a departmental reorganization because of differences on racial matters between Mrs. Spaulding and Mrs. Hobby." In fact, there were three problems, all dealing with racial issues, that led to Spaulding's forced resignation. First, after the NAACP and Adam Clayton Powell publicized Oveta Hobby's effort to delay integration of schools on military bases, Spaulding was asked to distribute a letter repudiating these charges. Spaulding would not sign the letter, creating a particularly tense situation since fifteen of the twenty-one military bases still had segregated schools, including those at Fort Hood, Texas, in Oveta Hobby's home state. Second, Spaulding made several antidiscrimination speeches. Third, she supported the NAACP's position that a hospital in Houston, Texas, should not receive a $1,500,000 grant unless it extended full privileges to African American doctors. Oveta Hobby sided with the hospital, which happened to be in her home city. It is clear that the same sterling character that suited Spaulding for positions of high responsibility also informed her attitudes, decisions, and actions in those positions.

While Spaulding's move from HEW to the War Claims Commission increased her annual salary from $9,600 to $10,800, it brought no security. After less than one year, she was notified that she was losing the War Claims position as of December 31 because the department was downsizing its staff. NAACP director Clarence Mitchell charged that the Eisenhower administration promoted Spaulding "with the idea of dropping her later," as reported in the *New York Times* in December of 1954. Whatever the reason for her being dropped, Spaulding's considerable abilities made her a viable candidate for yet another government position.

On Christmas Day, 1954, the *New York Times* reported that Spaulding was under consideration for appointment as a consultant with the Foreign Operations Administration (F.O.A.) in India. F.O.A. officials, well aware of her varied social welfare experiences, said that they wanted her "to help in efforts to get more Indian women to participate in the development programs in that country," and that they anticipated her "valuable aid to this phase of the Indian program." Appointed to a third position in the Eisenhower administration in less than two years, Spaulding remained in the states and immediately began working on the Point Four program for underdeveloped countries. In the *New York Times* of December 24 and 25, 1954, an F.O.A. spokesman explained, however, that she might work overseas for the agency at a later time. *Ebony* magazine's May 1955 characterization of Spaulding as "constantly traveling" certainly suggests a busy schedule whether stateside or abroad.

This trailblazing, powerful, and sometimes controversial leader apparently spent the last years of her life rather quietly. Indeed, records of her activities after 1955 are difficult to find. The few available biographical entries are brief, often mentioning only her social welfare and government work of the 1940s and 1950s. *Jet* magazine, April 19, 1962, cited her groundbreaking appointment as assistant to the secretary of HEW, "the first Negro woman to hold such a position," in a one-sentence summary of her achievements. But Spaulding's influence extended far beyond social welfare work and political appointments. Young women, long before women's liberation became a movement, must have admired and tried to emulate her full-time engagement as wife, mother, social worker, clubwoman, and political activist. In fact, Jane Spaulding's life provides documentation of the complex roles African American women have played and continue to play successfully, combining marriage, maternity, and social action. Having thus ensured a lasting legacy, Jane Morrow Spaulding will be remembered. She died in Chicago, Illinois, on September 10, 1965.

REFERENCES:

"Brotherhood Urged: Mrs. Roosevelt Demands Action Instead of Promises." *New York Times,* February 27, 1954.

Christmas, Walter. *Negroes in Public Affairs and Government.* Yonkers, N.Y.: Educational Heritage, 1966.

Congressional Quarterly's Guide to U.S. Elections. 2d ed. Washington, D.C.: Congressional Quarterly Inc., 1985.

Davis, Elizabeth Lindsay. *Lifting as They Climb.* Washington, D.C.: National Association of Colored Women, 1933.

"F.O.A. Job Studied for Negro Aide." *New York Times,* December 25, 1954.

Jenkins, Maude T. *The History of the Black Women's Club Movement in America.* Ann Arbor, Mich.: University Microfilms, 1984.

"Mrs. Spaulding Gets Position with F.O.A." *New York Times,* December 30, 1954.

"Negro Group Head Scores Mrs. Hobby." *New York Times,* December 24, 1954.

Posey, Thomas E. *The Negro Citizen of West Virginia.* Institute, W.Va.: Press of West Virginia State College, 1934.

Randall, James D., and Anna E. Gilmer. *Black Past.* Charleston, W.Va.: Colorcraft, 1989.

"Ten Best Dressed Women." *Ebony* 10 (May 1955): 94-95.

"Welfare Worker Named Hobby Aide." *New York Times,* April 15, 1953.

Wesley, Charles Harris. *The History of the National Association of Colored Women's Clubs.* Washington, D.C.: NACW, 1984.

"Yesterday in Negro History." *Jet* 21 (April 19, 1962): 11.

Patsy B. Perry

Vaino Hassan Spencer
(1920-)
Judge, lawyer

Vaino Hassan Spencer, currently an appeals court judge in Los Angeles, became California's first black judge when she was appointed to the municipal court for the Los Angeles District in 1961. With the appointment, she also became the third black woman judge in the United States. Having already been a highly successful real estate agent, she was equally successful on the bench and became known for her impartiality and concern for those who worked with her as well as those who appeared before her in court.

Born in Los Angeles on July 22, 1920, Vaino Hassan Spencer was the daughter of Abdul and Nona Taylor Hassan. After graduating from Los Angeles Polytechnic High School, she entered Los Angeles City College, eventually receiving her bachelor's degree summa cum laude in 1949. On October 15 that year she married Lorenzo V. Spencer; they were divorced in 1967. Prior to her marriage, she had obtained a California real estate license, and from 1938 to 1947 she was active in the real estate business. Possessed with a strong determination to be outstanding in whatever she did, she was one of the top salespersons in the profession, rapidly selling homes for the expanding Los Angeles population. It was through selling real estate that she developed the interest in law that eventually led her to become a judge.

She told *Sepia,* January 1963, "I had never given law much thought until a good friend of mine, George Cannady, with whom I was working in the real estate business, began studying for his bar examination. I became interested and decided to study law." Spencer began her law studies and in 1952 graduated from Southwestern School of Law in Los Angeles. Immediately after passing the state bar examination in 1952, she entered general law practice. Her friend from the real estate business, George Cannady, was one of her early law associates.

Spencer had a successful practice on her way to a judgeship. While in law practice from 1952 to 1961 she served on various appointive commissions and boards that involved her in the courts. During this time she also became involved in politics and the Democratic party. Her name became associated with state politics in 1958 when she became an ardent supporter of Edmund G. "Pat" Brown, a little known district attorney from San Francisco and later state attorney general. In that year he defeated former U.S. Senator William Knowland to become governor. Brown appointed Spencer to an important and influential position on the California Law Revision

Vaino Hassan Spencer

Committee which she held from 1960 to 1963. The nine committee members representing the state bar association examined statutes and made recommendations for change.

Named California's First Black Woman Judge

Governor Brown was well aware of Spencer's professional skills. In 1961 the California State Legislature voted to expand the judicial system to help alleviate the crowded conditions of the state's courtrooms. Brown then appointed Spencer to the newly created position of municipal court judge for the Los Angeles Judicial District, as this small claims court was known in California. She was to handle the overflow cases from the People's Court. She took office on October 6, 1961, becoming the first black woman judge in California's history. Since Spencer was assuming a new post rather than an unexpired term of a judge already seated, she would not run for reelection until 1964, when she would run for a six-year term.

Although she remained a staunch Democrat, the appointment brought an end to Spencer's political activism. A judicial code of ethics in California prevents judges from becoming involved in partisan politics. However, Spencer still exercised her right to become involved in voter registration and in encouraging people to vote.

When appointed, Spencer was only the third black woman judge in U.S. history. The first was Jane M. Bolin, who became judge of the Domestic Relations Court of New York City in 1939. The second black American woman judge was Juanita Kidd Stout, who in 1959 was the first black

woman elected to a court of record, the Municipal (later changed to County) Court of Philadelphia. Spencer was soon joined by Marjorie McKensie Lawson, whom President John F. Kennedy appointed to the juvenile court in Washington, D.C., and Edith Sampson, who was elected associate judge of the municipal court in Chicago in 1962. Notwithstanding Spencer's excellent background and qualifications, her judgeship came early in black women's involvement on the bench. There were people who wondered if she confronted racial and gender discrimination while carrying out her duties. Spencer said in the *Sepia* article,

> I have yet to see any reaction whatsoever to my being either a Negro or a woman and presiding in a courtroom. I have had no indication from the attitude of those who have appeared before me as to any reason why they have felt any difference toward me than they would toward another judge they might be appearing before.

While serving the municipal courts, Spencer for a while also acted as a traffic judge. She was especially concerned about the alarming traffic death rate and saw a need for a more rigorous education program as a requirement for obtaining a driver's license to enable the public to become more knowledgeable about traffic laws. She found that some offenders did not know they were breaking a law and concluded that driver's license examinations should be more difficult and should cover additional areas of traffic law. Altogether, she found traffic court gratifying. She told *Sepia*,

> There are so many new by-products of being convicted of a traffic offense—civil suits, insurance claims, jail sentences—that such a conviction could lead to serious consequences. Too, the large death toll and number of people being permanently injured puts more importance on traffic cases. So, in this area the discretion of the judge can be carried out for some good.

In either court, small claims or traffic, Spencer was known for her great sense of fairness, patience, and understanding. *Sepia* quoted A. E. Albu, the deputy county clerk assigned to Spencer's division, who said, "Judge Spencer is extremely kind and considerate to those who work with her and those who appear before her." Spencer continues to serve the legal system as a judge in the Los Angeles Court of Appeals, Second District, Division 1.

Spencer became involved in a number of community, civil rights, and legal activities prior to becoming a judge. From 1959 to 1961 she was on the board of directors of the Southern California chapter of the American Civil Liberties Union. She received several appointments, including membership on the Attorney General's Advisory Committee on Constitutional Rights, which came during the term of Stanley Mosk. She held the appointment for two terms—1959-61 and 1961-63. She served the NAACP as chair of the legal redress committee and a member of the executive board from 1955 to 1956, and she was a member of the life membership committee from 1962 to 1964. She was adviser to the integrated housing Consolidated Realty Board from 1961 to 1965.

Spencer was also a member of the board of directors of the National Committee against Discrimination in Housing. From 1963 to 1967 she served on the advisory committee of the Bank of Finance in Los Angeles.

Spencer's interest in politics led her to become president of the Democratic Minority Conference between 1955 and 1960 and to her membership on several committees and boards, including the California Democratic Central Committee, 1958-60 and 1960-62; the executive board of the Democratic County Central Committee, 1958-60; and the executive board of the Community Groups Political Action, 1960-62. Spencer's committee involvement expanded to other areas as well. She was director-at-large of the California Mental Health Association from 1962 to 1964. She was also elected to the Public Affairs Division of the California Department of Mental Hygiene.

Active in legal associations, Spencer has held memberships in the American, National, and Los Angeles bar associations, the California Conferences of Judges, the Langston Law Club, and the American Judicature Society. The first black president of the National Association of Women Judges, she was elected to office in 1979.

Spencer has received wide recognition for her work in the Los Angeles community. She was named Woman of the Year by the *Pittsburgh Courier* in 1946 and again in 1953 and by the *Los Angeles Sentinel* in 1952, 1957, and 1962. Other awards include the Civil Rights Service Award, Democratic Minority Conference, 1960; Equal Opportunities Honoree, Urban League, 1961; Distinguished Citizen in the Field of Civil Rights, the Coca Cola Company, 1962; Trailblazer Award, National Association of Business and Professional Women, 1962; and honorary citizen of Omaha, 1962.

A woman with a sense of civic responsibility beyond the bench, Spencer is active in civic affairs in Los Angeles and throughout the state. She is also a life member of the NAACP. A compassionate woman with a quiet, well-modulated voice, she has on occasion been voted one of the best dressed women in Los Angeles. Impartial, articulate, and sensitive, she is important in legal history as well as in American history for her work as a black woman pioneer on the bench in California.

Current Address: Court of Appeals, Second District, Division 1, 300 South Spring St., Los Angeles, CA 90013.

REFERENCES:

"America's Prettiest Judge." *Sepia* 12 (January 1963): 52-55.

"Chicago Judge Sophia Hall Heads Women Judges Group." *Jet* 77 (December 4, 1989): 6.

Clayton, Edward T. *The Negro Politician.* Chicago: Johnson Publishing Co., 1966.

"The Negro Woman in Politics." *Ebony* 20 (August 1966): 96-100.

Smith, Jessie Carney, ed. *Black Firsts.* Detroit: Gale Research, 1994.

Who's Who among Black Americans, 1980-81. 3d ed. Northbrook, Ill.: Who's Who among Black Americans, 1981.

Who's Who in America, 1970-71. Vol. 36. Chicago: Marquis Who's Who, 1971.

Who's Who of American Women, 1974-75. 8th ed. Chicago: Marquis Who's Who, 1975.

Jessie Carney Smith

Carrie Steele
(?-1900)
Children's home founder

Carrie Steele Logan was one of a number of underprivileged, uneducated African Americans who attacked religious, educational, and social problems in nineteenth-century America. The founder of the Carrie Steele Orphan Home, she performed a role much like that of today's volunteer probation officers. She filled that role in the city of Atlanta in the 1880s, and in her self-appointed task she earned the respect of Atlanta police officers and both black and white residents who were interested in the welfare of underprivileged children.

Carrie Steele did not work through the courts, but through the home for orphans that she founded. Employed as a maid in Atlanta's Union railroad station, she cared for abandoned babies and children she found in railroad waiting rooms by placing them in a boxcar during her workday. In the evening she took the children home to sleep, eat, and live under her own roof. She raised funds for the orphanage by writing her life story, by selling her home, by appealing to both southern and northern friends, and by getting the cooperation of the city of Atlanta and Fulton County.

Concerned citizens brought youthful offenders, recalcitrants, and neglected children to Steele, and she assisted in solving the problems of black waifs. Steele's interest in neglected black children was so great that she was known to many residents of Atlanta and every policeman as "Aunt Carrie." Steele was a ready listener and was very sympathetic with these children in helping to solve their problems.

The few records available on Steele are silent on the early years of her life. She was born a slave and became an orphan at an early age. After enduring many difficulties as a child, she reached womanhood and was employed as a maid at the Atlanta Union Depot.

Steele saw the suffering of orphans and neglected children as she went about her work, and she was moved to do something for these unfortunates. Her mission was to build an orphan asylum. Without funds, however, she did not know how to fulfill her dream of founding an orphanage for black

Carrie Steele

children to prevent them from becoming delinquents and criminals.

In the mid-1880s Steele bought four acres of land on the outskirts of Atlanta and began her work in a two-room house with five children. To finance the purchase, Steele had continued to work at the railroad station, and she earned additional income from the proceeds of the sale of a booklet she wrote about her life.

Part of the money for the investment also came from the sale of her home in Atlanta. With her wages she had bought a home at the corner of Auburn Avenue and Piedmont Avenue in the heart of the city. This site is of great importance to the social and economic history of black Atlanta. Steele sold her home to Henry A. Rucker, who in 1880 served as a delegate to the Republican National Convention. In 1897 Rucker was appointed the Internal Revenue collector of Atlanta by President McKinley, the only person of color to hold this position. In 1904 Rucker constructed on the site he had purchased from Steele the five-story Rucker Building, the first business office complex for black professionals.

Carrie Steele Orphanage Founded

With her finances greatly boosted by the sale of her home, Carrie Steele started what is now a monument to the history of child welfare among African Americans—the Carrie Steele Orphan Home. The home was chartered by the state of Georgia in 1888 as a nonprofit organization. Steele had great business acumen. She negotiated with the city of Atlanta to set up the orphanage with the stipulation that the

home would always be in the hands of a board of black trustees that she would name. The first board was chosen by her and afterwards it became a self-perpetuating board which elected members to fill vacancies.

Steele's shrewdness was further demonstrated when she entered into a contract with the city of Atlanta and Fulton County to care for their pauper children in exchange for monetary compensation to support the youngsters. This forethought assured some financial stability and the orphanage's maintenance until 1923; the home was then included among the beneficiaries of the Atlanta Community Chest, a community fund-raising effort.

A report of the Atlanta University Conference of 1898 on the "Welfare of the Negro Child" noted that through the aid of friends Steele had constructed a three-story brick structure, a hospital, and a schoolhouse. The report further stated that the number of children sheltered at the home had increased from the 5 who originally lived there to 225. Since there were no state reformatory facilities for black youths, reformatory work was performed at the orphanage.

Carrie Steele married a Mr. Logan sometime in the 1890s and the name of the institution was changed to the Carrie Steele Logan Home. The *Atlanta Constitution* of November 4, 1900, carried a front-page article chronicling the death of Carrie Steele Logan of a stroke on the previous day. Her funeral was held at Big Bethel African Methodist Episcopal Church and her remains were interred at Oakland Cemetery.

The Carrie Steele-Pitts Home, Inc. (the name was subsequently changed to honor Clara Pitts, a later administrator of the home) is now a private, nonprofit, and nondiscriminatory child development agency that provides state-approved residency and full-time services for neglected, abused, abandoned, and orphaned children. It is a fitting memorial to a former slave and orphan.

REFERENCES:

Du Bois, William E. B., ed. "Welfare of the Negro Child." In *Proceedings of the Third Conference for the Study of Negro Problems.* Atlanta: Atlanta University, 1898.

Mason, Herman. *Going against the Wind: A Pictorial History of African-Americans in Atlanta.* Atlanta: Longstreet Press, 1992.

Obituary. *Atlanta Constitution,* November 4, 1900.

100 Years, 1888-1988: Carrie Steele-Pitts Home, Inc. Atlanta: Carrie Steel-Pitts Home, 1988.

COLLECTIONS:

Records of the Carrie Steele Home and Records of the Neighborhood Union, both containing information about Steele, are located in Special Collections, Woodruff Library, Atlanta University Center, Atlanta, Georgia.

Casper L. Jordan

Charlotte Andrews Stephens
(1854-1951)
Educator, principal, librarian, reformer

Historical accounts of Charlotte Andrews Stephens's life portray a strong, spirited, loving, and remarkable woman. Because of her father's commitment to teaching blacks, Stephens was nurtured in and influenced by an environment rich in learning opportunities. Constantly battling racial prejudice and social inequity, Stephens fulfilled her dream of going to college and then became one of the most notable teachers in the South. Her seventy-year teaching career has been proclaimed the longest in the United States. According to *Ebony* magazine, January 1950, "For 70 years, from 1869 until retirement in 1939, she taught at every grade level in the schools of Little Rock, Arkansas." Her dedication to education ultimately led to her being the first woman in Little Rock to have a school named for her.

The third child of Wallace and Caroline Andrews, Charlotte Andrews Stephens was born in 1854 in Little Rock. Caroline Andrews had previously given birth to two boys, but one of them died shortly after birth. Stephens was named after her mother's best friend, known to the family as Aunt Charlotte, who lived across the street from them. Lottie was the nickname given to Charlotte by family and friends. Charlotte Stephens and her parents began the pioneer work of establishing a school to educate blacks in Little Rock as early as 1864. Her father's small Methodist church became the site of the first black school in Arkansas, which created groundbreaking educational opportunities for slaves and free blacks.

Although Charlotte Stephens's parents were slaves most of their lives, the two were uncommonly dynamic and enterprising. Caroline Andrews opened a home laundry business that supported the family. Stephens's father did several odd jobs in addition to working for his master. Aunt Charlotte operated a "wash house." Despite the hard work and conditions of slavery, Wallace and Caroline Andrews never lost an opportunity to teach lessons to Stephens and others in the community.

When Stephens was seven, she was taken away from her parents and enslaved as a housemaid on a plantation ten miles away from them. Two years later the fall of Little Rock to the federal army ended slavery in parts of the state, and Stephens was reunited with her parents. According to Adolphine Terry in her biography of Stephens,

> Two days after the fall of Little Rock, an old friend of Wallace Andrews from the plantation where Lottie had been living for two years put the child on a horse behind him and started for town to restore her to her parents. She was riding uneasily holding on with both arms around the man's waist, not able to see anything because of the broad back in front of her when her guardian suddenly reined in the horse exclaiming "Why there's Brother Andrews him-

Charlotte Andrews Stephens

self." Lottie peeped around his back to see her father and another friend driving toward them in a trim light wagon. They were coming to take her home.

Armed with bits and pieces of knowledge she gained discreetly while living on the plantation, along with her father's lessons, Stephens trained to be a teacher. Stephens's first assignment as a teacher came about as the result of her father's missionary work. While traveling, Wallace Andrews discovered a large population of blacks in the Pine Bluff, Arkansas, area who were desperate for teachers. Stephens and her brothers journeyed 150 miles up the river to reach the school. According to Terry, "The school was opened with John as principal, Jimmy and Charlotte as staff." Stephens later recalled that people from this area were so eager to learn that having two sixteen-year-old boys and twelve-year-old Charlotte as teachers did not reduce their fervor in the least. Countless adults and children poured into the small school for the opportunity to learn. Stephens and her brothers operated the school until their father died a few months later.

Stephens Excels as a Teacher

Charlotte Andrews Stephens returned home after her father's death and resumed the lifestyle of a twelve-year-old, playing, doing chores, and studying. Three years later she had her second chance to be a school teacher. In 1869 free schools were opened to blacks. Stephens, being the brightest student in her class, had the opportunity to fill in when one of the regular teachers became ill. Stephens's experience led to her entrance into the mainstream of the teaching profession.

While Stephens was successful as a teacher, she was dissatisfied with the limited preparation she had for her chosen career. Stephens made a major decision—to pursue a college education. Her efforts were not without the usual trials and tribulations faced by blacks seeking higher educations—financial woes, family separation, and racial prejudice. To give an example of the racial inequality existing at the time, Stephens's only choice for college was Oberlin in Ohio, where black students had been accepted and black women had already graduated with bachelor's degrees. Stephens paid her own way through college by saving money from her teaching job, and whenever her tuition money ran out, she went back to work again full time. College was a very enlightening experience for Stephens, both intellectually and socially.

As her level of social awareness rose, Stephens discovered that the blacks in Little Rock were starved for entertainment and recreation. She addressed this need by organizing in Little Rock activities similar to the ones she was introduced to at Oberlin, such as dramatic skits, musical concerts, and games designed for the entertainment of large groups. These programs were highly successful. Stephens was author, director, musical conductor, costume designer, and whatever else the occasion called for.

By 1877 Charlotte Stephens was principal of Capitol Hill School in Little Rock. That same year she married John Herbert Stephens on February 21. She continued to work as a reformer, challenging the educational and social traditions of her community. Her energy and popularity led to her participation in both local and national organizations. The Women's Christian Temperance Union and the Federated Women's Club were two national organizations that Stephens joined as a charter member. She joined other groups as well, including Lotus, the Bay View Reading Club, and the YWCA. Stephens selected organizational affiliations based on their commitment to the enhancement of people's lives. It was not long before Stephens took on another challenge—motherhood. As with many professional women, Stephens's life became structured to accommodate both her family and her career.

Stephens had eight children, two of whom died shortly after birth. Since Stephens and her husband both worked away from home, her mother and friends of the family looked after the children, ensuring that they received love and proper care. All of Stephens's children were intelligent. They were first in their classes and went on to make good lives for themselves.

Charlotte Andrews Stephens's competence as a teacher and administrator, along with her high level of energy, led to offers from schools such as Philander Smith College in Little Rock and the University of Arkansas at Pine Bluff, but she was adamant about her preference for teaching younger students, whom she felt could best benefit from her knowledge and guidance. She preferred the third and eighth grades. Stephens also worked as a librarian for a time. In recognition of her significant accomplishments, in 1909 a black school in Little Rock was named in Stephens's honor. A larger school

built on the site and also named in her honor was dedicated on October 8, 1950.

Charlotte Andrews Stephens continued to work even after she retired, when, during the summer months, friends and neighbors sent their daughters over to her house for lessons. Stephens stayed alert and active by traveling with her youngest daughter and studying. At this stage in her life, Stephens was elated about traveling to various cities, historical landmarks, museums, and other cultural attractions, many of which she had only read about before. At various times throughout her remarkable career, Stephens had visions of writing a novel about the progress and achievements blacks had made since their emancipation, but instead of writing the novel, she lived the life of an extraordinary role model. Stephens's tremendous influence on her students, and others with whom she came into contact, is documented in Terry's *Charlotte Stephens: Little Rock's First Black Teacher,* which also attests to Stephens's importance in the educational history of this country.

REFERENCES:

Anthony, Mary. "Dean of the School Marms." *Negro Digest* 9 (May 1951): 31-32.

Jackson, Barbara G. "Florence Price: Composer." *Black Perspective in Music* 5 (Spring 1977): 33.

Johnson, John H. "Speaking of People." *Ebony* 5 (January 1950): 5.

Terry, Adolphine F. *Charlotte Stephens: Little Rock's First Black Teacher.* Little Rock: Academic Press of Arkansas, 1973.

Thura Mack

Ellen Stewart

(c. 1920-)

Stage producer, fashion designer

No one could have predicted that a young African American girl growing up in pre-World War II America would become a major force in theater in the United States and in the world. Even an ambition to become a clothes designer could have seemed unrealistic for such a girl. Yet events spurred Ellen Stewart to fill these roles. After her arrival in New York City in 1950, she first became a designer. Success in this field funded her efforts in the theater. Her skills, perseverance, and devotion resulted in the creation and maintenance of the La Mama Experimental Theater Club, a major force in world theater for more than forty years.

Little is known about Ellen Stewart's background; she does not discuss her personal life except as it is connected with her theatrical projects. Thus, to outsiders her life is almost entirely the institutional history of La Mama. The uncertainty extends to such basic information as the date and place of her birth. Some sources give 1920 as her birthdate. Her birthplace is sometimes given as Alexandria, Louisiana, but a recent article places the event in Chicago and says she is the daughter of a southern tailor and a schoolteacher. At one point, in connection with her early interest in theater, Ellen Stewart stated without elaboration that some of her family members were in vaudeville and burlesque. She had a foster-brother, Frederick Lights, whose experiences in the New York theater inspired her to create her own theatrical group. Her former husband was a postman. She has a son who is a car salesman, and she is a great-grandmother.

Stewart admits to an interest in the theater from an early age when she and Frederick Lights played with a miniature theater made from shoe boxes and used spool people. She then had no personal experience of the theater. Lights is said to have studied theology at Howard University and, with the encouragement of *New York Times* drama critic Walter Kerr, drama at Yale University. The difficulties Lights experienced trying to gain a foothold in the New York theater became an important element in Stewart's determination to found an experimental company willing to give chances to new playwrights.

Details about Ellen Stewart's life as a young woman before she moved to New York are just as sketchy as those about her childhood. Her youthful ambition was to be a fashion designer. This was unthinkable as a field of study in the south at the time, so she studied education at Arkansas State University. In 1950 she came to New York City with the aim of studying at the Traphagen School of Design. Stewart is Catholic, and on her third day in the city, she lit a candle in Saint Patrick's Cathedral asking for help. As she came out of the cathedral she spotted Saks Fifth Avenue department store and applied for work; twenty minutes later she had a job cutting threads off bras.

Traveling on the subway and visiting neighborhoods was a cheap diversion. While Stewart was visiting the street market at Orchard and Delancey, she struck up a friendship with an old Jewish merchant, Abraham Diamond, a former pushcart salesman. He encouraged her ambition to design and helped by supplying her with fabrics. The clothes Stewart sewed at home and wore to work soon landed her a job as a designer at Saks. She held this job until about 1957 when she had to have surgery. Upon her recovery, she became a freelance designer. In the meantime her brother had been involved in a major musical flop of the 1955-56 season, *The Vamp*. Stewart claims that he was the real author of the musical, but that it was taken from him and rewritten by others. A money settlement was little compensation for the injury to his spirits.

In 1961 during a vacation in Tangiers, Stewart's discontents were coming to a head. There she met a friend, Theresa Klein, who began talking in a such way that Stewart believed Abraham Diamond was speaking through her mouth. Both used the metaphor of always having a spiritual pushcart, that is, a dream project separate from one's job. She thought of her

brother and another friend, Paul Foster, both of whom wanted to be playwrights. They became her pushcarts, and a pushcart wheel became La Mama's trademark.

Shortly afterwards, Ellen Stewart was humiliated by a midtown shop that refused to believe that she was a designer or even look at her sketches. Stewart found that meditating in front of a work by her favorite painter, Marc Chagall, was a way of restoring her inner peace, and so she made her way to Greenwich Village to see a friend who was a picture framer. He had occasional jobs framing Chagall lithographs, and she hoped to find one there. On the way she discovered at 321 East Ninth a basement for rent, and she determined that this was where she would begin her work to help theatrical neophytes and experimentalists. She was able to lease the space for fifty dollars a month. There she set up a business that was to be a dress boutique by day and a coffeehouse theater by night. She also began an occupation that gave her a consummate knowledge of New York City fire, health, and building codes. A sympathetic city health inspector—a retired actor—made it possible for her to get a restaurant license. A license requires a name. Paul Foster tossed up Stewart's nickname, Mama. That suggestion was adopted with the addition of La to make it sound fancier—Cafe La Mama.

Experimental Theater Founded

Cafe La Mama opened in July 1962 with an adaptation of a Tennessee Williams short story, *One Arm*. The space was very small, with room for some twenty-five spectators and a playing area about as big as a single bed. In a *New York Times* interview quoted in *Current Biography*, Stewart said, ''In fact, the only prop we had was a single bed. All the plays we did concerned a single bed. . . . We also had a lot of ketchup because we put on a lot of gory murder plays.'' In August 1962 La Mama put on its first original play, Michael Locasio's *In a Corner of the Morning*. In November La Mama presented the first New York production of a Harold Pinter play. La Mama and a few other places, like Cafe Cino, were launching what became known as the off-off-Broadway movement. La Mama was the first to do original plays and proved to be the most enduring. Stewart said in *Backstage*, December 21, 1990:

> But people should remember, if Joseph Cino was the Papa of Off Off Broadway, I'm the Mama. From the get-go we had to find ways to survive. If we couldn't go get a chair, we had to find one in the streets. But we still put the show on.

The city put difficulties in the way of the fledgling organization. A zoning ordinance forced it to move to a loft at 82 Second Avenue in 1963. Six months later the city found more violations of building ordinances and forced a move to 122 Second Avenue, where there was room for seventy-four spectators. Stewart's resilience and ability to improvise a solution was on call at this time. For example, during the move from 82 Second Avenue, Stewart asked the last audience to pick up something and carry it out as they left. Hassles with restaurant regulations resulted in the formation of a private, nonprofit club, La Mama Experimental Theater Club.

The net effect of this was that the patron purchased a short-term club membership rather than a theater ticket. As if the city regulations were not trial enough, yet another challenge came from Actor's Equity in 1966. The union was upset by its members working for no pay in coffeehouses and banned the practice. Stewart was able to persuade the union to waive its rule for La Mama on the basis of its status as a private club.

Until 1967 the principal benefactor of La Mama was Ellen Stewart herself. She earned her money by designing swimsuits and sports clothes for a New York clothing manufacturer. Fortunately, production costs were kept very low in the early days; a hundred dollars or less was a typical figure, and no one received a salary. Then it became fashionable for major foundations to give grants in support of the arts, and she persuaded the Rockefeller, Ford, and Kaplan foundations and the National Endowment for the Arts to give her theater club money. With these funds she was able to buy a building on East Fourth Street. There was a 144-seat theater on the first floor, another acting space and work and storage rooms on the second floor, and an apartment for Ellen Stewart on the top floor. The apartment has been described as essentially one large room that also serves as a place for the members of the La Mama company to discuss matters. The building at 74A East Fourth Street became the company's permanent location. In 1974 came the addition of an annex two doors away at 66-68 East Fourth Street.

The company opened in its new home on April 3, 1969. The acquisition of a building by no means assured La Mama's continuing physical existence. Its entire history is marked by the search for funds to stay afloat. Even today Ellen Stewart faces a constant fund-raising effort in order to keep La Mama open. In the December 21, 1990, *Backstage* article she said:

> Certainly, we have much more monies than we had in the beginning. Certainly, I am not the one working at four jobs like I used to have to do to pay all the bills. I don't do that anymore.
>
> But for the scope of our activities and what we attempt to do, and what we *do* do, we don't nearly have the monies. And on occasion, I do lament a light that I wish we had, or a sound system that I wish we had, or things like that. But that doesn't stop the show, honey.

Two years later, in 1992, La Mama was again in very dire straits because there was an accumulated deficit of $340,000 and the New York State Arts Council and the National Endowment for the Arts had cut their grants. Stewart privately borrowed $25,000, which she could not pay back. She could neither pay her staff nor the electric bills. Somehow this crisis, like the earlier ones, was overcome.

Ellen Stewart is a charismatic woman who is fierce in defending her theater. In the early years she established a tradition of appearing in front of the audience before every performance to ring a cowbell and say, "Good evening, ladies and gentlemen. Welcome to La Mama ETC dedicated to the playwright and all forms of the theater." It is this dedication that has made La Mama important in the theater. It started by

offering a forum to new playwrights. In the first four and a half years the organization mounted more than two hundred new plays. The plays mixed failures and successes. Playwrights can learn their craft only by seeing their work staged before an audience, and only an experimental theater can afford the luxury of failure. One notorious example of this was the early play *Futz!* by Rachel Owens. The subject matter—the love of a man for a pig—was shocking and Tom O'Horgan's direction further exaggerated the outrageousness of the text. The play was moved to an off-Broadway theater, where it received extremely divided reviews and an Obie. O'Horgan himself directed some forty plays during La Mama's first four years and went on to direct *Hair* and *Jesus Christ Superstar* on Broadway. The American Sam Shepard is only one of a group of well-known playwrights whose first production was at La Mama. *Viet Rock* and *Godspell* originated there as did the more recent *Torch Song Trilogy* of Harvey Fierstein.

The emphasis at La Mama has changed over the years. In the seventies Stewart built up ensemble companies, some of which were ethnic. To support the ensembles, she developed repertory seasons at La Mama. Even today La Mama is putting on an average of sixty presentations a season.

Ellen Stewart's first aim—presentation of new plays—was being fulfilled in the early years. The next step was publication. Publishers would not accept plays that had not been reviewed, and reviewers did not cover off-off-Broadway. The situation was different in some European capitals, where all plays presented were reviewed. So, with a decision that had surprisingly happy consequences, she sent a troupe abroad in 1965 for the first of La Mama's tours. The glowing reviews led to publication for twelve of the twenty-one productions sent to Europe, including *Chicago* by Sam Shepard and *Black Mass* by Adrienne Kennedy.

The success of the first tour led to traveling companies as a permanent feature of La Mama and fruitful contacts abroad. Troupes from La Mama went everywhere possible from Japan to South America to Europe. La Mama became an agent through which American avant-garde theater reached the world. In turn the international connections which were made led to La Mama's involvement in bringing foreign theater to this country. Many foreign companies came to perform in their native languages at La Mama.

The continuing international influence of La Mama was manifest in 1990. Romanian exile Andrei Serban had begun mounting a classical trilogy at La Mama in 1972. The work continued for the next seventeen years. With the overthrow of the communist regime, Serban was invited back to Bucharest to take charge of the National Theater, where he stunned audiences with his audacious project.

Ellen Stewart's life has centered on La Mama. Her work has won much acclaim, and among the awards are: American Theater Association/International Theater Institute Award in 1975; for her encouragement of new playwrights, the Margo Jones Award in 1979; in 1980 a *Village Voice* Off-Broadway Award (Obie) and Special Citation for her career; the Edwin Booth Award of the Graduate School of the City University of New York in 1984; and in 1987, for her and La Mama, a special citation from Dance Theatre Workshop. She has received ten honorary doctorates. In 1985 she received encouragement in the form of a John D. and Catherine T. MacArthur grant, an unsolicited award with unrestricted use of the generous funds. The prestigious award has the nickname of "genius" fellowship.

Ellen Stewart's contribution to theater is immense. The creator, leader, fund-raiser, and exponent and defender of La Mama, she has concentrated her efforts on this company and given it a longevity that is extraordinary among groups of this kind. She gave some of today's most famous playwrights their first start and became an important agent for international cultural exchange.

Current Address: La Mama Experimental Theater Clubs, 74A East Fourth St., New York, NY 10003.

REFERENCES:

Current Biography. New York: H. W. Wilson, 1973.

Elsom, John. *Cold War Theatre.* London: Routledge, 1992.

Heilpern, John. "La Mama Courage." *Vogue* 182 (August 1992): 138-42.

Henderson, Mary C. *Theater in America.* New York: Abrams, 1986.

Little, Stuart W. *Off-Broadway: The Prophetic Theater.* New York: Coward, McCann and Geoghegan, 1972.

Mapp, Edward. *Directory of Blacks in the Performing Arts.* 2d ed. Metuchen, N.J.: Scarecrow Press, 1990.

Robinson, Alice M., Vera Mowry Roberts, and Milly S. Barranger, eds. *Notable Women in the American Theatre.* New York: Greenwood Press, 1989.

Stewart, Ellen. "Finding Ways to Survive." *Backstage* 39 (December 21, 1990): 28.

Wilmeth, Don B., and Tice L. Miller, eds. *Cambridge Guide to American Theatre.* New York: Cambridge University Press, 1993.

Robert L. Johns

Maxine Sullivan

arrangement, with bassist John Kirby's Quintet providing the accompaniment. Thirty-five years later, a March 16, 1972, *Down Beat* review of a new Sullivan recording stated, "This kind of simple self-contained art-singing is the closest thing to Lieder singing Americans have ever developed and Maxine is one of our few but most successful exponents." *New York Times* journalist John S. Wilson reported on December 15, 1985, less than two years before Sullivan's death, "Whether the 50-year mark is tied to singing in an after-hour club, gaining momentum with recognition or exploding with "Loch Lomond," Miss Sullivan has been singing with consistent success since the mid-30s. . . . From the start, she had a vocal style that distinguished her from all her contemporaries." She had by this time outlived the "Loch Lomond Girl" label and proved wrong those who doubted her ability to sing jazz.

Born in Homestead, Pennsylvania, on May 13, 1911, Maxine Sullivan was surrounded by music from an early age. Her father played the mandolin. He and several of Sullivan's uncles, who also played musical instruments, including the banjo, violin, and tenor saxophone, sang barbershop harmony. When she was very young, Sullivan began to sing around the house. At the age of six she sang at a library show, upon the insistence of her grandmother. In junior high school she formed a trio with two male classmates. Jazz historian Sally Placksin, in her *American Women in Jazz,* quotes Sullivan as saying, "We used to book ourselves out of the other classes, so we were doing our circuit in school there." Before she reached her teen years, victrolas were popular, and, as a purchasing enticement, stores offered "give away" recordings featuring many of the leading vocalists of the day, mostly

Maxine Sullivan
(1911-1987)
Singer

Born Marietta Williams, Maxine Sullivan's career as a singer spanned fifty years. Wrote the *Los Angeles Times*'s Burt Folkart, the name changed "soon after going on the road during the latter days of Prohibition." For over half a century she sang folk, jazz, and pop in nightclubs and made a name for herself in radio, film, and the theater. She first came to national attention in 1937 with her recording of the Scottish folk song "Loch Lomond," sung to a Claude Thornhill those who were white. But as Sullivan later recalled in Placksin's book, "I wasn't into that kind of bag." Neither was she attracted to the blues when blues women made their appearance on records. Sullivan continued to sing in high school, performing with the glee club.

Her father's youngest brother, Harry Williams, was a drummer in vocalist Lois Deppe's popular Pittsburgh band. Unhappy as a drummer, he returned to Homestead and formed his own group, the Red Hot Peppers. It was with this band that Sullivan made her debut, which was followed by other engagements with the group. As she remembered during an interview with Placksin,

> Before I started tagging along behind the band, I had different little odd jobs, waiting tables and things like that. . . . Downtown Pittsburgh was jumping, but the singers that were tops were those gals with these big voices. . . . My handicap was that my voice was just a little bit too soft, and I wasn't into the repertoire that most of the singers were into.

Her repetoire included such selections as "I'm Forever Blowing Bubbles," "Molly Malone," and "If I Was a Ribbon Bow," folk songs requiring a lighter voice, but sung in her swinging style.

Singer Begins Professional Career

Sullivan began her professional singing career in a Pittsburgh speakeasy, a small private establishment curiously named the Benjamin Harrison Literary Club that had perfect acoustics for the size of Sullivan's voice. Sullivan's Uncle Harry had introduced her to the pianist Jeannie Dillard, who worked at the club, and arranged for her audition. Since another singer was already performing there, Sullivan had to go through a probationary period. After one week, she was hired as the official club singer at fourteen dollars a week. She remained there for a year.

Top jazz artists often visited the Benjamin Harrison Literary Club. It was a popular meeting place because it did not have to conform to the two A.M. curfew and was open in the early morning hours. It was at the Harrison Literary Club that members of Chick Webb's orchestra heard Sullivan. Two members of the band were John Kirby, bassist, and Cliff Jackson, pianist, both of whom she later married. Visiting the club one evening was Gladys Mosier, pianist with Ina Ray Hutton's band. Mosier recommended Sullivan to pianist and arranger Claude Thornhill in 1936 and urged Sullivan to move to New York City.

After arriving in New York, Sullivan sang, as she told jazz writer Dempsey Travis, in "every gin mill from 155th Street all the way down to 52nd Street." Two days following her audition at the famous Onyx Club on 52nd Street, she became the intermission entertainer at a salary of forty dollars a week. Mosier and Thornhill became her managers. Both realized that because of the timbre of her voice, a unique presentation was required. Thornhill was interested in adapt-

ing the classics and folk songs to a swing beat, particularly since they were in the public domain and therefore all royalties would go to the adapter.

On August 6, 1937, Sullivan recorded the Thornhill-arranged "I'm Coming, Virginia," "Annie Laurie," "Blue Skies," and "Loch Lomond." She had earlier recorded "Gone with the Wind" and "Stop You're Breaking My Heart." Only in the late 1970s did she discover that these two records had been released. The John Kirby Quintet backed Sullivan on "Loch Lomond," which brought her to national attention.

Controversy arose over Sullivan's swinging the classics. Several radio stations placed a ban on swing renditions of old-time songs. Other stations chose to give the public what it wanted—and what it wanted was Sullivan's rendition of "Loch Lomond." CBS radio's Saturday Night Swing Club, which elected to air the tune, staged performances at Loew's State Theater with Sullivan as featured vocalist. Said Sullivan to Placksin, "For years I was stuck with the folk material, you know. But it didn't hurt a bit." Her salary at the Onyx went from $40 a week to $80 and eventually to $150.

Sullivan's recording success brought her offers to appear on screen and the stage. She appeared in two Hollywood films in 1938: *Going Places,* opposite Louis Armstrong and Ronald Reagan, and *St. Louis Blues,* with Dorothy Lamour and Lloyd Nolan. Also in 1938 she married John Kirby. In 1939 she performed on Broadway with Louis Armstrong and Benny Goodman in *Swinging' the Dream,* a jazz version of *A Midsummer Night's Dream.* She began enlarging her repertory to include such pop tunes as "I've Got the World on a String," "Wrap Your Troubles in Dreams," and "I Got a Right to Sing the Blues." Many critics believed that a sense of the blues was even beginning to creep into her delivery.

Sullivan and Kirby worked as a team for her radio show, *Flow Gently, Sweet Rhythm.* The program, which often featured jazz interpretations of classical themes, was produced by a CBS network and remained on the air for two years. But as the Kirby band's popularity increased and Sullivan's movie, theater, hotel, and club engagements expanded, their marriage fell apart, and the two divorced in 1941.

Sullivan joined the Benny Carter orchestra for one tour and then launched a solo act. Highlights of her career were her tours of Great Britain in 1948 and 1954. In the mid- and late 1940s Sullivan performed with Johnny Long and Glenn Miller. She then worked for six years at Le Ruban Bleu on New York City's East Side, followed by four years at the Village Vanguard.

Sullivan wed stride pianist Cliff Jackson in 1950, a marriage that lasted until Jackson's death in 1970. In 1956 she retired from show business in order to devote her time to her family. Other activities included working with the local school board and serving as president of the Parent-Teachers Association of P.S. 136 in the Bronx. She also studied to be a nurse and began learning to play the valve trombone. Utilizing her nursing training, she spent time working as a health counselor. She had grown tired of both the road and "Loch Lomond."

Sullivan established the House That Jazz Built, a community center that she dedicated to her husband. It is headquartered in a building that Sullivan purchased in the South Bronx in 1956. Supported by memberships and grants, the House that Jazz Built is operated with the help of senior citizens. Sullivan explained to Placksin,

> It took us a little while to arrive at a formula . . . because I had no idea what I was doing; it was just an idea. And of course, in the beginning, it was a lot of my own money that went into fixing the house up. But then it's my own property; I had to do this.

Singer Comes Out of Retirement

In 1967 Sullivan went to Washington, D.C., to participate in the opening night festivities for the now-famous Blues Alley club. The following year cornetist Bobby Hackett persuaded her to join him at the Riverboat jazz club in New York City. She appeared there with Hackett's World's Greatest Jazz Band, frequently playing the valve trombone or flugelhorn. Her performance in the 1979 Broadway musical *My Old Friends* brought her a Tony Award nomination. There were more recordings—all of which received excellent reviews—and three Grammy nominations, in 1982, 1985, and 1986. The early 1980s saw appearances by Sullivan at jazz festivals in France, Holland, and Denmark, and in 1985 she toured Japan.

Maxine Sullivan was always a true professional and a master of her craft. Her voice was timeless, with "straight-ahead" delivery and musical integrity. As jazz encyclopedist Leonard Feather wrote during Sullivan's post-retirement years as quoted by Folkart, "The Sullivan sound . . . remains one of those immutable wonders in which simplicity, understatement and a lightweight sound that matches her dimensions have always been the bench marks."

Though her health was failing by the mid-1980s, Sullivan refused to slow down. She celebrated her fiftieth year in show business and at the time of her death was preparing for a return visit to the Provincetown, Massachusetts, Universalist Meeting House. Billed as a "legendary swing singer," she first appeared there before a capacity audience in September 1985. According to *Airwaves,* the program guide of radio station WOMR, Provincetown, Maryland,

> Some came to celebrate their own youthful memories and some, perhaps, were there from sheer curiosity. . . . She got down to business in a simple, friendly way and delivered two solid sets of music. And the applause was long and loving.

Sullivan made a return visit to Provincetown in August 1986. She was a bit smaller in stature but no less musically talented. She was scheduled to appear there in July 1987 but died three months earlier. In February 1987 she performed at Roosevelt Hotel's Cinegrill in Los Angeles and in March 1987 she performed in Connecticut. Between 1981 and 1987 Sullivan recorded eleven albums, four of which were titled *The Queen,* as well as two albums for the Stash label, two for Concord Jazz, one for Tono, one for Audiophile, and one for Atlantic. On her schedule at the time of her death was an ocean cruise devoted to jazz, a charity concert in London, and a return engagement at Los Angeles's Cinegrill.

The four-foot, eleven-inch Maxine Sullivan entered Westchester Square Hospital in New York City after suffering a seizure on April 1, 1987. She died on April 7, 1987. The cause of death, according to one report, was heart failure; another source attributed her death to lung cancer. She was survived by a daughter, Paula Morris, and a son, Orville Williams. Her death brought to a close the illustrious career of a versatile artist who sang jazz, pop, and folk on the radio and in movies, theaters, hotels, and clubs.

REFERENCES:

Chilton, John. *Who's Who of Jazz.* Chicago: Time-Life Records Special Edition, 1978.

Cullen, Frank. "Maxine Sullivan 1913 [sic]-1987." *Airwaves.* WORM (Provincetown, Md.) Program Guide and Magazine. May 1987.

Folkart, Bert A. "Singer Maxine Sullivan of 'Loch Lomond' Fame Dies." *Los Angeles Times,* April 9, 1987.

Levin, Michael. "Maxine Sullivan/Dick Hyman." Record review of *Sullivan, Shakespeare, Hyman. Down Beat* 39 (March 16, 1972): 30.

Placksin, Sally. *American Women in Jazz.* New York: Seaview Books, 1982.

Shaw, Arnold. *Black Popular Music in America.* New York: Schirmer Books, 1986.

Travis, Dempsey J. *An Autobiography of Black Jazz.* Chicago: Urban Research Institute, 1983.

Wilson, John. "Maxine Sullivan: 50 Years a Singer and Still Growing." *New York Times,* December 15, 1985.

———. "Maxine Sullivan, 75, Is Dead; Jazz Singer Won Tony in '79." *New York Times,* April 9, 1987. (A correction regarding this article appeared in the *New York Times,* May 18, 1987: Sullivan was a nominee rather than a winner.)

D. Antoinette Handy

Talbert, Florence O. Cole
See Cole-Talbert, Florence O.

Clara Smyth Taliaferro
(1873-?)
Pharmacist, educator, clubwoman

Important as an early black female pharmacist and drugstore owner, Clara Smyth Taliaferro is better known for her involvement in the black women's club movement. She was a founding member, and the first president, of the Tuesday Evening Club of Social Workers, which was established by a group of black women in Washington, D.C., with the aim of bettering the lives of black children and young adults. Taliaferro was also an active member of the National Association of Colored Women and the Federation of Women's Clubs in the District of Columbia.

Clara Smyth Taliaferro was born in 1873 to John Henry and Fannie W. Shippen Smyth. John Smyth, upon the recommendation of the Law Department faculty at Howard University in Washington, D.C., was awarded a master of laws degree in 1871. This was an academic milestone because Howard's first postgraduate degrees had just been awarded the previous year—to four members of the Medical Department faculty. Taliaferro had two marriages. Her first husband was James Fraction, whom she married on June 25, 1901, at St. Luke's Parish in Washington, D.C. On May 9, 1917, she married Alexander A. Taliaferro and became stepmother to his daughter, Louise E. Taliaferro; she was also the child's godparent at Louise's baptism on September 9, 1917.

Taliaferro was educated in the Washington, D.C., public schools and at Myrtilla Miner Normal School. She earned a doctor of pharmacy degree from Howard University in 1904. Taliaferro taught in the Washington public schools for nine years. She also owned drugstores in Washington and Richmond, Virginia, after completing her pharmaceutical studies and worked as a clerk in the Treasury and War departments of the U.S. government.

Social Center for Children and Young Adults Founded

Nothing more is known of Taliaferro's activities as a pharmacist. However, her role as a Washington clubwoman is better documented. One of a group of dedicated women interested in the problems of the black community in the District of Columbia, she was involved in prominent organizations founded to provide a voice and leadership opportunities for black women at the turn of the century. Taliaferro discovered that other women shared her interest in attending to the social needs of black children and young adults. She had long wanted to take children off the streets and place them in a home where recreational facilities would be provided and where adolescents and young adults could find a social outlet. In 1909, these women met in the Satterlee House on Wiltberger Street, Northwest, and formed the Tuesday Evening Club of Social Workers with Taliaferro as organizer. The organization was later chartered under that name. For over fifty years the club's facilities served as a social center for black youth and young adults and provided a wholesome outlet for their social and recreational needs. For fifteen years Taliaferro served as club president; for five years she was the head worker at the social center of Satterlee House.

The Tuesday Evening Club of Social Workers continued its work in shared quarters until 1935, when the members purchased a house at 515 M Street, Northwest, where its programs could be better implemented. A schedule of activities was then established under the supervision of the Community Chest and carried on as a United Givers Fund program. The house no longer exists. On May 1, 1960, the club celebrated its fiftieth anniversary at the National Association of Colored Women (NACW) headquarters, located at 1601 R Street, Northwest, in Washington. The only two founding members living then were Nannie Helen Burroughs and Imogene Wormley.

As a member and officer of the NACW and the Federation of Women's Clubs representing Washington and the nearby vicinity, Taliaferro participated in two of the District's premier organizations. The federation was founded on November 9, 1924, by the national president of the NACW, Mary McLeod Bethune. The organizational objective was to create interest in women's clubs and the programs of the NACW. As a measure of its prestige, the new federation entertained the national executive board of the NACW during the quintennial session of the International Council of Women, hosted a biennial session of the NACW, and entertained the body when it met on the thirty-second anniversary of its founding in Washington. Taliaferro served on the Child Welfare and Headquarters committees of the federation. Taliaferro was also a member of the Order of the Eastern Star, the NAACP, the YWCA, and the National League of Republican Colored Women Political Study Club.

A lifelong Episcopalian, Taliaferro was a member of St. Luke's Parish, located at 1514 Fifteenth Street, Northwest, Washington, D.C. She was confirmed there on April 3, 1901, shortly before her first marriage. Taliaferro was president of the Women's Guild and editor of St. Luke's *Parish Review*. Although information about this clubwoman, entrepreneur, and pharmacist is scarce, she stands as a shining example of the early twentieth-century black professional woman who used her education and social skills to make conditions better for the black community.

REFERENCES:

Davis, Elizabeth Lindsay. *Lifting as They Climb*. Washington, D.C.: National Association of Colored Women, 1933.

Dyson, Walter. *Howard University—The Capstone of Negro Education: A History, 1867-1940*. Washington, D.C.: Walter Dyson, 1941.

Peace, Joan [of St. Luke's Parish, Washington, D.C.]. Telephone interview with Dolores Nicholson, August 8, 1994.

Wesley, Charles Harris. *The History of the National Association of Colored Women's Clubs*. Washington, D.C.: NACW, 1984.

Who's Who in Colored America. 5th ed. New York: Thomas Yenser, 1940.

Dolores Nicholson

Alethia Browning Tanner

Alethia Browning Tanner
(17??-18??)
Slave, gardener

Determined not to spend her life in bondage, the ambitious, enterprising, and selfless Alethia Tanner earned enough money working as a hired-out slave to buy her freedom. Beyond that, she purchased the freedom of seventeen other family members and several friends. She therefore made it possible for her family to become outstanding citizens in the Washington, D.C., area. Also highly religious, after freedom she became known as the mother of the African Methodist Episcopal Church and was co-owner of a mortgage on her church.

Alethia Browning Tanner and her sisters Sophia and Laurena Browning were slaves on Rachel Bell Pratt's plantation in Prince George's County, Maryland. Sophia married George F. Bell (Beall), who later was one of three former slaves who in 1807 started the first school in Washington, D.C., for black children. Bell had been a slave in the home of Anthony Addison near the eastern boundary of the District of Columbia. He had purchased his wife Sophia's freedom from Rachel Pratt in 1809. Later, Sophia worked as a truck gardener and saved enough money to purchase his freedom.

Tanner was one of the most foresighted and enterprising women of her time. She worked as a hired-out slave and opened a vegetable market at Lafayette Square. One of her customers was Thomas Jefferson. By 1810 she had saved fourteen hundred dollars, enough to buy her freedom. In 1826 Tanner purchased the freedom of her older sister Laurena Browning Cook for eight hundred dollars. She also purchased the freedom of five of Cook's children (four sons and one daughter) that year, paying an average of three hundred dollars for each child. One of the children was John Frances Cook, Sr., who was fifteen years old when freed. In 1828 Tanner is said to have purchased the other Cook children and their offspring, including Hannah Ferguson and her four children, Annette and her child, and Aletha Cook and one child.

Anxious to earn enough money to reimburse his aunt Alethia Tanner for purchasing his freedom, John Cook, Sr. drew upon the trade he had learned in his childhood and for five years after freedom was an apprenticed shoemaker. With Tanner's assistance, he received an education from Columbia (or Columbian) Institute and became a successful educator, minister, and community leader before the Civil War. About August 1834, he was in charge of the school, located at Fourteenth and H streets northwest, that Henry Smothers built in 1822. The school was known then as the Columbian Institute, but Cook renamed it Union Seminary. Smothers conducted the school for three years, then was succeeded by

John Prout. Cook became the third schoolmaster and conducted the school for more than twenty years before he died. He helped establish two black churches in the District of Columbia—Union Bethel Church (1838), now known as the Metropolitan AME Church, and the First Colored Presbyterian Church (1841), later known as the Fifteenth Street Presbyterian Church. He married Helen Appo, the subject of a biography in this book. The Cook family became one of the most prominent and wealthy families in the District of Columbia, and family members were known throughout the nineteenth century for their contributions to education, politics, and community service.

Altogether, Tanner purchased the freedom of ten Cook children and seven grandchildren and, including herself and her sister, was responsible for the freedom of nineteen family members. After 1836, when all family members and their children had been freed by purchase, Tanner turned her attention to her neighbors. She purchased the freedom of Lotty Riggs and her four children; John Butler, who later became a Methodist minister; and Charlotte Davis.

According to *Alexander's Magazine,* March 1906, she extended her purchasing power elsewhere:

> Having apparently smashed the slave market, and seeing no more bargains in that direction she turned her attention to buying churches, and when the first Bethel church on Capitol Hill was sold out by the bank which held a mortgage against it, she with her brother-in-law, George Bell, bought it and gave it in and gave the society time to pay for it.

At some point Alethia either married or changed her name to Tanner. She continued to live in the Washington, D.C., area and, according to the *Cyclopedia of African Methodism,* which was published in 1882 and which identifies her as "Lethia," she was a "remarkable Christian woman." She was regarded as the mother of the African Methodist Episcopal Church. When she died, she was a member of Union Bethel Church, which her nephew John Frances Cook, Sr. had helped to establish. According to *Alexander's Magazine,* "She left a handsome property at her death. There is no telling what a woman like this might have accomplished if she could have lived long enough."

REFERENCES:

Joyner, William A. "Making a School System." *Alexander's Magazine* 1 (March 1906): 35-43, 50-51.
Logan, Rayford W., and Michael R. Winston. *Dictionary of American Negro Biography.* New York: Norton, 1982.
Major, Gerri, with Doris E. Saunders. *Black Society.* Chicago: Johnson Publishing Co., 1976.
Wayman, Alexander W. *Cyclopedia of African Methodism.* Baltimore: Methodist Episcopal Book Depository, 1882.
Williams, George W. *History of the Negro Race in America.* Vol. 2. New York: G. P. Putnam's Sons, 1883.

COLLECTIONS:

Information on the Cook family may be found in the Cook Family Papers, Moorland-Spingarn Research Center, Howard University, Washington, D.C.

Jessie Carney Smith

Mary Magdalena Lewis Tate
(1871-1930)
Minister, religious leader, healer, church founder

A leader in the Holiness-Pentecostal movement among black Americans, Mary Magdalena Lewis Tate established the Church of the Living God the Pillar and the Ground of the Truth without Controversy, popularly known as the House of God. She was general overseer of the church from 1903 until her death in 1930. She founded churches in dozens of states in the eastern half of the nation and influenced their development in foreign countries. She established the first great Pentecostal revival. Mother Tate, as she was known, is said to have saved thousands of souls and healed hundreds of her followers. She wrote much of the church's early literature and possibly some of its early music. She further influenced the development of the church by supervising the composition of the *Constitution, Government and General Decree Book,* containing church rules and bylaws, and she also wrote much of the book and edited it. Her life was a great spiritual journey, and in turn she had a profound effect on the development of the spiritual lives of others.

Mary Magdalena Bell-Street Lewis Tate, or Mother Tate, was born on January 3, 1871. She had two sisters, Dora O'Neal and Esther Edwards. Because of her pure character, as a youth she was called "Miss Do Right," and later, her followers were known as "The Do Righters." After marrying, Mother Tate lived for a time in Dickson, Tennessee, with her husband, David Lewis. Then in 1903, when Mother Tate was in her early thirties and the mother of two sons, Walter Curtis Lewis (1890-1921) and Felix Earl Lewis (1892-1968), she founded and established the House of God, Which Is the Church of the Living God, the Pillar and Ground of the Truth, without Controversy. According to John Michael Spencer in *Black Hymnody,* her Holiness congregation at Chattanooga, organized in 1903, may have been initially associated with another black Holiness church founded in 1889 and known as the Church of the Living God (Christian Workers Fellowship). William Christian organized the older group in Wrightsville, Arkansas.

Mother Tate was compelled to leave her home and go out with her children to spread the gospel. Starting in a small

Mary Magdalena Lewis Tate

community, Steel Springs, Tennessee, she appears to have spread the gospel extensively. Mother Tate went to Paducah, Kentucky, where she joined her two sisters and gave them religious instruction. Her first missionary journey was from Paducah to Brooklyn, Illinois, near East Saint Louis. Her sons did not accompany her but afterwards they became her helpers and constant companions on her journeys. While in Brooklyn, Illinois, she seems to have preached her first sermon. She taught and preached there a number of days, then returned to her sons and her sisters in Paducah. She appears to have had no further contact with her husband, and later she became Mary Magdalena Tate, affectionately called Mother Tate.

Mother Tate's second missionary journey was to Paris, Tennessee, this time with her two sons by her side. She preached to white and black audiences on the streets and in homes of the residents. She also preached in a Presbyterian church there, where "grown men shouted, leaped, and wept for joy." As early as 1905 Mother Tate and her sons traveled extensively in Alabama, teaching and preaching the gospel. By 1907 she was still traveling in Alabama and was said to have converted over three hundred people and baptized a number of them by immersion.

Mother Tate organized her followers in Alabama and Tennessee into bands, who would teach the gospel to others. In 1908 she contracted a serious illness that was considered incurable, yet it did not stop her career; when she spoke in tongues and claimed that she was "healed and sealed" and "baptized of the Fire and Holy Ghost," at first her followers

considered her insane, but her Pentecostalism prevailed. Mother Tate's triumph over illness inspired her to read the Bible more and demonstrate to her people the importance of being baptized "of the Holy Ghost and Fire." The church traces its founding to 1903, when Mother Tate also began to preach. The formal organization of the denomination as a Pentecostal church took place in 1908.

Church of the Living God Established

After her spiritual baptism in 1908, Mother Tate became chief apostle elder, president, and first chief overseer of the church, which was formally organized in Greenville, Alabama. On or near June 25, 1908, Mother Tate called for the first great Pentecostal revival to be held in Greenville. The newly saved, converted, and others attended, some who walked twenty-five and thirty miles to the meeting. As Mother Tate presided over the meeting, nearly one hundred people were baptized. Mother Tate organized the church with ten or more designated ministers, and together they formed the church's corporate body: the bishops and the board of trustees. The trustees ordained Mother Tate to the bishopric. The organization was then named The Church of the Living God, the Pillar and Ground of the Truth, which took its title from the Bible (I Timothy 3:15). Several preachers were ordained, and pastors were appointed to the local church bands that Mother Tate had already established.

During the first few years of its existence, the church was established in Tennessee, Kentucky, and Florida. In 1910 Mother Tate established the church in Waycross, Georgia, where three hundred people were baptized. Her son Felix was her chief assistant. By 1911 presiding elders had been introduced in the church and the general church provided financial support to the pastors. A significant development in the first Church of the Living God occurred during the 1914 general assembly held at Quitman, Georgia. Church rules and bylaws had been printed earlier, but in 1914 the *Constitution, Government and General Decree Book* was issued in book format. Mother Tate had written much of the literature. During the assembly four state bishops were appointed to serve in Georgia: J. D. Pagitt, B. J. Scott, and her two sons, Felix Earl Lewis and Walter Curtis Lewis. In this year Mother Tate also organized the first Church of the Living God in Florida, located in Ocala, where the first Florida state general assembly was conducted. Felix Earl Lewis became state bishop of Florida and, with the assistance of several elders who lived in Florida, he established local bands throughout the state.

Between 1916 and 1924 the church grew rapidly and bands were formed in more than twenty states, the District of Columbia, and several foreign countries. In 1923 the church established a publishing house in Nashville, Tennessee, known as the New and Living Way Publishing House, which published most of the church's literature. By 1924 seven bishops were active, including Mother Tate, and they presided over the assemblies held in the various states. Between 1930 and 1962 fourteen state charters were granted to establish additional churches and four more were added to the Church of the Living God roster by 1981. In 1992 the Church of the Living

God had on its roster charters in forty-three states and Jamaica.

Growing Discord

As the church developed, so did dissension and jealousy. In 1919 some members of the church in Philadelphia, Pennsylvania, left to found the House of God, Which Is the Church of the Living God, the Pillar and Ground of Truth. Mother Tate's loyal followers still believed in her, however. Witnesses to her healing powers said that she cured the sick by laying her hands on them and praying. According to testimonies of her believers, published in the *Seventy-fifth Anniversary Yearbook of the Church of the Living God,*

> She would pray for the sick and they would be healed; for the lame and they would walk; for the brokenhearted and they would recover! Such healing power was evidenced so miraculously that people walked away healed and sealed after Mother Tate had layed hand on and prayed for them.

Mother Tate was well aware of all the turmoil in the church, particularly in the eastern states, and the *Yearbook* reported that she was able to foretell her death: "Because of sin and jealousy, so much trouble will come on the church that I'll be glad that I'm asleep in Christ."

Another major event in the church's history came in 1931, the year after Mother Tate's death. The church reorganized and three persons became overseers: Mother Tate's son Felix Earl Lewis; M. F. L. Keith, the widow of Bishop Walter Curtis Lewis; and B. L. McLeod, all of whom eventually became leaders of distinct church bodies. The Lewis following continued as the Church of the Living God, the Pillar and Ground of Truth. Keith's following was the House of God Which Is the Church of the Living God, the Pillar and Ground of Truth without Controversy. McLeod's following was known as the Church of the Living God, the Pillar, and Ground of Truth.

In 1924, the Church of the Living God located its headquarters on Heiman Street in Nashville, where the original building is no longer used for service but still stands. The cornerstone reads: "Founded by Bishop Mary Magdalena Tate, 1903. Bishop Mary F. L. Keith is one of the Successors to the Founder, Ordained and Appointed to Office, June 1931." A new headquarters facility was dedicated in another Heiman Street location in 1981.

Mother Tate died on December 28, 1930, and was buried in Dickson, Tennessee, in a family plot. Her remains were moved to Greenwood Cemetery in Nashville in 1964 and placed in a conspicuous memorial site near the entrance. Her eldest son, Walter Curtis Lewis, died of pneumonia in 1921. Her second son, Felix Earl Lewis, had at least two children, both daughters. Gladys Lewis Sherrod, his second daughter, was also a bishop in the church and a constant companion and apprentice of Mother Tate. Sister Gladys, as she was known, married Lucien Sherrod and lived in Washington, D.C. She died during childbirth in 1931 when she was about nineteen years old. Buried beside Mother Tate in Dixon, Tennessee,

she too was relocated to the Nashville cemetery where her father, who died in 1968, is also buried.

Spiritual Songs and Hymns, the denomination's first hymnbook, was privately published in Chattanooga around 1944. The book names Mother Tate as composer and compiler of many of the songs. However, according to Spencer, she by no means composed all or even most of the songs. Yet, notations illustrate the way Mother Tate and her "saints" sang hymns over the years and confirm that they had learned the songs through the oral tradition.

The Church of the Living God had a membership of two thousand and approximately one hundred ministers in 1988. Its chief overseer is Bishop Helen M. Lewis, who succeeded Bishop Felix E. Lewis in 1968. The church publishes *The True Report* and continues to operate the New and Living Way Publishing House.

Mother Tate is known for her dedication and perseverance and for giving spiritual guidance to thousands of followers through her ministry and the founding of a church in the Holiness-Pentecostal tradition.

REFERENCES:

DuPree, Sherry Sherrod, ed. *Biographical Dictionary of African-American Holiness-Pentecostal, 1880-1990.* Washington, D.C.: Middle Atlantic Regional Press, 1989.

Lewis, Helen M., and Meharry H. Lewis. *Seventy-fifth Anniversary Yearbook of The Church of the Living God, the Pillar and Ground of the Truth, Inc., 1903-1978.* Nashville: Church of the Living God, 1978.

Melton, J. Gordon, ed. *The Encyclopedia of American Religions.* Vol. 1. Tarrytown, N.Y.: Triumph Books, 1991.

Shuford, F. Dovie. "Mother Mary Magdalena L. Tate, 1891-1930." *Leaders of Afro-American Nashville.* Nashville, Tenn., 1992.

Spencer, John Michael. *Black Hymnody: A Hymnological History of the African-American Church.* Knoxville: University of Tennessee Press, 1992.

Jessie Carney Smith

Merze Tate

(1905-)

Scholar, educator, writer

Merze Tate is a distinguished scholar of history and political science. She is also an important trailblazer, opening many doors previously closed to America's black citizens by becoming the first African American woman to

Merze Tate

earn advanced degrees in her field at both Oxford University and Harvard University. Throughout her career, she has contributed to the growing voice of black America through teaching, academic research, and publication.

Merze Tate was born on February 6, 1905, in Blanchard, Michigan, where she received her early education. Her parents were Charles and Myrtle K. Lett Tate. According to Irma Guy, in 1869 Charles Tate and his five siblings traveled with their parents from Ohio to relocate in Isabella County, Michigan, riding in a covered wagon to the forests where they made their new home.

Tate attended Blanchard High School and Battle Creek High School. At Blanchard High School she was valedictorian, and at Battle Creek High School, to which she walked eight miles a day, she achieved distinction by winning the Hinman Oratorical Contest.

Tate's higher education is extensive. Between 1921 and 1923, and also from 1926 to 1927, she attended Western Michigan State Teachers' College (now Western Michigan University), where in 1927 she achieved her bachelor of arts degree, becoming the first African American to do so there. Tate's determination to achieve scholarly proficiency led her to take courses when she was not teaching, and she eventually earned a master's degree at New York's Columbia University in 1930. In 1932, the American Association of University Women's Committee on Selections unanimously recommended her for admission to Oxford University. Between 1932 and 1935, under the supervision of professors J. L. Brierly, Agnes Headlam-Morley, and Sir Alfred Zimmern, she studied

International Relations at Oxford University in England, where she received a research degree in letters, the B.Litt., in 1935. This was the first advanced degree awarded to an African American woman by Oxford. Between 1931 and 1935, she attended summer courses at Switzerland's Geneva School of International Studies and at Germany's University of Berlin. In 1939, she began study at Radcliffe as a recipient of a Julius Rosenwald Fellowship. In 1941 Tate received her doctor of philosophy degree in government and international relations from Radcliffe College, Harvard University—another first as an African American woman. In addition to these accomplishments, Tate received an honorary D.Litt. in 1948 from Western Michigan University and an honorary D.Laws from Morgan State College. Howard University awarded her an honorary D.H.L. degree in 1981.

Tate's career as an educator is no less impressive. From 1925 to 1926 she was an elementary school teacher at Calvin Center School in Cassopolis, Michigan, and from 1927 to 1932, she taught history at Crispus Attucks High School in Indianapolis, Indiana. From 1935 to 1936, Tate was a history instructor and dean of women at Barber-Scotia Junior College (now Barber-Scotia College), in Concord, North Carolina. During the summer of 1936, she taught history at North Carolina State College in Durham, and from 1936 to 1941, she chaired the department of history and social science at Bennett College in Greensboro, North Carolina. During the 1941-1942 school year, Tate was a political science professor and dean of women at Morgan State College. From 1942 until her retirement thirty-five years later, Tate was a history professor at Howard University in Washington, D.C. In the course of her career, Tate was a visiting professor and lecturer at numerous colleges and universities in the United States and abroad. She was a Fulbright lecturer in India (1950-1951), and she held a civil service rating of GS-18 with the federal government, often serving as consultant on international relations and performing ambassadorial duties.

Tate's legacy is perhaps most concrete in her publications, which represent unfaltering scholarship. At Radcliffe College, Tate's Ph.D. dissertation focused on disarmament, and in 1942, the Bureau of International Research of Harvard University and Radcliffe College published her dissertation. *The Disarmament Illusion: The Movement for a Limitation of Armaments to 1907* was Tate's first book. She published four other books: *The United States and Armament* (1948); *The United States and the Hawaiian Kingdom: A Political History* (1965); *Hawaii: Reciprocity or Annexation* (1968); and *Mineral Railways in Africa* (1989).

Career Seasoned with Honors

Tate's education and career have been well-seasoned with honors. In 1931, she a received $1,000 Alpha Kappa Alpha Fellowship. In 1948, she received the Outstanding Achievement Award from the National Urban League, and in 1953, she was honored with the Radcliffe College Alumni Association's Distinguished Professional Service medal. Her father's home county of Isabella in Michigan honored her as its Most Distinguished Citizen in 1969, and in 1970, she received a Most Distinguished Alumnae award from her undergraduate alma mater. In 1978, she received the Spirit of Detroit Award of Merit and the American Black Artist's Pioneer Award. Radcliffe College honored her again in 1979 with the College Alumnae Achievement Award. In 1980, she became the only woman to receive the Promethan Plaque of Honor and Life Membership. The next year Tate was awarded the Distinguished Alumnus Award of the American Association of State Colleges and Universities.

In 1932, she coordinated a Bicentennial pilgrimage to Washington, D.C., for members of the Travel Club at Crispus Attucks High School. Subsequently, she held membership and office in a great number of organizations, including the North Carolina Teachers Association, Alpha Kappa Alpha Sorority, the Red Cross, the Young Women's Christian Association, the British Federation of University Women, the Oxford Homes Students' Society, the Association for the Study of Negro Life and History, Phi Beta Kappa, Phi Delta Kappa, Pi Gamma Mu, Phi Alpha Theta, the American Historical Association, the American Academy of Political and Social Science, the League of Nations Union, and the National Board of Radcliffe College.

On a more personal level, she was a member of several bridge and writers clubs. She was a member of the African Methodist Episcopal Church. She remained independent of political party affiliation. Upon retirement, she made her altruism even more pronounced by endowing Howard University with an annual Tate Seminar in Diplomatic History.

Through her scholarship, teaching, writing, and community involvement Tate has contributed to the growth of the African American voice in American and international affairs. Her international relations work has made a place for her in American history, just as her example as a pioneering African American in academia has secured her role in black history.

Current Address: 1314 Perry Street, N.E., Washington, DC 20017.

REFERENCES:

Greene, Harry Washington. *Holders of Doctorates among American Negroes.* Boston: Meador Publishing Co., 1946.

Guy, Irma. "Pioneer Days in Isabella County, Michigan." *Negro History Bulletin* 23 (February 1960): 102.

Hine, Darlene Clark, ed. *Black Women in America.* 2 vols. Brooklyn: Carson Publishing, 1993.

Shockley, Ann Allen, and Sue P. Chandler. *Living Black American Authors.* New York: Bowker, 1973.

Thorpe, Earl E. *Black Historians: A Critique.* New York: William Morrow and Company, 1979.

Who's Who among Black Americans, 1994-95. 8th ed. Detroit: Gale Research, 1994.

Who's Who in Colored America. New York: Thomas Yenser, 1944.

Who's Who in Colored America. New York: Christian E. Burckel, 1950.

Laura C. Jarmon

Mildred D. Taylor
(1943-)
Children's author

Mildred D. Taylor is one of the foremost African American writers of children's literature. She has transformed her own experiences of a warm and close-knit family and the stories told by relatives of African American survival against tremendous odds in a racist society into fiction with a worldwide audience. Her juvenile novel *Roll of Thunder, Hear My Cry* has become a classic, winning the prestigious Newbery Medal in 1977.

Mildred Delois Taylor was born September 13, 1943, in Jackson, Mississippi. Her immediate family consisted of her parents, Wilbert Lee and Deletha Marie Taylor, and one older sister, Wilma. When she was just three months old, the Taylor family relocated to Toledo, Ohio. She grew up in a warm and supportive home environment, the locus of relatives and friends escaping the harsh realities of Southern life. Her family experiences have provided the prototype of the close-knit, intact African American family found in her fiction.

One of the most profound influences on Taylor's childhood was her father, Wilbert. In her Newbery Award acceptance speech, published in *Horn Book,* Taylor said:

> I was blessed with a special father, a man who had unyielding faith in himself and his abilities, and who, knowing himself to be inferior to no one, tempered my learning with his wisdom. . . . A highly principled, complex man who did not have an excellent education or a white-collar job, he had instead strong moral fiber and a great wealth of what he said was simply common sense. Throughout my childhood he impressed upon my sister and me that we were somebody, that we were important and could do or be anything we set our minds to do or be.

Taylor describes her father as "a master storyteller." Throughout her childhood she heard stories of his strong, proud relatives in rural Mississippi.

Taylor attended the public schools of Toledo, segregated on the elementary level but integrated by the time she reached high school. She early formed the ambition to become a writer, an ambition fed by the disparities she found between the stories of her father and other relatives in Mississippi about African American people and the depiction of these same people in her history textbooks. She achieved academically, often being the only African American in college preparatory classes, and she also took part in various extracurricular activities. She attended the University of Toledo, graduating with a B.Ed. in 1965. For the next two years she served in the Peace Corps as a teacher of English and history in Yirgalem, Ethiopia. She fondly recalls these years as one of the happiest periods in her life. For a year after her return to the States, she served as a Peace Corps trainer and recruiter.

Taylor then pursued graduate studies at the University of Colorado, where she helped to found the Black Student Alliance and lobbied successfully for a black studies department. She graduated in 1969 with an M.A. in English. She remained at the University of Colorado for another two years as the coordinator of its study skills center.

During these important formative years of becoming formally educated and learning about the world through travel and work, she never forgot the stories she heard as a child nor abandoned her ambition to write. Taking steps to realize this ambition, she quit her job at the University of Colorado and moved to Los Angeles. From 1971 to 1973 she did temporary office work, which left her time and energy to write.

Taylor's first piece of fiction was a novella, *Song of the Trees*. The manuscript of this work won first prize in the African American category in a competition sponsored by the Council on Interracial Books for Children. It was published by Dial Press two years later, in 1975. In this year the *New York Times* cited it as Outstanding Book of the Year. *Song of the Trees* is based on an anecdote told by Taylor's father of the efforts of a Depression-era rural African American family to keep mercenary whites from grabbing their four hundred acres of land. In her Newbery Award acceptance speech, Taylor describes the genesis of the work:

> It was ... on a well-remembered day in late September a little girl named Cassie Logan suddenly appeared in my life. Cassie was a spunky eight-year-old, innocent, untouched by discrimination, full of pride, and greatly loved, and through her I discovered I could now tell one of the stories I had heard so often as a child.

From that meeting came her first published work. David Logan, Cassie's father, was modeled on Taylor's own father, and the Logan family on the Taylor family. Taylor said in her Newbery Award acceptance speech, "If people are touched by the warmth of the Logans, it is because I had the warmth of my own youthful years from which to draw. If the Logans seem real, it is because I had my own family upon which to base characterizations."

Best-Selling Classic Produced

In 1974 Taylor decided to write another book about the Logans. Two years later her classic *Roll of Thunder, Hear My Cry* was published. Taking place in 1933 and 1934 when Cassie is nine years old, the book continues the Logans'

struggles to hold on to their land. Taylor uses this ambitious work to dramatize the values instilled in her during her childhood and also interweaves many of the stories about her family and other families she had heard in her childhood. In this novel, Cassie, on the verge of puberty, undergoes significant growth as she learns how to cope constructively with the indignities and injustices of a racist society.

Roll of Thunder, Hear My Cry has been an overwhelming critical and commercial success. In 1976 the American Library Association cited it as a Notable Book, and in 1977 it received the Newbery Medal and became a finalist for a National Book Award. A dramatization was recorded by Newbery Awards Records, and it was also adapted for television in 1978. In 1985 it received the Buxtehuder Bulle Award in Germany for excellence in children's literature. The book has been published in eleven countries. In 1990, sixteen years after its initial publication, *Roll of Thunder, Hear My Cry* was still among the bestsellers in children's literature.

Between 1981 and 1990 Taylor added four more novels to the Logan family saga. *Let the Circle Be Unbroken* (1981), with its child characters and trial scenes, has been compared to Harper Lee's *To Kill a Mockingbird.* This book was nominated for the American Book Award in the hardcover fiction category in 1982 and received the Coretta Scott King Award in 1983. The second novel in the series is *The Friendship* (1987). The last two Logan family books, *Mississippi Bridge* and *The Road to Memphis,* both published in 1990, take the Logans through World War II. These two works were named Notable 1990 Children's Books in the Field of Social Studies. In addition to her series on the Logan family, Taylor published *The Gold Cadillac* (1987) about the trials of a family visiting the South in a gaudy gold Cadillac.

In her Newbery Award acceptance speech Taylor summed up the significance of her fiction:

> It is my hope that [this series of books about the Logan family], one of the first chronicles to mirror a Black child's hopes and fears from childhood innocence to awareness to bitterness and disillusionment, will one day be instrumental in teaching children of all colors the tremendous influence of Cassie's generation—my father's generation—had in bringing about the great Civil Rights movement of the fifties and sixties. Without understanding that generation and what it and the generations before it endured, children of today and of the future cannot understand or cherish the precious rights of equality which they possess, both in the North and in the South. If they can identify with the Logans, who are representative not only of my family but of the many black families who faced adversity and survived, and understand the principles by which they lived, then perhaps they can better understand and respect themselves and others.

Mildred D. Taylor in her fiction indeed educates children of all races about the strength and pride of African American families and their role in the survival of the race. Taylor presently lives in Colorado and continues to write.

Current Address: c/o Dial Books, 2 Park Avenue, New York, NY 10016.

REFERENCES:

Contemporary Literary Criticism. Vol. 21. Detroit: Gale Research, 1982.

Estes, Glen, ed. *Dictionary of Literary Biography.* Vol. 52: *American Writers for Children Since 1960: Fiction.* Detroit: Gale Research, 1986.

Hine, Darlene Clark, ed. *Black Women in America.* Brooklyn: Carlson Publishing, 1993.

Rees, David. "The Color of Skin: Mildred Taylor." In *Marble in the Water: Essays on Contemporary Writers of Fiction for Children and Young Adults.* Boston: Horn Book, 1980.

Taylor, Mildred. "Newbery Award Acceptance Speech." *Horn Book* 53 (August 1977): 401-09.

                                        Phiefer L. Browne

Rebecca Stiles Taylor

Rebecca Stiles Taylor
(1880-1970)
Educator, principal, club leader, journalist, humanitarian

Known for her professional versatility and talent, Rebecca Taylor focused her energies on the needs of children and health care among blacks in Savannah, Georgia. She became an outstanding teacher and school administrator, devoted most of her life to promoting the work of black women, and gave her latter years to the cause of women at the international level. Her work with women's clubs in Savannah led a local group, the Savannah Federation of Colored Women's Clubs, to achieve national stature, while her organizational and management skills led her to become the first executive secretary of the National Association of Colored Women.

Thus far many of the details of Rebecca Stiles Taylor's early life and family are unavailable to researchers. Records show, however, that she was born in Savannah, Georgia, in 1880. She completed her elementary and high school education in Savannah and later studied at or graduated from Atlanta University, Hampton Institute, and Columbia University.

Taylor's maiden name, Stiles, was commonly misspelled "Styles," a practice that she deplored. "I hate that y," she wrote to Jeanetta Welch about July 1944, when transmitting her an article for the National Council of Negro Women's journal. She asked Welch to make certain her name was spelled correctly.

Taylor was family-oriented. When her brother died she became a guiding force in the lives of his eleven children—nine boys and two girls—watching over them and encouraging them to read. John Stiles, Sr., one of the eleven, credits "Auntie Beck," as she was known in the family, with giving him his first book and adding a bookcase in his bedroom to house the collection that she helped him to build. She was known also as very race-conscious—concerned with what was best for the black race and with political ideals.

When Taylor was appointed Savannah's first black probation officer of the juvenile court, which probably occurred between 1909 and 1914, local white residents were resentful. A conscientious white citizen named Wright, who worked toward the solution of racial and social problems, felt strongly that the city needed a black in the position and offered to pay Taylor's salary from his own funds. Robert E. Perdue, chairperson of the Board of Commissioners of Georgia State Industrial College (now Savannah State University), said in *The Negro in Savannah 1865-1900,* Wright "was fighting a 'foolish and futile' battle" on Taylor's behalf. Wright was determined, however, and after city officials appointed Taylor to the position, Wright did, in fact, pay a large part of her salary.

Taylor taught in the Savannah schools for at least twenty-three years, becoming known as a very effective and outstanding teacher. Describing Taylor's reputation and competence as a teacher, her nephew John Stiles, Sr., said in Louise Lautier Owens's radio profile, "How Well We Remember Her!," "Anybody who didn't take English from her didn't take any English!" So outstanding was her work that her

English course at Cuyler Junior High School became known as "Stiles's English." Albert S. Otto's "Honor Roll of Negro Teachers" lists her as an outstanding educator. The chronology of Taylor's tenure in the Savannah Schools lists her at Tatemville, 1897-1901; East Broad Street School, 1901-09; East Savannah, 1914-16; Port Wentworth, 1916-1917; Maple Street School, 1917-19; Cuyler Street Elementary School, 1919-1921; and Cuyler Street Junior High School, 1921-22 and 1923-26. Her whereabouts from 1922 to 1923 are unclear. In Owens's radio profile of Taylor, Nancy Houston Walker said that Taylor "made a great impression upon all her students. She was totally involved in her subject and was quite competent." In addition to being a grammarian and teacher of English, she taught her students social graces and how to preside at meetings.

In 1914, Taylor was among the local educators who persuaded the Savannah Board of Education to build Cuyler Street School, the first junior high school for blacks in the city. For a time she was principal of the Mayesville Educational and Industrial Institute in Mayesville, South Carolina, better known as the Emma Wilson School. Taylor was the first state supervisor of primary education for blacks in Georgia, a position she held for fifteen years. She was also secretary of the Georgia Teachers Association.

Writes History of Club Movement in Savannah

Taylor was known also for her civic work and her success in promoting black women's causes. She wrote "A Sketch of the History of Club Life among Colored Women of Savannah, Georgia," published in the 1932 *Yearbook of Colored Savannah*. Here she noted that club life among the black women of Savannah dated back to the Civil War. She credited these early efforts to the Northern women who were pioneers in the culture and refinement of the city's former slave and free population. Savannah also maintained more clubs than most cities: the Urban League, the Civic League, and the Protective League were among the early black organizations there. Thus, the local climate was ripe for a successful black women's club movement and the abundance of organizations provided rich ground for the Savannah Federation of Colored Women's Clubs to grow.

According to the *Minutes of Meetings of the Savannah Federation of Colored Women's Clubs, 1928-1969*, quoted in Owens's radio profile, Taylor was one of seven women who in 1917 founded the Toussaint l'Ouverture branch of the Savannah Chapter of the American Red Cross. A group of local white women who acknowledged the contributions of blacks to the war called on Sol C. Johnson, editor of the *Savannah Tribune* and civic leader, to bring together a group of black women to form an auxiliary to the Red Cross movement in the city. According to these sources, at a meeting held at St. Philip's Church, located on West Broad and Charles streets, an organization was formed that later became known as the Toussaint l'Overture branch of the Savannah Chapter American Red Cross. The officers were Taylor, president; Mary Sheftall Belcher, secretary; and Mamie

L. Williams (known also as Mrs. George S. Williams), treasurer.

In time, the work of black women in Savannah reached national stature. According to Taylor's "A Sketch of the History of Club Life Among Colored Women of Savannah, Georgia," "[Red Cross work] was indeed the school for the colored clubwomen of Savannah, for at the close of the war, they were prepared to organize among themselves the Savannah Federation of Colored Women's Clubs and with this organization they have opened doors that were hitherto closed to their people." The women secured more than five hundred dollars per month from the city's and county's budgets. The federation was responsible for uniting the classes and masses in black Savannah in May 1918 by bringing together forty-one different clubs. Soon the forty-one clubs grew into one hundred, becoming "a potent factor in the life of the community."

First President of Savannah Federation of Colored Women's Clubs

Taylor and eleven other women founded the Savannah Federation of Colored Women's Clubs in 1918 and Taylor was its first president. It was chartered in 1924 by the state of Georgia, becoming an affiliate of the National Association of Colored Women's Clubs. The federation, which by the 1930s was comprised of as many as one hundred separate clubs, became well known for its community activities, in particular the hiring in 1921 of a black nurse for its Health and Nutritional Program for children and adults (founded a year earlier) and for establishing in 1922 the Cuyler Children's Free Clinic. The federation managed the clinic fully and was responsible for its financial obligations. The women were successful in persuading community professionals and leaders to contribute to the clinic: they persuaded black and white physicians to donate their services, and, after lobbying city and county commissions, they were successful in receiving funds to support the clinic and to pay the salary of a nurse. During the 1920s the clinic provided free services to about four hundred poor children each month, and on Tuesdays it served expectant women, most of whom were domestics, laborers, or unemployed.

The Savannah Federation, under Taylor's leadership, also owned the Chatham Protective Home for delinquent girls located at Thunderbolt, Georgia, and saw that black workers were active in Savannah's Associated Charities. Through its members' work the federation established a home for the aged and infirm—a $50,000 residence donated to the local black women by a white woman from Tennessee, who also endowed the home for $150,000.

Continuing her service to black women, Taylor was corresponding secretary of the Georgia Federation of Colored Women for five years, beginning in 1920, then president for two years. Taylor was the organization's seventh president and held the position from 1926 to 1928. According to her statement in the *Yearbook of Colored Savannah*, the Savannah association took control over the state federation, which may have occurred during Taylor's administration, and enlarged the state group to twenty-one city federations and forty separate clubs in forty other counties, making a total of sixty-one in Georgia. The Savannah association also became a prime factor in the establishment of the national headquarters.

During her tenure as president of the state federation Taylor toured the state, organized districts, and placed capable women in their charge. Both Mamie Williams and Taylor worked with the Training School Committee to raise substantial funds for the State Training School for Girls, which was located on the campus of Savannah State College. Taylor resigned the presidency of the Savannah association to become the second president of the Southern Association of Colored Women's Clubs (SACWC) in 1923.

Shares Interests with Mary McLeod Bethune

A contemporary of Mary McLeod Bethune (1875-1955), Taylor demonstrated through her work that she was clearly in the Bethune camp. Both women had a keen interest in education, opportunities for black women, and the black women's club movement, particularly the National Association of Colored Women's Clubs (NACW), the Southern Association of Colored Women's Clubs (SACWC), and the National Council of Negro Women (NCNW). When Bethune became president of NACW in 1924, she recruited Taylor to join the faculty at Bethune Cookman College, which she headed, and to become her aide for NACW work. The dates of Taylor's tenure at the college are unclear, although she might have gone there in 1926 after she left Cuyler Street Junior High School. At Bethune Cookman College Taylor taught English and served as dean of women. She also became Bethune's full-time paid executive secretary of NACW. Their friendship and mutual respect for each other continued until Bethune died.

In 1919 Bethune began efforts to organize women in the South and to found a strong, effective organization of Southern women which would be known as the Southern Association of Colored Women's Clubs. SACWC was established at Tuskegee Institute the next year with Bethune as its founding president. Other office holders were premiere black women, including Charlotte Hawkins Brown, chair of the executive board; Marion B. Wilkerson, vice president-at-large; state presidents from eight southern states who served as vice presidents; and Taylor, who was corresponding secretary. Taylor succeeded Bethune as head and remained in the post from 1923 to 1927.

During her presidency Taylor reported on the SACWC's activities in *National Notes,* the official organ of the National Association of Colored Women. In her first report, published in the February 1926 issue, she stressed the three planks of the federation—organization, interracial cooperation, and citizenship. As retiring president, her biennial address, published in the September 1927 issue of *National Notes,* was much more pointed. Dissatisfied with the progress the federation had made in developing its triple-planked platform, she cited specific areas of need and suggested how the needs might be met. "The new day of the South will be brought about almost entirely by the women of the South—white and black," she said. She called for a Home Mission Project in every church club and fraternal organization. While blacks had been emancipated from chattel slavery, Taylor argued, they were still mentally enslaved; therefore, survival was menaced and permanent progress hindered. She also urged women to vote and help out the best political candidate in office. "Let us use what we have, and work for more. . . . Our group welfare is at stake. Our children's welfare is our first thought."

Taylor was succeeded as head of the SACWC by another noted leader, Ora Brown Stokes of Virginia, who held the position a few months. Although the SACWC became inactive from 1927 to 1940, Taylor never lost sight of its importance. In 1940, at a meeting held at Tuskegee, Stokes and Taylor revived the group and Bertha L. Johnson of Mississippi became president.

Taylor's superior ability as an organizer and leader caught national attention. During Bethune's presidency of the National Association of Colored Women from 1924 to 1928, of which the Georgia Federation was a part, Taylor was twice unanimously elected corresponding secretary of the NACW. The NACW also created the position of executive secretary, making Taylor the first to hold the position.

In addition to her service to the local, state, and national associations of black women, Taylor was active in the local political arena. Taylor and Mamie Williams, who worked together in a number of organizations, were Republicans, and Taylor became a Republican national committeewoman from Georgia. Kermit O. Smalls, also a Republican, noted in *Yearbook of Colored Savannah* that the two women were among a number of black Savannahians who played an important part in politics, although accounts of their full contributions are unspecified.

At the depth of the Great Depression, Williams approached some seventy-five organizations in Savannah to come together and discuss the urgent and serious problems affecting blacks. Several strategy meetings were held at the Carnegie Library; then on Saturday night, April 29, 1933, the Chatham County Colored Citizens Council was organized with Williams as president and Taylor recording secretary. Among the organization's numerous accomplishments were increased employment of blacks in private industry, improved housing and sanitation, improved recreational facilities, a swimming pool for blacks, and a voter-registration drive.

Taylor Becomes Journalist

During her years in Savannah, Taylor edited the *Savannah Journal,* a weekly newspaper, and in her editorials often criticized the board of education for the inequities in education for blacks. Issues of the newspapers that published her work appear to be no longer extant. In the late 1930s Taylor moved to Chicago and was a columnist for the *Chicago Defender* which published her column called "Federated Clubs" from that time until the mid-1950s. She also remained active in women's club activities and gave firsthand accounts of the women's clubs in her articles.

By this time there was some tension between the leaders of the National Association of Colored Women and the National Council of Negro Women. Bethune had founded a new headquarters for the National Council of Negro Women, a move vital to the organization as a center from which Bethune and her staff could extend their work. Apparently other women did not share Taylor's enthusiasm for the new headquarters or Bethune's success. Taylor's comments on the matter also suggests that, notwithstanding Taylor's professionalism and talents, she was not void of human frailties. She wrote to Bethune on December 29, 1943, perhaps in reference to Sally Wyatt Stewart, Hallie Quinn Brown, and Nannie Helen Burroughs:

> But, Mary, dear (between you and me) it must be a terrific blow to Sally, Hallie and the rest of her gang . . . even Nannie . . . a blow from which they will never fully recover. I suppose it is wrong for me to be glad, but after all, I am human, and looking at it from any angle . . . I just can't be sorry, for after all is said and done "You can't make a silk purse from a sow's ear."

Jeanetta Welch, the executive secretary of NACW, wrote to Taylor at her Chicago address on May 11, 1943, at the request of Sue Bailey Thurman, editor-in-chief of the *AfraAmerican Woman's Journal* (in 1949 the name was changed to *Woman's Journal*). The official organ of NACW, the journal kept women informed of legislative matters and major issues affecting black women and reported on accomplishments of individual women. Welch persuaded Taylor to write an article on the role of black women's clubs in the World War II efforts.

Taylor became a life member of the National Council of Negro Women (NCNW) when she completed her fifty-dollar fee with a ten-dollar money order payment to the organization transmitted to Bethune by letter on December 29, 1943. She also discussed with Bethune her interest in editing a "Woman's Digest" column for the journal. The December 29 letter shows clearly a continuation of the warm relationship and mutual respect that had developed at least as early as 1920. Taylor proposed to include in the column items on the current advancement of women at the local, state, national and international levels regardless of race, creed, or nationality. While she was keenly concerned with the fight for democracy, she was more concerned with women's rights, asserting that the struggle was "tied up in the fight for total emancipation of women." She observed that men totally controlled the world and that peace among nations would be consummated only when women entered meaningful positions in government. She continued,

> The fight has two distinct fronts: that which deals with men, and that which deals with women, themselves, for the majority of women have been "down so long, that down don't worry them." Our journal can quietly and intelligently spread the gospel of total emancipation for women to the women and peoples of the world. Negro women suffer most, hence they should fight hardest.

By 1950 Taylor had become concerned with the universal plight of women and worked to raise the status of women in the world, to help secure lasting peace and true democracy. In her column "Federated Clubs" published in the January 7, 1950, issue of the *Chicago Defender*, she acknowledges her concern for the plight of foreign women. She said,

> I have become interested in all women of all races of all countries, and of a consequence, I recognize the fact that the struggle of the colored woman in the United States is the same as the struggles of all women—the world over. The only difference is that all other women face a SEX fight, while the colored woman in the U.S.A. and elsewhere faces a RACE as well as SEX fight.

The exact dates of Taylor's first and second marriage are unknown; she continued to write under the name Taylor until the mid-1950s, when she began to use Dodson. According to Samuel Stiles in an interview with Louise Owens for her radio profile, she married after she moved to Chicago in the 1930s. She appears to have been a Congregationalist, yet some sources say she was active in the Baptist Church. She died in Chicago in 1970. Among Taylor's living descendants are her nephew John Stiles, Sr. and grandnephews John Stiles, Jr. and Samuel Stiles. The Souvenir Program of the Twenty-ninth Biennial Convention of the Southeastern Association of Colored Women's Clubs and the Southeastern Association of Girl's Clubs, which was held in Savannah in 1977, was dedicated to Taylor. A fearless, straightforward, persuasive, and thoroughly competent organizer, journalist, and clubwoman, Taylor was an influential figure in black women's history. As Owens said, "she was not a woman to be ignored or easily forgotten."

REFERENCES:

"Biennial Address of Mrs. Rebecca Stiles Taylor." *National Notes,* September 1927, 7-12.

"Federated Clubs." *Chicago Defender,* November 20, 1937-December 31, 1956.

Gaillard, Margeret B. *History of the Southeastern Federation of Colored Women's Clubs.* Grenada, Miss.: Southern Federation of Colored Women's Clubs, 1967.

Greene, Gertrude. Telephone interviews with Jessie Carney Smith, November 1, 1994; November 15, 1994.

Hine, Darlene Clark, ed. *Black Women in America.* Brooklyn: Carlson Publishing, 1993.

Lee, Thelma. "Mrs. Rebecca Stiles Taylor: 1880-1970." Souvenir Program. Southeastern Association of Colored Women's Clubs and Southeastern Association of Colored Girls' Clubs. Twenty-Ninth Biennial Convention, 1920-1977. Savannah, Ga., DeSota Hilton Hotel, July 30-August 3, 1977.

Otto, Albert S. "Honor Roll of Negro Teachers." In *The Public School System of Savannah and Chatham County.* Vol. 3. N.p., n.d.

Owens, Louise Lautier. "How Well We Remember Her!" Radio Profile of Rebecca Stiles Taylor Dodson, prepared for public radio (WSVH) as part of the project "Great Women in Georgia History." N.d.

Perdue, Robert E. *The Negro in Savannah 1865-1900.* New York: Exposition Press, 1973.

Smalls, Kermit O., ed. *Yearbook of Colored Savannah.* Savannah: *Savannah Tribune,* 1934.

Stiles, John Sr. Telephone interview with Jessie Carney Smith, September 9, 1994.

Taylor, Rebecca Stiles. "Southeastern Federations Program for 1925-26." *National Notes,* February 1926, 14.

Wesley, Charles Harris. *The History of the National Association of Colored Women's Clubs.* Washington: NACW, 1984.

COLLECTIONS:

Information on the history of the Savannah federation, including a leaflet by the Savannah Federation of Colored Women's Clubs, is in possession of Gertrude Greene in Savannah. Papers of the Stiles family and some biographical information on Rebecca Stiles Taylor are in possession of John Stiles, Sr. in Savannah. Letters between Taylor and Jeanetta Welch and Mary McLeod Bethune are in the Records of the National Council of Negro Women located in the Bethune Museum and Archives, Washington, D.C.

Jessie Carney Smith

Debi Thomas

Debi Thomas
(1967-)
Figure skater

" "I guess I'm a pioneer, because I'm the first Black to make the world team," said Debi Thomas in *Jet,* March 19, 1986, after winning the United States National Women's Figure Skating Championship in 1986. Among the top American women contenders in figure skating competition, Thomas is no stranger to pioneer roles. She has had a stellar career filled with landmark accomplishments. She made history at the 1983 Criterium International du Sucre contest in France as the first African American ever to win a international senior-level singles competition. By 1985 Thomas was ranked second in the nation and fifth in the world ratings. At the age of nineteen, Thomas captured the 1986 United States International Figure Skating Championship "with a dazzling display of jumps bigger than many of the men's and a personal exuberance that won the crowds. . . . She made skating look fun," exclaimed Amy Engeler in *Rolling Stone.*

One month later, in March 1986, Thomas won the World Championship in Geneva, Switzerland, upsetting the reigning Olympic champion, Katarina Witt of East Germany. She won

the bronze medal at the 1988 Olympics. Not only is Thomas the first black woman ever to make the United States Olympic figure-skating team, she was also the first champion in thirty years to balance full-time university studies with competition.

Born in Poughkeepsie, New York, on March 25, 1967, Debi Thomas is the youngest of two children of Janice Thomas. She grew up in San Jose, California, where she and her brother, Rick, were raised by their mother after her divorce from Debi's father, McKinley Thomas. Exposing her children to opera, ballet, and ice shows, Janice Thomas encouraged her daughter's interest in figure skating, which was sparked at age four when Debi attended an Ice Follies performance starring the Swiss skating comedian Werner Groebli, also known as Mr. Frick. She began taking skating lessons at age five and quickly demonstrated her natural talents for the sport. Participating in local competitions, Thomas caught the attention of Janet Signorello, co-owner of the Redwood City, California, Ice Lodge, who recommended to Janice Thomas that she get Debi a professional coach. She took part in her first competition at age nine, winning with a routine choreographed to "Matchmaker" from *Fiddler on the Roof.* "From then on I was hooked on competing," says Thomas in *Ms.* "To this day, I skate because I'm very competitive." By ten years of age, Thomas was studying with coach Alex McGowan, with whom she worked closely for many years. He doubted her ability to become a world champion and found the odds against it astronomical. But Debi's love of skating, talent, and determination eventually changed his mind. She and McGowan have a close working relationship. She said in *Time* magazine, February 18, 1988, that, although McGowan had been and would always be her coach, she was not a string puppet.

Rigorous Preparation

Thomas began a rigorous training program under the tutelage of McGowan at the Redwood City Ice Lodge that required a grueling schedule for her mother and herself. Janice Thomas had to drive from their San Jose home to Sunnyvale, where she worked as a computer programmer analyst, back to San Jose to pick up Debi from school and take her to Redwood City Ice Lodge to practice for six hours a day, drive back to work, and then back to Redwood City to pick up Debi—a total of one hundred and twenty miles a day.

At age fourteen, Thomas had passed the United States Figure Skating Association's required tests. Thomas was a formidable competitor at local, national, and world skating meets. She skated in sixteen competitions from 1986 to 1989, won eight and placed second in three. But preparation and training were a financial burden for her family, and she found it costly and exhausting. At various times her family and friends contributed financially to her yearly budget. Even so, at times Thomas had to break training for a few months for financial reasons. It was not unusual for her skates to be completely worn out before her mother was able to buy her a new pair. Although her father helped, it was her mother and her brother who paid the bills—about $25,000 a year. Thomas entered Stanford University in 1986, and keeping her skating and schooling paid at the same time was a major financial drain for the Thomas family. In addition to the yearly expenses for training a world-class champion, Thomas's tuition, room, and board at Stanford University were more than $16,000 annually.

Until after the 1986 Denver Nationals, Thomas had no sponsor other than her family. According to *Ebony,* McGowan told the media: "It was 'sad' that the U.S. female skating champion, the No. 1 athlete in her sport had no sponsor while her two toughest competitors from Russia and East Germany were sponsored by their governments and skate full time." Soon after this pronouncement, a cosmetic company offered to sponsor Thomas, and other companies and organizations wanted her to represent their products. Thomas, in the fall of 1988, became the first member of the U.S. Skating Association to receive corporate sponsors when she signed with an agent of the International Management Group in New York. Since that time, Campbells, Raytheon, and Revlon commercials have provided for her financial support. For the first time, she could concentrate on both skating and school.

A freshman at Stanford in 1986, Thomas was advised to drop out of school and concentrate solely on skating until after the 1988 Olympics, but she refused. "I'm not going to make a choice between school and skating, they are both on an equal basis for me. I don't want to pursue one without the other," she said in *Ebony.* A fiercely competitive skater who believes that skating is fun, Thomas loves her sport and is serious about her amateur career, but will not let it dominate her life. She said in *Macleans* magazine, "People who live nothing but skating are in a dream world." Instead, she said in the December 1985 issue of *Essence* that she saw both her studies and skating as bringing balance to her life and attributes her love of ice skating to her success in both careers:

> Skating has given me self-discipline and a lot of drive. It's taught me how to work for things, to know what needs to be done to accomplish what I want, like getting the grades to be accepted by Stanford. . . . I know medical school will be hard, and skating has prepared me for that.

While juggling a rigorous training and competition schedule with full-time studies in premedicine, Thomas was secure in her success and in her future goals; she wanted to be an orthopedic surgeon, specializing in sports medicine. She did not want to devote her life to skating. In the March 17, 1986, issue of *Sports Illustrated* she stated, "I know too many skaters who don't get the gold medals or the big skating contracts and their lives are over." For her both pursuits balance each other. "I want to leave this sport willingly," she said in the *Sports Illustrated* article. Her dream is to own a sports training center in the San Francisco Bay area—a huge complex with an ice rink, a swimming pool, a ballet room, a weight room, and a sports medicine clinic; she also planned on teaching ice skating.

Thomas Wins Skating Crowns

Given Thomas's ability, during her first years of national competition, her scores were lower than they should have been, which caused coach McGowan great concern: "Because Debi was the first black skater, there may have been some doubt in the minds of the U.S. judges whether the international judges would accept her," said McGowan in *Ms.* magazine. But, he noted, "she won international acceptance before she was accepted here." Between 1985 and 1986, Thomas scored her first successes and greatly improved her standing as she moved from second place in the nation and fifth in the world to first place in each of three competitions—the National Sports Festival, the St. Ivel Competition, and Skate America 85—the last two occurring during her freshman year as a student at Stanford.

In 1985-86, what *Vogue* called "her year of miracles," she captured the crown in both the U.S. Nationals and World Championship. Describing Thomas's performance at Nationals as one of the best free-skate performances of her career, one critic wrote in *Sports Illustrated,* March 17, 1986, "Thomas 19, completed five triple jumps in all—an extraordinary feat in figure skating." Her spectacular performance placed her above former champion Tiffany Chin as the United States Women's champion. "Thomas put on the performance of her life," stated E. M. Swift in *Sports Illustrated.*

> In the opening dramatic interlude, she landed all three triples as if she had never missed one in her life. From then on she skated with a grin from ear to ear. The crowd loved her, and Thomas seemed to grow in stature with each new pass around the ice. She was having a ball, totally in command, urged on

by the adoration of the crowd and [her coach] McGowan's cheerleading.

Lynn Norment of *Ebony* added, "she had skating, not studying on her mind as the enthusiastic crowd cheered her on to victory at the Nassau Coliseum in Uniondale, N.Y., . . . she was self-assured and determined to do her best." In what the May 1986 *New York Times* called an "almost flawless free-skating program," Thomas bedazzled the judges with one of the most difficult programs attempted by a woman skater, in spite of burnout from the pressures of keeping up with both skating and school.

At the 1986 World Championship competition a month later in Geneva, Switzerland, she added yet another gold crown to her victories when she upset the reigning Olympic champion, East Germany's Katarina Witt. Thomas, at eighteen, had captured the World Championship. *Sports Illustrated,* March 31, 1986, described her win:

> With grace as usual, starting slowly, her first two triples were a bit jolting—Thomas relaxed as she landed her third and fourth while her teammates screamed encouragement. . . . But, with the guts of a burglar, she suddenly and spontaneously improvised a triple-double combination in place of the four triples. . . . She was having fun, right up until the double axel at the end—the same one that troubled her at the U. S. Nationals last month—and when she nailed that, it became clear to everyone that they were applauding the gold medal winner.

After the World Championship competition, Thomas had a rigorous round of interviews, award ceremonies, and exhibitions. She participated in Sport Aid in England and the Goodwill Games in Moscow. She lost the U.S. National title to Jill Trenary in 1987 and, although she skated a rousing long program, she was runner-up to Witt at the World Competition.

The 1988 Winter Olympic Games

Taking a leave from Stanford in the fall of 1987, she moved to Boulder, Colorado, to prepare for the 1988 Winter Olympics in Calgary, Alberta. That summer, she worked to strengthen her artistic skills, and to add new style to her athletic technique by consulting with dancer Mikhail Baryshnikov in New York, who gave her tips and assigned his assistant choreographer, George de la Pena, to work with her. "She is a spitfire," said de la Pena in the February 18, 1988, *Newsweek.* "She's lusty, she's fun and she has a great sense of humor. She's open to growing."

The Olympic competition among the world's leading female figure skaters was intense. In compulsory figures, Witt finished third, Thomas second, and Elizabeth Manley fourth. The following night, Thomas and Witt both had high scores, but with a clear contrast. Witt's closing dance routine was vintage Witt—showy, engaging, and stylish. While Thomas executed the technically difficult double loop-triple loop combination and skated flawlessly, she received high marks for technical merit but lower ones for artistic presentation. Although Witt won the short program, Thomas gained first

place and Witt second. In the final stage of the competition, the United States contingent—Debi Thomas, Jill Trenary, and Caryn Kaday—did not fare well. Trenary finished fourth, while Kaday had to withdraw because of the flu. Thomas not only failed in her attempt to capture the gold medal from Witt, but she faltered so badly during her free skating—missing three triple jumps—that Manley edged her out of the silver. Thomas won the bronze medal, the first black woman athlete to win a medal in the Winter Olympic Games.

Obviously disappointed yet undaunted, she competed in the World Championship in Budapest, where she also won a bronze medal. After the competition, Thomas announced she had secretly married Brian Vander Hogen on March 15 in Boulder, Colorado. "I will get on with my life," she said in the March 14, 1988, *Jet.* "And, now it's probably going to be a lot easier to finish school." Thomas, who retired from skating after the Olympics, continued her studies at Stanford University to become an orthopedic surgeon.

Considered an athletic skater, Thomas is perhaps the most powerful woman skater in the history of American women's figure skating. *Ms.* magazine describes Thomas's superior technical skills and tremendous talent:

> She's perhaps the most physically powerful performer women's figure skating has ever seen, racing along the ice at a breath-taking pace before translating that motion into a spectacular vertical leap and speed-of-light midair spin, she then lands effortlessly with the elan of a ballerina, and completes the seamless meld of artistry and athleticism that the sport has come to demand. Watch her skate for a few minutes and you quickly forget about color or academics.

REFERENCES:

"As Ice Skating Champ Debi Thomas Says the Goal is Gold in '88." *Jet* 69 (March 10, 1986): 48.

Austen, Ian. "Chasing a Crown." *Macleans* 101 (February 1988): 3.

Burazil, Bryan. "With Style and Grace." *Black Enterprise* 16 (June 1986): 86.

Callahan, Tom. "The Word She Uses Is Invincible." *Time* 131 (18 February 1988): 46.

Engeler, Amy. "Blade Runner." *Rolling Stone* (February 25, 1988): 72-84.

"Figure Skating Debi Thomas." *Newsweek* (February 18, 1988): 79.

Kort, Michelle. "Debi Thomas: Skater Extraordinaire." *Ms.* 15 (February 1987): 33.

Norment, Lynn. "The Nation's No. 1 Skating Sensation." *Ebony* 41 (May 1986): 147-51.

Slate, Libby. "Show Stopper." *Essence* 16 (December 1985): 31.

Swift, E. M. "Lashing in on the Lollywobbles. *Sports Illustrated* 64 (February 17, 1986): 29.

———. "Another Miracle on Ice?" *Sports Illustrated* 64 (March 17, 1986): 36.

Who's Who among Black Americans, 1994-95. 8th ed. Detroit: Gale Research, 1994.

Jacquelyn L. Jackson

Verneice D. Thompson
(1926-1993)
Social worker, psychotherapist, consultant, educator, administrator

Verneice D. Thompson

A clinical social worker and psychotherapist, Verneice Thompson devoted her life to teaching. She lovingly hounded her students to push their own boundaries in perpetual pursuit of personal and professional development. Much of her career was spent studying and educating people about power, authority, and leadership in organizations, especially in relation to age, gender, and ethnicity. She grappled with major social issues and their impact on individual experience and expected nothing less from her students.

Verneice D. Thompson was born in Waco, Texas, on May 25, 1926, and died of cancer in Berkeley, California, on September 26, 1993. Her parents were Albert and Geraldine Hunt. Her father was a carpenter and her mother worked at a variety of jobs, from domestic day work to running a food stand for citywide church revivals. Thompson is survived by one brother, Jerome Hunt, a daughter, Jann Thompson, and a grandson, Malik Thompson, all of Oakland, California.

Thompson's second husband, Jim Hammond, died in 1991, and his death coincided with the beginning of her struggle with brain cancer. Theirs was an extraordinary and passionate marriage that Thompson once described in conversation with Katherine Csezak as "twenty-five years of living it up." Jim Hammond was a man of many interests. He worked as a filmmaker, Audubon wildlife photographer, writer, manufacturer, and publisher of fine handmade books. He was also a world traveler.

Thompson strongly believed that the family of origin is the most influential organization that exists and that, as such, it shapes the way people work with others. Her mother and father were outgoing people who valued independence and saw it as necessary to achievement. Jerome Hunt remembers Thompson telling him that her mother was especially fond of saying, "Don't wait for anyone to do it for you. Do it yourself." As the oldest child and only girl, Thompson functioned as a surrogate mother to her two younger brothers during the many hours her parents were at work. This was her first venture as an authority figure and she credited the experience with having contributed to her feisty and assertive

personality. Thompson also was a leader in school. She was captain of the debating team for three years at Moore High School, from which she graduated at the age of fifteen.

Clinical Social Work Professionalized

Thompson attended Wilberforce University in Wilberforce, Ohio, and graduated in 1945. While there, she was among the first students to sit in at the local segregated lunch counter. She received her master's degree in social welfare from the University of California at Berkeley in 1951 and her Ph.D. in psychology in 1976 from the Wright Institute in Berkeley. The Wright Institute is an independent graduate school granting Ph.D. degrees in psychology. It was founded in 1963 by Novitt Sanford. It is unique in its emphasis on integrating social issues and clinical psychology. She began her career as a social worker with the Travelers Aid Society of Oakland, California, where she worked from 1953 to 1958, and she was chief clinical social worker and director of group programs and special projects at the Family Guidance Clinic of Children's Hospital Medical Center in Oakland from 1958 to 1976.

In 1961 Thompson became one of the first Bay Area clinical social workers to enter the private practice of psychotherapy. She initiated a group effort that resulted in the licensing of clinical social workers and the awarding of confidentiality to their clients. She was instrumental in establishing the California Society for Clinical Social Work and from 1971 to 1973 was its first president. This society was the prototype for a national movement in clinical social work.

From 1972 to 1973 Thompson was president of the National Federation of Societies for Clinical Social Work. She was dean of the California Institute for Clinical Social Work from 1979 to 1983. She was an associate clinical professor in the Department of Psychiatry at the University of California at San Francisco (1981-92) and served on the faculties of the Wright Institute (1976-86) and the California Institute for Clinical Social Work (1977-79). She held memberships in and served on the boards of numerous organizations, including the A. K. Rice Institute for the Study of Group Relations and its California affiliate, GREX. She was the first African American trustee of the Zellerbach Family Fund, which supports a variety of community service projects, and served on its board for more than a decade. From 1963 to her death, she headed an independent organizational consulting firm.

Lifetime Dedicated to the Study of Group Relations

The overriding focus of Thompson's studies was the work environment, specifically the study of power and authority in groups. She taught students and organization managers how to concentrate on systemic issues rather than on the individuals who symbolize such issues. She acknowledged how compelling an activity it is to focus on individual personalities, but she would always restore the larger systemic picture by asking, "Why does the group need this individual to behave in this way at this point in time?"

Much of her thinking and teaching spoke to the experiences of "outsiders" in mainstream America and she challenged her colleagues to "deliver on diversity," even in its absence. In an address before the Psychotherapy Institute in Berkeley, California, in October 1991, she said:

> There is no excuse for the short-sighted thinking . . . that cultural influences in the therapy relationship can't be addressed except in the presence of Third World members. Are we to assume that Caucasians have a monolithic cultural background? Does whiteness homogenize cultural experiences? I think not. What is needed to enrich teaching and learning about cultural diversity is just as much clear thinking as there is hand wringing about the absence of Third World staff or clients. . . . There is no reason to assume that programs could not still be planned to open up the discussion for those who are present. . . . Sooner or later the word will get out and Third World people will come.

As a consultant, her goals were to ensure that organizational leadership at all levels clearly understood the work task as well as the procedures that needed to be followed to maintain a competent work force, encourage widespread participation in decision making, and properly train emerging leadership. She worked closely with leadership to connect all parts of an organization to its stated task or mission. As an African American woman, she frequently was expected to align herself with minority groups within an organization. She resisted these pressures by stating that she was more effective working with leadership, who had the power and authority to create widespread change, than she was working to empower specific groups. While she refused to align herself with group factions, she also vigorously opposed the homogenization of group members. The object of diversity, she believed, was for different groups to be able to work together while maintaining their differences, rather than disguising or ignoring them.

Advocates Group Relations Conference

One of Thompson's favorite vehicles for teaching was the group relations conference, modeled after those first developed at the Tavistock Institute of Human Relations in London. Thompson encountered these conferences during her doctoral training at the Wright Institute and they greatly influenced her thinking and practice. In a December 18, 1985, in a memorandum to staff members for an upcoming group relations conference she was directing and sponsoring independently, she said,

> In my first . . . experience, it was shattering to learn how group dynamics influenced my behavior. Prior to that time, I would have maintained that my professional behavior was largely under my control!. . . I also gained perspective about others' reactions to me as a competent Black woman. When individuals were threatened by my competence (imagined or real), it was easier for them to focus on some aspect of race or gender. To experience these reactions emotionally validated what I knew intellectually. This was liberating, to say the least!

Group relations conferences operate as temporary organizations in which learning occurs through direct experience of overt and covert group dynamics rather than by the study of theory. This approach views a group or organization as an organism with a life of its own and a unique culture. Thompson described this phenomenon in 1987:

> The invisible side of the organization functions as if it has needs, wishes, fears and defensive strategies that often operate outside of conscious awareness. Because these elements affect the ways that tasks are organized and work is structured, they can either facilitate or interfere with the achievement of the stated organizational or group objective. . . . Management of this invisible culture requires leaders to develop the capacity to draw on unconscious sources of strength in themselves as well as in the organizational culture.

It was at conferences that Thompson was at her best and most intense, worrying over the learning experiences she promised to as many as one hundred participants of diverse backgrounds, ages, professions, and stages of career development. It was a large undertaking to facilitate the experiential learning of so many and then assist them in studying their own process. This was time for high drama, and her fiery directorship created a living laboratory in which the conference staff could examine their own responses to power and authority.

Nicknamed Einstein

While Thompson was brilliantly intuitive, she often was overwhelmed by the practical realities of everyday life. She frequently misplaced keys or important papers and would pace fretfully in her office, dressed in her characteristic silk slacks and tailored top with pearls. Her brother Jerome used to call her Einstein because she could do complicated things but not simple ones, to which she would reply, "Things that are not difficult are not important." Her impracticality was well known, and her affectionate dedication to those who had mastered what was to her the mysterious realm of technology softened her fierce preoccupation with having the upper hand in her own surroundings. A colleague with whom she co-owned an office building for two decades recalls having to restrain her from calling an electrician whenever a light bulb burned out, persuading her to call him instead. According to Garrett Hill's remarks at a memorial for Thompson, her grasp of technology was so limited that she could not bring herself to throw away used bulbs, and her supply of new bulbs was always mingled with her supply of burned out ones.

Teaching Style

Thompson held classes at the Wright Institute in her off-campus private office in order to ensure the integrity of a class's boundaries and protect student learning from institutional politics. In another example of her advocacy of learning by doing, she taught the value of being clear about boundaries by locking her office door at the start of class. Her students all remember the humiliation of having to knock on the door and disrupt class to gain entrance. Once inside, the tardy student would be subjected to a brief, incisive interpretation of his or her tardiness and then be offered coffee and pastries that Thompson had set out before class. In the middle of class or group consultation, Thompson, appearing to be more interested in food than the subject at hand, would rise from her chair, gather up the food tray for replenishing, and leave her students to carry on alone. When she returned ten minutes later, she would have worked out the core dynamics of the problem being discussed. She had a special talent that allowed her to concentrate on the specific learning needs of each student, remember the personal dynamics that influenced their work as a therapist or consultant, hold them to task in their own development—and feed them—all in one session. A colleague, Lowell Cooper, described her in a 1994 communication as uniquely able to mix formal intent with informal style, something she did often in fine restaurants, working and eating with equal gusto.

Thompson's teaching style was one of gentle pressure relentlessly applied, and she pushed colleagues and students alike to do things on their own, often before they thought themselves ready. She did not like people hanging onto her, but wanted them to go out on their own and use the strengths that sometimes only she could see. She was ruthless in pushing others to develop themselves. Her vision about individual potential was always connected to the development of humanity. According to Claire Allphin, she stayed connected to hundreds of people through telephone calls and letters, often including clippings with her correspondence.

While Thompson mentored hundreds of people, she made each feel unique and special. In his remarks at a memorial for Thompson, Calvin Sturgis described her as a "giant switchboard helping people make the most marvelous connections with themselves and to one another."

While Thompson was generous in her support of others, she lacked the ability to accept compliments herself. Her standard reply to clients' praise was "I certainly hope you'll be equally frank with me when you're not pleased." She was modest and never boasted about her achievements. It was only when her brother Jerome happened upon one of her business cards that he discovered she had a doctorate. She explained in a personal conversation with Garrett Hunt that she had earned her Ph.D. degree in 1976, seven years before, but had not considered it worthy of special mention.

Thompson died regretting that she had spent so little time writing. Her doctoral dissertation, along with most of her other papers, is located at the Wright Institute in Berkeley, California. A fellowship established there in her name will provide a work-study student with funds to collect class notes, handouts, and letters saved by her students and associates. Her true legacy, however, is the place of honor she occupies in the hearts and minds of so many who carry her work forward.

REFERENCES:

Allphin, Claire. Remarks at memorial for Verneice D. Thompson, Kensington, Calif., November 14, 1993.

Cooper, Lowell. Personal communication with Ellen Freeman Kirschman, 1994.

Csezak, Katherine. Personal communication with Ellen Freeman Kirschman, 1994.

Hill, Garrett. Remarks at memorial for Verneice D. Thompson, Kensington, Calif., November 14, 1993.

Hunt, Jerome. Personal communication with Ellen Freeman Kirschman, 1994.

Sturgis, Calvin. Remarks at memorial for Verneice D. Thompson, Kensington, Calif., November 14, 1993.

Thompson, Verneice. Class handout, Wright Institute, Berkeley, Calif., April 15, 1979.

———. "Marketing a Group Relations Conference." Memorandum to Group Relations staff members, Berkeley, Calif., December 18, 1985.

———. "Using Group Relations Conferences for Leadership Assessment and Personal Development." Announcement of training program for Group Relations staff, 1987.

———. Memorandum to staff members on Post-Conference Reflections of the March 1989 Group Relations Conference, Berkeley, Calif., June 20, 1989.

———. Address to the Psychotherapy Institute, Berkeley, Calif., October 1991.

Ellen Freeman Kirschman

Willie Mae Thornton
(1926-1984)
Blues singer, musician, songwriter, dancer

B lues singer Willie Mae "Big Mama" Thornton was known for her earthy voice, outspoken lyrics, and eccentric lifestyle. A gifted musician who sang gospel music as a child, Thornton also performed on harmonica, drums, and guitar. She left behind a legacy of recordings, many of which influenced better-known recording stars such as Elvis Presley and Janis Joplin.

Willie Mae Thornton was born on December 11, 1926, in a rural area outside Montgomery, Alabama. She was one of seven children. Her earliest musical experiences took place in the church where her father served as minister and her mother sang in the choir. She learned to play harmonica and drums at an early age and performed as a teenager throughout the Montgomery area in a variety of blues styles. At age fourteen, following the death of her mother, Thornton went to work in a local saloon washing floors to help support her family. It was here that she got her first opportunity to perform blues in public. The chance came unexpectedly around 1939 when she was asked to substitute on short notice for the tavern's regular singer. A short time later she won first prize in a local amateur music contest at which she attracted the attention of promoter Sammy Green of Atlanta.

Green engaged her to tour with his show, *The Hot Harlem Revue,* and by the early 1940s, Thornton was singing and dancing throughout the southeastern United States. Because of her powerful voice and mature interpretation, the revue initially billed Thornton as "the new Bessie Smith" or "Bessie Smith's younger sister." But while Thornton was undoubtedly influenced by Smith, her authoritative stage persona was already uniquely her own and not subject to manipulation by promoters.

Thornton later recalled her difficult start in the music business with authors Anthony Connor and Robert Neff:

> I had a hard way to go when I come up. Sometimes had to go to somebody's back door and ask for bread or something cool to drink. "Mister, could I have a drink of your water?" Sometimes they said no. I just kept on walking. I just made myself happy. People didn't know I was worried a lot of times. I always kept a smile on my face: I always be round friends, buy drinks, laugh. But they didn't know it. I was smiling. Didn't have nowhere to stay. They didn't know that. I slept in all-night restaurants and barrooms. Course it don't make no difference now. It's all the past. Anyway, I couldn't express what I went through. It don't make no sense to people today.

Thornton was self-taught, and her style reflected her humble rural upbringing. "My singing comes from my experience," she once said, according to author Arnold Shaw.

Willie Mae Thornton

"My own experience. My own thing. I got my feelin's for everything. I never had no one teach me nothin'. I never went to school for music or nothin'. I taught myself to sing and to blow harmonica and even to play drums by watchin' other people. I can't read music but I know what I'm singing. I don't sing like nobody but myself." Nonetheless, Thornton did, at times, acknowledge the influence of Ma Rainey, Bessie Smith, Junior Parker, and Memphis Minnie. Her style inspired a new generation of singers, including Elvis Presley, Janis Joplin, and Angela Strehli.

Recording Career Begins

In 1948 the *Hot Harlem Revue* arrived in Houston, Texas, where Thornton signed a five-year exclusive contract as a nightclub entertainer under the entrepreneurship of Don Robey. Thornton's recording debut came in 1951 when Robey arranged for her to work with Joe Scott's band for the Peacock label. Six feet tall and already approaching 350 pounds, she celebrated the recent acquisition of her nickname "Big Mama," in an early recording session with her song "They Call Me Big Mama."

In 1952 Johnny Otis, the "Godfather of Rhythm and Blues," negotiated a contract to record with his band in Los Angeles and sent the master tapes to Robey in Houston. Robey added Thornton's voice and distributed the final pressing on his Peacock label. Among these recordings was Thornton's version of "Hound Dog"—the song later immortalized by Elvis Presley. Usually attributed to the Jerry Leiber-Mike Stoller songwriting team, this classic rock 'n' roll tune may actually have been written by Otis and Thornton. In fact, Otis is listed as cowriter with Lieber and Stoller on Thornton's first pressing, though not on Presley's version, which is attributed only to Lieber and Stoller. Thornton maintained, however, that she did not write "Hound Dog"— at least she never laid claim to Presley's version. "Lieber and Stoller wrote it," she said in Shaw's *The World of Soul.* "They were just a couple of kids then and they had this song written on the back of a brown paper bag. So I started to sing the words and put in some of my own. All that talkin' and hollerin'—that's my own." Regardless of its origin, "Hound Dog" was a peculiar choice for the fledgling Presley, especially given the female orientation of its lyrics.

A nearly perfect vehicle for Thornton, "Hound Dog" was released in 1953 and hit number one on the rhythm and blues charts in 1955. Author Ian Whitcomb described a Thornton performance of "Hound Dog" in *Repercussions:* "When Big Mama sings 'Hound Dog' she's slow and easy and also menacing, smiling like a sabre-tooth tiger, her black diamond eyes glinting fiercely. Then, with the band in full roar, she leaves her chair to ambulate off in a swaying promenade that has a certain military regality, and the whole house cheers like royal subjects." "Hound Dog" was Thornton's biggest studio success, selling over 500,000 copies. Still, Thornton often expressed bitterness over the credit Presley received for his recording. "That song [Presley's version] sold over two million records. I got one check for $500 and never saw another," the August 13, 1984, issue of *Jet* magazine quoted her as once stating.

Thornton continued to perform with Otis until 1955, after which time she returned to Houston to record with Bill Harvey and his band. In 1956 her contract with Robey expired and she moved to San Francisco to tour with Gatemouth Brown. A year later Thornton experienced a slow period, with no regular back-up band, no recording contract, and only sporadic playing engagements. The blues revival of the 1960s brought renewed interest in her work and she was invited by Horst Lippmann to appear with the American Folk Blues Festival, which embarked on a European tour in 1965. While in England, Chris Strachwitz, representing Arhoolie records, produced an album, "Big Mama in Europe," featuring Thornton and a back-up band of Buddy Guy, Walter Horton, and Freddy Below.

"Ball and Chain" Record a Hit

While the authorship of "Hound Dog" has always been debatable, no one ever attempted to deny Thornton credit for the classic "Ball and Chain." A hit for Janis Joplin in 1969, Thornton first recorded the tune in 1967. Whitcomb recounted in *Repercussions,*

> Whereas Joplin's performance was always cultivated and labored, Thornton's is straight from the heart with a punch to the belly. From out of the chaos of messy real life she fashions a beautifully structured and controlled performance that always contains an element of danger: whatever will she do next? It's a cliffhanger.

In her later years, Thornton's appetite for whiskey and corn moonshine began to take its toll. Several years before her death she was diagnosed as having cirrhosis of the liver. She continued to perform but often had to be helped on stage and then remained seated while singing. In 1979 she appeared at the San Francisco Blues Festival. "Big Mama Thornton had to be led to the bandstand," wrote reviewer Richard Cohen for *Living Blues.* He continued,

> She'd been ill for some time and has a difficult time keeping her music together. The standing ovation that greeted Big Mama touched something deep in her and with tears in her eyes she thanked everyone for being there and thanked God for letting her come. In the next 50 minutes, she gave one of her best performances in recent years. While it sounded good at the festival, it was only when I listened to the tapes later that the stunning nature of her show became apparent. . . . *Ball and Chain* was the highlight of her set, and indeed, of the whole festival. Big Mama sang, moaned, yelled and did about everything there is to do to the song.

In recognition of her contributions over a period of three decades to the blues, she received the San Francisco Blues Festival Award.

At other performances, Thornton remained seated behind a table upon which she laid her harmonicas, cigarettes, and a fruit jar containing a concoction of milk and bourbon. Her health failing, she lost a great deal of weight, plunging from 350 to an emaciated 95 pounds. Refusing to cease performing altogether, Thornton disguised her frailness by cultivating two new stage "looks": one for which she wore a voluminous African robe, and for the other, an oversized man's business suit, cowboy boots, and a Stetson hat.

In 1981, Thornton was in a serious auto accident and her injuries required major surgery. After recovering she performed at a cabaret club in Pasadena, California, with the veteran Big Joe Turner, "The Boss of the Blues." Neither performer was able to walk, with Thornton using a cane and Turner on crutches. Whitcomb recalled the show:

> The audience was all ages but all white. This whiteness is typical of today's R & B following. At the cabaret, Turner and Thornton, being no longer ambulatory, did their respective acts from chairs on the stage. During the second set they actually performed from a bench in the auditorium.

In addition to "Ball and Chain" and "They Call Me Big Mama," Thornton wrote twenty other blues songs. She also recorded dozens of blues classics on such labels as Arhoolie, Baytone, Kent, Mercury, and Vanguard. Her television appearances included those for *Black, White and Blue* on PBS in 1967; *Della* in New York, 1969; *Rock I* in Toronto, 1970; the *Dick Cavett Show* in 1971; and *Midnight Special* in 1974. She recorded portions of the sound track for the Hollywood film, *Vanishing Point,* released in 1971, and participated in "From Spirituals to Swing" at Carnegie Hall in 1967, and "Blues Is a Woman" at Avery Fisher Hall in 1980. Throughout her career, Thornton appeared at numerous jazz and blues festivals and on many college and university campuses.

On July 25, 1984, Thornton died in her home in Los Angeles of a heart attack and complications from cirrhosis of the liver. She had been largely inactive professionally for a few months. Her body was discovered by paramedics responding to a call from concerned neighbors who had not seen Thornton in several days. The funeral was held in Los Angeles and, at Thornton's request, presided over by Reverend Johnny Otis. Jimmy Witherspoon and Margie Evans sang spirituals, and Tina Mayfield, wife of songwriter Percy Mayfield, read the obituary. A special benefit concert, scheduled to take place a week after the funeral to pay for funeral expenses, was organized by the Southern California Blues Society. Thornton, who never married and had no children, was survived by her sister, Mattie (Thornton) Fields of Los Angeles, California.

REFERENCES:

Aldin, Mary Katherine. "Willie Mae Thornton." *Living Blues,* 60-61 (Summer/Fall 1984): 68.

"Big Mama Thornton Dead at 57; Singer Influenced Early Rockers." In *Variety Obituaries.* Vol. 10. New York: Garland, 1988.

Bolcom, William, Max Harrison, and Paul Oliver. *The New Grove Gospel, Blues and Jazz.* New York: Norton, 1986.

Budds, Michael J. "African-American Women in Blues and Jazz." In *Women and Music: A History.* Edited by Karin Pendle. Bloomington: Indiana University Press, 1991.

Clarke, Donald, ed. *The Penguin Encyclopedia of Popular Music.* New York: Viking Penguin, 1989.

Cohen, Richard. "San Francisco Blues Festival." *Living Blues* 44 (Autumn 1979): 29-30.

Connor, Anthony, and Robert Neff. *Blues.* Boston: David R. Godine, 1975.

Gaar, Gillian G. *She's a Rebel: The History of Women in Rock and Roll.* Seattle: Seal Press, 1992.

George, Nelson. *The Death of Rhythm and Blues.* New York: Pantheon Books, 1988.

Govenar, Alan. *Meeting the Blues.* Dallas: Taylor Publishing, 1988.

Gregory, Hugh. *Soul Music A-Z.* London: Blandford, 1991.

Harris, Sheldon. *Blues Who's Who.* New Rochelle, N.Y.: Arlington House, 1979.

"Heart Attack Claims 'Big Mama' Thornton, 57." *Jet* 66 (August 13, 1984): 63.

Herzhaft, Gérard. *Encyclopedia of the Blues.* Translated by Brigitte Debord. Fayetteville: University of Arkansas Press, 1982.

Hitchcock, H. Wiley, and Stanley Sadie. *The New Grove Dictionary of American Music.* 4 vols. New York: Macmillan, 1986.

Hoke, S. Kay. "American Popular Music." In *Women and Music: A History.* Edited by Karin Pendle. Bloomington: Indiana University Press, 1991.

Larkin, Colin, ed. *The Guiness Encyclopedia of Popular Music.* 4 vols. London: Guiness Publishing, 1992.

Oakley, Giles. *The Devil's Music: A History of the Blues.* London: British Broadcasting Corporation, 1976.

Scott, Frank. *The Down Home Guide to the Blues.* Chicago: Down Home Music, 1991.

Shaw, Arnold. *The World of Soul.* New York: Cowles Book, 1970.

Southern, Eileen. *The Music of Black Americans.* 2d ed. New York: Norton, 1983.

———, ed. *Biographical Dictionary of Afro-American and African Musicians.* Westport, Conn.: Greenwood Press, 1982.

Strachwitz, Chris. *Big Mama Thornton: Ball and Chain.* Arhoolic CD-305, 1989.

Whitcomb, Ian. "Legends of Rhythm and Blues." In *Repercussions: A Celebration of African-American Music.* Edited by Geoffrey Haydon and Dennis Marks. London: Century Publishing, 1985.

Juanita Karpf

Amelia L. Tilghman
(1856-1931)
Singer, educator, writer, editor, composer

Performer, composer, and music teacher Amelia Tilghman is best known for editing the first periodical in the United States devoted to African American music and musicians. As a singer and composer, Tilghman contributed much to concert life in her native Washington, D.C. Her compositions are among the earliest published in the United States by a black American woman musician.

Amelia L. Tilghman was born on September 6, 1856, in Washington, D.C., to Margaret A. and Henry H. Tilghman. As a child she displayed an unusual talent for music. Upon hearing her perform the song "Departed Days" at a memorial service, the noted Bishop Daniel A. Payne of the African Methodist Episcopal (AME) Church was quoted by author Lawson Scruggs, in his *Women of Distinction,* as declaring, "That child's parents had better spend a hundred dollars on her voice now than leave her a fortune when they die." Tilghman's formal education included teacher training and music instruction at the Normal School of Howard University, where she graduated with high honors in 1871. In addition, she studied piano with Samuel Jamieson at the Boston, Massachusetts, Conservatory of Music in 1885.

Following her graduation from Howard University, Tilghman taught public school for fourteen years in Washington, D.C. She began to sing professionally in the choir of the Fifteenth Street Presbyterian Church in Washington, and she appeared at local concerts, sharing the stage with celebrated singers Anita Patti Brown, Nellie Brown Mitchell, Marie Selika, and Adelaide G. Smith.

Amelia L. Tilghman

On December 30, 1880, Tilghman made her New York City debut as a singer at Steinway Hall and received favorable reviews. Journalism historian I. Garland Penn, in his *The Afro-American Press and Its Editors,* reprinted this comment from the *National Era:* "Miss Tilghman's appearance in New York City was the bursting forth of a musical star, whose singing completely captivated the praise and admiration of the critics of the metropolis, and elicited their concession to her richly earned title of 'Queen of Song.'" In June 1881 she was engaged as the leading soprano in the *Sängerfest* held at the Grand Opera House in Louisville, Kentucky. In 1882, Tilghman produced a performance of the oratorio *Esther the Beautiful Queen,* written by William B. Bradbury. Tilghman sang the title role and was responsible for rehearsing the chorus of one hundred voices. The performance took place in Washington, D.C., at Lincoln Hall.

Singer Tours with Musical Troupe

In 1883, Tilghman became the leading soprano with the Washington, D.C., Harmonic Musical Concert Troupe. Sometimes billed as the Washington Harmonic Company, the ensemble usually consisted of eight singers, accompanied by a pianist. They performed at benefit concerts for the Metropolitan AME Church to support various building and improvement projects. An extensive new hall, proposed for the church in 1880, was dedicated in 1885, with an inaugural concert on the newly installed pipe organ occurring in 1886. This ambitious project actually included two separate facilities: one that could accommodate eighteen hundred people, and a smaller space with seating for one thousand. Fund-raising for this facility took place between 1883 and 1885, supported in part by performances of the troupe. Recitals were given in Maryland, Pennsylvania, and New York, raising as much as forty dollars per performance.

Sometime early in 1883, while on tour with the troupe in Saratoga, New York, Tilghman suffered a fractured skull in a freak accident. The mishap occurred when Tilghman was walking near a construction site and was struck in the head by a falling brick. Surgery was required to remove sixteen bone fragments. The *Washington Bee* issued regular bulletins on Tilghman's condition. The February 24, 1883, *Bee* said Tilghman was reportedly "worse, she is now unable to sit up." She continued to decline further, and on March 10, 1883, the *Bee* reported, "Miss Amelia L. Tilghman is still lingering. It is rumored that there is not much hope for her. It is greatly to be regretted." A final, more encouraging statement appeared a month later, on April 7, 1883: "Miss Amelia L. Tilghman, one of our favorite vocalists, is fast recovering."

By July 1883 Tilghman had recovered sufficiently to rejoin the troupe, and she was listed as one of the singers in a performance that took place on July 14th. A complimentary review of the performance appeared in the July 14, 1883, *Bee:*

> The concert last evening by the Harmonic Company, composed of persons of color, possessed of the highest order of musical culture, in Bethel Church on Short Street, was a decided musical treat and success. The audience was large and appreciative, and the higher order of pieces were selected and artistically rendered. The applause which greeted the artists and followed the pieces was hearty, and the encores were numerous. . . . The success of the concert is an evidence that musical talent of undoubted worth will attract a numerous audience [even] in an unfavorable season.

Mention of Tilghman's performance activities appeared regularly in the press and she continued her reign as "Washington's favorite prima donna." Her selection of repertoire did not always please the critics, however. Writing for the "Musical and Dramatic" column in the May 10, 1884, *Bee,* a reviewer commented,

> There is one suggestion we desire to make and that is, if Miss Tilghman will make some new selections and keep up with the advanced age in the musical art, she would become one of the most popular singers in the country. While she sang well what she did sing, her selections were too old.

Tilghman may well have responded to this very comment, for in the September 27, 1884, *Bee* it was noted, "Miss Amelia L. Tilghman will have new selections this winter."

In September 1884 Tilghman resigned her position with the choir of the Fifteenth Street Presbyterian Church and joined the choir at the Union Bethel Church. Reacting to this change, the press was again not entirely sympathetic. The September 27, 1884, *Bee* reported: "Miss Tilghman will find what she is looking for shortly, and that is empty notoriety." As if to apologize, the *Bee* reassured its readers a month later, on October 25, 1884, that Tilghman was still "one of the favorites."

Teaches Music in Montgomery, Alabama

In 1885, Tilghman accepted a teaching position in Montgomery, Alabama. Before beginning her new assignment, she enrolled briefly at the Boston, Massachusetts, Conservatory of Music to study methods for teaching piano. The *Bee* reported on September 12, 1885,

> Miss Amelia L. Tilghman, one of Washington's prima donnas, will leave this city in a few weeks for the South. This lady is one of our favorite vocalists, and her absence from this city will be regretted by her many friends and acquaintances. We wish this young lady much success in her new field of labor and hope her serene voice will echo throughout the South.

While in Montgomery, Tilghman produced another performance of *Esther,* preparing a chorus of sixty singers and again singing the lead role. According to Penn, the press commented,

> Miss Tilghman represented the beautiful queen, and she manifested that solemn, pathetic, and dramatic force throughout the play, which gave it lifelike appearance, as one would picture it as he reads it in the Bible. The highest praise is due her for the presentation of this cantata. She was the sole organizer, and deserves the thanks of the citizens generally for her interest in everything which tends to the improvement and elevation of our race.

The oratorio remained popular among Washington audiences, with at least one performance reported after Tilghman's departure—in January 1886 at Shiloh Baptist Church.

Tilghman met with immediate success in Montgomery, teaching piano and assisting with music instruction at Tuskegee University. A review in the *Southern Christian Recorder,* cited in Scruggs, lauded her accomplishments:

> Miss Tilghman is truly building monuments of music in the homes of the colored people. A few years ago there were no colored pianists in Montgomery, and in no house where colored people lived did one hear in passing the artistic rendition of music as is now heard in almost every two or three squares. Nowhere had such a thing as a musical recital ever been heard of until Miss Tilghman went to Montgomery and parents sat and listened to their own children perform in public on the piano, and their hearts swelled with pride as they looked and listened. This young lady is doing a grand and noble work in that city. She has not been without her trials and afflictions in life, but no woman has ever fought through them more nobly and womanly than she. No woman has ever taken a truer stand for the right. She has won the highest esteem and respect of all who have met her and witnessed her work, and in years to come the young ladies who have been under her instruction and watched her womanly learning will rise up and "call her blessed."

Tilghman's reputation traveled far beyond Montgomery, and word of her activities continued to appear in the press of the northeastern part of the United States. Writing from Montgomery in August 1886, in a letter to the editor of the *New York Freeman,* someone identified only as R. O. Bedford included this comment about a recent recital given by Tilghman's students:

> No public event of any kind has occurred in the history of the colored people of Montgomery more inspiring in its nature or more promising of good results in the higher planes of life for the future. The modest, gentle bearing of the pupils and Miss Tilghman's own self-possessed and lady like manner gave great satisfaction and encouragement to parents and all friends of the best interests of the colored people.

In December 1887 Tilghman left Montgomery to accept an invitation to teach in the music department of the Howe Institute in New Iberia, Louisiana. Her stay in New Iberia lasted only a few months and was cut short by a summons to return to Washington to be with her mother, who was seriously ill. Tilghman's mother recovered and lived several more years. Her death occurred in December 1903, shortly after the *Washington Colored American* of December 19, 1903, reported, "Mrs. Tilghman of 806 M St. N.W., mother of the well-known singer and composer is very ill."

Publishes *Musical Messenger*

Sometime in the late 1880s, Tilghman began publishing a journal, the *Musical Messenger.* With its inaugural issue, Tilghman became the first black woman in the United States to edit a periodical devoted specifically to African American music and musicians. She most likely began her publication while still residing in Alabama, perhaps as early as 1886. After returning to Washington, she resumed her work with the *Musical Messenger,* beginning with the July 1888 issue, which appeared as Vol. 1, No. 1. All subsequent issues were printed in, and distributed from, Washington, D.C. A review in the *Richmond Critic,* quoted by Tilghman in the May 1889 issue of the *Musical Messenger,* spoke highly of her efforts: "We have received a copy of the *Musical Messenger,* edited by Miss A. L. Tilghman. It is a perfect sheet, of good form, and we congratulate the editor, and hope our people will take advantage of this opportunity to learn something of music." Tilghman printed other reviews as well, including this comment from the *Montgomery Herald:* "The *Musical Messenger* is the finest journal of the kind ever issued in the south. It is full of good matter, written by some of the best people in the country."

Tilghman's goal as editor was to establish a format for articles about black concert music. She reported on the activities of prominent black musicians, reviewed performances, and even occasionally printed original pieces by black composers. Penn observed that Tilghman sometimes advised her readers in nonmusical matters as well, such as, "Stand fairly and squarely for the race to which you belong, and whenever there comes a moment when principle and money clash, then stick to principle and let the money go, and in the end you will reap rich reward."

Full-length editorials written by Tilghman were not uncommon, such as her rather direct essay in the May 1889 issue, "Colored Loafers: To the Young Colored Men of America." In it she admonished the "young men who have completed a grammar and high school education; whose mothers have toiled late and early, day and night, for the education of their children; and these sons repay them for their years of hard toil by becoming street loafers instead of seeking out some honest employment." She continued, "We have no respect or sympathy for a man or woman who will do nothing because race prejudice debars them from doing what they desire to do. It is time we had stopped depending upon the whites to open a way of employment for us, and carved a way for ourselves."

Circulation of the *Musical Messenger* grew, requiring an additional staff person. Tilghman turned to Lucinda Bragg Adams, a well-known singer in the Charleston, Virginia, area, for assistance. Penn described Adams as "a woman of indomitable will and a writer of superior ability." In addition to her work as the associate editor of the *Musical Messenger,* Adams contributed articles to other periodicals as well, especially the *A.M.E. Review.*

Adds Composing to List of Musical Achievements

Both Tilghman and Adams were also known for their work as composers, particularly in local Washington circles. The song "Old Blandford Church" by Adams appeared in 1886 and is one of the earliest compositions published by a black woman in the United States. Two compositions by Tilghman were published by the Sanders and Stayman Company in Washington in 1903. The first of these is a piano solo, "Hiawatha March," dedicated to the Coleridge-Taylor Choral Society, of which Tilghman was a member. A critic writing for the October 10, 1903, issue of the *Washington Colored American* called the work "a musical gem." In it Tilghman pays homage to the poem *Song of Hiawatha* by Henry Wadsworth Longfellow, especially in her musical versions of various sections of the poem. After a brief introductory passage, the Tilghman version of the story unfolds with "Wedding March," followed by "Death of Minnehaha," "Burial of Minnehaha," and "Hiawatha's Farewell." Tilghman was undoubtedly influenced in her choice of subject for this piece by the work and popularity of the Anglo-African composer Samuel Coleridge-Taylor. Several works by Coleridge-Taylor were inspired by the Hiawatha legend, and he won considerable acclaim when he toured the United States on three separate occasions (1904, 1906, 1910) conducting his various Hiawatha compositions.

A second song by Tilghman, "Come See the Place Where the Lord Hath Lain," was also published by the same company in 1903. It is scored for voice and piano with violin obbligato, and was, according to the March 28, 1903, *Colored American,* "a soulful, sacred soprano solo intended for Easter services." The cover of the sheet music for this song lists a third piece, "Trust Him, Do Not Fear."

Musical composition seems to have occupied Tilghman during a rather protracted period of illness and convalescence in 1903. On March 28 the *Washington Colored American* lamented her absence from the stage.

> Miss Amelia L. Tilghman, one of our finest vocalists, is being sadly missed from her accustomed place in the choir of the 15th Street Presbyterian Church. For several months her physicians have forbidden her to sing on account of the condition of her throat.

She did not remain idle, however, and instead, as reported by the *Colored American* for March 28, 1903, she readied her music for publication and sale: "Miss Tilghman is not only a singer of note but has a high rank as a composer. She has at present time three compositions in the hands of her publisher. They will shortly be on sale at our leading music stores."

Towards the end of the nineteenth century, Tilghman also served as a correspondent for the magazine *Our Women and Children,* published by William J. Simmons. In addition, she published poetry, and in honor of Queen Victoria's seventieth birthday in 1889, Tilghman printed a seven-verse poem in the *Musical Messenger* praising Her Majesty's antislavery sentiments: "Reign on! unequaled Queen / Till man to man is free / Till not one shackle shall be seen / and nowhere slaves shall be."

At the turn of the century, Tilghman accepted employment at the Government Printing Office in Washington. She continued teaching private music lessons in her studio through the 1920s. In the late fall of 1931 she developed pneumonia; she died on December 12, 1931, in Freedman's Hospital in Washington, D.C. She was buried in Harmony Cemetery in the Tilghman family plot.

Tilghman's work as a composer, music teacher, singer, and journalist served as a model for aspiring black women musicians in the late nineteenth and early twentieth centuries. Her impact on music journalism has proven to be most significant, and writers for the black press perpetuated a style of music reporting modeled after Tilghman's publication. In all her activities Tilghman was unselfishly devoted to community service, social activism, and artistic and educational excellence.

REFERENCES:

Cleveland Gazette, April 9, 1887.

Dann, Martin E. *The Black Press, 1827-1890: The Quest for National Identity.* New York: G. P. Putnam's Sons, 1971.

Death Certificate. District of Columbia Vital Records. Certificate #339791.

Dunningan, Alice E. "Early History of Negro Women in Journalism." *Negro History Bulletin* 28 (Summer 1965): 178.

Majors, Monroe A. *Noted Negro Women.* Chicago: Donohue & Henneberry, 1893.

McGinty, Doris Evans. "Black Women in the Music of Washington, D.C., 1900-20." In *New Perspectives on Music: Essays in Honor of Eileen Southern.* Edited by Josephine Wright with Samuel A. Floyd, Jr. Warren, Mich.: Harmonie Park Press, 1992.

Musical Messenger 1 (May 1889); 2 (July 1889).

"Musical Progress." *New York Freeman,* August 21, 1886.

New York Age, June 30, 1883; August 18, 1883.

New York Freeman, March 14, 1886; August 21, 1886.

New York Globe, September 1, 1883.

Penn, Irvine Garland. *The Afro-American Press and Its Editors.* Springfield, Mass.: Willey and Co., 1891.

Scruggs, Lawson Andrew. *Women of Distinction.* Raleigh, N.C.: Lawson Andrew Scruggs, 1893.

Snorgrass, J. William. "Pioneer Black Women Journalists from the 1850s to the 1950s." In *Black Women's History: Theory and Practice.* Vol. 2. Edited by Darlene Clark Hine. Brooklyn, N.Y.: Carlson, 1990.

Southern, Eileen. *Biographical Dictionary of Afro-American and African Musicians.* Westport, Conn.: Greenwood Press, 1982.

————. *The Music of Black Americans.* 2d ed. New York: W. W. Norton, 1983.

Walker-Hill, Helen. *Piano Music by Black Women Composers.* Westport, Conn.: Greenwood Press, 1992.

Washington Bee, November 3, 1879; January 13, 1883; February 10, 1883; February 24, 1883; March 3, 1883; March 10, 1883; April 7, 1883; July 14, 1883; August 11, 1883; May 3, 1884; May 10, 1884; May 17, 1884; September 13, 1884; September 27, 1884; October 25, 1884; January 31, 1885; September 12, 1885; September 19, 1885.

Washington Colored American, March 28, 1903; October 3, 1903; October 10, 1903; December 19, 1903.

Wright, Josephine. "A Preliminary Bibliographical Guide to Periodical Literature for Black Music Research." *Black Music Research Journal* 10 (Spring 1990): 14-17.

Juanita Karpf

Dorothy Wright Tillman
(1947-)
Politician, civil rights activist

Chicago alderwoman Dorothy Wright Tillman's political career, rooted in the activism of the civil rights movement of the 1960s and nourished in community organizing in San Francisco and Chicago in the 1970s, flowered during the administration of Chicago mayor Harold Washington. Washington, who was elected Chicago's first black mayor in 1983, often turned to Tillman for advice and support.

Dorothy Wright Tillman

In the changed political climate that followed Washington's death, Tillman has emerged as a major spokesperson for the interests of Chicago's black community and a leading critic of the administration of current mayor Richard M. Daley.

Dorothy Jean Wright Tillman, born in Montgomery, Alabama, on May 12, 1947, is the daughter of James Wright and Edna Sanders Wright. Her father installed shades and venetian blinds for a rug and shade company; her mother worked as a domestic. Tillman's father and mother divorced when she was very young. After the divorce, her mother married Willie Struggs and the couple moved to Pensacola, Florida. Tillman's childhood years were divided between periods with her father in Montgomery and with her mother and stepfather in Pensacola. While in Pensacola, she attended J. Lee Pickens Elementary School and Booker T. Washington School. In Montgomery, she attended Booker T. Washington High School.

Tillman's early years were marked by the experience of the Montgomery bus boycott. She vividly recalled its impact in the *Chicago Defender* in 1982:

> I can still see the color codes that in effect kept us in our place. A red stripe meant for colored only, and a heavy white stripe for whites. These stripes were over water fountains, restrooms, and modes of transportation. I remember when my church was burned during the boycott. It made me very angry, and I was so glad that no one got hurt. I remember listening to Dr. King's speeches, and I'll never forget when his porch was bombed.

Tillman Becomes Civil Rights Activist

During her teenage years the civil rights movement continued to intensify in Alabama. Tillman was prevented from completing high school in 1964 after helping to lead a student civil rights boycott. She later finished high school in Chicago. At age sixteen, she became first a trainee and later a field staff organizer for Martin Luther King, Jr.'s Southern Christian Leadership Conference (SCLC). In the spring of 1965 she was among the first SCLC staff members sent to Selma during the campaign for voting rights. After the Selma-to-Montgomery march, James Bevel assigned Tillman to organize for the Summer Community Organization and Political Education (SCOPE) project in Choctaw County, Alabama. This multistate voter registration and education project became the focus of the SCLC's drive for implementation of the 1965 Voting Rights Act.

Deeply immersed in her work in Choctaw County, Tillman received a telegram telling her to come to Chicago to join Martin Luther King, Jr.'s campaign against segregation and slum housing in the North. "Like a good soldier," she recalled later in an interview with Henry Hampton, "I packed up and came to Chicago—kicking and screaming." She was not impressed with what she found on her first trip to a large northern city. She continued:

> Blacks in this city were worse off than any plantation down south that we had to deal with. . . . Up here they lived on a plantation with Boss [Richard J.] Daley as slave master. Their jobs, their clothes, their shelter, food, that all depended on Boss Daley.

As noted in Dempsey Travis's book *An Autobiography of Black Politics,* Tillman and others on the SCLC staff immediately ran into opposition from prominent blacks tied to the Daley administration:

> Chicago was the first city that we ever went to as members of the SCLC staff where the black ministers and black politicians told us to go back where we came from. . . . Although there were Uncle Toms in every city that we went to across the country, nobody ever had nerve enough in any other town to stand up and tell Dr. King and his staff members to leave.

Tillman's experience in the SCLC's 1965-66 Chicago project deeply marked her later political perspectives; it also provided her with the opportunity to meet and marry Jimmy Tillman, a well-known Chicago blues drummer. She announced a SCLC open housing march into Gage Park, an all-white Chicago neighborhood, at a South Side club where Jimmy Tillman was performing, and she challenged him to participate in the march. They were married in 1967 and attempted to move into a house in a previously segregated area, not far from where the open housing marches had taken place. Met with flying bricks and racist graffiti, they were eventually forced to leave.

In 1969, Jimmy Tillman's travels resulted in the family relocating to San Francisco. There Dorothy Tillman became involved in a 1970 struggle over public transportation along with other residents in the Alemany public housing project where she lived. Angered because they had to walk long distances for shopping and other services, community residents conducted a successful series of protests that resulted in a permanent bus route serving the project.

By 1971, the family, now including five children—Jimmy, Ebony, Gimel, Denaji, and Jimilita—returned to Chicago. Three of the five children were enrolled at the Mollison Elementary School when parents of students there staged protests against low achievement test scores. According to the *Chicago Defender* of 1989, in the spring of 1981, Mollison parents marched to the office of school principal Dorothy Stevens and served her with an eviction notice, charging that she was producing "functional illiterates." Tillman's leadership of the Mollison school protest led to the formation of a city-wide organization, Parent Equalizers of Chicago, involving over three hundred schools. A suit against Tillman backed by the Chicago Principals Association eventually reached the United States Supreme Court before Tillman was vindicated.

The following year, as Harold Washington launched his mayoral campaign against Mayor Jane Byrne, Tillman organized the Chicago Housing Authority (CHA) residents to fight Byrne's nomination of three white candidates with no ties to any of the CHA's housing projects as members of the CHA board. The resulting uproar both energized Washington's campaign and became the springboard that launched Tillman's candidacy for alderwoman from Chicago's Third Ward, in one of the poorest neighborhoods in the city.

Tillman Seated on City Council

Tillman's opponent, Tyrone Kenner, was a longtime supporter of Daley and under indictment on extortion charges. Tillman lost by the razor-thin margin of 134 votes, but was nominated by Washington in December 1983 to fill Kenner's unexpired term after his conviction. Confirmation of her appointment by the city council, normally a routine matter, became a six-month-long battle between Washington supporters and foes before Tillman finally was able to take her seat.

A 1985 special election pitted Tillman against another soldier in the former Daley machine, James "Skip" Burrell. In a private meeting with Mayor Washington, Burrell secretly recorded a number of unflattering and ribald comments by Washington about Tillman and leaked them to the *Chicago Tribune,* via Washington's most intransigent foe, Ed Vrdolyak. The "Vrdolyak tapes" became a cause célèbre; Tillman's adroit handling of the episode won her national attention.

On the eve of the election one thousand black women, participating in the founding convention of the National Political Congress of Black Women for Illinois, made their first act: the endorsement of Tillman for alderwoman of Chicago's Third Ward. Speaking for the group, People United to Serve Humanity (PUSH) leader Reverend Willie Barrow told the *Chicago Defender* in 1985: "The movement to elect Harold Washington mayor of Chicago did not begin from the top down, but from the bottom up. The campaign to retain and elect Tillman is a continuation and part of the same Chicago movement which is for the purpose of empowering the locked out.''

When Tillman swamped Burrell and seven other candidates, winning 81 percent of the vote, the *Chicago Defender* in February 1985 headlined: ''Tillman Swats 'Bugger' Burrell.'' In subsequent elections, she has won handily, and now serves as the senior alderwoman on the city council. She remains one of the most controversial figures in a Chicago political landscape that is anything but placid. Political analyst David Fremon noted just before Washington's 1987 death: ''Tillman is known for two things: her hats (she is always seen wearing one of more than two hundred that she owns) and her aggressive defense of the Washington administration.''

When the coalition of blacks, Hispanics, and white liberals built by Mayor Washington fractured after his death, with deep divisions appearing within the ranks of black elected officials, Tillman stridently called for continued adherence to Washington's policies. In April 1989, she told the *Chicago Defender* that ''the Black community needs to purge traitors from the movement.''

Washington's interim successor, Mayor Eugene Sawyer, was often the focus of Tillman's critiques, most notably during the controversy over anti-Semitic speeches given by a top Sawyer aide, Steve Cokely. According to Lou Turner, Tillman, speaking out with her usual combativeness, denounced Cokely as ''a chief among a small band of Blacks who were Washington haters. This group of Washington haters, like their white counterparts . . . use race baiting and anti-Semitic rhetoric in the Black community as a political strategy designed to confuse and divide Harold's base.''

Tillman's persistent opposition both to current mayor Richard M. Daley's policies and to black officials allied with him has made it difficult for her to exercise the kind of political ''clout'' often associated with council members with her seniority. She has nevertheless managed to bring several significant new economic developments to her impoverished ward and to sponsor beautification programs that Fremon calls ''a positive example of what cleanup programs can accomplish.''

Among the few women veterans of the Southern Christian Leadership Conference staff to enter electoral politics, Dorothy Tillman has made her mark on Chicago, and perhaps national, political affairs.

Current Address: 4645 South Martin Luther King, Jr., Drive, Chicago, IL 60653.

REFERENCES:

Anderson, Alan B., and George W. Pickering. *Confronting the Color Line: The Broken Promise of the Civil Rights Movement in Chicago.* Athens: University of Georgia Press, 1986.

''Biography of Dorothy Tillman.'' Brochure. Chicago: Third Ward Service Office, n.d.

Fairclough, Adam. *To Redeem the Soul of America: The Southern Christian Leadership Conference and Martin Luther King, Jr.* Athens: University of Georgia Press, 1987.

Fremon, David K. *Chicago Politics Ward by Ward.* Bloomington: Indiana University Press, 1988.

Hampton, Henry, and Steve Fayer. *Voices of Freedom: An Oral History of the Civil Rights Movement from the 1950s through the 1980s.* New York: Bantam Books, 1990.

Miller, Alton. *Harold Washington: the Mayor, the Man.* Chicago: Bonus Books, 1989.

''School Ruling Favoring Ald. Tillman Upheld.'' *Chicago Defender,* March 7, 1989.

''They Vow to Help City Become Safe.'' *Chicago Defender,* July 20, 1982.

''Tillman Swats 'Bugger' Burrell.'' *Chicago Defender,* February 27, 1985.

''Tillman Urges Community to Purge 'Traitors' from Ranks.'' *Chicago Defender,* April 17, 1989.

Travis, Dempsey. *An Autobiography of Black Politics.* Chicago: Urban Research Press, 1987.

———. *'Harold': The People's Mayor.* Chicago: Urban Research Press, 1989.

Turner, Lou. ''Black Anti-Semitic Disorder.'' *News & Letters* 33 (June 1988): 10.

''Women Mobilize for State Politics.'' *Chicago Defender,* February 11, 1985.

Michael Flug

Katherine Davis Chapman Tillman

(1870-?)
Writer

Katherine Tillman was one of many black women writers of her period who were very much involved in writing and publishing black religious and secular periodicals. Some of these women, like Mary Cook Parrish, Susie Lankford Shorter, and Tillman, were closely connected through their work. These three, for example, were only some of the women connected with the short-lived magazine *Our Women and Children,* which was based in Louisville, Kentucky. No copies of this magazine survive, and it is still difficult to locate what does remain of the scattered writings of the numerous women who were making contributions to defining the African American experience at this time. Recent work has resulted in the rediscovery of some of these writings. Claudia

Katherine Davis Chapman Tillman

Tate, editor of a 1991 collection of Tillman's published works, does not claim that Tillman is a major writer. In her preface to the collection, she writes:

> She remains a minor writer. This label is by no means used to demean her talent, though it has served to obscure many writers whose careers constitute large and important parts of literary history, parts without which we can achieve only a limited understanding of the undisputed major writers and of specific periods in literary history. . . . Her work approximates that of many early, minor, black authors, heretofore obscure, who similarly asserted their authority to interpret black culture, question its values, and preserve its integrity through the dissemination of the written word.

Katherine Davis Chapman Tillman was born on February 19, 1870, in Mound City, Illinois. She was the daughter of Charles and Laura Chapman. Her parents were poor and she had no formal schooling until she was twelve, although she had learned to read before then. Her parents then moved to Yankton, South Dakota, where she entered school and eventually graduated from high school. Little else is known about her family background.

Tillman also spent time at State University, Louisville, Kentucky, and at Wilberforce University. Sometime prior to 1893, when she was published under the name Katie D. Tilman [sic] in Monroe A. Majors's *Noted Negro Women,* she married George M. Tillman, an African Methodist Episcopal (AME) minister.

George Tillman was born in York County, Pennsylvania. He spent four years at Wilberforce University, where he lived part of the time in the home of Bishop James L. Shorter, the father-in-law of Susie Lankford Shorter. George Tillman, who underwent a conversion experience at seventeen, entered the active ministry in 1890. His first assignment was in Yankton, South Dakota, where he probably met Katherine Tillman. Since she attended Baptist-run State University for a time and then attended the AME-affiliated Wilberforce for a while, it is plausible that Tillman changed denominations in connection with her marriage.

George Tillman was an active and successful minister. After spending time at several churches in Iowa, he pastored St. John's AME Church in Chicago, where he paid off the mortgage and tripled the membership. He then served successively in Colorado Springs, Colorado; Oakland, California; and Pasadena, California; he subsequently became a presiding elder of the St. Joseph district in the North Missouri Conference. At present, knowledge of his career ends in 1916 with the publication of the *Centennial Encyclopedia of the African Methodist Episcopal Church,* which has articles on both George and Katherine Tillman.

A separate account of Katherine Tillman's life in these years is at present fragmentary. She wrote and she was active in church associations in the various cities in which her husband was a minister. She was editor of the *Women's Missionary Recorder.* She served as secretary of the Iowa Branch of the Women's Mite Missionary Society for twelve years, and she became president of the North Missouri Conference branch. In addition to her writing and her work in religious associations connected with her church, she was active in the women's club movement. She was honorary president of the City Federation of Colorado Springs and honorary president of the California Federation. Tillman also served at least six years, beginning around 1910, as an officer of the National Association of Colored Women.

Although the death dates of both George and Katherine Tillman are unknown, both were alive in 1916 but dead in 1947 when the second edition of the *Encyclopedia of the African Methodist Episcopal Church* was published. Katherine Tillman's last publications appeared in 1921 and 1922.

Tillman Establishes Career as Writer

Tillman began to write early; there is record of a lost poem, "A Dying Child's Fancy," which she wrote at the age of fourteen. In the summer of 1888 she began contributing articles and poems to various religious publications, including the *Christian Recorder* and *American Baptist.* She was a regular contributor to *Our Women and Children* magazine and was also published in the *Indianapolis Freeman.* After this early start, Tillman continued to write and publish for many years. Although some of her publications are lost, much remains. Claudia Tate, who edited her works for Oxford University Press, was able to assemble a considerable body of work, including poems, fiction, essays, and drama. Throughout her career, Tillman's works appeared most frequently in the *AME Church Review* and the *Christian Recorder;* her books and pamphlets were published by the AME Book Concern or, in the case of some later work, self-published.

Between 1888 and 1902 Tillman published some eighteen poems in the *Christian Recorder;* some of them appear in revised versions in her collection, *Recitations,* of 1902. This substantial collection of forty-four poems contains her last known poetic work. She produced four extant works of fiction: two novellas—*Beryl Weston's Ambition: The Story of an Afro-American Girl's Life* (1893) and *Clancy Street* (1898-99)—and two shorter works—"Miles the Conqueror" (1894) and "The Preacher at Hill Station" (1903).

Tillman's dramatic works are a one act play, "Aunt Betsy's Thanksgiving" (n.d.); a very short pageant, "Heirs of Slavery" (1901); a short four-act play, *Thirty Years of Freedom* (1902); a five-act play, *Fifty Years of Freedom, or From Cabin to Congress* (1910); and *The Spirit of Allen: A Pageant of African Methodism* (1922). Her remaining works are a brief anthology, *Quotations from Negro Authors* (1921), and seven essays: "Some Girls That I Know" (1893), "Afro-American Women and Their Work" (1895), "Afro-American Poets and Their Verse" (1898), "The Negro Among Anglo-Saxon Poets" (1898), "Alexander Dumas, Père" (1907), "Paying Professions for Colored Girls" (1907), and "Alexander Sergeivich Puskin" (1909). All of these essays appeared in the *AME Church Review,* except for "Paying Professions for Colored Girls," which appeared in *Voice of the Negro.*

Tillman's work is often fairly conventional. She does have a sense of humor, as in this statement about the role of women in the church from the essay "Afro-American Women and Their Work,"

> It is the women in our churches who assist the perplexed pastor in devising plans for the annihilation of state and church debts, and who assume the charge of clothing the pastor and his needy family in a little purple and fine linen occasionally; who prepare at home, little feasts and invite this everyday hero, that he may fare sumptuously at least one day a week, and who often seem to their pastor angels in disguise.

Katherine Tillman is an exemplar of the women of her generation who pursued reform as a means of strengthening the position of African Americans at a particularly difficult moment in black history. Characteristic of her vein of uplift and reform is the conclusion of this essay:

> Let us as Afro-American women pledge ourselves to the elevation of our home. Let us war against intemperance, against infidelity, against gambling in saloons or parlors, against bad literature and immorality of all kind, for these are the demons that destroy our homes. Let us enlist under the banner of Christ and help subdue these evils. The world needs our efforts and let us go forth in His name to conquer.

REFERENCES:

Majors, Monroe A. *Noted Negro Women.* Chicago: Donohue and Henneberry, 1893.

Penn, I. Garland. *The Afro-American Press and Its Editors.* Springfield, Mass: Willey and Company, 1891.

Tillman, Katherine Davis Chapman. *The Works of Katherine Davis Chapman Tillman.* Edited by Claudia Tate. New York: Oxford University Press, 1991.

Wright, Richard R., Jr., comp. *Centennial Encyclopedia of the African Methodist Episcopal Church.* Philadelphia: Book Concern of the AME Church, 1916.

———. *The Encyclopedia of the African Methodist Episcopal Church.* 2d ed. Philadelphia: Book Concern of the AME Church, 1947.

Robert L. Johns

Melba Tolliver
(1939-)
Broadcast journalist, writer, producer

Melba Tolliver entered the field of broadcasting at a time when television, especially news broadcasting, was overwhelmingly white and male. Beginning with reporting and anchoring news at the American Broadcasting Company (ABC) flagship station, WABC in New York, during the late 1960s, Tolliver has maintained a presence in New York news telecasting for over two decades, demonstrating her skills in writing, reporting, producing, and anchoring in a wide variety of television programming. Today she is primetime coanchor on NEWS 12, a Long Island, New York, twenty-four-hour news channel.

Tolliver has honed and advanced the communication skills she first developed in the acting classes in which she enrolled when she arrived in New York from Akron, Ohio. Born December 8, 1939, in Rome, Georgia, Melba was one of two daughters of Susan Turner Tolliver, a housewife, and Emory Leonard Tolliver, a hotel bellhop. She grew up in Akron, Ohio, with her mother and sister, Constance Louise. After high school, she moved to New York and came under the influence of an aunt who was a nurse. Tolliver enrolled in New York University-Bellevue School of Nursing, receiving a relatively inexpensive education—one financed in large part by scholarship money. Her training included work at Bellevue, a city hospital. She graduated from nursing school in 1959 with honors. She said in the *New York Times,* February 18, 1973, "Academically, I was a Florence Nightingale. But I found that I really didn't like being around sick people." She became an operating room nurse and sometimes had to nap on available operating tables because she spent all her spare time studying acting at the American Academy of Dramatic Arts and HB Studio. She also tried her hand in the

Melba Tolliver

competition for "Miss New York Is a Summer Festival," sponsored by the New York Visitors and Convention Bureau.

By 1967 Tolliver had left nursing, and when she answered an advertisement in the *New York Times,* she landed a job as a secretary and girl Friday at ABC network television. The new position was, in her mind, a chance to look around the television business and an opportunity to "make something" of herself. She had intended to keep the job only for six months. She said in the *New York Times* article, "I figured I could look around once I got in. But I was so busy with my secretarial job that my six months was almost up and I hadn't even been down to the newsroom."

Tolliver Seizes Opportunity

A strike of the American Federation of Television and Radio Artists (AFTRA) in 1968 gave Tolliver an unexpected opportunity. Having done some work in commercials during her nursing days, she had gained some experience before the camera, and she was asked to fill in on short notice for a striking newscaster on a five-minute afternoon network news show. She said in the *New York Times,* "I wasn't afraid or worried. I didn't think about the millions of people looking at me. I was ab-so-lute-ly fearless. Besides, what did I have to lose?"

Tolliver's assessment seems to have been correct. Shortly after the strike ended, she was invited to enter an ABC reporter trainee program as its only trainee. Tolliver feels that she was fortunate to have been the right person at the right time. "TV was under heavy criticism because of the absence

of blacks and other minorities on staffs," she said in the *Akron Press,* May 5, 1977. After completing the training program, including attending New York University School of Journalism for the summer, she became a TV news reporter for WABC in October 1968, on what was then called *Channel 7 News.*

In addition to her work as a reporter, Tolliver served as weekend news coanchor and as a cohost for a morning talk show and for public affairs programs. She wrote and produced *Gordon Parks: A Man for All Seasons,* a half-hour profile of the award-winning photographer, writer, and filmmaker. All of this was at a time when few women reporters' faces found their way to the television screens of America. Tolliver was virtually alone as a woman of color on New York television news.

In the summer of 1971, the day before she was supposed to cover Tricia Nixon's wedding at the White House, Tolliver changed her hair to a natural. Previously, her hair had been straightened. She was told that she couldn't appear live in the studio unless she changed her hair back. She said in the *New York Times,* "They said I looked less attractive—less feminine. But it was *their* standard of femininity, not mine." Tolliver refused to straighten her hair, and finally, after the pressure of some publicity about their mandate, the station relented and permitted Tolliver to appear on the air with her hair as she wished it.

After eight years at WABC, Tolliver took a year's leave from New York television to study at the University of Michigan in Ann Arbor, where she was a National Endowment for Humanities Fellow. At Michigan, she codirected a conference on minorities and the media ten years after the Kerner Commission Report, which documented government research on civil disorder. It was called "Kerner Plus 10." Findings from this conference, published in a report that she coauthored, have been cited by the U.S. Commission on Civil Rights.

Return to Broadcasting

On her return to New York, Tolliver moved to the National Broadcasting Company (NBC) flagship station, spending four years at WNBC-TV Newscenter 4. There, she was first a reporter-producer on her own feature series, *Melba and Company.* Then she coanchored the news on weekdays with Pia Lindstrom. At WNBC, Tolliver also hosted a public affairs show, *Meet the People.* Tolliver's television appearances outside of news have included a stint as a regular panelist on *What's My Line?* and acting as cohost of the Emmy Awards with actor Robert Klein.

In addition to work in television, Tolliver has written feature articles for *Good Housekeeping* magazine and for the newspaper *USA Today,* where she wrote profiles for the business section.

During the 1983-84 presidential political race, Tolliver served in the Jesse Jackson campaign as media director for the candidate in New York state. Her experience in the news business and familiarity with New York allowed her to organize press conferences, write press releases, respond to media editorials, and coordinate appearances by the candidate throughout New York City, which Jackson won, and New York State, where he also did well.

Honors and Awards

Tolliver has received several awards for her work. In 1975 she was named Outstanding Woman in Media by the National Association of Media Women. Tolliver was honored with the Matrix Award for Television Journalism by New York Women in Communication, and the New York Urban League awarded her the John B. Russwurm Award. Also, Lincoln University (Missouri) honored her with the Unity Award for Political Reporting.

Today Tolliver is prime-time coanchor for NEWS 12 Long Island, the nation's first twenty-four-hour regional news network. She is an on-air personality who writes and broadcasts news and who anchors coverage of events as they happen, from plane crashes to terrorism to weather-related phenomena on Long Island (Nassau and Suffolk counties), the region adjacent to New York City from which NEWS 12 broadcasts. The Anti-Defamation League of the Five Towns of Long Island has given her its Torch of Liberty Award. Tolliver has also been honored by Long Island's Molloy College, which conferred on her an honorary doctorate of humane letters. She was named Woman of the Year by the thirty thousand-member Long Island Association, the largest business and civic association on Long Island. She is also a recipient of the prestigious award for Lifetime Achievement by the New York Association of Black Journalists. Tolliver piloted the "Communication Dynamics" program, a one-day effort to provide high school students with the opportunity to improve their communication skills and to interact with business people in order to get a sense of what they will be facing in the world of work. Tolliver said in *Newsday*, May 9, 1993, "We wanted to bring in the business side of it . . . to talk to kids about how they can expect the workplace to be when they enter it and the value of good communication skills." In addition, Tolliver has special interests in breast cancer education and in mentoring programs.

Melba Tolliver is a seasoned television journalist who reaches audiences in the area of New York but whose pioneering work as a black woman is even more widely known and recognized. She is also praised for sharing her expertise as a journalist with the community.

Current Address: NEWS 12 Long Island, One Media Crossways, Woodbury, NY 11797.

REFERENCES:

"Any Road Will Take You There." *Akron Press,* May 5, 1977.

"Friends Toast and Roast Melba Tolliver." *Networking, Newspaper for Women,* Holiday Issue, 1992.

"Learning to Communicate, Not Just Talk." *Newsday,* May 9, 1993.

"Melba? She's the Toast of the Town." *New York Times,* February 18, 1973.

Tolliver, Melba. Interview Martia Graham Goodson, June 1993.

Martia Graham Goodson

Gloria E. A. Toote
(1931-)
Lawyer, writer, entrepreneur, government official, politician

A self-directed trailblazer, Gloria E. A. Toote has several accomplishments to her credit. In 1954, she became the youngest graduate in the history of the Howard University School of Law in Washington, D. C. After several years as a practicing attorney, she founded the Town Sound Studios in Englewood, New Jersey, the only black-operated recording studio in the United States that wasn't allied with a record company. Toote's studio stood as a positive example for other black entrepreneurs who wanted to enter the white-dominated music industry. Toote is also interested in politics and government affairs, and in 1973 she was appointed assistant secretary for equal opportunity of the U.S. Department of Housing and Urban Development. The appointment made her the highest-ranking black woman in government service during the Nixon and Ford administrations.

Gloria E. A. Toote was born in New York City on November 8, 1931. She is the daughter of Lillie Toote, who was a park technician, and Frederick Augustus Toote, a former leader in the black nationalist Marcus Garvey movement. Some of Gloria Toote's drive and initiative can probably be traced to her father, who held a doctorate in theology and was the archbishop of the African Orthodox Church. The February 16, 1974, *New York Post* described him as "a fiery black man who took over the United Negro Improvement Association when its head, Marcus Garvey, was deported to Jamaica in the late 1920s." In the same *New York Post* article, Toote reflected on her relationship with her father: "We were always at odds because I was so much like him. . . . He was demanding. He insisted upon professionalism, and I strive to be a professional in whatever I do."

Toote attended Howard University School of Law and became the youngest graduate in the history of the school, receiving her J.D. degree in 1954. In 1956, she received her LL.M. degree from Columbia University Graduate School of Law and later passed the New York Bar. According to *Sepia,* June 1968, she "became a full-fledged practicing attorney

Gloria E. A. Toote

even before she was old enough to vote," which prompted some judges to call the county clerk's office to confirm that she really was licensed to practice law. When Toote reached the age of majority, she registered to vote as a Republican, which was not a very popular choice among African Americans living in New York City at that time. Toote told the *New York Post,* February 16, 1974, that an earlier experience with politics had steered her away from the Democratic party:

> I would have been a Democrat . . . but the year I finished law school, I got involved in one of Adam Clayton Powell's re-election campaigns and I became so disillusioned by practical politics that I said no more politics for me. . . . This was during a time, somewhere around the mid-'50s, when . . . the liberal element in the Republican Party was beginning to emerge. They were seeking an identification with minorities then within the county and state—John Lindsay was in Congress, Nelson Rockefeller's commitment was clear at that point, during that stage before he became Governor, and we always had the leadership of Jacob Javits—and I could talk to the New York County leader, tell him about our lack of money and the lack of political support for the black republicans and he tried to effectuate change.

Toote strongly believed that African Americans had to become active in both parties in order to effect change.

After passing the bar examination in 1955, Toote was recommended to Morris Ernst, the renowned civil and human

rights lawyer with Greenbaum, Woolf, & Ernst. She worked for the law firm until 1957 and then joined Governor Nelson Rockefeller's staff. Following that, she entered private practice. She also served as an editorial staff writer for *Time* magazine from 1957 to 1958.

Recording Studio Opened

After eleven years of practicing law, Toote took up another challenge; she decided to open a recording studio. Toote's introduction to the music business came from her legal representation of black recording artists who constantly complained about their inferior status in the white-controlled recording industry. Many artists were being cheated out of their royalties and knew little about management practices. Seeing the need for a recording studio that would treat blacks fairly and wanting to prove that blacks are capable of working "in other capacities than performing," Toote founded Town Sound Studios in Englewood, New Jersey. She explained her motivation in an interview for *Ebony,* May 1969:

> Negroes have been part of the entertainment industry since slavery . . . and we sing and dance well. We don't learn the techniques of the trade—many of us cannot even read music. So we're exploited. I want to make Negroes aware of and train them for the many existing, lucrative jobs in this industry.

Toote's quest to build a recording studio began in 1966. She took her first step by securing an old low-rent building in Englewood, New Jersey. The majestic four-story red brick building, which once served as Englewood's City Hall, had been unoccupied since 1928 and had no lights or electricity. Although the renowned Town Sound Studios had humble beginnings, it later was described as a state-of-the-art, twenty-first century facility. The twenty-four hundred-square-foot building was one of the largest recording studios in the New York area.

By building the recording studio, Toote wanted to show other African Americans who aspired to careers in business that their dreams were possible. She told *Sepia,* June 1968:

> Our kids grow up thinking the neighborhood numbers banker is the greatest big-shot around. And there's really nothing at all wrong with that job. A few of our children do manage to see doctors and lawyers as a goal to shoot for but they aren't really the top either. Society has set up businessmen to be the big-shots, like it or not, and somebody's got to be an example so our kids can set their goals on being big-shots too.

Toote also wanted to make other African Americans a part of her own dream. Thus, she decided to use dropouts from an antipoverty work program to help build Town Sound Studios. According to *Sepia,* "Recalling the lessons her preacher-father showed her when he puttered around the house, she taught the young dropouts how to build a recording studio. . . . She and the kids learned how together."

Through creative financing and the help of these young people, Toote built an eight-track recording studio with high-tech equipment and remote console controls. This type of facility was state of the art during the 1960s. *Ebony* magazine, May 1969, reported,

> The electronic equipment is the most modern available and cost more than a quarter of a million dollars. One hundred thousand dollars came from a Small Business Association-sponsored loan with Harlem's Freedom National Bank, the rest from savings and personal loans from friends. The studio is also furnished with two pianos, a Hammond organ, drums, vibes and bass and guitar amplifiers that are at the disposal of artists who book the studio.

Besides the state-of-the-art equipment, *Ebony* noted that Town Sound Studios was the "only black-owned professional recording studio not connected with a record company in America." Several artists recorded at Town Sound Studios, including Miriam Makeba, Lon Courtney, Donald Height, Gloria Lynn, The Animals, The Blues Project, Don Gardner, and Lloyd Price.

In addition to being the founder and owner of Town Sound Studios, Toote taught herself all of the technical functions involved in recording, including cutting master tapes. She then shared these skills with the young people she trained, who later built studios for others.

Toote Enters Government Service

After her success as an entrepreneur, Toote returned to law and also began a career with the government. Having campaigned for President Richard Nixon, in 1971 she was rewarded with an appointment as assistant director of ACTION, the umbrella agency for federal volunteer programs. She remained in this position for two years, overseeing the Office of Voluntary Action Liaison, which assisted in placing former Peace Corps and Vista workers in jobs and in school. In 1973 she was appointed as assistant secretary for equal opportunity of the U.S. Department of Housing and Urban Development (HUD). This launched her career to the highest ranking African American woman in the administrations of Presidents Nixon and Ford. Toote remained in this position until 1975, and in 1976 she entered the real estate business to become a housing developer, serving as president of Trea Estates and Enterprises.

In 1978, Toote declared herself to the *New York Times* as a "candidate to become the first black co-chairman of the Republican National Committee." She made the following statement during her interviews:

> My election can lift the last tinge of racism, however false that accusation may be, from the back of our party. . . . My election will tell those who have left our party because they feel that we are the party of closed doors, that we are indeed opening those

doors. Surely no one could reach any other conclusion from the election of a black woman from Harlem to the co-chairmanship.

Although she campaigned vigorously, Toote did not achieve this particular goal. She was later appointed to the President's Advisory Council on Private Sector Initiatives, serving from 1983 to 1985.

Gloria E. A. Toote has made her mark in history by achieving success in not just one career but several. She has also devoted much of her time to community work and political affairs. She has served on the boards of various organizations and companies, including Fanny Mae, Citizens for the Republic, National Black United Fund, Executive Women in Government, American Arbitration Association, Consumer Alert, and the Hoover Institute. She was also vice-chair for the National Political Congress of Black Women and president of the New York City Black Republican Council. Toote has received several honors and citations from a number of organizations, including the National Business League, Alpha Kappa Alpha, National Association of Black Women Attorneys, National Real Estate Brokers, National Federal Mortgage Association, National Bar Association, and Delta Sigma Theta Sorority.

REFERENCES:

"An Even Chance." *New York Post,* February 16, 1974.

"Lawyer Tries a World of Sound." *Ebony* 24 (May 1969): 73-80.

"New HUD Chief, Aide Differ on Resignation." *Washington Post,* March 17, 1975.

"New Sound at Town Sound." *Sepia* 17 (June 1968): 72-78.

Who's Who of American Women, 1993-94. Vol. 18. New Providence, N.J.: Reed Reference Publishing Co., 1993.

Dhyana Ziegler

Rosina Tucker
(1881-1987)
Labor organizer, social and civil rights activist, educator

As founder and secretary-treasurer of the International Ladies' Auxiliary and a force in the establishment of its parent organization, the Brotherhood of Sleeping Car Porters, Rosina Tucker helped to raise the economic level of large numbers of black people in the United States and

Rosina Tucker

Canada. She organized porters' wives in activities to support the auxiliary and the union, and their efforts helped to ensure the men of adequate pay, decent working conditions, and new benefits. The brotherhood focused on battling racism and, with Tucker's assistance, organized civil rights marches in 1941 and 1963.

Rosina Budd Harvey Corrothers Tucker, one of nine children, was born on November 4, 1881, on Fourth Street in northwest Washington, D.C. Her parents, Lee Roy and Henrietta Harvey, had been slaves in Virginia before they relocated to Washington after their emancipation. As was the case with many former slaves, they found the brutal memories of bondage painful to recount. Although the Harveys never told their story to their children, Rosina Tucker overheard them discussing their experiences with each other. Tucker remembered her father talking about the meager amounts of food he received as a slave. On Thanksgiving Day he and other slaves on their Virginia plantation were denied turkey but were allowed to chew on the string with which the turkey had been tied. After he married and his children were born, Lee Roy Harvey never invited guests to dinner to ensure that enough food would always be available to his children. On the other hand, Tucker's grandmother, also a slave, ate well. She was assigned to the master's house and whenever she wanted or needed food, she took it.

Notwithstanding the harsh realities of his upbringing, at some point in his life Lee Roy Harvey taught himself to read and write. He surrounded himself with the books he loved and read to become more familiar with the world around him and

to learn history, which he particularly enjoyed. He became a shoemaker by trade. Doubtless his slave experiences affected the way he reared his children; he was very protective of them and prevented them from working as service employees or in white people's kitchens. Rosina Tucker had pleasant memories of her early childhood and fondly reminisced about her musical training and her father's teachings. Lee Roy Harvey provided an organ at home, which he learned to play, and saw to it that his children studied music and played the organ as well. By the time the children entered school, they already had a more than rudimentary musical education and were able to read and write. When she was twelve years old Rosina Tucker played piano for her Sunday school and also taught in the infant department.

When Tucker was a child, segregation existed everywhere in the District of Columbia except on the street cars and in public buildings. She began school at the old Banneker School Building on Third Street in northwest Washington. She completed the eighth grade, then entered the old M Street School, the predecessor of Dunbar High School. In 1897, while still in her junior year of high school, Tucker visited an aunt in Yonkers, New York, where she taught Sunday school at the Colored Baptist Church and met James D. Corrothers, a guest minister. A graduate of Northwestern University, Corrothers became known as a poet and writer of short stories, particularly his sketches on black humor and folklore. His poems and stories were published in leading newspapers for 25 years. Rosina Harvey and James Corrothers married on December 2, 1899. The couple had one son, Henry Harvey Corrothers, who later became a fine athlete and graduated from the American International College in Springfield, Massachusetts. He directed the physical education program at Wilberforce University in Ohio before he died of heart disease in 1945. Rosina and James Corrothers also raised a son from his previous marriage.

After marrying, the couple lived first in New York City, then in South Haven, Michigan, where James had lived as a child. He continued to practice his ministry and to write and publish poetry. Rosina occupied herself by teaching music to some thirty students. The family moved to Washington, D.C., in 1904, when James Corrothers took a position with the National Baptist Convention. Rosina continued to share her musical talent with others, becoming organist for Liberty Baptist Church in the Foggy Bottom section of the District. Two years later James Corrothers became pastor of the First Baptist Church in Lexington, Virginia. In their new town the couple often appeared in church, with James telling stories and reading poetry while Rosina played classical pieces. About this time she composed "The Rio Grande Waltz."

After James Corrothers died in 1917, Rosina returned to Washington, D.C., where she worked as a file clerk with the federal government and became involved in civic activities. Through friends she met Berthea J. Tucker, known as B. J., who had worked as a carpenter's helper before becoming a Pullman car porter. They married on Thanksgiving eve in 1918, when she was thirty-six years old, and moved into a two-story brick house on Seventh Street northeast near Gallaudet College, where she remained the rest of her life.

Porter's Union Established

In the 1920s the Pullman Company had a virtual monopoly on railroad sleeping-car facilities throughout the United States. The company was a major employer of black men, and those who had jobs as Pullman porters were held in considerable esteem in the black community. Rosina Tucker said in the November 8, 1984, *Washington Post* that, in the early days, a job as a Pullman porter was perhaps one of the best available for a black man. By working the sleeping coaches, making beds, and shining shoes, they collected hefty tips. "To be a Pullman porter in those days meant respect, prestige, social status and prominence." Nonetheless, porters were poorly paid, and charges for any damage to Pullman equipment were deducted from their small salaries. They were required to work long hours without overtime pay, sometimes working up to four hundred hours a month with "deadheading" and "doubling out" responsibilities. In the absence of a union to protect the men's rights, the company took full advantage of its black labor force.

Although the black porters were restless at the beginning of the twentieth century, it was not until some years later, in 1909, that the porters formulated their grievances and made efforts to organize. While the attempt was unsuccessful, the Pullman Company made faint gestures to address some of the men's concerns. Driven by the abuse of the black Pullman workers and an accumulation of grievances, Ashley Totten, a militant New York porter, made a bold move in 1925 to stimulate the organization of a porter's union. He engaged A. Philip Randolph, a radical journalist and social theoretician who was later prominent in the civil rights movement, to organize the union. On August 25 that year, in the Imperial Lodge of Elks, 160 West 129th Street, the Brotherhood of Sleeping Car Porters was launched and Randolph began what was to be a long tenure as president. The union also established the Women's Economic Councils, an organization through which women could work for the rights of the brotherhood. To protect the workers who could be fired for their connection with the union and their criticisms of the Pullman Company, Randolph surprised the stool pigeons present by handling the entire discussion himself. The next day some two hundred porters came to his office, the brotherhood's headquarters, to join the union.

Randolph and Totten tried to bring the union to Washington, D.C., where they had a big meeting at John Wesley Church for the porters as well as their wives. But the porters were reluctant to join for fear of losing their jobs. B. J. Tucker joined the union immediately—in time he became a member of the executive board—and then he and Rosina took up the cause in the District. At first the men's work was so demanding that they had little time for union activities; therefore, their wives did much of the work for them and held secret meetings so that the men's positions would not be threatened. When Rosina Tucker met with Randolph and Totten, they did so in private and secret places, including Tucker's home, so that informers would be unable to report on the sessions to the company. To organize unions in the South, Tucker visited the homes of some three hundred porters who lived in the Washington area, distributed literature, discussed the organization with prospective members and their wives, and collected dues from the women as well as the men.

International Ladies' Auxiliary Formed

The next step for Tucker was to organize the local Ladies' Auxiliary, which, over the years, provided financial and emotional backing for the brotherhood. From the start, the women raised a great deal of money by hosting parties, dances, dinners, and other activities. Tucker called upon her church and social service background to help families experiencing illnesses and other difficulties, including loss of employment. In time the Pullman Company learned about her work and reacted by firing her husband. When she heard about the company's punitive action, she declared, "I'm not going to take that." She told Susan Ellen Holleran for *about. . .time,* May 1985, that she tried to contact the company superintendent, who was always "in conference." Then she went to his supervisor and said, "I'm Mrs. B. J. Tucker and I came over to see you about why my husband lost his job." When the man asked why B. J. Tucker was not there to see about it himself, Rosina reacted by banging on his table and saying, "You brought me into this thing, and you have nothing to do with what I do." B. J. Tucker was rehired.

In 1937, when the porters and the Pullman Company signed a contract, for the first time there was a formal agreement between a union of black workers and a major American corporation. The next year Rosina Tucker attended the union's national convention in Chicago and chaired the Constitution and Rules Committee. Immediately after the brotherhood's convention, the International Ladies' Auxiliary was established and held its first meetings on September 24-27. Since it was a support organization, the group was intentionally designed to be subordinate to the brotherhood. Officers included an international president, Halena Wilson of Chicago; four international vice-presidents; and an international secretary-treasurer, Rosina Tucker. Program visitors included Mary McLeod Bethune, the most influential black woman in the United States, who represented the Division of Negro Affairs of the National Youth Administration, Washington, D.C. There were 1,446 members of the auxiliary by August 1940. Tucker traveled to railroad centers throughout the United States and Canada to unite workers, often coming in contact with such prominent women as Eleanor Roosevelt and Bethune.

Over the years, the Brotherhood of Sleeping Car Porters and the Ladies' Auxiliary became more powerful. Through its official presence in the House of Labor, a speaking platform for the workers, the union could focus on the evils of racism, the need for civil rights legislation, the protection of minority voting rights, and the preservation of dignity on the job. The auxiliary remained a consistent part of the effort. Some sources report that although the brotherhood is generally given credit for the work, Tucker helped the group organize its first March on Washington, scheduled to occur in 1941. The march was called off when A. Philip Randolph convinced

President Franklin D. Roosevelt to issue Executive Order 8802, which addressed fair employment practices and discrimination in government offices and defense plants. In 1963, again with Tucker's assistance, Randolph and the brotherhood organized another March on Washington. However, technological change was undermining the union as rail passenger service declined. In 1978 the Brotherhood of Sleeping Car Porters merged with the Brotherhood of Railway and Airline Clerks.

Tucker told her story and that of the work of the brotherhood and the auxiliary in the 1981 award-winning, hour-long documentary *Miles of Smiles, Years of Struggle,* produced and directed by Paul Wagner and Jack Santino and aired on public television. In the documentary she also sang "Marching Together," which she wrote in 1939 in honor of the Pullman porters.

Unfaltering Devotion to Social and Civil Rights

Tucker's interest in civil rights never wavered. In 1985 she participated in an unsuccessful picket at a Safeway market, located at 6th and H Street, N.E., to stop the store from moving out of the black community. In 1986, when she was 104 years old, Tucker was still giving lectures across the country, primarily recounting the history of the brotherhood and the Ladies' Auxiliary. She had completed a book-length manuscript about her life when she was 96 years old entitled *Life As I Have Lived It.* She often participated in discussion groups in the Fifteenth Street Presbyterian Church, where she had held membership since 1917 and was affectionately called Mother Tucker. Over the years she testified before Senate and House committees on education, day care, labor, and voting rights for the District. She lobbied Congress for legislation on labor and education and helped organize unions for laundry workers and domestics. When she was 102 years old, she testified before a Senate Labor and Human Resources subcommittee on aging. Her community activities extended to other areas as well; for example, she worked with the Board of Public Welfare, NAACP, Northeast Women's Club, and the Sunday school.

During her life and after her death, Rosina Tucker was honored for her work with the brotherhood and for her civil rights activities. In 1983 she received a humanitarian award from the Leadership Conference on Civil Rights and the Candace Award for leadership from the National Coalition of 100 Black Women. In 1985 the Coalition of Labor Union Women honored Maida Springer-Kemp, Addie Wyatt, and Rosina Tucker for their contributions to the American labor movement. In 1993, during its sixth year of operation, the District of Columbia Hall of Fame selected five women who had made significant contributions in local public service, health care, labor initiatives, housing, and education. Rosina Tucker, who died on March 3, 1987, at the age of 105, was honored posthumously for her role as a founder of the Brotherhood of Sleeping Car Porters in 1925 and as a founder and international secretary-treasurer of the union's Ladies' Auxiliary.

Toward the end of her life, Rosina Tucker was still iron-willed, robust, and healthy. She laughed easily and was overflowing with wit and wisdom. Commenting on her longevity and the fact that all of her close relatives had died, she told Dave Pitts for *Washington Living,* July 1986: "Being alone is an inevitable consequence of living long enough." Tucker's great-grandmother lived to be 101 and her grandparents lived to their mid-90s. "I don't know why we live so long," she told the November 8, 1984, *Washington Post.* Most of the neighbors from her once elegant neighborhood had died or moved away, yet she enjoyed life to the fullest. She added, "I've been almost every place I wanted to go, met many interesting people and basically had a good life. But that doesn't mean I'm ready for the Man to come get me!"

Perhaps the best summation of Tucker's life can be found in her autobiography, which Dave Pitts quotes in the July 1986 *Washing Living* article. Responding to a young man who had asked what it was like in her day, she wrote, "In my day. This is my day." The autobiography continues:

> Today is my day as it is your day. Although I live far removed from the time I was born I do not feel that my heart should dwell in the past. It is in the future. Each day for over a century added to another has culminated in growth that has led to my present experience and has made the person I am today and will be tomorrow. . . . While I live let not my life be in vain. And when I depart may there be remembrance of me and my life as I have lived it.

Rosina Tucker devoted her life to her community, her church, piano instruction, civil rights, education causes, and the labor movement, particularly the Brotherhood of Sleeping Car Porters and its auxiliary. She will continue to be remembered for her life and the way she lived it.

REFERENCES:

Brazeal, Brailsford R. *The Brotherhood of Sleeping Car Porters.* New York: Harper and Brothers, 1946.

Cole, Harriette. "Saluting the Spirit of a Centenarian." *Essence* 16 (May 1985): 168, 170.

"Hall of Fame Recognizes Five Women Who Made a Difference in D.C." *Washington Post,* April 1, 1993.

Holleran, Susan Ellen. "Rosina Corrothers-Tucker: A Bedrock in the Union Movement." *about. . .time* 13 (May 1985): 10-13.

"Labor Group Cites Three Black Women." *Jet* 68 (March 25, 1985): 23.

"Long Life and Civil Rights." *Washington Post,* January 25, 1983.

Pitts, Dave. "A Century of Struggle." *Washington Living* 5 (July 1986): 38-41, 61.

Salem, Dorothy, ed. *African American Women.* New York: Garland Publishing, 1993.

"Still Vocal and Active at Age 103." *Washington Post,* November 8, 1984.

"Tracing Her Roots: Rosina Tucker's Work for the Pullman Porters." *Washington Post,* May 26, 1982.

"A Word from the Wise." *Jet* 67 (October 22, 1984): 22.

Jessie Carney Smith

Carmen Pawley Turner
(1931-1992)
Transportation official, government official

" "S he and she alone was the critical component that made it possible," said Representative Steny H. Hoyer (D-MD) in the *Washington Post,* referring to the person who persuaded federal, state, and local officials to work together towards completing the Washington, D.C., subway system. "She was the best thing Metro ever had," said Janice Onque, a Metro bus driver in Washington, D.C., in the same issue of the *Washington Post.* "Being a grandmother. That has been my most satisfying role," said a woman with power that influential men envied and elegance that graceful women desired and emulated. The woman in question is Carmen Pawley Turner, who worked with a powerful Democrat to secure $1.3 billion to finish the rail system, who opened up employment opportunities to district residents, and who was most satisfied when tending to her greatest legacy, her "grandbabies."

Turner was born in 1931, in Teaneck, New Jersey, to James and Carmen Pawley. The family moved to Washington, D.C., where Turner and her sister, Dolores, were raised. Turner attended Morgan School and Dunbar High School in the district before enrolling at Howard University. She left college to elope with Frederick Turner, Jr., to whom she was married for forty-one years. The couple had two sons, Frederick and Douglas. In 1968, Turner received a B.A. degree in government and history from Howard University. She later earned an M.A. degree in public administration and political science from American University and completed coursework toward a doctorate in American government. The Pawley sisters' academic and professional success mirrored that of other family members. Their parents expended great efforts towards their own college educations, and one grandfather was instrumental in the founding of the Bergen County, New Jersey, Urban League.

Begins Career with Federal Government

In July 1983 Turner was appointed general manager of the Washington, D.C., Metropolitan Area Transit Authority (WMATA), the first black woman to assume such a position. During her seven-year tenure, the Metro rail system grew from forty-two miles and forty-seven stations to seventy miles and sixty-three stations. The WMATA transported

Carmen Pawley Turner

nearly a million people a day and in 1990 had an operating budget of $612 million.

The ascent to such a heady and challenging position was a circuitous and long journey for a black woman who began her federal government career as a clerk typist. Her reputation as a conscientious and hardworking professional who always did her homework was bolstered by a solid educational background and interpersonal skills. Maryland representative Steny Hoyer, "an unabashed member of the 'Carmen Cult,'" described Turner in the *Washington Post* as "a warm and gracious individual who engenders a warmth that diffuses confrontation. Her objective is not to beat people, it's to convince people."

After working in the Department of the Treasury and at the Veterans Administration, Turner obtained her first major federal position. She was appointed to work with the United States Army Material Command as administrative officer to a project management staff. In this capacity, she was the liaison officer between the Deseret Test Center in Fort Douglas, Utah, and the Washington, D.C., Material Command Headquarters. Turner then moved to the Department of Army in 1952 as chief of internal programs for the Urban Mass Transportation Administration (UMTA) Office of Civil Rights. This position entailed responsibility for minority recruitment; supervision of the Women's Program and Summer Youth Program; generation of reports on minority employment and civil rights as requested by the President, Congress, and the Secretary of Transportation; and provision of assistance to the Service Development Program. The latter assignment involved working directly with cities to draw up plans to provide improved public transit services for those citizens most in need of them. Turner's successful tenure in this position led to subsequent promotions to deputy director of civil rights for UMTA and, beginning in 1976, acting director of civil rights for the Department of Transportation.

Turner Heads Transit System

In 1977 Turner was hired as the first assistant general manager for administration at WMATA. Her duties often required the exercise of her expertise in handling civil rights and labor relations issues. In May 1983 Turner agreed to become acting general manager of WMATA during the search for a permanent general manager. After reviewing the list of candidates, the board of directors concluded that Turner was the best choice. When approached as to her interest and availability, she exhibited another of the qualities that characterized her as being a top-flight administrator, the ability to make a quick, but critical decision. Within five minutes, the board received an affirmative answer and WMATA had a new general manager. The irony was that Turner, in agreeing to serve as acting general manager, had no intention of applying for the top position and did not want it because of the internal struggles that had plagued her predecessors. Turner's strong point as a transit administrator was her ability to plan workable strategies, lobby for federal dollars in coalition with key congressional leaders, and implement programs after making critical decisions based on logical, analytical thinking.

Turner's first task as general manager was to change the thrust of WMATA. When she was second-in-command and then acting head, the emphasis had been on construction. As first-in-command, Turner initiated the shift to the next critical phase of running the nation's second largest rail and fourth largest bus transit system, that of operating and maintaining WMATA. Completing the remainder of the 103 miles of rail line would still be a priority, but now WMATA would focus on improving bus maintenance facilities, establishing a bus replacement program, and developing the public relations skills of personnel.

By 1986 the rail system had expanded by 30 percent; in 1987 the operating budget was $458 million, the annual capital construction program budget was $381 million, and there were eight thousand full-time employees. Turner's formidable diplomatic skills were needed to persuade U.S. senators and representatives to provide federal monies for mass transit in the Washington, D.C., area since their first priorities were always to their constituents and congressional districts. There were also local problems to be addressed since the transit system provided services not only for the district but also for neighboring counties in Maryland and Virginia. Turner testified before Congress many times, especially to address the need for continued federal funding. She also kept a watchful eye over local and state governments that provided operating funds as well as the district government because their treasuries were always in financial distress. In 1988 WMATA won the transit industry's highest award when it was named the best bus and rail system in North America, and

in 1989 Turner was named Transit Manager of the Year by the American Public Transit Association. She was honored as the manager who had most advanced the urban transit industry in the United States and Canada. By 1990 only 13.5 miles of the 103-mile system were left to be completed, but WMATA still needed a federal monetary allotment of $2.1 billion from Congress. It was fully expected that Turner would again work miracles, but this time it was not to be.

Position at Smithsonian Institution

In December 1990 Turner made a decision that according to the October 3, 1990, *Washington Post,* "caught board members by surprise." She accepted the position of second-in-command at the Smithsonian Institution. As undersecretary, she was the chief operating officer of an agency then suffering from managerial and financial problems and internal tensions. The Smithsonian secretary, under pressure because of his management style and slowness in hiring minorities, praised Turner as a career administrator and public servant with the special insights and abilities needed to manage the complex institution. She was also cited as an administrator who was politically astute and who possessed interests and experiences beyond those of average administrators. Unfortunately, Turner was unable to implement envisioned changes on a scale with those at WMATA due to a 1991 diagnosis of cancer, the disease that caused her death on April 9, 1992.

Despite her busy career, Turner found time to join a number of professional, service, and civic organizations. She was a member of the Women's Forum of Washington, D.C., the National Academy of Administration, the Howard University Board of Trustees, the Washington Urban League, the District of Columbia Committee on Public Education, the Vestry of Saint George's Episcopal Church, and the American Public Transit Association Board of Directors (vice president of rail transit). Turner was also cofounder of the Conference of Minority Transit Officials (COMTO) and was once president of COMTO's Region Two.

Some of Turner's awards and honors include the Department of Transportation—Secretary's Outstanding Achievement Award, and Superior Achievement Award, UMTA (1977); the WMATA Affirmative Action Award (1981); and Woman of the Year awards from Iota Phi Lambda Business Sorority, YMCA National Capitol Region, and Phyllis Wheatley YWCA (1985). She was named Distinguished Black Woman of the Year by Black Women in Sisterhood for Action (1986) and "Washingtonian of the Year," by *Washingtonian Magazine* (1987).

One of the greatest tributes to Turner was given at a memorial "Service of Thanksgiving" held for her at the National Cathedral. Her sixth-grade teacher, Inez Brown, came to pay homage to one of her best students, as quoted in the *Washington Post:* "She turned out to be exactly what she was then, a studious little girl who was a perfectionist." Often described as regal in appearance, Turner was well tailored and immediately recognizable by her "crown of silver-gray hair" and beautiful smile. Her smile is what the general public saw long before she spoke a word and this is what her family, friends, and colleagues will also remember, especially her two grandchildren, Morgan and Lindsay. Despite her successes at WMATA and the Smithsonian, Turner considered her family and friends her greatest accomplishments.

REFERENCES:

"Carmen Elizabeth Turner." *Washington Post,* April 11, 1992.

"Carmen Turner Tells How She Keeps Wheels Rolling as D.C. Mass Transit Head." *Jet* 65 (March 5, 1984): 38.

"Deaths." *New York Times,* April 12, 1992.

"Metro's Top Official to Join Smithsonian." *Washington Post,* October 3, 1990.

Noel, Pamela. "First Black Woman Transit Boss." *Ebony* 39 (March 1984): 93-94, 98.

"On the Move with Carmen Turner." *Washington Post,* October 4, 1990.

"Smithsonian Administrator Dies of Cancer in D.C." *Jet* 82 (May 4, 1992): 53.

Turner, Carmen P. Professional Resume. Urban Mass Transportation Administration, Department of Transportation, Washington, D.C., 1972.

———. Professional Resume; Honors and Awards. Washington Metropolitan Area Transit Authority, Washington, D.C., 1986.

"Turner Remembered as 'the Best Thing' Metro Had." *Washington Post,* April 14, 1992.

Who's Who among Black Americans, 1990-91. 6th ed. Detroit: Gale Research, 1991.

Who's Who among Black Americans, 1992-93. 7th ed. Detroit: Gale Research, 1992.

COLLECTIONS:

Information on Carmen Turner may be obtained from the American Public Transit Association, 1201 New York Avenue, N.W., Washington, D.C. 20005.

Dolores Nicholson

Wyomia Tyus
(1945-)
Track athlete, educator, coach

Track star Wyomia Tyus has been called "the fastest woman on land." This label resulted from her phenomenal speed—she was clocked in 1963 running at twenty-three miles per hour and she made record times in many of the events in which she competed. She was the first Olympian,

Wyomia Tyus

male or female, to successfully defend the 100-meter title. Her best events were the 100-meter, 200-meter, and 60-yard races. Ed Temple, her coach at Tennessee State University, said in his *Only the Pure in Heart Survive* that she deserves more recognition because she not only successfully defended the 100-meter gold but also set both world and Olympic records with each of these wins.

Tyus was born on August 29, 1945, in Griffin, Georgia, to Willie Tyus, a dairy worker, and Marie Tyus, a laundry worker. She was the youngest of four children and the only girl. She moved to Los Angeles after her marriage to Art Simburg and is now the mother of two children: a daughter, Simone, and a son, Tyus Tillman.

Tyus is a graduate of Annie Shockley Elementary School and Fairmont High School, both in Griffin, Georgia. When she was growing up, her primary sport was basketball; even though she was the top sprinter at her high school, she only pursued track as a sideline. She came to the attention of Tennessee State University track coach Ed Temple at a Georgia high school championship. Following this, Temple invited her to participate in the Tennessee State Track and Field Clinic. She participated in the clinic for two consecutive summers prior to entering the university as a recreation major. During this period, Temple took her to the Amateur Athletic Union (AAU) Girls' National Championships. In 1962, she won the 50-yard, the 75-yard, and the 100-yard dashes and broke two American records. In 1963, she won the 75-yard and 100-yard races, and the 100-yard heat; that fall, she entered Tennessee State and continued to set records on the field.

Runner Sets Olympic Record

In 1964, Tyus performed exceedingly well. In the Mason Dixon Games in Louisville, Kentucky, she set a new meet and world record in the 70-yard dash. She won the 100-meter dash in the National AAU Women's Outdoor Track and Field Championships at Hanford, California. At the USA-USSR Track and Field Meet at Los Angeles, California, she placed second. Tyus won a gold medal in the 100-meter dash and established a new Olympic record at the Olympic Games in Tokyo, Japan. In the same games she won the silver medal in the 400-meter relay. One of the rewards of this year-long string of achievements was the declaration by Lester Maddox, governor of Georgia, of November 21, 1964, as "Wyomia Tyus Day" in her hometown of Griffin, Georgia.

In 1965, Tyus again made track history. In the 60-yard dash at the Los Angeles Invitational Meet, she set a new American record; she was a member of the winning 440-yard relay team in the Mason Dixon Games at Louisville; and she set new world and indoor records. At the USA-USSR meet in Kiev, Russia, she set a new world record in the 100-meter dash. In 1966, Tyus won the 100-meter dash in the USSR-British Commonwealth Track and Field Meet at Los Angeles, the 100-yard dash in the All-American Track and Field Meet at Berkeley, California, and the 100-yard dash at the National AAU Outdoor Track and Field Championships at Frederick, Maryland. At the National AAU Women's Senior Track and Field Championships, also in Frederick, Maryland, she was a member of the winning relay team. Other wins for 1966 include the 100-yard dash in the Ohio AAU Track and Field Meet and the 100-yard dash in the Southeastern Track and Field Meet.

Because of these accomplishments, in 1966, Tyus, her teammate Edith McGuire and their coach Ed Temple became U.S. goodwill ambassadors to Ethiopia, Kenya, Uganda, and Malawi. They attempted to inspire and encourage African women athletes, demonstrating their talents and giving pointers on track basics like starting and baton passing.

Like previous years, 1967 proved to be one during which Tyus excelled in competition. She won the 70-yard dash in the Mason Dixon Games in Louisville, the 100-meter dash in the Europe-America Track and Field Meet at Montreal, the 200-meter dash in the Pan American Games in Winnipeg, the 60-yard dash in the National AAU Indoor Track and Field Championships in Oakland, and the 50-yard dash in the Maple Leaf Games at Toronto.

Tyus Wins Second Olympic Gold Medal

The following year, Tyus won the 100-meter dash at the Twelfth Venados, Mexico, Track and Field Tournament, tying the world record. She placed first for the 100 meters and second for the 200 meters in the Olympic trials for the nineteenth Olympic Games to be held in Mexico City. Her Olympiad performance in Mexico secured Tyus's place in the annals of track and field, for she became the first sprinter to win gold medals in the same event in consecutive Olympics by winning the 100-meter race; she also set new Olympic and world records. In the same games, she ran anchor on the U.S. 400-meter relay team and won a gold medal; in this relay, new world and Olympic records were established.

The decade of the sixties was a turbulent time of racial unrest in the United States. Some prominent black athletes in this country attempted to use their status in an effort to raise racial consciousness. At one point, there was a call for African Americans to boycott the Olympic Games in Mexico. In the end, they did participate, however, and the actions of African American athletes Tommy Smith and John Carlos were representative of the racial climate of the country. Smith won the 200-meter race and Carlos came in third. On the victory stand, they raised their gloved, clinched fists and bowed their heads during the singing of the national anthem. The outcry resulting from their actions was so great that they were expelled from the Olympic Village. In an interview in Brian Lanker's *I Dream a World: Portraits of Black Women Who Changed America,* Tyus said that the other black American athletes attempted to show solidarity by wearing "black arm bands, black socks, something dark. I wore dark shorts after winning my gold medal . . . and dedicated my medal to them for what they did."

Tyus graduated from Tennessee State University in the spring of 1968, and, after the conclusion of the 1968 Olympics, she retired from amateur sports. She said in Michael Davis's *Black American Women in Olympic Track and Field,* "After the Olympics I did not even run across the street." Following her marriage, her move to Los Angeles, and the birth of her daughter, the International Track Association was formed, and she returned to track competition as a professional. In her first year in professional competition, according to the Temple Papers, she "had won eight of 18 races and she was the leading money winner in the women's event. By the 1974 season, Tyus had . . . won all 22 races on the tour. Once again she was the top women's money winner."

Tyus enjoyed her Olympic experiences and the recognition that came with it, but she also knew the importance of education. She was aware that she could not perform as an athlete all of her life. Accordingly, since her retirement, she has taught physical education in junior and senior high school, coached at Beverly Hills High School, and acted as consultant to the Olympic Experience Group. She does public speaking engagements and is involved with youth groups, working to support and promote women in all sports. She served on the Advisory Board of the Women's Sports Foundation and participated in Colgate-Palmolive's Help Young America Campaign. She is currently involved with the United States Olympic Committee and the Black Studies Center at the University of California, Los Angeles.

In addition to the medals she won on the field, Tyus has earned other forms of recognition for her accomplishments. She was inducted into the Tennessee Sports Hall of Fame, Women's Sports Hall of Fame, Black Athletes Hall of Fame, Georgia Athletic Hall of Fame, and Olympic Hall of Fame. Track and field sportswriters and statisticians chose her as woman sprinter for the All-Time Team. Additionally, she received the Saettel Award, which is given annually by the

Women's Track and Field Committee to the woman who exhibits the most outstanding performance of the year, and the NCAA Silver Anniversary Award. According to the Temple Papers, Tyus was "ten times AAU National Champion and All-American Athlete in both indoor and outdoor competition and five times world record holder in 50, 60, 70, and 100-yard dashes and meter sprint."

Tyus is described in Edwin Henderson's *The Black Athlete* as "a quiet, shy girl, 5ft.-7in. and 134 pounds [who] runs with power." As an athlete she made major contributions to the field of track in general and to the Tennessee State University track program in particular. She credits Ed Temple, her coach at Tennessee State, for much of her development as a world-class sprinter. Throughout her career, she has demonstrated the ability to give credit where it is due, to share her glory, to support others, and to be concerned about the world around her.

Current Address: 1102 Keniston Avenue, Los Angeles, CA 90019.

REFERENCES:

Ashe, Arthur R., Jr. *A Hard Road to Glory: A History of the African-American Athlete since 1946.* New York: Warner Books, 1988.

Bentley, Ken. *Going for the Gold: The Story of Black Women in Sports.* Los Angeles, Calif.: Carnation Co., 1983.

Davis, Marianna W., ed. *Contributions of Black Women to America.* Vol. 1. Columbia, S.C.: Kenday Press, 1982.

Davis, Michael D. *Black American Women in Olympic Track and Field.* Jefferson, N.C.: McFarland, 1992.

Henderson, Edwin B., and the editors of *Sport* magazine. *The Black Athlete: Emergence and Arrival.* New York: Publishers Co., 1978.

Laklan, Carli. *Golden Girls: True Stories of Olympic Women Stars.* New York: McGraw-Hill, 1980.

Lanker, Brian. *I Dream a World: Portraits of Black Women Who Changed America.* New York: Stewart, Tabori and Chang, 1989.

"NCAA Honoree Tyus Grateful to Temple." *Tennessean,* January 14, 1983.

"Olympic 'Triple' Wyomia's Goal Now." *Tennessean,* April 14, 1969.

Page, James A. *Black Olympian Medalists.* Englewood, Colo.: Libraries Unlimited, 1991.

Temple, Ed. *Only the Pure in Heart Survive.* Nashville, Tenn.: Broadman Press, 1980.

COLLECTIONS:

Information on Wyomia Tyus may be found in the Ed Temple Papers, Brown-Daniel Library, Tennessee State University, Nashville, Tennessee.

Helen R. Houston

Leslie Uggams

(1943-)

Actress, dancer, singer

When Leslie Uggams was in her teens she was the only black appearing on a regularly scheduled television program. She had been performing in public since she was six and would go on to make the transition to adult star successfully. Uggams's seemingly easy early success came at a higher cost than many of her fans knew. The desire to please is part of her character, but she faced tremendous pressure from producers determined to mold her into their vision of a black who would be acceptable to white audiences. Nonetheless, it was her genuine ability to draw an audience that made her into an effective pioneer for blacks in the field of television.

Leslie Marian Uggams was born in New York City's Washington Heights area on May 25, 1943, to Harold C. and Juanita Smith Uggams. She has an older sister, Frances. Her family name is said to be Native American, reflecting that strand in her mixed heritage. At the time of her birth Harold Uggams was an elevator operator and floor waxer. Both of her grandfathers were ministers, but other members of her family had been in show business. Her aunt, Eloise Uggams, had appeared in the Broadway production of *Porgy and Bess.* Her mother had been a chorus girl at the Cotton Club, and her father had been a member of the Hall Johnson Choir. With this background, Uggams began to sing very early; she sang in public for the first time at the St. James Presbyterian Church in 1949, and she acted for the first time in that year in a supporting role on the television program *Beulah.* Through *Beulah* and other television work, she became a child star.

Uggams started her education in public schools but transferred in the fourth grade to the Professional School for Children, from which she graduated in 1961. She then entered the Juilliard School of Music. She dropped out of Juilliard in 1963, a year before graduation, because of the demands of her career. In addition to her formal schooling, she also took dancing lessons to develop poise.

From the time of her debut on *Beulah,* Uggams continued to appear on television in programs like Johnny Olsen's *TV Kids* and the shows hosted by Milton Berle, Arthur Godfrey, and Sid Caesar and Imogene Coca. In 1952, at the age of nine, she performed at the Apollo Theater in Harlem, and in 1954 at New York's Palace. Her career then paused as she passed through an awkward phase during adolescence.

Uggams came to public attention again when she was almost fifteen. Her extensive knowledge of popular music

Leslie Uggams

enabled her to win twenty-five thousand dollars on the television quiz program *Name That Tune.* It also brought her singing ability to the attention of Columbia Records producer Mitch Miller, who signed her. Her first album appeared in October 1959, and in less than a year she had a solo spot in a Radio City Music Hall stage production.

Uggams Reaches Stardom

Major stardom came when Uggams began work on a new television show with Mitch Miller, *Sing Along with Mitch,* in January 1961. She was on the program for three years. For two of the three years several polls rated her as the best female singer on television. She had the distinction at the time of being the only black regularly featured on television. Uggams also exemplified the wholesome image Miller insisted on for the show and the performers.

In late 1963 Uggams began her career as a nightclub entertainer, a process that involved gradually shedding her wholesome image. *Sing Along with Mitch* went off the air in March 1964, and she undertook a national tour of nightclubs to great acclaim. That year, between engagements, she made six appearances on the *Ed Sullivan Show.* At one point in 1965 she was using in her nightclub act a large picture of Mitch Miller, who blushed and frowned as she sang her sexy songs. She had now made the transition to being viewed as an adult performer although many still continued to feel she was wholesome—sexy, granted, but nonetheless wholesome. Capitalizing on her fame and glamour, she published *The Leslie Uggams Beauty Book* in 1966.

Uggams also made the transition to married woman. She met a young Australian businessman named Grahame Pratt in 1963 during a tour of that country. A year would pass before they saw each other again, and Uggams was involved in a close relationship with singer Billy Ekstine's son, Ronnie, when they renewed contact. Other problems between Uggams and Pratt were worked out—for example, he had to establish a career in the States—and they were married on October 16, 1965. They settled in New York City. The union has proved to be remarkably stable for a show business marriage. The couple has two adopted children. In the late 1970s, when her husband declared bankruptcy and took the position of her business manager, there were unfounded rumors that the marriage was ending.

Appearances on Broadway

After her enormous success, Uggams was ambitious to star in musical comedy. Her first step was to take the lead in a West Coast revival of *The Boy Friend,* for which she won rave reviews. Her New York opportunity came in 1967 when Lena Horne walked out of *Hallelujah, Baby!* before it opened. Uggams was hired as a replacement for the musical, which officially opened at New York's Martin Beck Theater on April 26, 1967. The reviews of this attempt to present sixty years of black history were mostly negative, but Uggams herself received praise. *Variety*'s poll of New York theater critics named her the most promising new Broadway actress for the 1967-68 season. She also won a Tony and the Drama Critics Award. Her second Broadway musical, *Her First Romance,* was less successful. A musical version of Shaw's *Caesar and Cleopatra,* it opened in New York on October 20, 1968, but lasted only two weeks. Her other Broadway appearances include *Blues in the Night* (1982), *Jerry's Girls* (1985), and *Anything Goes* (1987).

Uggams's success in *Hallelujah, Baby!* led to her own network television program in 1969, when she replaced the *Smothers Brothers Comedy Hour.* Her show lasted only to mid-season. Her singing was stunning, but her skits were less successful. She was much criticized for a continuing segment that featured her as a bossy black wife with a weak husband. Jeanne Noble in *Beautiful, Also, Are the Souls of My Black Sisters* states that, because of Uggams's middle-class and show-business backgrounds, "her black 'situations' lacked emotional conviction," and Noble suggests this was a major reason for the cancellation. Noble also repeats the cruel remark some people were making about Uggams's role as Georgiana in *Hallelujah, Baby!:* "How can she possibly play a Negro? She's never been one."

This sort of disparagement was reaching a crescendo in the late 1960s and early 1970s with the rise of a militant civil rights movement. Uggams feels that this criticism is unfair and that it overlooks the burden she faced as a pioneer lone black in television. In a March 1978 *Essence* interview, she said, "I'd like a little credit. I was always involved. I was a pioneer and nobody knew it. And now suddenly it bothers me that I got what I *didn't* deserve and never got what I *did.*" Uggams denies that she had a white, middle-class upbringing. She points out that while her grandparents, uncles, and aunts were professional people, both parents had to work. She added, "I always knew I was Black. I grew up with a positive identity. My parents gave me that." She further points out that she does not seek publicity for her struggles on behalf of African Americans and that her achievements were not unmarked by burdens imposed by race. For example, only Mitch Miller's insistence kept her on his show in the face of the reluctance of southern stations to carry a black performer, and the Brooklyn television studio where the show was produced had to be evacuated more than once because of bomb threats. Even when she had her own show, she was angered because the network spent two weeks on her hair to produce an "acceptable" style and falsely claimed that some black guests she wanted were unavailable. In the March 1978 *Essence* article, she commented on the behind-the-scenes struggles on the show:

> I also sneaked in my Afro. They in turn sneaked in Andy Griffith. Back and forth we went. I won the fight to have a Black conductor on my own show, and in exchange I gave them the bulk of my hairstyles. It sounds funny now but it wasn't funny then. Nor was it funny to me that up and down the line my people were thinking, she's not concerned. I was never apolitical. I'm just not a shouter. But I have been out there fighting all my life.

In this *Essence* interview she was also adamant in defending her marriage to a white man:

> I didn't give a damn whether people understood or not. My marriage was *my* marriage. Nobody's business but mine. And that remains true today. My private life belongs to me. I'm the one who has to be happy. What I give at the office, so to speak, is in the public domain. What occurs at home belongs to no one other than me and mine.

This type of criticism subsided after Uggams appeared as Kizzy in the ABC miniseries *Roots* in 1977. She won wide acclaim and was nominated for an Emmy. She did not win, but the Television Critics Circle gave her the award of best supporting actress for her performance. Uggams continued to appear on television from time to time on specials and in guest appearances. In 1979 she won praise for her performance in the miniseries *Backstairs at the White House.* Uggams's work in theatrical films includes a bit part in *Two Weeks in Another Town* (1962) and roles in *Black Girl* (1972), *Skyjacked* (1972), and *Poor Pretty Eddy* (1975). Some critics feel her most successful role in these movies was in *Black Girl.*

Although Uggams has less exposure as an adult performer than she had in her childhood and youth, she continues to be a popular star. Television and club performances keep her busy, and her singing still delights many people. Her pioneering role has been key in opening doors for blacks in show business.

Current Address: c/o Glen Rigberg, William Morris Agency, 151 South El Camino Drive, Beverly Hills, CA 90212-2775.

REFERENCES:

Bogle, Donald. *Blacks in American Films and Television: An Encyclopedia*. New York: Garland, 1988.

Bordman, Gerald. *American Musical Theatre: A Chronicle*. 2d ed. New York: Oxford University Press, 1992.

Current Biography 1967. New York: H. W. Wilson, 1967.

Ebert, Alan. "Coming to Terms." *Essence* 8 (March 1978): 84-85, 156-57.

Klotman, Phyllis Rauch. *Frame by Frame—A Black Filmography*. Bloomington: Indiana University Press, 1979.

Noble, Jeanne. *Beautiful, Also, Are the Souls of My Black Sisters*. Englewood Cliffs, N.J.: Prentice-Hall, 1978.

Randolph, Laura B. "Black Women, White Men: What's Goin' On." *Ebony* 44 (March 1989): 154-62.

"School for Child Entertainers." *Ebony* 8 (August 1953): 62-66.

"She Sings Along with Mitch." *Ebony* 17 (March 1962): 40-46.

Uggams, Leslie. "Why I Married an Australian." *Ebony* (May 1967): 140-49.

Who's Who among Black Americans, 1994-95. 8th ed. Detroit: Gale Research, 1994.

Who's Who in America. 48th ed. New Providence, N.J.: Marquis Who's Who, 1994.

Robert L. Johns

Shirley Verrett
(1931-)
Singer

S hirley Verrett combined beauty, intelligence, and above all a remarkable voice in a career in opera and recital that made her into a major star. She has appeared in most of the world's principal opera houses to great acclaim, at first as a mezzosoprano and then as a soprano. Her voice defies categorization, and she would prefer to be known simply as a singer.

Shirley Verrett was born in New Orleans on May 31, 1931, to Leon Solomon and Elvira Harris Verrett. Her father was a building contractor. She had four brothers and a sister. Her parents were fervent members of the Seventh Day Adventist Church, an affiliation that would play a role in the development of Verrett's career. When Verrett was five, the family moved to Oxnard, California, where Leon Verrett established the Verrett Construction Company.

Verrett and her siblings were educated in Adventist schools, and for a short time she was a student at Adventist-affiliated Oakwood College in Huntsville, Alabama. Although Verrett chafed at the church's restrictions, it would take a long time for her to break away. The quality of her voice was apparent from an early age. By the time she sang her first solo, "Jesus Loves Me," in the Ephesus Seventh Day Adventist Church in New Orleans at the age of five, her voice sounded like that of a ten- or twelve-year-old. The family was musical. Her mother was a fine soprano, and her father sang in church, where he also directed choirs. The whole family gathered to sing religious music at home on Friday evenings, the beginning of their Sabbath.

In 1948, when Verrett was seventeen, her father, who was sure of her ability to do anything, encouraged her to enter a local talent competition for a John Charles Thomas Scholarship. Thomas was a popular baritone noted for his concert, radio, and film appearances as well as his support of young singers. Thomas's attention was caught by one of her songs, and he offered to pay for her to study with the celebrated singer and teacher Lotte Lehman at the Music Academy of the West. Verrett turned the offer down, saying that she was not yet ready for serious study. This would not be the last time that she chose her own path.

At the age of eighteen, Verrett married a man fourteen years her senior. The marriage lasted only a short time and would have legally ended much earlier had it not been for her church's ban on divorce. Until 1963 she combined her husband's name with hers and was known professionally as

Shirley Verrett

Shirley Verrett-Carter. Verrett studied real estate law and accounting at Ventura Junior College, where she earned an A.A. degree in 1951. After earning her associate's degree, Verrett began a successful career selling real estate, but she began having doubts about her career choice and sought out a music teacher in the Yellow Pages of the telephone directory. The teacher she chose recognized her potential, and she eventually went on to train with Anna Fitziu. For five months she studied intensively with Fitziu several hours a day. Verrett also made contact with the noted black musician and choir director Hall Johnson to talk about spirituals. Johnson helped her with them but also became her German teacher and worked with her on lieder singing. In 1955 Verrett won two competitions sponsored by a California organization called the Young Musicians Foundation. She also won a chance to appear on Arthur Godfrey's television show *Talent Scouts,* in New York, on which she sang the contralto aria "Mon coeur s'ouvre à ta voix," from Saint-Saëns's opera *Samson and Delilah.*

This television appearance led to a chance to study with Marian Szekely-Freschl, a celebrated voice teacher, at Juilliard, where Verrett studied for six years. Both teacher and pupil were strong-minded women, and they eventually clashed often, especially concerning Szekely-Freschl's advice about Verrett's personal and professional life. The very first clash, however, had to do with music. Szekely-Freschl felt that Verrett had a mezzo voice. Verrett yielded on that point. She also came to agree with Szekely-Freschl that it was time to end her marriage. Verrett characterized her teacher as being a very strong mother figure with whom she had to break to establish her own independence.

The Juilliard years were important to Verrett for more than vocal training. She developed a solid foundation in music that enabled her to learn her parts by herself, playing from the orchestral score on the piano. She said in an April 14, 1975, *New Yorker* profile by Winthrop Sargeant, "The only way I can memorize is to analyze chords and melodies. Knowing the technique of composition has helped me a lot." She learned the role first by herself and then went to her accompanist to work on characterization. Verrett is also highly knowledgeable about voice technique, especially in relation to her own voice. Her conscious attention to this area led to her independence from her teachers and her decision to dispense with voice coaches. Despite her knowledge of vocal technique, she has no desire to teach. Concerned with all aspects of her profession, she also has strong feelings about opera production.

The divorce from her first husband marked a major rupture between Verrett and her church. The final break was precipitated by her study of opera, since anything having to do with the secular stage was anathema. A career as a recitalist was possible for her as a church member, but not one in opera. Her parents had mixed emotions about the direction of her life. They were staunch church members, but they were proud and supportive and broke church rules to attend her performances.

Professional Career Begins

Verrett credits a summer's study at Tanglewood in the Berkshire mountains of Massachusetts with Boris Goldovsky with being a major influence in her turn to opera, although she deplored the intensity of the competition between singers. While she performed opera, Verrett did not see herself primarily as an opera singer until 1967. Before her graduation from Juilliard in 1961, she sang the title role in Britten's *Rape of Lucretia* and the role of Irina in Kurt Weill's *Lost in the Stars* in 1957 in Yellow Springs, Ohio. In 1958 the latter role was her New York debut, with the City Center Opera; a vocal recital soon followed. She also spent a summer in Cologne, Germany, working on the premiere of a new opera, taking the role of a gypsy in Nicolas Nabokov's *Rasputin's End*. She was engaged by Leopold Stokowski to sing Schoenberg's *Gurrelieder* with the Houston Symphony, but the symphony board refused to allow a black singer to appear. (She has since triumphed in productions of the Houston Opera.) A few months later Stokowski was able to have her sing Falla's *El Amor Brujo* in his first concert with the Philadelphia Orchestra in nineteen years.

The year 1961 marked Verrett's graduation from Juilliard and her return to the South on her first concert tour. She demanded that she not sing to segregated audiences and that she be met at the airport by a private car. In the end she enjoyed the concert tour more than she expected since she found the experience of singing at many black colleges very rewarding. It was about this time that she began a relationship with Louis LoMonaco, a painter and magazine illustrator of Italian ancestry born in Brooklyn. They met when he designed a brochure for her, and they were married on December 10, 1964. They have an adopted daughter, Francesca, who joined the family in 1973. Verrett told Rosalyn Story of the marriage for the book *And So I Sing,* "I had lots of black friends, but the people I saw all the time were of another race. It just goes to show, you fall in love with the people that you know and who you are around all the time."

In the early 1960s the Metropolitan Opera offered Verrett small parts that she considered unsuitable—and she did not have much rapport with the current manager, Rudolph Bing. She turned the parts down and concentrated on building her career abroad, with her major bases after the mid-1960s being Covent Garden in London and La Scala in Milan. At Covent Garden she sang the standard mezzo roles, Amneris, Azucena, Eboli, and Ulrica, with great success. She also built a major reputation singing the role of Carmen, although she was fully satisfied with only one production, the 1969 one at the Maggio Musicale in Florence, which presented the opera as an ensemble rather than a star vehicle. She triumphed as Carmen at Spoleto in July 1962—her first public performance of the role—at the Bolshoi in 1963, at the City Center Opera of New York in 1964, and at La Scala in December 1966, where a special production was mounted for her. At the same time she was building a substantial reputation as a soloist with orchestras and as a recitalist.

Current Biography said of her voice in 1967, "Miss Verrett has a remarkable range, and her steady low register provides fine support for her velvety middle register and her clear striking top register." Winthrop Sergeant said in the April 14, 1975, *New Yorker* article:

> Miss Verrett's voice is a remarkable one. Its range is enormous. She is one of those spectacular mezzos ... who not only tackle the mezzo-soprano range with the utmost ease but have an upper extension into the soprano area, with unusual agility in coloratura and high notes around C, D, and E. ... Certainly there are few roles for female voice that she cannot approach with complete confidence. She is, if anything, a supersinger, of a type that is rare indeed.

Opera Star Sings at the Met

The Met offered Verrett a contract to sing Carmen during the 1968 season. Verrett rather reluctantly accepted the offer. She was not enamored with the role in the general run of productions although she may have sung it more often than any other American singer by 1964, with the possible exception of Risë Stevens, and the new production did not appeal to her. In the event, critics for the most part did not like French actor and producer Jean-Louis Barrault's production, and some found Verrett ill at ease in it. Verrett left the Met after this season, not returning until she sang in *Les Troyens* in 1973 when the house was under new management. Her relations with the Met would be on and off during the rest of her career—there were several seasons she did not sing there, and some of her most important roles were never performed there.

Verrett's dissatisfaction with a constant string of Carmens in mediocre productions may have been a factor in her decision to take on soprano roles. She told Winthrop Sergeant, "I feel I am probably one of the greatest Carmens in the world. But I don't think that I am ever going to be able to prove it. In fact, I've taken it out of my repertoire." Even before her Met debut she had sung the soprano role of Queen Elizabeth in Donizetti's *Maria Stuarda*. Just as in the case of Grace Bumbry, who made the same switch from mezzo to soprano, there were critics who predicted that Verrett would wreck her voice.

Verrett proved the critics wrong in spectacular fashion on October 22, 1973. On the opening night of the Metropolitan's first production of Hector Berlioz's *Les Troyens*, she sang the soprano role of Cassandre in the first act and after intermission the mezzo role of Dido, both very long and demanding roles. She is the first singer ever to sing both roles in a substantially uncut performance of the four-and-a-half-hour opera. After repeating the feat once more, she wisely declined to continue. The accomplishment was not only vocal; she won praise for acting the parts of two very different women. She also became a genuine superstar in the United States, a status she has maintained here, as well as throughout the world.

Verrett's preeminence in the world of opera meant her fees were high, and her audiences eager to hear her. However, Verrett has had bouts of poor health, and she was sometimes exposed to spiteful criticism when illness forced cancellations. She is highly susceptible to colds, which are aggravated by a chronic sinus problem, and even her extraordinary technique cannot always allow her to perform. For example, although she is a celebrated Lady Macbeth in Verdi's opera, she was able to sing only one of her scheduled performances in New York due to a persistent ear infection. It was not until late in her career that the underlying problem was identified as a severe allergy to mold spores.

Verrett has made a number of opera recordings over the years, including Donizetti's *Maria Stuarda, Lucrezia Borgia,* and *La Favorita,* Verdi's *Macbeth* and *Rigoletto*—and also his nonoperatic *Requiem Mass*—Rossini's *Siege of Corinth,* Saint-Saëns's *Samson et Dalila,* and Berlioz's *Les Troyens.* She has also appeared on television, most notably in a Great Performances presentation of *Samson and Delilah* in 1984.

Despite her acting ability and beauty, she has appeared only rarely on film. Her two major movie roles were in a 1987 version of Verdi's *Macbeth,* set in a tenth-century castle and directed by Claude D'Anna, and 1989's *Maggio Musicale,* which offered Verrett her first speaking role. In this film she played a temperamental soprano who has a tumultuous relationship with her director during a production of *La Bohème* for the Maggio Musicale music festival in Florence, Italy.

In *Opera News,* February 17, 1990, Verrett talked about the "winding down" of her career and exploring new options. She came close to suggesting that her Dalila at the Met in that season might be one of her last performances in that role. She said, "When the Met asked me to sing Dalila this season, I wasn't sure it was something still for me, but the morning I had to let them know my decision, I sang through the whole opera twice and decided it would be OK." One of her most recent New York stage appearances was in a new type of venture. In the spring of 1994 she sang the maternal role of Nettie Fowler in a multiracial production of the musical *Carousel.*

Verrett's fame as a singer and performer is secure. Equipped with an outstanding voice, she leaves on record a legacy of musically interesting and well-thought-out performances to inspire later singers and listeners. She also sets an example of professionalism and adherence to the highest standards in her chosen field.

Current Address: c/o IMG Artists, 22 East 71st Street, New York, NY 10021.

REFERENCES:

Current Biography 1967. New York: H. W. Wilson, 1967.

Dyer, Richard. "Characteristically Verrett." *Opera News* 54 (February 17, 1990): 8-12, 52.

Hitchcock, H. Wiley, and Stanley Sadie, eds. *The New Grove Dictionary of American Music.* New York: Macmillan, 1986.

Mapp, Edward. *Directory of Blacks in the Performing Arts.* 2d ed. Metuchen, N.J.: Scarecrow Press, 1990.

Sargeant, Winthrop. "Profiles—Doing Something." *New Yorker* 51 (April 14, 1975): 42-58.

Simon, John. "No Brass Ring." *New York* 27 (April 4, 1994): 73.

Story, Rosalyn M. *And So I Sing.* New York: Warner Books, 1990.

Robert L. Johns

Yvonne Walker-Taylor
(1916-)
Educator, college president, humanitarian

"Wilberforce Sets Hefty Goals under New Leader" was the headline in the *Xenia Daily Gazette* on Tuesday, March 15, 1984, when Yvonne Walker-Taylor became the sixteenth president of Wilberforce University. Located in southwestern Ohio, Wilberforce University is the nation's oldest private historically black liberal arts college. It was founded in 1856 by the early leaders of the African Methodist Episcopal (AME) Church. With many years of experience as a teacher and administrator at Wilberforce, Walker-Taylor was more than capable of executing her presidential responsibilities. Coupled with her professional qualifications were her ambition and desire to follow in her father's footsteps (Bishop D. Ormonde Walker was the tenth president of Wilberforce from 1936 to 1941) and to fulfill a lifetime dream. When she was invested as the first woman president of Wilberforce, she was also the first woman in the nation to follow her father in becoming president of the same university.

The only child of Dougal Ormonde Beaconfield Walker and Eva Reviallion Walker, Yvonne Walker-Taylor was born on April 17, 1916, in New Bedford, Massachusetts. Her father was an AME minister, and later a bishop; given her father's status in the church, Walker-Taylor grew up in a relatively privileged household.

Walker-Taylor has maintained strong ties with the AME Church. She was executive secretary of the Fifth Episcopal District of the AME Church from 1948 to 1956. While president of Wilberforce, she strengthened the bond between the university and the church by representing the university at all AME conferences. She is frequently a speaker at AME churches across the United States and has spoken in Hamilton, Bermuda. As president, she established the Adopt-A-Student Program, which encourages churches to sponsor Wilberforce students. Her active involvement in the AME Church has earned her many awards, including the 1985 Sarah Allen Award from the Woman's Missionary Society of the AME church in Washington, D.C. Thus, Walker-Taylor's participation in the AME Church is another example of her following in her father's footsteps. She is a member of the Trinity AME Church in Wilberforce, Ohio, where she is chairperson of the Commission on Membership and sings tenor in the choir.

One can conjecture that Walker-Taylor's vocal ability is not the ordinary "sing every Sunday voice" because she once

Yvonne Walker-Taylor

considered a career as a jazz singer. She told Karen Farkas for the July 8, 1984, issue of the *Cleveland Plain Dealer,* "In college I was a singing sensation and knew I was as good as Ella Fitzgerald." She recalled, "I had a little radio program called 'Yvonne and Van' which ran for a half hour every Thursday from Dayton."

Walker-Taylor is the widow of Robert Harvey Taylor, who died December 15, 1983, just three months before her inauguration as president of Wilberforce on March 15, 1984. She recalls how supportive her husband was during their twenty-two years of marriage. She also affirms how blessed she is to have had two such supportive, loving, and caring men in her life.

Walker-Taylor was educated in the elementary schools of Chelsea, Massachusetts, and the high schools of Cleveland, Ohio, where her father was minister of Saint James AME Church. She received a bachelor of science in education degree from Wilberforce with a major in English and a minor in sociology. During her senior year at Wilberforce her father was appointed its tenth president. She earned a master of arts in English from Boston University in 1938 and an educational specialist degree with a major in curriculum and administration from the University of Kansas in 1964.

Prior to joining the Wilberforce faculty in 1955, Walker-Taylor taught French at the Wilberforce Academy and history and English at Girls' Latin High School in Boston. She also worked at the Bronx School for the Retarded and taught English at the United States Air Force High School in Bad Nauheim, Germany.

Elected First Woman President of Wilberforce

During her career at Wilberforce, which ended after thirty-two years when she retired as president in 1987, Walker-Taylor held numerous academic and administrative positions. She was appointed in 1955 as assistant professor of English and organized the first reading clinic at the university. She thereafter served in such positions as administrative assistant to the president, 1956-67; supervisor of work aid, 1957-63; and secretary of faculty, 1957-64. In 1964, she was promoted to associate professor of English and that year initiated a Cooperative Education Program, which allowed students to gain work experience in their chosen career fields while pursuing their undergraduate degrees. The program distinguished Wilberforce as the first black college to mandate such a plan.

Other positions held by Walker-Taylor include chair of the division of education, 1963-67; supervisor of student teachers, 1964-67; assistant academic dean, 1967-68; acting academic dean, 1968-69 (she was elected to the position again by the faculty for 1971-72); and dean of instruction, 1969-71. From April to September 1973, by action of the board of trustees, she was acting president. When, in 1973, Walker-Taylor was appointed permanent academic dean and vice president, she became the first woman to hold both positions. She kept both positions until January 1, 1983, when she became the first provost in the history of the university. On March 15, 1984, she was elected by the board of trustees to be the first woman president of Wilberforce. She was the only female candidate among the more than one hundred applicants screened for the position.

Having served in so many different positions at Wilberforce, Walker-Taylor was more than qualified to serve as president. Not only was she capable, she was willing and ready. Walker-Taylor told *Plain Dealer* reporter Karen Farkas, "I had my eyes set on the presidency and was close to it so many times, but it eluded me. . . . I have played second banana for 20 years, and last year when I was appointed provost, I thought it was close as I'd ever get. I said, 'Daddy, I'm close.'"

At the onset of her presidential tenure, she launched a ten-million-dollar Major Gift Campaign to be realized in three years. This campaign would provide new money for capital improvement, the university's endowment, and the current operations annual fund. Other funding efforts that she established were the Women for Women and Wilberforce Endowment, which provides financial assistance to outstanding female students, and the Adopt-A-Student Program.

Academic Innovations

Academically, Walker-Taylor worked to create both the Rehabilitation/Health Care Administration Program and the

dual degree engineering program with the University of Dayton. Walker-Taylor was also cofounder of Sigma Omega Honor Society on campus. During her presidency, the Academic Computer Center was enlarged and a new Cooperative Education Center wing was added to the Walker Center. Walker-Taylor's concern for the "total" student motivated her to improve not only the curriculum, but campus life as well. She enhanced the quality of student life with several beautification projects, such as painting the dormitories and renovating the cafeteria.

As a result of her dedicated service to academia, church, and community, Walker-Taylor is much sought after as a speaker. Between 1982 and 1987, she had more than eighty-five speaking engagements, appearing before such diverse organizations as the United Negro College Fund, Christian Education Congress, NAACP, Kiwanis Club, National Council of Negro Women, Phi Delta Kappa Sorority, National Urban League, and American Association of University Women. Topics of her speeches have run the gamut from "Empowerment of Black Women" to "Minority Opportunities/Problems in the Workforce" to "With God, All Things Are Possible."

She has appeared on numerous television shows, including the *MacNeil/Lehrer Report*. She has also testified before the House Subcommittee on Labor, Health and Human Services and Education on behalf of the National Afro-American Museum and Cultural Center Planning Council. In Chicago in 1987, she testified before the Task Force on Women, Minorities and the Handicapped in Science and Technology about Wilberforce's dual-degree engineering program.

Walker-Taylor's accomplishments have been recognized by many organizations. In 1984, she was awarded the Woman of the Year Award from the Metropolitan Civic Woman's Organization and was named one of the Top Ten Women by the Dayton Newspaper and Women Coalition. In the same year, she was also honored by Black Business and Professional Women of Los Angeles County and received the Recognition Award from the Chicago Inter-Alumni Council of the United Negro College Fund, the Bethune-Tubman-Truth Award from the Chicago Teachers Guild, and the Southern Christian Leadership Conference Drum Major Justice Award in Education.

Because of her outstanding work as an educator and college administrator, Walker-Taylor was awarded three honorary degrees in 1985: a doctor of humane letters from Morris Brown College, Atlanta, Georgia, and doctors of pedagogy from Medialle College, Buffalo, New York, and Northeastern University, Boston, Massachusetts. She has also received an honorary degree from the University of Monrovia, Liberia.

Upholds the Interests of Low-Income Students

Again displaying her concern for the welfare of students, Walker-Taylor in 1987 admonished the federal government for its conversion of work study and Supplemental Educational Opportunity Grant Assistance to a loan formula. She said in

Higher Education and National Affairs that such a shift will "increase the average indebtedness of a student to as high as $16,000. This threat of loan burdens of this magnitude will certainly discourage low-income young people from even considering college as a viable option in their lives."

Despite her academic responsibilities, Walker-Taylor finds time for involvement in professional organizations, including the American Association of University Women, American Association of Higher Education, National Association of Academic Deans (she was elected to the board of directors in 1977), Black Women Academicians, Council of Independent Colleges' Academic Task Force, Board of Directors of the National Commission on Cooperative Education, and State Advisory Committee on Issues Facing Women and Black Faculty and Administrators in Higher Education.

In the community, she is a member of the board of directors of the Afro-American Museum, the board of trustees of the Dayton Art Museum, the board of directors of the Unity Bank of Dayton, and the NAACP. Walker-Taylor is also active in the Alpha Kappa Alpha and Phi Delta Kappa sororities and the Links.

Yet, Walker-Taylor has long realized that all work and no play is not healthy. Therefore, she swims, bicycles, plays racquetball, and water-skis in Hawaii and the Bahamas. She said in an August 1993 interview: "I would miss my swimming pool, my fifteen-year-old husky and my friends if I were to accept the interim presidency at Allen University in Columbia, South Carolina, this fall."

An advocate for women and their pursuit of nontraditional career goals, Walker-Taylor told the *Wilberforcean* in February 1984 that her appointment to the presidency of Wilberforce was "a dream come true" and the fulfillment of a lifelong career ambition. "My father wanted a boy to follow after him. He only had one child, yet I am able to follow in his footsteps. It epitomizes what I have preached for years as an instructor and otherwise. You don't have to be a man to qualify for areas previously held only by men."

Walker-Taylor has been a guiding force in higher education in general and to Wilberforce and the state of Ohio in particular. As an educator, administrator, and humanitarian, her accomplishments confirm that she believes in the pursuit of peace and happiness for all people, with higher education as the key to mobility. Students as well as faculty at Wilberforce and now at Central State College, where she has been Presidential Professor of Education since 1990, have benefitted from her innovative projects for curriculum improvement. The belief that students are a school's most important product might very well be the guiding force behind Walker-Taylor's illustrious career as educator and administrator.

Current Address: P.O. Box 336, Wilberforce, OH 45384.

REFERENCES:

"Central State Appoints Dr. Walker-Taylor to Post." *Jet* 78 (April 30, 1990): 37.

Eckhart, Roger. "Wilberforce Sets Hefty Goals under New Leader." *Xenia Daily Gazette,* April 3, 1984.

Farkas, Karen. "Proudly Carrying Torch of Academia." *Plain Dealer,* July 8, 1984.

Walker-Taylor, Yvonne. "Society Will Pay a High Price for the Continued Shift from Grants to Loans." *Higher Education and National Affairs* 36 (March 9, 1987): 7.

————. Telephone interview with Margaret Ann Reid. August 2, 1993.

Who's Who among Black Americans. 5th ed. Lake Forest, Ill.: Educational Communications, 1988.

"Wilberforce Gets First Woman President." *Jet* 66 (April 2, 1984): 23.

"Woman Gets WU Position." *Xenia Daily Gazette,* April 6, 1973.

COLLECTIONS:

Yvonne Walker-Taylor's papers are housed at Wilberforce University and at her home.

Margaret Ann Reid

Fannie Franklin Wall
(c. 1860-1944)
Clubwoman, civic leader, children's home founder

The influence of Fannie Wall remains strong in the San Francisco East Bay area of California through the existence of the Fannie Wall Children's Home, now the site of a Head Start program in Oakland, where children aged one through four from economically disadvantaged families receive educational, medical, and social service support to prepare them for admission into preschool. Although the activities of the home have been well chronicled, there is a dearth of information about Fannie Wall herself. Since she died a half century ago, most of her peers are either no longer alive or their recollections have dimmed with the passage of time.

Fannie Franklin Wall was born in Gallatin, Tennessee, in about 1860. She came to San Francisco with her husband, Archy H. Wall, a staff sergeant in the U.S. Army, when he was transferred from Silver City, New Mexico, to the Presidio of San Francisco during the Spanish-American War. Archy Wall had been recruited as a musician into the all-black Twenty-fourth Infantry by Major Walter H. Loving, the first African American bandmaster. After Archy retired on July 13, 1900, he and Fannie settled in Oakland, and Archy worked for a time at the San Francisco post office, commuting by ferry across the San Francisco Bay. Years later he described to his grandchildren the horrible trauma of trying to return to his

Fannie Franklin Wall

home in Oakland from his work in San Francisco after the earthquake and fire of 1906.

At first the Wall family lived on Sixtieth Street in North Oakland. But when Fannie Wall died, she was living at 6114 Telegraph Avenue, just a few blocks from the original address. The house on Sixtieth Street was the center for family holidays. Friends and relatives came for Christmas and Thanksgiving celebrations, and in those days when hotels were not open to African Americans, fellow clubwomen who visited Oakland were house guests.

Archy Wall died on May 11, 1931, and was buried three days later in the San Francisco Presidio cemetery, section B, plot number 1179. Fannie Wall died on April 14, 1944, at age eighty-four, and was laid to rest on April 18 in the same grave. An American Legion post in San Francisco has been named in honor of Archy Wall.

Archy and Fannie Wall had two daughters, Lillian and Florence, and one son, Clifton. Daughter Lillian had three children: Archie, Florence, and William (Fritz). Even though Archie was named after his grandfather, there is a slight variation in the spelling of his first name. In her will Fannie Wall left the Telegraph Avenue residence to her two daughters. Both of Wall's daughters, the grandchildren, and the cousins all lived or visited in the family home in Oakland during the lifetimes of Fannie and Archy.

Grandson Archie Williams, the best known of Wall's family, died on June 24, 1993. While a student at the University of California, Berkeley, where he obtained a bachelor of science degree in mechanical engineering, Williams won a gold medal in the four hundred meter track race in the 1936 Olympics in Germany. He remembered his grandmother's pride when Oakland feted him, the returning athlete, with a parade down Broadway, the city's principal thoroughfare. From 1941 to 1945 Williams was a member of the Flying Ninety-ninth Squadron of Tuskegee, Alabama, the celebrated African American Army Air Force aviators who distinguished themselves in World War II as the Tuskegee Airmen. He left the military in 1946 as a lieutenant colonel. In civilian life Williams operated a flying service from the Oakland airport, and then taught mathematics and computers in San Anselmo, a suburb of San Francisco, until he retired in 1987.

Extensive Civic and Social Activities

Fannie Wall was an active member of Oakland's First African Methodist Church, which is now located on the corner of Telegraph Avenue and Thirty-seventh Street. This church, one of the first organized by African Americans in the East Bay Area, was the center of community activities and the religious home of black Americans prominent in the civic and social affairs of Oakland.

Although it seems that Wall's energies were primarily given over to the California Federation of Colored Women's Clubs, where she repeatedly held the office of president and in renewed terms as treasurer increased its funds and oversaw its prudent investments, she had an important role in other groups with similar goals. Wall was an enthusiastic member of the National Association of Colored Women. She also joined and was an officeholder in the King's Daughters Circle, the Art and Industrial Club of Oakland, the Sisters of the Mysterious Ten, the Urban League, and the NAACP. In addition, she organized, developed, and chaired the Spanish-American War Auxiliary.

Through her involvement in a variety of organizations, she sought to influence the white power structure to make financial contributions and take political and social action to improve not only the quality of life for African Americans in the East Bay area but also relations between black and white residents. She was an outspoken woman, constantly involved in community projects. Many times Wall entered the office of Mayor John L. Davies of Oakland and refused to leave until he addressed her concerns and promised to take corrective action.

During the Fifteenth Biennial Session of the National Association of Colored Women, July 30 to August 6, 1926, held in the Civic Auditorium of Oakland, Wall was a prominent participant and served on the local committee to organize the sessions. The program of the event paid tribute to past and present members and delegates like Hallie Q. Brown, Mary McLeod Bethune, Mary Church Terrell, and Margaret Murray Washington. Bethune and her secretary, along with other out-of-town delegates, were houseguests of Wall. Amid the bustle of the usual family members and the added visitors, two incidents occurred that added to the excitement. Grandson Archie fell out of a tree, breaking his arm, and his cousin Yancy, brother of Alfreda, came down with an attack of appendicitis.

Home for Black Children Established

In 1916 Wall was the motivating spirit behind the establishment of a home for black children in Oakland by the northern California section of the California Federation of Colored Women's Clubs. Because local charities had failed to provide adequate services for black children, it was the only institution for the care of African American children in that part of the state. The home provided a family environment for boys and girls ages four to fourteen, for day care or twenty-four hour living. Orphans were accepted, as were children of working parents and those referred by social agencies of the counties of Alameda, San Francisco, and Solano. Among the paid staff and volunteer professionals were social workers, dieticians, recreation leaders, teachers, and psychiatrists. To reward her untiring efforts as president in its period of conception, the new venture was ultimately named the Fannie Wall Children's Home.

Funding came from three major sources: the Community Chest, a bequest from the estate of writer Theodore Dreiser, and income derived from the sale of a sixteen-room house located at 1515 Fairview Street in Berkeley, the generous gift of a former board member, Josephine Hutton. These finances were augmented by donations from other individuals and local organizations and by various community fund-raisers, including banquets, concerts, balls, and dinners.

Probably the most severe financial crisis developed when the Community Chest questioned the leadership of the home's board of directors and threatened to withhold its contributions. Other major challenges came from some members of the black community who would not support the home because they believed it was encouraging the segregated care of African American children and from the city's persistence in seeing that the physical structure of the home was brought into compliance with safety codes. Despite the absence of records to document the details, it appears that workable solutions to the dilemmas were devised, including an innovative agreement stipulating that the city administration and the home's board of directors would share responsibilities. After various periods of suspended operations, the home reopened in 1978 as a child-care center and has continued to make a contribution to the welfare of the children of Oakland.

The first two sites of the Fannie Wall Children's Home, 1215 Peralta Street and 815 Linden Street, were in West Oakland, the section of the city where most of its African American residents lived. In 1964, the board of directors purchased a house at 647 Fifty-fifth Street, its present location, in North Oakland. The front of the building that houses the Head Start Center on Fifty-fifth Street bears the inscription "Fannie Wall Children's Home," a lasting reminder of her contributions.

REFERENCES:

Beasley, Delilah L. *Negro Trail Blazers of California.* 1911. Reprint. New York: Negro Universities Press, 1969.

Davis, Elizabeth. *Lifting As They Climb.* Washington, D.C.: National Association of Colored Women, 1933.

"Fannie Wall Will Probated." *Oakland Tribune,* March 30, 1954.

Hausler, Donald. "The Fannie Wall Children's Home." *Oakland Heritage Alliance News* 6 (Summer 1986): 1-4.

Jackson, George F. *Black Women Makers of History, a Portrait.* Windsor: G. R. T. Printing, 1975.

Robinson, Alfreda. Interview with Dona L. Irvin. March 11, 1993.

Williams, Archie. Interview with Dona L. Irvin. February 26, 1993.

COLLECTIONS:

Information on Fannie Wall can be located in the Northern California Center for Afro-American History and Life, Oakland, California.

Dona L. Irvin

Aida Ward
(1903-1984)
Entertainer

Aida Ward was a popular nightclub, stage, and radio singer of the 1920s and 1930s. She was already a star in her own right when she succeeded Florence Mills in 1928 as the star of *Blackbirds.* She made famous the hit song "I Can't Give You Anything But Love, Baby." She was called the prima donna of Harlem's Cotton Club and was a featured vocalist with the Duke Ellington and Cab Calloway bands.

Aida Mae Gist Ward was born on February 11, 1903, a few blocks northwest of the Capitol building in Washington, D.C. She was the daughter of Susie Wallace, a prominent patron of local clubs, civic causes, and charities. Aida Mae, as she was called, fit the adult definition of a proper child; she was quiet, good, and obedient. After graduating from M Street School, she began to prepare for a musical career. She studied voice with Madame Lillian Evanti, a local teacher and later a noted classical singer. Ward may have been a stage name; although she was married several times, there is no record of when or how she assumed the name.

Ward gave her first music recital at Second Baptist Church in Washington, D.C., and was well received by critics. Later she appeared in concerts and amateur productions. By 1922 she had married Walter Gist, a tall, heavyset man from Buffalo, New York, and they had one son, Jerome. The couple's marital difficulties and later estrangement are said to have led Ward to seek employment at Washington's Dunbar Theatre, where she was to have her first theatrical experience as a pianist and perhaps as an organist. Raymond Murray, owner and manager of the Dunbar Theatre, told the *Afro-American* that Ward sought a position at the Dunbar, but he

Aida Ward

discouraged her on the grounds that he had no opening and considered her unable to do the work. The persistent, determined Ward assured him that she was as competent as anyone else and that all she needed was a chance. Murray was persuaded to give her one. A Howard University student named Fullerton had become unsatisfactory as organist in the production of *Great Day* playing at the Dunbar, so Ward replaced him. She played well, and agreed to sing in future productions for no additional compensation.

When Ward went to the Dunbar she became friendly with another employee, Malcolm Thomas, son of Charles M. Thomas, a teacher at Armstrong High School in the District of Columbia. Their friendship grew, as did Ward's estrangement from her husband. The Gists separated and Walter Gist died in about 1926 in Buffalo. Ward saw greater opportunities in New York City and decided to move there in 1923. She told Raymond Murray of the Dunbar that the next time he would hear from her she would be on Broadway. Ward's prediction was fulfilled in 1928 with *Blackbirds.* Although Ward had lost contact with him for a time, she saw Murray again at the Eltinge Theatre, where she appeared in *Blackbirds.* Their friendship was reestablished.

Ward Rises to Stardom

Ward's first professional engagement in New York was at the Hollywood Cafe, Forty-ninth Street and Broadway, with Duke Ellington. Leonard Harper, who was to become Ward's director, was in charge of the show. She also had small parts in the *Frolics* in 1923. In 1924 Lew Leslie cast her as

little "Blackbird" in the show *Dixie to Broadway,* in which Florence Mills was also featured, and Ward rose to stardom. She played in subsequent productions of the show, which had a successful run in London and Paris. From 1926 to 1939 *Blackbirds* was an annual series of entertainments that Lew Leslie staged. Will Vodery usually arranged the shows while a number of people provided skits and songs to produce a successful formula of racial clichés. Careers of several talented performers were launched through *Blackbirds,* and certainly Florence Mills's career was enhanced by it. *Blackbirds* of 1926 ran six weeks at the Alhambra Theatre in Harlem. Starring Mills, the show played six months in Paris before moving to London. Ward was one of the performers. *Blackbirds* of 1928, which included such songs as "I Can't Give You Anything But Love" and "Diga Diga Do," opened on May 9 for an extended run at the Liberty Theatre. Here the cast included Elisabeth Welch, Adelaide Hall, Tim Moore, Bill "Bojangles" Robinson (for a single number only), and Ward. Ward was replacing Mills, who had died the previous year. (Ward had been an honorary pallbearer at Mills's elaborate funeral, along with Edith Wilson, Cora Green, Evelyn Preer, Gertrude Saunders, Maude Russel, Lena Wilson, and Ethel Waters.) Ward toured abroad a second time in Lew Leslie's show at the Moulin Rouge in Paris.

Ward had become a popular and successful entertainer who was recognized for her brilliant work. She was an outstanding figure in the long Broadway run of *Blackbirds.* In 1930 she played in *Brown Buddies* and later in revues held at the Apollo Theatre. She toured the United States and Canada, sang on national radio, and helped popularize the tune "I Can't Give You Anything But Love." She appeared at the Beacon Theater on Broadway in 1934 with Jack Benny, Milton Berle, George Burns and Gracie Allen, and other well-known performers. While in New York, Ward also performed at the Cotton Club as a regular entertainer, where she appeared with the Duke Ellington and Cab Calloway orchestras. She had an indefinite engagement at Connie's Inn, one of Harem's brightest night clubs. She also performed at the Ambassador and at benefit shows, special concerts, and private shows held in elite hotels.

According to Raymond Murray, in 1929, Ward was engaged to Malcolm Thomas, her friend during her stay at the Dunbar Theatre, who later became an electrician in New York City. Whether or not the two ever married is unclear. At some point, however, she married and divorced a man named Edward Chavers. By 1936 Ward was married to Anderson Gilmer, a Detroit, Michigan, mortician who planned to open a business in New York City. Ward had purchased a palatial home in Washington, D.C., which her mother and grandmother occupied. Ward and Anderson Gilmer lived in an apartment at 80 Saint Nicholas Place, New York City, and she was said to have been an efficient housewife. Apparently Ward was also artistic, which was reflected throughout her well-appointed, modern apartment. She was delighted with home life and was especially fond of cooking plain, tasty foods. The multitalented Ward enjoyed books and literature, playing the piano, and entertaining friends at home. She did not smoke cigarettes, and wine was her favorite drink. Though a simple dresser, Ward had a mania for collecting dainty lingerie and had gathered an unusual variety from Paris and London. She had few other hobbies or pastimes, but was an excellent whist player. Ward was small in stature, standing five feet, four inches tall and weighing 115 pounds. She wore size three-and-a-half shoes.

Ward retired from show business in the late 1940s to operate a nursing home in Washington, D.C. She too spent her final years in a nursing home there, eventually dying of a respiratory ailment at Howard University Hospital in July 1984, when she was eighty-one years old. Her son, Jerome Gist, had died a year earlier.

After a stellar career, history placed Aida Ward in obscurity. She is greatly overlooked and referred to only briefly in historical literature. She is a woman whose achievements in the entertainment field as a popular nightclub, stage, and radio singer deserve reexamination.

REFERENCES:

"Aida Ward, 84, Popular Singer of '20s and '30s." *Baltimore Afro-American,* July 7, 1984.

"Aida Ward's Real Name Is Gist—Engagement Hinted." *Afro-American,* November 16, 1929.

Anderson, Jervis. *This Was Harlem: A Cultural Portrait, 1900-1950.* New York: Farrar, Straus & Giroux, 1981.

Bogle, Donald. *Brown Sugar.* New York: Harmony Books, 1980.

Cunard, Nancy, ed. *Negro Anthology, 1931-1933.* Reprint. New York: Negro Universities Press, 1969.

Fox, Ted. *Show Time at the Apollo.* New York: Holt, Rinehart and Winston, 1983.

"Harlem Limited Broadway Bound." *Pittsburgh Courier,* November 29, 1930.

Hughes, Langston, and Milton Meltzer. *Black Magic: A Pictorial History of the Negro in Entertainment.* Englewood Cliffs, N.J.: Prentice-Hall, 1967.

Kellner, Bruce, ed. *The Harlem Renaissance: A Historical Dictionary of the Era.* New York: Methuen, 1984.

Obituary. *Variety,* July 11, 1984.

"Singer at Cotton Club, Aida Ward, Dies at 84." *Jet* 66 (July 16, 1984): 95.

Jessie Carney Smith

Gertrude Mae Murphy Ward
(1901-1981)
Gospel singer, road manager, publishing firm founder

Gospel singer Gertrude "Mother" Ward performed with the Ward Singers, a renowned gospel group she organized, from the early 1930s through the early 1970s. Benefiting from Ward's incomparable managerial and promotional skills, the Ward Singers became entertainment's most highly paid gospel attraction, performing and recording to great acclaim throughout the United States.

Gertrude Mae Murphy Ward was born to a poor family in Anderson, South Carolina, in 1901. As a child she sang in church and was introduced to the hymns of the Methodist minister Isaac Watts. Best known for popularizing the hymn "Amazing Grace," Watts cultivated in his church the a cappella moaning style and flowing improvisation that would influence all subsequent black religious music. In 1920 Gertrude married George Ward and shortly thereafter she and her husband moved to Philadelphia. Their first daughter, Willa, was born in 1921, followed in 1924 by a second daughter, Clara. The family struggled during the depression, changing residences several times. With no regular employment available, Gertrude Ward stood on street corners in the early morning hours waiting to be hired out to do domestic work for the day. In *The Gospel Sound,* written by gospel music critic Anthony Heilbut and published in 1985, she recalled, "These old feet, these feet can remember where there was holes in the shoes. Clara Ward used to walk on cardboard. Glory!"

Founds Gospel Singing Group

Ward's career in gospel music began dramatically in the early 1930s. In an interview with *Ebony* in October 1957, Ward told of a trance she experienced in 1931 while working at a dry-cleaning establishment. A voice instructed her to "go sing my gospel and help save dying men and women." It was the first of many visions that would guide her in the following decades. With only pennies to her name, Ward started a vocal trio with her daughters—the Ward Singers—and they began performing in area churches. Clara Ward was the lead singer, doubling as piano accompanist. Her first solos were memorable occasions, as an anonymous observer recalled for *Ebony,* "To this day, old timers in Philadelphia remember Sister Ward's little girl [Clara] clapping her hands and shouting *When the Saints Go Marching In* at local church services." Clara Ward later admitted to *Ebony* that the early days of the trio demanded long hours of practice. "In the evenings when other girls were going out or sitting on the steps with their boy friends, I was on my way to church. Sometimes I wanted to give it up and do the things other girls do. But I didn't and I'm glad. I've done so many things that I thought were impossible."

In 1935, Ward and her daughters caught the attention of prominent gospel music composer Thomas Andrew Dorsey

Gertrude Mae Murphy Ward

and his protégé, Sallie Martin, who were visiting Philadelphia. Known as the "Father of Gospel Music," Dorsey persuaded Ward to select and develop a repertoire for her group that featured gospel tunes. Dorsey was a prolific composer—he had written over five hundred gospel songs—and many of his compositions found their way into the Wards' programs. In his essay "Take My Hand," gospel music scholar Horace Clarence Boyer observed that Dorsey's music reflected "the anxieties, joys, and aspirations of the poor, rejected, and often uneducated African American population and express[ed] them in lyrics that not only captured the very essence of the Christian movement but also spoke for each Christian as if he or she were making a personal statement." Ward became an early exponent of Dorsey's style and philosophy and by the late 1930s, the Ward Singers were performing his music throughout the southeastern United States.

Sallie Martin also made a significant impact on the direction Ward's career took in the late 1930s. Together with Dorsey, Martin traveled from church to church throughout the East, South, and Midwest in the early 1930s, organizing and training choirs to sing gospel—especially Dorsey's songs. Headquartered in Chicago, the Martin-Dorsey sound became known as the Chicago School of Gospel. In addition to the "discovery" of the Ward Singers, the Chicago School also launched the careers of several other well-known performers, including Mahalia Jackson and Roberta Martin (no relation to Sallie Martin). The practice of accepting "offerings" of money to be distributed among gospel singers was begun by Dorsey around 1936, thus enabling Jackson, the Wards, and

others to launch professional careers. Gospel performances were still exclusively church activities, however, and it would be another two decades before gospel music would become commercialized.

Prior to Dorsey's rise in gospel music, the unaccompanied male vocal quartet, called "quartet singing," had been the only small singing ensemble in black churches. When Dorsey teamed up with Sallie Martin, he began experimenting with the use of female voices in his own song arrangements. The higher pitched sound of women singers evoked an angelic quality and heightened emotional excitement; it held immediate appeal for Dorsey's congregations. When Ward met Dorsey in 1935, she recognized a golden opportunity to share in the development of a whole new approach to religious singing—gospel singing that involved only women's voices.

In spite of the increasing fame and success of the Ward Singers, Clara Ward experienced much frustration during her teenage years. At age seventeen, she decided to get married. "It was a mistake," she recalled to *Ebony* in October 1957. "We were both kids. It lasted only two years." Undaunted by her daughter's temporary lack of interest in the singing group, Gertrude Ward persevered with dignity and determination in her role as what Heilbut called a "Baptist show-business mother." Ward's patience paid off. After the dissolution of her marriage, Clara moved back to her mother's house and began singing again.

After a stunning performance—their debut at the National Baptist Convention in 1943—the Ward Singers found themselves much sought after as performers. By popular demand, Gertrude Ward began producing and distributing short souvenir booklets that detailed her discovery of gospel music and offered suggestions to church parishioners and clergy for promoting gospel programs. By this time, Clara Ward had developed into a consummate solo artist and began assuming more and more of the trio's leadership responsibilities.

The Ward Singers Reorganize and Expand

In 1947, the group reorganized as the Clara Ward Singers, and under Gertrude Ward's supervision, two new singers—Henrietta Waddy and Marion Williams—were recruited. Waddy, a middle-aged singer from Philadelphia, brought to the group a sound reminiscent of the classic blues performers of the 1920s and 1930s, especially Ma Rainey. Williams was a teenager from Miami, Florida, whose wide vocal range and varied timbral palette would become one of the group's trademarks. In his 1985 book, Heilbut called Williams "the best singer Miss Ward ever had," and described her voice as "ranging from a growling [male] quartet bottom to the airiest, most floating high soprano."

Reinforced by the talents of additional performers, Ward encouraged the singers to experiment with new sounds. With one of their biggest hits, "Surely, God Is Able," they became the first gospel group to arrange a well-known religious song as a waltz. They often featured more than one lead singer—usually an exchange between Clara and Williams—a practice previously associated only with male quartets. When Williams sang lead by herself, the group supported her highly inventive style with great sensitivity. Capitalizing on her exceptional range and unusual vocal agility, Williams sometimes incorporated into her interpretations passages on par with those sung by operatic coloraturas. She developed a uniquely expressive breathiness of tone that added to the emotional intensity of her performances. Pearl Williams-Jones, writing in *Ethnomusicology,* identified this technique as a characteristic of the gospel genre in which "audible breath intake and expulsion of air acts as a rhythmic factor and is an essential part of black timing and rhythmic pacing. It is a distinctive ethnic phenomenon firmly rooted in tradition. The melismatic embellishments of gospel singing can achieve dizzying heights of virtuosity."

The addition of new songs also enhanced the group's reputation. Ward began to mine the huge collection of music written by William Herbert Brewster for appropriate material. Brewster was one of the most prolific gospel composers and a major force in the evolution of the gospel idiom. Eventually he started writing tunes expressly for the Wards.

Beginning in 1948, the Wards made a series of now-classic recordings. Their 1950 release of "Surely, God Is Able" featured Williams as lead singer and Clara Ward as pianist and became the first gospel million seller. Though conservative in style, Clara Ward's piano playing proved highly effective and influential, especially during the 1950s and 1960s. Clara Ward had no need to rely on thick sonority: she provided ample supporting chordal structure with the right hand, and octaves or single tones with the left hand. Her most significant contribution to gospel piano was her practice of interrupting a basic harmony by unexpectedly inserting another harmonic scheme and then immediately returning to the initial harmony—adding to the tone of religious fervor. At no time did her playing cover the voices; instead, her arrangements complemented the singers, allowing them freedom to vary both words and music.

As other gospel groups became well known, Gertrude Ward responded to her new competition with heavy doses of religious theatrics. Each member of the Clara Ward Singers took turns striving to elevate the level of their audience's emotional frenzy. Shouts from listeners were considered to be the most flattering of reactions. With a less responsive audience, the singers called upon Ward to perform her specialty, a congregational hymn. Later, the group traded in their choir robes for evening attire. They sported lavish gowns, furs, and fancy wigs, drawing huge audiences who often appeared just to catch a glimpse of the latest Ward costume.

Music Publishing Firm Established

Gertrude Ward extended her activities beyond the Clara Ward Singers, gradually becoming involved in promoting various gospel acts and other related enterprises. She established the highly successful Big Gospel Cavalcades, which featured several groups and quartets and attracted audiences of up to twenty-five thousand at a time. With Clara Ward's assistance, she opened a publishing firm, Ward's House of

Music, in Philadelphia in 1954. They built their business exclusively on gospel sheet music sales, most notably songs by Brewster and Clara Ward, who had begun to compose and arrange her own material. After 1958, all of Brewster's new music was available only through Ward's House of Music. It was a highly successful and mutually beneficial arrangement, and by the mid-1950s almost every Clara Ward Singers recording was a Brewster song.

Changes continued to occur in Ward's relationship with Clara and the singers that considerably altered the artistic and religious mission of the group. By 1955 Clara had completely replaced Ward as leader and manager of the singers. They began to tour with the Reverend C. L. Franklin of Detroit, father of Aretha Franklin. C. L. Franklin became Clara Ward's constant escort and at his urging, Clara traveled with him to Europe and Israel. Gertrude Ward produced a souvenir book recounting Clara's visit to the Holy Land, which was sold at church performances. According to Heilbut's 1985 book, Gertrude Ward would implore her audiences, "I wish everybody in this church would buy this book . . . I wish everybody in America would buy this book."

In an article written for *Color* magazine after her return from the Holy Land, Clara Ward delivered a fervent spiritual message, yet never denied her commercial success. Calling herself "Queen of Gospel Singing," she boasted of her record sales and proposed that the Clara Ward Singers perform in theaters as well as churches. In fact, the group had appeared in Harlem's Apollo Theatre in 1955, in spite of the strong objections of Gertrude Ward and religious leaders who objected to the performance of gospel music in secular settings.

Clara Ward Singers at Newport Jazz Festival

The Clara Ward Singers further blurred the distinction between religious and secular music when in 1957 they performed at the Newport Jazz Festival. The possibility of a wider and different audience and more money proved too tempting for Clara Ward to resist.

Gertrude Ward showed no signs of her initial opposition to performing gospel music outside the church when she saw the positive press reviews after the Newport Jazz Festival appearance. She declared to *Ebony* in October 1957, "We made it [the Festival] Newport Church," describing in this way her feeling that the performance at the Newport Jazz Festival was of a spiritual level sufficient to turn the highly secular festival into a religious experience. The successful theater and festival concerts only inspired Ward, who was now acting as general manager of all Ward enterprises, to tighten her grip on the singing group's finances. Most of their considerable earnings were divided between Ward and Clara, while the other singers received substantially lower salaries. Ward kept Clara outfitted in a fifty-thousand-dollar wardrobe that included, according to the October 1957 issue of *Ebony,* "dazzling gold gowns, bare-backed slippers, mink-trimmed shoes and creations by Dior, the Paris designer." In 1957 alone, Clara Ward earned two hundred thousand dollars from performances, fifty thousand dollars from her share of

Ward's House of Music, and was transported about in a twenty-five-foot-long eight-door Chrysler limousine owned by Clara and designed to her specifications. Gertrude Ward invested in real estate and insisted that the other Ward singers live in the apartment buildings she owned, paying her rent.

In protest over their meager wages, Marion Williams and the other singers quit the group in September 1958. "It's a sit-down strike," Gertrude Ward lamented in *Jet* magazine, September 11, 1958. She recruited the Imperial Singers of Philadelphia as replacements, but the old magic couldn't be recaptured. Squabbles over money continued to plague the singers and in October 1958 one of the new recruits, Mildred Gay, complained to Gertrude Ward about her salary. When Gay questioned the amount she had been paid for a recent performance, Ward allegedly cursed and physically threatened her.

Clara Ward sought out other places to perform, and in 1961, she signed a contract with nightclubs in Las Vegas guaranteeing her five thousand dollars a week for forty weeks of the year. At first Clara performed in clubs alone, but eventually Gertrude Ward yielded and joined her daughter. Success returned to the Wards and Gertrude negotiated a performance contract with Disneyland in 1962. In the mid-1960s Ward took time off to travel to Israel. After her trip, she sold photographs and slides of her Holy Land excursion, proclaiming to her audiences, as Heilbut quotes in his 1985 book, "Yes, children, Mother finally made it over."

In 1967, Clara Ward suffered a stroke while performing. As Heilbut remarked, "She survived, and Gertrude began making public announcements about 'God's miracle girl.' They returned to Philadelphia for a special testimonial program, and when Marion Williams got up to sing 'Surely, God Is Able,' Mrs. Ward ran and jumped and hollered 'Sing, sing' as if it were the old days."

Clara Ward continued to perform, but largely as a solo act. Gertrude Ward's singing career had been interrupted by surgery for removal of a goiter and her voice never completely returned. Heilbut described Ward's post-operative voice as "a great, big, cracked instrument, leaping octaves from word to word. It may start out a loud, shaky baritone and then soar to a gravelly falsetto in an anomalous manner that has inspired scores of party imitations."

On December 8, 1972, Clara Ward suffered a second stroke at the Baldwin Hills, California, home she shared with Gertrude Ward. A heart attack and another stroke occurred on January 9, 1973, and she died on January 16, never having regained consciousness. Clara's funeral was Ward's last, and perhaps most lavish, spectacle. Two funerals took place, one a "Service of Triumph" in Philadelphia, and the other a "Going Home Service of Praise and Thanksgiving" in Los Angeles. Sparing no expense or extravagance, Ward announced, "I won't give my child, the world's greatest gospel singer, a pitiful funeral. Clara gave me everything I wanted. I'm saying 'thank you Clara,'" as Heilbut related.

After 1973, The New Ward Singers continued to perform, but without Gertrude Ward, who had retired to private life. Whenever friends visited, she insisted on taking them to the cemetery where Clara lay buried. Ward died on November 27, 1981, in Los Angeles. The cause of death was never made public. She was survived by her eldest daughter, Willa Ward Royster, of Philadelphia.

REFERENCES:

Banks, Lacy J. "Gospel Music: A Shout of Black Joy." *Ebony* 27 (May 1972): 161-68.

Bolcom, William, Max Harrison, and Paul Oliver. *The New Grove Gospel, Blues and Jazz.* New York: Norton, 1986.

Boyer, Horace Clarence. "Gospel Music." *Music Educators Journal* 64 (May 1978): 34-43.

———. "Contemporary Gospel Music: Part 1: Sacred or Secular?" "Contemporary Gospel Music: Part 2: Characteristics and Style." *The Black Perspective in Music* 7 (Spring 1979): 5-11, 22-36.

———. "A Comparative Analysis of Traditional and Contemporary Gospel Music." In *More Than Dancing.* Edited by Irene V. Jackson. Westport, Conn.: Greenwood Press, 1985.

———. "Take My Hand, Precious Lord, Lead Me On." In *We'll Understand It Better By and By.* Edited by Bernice Johnson Reagon. Washington, D.C.: Smithsonian Institution Press, 1992.

Burnim, Mellonee V. "The Black Gospel Music Tradition: A Complex of Ideology, Aesthetic, and Behavior." In *More Than Dancing.* Edited by Irene V. Jackson. Westport, Conn.: Greenwood Press, 1985.

"Clara Ward." *Variety Obituaries.* Vol 7. New York: Garland, 1988.

Cleveland, J. Jefferson. "A Historical Account of the Black Gospel Song." In *Readings in Black American Music.* Edited by Eileen Southern. 2d ed. New York: Norton, 1988.

"Death of Clara Ward Saddens World." *Jet* 43 (January 16, 1973): 16-17.

Gehman, Richard. "God's Singing Messengers." *Coronet* 44 (July 1958): 112-16.

"Glamour Girl of Gospel Singers." *Ebony* 12 (October 1957): 24-28.

Heilbut, Anthony. *The Gospel Sound.* Rev. ed. New York: Limelight Editions, 1984.

Hillsman, Joan R. *Gospel Music.* Washington, D.C.: Middle Atlantic Regional Press, 1990.

Hine, Darlene Clark, ed. *Black Women in America.* Brooklyn: Carlson Publishing, 1993.

Hoke, S. Kay. "American Popular Music." In *Women and Music: A History.* Edited by Karin Pendle. Bloomington: Indiana University Press, 1991.

Jet 14 (September 11, 1958): 60; (October 2, 1958): 64; (October 23, 1958): 59.

Larkin, Colin, ed. *The Guiness Encyclopedia of Popular Music.* 4 vols. London: Guiness Publishing, 1992.

Mapp, Edward. *Directory of Blacks in the Performing Arts.* Metuchen, N.J.: Scarecrow Press, 1990.

Obituary. *The Black Perspective in Music* 10 (Fall 1982): 233.

Reagon, Bernice Johnson, ed. *We'll Understand It Better By and By.* Washington, D.C.: Smithsonian Press, 1992.

Shaw, Arnold. *The World of Soul.* New York: Cowles Book Co., 1970.

Southern, Eileen. *The Music of Black Americans.* 2d ed. New York: Norton, 1983.

Spencer, John Michael. *Protest and Praise.* Minneapolis: Fortress Press, 1990.

Ward, Clara. "How a Visit to the Holy Land Changed My Life." *Color* 11 (May 1956): 15-17.

Williams-Jones, Pearl. "Afro-American Gospel Music: A Crystallization of the Black Aesthetic." *Ethnomusicology* 19 (September 1975): 373-85.

Juanita Karpf

Mary Fitzbutler Waring

Mary Fitzbutler Waring
(c. 1870-?)
Physician, educator, clubwoman, activist, writer

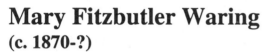

At a time when black female physicians faced tremendous obstacles, Mary Fitzbutler Waring used her medical training to improve the lives of thousands of black people in the United States. Through her leadership in the National Association of Colored Women's Clubs (NACW) from the second decade of the twentieth century through the third, Waring traveled extensively, and her lectures and writings reached a wide audience of black people, supplying them with vitally necessary health-care information. Waring also solicited support for the establishment of health-care training programs that provided opportunities for black women who wished to enter the medical profession. She was active in church, social, educational, and civic work and held important offices in women's clubs at the local, state, and national levels. Her leadership also shepherded the NACW through its most critical period, the depression years. The tireless, selfless work of Waring truly embodied the club motto, "Lifting as We Climb."

Mary Fitzbutler Waring was born in Louisville, Kentucky, around November 1, 1870. (Some sources say she might have been born in Amherstburg, Ontario, Canada.) The date and circumstances of her death are unknown. When she was young her desire to be a doctor was strong: her parents, Sarah and Henry Fitzbutler, were both physicians at a time when few African Americans practiced medicine. Her father founded and ran a hospital in Louisville and Waring assisted him in his practice while she was growing up. She attended public schools in Louisville and then went on to normal school in preparation for a teaching position. She taught for a time but then pursued a degree in medicine, graduating from National Medical College of Chicago in 1923. She met her husband, Frank Waring, an educator from Chicago, Illinois, in Louisville, where they got married. After the wedding, the Warings moved to Chicago.

Becomes Activist and Clubwoman

After first arriving in Chicago, Waring taught in the public school system but she later resigned to practice medicine. It was in Chicago that she began her lifelong career as an activist and clubwoman. Waring organized and was president of the Necessity Club, one of many women's clubs that focused on the needs of the black community. These organizations provided critical support to black citizens. The Phillis Wheatley Club, for example, had branches in cities across the nation and provided charitable services for the needy, often in the form of housing for young girls or day care for their children, social space, and training activities. Waring was a member of the Phillis Wheatley Club and also served as its vice president for a time. Other clubs focused on political activism at the local level.

On March 12, 1906, the Necessity Club became one of fifteen women's clubs in Chicago to form the city federation of Colored Women's Clubs, later to be known as the Chicago and Northern District Association. In November 1911, Waring was selected as an alternate for fellow clubwoman Fannie Barrier Williams to represent the NACW at the National Council of Women's (NCW) Executive Session. The NCW was a predominately white women's organization founded in 1888 by suffragists and temperance workers. This appointment was one of the first of many national roles for Waring.

The eighth biennial convention of the NACW assembled at Hampton Institute in Virginia on July 23, 1912. When the Illinois delegation was called, delegates responded with a state song that Waring had composed—giving yet another example of her talent.

In 1913, Waring was elected to statewide office in the Illinois Federation of Colored Women's Clubs as the corresponding secretary. Although she still remained active in local and state club activities, she was gaining prominence nationally. The next step in Waring's development as a national figure was her appointment as chair of the NACW's Department of Health and Hygiene. Although *Who's Who in Colored America, 1927* lists the beginning of this appointment as 1911, she first appears in *National Notes* bearing the title of department head in November 1913. Waring was to hold this position for the next seventeen years.

The Department of Health and Hygiene played a crucial role in informing the members of the NACW of the health challenges facing the black community. Waring sponsored many programs and training sessions on health at national and regional meetings around the country. In these settings and in her column in *National Notes,* the NACW's official publication, Waring stressed preventive care and sanitation and provided critical information about prevalent diseases and their treatment. At the time of her appointment to office, the country was in the grip of a tuberculosis epidemic that struck down thousands. Tuberculosis was particularly pernicious because, as of 1913 and 1914, there was not yet a cure for the disease. At the November/December national meeting, the NACW passed a resolution supporting the National Tuberculosis movement, making this issue a priority for the organization and for Waring's department.

In August 1914, the NACW passed a resolution calling for the appointment of a "colored woman" to the Board of Commissioners of the Illinois Exposition Celebrating Fifty Years of Freedom of American Negroes. The Illinois state legislature had appropriated twenty-five thousand dollars to commemorate the event, which was to be held the following year. The Illinois federation chose Waring to be its representative and the governor of Illinois subsequently appointed her. In Waring's view, the purpose of the exposition was to illustrate how successfully black men and women had educated themselves and assimilated into American culture. She stated in the April/May 1915 edition of *National Notes:*

> How well the condition was met and how accurately the problem was solved can hardly be realized by even the best people. That the American people may better understand the progress that has been made; that all nations may form a conception of the present development; that, knowing their mental, and financial progress, all people may accord the Negro the respect he deserves.

Waring went on in the article to urge her colleagues to participate actively in amassing "quality" work to display the gains made by the race in business, education, and manufacturing.

Waring's insistence that the Illinois Exposition stress the positive aspects of black life reflects the NACW's central theme of racial uplift. It was the desire of the club movement to dispel the stereotypical image of blacks as lacking intelligence, resources, and culture. By combatting this image as well as creating community-help programs, clubwomen not only improved the quality of life in the black community but also fought racism. The exposition, then, was a marvelous opportunity for the clubwomen to see their goal realized.

Waring was often acknowledged for her fund-raising capabilities as well as her other club work. She had been a longtime financial supporter of *National Notes* and was recognized as such in the May/June 1915 edition. In October 1916, she and another clubwoman, Elizabeth Lindsay Davis, were honored for their role in supporting the Phillis Wheatley Home. And, on Frederick Douglass Memorial Day the following year, she was noted for "sen[ding] out 400 notices and sen[ding] a big sum to the Fund."

Club Work Intensifies

During 1917, Waring's activities at the state and national levels intensified. The year before she had addressed the national convention in Baltimore, Maryland. She was now treasurer of the Illinois federation. She wrote a number of articles on health for *National Notes,* including lengthy pieces on tuberculosis, sanitation, and dentistry. Waring's columns were notable not only for their information but also for their calls to political and social action. In her January 1917 article, "Movement for Extermination of Tuberculosis," she urged clubwomen to

> get busy.... Require physicians to register all cases of tuberculosis, make public provisions for sanitariums camps or hospitals for the proper care for poor patients ... insist upon better regulations and stricter inspection of light, air, heat and sunshine in schools, factories, stores, theatres, and churches.

In 1917 the United States entered World War I. Black women who had been working in the textile, clothing, food, and tobacco industries now began to enter war industries. At the eleventh biennial convention in 1918, the NACW took up the issue of the role of black women in the American war effort. In addition to working for the acceptance and representation of black women in labor unions, the NACW stressed the importance of supporting the efforts of blacks in the armed forces and fighting racism: President Mary B. Talbert also urged the women to help with Red Cross and relief work.

Waring's contribution to this effort was tremendous. During the conference she introduced a petition that called for the inclusion of black Red Cross nurses in the war effort and asked for signatures. Later in the convention, she led a group of Red Cross nurses, in full uniform, into the room to make her idea concrete. Back in Chicago, she organized the first classes for nurse training under the auspices of the National Nurse Training Service and later established Red Cross training and home-care training classes in Saint Louis, Missouri.

Waring's work as an activist led to her appointment as a trustee of the board of the Frederick Douglass Memorial Home in Cedar Hill, Washington, D.C. The preservation of the Douglass estate symbolized the efforts of abolitionists and black organizers to uplift the race.

Compares Race Relations in Europe and U.S.

In 1920, Waring was elected one of three alternates to Mary B. Talbert, president of the NACW, at the September 8-16 meeting of the International Council of Women in Christiana, Norway. Waring was selected as an alternate amidst some controversy; originally Margaret Murray Washington was to be an alternate to Talbert. When Washington could not attend due to illness, the executive board selected Waring. This was done, in part, to allay the concerns of some NACW members that there was a bias towards Washington, D.C., members in selecting representatives of the organization.

On October 5, 1920, Waring reported on the trip in a letter to the *Competitor* from Christiana. She discussed some of the highlights of her trip and how the delegation was treated because of their race. She wrote:

> We have had to be constantly confronted with the accursed American prejudices; for instance, everywhere in Europe all hotels and restaurants; all porters and waiters, have treated the members of the darker race with exactly the same courtesy as other guests, except at a hotel in Paris, known as the American Women's club and managed by the Y.M.C.A. Here the door was closed in our face and we were told that there was room for the other members of the American party, but it would be impossible to entertain colored people. . . .
>
> Now the prejudice of the United State is a disgrace to the country and the Y.M.C.A. should let it be washed out by the broad expanse of water of the Atlantic and not introduce it into their private hostelries of Europe under the false name of the Y.M.C.A. In Norway the women cannot understand this sort of thing and we have been treated with the greatest courtesy everywhere.

Thus, the ugly face of American racism confronted the black women delegates, regardless of their recognition as equals by other nationalities.

During the 1920s Waring continued to write for the *National Notes,* maintained a speaking schedule, and supervised programs for the Department of Health and Hygiene. In a 1920 issue of the *Competitor,* a national black news magazine, she, along with other NACW department heads, wrote of their plans for the upcoming year. Waring encouraged young women to take classes in chemistry and biology to improve their knowledge of dietary health. She also pressed readers to get involved with local health-care agencies to promote information sharing about health care, once again linking health concerns with community and political action. To facilitate this endeavor, Waring offered the services of the Red Cross organizations she had helped get established.

Her fund-raising activities during this time focused on the Frederick Douglass Memorial Home. In 1922 she personally raised nearly three hundred dollars for the restoration of the estate. She was appointed to the Advisory Board of the Frederick Douglass Memorial and Historical Association in 1923.

Later that year, tragedy struck. Waring's husband Frank died in November after a long and painful illness. Frank Waring had been the principal of a high school in Chicago. Like his wife, he had been very involved in community activities, including the Amateur Minstrel Club, which raised money for the Old Folks Home, the Appomattox Club, and the Grand Lodge of the Knights of Pythias.

After her husband's death, Waring continued to travel to other cities, giving talks and demonstrations for the Department of Health and Hygiene. From 1927 to 1930, she wrote several articles for *National Notes* emphasizing the role of education in the fight to prevent disease. In a February 1927 article, she wrote, "Health and Hygiene must have a good part of real study to be effective." She urged women to make use of pamphlets distributed by the U.S. government to find out about such topics as infant care, general health, and common diseases.

Poverty and racism left the black community more susceptible to fatalities from preventable diseases than the white community; blacks simply did not have access to health-care information. Disseminating this information was crucial to the community's survival. Literacy, therefore, was an equally important issue. Waring sponsored health drives, promoted radio shows, and recruited clubwomen to include churches and schools in their efforts to improve community health. She also continued her specific quest to prevent the spread of tuberculosis, which declined as more and more people learned how to avoid it.

Waring married Charles F. Cantrell on August 14, 1930. That year she was elected vice president-at-large of the NACW. The year marked a dramatic shift in her focus and that of the organization, as well as in the direction of the country. The stock market crash and the onset of the Great Depression affected every part of the country, but the black community was devastated. Financial support for the NACW, which had begun to dwindle towards the end of the previous decade, shrank even more as people felt the economic pinch. Moreover, former NACW president Mary McLeod Bethune felt that the NACW's priorities were misplaced and had begun in 1928 to recruit supporters to form a new national organization. By 1930, plans for this group, which was to become the National Council of Negro Women (NCNW), were underway.

During Waring's tenure as vice president, the NACW's internal organization changed from having thirty-eight different departments to two; the National Association of Colored Girls, which was created to attract younger members to the group, and Women in Industry, Mother, Home and Child. Waring's columns now expanded beyond her previous scope of health as she sought to address the needs and goals of the organization. She regularly pointed out the achievements of women in local clubs around the country and called on the women to be strong in trying times. She also urged the clubs to continue their work.

Elected President of the NACW

In 1933, after twenty-seven years of club activity, Waring was elected president of the NACW. The mantle of leadership was passed on to her at a critical moment in the organization's history. The nation was now in the middle of the Great Depression. Nevertheless, Waring and the NACW remained positive. According to *Black Women in America,* edited by Darlene Clark Hine, the discussion at the 1933 convention focused on "traditional women's issues: standardize the home; create a good environment for the child, train girls to be industrious, artistic and gracious; improve working conditions for women and girls, and increase community service." The continued focus on these issues is revealing. It shows a recognition on the part of the clubwomen that black womanhood remained plagued by negative images. Yet it also shows that they were not as flexible as they could have been in examining the needs of the community.

At the same time, however, Waring's columns in *National Notes* as president dealt with the difficulties all blacks faced. She wrote extensively about the horrors of lynching and the injustice of segregation. In March 1934, she urged members to actively support the antilynching measure that was pending in the U.S. Senate and to join efforts to make segregation illegal. She asked readers, "Do you notice that we're doing everyone's work but our own," a charge leveled at the NACW by Bethune. She demanded that women "not be weaklings" and that they help organize for better wages, better living conditions, and better jobs. She also asked repeatedly for much-needed financial assistance for the NACW, reminding the women of their responsibility to support the movement.

Waring was elected to a second term in 1935. At that year's convention, her address focused on the traditional platform of mother, home, and child; women in industry; and the role of the NACW. While imploring the clubwomen to work together to accomplish their goals, she also made a pointed reference to the imminent formation of the NCNW:

> Women, we can do it, if we will do it, we can not do it by fighting, we can not do it by keeping up petty jealousies, we can not do it by traipsing around sowing discord.... Let human unity and honest helpfulness of each other keep out the feeling of strife, envy and hatred. Look with charity on mistakes and not by being overconfident. Remember that sometimes you may have the wrong view. Remember that the organization is bigger than any state or club or woman.

Waring was vehemently opposed to the NCNW and, according to *Black Women in America,* criticized the founders, arguing correctly that it would weaken the national club movement. Nonetheless, Waring was undaunted and fought to keep the NACW intact and growing. In the last year of her presidency, she organized new clubs and federations in three states.

In addition to her untiring efforts with NACW, Waring was a member of the National Medical Association, the Chicago League of Women Voters, the National Republican League of Colored Women, the NAACP, and Delta Sigma Theta Sorority. For her work in health care and in promoting the work of black women, Waring has often been called a humanitarian who was generous with both her time and service.

REFERENCES:

The Competitor, c. October 1920.

Davis, Elizabeth Lindsay. *The Story of the Illinois Federation of Colored Women's Clubs, 1900-1922.* The Federation, 1922.

———. *Lifting as They Climb.* Washington, D.C.: National Association of Colored Women, 1933.

Hine, Darlene Clark, ed. *Black Women in America.* Brooklyn: Carlson Publishers, 1993.

National Notes, April/May 1915; May/June 1915; January 1917.

Salem, Dorothy. *To Better Our World: Black Women in Organized Reform, 1890-1920.* Brooklyn: Carlson Publishing, 1990.

Simms, James [Nelson]. *Blue Book and National Business and Professional Directory.* Chicago: James N. Simms, 1923.

Wesley, Charles Harris. *The History of the National Association of Colored Women's Clubs.* Washington, D.C.: NACW, 1984.

Who's Who in Colored America. New York: Who's Who in Colored America Corporation, 1927.

Who's Who in Colored America, 1928-29. 2d ed. New York: Who's Who in Colored America Corporation, 1929.

Who's Who in Colored America. 3d ed. Brooklyn: Thomas Yenser, 1932.

Nadya J. Lawson

Fanny Smith Washington
(1858-1884)
Housekeeper, educator

Fanny Smith Washington's name is generally found in works on the early history of Tuskegee Institute, both as the first wife of the school's founder, Booker T. Washington, and as the school's housekeeper, who ensured its cleanliness and order. A relatively obscure woman who has been overshadowed by the two more prominent wives of Booker T.

Fanny Smith Washington

Washington, Fanny Smith Washington is nevertheless important for helping her husband begin his work at Tuskegee Institute and for her own contribution to the school's early life. She is also an example of a black woman from a small, rural area in the South who valued education. With meager funds, she managed to begin her college education at the historically black Hampton Institute; when her money ran out, she left school and worked as a teacher, saving money to pay her outstanding account with Hampton and to finance her remaining years there.

While information on Washington is scarce, it is known that she was born Fanny Virginia Norton Smith in Malden, West Virginia, in 1858, the daughter of Samuel Smith, who was part Shawnee, and Celia Smith. As a young woman she attended the local school and attracted the attention of her teacher, Booker T. Washington, who fell in love with her. Booker T. Washington was only two years older than Fanny, but from 1875 to 1878 he was a schoolteacher in Malden, where eighty to ninety students were enrolled in the day program. He gave special attention to his brightest pupils and prepared them to enter Hampton Institute in Hampton, Virginia, where they were known as the "Booker Washington boys." Fanny was the only young woman in the group at the time. Booker T. Washington also began a reading room, or public library, for the community.

Washington arranged to send his brother John and adopted brother James to Hampton. He also helped his sweetheart Fanny get accepted at Hampton and sought some scholarship aid for her from the school. However, Washington and the school's principal, General Samuel Chapman Armstrong, had different views on Hampton's share of the obligation. Responding to a letter from Booker T. Washington dated February 6, 1877, published in the *Booker T. Washington Papers,* Armstrong wrote to Washington on February 12 that John and Fanny came to him as "full pay students" and made no mention of a prior arrangement for a scholarship. Yet Louis Harlan says in *Booker T. Washington* that Fanny did, in fact, receive a scholarship. In any case, Fanny Washington became delinquent in her payments and left the school in 1878 to earn money to pay her existing school bills and to cover her expenses when she returned.

For two years, 1878 to 1880, she lived with her mother to save money and walked three miles to and from a school near Malden where she taught. She struggled to settle her account at Hampton and support her mother as well. By 1880 Fanny Washington was earning $32.50 a month, with most of her salary being used for household expenses. She had made her final payment of $48.00 to Hampton in January of that year, at which time when J. F. B. Marsh placed her on the school's honor roll, a designation for students who left school with delinquent payments but who later paid their bills in full.

According to Harlan in *Booker T. Washington,* "The census taken in 1880 found her at Hampton ready to enter school, a mulatto of twenty-two." Booker T. Washington worked at the school as director of the Indians' dormitory and teacher in the night school. With Fanny back at Hampton, the personal relationship between her and Booker T. developed more fully, and by the end of the school term they were openly courting. In spring of 1881, Booker T. Washington accepted the principalship of a new normal school for blacks in rural Tuskegee, Alabama. That school was the infant Tuskegee Institute. Three days after he opened the school he wrote to Olivia Davidson, a Hampton graduate who had superior academic talent, grace, and maturity, asking her to serve as lady principal. His need for help was immediate; Fanny had another year before graduation and lacked the teaching experience that Davidson had. She also was not as academically talented. Fanny completed her education and graduated from Hampton in June 1882.

Fanny, then twenty-four years old, and Booker T. Washington, twenty-six, married on August 2, 1882, in Rice's Zion Baptist Church in the Tinkersville section of Malden. Booker T. Washington had not yet made his way in the world and brought little financial security to the marriage. Fanny's mother, Celia Smith, had been unenthusiastic about the marriage for this reason and also because Fanny would move so far away from home.

Immediately after their marriage, Fanny and Booker T. Washington moved to Tuskegee, where they shared a big house, the Teachers Home, with four of Tuskegee's teachers. Although this was not the best way to start a marriage, it was a tremendous help to Booker T. Washington. He had a new school, a new bride, a faculty dormitory, and a college housekeeper. By 1883, the Washingtons had increased to eight the number of teachers boarding with them.

On June 6, 1883, Fanny Washington gave birth to Portia Marshall Washington, the first child born on the Tuskegee campus. Completely devoted to her husband and the school, the young mother also organized one of the first home economics classes for women. Fanny Washington was kind, gentle, and apparently well accepted. She also provided important services that both Washington and Tuskegee needed. Her primary task was that of housekeeper, certainly a significant function though not equal to her level of training. Booker T. Washington acknowledged in his *Up from Slavery* that "from the first, my wife most earnestly devoted her thoughts and time to the work of the school, and was completely with me in every interest and ambition."

Fanny Washington died suddenly on May 4, 1884, at age twenty-six and after only twenty-one months of marriage, and was buried in the campus cemetery. The cause of her death was never exactly determined. A local newspaper attributed her death to "consumption of the bowels," yet some family members cited the cause as internal injuries she suffered when she fell from a wagon on campus.

By the time of Fanny's death, the Washingtons had gained some recognition in the community, which was evidenced by the published notices of her death. When Fanny Washington died, *Simms' Blue Book* published Booker T. Washington's summary of her contributions:

> Perhaps the way in which Fanny was able to impress her life upon others most was in her extreme neatness in her housekeeping and general work. Nothing was done loosely or carelessly. In this respect, she taught our students many valuable lessons. Her heart was set on making her home an object lesson [for] those about her, who were so much in need of such help.

Fanny Washington's life was obscured by that of Olivia Davidson, who would become Booker T. Washington's second wife, and Margaret Murray Washington, who would become his third. Each wife occupied her own place in history and in the life and work of the school. But it was Fanny Norton Smith Washington who was at Tuskegee from its beginning and helped her husband and the school in its initial critical years, although she died before the school had established its later prominence.

REFERENCES:

Bennett, Lerone. "The Three Wives of Booker T. Washington." *Ebony* 37 (September 1982): 29-31.

Harlan, Louis R. *Booker T. Washington: The Making of a Black Leader, 1856-1901.* New York: Oxford University Press, 1972.

Harlan, Louis R., ed. *The Booker T. Washington Papers.* Vol. 2. Urbana: University of Illinois, 1972.

Hunter, Wilma King. "Three Women at Tuskegee, 1882-1925: The Wives of Booker T. Washington." *Journal of Ethnic Studies* 3 (September 1976): 76-89.

Simms, James Nelson. *Simms' Blue Book and National Negro Business and Professional Directory.* Chicago: James N. Simms, 1923.

Washington, Booker T. *The Story of My Life and Work.* Naperville, Ill.: J. L. Nichols and Co., 1900.

————. *Up from Slavery.* New York: Doubleday, Page and Co., 1905.

Daniel T. Williams

Ora Washington
(1898-1971)
Tennis player, basketball player

Ora Washington was one of America's most outstanding black female athletes. She is famous for her accomplishments in both tennis and basketball. Her greatness of performance and longevity in tennis has led some to compare her early achievements to those of Althea Gibson, one of the greatest tennis players of her time. During her career, Washington played throughout the northeastern and midwestern United States, including Massachusetts, New York, Maryland, Pennsylvania, Ohio, Illinois, and Indiana. Among her competitors were Lula Ballard, Catherine Jones, Lillian Hines, Emma Leonard, Frances Giddens, Flora Lomax, and Isadore Channels. According to Marianna Davis in *Contributions of Black Women to America,* Ora Washington "earned lasting recognition as one of the greatest pioneering inspirations for Black women athletes."

Washington began playing tennis when, according to Wally Jones and Jim Washington in *Black Champions Challenge American Sports,* she was urged on to this endeavor by "a YWCA instructor in Germantown, Pennsylvania, who attempted to relieve Ora's grief over the death of a sister by suggesting she take to some sport." Washington's gift for tennis was soon obvious. The first African American National Tennis Tournament was held in Baltimore, Maryland, in 1917, and it was at Baltimore's Druid Hill Park in 1924 that Washington won her first national championship, when she defeated Dorothy Radcliffe. For the next twelve years, Washington was undefeated among players of the American Tennis Association (ATA) and the African American National Tennis Organization, founded in 1916. She won her first women's singles trophy when she defeated Lula Ballard, a teacher from Cleveland, Ohio; Ballard later defeated Washington in 1936, when Washington suffered a sunstroke and her twelve-year reign as champion came to an end.

During her twelve years as champion, Washington excelled in both individual and team tennis. She held the ATA singles title from 1929 through 1935, but lost it to Ballard in 1936. In 1937, she regained her championship title with her defeat of Catherine Jones. Washington also gave outstanding

Ora Washington (second from right) and the other finalists of the 1947 American Tennis Association Women's Doubles Championship.

performances in the women's doubles championships from 1930 through 1936. For a total of eight years, seven consecutively, Washington held the ATA singles championship. She was also a member of the championship ATA women's doubles team for seven years in a row.

Washington's tennis career and her public acclaim were marked by segregation. Parallel to her twelve-year career of unprecedented championship in the ATA was the career of Helen Wills Moody, a player in the United States Lawn Tennis Association. Moody, who was white, held her championship for seven years, but because of segregation and personal preference, refused to meet Washington's desire to play a match to determine America's best in women's singles. According to Jones and Washington, in 1962 Malcolm Poindexter said, "If history were able to repeat itself and the tennis world could have seen fit to drop its racial behavior 40 years ago, Philadelphia would probably have the distinction of honoring Miss Ora Washington as the holder of the national women's singles title and the woman who held it longer than any other in American history."

Washington's tennis style is generally qualified by references to her speed and particularities of tennis play for her era.

According to Arthur R. Ashe, Jr.'s *A Hard Road to Glory,* Washington's approach was unorthodox: "She held the racket halfway up the handle and seldom took a full swing. But no woman had her foot speed, which she honed while playing basketball for the *Philadelphia Tribune* team. She was clearly the first black female to dominate a sport." In addition to this, Washington's style was characterized by a form of play developed by such African American tennis pioneers as Edgar Brown and James Stocks. A. S. Young in *Negro Firsts in Sports* quotes Poindexter, stating:

> She had the strategy and was dynamic to watch . . . and her overhead game was terrific. She played an entirely different style—using mostly forehand, backhand drive, and slice. . . . Ora had a dependable service—she seldom waited to get the first ball in play. She had moderate speed and her court game was a bit outmoded.

Washington did not believe in warm-ups; Young reports her explanation: "I'd rather play from scratch and warm up as I went along." Ashe cites the *Chicago Defender* of March 14, 1931, as stating, "Ora Washington, now of Chicago, again holds her position as national champion, having gone through the season without a defeat. We don't even recall her losing a set. . . . Her superiority is so evident that her competitors are frequently beaten before the first ball crosses the net.'' Ashe places Washington first among five different ATA winners between 1917 and 1937, ''the first twenty years of the ATA's history.''

Washington's retirement as an active tennis player in the ATA occurred twice. Jones and Washington cite Malcolm Poindexter's note that the first occasion of Washington's retiring ended in response to a challenge from Flora Lomax of Detroit, who upon winning the women's singles title, publicly ''expressed her great anger over Miss Washington's refusal to defend her title again.'' Washington defeated Lomax in the challenge match. Her final retirement was a decision to resign and yield to the spirit of younger competitors. *Sepia* magazine describes this as a decision based on a tennis official's complaint ''that her continued presence in the sport 'killed the spirit of young hopefuls who shied away from tennis rather than meet her.'''

Basketball Career Launched

For many years Washington was an outstanding basketball player. She was the star center for the *Philadelphia Tribune* girls squad for eighteen years and for a while was top scorer. She played as well for the Germantown Hornets, where she was also top scorer. The Philadelphia girls team was begun in 1931, sponsored by its namesake, a prominent black newspaper. Ashe describes the era's playing style as ''the typical six players per team style which had separate threesomes for offense and defense at opposite ends of the court.'' Among Washington's teammates were Marie Leach, Sarah Latimore, Gladys Walker, Lavinia Moore, Virginia Woods, Rose Wilson, Myrtle Wilson, and Florence Campbell. Throughout the thirties, Washington and her teammates were champions, losing only six games to the opposing teams. For part of this period, they traveled, presenting clinics and demonstrations. Ashe called them ''black America's first premier female sports team.'' Washington was captain of the team. In *The Negro in Sports,* Edwin Bancroft Henderson states,

> Each year the team traveled thousands of miles in playing a schedule with the best colored and white teams. They played the boys' game. In February and March of 1938, they made a three thousand mile tour of the South covering nearly a dozen states. In the nine years of activity, they made an outstanding record of having lost only six games to colored teams that played boys' rules.

In the 1929-30 season, while with the Germantown Hornets, Washington served as team captain with Joseph Rainey as coach, and the Hornets defeated Inez Patterson's Philadelphia Quick Steppers.

Ora Washington, although an outstanding basketball player and team captain, is most famous for her skill as a great tennis player. According to A. S. Young, she states, ''Courage and determination were the biggest assets I had.'' She is described as a powerful woman, for both her physical stamina and her athletic accomplishment. In another testament to her fame and honor, Jones and Washington state: ''No one who ever saw her play could forget her, nor could anyone who ever met her. She was a quiet person, gracious, yet a fierce competitor on the tennis court.''

In 1961, thirty-seven years after she began her tennis career, she was described in *Sepia* as being ''as slender and attractive'' as she was during her career as a champion. At that time she was not only the owner of an apartment building purchased with earnings from work in domestic service, but more importantly, she was enthusiastically performing community service by conducting free training and coaching for youngsters at the community's tennis courts in Germantown. In her career in tennis and basketball, she won two hundred and one trophies. Washington's athletic stature marks her as one of black America's treasures.

REFERENCES:

Ashe, Arthur R., Jr. *A Hard Road to Glory: A History of the African-American Athlete 1919-1945.* New York: Warner Books, 1988.

Davis, Marianna W., ed. *Contributions of Black Women to America.* Vol. 1. Columbia, S.C.: Kenday Press, 1982.

''Women in Sports.'' *Ebony* 32 (August 1977): 62.

Henderson, Edwin Bancroft. *The Negro in Sports.* Washington, D.C.: Associated Publishers, 1949.

Jones, Wally, and Jim Washington. *Black Champions Challenge American Sports.* New York: David McKay, 1972.

''*Sepia* Salutes.'' *Sepia* 9 (August 1961): 51.

Young, A. S. *Negro Firsts in Sports.* Chicago: Johnson Publishing Company, 1963.

Laura C. Jarmon

Maxine Waters
(1938-)
Politician

Feisty, articulate, passionate—these are words used to describe politician Maxine Waters, a former member of the California State Assembly and a legislator in the United States House of Representatives. Growing up poor, Waters learned as a child to work hard and strive for success in all of her endeavors. A high school classmate predicted a bright

Maxine Waters

political future for Maxine Waters, whose leadership skills were apparent at an early age. Ron Harris noted in *Essence* magazine, March 1984: "If Maxine Waters maneuvers as easily among the makers and shapers of public policy on Capitol Hill as she does among the welfare mothers, blue-collar workers and street toughs in Watts [suburb of Los Angeles], it's because she knows, firsthand, what it's like at both ends of the spectrum."

Maxine Moore Waters was born in St. Louis, Missouri, on August 15, 1938, to Remus Moore and Velma Lee Carr Moore, who divorced when Maxine was two years old. The fifth of thirteen children (Maxine's mother remarried), Waters grew up determined to make her mark in the world. A conscientious student, she also participated in extracurricular activities such as musicals, track, and swimming. At thirteen, she secured her first job as a busgirl at a segregated restaurant.

After graduating from high school in 1956, Waters married her childhood sweetheart, Edward Waters. They had two children, first a boy, Edward, and then two years later a girl, Karen. While married and living in St. Louis, Maxine Waters worked in factories. After a stint in the armed services, Edward Waters also obtained factory work. In 1961 the couple decided to move to Los Angeles, where Maxine found work in a garment factory and later at the Pacific Telephone Company as an operator. After suffering a miscarriage in the mid-1960s, she had to quit her job at the telephone company. In the aftermath of the 1965 Watts riots, she took a job as an assistant teacher in the newly created Head Start program, a nationwide project sponsored by the federal government that

was designed to give children from poor families a more advantageous start in school and life.

Velma Lee Moore, Maxine Waters's mother, had a keen interest in local politics; she worked at the polls and contacted officials for help. Her daughter, who inherited this interest, would later break new ground in California and national political circles. Just as Maxine Waters was often selected spokesperson for her high school class, she also became the voice for frustrated parents whose children attended the Head Start program. She recalled in *Essence* magazine her efforts to encourage parents to make federal budget requests, to contact legislators and agencies for increased funding, and to lobby for Head Start program components tailored for their community. She said, "I was really teaching parents how to grab control, and the project directors didn't like it. . . . They began to see the parents as a threat."

Waters's concern for the parents' rights led her to become involved with local elections, leading to a position as chief deputy to city council member David Cunningham from 1973 to 1976. She also campaigned for Wilson Riles, superintendent of instruction for the California school system, U.S. Senator Alan Cranston, Los Angeles Mayor Tom Bradley, and city council members David Cunningham and Robert Farrell.

In 1968, while working at Head Start, Waters decided to attend college. Three and a half years later, in 1972, she graduated from California State University at Los Angeles with a degree in sociology. That year she also divorced Edward Waters.

Heads To the California State Assembly

Sidney Williams, a Mercedes-Benz salesman in Los Angeles and a former Cleveland Browns football player, wooed Maxine Waters for five years before they wed in 1977. He supported her candidacy for the California State Assembly in 1976 after she quit her job to run for election. She was elected and served in the state assembly for fourteen years. She kept a small apartment in Sacramento, where she stayed during the week, and returned home on weekends to attend functions and to meet with constituents. Her husband has no problem with his wife being in the limelight. Sidney Williams told Aldore Collier in a January 1991 interview for *Ebony*, "I have my career and she has hers. . . . I'm an ex-professional football player. So all the accolades she's getting right now I've gone through. So it's not a big deal. It's her time to be the shining light. I admire her for that. She has worked very hard to be in the position that she's in right now. I enjoy every minute of it that she's happy."

During her tenure in the state assembly, Maxine Waters became the chairperson of the Ways and Means Subcommittee of State Administration. She was the first woman to serve on the Joint Legislative Budget Committee, the Judiciary Committee, the Elections Reapportionment and Constitutional Amendments Committee, the Natural Resources Committee, the Joint Committee of Legislative Ethics, and the California Commission on Status of Women.

Concerning her interaction with the other eleven women in the assembly in 1984, Waters in a January 1984 *Ms.* magazine article noted their reluctance to caucus to discuss political issues:

> I tend to relate to people around issues. For the most part, women legislators are afraid to be called a caucus of women. They meet informally, at dinner or whatever. I don't go any more. They don't talk about issues or politics or strategizing. And I don't know a lot else to talk about. My children are grown. I don't redecorate my house every year.

This attractive, self-assured woman boldly confronted the male-dominated system in the assembly. She made her presence known on often controversial issues with her knowledge and self-confidence, and, in order to underscore her demand to be heard, she would power-dress in red suits and beautiful jewelry.

While serving as a member of the Select Committee of Assistance to Victims of Sexual Assault, Waters sponsored legislation to prohibit policemen from conducting strip searches and body-cavity searches of persons arrested for misdemeanors. Her membership on the Joint Committee on Public Pension Fund Investments also led to groundbreaking legislation. She lobbied for eight years and submitted a bill to the assembly six times before getting it passed. This landmark law required California to divest state pension funds from firms doing business in South Africa. She also worked tirelessly to get other United States companies to get out of South Africa.

As she became known as the conscience of the California legislature, Waters was also evolving into a powerhouse in the state Democratic party. In 1981, she was influential in garnering the speakership position for Willie Brown, Jr. A close friend and ally in the assembly, Brown, in turn, supported her successful bid to become the majority whip. She thus became the first woman in the state to be elected chair of the Democratic Caucus, ranked number four on the leadership team.

One of Maxine Waters's primary concerns was women's rights, an issue often not given much consideration at the state assembly. To involve more women in Los Angeles in this issue, she, along with Ethel Bradley (wife of Los Angeles's Mayor Bradley) and publisher Ruth Washington, formed the Black Women's Forum, which now numbers over one thousand women. This organization sponsors lectures and strives to motivate women to develop their own lists of important concerns. On a national level, Waters joined Dorothy Height, Coretta Scott King, Eleanor Holmes Norton, Barbara Rose Collins, Cardiss Collins, Antoinette Ford, Willie Barrow, Gloria Lawlor, Barbara Williams Skinner, Leslie Baskerville, and Gloria E. A. Toote in founding the National Political Congress of Black Women in 1984. The *Washington Informer* of September 30, 1992, noted the primary mission of this

nonpartisan, nonprofit organization: "to promote and encourage the participation of Black women in the political process to gain the social, educational and economic empowerment needed to enhance the quality of life for Black women, their families and community."

Waters's commitment to job training for her constituents has been demonstrated through her efforts to build the Maxine Waters Employment Preparation Center, an extension of the Watts Skills Center, founded in 1966. The center was renamed by the Los Angeles Unified School District Board of Education in 1989. At the center, approximately 2200 students and young adults receive training lasting from three to six months in vocational occupations such as computer technology, bank telling, nursing, welding, telecommunications, electronic assembly, and auto and diesel mechanics.

Waters also created Project Build, a program to provide much-needed information regarding child care, health, and day care, as well as educational and job-training services to families in six Los Angeles housing projects.

Among other acts of legislation she sponsored were the first child abuse prevention training program and the nation's first plant closure law. Waters also supported an environmental protection bill, a bill that would provide assistance to victims of sexual assault, and the *State Contracts Registry.*

Waters was a state delegate to the 1972, 1976, 1980, 1984, 1988, and 1992 National Democratic conventions. In 1984 and 1988 she served as a key advisor to Jesse Jackson in his campaign for the presidency. As co-chairperson of the board for the Center for National Policy, she advised congressmembers and senators regarding key issues. She also served on the Rules Committee.

Waters Becomes U.S. Representative

After fourteen years in the California State Assembly, Waters ran for the seat vacated by retiring congressman Augustus Hawkins in the Twenty-ninth Congressional District of California. Although her opponent in the June 1990 primary was endorsed by the Democratic machine, Waters soundly defeated him, garnering 88 percent of the vote. She also won the general election handily, with 37,396 votes, or 80 percent of the votes cast.

In a January 1991 article in *Ebony* magazine, Waters made the following remarks concerning her joining Cardiss Collins of Chicago, then the lone black female representative in Congress:

> The women of this country, the Black women,... have wanted very much to increase their numbers. So I think our voices are going to be extremely important, not only to articulate the aspirations of Black women, but to add our voices to the voices of Black men.

In 1992, running in the much larger Thirty-fifth Congressional District, Waters accrued 98,338 votes, or 83 percent of the votes cast, to win reelection for a second term. Ranked as one of the most liberal members of Congress, she serves on the Banking, Finance and Urban Affairs Committee, the Small Business Committee, and the Veterans' Affairs Committee. During a 1992 meeting, Waters demonstrated her vigilance in regard to job opportunities for minorities when she chided Congressman Sonny Montgomery, the chair of the House Veterans' Affairs Committee, for not having a single minority staff person on his committee.

Waters is a member of the Congressional Black Caucus, the Congressional Caucus for Women's Issues, the Democratic Study Group, the Congressional Human Rights Caucus, and the Congressional Arts Caucus. She also is an associate member of the Congressional Hispanic Caucus. In addition to her congressional responsibilities, Waters still actively involves herself in California politics, where her constituency is predominately African American and Latino American. Her congressional district includes South Central Los Angeles, Inglewood, Hawthorne, and Gardena.

Waters's district office burned in the Los Angeles riots that broke out in 1992 after four white policemen were found innocent of using unnecessary force in the beating of black motorist Rodney King. Waters invited herself to a meeting at the White House where President George Bush and top advisors were consulting about how to aid the city. Since the primary people involved were Congressman Waters's constituents, she felt obligated to offer concrete suggestions to improve the quality of life not just in South Central Los Angeles, but in urban communities across the nation. She was also instrumental in preventing riots after a second criminal trial of the four policemen, this time in federal court, in which two of the officers were given thirty-month sentences.

Although Waters has a very hectic schedule, she finds time to relax by reading, playing tennis, swimming, and enjoying her two grandchildren. She also loves to shop for antiques and add to her large collection of black dolls.

This able politician lends her support to diverse corporate and private organizations, including the National Women's Political Caucus, the Elizabeth Jackson Carter Foundation of Spelman College, the National Minority AIDS Project, and the National Council of Negro Women. She is also a member of the National Select Committee on Education for Black Youth, the National Steering Committee for the Center for the Study of Youth Policy, and the National Commission for Economic Conversion and Disarmament. She was one of the founders of the TransAfrica Foundation. She serves on the board of *Essence* magazine and is a board member of the Overseas Education Fund of the League of Women Voters, which provides Third World women with financial support.

Maxine Waters has received honorary doctorates from Spelman College, North Carolina Agricultural and Technical State University, and Morgan State University. Earl S. Richardson, president of Morgan State, issued a citation in 1992 in which he praised her for "her inspired and inspiring leadership, for her commitment to justice at home and abroad, and for her fine example."

Maxine Waters is deeply committed to the concerns of the American people. She offered justification for her forthright manner as a legislator in a speech she made to second the nomination of Bill Clinton at the 1992 Democratic National Convention, quoted in the *Los Angeles Sentinel:*

> I'm a member of the House of Representatives of the U.S. Congress and I take my job seriously. I'm not known as one who vacillates, or hesitates. I know what I'm doing and I know why I'm doing it.

REFERENCES:

Beyette, Beverly. "Maxine Waters." *Ms.* 12 (January 1984): 42-46.

Collier, Aldore. "Maxine Waters Elected to Fill the Seat of Augustus Hawkins." *Ebony* 46 (January 1991): 105, 108.

———. "Maxine Waters: Telling It Like It Is in L.A." *Ebony* 47 (October 1992): 35-36.

Congressional Quarterly 49 (January 12, 1991): 91.

Dowd, Maureen. "Fresh Faces for an Old Struggle." *Time* 122 (August 22, 1983): 31.

Grier, Roosevelt. *Rosey Grier's All-American Heroes: Multicultural Success Stories.* New York: MasterMedia Limited, 1993.

Harris, Ron. "Maxine Waters: The Most Powerful Woman in Politics." *Essence* 14 (March 1984): 79-80.

Hine, Darlene Clark, ed. *Black Women in America.* Brooklyn: Carlson Publishing, 1993.

Los Angeles Sentinel, July 30, 1992; October 29, 1992.

Los Angeles Times, November 7, 1990; November 5, 1992.

Malveaux, Julianne. "Maxine Waters: Woman of the House." *Essence* 21 (November 1990): 55-56, 116-17.

Marshall, Marilyn. "Maxine Waters: America's Most Influential Black Woman Politician." *Ebony* 39 (August 1984): 56.

"Maxine Waters Rips Vet Committee Chief for Lack of Black Staffers." *Jet* 79 (October 22, 1990): 38.

National Journal 24 (January 18, 1992): 134, 136, 143.

Sweet, Ellen. "Women to Watch in the 80's." *Ms.* 12 (January 1984): 42-46.

Washington Informer, September 30, 1992.

Who's Who in American Politics, 1991-92. 13th ed. Vol. 1. New Providence, N.J.: Bowker, 1991.

Who's Who of American Women, 1993-94. 18th ed. New Providence, N.J.: Reed Reference, 1993.

Women in Public Office. Metuchen, N.J.: Scarecrow Press, 1978.

Zia, Helen. "The King Verdict: Making Sense of It." *Ms.* 3 (July/August 1992): 41-43.

Jacqueline Brice-Finch

Watkins, Gloria Jean
See Hooks, Bell

Barbara Watson
(1918-1983)
Ambassador, state department official, lawyer, entrepreneur

A career diplomat, Barbara Watson rose from the position of special assistant to a deputy undersecretary of state to that of director of the Bureau of Security and Consular Affairs, Department of State, in only two years. After serving in the latter position for six years (1968-1974), she resigned. In 1977, President Jimmy Carter named Watson assistant secretary for consular affairs with the rank of assistant secretary of state. With this presidential appointment, Watson became the first black and first woman to achieve this diplomatic rank. She ended her diplomatic career as ambassador to Malaysia after retiring from federal service in 1981.

Barbara Mae Watson, born November 5, 1918, in New York City, was the oldest of four children born to James S. and Violet Lopez Watson. Although Watson's mother came from a prestigious family whose wealth had been accrued in real estate and retail operations, her father studied law while working as a New York bellhop. As parents, James and Violet were determined to teach their children the substantial benefits of being well-mannered and well-read, and they exposed them to black role models whose success was proof of their lessons. Family conferences were held each Wednesday night in the library of their fifteen-room greystone townhouse on 120th Street, Harlem's "Millionaire's Row," to which prominent blacks were regularly invited. Among the visitors were Kwame Nkrumah and Nnamdi Azikiwe, later presidents of Ghana and Nigeria respectively, and writer and poet James Weldon Johnson. The four children were expected to hold their own in family discussions with these important and successful individuals. These weekly meetings not only served to cultivate the children's moral and aesthetic values, but also to foster independent thinking, a thirst for higher knowledge, and the drive to excel.

Barbara Watson's parents held high standards of conduct, which they ingrained in their four children. According to *The Annual Obituary 1983,* her mother, Violet Lopez Watson, always reminded her children, "[You are] not on this planet just to take up space. You must justify your existence." Her father, James S. Watson, the first black New York municipal court judge, constantly admonished Watson and her three siblings to "look to the world" and not limit their vision. Watson's wealthy Jamaican-born parents expected their children to excel, believing that "honor through distinction" was the norm by which their achievements should be measured. At her death on February 17, 1983, Watson was described in *The Annual Obituary* as a distinguished public servant. Barbara Watson's life work clearly met her parents' expectations, for she did indeed justify her existence and look to the world.

Barbara Watson

All the Watson children were achievers. Arna Bontemps's *We Have Tomorrow* includes a biographical sketch of Watson's brother Douglas, an aeronautical engineer. A prize-winning student at New York University's Guggenheim School of Engineering, Douglas ranked third among graduating engineering students. Despite his outstanding academic achievements, he was the only student still jobless before graduation. With the help of former teachers who were respected in the burgeoning field of aeronautics, Douglas was finally hired by the president of a young, upcoming company. His expertise was important to the design of a revolutionary military aircraft that won an Army contract, and his involvement in the project launched him on a brilliant career in engineering.

Watson's other brother, James Lopez, followed their father in the field of law. He served a nine-year term as New York state senator from the Twenty-first District and a three-year term as a New York City civil court judge. From there, he went on to become a U.S. customs judge for the Court of International Trade. Barbara Watson's sister, Grace, shared a home with her, and also worked on Capitol Hill in close proximity to her. The sisters closely resembled one another. Grace, in particular, was frequently mistaken for her sister, so she always had to be careful not to unintentionally offend someone with whom her sister had a working relationship. Grace was an attorney who served as director of volunteers for the Department of Health, Education and Welfare's Bureau of Educational Personnel Development and later as chief of the New Careers and Education Program in the Department of Education.

Watson Prepares for Public Service

After graduating from Hunter College elementary and high schools, Watson attended Barnard College in New York City. She graduated in 1943 with a bachelor of arts degree. She immediately enrolled in law school at St. John's University but withdrew after a short time because she was bored and didn't feel challenged. Before entering into a three-year stint with the United Seaman's Service of New York, Watson worked as a music research assistant with the National Youth Administration, as a clerk with the New York State Unemployment Insurance Office, and as a clerk and interviewer for the New York State Employment Office. During World War II, she made broadcasts in French and English for the Office of War Information and produced a weekly half-hour show for radio station WNYC in New York City.

In 1946 Watson made a career move that met her need to be challenged on both personal and professional levels. Ever the visionary, she foresaw a trend in marketing strategies for consumer products that would place more emphasis on the black market. As a result, she opened a charm school and modeling agency to recruit young black women for fashion and photographic assignments. Edward Brandford, a commercial artist, was Watson's partner. Their models were some of the first women to appear in magazine advertisements that featured blacks. After assuming full ownership of the firms, Watson renamed them Barbara Watson Models and Barbara Watson Charm and Model School. Before closing the agencies in 1956, Watson worked for the New York State Democratic Committee as assistant director of research. In this position she assisted organizations and political candidates needing information and materials; she also lectured women's groups on campaign issues.

In 1958 Watson assumed dual positions as coordinator of student activities and foreign student advisor at Hampton Institute (now Hampton University) in Virginia. Hampton presented no more of a challenge to Watson than any of her former positions. She soon found herself ready to resume law studies and entered New York Law School, from which she graduated third in her class in 1962 at the age of forty-four. She then began a four-year stint in city government, first as attorney and statutory aide for the New York City Board of Statutory Consolidation and then as assistant attorney in the office of the Corporation Counsel of the City of New York— Opinions and Legislation Division and Appeals Division. After this, she served as executive director of the New York City Commission to the United Nations, the official liaison agency between the city and its United Nations personnel and diplomatic representatives. As the mayor's representative, Watson monitored the provision of a wide range of services to permanent missions at the United Nations. The critical job of alleviating problems arising between visiting diplomats and the city required great tact and diplomacy.

Diplomatic Career Training and Advancement

Only four years after graduating from New York Law School, Watson was invited to the State Department to explore employment options. This initial talk was followed by a more formal interview with Secretary of State Dean Rusk. In 1966 Watson began her State Department career as special assistant to the deputy undersecretary of state for administration, William Crockett. Later that year, President Lyndon Johnson appointed her to the Bureau of Security and Consular Affairs as deputy administrator for a seven month period, and then as acting administrator for sixteen months. In August 1968, Watson became director of the bureau and served in that position until December 1974. When asked why she accepted this difficult post, she replied in *Ebony,* June 1968: "Because I viewed it as a challenge, not only for me personally, but for my race and my sex. I'm only a symbol of what can be accomplished. Now we move on to greater things."

As the director of the Bureau of Security and Consular Affairs, Watson monitored the implementation of laws and policies relating to visas, passports, and nationality status and supervised the protection of U.S. citizens living and working abroad. While administering a sixty-million-dollar annual budget, she was responsible for 3,000 employees in the United States and 250 Foreign Service posts abroad. Learning how to address potential crises abroad was not the first agenda item for Watson; she would first deal with problems at home. As chief of Security and Consular Affairs, Watson frequently interacted with the head of the U.S. Passport Office, who at the time was Frances Knight, a woman who had held the position for thirteen years with the backing of powerful conservatives. The two women held decidedly different positions about alien status and passport procedures. Because of Frances Knight's specific rules about what personnel were eligible to process passport applications, American citizens were regularly inconvenienced. Watson finally prevailed by authorizing post offices to accept passport applications; the new procedure saved time and did not cause any increase in fraud. This is only one example of how Watson strived for efficiency in a bureaucracy known for its task duplication and constant tension among staff members. She was later able to say in the June 1968 issue of *Ebony:* "Organization and tranquillity now reign—much to everyone's astonishment."

Efficiency has its drawbacks, and Watson, like many other capable administrators, always had detractors. Her enemies could not attack her competency, so they offered her ambassadorships in the Caribbean and South Pacific, in Central America and sub-Saharan Africa, in the hope that these posts would entice her to leave her job. However, what they could not accomplish, a Republican president could, and in 1974 her pro-forma end of term resignation was accepted. Although the resignation had been tendered in 1972, it was not accepted until Richard Nixon had left office and Gerald Ford had assumed the presidency, despite formal complaints by the Congressional Black Caucus and the NAACP. During the next two years, Watson worked as an attorney in private practice and served as a legal consultant and college lecturer.

Jimmy Carter assumed the presidency of the United States of America in 1976, and one year later he appointed Watson assistant secretary of state for consular affairs with the rank of assistant secretary of state. She then became the first black and first woman to achieve this diplomatic rank. The scope and tenor of Watson's duties were largely the same as she had performed as director of security and consular affairs because the rank of director is at nearly the same level as that of an assistant secretary of state. Watson now had the title and the "perks" to compensate for the work she had done as director, much of which was refining the duties of that position. She had already proven herself as a highly capable and efficient administrator, and now she had her reward. Watson held this position until 1980 when she was named ambassador to Malaysia. As the ranking American official in Malaysia, Watson was responsible for all U.S. mission operations and was also chair of the American Business Council. She retired in 1981 when Ronald Reagan became president.

Retirement simply afforded Watson more opportunities to benefit a wider array of constituents. She maintained close ties with the State Department as a consultant and worked with two District of Columbia law firms as international law counsel and senior associate in charge of international business development. At the time of her death, Watson was ready to assume new duties with the State Department as a member of the Special Selection Board, the body responsible for reviewing the qualifications of Foreign Service officers.

Watson's professional and civic affiliations were numerous. She sat on the Women's Advisory Board of the Office of Economic Opportunity and the board of directors of the Wolf Trap Foundation for Performing Arts. She held memberships in a number of other organizations such as the Museum of African Art (Washington, D.C.), the Greater Washington Educational Telecommunications Association, the American Bar Association, the New York County Lawyer's Association, the International Women Lawyer's Association, the American Foreign Service Association, the Harlem Lawyer's Association, and the Urban League Guild. She served as a board member of Fordham University, Barnard College, Georgetown University School of Foreign Service and Center for Strategic and International Studies, the World Trade Institute, United Mutual Life Insurance Company, and the Girl Scouts of America. She was also an honorary member of Delta Sigma Theta Sorority.

Watson received many honors and awards, including the Hadassah Myrtle Wreath Achievement Award (1968), American Caribbean Scholarship Fund Award (1969), and United Seaman Service Award (1970). In 1971 she received the Award of Merit from the International Aviation Club, the National Council of Negro Women's Distinguished Service Award, and a Certificate of Recognition from the Washington Urban League; also in 1971 she was named Woman of the Year by the Deliverance Evangelistic Center. In 1973 she was decorated as a commander in the National Order of the Ivory Coast Republic. Watson received an honorary doctor of laws degree from the University of Maryland and an honorary doctor of humane letters degree from Mount Saint Mary College in New York.

Despite her formidable talents and high-pressure jobs, Barbara Watson was usually seen displaying a dazzling smile. A proud and stately woman, she was always well groomed and tastefully dressed. Her success as a diplomat was based largely on her capabilities as a political problem-solver and

efficiency expert. According to *The Annual Obituary 1983,* Watson once told an interviewer: "Life is a compromise. The important thing is not to be so stubborn you don't give an inch. The minute you become rigid, you lose your effectiveness. But if you bend too much, you lose your bargaining power."

REFERENCES:

"Barbara M. Watson Is Dead; Former U.S. Diplomat Was 64." *New York Times,* February 18, 1983.

Bontemps, Arna. *We Have Tomorrow.* Boston: Houghton Mifflin, 1945.

Booker, Simeon. "Washington Notebook." *Ebony* 29 (September 1974): 28.

"Cool Headed Lady of the 'Crisis Bureau.'" *Ebony* 23 (June 1968): 56-62.

Devine, Elizabeth, ed. *The Annual Obituary 1983.* Chicago: St. James Press, 1984.

The Ebony Success Library. 2 vols. Nashville: Southwestern Co., 1973.

Gilliam, Annette. "Essence Woman: Barbara Watson." *Essence* 3 (October 1972): 8.

Poinsett, Alex. "Women in Government: A Slim Past, but a Strong Future." *Ebony* 32 (August 1977): 94.

Schoener, Allon, ed. *Harlem on My Mind—Cultural Capital of Black America: 1900-1968.* New York: Random House, 1968.

Smith, Jessie Carney, ed. *Black Firsts: 2000 Years of Extraordinary Achievement.* Detroit: Gale Research, 1994.

Who's Who among Black Americans, 1990-91. 6th edition. Detroit: Gale Research, 1991.

COLLECTIONS:

The Barbara Watson Papers, including biographical materials, are in the Schomburg Center for Research in Black Culture, New York City.

Dolores Nicholson

Joann Watson
(1951-)
Organization executive, social activist, writer, radio producer and host, educator, social worker

Joann Watson is a highly visible black woman in the community of Detroit, Michigan. Her commitment to civil rights, women's issues, youth, and economic development, among other concerns, is well documented by her work experience as well as by her countless volunteer activities, which consume a great deal of her time. Currently, Watson is executive director of the Detroit branch of the NAACP, and

Joann Watson

she is very involved in Detroit's Human Rights Commission and the Coalition of Labor Union Women, among other groups. She has also contributed much to the YWCA, both at the local and national level. Although her career was unplanned, Watson values it highly and has successfully balanced work, volunteer activities, and family.

Born April 19, 1951, in Detroit, Michigan, Joann Watson is the daughter of Jefferson Nichols, Sr. and Lestine Kent Nichols and the oldest of ten children. Jefferson Nichols retired from his position with the city of Detroit in 1988 but continued to work as a master gardener and automobile mechanic. In an October 27, 1994, interview, Watson praised her father for his influence on her life. She called him a "doting father" and "supreme protector," a community servant, and a devoted churchman. "The church loved him," she said. Watson called her mother a "goal setter" who postponed her education to devote time to her family. After her children were grown, she resumed her studies, earning a bachelor's degree and in 1994 completing her master's degree at Cambridge University. She is now a minister in Detroit's R. R. Wright African Methodist Episcopal (AME) Church. Both parents were strong supporters of the family and the church and were known in both institutions as "Big Daddy" and "Big Momma."

Watson received her bachelor of arts degree in journalism from the University of Michigan in 1972. From 1974 to 1975 she studied at Michigan State University, receiving graduate credits in education. She was a fellow at New York University's Institute for Educational Leadership from 1987 to 1988, and in 1988 she founded the Alumni Organization

there. She is also a licensed social worker for the state of Michigan.

Watson's work experience began with her position as executive director of the Community Parents Child Care Center, which she held from 1973 to 1975. From 1975 to 1976 she was an instructor at Lake Michigan College, Benton Harbor, where she taught a course in racism and sexism. During this time she cofounded the Benton Harbor chapter of the Association of Black Social Workers. In 1976 and 1977 she was a social worker for the Coalition for Peaceful Integration, and in 1978 she worked as coordinator of Focus Hope, both in Detroit. From 1976 to 1987 Watson was branch executive director of the YWCA of metropolitan Detroit. She then served as assistant executive director of the YWCA of the USA, based in New York City, from 1987 to 1990. In an October 27, 1994, interview Watson credited Dorothy Height of the National Council of Negro Women with creating this position while Height served the national YWCA. She further said that Height gave her the ultimate compliment when Watson took the position: "Finally there was a real successor to her at the [YWCA]."

Since 1990, Watson has been executive director of the Detroit branch of the NAACP. In this position she has administrative and advocacy responsibilities for the largest NAACP branch in the nation. She spends her time enforcing affirmative action programs and training others in economic employment opportunities and advocacy, public speaking, race relations training, volunteer development, civil rights redress and litigation, educational reform, youth leadership development, and multicultural and diversity training.

Busy Schedule as Community Activist

When she isn't working, Watson focuses her energies on community activities, particularly those involving women's issues, civil rights and race relations, and programs for youth. While a student at the University of Michigan she became active in the civil rights movement and has remained loyal to the cause ever since. She was involved with the movement when it was at its peak, and she became so caught up in the struggle that she wonders how she managed to graduate with honors. Her work in the area of civil rights escalated once she entered the work force. Since 1979 she has been a member of the Woman's Conference of Concerns, since 1981 a member of the Detroit Women's Forum, and since 1985 a member of the Minority Women's Network. Most years since 1985, Watson has served as a judge and nominator for the Michigan Women's Hall of Fame. From 1985 to 1987 she chaired the Women's Committee and Women's Equality Day for Detroit's Human Rights Commission; she resumed these responsibilities in 1991 and continues to chair both committees. In 1988 she organized and cosponsored the Women in Civil Rights Movement Conference. Since 1991 she has been a member of the Pay Equity Network of the Coalition of Labor Union Women. From 1992 to 1993 she was a committee member of the Michigan Women's Foundation. Her projects for youth include the Martin Luther King First Annual Youth Conference, which she organized and cosponsored in 1988.

That same year she was vice-chairperson of the Twenty-fifth Commemorative March in Washington, and in 1989 she cosponsored the NAACP Silent March on Washington.

Watson has held memberships on numerous boards, including the Twin Cities NAACP, Benton Harbor (executive board), 1973-76; *Detroit Reporter* (executive board), Detroit branch NAACP, mid-1980s; Michigan Coalition for Human Rights (and executive committee), 1986-87 and 1991 to present; National Project Equality of EEO (executive board), 1988; Project Equality (Interfaith EEO Validation Agency), 1988-90; Detroit Association of Black Organizations (executive committee), 1990-93; Virginia Park Community Investment Association, 1990-94; United Community Services, 1990 to present; Black Family Development, 1991-93; Center for the Study of Harassment of African Americans (cofounder and vice-president), 1991 to present; National Council on Alcoholism and Other Dependencies, 1991 to present; Detroit Women's Forum, 1991 to present; American Red Cross, Southeastern Michigan, 1992; American Civil Liberties Union, 1992; National Alliance against Racism and Political Repression, 1992 to present; Center for Democratic Renewal, also known as the National Anti-Klan Network (national board president), 1994; and Self Help Addiction Rehabilitation, 1994 to present.

Organizational affiliations include the National Council of Negro Women, Michigan Women's Hall of Fame Review Panel, Affirmative Action Top 10, Racial Justice Working Group of the National Council of Churches, Association of Black Women in Higher Education, Black Child Development Institute, Michigan NAACP (vice-president, 1982-87), City of Detroit Human Rights Commission, New York Alumni of NYU Institute for Educational Leadership (president, 1988), National Interreligious Civil Rights Commission, and YWCA of Detroit.

Watson's Message Carried in the Media

A writer on a variety of topics, Watson's works include *The ABC's of School Finance* (1977); the monthly newsletter *On the Cutting Edge,* YWCA of the USA, 1987-90; *Action Audit for Change* (1990); and "Harassment of African American Elected Officials," in the *Journal of Intergroup Relations.* She has also served as the editor of the *Michigan Mobilizer,* Michigan NAACP news organ, 1978-87, and the *Detroit Reporter,* Detroit Branch NAACP news organ, mid-1980s.

A television journalist as well, Watson was editorial commentator for WGPR television, Channel 62 in Detroit, for which she prepared and taped two-minute editorials on a biweekly basis from 1991 to 1992. Watson also hosted and produced a weekly radio broadcast called "NAACP in Action," which aired on WCHB/WJZZ in Detroit, from 1990 to 1992.

Since 1992 Watson has hosted a daily newstalk program, "Newstalk Radio," on WCHB, AM 1200, in Detroit. Her show attracts a sizeable audience, who may call in to question her guests or to discuss timely topics. Her show focuses on black economic development, black self-help, and black unity and organization. An avid promoter of the race, she condemns petty jealousies among blacks.

Watson has been widely recognized for her extensive volunteer work and contributions at local and broader levels. Her honors include the Distinguished Service Award, U.S. District Court Monitoring Commission, 1984; Certificate of Appreciation, Top Ladies of Distinction, 1987; Detroit Human Rights Award, 1987; Mayoral Proclamation, City of Detroit, 1987; Governor's Proclamation, State of Michigan, 1987; Contribution Award, Detroit branch of the NAACP, and Appreciation Award, NAACP of the State of Michigan, both in 1987; and YWCA Outstanding Achievement Award, 1989-90. She was also named one of the Top 100 African American Business and Professional Women, 1989-90.

In the 1990s her honors have included the Civil Rights Activist Award, Minority Women's Network, 1990; National Sojourner Truth Meritorious Service Award, National Association of Negro Business and Professional Women's Clubs, 1991 and 1992; Wayne State University Peace Activist Award, 1992; and Union of Palestinian Women Award for Peace and Justice, 1992. In 1994 she received the Woman of the Year Award, Zeta Phi Beta Sorority; the Distinguished Award, Michigan Civil Rights Commission; the National Council of Negro Women's Tribute to Women Award; and the Black Women Community Leaders Award. Also in 1994, she was recognized for her outstanding achievements by the National Lawyers Guild.

In September of 1989 Watson was named to the American contingent of twenty women who traveled to the former U.S.S.R. to promote peace and human rights. She has also lectured widely, speaking to such groups as the Congressional Black Caucus, NAACP, National Bar Association, National Association of Black Social Workers, National Council of Negro Women, National Political Congress of Black Women, Women's Conference of Concerns, Women's International League for Peace and Freedom, and YWCA. In addition she has given commencement addresses and talks on occasions such as Black History Month in the Detroit Public School system.

Watson is a member of Greater Quinn AME Church in Detroit, where she serves on the trustee board, and is a member of the Effie Baber Missionary Society. Proud of her family's long-standing connections with the church, she said in an October 27, 1994, interview, "I am a fifth-generation AME member, and I truly love the black church."

Joann Watson has characterized herself as family-, church-, and community-oriented, a description thoroughly attested to by her activities. In addition to the strong influence of her grandparents and parents, she identified in her 1994 interview the key women role models in her life: Ella Baker, Fannie Lou Hamer, Dorothy Height, and Rosa Parks. "I marvel at their leadership, coupled with humility and grace," she said. Watson is a staunch advocate of volunteer service. Every professional position she has had, she said, "shadowed or followed some volunteer role." Though highly accomplished, her professional career was totally unplanned.

Now divorced, Watson is the mother of Damon Gerard, who attended Lincoln University in Pennsylvania; Celeste Nicole, an honors graduate of Lincoln; Stephen Bernard, a student at Central State University in Ohio; and Maya Kristi, a student at Renaissance High School in Detroit. She has supervised and financed her children's educations on her own. Watson commented in the interview that her children are the light of her life. "They do not take a back seat to my work." She admits that she is a doting and protective mother and also said that she enjoys cooking very much.

Joann Watson is an assertive, articulate, and talented black woman who is fully committed to curing the ills of society, particularly those that impact on black people. Just as black women role models influenced the direction her life would take, Watson herself has become a role model, not just for young women but for all young people familiar with her work.

Current Address: Detroit Branch, NAACP, 2990 East Grand Boulevard, Detroit, MI 48202.

REFERENCES:

Watson, Joann. Resume. N.d.
————. Telephone interview with Jessie Carney Smith, October 27, 1994.
————. Letter to Jessie Carney Smith, November 8, 1994.
Who's Who among Black Americans, 1994-95. 8th ed. Detroit: Gale Research, 1994.

Jessie Carney Smith

Elisabeth Welch

(1908-)

Singer, actress

A masterful cabaret singer and stage performer, Elisabeth Welch was one of the African Americans born near the turn of the twentieth century who made their careers abroad. In her case, this decision to work overseas seems not to have been so much a deliberate choice as it was a matter of the availability of work. Until the 1980s many Americans were only partially aware of her work, knowing her as a singer in shows and cabarets in the United States in the 1920s and early 1930s. However, she later became a genuine star in England with a substantial career. Only when she returned to New York in 1980 to begin performing again in this country did Americans become really aware of the quality of her work

Elisabeth Welch

and discover a living link with some of the great names in American musical theater—a link, moreover, whose performing abilities were still substantially intact at an advanced age.

Elisabeth Welch was born on February 27, 1908, in New York City and raised at Sixty-third and Amsterdam, in the old San Juan Hill area, the neighborhood of the present-day Lincoln Center. Her mother was a Scot from Leith, and she grew up hearing the recordings of the Scottish entertainers Harry Lauder and Will Fyffe. Her father, whom she described in a May 16, 1980, *New York Times* interview as "Negro and red Indian from a tribe in the Wilmington section of Delaware," was a fan of Gilbert and Sullivan. She has a younger brother who became a classical musician. In a June 18, 1983, interview for the *London Times,* Welch said that her father was a strict Baptist who frowned upon girls who whistled and who reproved her constant whistling with, "Whistling girls and crowing hens never come to good ends." However, he approved of her first stage appearance in *HMS Pinafore* at the age of eight. She later sang in the choir of Saint Cyprian's Episcopal Church, and she attended Julia Richards High School.

Even before she graduated from high school, Welch was singing in the choruses of shows. In the *London Times* interview, Welch said that when her father discovered that she was participating in real stage shows with the silent support of her mother, he walked out on the family, saying, "Girlie's [Welch's nickname] on the boards—she's lost." Her first appearance was in a short-lived musical called *Liza* in 1922. It introduced the Charleston to New York when it opened on

November 27, but the dance made little impression at the time. In 1923 Welch won a spot in the chorus of *Runnin' Wild,* which made the Charleston into a craze. Welch was picked out of the chorus to sing "The Charleston." However, as she pointed out in the 1980 *New York Times* article, "Singing 'Charleston' meant nothing to me. It's really a dance. It's not a song you can get up and sing." She continued to work in choruses of shows, including *Chocolate Dandies* and *Velvet Brown Babies* of 1924.

Welch was studying social work when she landed a job in *Blackbirds of 1928,* which she counts as her real professional debut. She sang with the chorus in a scene adapted from the novel *Porgy* and played in a sketch with comedian Johnny Hudgins, whose persona was always mute. In their routine, Welch was in bed with Hudgins when she answered the phone. All she said was "Yes, Mose" and "No, Mose" in varying inflections while Hudgins reacted to the tone of her voice. Her final line, after she hung up, was, "That was Mose." When the play went to Paris, Welch received some press notice for the first time and decided that her vocation lay in the field of entertainment.

In Paris Welch soon was singing at some notable cabarets, such as the Moulin Rouge and Le Boeuf Sur Le Toit. She followed Mabel Mercer at Chez Florence. In the summer of 1930 she returned to New York to open a new club, the Royal Box. Peggy Joyce Hopkins, a café habitué celebrated for her many marriages, had obtained a copy of Cole Porter's "Love for Sale," and Welch added it to her repertoire as soon as the revue *The New Yorkers* opened in December. The song, as it was originally presented on stage in the revue, was roundly condemned by the critics as scandalous. The show's producer, Ray Goetz, co-producer Monty Woolley, and Irving Berlin heard Welch sing it and chose her to replace the original singer, changing the production to accommodate her. She continued her nightclub performances and sang "Love for Sale" in the show from January 1931 until the show closed in May. Welch brought the house down with one song, and she would eventually call herself "One-song Welch," a reflection of the number of times she appeared in shows singing only one song, but one that was a showstopper.

Welch Establishes Herself in England

Welch then returned to England at the invitation of Cole Porter to appear in the show he was putting on in London. It was in England she made the rest of her career. This was not part of a plan. She explained to David Lida for *Women's Wear Daily,* January 28, 1986, "I never intended anything in my life. People don't understand that, but I've just drifted in and out, in and out. I had no star that I looked for or followed. My whole life has been—an event." In London Welch was first principal singer in *Dark Doings* in June 1933, a show she performed in while waiting for Porter's show to open. She stopped the show four times a day with "Stormy Weather," introducing the song in England just a week before Duke Ellington's first appearance there. That same year Cole Porter wrote the song "Solomon" for her. She performed it in his

Nymph Errant, starring Gertrude Lawrence, to such success that the song became identified with her and was played for her wherever she went.

Ivan Novello, the great star of prewar London musicals, wrote "Shanty Town" for her in *Glamorous Night,* and she continued a brilliant career on the London musical stage. Some shows were successes, like *Happy and Glorious,* which ran for twenty months, and there were a few flops, like *Arc de Triomphe.* During the war she entertained British troops in various capacities, once with Sir John Gielgud's theatrical company. After the war she appeared in a famous series of revues produced by Laurier Lister, *Tuppence Colored, Oranges and Lemons,* and *Penny Plain.* In 1976 she appeared in *I Gotta Shoe.* She performed her first one-person show, *A Marvelous Party,* in 1969.

Before the war Welch appeared regularly in a series of mediocre British films, beginning with *Death at Broadcasting House* of 1934. She was usually called upon to enliven the proceedings with a song. She told David Robinson for the *London Times,* June 18, 1983, "I'd do a number while the rest of them would be rushing about getting murdered and detecting and things." She also appeared in two British-made films with the famous American actor and singer Paul Robeson, *Song of Freedom* (1937) and *Big Fella* (1938). Welch remembers refusing to discuss politics with him on the set of the first picture and being quite puzzled about his reason for agreeing to appear in such a poor film as the second. She suspects part of the reason may have been the desire of Robeson's wife, Eslanda, to play the role offered her by the producers. Welch was also active on the radio, being, for example, a principal singer on the series *Soft Lights and Sweet Music,* which began in 1935.

Welch appeared in the movie *Revenge of the Pink Panther* (1978) and in Derek Jarman's strange film *The Tempest* (1979), playing the Goddess and singing "Stormy Weather." She explains the film by saying, "It's Shakespeare's lines, but a lot of it was cut, and there's a lot of nakedness in it. Jarman always likes to have naked boys in there. I didn't appear naked, but a very big lady did— Caliban's mother."

By 1973 Welch was gravely crippled by arthritis; Bob Fosse arranged the role of the Grandmother in the London production of *Pippin* so that she could sit most of the time. She had operations on both hips and recovered her agility. She spent the next decade primarily appearing in cabarets, concerts, and musicals.

In 1980 Welch returned to the United States to perform for the first time in nearly fifty years in the *Black Broadway* segment of the Newport in New York Jazz Festival. She had been asked to participate the year before, but the date conflicted with a tribute given her at Festival Hall in London. In 1982 Welch was drawing young audiences in a strenuous one-person show. In January 1986 she appeared on Broadway in a revue called *Jerome Kern Goes to Hollywood,* an import from London, which was not a success although she won a Tony nomination for her work. Her personal success in this endeavor led to her performing *Time to Start Living,* a one-person show, which opened for a limited run at the Lucille Lortel Theatre on March 20, 1986. For this show she won an Obie. She later took it to Australia and continued to perform it on occasion although she no longer was physically capable of doing the normal theater schedule of eight performances a week.

Welch entered the recording studio in 1987 to record *The Irving Berlin Songbook* for Verve; the record was released in 1988 to high praise. There was also a retrospective compilation, *Miss Elisabeth Welch (1933-40),* in 1979. Three other albums appeared in the 1980s: *Elisabeth Welch in Concert* (1986), *Where Have You Been* (1987), and *This Thing Called Love* (1989). In 1989 she appeared in a one-night concert performance of *Nymph Errant,* in which she had first sung "Solomon" fifty-six years earlier.

In 1988 Welch appeared in the film *Far from Lazy after All These Years,* a combination of performance and oral history. On October 19, 1989, she was one of the recipients of the first Cabaret Classic awards at New York's Town Hall, and the following Sunday she performed at a gala benefiting the Mabel Mercer Foundation, the host of the Cabaret Convention.

Elisabeth Welch has had an outstanding and long-lasting career. She reminds her listeners of the great show and cabaret singing tradition that flourished in the years Irving Berlin and Cole Porter were writing for the stage, but at the same time she has survived into very different times. Only the onset of old age has been able to slow her down. Clive Barnes, the New York critic who also heard her while he was growing up in London, summed up his impressions in the *New York Post,* March 24, 1986:

> Welch is an original. With her sweetness, her gentility, arsenic-laced with a sense of roguish innuendo and pagan sensuality, she is like no one else. . . . She has class, and class, and class. A saloon singer who would make any saloon into a salon.

REFERENCES:

Barnes, Clive. "To Keep Our Love Alive." *New York Post,* March 24, 1986.

Canby, Vincent. "For Elisabeth Welch, Life Is a Dark Cafe." *New York Times,* February 13, 1988.

Duberman, Martin Bauml. *Paul Robeson.* New York: Knopf, 1988.

Gerard, Jeremy. "The Ageless Elisabeth Welch." *Newsday,* March 21, 1986.

Green, Blake. "Still Runnin' Wild Here and Abroad." *Newsday,* October 17, 1989.

Kellner, Bruce. *The Harlem Renaissance.* New York: Methuen, 1984.

Larkin, Colin, ed. *The Guiness Encyclopedia of Popular Music.* Chester, Conn.: New England Publishing Associates, 1992.

Lida, David. "The Return of an American Diva." *Women's Wear Daily,* January 28, 1986.

McDonough, John. "Three for Berlin." *Down Beat* 55 (August 1988): 40.

Robinson, David. "A Woman with Something to Sing About." *London Times,* June 18, 1983.

Troup, Stuart. "For Elisabeth Welch, Life Is a Cabaret." *Newsday,* March 30, 1988.

Wilson, John S. "Welcome Home, One-Song Welch." *New York Times,* May 16, 1980.

Robert L. Johns

Verda Freeman Welcome
(1907-1990)
Educator, state senator

Verda Mae Welcome was one of the first two black women elected to the Maryland House of Delegates and later the first African American woman elected to the state senate. During her career as senator in Maryland, she sponsored a bill to repeal the ban on interracial marriage, and she was involved in the revolution to open public accommodations in Maryland to all persons, regardless of race, creed, or color.

Born in 1907, Welcome was the third of sixteen children born to John Nuborn and Ella Thodocia Freeman. The farm on which she was born was located in the Blue Ridge Mountains of western North Carolina in Uree, now Lake Lure, a resort town. After her mother's death, Welcome was faced with family responsibility at an early age. Welcome attended Mary B. Mullen Elementary School and graduated about 1910. Although the dates of attendance are not known, she studied at a junior high school in North Carolina known as the Peabody Institute, and at Delaware High School in Wilmington. She moved to Baltimore, Maryland, in 1929, and enrolled in classes at Coppin State Teachers College, graduating in 1932.

Verda Welcome married Henry C. Welcome, affectionately referred to as Palie, in 1935. He was from La Ceiba, a seaport town in Honduras, and had come to the United States in 1926 to attend high school at Straight University, now known as Dillard University, in New Orleans. By the time they met, Henry Welcome had entered medical school at Meharry Medical College in Nashville, Tennessee. He graduated in 1936. Verda Welcome always loved children, frequently having them as guests at her home. Mary Sue, one of these children, was adopted by the Welcomes.

From 1934 to 1945, Welcome taught in the Baltimore city schools. During this time, she continued her education, graduating from Morgan State University in Baltimore, Mary-

Verda Freeman Welcome

land, in 1939. She also received her M.A. degree from New York University in 1943.

Begins Political Career

Welcome's political involvement began after she became president of Baltimore's Northwest Improvement Association, which in the 1950s spearheaded the fight to lower racial barriers in public places. With the assistance of a group of fellow activists called the Valiant Women, she ran for the Maryland House of Delegates in 1958 and defeated the powerful Jack (James H.) Pollack political machine in the predominantly black fourth district in Baltimore. She was the only Democrat not backed by Pollack.

Welcome ran as part of a coalition ticket that had been formed; it was a combination of black Democratic and Republican candidates from the Fourth District who ran for election to Maryland's General Assembly. The coalition had been charged with "self-imposed" segregation and insisted that their aim was to bring about greater integration to the legislature. Their advertisements called the ticket "all colored by accident." Edward T. Clayton wrote about the new cry for leadership in *The Negro Politician* and quoted Welcome's position on the issue:

> Because I am so dedicated to the "one world" idea and work with so many interracial groups I took care to ascertain if the members of the coalition were moved by any racial prejudice. I am satisfied that there are no anti-white sentiments in the coalition.

Against the wishes of her advisors, Welcome used the door-to-door approach in the white neighborhoods—something the other coalition candidates did not do. She would not "write off" white voters. She greeted her listeners with her typical plea:

> I am Verda Welcome. I am a candidate for state legislature from this district. I am a Democrat. I feel myself a candidate for the entire Fourth District, and when I am elected, I shall represent all the people of the Fourth District.

Both Welcome and the regular Pollack-backed Democratic candidate, Irma Dixon, unseated white veteran politicians. Welcome was a member of the Maryland House of Delegates from 1959 to 1962; then she was elected to the state senate, the first African American woman to serve in the Maryland State Senate. She was a delegate to the Democratic National Convention in 1968, 1972, and 1976.

Her legislative achievements include leading fights for passage of a state public accommodations law, sponsoring the bill which brought Maryland's public accommodations law into conformity with the broader federal law, and sponsoring legislation which repealed Maryland's 100 year old miscegenation law, removing the prohibition against mixed marriages. Welcome also assisted in the passage of gun control and antismoking legislation. The *Washington Post* said of Welcome:

> As a senator, she helped vote down the state's century-old miscegenation law, sponsored bills establishing equal pay for equal work and voter registration by mail, and was instrumental in the passage of a measure that provided $4.8 million to build Baltimore's Provident Hospital.

The *Post* also commented that Welcome's work to end racial discrimination in public places was inspired by her own experiences. She herself had experienced "the stinging rejection of racism and being denied restaurant privileges and given a room in a basement of an Ocean City hotel while attending a Young Democrats convention."

While remembered as a mild-mannered presence in the legislature, Welcome was also known for her strong stands on the issues most important to her. Former governor of Maryland Harry R. Hughes, once a colleague of Welcome in the state Senate, remembered in the April 27, 1990, issue of the *Baltimore Sun* the turbulent years of the civil rights struggles of the 1960s, during which time he and Welcome shared "very bitter and not very pleasant battles."

It was apparent that Welcome, a feminist, loved politics. She acknowledged her husband's encouragement in her political and educational careers. She told James Abraham in *My Life and Times,*

> Palie was so supportive. He urged me to go back to school, because he understood my dream of continuing my education. . . . Palie was a pretty modern husband for his times. When I first entered politics, it was a masculine field. Few men would

allow their wives to participate, especially as candidates. But Palie was different. We trusted and respected one another, and that encouraged mutual success. He was willing to remain in the background and yet stepped forward whenever I needed him.

Welcome also credits her family and friends for her success. She told Abraham,

I believe that the key to personal happiness, regardless of profession, is a loving family. I certainly know that without Mary Sue, and our friends, I would not have survived the pressures of my career. Politics never made me bitter and I never lost sight of my priorities, because I knew I was loved.

In addition to her political career, Welcome maintained memberships in the NAACP, United Negro College Fund, Americans for Democratic Action, and Delta Sigma Theta Sorority. She was a strong impetus in the establishment of the Banneker-Douglas Museum in Annapolis, Maryland.

Her civic activities included instituting a suit against the Mayor and City Council of Baltimore to prevent the Civic Center from being placed in the Druid Hill Park, the largest of Baltimore's parks. She took responsibility for an ordinance preventing fire escapes from being constructed on the fronts of homes in residential neighborhoods and other buildings on the main streets of Baltimore. Welcome received many honorary degrees, including Doctor of Social Science, University of Maryland, 1970; Doctor of Letters, Howard University, 1972; and Doctor of Law, Morgan State University, 1976.

Welcome died on April 22, 1990, at the age of 83. Her unflinching dedication to ending racial discrimination earned her the respect of lawmakers and the public alike. She was remembered in the *Baltimore Sun* as:

a quiet pioneer, but a trailblazer, nonetheless. . . . [A]s a state legislator, Verda F. Welcome made an enormous difference in the fight for civil rights and an array of other social causes. She never hesitated to lead the way. . . . Throughout her years in the rough and tumble legislature, Mrs. Welcome remained a gracious but persistent lawmaker who rarely raised her voice.

REFERENCES:

Abraham, James M. *My Life and Times*. Englewood Cliffs, N.J.: Henry House Publishers, 1991.

Baltimore Afro-American, May 9, 1972; July 10, 1982; April 28, 1990; May 9, 1992; August 8, 1992.

Baltimore Sun, April 24, 1990; April 27, 1990; April 29, 1990.

Clayton, Edward T. *The Negro Politician*. Chicago: Johnson Publishing Co., 1964.

Hine, Darlene Clark, ed. *Black Women in America*. 2 vols. Brooklyn: Carlson Publishers, 1993.

Ploski, Harry A., and James Williams. *The Negro Almanac*. 5th ed. Detroit: Gale Research, 1989.

Washington Post, April 24, 1990.

Who's Who among Black Americans, 1990-91. 6th ed. Detroit: Gale Research, 1990.

Who's Who among Black Americans, 1992-93. 7th ed. Detroit: Gale Research, 1992.

COLLECTIONS:

Personal correspondence and papers of Verda Freeman Welcome are at the Maryland Historical Society and Morgan State University, Baltimore, Maryland.

Simmona E. Simmons-Hodo

Frances Cress Welsing
(1935-)
Child psychiatrist, lecturer, writer

Frances Cress Welsing is a child psychiatrist and lecturer who is best known as the proponent of a controversial theory of racial superiority. For over twenty years, she has counseled her patients and audiences that if blacks are to vanquish global racism and comprehend the magnitude of the hopelessness that it engenders, they must learn to recognize and thoroughly understand racist beliefs and the great extent to which they are part of the social fabric worldwide. Welsing hypothesizes that white supremacy is a defense mechanism that developed out of a genetic inferiority that causes whites to produce lower levels of the skin pigment melanin than nonwhites. In the January 17, 1991, *Atlanta Journal-Constitution,* she instructs blacks on how to counter racism:

Once you decode the plays that your opponent is going to move, then all you have to do is counter the moves. For years blacks have not understood the depth of racism and prepared for the wrong "game," and then operated defensively, falling down, crying, and saying, "Oh, save us Jesus, save us," as opposed to mastering and understanding what the "game" is all about and playing our best hand.

Frances Cress Welsing was born in Chicago on March 18, 1935. She would later become a third-generation physician in her family, following the path of her grandfather, Henry Clay Cress, and her father, Henry N. Cress. Welsing received a B.S. degree from Ohio's Antioch College in 1957 and an M.D. degree from the Howard University College of Medicine in 1962.

She interned at Chicago's Cook County Hospital from 1962 to 1963, then moved to Washington, D.C., and undertook a residency in general psychiatry at St. Elizabeth Hospi-

Frances Cress Welsing

tal from 1963 to 1966. She held a fellowship in child psychiatry from 1966 to 1968 at Children's Hospital, Washington, D.C. From 1968 to 1975 Welsing was an assistant professor of pediatrics at the Howard University College of Medicine. She served as clinical director of the Hillcrest Children's Center, Washington, D.C., from 1975 to 1976, and since then she has been in private practice as a child psychiatrist. Welsing holds professional memberships in the National Medical Association, the American Medical Association, and the American Psychiatric Association.

Welsing Advances Theory of Color Confrontation and White Supremacy

The author of *The Cress Theory of Color Confrontation and Racism,* a theory first formulated in 1969, Welsing has stirred considerable discussion and controversy in the medical and behavioral science fields because of her views. Welsing conjectures that blacks cannot understand anything as black people until they begin to understand all of those forces that determine their being. Nine-tenths of the people in the world are nonwhites; one-tenth are white. Welsing perceives that power is in the hands of people who are classified as white. All of the nonwhite people in the world have a power portion that is effectively zero. A few black behavioral scientists who adhere to this theory assert that blacks are in a global system that is organized to sustain white supremacy. It is a behavioral system of logic, thought, speech, action, and emotional response, the goal of which is white domination over nonwhites. The behavior that sustains this system operates in all aspects of life. According to Welsing in *Essence:*

The total spectrum of function becomes power—what you are able to do in economics, education, entertainment, labor, law, politics, religion, sex, and war. Whether you can determine what happens to you in all nine areas of your life activity, not just one. The system refines itself by saying, "OK, they are asking for power, we'll give them a better job. But, then we will manipulate their activities on all other areas so the fact that they've got jobs doesn't mean anything."

Welsing theorizes that white people have organized themselves in this behavioral system because they are color deficient and because they are outnumbered by nonwhites. Welsing considers white skin a form of albinism, which, to her mind, is a condition of genetic deficiency that can be demolished by anyone with the potential to produce color. If white people are to survive as a group, Welsing states, they must maintain [genetic] control over people who are classified as nonwhite. She commented in *Essence* magazine, October 1973, "This system has evolved as a sort of psychological defense to deal with their sense of inadequacy." As long as whites have privileges, as long as they appear to be functionally superior to people with color, they say in effect, "Even though we don't have color, we are superior."

As a black psychiatrist, Welsing believes that racism is the number-one health problem. She has called for the establishment of an institute of mental health to study racism and white behavior. Her suggestion has largely fallen on deaf ears, and she believes that she and her supporters are victims of system manipulation.

Welsing speculates in the October 1973 *Essence* article that suntanning is defensive behavior on the part of people who lack color. "Biology and dermatological textbooks say that white skin is normal. How can white skin be normal if nine-tenths of the people in the world produce color?" asks Welsing.

Welsing would like to see whites and nonwhites live in harmony with each other as well as with nature. The challenge for white behavioral scientists, in Welsing's view, is to help white people come to terms with their feelings of inadequacy about their lack of color. Once this is accomplished, Welsing speculates, whites will not feel such an urge to dominate nonwhites.

Welsing also believes that in order for racial harmony to be achieved the mental health of blacks must be improved through increased self-respect. She told the *Atlanta Journal-Constitution,* January 17, 1991, that blacks can increase their self-confidence if all black children are taught the following fundamental guidelines for life before they reach the age of six:

Stop name-calling one another
Stop cursing one another
Stop squabbling with one another
Stop gossiping about one another
Stop snitching on one another
Stop being discourteous toward one another

Stop robbing one another
Stop stealing from one another
Stop fighting one another
Stop making black children think as black children
    they can't be adequate mothers and fathers.
And stop pretending white supremacy does not
    exist.

These guidelines must also be reinforced by adult example in the home, church, and neighborhood.

Frances Welsing uses both her practice and her lectures to advance her theory of color confrontation and race. One of her primary concerns is that black children achieve a positive attitude toward self, but she fears that their health and well-being could easily be destroyed by racism.

Current Address: 7603 Georgia Avenue, N.W., Washington, D.C. 20012.

REFERENCES:

"Blacks Need to Know Racism, Author Tells Workshop." *Atlanta Journal-Constitution,* January 17, 1991.

"A Conversation with Dr. Welsing." *Essence* 4 (October 1973): 51.

Ebony Success Library. Vol. 1. Nashville: Southwestern Co., 1973.

"The Isis Papers: The Keys to the Colors." *Ebony* 46 (March 1991): 109.

Sammons, Vivian Ovelton. *Blacks in Science and Medicine.* New York: Hemisphere Publishing Corporation, 1990.

Welsing, Frances Cress. "The 'Conspiracy' to Make Blacks Inferior." Vertical file, Woodruff Library, Atlanta University Center.

———. "The Cress Theory of Color Confrontation." *The Black Scholar* 5 (May 1974): 32-40.

———. "On 'Black Genetic Inferiority.'" *Ebony* 29 (July 1974): 104-5.

Who's Who among Black Americans, 1992-93. 7th ed. Detroit: Gale Research, 1992.

Casper LeRoy Jordan

Emma Rochelle Wheeler
(1882-1957)
Physician, hospital and nursing school founder

A woman of diverse interests, Emma Rochelle Wheeler was a trailblazing physician, hospital and nursing school founder, and an initiator of an unparalleled, prepaid hospitalization plan. Wheeler practiced medicine for almost fifty years and was well known for her assistance to young

Emma Rochelle Wheeler

African Americans in their academic and business undertakings. An organizer of a chapter of the Alpha Kappa Alpha Sorority, she was among the early most notable and distinguished African American women leaders in Chattanooga, Tennessee. Wheeler was the founder and operator of Walden Hospital. Dedicated on July 30, 1915, Walden was the first and only African American-owned and operated medical facility in Chattanooga.

A native Floridan, Wheeler was born near Gainesville on February 7, 1882. According to an interview given by Wheeler that appeared in the *Chattanooga Times,* her father was a farmer and veterinarian. In a telephone interview in 1993, Bette Wheeler Strickland indicated Wheeler had two siblings, William Rochelle and Ella Rochelle Stamps, both of whom are now deceased.

Wheeler grew up in Florida and her intrigue with the medical profession was aroused at the early age of six, when an eye problem prompted her father to take her for treatment to a white female physician. According to the interview in the *Chattanooga Times,* Wheeler said, "Back in 1888 a little Florida farm girl, with eye trouble was taken to a doctor who turned out to be the prettiest little white lady I ever saw—and I made up my mind then and there I was going to be a doctor too." Young Emma and the woman physician became friends and when she went to school in Gainesville the doctor's abiding concern for and interest in her continued. She visited Emma at Cookman Institute in Jacksonville. At age seventeen, Wheeler finished Cookman, and in 1900 she married Joseph R. Howard, a teacher. Howard died a year later of typhoid fever, never seeing the son named for him.

Shortly after Howard's death, Emma Wheeler and young Joseph moved to Nashville, Tennessee, where she pursued her childhood dream of becoming a physician. She attended Walden University, and in 1905 she graduated from Walden University's Meharry Medical, Dental, and Pharmaceutical College. She married John N. Wheeler, also a physician, during the week of Meharry's commencement. The marriage ceremony was held on Tuesday afternoon, February 28, at two o'clock in the Meharry auditorium. The Wheelers had two daughters, Thelma Wheeler and Bette Wheeler Strickland, and an adopted son, George Wheeler, who was Emma Wheeler's nephew. John N. Wheeler died in 1940 and is buried in Chattanooga's Highland Cemetery.

Wheeler Begins Medical Practice

Following Emma's graduation from Meharry, the Wheelers moved to Chattanooga and set up their medical practice on Main Street. Based on the census of 1900, Chattanooga had a total population of 30,154 of which 13,122 were African Americans.

In Chattanooga, as in other parts of the state and the South, the Wheelers found a rigid, racially discriminating social system. Health care in Chattanooga presented a rueful picture. Horrendous, unsanitary surroundings contributed to a menacing tally of tuberculosis cases. Poor health and high mortality scourged the black community, more so than the white community. African Americans needing hospital care were consigned to the basements of existing white hospitals. For ten years, John and Emma Wheeler practiced together and labored assiduously to provide African Americans in their hometown with health care services and to help them improve their physical well-being.

Walden Hospital Founded

After practicing medicine for ten years with her husband, Emma Wheeler was painfully aware of the need for a facility where both the acutely and chronically ill patient could receive more intensive care. She envisioned a facility that not only attended to the medical needs of a rapidly growing African American population, but one that also granted admitting privileges to African American physicians. Additionally, she visualized the hospital serving as a practical training school for student nurses.

In 1915, with money she had put aside, Emma Wheeler purchased two lots on East Eighth Street at the corner of Douglas, where she had a three-story building constructed. After the structure's completion, Wheeler's vision of a hospital for Chattanooga's African American populace became a reality. On July 30, 1915, when the facility, Walden Hospital, was dedicated, it had a thirty-bed capacity, with nine private rooms and one ward of twelve beds. The afternoon dedication ceremony was held just up the street at the neighboring First Baptist Church on East Eighth Street. The evening ceremony was conducted in the parlors of the newly inaugurated hospital. On the day Walden Hospital was dedicated, the *Chattanooga Times* stated: "The completion of this hospital is a work of which the colored people feel justly proud. It will be conducted by colored people, for the benefit of colored people and will enable the colored physicians to render better service to patients needing the advantages which a hospital affords than has heretofore been possible."

Walden Hospital had surgical, maternity, and nursery departments. It was staffed by two house doctors and three nurses. Seventeen physicians and surgeons from the Mountain City Medical Society used the new facility and admitted their patients. The median monthly patient load was twelve. Although John N. Wheeler used the facility, it was managed, operated, and paid for entirely by Emma Wheeler. She told the *Chattanooga Times* in an interview: "I'd saved about half enough money to pay for the building, and the hospital succeeded so well that all the notes were paid off in less than three years." Thirty-two years later, a staff writer for the *Chattanooga Observer,* an African American newspaper, said: "The Walden Hospital has stood out through the years as a beacon and ray of hope to the sick, wounded and afflicted. . . . It gives physicians of all races an opportunity to improve their medical knowledge and skill."

While maintaining long office hours and serving as superintendent of Walden Hospital, Emma Wheeler personally performed a number of surgical procedures. However, she found surgery too exhausting to continue in addition to her other responsibilities. For more than twenty years, Wheeler maintained a school for nurses. With the assistance of her husband, she taught and trained many students who were interested in becoming nurses.

In 1925 Wheeler initiated the Nurse Service Club of Chattanooga, an innovative, prepaid hospitalization plan. The Nurse Service Club, the only one of its type in Chattanooga, was entirely separate from the hospital's operation. Membership in the organization offered two weeks of free hospitalization, if needed, and at-home assistance given by a nurse after discharge from the hospital.

A second hospital was established in 1947 to care for the city's African Americans. The city of Chattanooga, Hamilton County, and Erlenger Hospital (for whites) established Carver Memorial Hospital. Carver, a tax-supported and segregated institution, had fifty beds and was staffed by personnel of African American heritage. The hospital was named for George Washington Carver, the esteemed African American scientist, botanist, researcher, and agronomist.

Considered a foster mother to many young African Americans, Wheeler was known for her support of young people pursuing their academic and entrepreneurial aspirations. In 1949 the Chattanooga branch of the NAACP voted her "Negro Mother of the Year." An active professional and community person, Wheeler was a member of the Mountain City Medical Society, the State Volunteer Medical Association, and the Wiley Memorial Methodist Church, as well as treasurer and member of the board of trustees of Highland Cemetery. In January 1925 she, along with Emma Henry, Zenobia House, and Marjorie Parker, organized the Pi Omega

Chapter of Alpha Kappa Alpha sorority, Chattanooga's first AKA chapter.

Wheeler Retires from Hospital Management

Wheeler's health began to decline in 1951 and two years later, in June 1953, she retired from operating and managing Walden Hospital. Wheeler stated in the *Chattanooga Times* interview:

> It is difficult to find words that adequately express my deep appreciation to the fine white and Negro doctors here who have used Walden Hospital and helped to make it so successful in community service through all these years. . . . I have tried to encourage many young men to study medicine— and many young women, too, for although few women of my generation became doctors, it always seemed to me a natural career for women.

With her retirement, Chattanooga's first and only African American-owned and operated hospital ceased operation on June 30, 1953, after thirty-eight years of service. Because of the hospital's closing, members of the Nurse Service Club of Chattanooga disbanded. For a while, Wheeler continued to practice general medicine, receiving her patients on the first floor of the former hospital building.

Out of all of the cases Wheeler handled, she had the greatest fondness for the obstetrical ones. Because a fire destroyed Walden's records, she had no idea how many babies were born at the hospital. However, she estimated that the total number ran beyond two thousand. In a June 14, 1953, interview with the *Chattanooga Times,* Wheeler noted that many of the "Walden babies" became successful adults. But she also noted, "I never had as many doctors as I would have liked from them." A great number of her "babies" took the time to pen their heart-felt appreciation and to let her know how much of an inspiration she had been to them. Wheeler cherished their numerous letters. "God has certainly been good to me and I hope he [sic] gives me many more years to serve my people," she said.

Although of demure demeanor, Wheeler was of strong character and determination. Wheeler saw a void in the delivery of health care services for African Americans in Chattanooga. She met the challenge and filled the vacuum. A woman of vision and compassion, Wheeler helped to ease the discomfort of the medically distressed and placed health care for Chattanooga's citizens of African descent on a higher plane.

At age seventy-five, on September 12, 1957, Emma Rochelle Wheeler died in Nashville's Hubbard Hospital. Her body was taken back to Chattanooga, and funeral services were held on September 17 at the Wiley Memorial Methodist Church. She was buried in Highland Cemetery. At the time of her demise, Wheeler was survived by a son, Joseph R. Howard (now deceased), and two daughters, Bette and Thelma Wheeler of Chattanooga; a sister, Ella R. Stamps of Rome,

Georgia; and four nephews, George Wheeler of New York City, George Wheeler, Jr., William Rochelle Wheeler, and Joseph J. Wheeler, all of Chattanooga.

Five years after her death, the Chattanooga Housing Authority named the city's newly completed housing project the Emma Wheeler Homes. Ten years later, as a part of its Black History Week celebration, the Chattanooga branch of the Association for the Study of Negro Life and History paid homage to the life and contributions of Wheeler as one of the city's pioneering African American women. On February 16, 1990, through the sponsorship of the Chattanooga African American Museum, the Tennessee Historical Commission approved the placement of a state historical marker at the site of Walden Hospital. Three months later, on May 16, dedicatory ceremonies were held for Chattanooga's newest historic site.

REFERENCES:

Chattanooga News-Free Press, August 10, 1986.

Chattanooga Observer, July 25, 1947.

Chattanooga Times, July 30, 1915; June 14, 1953; September 15, 1957; February 22, 1990; May 17, 1990; February 25, 1993.

Fields, Velma. Interview with Linda T. Wynn. August 10, 1993.

Livingood, James W. *Hamilton County.* Tennessee County History Series, vol. 33. Edited by Joy B. Dunn and Charles W. Crawford. Memphis: Memphis State University Press, 1981.

———. *A History of Hamilton County, Tennessee.* Memphis: Memphis State University Press, 1981.

———. *Chattanooga and Hamilton County Medical Society: The Profession and Its Community.* Chattanooga: Chattanooga and Hamilton County Medical Society, 1983.

Strickland, Bette Wheeler. Interview with Linda T. Wynn. April 29, 1993.

Wheeler, George. Interview with Linda T. Wynn. May 3, 1993.

COLLECTIONS:

Many of the papers of Emma Rochelle Wheeler are in the possession of her daughter, Bette Wheeler Strickland of Chicago, Illinois. Strickland is in the process of donating Wheeler memorabilia to the Chattanooga African American Museum, which already has some information on John N. and Emma Rochelle Wheeler and Walden Hospital. Additional information can be obtained from the Chattanooga-Hamilton County Bicentennial Library. Walden Hospital Historical Marker File is on file in the offices of the Tennessee Historical Commission, Nashville, Tennessee.

Linda T. Wynn

Frances Anne Rollin Whipper
(1845-1901)
Writer, political activist

Frances Anne Rollin Whipper wrote the first biography of a free-born black, *The Life and Public Services of Martin R. Delany*. In accord with the prejudices of the time, the book bore the name of a male author, Frank A. Rollin. This 1868 publication had a modest success and was reissued in 1883. Even today it is a valuable resource for the investigation of the life of Martin Delany, one of the most significant black leaders of the nineteenth century. Growing up in a free black community in Charleston, South Carolina, Whipper came to maturity as the practice of slavery was ended. She participated in Reconstruction in her native state, especially through her marriage to the prominent black politician William James Whipper. After separating from her husband, she continued her involvement in politics in Washington, D.C., and continued to write. Unfortunately, her career as a writer for magazines and newspapers is difficult to trace because she used numerous pseudonyms.

Whipper was born on November 19, 1845, on America Street in Charleston, South Carolina. She died in Beaufort, South Carolina, on October 17, 1901. Her parents, Margarette and William Rollin, were free persons of color. Little is known of Margarette—not even her maiden name—except that in later life she signed legal documents with an X, suggesting illiteracy and that she or her family came from one of the Caribbean islands, presumably Saint Domingue (now Haiti), as did her husband's family. She was also of somewhat darker complexion than William Rollin, who was so fair that he could pass for white.

William Rollin was a member of the mulatto side of the De Caradeuc family, which had left Saint Domingue in 1792 to escape the slave rebellion and which had settled on a plantation near Charleston and entered the lumber trade. The family was French, noble, and well-off. Whipper identified Jean Achille de Caradeuc (1816-1895), a prominent white Charlestonian, as her father's nephew from a clipping of his death notice. William Rollin's father and mother cannot be identified, but he benefitted from the protection of his white family; in particular he seems to have become involved in lumber through the family connection, and when Jean Achille set up house in 1850 with his new bride, William Rollin moved next door. By 1860 Rollin had become very prosperous by the standards of the free black community. He was buying property, owned three slaves, and had trading connections as far away as Philadelphia. His prosperity was compromised during the war, and he was wounded by a Union soldier as he was trying to protect it.

William Rollin's family increased along with his wealth. It is known that four more daughters survived infancy: Charlotte (b. 1849), Katherine (1851-76), Louisa (b. 1858), and Florence (b. 1861). The daughters received good if quite

Frances Anne Rollin Whipper

illegal educations, as educating blacks was officially forbidden at that time. Whipper went to a French-speaking woman for her first instruction and learned French as she learned to read. The family seems to have retained its Catholic heritage.

As the Civil War approached, the rising tension rendered the position of the free blacks precarious. There was talk of general reenslavement of all persons with African ancestry and increasingly careful scrutiny of the proofs of freedom. Free families began to leave the South or at least send their children to the safety of the northern states. In 1859 Whipper was taken to Philadelphia and placed in the Institute for Colored Youth. Charlotte, Katherine, and Louisa soon followed her north, going to school first in Boston and then in Philadelphia. Whipper was to remain in Philadelphia for six years, for much of them completely cut off from her parents. Nothing is known of the arrangements made to support the children or how well they fared. Since Frances did not graduate from the Institute, she and the older daughters may have had to work. It is known that the Rollin daughters impressed contemporaries with their intelligence and their educational achievements, however attained. During this time, Whipper regularly attended Saint Thomas's Episcopal Church. She became a life-long Episcopalian, although her confirmation card was not signed until she was a parishioner of Alexander Crummell at Saint Luke's in Washington, D.C., in the 1880s.

At the end of the war, Whipper seized the opportunity to return to Charleston as a teacher for the newly freed blacks. She worked first for the Freedmen's Bureau and then for the American Missionary Society, which paid more. Even though a supervisor recognized her superiority as a teacher by recommending a high salary of thirty dollars a month for her, gender inequity still prevailed. Another teacher was recommended at the same time for sixty solely because he was male.

Martin Delany's Biography Written

At the time of Whipper's return, Charleston was still under martial law; the legal consequence of this circumstance allowed her to bring suit against the captain of a steamer who denied her first-class accommodations. In this early civil rights case she won $250. She also met Martin Delany (1812-1885), one of the most notable black leaders of the nineteenth century. Delany was then a major in the army and worked for the Freedmen's Bureau as subassistant commissioner with special responsibility for the Sea Island blacks. Whipper agreed to write his biography. He furnished her with a suitcase full of materials and promised her a stipend. She decided to establish herself in Boston to write the book. Her surviving diary dates from 1868 and covers the end of the period in the North.

In Boston she took advantage of the intellectual opportunities of the city, meeting prominent blacks and whites. As a rule she spent her Sundays visiting different white churches, and she seems to have been the only African American at a reading by Charles Dickens, the English novelist. She frequented black elite circles and weighed the merits of her suitors—among them Richard Greener, the first black to graduate from Harvard ("too intellectual" she wrote in her diary). At times, especially toward the end of her stay during the first part of 1868, her situation became difficult. Snow seemed to linger on and on that year, her mother was found to have dropsy, she herself was ill, and Delany did not continue to send money. (In fairness, he had a large family to maintain in Wilberforce, Ohio, and could easily have overextended himself.) She supported herself by sewing and copying, and by July the *Life and Public Services of Martin R. Delany* was published under the name of Frank A. Rollin. Ironically, this masculine first name was the family nickname for Frances.

Whipper left Boston for Columbia, South Carolina, on July 28, 1868. She had accepted a job as copyist offered by William James Whipper, a Northern lawyer who had moved to South Carolina after the war and who had recently been elected to the South Carolina legislature. William James Whipper (1835-1907) was the nephew of William Whipper (1804-1876), the noted Philadelphia merchant, abolitionist, magazine writer, and editor. According to family tradition, William James Whipper failed the Ohio bar examination, went to Michigan where he passed, and then returned to Ohio to marry and practice law. When the war was over, he seized the opportunity to try his fortune in South Carolina. Beginning as a lawyer in Beaufort, he accumulated property and entered politics. Ambitious and idealistic, Whipper was a tall, handsome man of great merits and some defects. He had at that time an alcohol problem, or developed one later, and was an inveterate gambler. According to one story he lost $75,000 in a single sitting, most of it on one hand when his four aces were beaten by a straight flush. At the time of his job offer to

Frances Rollin, Whipper was married and had charge of three children: a recently born child, the son of a brother, and an adopted older boy. By the time Frances Rollin arrived in Columbia, William Whipper was a widower.

Columbia was an exciting place to be. The legislature was meeting with a black majority in the house. It was conservative in its actions, but there was room for discussion of radical proposals like woman's suffrage—Charlotte Rollin spoke for it on the floor of the house in 1869. There was also a strong undercurrent of violence and danger; men went armed and weapons were used. Charlotte and Katherine Rollin had settled in the city, ostensibly to lobby for funds for a school, and their salon attracted the attention of northern reporters whose stories contributed to their celebrity. They eventually found jobs in the state government due to the patronage of William Whipper, and both would later buy houses in the city but lose them because of difficulty meeting mortgage payments.

Francis Rollin arrived in Columbia on August 2, and William Whipper proposed to her by August 14. After some hesitation, she accepted, and they were married in Columbia on September 18, 1868. There was opposition from William Rollin, whom she did not see until after she accepted Whipper's proposal. Some members of the family may have been unhappy because of the darkness of William Whipper's skin. In a newspaper article Charlotte Rollin was quoted as saying, "Our family never condescended to notice such small people as Elliott or Whipper, although Whipper married our sister. . . . They are both negroes, and our families are French." She is apparently describing the past since at the time the newspaper article appeared she was working for Robert Brown Elliott, who was adjutant general of the state militia.

Frances Rollin Whipper immediately fell into the pattern of repeated pregnancies at close intervals. Alicia was born and died in 1869. Then came Winifred (1870-1907), Ionia Rollin (1872-1953), Mary Elizabeth (1874-1875), and finally a son, Leigh (1876-1975). In addition, she had to cope with the fluctuations of her husband's political career and his business dealings. For example, she had property placed in her name to protect it from creditors. A major change in family life is directly attributable to a political setback. In 1875 the family moved to Beaufort. Earlier that year William Whipper had been elected circuit judge in a hastily arranged election, and blacks again discovered the unreliability of their white allies when Governor Daniel H. Chamberlain, himself a carpetbagger, refused to sign the commission. The high tide of black influence in state government was rapidly ebbing. Wade Hampton was the candidate of the white supremacists in the fall election, and violence and fraud accompanied the resumption of power by whites who opposed the newfound rights of blacks in society.

In 1880 William Rollin died. Margarette Rollin appears to have left him in 1870 to live with Charlotte and Louisa. Frances Rollin Whipper began to administer the estate, only to have her administration challenged by her mother. Frances Rollin Whipper did not persist, and the suit did not reach trial. There is no way to know exactly what was salvaged from the estate, but it appears to have been less than expected. In 1882 several properties of William Rollin were foreclosed. By the end of 1880 Louisa and Charlotte Rollin were operating a boarding house in Brooklyn, a city not yet part of New York City, and their mother was living with them—the sisters had been discussing a move to Brooklyn as early as 1871. Francis Rollin Whipper was living in Washington, D.C., with her children, but without her husband. It is impossible to untangle the family imbroglio, but part of the problem with her husband was his open maintenance of a mistress.

Frances Rollin Whipper found a job as copyist in the U.S. Department of Lands. She also oversaw the education of her children, all of whom graduated from Howard University. Winifred became a nurse and teacher in Washington. Ionia Rollin Whipper became a noted physician and founder of a home for unwed mothers. Leigh Whipper entered show business and had a long and distinguished career on the stage and in the movies. Frances Rollin Whipper maintained her keen interest in politics, working for the Republican party, and seems to have continued to write, although under now unidentifiable pseudonyms. There is evidence that she wrote at least one unidentified story at the request of a national magazine.

William Whipper practiced law in Washington from 1882 to 1885, when he returned to Beaufort to win election as probate judge, a position from which he was turned out in a rigged election in 1888. He made off with all of the office records and refused to surrender them until he had been imprisoned for eighteen months. An immediate result of the election of 1885 was that Frances Rollin Whipper lost her government job because of her husband's position in state government. She was rescued by Frederick Douglass, who was recorder of deeds for the District of Columbia. He gave her a place in his office, a position she held until 1893.

In 1889 Frances Rollin Whipper's health began to deteriorate rapidly, and she returned to Beaufort. Her husband had had a religious conversion that ended his drinking and womanizing. He was now a tall thin man who often wandered the streets at night because attacks of asthma prevented him from sleeping. Frances Rollin Whipper died of tuberculosis on October 17, 1901. Her children arrived in time for the Episcopal service. Her grave cannot be identified, but it is probably in the Craven Street A.M.E. graveyard in Beaufort.

REFERENCES:

Foner, Eric. *Reconstruction: America's Unfinished Revolution 1863-77.* New York: Harper and Row, 1988.

Ione, Carole. *Pride of Family: Four Generations of American Women of Color.* New York: Avon Books, 1991.

Johnson, Michael P., and James L. Roark. *Black Masters: A Free Family of Color in the Old South.* New York: Norton, 1984.

Shockley, Ann Allen. *Afro-American Women Writers: 1746-1933.* Boston: G. K. Hall, 1988.

Sterling, Dorothy, ed. *We Are Your Sisters: Black Women in the Nineteenth Century.* New York: W. W. Norton, 1984.

COLLECTIONS:

Frances Anne Rollin Whipper's diary and other memorabilia are in the possession of Carole Ione. Other items are in the Leigh Whipper Collections of the Moorland Spingarn Research Center, Washington, D.C., and the Schomburg Center for Research on Black Culture, New York, New York. There are two known photographs, both in the Schomburg Collection.

Robert L. Johns

The Whitman Sisters
Mabel Whitman
(?-1942)
Essie Whitman
(1882-1963)
Alberta Whitman
(?-1964)
Alice Whitman
(?-1969)
Entertainers, theatrical entrepreneurs

The period from the time ten-year-old Essie Whitman won a talent contest in a Kansas City, Missouri, theater until the Whitman Sisters Theater Company finally broke up was over fifty years. For more than twenty of these years the company was the top attraction in the theaters of the Theater Owners' Booking Association, and the Whitman sisters were in full charge of running the group. They hired as children a whole generation of dancers, including Aaron Palmer, Maxie McCree, Pops Whitman (the son of Alice), Billy Adams, Joe Jones, and an extremely talented but little known tap dancer known only as Groundhog. The Whitman sisters were all notable performers during their time. Unfortunately, their names are now largely forgotten. Some of the reasons for their obscurity today can be explained. First, while the sisters appeared on the major white vaudeville circuits until 1920, in the latter part of their careers, they based themselves in Chicago, away from the publicity centers of New York and Los Angeles, and concentrated on entertaining black audiences. Second, the strengths of their company were primarily in the area of dance, which tends to be underdocumented and neglected as a field of study, rather than in music and song, which in the Whitmans' time was more likely than dance to be preserved and which fans and scholars tend to study very closely.

Mabel Whitman

Mabel (May), Essie, Alberta (Bert), and Alice Whitman were the daughters of Albery Allson Whitman (1851-1901) and Caddie Whitman (?-1909). On the basis of the age given on Alice Whitman's death certificate in 1969, sixty-one (which would make her date of birth around 1908), it has been suggested that the two youngest sisters were born to Caddie Whitman during a second marriage, an assertion that appears in several biographical sketches of their father. This contention is almost certainly wrong. Alice Whitman is the youngest sister, but 1908 is not her birth date. From other sources it is known that she joined the sisters' act in 1909 after Caddie Whitman's death and gave birth to a child in 1919, Albert Palmer, better known as "Pops" Whitman. Alice married dancer Aaron Palmer (c. 1897-?), who joined the Whitman troupe in 1910 and remained until 1922. In addition there is no indication of a second marriage in information about Caddie Whitman's death in 1909. These circumstances establish a birth date for Alice early enough for her to be Albery Whitman's daughter.

Albery Whitman was a person of considerable stature: he is now recognized as a major black poet of the nineteenth century—and one of the most prolific. Whitman was born May 30, 1851, to slave parents in Hart County, Kentucky. His mother died in 1862, and his father in 1863. He held a variety of jobs and secured a few months' education before spending six months around the year 1870 at Wilberforce University, where he came under the influence of Daniel A. Payne. Payne, who served as president of Wilberforce, was an African Methodist bishop who was responsible for the development of the school as a wholly black-controlled institution. In 1877 he

published *Not a Man and Yet a Man,* his earliest extant poetry. He was then pastor of a Springfield, Ohio, African Methodist Episcopal (AME) church. In his own lifetime, Whitman was most famous for his abilities as a preacher, in spite of his being handicapped by the alcoholism that shortened his life. He was often moved from church to church, serving in Ohio, Kansas, Texas, Savannah, Georgia, and then finally in Atlanta, where he died. There is little known about Caddie Whitman, his wife, who was so fair skinned that the suggestion has been made that she was legally white. Albery Whitman was also very light, and his daughters inherited their parents' complexions. (Essie Whitman claimed that Albery was poet Walt Whitman's first cousin.) Caddie Whitman may have had some dramatic flair herself since her husband called upon her for assistance at public readings of his poetry. While they were living in Lawrence, Kansas, Albery Whitman taught the girls a dance called the Double Shuffle, "just for exercise," according to Marshall and Jean Stearns in their *Jazz Dance,* but there is no record of his feelings about their involvement in show business, which began well before his death. George Walker, later of the famous vaudeville team of Williams and Walker, was a Kansas neighbor for whom Essie cooked greens. Walker was already displaying his abilities as a dancer as the Whitman girls were growing up.

Whitman Sisters Go on Stage

The daughters started by singing in churches and entertaining locally but early began their professional careers. In 1899 The Whitman Sisters' Comedy Company played to both black and white audiences in Savannah, Georgia. On October 22, 1902, Mabel, Essie, and Alberta began a mid-winter tour at the Grand Opera House in Augusta, Georgia. Henry T. Sampson in his history of blacks in show business, *The Ghost Walks,* quotes a review from the *Birmingham (Alabama) News* that calls them "bright, pretty mulatto girls" and continues,

> They have wonderful voices, that of Essie being the lowest contralto on record. The sisters play banjoes and sing coon songs with a smack of the original flavor. Their costuming is elegant; their manner is graceful and their appearance is striking in a degree as they are unusually handsome.

Early records of the sisters' activities are not complete, but they were successful enough to travel on the Pantages circuit, a second-tier circuit in the West, and to work abroad with their mother as chaperone. They seemed to have occasionally worked as a white act and often had to use blackface at the insistence of theater managers. In the summer of 1904 they formed The Whitman Sisters' New Orleans Troubadours. The appearance of this group at the Jefferson Theater in Birmingham, Alabama, in November 1904 marks the first time blacks were allowed to buy dress circle and parquet seats in this theater, and possibly the first time anywhere in Birmingham. In 1904 the sisters were still based in Atlanta, but by October 1905 they gave their home address as 2726 Wabash Avenue in Chicago. Chicago would remain their primary headquarters for the rest of their lives, and they were long-term residents in a fine stone home around the corner from the Regal Theater on the city's South Side. Even Alberta, who had moved to Arizona for several years, returned here a short time before her death.

The engagements continued along with their success, although they seemed to be playing as an act now, only part of a larger vaudeville bill. In March 1906 they played the Waldorf Astoria with Little Willie (Willie Robinson), who was, in the words of a *Springfield (Massachusetts) News* reporter quoted by Sampson, "a little fellow, about as big as a couple of bunches of toothpicks [whose] drollery would make a cow smile." By this time the three sisters were very accomplished dancers, as well as uncommonly able singers. In 1908 they spent two weeks in Washington, D.C., singing to overflow crowds in churches; Little Willie also appeared with them.

Caddie A. Whitman died in Atlanta, Georgia, in early June 1909 and was buried from Big Bethel AME church, the last church her husband pastored. It was at this point that Alice Whitman, long known professionally as Little Alice, along with an "adopted" sister, Mattie, joined her sisters. Mattie may have been a replacement for Mabel, who was billed as amusement director and manager of the troupe, which by mid-1910 was called The Whitman Sisters' Own Company. This troupe listed eighteen persons on its roster, including a stage manager, a director of music, and manager Mabel Whitman. By November of this year Mattie was gone, and Mabel was again performing. Sometime soon after this she took an act, Mabel Whitman and the Dixie Boys, on tour to Germany and Australia, while the other sisters stayed home. After this tour the sisters organized road show companies on a regular basis. Mabel was business and booking manager, Essie worked on designing and making costumes, and Alberta handled the music and was financial secretary.

The Whitman sisters seemed to have discovered the secret to a successful career in show business—they gave an exciting show featuring lots of dancing. Performers from the family starred with backup from the dancing of talented children. In Pittsburgh in 1911 their success as an act was so great that the following act could not go on as scheduled because audience enthusiasm would not die down. In using child performers, the Whitman sisters trained a number of black performers of the next generation. By about the time of World War I, when they began appearing solely for the black-operated Theater Owners' Booking Association (TOBA), they had established the pattern that would enable them to continue with great success until Mabel Whitman's death in 1942.

In the 1920s and 1930s the company regularly had between twenty and thirty performers, including dancing comedians, women singers, a chorus line of twelve or fourteen women, and an excellent five- or six-piece jazz band, led for nine years by Lonnie Johnson. There were always outstanding dancers, who were, however, never allowed to upstage the family performers. Among the attractions in the 1920s was a talented midget called Princess Wee Wee. It was natural to team her in 1926 with sixteen-year-old dancer Willie Bryant, who was already very tall. The top of Princess Wee Wee's head reached his waist.

The format of the shows varied, but they were always fast paced. When silent movies became a threat, the Whitmans simply cut the show to an hour and fifteen minutes to fit between screenings and carried on. It was the death of Mabel in 1942 that caused the show to succumb to changing conditions. The company struggled on only for another year, disbanding in 1943. Alice's son, known as Pops Whitman, then teamed with Louis Williams, who had been with the show. They went on to dance with big swing bands, and white audiences who had never heard of the Whitman Sisters knew of Pops and Louis. In 1950 the early death of Pops Whitman marked the end of an era.

Whitmans Had Distinct Roles

Each Whitman sister had a distinct personality and role. Mabel Whitman, the eldest, was a formidable woman; few except sister Alberta dared cross her. In *Jazz Dance,* Marshall and Jean Stearns tell of her run-in with the Regal Theater in Chicago, which refused to pay the agreed-upon price for the act. Mabel led her company to the Metropolitan Theater across the street, had a new stage built, put on her show, and ruined the Regal's business for two weeks. She had a loud voice and an unmerciful frown. According to the Stearnses, each time the company moved she said something like, "Now when we get to Cuthbert, the married couples will live together and the unmarried will not. It's a mortal sin, and I don't want to catch any of you young girls staying with any boys. Is that clear?" Both Mabel and Essie, who both had speaking voices as low as a man's and who were not adverse to spanking children, were more than capable of keeping the young performers in the show in line. Parents who entrusted youngsters to the Whitman sisters could be assured that they were not getting into trouble and that they were diligently doing their schoolwork, as well as being drilled as performers. Mabel's husband, "Uncle" Dave Payton, served as private tutor to the children.

Essie Barbara Whitman was born on July 4, 1882, in Osceola, Arkansas. She won a talent contest in a Kansas City, Missouri, theater about 1892. At age ten, her voice was clearly audible in the most remote regions of the theater as she sang "God Won't Love You if You Don't Be Good." She married three times, to Prince Ismael, Johnnie Woods, and Carter Hayes. Her specialties were as a comedian in a drunk act and as a singer—her voice was loud and very low-pitched. The Stearnses characterize her "resonant contralto" as making "Sophie Tucker sound like a soprano." She was so careful about how she looked that Alice remembered spinning out encore after encore while Essie was arranging the last errant curl before finally making her entrance. She retired from the act about 1926 and became a lay preacher at the Metropolitan Church. In addition, she worked on design and costumes for the show during the 1920s and appeared with the sisters in a review at New York's Lafayette Theater in 1930. She was an active evangelist until her death, caused by smoke inhalation in a home fire, on May 7, 1963, at Chicago's Provident Hospital.

As with Mabel and Alice, Alberta's birth date is not known for certain. For a time she was married to Maxie McCree. She wore her hair short and became a noted male impersonator. In her retirement she lived for several years in Arizona but died in Chicago in 1964. The only surviving sister, Alice, moved the bodies of Essie and Alberta to Atlanta for burial.

Alice Whitman was much younger than her other sisters. Billed as "The Queen of Taps," dancers who knew her and worked with her said she deserved the title. With her talent and youth, she was the unchallenged star of the shows for many years. The Stearnes quote her as saying,

> "I'd make my exit with the Shim-Sham-Shimmy, mostly from the waist down—along with more squeals—wearing a shawl and a little flimsy thing around my middle with a fringe and a bow on back. If I ever lost that bow, they used to say, I'd sure catch cold." Alice has no false modesty. "I could swing a mean . . ."—and she whistled to indicate the part of her anatomy and the general effect—"around."

Alice Whitman died in 1969. As mentioned earlier, her marriage to Aaron Palmer produced a son, Albert, born in 1919. A very talented dancer and sometime star of the shows, he worked under the stage name Pops Whitman and died young in 1950.

The Whitman sisters had a show business career that was remarkable in its length and success. Not only were they notable performers in their own right, they were accomplished on the business side of show business. Considering their remarkable achievements, it is unfortunate that they seem to belong to a nearly forgotten chapter of African American entertainment.

REFERENCES:

"Census." *Jet* 35 (January 30, 1969): 44.
"Beautiful Whitman Sisters Won International Acclaim on Stage." *Ebony* 9 (March 1954): 57.
Harris, Sheldon. *Blues Who's Who.* New York: Da Capo, 1981.
Kellner, Bruce. *The Harlem Renaissance: A Historical Dictionary for the Era.* New York: Methuen, 1984.
Sampson, Henry T. *The Ghost Walks: A Chronological History of Blacks in Show Business.* Metuchen, N.J.: Scarecrow Press, 1988.
Sherman, Joan R. *Invisible Poets: Afro-Americans of the Nineteenth Century.* Urbana: University of Illinois Press, 1974.
Stearns, Marshall, and Jean Stearns. *Jazz Dance.* New York: Macmillan, 1968.

Robert L. Johns

Marion Birnie Wilkinson
(1870-1956)
Humanitarian, educator, clubwoman

A skillful leader and producer of numerous statewide clubs and projects, Marion Birnie Wilkinson improved the quality of life for many, uplifted her race, and served humankind. The seeds she planted throughout the state of South Carolina, and the nation, continue to flourish and grow today.

Marion Raven Birnie Wilkinson was born June 23, 1870, to Richard and Anna Frost Birnie in Charleston, South Carolina. Her five sisters and brothers were Charles Wainwright, Lawrence, Richard, Hilda, and Florian. Later, Richard Birnie married Grace Hope and another child, James Hope Birnie was born from this marriage. The Birnies were well-to-do blacks, having received their status from earlier family members characterized as free blacks in Charleston. The father, Richard, was a cotton classer, who traveled in the South and Southwest following the cotton markets during that season.

The Birnie children began their education at Avery Institute in Charleston. While there, Wilkinson became interested in the advancement of her people. When she returned to the historic institution as a teacher, much of her money from her salary was channeled to worthy causes.

Education and service came naturally to Wilkinson, for her forefathers had also followed this path. Her maternal great-grandmother, who is known simply as Mrs. Stromer, founded a school in Charleston for blacks in 1820 and taught in schools established for freed blacks after the Civil War. Henry Frost, her maternal grandfather, operated a school on Magazine Street.

Wilkinson married Robert Shaw Wilkinson, also from Charleston, on June 29, 1897. Robert Shaw Wilkinson was the son of Charles Henry and Lavinia Robinson Wilkinson. He was educated at the Robert Shaw Memorial School, Avery Institute, and West Point, and received his B.A. from Oberlin College. His career as an educator began at Kentucky State University, and he later moved to South Carolina State University as professor of physics and chemistry on its first faculty in 1896. After Thomas E. Miller, a former African American congressman, resigned his presidency of the university in 1911, Wilkinson became president. As his wife, Marion Birnie Wilkinson became "first lady" and leader of students, faculty, and community. The Wilkinsons had four children: Helen Raven, Robert Shaw, Frost Birnie, and Lula Love.

On the campus of South Carolina State, Marion Birnie Wilkinson, affectionately known as "Mother Wilkinson," guided the work of the YWCA for many years. Through this organization, young women developed many characteristics that would serve them well in the workplace and in the community, such as leadership, character, and service. In

Marion Birnie Wilkinson

1928, Marion Birnie Wilkinson's leadership led to the construction of the only YWCA building on a college campus during that era. Funds were raised by the students for the construction of that building, later named the Marion B. Wilkinson Y-Hut. It served the Y organizations for years and is still being used on the college campus.

Wilkinson headed the College Boarding Department for many years. Auxiliary services like this department were not provided by the state of South Carolina; therefore, faculty and staff led the way for the students to have full college-wide services similar to those in other institutions.

The Wilkinsons began an Episcopal church in their home in 1912, both having practiced that faith in Charleston. St. Paul's Episcopal Church, located next to the college, had its early beginning in the president's residence, moved later to the Y-Hut, and in 1950 moved to its permanent home next to the college campus. Marion Wilkinson's brother, Charles W. Birnie, while practicing medicine as the first African American doctor in Sumter, South Carolina, founded Good Shepherd Episcopal Church for blacks in Sumter. Religion played an important role in Marion Wilkinson's family, and evidence shows family activity in the Episcopal church through several generations.

Women's Clubs Founded

Community and social uplift were Marion Wilkinson's primary concern. She became widely known for her work in these areas in Orangeburg, South Carolina, and nationwide.

Cited as a "gift of womanhood in Ebony," by historian Asa Gordon, she was in the initial group of women at Sidney Park Colored Methodist Episcopal Church (now Christian Methodist Episcopal Church), who in 1909 founded the South Carolina Federation of Negro Women. Others in the group were Sara B. Henderson, Celia D. Saxon, and Lizella A. Jenkins Moorer. These women spearheaded the growth of the federated clubs in the state such as the Uplift Club (Camden), Louise F. Holmes Literary and Art Club (Charleston), Sunlight Club (Orangeburg), and One More Effort (Sumter). During Wilkinson's leadership as president of the state organization, she received support from all the South Carolina federated clubs for the organization's projects. She gained further support for the projects of the South Carolina Federation of Colored Women from students, faculty and staff at the college.

During its infancy, a primary purpose of the South Carolina Federation of Colored Women was to found and support a reformatory school for delinquents. Later, the school was used for girls who lacked proper family protection. Known initially as Fairwold, the school later became the Marion Birnie Wilkinson Home for girls. Wilkinson, along with other citizens, headed committees to appear before the state legislature to gain annual financial support for the Fairwold School, having taken its name from the Fairwold, South Carolina, train station stop. The state withdrew financial support in 1929, placing the burden of all of the fundraising for the home on the local clubs. Fire destroyed the home, but under the leadership of Wilkinson the home was rebuilt in Cayce, South Carolina, on land donated by the Upper Diocese of the Episcopal Church of South Carolina. The Duke Foundation, which would not support the home when it served delinquents, funded the home after it was made an orphanage. The Marion B. Wilkinson Home for Girls was a model for a similar establishment in Virginia.

Etta B. Rowe, in a statement about the history and success of the South Carolina Federated Women's Club published in *Our Book of Gold*, declared:

> Why this interest, Why this success: Why this movement to the heroic effort of our women? To this question we exclaim in one, united voice—the great inspiring leadership of the sainted Marion Birnie Wilkinson. Real leadership does not mean standing at the head of an organization—real leadership is that technique so lofty, so skillful, that it induces others to work and perform in like manner.

Rowe also described Marion B. Wilkinson's personality. She describes the clubwoman's popularity on the national level: "So peculiarly sweet and delicate was her ambition that at a National Association meeting in Washington, when the crowd was yelling, 'Make Marian Wilkinson President,' she declined with modesty in favor of Mary McLeod Bethune, giving as her reason that Mrs. Bethune had far more struggles than she, let's honor her."

Wilkinson was instrumental in the founding of the Sunlight Club, an affiliate of the South Carolina Federation of

Negro Women in Orangeburg, South Carolina. In 1909, at the founding of the organization, the Sunlight Club promoted cultural enhancement, education, good character, and better human relations. Charter and early members came from faculty wives, staff of South Carolina State, Claflin College, and the Orangeburg community. The club continues to function, serving various aspects of the community. One of its main fund-raisers is the annual Wilkinson Tea held in February.

Wilkinson made many notable contributions at the state level. She organized recreation centers at Camp Jackson for African American soldiers during World War I. She was responsible for the Better Homes Project, a statewide project to improve homes of the less fortunate, and for the establishment of the Rosenwald Schools in South Carolina, part of a multistate effort in the South funded by the Julius Rosenwald Fund to build schools in rural communities. She worked with the Red Cross. She also set up a WPA training school and day nursery during the late 1930s. President Hoover sought her advice on the child welfare program.

Asa Gordon described the accomplishments of this formidable woman:

> The finest contribution Mrs. Wilkinson has made to the state is that of her life as a model mother for her family of four children. Mrs. Wilkinson has demonstrated in her life the possibility of a woman taking an active part in the work of the world and yet being true to her family obligations and bringing up a family in the way that it should go. She has been of inestimable aid to her husband as executive of the college at the same time that she trained her sons and daughters. . . . The career of Mrs. Wilkinson and others like her in this state proves that the progressive colored woman has shown herself capable of using the new freedom in such a way as to preserve the old family life and at the same time give the woman a chance to function as a productive member of the social order.

The Wilkinson children were well-educated and made important contributions to society. Helen Raven was professor of chemistry at the college and a follower in her mother's footsteps, serving the community of Orangeburg, the Sunlight Club, other civic organizations, and St. Paul's Episcopal Church. Robert Shaw Wilkinson, Jr., and Frost Birnie became outstanding physicians, and Lula Love, a social worker, was active in civic and welfare organizations.

Serving as the wife of the second president of South Carolina State, known then as State Agricultural and Mechanical College, Wilkinson was a gracious, knowledgeable, and intelligent woman. She and her husband were friends of many well-known persons, including Mary McLeod Bethune, Charlotte Hawkins Brown, and Benjamin E. Mays. They were influential on campus, in the city, state, and nationwide. Marian Birnie Wilkinson died on September 19, 1956. She is remembered for her tireless efforts to uplift the black community, particularly in South Carolina.

REFERENCES:

Birnie, C. W. "Education of the Negro in Charleston, South Carolina, Prior to the Civil War." *Journal of Negro History* 12 (January 1927): 13-21.

Caldwell, A. B. *History of the Negro.* South Carolina Edition. Atlanta: A. B. Caldwell Publishing Co., 1919.

Drago, Edmund L. *Initiative, Paternalism, and Race Relations—Charleston's Avery Normal Institute.* Athens: University of Georgia Press, 1990.

Fitchett, E. Horace. "The Origin and Growth of the Free Negro Population of Charleston, South Carolina." *Journal of Negro History* 26 (October 1941): 421-37.

Gordon, Asa H. *Sketches of Negro Life and History in South Carolina.* Columbia: University of South Carolina, 1929.

McDonald, Anna Birnie. Interview with Barbara Williams Jenkins, Sumter, South Carolina, January 1994.

National Negro Digest 4, Special Issue (1940): 28-29.

Nix, Nelson C. *A Tentative History of State A & M College.* Unpublished. Orangeburg, S.C.: 1940.

South Carolina Federation of Colored Women's Clubs, 1909-1959. *Fiftieth Anniversary, "Our Book of Gold."* Souvenir Journal, 1959.

Who's Who in Colored America, 1930-1932. Edited by Thomas Yenser. Brooklyn: Who's Who in Colored America, 1933.

Wilkinson, Lula Love. Interview with Barbara Williams Jenkins, Orangeburg, S.C., January 1994.

Zimmerman, Geraldyne Pierce. Interview with Barbara Williams Jenkins, Orangeburg, S.C., January 1994.

COLLECTIONS:

Articles, photographs, and memorabilia are available in the Miller F. Whittaker Library, South Carolina State University Historical Collection, Orangeburg, South Carolina.

Barbara Williams Jenkins

Camilla Williams
(1919-)
Opera singer, educator

Camilla Williams is one of the most important black opera singers in the twentieth century. With her remarkable voice and talent, she became a pioneer in the world of opera during her long and illustrious career. She paved the way for other black performers and premiered several important operas in the United States.

Camilla Williams was born in Danville, Virginia, on October 18, 1919. Her parents, Fanny Carey Williams and Booker Cornelius Williams, encouraged the musical educa-

Camilla Williams

tion of their four children: Camilla, Cornelius, Mary, and Helen. Music and culture were important to the Williams family as well as to the town of Danville. Camilla's development as a singer began in the Calvary Baptist Church choir. Even in these early days, the people she came in contact with recognized her outstanding talent. When she was only nine, the minister of the church predicted, "We have heard a voice today that is going to be heard around the world one day."

Williams attended the Presbyterian school in Danville until the fourth grade, when she transferred to public school. She was a gifted student who graduated as valedictorian from high school in 1937. She then studied at Virginia State College. There she earned a B.S. degree with a special recognition as the outstanding graduate of 1941. Throughout her early school days, mentors nurtured her potential and encouraged her to study music. Her first music teacher was Jemima Fliepen, who taught piano. When she was twelve, she and several other choir members from Calvary Baptist were selected to study with Raymond Aubrey, a noted voice professor from Wales. Aubrey taught at some of the most prestigious colleges in Virginia, which were closed to black students at the time.

During her college years, Williams sang frequently and toured with the Virginia State College choir. After graduating, she sought out Raymond Aubrey for further study. As she explained in a May 7, 1993, interview, he was one of the most important influences in determining the direction her career would take. She credits him with introducing her to the music of Mozart, which would become a lifelong passion for which she would win many awards. Aubrey also introduced her to

the music of Puccini, whose opera *Madame Butterfly* would make her famous many years later.

For a year after graduation, Williams taught third grade in Danville. In 1942 she moved to Philadelphia to begin a three-year course of study with the renowned voice teacher Marian Szekley-Freschi. Shortly after, in 1943, Williams became one of the first recipients of the newly established Marian Anderson Award, which she again won in 1944. This honor was among the many firsts in a singing and teaching career that has spanned almost half a century. Also in 1944, she won the Philadelphia Orchestra Youth Award, performing with the orchestra as her prize.

Successful Opera Singer Emerges

Camilla Williams made her professional debut with the Chicago Symphony. In the interview she described this period as her "Hungarian era," when she worked with Eugene Ormandy and Zoltan Kodaly. In 1944, during the war, she became the first unknown singer to be signed by RCA Victor. She made one recording on the Red Label of two Negro spirituals, "Oh, What a Beautiful City" and "A City Called Heaven."

Williams noted quite correctly in the interview that *Madame Butterfly* followed her throughout her career, from the day in the Calvary Baptist Church when Raymond Aubrey gave her a booklet with a beautiful Japanese woman on the cover to the time when Geraldine Ferrar, then the world's greatest Madame Butterfly, would tell her, "You have the voice for opera." After hearing Williams sing in Connecticut, Ferrar wrote to Columbia Records about her, prompting an invitation to audition for Laszlo Halasz, music director of the New York City Opera. Halasz thought Williams had the perfect voice for *Madame Butterfly*. After the war, on May 15, 1946, he sent for her to play the lead role of Cio Cio San. Williams's contract with the New York City Opera was also a first for black performers, since she was the first to have a steady contract with a major opera company. She sang the first *Aida* for New York City Center in 1948, the first New York performance of Mozart's *Idomeneo* for the Little Orchestra Society in 1950, and the first New York performance of Handel's *Orlando* in 1971.

Following an auspicious professional debut, Williams was on her way to becoming one of the most successful black opera singers of her time, singing with the world's greatest orchestras both at home and abroad. In 1947 the Newspaper Guild named her the First Lady of American Opera. She became Columbia Records' most traveled artist, touring the country extensively in the late 1940s and adding Alaska in 1950. Encouraged by Geraldine Ferrar to go abroad, she went to London in 1954 to begin a highly successful international tour that included the first Viennese performance of Menotti's *Saint of Bleecker Street* in 1955 and the first American Festival in Belgium. In the late 1950s, on behalf of the Department of State, she participated in the first African tour, which included fourteen countries. In 1959 she was the first American singer to tour Israel. She continued to tour internationally in the 1960s as a guest of President Dwight D.

Eisenhower. In 1960 she sang a concert for the crown prince of Japan. An eight-country tour in 1962 included Formosa, Australia, New Zealand, Korea, Japan, the Philippines, Laos, and South Vietnam. During that tour she received a gold medal from the emperor of Ethiopia.

Camilla Williams was married to Charles Beavers for nineteen years until his death in 1969. She described their life together as "one of the best marriages of any singer," and it sustained her throughout her career. In the 1970s, after a long and distinguished professional singing career, Williams turned her attention to teaching. She taught first in New York as a professor of voice at Brooklyn, Bronx, and Queens colleges. In 1977 she was invited to teach at Indiana University. She accepted the position as Indiana University's first black professor of voice and embarked upon a second career, which, in her own words, was one of the highlights of her life. She taught at Indiana University until her retirement in 1990. She continues to live in Bloomington and teach privately.

Current Address: School of Music, Indiana University, Bloomington, IN 47405.

REFERENCES:

Williams, Camilla. Interview with Robert W. Stephens, May 7, 1993.

Robert W. Stephens

Ella V. Chase Williams
(1852-?)
Educator, school founder, organization leader

Ella V. Chase Williams was a crusader for education who, along with her husband, founded two schools for blacks in Abbeville, South Carolina, that were connected with the Presbyterian church. Working in the newly reconstructed Deep South, the Williamses were forced to confront the racism of white Presbyterians. Yet they refused to be intimidated. Ella Williams's spirit of resistance and perseverance in the face of hardships made education a reality for African Americans in Abbeville.

The daughter of Lucinda Seaton Chase and William H. Chase, Williams was born in 1852 at 1109 I Street, N.W., Washington, D.C. Her mother was a free-born African American from Alexandria, Virginia, whose family was described by Lawson Scruggs in *Women of Distinction* as one of "the best and purest families in the Commonwealth of Virginia." Her relatives were wealthy and politically prominent, and she possessed a strong sense of family pride. William H.

Chase was a blacksmith and prestigious citizen in the District of Columbia. He moved to the district from nearby Maryland around 1835. By 1839, he had acquired the three-story brick house on I Street. Little is known about his side of the family, and he seems to have derived his social status from his marriage to Lucinda Seaton.

Williams was the first child born to Lucinda and William Chase in the imposing residence in northwest Washington, D.C. In 1854 her only brother, William Calvin Chase was born, followed by the birth of four sisters, Frances, Lucinda, Evelyn, and Ida. The Chases were members of the Fifteenth Street Presbyterian Church, where Lucinda and William had married in 1844, just three years after its founding.

In 1863 William Chase died, leaving his wife to raise their six children. Lucinda Seaton Chase, described by Hal Chase as a "strikingly tall and beautiful woman," did not remarry following her husband's accidental death. She kept the home on I Street and devoted herself to rearing her children. She exerted a great influence on them. In fact, neither Ella nor her sisters and brother left home before they were thirty years old. Lucinda Chase's commanding presence, independent thinking, service to the Fifteenth Street Presbyterian Church, and regular teas and open houses brought her children in contact with the most notable persons in the Washington, D.C., area. She made sure that all of her children received good educations and she encouraged her daughters to pursue careers. Her belief in the importance of education influenced three of her five daughters to become teachers.

Williams, along with her brother, began her education in the basement of the Fifteenth Street Presbyterian Church. The John F. Cooke School, named for its founder and teacher, John F. Cooke, Jr., an abolitionist from Oberlin, Ohio, educated her in the tradition of protest. Following the death of her father, Williams enrolled in the public schools of Washington. She completed the Preparatory Division of Howard University and must have completed her college education by 1879, for in that year she began her teaching career in the public schools of Washington.

At Howard University Williams had met a young, ambitious Presbyterian minister, also educated at Howard, with whom she fell in love. On December 1, 1882, she married Emory W. Williams in a large formal ceremony presided over by minister Francis J. Grimké, in the Fifteenth Street Presbyterian Church.

Following her marriage, Williams moved with her husband to Abbeville, South Carolina, fourteen miles west of Greenwood, South Carolina. Williams had never before been south of her native Washington. The reconstructed South was quite a contrast to the genteel society world of the African American elite in Washington.

The Williamses were sent to Abbeville by the Board of Missions for Freedmen of the Presbyterian church to build a church and school. But racism had created an extremely tense atmosphere in South Carolina, and they were met with strong opposition from the white Presbyterian congregation there. The African American Presbyterians, led by Emory Williams, separated from the South Carolina Synod, by whom they were not welcomed or financially supported, and formed the Colored Presbyterian Church (CPC).

Williams and her husband were forced to return to the North to solicit money from the northern Presbyterians. After three months they had secured fifteen hundred dollars, which supplemented the five hundred dollars received from the Board of Church Erection in New York City. They returned to Abbeville with the funds to build a church and school.

School Founded in Abbeville

A handsome church and adjoining school were constructed one year after the Abbeville congregation had organized. Williams opened the school in January 1884. It was named Ferguson Academy, after a Reverend Ferguson of New Jersey, one of the generous contributors to the building fund. Williams's success with the school was impressive. During the first year the school taught all elementary grades and maintained an average daily attendance of about sixty-five students. The academy offered grammar, history, geography, and arithmetic—all taught by Williams and her husband.

In the beginning the McClelland Presbytery, consisting of twelve counties in the upper part of South Carolina, had simply wanted to sustain a small parochial school as an auxiliary to their church. But by 1885, Williams's success caused them to reconsider. They decided to make Abbeville an educational center for African American children of both sexes. Previously it had only been open to boys. The plan to expand brought more trouble from racists within the church and in the Abbeville community. African American families were threatened and a fire of unknown origin damaged the school.

Again Emory Williams traveled north to raise funds for the project. This time Ella Williams remained behind to run the school, where she functioned as both principal and teacher. Emory Williams returned with one thousand dollars to build the extension which would include a college. By 1890, they had expanded the school with the addition of a forty-five by sixty foot brick building located on the church lot. According to Lowry Ware, in *Old Abbeville*, the *Abbeville Press and Banner* described the school as a "splendid three story structure with mansard roof—a monument to the seal of [African Americans] and the liberality of his [Emory Williams's] Northern sympathizers. . . . The institution is practically out of debt and the work in the college, and on the farm which is connected with the school, progresses in a satisfactory manner." The building could accommodate three hundred children. The academy included boarding and day students and had an industrial department. Students could work on the farm and in the department in order to earn their way.

Although she taught full-time at the school, Williams remained active in the church. In the spring of 1885, she traveled to Cincinnati, Ohio, where she represented the women of the South at the Woman's Missionary Meeting in connection with the General Assembly of the Presbyterian Church of America. She was reelected representative and

traveled to Minneapolis, Minnesota, the following year and was sent to the Centennial Assembly in Philadelphia in 1888.

Both Williams and her husband persistently worked to meet the needs of the church congregation and the school. In 1891, they had 115 students. The Abbeville farm on which Williams resided was austere compared to her childhood home on I Street in the capital city of the United States. Yet, she willingly sacrificed personal comforts in her effort to contribute to the welfare and advancement of her people. The sacrifice of the Williamses was met with resentment. Not all of Emory Williams's congregation backed his efforts to expand, nor did they appreciate the activity of Ella Williams, who did not conform to their notion of a minister's wife.

Time of Sorrow and Change

Ella and Emory Williams celebrated their tenth wedding anniversary in December 1892 and enjoyed Christmas, but the new year started off badly. Ella's mother became ill and died before the end of January. Lucinda Chase's funeral sermon was delivered by Francis J. Grimké on January 28, 1893, at the Fifteenth Street Presbyterian Church in Washington, D.C. Not long after Ella Williams's return from Washington, Emory Williams, as editor-in-chief of the *Atlantic Beacon*, Ferguson Academy's weekly newspaper, wrote an editorial regarding the management and general control of the work taken on by the Board of Missions for Freedmen. The article apparently offended the Board of Missions for Freedmen of the Northern Presbyterian Church, who insisted that Emory Williams retract his statements. When he refused, he was removed from the presidency of the school he and Ella had founded. Ella Williams lost her principalship and her position in the classroom. The Williamses were replaced by Thomas Amos, a minister from Baltimore, who became president of the academy. The CPC retained Emory Williams as their pastor. However, conditions did not improve. People were disgruntled, some because Williams was retained by the church, and others because, after all of the Williamses' efforts on behalf of the school, they were booted out.

The situation came to a head on April 27, 1893, when the McClelland Presbytery sent a committee to investigate the contention in the Second Presbyterian Church. At this meeting the members of the CPC voted forty-eight to forty-six to remove Williams as pastor of the church.

Ferguson and Williams College Founded

If Ella and her husband were depressed by the events of 1893, they did not allow their feelings to interrupt their work. Together they established another institution to promote the industrial, literary, musical, and religious advancement of African Americans in Abbeville. Within a year Ella Williams was again presiding over a large and flourishing school and her husband was pastoring a church. Many of the members of the original congregation supported the couple and helped them build the new school, which they named Ferguson and Williams College.

Ferguson and Williams College was dedicated in June 1894, and in 1895 the new church, Third Presbyterian Church of Abbeville, became the first African American congregation to join the South Carolina Presbytery of the Southern Presbyterians. The *Minutes of the Presbyterian Church, Convened in Abbeville, South Carolina, Thursday, November 17, 1904,* report that the Williamses were dismissed from the church in 1897, and that Emory Williams was presumed dead. However, he was still alive, and Ella continued to run the school.

The Williamses wanted to form a separate African American church. In 1897, Ella traveled with her husband to Charlotte, North Carolina, where he presented their case to the Southern General Assembly. In November 1897, a religious convention took place in Birmingham, Alabama, where the need for a separate church and school was discussed. For the next two years Ella Williams and an assistant continued to run Ferguson and Williams College with the support of the southern Presbyterians. Her husband traveled extensively, garnering support for the separate church.

On Thursday, November 17, 1904, the Afro-American Presbyterian Church Synod convened at Ferguson and Williams College. For all of their energy and hard work to bring the church into being, it did not last. Nor did the school. Emory Williams apparently died around 1910. Ella Chase Williams continued to live in Abbeville and to direct the school until she died. The year of her death is not known. A 1915 Government Survey lists her as principal of the school, which had an enrollment of twenty-five pupils. The school officially closed in 1919, and the buildings became Abbeville Memorial Hospital.

Ella V. Chase Williams devoted her life to the uplift of African Americans through education and religious training. She worked with young people daily as teacher and Christian leader. In 1906 she was among the honorees at the Negro Young People's Christian and Education Congress in Washington, D.C. Williams edited the woman's section of the *Atlantic Beacon* and often contributed to her brother's newspaper, the *Washington Bee*. She was president of the Women's Synodical Missionary Society, the Atlantic Synod. She was also president of the Women's Christian Temperance Movement of South Carolina.

REFERENCES:

Chase, Hal. "William C. Chase and the *Washington Bee*" *Negro History Bulletin* 36 (December 1973): 172-74.

Minutes of the Seventh Annual Meeting of the Synod of the Afro-American Presbyterian Church Convened in Abbeville, South Carolina, Thursday, November 17, 1904.

Parker, Inez M. *The Rise and Decline of the Program of Education for Black Presbyterians of the United Presbyterian Church, USA, 1865-1970.* San Antonio, Tex.: Trinity University Press, 1977.

Penn, Irvin Garland. *Souvenir: Official Program and Music of the Negro Young People's Christian and Education Congress.* Washington, D.C.: N.p., 1906.

Scruggs, Lawson A. *Women of Distinction.* Raleigh, N.C.: Scruggs, 1893.

Tindall, George Brown. *South Carolina Negroes.* Columbia: University of South Carolina, 1952.

U.S. Bureau of Education. *Negro Education: A Study of the Private and High Schools for Colored People in the United States.* Vol. 2. Washington, D.C.: Government Printing Office, 1917.

Ware, Lowry. *Old Abbeville.* Columbia, S.C.: SCMAR, 1992.

Nagueyalti Warren

Marion Williams
(1927-1994)
Gospel singer

Marion Williams, the grande dame of gospel music, delighted audiences throughout the world for half a century. As gospel music historian Bernice Johnson Reagon was widely quoted as stating, "She is simply the best we had during the gospel era of the '40s and '50s." Critics and journalists noted her importance: *Down Beat* magazine called her "the finest artist gospel has produced"; *Broadside* said that she was "the most creative singer alive"; *Jazz Journal* labeled her "the greatest singer ever"; *Rolling Stone* saw her as "the equal of any blues singer"; the *New York Times* recognized her as "one of the greatest jazz singers"; and following the death of Mahalia Jackson in 1972, *New York Newsday* named her "gospel's reigning queen." Secular references in her music notwithstanding, Williams never performed songs with "worldly" texts.

Born in Miami, Florida, on August 29, 1927, Marion Williams was the youngest of eleven children, a group that included three sets of twins. Williams was one of only three children who survived past the first year. (Some sources indicate that she was the tenth of eleven children.) Williams's father was a West Indian who worked as a barber and also taught music. Her mother, originally from South Carolina, worked as a laundress and sang in a choir. Williams referred to her mother as a saint and related to gospel historian Tony Heilbut, as quoted in his book *The Gospel Sound,* "She used to go from fence to fence, spreading good news." Williams's father died when she was nine years old. Because of the family's poor financial circumstances, Williams dropped out of school at age fourteen to work as a maid and child nurse. Subsequently she worked in a laundry, "from sunup to sundown."

Williams was only three years old when she began singing with her mother, a soloist in the church choir. Williams's roots were in sanctified singing in the Church of God and Christ, a denomination to which she remained faithful

Marion Williams

throughout her life. From her local Pentecostal church, she branched out to other churches in Miami, tent revival meetings, and street corner revivals. Her life's ambition was to become a traveling gospel singer, like the many male quartets, the sanctified shouter Rosetta Tharpe, and the Baptist mourner Mary Johnson Davis. Her young ears also came in contact with the sounds of blues and jazz, played by her older brother on a jukebox.

Gospel Performer Joins Ward Singers

While visiting her sister in Philadelphia, Pennsylvania, in the mid-1940s, Williams encountered the famous Clara Ward Singers, the preeminent gospel group of the 1940s and 1950s, at the Ward African Methodist Episcopal (AME) Church. Upon invitation, Williams sang "What Could I Do (If It Wasn't for the Lord)" at the church. The teenager's stunning performance amazed and captivated the audience. Clara Ward immediately asked Miami's premier gospel soloist to join her group.

After about a year, she accepted the invitation. Between 1947 and 1958, Williams, as one of the now-famous Ward Singers, stood out as a backup member and excelled as a vocal leader. In 1948 the group began recording for Savoy Records. According to Heilbut, the verse that Williams sang on W. Herbert Brewster's "Surely God Is Able" made the record a hit: "Marion's 'Surelys' were the most terrifying blast out of gospel in the fifties." Other Ward Singers recordings featuring Williams followed; "Packin' Up" and "I'm Climbing Higher and Higher" were perhaps the most notable.

Williams left the group in 1958, taking group members Frances Steadman, Kitty Parham, and Henrietta Waddy along with her. She organized another gospel group, the Stars of Faith. Nine years later, she joined the Wards for a one-night appearance. The number that caused the Philadelphia congregation to shout was once more Williams's rendition of "Surely."

Heilbut states that all Ward Singers were on salary, except family members. He reminds his readers that "no group ever made money like the Wards." When it was later suggested to Williams that the Ward Singers acquired their wealth primarily from her singing, she responded, "That's all right. If it wasn't for Gertrude Ward, I'd be taking care of somebody's children, and singing on Sundays." And, though the Stars of Faith enjoyed tremendous success, Williams recognized that the group lacked the managerial skills of Gertrude Ward.

Williams made her theatrical debut in 1961 in the gospel song-play *Black Nativity,* the text of which was written by the noted black author Langston Hughes. Hughes wrote the songplay especially for Williams, and he chronicled its success in his frequent letters to another noted black writer, Arna Bontemps. These letters were edited and published by Charles H. Nichols in 1980. Following an outstanding three-year run in the United States, *Black Nativity* and its star enjoyed fantastic success in Europe. Appearing along with Williams were costars Alex Bradford and the Stars of Faith. During the Christmas season of 1963, *Black Nativity* was produced for national television.

Williams Goes Solo

Gospel diva Williams made her debut as a soloist in 1966 and continued in that capacity until her death. During the late 1960s, she covered the college circuit, appeared at the Antibes Jazz Festival in France and the Dakar Festival of Negro Arts in Africa, did several television specials, and received from Princess Grace of Monaco one of Europe's top achievement honors, the International Television Award. Though the popularity of contemporary gospel rose in the 1970s, Williams, a gospel traditionalist, performed less frequently. Through the efforts of Heilbut and his Spirit Feel label, however, this gospel legend was not out of the public's mind for long. From the mid-1980s until her death, her concert career thrived, limited only by the physical disabilities she experienced from diabetes.

Though financial success seemed to evade her, one year prior to her death, Williams was rewarded with $374,000 as a MacArthur Foundation award recipient. The same year, 1993, she dined at the White House and shared the Presidential Box at the Kennedy Center Opera House with President Bill Clinton, Hillary Rodham Clinton, and other Kennedy Center honorees: Johnny Carson, Stephen Sondheim, Arthur Mitchell, and George Solti.

Heilbut devoted an entire chapter to Williams in his definitive study of gospel music, *The Gospel Sound.* Of Williams he wrote,

Her style is to respond to the moment ... an overwhelming showman ... retiring and flamboyant ... Marion is simply the most lyrical and imaginative singer gospel has produced. ... Hers is thrilling musicianship. ... She's a fat sweet-faced woman whose physical graces belie her size. When she sings, she may strut, run, Suzy-Q, sashay, sit or kneel. ... Marion's ability to incorporate the best traditional approaches in a uniquely personal way, her vocal range from growl to whoops, from big-mama holler to little girl trill, should impress anybody.

Music critics, in addition to praising Williams's singing, usually remarked that she was also a great entertainer. In his "Appreciation," written for the *Washington Post* one week following her death, Richard Harrington commented, "She could shout a church into submission, leaving fans faint, falling into faith." He further remarked, "Untrained but unlimited, she sang with astonishing rhythmic acumen and perfect timing, displaying a gift for ornamentation to rival makers of illuminated Bibles. ... [W]hen Williams sang, she was illuminating the Bible in her own inimitable way." He also recalled a Williams appearance at the old Griffith Stadium in Washington, D.C. "She ran around the infield in the middle of her performance. When it came to God, Marion Williams touched all the bases."

Missionary Faithful to Gospel Music

Williams received abundant recognition and praise throughout her professional career, but she never lost her humility or let the adulation go to her head. In her eyes, as she frequently remarked, she was simply doing the Lord's work: "Thank you Lord for all you've done for me." She referred to herself as a missionary, one who ministered through her renditions of "We Shall Be Changed," "Standing Here Wondering Which Way to Go," "Packin' Up," "Prayer Changes Things," and "How I Got Over." Never was the delivery of a song the same twice, since she was a marvelous improviser, shifting rhythms and embellishing melodies, adding surprising whoops and hollers to her songs.

Promoters and producers who envisioned Williams's ascension to the top of the pop charts made efforts to persuade her to sing more secular material and offered her lucrative contracts, but she remained faithful to gospel music. She told Sharon Fitzgerald for *American Visions,* December/January 1994: "Secular artists sing about the lovers of their bodies—their baby, their honey, 'my woman' and all that. I sing about Jesus Christ, who is the lover of my soul."

Williams's performing venues included nightclubs, jazz festivals, and summer park extravaganzas. She believed that people who refused to go to church also needed to hear the gospel. It was her firm conviction that if she could reach listener's ears, she stood a good chance of reaching their spirits. She did not object, however, to appearing on the same bill as secular singers and was not envious of those who made fortunes in the world of popular music. As she said to journalist Steve Bloom of *New York Newsday* just prior to her appearance at New York City's Central Park Bandshell in August 1988,

It don't bother me. ... I feel like what's for me I'll have. In earlier years I might have worried about it. As you grow older you find out that you don't need what you thought you needed to take you over. I'm not singing like some people who want to make a living off it. It's just a part of me that wants to see souls being saved. And I don't care who know that. ... If they don't want to book me because of that, they can forget it.

The owner of Savoy Records wanted to make Williams another Big Mama Maybelle, a popular 1950s blues shouter, and she was offered $100,000 to cut one blues album. The offer was not at all appealing to Williams. She said in *New York Newsday,* "I've been eatin' all these years. I often tell them, if they don't book me, I'll just sit home and eat my rice and beans. ... And enjoy it."

All that Heilbut and others have written about Williams's artistry, versatility, vocal agility, and improvisational skills is clearly illustrated on an album rarely listed in her discography. Williams was persuaded by bassist Ray Brown and vibraphonist Milt Jackson, two jazz legends, to join them and several other jazz artists on a 1964 Verve recording. The album was appropriately titled *Much in Common.* Brown had come under Williams's vocal spell when she appeared in London, England, in *Black Nativity* in March 1963. He wrote that he never forgot the sound.

Brown contacted Williams and proposed the idea. He later recalled,

She sounded a little apprehensive, but said she would be glad to come and meet us. I thought that maybe I could get her to sing a few blues. ... However, upon arriving at the studio she informed me that she did not sing any popular music, jazz or blues. After finishing the five spiritual tunes ... I think that it doesn't matter whether we did blues or whatever type tunes we would have done, as the background of the singing of Marion Williams to show we have so much in common.

Her five spiritual tunes were "When the Saints Go Marching In," "I've Got to Live the Life I Sing About in My Song," "Swing Low, Sweet Chariot," "Sometimes I Feel Like a Motherless Child," and "Give Me That Old Time Religion." Williams was backed by Brown, Jackson, organist Wild Bill Davis, guitarist Kenny Burrell, and drummer Albert "Tootsie" Heath. Brown insisted that they play the same on the spirituals as they did on their jazz tunes, "because the feeling of the music is the same." The compatibility of the two genres is clearly evident on the album, as is Williams's enormous talent.

In total, Williams recorded ten albums. She can also be heard on the 1991 film soundtrack for *Fried Green Tomatoes,* which was dedicated to her, and the 1992 movie soundtrack for *Mississippi Masala.* Williams was guest soloist for the 1992 premiere of trumpeter and composer Wynton Marsalis's gospel-influenced jazz suite, "In This House/On This Morning." She was also featured in the PBS presentation *Amazing Grace.*

Honored with Award from the MacArthur Foundation

1993 was a banner year for the pioneering gospel singer because she became the first singer to be honored with a "genius" award by the MacArthur Foundation. When the word reached her, she was preparing an after-service meal in the soup kitchen at her Philadelphia church. "I thought I was in heaven and the angels were talking to me," she told Sharon Fitzgerald for *American Visions.* She cried loudly, leading the church mothers and daughters to assume that a family member had died.

It was the chair of the National Endowment for the Arts, Jane Alexander, who introduced the segment honoring Williams at the Kennedy Center Award Ceremony on December 5, 1993. Alexander described Williams as the owner of the "golden voice of gospel's golden age." Williams's tribute included performances by a few of the many singers she had inspired, namely, Aretha Franklin, Little Richard, and Billy Preston, as well as a one-hundred-voice gospel choir.

On the day of the Kennedy Center for the Performing Arts event and the White House reception, Williams was asked to comment on the major changes in her field during her career and her outlook on the future of her art form for the *Washington Post.* She responded,

> When I first started out, gospel music was in its infancy. People didn't pay attention to it, really. That didn't bother me; I kept on singing. I loved it and the spirit that I got from it. It just tugged at the very soul of folks. It made me want to live what I sing. I think around 1940, '45 was when people really started to take heed of gospel and know it was an art form. . . . I think gospel will just bloom. It's opening up more than ever.

There was national press coverage announcing Williams's death on Saturday, July 2, 1994. Williams, who had long suffered from diabetes and kidney ailments, died of vascular disease. As reported by the *Chicago Tribune,* July 4, 1994, she was survived by a son, Robin, of Philadelphia, a brother, Isaac, of Miami, and three grandchildren.

Marion Williams arrived on the gospel scene when the art form was still in its infancy but lived to see it acquire great popularity and respect, largely because of her outstanding contributions. She brought to gospel a sense of dignity, a capacity for entertaining that exceeded that of most of her peers, a vocal range that few could duplicate, and a humility that was supported by personal and artistic security. In so doing, she was in a class by herself.

REFERENCES:

"Amazingly Graced." *Washington Post,* July 10, 1994.
Brown, Ray. Liner Notes. *Much in Common.* Verve Records, 1964.
Fitzgerald, Sharon. "The Glorious Walk of Marion Williams." *American Visions* 8 (December/January 1994): 48-51.
Heilbut, Tony. *The Gospel Sound: Good News and Bad Times.* New York: Simon and Schuster, 1971.
Hine, Darlene Clark, ed. *Black Women in America.* Brooklyn: Carlson Publishing, 1993.
"Marion Williams, 40 Years on the Road to Salvation." *New York Newsday,* August 5, 1988.
Nichols, Charles H., ed. *Arna Bontemps-Langston Hughes Letters, 1925-1967.* New York: Dodd, Mead, 1980.
"Singer Marion Williams Influenced Gospel Music." *Chicago Tribune,* July 4, 1994.
Southern, Eileen. *Biographical Dictionary of Afro-American and African Musicians.* Westport, Conn.: Greenwood Press, 1982.
"2 Worlds Meet at Kennedy Center." *New York Times,* December 6, 1993.
"Views from the Top." *Washington Post,* December 5, 1993.

D. Antoinette Handy

Blenda Jacqueline Wilson
(1941-)
College president, administrator, educator

An insightful and visionary educator and school administrator, Blenda Wilson is a model for twenty-first-century leadership in academia. Her African American heritage provides the historical perspective needed for embracing diverse populations and shifting power structures; her experience as a woman produces alternate ways of knowing how to manage people and problems; and her educational background and training equip her with the knowledge to address the needs of an expanding multicultural society. As president of California State University at Northridge, Wilson has proven herself capable of preparing for the future while also dealing effectively with current major crises.

Born in Perth Amboy, a small urban town in New Jersey, on January 28, 1941, Blenda Jacqueline Wilson was the middle child in a family of three, with an older sister and a younger brother. Wilson's father, Horace Lawrence Wilson, attended trade school in New Jersey and became an electrician. However, the trade unions of this northern state refused to admit him. He therefore earned a living by working as a presser in a dry cleaning establishment. Wilson's desire to teach and her ambition to lead and to change the inequities in education were dreams passed down to her by her mother. Margaret Brogsdale, Wilson's mother, grew up in south Georgia and attended Seldon Normal School, where she trained to be a teacher. But when she married and moved north to New Jersey, her southern education was scoffed at. Marga-

Blenda Jacqueline Wilson

ret Brogsdale Wilson worked a variety of white-collar jobs but never was able to enter the teaching profession.

Although she was born in Perth Amboy, Wilson actually grew up in Woodbridge, a small, village-like community that was mostly white. In 1946, when Wilson entered the New Jersey public school system as a student at PS #1, she was one of only two African Americans in her kindergarten class. She recalls that the school was a good one with mostly women teachers, all of whom were white and most of whom had high expectations of the students. Wilson was a happy, active child who participated in the Brownie troop at her school, fought and played with her sister and brother, and developed a love for reading.

At Woodbridge High School, Wilson campaigned for secretary of the student government association and won, worked on the yearbook staff, and was a cheerleader and a debater. She might not have been exposed to black culture had it not been for her family's Sunday trips into Perth Amboy to attend an African American Baptist church. Wilson sang in the youth choir and worked in the Baptist Student Union.

In 1958 Wilson graduated from Woodbridge High School and began what was to become an educational journey leading to a college presidency. As a high school senior Wilson learned that several women's colleges were offering scholarships to bright young women of any race. She researched the colleges at her local library and came up with a list. Her top choices were Smith and Cedar Crest. She chose Cedar Crest, perhaps because of the financial assistance it offered; however, unlike Smith, Cedar Crest was not highly competitive.

Located in Allentown, Pennsylvania, the liberal arts college of only five hundred students was situated on eighty-eight wooded acres with part of the campus designated as an arboretum. Only 22 percent of Cedar Crest students graduated from the school. As it turned out, Wilson became one of the college's most prominent alumnae. She is listed along with Claudia Marshall, vice president of Travelers Insurance, in *The Right College,* published by Arco, and in various other publications about the college.

At Cedar Crest Wilson found a nurturing environment that was woman-centered and that allowed for her continued growth and development. Wilson majored in English education because she loved reading and language. Following in her mother's footsteps, she prepared to teach, specializing in secondary school English and elementary school reading.

Begins Career in Education

Wilson graduated from Cedar Crest in 1962, having earned a bachelor of arts degree in English education. She began her teaching career in her hometown with the Woodbridge Township Public Schools in the fall of 1962. While teaching, Wilson continued her education in order to increase her salary. In 1965, she earned a master's degree in education from Seton Hall University.

While Wilson was not an active participant in the civil rights movement and the black power movement in New Jersey, these movements and the Newark riots influenced the politics that touched her life. They helped kick open doors previously closed to African Americans. When the doors opened, she was prepared to walk through. In 1966, Wilson accepted one of the first War on Poverty jobs created by the Lyndon B. Johnson administration and moved to New Brunswick, New Jersey. She wrote a grant for the first Head Start program in the state. It was funded, and she served as Head Start director and education specialist for one year. In 1967, she became associate executive director and education director of Head Start. Wilson quickly rose to the top, and in 1968, she became executive director of Middlesex County Economic Opportunities Corporation (MCEOC), one of the War on Poverty programs.

Wilson's stint in federally funded jobs was short-lived, as was the actual War on Poverty. In the fall of 1969, Wilson became assistant to the provost at Rutgers University. Once again she was on a fast track to success, becoming assistant provost in 1970 and executive assistant to the provost in 1971. As executive assistant to the provost, Wilson reported directly to the university president. Primarily responsible for policy development and supervision of Rutgers's affirmative action program, Wilson managed the Educational Opportunity Fund programs at fourteen schools and colleges. During the summer of 1970, Wilson participated in the Institute for Educational Management at Harvard Business School, which tremendously enhanced her administrative skills.

Wilson's wide-ranging experience and personable manner brought her to the attention of recruiters seeking talented minorities. In 1972, Harvard wooed her away from Rutgers with an offer to become associate dean for administration. Moving to Massachusetts, Wilson remained in this position for three years before her promotion to senior associate dean in the Graduate School of Education in 1975. As senior associate dean Wilson's primary responsibilities were planning and coordinating the decision-making process at the Graduate School of Education and acting in the dean's absence. She also developed and supervised fiscal affairs and budget management, academic and administrative personnel, student and alumni affairs, facilities planning and maintenance, and grants and contracts.

While working as senior associate dean, Wilson enrolled in a graduate program of Higher Education Administration at Boston College. She completed her Ph.D. degree, graduating in 1979. In 1982, Wilson moved to Washington, D.C., where she worked for two years as vice president for effective sector management at the Independent Sector, an association of national charitable, voluntary, and philanthropic organizations whose purpose is to enhance and encourage nonprofit initiative. As vice president Wilson planned and implemented the first Independent Sector division designed to improve the management capabilities of nonprofit organizations.

Manages Colorado's $424 Million Education Budget

Looking for challenge and change, Wilson moved to Denver in 1984 to accept concurrent appointments as executive director of the State Department of Higher Education and state cabinet officer. As director of the Colorado Commission on Higher Education, Wilson supervised six higher education governing boards and twenty-eight campuses. She managed a state budget of $424 million, 21.6 percent of the state's general fund budget, and $85 million in capital construction in 1987.

Wilson met her husband, Louis Fair, Jr., also an educator, in Colorado and they were married in 1985. Having met the challenge in Colorado, Wilson set her sights on Michigan. In 1988, she became chancellor of the University of Michigan-Dearborn campus and a professor of public administration and education there. She was the first woman to head a public university in the state of Michigan. The University of Michigan-Dearborn campus is a comprehensive state university with an undergraduate college and graduate and professional programs leading to the master's degree level. The Dearborn campus serves eight thousand students in the southeastern part of Michigan. It is one of three campuses in the University of Michigan system.

As chancellor, Wilson was credited with providing extraordinary vision and energetic leadership. Under her supervision the Dearborn campus became an option for many inner-city youth who might not have considered college a possibility. Minority enrollment was 5.7 percent when Wilson took office in 1988. By 1992, it had grown to 6.9 percent. The *Detroit Free Press,* May 21, 1992, noted that "students, faculty and alumni credit Wilson with making the Dearborn campus, which long had stood in the shadow of its Ann Arbor sister, more visible."

Wilson Heads West

California lured Wilson and her husband, who was director of Detroit City Airport, to its golden shores. The rapidly changing demographics and ethnic diversity in southern California were appealing challenges to Wilson, who accepted the presidency at California State University-Northridge in 1992. She was appointed by the board of trustees on May 20, becoming the first African American and the third person to preside at the university. Wilson says that she plans to remain at Cal State-Northridge until she retires. She wants to make the 353-acre commuter campus with more than one thousand faculty and twelve hundred staff ready for the twenty-first century.

Wilson, the only woman to preside over a branch of the largest public university system in the United States, was in effect forced to become commander-in-chief of the campus on January 17, 1994, when California State-Northridge found itself at the epicenter of one of southern California's most destructive earthquakes. The early morning earthquake killed fifty-five people, including two of Wilson's students. Although the earth was quaking, Wilson's faith remained unshaken. "I have a deep abiding personal faith," she said in *Black Issues in Higher Education* February 10, 1994, "and I believe that you can accomplish what you need to accomplish." Wilson amazed her faculty, students, staff, and the chancellor for the state university system, Barry Munitz, with her grace under pressure. One board of trustees member stated, "Her leadership skills had been well documented before the quake, and are validated even more because of this crisis." Wilson used the earthquake as an opportunity to create a better and more modern campus.

Wilson serves on the governing boards of several organizations, including the Children's Television Workshop, the J. Paul Getty Trust, Union Bank, the Achievement Council, and the International Foundation for Education and Self-Help. She is past chair of the American Association of Higher Education and a commissioner of the Education Commission of the States. Wilson serves on both the Advisory Council of Presidents and the Program Advisory Group for State Governing Boards.

Wilson was selected as one of the one hundred "Emerging Leaders in American Higher Education" by *Change Magazine* and the American Council on Education, October 1978. In 1989, Wilson won the Michigan Bell Living the Dream Award and the Ebony Excellence Women on the Move Award presented by the Renaissance chapter of the Links. A Community Service Award was presented to Wilson in 1990 by the Detroit public schools' Student Motivational Program, and this same year she was selected as one of the ninety "Leaders for the 1990s" by *Crain's Detroit Business* magazine. Wilson was chosen as Distinguished Alumna of the Year by the College of Education and Human Services Alumni Association, Seton Hall University, in May 1991. She is also the recipient of numerous honorary degrees.

Wilson's ability to make headway in seemingly impossible situations is a legacy passed down to her from her African American foremothers, who were candles in the dark for their families. Inspired by the setbacks and challenges her family faced, Blenda Wilson has made her mark in a field that opens doors of opportunity to all who seek knowledge. As president of a branch of the largest system of higher education in the country, she is positioned to steer the university into the next century. She is a leader who promotes educational opportunity as a rite of passage available to all.

Current Address: Office of the President, California State University, 18111 Nordhoff Street, Northridge, CA 91330.

REFERENCES:

Hayes, Dianne Williams, and Mary-Christine Phillip. "Quake at the Epicenter, A President Stands Her Ground." *Black Issues in Higher Education* 10 (February 10, 1994): 20-23.

Wilson, Blenda. Telephone interview with Nagueyalti Warren. March 15, 1994.

"Wilson Leaving Dearborn Campus." *Detroit Free Press,* May 21, 1992.

Nagueyalti Warren

Emma J. Wilson

Emma J. Wilson

Educator, school founder, missionary, fund-raiser

" "W hy you are crazy child, you can't go to school. Only white children go to school." These words, published in the *National Cyclopedia of the Colored Race,* are said to have been spoken by the mother of Emma J. Wilson. They became the inspirational seed that nurtured Wilson's desire to start a school for black youth, a dream that was fulfilled with the creation of the Mayesville Educational and Industrial Institute in Mayesville, South Carolina. At its height, this institution enrolled approximately five hundred students, one hundred and fifty of whom were boarders while forty were orphans. The Mayesville Institute was accredited in 1896 but never received the type of financial support needed to keep it active. Today, this renovated facility is used as an elementary school in the Mayesville District of Sumpter County, South Carolina. While the Mayesville Institute no longer exists, Wilson's desire to provide an educational framework and resource for the children of her race is still being honored.

Emma J. Wilson's family background is poorly documented. The most cited source of information, *National Cyclopedia of the Colored Race,* indicates that she was "born in the days bordering on slavery . . ." and that she got "three

little white children to teach her" the basic alphabet. From this basic knowledge, Wilson then taught herself to master "the big words" and learned to read. She attended a Mission School taught by Northern women and from there enrolled and graduated from the Scotia Seminary at Concord, North Carolina.

Addresses Needs of Rural Black Youth

While planning and praying to go to the Scotia Seminary, Wilson promised the Lord that, if it were His will, she would go to Africa as a missionary. After finishing her course work at Scotia, however, she returned to her hometown of Mayesville, South Carolina, where she found a "village without a Negro school building or any one to teach." This became her Africa.

Wilson opened school with ten pupils in an abandoned cotton-gin house, accepted eggs, chickens, and produce as tuition, and persuaded the County Board of Education to allot her forty-five dollars a year in aid. With this munificent sum she hired an assistant, accepted more students, and began to build a schoolhouse. When Mayesville Institute was opened, the segregated school system was well entrenched; poverty generally prevailed in the South, among blacks in particular; and white hostility was evident. Educating southern black children was considered an unnecessary luxury, if not a dangerous indulgence, by state and county governments. In many rural counties, schools for black children were kept open only a few months of the year. Expenditures for buildings, supplies, and teacher's salaries were a fraction of that spent for white schools and there was little pretense that a thorough education was being offered to black children. Southern blacks were forced to develop their own educational institutions in order to overcome some of these inadequacies.

The black educator, male or female, was normally young and very committed but limited in educational background and lifetime experiences. Armed with exceptional leadership qualities and an education from one of the black seminaries or normal schools, these young people would return home eager to start a school of their own that would provide education to other black youth. The black educator had to teach, administer, and do extensive fund-raising just to keep a facility open, since there was little to no support from the state or county and financial resources were derived from local churches and northern white philanthropists.

For Wilson, fund-raising meant extensive traveling throughout southern and northern states. Alone but unafraid, she spent many years explaining her dream and soliciting contributions. William Lloyd Garrison and Richard H. Dana became her northern financial contacts. They investigated her work and pronounced it sound and deserving. With their support and contacts, and her perseverance, Wilson was able to obtain funds needed to establish the school and keep it going for quite a while.

The school provided courses in agriculture (farming, gardening, dairy) and the mechanical and domestic arts (carpentry, shoe-making, brick-making, tailoring, sewing, cooking, nursing, and housework). Mayesville Institute received no more than two hundred dollars annually from the State of South Carolina. To sustain themselves and the school as well, the students raised their own food, built their own buildings, and derived some income from their brickmaking establishment.

Wilson was one of many unsung black female educators of her time. Strangely enough, much that happened to her parallels the experiences of another well-known black woman educator, Mary McLeod Bethune (1887-1955). Like Wilson, Bethune was born in Mayesville, South Carolina, graduated from the Scotia Seminary in Concord, North Carolina, and offered to become a missionary to Africa. But her request to become a missionary was turned down twice by the church and she had to move on to other things. Bethune taught at the Haines Institute and in 1904 founded her own school, Bethune-Cookman College in Daytona Beach, Florida. This historical institution still exists today.

Other black female educators who followed a similar road and founded institutions to educate black youth include: Charlotte Hawkins Brown, founder of Palmer Memorial Institute, Sedalia, North Carolina (1902); Cornelia Bowen, a Tuskegee graduate who founded Mount Meigs Institute in Alabama (1888); Lucy Laney (sometimes spelled Lainey), a slave born in Macon, Georgia, founder of Haines Normal Institute in Atlanta, Georgia (1886); and Mary S. Peake who, in the 1860s, opened a day school for fifty pupils in Hampton, Virginia, near Fortress Monroe. Like these women, Emma J. Wilson deserves recognition for founding a school in the South for rural black youth who otherwise might have remained uneducated.

REFERENCES:

Lerner, Gerda, ed. *Black Women in White America.* New York: Pantheon Books, 1972.
————. *The Majority Finds Its Past.* New York: Oxford University Press, 1979.
Line, Faith. Telephone interview with Marva L. Rudolph. May 11, 1993.
Richardson, Clement, ed. *National Cyclopedia of the Colored Race.* Vol. 1. Montgomery: National Publishing Company, 1919.

                                        Marva L. Rudolph

Addie L. Wyatt

(1924-)

Labor executive

Addie L. Wyatt was the first black woman to sit on the board of an international union. Given the long history of hostility toward blacks in much of the labor union movement and the perhaps even stronger bias towards male leadership, this was a remarkable achievement. Her position enabled her to work for equality of opportunity and pay for both blacks and women. In addition, she was much involved with the Chicago community and with her church, to both of which she rendered notable service.

Addie L. Wyatt was born in Brookhaven, Mississippi, on March 28, 1924, to Ambrose and Maggie Nolan Cameron. There were five younger brothers and sisters in the family. During Wyatt's childhood, the family moved to Chicago in search of a better way of life, and Wyatt was educated in the public and private schools of that city. Her mother was a very strong influence on her family; she nurtured the faith of her children and refused to let them fight, even in the face of strong provocation. This led to Wyatt's own strong and abiding faith. Wyatt became minister of music in the church where her husband was pastor, Vernon Park Church of God, and was active in organizations like the Women's Organization of the National Association of the Church of God. Wyatt attributes her perseverance in the face of obstacles and her achievements in life to her faith.

On May 12, 1940, at the age of sixteen, she married Claude S. Wyatt, Jr. She soon had two children, Renaldo Wyatt and Claude S. Wyatt III. Trying try to break out of poverty, she initially applied for a job as a typist, but was denied the white collar job. She found a job in a meat packing house at sixty-two cents an hour in 1941 and dealt with the problems of working early hours and finding a sitter for her children. Ironically, because of the union, the factory job paid more than the clerical position would have. Somewhat later during World War II, just before Wyatt's husband was drafted

Addie L. Wyatt

into the Navy, Maggie Cameron died. Wyatt granted her mother's deathbed wish that she raise her brothers and sisters because her father was in very poor health. She became responsible for Emmet Cameron, Willie Cameron, Bluett Cameron, Audrey Cameron Dandrige, and Maude Cameron Parker. Fortunately, she was soon able to find better housing for the family in a federally subsidized Chicago housing development. She continued to work in various packing houses around the city until 1954.

Wyatt Becomes Union Leader

In 1953 Wyatt was elected vice president of the United Packinghouse Food and Alliance Workers Union Local 56. She was the first woman of any race to be on the board of her union. She reported in *Guideposts* her feelings of uncertainty as she attended her first grievance meeting and the gender bias reflected in questions she was asked by her fellow workers:

> Although I had prayed and read my contract over that morning, and even felt calm as I walked toward the meeting room, I was still unsure of myself as the newly elected union vice-president. . . . I recalled the words of some men at the plant. *You're a woman. How can you do a man-sized job? You're a Christian. How can you handle a room full of roughtalking union and management reps?*

Wyatt found the strength that day to directly challenge the plant management and win her point. This strength led her onward. Her position as local vice president continued through 1955. She became a full-time union worker when she became

an international representative in her union, which merged with the Amalgamated Meat Cutters Union in 1968. (In 1979 the union again merged, this time with the Retail Clerks International Union, to form the United Food and Commercial Workers International Union, AFL-CIO and CLC.) She worked in such positions as organizer, negotiator, and program coordinator. Wyatt held the position of international representative until 1974 when she became director of the Women's Affairs Department of the union. This department was formed to further the full equality and participation of women in the union and held its first conference in July 1974. Seventy local women union members attended the conference. The concerns of the women ranged from local union bargaining problems and equal pay to passage of the Equal Rights Amendment. In 1976, Wyatt became an international vice president while remaining director of the Women's Affairs Department. This landmark position made her the first black woman member of the leadership of an international union.

Her abilities and visibility earned Wyatt prominent leadership roles outside the union. She was a national vice president of the Coalition of Labor Union Women. She served as advisor to the Chicago Urban League and labor advisor to Martin Luther King's Southern Christian Leadership Conference (SCLC) and to Jesse Jackson's PUSH (People United to Save Humanity). A member of the National Council of Negro Women, she also served as a board member at-large for the Americans for Democratic Action and as an at-large member of the Democratic National Committee in 1976. President John Kennedy made her a committee member of the Commission on the Status of Women, and President Jimmy Carter appointed her to the National Commission on the Observance of International Women's Year. She has also been involved in many church, school, and community activities.

Wyatt's numerous awards include the Image Award from the League of Black Women (1973); selection as one of twelve Women of the Year by *Time* magazine (1976); selection as one of nine Women of the Year by *Ladies Home Journal* (1977); International Women's Year Award from the University of Michigan; and a citation from the Michigan House of Representatives. She has also received the Volunteer Youth and Community Service Award of the Chicago Housing Authority; a citation as one of Chicago's Mothers of the Year from the Chicago State Street Council; a Certificate of Appreciation from the Chicago Black Caucus, American Federation of Teachers; an award as Outstanding Woman Western Region from Iota Phi Lambda Sorority; and the Award for Outstanding Achievement from the Ministers' Wives Association, Church of God. In 1981, 1982, and 1983, *Ebony* magazine listed her as one of the 100 Most Outstanding Black Women in America. She received honorary doctorates from Anderson College, Anderson, Indiana (1976), and from Chicago's Columbia College (1978).

Biographical material provided to the Fisk University Library declares that Wyatt fought for ''equality, economic security, justice, peace, and full participation, not only in the world of work but also in the total society, especially on behalf of women and blacks.'' Wyatt is quoted as stating:

We have a real chance to move our world a few steps nearer to closing the gap between the promise of these goals and their fulfillment. My union, the Amalgamated Meat Cutters, my church, the Vernon Park Church of God, and my family have been my most effective vehicles to collectively accomplish these ends. They have been the strengthening and stabilizing forces which have encouraged and sustained me during the days of greatest travail. When things appear at their discouraging worst, God, who has never failed me, reveals the way.

Addie Wyatt retired as vice president of the United Food and Commercial Workers Union on September 30, 1984, and has entered the ministry.

Current Address: Vernon Park Church of God, 9011 Stony Island, Chicago, IL 60617.

REFERENCES:

Addie L. Wyatt. Biographical Statement. Fisk University Library, Nashville, Tenn.

"Addie Wyatt, Labor Union Executive." *Ebony* 32 (August 1977): 72.

Davis, W. Marianna, ed. *Contributions of Black Women to America.* Vol. 2. Columbia, S.C.: Kenday Press, 1982.

"Labor Group Cites Three Black Women." *Jet* 68 (March 25, 1985): 23.

"Labor Union Pioneer Addie Wyatt Retires." *Jet* 66 (August 27, 1984): 34.

Who's Who among Black Americans, 1994-95. 8th ed. Detroit: Gale Research, 1994.

Who's Who in America. 43rd ed. Chicago: Marquis, 1984.

"Women's Affairs Director: Addie Wyatt." *The Butcher Workman* 61 (May 1975): 2-3, 19.

Wyatt, Addie. "Look for the Best, Addie." *Guideposts* 31 (October 1976): 32-34.

COLLECTIONS:

An oral history of Addie Wyatt and her trade union work was made for Roosevelt University, Chicago, Illinois.

Robert L. Johns

Madie Hall Xuma

(1894-1982)

YWCA founder, educator

Madie Xuma developed an interest in YWCA activities while she was a young woman and it continued throughout her life. She is remembered for her involvement in the YWCA in North Carolina and Virginia, but more particularly for her courageous and intense work in South Africa to found one of the world's leading YWCA branches.

Madie Hall Xuma, one of four children and the first girl in her immediate family, was born in 1894 in Winston-Salem, North Carolina. Her parents, Ginny Cowan Hall and H. H. Hall, met in Salisbury, North Carolina, and studied together at Shaw University in Raleigh. At that time Shaw operated Leonard Medical School, which later closed. H. H. Hall graduated from the medical program there and in 1891 married Ginny Cowan. They moved to Winston-Salem, where Hall was the first black physician. He also organized the black medical community and planned the city's first black hospital.

Xuma (she continued to be known by the name Hall in Winston-Salem after her marriage) knew about racism early on from witnessing the white medical community's rejection of her father in his early years of practice. After many white patients died during an influenza epidemic, other white families turned to Hall for health care. None of the patients he treated for influenza died. After that, he became very well respected by both races.

Ginny Cowan Hall, who was born in Whiteville, North Carolina, had a white grandfather. She grew up in Salisbury under the care of her mother and a Baptist minister named Cowan and his family. Ginny Hall invested widely in real estate, particularly in Salisbury, where she bought and built houses. She also owned property in Asheville. While for a time she kept her business dealings a secret from her husband, later she revealed her secrets and became full business manager of the home and the family property. She taught sound business procedures to her daughter Madie, who used her training wisely later on.

Ginny Hall taught her daughter to care for the sick, poor, and needy. When young Xuma received her first paycheck from her first job, Ginny Hall persuaded her to share it with someone in need, in this instance an old lady in the neighborhood. According to Xuma, who recounted the experience in Emily Herring Wilson's *Hope and Dignity,* her mother said,

"You can help that old lady get enough coal for the winter, so she'll have fire. . . . I'll feed her and you keep her warm." With a portion of her check Xuma bought coal for the woman and watched her parents repair the woman's house and attend to her other needs. "And that was one of the greatest things she taught me, helping people," said Xuma.

Early on, Xuma, who had tremendous love and respect for her father, wanted to become a doctor; she had been influenced by his profession and enjoyed the experience of carrying his black bag when she was a child. Her father dissuaded her, saying that "no girl can be a doctor." While a student at Shaw University, Xuma was accepted into medical school at Howard University, Washington, D.C., as was her brother Leroy, who had completed his studies at Livingstone College in Salisbury. Her father agreed that son Leroy could attend, but not his daughter. When questioned further about his decision, he discussed the experiences of the one or two women in his medical class in 1890 and gave follow-up accounts of their work after graduation. Xuma said in *Hope and Dignity,* "They had a hard time, going out, country practicing, winter time, and women molested." Her father would rather she study any other subject instead. In time, Leroy Hall finished medical school and joined his father's practice.

After completing two years at Shaw University, Xuma taught for a while in Winston-Salem. Her illness during an influenza epidemic caused her parents to send her to Miami for recovery. She accepted a temporary teaching assignment at Booker T. Washington High School, during which time she met Mary McLeod Bethune, founder and head of Bethune Cookman College in Daytona Beach, Florida. Since Xuma was a pianist as well as a teacher, Bethune offered her a position at her school. She was there when benefactor John D. Rockefeller visited the college and gave Bethune fifty thousand dollars. She spent one year on the staff, then returned to Winston-Salem. After her mother died in 1930, Xuma managed affairs at home and cared for her father until he died. Now she could complete her studies as her parents had wished. She had graduated from Winston-Salem Teachers College and in 1937, when she was forty-three years old, she completed her master's degree at Columbia University in New York.

While studying in New York she met Alfred B. Xuma, a physician from Johannesburg, South Africa, whose marriage proposals to her continued after she returned to Winston-Salem. After three proposals by mail, she accepted. World War II delayed her passage to South Africa for a year. The U.S. government approved her travel in April 1940 and she gave up the first grade class she was teaching and left for Africa. The cargo ship that she had taken from Holland to

Cape Town, where she disembarked, was destroyed by the Germans when it reached the Indian Ocean. When she learned the ship's fate she said, "God was with me all the way, all the time I was there." Alfred and Madie Xuma married in Cape Town, then moved to Sophiatown, near Johannesburg, where they lived until the South African government forced them, along with other residents, to give up their homes and move to the Soweto area where other blacks had settled. The government declared Sophiatown a "white area."

YWCA Founded in South Africa

After winning acceptance from the residents of Soweto, including some who had been hostile toward the idea of an African doctor's marriage to an American, Madie Xuma invited into her home housewives, teachers, and church workers and formed the African Self-Improvement Organization. Later she converted the organization into the Zenzele (which means "people helping themselves") YWCA. Her interest in the Y began in North Carolina while she was a student at Shaw. She had worked with the Y in Lynchburg, Virginia, and later set in motion the establishment of a Y for black girls and women in Winston-Salem. But her efforts in South Africa were much more daring; she faced bitter opposition from the government and the white Y and discouragement from local black women. In 1981 the Zenzele YWCA, which had become one of the world's strongest Y branches, celebrated its fortieth anniversary. The group named the administration building in her honor. Xuma's contributions to the Y were widely known and for eight years she served on the executive board of the world organization.

Xuma saw apartheid in practice in South Africa and experienced more extreme prejudice than she had known in segregated North Carolina. "I had more freedom in America. I could go many places here I couldn't go there, to theaters and picture shows," she said.

In December 1940 Alfred Xuma was elected president of the African National Congress. She joined her husband in protest activities by marching the Market Place to Gandhi Hall. The demonstration was allowed to occur on Sunday, when the streets were free of people. Little else is known about her South African experiences. After Alfred Xuma died, Madie Xuma returned in 1963 to the United States, where she felt that she would be safer. She had spent twenty-three years in South Africa.

Madie Xuma spent her final years active with local and state garden clubs for black women, but generally lived quietly in Winston-Salem until her death in 1982. She had established a world network of friends in Mexico, the Caribbean, England, Africa, and elsewhere, whom she met during her trip around the world in 1966. She had also become widely known as a YWCA worker and founder.

REFERENCES:

Wilson, Emily Herring. *Hope and Dignity: Older Black Women of the South*. Philadelphia: Temple University Press, 1983.

Jessie Carney Smith

Jean Childs Young
(1933-1994)
Civil rights activist, educator, children's welfare advocate

Jean Young was a prominent activist for civil rights, education, and children's welfare whose work spanned more than three decades. In 1978 she became widely known as the chairperson of the International Year of the Child. She was a strong, independent woman who was both career and family oriented. She was never overshadowed by her husband, famed civil rights leader and politician Andrew Young, but worked beside him, helping to further his causes, many of which she supported, while actively defending her own as well.

The youngest of five children, Jean Childs Young was born during the Depression on July 1, 1933, in Marion, Alabama. Her father, Norman Childs, and his family owned a combination grocery, soda fountain, and candy store. The family made candy that Norman Childs sold throughout the South. Her mother, Idella Childs, was an elementary school teacher. Andrew (Andy) Young, whom Jean Young would later marry, wrote in his spiritual memoirs, *A Way Out of No Way,* "Norman Childs was a black Clark Gable and Idella as fiery, independent, and as passionate a woman as Miss Scarlett ever hoped to be. This was a wonderful family."

The school system in Marion, Alabama, was characterized by the racial discrimination commonly practiced throughout the South. A potbellied stove was the only source of heat in the one-room school where Idella Childs taught, and the children sat on benches without backs. Unlike the freshly painted white school, the black school was rough clapboard, and it could only provide students with used books handed down from the white school. The situation may have agitated young Jean and perhaps she showed it. Her parents became concerned about her behavior and thought that she was developing a chip on her shoulder.

Mr. and Mrs. Childs provided a comfortable living for the family and helped to make life for the children happy. A family garden was an additional source of food and Idella Childs, who was also a seamstress, made all of the children's clothes. Young's solid upbringing, coupled with the positive attitude of the black community, helped her to develop a strong sense of pride. She was very affected by the tightly knit black community in Marion. She told A. Victoria Hunter *for Essence* magazine, October 1979,

Jean Childs Young

The problems of segregation forced people into closer-knit communities. . . . The fact that you could not live in certain areas, that you could not attend certain schools, that you could not go to movies or public facilities created a closer family unit and a closer community unit. . . . It . . . tended to bind us . . . in a rather unique way to one another. We were living in a hostile environment, but we had . . . a closer-knit group to cope with the hostility.

Doubtless Young's parents also helped her to develop a positive attitude. For example, they refused to allow her to work as a babysitter, as her schoolmates did, so she would avoid getting into "that maid relationship." Mr. and Mrs. Childs expected that all of their children would attend college. "That was a route out of the social dilemma," she continued in *Essence.*

From her early days Young knew who she was and accepted her blackness. Her passage through childhood might have been eased by her light skin and "good" hair—a possibility that she acknowledged. Young took steps to be as inconspicuous among her peers as possible and to be accepted on the basis of her appearance; therefore, instead of wearing her "good" hair loose, she wore it braided and tied with ribbons, or pinned back, as if to draw attention away from her hair. Later, in *Essence,* Young reflected, "Black never has been the color of skin" but "a culture."

Young attended Lincoln High School, which the American Missionary Association operated. After graduating, she enrolled at Manchester College in North Manchester, Indiana, a school affiliated with the fundamentalist Church of the Brethren. Although she planned to become a missionary to Angola and applied to the school for missionary status, the American Board of Commissioners for Foreign Missions denied her request because of their policy against accepting missionaries who were single.

When she was a college student, Jean Childs met Andy Young, a graduate of Howard University, Washington, D.C., and for a short time pastor of the church in Marion where the Childs family held membership. The New Orleans native, who had entered Hartford Seminary in Connecticut, had returned South on a summer internship and hoped to mingle with "plain, wise black folk." Since the church membership was so small, ministers came only for the summer. Andy Young received no pay for his services but was given housing and meals with different families on a weekly basis. Norman and Idella Childs provided meals for Young during his first week in Marion. Although Jean Young was not yet home for the summer, Andy Young saw evidence of her everywhere in the home. He saw a revised standard version of the New Testament, a Thomas Nelson study version underlined and filled with notes in the margin on some of his favorite passages. He observed a Red Cross Senior Life Saving certificate and, as he wrote in his spiritual memoirs, he "was not accustomed to young black women who studied the Bible seriously and who were good swimmers." He knew about Manchester College, where she studied, through one of its former students, who introduced Young to the concept of nonviolence and Mahatma Gandhi's teachings.

Andy Young had come to Marion at a time when he was totally committed to the church and felt that he had no room in his life for marriage or a family. He began to suspect, however, that the Lord had sent him to Marion to meet his wife. Andy and Jean first met at a family meal at the Childs home. The initial meeting of Jean and Andy Young was warm and friendly and led to easy conversation. On their first date they drove thirty miles to Selma to a swimming pool for blacks because Marion offered no such facility. Later they developed a romantic relationship, but marriage took a back burner to their educations. In his memoirs Andy Young wrote an account of his wife as a young woman. His description is an apt characterization of her later life as well.

> I had never met a young woman quite like Jean. There was a simple elegance about the way she did things. She was wise beyond her years, and she possessed a sense of mission about teaching in the South which impressed me more than her charm and beauty. I had known many beautiful women, but with Jean, the beauty was not just external. It was her spirit, her dedication, and her purpose to serve others which made her the "one in a million, chance of a lifetime."

They returned to their separate schools and in 1954, Jean Young graduated from Manchester. They married in June of the same year. This was a critical time in the civil rights movement because of the Supreme Court ruling that outlawed school segregation. Their interests, however, were in the church, not the political activities that would consume them later on.

The Youngs headed for Thomasville and Beachton, Georgia, to two small churches that Andy Young was to pastor. Andy Young outraged the Ku Klux Klan when he started a voter registration drive in the area. He admitted in his memoirs that he had his own hidden agenda when he went to Thomasville. He had studied about Gandhi and India's non-violent struggle and hoped to stir up "a similar movement among southern Negroes." Soon they moved to the New York area, where Andy Young became affiliated with the National Council of Churches (NCC) Department of Youth Work.

Civil Rights Movement Begins

While in the New York area, Jean Young taught school in Hartford and at the same time earned a master's degree from Queens College in Flushing, New York. But she knew there was a need for black teachers in the South and that education was one way to address racial problems. In 1960, as they watched NBC's *White Paper* give an account of a racial demonstration in Nashville, Tennessee, in which students from Fisk University, the American Baptist Seminary, and Tennessee State University were arrested, they knew immediately that, although they were not students, they would return to the South and join the civil rights movement. They felt the call although the solution to racial strife was not yet clear to them. Jean Young had studied with committed pacifists at Manchester College and Andy Young had studied Gandhi; therefore, nonviolent protest must have appealed to them. "We didn't know what the Civil Rights Movement would involve, but I can remember thinking this was the most important place in the world to be," she told A. Victoria Hunter for the *Essence* piece.

The Youngs returned to Atlanta, where Andy Young served as a staff member of the Board of Homeland Ministries of the United Churches of Christ and administrator of its Dorchester Citizenship Education Project. He was also a staff member of the Southern Christian Leadership Conference (SCLC) from 1961 to 1970. By 1964 he was SCLC's executive director. He was a top strategist and theorist for the movement and assisted in drafting the Civil Rights Act of 1964 and the Voting Rights Act of 1965.

Jean Young had great respect for Martin Luther King, Jr. and the entire civil rights movement. As she stated in her interview with Victoria Hunter for *Essence,* she knew then that the movement was right, that those involved in it were totally committed, and that the masses of people in the streets were there because they knew too that "this is the right time and the right place and we've got to be here."

The Youngs' Atlanta home became a meeting site for civil rights strategy sessions and a hotel for participants in the movement. Those passing through who needed a place to stay often slept on the floor, in the basement, or wherever they could in the Youngs' home. Jean Young's involvement began at this level and advanced to public demonstrations. Personal circumstances prevented her from sustained involvement in the movement; she had young children and was a school teacher in Atlanta. But Jean Young did what she could. She participated in the 1961 boycott of downtown lunch counters and marches in Birmingham, Alabama. She attended the meetings in St. Augustine, Florida, where in 1964 for the first time she joined in a march, at a site where Andy Young worked. In fact, she participated in all of the major civil rights marches: the 1963 March on Washington, the 1965 march from Selma to Montgomery for voting rights, the 1966 march in Mississippi, and the 1968 Poor People's Campaign. Meanwhile, Andy Young marched with King wherever he went and was with him when King was assassinated in 1968.

Young saw an important role for black working women in society and a position for herself in the workforce that would not interfere with her family responsibilities. She told Hunter for *Essence* magazine, "Being a Black woman, having to grow up in a society in which my parents worked and in which many of my friends' parents worked, the idea of women working was not something new. What was new was women working in jobs that paid well—creative jobs, meaningful jobs within the context of the Black community."

Young became coordinator of school programs for the Atlanta system and was a lead teacher in the Teacher Corps. She was appointed to the team that developed Atlanta Metropolitan College and was the school's first public relations officer. Later on she served on its board of advisers. She worked with IBM Educational Systems in the development of *The Illuminated Books and Manuscripts,* a multimedia software program.

Young Becomes Children's Welfare Advocate

The world knew the work of Andy Young, the civil rights leader, minister, congressman (1972-76), U.N. ambassador (1977-79), and mayor of Atlanta (1982-90), yet Jean Young, a widely accomplished woman in the areas of education and civil rights, received little notice in some communities. In an interview with Maria Saporta published in the *Atlanta Journal and Constitution* on September 17, 1994, she said that "she did not see herself as the woman behind the man, but 'beside' the man. 'Whatever role I have in relationship to Andy will be one that I determine.'" She was a staunch advocate of children's welfare, as demonstrated through her role as chair of the U.S. Commission on the International Year of the Child. President Jimmy Carter named her to the volunteer position in 1978. Sponsored by the United Nations, the program was designed to enhance the lives of children around the world. While chairing the commission, she developed a network of child welfare advocates in each state in the United States.

As she discussed the commission's work with *Essence*'s Victoria Hunter, Young spoke of its efforts to get the corporate world, professional and social organizations, labor unions, the government, and other groups and individuals more involved in children's causes. "What we're really asking is that these groups begin to examine . . . their social responsibility . . . to the future of this nation. . . . That's what our children represent."

Jean Young also served on a number of boards. She chaired the board of directors of the African American Panoramic Experience Museum in Atlanta. She was a member of the advisory boards of Outward Bound, UNICEF, Families First, the Georgia Woman of Achievement Museum, and Habitat for Humanity. During Andy Young's tenure as mayor of Atlanta, Jean Young established the Atlanta Task Force on Education and was its chair for seven terms. The task force sponsored the Mayor's Scholars and the "Dream Jamboree," which brought together in Atlanta's Civic Center high school seniors and recruiters from colleges and trade schools. These two programs are an enduring legacy to her dedication to young people. Jean Young most recently demonstrated her concern for children with the Atlanta-Fulton Commission on Children and Youth, which she cofounded in 1990 and which began to implement its programs in 1992.

In recognition of her work, Jean Young has received numerous awards and honors. She was awarded honorary doctorates from Loyola University in Chicago, Manchester College, and New York City Technical College of the City University of New York. She received the NAACP Distinguished Leadership Award in 1989, the YWCA Woman of Achievement Award in 1993, and the Community Service Award in 1993 from WXIA-TV, Channel 11, in Atlanta.

Young enjoyed athletics as much as she supported athletic programs. She had been a five-foot-three-inch guard on her high school basketball team and a swimmer as well. She became a "B" level player in the Atlanta Lawn Tennis Association, winning several trophies. Andy and Jean Young were friends with Arthur and Jeanne Ashe and the couples often played tennis doubles together. Jean Young helped boost Atlanta's successful bid for the 1996 Summer Olympics by traveling through Africa, the Middle East, and Europe to garner support from members of the International Olympic Committee.

In 1991 Jean Young was diagnosed with liver cancer, which led to her death at Crawford Long Hospital of Emory University in Atlanta on Friday, September 16, 1994. In addition to her husband, she was survived by four children—Lisa Alston, Paula Shelton, Andrea Young, and Andrew Young III—her mother, four sisters, and seven grandchildren. A three-hour ceremony celebrating her life was held before thousands of friends and well-wishers at the Civic Center, with the pastor of First Congregational Church of Atlanta, where Young held membership, officiating. The ceremony was filled with tributes to Jean Young, including a handwritten note from President Bill Clinton, a poem recited by Maya

Angelou, a personal remembrance from Coretta Scott King, and a moving message from daughter Lisa Young Alston. Commenting on the services, Casper Jordan wrote: "This city has been obsessed with her since her death. . . . As we say, 'she was put away in grand style.'"

Both in her life's work and in selections from her memoir, "What to Remember about Me," published in her funeral program and in the *Atlanta Journal and Constitution* on September 20, 1994, Jean Young expressed how she wished to be remembered. These selections showed that she was caring and understanding; she loved reading, especially historical novels; she was a problem solver for her children; she was an advocate for her children, family, friends, and all just causes; she was a loving mother and wife who believed that each member in a relationship should give more than half; and she believed in the grace of forgiveness and was a forgiving person. According to the selections from her memoir, she wanted people to remember, "Jean Young, now that was a woman!"

REFERENCES:

Bims, Hamilton. "A Southern Activist Goes to the House." *Ebony* 28 (February 1973): 82-90.

Hunter, A. Victoria. "Jean (the Other Activist Named) Young." *Essence* 10 (October 1979): 92-93, 154-61.

"Jean C. Young, 61, Educator, Activist and Wife of Former Atlanta Mayor Andrew Young, Dies of Cancer." *Jet* 86 (October 3, 1994): 6-7.

"Jean Young Dies; Battled Racial Bias." *Washington Post,* September 17, 1994.

"Jean Young (1933-1994). Graced City as Advocate for Children, Human Rights." *Atlanta Journal and Constitution,* September 17, 1994.

"Jean Young (1933-1994). Character, Compassion Marked Her Life." *Atlanta Journal and Constitution,* September 17, 1994.

"Jean Young Set a Fine Example on Independence." *Atlanta Journal and Constitution,* September 17, 1994.

Johnson, Herschel. "A Close Encounter with Andrew Young." *Ebony* 33 (April 1978): 110-22.

Jordan, Casper L. Letter to Jessie Carney Smith, September 20, 1994.

Obituary. *Atlanta Journal and Constitution,* September 18, 1994.

"Remembering Jean Young." *Atlanta Journal and Constitution,* September 20, 1994.

Who's Who among Black Americans, 1994-95. 8th ed. Detroit: Gale Research, 1994.

Young, Andrew. *A Way Out of No Way.* Nashville: Thomas Nelson Publishers, 1994.

Jessie Carney Smith

Geographic Index

Geographic Index

Subject Index

Personal names, place names, events, institutions, and other subject areas or key words contained in *Notable Black American Women, Book II,* entries are listed in this index with corresponding page numbers indicating text references. Inclusive page numbers are also given in **bold** type for each of the volume's main entries. Also cited are the names of people with main entries in the original *Notable Black American Women,* as indicated by the abbreviation **"NBAW"** in bold type after a name.